All Men Are I

ALL MEN ARE BRETHREN

French, Scandinavian, Italian, German, Dutch, Belgian, Spanish,
Polish, West Indian, American, and other prisoners of war in Scotland
during the Napoleonic Wars, 1803–1814

IAN MACDOUGALL

First published in Great Britain in 2008 by
John Donald, an imprint of Birlinn Ltd

West Newington House
10 Newington Road
Edinburgh
EH9 1QS

www.birlinn.co.uk

ISBN 10: 1 904607 72 1
ISBN 13: 978 1 904607 72 4

British Library Cataloguing-in-Publication Data
A catalogue record for this book is available on request from the British Library

Typeset by SJC
Printed and bound in Britain by Cromwell Press, Trowbridge, Wiltshire

Contents

ILLUSTRATIONS

ABBREVIATIONS AND CONTRACTIONS

ADM	Admiralty
Adm.	Admiralty
arr.	arrived
b.	born
Bn/bn	Battalion/battalion
capd	captured
CM	*Caledonian Mercury*
d.	died
dischgd	discharged
Eb	Edinburgh bridewell
EC	Edinburgh Castle
EEC	*Edinburgh Evening Courant*
EM	Esk Mills
frig.	frigate
G	Greenlaw
h.	height
HO	Home Office
ltr(s)	letter(s)
M	Merchant vessel
ML	Midlothian Libraries
m.o.w.	man-of-war
m.v.	merchant vessel
N	Naval
NAS	National Archives of Scotland
n.d.	no date given
n.k.	not known
NLS	National Library of Scotland
n.p.	no place given
NWMS	National War Museum of Scotland
P Perth	(*except* in Appendix 5, where P stands for Privateer)
p.o.b.	place of birth
POW(s)	prisoner(s) of war
priv.	privateer
PRO	Public Record Office (now retitled The National Archives (TNA))
recapd	recaptured
regt	regiment
rel.	released
RN	Royal Navy
T	Transport vessel
TB	Transport Board
TNA	The National Archives (formerly the Public Record Office (PRO))
TO	Transport Office
trans.	transport vessel
U/u.	Uncertain/unspecified
V	Valleyfield
WO	War Office

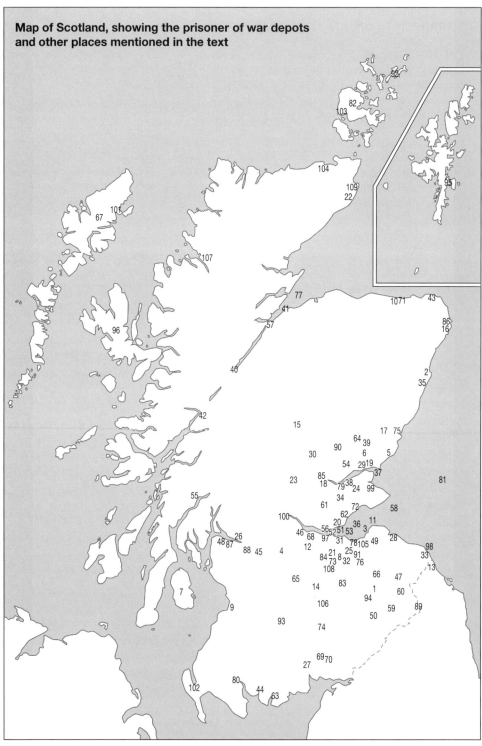

Map of Scotland, showing the prisoner of war depots and other places mentioned in the text

Key to places marked on map

D Depot
PT Parole town

Abbotsford	1	Floors Castle	60	Midlothian	73
Aberdeen	2	Forfar	39	Moffat	74
Aberlady Bay	3	Fort Augustus	40	Montrose	75
Airdrie	4	Fort George	41	Moorfoot Hills	76
Arbroath	5	Fort William	42	Moray Firth	77
Angus	6	Fraserburgh	43	Musselburgh	78
Arran	7	Galashiels	1	Neidpath Castle	83
Auchencorth Moss	8	Gatehouse of Fleet	44	Newbattle Abbey	25
Auchendinny	8	Glasgow	45	Newburgh on Tay	79
Ayr	9	Grangemouth	46	Newton Stewart	80
Banff	10	Greenlaw (D)	32	North Queensferry	56
Bass Rock	11	Greenlaw,		North Sea	81
Bathgate	12	Berwickshire (PT)	47	Orkney	82
Belhaven	28	Greenock	48	Peebles (PT)	83
Berwick on Tweed	13	Haddington	49	Penicuik	8
Biggar (PT)	14	Hawick (PT)	50	Pentland Hills	84
Blair Atholl	15	Huntingtower	85	Perth (D)	85
Boddam	16	Inchcolm	51	Peterhead	86
Brechin	17	Inchgarvie	52	Pettycur	20
Bridge of Earn	18	Inchkeith	53	Polmont	68
Broughty Ferry	19	Inchture	54	Port Glasgow	87
Burntisland	20	Inveraray	55	Prestonpans	78
Camelon	46	Inverkeithing	56	Renfrew	88
Castlelaw	21	Inverness	57	River Tweed	89
Clyth	22	Isle of May	58	Roslin	8
Craigmillar Castle	31	Jedburgh (PT)	59	Ruthven	90
Crieff	23	Kelso (PT)	60	Saltoun	91
Cupar Fife (PT)	24	Kinross	61	Sanday	92
Dalkeith	25	Kirkcaldy	62	Sanquhar (PT)	93
Dumbarton	26	Kirkcudbright	63	Selkirk (PT)	94
Dumbarton Castle	26	Kirkhill	8	Shetland	95
Dumfries (PT)	27	Kirriemuir	64	Skye	96
Dunbar	28	Lanark (PT)	65	South Queensferry	97
Dundee	29	Lasswade	25	St Abbs Head	98
Dunkeld	30	Lauder (PT)	66	St Andrews	99
Edinburgh	31	Leith	31	Stirling	100
Edinburgh Castle (D)	31	Lerwick	95	Stornoway	101
Esk Mills (D)	32	Lewis	67	Stranraer	102
Eyemouth	33	Linlithgow	68	Stromness	103
Falkirk	46	Loanhead	25	Thurso	104
Falkland	34	Lochmaben (PT)	69	Tranent	105
Fife	24	Lockerbie (PT)	70	Tweedsmuir	106
Findon	35	Lomond Hills	34	Ullapool	107
Firth of Forth	36	Macduff	71	Valleyfield (D)	32
Firth of Tay	37	Melrose (PT)	1	West Linton	108
Flisk	38	Methil	72	Wick	109

Introduction

This book is about the thousands of men, youths and even, in some cases, mere boys of primary school age who during the Napoleonic Wars in 1803-1814 found themselves prisoners of war in Scotland. Most of them were French, but several thousands of them came from virtually every other country in Europe, and a few even from the Americas, the West Indies, and the Middle East or one or two other parts of Africa and Asia.

The Napoleonic Wars, dragging in as they did so many of the peoples of Europe and even some from other continents, cost myriads of lives among the soldiers and seamen of the belligerent states. Precise figures are difficult to establish but up to perhaps a million of those who died in those Wars were French soldiers and seamen. A further 400,000 or so of the dead were combatants who came from Napoleon Bonaparte's allied or subject states in Germany, Italy, Holland, Belgium, Switzerland, Scandinavia, Poland, or elsewhere in Europe. The armed forces of Britain and of states such as Austria, Prussia, Russia, Spain, and some others which at one stage or another in the war fought against those of Napoleon, likewise suffered a multitude of casualties. Losses on both sides were by no means all in battle: many were the result of disease, inadequate medical provision, climate, or other causes. Not a few among some civilian populations, too, lost their lives in or as a result of the fighting, as for example in Spain and Portugal, and in 1812-13 during the French invasion of Russia.[1]

Among the other categories of casualties in the Napoleonic Wars were the hundreds of thousands of those who became prisoners of war. The aggregate number of French and French allied prisoners of war held in captivity in Britain between 1803 and 1814 was 122,000. Of several hundred thousand prisoners of war from other European armies and navies who at one time or another during those years languished likewise in captivity in France, or at least in French hands, some 16,000 were British. The striking imbalance between the number of French prisoners of war in Britain and of British in France contributed, as will be shown in the pages below, to the painful prolongation of captivity for thousands of those prisoners in both countries. In some cases their captivity lasted as long as eleven years.[2]

Some comparison is attempted in the pages below, too, between the conditions and experiences of prisoners in Scotland during the Napoleonic Wars and those of their fellow prisoners in England, and also with those of British prisoners in France. If similarities predominated there were also some dissimilarities. In Scotland there were, for instance, no prisoners of war who spent their captivity on floating prisons such as those in England at Portsmouth, Plymouth and Chatham, where thousands of prisoners throughout the Napoleonic Wars were confined aboard the hulks of old warships. And, as will be seen, it was the view of one much quoted among the captives in Scotland that on his arrival there in 1811 along with hundreds of others, 'The people appeared to us more sympathetic than in England.'

If the Napoleonic Wars were to be described, from the point of view of Britain, as the last phase in a second Hundred Years' War with France, that description would call for some correction. In the Hundred Years' War in the middle ages it had been England, not Britain, that fought France, for Scotland had then been the ally of France. And in the French Revolutionary Wars from 1792 immediately preceding the Napoleonic Wars, the landing or attempted landing in 1796, 1797 and 1798 of French troops in Ireland was not least intended to prompt or support Irish nationalist risings against British control of that island, as in earlier wars of the 18th century French troops had at least been expected to land in Scotland to support Jacobite risings there. That said, there certainly was during the century and a quarter from 1689 to 1815 frequently recurring warfare between Britain and France. In all those wars (of the League of Augsburg, 1688-97, of Spanish Succession, 1703-13, of Austrian Succession, 1740-8, the Seven Years' War, 1756-63, of American Independence, 1775-83, and the French Revolutionary and Napoleonic Wars, 1792-1815), whatever changes occurred in alliances among some of the other states involved, Britain and France were consistently antagonists. During that protracted period of warfare the two states fought each other in one campaign or another not only in Europe but also in India, North America, the West Indies, Egypt, and not least at sea. These Franco-British struggles were over colonies, trade, threats of invasion, and naval supremacy, as well as over other territorial issues and the balance of power in Europe.

The French Revolutionary Wars from 1792, into which Britain entered the following year, had introduced at least in their opening years ideological aspects in that recurrent warfare: the early French revolutionary armies were defending not only the territory of France but also the ideas and ideals of the Revolution itself. If, however, patriotism is love of one's country whereas love of other people's country is imperialism, then it was the latter which by the mid-1790s became an increasingly significant part of official French aims and achievements. The seizure of power in France by Napoleon Bonaparte on 18th Brumaire (9 November) 1799 hugely strengthened during the following decade and a half the tide of French imperialist expansion. Yet borne along on that tide of French bayonets into, for example, Italy, Germany, and Spain, there remained some ideals or principles of the Revolution which, some temporarily, others more permanently, were implanted at least sporadically in those territories. Among those ideals or principles were the career open to talents, the civil code of law, sequestration and sale of church estates and, in Spain, those which resulted in the abolition of the Inquisition.

Even this bare outline of those recurrent wars between Britain and France from 1689 to 1815 may indicate why it seemed to some in both countries that the Treaty or Peace of Amiens signed by their two governments in March 1802, although it appeared to bring to a close the French Revolutionary Wars, was nonetheless unlikely to establish a lasting peace between those two states.

For such scepticism there were at least five reasons. First, some war aims in pursuit of which the British government had entered the Revolutionary Wars in 1793 remained in 1802 unachieved. Thus France still held, and moreover had apparently won the recognition of the other European powers for its acquisition of, the Austrian Netherlands (in later years retitled Belgium). France also retained the 'natural frontiers' to which during the Revolutionary Wars it had expanded on the Rhine and in the Alps. In addition, having in 1795 overrun Holland France dominated it still in 1802 as the Batavian Republic, a client state. Historically, the occupation of the whole of the Low Countries by a powerful and hostile, or potentially hostile, continental state had rung alarm bells for British governments. Second, under the terms of the Peace of Amiens British conquests of territories, especially colonies, during the war were, with the two exceptions of Ceylon and Trinidad, returned to their previous holders: thus to Holland, Cochin in India, Cape Colony in South Africa and the Spice Islands in the East Indies; to Spain, Minorca; and to France, some trading stations in Africa and India, and several West Indian islands, including Martinique. Egypt, where the remnant of the French troops landed in 1798 by Napoleon had capitulated in 1801 to British forces, was returned to Turkey. These were aspects of the Peace of Amiens that hardly reconciled to it thrustful merchants, colonisers, and other influential groups in Britain. Third, for their part French merchants, manufacturers, and colonisers continued to see their British counterparts as their main and inveterate rivals, and sought the protection of their own government against imports, especially textiles, from across the Channel. Continuing friction on such issues between the two states appeared inevitable. Fourth, the Consulate government established in France following his coup d'état of 18th Brumaire 1799, was headed by that military genius Napoleon Bonaparte. By 1801-2

Napoleon seemed to have brought peace at last to France through its victories on the battlefields and the successive withdrawals between 1795 and 1801 from the war of hostile, or formerly hostile, states such as Prussia, Russia, Austria, Holland, Spain, and several lesser ones. Yet even while preliminary Franco-British negotiations that led to the Peace of Amiens a year later were underway by March 1801, Napoleon's restless ambitions for further acquisitions by France of territory and power were surging. Examples then or in the following months included his decision to annex Piedmont, the extension of French power elsewhere in northern and central Italy, establishment of French influence over Switzerland, and his sending of an expedition to reconquer St Domingo (Haiti) from a black slave rebellion. That reconquest was to be a step toward implementing his larger scheme for colonial expansion and the consequent establishment of bases valuable in any renewed naval struggle with Britain—a scheme that had included his purchase in October 1800 from Spain of the vast territory in America of Louisiana. Fifth, by the end of 1802 Napoleon had declared the exclusion of British exports from France, Holland and Italy, and he had also undertaken to increase by half the number of French major warships—men o' war or ships of the line. Events such as these thus seemed hardly likely to ensure a lasting peace between Britain and France.

On the contrary, they intensified surviving mutual distrust in Britain and France as well as dissatisfaction among influential sections in both countries with the Peace of Amiens. And just as Napoleon undermined some terms or expectations of the Peace Treaty by establishing or tightening his control over Holland, Switzerland and Piedmont, so the British government, which Napoleon considered had also undermined the Peace by its failure to prevent scurrilous criticism of him in the British press, defaulted on a Treaty commitment concerning Malta. Captured by British forces in September 1800 from the French garrison installed there two years earlier during Napoleon's expedition to Egypt, Malta by the terms of the Peace of Amiens was to be returned by the British government to the sovereignty of the Knights of St John. The British government, however, dragged its feet. It regarded Malta as an invaluable naval base in the event of relations with France, as seemed more and more likely by spring 1803, again erupting into war. In May 1803, after fourteen months of increasingly unstable peace, what to influential groups on both sides of the Channel had come to appear unavoidable duly occurred. With the declaration then of war by the British government, hostilities with France were resumed. As that great French historian Georges Lefebvre put it (although by England he meant Britain): 'The conflict between Bonaparte and England was in reality a clash between two imperialisms.'[3]

❖

The breakdown of the Peace of Amiens and the resumption and spread of hostilities from May 1803 thus came to transform or disrupt, and in several hundred cases even to end, the lives of the mass of men and youths who between then and 1814 found themselves prisoners of war in Scotland. The overwhelming majority of those prisoners in Scotland were the ordinary rank and file of the armies and navies and merchant and privateering vessels of Napoleonic France or its allies or subject states. Like most of the rest of mankind, these prisoners of war have left almost no footprints in the sands of time. Beyond the pages of entries in the large official General Entry Books or ledgers of the prisoner of war camps (or depots, as they were termed in the Napoleonic Wars) where they were held, which recorded such basic information as their names, their regiment or ship, their rank, where and when they were captured, their age and place of birth, and their physical description, almost nothing is known about them—especially about their experiences in the Napoleonic or earlier wars or about their pre- or post-war lives. Exceptions to that paucity of information occur to some extent where prisoners breached depot rules, or submitted applications, or escaped, or died, or otherwise caught the eye of the British authorities responsible for confining and guarding them. On the other hand, one aspect which, although for the most part of little or no historical significance, was recorded in great detail in the Entry Books was their physical appearance. That record was made so that, in the event of escape, descriptions of the escapers could be swiftly circulated. The descriptions were of the prisoner's build or physique, the shape of his face, even the colour of his complexion, hair and eyes, whether he had any marks or wounds, and his height to the nearest quarter or half inch. The first and the two last entries, unlike the others, do contain at least some historical or socio-medical significance. An attempt has therefore been made in the pages below to present as comprehensive an account as surviving sources permit not only of the physical and other conditions of captivity of these men, youths and boys in the prisoner of war depots in Scotland during the Napoleonic Wars, but also, where it has proved possible to discover them, of the personal experiences and characteristics of at least some of the prisoners themselves—in short, to try to ensure they do not remain forgotten casualties of war.

That so many of the official records of the Admiralty and particularly of its Transport Board and Office concerning these prisoners have been preserved at The National Archives (formerly the Public Record Office) at Kew in London has enabled a much more detailed account of the prisoners and their experiences to be presented in the pages below than would otherwise have been possible. Other invaluable sources have been the personal (and here much quoted) accounts left by three of the prisoners themselves: Sergeant Major Philippe Beaudoin of the French 31st infantry demi-brigade, Captain Paul Andreas Kaald, a Norwegian privateersman, and Lieutenant Henri-Ferdinand Marote, alias Jean Baptiste Carrier, a Belgian privateersman. Beaudoin and Kaald were prisoners at Greenlaw (now the site of Glencorse Barracks), Penicuik, near Edinburgh; Marote-Carrier was successively at Esk Mills and Valleyfield Mill, both also at Penicuik, and then at Perth. These three witnesses therefore provide insiders' accounts of the conditions, attitudes, and activities of prisoners in four of the five main places of confinement which at one time or another during the Napoleonic Wars held the vast majority of all the captives in Scotland. An attempt has been made throughout to relate, compare and exemplify those conditions, attitudes and activities of the prisoners, as well as other aspects of their captivity, in each of the Scots depots. A projected separate volume will attempt to deal with the minority (very small until 1810-11) of prisoners, almost all of them commissioned army or naval officers or some of their equivalents among merchant seamen and privateersmen, plus a few civilians, who during the war enjoyed the greater freedom of captivity on parole in one or other of some 15 Scots parole towns such as Peebles, Kelso, Selkirk, Hawick, Lauder, Lanark, Biggar, Dumfries, and Cupar Fife. A further indispensable source of information has been the contemporary press, especially the *Edinburgh Evening Courant*, the *Caledonian Mercury*, and the *Perth Courier*. Other useful sources have included some official and non-official papers preserved in the National Archives of Scotland (formerly titled the Scottish Record Office), the National Library of Scotland, the National War Museum of Scotland, and in several other libraries, museums and archive centres, including especially Perth Museum and Art Gallery, Midlothian Libraries, Orkney Library, and the Service historique de l'Armée de Terre et de la Marine, Vincennes. The range of sources, published or unpublished, consulted is indicated in the bibliography and notes.

An attempt such as this to recount for the first time comprehensively the experiences of the prisoners in Scotland during the Napoleonic Wars is necessarily deeply indebted to two groups. The first consists of those historians who have previously tilled either at least parts of this particular field in Scotland, or in England or France, or, as in most cases, of other adjoining and relevant fields and not least the vast acreages concerned with the campaigns, battles, and armed forces engaged in those Wars; the second, of those librarians, museums and archives staffs and the many other persons and institutions that have provided information, advice, illustrations, funding, practical help or encouragement, or granted copyright permission.

To all those in the first group it is hoped that necessary and adequate specific acknowledgement is given below in the introduction, notes, and bibliography.

Among all those in the the the second group, particular thanks for permission to quote from or cite sources indicated in the notes below are due to The National Archives, London; National Archives of Scotland; National Library of Scotland; Trondelag Folkemuseum, Trondheim, (Joh. N. Tonnessen, ed., *Pa Kapertokt og i prisonen 1808-1810* (the diary of Captain Paul Andreas Kaald) (Trondheim, 1950), and to Peter Sorholt, Randi Larsson and Arnstein Lund of the Folkemuseum for allowing me freely to reproduce illustrations from Kaald's published diary, and presenting me with one of the few remaining copies of it still in print; Dr Roy Bennett, ('French Prisoners of War on Parole in Britain (1803-1814)', unpublished Ph.D thesis, University of London, 1964); M. Guillaume Lévêque, ('Les Prisonniers de Guerre Français en Grande Bretagne, 1803-1814', 2 vols, Mémoire de Maitrise, 1986-7, University of Paris, Panthéon-Sorbonne); Katholieke Universiteit Leuven, Belgium, (Léon Wocquier (ed.), *Les Souvenirs d'Un Corsaire* (Liège, 1845); The Old Edinburgh Club (N.G. Allen, 'The French Prisons in Edinburgh Castle', in *Book of the Old Edinburgh Club* (Edinburgh, 1985), Vol. XXXV, Part II); Princeton University Press (Louis Bergeron, *France under Napoleon* (Princeton, 1981); Dr M.J.T. Lewis, (Michael Lewis, *Napoleon and his British captives* (London, 1962), and Michael Lewis, *A Social History of the Navy, 1793-1815* (London, 1989); Editions Robert Laffont, (Georges Blond, *La Grande Armée* (Paris, 1979); Pearson Education Ltd, (Antony Brett-James, ed. *Edward Costello. The Peninsular and Waterloo Campaigns* (London, 1967), and Piers Mackesy, *The War in the Mediterranean, 1803-1810* (London, 1957); Mrs Gillian Chandler, (David G. Chandler, *Dictionary of the Napoleonic Wars* (Ware, 1999); Greenhill Books, (David G. Chandler, *On the Napoleonic Wars. Collected Essays* (London, 1994); Ashgate Publishing Ltd, (Patrick Crowhurst, *The French War on Trade: Privateering 1793-1815* (Aldershot, 1989); Oxford University Press, (E.H. Kossman, *The Low Countries* (Clarendon Press, Oxford, 1978); Oxford University Press, New York, (Alan Forrest, *Conscripts and Deserters: The Army and French Society during the Revolution and Empire* (New York, 1989); Merlin Press Ltd, (Louis Garneray, *The French Prisoner* Trans. by Lawrence Wood (London, 1957); Constable & Robinson Ltd, (H.J.C. Grierson, ed. *The Letters of Sir Walter Scott* (Constable & Co. Ltd, London, 1932); Christopher Hibbert, (*The Recollections of Rifleman Harris* (London, 1970), and *A Soldier of the 71st. The Journal of a Soldier in the Highland Light Infantry* (London, 1975); Presses Universitaires de France, Paris, (Georges Lefebvre, *Napoleon* (London, 1969), Vols I and II); Editions Historiques Teissèdre, Paris, (Jean Morvan, *Le Soldat impérial* (Paris, 1904); *Les Carnets de la Sabretache*, Paris, (*Carnet d'Etapes et Souvenirs de Guerre et de Captivité du sergent-major Philippe Beaudoin, de la 31e demi-brigade de ligne* (Paris, 1909); Birlinn Ltd, (I.M.M. MacPhail, *Dumbarton Castle* (Edinburgh, 1979); Cambridge University Press, (B.R. Mitchell and P. Deane, *Abstract of British*

Historical Statistics (Cambridge, 1962); Julian Rathbone, (*Wellington's War* (London, 1984); Tom Donovan Publishing, (Antony Brett-James, *Life in Wellington's Army* (London, 1979); Oman Productions Ltd, (Sir Charles Oman, *A History of the Peninsular War* (Oxford, 1902-1930); The Free Press, a Division of Simon & Schuster Adult Publishing Group, New York, (John R. Elting, *Swords Around a Throne: Napoleon's Grande Armée* (London, 1989) © 1988 by John R. Elting); Archives de l'Etat à Liège, (Emile Fairon and Henri Heuse, *Lettres de Grognards* (Liège and Paris, 1936); W. Bro Walter Glover and the Lodge of Research No.2429, Leicester (John T. Thorp, *French prisoners' lodges: A brief account of fifty lodges and chapters of freemasons, established and conducted by French prisoners of war in England and elsewhere, between 1756 and 1814* (Leicester, 1935); Sir Halley Stewart Trust (*The Life of Alexander Stewart, Prisoner of Napoleon and Preacher of the Gospel, Written by himself to 1815, abridged by Dr Albert Peel to 1874* (London, 1948); the Governor and Company of the Bank of Scotland (Directors' minute book, 24 Feb. 1812); Joy Deacon and Penicuik Historical Society, ('History of Penicuik', n.d., vol. 5: 'Penicuik—Napoleonic Prisoner of War Camp').

Every effort has been made, although without success, to trace the copyright owner of each of the following books from which words or passages have been quoted in the pages below; anyone claiming copyright should get in touch with me: T.K. Derry, *A History of Scandinavia* (George Allen & Unwin, London 1979); B.H. Liddell Hart, ed., *The Letters Of Private Wheeler 1809-1828* (Michael Joseph, London, 1951); Christopher Lloyd, The British Seaman 1200-1860 (Collins, London, 1968); J. Lucas-Dubreton, *Napoléon devant L'Espagne* (Arthème Fayard, Paris, 1946); Basil Thomson, *The Story of Dartmoor Prison* (William Heinemann, London, 1907).

Other persons and institutions in the second group form almost another Grande Armée, and to thank them all by name would take several pages. It is hoped it will not appear invidious to name those, however, to whom or to which particular thanks are due, thus: Monica Gribben, post-graduate student, Department of Scandinavian Studies, University of Edinburgh, who translated Kaald's diary into English for me, and Finn Andersen, former Director, Danish Cultural Institute, Edinburgh, for related help; Sir Gerald Elliot, chairman, The Binks Trust, Hugh McCaig, Glencorse House, Fred Mehlsen, Lasswade, and Dr Maurice Wright, Dalkeith, all of whom made generous donations toward the cost of that translation; and the Scottish Arts Council for an indispensable travel and research grant. The path of research was greatly smoothed throughout by the unfailing courtesy and helpfulness of members of staff of archive centres, libraries and museums in Scotland and elsewhere in Britain, as well as in several countries in Europe some of whose then natives were prisoners of war in Scotland during the Napoleonic Wars. Among numerous other people and institutions owed special thanks for advice, information, funding, practical or other forms of help, are: Iain Anderson, Professor Robert Anderson, Barbara Arkless, Phil Astley, Elspeth Attwooll, MEP, Paul Baillie, Bruno Baudry, Andrew Bethune, Beveridge & Kellas, SSC, John Beveridge, Terry Blundell, Dr Ken Bogle, Dr Alan Borthwick, the Broadcasting Entertainment Cinematograph & Theatre Union, Dr Iain G. Brown, May Buchanan, Tommy Burke, Patrick Cadell, Alan Cameron, Dennis Canavan, MSP, Dr Tom Carbery, Michael Clapham, Dr Martin Clark, Gordon Craig, Sir John Crofton, Stéphane Crouzat, The Rt Hon. The Lord Cullen of Whitekirk, Fiona Cuthill, Kathleen Dalyell, Helen Darling, the late Margaret Deas, Professor I. M. L. Donaldson, Lieutenant Colonel Tobin Duke, Jeremy A.C. Duncan, Dr William Ferguson, the late Dr Bill Findlay, the Franco-Scottish Society of Scotland, Ruth Calvert Fyfe, Trish Godman, MSP, and Dr Norman Godman, Dr Julian Goodare, Professor Tony Goodman, Donald Gorrie, MSP, Olive Graham, Nigel Griffiths, MP, and Mrs Sally Griffiths, Ivor Guild, Dr Hugh Hagan, Sally Harrower, Dr Diana Henderson, James Hogg, Dr Barbara L. H. Horn, Richard Hunter, Norman Irons, Rev. James A.P. Jack, F.P.M. Johnston, Professor V.G. Kiernan, Dorothy Kidd, Janet Klak, Ian Landles, Anne Brit Larsen, The Rt Hon. Mrs Helen Liddell, Baroness Linklater of Butterstone, The Hon. Lord McCluskey, Alan MacDougall, Rev. Alistair McGregor, the late Iain F. Maciver, Hugh K. Mackay, Neil Macvicar, Lord Maxton of Blackwaterfoot, Ailsa Maxwell, Fred Mehlsen, Sheila Millar, Professor Karl Miller, Dr Alex Murdoch, Rt Hon. Lord Ronald King Murray, Ian Nelson, Archie Pacey, Bill Paterson, Dr Irene Paterson, Susan C. Payne, Mrs Ethel D. Philip, Bernadette Pic, Alan Reid, Professor Sian Reynolds, Marion Richardson, Trevor Royle, Colonel Aidan Sprot, Catherine Stihler, MEP, Dr Gavin Strang, MP, Andrew Swanston, Paul Taylor, Jacob Thomsen, Rt Hon. Lord Thomson of Monifeith, the late W.A. Thorburn, Helena Turner Gaffney, UNISON Scotland, Madame Anne-Marie Usher, Phil Watson, Tor Weidling, David Weir, West of Scotland Swiss Club, Dr Richard Wilson. The commitment and skills of Mairi Sutherland, Seán Costello and Tom Johnstone of Birlinn Ltd have been indispensable. Given the size of the book, and the need for a subvention to help meet the costs of its publication, the grant-giving bodies among all those persons and institutions that made donations or awarded grants toward securing publication and which are also owed special thanks are: the Baron Court of Prestoungrange, Scottish Society of the History of Medicine: The Douglas Guthrie Trust, The Binks Trust, The James Thom Howat's Charitable Trust, Scotland Inheritance Fund, Scottish International Education Trust, and The Strathmartine Trust. For the opinions or interpretations expressed in this book, none of those persons or institutions bears any responsibility whatever since that is mine alone, as it is for any sins of commission or omission that may remain in the work.

Finally, without the constant encouragement, patience, and practical help of my wife Sandra, and the hospitality in London provided during the past two decades by my sister-in-law Ruth Campbell, the work would have taken even longer to complete.

Ian MacDougall,
Edinburgh.

1

The First Year of the War, 1803–1804

No sooner had the British government on 18 May 1803 repudiated the Peace of Amiens and declared war on France, and also in effect on France's client state Holland, than prisoners of war began to be taken. Indeed, even before the formal declaration of war French and Dutch ships in British ports were seized on 16 May and their crews made captive. Next day the British Channel fleet set sail to blockade Brest and on 18 May took the first prisoners outside Britain itself—about 80 of the crew of the French naval lugger *Affronteur* who survived an encounter with HMS *Doris* off Ushant, and the crews of two French merchant vessels made prisoner either that day or the next in the bay of Audierne, 25 miles south of Brest. The first prisoners taken into Scotland appear to have been the crew of an unnamed Dutch merchant vessel bound for Leith that was seized by the frigate HMS *Clyde* on 21 May in the Firth of Forth.[1]

Responsibility for dealing with prisoners of war in Britain (and for captive Britons abroad) lay with what was known for short as the Transport Board, a department of the Admiralty. The Board was composed of between five and seven Commissioners for Conducting His Majesty's Transport Service and for the Care and Custody of Prisoners of War. Under the direction of its secretary Alexander M'Leay the Board's Office in London was staffed by clerks and accountants whose numbers grew in the course of the war from about 50 to 90.[2] They, along with the Board's appointed agents at the prisoner of war depots and parole towns, carried out the Board's policies, as directed or approved by their Right Honourable the Lords Commissioner of the Admiralty, concerning the accommodation, guarding, feeding, clothing, exchanging, hospital provision, transfers, escapes, and innumerable other aspects of administering what in the course of the decade of war from 1803 became the tens of thousands of captives held in various parts of Britain including, particularly from 1811, Scotland. In earlier wars, including the French Revolutionary Wars, that work had been carried out by what was popularly known as the Sick and Hurt Office of the Admiralty—more formally titled the Commissioners for taking Care of Sick and Wounded Seamen and for exchanging Prisoners of War. But in 1799 responsibility for prisoners of war had been transferred to the newly created Transport Board and remained with it until the Board's abolition soon after the Napoleonic Wars, in 1817. The large letters TO (for Transport Office) indeed were stamped on the special clothing issued to prisoners of war in Britain, other than parole prisoners.[3]

As barbed wire was not invented until half a century after the Napoleonic Wars, the Transport Board from the outbreak of war in May 1803 had to find what the *Edinburgh Evening Courant* described as 'receptacles' that were or could be made sufficiently secure to hold the vast majority of those who during the following decade became prisoners of war in Britain.[4] That vast majority of prisoners were private soldiers, non-commissioned and warrant officers of the French and French allied armies, and the men and youths of equivalent rank in their navies, merchant navies and privateering ships—privately owned ships licensed by their governments to attack British merchant or other shipping. A small minority of the prisoners of war, less than ten per cent of the total, were parole prisoners—commissioned officers in the French or French allied armies and navies, or officers of the most senior rank from captured merchant ships or privateers, or civilians considered eligible for parole. Parole prisoners were sent to specified towns in certain parts of Britain, including Scotland, upon giving a written undertaking not to attempt escape. In those towns they lived in civilian lodgings, although subject to a nightly curfew, restriction on their movements to within a mile or so of the town, and certain other limitations on their freedom. It is intended that parole prisoners in those Scots towns where they spent their captivity will be the subject of a forthcoming volume.

For the mass, or rank and file, of the prisoners of war held in England two sorts of 'receptacles' were provided by the Transport Board. One was the hulks, old wooden warships (including some captured from enemy fleets) no longer otherwise usable by the Royal Navy and anchored in line astern at the naval bases of Chatham, Portsmouth and Plymouth. The use of such hulks to hold prisoners of war had begun in the Seven Years' War, 1756-63, when the *Royal Oak* had served that purpose first at Plymouth, later at Portsmouth. Greater use of hulks had been made by the British authorities during the American War of Independence, 1775-83, when no fewer than 42 ships holding prisoners of war were anchored at one time or another at Long Island and in the Hudson and East Rivers. But it was in the French Revolutionary Wars from 1793 that increasingly large numbers of prisoners of war were held on the hulks moored at the three bases on the southern coasts of England itself—eventually six hulks at Chatham, nine at Portsmouth and one at Plymouth. On the resumption of war in May 1803 the Transport Board at first sent prisoners on board two hulks, the *Bienfaisant* and the *Europa*, at Plymouth. By the end of the Napoleonic Wars in 1814-15 thousands of French and other prisoners of war had been held captive at one or other of those three naval bases, where there were in use for the purpose at one stage or another no fewer than 30 hulks.[5] Hulks were never used in those wars to hold prisoners of war in Scotland.

The second kind of 'receptacle' in England for rank and file prisoners of war from 1803, as before then, consisted of prisons—or depots, as they were termed—on land. In Scotland that was the only kind of 'receptacle' used. There were two sorts of land prison or depot: first, old castles (Portchester Castle at Portsmouth, for example) or town jails (as at Liverpool) or other existing buildings considered suitable which were pressed into service for holding prisoners of war; and, second, depots (such as Norman Cross in Huntingdonshire and Stapleton at Bristol) that had been specifically built in the later 18th century to hold prisoners of war. There were no such purpose-built depots in 1803 in Scotland. During previous wars in the 18th century, including the French Revolutionary Wars, prisoners of war had languished in Edinburgh Castle or, in the case of some parole prisoners in the later 1790s, at Peebles.[6]

Within a month from the resumption of war in May 1803 the Transport Board had appointed, or in some cases reappointed, agents to administer on its behalf the hulks and four land prisons or depots in England at Norman Cross, Stapleton, Liverpool, and Forton at Portsmouth into which prisoners of war began to trudge.[7] As its agent at Edinburgh, the Transport Board recommended to the Admiralty on 9 June 1803 the reappointment of Malcolm Wright. Wright, an Edinburgh merchant and city magistrate, had first been appointed government agent for prisoners of war there in the mid-1790s. After some enquiries by the Admiralty about Wright's previous salary and about the number of prisoners of war held captive in Edinburgh Castle in the French Revolutionary Wars, he was formally reappointed on 1 September. William Ker (or Kerr) of Kerfield, a distiller and former provost of the town, who had been the Board's agent at Peebles for parole prisoners during the French Revolutionary Wars, was likewise reappointed there on 23 August.[8] At Greenock, where on 21 July the first two prisoners to land came from a French vessel captured by a British privateer, David Colquhoun, a surgeon, had already written to the Transport Board a fortnight earlier, applying for appointment as its agent there. He was told the Board was not then in a position to grant his request, but after further correspondence between Colquhoun, the Board, Malcolm Wright, and Captain Tatham, senior naval officer at Greenock, concerning those two French prisoners (a merchant ship captain and his nephew aged 15), and also a further three from the West Indies landed three months later, Colquhoun was formally appointed in mid-October by the Board as its agent at the port and instructed to send all further prisoners landed there to Malcolm Wright, its agent at Edinburgh.[9]

In the first weeks, however, following the resumption of war in May 1803, the Admiralty decided to change its previous policy on holding rank and file prisoners of war in Scotland. Prisoners eligible for parole who were landed in Scotland from ships putting in at Leith, Greenock or other ports north of the Border were to be sent as before to Peebles. But prisoners—the great majority—not entitled to parole who were captured off the coasts of Scotland or otherwise landed in Scotland were not to be held in Edinburgh Castle as in previous wars. They were all to be sent to the purpose-built depot at Norman Cross in Huntingdonshire. At the end of July, however, as the number of prisoners of war arriving in Scotland by sea began to increase, the Transport Board again sought to persuade the Admiralty of the need to establish a depot at Edinburgh. Their lordships of the Admiralty allowed themselves reluctantly to be persuaded. On 4 August they conceded to the Transport Board 'that if it be found absolutely necessary some temporary depot must be made at Edinburgh.'[10]

The Board immediately directed Malcolm Wright, its agent at Edinburgh, to report what accommodation at the Castle could at once be prepared for prisoners of war, and at what cost, and also 'whether any other place more suitable for a Prison could be procured and on what terms.' The Board wrote again to Wright on 23 August, urging him to respond promptly to the latter question. He did so two days later, enclosing a copy of a letter he had written to Lieutenant General Richard Vyse, army commander in North Britain, about accommodation in Edinburgh Castle, and of a reply from a senior officer of the Barrack Department, which was responsible for army quarters there as elsewhere. Though this latter reply appears not to survive in the archives it clearly amounted to a refusal by the army authorities to grant accommodation at the Castle for prisoners of war.[11] Wright also enclosed a separate offer he had received for using, at a price of £2,500, Queensberry House in the Canongate, Edinburgh, as a depot for prisoners of war. The House, built in the 17th century, had been sold in 1801 to the government by the Duke of Queensberry. The Board decided at least for the time being to ignore this last proposal.[12]

Other proposals, or rumours of proposals, then circulating about further historic buildings in Scotland being pressed into service as depots were reported in the *Caledonian Mercury*. 'It is, we understand,' the paper reported in jingoistic overtones on 5 September, 'in agitation to convert the palaces of Linlithgow and Falkland, Craigmillar Castle and Queensberry House in Canongate into receptacles for prisoners of war. "To what base uses may we not return?" It is grating to the feelings of a Scotchman to see the ancient abodes of his monarchs converted into "dens of thieves". Linlithgow, the birth place of Mary [Queen of Scots], and Craigmillar, her favourite residence, correspond only with the residence of such vermin.'[13] This was not the last occasion during the Napoleonic Wars when the feelings of at least some

Scots were to be 'grated' by similar proposals for the creation of prisoner of war depots.

Simultaneously other issues, often to recur during the war, were arising in Scotland about prisoners of war, and another possible place of confinement for them had been suggested: Fort George, on the shores of the Moray Firth and nine miles east of Inverness.[14] On 24 August some 87 prisoners of war at first reported to be Dutch had been marched into Fort George after being landed by a Liverpool privateer fifty miles away on the west coast at Ullapool. The Admiralty promptly informed the Transport Board on 2 September that 'instructions had been given to all [privateers] not to land any prisoners in future, under the usual Penalties, excepting at the regular Depots.' After further reports from Fort George and correspondence between the army authorities there, the Transport Board, the Admiralty and Malcolm Wright, it was established that only two of the 87 were in fact Dutch, 'one of whom is blind, and that the rest, excepting the Negroes, are subjects of Neutral States.' Denmark (of which kingdom Norway was then part) and Prussia chiefly, but also Sweden and several small German states, soon proved to be the neutral states concerned. Short of men to crew His Britannic Majesty's warships, the Admiralty told the Transport Board that it 'desired that the Neutral Prisoners therein mentioned should be encouraged to enter into HM's Service.' Lieutenant John Flinn, Royal Navy, the Board's agent for transports at Leith, was therefore sent up to Fort George and succeeded in persuading seven of the prisoners (from Hamburg, Bremen, Emden and Danzig) to enter HM's Service. Flinn reported, however, 'that no more could be prevailed upon to enter after the receipt of a letter from the Danish Vice Consul promising to apply for the release of such of them as are natives of Denmark.' Shortly afterwards a similar intervention on behalf of prisoners from a neutral state held at Fort George was made by the Russian consul general.

Flinn's attempt to persuade these prisoners at Fort George to volunteer themselves into the Royal Navy was the first of innumerable similar attempts by the naval and army authorities in Scotland during the Napoleonic Wars. Flinn's report to the Transport Board on 3 October gives an unusual, if not unique, glimpse of the arguments used. '… every encouragement was held out to the men,' he wrote. 'The probability of a long confinement, a very severe winter, and at the best very little comfort to be found in a prison, contrasted with friendship, good food or provisions, comfortable lodgings, good pay, and a chance of prize money, and when paid off money in their pockets to assist their friends on their return home, which could not be expected coming out of prison; every argument was made use of to induce them to enlist into His Majesty's Service …'[15]

In an attempt evidently to steer the Admiralty and the Transport Board away from their wish to recover their previous use of part of Edinburgh Castle for prisoners of war, General Richard Vyse, army commander in North Britain, with the approval of General Robert Brownrigg, Quartermaster-General at the War Office, proposed to the Admiralty on 25 September that Fort George could be fitted up to hold prisoners of war. The Transport Board commissioners, however, in their response on 1 October to the Admiralty, fired a broadside at the generals' proposal and sank it: '... it appears to us that on account of the great distance of Fort George from Leith, where prisoners are usually carried in His Majesty's ships, and from Greenock, to which port some prisoners are occasionally brought from the West Indies in merchant vessels, the constant movement of prisoners to that garrison from those places would be attended with very great difficulties and extraordinary expense ...' Moreover, the Board argued, if exchanges of prisoners of war took place as in the French Revolutionary Wars, their lordships of the Admiralty would realise 'that the expense and inconvenience which must inevitably attend the conveyance of prisoners in small numbers, and sometimes singly, from Fort George to France, would not by any means be compensated by the advantages held forth by Lieutenant General Vyse of the prisoners being more securely guarded and having less communication with the inhabitants at Fort George than in the neighbourhood of Edinburgh.' The Board added that all its agents had very strict instructions to allow no one except the officer of the guard to communicate with prisoners of war. Although in autumn 1803 a few and diminishing number of prisoners—probably those remaining from the original 87 who had arrived in August from Ullapool—continued to be held at Fort George until the last of them were repatriated in December, no more was heard for several years afterward of the Fort as a possible prisoner of war depot.[16]

If the Transport Board had won the argument over Fort George it was meantime losing the more important and urgent one with the army authorities about recovering the use of part of Edinburgh Castle for holding prisoners of war. In the Castle French and French allied prisoners of war had been confined during all the wars in at least the half century before 1803. At the end of the Seven Years' War in 1763, for instance, some 500 captives, many of them from privateering ships, had been repatriated from the Castle to France; and during the American War of Independence about 1,000 American, French, Spanish and Dutch, as well as Irish, prisoners had languished in the Castle at one time or another between 1778 and 1782. During the French Revolutionary Wars at least 1,100 prisoners of war in aggregate had been confined there between 1796 and 1801.[17]

In July 1799, toward the end of the French Revolutionary Wars, Ambrose Serle, one of the Transport Board commissioners, had inspected the prisoners' quarters at Edinburgh Castle. His report to the Board was critical of Malcolm Wright, its agent at Edinburgh, for his failure to carry out some of his duties. About the conditions in which the prisoners were confined Serle was scathing.

'The Depot,' he reported, 'is divided into two parts, the one consisting of ancient caverns or cells under the Castle, and the other of the vaults, probably intended for stores, under the new Barracks lately erected within the precincts of the Fortress for the reception of troops. The cells under the Castle are for the most part miserable holes, fit only for the reception of the worst malefactors, and are dark, long and narrow, capable of admitting little light and air and, in their present state, very offensive if not dangerous in point of health. The vaults under the barracks are less noxious indeed but, in my opinion, too subterranean for the long confinement of men, having only a narrow front open to the air, and filled at this time beyond all proportion to their size. The airing grounds appropriate to both of these Depots, though well-exposed on account of their height, being elevated upon the Castle rock at a great distance from the lower ground, are much too small and narrow, and especially when the bedding and cloathes are brought out to the wind, for the common exercises necessary for health. It is, upon the whole, not only an unpleasant but an inconvenient situation; and the best that can be said of it is, the Government pays no rent for it, though the repairs and alterations which have been made (chiefly under the direction of the military, who, I understand, are not over much pleased with our tenants) have rendered the place sufficiently expensive.' Serle reported that these alterations would cost the Transport Board the then considerable sum of at least £1,400, part of that cost being attributable to Malcolm Wright's failure to obtain further estimates for additional work carried out or to seek the approval of the Board for it. 'With respect to the present crowded state of these prisons,' continued Serle, 'I am decidedly of opinion with the Agent and others upon the spot, that some measures should be taken, as soon as may be, either for the entire removal of the prisoners or of such a proportion of them as may give relief to the rest. The number now amounts to nearly 750; but if the place were fitter than it is for the reception of such men, there ought to be, upon a fair calculation, not more than 400 for both of the Depots within the Castle, at least for continuance.'[18]

Having expended so much money on making those parts of the Castle more suitable, or less unsuitable, for confining a smaller number of prisoners of war than in the preceding wars, the Transport Board was therefore chagrined when on the resumption of war in 1803 it found its expectation of again being able to confine prisoners there was rebuffed by the army authorities. With the need for a depot in Scotland for rank and file prisoners of war becoming more urgent week by week as their numbers began to increase, the Board nonetheless for some time remained hopeful that its arguments for being allowed to use parts of the Castle would prevail.

The refusal in late August 1803 by the Barrack Department to agree to the Board's request was certainly not accepted by the Transport Board as a final decision. In early September the Board wrote to General Vyse expressing the hope that 'he would afford Mr Wright every facility in his power in procuring a place proper for the confinement of prisoners-of-war, and that he would allow such prisoners as might in the meantime be brought to Edinburgh to be confined in some of the appartments occupied by prisoners during the late war.' Nor did a statement, probably released by the army authorities and widely published in identical language in the press on 22 September, that 'No prisoners are in future to be confined in the Castle', finally crush the hopes of the Transport Board.[19] As late as January 1804 the Board, confronted with a growing number of rank and file captives in Scotland and the continued absence of a permanent depot there in which to confine them, made another effort to regain its former use of parts of the Castle. On or about 8 January the Board wrote to General the Earl of Moira, a distinguished soldier, close adviser to the Prince of Wales, and by then successor to General Vyse as commander of the Forces in North Britain, to try to enlist his support for its being granted even temporary use of some of the quarters in the Castle that had previously held prisoners of war.[20] But the Board's efforts failed. So apart from holding overnight, or otherwise briefly, prisoners of war landed at Leith or Greenock and in transit elsewhere, Edinburgh Castle did not become a depot for captives during the Napoleonic Wars until as late as 1810-11.

The growing number of prisoners of war—even if as yet they were only a trickle into Scotland, not a flood as they became later on in the war—had, however, to be confined somewhere in or about Edinburgh and Leith, if not in the Castle. The place of confinement found in later September for the Board by its agent Malcolm Wright had already been suggested in Ambrose Serle's report of July 1799. This was the Edinburgh bridewell or gaol. Serle, in arguing then that the Castle should contain not more than about 400 prisoners of war, had urged there was a need, if the war continued, for a larger depot in Scotland, which would not only prevent 'the danger of epidemical disorders from close and crowded confinement' (as in the Castle) but also might prove easier and less costly to maintain. He had therefore visited the Edinburgh bridewell. 'I acknowledge,' Serle reported, 'that it appears to me one of the completest structures … for a place of confinement that I have yet seen. It is so disposed that a person from the Centre can perceive every thing that is going on in the prisoners' compartments at the same instant. There is a house for the keeper, convenient rooms for cooking, outhouses, and other conveniences for an hospital; Guards and stores. It could contain … nearly 2,000 prisoners and is surrounded by a wall, with a parapet for the walking of the guard, of considerable height. Its situation is upon an eminence, at a little distance from the town, and has convenient space for airing grounds within itself.' Serle added that the bridewell 'was built at a great expence by the city upon a scale beyond calculation for the number of occupants who now do not exceed 40, and appears ... to have been adopted upon the plan of philanthropy proposed by the late Mr Howard, from the striking ingenuity of the scheme, and the warmth of the moment, rather than from considerations of absolute emergency.'[21] Serle had at that time therefore told Malcolm Wright, the Board's agent and himself a city magistrate, to sound out the lord provost about the cost if the Board were to decide to seek to hire the bridewell as a prisoner of war depot. A rent of £500 a year for two years (which Serle believed might be reduced to £400) was consequently proposed by the city authorities, with an option for the Board to retain the building as long as it wanted it, subject to giving three months' notice. The French Revolutionary Wars ended, however, and the prisoners of war in Edinburgh Castle were repatriated before any further steps were taken to use the bridewell as a depot.

The Edinburgh bridewell was first mentioned again as a possible depot in a letter of 17 September 1803 from Malcolm Wright to the Transport Board. Wright explained that, asked to take charge of some prisoners landed at Leith from the frigate HMS *Ethalion*, he had applied for permission to confine them in the bridewell. Wright wrote again next day to report that the sheriff had agreed that part of the bridewell be given over free of charge to the temporary confinement of prisoners of war. The Transport Board approved of Wright's arrangements and instructed him to give each prisoner a hammock and one blanket and to provide them with food in accordance with his standing instructions as agent. The appointment of a clerk for Wright was also approved. He was Alexander Fraser, who had been Wright's clerk during the French Revolutionary Wars. Two turnkeys or jailers, Peter Cameron and Alexander Clark, were also appointed as assistants to Wright at the bridewell. Both these men had served under Wright as turnkeys at Edinburgh Castle in the preceding war.[22]

Not a great deal is known about the prisoners of war who from the second half of September were confined in the Edinburgh bridewell, even less about the conditions of their captivity during the six months the bridewell served as a depot. If only one blanket was issued to each captive, as the Transport Board instructed, then all of them must have suffered a cold autumn and winter. Malcolm Wright contracted with local suppliers to provide to the prisoners of war rations that cost 6d. a head per day.[23] One of the few other scraps of information surviving about the regime at the bridewell and which illustrated the kind of petty departmental disagreements that often arose from the administration of the prisoners of war, was when Wright reported he had received a formal complaint, presumably from the army authorities, 'for not providing the Guard with Fire, Benches and Blankets', and that he had been obliged to provide a fire for them 'although not regularly entitled thereto until the 1st of October.'[24]

More significantly, the Transport Board ordered Wright at the end of September 'to permit Major Halket to recruit from among the prisoners under his care.' As a result seven Dutchmen were released a week later into Halket's corps. But the Board approved Wright's refusal to release some prisoners enlisted by Halket's recruiting agent, 'they being the Crews of 2 Ostend Fishing Vessels and chiefly Flemings.' Simultaneously, Wright informed the Board that ten of the prisoners 'were willing to enter into the Navy on receiving a Bounty.'[25]

A few years later Louis Simond, a Frenchman who had lived for over twenty years in the United States of America, visited the Edinburgh bridewell and left a description of it that adds a little to Ambrose Serle's in 1799. Simond says the bridewell was a semi-circular building, seven storeys high, each storey containing fourteen cells, all of them open toward a common centre 'which is like a great well, open from top to bottom. A bow window, with lattices, repeated at each storey, overlooks them all, and nothing can be done by the prisoners without being seen ... they [i.e., the civil prisoners Simond saw, not the prisoners of war there in 1803-04] work solitary, and in silence, in these 98 cells; and at night sleep in other little rooms behind them ... This tower, or rather section of a tower, is lighted by a sky light, and well ventilated. No bad smells, no noise, great order, all as well as possible...'[26]

Between September 1803 and the end of March 1804, when they were all transferred to a new depot opened ten miles south of Edinburgh, it appears that 105 prisoners of war were confined in the bridewell.[27] All of them were seamen. The first 67 of them were marched into the bridewell on 19 September. They, and 14 more out of a further 27 who arrived there successively in smaller groups by 3 October, had been captured at sea by HMS *Ethalion*, which landed them at Leith. Several of the other prisoners arrived in the bridewell after spending some time as captives on board a prison ship in Jamaica, and some of them had been obliged to help man the British merchant ships on which they had been brought from Jamaica.[28]

The melancholy distinction of being the first prisoner of war in Scotland during the Napoleonic Wars entered in the 'French' General Entry Book or register for the bridewell belonged to Jean Jacques Andriesen, a seaman captured on the merchant ship *Elizabeth* in the North Sea on 11 July 1803. Andriesen remained a prisoner of war in Scotland until he escaped (not from the bridewell but from Greenlaw) seven years later in December 1810.[29]

That no fewer than eleven of the 105 prisoners of war in the bridewell escaped during its six months' use as a depot indicates it was a far from secure place. The first escapers from it—the first rank and file prisoners to escape in Scotland during the Napoleonic Wars—were five Belgian seamen. Their case provides an early illustration of routine procedures followed by the

Transport Board and its agents in dealing with escapes. The five men, two of them brothers, escaped from the bridewell on the morning of 25 October. That same day Malcolm Wright inserted an advertisement in the *Edinburgh Evening Courant*, thus: 'FRENCH PRISONERS. Whereas the five Seamen, Prisoners of War, named and described below, effected their escape from the place of confinement here this morning, THIS IS TO GIVE NOTICE That a Reward of One Guinea, over and above all necessary and reasonable expenses, will be paid by the Agent, for retaking and bringing back each of these prisoners. Names and Descriptions are: JEAN DE RYCKE, native of Nieuport, 39 years of age, 5 feet 7 inches high; PAUL DE RYCKE, brother of the former, 37 years of age, and nearly of the same stature; JACQUES DECHAINE, native of Ostend, 34 years of age, 5 feet 8 inches high, or thereby; PHILLIP WAELLINCK, native of Ostend, 20 years of age, about 5 feet 6 inches high; PETER VOLKERYERX, native of Ostend, 22 years of age, about 5 feet 6 inches high. These men are habited as sailors, and all of them talk more or less English; and as they had lately expressed a strong desire to enter into our navy, it is thought that unless they can immediately get away in some neutral vessel, their next object will really be to get on board a tender or ship of war, passing themselves off for subjects of neutral powers.'

None of these five escapers appears, in the absence of any entry to that effect in the General Entry Book, to have been recaptured.[30] Of the other six prisoners of war who escaped from the bridewell—two on the night of 3-4 December, two on 24 February, one on 4 March and one on 16 March—all but one were recaptured. The escaper on 16 March, a merchant vessel junior officer named Henry Le Hure, whose attempt appears to have resulted from the rejection of his application for parole, was punished on recapture by being sent to the hulks at Chatham.[31] Of the two escapers on 3-4 December one was Charles Cottier or Cotier, a seaman, aged 17. Cottier was recaptured. His death in captivity by shooting three years later became a *cause célèbre*.[32] As in the case of the five Belgians, an advertisement was inserted by Malcolm Wright in the *Edinburgh Evening Courant* on 5 December about the escape of Cottier and his fellow prisoner Jean Lisessoone, also a seaman, aged 48. On this occasion, as usually on later such occasions, not only were the heights of the escapers given, but also fuller physical descriptions. Thus Cottier was described as having 'black hair, brown eyes, round visage, good complexion, stout person', and Lisessoone 'dark brown hair, grey eyes, long visage, pale complexion, stout person, and much pitted with the small pox.' It was added that 'Both speak English tolerably well, and there is reason to believe they are yet lurking about Leith, Cottier being seen in North Leith yesterday afternoon.' When Joseph Gascourin, a seaman, escaped from the bridewell 'by leaping the wall' on 4 March the sentry on duty 'fired his piece, but missed him, and notwithstanding he was immediately pursued, he got clear off.' But not for long—Gascourin was recaptured and reconfined in the bridewell two days later.[33]

The bridewell had been in use as a depot for only three weeks when Malcolm Wright reported to the Transport Board an offer to lease for use as a depot at a rent of £190 per annum for two and a half years some premises at Drumsheugh in Edinburgh. The Board told Wright two and a half years was too short a period and to ask whether the lease could be extended and also to estimate the cost of preparing the premises as a depot. The following month Wright reported to the Board 'the result of his enquiries for a place proper for a prison and recommended the erection of wooden barracks for the purpose....' The Board sent no answer.[34]

Early in December the Board asked Wright to find out whether the entire bridewell could be let to the government for the duration of the war, and if so on what terms. Not only did the commissioners for the bridewell refuse, however, to let it for the duration but also they told Wright that the Board's use of part of the building for prisoners of war would have to be discontinued.[35] It was at that point that the Board sought the intervention of Lord Moira in the hope it could recover use of part of the Castle.

A solution to the Board's difficulty in finding a more permanent depot for the prisoners of war was, however, at last in sight. At the end of January the Board instructed Wright to lease the old mansion house at Greenlaw, ten miles south of Edinburgh near the village of Penicuik, on the terms offered by its owner, Robert Trotter of Castlelaw, to send the Board promptly a plan of the premises, and 'to cause the Buildings to be prepared with as little Delay as possible' at an estimated cost of £750.[36] By mid-February the lease had been duly signed. A house at Roslin, two miles from Greenlaw, suitable as a residence for the agent, was agreed on at a rent of £65 a year. And on 31 March, escorted by a detachment of the Inverness and Argyllshire militia, all seventy or so remaining prisoners of war in the Edinburgh bridewell were marched out from the city to the new depot at Greenlaw.[37]

2

Greenlaw

The decision in 1804 to make Greenlaw mansion house a depot for prisoners of war had been foreshadowed in his report to the Transport Board by Commissioner Ambrose Serle in July 1799. Serle had argued that if Edinburgh Castle and the city bridewell proved unable to house the prisoners landed in Scotland then the Board would either have to ship them to King's Lynn on the Norfolk coast and from there send them 35 miles inland to Norman Cross depot, 'or we must engage some additional place of safety in the neighbourhood of Edinburgh, which perhaps would be more durably expensive to Government though a more certain or continual reception for prisoners.'

From its opening in the spring of 1804 until the influx to Scotland in the winter of 1810-11 of much larger numbers of prisoners of war Greenlaw remained the only 'continual' depot for rank and file prisoners north of the Border.[1]

The old Greenlaw mansion house appeared well situated as a place of confinement for prisoners landed from the sea at Leith and, to a lesser extent, Greenock and occasionally other Scots ports. Only eight miles south of the centre of Edinburgh and ten from Leith, Greenlaw was within easy marching distance for prisoners of war landed at the port or sent on after an overnight staging at Edinburgh Castle. Those miles, conversely, might prove a hurdle for any escapers fleeing north from Greenlaw to surmount before they might find any refuge in the wynds and closes of Edinburgh or on a neutral ship at Leith. More important, Greenlaw appeared able to hold considerably more prisoners than the Board had been allowed to confine in the Edinburgh bridewell, and perhaps at least as many as it had hoped to hold in Edinburgh Castle. And Greenlaw could also form a staging post for the much smaller number of prisoners of war sent on parole to Peebles, a dozen miles south of Penicuik.

Although Greenlaw mansion house was demolished after the Napoleonic Wars four contemporary sketches of it as a prisoner of war depot survive. Two of these are of the outside of the house. One, probably by Robert Reid, crown architect in Scotland, shows the mansion to have been L-shaped, the longer wing with two storeys and the shorter with three. Behind the junction of the two wings there stands also a short abutment or wing from the three-storey section. A double palisade, the one separated from the other by perhaps twenty yards, surrounds the house. In the exercise yard or airing ground formed by the inner palisade in front of the house a dozen prisoners are depicted. Between the outer palisade and what appear to be encircling stone walls three (probably of four) sentry boxes and several armed sentries are visible. On the outside of the walls are five other figures who may represent officers of the guard or depot officials. In the background, beyond the mansion house, is a long line of trees, and within one of the stone walled enclosures young trees also appear to be growing.[2]

The accuracy of that sketch of the house appears confirmed by a second one drawn in August 1809 by Paul Andreas Kaald, a Norwegian privateer captain then a prisoner of war at Greenlaw. Kaald's sketch is a close-up of what is evidently the front of the house, with its heavily barred windows and its two doors opening on to the airing ground. Part of the inner palisade is shown and so are two lamps on the top of poles perhaps eight or nine feet in height, one in front of the larger of the two doors, the other at the inner palisade to the left of the three-storey wing of the house. At most of the windows prisoners are depicted looking out through the heavy bars. Outside the smaller of the two doors is what seems to be a pile of coal. In the small part of the airing ground or exercise yard that is visible are shown wooden trestles and troughs in which the prisoners washed their clothes, and also a clothes line with some washing on it. A dozen figures, presumably all prisoners, and all evidently wearing broad brimmed and high crowned hats, stroll or go about their various tasks in the airing ground or in the narrow space enclosed by what appears to be an open paling fence between the airing ground and the house itself.

A third surviving depiction of part of Greenlaw depot is a faded sketch by Robert Reid, dated July 1813 (by which time very substantial extensions to the depot were being made), showing what seems to be a section of the airing ground, bounded by iron railings, a line of four sentry boxes with their armed sentries, and the 'military way' between the railings and the sentry boxes. In the airing ground about thirty prisoners of war are depicted at recreation, one with a pet dog, one evidently dancing, one throwing a ball in the air, and further off a group of five who appear to be playing cricket.

Finally, a unique sketch by Captain Paul Andreas Kaald in 1809 shows the inside of one of the rooms in Greenlaw depot. Seated in the room are six named prisoners (including Kaald himself at one of the two heavily barred windows) engaged in various tasks or pastimes. Pots and pans and prisoners' boxes or chests, and other items, rest on the floor, items of clothing, etc., hang on the walls, and several hammocks are shown suspended from posts that rise from floor to ceiling.[3]

Some of the features of the house and its grounds can be gathered also from the tack or lease agreed between the owner, Robert Trotter of Castlelaw, and the Transport Board. The lease allowed the Board to convert the property into a depot from Candlemas term 1804 until Whitsun term 1809 and, if the war was not by then ended, afterward until the Whitsun after the signing of a formal peace treaty. Trotter agreed to lease 'All and whole the Mansion House of Greenlaw, with the stables and coach house, poultry house and washing house, as also the garden and small plot of grass immediately round the house, and the ground betwixt the garden and the house, together with the four parks or fields called the Cow Park, the Wood Park, the Dovecot Park (but not the strip of planting at the bottom thereof) and Pond Park; and lastly the two houses at the gate with the yard presently possessed by David Robertson and Alexander Henderson.' The area leased appears to have amounted to about 42 acres.[4] The lease (later described by the Admiralty law agent in Scotland as containing some 'very singular clauses and obligations')[5] reserved to Trotter and his heirs the right to 'carry a level under ground for the purpose of drawing the coal or minerals on the other parts of his estate', and gave him full power to 'set down pits or shanks as air holes on any part of the lands hereby set … but the same shall not be done on any part of the premises where any buildings or enclosures for airing the prisoners or other purposes shall be erected by the … Commissioners'. All trees, wood and under-wood and shrubs on the lands were also reserved to Trotter, 'with liberty at all times to top, dress, fell, cut down and root up the same.' The Transport Board was debarred from ploughing or digging up the four parks named, which were let for 'the peculiar uses and purposes of the Depot or for pasture only …'[6] The lease asserted that the mansion house 'in its Roof, Walls, Timber, Plaster and inside finishing is all at present in good and sufficient repair, and had all been lately papered and painted.' The Commissioners consequently undertook at the end of the lease to 'reinstate and leave the same in the like good order and condition', and likewise the stables and two houses at the gate, which are also said to be in good condition. The Commissioners were not permitted to 'slap, break down or remove any of the stone and lime walls or subdivisions of the mansion house' without first securing Trotter's permission, and any alterations made must be 'exactly replaced' at the end of the lease. Finally, Trotter agreed that wherever there were no existing buildings or trees the Transport Board could build barracks or buildings found necessary to further accommodate prisoners of war at the depot, 'which Depot it is hereby expressly stipulated shall not exceed at any time three thousand Prisoners' without Trotter's consent to a further extension.[7] Later correspondence between the depot agent and the Transport Board refers to 'the Road to the Pond where the prisoners fetch their water.'[8]

The old mansion house, where troops of Prince Charles Edward Stuart had been billeted during the Jacobite rebellion in 1745, soon began to contain more prisoners of war than the original 70 or so who arrived on 31 March 1804 from the Edinburgh bridewell. The first newcomer was Louis Anghen, a seaman, captured in the Mediterranean off Cartagena on board the privateer *L'Espérance*. Anghen was brought first to Hull then sent to Newcastle, and from there he arrived at Greenlaw on 1 May.[9]

Six weeks later the next batch of French prisoners arrived, this time six of them. One of the six proved especially notable: Philippe Beaudoin or Baudouin. Beaudoin was one among only a tiny handful of prisoners of war in Scotland who are known to have kept a diary, or at least a note, of events and of observations during their captivity or to have recorded recollections in later years. Taken prisoner off Cuba in April that year by a British naval squadron while he was on board a troop ship sailing back to France from Saint Domingo, Beaudoin, a sergeant-major in the 31st infantry demi-brigade, was landed with some other prisoners at Greenock. Marched under guard from Greenock on 6 June he and five other captive French soldiers—a sergeant and four privates—passed through Port Glasgow and Renfrew and spent the night in custody in a militia barracks in Glasgow. 'What is striking,' Beaudoin observed in his diary about his passage to Glasgow, '... is that the women walk about almost always bare-footed. The number of beautiful women is not great ... besides, in general they have mouths like ovens.' Marching eastwards through Airdrie and Bathgate the prisoners arrived on 9 June at Edinburgh Castle, where they spent the night in the guard house. Next day they arrived at Greenlaw depot. 'This house,' Beaudoin noted in his diary, 'is surrounded by two rows of palisades, with sentries all around; at the side is a little wood that sometimes benefits escapers. We entered the said prison at two o'clock in the afternoon; we were lodged among the Dutch [prisoners].' Beaudoin and his five companions from Greenock became respectively Nos 98 to 103 in the depot's register of French prisoners.[10]

Beaudoin's reference to Dutch prisoners illustrates a distinctive feature of the administration of Greenlaw as a depot under Malcolm Wright, its agent from 1804 to 1810-11. Greenlaw had, or by 1810-11 had come to have, eight separate registers or General Entry Books for prisoners confined there who were ostensibly grouped in one or other of four main nationalities. It had three successive registers apparently listing French prisoners, two Dutch registers, one Spanish, and two Danish (which included many Norwegians). But some of the entries are duplicated between one register and another. For example, the first 351 men listed in the second Danish register for 1808-11 were already listed in the first register for 1807-11. The confusion is enlarged by a register, the first 38 pages of which list 214 Dutch prisoners said to be in captivity at Edinburgh, of whom the first 97 constitute also all those listed in a second Dutch register said to be of prisoners at Greenlaw. In fact, the first 13 of the 97 arrived in custody on 29 September 1803 and the 14th on 14 February 1804—so these 14 had originally been held in the Edinburgh bridewell; whereas of the remaining 83, one had arrived at Greenlaw on 11 May 1804, 77 on 16 May, and five on 9 August 1804. Information in the Greenlaw registers has therefore to be treated with particular caution.[11]

Nonetheless there is no question but that the number of prisoners arriving at Greenlaw increased steadily, if not spectacularly, between 1804 and 1811. Sometimes they arrived singly. Examples of the latter were Pierre Corbeau, a seaman, who was marched into Greenlaw on 19 September 1804, having been captured in Demerara in South America; and Pierre Gerrin, alias Jean Brilbord, also a seaman, who entered Greenlaw in December that year, having been 'Taken in the North Sea on Board a British Coals Vessel Captured by a Privateer of Flushing and sent to Leith.' Sometimes they came in twos and threes or small groups of a dozen or so, such as ten who arrived on 7 October 1806: 'One Boy and nine Sailors, Taken in the West Indies at different Times, Particulars not received.'[12]

But sometimes almost entire crews of captured ships trudged into Greenlaw in those years. That was the fate of 77 of the crew of the Dutch 16-gun brig *Union*, for example, captured on 10 May 1804 in the North Sea near Bergen by the frigate HMS *Ethalion*. Most of the 77 were landed at Leith and under an escort of the Argyllshire militia marched out on the 16th to Greenlaw. A further 13 members of the *Union*'s crew were detained on board the *Ethalion* 'until they can furnish certificates of their birth, and it is said will be sent to London.'[13] A similar fate befell many of the crew of the *Adolphe*, privateer, who arrived at Greenlaw on 3 and 4 February 1807 after their ship's capture in the North Sea a few days earlier. The captain, 2nd captain, four lieutenants, surgeon, écrivain (writer or clerk), conducteur des prises (prize master), maître d'équipage (bosun), contremaître (bosun's mate), quartermaster, gunner, two carpenters, maître voiles (master sailmaker), capitaine d'Armes (master-at-arms), armourer, distributeur des vivres (seaman in charge of victuals or rations), cook, seven seamen, two novices, three volunteers, and four boys, shared, at least for a time, their captivity there.[14]

On the other hand, 159 officers and crew of the Dutch frigate *Utrecht* who arrived from Leith at Greenlaw on 29 and 31 March 1807, did not long remain captives at the depot. One of a squadron of three Dutch warships voyaging from Helvoetsluys in Holland to Curaçao in the Dutch West Indies with troop reinforcements, evidently unaware that the island had already fallen to British forces, the 38-gun *Utrecht* was shipwrecked on its maiden voyage during a storm on 26 February on the northern Orkney island of Sanday.[15] Of the 450 crew and troops on board about 100 were drowned or died after they had struggled ashore on the island. The survivors immediately surrendered to the islanders and, taken to Kirkwall, the officers were lodged in inns on their parole or word of honour not to try to escape, and the crew and the soldiers were confined in the town-house. Another version of events and numbers reported in the *Caledonian Mercury* was that the *Utrecht* had 40, 42 or 44 guns, 37 men perished in the shipwreck, the survivors were housed in small groups in the houses of the islanders but had threatened to break into a store-house on the island containing a hundred muskets and other weapons, and had only surrendered on the arrival of 300 armed men from the Caithness Volunteers. A further contingent of survivors was reported to have landed at Leith early in April. A letter of 14 April from James Watson, Vice Admiral Depute of Orkney and Shetland, to William Marsden, Admiralty Office, reported that he had completed the salvage of the wreck of the *Utrecht*, and had 'sufficiently secured it from any further depredations on the part of the inhabitants of the island of Sanday.' Watson said bad weather had prevented him reaching Sanday with a detachment of 50 men from the Caithness Volunteers until 10 March. By then they found the wreck had been 'completely plundered by the inhabitants of Sanday, who as soon as they discovered the ship had taken possession of it and seized and carried off every thing of value belonging to it that they could possibly remove and secrete. They were even barbarous enough to rob the unfortunate officers and crew of their private property, and in some instances of their clothes. A few of the islanders with the most shocking inhumanity refused to give shelter in their houses to some of the crew, whom they turned out, and who in consequence perished in the night and were found dead next morning.'[16] Landed at Leith on 29 March from British warships, François le Maire, captain of the *Utrecht*, and eight of his officers, guarded by an escort of Scots Greys, journeyed in a coach to Greenlaw. But from there they were immediately sent on parole to Peebles.[17]

When news of the shipwreck had reached him early in March Malcolm Wright, agent at Greenlaw, wrote to the Transport Board in London asking for an immediate supply of bedding for the survivors and the Board replied on 17 March that 400 sets of bedding had been ordered. The Transport Board, moved it seems by humanitarian considerations for the shipwrecked Dutchmen, instructed Wright on 2 April that all the officers of the *Utrecht*, including the midshipmen, were to be repatriated to Holland in a hired vessel from Leith under a flag of truce. The rank and file survivors held at Greenlaw were subjected to efforts, undertaken for the army by Lord Robert Ker, to recruit them into His Britannic Majesty's armed forces. Consequently 21 of them enlisted in the army and six in the Royal Navy. Though there is conflicting evidence about actual numbers, it appears that all the remainder of the shipwrecked men from the *Utrecht* were then repatriated to Holland on 18 April. Amid so much brutality (including that apparently demonstrated by some inhabitants of Sanday) and slaughter in that decade of spreading warfare, it was an example of humanitarianism. A letter of thanks from the repatriated prisoners, which was sent on to it by Malcolm Wright, 'afforded the Board much satisfaction.'[18]

The arrival of some other groups of prisoners at Greenlaw in the years before 1811 illustrated how after its resumption in 1803 the war had engulfed other states than Britain and France. The declaration of war on Britain in December 1804 by Spain as an ally of France was followed within a few months by the arrival of the first Spanish prisoners at the depot. Five passed through its gates on 21 July 1805, a further 27 by the end of October, and altogether 36 were in captivity there by the end of that year. By March 1806 the total had reached 48. All were seamen. Of the first seven listed in the General Entry Book for Spanish prisoners it was written: 'The particulars of these seven prisoners communicated cannot in any degree be relied on. They were confined in the prison ship at Jamaica, whence they were obtained (on obligation to deliver them in this country as prisoners of war) to assist in the navigation of certain merchant vessels bound from thence to the Clyde.'[19]

The next 11 prisoners in the Spanish register were captured on the *Gasconay*, a privateer, off Newfoundland in August 1805; and the remaining 30 were brought from prison ships in Jamaica on board merchant vessels bound for Britain. Two of the prisoners, Pedro Gomes, No. 1 in the register, and Jean Crevis, No. 22, were enlisted into the Royal Navy in autumn 1805, and two others, Joseph Costes, No. 38, and Joaquin Detarre, No. 44, were both released from Greenlaw to serve in the regimental band of His Britannic Majesty's 27th regiment of infantry. Thirty-four of the prisoners were transferred by boat from Leith to Portsmouth (presumably to the hulks there) on 2 January 1806. Of what became of the other 10 Spanish prisoners listed in that General Entry Book at Greenlaw nothing is there recorded.[20]

Within six months of the departure at the beginning of 1806 of those 34 or more Spanish prisoners from Greenlaw the war brought into the depot captives from another state: Prussia. After the crushing defeat by the French army at Austerlitz in December 1805 of the armies of Britain's allies Austria and Russia, Napoleon was able two months later to impose on Prussia, hitherto neutral but inclined toward alliance with Britain and its allies, the Treaties of Schonbrunn and Paris by which Prussia was pushed from neutrality into war with Britain. Prussia, in accepting Hanover (long associated with Britain) as a gift from Napoleon, was obliged to enter his Continental System and to close the ports of north Germany to British trade. The response by the British government in early April 1806 was to seize about 400 Prussian merchant ships at that time loading or discharging cargoes in British ports. The outcome was that for several months a state of war existed between Britain and Prussia.[21]

'Saturday,' reported the *Caledonian Mercury* on Monday, 9 June, 'about 160 Prussian sailors, the crews of the different ships detained and brought into

Leith, were marched from that place to Greenlaw ... under the charge of a captain's guard from the regiments quartered in the Castle.' And twelve days later some more Prussian prisoners brought from Aberdeen and Dundee were confined for four days in Edinburgh Castle then marched out to Greenlaw.[22] These Prussian seamen at any rate did not languish long at Greenlaw. The tides of war again turned—this time in their favour. Prussia having at last entered the war, unwisely as it proved, against Napoleon in October 1806 its army was overwhelmed that month by the French at Iena and Auerstadt. In January 1807 Prussia and Britain made peace with each other, and the following month all the Prussian prisoners at Greenlaw were released.[23]

The entry into the Napoleonic Wars by Spain in 1805 and Prussia in 1806 was followed in 1807 by that of Denmark, a kingdom which then included Norway. Denmark, until then a neutral state with a significant fleet of warships that was a subject of concern to both Napoleon and the British government, was mistakenly reported to the latter to be preparing to take naval action, to close its ports to British trade, and to accept occupation by French troops. The consequent bombardment and burning down of central parts of Copenhagen in September 1807 by a British expeditionary force, and its seizure of the Danish fleet at anchor there as well as of £2 million worth of naval stores, ended Denmark's neutrality. The following month Denmark entered into an alliance with France which lasted until virtually the end of the war in 1814.[24]

Within a few weeks of the outbreak of war between Britain and Denmark Danish prisoners began to arrive at Greenlaw. The first batch of 87 were marched into the depot on 12 November. All of them, apart from nine passengers, were seamen on merchant vessels captured off the coasts of Norway. In the following three years to the end of December 1810 no fewer than 869 'Danes' (who included Norwegians) passed into captivity at Greenlaw. All these captives, again with the exception of a few passengers, were seamen. There appear to have been no soldiers at all among them.[25]

From April 1808 Danish prisoners taken while serving on board privateers began to arrive at Greenlaw. The first to do so were 57 members of the crew of the privateer *Gordenskiold*, captured the previous month off the coast of Norway. There were also occasional prisoners captured on Danish naval vessels, the first three of whom to arrive at Greenlaw in September 1808 were members of the crew of the man-of-war *Fama*, captured the previous month off Jutland.

A captive of particular interest among these Danes was one already mentioned: Paul Andreas Kaald. One of very few prisoners in Scotland during the Napoleonic Wars known to have kept a diary of his captivity Kaald, like so many others among the 'Danish' prisoners, was not a Dane but a Norwegian. Born at Trondheim in 1784, the son of a police sergeant there, Kaald had gone to sea at the age of 14 and in 1803 became a ship's mate. But the war between Denmark and Britain deprived many merchant seamen like Kaald of employment, so early in 1808 he became mate on a privateer sloop *Den Kjaekke*, sailing out of Trondheim. Fortunately for Kaald he was sailing as prizemaster into Bergen in May that year on board the *Eliza*, a British sloop captured off Orkney, when his own ship *Den Kjaekke* was captured by the British navy. The *Eliza* was promptly converted into a privateer named *Den Flinke*, with Kaald as captain. But on his first voyage on her Kaald and his crew were taken prisoner at the end of September off the northern coasts of Scotland and five weeks later were landed at Leith. 'At 2 p.m.,' Kaald wrote in his diary on 8 November, 'we were 46 men altogether, and were transported, guarded by 31 soldiers with loaded weapons, 13 English miles to the prison called Greenlaw Depot by Penicuik. We arrived there at 6.30 p.m. and were shown to our respective cells.' Two days later he recorded: 'We heard that now there are altogether 252 prisoners here, French and Danish.' Kaald remained a prisoner at Greenlaw for the following two years, his diary, which he wrote daily, a unique source of information about aspects of life in the depot.[26]

Until late in 1810 almost all the prisoners arriving at Greenlaw were, like Paul Andreas Kaald, seamen. But from that time major land campaigns, not least the Peninsular War in Portugal and Spain which had begun more than two years earlier, resulted in the depot receiving more and more prisoners from Napoleon's armies. During ten days in November that year there was a large intake of captive soldiers at the depot. Of 214 soldiers who arrived between 8 and 17 November, 134 were officers from the French army in Spain commanded by General Dupont, whose ignominious surrender in July 1808 to Spanish forces at Baylen in Andalusia appeared to end what until then had been regarded as the virtual invincibility of Napoleon's armies. Within a few days of their arrival at Greenlaw, however, these 134 officers were sent on parole to Peebles. The sixteen officers among the other 80 soldiers, who were all apparently from Marshal Massena's army in Portugal, were also promptly sent on parole to Peebles, while the rank and file remained in captivity at Greenlaw until early in 1811.[27]

The number of prisoners sent to Greenlaw mounted as the war continued. In the first of the two registers of 'Danes', for instance, Paul Andreas Kaald was entered in November 1808 as No. 410. By the end of December 1810 their number had risen to 869. But in addition of course two or three hundred Dutch, Spanish and 'Prussian' prisoners had passed by then into captivity at Greenlaw since 1804. And the two French registers list a further 650 or so prisoners who had arrived at the depot between May 1804 and November 1810. Altogether, then, by the end of 1810 it appears from its registers that around 1,700 to 1,800 prisoners had entered Greenlaw during the previous six and a half years.

Yet at no time did, or could, the depot hold anything like that aggregate number of prisoners. In autumn 1810 Greenlaw was officially stated to be able to hold a maximum of 570.[28] Within those years 1804-10, therefore, a high proportion of those who entered Greenlaw also left it.

They left it for one or more of a variety of reasons. Almost 200 officers and officers' servants, or civilians such as shipboard passengers, within a few days of their arrival passed back through Greenlaw's gates on their way to parole at Peebles. Around the same number, as has been seen, of the shipwrecked crew of the Dutch warship *Utrecht* was repatriated in 1807; some 100 Prussians were released in February 1807, and about 85 Spanish either sent to the hulks at Portsmouth in January 1806 or repatriated from Greenlaw in July 1808.

In November 1808 and again in October 1809 the Transport Board reported to the Admiralty that Greenlaw was full. The Board asked on the first occasion that all 218 French prisoners then at the depot be removed by sea to the Nore; on the second, that some of the French prisoners be transferred to the hulks at Chatham. Indeed, from 1808 to 1810 the Board appeared uncertain whether to make Greenlaw a depot for French prisoners to the exclusion of Danes, or the converse. During those three years several hundreds of both nationalities (or Danes and Norwegians, in the case of the 'Danes') were transferred from Greenlaw to captivity in England. The General Entry Books indicate that two or three hundred Danes were sent to the hulks at Chatham; and to there also the diarist Sergeant Major Beaudoin noted the departure successively on 30 March, 18 April and 25 July 1809 of 171 French prisoners. On 31 October that year Beaudoin himself and the remaining 39 French captives were marched from Greenlaw to Leith and put on a corvette which set sail for Chatham.[29]

But there were other reasons, too, for prisoners leaving Greenlaw. One was through their enlistment in the British armed forces. Most of the depot's Entry Books show prisoners who volunteered to serve in the Royal Navy, Royal Marines, various army corps or regiments, on merchant vessels, and even in the militia.

Medical certification as 'unserviceable'—that is, as a result of wounds or chronic incapacitating illness, being unable to take any further active part in the war—was another reason for release from captivity at the depot, as was age. In the first Danish register, for instance, 19 prisoners are said to have been discharged as unfit for service. A further 44 had 'To go home' entered against their names, of whom two are described as 'old man'. The same register lists 24 'Boys under age' repatriated—the age of 12 was normally considered by the Admiralty and the Transport Board that from which boys could justifiably be held as prisoners of war. No fewer than 53 prisoners in this register were discharged for reasons unspecified. Five others left Greenlaw 'To serve on a merchant vessel', three more because they were 'native of Iceland', seven because they were Swedish subjects, two because they were Americans, five 'To join their ships', and a further 125 or so were sent to Bergen, Stavanger or other places in Norway or Denmark but without reasons for their release being stated in the register.

There was also almost a score of prisoners who succeeded in escaping from Greenlaw between 1804 and the end of 1810—some of them 'Danes', others French, Dutch, Belgian, or Prussian—although some were recaptured. There were moreover some 26 prisoners who died in captivity at Greenlaw in those years. One of these deaths became something of a *cause célèbre*—the shooting in January 1807 of a young French prisoner named Charles Cottier or Cotier.[30]

3

Shootings and 'Serious Abuses' at Greenlaw

'My Lord,' wrote Lieutenant General Lord Cathcart, Commander of the Forces in North Britain, to Earl Spencer, Home Secretary in the 'Ministry of all the Talents', on 11 January 1807, 'I think it my duty to acquaint your Lordship that on the night of the 7th instant between the hours of ten and eleven, one of the French prisoners confined in the prison at Greenlaw House seven miles from Edinburgh was shot in his hammock, and has since died of his wound.

'A noise having been heard, and a light perceived in one of the rooms, during the absence of the turnkey, the officer on guard was called, who perceiving the noise and the light, and having repeatedly called to the prisoners to be quiet, and to extinguish the lights, without being obeyed, and conceiving that they were about to make an escape, ordered the nearest centinel to fire into the room. On the arrival of the turnkey the deceased was found wounded in his hammock, and although the surgeon attended without delay, he expired the following day.

'An officer of rank was sent as soon as the report was received to meet the Sheriff Depute of the county of Edinburgh who went to the spot to make the sort of inquest established by the law of Scotland, and the officer who was on guard, viz., Ensign Hugh Maxwell of the Lanark Militia, and Private John Gow, the centinel who fired the shot, and who belongs to the Stirlingshire Militia, have been delivered to the Civil Power, and are lodged in the Tolbooth of Edinburgh, until the Crown lawyers shall have decided whether they may be bailed.

'As the rumour of the death of a prisoner under such circumstances might give rise to misconstructions of a dangerous tendency to the lives of some of His Majesty's subjects who are prisoners of war, I judged it expedient to state the accident to your Lordship as soon as the facts were understood, together with the steps which have in consequence been taken. I must, however, beg leave to remark that although no proof has appeared that an escape was on this occasion actually meditated by the prisoners, who have very frequently succeeded in such attempts, yet it does not seem that the officer was actuated by any other motive than a deliberate belief that the order he gave was absolutely necessary for securing the prisoners under his charge.'[1]

The shooting of the young French seaman Charles Cottier or Cotier thus aroused concern about possible retaliation by the French authorities on British prisoners of war. But Cottier's death also raised several other questions, including the treatment of the prisoners at Greenlaw and the manner in which the depot was administered and guarded.

Lord Cathcart's concern that there might be retaliation on British prisoners of war in France proved unfounded. Nonetheless the trial of Ensign Maxwell in the High Court in Edinburgh on 15 June attracted widespread interest. Even *The Times* carried a report of the trial, one of the relatively few occasions on which that paper reported anything about the prisoners of war in Scotland.[2] Indicted for murder, Maxwell had eminent counsel to defend him in Adam Gillies and Francis Jeffrey. Counsel for the crown were the Lord Advocate, the Solicitor-General, and William Erskine.[3] Maxwell's defence was that 'if any person was killed in consequence of a shot fired by his order, he was justified in giving that order by the circumstances in which he was placed, and his duty as officer upon guard.'[4]

The trial—at which the witnesses included Malcolm Wright, agent, and five of the Greenlaw prisoners (one of whom was Jean Jacques Andriessen), who gave evidence through an interpreter—lasted from 10 a.m. until 6 p.m. Next day the jury unanimously found Maxwell not guilty of murder but, by a majority, guilty of culpable homicide. The jury's verdict was accompanied by a recommendation to mercy. Maxwell, who was aged about 22 or 23, was sentenced to nine months' imprisonment in the Canongate tolbooth.[5]

No detailed account of the trial has been found but the indictment, precognitions by Maxwell and the Penicuik surgeon who attended Cottier on his death-bed, orders dated 30 September 1805 issued by the Deputy Adjutant General for the guard at Greenlaw, lists of crown and defence witnesses, a petition (evidently successful) by Maxwell for postponement of his trial from 2 March 1807 because one of his fellow officers who was a witness had gone on leave to Mull, and some other papers are preserved in the National Archives of Scotland.[6]

Maxwell's precognition coincided fairly closely with the account given by Lieutenant General Lord Cathcart in his letter of 11 January. Maxwell stated 'That he did not intend to kill any person and he is sorry that the shot has had so fatal an effect.' He admitted that the sentinel had fired on his orders. He said there were written orders in the guardhouse for the guard concerning the prisoners, and that besides those orders he understood there was a verbal order that if the prisoners did not put out their lights after twice being called to do so they might be fired on. He could not say from whom the verbal order came for he had not received it from his immediate superior or any of the commanding officers but he 'understood that it had passed from guard to guard and that there was no other compulsion to make the prisoners put out their lights.'

The Penicuik surgeon, Robert Renton, declared that, on being called to the depot within half an hour or so of the shooting, he had found Cottier lying in the room for sick prisoners where he had been carried. Renton found a musket ball had entered Cottier's left hip and lodged in his belly where it would have been dangerous to extract it. He considered Cottier's case 'desperate' and his death had occurred the following afternoon.

A letter dated 7 January written, with some spelling errors, by Ensign Maxwell to his superior officer Captain Rowan of the Lanarkshire Militia apparently immediately after the shooting, said: 'I am sorry to mention to you that 10 minutes after ten o'clock being called upon by Sergeant Wardrop saying their was a noise in the jooils [jails] I went out examaning whate the case was, found lights in the room which I mentioned to be out twice which was not complyed with. I then ordered the Sentry to fire and sory I am to say that the Shot has been fatal.'

A copy of the orders produced by Captain Rowan when examined on 9 January by the Sheriff enquiring into the shooting, showed that they had been issued on 30 September 1805 by the Deputy Adjutant General Alexander Mackay for the guard at Greenlaw. The orders declared: 'At each relief of the guard the officers of the old and new guard will minutely inspect the whole of the prison in every part of the house, attended by one of the officers (employed under the agent) to see that all the doors, locks, etc., are secure and sufficient, and take notice of any damages done by the prisoners, and report the same to the captain of the detachment. The charge of the prisoners within the house, and all the interior economy being under the orders and management of the agent for prisoners, all and every assistance that he may require of additional sentinels, etc., to be furnished at his requisition, and in case of any disturbance, riot, or attempt to escape, the same assistance to be given to the jailor or keeper and if necessary to be repelled by force. The sentinel will fire at any prisoner in the act of escaping or attempting to run off and not immediately stoping [sic] when so challenged or called to by the sentinel. The officer of the guard will frequently during the night visit his sentinels, to see that they are alert, and to learn if any noise has been heard by them such as might denote any attempt at breaking out or undermining the wall. The non-commissioned officers will observe the same each time they go round with the reliefs, at which time they are to be accompanied by one of the turnkeys and immediately report any thing they see, or conceive anything wrong, to the officer of the guard. No spirits of any kind to be allowed to be brought into the prison or any communication to take place with any of the prisoners but such as is permitted by the agent or his keepers, and no soldiers or women belonging to the detachment to be allowed to sell any spirits to the prisoners or soldiers on duty. No soldier or any other persons whatever to be allowed to walk or loiter near the pallisades [sic] or the prison within the sentinels posts, or inside where the sentry boxes are now placed, excepting when the keepers are going round, or other wise allowed by the agent. The agent for prisoners having agreed to supply what may be necessary to put the officers and other guard rooms into complete repair and to furnish them according to custom, an inventory will be delivered to the captain of the detachment of everything, and another left with the officer of the guard, who will deliver the same in good order to the officer relieving them, a copy of this inventory to be given to the Barrack Masters Department. No non-commissioned officer of the guard is to go further from their guard than the avenue in front of the house and not without the gate, and the men are on no account to go through the neighbouring fields or parks as they are let to other individuals. No person whatever to be allowed to come within the avenue near the prison (the officers of the navy and army being in uniform excepted) without the permission of the agent for the prisoners. A sergeant of the guard attended by one of the turnkeys is to attend the markets usually allowed and follow such regulations as the agent for the prisoners will give.' It is not clear whether the markets mentioned, which by implication appear to have been open to members of the public, were the same as those described thus by the Greenlaw diarist Captain Paul Andreas Kaald: 'At the edge of the courtyard nearest to the prison, are numerous small tables which belong to some of the prisoners, who purchase cigarettes and tobacco, butter, meat, bread, pepper, salt, onion, small clay pipes and candles, and sell them to the others, in ha'penny and penny worths, just as much as we can afford to buy.'[7]

Maxwell's conviction was significant in military law. The case was quoted in *The Manual of Military Law*, where it was stated that: 'The general instructions issued from the Adjutant-General's office for the conduct of the troops guarding the prison contained no such order as that upon which Ensign Maxwell had acted; and it appeared to be a mere verbal one which had from time to time in hearing of the officers been repeated by the corporal to the sentries on mounting guard and had never been countermanded by those officers, who were also senior to Ensign Maxwell.' *The Manual* said the Lord Justice Clerk's ruling at the trial had been that: 'A mistaken impression of duty will not excuse an officer, if he, without being justified by other circumstances, orders his men to fire, and someone is thereby killed … The Lord Justice Clerk laid it down that Ensign Maxwell could only defend himself by proving specific orders, which he was bound to obey without discretion, and which called upon him to do what he did.'[8]

Charles Cottier, born at Dunkirk and aged about 19 or 20 at the time of his death, had been a seaman captured on board the merchant ship *Elizabeth* in the North Sea in July 1803, and was one of the first prisoners of war to arrive in Scotland that year. Cottier had escaped from the Edinburgh bridewell in

December 1803 but had been recaptured and was among the first prisoners to enter Greenlaw in the spring of 1804. Unlike other prisoners who died in captivity at Greenlaw and who were buried at the back or south-east side of the depot on the banks of the North Esk river, Cottier was interred half a mile away in Glencorse parish churchyard. There, two centuries after his death, the inscription on his tombstone is barely legible: *Ici repose Charles Cotier de Dunkerque, mort le 8 janvier 1807.*[9]

Cottier was hardly in his grave when there was another murder trial at the High Court in Edinburgh as a result of a shooting at Greenlaw. This time the shooting was of one militiaman by another. William Dreghorn, a corporal in the Stirlingshire militia, had been sent from Penicuik on 26 November 1806 with another corporal to deliver a message to the officer in command at Greenlaw a mile or so away, but on the way the two NCOs became embroiled in a scuffle with soldiers in the Lanarkshire militia. Returning to Penicuik Dreghorn was again ordered by his commanding officer to go to Greenlaw, this time accompanied by a sergeant in the Lanarkshire militia. Dreghorn took his loaded musket with him, despite the advice of the sergeant not to do so. When the two NCOs on their way to Greenlaw met several soldiers of the Lanarkshire militia an altercation took place. Dreghorn fired his musket and mortally wounded William M'Leay, one of the Lanarkshire militiamen.

When the trial of Dreghorn, one of whose counsel was Henry Cockburn, later Lord Cockburn, took place on 16 February his defence was that he had been violently obstructed while he was on duty carrying orders. The jury unanimously found Dreghorn not guilty of murder or culpable homicide.[10]

Three and a half years afterwards there was another shooting of a prisoner at Greenlaw in circumstances to some extent similar to those in the case of Charles Cottier. The victim was Simon Simonsen, a Danish seaman captured on the privateer *Gordenskield* off Norway in March 1808. Since then he had been a captive at Greenlaw. On 27 July 1810 Simonsen was standing at a window in the depot having a quiet conversation with a fellow prisoner when a musket shot fired by Private James Inglis, a member of the guard from the Edinburgh militia, mortally wounded him in the head.

The trial of Inglis for murder took place at the High Court in Edinburgh a month later on 28 August. In evidence the prisoners were said to have been 'very riotous and disorderly' for some days and particularly on the day Simonsen was shot. They 'had frequently pelted the sentinels with stones, pieces of wood, bones, etc., from the windows of the House ... several of the soldiers had been struck with these.' The soldiers had complained to the officer and sergeant of the guard and had threatened to fire on the prisoners in the House if the throwing of missiles continued. Inglis, who was posted as a guard on the south side of the House outside the palisade, complained that stones, bones and sticks were being thrown at him by the prisoners. He was heard to call repeatedly to them to keep back from the windows. When one of the turnkeys went into the House to warn the prisoners Inglis had fired his musket through the window of the staircase of the third flat, mortally wounding Simonsen. Evidence given by officers and NCOs of the guard was that complaints had often been made to them by militiamen on guard about the behaviour of the prisoners, and that they did all they could to prevent such behaviour and identify the offenders. Strict orders had been given not to fire on such occasions but to call the sergeant of the guard. The general orders read to the guard made it clear that the sentries were not to fire except when prisoners were escaping or attempting to escape. Inglis declared that 'he had not called the sergeant of the guard nor received orders to fire, but that he was severely pelted by the prisoners from the staircase window of the third flat; that he repeatedly called on them to keep back from the window, that they laughed at him and said he had no ball in his piece; that he cocked and presented, but not wishing to fire he recovered his arms, and that it was not till after repeated insults that he fired. He considered himself entitled to do so, being insulted at his post.' The jury found Inglis guilty of culpable homicide. Inglis was 'about 20 years of age and had not been full twelve months a soldier, and his captain gave him the character of a steady quiet man.' The sentence imposed on him was 14 years' transportation.[11]

The contrast between the sentences imposed on Ensign Maxwell and Private Inglis after their conviction for the same offence is striking. Was that contrast a result mainly of the difference in their social class and their military rank? Or was it that, given his was the second such shooting of a prisoner at Greenlaw within a few years, Inglis's punishment was intended by the court so to impress enemy governments by its severity that they would feel no need to retaliate on British prisoners of war in their hands? Whatever the explanation the two cases may be seen as a reminder, if any were needed, that as in all wars prisoners of war on either side were, or could be regarded as, hostages for the reasonable treatment of captives by enemy governments and their armed forces.

The shooting of the prisoners Cottier and Simonsen also raised critical questions about the efficiency and suitability as agent at Greenlaw of Malcolm Wright. The shooting of Simonsen more or less immediately prompted a letter to the Transport Board from Lieutenant General Lord Cathcart, commander of His Majesty's Forces in North Britain. This letter does not seem to have survived, but its message is clear from the reference to it in one of 14 August 1810 from the Board to J.W. Croker, secretary to the Admiralty. Lord Cathcart, said the Board, 'having represented to us that in consequence of riotous and outrageous conduct among the people confined at the Depot at Greenlaw a sentinel on duty there fired and wounded one of the prisoners, who is since dead; we request you to communicate the same to the Right

Honourable the Lords Commissioner of the Admiralty. And as Lord Cathcart attributes the described conduct of the prisoners on the present occasion, as also on other occasions, to the absence of the agent at Greenlaw, who holds a public situation in Leigh [i.e., Leith] which prevents him from paying proper attention to the prison, we submit to their Lordships the propriety of appointing a Lieutenant of His Majesty's Navy to supercede [sic] him, who may reside constantly on the spot.'[12]

If Malcolm Wright held a public position in Leith it has not been identi-fied. He was a bailie in 1793-4, 1796-7 and 1800-1 in Edinburgh, and the Scots saying 'aince a bailie, aye a bailie' meant that Wright, like other bailies, was 'always thereafter considered to be a person of importance in local society.' A charter granted by king James III gave the provost and bailies of Edinburgh a jurisdiction unique in Scotland to impose the death penalty, banishment, 'or any other punishment' on convicted criminals, according to the nature of their crimes.[13] Wright was a merchant with his address in the Lawnmarket at the Luckenbooths in 1790-2 and 1794-6, at the head of Warriston's Close in 1793-6, at Gosford's Close in 1797-8, and at the head of Stevenlaw's Court in 1800. No further trace of him has been found, except for the frequent references in the Transport Board archives to his work as its agent.[14]

These shootings, the treatment of the prisoners and the general manage-ment of Greenlaw did not, of course, pass without comment from the two resident diarists among the prisoners at Greenlaw, Sergeant Major Beaudoin and Captain Paul Andreas Kaald. But a third witness to these and other as-pects within the depot who many years later published some recollections of them was a Scots militiaman, James Anton. His testimony indicates a lack of discipline among some, perhaps many, of the guards. Anton had enlisted in the militia in 1803, and after three years of service at Edinburgh Castle and Haddington had been posted with his battalion to Musselburgh 'from which we sent detachments to do duty over the prisoners of war at Greenlaw. This,' Anton recalled, 'was a light and in some respects even an amusing duty. ... The prisoners were locked up at sunset, and then the sentries, who were out of immediate view of the guard-house, laid their firelocks against the sentry-boxes and amused themselves by playing at putting-stone, pitch-and-toss, and such-like amusements, without fear of detection; for a cordial unity of feeling existed throughout the corps, so that as soon as the officer, sergeant, or corporal of the guard made his appearance, it was notified in an instant to the remotest corners, without his being aware of the communication, and our gambling amusements instantly ceased. While our duty was thus easily and pleasantly performed the prisoners of war under our charge were far from being severely treated, as some have stated.'[15]

Among those who did complain of severe treatment of the prisoners was the diarist Sergeant Major Beaudoin, a prisoner at Greenlaw from June 1804 until October 1809. 'In this prison,' wrote Beaudoin about the time when Cottier was shot, 'they have perpetrated on us all the atrocities possible. As the order is to put out the candles at nine o'clock in the evening, the rolling of the drum sounded all round the prison. As soon as the rolling finished, if you had the misfortune not to hear the drum on account of the noise we all made, shots were at once fired at us through the casement windows without warning. That made us keep quiet pretty quickly and put out the candles. Several of us have been victims of this barbarous treatment. Fortunately, a capable man was among us; he wrote a letter in the name of all the prisoners that described how we were treated and begged the government to have regard for our unhappy fate. It was put in the post on the quiet by an Englishman whom we paid generously. A fortnight later the agent came to the prison in an angry state, saying: "I want to know who gave himself permission to write to the government. I'll put him in the black hole until he tells me who put the letter in the post." But he did not find out who it was. He received a severe reprimand and came near even to being dismissed.' In an evident reference to the case of Cottier and Ensign Maxwell, Beaudoin noted that 'An officer of the guard was cashiered and remained in prison a long time; several prisoners went to Edinburgh to give evidence in this affair. Posters were put up at once by order of the government forbidding any firing on the prisoners; and that, in the event of noise, the guard was obliged to enter the prison to put out the candles and establish good order. Besides, if there were unruly prisoners there was the black hole for punishing them, and it was strictly forbidden to strike [them]. They were now allowed to fire at a prisoner only when he was escaping, and even then he had to be outside the prison or mutinying. That letter made things a lot easier for us.'[16]

Captain Paul Andreas Kaald's diary of life at Greenlaw during his captivity there from November 1808 until August 1810 was, unlike Beaudoin's notes, entirely contemporaneous and also much more detailed. Though Kaald arrived at the depot almost two years after the shooting of Cottier and the trial of Corporal Dreghorn for shooting a fellow militiaman, he provides in his inimitable style a detailed account of the shooting of Simon Simonsen in 1810:

'Friday, 27 July. Today some of the boys here in the prison have thrown some meat bones and stones out of the window from the 3rd floor on the passage down to a guard who stood just outside. A sergeant came in, told the prisoners that such like things shouldn't happen since the guard had orders to shoot. At 6 pm a man by the name of Simon came up the stairs, and since the aforementioned window looks out on to a nice field, he remained standing there. He then started to speak to someone else and admired the beautiful meadow. The soldier who saw a man standing by the window, took hold of his gun and shouted—"Away from the window or I shoot!" Simon stepped back at this cry, but since every prisoner is allowed to go there and stand, he wasn't frightened in the slightest. This man is also a very quiet and calm person. But the soldier (either from excitement or from a strict order) aimed and fired bullets in through his head, so the poor man fell backwards down the stone stairs. And when some prisoners came to his aid, the other guards would have fired if they hadn't moved away from the window. The bullet went into the left eyebrow and out the middle of the head where it blew the skull to bits. He was bandaged and brought to hospital. Since the guard commander now feared a rebellion and attack by the prisoners, he quickly divided up the entire guard—44 soldiers in all, all with loaded weapons—round about the prison, as well as having 6 men in the prison passage. He himself went round patrolling with a sword. When he was warned that a man had been shot and that a doctor had to be sent for, he answered angrily that he would shoot all of them. One of the guards also said to another that for tuppence apiece he would shoot all the prisoners. Very hard to hear this from those people, who ought to have had more sense, and that we here should be looked upon as almost unimportant creatures. When it was turning-in time he placed 12 soldiers with loaded weapons in the prison courtyard. He himself and two junior officers, all with sabres, counted the prisoners. A second officer had just arrived with 12-14 soldiers. The prison doctor had been at the hospital with the sick man until 11 o'clock. He was raving quite a lot.

'Saturday, 28 July: Today the patient is very poorly and raving so much that 4 men had to hold him down. The Doctor took a piece from his head that weighed 2 ounces.

'Sunday, 29 July: The patient still lives, but senses and eats absolutely nothing. Raves as strongly as usual.

'Monday, 30 July: Simon Simonsen died today, about 7pm.

'Tuesday, 31 July: In the afternoon ... I, Locke, Rohde, Cramer, Andersen and Meyer were called down to the office, with a guard of 9 soldiers and 1 junior officer, where we were one after the other questioned by certain great gentlemen from Edinburgh. The reason was about the shooting of Simon Simonsen last Friday. We answered what we knew.'[17]

Kaald had the good fortune to be released from captivity on 22 August, six days before Private Inglis was tried, and convicted and sentenced at the High Court in Edinburgh for the culpable homicide of Simon Simonsen.

But Kaald's diary—a unique and detailed day-by-day account written during his two years as a prisoner of war in a Scots depot during the Napoleonic Wars—contains many other references to events and routines, and to the sometimes idiosyncratic manner in which Greenlaw was administered under Malcolm Wright, the agent. Indeed Kaald's diary provides clear evidence of frequent and sometimes serious breaches by Wright and his assistants of the regulations issued by the Transport

Board and which were intended to be observed at every prisoner of war depot in Britain.

Two such breaches arose from what appears to have been Wright's personal sympathy for some at least of the officers (who were mainly from merchant or privateer ships) in his custody at Greenlaw. That sympathy seems to have moved him into allowing them not only a form of local parole but also visitors from outside the depot—both indulgences entirely unauthorised by and, for some time, unreported to the Transport Board. Kaald's diaries provide many examples of both these breaches of depot rules.

'Today,' Kaald writes, for instance, on Sunday, 25 June 1809, 'we had a visit from 2 Danish mates who are free and sailing with 2 ships that are in Leith. One of them by the name of Nyeborg is mate with Captain Smidt, commanding a Russian ship from Archangel. This same man lay alongside my ship in Bergen when I was there and therefore he recognised me. He was captured and brought to Leith on his voyage from Bergen, but is now free again. The other mate is with Captain Moller and is also free and … is going to Copenhagen. These two gave us much more news, among other things that a small privateer has been captured at Bergen and brought to Leith. I presume it is *Den Dristige*.'

Whether it was the same Captain Smidt of the Archangel ship or a namesake is not clear, but on 17 November that year Kaald records: 'In the evening Captain Smidt was up here from Leith and chatted with his acquaintances.' And a few days before his own release from captivity, Kaald writes on 7 August 1810: 'Captain Eeg from Kristiansund was up here today, but received only a few minutes' permission to stand at the palisade in order to speak to his son, which also had to be in English. But when Mr Wharton [the depot clerk] came up he received permission to get his son outside the prison for an hour. Two other Norwegian Captains were up here later in the afternoon and brought a number of letters from Norway.'

On no fewer than eighteen separate occasions between June 1809 and August 1810, Kaald records in his diary similar visits to prisoners at Greenlaw. All such visits were completely contrary to Transport Board rules.[18]

Nor was the clerk Wharton's grant of permission to Captain Eeg and his son to meet for an hour outside the depot unique. Three months after his arrival at Greenlaw, Kaald records on 23 February 1809: 'Today [Captain] Richelieu, Captain Griff and Captain Knudtzen received permission from the Captain on guard to go outside the prison.' And next day: 'Today the same Captains received the same permission to go out.' On 13 March, 'This morning at 6 o'clock Captain Richelieu went to Edinburgh and Leith after obtaining permission from Mr Fraser [the depot clerk]. He came back here this evening at 9 o'clock.' Afterwards it became clear that Captain Richelieu had used this and similar later visits (on one of which in July he was absent for three days) to the city to prepare his escape from Greenlaw. That, some months later, he duly succeeded in achieving, hidden in a chest.[19]

Kaald himself first received permission, along with Captain Griff, a fellow Danish prisoner, on 21 April 1809 to go out for an evening stroll. 'We ate supper (NB—for money) at one of the jailer's homes, and from there went back to the prison.' Two days later, a Sunday, Kaald again records, 'I was out and walked to Penicuik, where I drank tea and ate supper at the same jailer's house.' At the end of the following week he writes: 'Every day this week I have been out walking.' Kaald recounts how on 7 January 1810, along with three fellow prisoners, he was allowed to accompany officers of the depot guard to an inn or ale house and 'enjoy ourselves with two bowls of toddy'.[20] A few weeks later, on 20 February, 'I was so lucky to get permission to go to Penicuik, albeit under the guard of 2 big Grenadier soldiers. I nevertheless had the pleasure of skating for an hour on lovely ice, under the baronet's manor house. I came back [to Greenlaw] at 6 o'clock in the afternoon.' The baronet was Sir George Clerk of Penicuik.[21]

Perhaps the most remarkable of Kaald's jaunts outside Greenlaw depot was on Good Friday morning, 20 April 1810, when Malcolm Wright, the agent, granted him and his friend and former shipmate 2nd Captain H. Andreas Locke of the privateer *Den Kjaekke* permission to go to Penicuik. 'When we were near Kirkhill,' writes Kaald, 'Mr Wharton [clerk at Greenlaw] brought us in to his lodgings at Mistress Annadells [? Annandale's], where we ate a good breakfast together. After this he brought us, with this good woman's permission, into a very pretty garden belonging to Mr White [owner of Esk Mills], where we looked at this year's beautiful blooming flowers and plants. Near to their house we were very warmly greeted by the aforementioned gentleman's son Mr John White who, after having walked around the garden a bit, talking about our terrible situation, brought us finally to a very costly and beautiful papermill nearby, belonging to his father. He wanted to show us from the lowest and smallest to the highest and most important of the paper works—its finished product. From there we were led by Mr J. White to their house, where we were warmly welcomed by Mrs White and her 2 oldest girls (two most charming and civil ladies, in the bloom of their youth). We spent about 2 hours there in conversation about our terrible situation. At 11 o'clock we left this kind-hearted family, with Mr White walking a bit of the way with us. When we arrived at Penicuik I immediately went in to Mr Allan [a retailer], where I carried out my business. At the exit there we met Captain Miller [of the guard], a very honest man. We took a walk with him and had a conversation about our fatherland and its shipping. We finally left him and went to a retailer, Mr J. Niven, where we shopped a bit. While Locke bought some material for clothing there, I went with Mr Wharton into a room where we met the retailer's daughter, a young pretty girl, but not counted among the virtuous of her sex, as she is (so it is said) more than usual acquainted with the officers of the Aberdeen Militia and also much too fond of taking a glass of whisky. From there we went to a billiard room and while Mr Wharton played a game of billiards, I went to visit a good friend, Mr Jackson. Eventually we left town and when we arrived at Kirkhill on our way back, we went to Mrs Annadell, who told us that we were all invited to dinner by Mrs White. We accepted the invitation and went to Mr White's, where we were all warmly received. It was then about 3 p.m.'[22]

Almost a score of such outings, either by Kaald himself or by other captives at Greenlaw during the two years he spent there, are recorded in his diaries. There is no ground for doubting the accuracy of his account. Andrew Johnston, chief clerk successively at the depots at Esk Mills, Valleyfield and Perth, in his recollections written a quarter of a century after the Napoleonic Wars briefly confirms Kaald's account. 'Mr Wright was in the habit of granting some of the [captive] Officers under his charge their parole for the day. They were much attended to by the families of the neighbourhood, and frequently in Mr White's, Mr Cowan's [owner of Valleyfield paper mill at Penicuik], etc., at dinner, etc., etc. This was before Esk Mills or Valleyfield were converted into prisons. They were of course well acquainted with the localities of the neighbourhood of their confinement—the Cotton Mill [i.e., Esk Mill], etc., etc.'[23]

It was hardly surprising therefore, given that such outings were entirely in breach of Transport Board regulations for prisoners of war in depots such as Greenlaw, that when the Board got wind in September 1809 of Wright's unauthorised activities it told him it 'highly disapproved' of his 'permitting any prisoner not entitled to parole to go out of Prison under any Pretence whatever, and that if any similar instance should occur, the Board must take severe Notice of it.'[24]

A month later the Board sent Wright a letter of 29 September it had received from Lieutenant General Lord Cathcart 'on the subject of serious abuses prevalent at the Depot for prisoners of war under your charge at Greenlaw, and we direct you will report to us *immediately* on the subject. [Also] ... unless your Clerk reside at the Prison and remain there constantly, and unless you visit the Prison yourself every Day, we must immediately appoint other persons in your stead.' One of the abuses of which Lord Cathcart had been told by the major general in ultimate command of the troops at Greenlaw was that the jailers or turnkeys were 'in the habit of selling ale & spirits to the prisoners, & of allowing chests to be carried in & out of the prison without their being inspected by the officer on duty.' The reference to unsearched chests was no doubt to the one in which Captain Richelieu had recently made his escape. Two of the turnkeys were dismissed as a result of these incidents.[25] Another outcome a couple of months later was that Alexander Fraser, Wright's depot clerk, also fell, or was pushed, overboard.

One of the roots of Wright's peculiar administrative practices or malpractices at Greenlaw was that when the depot opened in 1804 he appears to have been provided with accommodation as agent two miles away at Roslin. But if ever he did live at Roslin there are indications that sooner or later he returned to living in Edinburgh and to making only sporadic visits to Greenlaw. At any rate Wright appears, as General Lord Cathcart complained following the shooting of Simon Simonsen in July 1810, never to have been resident at the depot itself. His clerk, Alexander Fraser, who had been his assistant also during the French Revolutionary Wars when Wright was agent for prisoners of war at Edinburgh Castle, appears also to have been often absent from his duties at Greenlaw. 'Mr Fraser has been up here every day during the last 14 days, which is something quite strange,' wrote Kaald in his diary on 6 November 1809. And a few months later, on 28 April 1810, Kaald wrote: 'We had the honour of seeing both commissioners [i.e., Wright and Fraser] up here. ... Mr Fraser we haven't seen over the last 2 months.'

The reason for Fraser's prolonged absence from Greenlaw at that period, however, was that he had yielded to an ultimatum from the Transport Board and resigned the previous December. This minor revolution in the administration of the depot began with the letter of 6 October 1809 from the Board to Wright, enclosing the one from General Lord Cathcart. The Board also ordered Wright 'to allow access to the Prison to the officer commanding the detachment ... in the neighbourhood of Greenlaw, and to furnish him regularly, as heretofore, with a copy of the surgeon's report of the Health of the Prisoners agreeably to Lord Cathcart's report.' Wright replied on 9 October, 'denying the existence of the abuses complained of in Lord Cathcart's letter, & respecting the attendance of himself & his clerk alleged that the duties of the Depot had constantly been fulfilled if not in the letter at least in the spirit of the Board's directions.' The Board promptly wrote him again on 12 October, demanding a 'positive Answer' to the question of his or his clerk's residing at Greenlaw. Wright replied four days later that he 'himself had resolved to conform to the proposed regulation respecting their residence and attendance, but represented it to be attended with much inconvenience and expense.' The Board sent a copy of this reply to General Lord Cathcart, 'requesting his opinion whether if a steady person as clerk were resident at the Prison at Greenlaw it would be sufficient for the Agent to visit the Depot daily, as is the present practice.' On 25 November Wright informed the Board that since the opening of the depot almost five years earlier 'Mr Fraser, not being able to attend there constantly, had been assisted by his clerk, Mr Francis Wharton.' Wright recommended to the Board the appointment of Wharton as 'an additional clerk to reside constantly at the depot.' The Board, hardly surprisingly, fired a broadside into Wright's recommendation and on 29 November 'Ordered that unless Mr Fraser can give up his time to the service and reside on the spot he cannot be continued in his present situation; and in this case, if Mr Wharton will actually give up the whole of his time to the service and reside constantly at Greenlaw so as not to be absent without the Board's special leave, he is to be appointed in Mr Fraser's room.' The Board also ordered that Wright himself 'be informed that it is fully expected and absolutely necessary that the Depot should be visited by himself as frequently as possible.' In his reply to the Board on 4 December Wright enclosed a letter from Fraser 'resigning his appointment as clerk, and stated Mr Wharton to be willing to devote his whole time to the duties of the situation.' The Board ordered that Francis Wharton be appointed accordingly.[26]

What seems extraordinary about the absences of Wright and Fraser from their duties at Greenlaw in those years from 1804 onward is that the Transport Board did not take action much sooner. The explanation may be partly that Greenlaw was in those years the depot in Britain most remote from the Transport Office in London, and therefore more difficult to oversee than the other land depots, all of which (except for Peebles as a parole town) were based in the southern half of England. But it would also appear that Wright, in the series of appointments he held as one of the Board's agents for a decade and a half from the 1790s, must have had a patron or patrons (whose identity, however, it has not so far proved possible to establish) sufficiently influential to be able to shield him so long from the recurring wrath of the Transport Board and of some other authorities, including General Lord Cathcart.

But Wright also weathered such storms by battening down Greenlaw's hatches, at least for a time. 'Everything,' wrote Kaald in his diary on 11 November 1809, for instance, during some fraught weeks then at the depot, 'now is, to the highest degree, strictly guarded and extremely restricted.' The crisis for Wright at that period passed, however, at least for the time being, and Kaald and some of his fellow officer captives were soon able to resume their outings from the depot with the permission of Wright or his assistants.[27]

Yet a year later, despite his surviving these controversies with the Board and General Lord Cathcart, a question mark appeared against Wright's continuation in office as the Transport Board's longest serving agent in Scotland. A letter of 29 October 1810 to the Board from the Admiralty 'Desired to know whether under the new arrangements the Board considered the present Agent at Greenlaw as competent to fulfil the duties of the Service.' The 'new arrangements' amounted to a far-reaching change in the policy hitherto of confining the mass of prisoners of war in depots and parole towns in the southern half of England. The trickle of prisoners into Scotland from 1803 that had become from 1807 a moderate flow rose rapidly almost into a flood in the winter of 1810-11.[28]

4

The 'New Arrangements'

Between 1804 and the end of 1810 Greenlaw remained the only prisoner of war depot, and Peebles the only parole town, in Scotland. In May 1804, a year after the resumption of the war, a Transport Office list showed a total then of 6,188 prisoners of war in Britain, of whom 5,663 were confined in depots or on hulks and 525 were on parole. Of those 6,188 prisoners only 73 were shown to be then in Scotland: 64 at Greenlaw, and nine on parole at Peebles.[1] Even as late as 1810 there had been at most only about 600 or 700 prisoners of war at any one time in Scotland. But between the end of 1810 and summer 1812 three new depots—each of them far larger than Greenlaw—and one former depot were opened and fourteen new parole towns established north of the Border. By August 1811, according to the Transport Office, the number of captives in Scotland had increased about fivefold to 3,350, of whom 2,744 were in confined depots and the other 606 were on parole.[2] In the three years from 1811 the total in Scotland came to be about 13,000 or 14,000. It has been estimated that in March 1810 out of all the prisoners of war in Britain only 0.05 per cent were in Scotland, but by May 1814 that percentage had increased to 17.6. In the same period the percentage of parole prisoners in Britain who were living in parole towns in Scotland has been estimated to have increased even more remarkably—from 1.1 per cent to 25 per cent.[3]

These developments were part of the 'new arrangements' referred to in the Admiralty letter of 29 October 1810. What exactly were these arrangements? What were the reasons for them? And why was there so much haste in carrying them out between autumn 1810 and summer 1812? The explanations appear to be at least fourfold.

First, by the second half of 1810 many more prisoners had fallen into the hands of British forces as a result of several major campaigns in Europe and the West Indies. The Peninsular War, begun in 1808, produced by 1810 thousands of French and French allied or satellite state prisoners. For example, the battle of Busaco in September 1810 and the capture of Coimbra a few days later together cost the French not only 4,000 killed and wounded but also 5,000 taken prisoner.[4] French prisoners taken in Spain and Portugal could not conveniently or safely be held in captivity there by Wellington's army. Many French and their allied or satellite troops who fell into the hands of Portuguese or Spanish peasants or guerrillas enraged by depredations and atrocities perpetrated by some of the invaders of their country, were massacred.[5] When in the winter of 1810-11 the Lords Commissioner of the Admiralty in London, alarmed by the growing number of prisoners arriving from Spain and Portugal, gave to Admiral Berkeley, the British naval commander at Lisbon, 'positive directions that you do not send another French prisoner to England on any consideration', Wellington commented to Berkeley that when prisoners of war in the Peninsula 'accumulate to such numbers as that it will become inconvenient to guard them, we must only send them back again to the enemy.'[6] In fact, however, Wellington continued to send prisoners of war from the Peninsula to Britain, and in 1811-12 alone he sent 20,000.[7]

Prisoners also arrived in large numbers in Britain in 1809-10 from Martinique and Guadeloupe in the West Indies, and from Walcheren in Holland. The capture of Martinique by British forces in February 1809 resulted in more than 2,000 prisoners being sent to Britain. Hundreds more joined them in captivity following the surrender on 6 February 1810 of French forces on Guadeloupe. In the major British expedition to Walcheren and the campaign fought there between the end of July and beginning of December 1809, almost 8,000 French prisoners were taken.[8]

Second, new depots opened in England and additional hulks brought into use there after the resumption of war in 1803 were already full or rapidly filling up by 1810. The 6,188 prisoners of war in all the depots and parole towns in Britain, including Greenlaw and Peebles, in May 1804 increased by mid-October 1809 to about 45,000.[9] Dartmoor, a purpose-built depot, construction of which (in granite) had begun at the end of 1806, received its first prisoners of war on 24 May 1809—and had already reached its planned capacity of 5,000 by the end of the following month.[10] Between 1808 and 1810 the number of French prisoners on parole in Britain almost doubled from 1,674 to 3,245.[11] It was therefore necessary to find still more 'receptacles' for the prisoners. And creating more depots and parole towns in Scotland appeared to have advantages in dealing with the problem of security which arose from the presence of tens of thousands of prisoners of war confined in the south of England at or near the great naval bases and arsenals at Portsmouth, Plymouth and Chatham.

A third reason for the 'new arrangements' made in 1810-12 was that whereas in wars in the previous century many prisoners, particularly those on parole, could reasonably expect to be exchanged not too long after capture, that was not, or was not nearly so often, the case in the Napoleonic Wars. That exchanges of French and British prisoners were relatively few between 1803 and 1814 was a result of several factors, including the imbalance in the numbers held by each side and the lack of trust between the two governments. Whereas Britain held in aggregate about 122,000 prisoners of war between 1803 and 1814 (although about a third of these were not French but were men from the allied or subject states of France), British prisoners in France totalled only about 16,000. Napoleon was convinced that if a general exchange were agreed the British government would cease to repatriate prisoners in its hands once the 16,000 British captives had been returned home. Several attempts by the two governments between the summer of 1803 and the autumn of 1810 to reach agreement on a general exchange had broken down.[12] Consequently, from 1809-10 onwards more and more prisoners of war in Britain, despairing of being exchanged, attempted to escape. The increase in escapes among parole prisoners was particularly significant, since (unlike the rank and file languishing in closed depots) these were officers and gentlemen whose *parole* or word of honour had been given not to escape or attempt escape.[13] Moreover, such serious breaches of the rules and conventions of the parole system—a system which had been developing, particularly between Britain and France, during the wars of the previous century—were not confined to junior officers but were committed even by some senior officers in captivity in Britain.[14] The British authorities became convinced that removing large numbers of parole prisoners from parole towns in the south and Midlands of England to new parole towns to be created in Scotland would reduce the number of escapes.

Finally, what appears to have brought these problems to a head and galvanised the Admiralty and the Transport Board into swift and at times almost frantic action was a report of a conversation that was said to have taken place among four or five prisoners at Portchester Castle depot near Portsmouth about eight o'clock on Sunday evening, 2 September 1810. The conversation was overheard there by Garçon Baptiste, a black prisoner from St Vincent in the West Indies, who was lying in his hammock within earshot. Baptiste informed Captain Paterson, the depot agent, of the conversation, his reason for doing so, he said, being that the prisoners concerned 'are very hostile to the Blacks and Americans and that in the event of a general rising he has but very little doubt but they would put them all to death.'[15]

It was Baptiste's report that the conversation he had overheard revealed the prisoners' intention at the end of that month to lead a general uprising of the 17,000 prisoners of war at Portchester Castle and on the hulks nearby at Portsmouth which so alarmed the British authorities. Writing on 5 September to the Transport Board commissioners with a summary of Baptiste's report to him, Captain Paterson declared: 'He states that it is the intention of the prisoners to make a desperate effort about the end of September to surprise the Guard, and take from them their arms, and finally to get possession of the arms of the whole regiment doing duty at this place, that by a certain

signal understood by the prisoners on board the prison ships in Portsmouth Harbour they are at the same time to make a corresponding movement to secure the Guard, and to take from them their arms, after which the whole are to make for Portsmouth, which they consider incapable of offering any effectual resistance from its insufficiency of strength. The man says at present about seven or eight persons are chosen as the principal leaders, all of whom are members of the Legion of Honour, but the person who appears to take the most active part is a Corsican and was a captain of a privateer.....
I shall endeavour to find out the Corsican he mentioned, and he [Baptiste] has promised to communicate any particulars from time to time which may occur, tending to throw any light on the subject.'

Baptiste had also reported that the four or five prisoners he had overheard said 'that they understood the French Government were preparing three different expeditions against this country, and that it was in contemplation amongst the prisoners at Bristol, Plymouth and Portchester Depots to make a general rising.' One of the four or five prisoners overheard had said he had learned this 'from a person outside the stockade, who also informed him that there had been already a rising at some of the Depots.'

On 6 September Major General Whetham, the army commander of the district, arrived at Portchester depot from Portsmouth, had Baptiste removed from his room on the pretence that he was sick, and questioned him closely. The general then summoned the Legion of Honour prisoners and spoke to one of them. Afterwards, when the general had gone, Baptiste reported he had heard these prisoners exclaim, 'We are betrayed. Why should the General ask so particularly for those of the Legion of Honour if he had not some information?' They had repeated they were betrayed, 'on which they laid great stress; but could not conjecture in which way or by whom.'[16]

Meantime, also under pretence of sickness, Catala, the Corsican privateersman said by Baptiste to be a leader of the projected rising, had gone into the Portchester depot hospital. 'Catala is described as violent in politics, calls himself a Freemason, and under cover of Freemasonry unnecessarily and clandestinely celebrated the birthday of Bonaparte.'[17]

Nothing has been found about whatever action was taken by the authorities against those other than Catala who were said to be concerned in the reported plot. That Catala himself was restored to parole at Odiham on 11 September (and a year later was sent from there on parole to Selkirk) suggests the authorities must have decided there was no reliable evidence of his complicity in any such plot. But a report of the whole affair was passed from the Transport Board to the Admiralty on 8 September and from the Admiralty to the Home Office two days later. It was not the first nor the last report of a projected uprising by prisoners of war in Britain. But there is little doubt that the authorities took this one seriously.

Within a fortnight the Lords Commissioner of the Admiralty had directed the Transport Board commissioners 'to cause preparations to be made with as little delay as possible for receiving prisoners in Scotland, in addition to the present establishment in that part of the United Kingdom, reporting to our secretary for our information when the same may be ready.'[18] And on 18 October the Admiralty informed the Home Office that 'as the number of French prisoners confined in the neighbourhood of the principal sea ports of the kingdom is much greater than appeared adviseable, that near Portsmouth being no less than 18,000 and near Plymouth 8,000 men, their Lordships directed the Transport Board by their order of the 24th September last to cause preparations to be made for receiving a certain number of prisoners in Scotland; that in consequence of this the Commissioners wrote to Lord Cathcart [army commander in Scotland] for information on the subject and received his Lordship's reply … by which it appears that a considerable number of the said prisoners may be confined in Scotland, that in consequence of this information their lordships have given directions to the Commissioners for Transport to send down one of their members (Commissioner Bowen), with instructions to cause such preparations and arrangements to be made, in concert with Lord Cathcart, as to admit of sending into that part of Great Britain 15,000 French prisoners.' Such arrangements, their lordships of the Admiralty told the Home Office, appeared to them 'of the utmost importance for the good of the public service.'[19]

Commissioner Bowen, as the Transport Board's emissary, had already set off for Scotland on or very soon after 10 October.[20] When Lieutenant General Lord Cathcart, commander of the Forces in Scotland, received the Transport Board commissioners' letter of 25 September concerning the Admiralty's instructions of the previous day to arrange for receiving more prisoners in Scotland 'in addition to the present establishment at Greenlaw, in consequence of the very great number in England,' he wasted little time in sending his opinion on where the additional prisoners might be held. The Transport Board had asked his opinion about their possible confinement in Fort Augustus, Fort George, Fort William, and Edinburgh Castle, or any other place 'so that Government may not be put to any considerable expense on account of building.'

In his reply of 3 October, which illustrated the problems the Board faced in finding, and finding quickly, suitable new depots in Scotland, Lord Cathcart told the Transport Board that 'the *permanent* barracks are the only public buildings I know of in Scotland in which it would be practicable immediately to lodge and secure prisoners on an extensive scale. All the buildings within the Castles and fortresses in North Britain, except those which are necessarily fitted with arms, ammunition and other military stores, and the apartments of the Governors, and of the Garrison staff, are in charge of the

Barrack Department, and are fitted and occupied as *permanent barracks*. There is no superfluous barrack accommodation in North Britain, on the contrary, there are, at this moment, two Regiments and part of a third in quarters. The Permanent Barracks at Fort George and at Edinburgh Castle are the headquarters of the 6th and 9th Royal Veteran Battalions, and each station requires to be occupied besides by troops of a more active description. The quantity of powder and stores at each place would render the introduction of a large body of prisoners extremely dangerous and detrimental to His Majesty's service. The objection to Fort George is greater than to Edinburgh Castle, because of the position of the fortress which is kept in a state of preparation for defence, and of the difficulty of quartering troops near it, to replace, if required, those removed to make way for prisoners, and the difficulty which would occur in removing prisoners by land, if that measure were necessary. There is no objection to the occupation of Fort Augustus by prisoners of war with some troops, except that the number it would contain is inconsiderable, and there would be considerable difficulty in securing prisoners on the march by land at the halting places, and in supplying them with fresh meat at a reasonable rate. Fort William is out of repair, and it would require some months to replace the roof of the buildings. It would not contain so many prisoners as Fort Augustus.

'From what has been stated,' Lord Cathcart's letter continued, 'it will appear that transferring permanent barracks, situated in Forts, to your department, would, except, in the instances last named, Fort Augustus and Fort William, be as inconvenient in the same respects as transferring those in open towns and places, and that there are additional objections peculiar to themselves. The expense of fitting Fort George would be very considerable, and it would require an [sic] high wall to divide the parade, and a stockade to surround the outward front of the whole range of barracks to be used as a prison—besides alterations of doors and windows and bars and fastenings. Edinburgh [Castle] is less objectionable, and would be sooner, and at a less expense, converted to the use in question. If permanent barracks are converted into prisons with a view to replacing them by temporary barracks to be occupied till the end of the war, there will be no saving to the public in the expense of the building; on the contrary, to a provision for the like number of temporary barracks, is to be added the expense of altering the permanent barracks to fit them for prisoners and that of restoring them at a peace for their proper use.'

Lord Cathcart then made a suggestion that proved to contain parts of the shape of things to come in Scotland in the two following years. 'If the necessity of sending prisoners to Scotland could be parried for six months, in that time I am assured it would be practicable to construct prisons to any extent on the extensive premises at Greenlaw, or at Perth or Linlithgow, both eligible stations, and where ground may be had, at Perth indeed without any outlay of money. Mr White's manufactory near Greenlaw might, as it is reported to me, probably be hired, and could in three months be fitted for 3,000 prisoners.'

His letter concluded: 'I have subjoined a statement of the greatest number of prisoners that can be confined at the several places named in your letter ... [thus:] Fort George 2,500, Fort Augustus 500, Fort William 450, Edinburgh Castle 2,800. N.B.: Two prisoners occupy the room of one soldier, where officers' rooms are not transferred with the men's rooms, and three prisoners occupy the room provided for one soldier in the construction of barracks, where officers' rooms are transferred with those of the men.'[21]

The allusion in the letter to 'Mr White's manufactory near Greenlaw' was to Esk Mills, and Lord Cathcart's estimate, once acted on, that these could swiftly be adapted to house 3,000 prisoners of war helps explain the crisis at those Mills five months later.

The anxious search for possible depots in Scotland included a request from the Transport Board on 29 September to Sir John Sinclair, the distinguished agriculturalist and the driving force behind the publication in the 1790s of the first *Statistical Account of Scotland*, 'in case it should be found adviseable to send any prisoners of war ... to point out any place in the North of Scotland fit for their confinement or that can be made so at a moderate expense.' Whatever reply came from Sir John appears not to survive.[22]

Meantime, Commissioner Bowen, the Transport Board's special emissary in Scotland, had arrived there about the second week in October.[23] The instructions he carried with him from the Board, which also gave him a copy of Lord Cathcart's reply of 3 October, were sixfold. He was to ascertain first whether the existing lease of Greenlaw could be extended, and if so on what terms, for how long, and what additional accommodation could thus be secured, the cost of this, and the earliest date that more prisoners could be sent there. Second, 'the fitness of Mr White's Mills [Esk Mills] for the reception of prisoners,' the terms on which the Mills could be acquired, the number of prisoners they could house, how soon, and the cost of adapting the buildings. Third, 'Linlithgow Palace and Stirling Castle, their fitness for the above purpose', and the same information about numbers, cost, etc. Fourth, 'The Castle of Edinburgh, its fitness, particularly with the view of confining, if necessary, about 1,000 superior refractory prisoners', and the same information as sought for the other places. Fifth, 'Whether any other, and what, place or places in Scotland, fit for the reception of prisoners of war can be procured, and if so upon what terms, etc.' Finally, Bowen was told that as other parole towns would also have to be established in Scotland, in addition to Peebles, 'we desire you to make enquiry for such towns as may be most eligible and for fit persons to act as the Board's agents there.' Once he had fully investigated all these questions Bowen was instructed to report the results of his enquiries to the Board. The Lords Commissioner of the Admiralty would also be kept informed.[24] The 'superior refractory prisoners' who might be kept in Edinburgh Castle were so-called *mauvais sujets*—prisoners who gave trouble in one way or another, by being involved in uprisings projected or actual, attempting escape, abusing or assaulting depot staff, damaging depot buildings or property, or committing other serious breaches of depot regulations. In this case there was an implication these *mauvais sujets* might include commissioned officers or senior other ranks—warrant officers and non-commissioned officers and their equivalents among merchant seamen and privateersmen.

Commissioner Bowen appears to have spent most of the following nine months in Scotland carrying out his instructions, so great was the work involved.[25] The magnitude of his task, far greater than the search for a depot by Malcolm Wright in Edinburgh and district in 1803-4, was illustrated by an instruction on 24 October from the Admiralty to the Transport Board, which the Board sent on next day to Bowen, 'that we should make preparation for sending all future prisoners, officers and men, to Scotland, except only such as from wounds or sickness may require to be allowed to land; and also to make arrangements for removing one fourth of the French officers now in South Britain into North Britain.'[26] A constant stream of letters, suggestions, and reports passed between the Board and Bowen during those nine months, but especially between October 1810 and March 1811.

More than a dozen possible buildings, islands, or other places, several of which have already been mentioned, that might be pressed into use as depots were suggested. They included Arran, Ayr, Edinburgh Castle, Esk Mills, Fort Augustus, Fort George, Fort William, 'any of the islands in the Firth of Forth' (presumably Inchkeith or the Isle of May were intended, but possibly not excluding Inchcolm, Inchgarvie, and even, towering 420 feet from out of the sea, the Bass Rock, that grim former state prison used in the later 17th century to confine Covenanter and Jacobite prisoners), Linlithgow Palace, 'a large cotton mill adjoining the town of Newton Stewart', some land at Penicuik offered by Sir George Clerk, the Hebridean islands of Lewis and Skye, Stirling Castle, and Valleyfield Mills at Penicuik. The building of a depot at Perth and of an extension to the existing one at Greenlaw had, as already noted, been suggested in October 1810 by General Lord Cathcart.[27] The comment that prisoners of war, 'these brave and honourable men', should have been placed in 'one or two of our western islands, which they could have cultivated, and whence they could not have escaped, if we had forbidden all boats to approach the islands, save an armed vessel or two to guard the coast', was said also to have been made long after the war by Sir William Napier, historian of the Peninsular War, who had himself fought in it. Sir William was quoted as saying that that suggestion had been made at the time, 'but there was in those days a desire to insult the French which prevented this humane proposal from being received.'[28]

Some of these suggestions sank at once without trace. 'Ayr is not by any means approved of for a depot for prisoners,' the Transport Board told Commissioner Bowen on 14 May 1811.[29] Although the Admiralty had instructed the Transport Board in November 1810 to report 'on the expedience of erecting prisons in any of the islands of the Firth of Forth', whatever response was made by Commissioner Bowen to this instruction when it was relayed to him appears not now to survive.[30] But the Board already had in its files a report submitted to it in 1799 by Commissioner Ambrose Serle, who in 1810 was still one of its members, on the impracticability of making Inchkeith island a depot for prisoners of war, and it may be that the Admiralty was reminded in 1811 of the insuperable and unchanged difficulties Serle had described a decade earlier. Inchkeith, he wrote then after visiting it, about five miles out in the Firth of Forth from Leith, 'is one vast rock of about one mile and a half long, and one mile broad, of a very broken surface, and covered in some few spots with a thin mould. The foundations of an old building of large dimensions and great thickness are upon the summit; and these foundations, some of which are several feet above the ground, would serve for another superstructure, if required. There is a well within the old walls, but now filled up with stones; and there is an excellent spring at some distance; but too far off for convenience, and possibly too small in its issue of water to be depended upon for a large number of people. But the great objection appears to me invincible. It stands in the midst of a large inlet or bay, into which an easterly wind tumbles a very heavy sea, and the shores are so inaccessible at such times, and so difficult of access at all times, from the rocks and shallows which entirely surround the island, that the prisoners would run the risque of being starved in winter, or the stores of being lost in their passage to the island. When I add to all this the expence of boat-hire, the inconvenience of attendance, the charge of new buildings, and the prospect of their inutility at the close of the War, unless for a lazarette, I must express my belief that such a measure as the establishment of a Depot for prisoners upon this dreary and almost inaccessible rock cannot be adviseable.'[31]

Arran was likewise dismissed by the Transport Board as a suggested depot. The suggestion was made in March 1811 by David Steuart of Milton House, Edinburgh, who argued that the island offered a solution for what he regarded as the turbulence and unruliness of the prisoners in depots and the attempts by those on parole 'to disseminate their political principles' among local inhabitants. One of Arran's chief attractions for the purpose, wrote Steuart, was that it was so far from the surrounding coasts of Ayrshire and Argyllshire 'as to render it impossible for prisoners to escape if it was guarded by a frigate, some sloops, and smaller vessels—especially if it was made a felony to approach the island or land in it without a proper passport … This island is sufficiently large to contain all the Prisoners of War in Great Britain even were they double the number they are at present; … no extra expense would be required in building habitations for them. Slight houses would answer for that purpose, for the building of which there are inexhaustible quantities of free stone, limestone and slate in the island, and large forests in Argyllshire. Here also the Prisoners would be removed at the greatest possible distance from the enemy coasts of Norway, Sweden, Denmark, Holland and France. The Magazines for their provisions might be erected on the opposite points in Ayrshire and Argyllshire nearest the island of Arran, by which means the prisoners could be victualled in all weathers …'[32] Asked by the Admiralty to comment on Steuart's suggestion, the Transport Board declared that 'from the situation of the Isle of Arran and the Account given of it by Mr Steuart the Board do not think that it would be adviseable to make use of it as a general Depot for prisoners of war as the expense attending it would be enormous; but if hereafter it might be judged proper to build another Prison for 5,000 or 6,000 Prisoners in Scotland the Isle of Arran might be a very fit situation for such an establishment. It is almost unnecessary to observe that it cannot be adviseable to have 50 or 60 thousand prisoners together in any part whatever of the British Dominions as proposed by Mr Steuart.'[33]

'A large cotton mill adjoining the town of Newton Stewart, which has not been wrought for some years', suggested as a possible depot by the adjutant of the Wigtown Militia, was left unwrought also by the Transport Board.[34] But the offer by Sir George Clerk, a prominent local landowner, to lease or sell some land at Penicuik as a site for a possible depot was considered by the Transport Board for some weeks during May and June 1811, although eventually declined because the land was no longer wanted.[35]

Lewis and Skye had been suggested as possible depots, along with the Isle of Man and Lundy, by that veteran and highly influential politician Henry Dundas, Lord Melville, 'King Harry the Ninth of Scotland', in a letter on 24 December 1810 to the brother of Sir Rupert George, chairman of the Transport Board. Lord Melville was not alone among members of the upper classes in seeing the presence of so many French prisoners of war in Britain as an actual or potential Trojan horse. 'It appears to be part of the policy of Buonaparte,' he wrote, 'to load England [by which Melville meant Britain] with the Burthen of keeping as many Prisoners as possible, by which means he not only wars against our Finances, but contrives to keep in Britain upwards of Fifty Thousand of his Military Executioners, ready in the event of either internal Commotion or Foreign Invasion, to act against us, so soon as arms are put into their hands.' Despite Lord Melville's advocacy, no evidence has been found that Lewis and Skye were considered by the Admiralty or the Transport Board as possible depots.[36]

Lord Melville, however, played an active and successful part in a campaign to defeat proposals by the Admiralty, Transport Board, and Home Office to create a prisoner of war depot out of Linlithgow Palace. The Palace had been considered at the beginning of the Napoleonic Wars in 1803 as a possible depot for captives, and four years earlier Commissioner Ambrose Serle of the Transport Board had likewise intended to examine its possibilities for that purpose during his tour of Scotland in 1799. '… but,' reported Serle then to the Transport Board, 'I was well assured that it was at once so large and so ruinous that it would not be proper to meddle with it …'[37]

The possibility of converting the Palace into a depot was raised again in General Lord Cathcart's response of 3 October 1810 to the Transport Board's request for advice on additional places where prisoners of war might be held in Scotland.[38] Commissioner Bowen, instructed by the Transport Board to see if the Palace might be suitable, made it one of the first places he visited after his arrival in Scotland in mid October. 'The ruins of Linlithgow Palace,' he reported to the Transport Board on 28 October, 'stand on ground well situated for a prison, but the walls are in a bad condition, and it is doubtful whether in their present state, they would bear roofing. Mr Reid, the architect, who visited the Palace with me, has my directions to form an estimate of the expence required to make it a secure prison for 5,000 men, with an hospital, guard room, and other necessary appendages for the establishment. The ground being situated near the town, the agent, surgeon and clerks may be accommodated near the prison gates without any additional expense of buildings for them; nor would there be any occasion for building barracks, as the soldiery for guard might be quartered in the town.'[39]

Within five days of Bowen's report the Admiralty asked the Home Secretary, Richard Ryder, 'to cause Linlithgow Castle [sic—Palace was meant] to be given up for that purpose.' The Home Office evidently told the Admiralty and the Transport Board that the latter would have to negotiate on the question with Sir Thomas Livingstone, Keeper of the Palace. Bowen was authorised by the Board to bargain with Sir Thomas to a maximum of £200 to compensate him for the loss of his annual income from his appointment, which was believed to be not more than £100. Once that were settled Bowen was instructed to 'immediately take the necessary measures for the requisite plan and specification to enable us to advertise for a contract to rebuild and fit the premises as early as possible in the spring.' The Board's instruction was reinforced by one from the Admiralty that Bowen should 'make as soon a bargain as you can with Sir Thomas Livingstone to induce him to relinquish his right to Linlithgow Palace.' Sir Thomas, impressed by the anxiety of the Board and the Admiralty to convert the Palace into a depot, appears to have had a larger payment in mind: '… you are not to allow Sir Thomas Livingstone more than £200 per annum for his life-interest in Linlithgow Palace and premises,' Bowen was warned by the Board on 29 November. A week later Sir Thomas was still proving difficult: 'Should Sir Thomas Livingstone not accept of the terms you may offer him,' the Board told Bowen, 'you are to call upon him for a statement of the yearly emolument derived by him from Linlithgow Castle [sic] at present.' Sir Thomas put his cards on the table on 7 December. In a letter that day to Bowen he offered to give up to the Transport Board 'my Interest in the Palace of Linlithgow, and adjoining grounds called the Peel, in consideration of their paying me a yearly rent of Two hundred and twenty five pounds during my life, Reserving to myself that small garden and stripe [sic] of ground pointed out to you upon the Plan, and a servitude of a free road along the shore of the Loch and other conveniences for the Fishing.' On 14 January Alexander Greig, solicitor at Edinburgh for the Admiralty and Transport Board, reported that Sir Thomas had agreed to sign a lease of the Palace and its adjacent grounds, but before doing so he had asked that the Transport Board should secure formal sanction from the government, a request endorsed by Greig 'as I do not think Sir Thomas's commission gives him any power or authority to authorise any kind of alterations on the Palace such as are intended.'[40]

But these plans went agley and Linlithgow Palace never did become a depot for the prisoners of war. The proposal to make it so had badly upset some influential members of the upper class in Scotland. The Earl of Aberdeen, for example, wrote on 31 March to inform Charles Yorke, First Lord of the Admiralty, of complaints he had received from Scotland about 'the intended destruction of the Palace of Linlithgow for the purpose of accommodating French prisoners about to be sent to that country.' The government's proposals, said the earl, had created a 'very considerable sensation' and there was deep feeling throughout the country about 'the destruction of this monument of ancient magnificence.' Aberdeen recognised the difficulty of finding a suitable depot for the prisoners of war, but 'from the state in which the palace actually is, I feel convinced that a new building might be erected for a less sum than it will take to accomplish the work of mutilation.' He asked Yorke to reconsider the proposal.[41]

A more intemperate letter on the subject was written that month by Henry Dundas, Lord Melville, to his son Robert: 'For this week past,' Melville wrote, 'I have never been in any society without hearing much discussion and complaints uttered upon the plan of converting the Palace of Linlithgow into a Prison for French prisoners, and I confess I was much pleased with the tone of sentiments which broke out upon the occasion. I should have thought that our Monarchical and Aristocratical Pride was much blunted and impaired if one of the Palaces of our ancient Sovereigns, one of the few Badges of our monarchical pride, had been, without creating any sensation in the country, converted into a den for the execrable vermin destined to be its future inhabitants. I don't disguise from you that for one I entered warmly into those feelings and could not help thinking that the measure had been adopted as a piece of mere official detail without attending to what feelings would naturally be exacted by it.' Melville said some 'of the most respectable Gentlemen of Linlithgowshire and Stirlingshire' had come to him to see if a meeting of those counties could not be called on the issue, and he believed that Midlothian might also be induced to follow their example and join with others 'in addressing the Regent and remonstrating against what they naturally, and I confess not inaptly, call an insult to the feelings of the country.'[42]

Melville had sent for the government architect Robert Reid, who had shown him the specifications for the alterations and buildings proposed. They showed that 'the whole appearance of the Structure of the palace is altered, much of it pulled down, and all the turrets and vestiges of antiquity annihilated and every traveller who passes to or from the western part of the Kingdom must be subjected to the mortification of no more enjoying the Beauty and dignity of one of our prouder monuments of antiquity, and of one of the greatest ornaments of an extensive and populous surrounding country.' The Lord President of the Court of Session, Melville said, joined 'warmly in the mortification he has to undergo in being deprived of the chief ornament of the spot he has selected as the seat of his retirement and solace from business.'[43] Reid, said Melville, had frankly admitted to him there was no particular reason for choosing the Palace as a depot for French prisoners 'with which we are now annoyed in every corner of this part of the Kingdom', and that Linlithgow was thought to be a good place for a barracks to be built, which would be the ultimate outcome of the project, but a barracks could equally well be built elsewhere near the town and would cost no more than the proposals to convert the Palace into a depot. Urging his son Robert Dundas to press the government, particularly the Treasury and the Admiralty, on the question, Melville said Acts of the Scots parliament in the reign of James VI had inalienably annexed the Palace and park of Linlithgow to the crown and the present proposals concerning the creation of a depot there could not proceed without another Act of parliament. He concluded by remarking that though the country had long accepted 'the loss of a Resident king and a local Parliament, with the sacrifice of all the Pomp and Morale and National Pride which such a change of Government necessarily produced' through the union of the crowns in 1603, before which the Scots parliament had sometimes met in Linlithgow Palace, it was nonetheless 'surely undervaluing our feelings too much to destroy for so trite an object as a Den for French miscreants, the Palace in which our last Resident monarch held his last Parliament out of …' [the last word of Melville's letter is illegible but the context indicates he meant Edinburgh.].[44]

Another combatant in the forces mobilised to prevent Linlithgow Palace becoming a depot may have been Sir Walter Scott. Though there is no evidence in *The Letters of Sir Walter Scott* Vol.III: *1811-1814* that Scott took part in the opposition to the project it is difficult to believe he did not use his influence, given the passage in his novel *Waverley*, published in 1814, paying tribute to Lord Melville: 'They halted at Linlithgow, distinguished by its ancient palace, which Sixty Years since, was entire and habitable, and whose venerable ruins, not quite *Sixty Years since*, very narrowly escaped the unworthy fate of being converted into a barrack for French prisoners. May repose and blessings attend the ashes of the patriotic statesman, who, amongst his last services to Scotland, interposed to prevent this profanation!'[45]

By the middle of April 1811 the Admiralty and the Transport Board had hauled down their colours and admitted the defeat of their proposal to convert Linlithgow Palace into a depot.[46]

Of the two Castles (Edinburgh and Stirling) and three Forts (George, Augustus, and William) at first considered in autumn 1810 as possible depots for prisoners of war only Edinburgh Castle consequently became one. General Lord Cathcart's discouraging comments in his reply of 3 October to the Transport Board's initial enquiries about four of these five places appear effectively to have removed Fort Augustus, Fort George and Fort William from the agenda.[47]

Lord Cathcart's reply of 3 October had made no specific mention of Stirling Castle as a possible depot for prisoners of war. The Transport Board's instructions a week later to Commissioner Bowen included one that he should report on the suitability of the Castle; and in the last week of October Bowen duly visited it. He reported to the Board on 28 October that 'Stirling Castle can be fitted to receive 2,500 prisoners without disturbing the new barracks, which would contain the guard or 500 troops. There is an hospital near the Castle which can be fitted at a small expense to receive 100 sick or more. In short, stauncheons may be fitted, the windows secured, and the whole be put into a secure state to receive prisoners in less than a month.'[48] Bowen added that if the problems indicated in Lord Cathcart's reply about the use of castles, forts and barracks in Scotland could be overcome then Stirling Castle and Edinburgh Castle could together hold 5,500 prisoners of war 'who might be sent to the Firth [of Forth] immediately or as soon as Hammocks, stores and provisions can be provided for them ... but if the temporary inconvenience and obstacles stated are considered as insurmountable no prisoners can be confined in this country (except in White's buildings) [i.e., at Esk Mills, Penicuik] until about the month of August next.' Three weeks later, however, doubtless because of the unwillingness of the army authorities to give up any part of the Castle to prisoners of war, the Transport Board told Bowen that 'No steps are to be taken at present concerning Stirling Castle.'

And by the last week of November the Admiralty had clearly given up hope of acquiring any part of the Castle for that purpose.[49]

Edinburgh Castle, or at least part of it, fell, however, to a steady offensive by the Admiralty and the Transport Board, despite stubborn rearguard action by the army authorities. This measure of success by the end of 1810 owed something to the previous use of part of the Castle as a depot for prisoners during the French Revolutionary and earlier 18th-century wars, and as an occasional overnight or otherwise brief staging post for some prisoners on their way to Greenlaw or Peebles during the first decade of the Napoleonic Wars. That the Transport Board had spent £1,884.3s.6d. at the end of the French Revolutionary Wars in fitting out quarters in the Castle for several hundred prisoners of war but had been denied the use of them by the army authorities on the resumption of war in 1803, still rankled with the Board.[50] The admission, however, by Lord Cathcart on 3 October 1810 that 'Edinburgh [Castle] is less objectionable' than Fort George, and 'would be sooner, and at less expense, converted to the use in question' [i.e., a depot for prisoners of war],[51] encouraged the Admiralty and the Transport Board to persevere with their efforts to acquire, or reacquire, the use of at least part of the Castle. The Board's instructions to Commissioner Bowen a week later had included one that he ascertain the Castle's fitness to become a depot, 'particularly with the view of confining, if necessary, about 1,000 superior refractory prisoners', and, if so, when and at what cost it could be made ready to accommodate them.[52] Bowen had reported on 28 October that the Castle 'could be fitted up to receive 3,000 prisoners immediately if the barracks were given up, and the troops quartered in the town, until White's buildings [i.e., Esk Mills] are ready.'[53]

On 12 November Bowen reported again to the Board: 'Notwithstanding the obstacles that have been stated against Edinburgh Castle, I think it very desirable to have the barracks that I have already pointed out for a Depot to be fitted immediately to receive prisoners upon their arrival in the Firth [of Forth], for it will often happen (owing to the state of the tides and bad weather) that prisoners may be landed too late in the day to be marched to Penicuik … in that case we should have a secure prison to arrange the healthy for marching and a good hospital to receive the sick, both of officers and men, incapable of marching immediately. Lord Cathcart is now in London and can give their Lordships [of the Admiralty] all the information necessary for removing or securing the ordnance stores in the Castle which are the only impediments to our occupying the New Barracks which is admirably suited for a prison.'[54] Thus the uses to which the Castle might be put by the Board now appeared to be threefold: as a 'permanent' depot, as a depot for confining 'superior refractory prisoners', and as a staging post for prisoners landed at Leith or elsewhere on their way to depots at Penicuik or to parole towns. The Board replied to Bowen on 15 November that 'We shall endeavour to procure a part of Edinburgh Castle for the purpose you mention',[55] and a week later added that 'it is intended to appropriate such part of Edinburgh Castle for the reception of prisoners as was occupied last war.'[56] On 30 November the Board wrote the Admiralty inviting their Lordships, who by then had given up the attempt to acquire the use of part of Stirling Castle, to agree that 'it will be adviseable that from 500 to 1,000 prisoners should be received in Edinburgh Castle, and that application should therefore be made to the Ordnance and Barrack Departments to cause the stores belonging to them in that part intended to be occupied by prisoners to be removed, and that the resident storekeeper and barrack master should be instructed to communicate with Commissioner Bowen on the subject.'[57] The Lords Commissioner of the Admiralty duly applied to the Treasury and the Board of Ordnance for that to be done, and on 14 December the Treasury assured the Admiralty that orders had been given to remove Ordnance stores from the Castle to make room for prisoners of war. The Board, after receiving a report from Robert Reid, government architect, on the question, informed the Admiralty on 21 December that 'The two lower floors of the New Barracks at Edinburgh Castle having been selected to be appropriated for the accommodation of from 500 to 1,000 prisoners ... we have given directions for their being fitted for this purpose with as little delay as possible.'[58]

The Board then proceeded to recommend that Malcolm Wright, 'the present agent for prisoners of war at Greenlaw Prison, in consequence of local knowledge and long experience in the detail of that service, be appointed agent at the prison in Edinburgh Castle, and that a lieutenant of the navy be appointed agent at Greenlaw prison in his room.' Wright was formally appointed agent at the Castle by order of the Admiralty on 28 December. He was also made responsible for receiving all prisoners of war and stores for their use arriving at Leith or its neighbourhood, 'and also facilitating as much as lies in your power all communications of this Department with its Agents in Scotland.'[59]

By this time the proposed confinement of hundreds of prisoners of war in the Castle was becoming public knowledge. 'We understand that accommodation is preparing in the Castle of Edinburgh for 500 French prisoners, which are soon expected to arrive here,' reported the *Caledonian Mercury* on 22 December. And on the last day of the year an advertisement in the press announced that the Transport Board Commissioners would be ready on 3 January 'to receive sealed Tenders and treat with such persons as may be willing to contract for Victualling prisoners of war, in health or sickness' at the Castle for a period of six months.[60]

Yet with Robert Reid, the government architect, anxious to get ahead with preparing the accommodation for prisoners of war at the Castle and complaining to the Transport Board as late as 25 December that no authority had yet been given him by the army authorities to take over the agreed part of the barracks, it was obvious that those authorities were still dragging their feet about giving it up. This reluctance was shown in a letter on 29 December to the Board from Major General the Honourable Alexander Hope, Deputy Quartermaster-General. General Hope claimed it had been agreed that 'the occupation of Edinburgh Castle should be restricted to the confinement of a limited number of refractory prisoners', and that the commander of the Forces in North Britain 'would be instructed to give up sufficient accommodation for the purpose, when prepared, and when it should be found necessary.'

Hope's letter prompted the Transport Board to appeal at once to the Admiralty to ensure that 'such parts of the Barracks Buildings at Edinburgh Castle ... be appropriated to the reception of prisoners of war as were appropriated in the last war.' These were the only parts of the Castle, the Board said, use of which was sought. '... but it was never intended to restrict it to the confinement of refractory prisoners only; ... a proper place for receiving from 500 to 1,000 prisoners at Edinburgh, previously to their being marched to the inland depots is absolutely necessary... We have to add that if Edinburgh Castle be only used for prisoners of war as proposed in General Hope's letter great distress and inconvenience must attend the landing of prisoners at Leith.'[61]

Some progress, though not as much as the Board would have wished, had been made in the matter by 21 January, when the Board appears to have told the Admiralty that 'we must for the present be satisfied with the accommodation already delivered up and now fitting for the reception of prisoners in Edinburgh Castle...' Instead of places being made available in the Castle for up to 2,800 prisoners of war, as Lord Cathcart in his letter of 3 October had estimated, the Transport Board found itself early in 1811 with accommodation there for a maximum of about 1,000.[62]

While the Board and the Admiralty were thus attempting to acquire accommodation at Edinburgh Castle, they were also pursuing the acquisition of two new depots at Penicuik that would be additional to Greenlaw.

At Greenlaw itself the building of a new depot or prison within the following six months had been suggested by Lord Cathcart in October 1810.[63] At that time Greenlaw's maximum capacity was 570 prisoners and it then held 332. In October the Transport Board arranged to send more than 200 prisoners from Forton depot at Portsmouth to Greenlaw, and in mid-November they were duly landed from four ships at Leith and marched out to the depot—though the 170 or so officers among them were promptly sent away on parole to Peebles. By March 1811 at least 145 more prisoners (mainly 'Danes') had arrived at Greenlaw, and by September 1811 the depot was said to have 624.[64]

When at the end of December 1810 Malcolm Wright was appointed agent at Edinburgh Castle, he was succeeded as agent at Greenlaw by Lieutenant Joseph Priest, Royal Navy. Priest was told by the Transport Board on his appointment on 3 January that 'it is indispensably necessary that he should reside constantly as near to Greenlaw as possible.' Priest took up his duties at the depot at the end of that month.[65]

The first of the Board's instructions on 10 October to Commissioner Bowen had been to ascertain whether its existing lease of Greenlaw taken in 1804 could be extended, on what terms and for how long, what additional accommodation for prisoners could be provided and at what cost, and the earliest date that prisoners could be received there.[66] Unfortunately, the minutes of the Transport Board between January and April 1811 appear not to have survived. But negotiations between Bowen and Mrs Trotter, widow of the owner in 1804, clearly proved protracted and difficult. She was obviously intent on making hay while the sun shone. On 25 April the Board sent Bowen a copy of a letter it had received from Mrs Trotter, arising from his negotiations with her, and the Board declared, 'we have to observe that we consider the terms on which she proposes to dispose of the said premises to be totally inadmissible.' Nonetheless negotiations dragged on with her. In response to further instructions from the Board on 1 April 1811 Bowen had asked the government architect Robert Reid 'to refit Greenlaw'. But on 14 May the Board told Bowen that 'all idea of purchasing the premises at Greenlaw is relinquished.' When at the end of that month Sir George Clerk proposed to lease the Board 10 or 15 acres near Penicuik, Bowen recommended 'the erecting additional Prisons at Greenlaw instead of Pennycuick' and enclosed a letter from Mrs Trotter 'proposing to reduce her terms for the sale or hire of the premises at Greenlaw.' The Board told Bowen on 4 June that it 'did not consider it desirable to extend the Premises at Greenlaw under the present lease, but they wish him to ascertain on what terms Mrs Trotter will dispose of a piece of ground.'[67]

'Exorbitant' was how Bowen described to the Board on 12 June her terms for the provision of land at Greenlaw. He reported that he proposed to try to negotiate the purchase of some freehold land being sold near Esk Mills, so that a depot might be built on it. The Board's response was to inform Bowen 'that it is not intended to build any more prisons at Greenlaw but to complete the present for 600 men, and that it is not intended to purchase the land from Mrs Trotter.' And later that month Bowen was told that neither the land offered by Sir George Clerk nor the freehold land for sale near Esk Mills was any longer wanted by the Board.[68] With the addition or adaptation of accommodation then to house a further fifty or so prisoners Greenlaw remained a depot until nearly the end of the war in 1814. But, as will be shown in a later chapter, a huge enlargement of its accommodation was being undertaken during the last year of the war. By that time ownership of Greenlaw had passed into the hands of the government.

The two new depots at Penicuik which the government did succeed in acquiring in the winter of 1810-11 were at Esk Mills and Valleyfield Mills.

Esk Mills, built between 1773 and 1777, perhaps the oldest cotton mill in Scotland and which in the mid-1790s had employed more than 500 workers, appear to have been partially converted to paper-making by the earlier years of the Napoleonic Wars.[69] The Penicuik local historian John Wilson says that by the beginning of the 19th century Esk Mills, 'whether resulting from excessive competition, or from want of enterprise in adopting the necessary machinery', had gradually fallen behind in the race with larger cotton mills such as New Lanark.[70] The Mills—described in the newspaper advertisement as 'the two cotton mills at Esk Mills'—had been advertised for sale in April 1804. After more than a dozen re-insertions the advertisement on 27 November that year announced the 'Upset price reduced from £9,000 to £7,000 or lease for 3 or 5 years.' The advertisement on 21 April, in announcing the sale of the mills by public roup or auction in June or July following, provided this description of them: 'The two COTTON MILLS of Eskmills of Penicuik, situated about nine miles to south of Edinburgh, with a most excellent dwelling place for a managing partner or overseer. There is a fall water [sic] of 22 feet and there are forty acres of land belonging to the mills. There are 3,432 spindles in both mills, with suitable machinery, and about 70 apartments for workers. The premises are held feu for payment of £50 sterling.' A year later the mills remained unsold or unlet and another newspaper advertisement, which added to the previous description that as well as the 3,432 water spindles 'there are also Nine Mull Jennies, containing 180 spindles', announced another public roup for them in Edinburgh on 10 April 1805, with the upset price now reduced to £5,000.[71]

Esk Mills, less than a mile up the North Esk river from Greenlaw depot, were still available for sale or lease in autumn 1810 when on 3 October Lord Cathcart suggested to the Transport Board the buildings could probably be hired and within three months made ready to hold 3,000 prisoners. Of the list of instructions given by the Board a week later to Commissioner Bowen the second was to check whether Esk Mills were a fit place to hold prisoners of war, the terms on which the Mills could be acquired, the number of prisoners they could contain, within what time they could be made ready and at what cost.[72]

Bowen wasted no time. By 6 November, along with the architect Robert Reid, he had twice inspected Esk Mills and sent back reports to the Transport

Board. Meantime, however, the Board was having doubts about the Mills as a possible depot, and submitted to the Admiralty on 23 October 'our opinion that the expence which would attend Mr White's premises ... if converted into a prison, although less perhaps than prison ships, would be so very great, that it is not by any means adviseable to incur it, if any other less expensive manner of confining the prisoners can be devised. To this may be added the great delay which must necessarily take place in any arrangement of this kind.' The Admiralty, however, did not share these doubts and on 12 November it ordered the Transport Board to instruct Bowen 'to agree with Mr White for the whole of his Buildings on the best terms in his power and to use all possible expedition in fitting them for the reception of prisoners of war.'[73] Two days later the government formally leased the mills. Both the cotton and the paper mill were leased for a minimum of three years or for the duration of the war, whichever was the longer, at an annual rent of £2,000. Certain parts of the paper mill, including the engine house and vat house, were reserved to the owners, and a stone wall was built to partition them off from the rest of the buildings. 'Both mills were speedily emptied. The Cotton Mill machinery was knocked up, and the Brass, Iron, Lead, etc., sold.' The Transport Board had instructed Bowen on 30 October not to offer more than £1,200 a year as rent for the mills. That the rent actually agreed proved to be 60 per cent greater was an indication of the desperation of the government to acquire depots in Scotland for the prisoners.[74]

On 16 November Captain Richard Pellowe, Royal Navy, was appointed agent for prisoners of war in Scotland, with his base at Esk Mills. Work began at once on preparing the mills to receive prisoners, and Robert Reid, the architect supervising the building works there, told the Transport Board on 22 December that the new depot should be ready for its first intake on 5 or 6 January. On 29 November an advertisement was issued by the Transport Board seeking tenders for victualling prisoners at Esk Mills for a six-month period from 1 January. Thus speedily Esk Mills was emerging as the first entirely new depot in Scotland since 1804.[75]

Almost as speedily, Valleyfield Mills at Penicuik was following in its wake. These mills, up the North Esk river half a mile from Esk Mills and a mile and a half from Greenlaw, had, unlike the two latter places, not been mentioned either in Lord Cathcart's letter on 3 October 1810 about possible depots or in the instructions a week later by the Transport Board to Commissioner Bowen. Valleyfield Mills, owned by the brothers Alexander and Duncan Cowan, had been producing paper since 1709. But by 1810-11, as Charles Cowan, son of Alexander, later recalled: '... trade was in a miserable state, no doubt in consequence of the protracted war and the famine prices of the raw material ...' Within three weeks of arriving in Scotland Commissioner Bowen reported that he hoped to arrange with the Cowan brothers the sale to the Transport Board of the mills for use as a prisoner of war depot, and on 7 December the mills were duly bought for £10,000.[76]

Work began at once on preparing the mills to hold prisoners of war, and on 18 December Captain Thomas Heddington, Royal Navy, hitherto the Board's agent at Yarmouth, was appointed its agent at Valleyfield, 'with the usual salary of thirty shillings per diem.' Like Lieutenant Priest, agent at Greenlaw, Captain Heddington was made subject to the orders of Captain Pellowe at Esk Mills. Eleven days later was published in the press the standard advertisement inviting tenders from contractors for victualling the prisoners at Valleyfield for six months from 1 February.[77]

Finally, in 1811-12 an entirely new purpose-built depot for 7,000 prisoners of war was constructed at Perth. The suggestion made by General Lord Cathcart in October 1810 about building a new depot there, 'where ground may be had … indeed without any outlay of money', was followed up by the Board and Commissioner Bowen as their representative in Scotland. By the end of that month Bowen had visited Perth and reported back enthusiatically to the Board: 'There is a piece of ground near the town of Perth, belonging to the [Board of] Ordnance, alluded to in [Lord Cathcart's letter], which he informs me is not wanted, and which is admirably situated to build a prison on, water and every other convenience for supplying the prison being near the spot. The prison might be so constructed as to be fit for barracks in time of peace.'[78]

The Board of Ordnance dragged its feet about giving up the eight or nine acres of ground the Transport Board sought for the new depot to be built on. The latter pressed the question during May and June, when it impressed upon the Admiralty that 'Commissioner Bowen is very urgent respecting the Commencement of the Works as soon as possible, in consequence of the Advanced Period of the Season.' But at last on 21 June the Ordnance Board agreed to transfer the ground to the Transport Board. Advertisements in the press beginning a week later and repeated during the first week of July invited tenders by 15 July from building contractors for the construction of the new depot, though the Admiralty's approval for building work to begin was withheld until an estimate was available of the cost according to the lowest tender. By mid-July Bowen, still in Scotland, had made the necessary arrangements, and on 2 September several hundred building workers began the construction of the new depot at Perth, the first to be built for that purpose north of the Border.[79]

Scotland from the end of 1810 was thus rapidly becoming a major place of confinement for prisoners of war.

5

Esk Mills, and the Voyage from England to Scotland

When Robert Reid, government architect in Scotland, told the Transport Board on 22 December that the new depot at Esk Mills should be ready to receive its first prisoners by 5 or 6 January 1811, his prediction proved over-optimistic. Reid admitted 'some matters' would remain then to be dealt with, but he said he was using every means in his power to urge the building contractors there and at Valleyfield 'to get on with despatch, and I shall use every possible exertion to hasten the speedy completion of the works. The weather has unfortunately become very unfavourable.'[1] Captain Pellowe, RN, who had arrived at the end of November at Esk Mills, his base as the Board's agent for Scotland, was less sanguine than Reid. 'I cannot positively state,' he told the Board on 20 December, 'at what earliest time this Depot will be ready to receive prisoners. Had the weather continued fair I should have had the whole line of the stockade fence levelled and ready for the captives. The posts are in and the fence up but it has snowed so incessantly ... that no man can stand out to work.'[2] Impressed by Pellowe's report, the Board asked the Admiralty on 24 December not to embark prisoners under orders for transfer to Scotland 'until we can ascertain when the prison will be ready for their reception.' The Admiralty agreed to the Board's request.[3]

The date for the opening of the depot was postponed several times during the following few weeks. As early as 27 December, however, the Board's optimism about the opening date had evidently returned and it told HM Treasury that it would be 'about the 5th of January'. The following day the Board, in asking the War Office to provide a guard of 200 soldiers at Esk Mills, declared the depot would be ready to receive prisoners on 6 January. The latter date had been given the Board a few days earlier by Captain Pellowe, whose optimism about it was beginning to overtake his earlier pessimism. The Admiralty had by then already told the Board that as many prisoners as HMS *Pompée* could take were to be put aboard her at Plymouth and sent to Scotland. The Board replied on 2 January that the prisoners could be embarked 'whenever their Lordships shall think proper'. Even earlier, the Board had informed Malcolm Wright, its agent at Edinburgh Castle, on 28 December that '300 French prisoners are to be immediately embarked at Portsmouth for Leith, and if Esk Mills is not ready to receive them, or some of them, those not taken in there are to go to Greenlaw or Edinburgh Castle.' Wright, who remained in charge also at Greenlaw until the arrival there at the end of January of his successor as agent, Lieutenant Priest, RN, was further instructed by the Board on 19 and again on 23 January that as Greenlaw was in future to be only for Danish prisoners all French prisoners there should be immediately removed to Esk Mills. When Priest did arrive at Greenlaw he too was instructed by the Board to send all French prisoners there to Esk Mills, which Captain Pellowe had meantime reported would be ready to take them on 2 February.[4]

Although the surviving evidence about the position at Esk Mills is scrappy, the impression it leaves is one of over-hastiness, problems with the fabric or construction of the buildings, and shortcomings in the arrangements to deal with the prisoners once they arrived. Thus on 21 December Captain Pellowe reported to the Board '... there is no room for the Hospital Mates in the Hospital, and that the Hospital is only large enough to contain 36 cradles for the sick.' The Board replied that accommodation for the mates, matron and stewards should be found in some of the houses attached to the mills, 'and they consider that each floor of the Hospital will contain 36 cradles and if it will not contain all the sick the upper of one end of the Prison is to be appropriated.'[5] As late as 25 February the Board sent Pellowe for his explanation a complaint by the Admiralty that 'HMS *Ardent* had arrived at Leith with 480 French prisoners but that in consequence of the defective state of the Prison at Esk Mills they could not be landed until the 22nd instant ...'[6]

It was on 4 February that the first intake of prisoners entered Esk Mills. There were 192 of them. All of them had been sent there from Greenlaw. It was not without significance for what proved to be the brief but troubled existence of Esk Mills as a depot that some, perhaps many, among those 192 were French prisoners who had taken part a month earlier at Greenlaw in what was described as an 'Insurrection' against Danish and Swedish prisoners volunteering into the British navy.[7]

The first prisoner enrolled on the Esk Mills General Entry Book or register was Nicolas Aucum, described as First Lieutenant of the merchant vessel *La Flore*. Aucum had already spent almost eight years in captivity at Greenlaw, as he and his ship had been captured on 11 July 1803, within a few weeks of the resumption of the war. On his entry to Esk Mills Aucum was aged 52. He was described in the Entry Book as 5ft 7ins in height, of stout build, with a long visage, dark brown hair, grey eyes, and with smallpox scars.[8] Aucum was unquestionably 'the worthy old mercantile gentleman from Nantes' recalled long afterwards by Charles Cowan, son of one of the Valleyfield millowners. He was, wrote Cowan, 'named "Aucamp". I know not how to write it, but it was pronounced Okang. He had been nine or ten years a prisoner, having been captured on board a merchant vessel, and a son had been born to him since his capture, whom he had never seen. Though he longed much to recover his liberty and his home, he was patient and resigned to his sad fate, and was much liked by my father and mother, whom he often visited, and from whom he received a hearty welcome so long as he was at liberty.' Aucum had apparently been given 'parole' at Greenlaw during the idiosyncratic regime there of Malcolm Wright, agent, but it had been withdrawn from him and others when certain prisoners had escaped.[9]

The first 192 prisoners to enter Esk Mills on 4 February were rapidly followed by a flood of others. Next day 256 more arrived from the hulks at Chatham, having been landed at Leith from the 74-gun warship or man-of-war HMS *Vanguard* after a seven-day voyage from Sheerness and then marched out at once the eleven miles to the depot, escorted by soldiers of the Ross-shire militia and a troop of dragoons.[10] A further 220 prisoners from the hold of the *Vanguard* were landed on 6 February, lodged for the night in Edinburgh Castle, then marched out next day to Esk Mills. From Chatham also there arrived at Leith on 4 February on the warships HMS *Dictator* and HMS *Ruby* about 900 more prisoners. There was some delay in landing them because of a strong south-westerly wind sweeping across the Firth of Forth which made conditions in Leith Roads very difficult. The wind worsened on 7 February into a violent gale. One naval lighter ferrying prisoners ashore at Leith from the frigates that day was forced by the weather to bear away with 150 of them to the Fife coast, and landed them safely at Burntisland. A strong escort of troops was sent over that evening to Burntisland to prevent their escape, and the following day brought them back over the Forth to Leith from where they were marched into Edinburgh Castle. On 9 February these prisoners and about 300 others who had been lodged in the Castle were marched out to Esk Mills, 'under a strong guard of the Perthshire militia and a party of dragoons.' And on 18 February the remaining 440 or so prisoners from HMS *Ruby* who had been lodged in the Castle since 9 February were also marched out there, similarly guarded en route.

Thus in its first two weeks as a depot Esk Mills had taken in almost 1,600 prisoners—only about 300 fewer than Greenlaw had held in aggregate during the seven years from 1804 to 1810.[11]

Before the gates of Esk Mills depot opened wide again to admit another flood of captives, two men arrived there on 20 February from Greenlaw: Jean Heudier, prize master of the privateer *Le Vengeur*, captured in the English Channel in October the previous year; and Jean Baptiste Lambare, a soldier from the French 15th line infantry regiment, who had been captured in Spain in 1810.[12] Then the torrent of intakes at Esk Mills resumed on 27 February and continued until 6 March. On the earlier date 480 prisoners arrived who had been brought in HMS *Ardent* from Portsmouth. Landed at Leith on 25 and 26 February and lodged overnight in Edinburgh Castle they then were all marched out to Esk Mills on the 27th. That same day HMS *Dictator* returned to the Firth of Forth with 450 more prisoners—this time from Portsmouth. The *Dictator* was accompanied by HMS *Gorgon*, of 64 guns like the other two, carrying about 300 prisoners, many of them officers, also from Portsmouth. Because of stormy weather both ships anchored at the back of Inchkeith island in the Forth, before landing the prisoners on 5 and 6 March at Leith, from where they were marched off to Esk Mills.[13]

Thus by 6 March, a month after its opening, Esk Mills held 2,817 prisoners. They were a mixture of seamen and soldiers of all ranks, including some officers, and a few civilian passengers from captured ships. There were ensigns, surgeons, clerks, bosuns, pilots, captains, interpreters, corporals, cooks, midshipmen, mates, drummers, sergeants, prize masters, a purser, lieutenants, sailmakers, masters-at-arms, carpenters, quartermasters, armourers, servants, coopers, artillerymen, stewards, masters' mates, a caulker, a trumpeter, ships' gunners, two chief apothecaries, storekeepers, carpenters' mates, sergeant majors, adjutants, and even a Customs House officer. More than 1,200 of the prisoners are simply described in the General Entry Book as 'Seaman', and a further 903 as 'Soldier'. No fewer than 71 are described as 'Boy'- almost all ships' boys.[14]

Inevitably the flood of arrivals into the new depot created new problems or compounded those already observed there. Basic details concerning each prisoner had to be entered in the large format register or General Entry Book for the depot. Each page of the heavily bound register was 14 inches wide and 19 inches long. Each double page was divided into 35 columns. From left to right the headings of the ten columns on the left page were: the prisoner's number in the Entry Book; By what Ship or how taken; Time when; Place where; Name of Prize [i.e., ship—or regiment]; Whether Man-of-War, Privateer, or Merchant Vessel; Prisoners' Names; Quality [i.e., rank]; Time when received into Custody; From what Ship or whence received. Then on the right-hand page there were altogether 25 columns: Place of Nativity [birth]; then under the heading Description, seven columns, thus: Age, Stature [height], Person [physique], Visage [shape of face] and Complexion, Hair [i.e., colour of], Eyes [ditto], Marks or Wounds. Then under the heading Supplies of Bedding and Clothing, there were fourteen columns: Date of Supply, Hammock, Bed, Paillasse, Bolster, Blanket, Hat, Jacket, Waistcoat, Trowsers, Shirt, Shoes, Stockings, Handkerchiefs. The last three columns on the right-hand page were headed: Exchanged, Discharged, Died, or Escaped; Time When; Whither, and by what Order, if discharged.

The writing into the General Entry Book of all this information for each prisoner was a major task for the depot clerks. Three of these had been appointed by the end of December: John White, First Clerk, at a salary of

£118 a year, John Lewis, as Extra Clerk and interpreter, and a Mr Leslie, Extra Clerk—both Lewis and Leslie to be paid 30s.6d. per week. As soon as the first prisoners arrived Captain Pellowe, the agent, sought the Board's approval for the appointment of more clerks to deal with the mass of work. In refusing its permission the Board told Pellowe on 12 February: 'Stapleton Depot [at Bristol] has over 4,800 prisoners but only two clerks.' Whether this refusal led to the resignation of John White is not certain but at any rate White resigned in mid-February. When Captain Pellowe again complained to the Board about the problem of clerks, the Board told him on 22 February: 'We consider that you can be at no loss to procure fit persons for Clerks ..., many applications having been made to Commissioner Bowen in that capacity, and we therefore direct you to nominate a first clerk and two Extra Clerks.' A week later Pellowe's appointment of Andrew Johnston as an Extra Clerk was approved by the Board.[15]

The Esk Mills clerks were clearly overwhelmed by the volume of their work and they never did succeed in entering all the information about each prisoner in the depot's General Entry Book. Only the depot number of each prisoner, his name, rank, date of arrival at Esk Mills and where he had come from, the name of his ship and whether it was a man-of-war, a privateer or a merchant vessel or, in the case of a soldier, his regiment, were entered throughout the register. Places of birth were entered for only two prisoners, ages for only 25, physical descriptions such as heights and marks and wounds only for the first 192, places and dates of capture and by what or whom for only the first half of the 2,817. Very few entries at all were made for prisoners exchanged or discharged, when and by what order, or for issues of bedding and clothing.

Such problems at Esk Mills were multiplied a fortnight after it opened as a depot by a mass escape of prisoners. It was the largest such escape until then in Scotland. 'Tuesday morning, about five o'clock', reported the *Caledonian Mercury* on Thursday, 21 February, 'the prison at Esk Mills near Pennycuick, in which a number of French prisoners are confined, was broke by undermining the wall, and 12 of them got out. The alarm was soon given, and the guard fired, by which one Frenchman was killed. The rest escaped, but we hear that some of them have since been retaken.' The *Edinburgh Evening Courant* in reporting the escape that same day had found more exciting sources of information than its rival paper, and declared: 'Twenty-seven effected their purpose, but we hear that they have almost all been re-taken. Four of them are stated to have been shot by the soldiers and one drowned attempting to cross the Esk.'

In fact, there were 23 escapers. One was shot and killed during the attempt, ten were recaptured sooner or later and the other twelve appear to have got clean away. The escape aroused the hunting instincts of at least one member of the local aristocracy. At Newbattle Abbey, seven miles north-east of Esk Mills, Lord Schomberg Kerr wrote next day to his brother Lord Newbattle, then in Wiltshire: 'Twenty eight french [sic] prisoners got out from Penicuik yesterday morning. I was awoke last night by the soldiers firing. They killed one and have taken five somewhere near Musselburgh. The rest are kicking about the country. It would be capital fun to go in the woods and beat for them like woodcocks. I dare say they have stowed themselves away in the woods somewhere.'[16]

According to further press reports a few days later the escapers had raised the floor of the room in which they were confined, worked their way into the mill lade, dug through an arch which had recently been thrown over the place where the axle of the mill wheel was formerly inserted, and came out on a narrow strip of ground where three sentinels were stationed between it and the river North Esk. 'The first sentinel's piece missed fire, the shot of the second did not take effect, but by that of the third, one of the prisoners fell.' Two of the escapers who had succeeded within two days in covering the 40 miles to Maxwellheugh near Kelso were recaptured there on 21 February.[17]

Andrew Johnston, appointed an extra clerk at Esk Mills at that time, believed that several of the escapers, having been granted parole while they were confined at Greenlaw before their transfer to Esk Mills, had used their opportunities then to familiarise themselves with the buildings at the latter and the prospects they presented for escape. It was the case that at least eight of the 23 had been among the prisoners transferred to Esk Mills from Greenlaw a fortnight before the escape. Johnston's recollections provide some details additional to and different from those presented in the press. 'They cut a hatch in the underfloor above the water wheel,' he wrote, 'and got into the mill lead from whence they made their way through the river and dispersed themselves—the night was very dark and [there was] only one sentinel in the rear of the prison at that spot. The escape was only known by this Sentinel firing his piece at a poor fellow who had mistaken the road taken by the others and came up the lead in place of down. Next morning early the body was lying in the ... shed, where I saw it, and a number of prisoners playing pitch and toss with the Gog within an inch of his head.'[18]

The most circumstantial account, however, of the mass escape from Esk Mills is provided by another prisoner, who had arrived via HMS *Vanguard* at the depot on 7 February from the hulks at Chatham, and whose recollections of his three years of captivity in three successive depots in Scotland are among the most informative and on the whole reliable surviving non-official sources for the subject.

Long after the Napoleonic Wars, in the winter of 1840, Léon Wocquier, secretary of the Literary Society of the University of Louvain in Belgium, made the acquaintance of 'an old man, still hale and hearty and sturdy,' with whom he struck up daily contact. 'A kind of intimacy grew up between [us],' Wocquier wrote, 'as a result of which the old man spoke to [me] of his past with that allurement and that marvellous sureness of memory that character-ises those who have seen and suffered a great deal.' From the outset of their acquaintance Wocquier began to write down each evening what the old man had told him that day, with the intention of publishing the material 'while preserving the anonymity of the hero; but the latter allowed [me] to cite his name and that of a number of persons still alive today in Belgium and in the north and west of France, and who finding themselves mentioned among the facts given in the book, can bear witness to its authenticity.' Thus came to be published at Liège in 1845 *Souvenirs d'un Corsaire 1811-1814. Souvenirs de H.F. Marote, Lieutenant du Corsaire L'Aventurier 1811-1814.* Marote's recollections ran to 195 pages. In publishing them Wocquier said that as author or editor he had 'scrupulously respected the substance and the detail of events; only the form has been added ... It is a simple story which must depend for its value ... on its novelty and on the truthfulness of him who recounts it.' There is no doubt that the official archives and other contemporary documentary sources bear out a great deal of what Henri-Ferdinand Marote recalled thirty years later of his experiences as a prisoner of war in Scotland. But also his recollections provide information about and insights into aspects of the prisoners' lives in captivity that the official and other sources, such as newspaper reports, do not. Marote does not appear to have kept a diary or made notes at the time of his experiences. It is hardly surprising, given the passage of so many years before Wocquier recorded his oral recollections, that Marote's memory is sometimes demonstrably mistaken—for instance, about dates. An example is his statement that he and his ship *L'Aventurier* had been captured at the end of 1811, when in fact it was on 17 December 1810.[19]

A search for Henri-Ferdinand Marote in the Esk Mills Entry Book would be in vain. For he failed to tell Wocquier (or, if he did tell him, Wocquier may have decided not to publish the fact, for fear perhaps of creating difficulties for Marote's family or for other surviving prisoners of war) that throughout his captivity, and perhaps throughout his years as a privateersman and even as a merchant seaman, he had used as an alias or *nom de guerre* the name Jean Baptiste Carrier. It is Carrier, and not Marote, who is No. 577 in the Esk Mills General Entry Book. The entry there describes him as 1st Lieutenant, *L'Aventurier*.

Marote-Carrier's account to Wocquier of his years before he became a prisoner of war was that he was born about 1784, son of an old seaman from Ostend. As a child he had had 'as a toy the oar, the boat of his father, as food the products of fish; the winds, the sea, the rocks, the clouds—such were the aspects of nature he had come to know. From the age of nine he had sailed to

Iceland; since then he had not left the sea and had passed his childhood and part of his youth on merchant vessels commanded by his brother. At the age of twenty he had seen Philadelphia, the North Pole, the West Indies.' But as with those of so many other merchant seamen Marote-Carrier's livelihood was badly affected by the mutual and extensive blockades on trade that were created both by the Berlin Decree issued by Napoleon in November 1806, which, reinforced the following year by the decrees of Fontainebleau and Milan, established the so-called Continental System, and also by the consequent British Orders-in-Council of 1807.[20] As for many other continental merchant seamen, for Marote-Carrier 'the stagnation of trade and the pointless dangers of merchant sailing led him to decide to give up [that] career ... Drawn along by the spirit of the age and the lure of the adventurous life of the privateers he signed on in 1807 on the lugger *L'Aventurier*.' He remained a privateersman until his capture at the end of 1810, by which time he had become lieutenant of his ship.[21]

Landed on 7 February at Leith from HMS *Vanguard* which had brought him and his fellow prisoners from the hulks at Chatham, Marote-Carrier trudged, as had so many others since 1804, and still more were to do until the end of the war, out to captivity at Penicuik. 'Always escorted by a strong detachment of soldiers,' he long afterwards recalled, 'we arrived at nightfall at our destination [Esk Mills]. We could hardly see the lay-out of our new prison. It was situated on the left of the route from Edinburgh. ... Darkness prevented us from taking clear note of the place that day; but the next day we had nothing more urgent to do than to go round everything and see if we could find some way out. Unfortunately nothing could favour an attempt at flight.' Unknown to Marote-Carrier, however, a score of other prisoners at Esk Mills were then reaching a very different conclusion.

'... the building which was to be our prison,' continued Marote-Carrier, in providing a rare description of Esk Mills as depot, 'was ... a square edifice, in stonework topped with slates, which had previously served as a papermill. At the two sides of the principal block rose two barracks made of wood where the garrison of about 700 men lodged. A curtain of walls enclosed the three buildings; outside these walls extended a line of wooden palisades. Numerous sentinels were on the lookout in the courtyard and on the outside. Outside the palisades were some houses built in wood and stone where formerly the mill workers lived, and which were then occupied by the people attached to the service of the prison. Behind the principal building and still outside the palisades stood another building—the hospital.'

Marote-Carrier then gives a more detailed description of the depot buildings. 'All the windows were grilled with solid iron bars; the door was clad in the same metal. I should have said the only door that opened, for only the principal entry was left. The others had been walled up. Each prisoner slept in a hammock that was distributed to us on our arrival. These hammocks were stretched out on the ground floor and on the two upper floors of the building, each of which consisted of only one big room. A stair that mounted from the ground to the attic established communication between the three floors. Two sentries were at the door when we presented ourselves in the morning to go out. They let only one man pass through at a time. A gaoler counted us as we entered the courtyard where, despite the cold, we had to pass a good part of the morning. We were allowed to remain in the building in the evening because of the snow, which fell in big flakes.'[22]

Afflicted with a feverish temperature, Marote-Carrier says he took to his bed on the evening of his first full day of captivity at Esk Mills. 'When I awoke next day I could not get up although I tried to do so. I was in a state of overpowering weakness and my head burned horribly. I slept on the first floor. When the round of the sleeping places was made to get us up, a soldier came to thump with his rifle butt at my hammock. I did not respond. He struck several times more, calling on me to get dressed. As he did not get any response, the turnkey hoisted himself up on a stool or step-ladder to learn the reason for my silence. He saw that my cheeks were feverishly inflamed and realised I was ill. I was allowed to remain in bed that day. The hospital doctor who came to see me found that I had a raging fever that demanded care, and recommended me not to leave my hammock for some days, and told me that when the bout passed I would be taken to hospital.

'I did not get up all day nor the day following. Condemned to diet absolutely I took no nourishment at all. Nothing tempted me to eat, and I was glad to drink tea that a former privateer captain who traded in it brought me. On the evening of the 21st [February],[23] the indisposition gave me some respite and I was gradually dozing off when I heard stealthy footsteps in the dormitory where I was lying and in which because of my presence prisoners were not allowed during the day. I did not know who could be visiting me at this hour. It proved to be a Dutchman named De Backen, one of the pupils from my navigation class who still today [c. 1840] commands a merchant ship.[24] I was going to speak to him and ask him the reason for his coming, when he signed to me to remain silent and leaning over me, he said into my ear: "Marote, do you want to get away?" "What's that?" I cried, forgetting the fever that gripped me and that I was too weak to take two steps without falling down. "What's that?" I repeated, grasping tightly at this hope of liberty which had so many times presented itself to me and which had always escaped me. "We have found a way out!" said De Backen. "That isn't possible! Didn't we check everything the day before yesterday?" "That's right!" said De Backen, "But yesterday … we discovered a sure way that no one had suspected." "How's that?" "You know," replied De Backen, "that the room at the bottom has a planked floor. While we were tapping the ground we

67

found a place that sounded hollow. We made good use of the evening, when we were free to walk about, to raise up some planks, which presented no great difficulty, and we discovered a drain built probably at the time of the papermill and of whose existence the English don't know." "And where does this drain lead to?" "A little patience! Don't speak so loudly or you'll give us away. Some of us—I'm one of them," continued De Backen, "after obtaining an old lantern, went into this drain. It's a kind of low, straight culvert which one could only pass along bent low and where mud comes half-way up your legs, but its width allows two abreast. We have passed along from one end to the other without finding any obstacles. It runs out on the other side of the hill that overlooks Penicuik: it's a valley where there are only woods to be seen and no sign of habitation."

"'And this drain—isn't it closed?" asked Marote-Carrier. "How have the English, who are so cautious and meticulous, not discovered …?" "It was closed by an iron grill," replied De Backen. "We have broken a bar of it and now it can be passed easily. The bar has been put back in place so that the break will not be noticed, and we have arranged the escape for tomorrow night. We are running no risk: you know that there is only a single sentry on that side, which is that of the hospital. If we do not make too much noise he will not be able to hear us, and once in the woods …'"

De Backen went on to tell Marote-Carrier that the plan was being kept close to the chests of those involved in the projected escape. "We are trying to form a group big enough to provide more resources," De Backen said, "but we don't want anyone who does not have money. That would only be a useless responsibility. We are already 21. Your purse must be quite well furnished. A more attractive chance of escape will never present itself. Do you want to be one of us?" "Yes, yes! I have ten louis. We leave tomorrow, tomorrow …!" "Speak more quietly," warned De Backen. "Stay very quiet in your hammock. Try to get back to full strength so you are quite recovered for getting away. Tomorrow I will come and call you at midnight precisely. Goodbye." "Adieu," I replied. "Be careful! Above all take good care that the outlet is not discovered." "Don't worry yourself about that," said De Backen. "All precautions are taken. During the day we roll our hammocks on the planks that have been put back in place, and we have filled the crevices with mud so that nothing could be seen."'[25]

Marote-Carrier that night forgot his fever and fell asleep with '… thoughts of happiness and freedom. I saw again in my dreams my family, my dear children. I hugged them and recounted to them my sufferings and my escape. Suddenly I awoke. The night was scarcely half gone. My sleep had been heavy and instead of restoring my strength had left me very, very tired. I didn't close an eye for the rest of the night. Sometimes I felt my pulse and deluded myself about its deep and irregular beats. Sometimes I got up, wanted to get dressed but fell back from weakness into my hammock. When I had lain down for a few minutes I felt quite calm, quite robust, but when I tried my strength again I could hardly sit up in bed. This moral agitation which tormented me, these violent and repeated physical movements, led to a complete prostration from which I was drawn at daybreak by a new bout of fever. It lasted the whole morning. I voiced the wildest words and made the wildest gestures and I do not understand how I did not give away the escape project.'[26]

When about midday Marote-Carrier came to, he overheard the doctor and a nurse say that the fever had at last left him and he could be taken next day to the depot hospital. 'I could no longer harbour any illusion about the state I was in,' he recalled thirty years afterwards. 'With despair I realised that my strength was not up to it and that it would be impossible for me to run away, no matter how hard I tried. I had to drain the cup of sorrows.' His only visitor that day was the officer prisoner who supplied him with tea. In the evening, by which time his condition had not improved, Marote-Carrier fell into a deep sleep, his eyes filled with burning tears at the knowledge of his physical weakness.[27]

At midnight he found De Backen at his bedside, as he had promised. But Marote-Carrier, broken hearted, had to admit his illness made it impossible for him to join the escapers. De Backen promised that if he himself succeeded in the escape he would deliver a fond message from Marote-Carrier to his wife and children, from whom he had not heard for some time past. After De Backen stole away Marote-Carrier fell into a leaden sleep.

'A musket shot woke me up with a start,' he recalled thirty years later. 'I heard the cry "To arms!" I opened my eyes, the night was still very dark. The first idea that came to my mind was that the fugitives had been surprised. All the prisoners were awakened like me, most of them not knowing what the matter was and unable to imagine the cause of this alarm. A dreadful tumult reigned throughout the prison. From every direction cries were heard, oaths, and musket shots. That went on until morning, and it was only then that I learned the cause of the alert.

'Hardly had De Backen left me than the fugitives entered the drain and to the number of thirty began their escape without anything giving them away. But on leaving the room, the last to go having imprudently left the opening uncovered, two other prisoners noticed it and slipped into it. One of them, my supplier of tea, had taken over the lead. The hospital sentry, thinking he heard a noise from the other side of the mound or hillock where the drain ran out, immediately ran there, saw one of the bars of the grill broken, and without stopping to think fired a musket shot into the shaft, and gave the alarm. My tea captain, who was near the opening, had no time to turn back and received the musket ball in his stomach. He dropped dead. The other fugitive had heard the sentry run along to the drain, where his footsteps echoed with a hollow sound as in any other excavated passage, and fearful of being noticed he wisely retraced his steps and was back in the dormitory before his absence was noticed.

'The English, roused by the cries of the sentry, made thorough searches throughout the night in the neighbourhood of the prison. The chase lasted until the evening of the next day. All the routes were followed, all the glens were explored, but in vain. De Backen and his companions had dived into the woods, as I learned later, and there every search had been unsuccessful.'

Taken next day into the depot hospital, Marote-Carrier says: 'In crossing the yard I saw the body of the tea captain stretched out fully clothed on a ladder. To provide a lesson for prisoners who might be tempted to imitate him the commandant [i.e., Captain Pellowe, RN, the agent] had had him put on public view. He was clothed, as in life, in a pair of trousers made of poor quality cloth, a half-worn jacket, and a hat covered in striped cotton. I can see him still: his chest was uncovered, blood from the wound had not been wiped clean and was clotted by the cold. I turned my gaze sadly away. The poor man had brought me a cup of tea the previous evening when he was still hale and hearty.'[28]

Marote-Carrier's recollection of the sequel to the escape was not entirely accurate as he failed to remember or to say that at least ten of the 22 who got away were recaptured within a few days. But, he says, these 22 escapers, more fortunate than the tea captain, 'dived into the woods, and from daybreak they were far from Penicuik … They hired without delay several carts from the highlanders,[29] saying that they had to be back in Edinburgh the same day, where they had to go on board a vessel in Leith Roads that was ready to sail. This need for urgency was enough to justify the haste with which they left and the increased price that they offered to those who wished to provide the service they asked for. The good peasants harboured no suspicion and conducted the fugitives to Edinburgh.[30] From there they set out southwards for Dover, walking only at night. Once arrived in that town they stayed over there some time, passing themselves off as other than they were and each lodging in separate quarters. … They hired two fishing smacks, and taking advantage of the dark, landed safely on the coasts of France. They went to Calais, where De Backen found my family again and to whom he gave reliable news of my situation and passed on the messages that I had confided to him.'[31]

Of the escapers recaptured, five privateersmen—David Fourneau and Antoine Morel, both lieutenants, Jean Simonsen, bosun, and Louis Lepine and Jean Francois Ruy, seamen—were said to have been retaken on 22 February. Where they were recaptured, and whether all five were retaken at the same time and place, is not certain; but if Lord Schomberg Kerr's reference to the recapture of five near Musselburgh was correct then it was presumably to them.[32] The two escapers recaptured 'by Mr Alexander Nelson' at Maxwell-heugh, Kelso, on 24 February, were Jean Baptiste Cabouche (or Caboche) and Pierre François Le Couche, alias Barbouche, both seamen. Marc Butel, privateer bosun, was retaken on 5 March—though the place of his recapture is unstated. The date of recapture of two other escapers—Jerome Favali and Frederik Reimer, both ensigns on the privateer *Le Vengeur*—is also not stated but both were sent to Valleyfield depot on 30 March, so they must have been retaken that month or, less likely, in the last few days of February. All the other recaptured escapers (except Marc Butel, who was sent to Valleyfield on 11 March) were sent on 4 or 5 March to Edinburgh Castle.

Of the 23 escapers from Esk Mills on 19 February at least 21 were privateersmen. Of the other two Charles Marechal, No. 428 on the Esk Mills register, was a soldier captured on the *Somnambule* privateer in October 1810 in the English Channel off Tréport; and the second, Etienne Duplessy, No. 246 on the Depot Register, had been captured on the corvette *Janet* or *Jenet* in October 1808 in the Bay of Bengal, which, in the absence of any other information about him, indicated he was in the French navy. Five or six of the 21 privateersmen were members of the crew of the *Vengeur*, captured in October 1810 in the English Channel; another two were from the crew of the *Mameluke*, captured off Dover in December 1810. The others were from several other privateers, including *La Josephine*, *Le Barbier de Seville*, *L'Aventurier*, *Le Phoenix*, *Le Sans Souci*, *L'Héro du Nord*, and *Le Général Tous-saint*. The 21 privateersmen had become prisoners of war between February 1805 and December 1810—16 of them during 1810. So whether in some cases their recent capture made them unable or unwilling to accept that fate, or in others it was that they had already endured captivity for several years, they shared the same resolve. At least 15 of the 23 escapees were officers or of equivalent rank: two captains, two 2nd captains, six lieutenants (of whom two are described as 1st and three 2nd lieutenants), two ensigns, two prizemasters, and one pilot. The remaining eight were two bosuns, four seamen, one sailor (Etienne Duplessy) of unknown rank, and one soldier (Marechal).[33]

Who among the 23 were the planners and leaders of the escape is not certain. But of the 23 some of those eight who had been transferred from Greenlaw to Esk Mills at its opening on 4 February—Cabouche, Favali, Iusset, Le Couche-Barbouche, Lepine, Nosten, Pagliano, and Reimer—may have provided that leadership, particularly if the recollection of Andrew Johnston, Esk Mills clerk, was correct that those among them who were officers had enjoyed 'Mr Wright's parole' at Greenlaw and had made themselves 'well acquainted with the building [i.e., Esk Mills] when a Cotton Mill' and no doubt had been for some time before 19 February drawing up plans for escape from it. Four of the escapers—Muller, Noets, Vanvelier and Vanveen—had arrived at Esk Mills only on the day before their escape.[34]

Such a mass escape (or at least, in the case of the one shot and ten re-captured men, attempted escape) had an unsettling and disturbing effect on many of the other 2,800 prisoners at Esk Mills. Half, as it proved, of the 23 escapers had got clean away: a relatively high success rate. No fewer than 48 prisoners 'of bad character' (*mauvais sujets*) at the depot—including those seven or eight of the 23 escapers who had by then been recaptured—were to be sent to Edinburgh Castle on 4 and 5 March 'to be confined in the cells there.'[35] It appears from the scrappy evidence available that one of the turnkeys, James Cuthbertson, was dismissed as a result of the escape; and a cryptic passage in a letter from the Transport Board to the agent suggests that the other prisoners had helped win time for the escapers to get clear away from the vicinity of the depot by carrying out delaying and diversionary tactics of a kind practised by prisoners in similar situations during many other wars: 'On account of what you state all the prisoners are to be put on Short Allowance [of food] three days for not answering their names and further until the damage done be made good.'[36] The prisoners appear also to have made a collective complaint about, and even carried out a boycott of, some of their rations of food. 'We direct you,' the Transport Board instructed Captain Pellowe on 4 March, 'to cause the Herrings refused by the prisoners put on short allowance to be sold ... You will send a sample loaf of the bread now issuing to the prisoners.'[37] Despite, or partly because of, these measures by the authorities the situation at Esk Mills appears to have remained tense. 'The behaviour of the prisoners at Esk Mills has, for these some days past, been very insolent and refractory,' reported the *Edinburgh Evening Courant* on 11 March.

The unsettling effect of the mass escape upon the inmates at Esk Mills was compounded by reports of an attempted rising among 300 prisoners being transferred in late February and early March on board the 44-gun warship HMS *Gorgon* from Portsmouth to Esk Mills. 'Tuesday,' reported the *Caledonian Mercury* on Thursday, 7 March, '300 French prisoners were landed at Leith from the *Gorgon* ... and marched off in three divisions for the depot at Greenlaw [in fact, Esk Mills was their destination] ... It is reported that there were some symptoms of mutiny among the prisoners while on board the *Gorgon*.' The *Mercury* provided more details two days later: 'The report of a conspiracy among the prisoners on board the *Gorgon* to rise on the crew, appears to have been well founded. Fifty of the prisoners were allowed to be on deck at a time [i.e., for fresh air and exercise] and these, on a given signal, were to seize the arms of the marines, while the remainder were to rush up and attempt to overpower the ship's company. The bulkhead was already cut through and everything prepared for putting their plan in execution, when a discovery was fortunately made by two of the prisoners. A lieutenant of marines [i.e., of *marins* or seamen: the French did not have marines as the British did] who was at the head of the conspiracy was sent off by himself under a serjeant's guard to Pennycuick. The *Gorgon* sailed from the [Leith] Roads for Portsmouth on Wednesday afternoon [6 March].'

Entries, though very bare, in the log of HMS *Gorgon* indicate that on 25 February, when the vessel was two days out into the English Channel or North Sea on its voyage from Portsmouth to Leith, 'Anthony Suett and Francis Goddard, French prisoners, came aft and gave information of a plot rase amongst them to brake out the Prison and take charge of the ship.' Shortly afterward another entry in the log says, 'Armed the Watch.' On Monday 4 March, the log records the safe arrival of *Gorgon* in Leith Roads, where she 'Came alongside the Boats of H.M. ships *Dictator* and *Adamant* to convey the French prisoners on shore.'[38]

An unnamed officer of the *Gorgon*, in a letter to the *Edinburgh Evening Courant* of 18 March, said he and the other members of the crew had had 'a narrow escape ... of being murdered by the French prisoners we took to Leith. On the 25th ult. an attempt was made to take the ship from us, and the murder of all the officers was to be a part of this horrible plan. Fortunately for us, one of the prisoners revealed the plot a few hours before it was to be put in execution. The number of prisoners on board was 300, and our crew consisted, including officers, of only 120, a half of the number foreigners and men of a very inferior description. The plan which they [the prisoners] had laid (and which, if it had not been discovered, would have put them in possession of the ship in a few minutes) was well concerted. Fifty of them, who usually had their parole on deck at one time, were to have been picked then, and headed by several officers of privateers. The time selected was when one watch of our men and the officers, except him who had the watch, were at breakfast. A rush was then to be made, the officer thrown overboard, and the arms to be seized upon at the same time. One of them was to have been sent down to the prison, on opening the door of which the 250 inside were to have pulled in the centinel [sic], and then have rushed through the door and up the fore hatchway, which to our surprise they had cut through the plank of, though three inches thick, and were only waiting the signal from the deck which was to be "It blows hard" (actually the case at the time). Profiting by the information we had, we armed ourselves with all the rusty swords and pistols on board, without creating any alarm, and sent for two of the principal ringleaders, as if the Captain merely wanted to speak to them, and quietly secured them in irons. The Captain then went into the prison and told the remainder of the prisoners that the least symptom of rising would be attended with the immediate shooting of the hostages on deck. This effectually quelled them, still leaving us an unpleasant duty during the remaining 10 days of our voyage, being obliged to walk the deck night and day armed, to guard ourselves against any renewed machinations of our hostile companions.'

A detailed account of a projected rising by prisoners, including himself, on the ship bringing them to Leith from Chatham in January-February 1811 is given by Marote-Carrier. But if Marote-Carrier's account is fundamentally accurate and reliable it cannot be of the rising or attempted rising on HMS *Gorgon*, for he arrived from Chatham at Leith on HMS *Vanguard*. It is true that his account lacks accuracy in some of the detail of his recall—hardly surprising, since his recollections were recorded thirty years after the events they dealt with. First, he does not name the ship he sailed on, though he does say it had 64 guns (HMS *Gorgon* had 44, *Vanguard* 74). Second, he says 29 January was the date it set sail from the mouth of the Thames, almost certainly Sheerness, and it was 18 February when he and the other prisoners were landed at Leith, after a very stormy voyage during which the ship was blown so far off course to the east in the North Sea that for several days it was within sight of Norway. Contemporary press reports say HMS *Vanguard* left Sheerness for Leith on 28 January and arrived on 4 February.[39] Third, since Marote-Carrier by his own account had been at Esk Mills for two or three days when the mass escape there took place on 19 February (actually he had been there a fortnight by that time), the shipboard rising or attempted rising he recounts cannot have been the one on HMS *Gorgon*, which arrived in the Firth of Forth on 27-28 February and disembarked its prisoners at Leith on 5 March. Fourth, HMS *Gorgon* sailed to Leith from Portsmouth and there is no evidence it picked up more prisoners en route at Chatham or Sheerness. Fifth, Marote-Carrier clearly states that he and the other prisoners landed with him at Leith marched out that same day to Penicuik and were not lodged overnight at Edinburgh Castle. Sixth, the only publicly reported rising attempted on board a ship bringing prisoners at that period to Leith was the one on the *Gorgon*.

In fact, Marote-Carrier is shown in the Entry Book to have arrived at Esk Mills from Chatham via HMS *Vanguard* on 7 February. The contradictory entry already observed, however, in the depot hospital register says that he was in the depot hospital from 5 until 10 February (as well as again later from 7 until 25 March).[40]

Unless, therefore, Marote-Carrier, having heard other prisoners at Esk Mills speak of the rising on the *Gorgon*, came years later to believe that he had himself taken part in it, the attempted rising which he recounts was a quite different one, occurred a week or two earlier than that on the *Gorgon*, and took place on HMS *Vanguard*. If indeed not merely one but two separate risings or attempted risings took place aboard ships bringing prisoners from the south of England to Esk Mills in February 1811, small wonder that by the first week of March feelings among them were running high at the depot.

Shipboard risings or attempted risings by French prisoners of war may have been more common, or less uncommon, than press reports alone suggest. Yet another such rising or attempted rising is referred to in a cryptic passage in a proforma report about the escape from Valleyfield depot on 4 January 1812 of a prisoner named Guillaume Mariote. The report was signed by the then agent at Valleyfield, Captain E.J. Moriarty, RN. Said to have been a soldier in the 66th line, or Basque, infantry regiment who was captured along with 28 other soldiers of his regiment on 13 November 1809 'off Ireland', Mariote, described as aged 20, born at Mussy, 5 feet 6 inches tall, of stout build, oval face, fair complexion, fair hair, grey eyes, and with no marks or wounds, was 'Supposed to have Escaped by the Gate in Workman's dress while the turnkeys were inside counting [the prisoners]. This man arrived in Scotland under the denomination of a Soldier, but from the information of his Comrades he is a Lieutenant in the French Navy, and is one of those who attempted to seize the *Brune* on passage—came from the *Generaux* Prison Ship at Plymouth.' Mariote had arrived at Valleyfield on 19 September 1811 from Plymouth on the *Brune*. Although Captain Moriarty's report does not specifically say it was on HMS *Brune's* passage from Plymouth to Leith that month that the rising or attempted rising took place, the context makes it perhaps unlikely the reference can be to any other passage by the *Brune*. The voyage from Plymouth and arrival at Leith of the *Brune* were reported in the press but not so the rising or attempted rising on board either it or, if Marote-Carrier is to be relied upon, on the *Vanguard*. Of course, according to Marote-Carrier, in the case of the projected rising on the *Vanguard* only the prisoners, and not the officers and crew of the ship, were aware of it. Those two cases contrasted with the press reports devoted to the rising on the *Gorgon*. Was the absence from the press of two such further newsworthy items due perhaps to a deliberate and successful (except in the case of the *Gorgon*) policy of suppression by the authorities of such news in case publication encouraged still more risings? An earlier attempt in September 1810 by French deserters from Napoleon's army in Spain to seize control of HMS *Latona*, on which they were sailing from Gibraltar to Britain as volunteers for enlistment in His Britannic Majesty's forces, was reported by the ship's captain, Thomas Sotheby. The prisoners, Sotheby said, had intended to sail the ship into a French port once they had control of her but they had been 'fortunately detected ... by the loyalty of the German soldiers (likewise deserters from the French army in Spain and volunteers for HM's service) whom I have on board but who are not to be persuaded to join with the French, and [who] immediately revealed the design to the commanding officer.'[41]

Marote-Carrier's is the only known detailed account by a prisoner of war about one of the many voyages made in 1811-13 by thousands of captives in successive contingents from the south of England to Scotland, and also about an attempt by prisoners during the voyage to seize control of the ship. His account, which aside from questions it raises about dates, names of ships, etc., appears authentic, is certainly detailed and circumstantial, and provides insight not only into the prisoners' conditions and treatment but also their hopes and fears.

It was after several weeks of captivity in the cramped and miserable conditions aboard the hulk *Glory* (the former French warship *Gloire*, captured in 1806) at Chatham that, Marote-Carrier recalled thirty years later, '... an unexpected event took place that changed my fate.[42] On 28 January [he says 1812, but it was in fact 1811] we had hardly risen from our beds than a report spread through the hulk that we were going to be visited by the military commandant of Chatham. Each of us wore ourselves out wondering about the object of his coming. Most dreaded it, some would not believe the report until it was shown to be true. Towards nine o'clock a launch came alongside our hulk. The commandant was in it, and a few minutes later he came into our prison. After silently examining the misery in which we were sunk, he spoke sharply to the officer of the hulk about the state in which he had allowed us to be in; and addressing himself to us, he announced that the British government, considering how very uncomfortable we were in such a cramped space, had been moved by a pious concern for us and that, wishing to avoid the disadvantages that could result for our health from a longer stay in that place, it had decided to propose to prisoners of goodwill to leave the hulks for Scotland. He ended by telling us to reach a definite decision that day, and if we wished to leave, to put our names on a list held by the commandant of the hulk. Finally, he advised those who agreed to this change of prison to make their preparations immediately, as the next day they would be put on board the vessel which was to take them to their new destination. The commandant went on to the other decks [of the *Glory*] to make the same proposal there. In this way he visited all the hulks.

'... Many of us, even most of us,' recalled Marote-Carrier, 'were afraid of finding in Scotland a still more miserable existence and of falling from Charybdis to Scylla. It was also further from France, and in case of escape the chances of arriving there were very much less. I did not, however, stop at these considerations ... Life on the hulks again seemed to me to contain so much misery and suffering that although the reduction in the number of prisoners on them could result in some improvement, I saw only advantages in the change of residence. For, admitting the worst suppositions, I could not believe that a fate more unhappy than that which presently overwhelmed me awaited me in Scotland. And then might not a favourable opportunity [for escape] present itself either during the voyage there or afterwards? ... It was only a vague hope ... but it was a hope; and on the hulks we hardly had the chance to avoid the keen watchfulness of our guards, nor to escape the harsh seclusion to which we were subjected. However imprecise the reasons I have just given they acted with no less force on me and on several of my companions who, after due reflection, took the same view and resolved to take whatever risks there were.

'I made ready what I wanted to take with me. I wore my best clothes, I took on me my purse still containing ten louis; and however slight and scanty my baggage I nonetheless found means of filling a small pine trunk I had bought. I stowed away my stuff in it and closed it firmly, taking care to put my name on it in big easily read letters: I was afraid some sailor might seize it for his own profit, and I put little faith in the success of protests ...'

Marote-Carrier was one of the first on the list of those leaving the hulks. 'I spent the rest of the day saying goodbye to those of my friends who were not coming with me, and when evening came I went to bed for the last time on the hulks, my heart full of hope and joy and blessing God and the English for taking pity on us.'

After a sleepless night, Marote-Carrier says that next day he boarded a 100 or 150 ton cutter which, together with three sloops, came alongside the hulks at 10 in the morning to take the prisoners on the first stage of their voyage to Scotland. It was, he says, 29 January 1812 [a mistake for 1811]. A crowd of local people on the right bank of the river Medway gathered to watch the prisoners leave the hulks: 'I thought I heard some exclamations of pity, but many more hostile shouts. We were threatened from afar by insulting gestures, for we had been allowed to remain on deck. I breathed in with delight the pure air of which I had been deprived for so long.' Some of the crew of the cutter seemed touched by the sad state to which the prisoners had been reduced during their time on the hulks; but when snow began to fall the crew wrapped themselves in warm cloaks or went below 'without bothering about us [prisoners] ... The snow fell so heavily that we were all covered with it ... We couldn't see ten paces beyond the cutter. However, a west wind enabled us to run quite easily, and our crossing [of the Medway] was made rapidly and without mishap to the ship of the line that was to transport us to Scotland, and that we found hove to at the mouth of the Thames.

'It was a fine vessel of 64 carriage guns [i.e., cannons] with a numerous crew and some marines. We were so exhausted and besides such good precautions had been taken that they were justified in having no fear of us. We were given a rude welcome. As we came on board we were thrown down into the hold. It was there that we all came together towards evening. There were about 600 of us of all ages and conditions, for apart from the seamen taken on board corsairs [privateers] there were among us very many prisoners from the army in Spain …

'It may well be imagined whether we were comfortable! It was much worse than on board the hulks: packed into this narrow space, we were choking in the soon tainted air. There were no portholes that enabled us to get fresh air. Only one opening gave entry into our *cachot* [prison]. Two members of the crew constantly stood guard at it, with their bayonets pointed toward us and threatening to thrust them into whoever attempted to go out.'

The food given the prisoners—salted meat, biscuit [or hardtack, a kind of hard saltless biscuit that was a staple food aboard ships], and a ration of wine for each man—seemed better than on board the hulks. But the soldier prisoners from Spain, unlike the seamen, were unaccustomed to biscuit and did not care for it. 'As for the bed on which we had to lie, it was far from being soft and downy. There were no longer over-short hammocks [as in the hulks], but quite simply the hard sharp stones that made up the ballast of the ship.' As the temperature in the hold, despite the wintry weather, was high enough to banish cold the prisoners were able to take off some of their clothes before going to sleep that night.

As soon as the wind became favourable in the morning the ship set sail for Scotland. 'Our prison,' recalled Marote-Carrier, 'then became one of a lamentable spectacle. A great number among us not being accustomed to the roll of the vessel were seized with that terrible and inevitable indisposition which grips whoever sails for the first time on the sea. They writhed in frightful convulsions, uttering cries of distress and believing themselves at the point of death. The warm and stinking atmosphere … added to their tortures. It upset me to see these poor people, and I was very upset to see some old sea dogs burst out laughing and making fun of their sufferings and contortions.' When at length Marote-Carrier approached the sentry guarding the entry to the hold and, using the few words of English he had learned in captivity, tried to persuade him to arrange for the seasick prisoners to be taken up on deck, the sentry kept repeating 'I do not understand you' and he eventually threatened Marote-Carrier with his bayonet. As Marote-Carrier was one of those responsible for fetching food for his fellow prisoners he bided his time until in mid-morning he was able to go up on deck. He then sought out 'a certain De Kuyper, former commissary of the town of Ghent. He was a prisoner like us; but, thanks to the favour he enjoyed with the commandant of the hulk and to his perfect knowledge of French and English, he had been recommended to the captain of the vessel, who had chosen him as interpreter between us and him. As a result of his work, De Kuyper enjoyed considerable privileges. He had quarters between decks, slept in a hammock, was free to come and go all over the ship, and could speak to the captain when he wished.'[43]

De Kuyper appeared impressed by the representations made him by Marote-Carrier about his approaching the captain of the ship to permit the sick prisoners to be brought up into the fresh air, and he went down to the hold with Marote-Carrier to see for himself. De Kuyper assured the prisoners of his concern, promised to speak to the captain and to do all he could to improve their lot. But nothing happened for several hours afterwards, though the seasickness abated. Then the lieutenant of the ship entered the hold toward evening, 'a man with a sour, sullen face. He examined us with a severe eye. All [the prisoners] were quiet. Only some suppressed cries, some groans here and there, were evidence of sufferings barely assuaged. ... "Damn your eyes!" the lieutenant cried, expressing at the top of his voice this untranslateable oath so common among the English. Then he began again to eye us from head to foot with an irritated expression. "Who the devil is complaining among these French beggars? Who says he's ill here? I don't see a single one with seasickness." He didn't understand the unspeakable suffering shown on those haggard distorted faces, who looked at him in fear and dared not open their mouths to implore his pity. None of us complained. We were sure of the uselessness of prayers addressed to such a man. He withdrew, muttering and cursing "the French buggers" who had made him come down into the hold without reason, and using the most drastic oaths that his repertoire could furnish him with.' It was only later that Marote-Carrier learned that De Kuyper had indeed spoken on behalf of the prisoners to the captain, who had ordered his lieutenant to visit them, accompanied by the ship's doctor, and to bring up to the sick bay those whose condition justified it. But the lieutenant had not called out the doctor and since by the time he entered the hold the prisoners' seasickness had abated he convinced himself they were swinging the lead.[44]

After two more days in the hold, during which some of those subject to seasickness suffered violent further attacks of it, 'the heat and bad air were stifling us and made us sweat continually'. A very fat prisoner named Arendt, from Nieuport, who had been a pilot on a privateer, became quite ill and appeared to be suffocating. Marote-Carrier was deputed by his fellow prisoners to intercede for Arendt with De Kuyper. The latter at once persuaded the ship's surgeon to examine Arendt in the hold, and Arendt was immediately carried out of the hold and up to the sick bay.

That same day and for the following couple of days the ship was severely buffeted by violent winds as snow fell heavily. 'The crew,' said Marote-Carrier, 'was occupied without respite in handling the ship, which, driven by the contrary wind, was blown off course despite their efforts to hold her to it. During the night of the 3rd-4th the tempest became more violent than ever. The bowsprit was broken clean off. The vessel plunged from wave to wave as if it were going to be engulfed: shipwreck seemed inevitable. What a frightening prospect that was, far from any coast as we were! For if the seamen of the crew could save themselves in the long boats, it was beyond doubt that we would not be allowed into them, hardly were they able to take all the Englishmen. Hour by hour we expected to be engulfed, without being able to get out of that hold where we were shut up, nor in any way to avoid death. Already we were saying sad farewells, we were ready to depart from life. We gave our last thoughts to God and our families.'

About two o'clock in the morning, with waves pounding on the deck and flooding it with water, there roared 'a gust of wind so violent that the vessel tilted to starboard'. Five cannons rolled from their mountings at the prow of the vessel and all the others followed them. It seemed that the vessel was turning turtle. Then the violence of the tempest seemed to abate, though the weather continued stormy and looked like remaining so, while the ship drifted considerably further off its course. 'From time to time the hurricane roared again and in the prison that might become our tomb we heard the gusts of wind growling and the angry waves beating against the sides of the ship, ready to crush it beneath their weight. The situation was frightful. The sea howled around us, as if it wished to play a long time with its prey before devouring it. This critical and terrifying situation inspired in us a project every bit as desperate.'

During the several days the tempest blew, the ship's crew had toiled ceaselessly. 'Our gaolers were worn out. The thought of revolt occurred to us. It was a bold idea but it seemed to offer some chances of success.' So preoccupied were they with handling the ship amid the storm that the crew seemed to have forgotten the prisoners and had even removed the sentry at the entrance to the hold as every hand was needed to help sail the ship. The only person who looked near the prisoners was De Kuyper. His agreement with their plan was assured.

'Taking advantage of night to make the crew prisoner, take possession of the vessel and set sail for Norway from which, in all probability, we could not be far distant so much had we been blown off course—such was our plan … Once we reached Bergen or Christiansund we would be safe and no longer have anything to fear from the English.' Meanwhile, as Marote-Carrier and the other prisoners made their plans to seize the ship, and De Kuyper at once agreed to join them, 'the exhausted English strove to control the ship that the tempest harried for eight days. The crew were worn out, exhausted. The vessel had suffered greatly: the bowsprit was broken, yardarms were in pieces, the sails torn or swept away. It was no longer possible to steer the ship.' The prisoners decided that if their uprising succeeded but the ship was wrecked they would make use of the longboats to escape to Norway.[45]

On the evening of 8 February the storm at last appeared to abate. The exhausted crew sought rest. Only those members of the crew on watch would be on deck that night, so De Kuyper told the prisoners that would be the time to carry out the uprising. They did not have any arms but De Kuyper undertook to provide them with some: he had stolen a skeleton key to the armoury. If the coast was clear De Kuyper was to come to the hold and give the signal at midnight, after the changing of the watch. 'We passed the evening in a state of great excitement. Then we ensured a deep silence in order not to arouse suspicion and went to bed without closing our eyes, ready to rise up in a body at the first call. Midnight sounded on the captain's big clock.'

But De Kuyper never came and the rising never took place.

At two o'clock in the morning Marote-Carrier crept out of the hold and explored the ship. All but two or three of the crew seemed to be asleep. He then proposed to his fellow prisoners that, despite the non-appearance of De Kuyper and the absence of the weapons he had promised them, the rising should go ahead. But few supported his proposal. Without arms or the means of obtaining them it seemed to most of the prisoners a forlorn prospect. 'It was,' said Marote-Carrier, 'a moment of dreadful sadness. My heart sank and I thought that despair would push me into some fatal resolution. But I thought of God and that gave me back the hope and the strength to bear my misfortune.'

The reason for De Kuyper's failure to appear was that he had lost the skeleton key for the armoury and his search for it had been in vain. Marote-Carrier at first doubted if he was telling the truth but later came to believe De Kuyper had no interest in deceiving the prisoners: 'He was bound like us to profit from success, and later he shared our fate.'

Next day the prisoners' chagrin increased as the coast of Norway was in sight—'hardly a few leagues separated us from Bergen'—and the storm ended and the sun shone 'as if to scoff at us.' As the crew busied themselves with repairs to the ship the sentry was put back on the entrance to the hold 'and we accepted that our project was for ever given up … We had to resign ourselves to our fate. The English [crew] continued to treat us as they had done until then, without diminishing our miseries, as also without making them more rigorous, which would have been difficult. Nothing indicated they had the slightest notion that so imminent a danger had threatened them and that only a thread had saved them from taking our place at the foot of the hold.'

After a further three days in sight of the coast of Norway, during which time the damage to the ship was being repaired, the wind shifted to the north-north east and they set sail again for Scotland. About seven in the evening of 17 February, Marote-Carrier recalled, they hove to in Leith Roads and next day the prisoners were disembarked and marched out to Esk Mills.[46]

❖

Given then the mass escape of 19 February, delaying or diversionary tactics practised by other prisoners to help the escapers get clear away, the decision to send on 4 and 5 March 48 'bad characters' to Edinburgh Castle, the dismissal of a turnkey, the placing of prisoners on short allowance of food for three days, an organised complaint about, or perhaps boycott of, some of the rations of food by the prisoners, and that one or, it would appear, even two shipboard risings had so recently been attempted by prisoners on their way to Esk Mills, it was hardly surprising the *Evening Courant* on 11 March should describe the behaviour of prisoners at the depot as for some days past 'very insolent and refractory'.

That same day a further dramatic and, as it proved, decisive event took place at Esk Mills. The crisis developed over the weekend of 9-11 March. 'On Saturday,' reported the *Caledonian Mercury* on Monday the 11th, 'an attempt at escape was made by the prisoners at Esk Mills, which although at first it seemed to threaten serious consequences, we are happy to learn was subdued without bloodshed. It appears that, some suspicion of their intention having arisen, the prisoners were ordered to turn out, which they did with considerable reluctance, when a hole was discovered to have been dug under the foundation of the wall, nearly communicating with the outside. The prisoners, upon learning their disappointment, became quite turbulent and vented their rage by demolishing the windows of the house occupied by the chief in command at the place; nor could they be brought to submission till an addition to the military force arrived. An increased supply of ball cartridges has since been delivered to the soldiers, and some field-pieces [artillery] have been got in readiness, in case of necessity. Several French officers, who were supposed to have been instigators of the disturbance, were brought to the [Edinburgh] Castle, to be confined by themselves. We hear that the cause of these discontents among the prisoners is the want of sufficient accommodation for so great a number of people in the place where they are confined; and to remedy this inconvenience we understand a detachment of militia was sent off this morning to remove 500 of them to the Castle.'

A further instalment of information about events at Esk Mills was added on 14 March by the *Edinburgh Evening Courant* as an 'authentic account of the cause of the mutiny among the prisoners.' As a result, the *Courant* reported, 'of a false alarm made by some of the prisoners at Esk Mill depot that part of the prison buildings was giving way, a general confusion and attempt to get out prevailed among the prisoners, when unfortunately, owing to the presence [sic] of the crowd, two of the prisoners were so much injured that we hear they died soon after. This matter made so strong an impression on the prisoners, although no insecurity whatever appears in any part of the building, that they expressed reluctance to occupy it immediately, and were removed for the present into an adjoining depot. 450, among whom are several officers, were marched for Edinburgh Castle (who had been previously ordered to be moved to the depot there in consequence of having shown a disposition to riot for some days past).'

The crisis of 9-11 March at Esk Mills thus appears to have been the result of an attempt at escape compounded by the instability of the building.

It was certainly true that two of the prisoners were trampled to death on the stair in the rush to get out of the prison building on 11 March. The two victims were Eloy, a soldier in the 4th Régiment de Marine, and Charles de Charles, a seaman captured on the privateer *Grand Napoléon*. Of them Andrew Johnston, a clerk at Esk Mills, wrote on the official death certificates that day: 'Trampled to death this morning by the Prisoners in rushing to the doors on an alarm that the Prison was falling.'[47]

Another version of events was provided in his recollections almost thirty years later by Johnston himself. '11th March, at one a.m., in consequence of a false alarm that the prison was falling—a *ruse de guerre* contrived and carried on by the officer prisoners from Edinburgh Castle (the particulars of this hoax I afterwards learned at Perth Depot from De Cuyper, who was himself concerned in the plot).[48] All the prisoners in the top flat, who were let into the secret, at least 300 men, leapt from their hammocks to the floor, from a height of 6 or 7 feet on a given signal, by which the floor was so shaken that the wooden supports, rails, etc., of that flat fell to the floor with a tremendous crash—by which those in the other flats not in the secret were so alarmed as to rush to the windows, stairs, etc., which were beat out, and increased the confusion. Even some made their exit into the yard by knocking out the iron stanchions of the lower windows. One poor fellow was left sticking fast between two bars, and was relieved by cutting the iron. The Prison doors were knocken [sic] open, and numbers got into the airing ground. I was upon the spot on the first alarm and went into the prison, flat by flat, endeavouring to persuade them there was no danger, otherwise I would not have come among them, etc., etc., but nothing would persuade them to remain in the house.'

A further aspect of the crisis that night was described by Johnston: 'Large detachments of Troops arrived on the alarm by Bugle first from Roslin where a small party was stationed and from Dalkeith Barracks, bringing with them two field pieces. While in the yard several attempts were made to level the Stockade by the Prisoners rushing in large bodies against it. The whole length of the inclosure next to the river was shook at the first onset, and another rush would have brought all down; this was prevented by the military surrounding the entire stockade with fixed bayonets pointed through the openings of the Palisade. The two field pieces loaded with grape were placed on the heights above the prison so as to command the whole yard.'[49] In a reference almost certainly to these events at Esk Mills Charles Cowan, son and nephew of the recent former owners of the nearby Valleyfield Mills, long afterward recalled that '… a battery of artillery, which on one dark night, was called out suddenly owing to an alarm that the prisoners in Esk Mills were about to make their escape … were ordered to move with their guns, to descend the steep hill, probably a descent of not less than 200 feet, to cross the Esk by the bridge below Esk Mills, and then take up their position opposite Esk Mills, in order to overawe the prisoners. From the steepness of the hill, the desire of the artillerymen to lose no time, and the sudden and sharp turn at the foot of the hill, the guns, with artillerymen and horses, went over the steep bank into the river—a fall of probably not less than twelve or fifteen feet, nearly perpendicular, and, strange to say, there was but little damage either to men or horses.'[50]

Still recovering from his fever in the depot hospital during these dramatic events at Esk Mills on 9-11 March was Marote-Carrier, who had been prevented by his illness from joining the score of escapers on 19 February. A wooden building with only a ground and an upper storey, in the latter of which Marote-Carrier lay in a wooden bed with, he says, a palliasse, a hair mattress and a thick wool cover, and the windows in which were high up, the hospital was across the yard and through the palisades from the prison buildings. He gives a different version of the events on 11 March. He says that he and other patients were sound asleep in the hospital when '… we were awakened with a start about the middle of the night by a dreadful uproar. There were cries, oaths, then terrible cracking sounds. In the blink of an eye we were up out of bed and looked out of the window. All the noise came from the prison. The darkness was profound and we could make out nothing, only from minute to minute the tumult grew without our being able to grasp what was happening. We thought at first the prisoners were in revolt, and we prepared to join them in their flight. But a moment of reflection removed that idea from us. No one went out of the prison. None of the English slept there except the turnkey, and anyway the exclamations we heard were rather an expression of distress than the signal for an uprising.

'Soon the guards turned out and torches lit up the yard. But we were ordered to get back from the window and back into bed otherwise we would be fired at. We were forced to obey and we got back into bed, tormented with a thousand anxieties and seeking in vain to account for the noise which kept on getting louder.

'The cries continued to be heard for quite a long time inside the building, mingled with those of the guards outside, the sound of picks against the walls, and the rolling of the drums. But what reassured us was that we did not hear a single musket shot. Although that circumstance calmed me a little, I was unable to get back to sleep and when day dawned I got up and went to the window. All the prisoners were in the yard in spite of the extreme cold, attested by the window panes that were covered in frost and by the snow that fell in abundance and covered the ground with a layer half a foot deep. Everyone appeared very agitated. They were gathered in groups and the conversation was everywhere very animated.'

At nine o'clock in the morning, when Marote-Carrier and the other patients in the hospital were still awaiting the appearance of a nurse or hospital mate, 'Suddenly we saw coming out from the prison a stretcher carried by soldiers and on which lay two bodies. They headed towards the gate and passed through the palisades. Some minutes afterwards they reappeared with the stretcher empty, went back into the prison and came out again carrying two more bodies. You can imagine our astonishment! It was so great that, no longer able to contain my anxiety, I was going out to seek news when the nurse came in. We bombarded him with questions and here is what he told us.

'It will be remembered that the prison had two storeys above the ground floor. The prisoners had slept in those three rooms [i.e., one big room or dormitory on each floor]. But as we had all arrived at the depot so recently a place had not yet been assigned to everyone. Each man had therefore chosen a place in his own way. That had worked well the first day. The three dormitories were little by little equally filled. But next day it had been noticed that it was very much warmer on top than in the lower rooms and above all than on the ground floor. The result was that that evening and the days following some on the bottom floor went upstairs. In the end, the cold having reached a new intensity the night before [the crisis], more than two thirds of the prisoners had taken refuge on the top floor, where they were more than four hundred strong, whereas hardly two hundred remained in the other dormitories. It was simply forgotten that the prison was a former paper mill, when the top floor had been used as a store for paper. And as nothing had been foreseen about its being later used for other purposes, the floor had not been given extra support. The joists were few and meagre, so they were hardly submitted to the enormous pressure of four hundred men moving about than they slowly began to bend. No obvious sign of this, however, aroused the concern of the prisoners, who went quietly to bed as usual. While they slept, unaware of the danger that threatened them, the floor slanted more and more. From time to time a muffled cracking, a groaning from the beams which were sagging under the burden, could be heard. About midnight a dreadful noise resounded, all the prisoners, awakened with a start, hurled themselves half-clad down from their hammocks without knowing what was happening. The pressure on the floor became greater. The floor was still noisily descending. Then the imminence of the danger was realised. Everyone hurled himself toward the narrow stairway that led to the ground floor. But each one wanted to get down first, so the entry became blocked. Hardly had some managed to get out than the mass of men, carried from a single side, upset the equilibrium and overloaded the floor, which fell several feet on to the second dormitory. Then the alarm was general. The cries of distress resounded on all sides and all the prisoners sought a way out to escape the danger. But the crowd was so tightly packed that a long time passed before everyone got down. Serious accidents were the result of this foolhardy rush.

'... The same scene was repeated when it was necessary to get out of the prison. The single doorway could hardly let out two men abreast. From when it was opened there was such a crowd that the prisoners could neither go back, so great was the crowd behind them, nor forward, so much were they crammed between the two sides of the door.

'The English, seeing the slowness with which the prisoners were getting out, feared that some catastrophe might be the result of this delay. The upper storey could collapse in a second ... [so] The guards began to demolish the wall in order to open up new exits, and to break the iron bars of the windows. Thanks to that expedient all the prisoners at last got out into the yard, not without some of them being stifled and succumbing in the press. Those were the four bodies we had seen carried out.'[51]

As the *Evening Courant* reported, 450 of the 2,800 prisoners at Esk Mills were marched off that morning to Edinburgh Castle. The remainder, but for 93, were marched to the new adjoining depot of Valleyfield, half a mile away up the North Esk river, which, says Andrew Johnston, 'they [the prisoners] knew to be a superior Depot.' The first detachments were marched by the rather longer route via the village of Kirkhill to Valleyfield. But, says Johnston, 'This was a tedious and fatiguing business. We then formed two lines of military and marched them by the nearest road (the water side) to the Depot. This operation took up the whole day from 6 a.m. to 10 p.m.'[52]

Of the remaining 93 left at Esk Mills, 35 were 'old men who remained all night in the yard' and were marched next day, 12 March, to Valleyfield. The other 58 were sick men, including Marote-Carrier, who were left for the time being in the Esk Mills hospital.[53] Marote-Carrier himself confirms Johnston's recollection about the emptying of Esk Mills depot, and adds: 'As for us, we remained as sick men in hospital. The doctor had declared us incapable of supporting the strain of passing from one depot to the other ... We passed several days further in the infirmary. The regime we had to follow was so agreeable to us that we sought to stay there as long as possible, when we were well enough restored to savour all the advantages of it. A good fire, excellent food in abundance, fine wines that were handed round us quite liberally, and not least a healthy and spacious lodging—how many reasons to be ill a little longer.' The doctor, however, proved deaf to the patients' continued appeals and they were all transferred to Valleyfield by 18 April.[54]

Although the minutes of the Transport Board have not survived for the period from January to April 1811 inclusive that was so crucial in the history of the Esk Mills depot, some of what must have been a considerable flurry of correspondence between the Board and its agents in Scotland does survive for those months. This correspondence shows that the initial reaction by the Board was a determination to repair the buildings at Esk Mills and continue its use as a depot for prisoners of war.

A letter the Board sent on 14 March, within three days of the crisis at Esk Mills, to Malcolm Wright, its agent at Edinburgh Castle, says: 'Having directed Captain Pellowe to send to Edinburgh Castle 30 prisoners who have been given up as concerned in outrageous proceedings at Esk Mills Prison, we direct you to keep these prisoners in solitary cells on short allowance of provisions, as also the four French officers who have been sent to you as Ringleaders on this occasion. We have also directed Captain Pellowe to release the Prisoner named in the margin, who has given him information relative to the intended Escape of Prisoners, and we desire that you will endeavour to procure a conveyance for him to the Continent, communicating with Captain Pellowe on that subject.'[55]

The Board wrote next day to Pellowe approving of his immediately reporting to it the removal on 11 March of prisoners from Esk Mills to Valleyfield. The Board added: 'We direct you to cause additional stairs to be immediately made [at Esk Mills] as suggested by Mr Reid [architect], and the damage done to the prison to be repaired.' And on 16 March the Board again wrote to Pellowe, approving 'of the measures adopted by you in consequence of the late Alarm among the Prisoners at Esk Mills. We desire to be informed in what manner you propose to enlarge the airing ground to the West of the prison and on whose ground. Lord Cathcart has represented to us the inadequate extent of the airing ground at present. ... The Foundation of the Prison at Esk Mills is to be particularly and carefully examined, in order to ascertain if it has been undermined.' But when Pellowe reported a proposal from a senior militiary source concerning future security at Esk Mills he was told by the Board: '... to keep a Guard inside of the Prison is totally inadmissible, and no such thing has been proposed at any other depot.'

For a further week or so the spate of decisions and orders about Esk Mills continued. Pellowe was told by the Transport Board as late as 25 March that '... only two thousand prisoners are in future to be confined at Esk Mills. We approve of the ground floor of the prison being given up to the military guard by night, as suggested by you. The subterraneous [sic] passages round the Prison are to be filled up.'

But next day the Board ordered Pellowe 'to discontinue all the Works carrying on at Esk Mills Depot until further orders.' Rear Admiral Otway at Leith had been instructed by the Admiralty on the 25th to 'exercise a general superintendence of the Depots for prisoners of war in the vicinity of Leith', and the Transport Board agents at Penicuik and Edinburgh Castle had been told to seek instructions from him 'in all cases of emergency.' On 29 March Admiral Otway was told by the Transport Board that two additional prison buildings were to be immediately erected at Valleyfield 'in order that the present building at Esk Mills may be converted into a barrack as recommended by Lord Cathcart.' That same day Captain Pellowe was informed by the Board: 'It being intended that the Building at Esk Mills be given up to the Barrack Department, to be converted into a Barrack and that Two additional Prisons be erected at Valleyfield capable of containing 1,200 prisoners each, we acquaint you therewith; and we have accordingly requested that an officer of the Barrack Department may be directed to meet you on the spot and point out what articles of fitting belonging to this Department may be necessary to be left for the use of the barracks and what may be removed to Valleyfield.'

It was the end for Esk Mills as a depot. Captain Pellowe, the Esk Mills surgeon John Macansh, and the depot staff, including four clerks, a dispenser, a hospital steward, a matron, a sempstress, six turnkeys, a steward, and a lamplighter and two labourers-cum-gravediggers, were transferred to Valleyfield.

'The large building alone,' Andrew Johnston, clerk there, long afterwards recalled of the demise of Esk Mills as a depot, 'was filled up with hammock rails, etc. The smaller Mill was turned into barracks for the soldiers on duty. A small shop was fitted up and used for the officers on duty and a separate building of three storics converted and appropriated for an hospital. What was the vat house was used as a guard room.'

Johnston concluded: 'Esk Mill was a very unfit building for a depot, from being four stories high, very narrow, and confined airing ground. When the prisoners were in the yard, which Captain Pellowe, strict to his orders, endeavoured to do weekly, you might have walked on heads for the whole length and breadth of it.'

Thus exactly five weeks after it had received its first prisoners of war Esk Mills had ceased to hold any at all, apart from a few temporary patients in its hospital.[56]

6

Valleyfield and Edinburgh Castle

The 2,250 or so prisoners marched the half mile from Esk Mills on 11 March 1811 were the first to enter the new depot at Valleyfield. The first prisoner enrolled in the Valleyfield General Entry Books was a privateer seaman, Thomas Paumier, captured on *Le Vengeur* in the English Channel in October 1810. Paumier belonged to Le Havre, was aged 20, and was described as 5 ft 6 ins tall, of slender build, sallow complexion, oval face, black hair and eyes, and with no marks or wounds. Like so many others he remained in captivity at Valleyfield until the general release of prisoners after Napoleon's first abdication in the spring of 1814.[1]

Work on preparing the depot for prisoners had been going ahead since the previous December, when the Cowan brothers had sold the paper mill to the government. But, as for Esk Mills, the original opening date for Valleyfield, which was to have been 'shortly after' 5 or 6 January, had proved distinctly over-optimistic.[2] The Transport Board's advertisement on 21 December seeking tenders for victualling prisoners at the new depot had given 15 January as the deadline for their submission and 1 February 'or as soon after as the prisoners shall be sent there', as the starting date for the successful contract.[3] As late, however, as 22 February the Transport Board wrote to Captain Heddington, its agent at Valleyfield, that: 'You may expect Prisoners to arrive in less than seven Days from this time. You will therefore hasten for their Reception as much as possible.' Heddington that same day complained to Malcolm Wright, the Board's agent at Edinburgh, that Valleyfield 'is not in a fit state for the reception of the Prisoners ...' His complaint reached the ears of the Board and he was asked by it on 27 February to explain why the depot was not ready 'and what is still wanting to be done thereto.' Heddington's reply has not survived.[4]

The fact that, apart from the hundred or so who were either 'old men' and arrived next day or like Marote-Carrier had been patients in the Esk Mills hospital and arrived later in March or in April, no other prisoners entered Valleyfield until September indicates the extent of the upheaval caused by the sudden and unexpected closure of Esk Mills depot and the transfer of around 2,400 prisoners from it to Valleyfield. A week before that closure the

Transport Board had been sent by the Admiralty copies of letters from Rear Admiral Otway at Leith and from General Lord Cathcart 'representing the unprepared state of the prisons at Esk Mills and Valleyfield'. The Admiralty had consequently told Admiral Otway that 'no more prisoners than those on board *Dictator* and *Gorgon* [both of which had arrived with prisoners in Leith Roads on 28 February] would be sent to Leith for some time.'[5]

Until mid-August building work was carried on constantly at Valleyfield upon the two further blocks, each to hold 1,200 prisoners, which had been made necessary by the closure of Esk Mills depot. On 10 August an advertisement in the *Edinburgh Evening Courant* invited builders to tender for contracts to fit up 'the large building at Esk Mills as a Barracks, and other outbuildings, and for erecting a guard House at Valleyfield.' Even as late as November a soldier of the Perthshire Militia 'lost his life while assisting at the public works at the Depot at Penicuik.' As Robert Reid, crown architect in Scotland responsible for the building work at Valleyfield, explained years later: 'The prisoners were lodged in the large buildings formerly used in the manufacturing of paper, and the agent, surgeon and other officers of the Establishment were accommodated in the dwelling houses of Messrs Cowans. This arrangement was accomplished without any very material alteration in the premises and embraced all that was in contemplation when the agreement for the purchase ... was entered into [at the end of 1810] with Messrs Cowans. It was, however, afterward judged expedient that a greater number of prisoners should be sent to Scotland and directions were given for the premises at Valleyfield being extended and altered so as to form a Depot on a much larger scale than originally intended. Various new buildings were accordingly erected, the dwelling houses of the Messrs Cowans were gutted and converted into an hospital for the sick. The gardens and grass grounds adjoining were wholly broken up and included in the airing grounds of the prisons. The course of the water run, formerly used for the machinery, which passed through the centre of the grounds was changed and continued by a new cut round the whole extent of the premises, serving in some measure as an enclave and boundary to the prison yards. Thus a complete change took place in the premises, by the erection of new buildings, dismantling and changing the appropriation of others, and converting the whole space of ground into prison yards, which were partly paved and partly covered with gravel, forming on the whole an extensive and suitable depot for the accommodation of upwards of five thousand prisoners, with barracks and guard houses for the troops on duty. The premises continued to be thus occupied until the conclusion of the War in 1814 ...'[6]

Thus by late summer 1811 Valleyfield had become a depot with capacity for double the number of prisoners originally envisaged for it and easily the largest depot in Scotland until the opening of Perth a year later. On 12 August the Transport Board, having been informed that the new prison buildings at Valleyfield were 'nearly ready', instructed Captain Pellowe, who on transfer from Esk Mills in March had become agent at Valleyfield with Captain Heddington as his assistant, to 'Remove the whole of the Prisoners into the new Buildings, in order to admit of the necessary work being done to those now occupied, previously to the arrival of an additional number of prisoners. The prisoners intended to be sent from Plymouth may be expected in a fortnight or three weeks.' The first intake since the original 2,400 from Esk Mills in March and April duly arrived on 2 September. Other intakes rapidly followed. By the end of that year 5,000 prisoners had entered Valleyfield. A handwritten note at the bottom of the flyleaf of its first General Entry Book says: 'There is no end of us.'[7]

Charles Cowan, son and nephew of the two former mill owners and himself a schoolboy at that time, long afterwards recalled that the level space in the valley was more than seven acres, and that 'The new prisons added at Valleyfield were about six in number, from 80 to 120 feet in length, chiefly of wood, and of three stories. They had no glass in the openings for light and air, which were closed at night by very strong wooden shutters, and secured by strong iron stanchions, nor were there any fireplaces or artificial heat, for it was expected that the animal heat would suffice for their comfort, the prisoners having been stowed away as close almost as herrings in a barrel ... The prisons and level ground on which they were erected were surrounded by a strong wooden stockade or palisade, with a carriage-road outside, and guarded by military—generally a regiment of militia.'[8]

Marote-Carrier, the privateer lieutenant who on 25 March 1811 left Esk Mills hospital and entered Valleyfield, recalled that at the latter '... it was the same system of imprisonment. It was again three wooden casemates in the middle of a big yard enclosed with walls and palisades, and divided into three parts. It was again of big bare cold rooms where hammocks were stretched. It was again the same food, niggardly and unwholesome like that of the hulks—worse even, if that was possible. It was in a word the same regime, the same kind of life.'

One difference at Valleyfield, however, Marote-Carrier, himself a lieutenant, pointed out was that 'the fate of the officers was more bearable than that of our companions of a lower rank. A large number of new prisoners having soon joined us, our number reached three or four thousand. The officers were separated from the crowd and given a separate quarter. It was a big room, very poorly furnished, in which about fifty of us were gathered. A notice placed above the door strictly forbade any prisoner to enter our place without permission. We granted a daily payment to a master of arms among us, so that he supervised the observance of this measure. His duty was to be on watch and to turn away anyone who sought to enter without authorisation.

His salary was a ration of bread and wine that we raised, collectively and in turn, from among a certain number of us.

'Thus isolated from the mass of people of all sorts who had rubbed shoulders with us formerly and made useless all care about cleanliness, we could establish a certain order in our common apartment. Each man was assigned the place where he slept. We ate regularly and without establishing a disgusting sharing out at meal times. Eventually thanks to the few resources that each of us had saved we came to enjoy a kind of comfort, compared with the misery that we had had to suffer before. It was thus that I equipped myself with a *cadre*, a frame or a kind of wooden hammock or bed without feet, suspended by cords above the floor. The bottom of it was made of planks and there was a wooden frame round it. I procured a mattress to fill it and two covers. The room was spacious enough to make it unnecessary to place the beds in tiers one above another. The freedom we had to open the windows when we wanted to do so enabled fresh air to come in to replace air our breathing had tainted. If the weather was bad we did not go out and each busied himself according to his tastes.'[9]

One of Marote-Carrier's 'companions of a lower rank' at Valleyfield, who did not enjoy these better conditions for officers, long afterward recalled his years of imprisonment at the depot as 'terribly cold, there were no windows, no warmth, no fruit, but the cabbages were very large.'[10] Such experiences must have been very common among thousands of those prisoners of war in Scotland who were accustomed to the warmer climates of their homelands but obliged to endure the colder temperatures north of the Border, not least at Penicuik, on the edge of the Pentland Hills, where the thermometer appeared often to be lower than in places a few miles away and where in winter snow could fall more frequently and more heavily, too.

Edinburgh Castle had been among the sights observed by Marote-Carrier and his fellow prisoners as they were marched through the city to their captivity at Esk Mills, after landing on 7 February 1811 at Leith. Their experiences and impressions were no doubt those of thousands of other captives who trudged the same route from Leith or Edinburgh to Penicuik during the Napoleonic Wars.

Of Leith itself what he saw did not impress Marote-Carrier. 'When we landed,' he recalled, 'we were received by the English troops drawn up in two lines which stretched as far as the shore. An immense crowd had rushed out from the town and the surrounding countryside to see us disembark. The soldiers had difficulty in holding back this mob which forced them despite their best efforts to give ground under its huge and tumultuous pressure. We were made to wait at the edge of the sea until the longboats had transported all our companions, which took till midday. We had time to trample the snow underfoot as it melted in the rays of the sun that had shone since morning, and to hear the exclamations of the Scots people around us. At midday we set off through Leith, marching in three ranks, always between three lines of troops. Several conveyances loaded with our baggage followed us. We did not yet know what place had been decided on as our prison.

'The people appeared to us more sympathetic than in England. The words of commiseration of a great number of the spectators proved to us their sympathy for our sufferings. Several of them threw over the top of the line of soldiers pieces of money of all kinds.

'We passed quite rapidly through Leith, which did not appear to me a very remarkable place. It was only a chaos of dirty and ugly houses, separated by tortuous and gloomy alleys and inhabited by wretched and coarse people. The basin of the port, however, was remarkable. It contained ships of every flag; and I did not fail to notice here and there some noteworthy buildings. Moreover, we could only form a very imperfect impression of the places where we passed, because of the speed of our march and the masses of people and soldiers who surrounded us and past whom we could not see. Some habitations already bordered the road that led from Leith to Edinburgh, and everything seemed to indicate that these two towns, only two miles apart, would one day become one.'

After passing up the High Street in Edinburgh the column of prisoners was halted briefly in Parliament Square, beside St Giles' Cathedral and the Tolbooth gaol. 'We remained [there] shivering and paralysed with cold ... The sight of Edinburgh Castle, which rose above us and crowned the central hill frightened us. We knew that many Frenchmen had already been shut up there, and we were fearful that we would also be imprisoned within those thick black walls ...' It was, however, Esk Mills to which Marote-Carrier and his fellow prisoners were bound, not the Castle.[11]

Edinburgh Castle, in fact, at the time Marote-Carrier looked at it with such foreboding was being used mainly as a brief staging post for some of the prisoners landed at Leith on their way to Penicuik. Malcolm Wright, the Transport Board's agent for the Castle, consistently failed to maintain records of the prisoners in his charge, whether there or earlier at Greenlaw, which were as clear, unambiguous and, within the obvious limits of the column headings of the General Entry Books, relatively comprehensive as those kept by other depot or parole agents in Scotland. Movements of prisoners in and out of Edinburgh Castle are therefore often more difficult to follow than was generally the case at other depots.

But what seems clear is that the first prisoners taken into the Castle in early 1811, for reasons other than overnight staging on their way between landing at Leith and confinement at Penicuik, were seven of the ten recaptured after the mass escape of 19 February from Esk Mills. The seven were recaptured on 22 or 24 February; the other three not until the following month, when they were sent to Valleyfield. Of the seven, five were sent to the Castle on 4 March and the other two next day. The prisoner entered as No.1 on the Castle General Entry Book was David Fourneau, a lieutenant captured on the privateer *Le Barbier de Seville* in November 1810.[12]

Thus from 4 March the Castle was also being used, as it continued to be until the end of the war, as a place of punishment or deterrence. It was to the Castle that were sent numbers of those prisoners in Scotland whose breaches of depot regulations were considered not serious enough to merit their removal to the hulks in the south of England but more serious than would be adequately punished by their being put into the cachot or otherwise dealt with at the depot where the breach had been committed.

After the seven escapers from Esk Mills who arrived on 4 and 5 March at the Castle four other *mauvais sujets* from Esk Mills arrived on 9 March. These four were all lieutenants—two naval, two army. The reasons for their transfer to the Castle are not given. But clearly they were considered by the authorities to have played a leading role in either the attempted rising on HMS *Gorgon* or in the reported attempt at an escape from Esk Mills on 9 March, or perhaps both.

Of the two naval lieutenants one was Hipolyte Decreuse (or Decroze or Decruise), whose apparent involvement in the rising on the *Gorgon* has already been noticed.[13] The other was Honoré Foucault, captured in July 1808 in the Persian Gulf on the sloop *Requin*. Born on the Ile de Ré, in the Bay of Biscay off La Rochelle, Foucault was aged 23. He may have been the other 'ringleader' of the *Gorgon* rising as reported in the *Edinburgh Evening Courant*, although the *Courant* had implied he was not an officer.[14]

Of the two army lieutenants sent on 9 March to Edinburgh Castle from Esk Mills, and who may have been leaders in the attempted escape that day from the latter, one was Louis De Beausset or Debasset, of the 5th Light Infantry regiment (or the 2nd Regiment of Artillery), who had been captured in February 1809 on Martinique. The other was Grandjean Duhenot (also known as Benoit P. Grandjean), 65th Infantry regiment, who had been captured in August 1809 at Flushing. Born at Nantes and aged 27, De Beausset had arrived on 27 February at Esk Mills from Portsmouth, via HMS *Ardent*. Duhenot or Grandjean, born in Paris and aged 25, was transferred on 14 August 1811 from the Castle to Greenlaw. From the latter he was discharged along with four other prisoners on 18 September, 'Delivered over to the Civil Power ... on account of the forging of Bank Notes.'[15]

After these eleven *mauvais sujets* sent to the Castle between 4 and 9 March inclusive came the 450 prisoners marched there on 11 March from Esk Mills as an immediate result of the crisis at that depot early that day. As already noticed, 30 of those 450 prisoners were said to have been 'concerned in outrageous proceedings' at Esk Mills and were to be kept at the Castle 'in solitary cells on short allowance of provisions, as also the four French officers who have been sent to you as Ringleaders on this occasion.'[16] Whether, as seems likely, the latter reference was to Decreuse, Foucault, De Beausset and Duhenot, who had been sent to the Castle on 9 March and therefore before the crisis at Esk Mills on 11 March, or whether it was to four other officers, is not certain. Nor is it clear who among the 450 prisoners marched from Esk Mills into the Castle that day were the 30 to be kept in solitary confinement.

What is clear, however, is that from 11 March Edinburgh Castle was no longer only or mainly an overnight staging post for prisoners landed at Leith or a place of punishment for *mauvais sujets* among prisoners at other depots. Because of the unexpected and sudden closure of Esk Mills and the inability of either Greenlaw or Valleyfield to house the surplus numbers, the Castle had apparently become a depot like any other. Certainly, it was much smaller than either Esk Mills or Valleyfield and could evidently accommodate only between 500 and 1,000 prisoners of war.

Their accommodation in the Castle, as in the French Revolutionary and earlier wars, appears to have been in the vaults or casements that had been largely built by the early 15th century and which formed part of one of the oldest structures in the fortress.[17] Of these vaults there were six and they ran from north to south as bases for the buildings on the south side of Crown Square. The three most westerly vaults were entered from a passageway north of the vaults and on the same level; the three easternmost vaults were entered from a parapet walk known as the Devil's Elbow.

But below these six vaults were a further seven sub-vaults—four of them below the western vaults and three below the eastern. It is very likely that the 30 *mauvais sujets* sent to the Castle from Esk Mills on 11 March were put into one or more of these sub-vaults.[18]

How far the vaults had been improved, from the prisoners' point of view, as a result of the £1,884 3s.6d. worth of building works carried out on them by the Transport Board at the end of the French Revolutionary Wars is unclear.[19] But any improvements would have had to be very substantial indeed to transform accommodation that had been so strongly denounced by Ambrose Serle, a commissioner of the Board, in his report on the Castle in July 1799.[20] The depots in Scotland were not, and were not intended to be, places of comfort and joy for the prisoners of war crowded into them. But of all the places of confinement north of the Border the vaults in Edinburgh Castle seem likely to have been the least agreeable, and the sub-vaults worst of all. That was why the latter were so often used as places of confinement for *mauvais sujets* from other Scots depots. But even prisoners who had given the authorities no trouble might also occasionally in 1811, because of the sheer numbers marched into the Castle, find themselves so unfortunate as to be lodged in some of the sub-vaults.

In February 1811, at a time when those parts of the Castle were being used mainly to confine some hundreds of prisoners of war for a night or two between their landing at Leith and their departure for Esk Mills, Edinburgh Castle was visited by a traveller born in France but who had lived during the previous twenty years or more in the United States of America, and whose wife was English. Louis Simond, who afterwards published his *Journal of a tour and residence in Great Britain during the years 1810 and 1811*, learned on his arrival that month in the city that 'New depots of prisoners of war are forming in the environs of Edinburgh, and detachments of these unfortunate people, transported by sea from the south of England to Leith, have arrived here; they are first lodged in the Castle. I have been informed that a great number of them have been seen marching barefoot in the half-frozen mud. Wishing to ascertain the fact and if possible to alleviate their sufferings, I procured an introduction to Colonel Maghee, commanding at the fort, who had the goodness to go with me among the prisoners.' Simond's visit took place on 14 February, four days before 450 prisoners were marched from the Castle to Esk Mills.

'I found,' Simond wrote, '3 or 400 men, nearly all seafaring people, in a small court, surrounded with palisadoes [sic], in front of that part of the building where they lodge at night; this esplanade, about 100 or 120 feet every way, had a very beautiful view of the town and country over the brow of the hill. I do not suppose, however, that these unfortunate people were much disposed to enjoy it. I found them walking to and fro in their narrow inclosure, most of them talking merrily enough, poorly clad, though not in rags. Those who have no clothes of their own receive certain yellow jackets which, by their remarkable appearance, render their escape more difficult; instead of shoes they had most of them a sort of galoches, the sole of wood and top of list. I understood that many had lost their shoes in the muddy road, and that 150 of them were really in great want of that important article, which Colonel Maghee assured me was to be supplied before they left the Castle to go to the depot.

'The daily ration is 1½ lb of bread, at 3d.; ½ lb of meat, at 6¾d. per lb; once or twice a week they have fish instead of meat; each man is provided with a hammock and two blankets. Many supplicating hands offered for sale the produce of their industry; watch-chains made of hair, and other trifling articles, most of them very ingeniously manufactured. A young man, his countenance all radiant with good humour, informed me he had been seven years thus engaged, having been one of the first taken at the renewal of the war. If he is proof against such a fate as this he need not envy any one. The richest gifts of fortune are poor indeed compared to an indestructible power of happiness.

'I observed, on the other hand, several prisoners traversing slowly, apart from the rest, the narrow and muddy area, or leaning back against the paling, with sunken eyes, fixed with dull looks, and earthy complexions—wrapt in meditation upon nothing; upon time, which does not pass for them; upon these eternal hours, which bring no other change than light and darkness; short light, at long and frightful intervals of night; dreaming on an existence of which nothing marks the duration, and which consumes nevertheless the best years of their lives—and on the final annihilation of a momentary hope of liberation. It is shocking to think that fifty or sixty thousand human beings should be in this deplorable situation! [21] Not so many, however, feel it. The abject crowd was seen here pressing with eagerness and loud clamour—all speaking at the same time—round a spot where some game was going on, with the same bursts of laughter, the same oaths and frantic gestures, as if their dearest interests had been in question. An aristocrat *à la lanterne*, the execution of Robespierre, or the news of a cartel for the general exchange of prisoners, could not have excited more bustle and agitation! This is the best possible school for idleness and vice, as well as an abode of unspeakable wretchedness, to all those whose feelings are not blunted. If the persons on whom the liberation of so many miserable men depends could be placed for a little while in the midst of them, it is scarcely possible to suppose that the negotiation for the exchange should not be facilitated thereby. Many of the prisoners seemed too old to be worth keeping, and might be sent back without any accession of strength to the enemy. I have heard of an [French] East India captain, who was taken [prisoner] in 1793, liberated in 1802, taken again the following year, and now a prisoner with a wife and family in France.'

Simond concluded that as the non-parole prisoners of war cost the British government about 10d to 1s. a day, or nearly £1 million a year for 50,000 prisoners, apart from the cost of troops employed in guarding them, 'An exchange on any terms would be better than this. I cannot help thinking that some useful employment might be found for these men, such as roads and canals, or the tillage of waste lands. The greatest part of them would prefer the lowest salary, with some degree of liberty, to their present confinement; the difference of dress and language, and the insular situation of the country would, with certain precautions, render their escape very difficult; and in a country so often short of grain, it cannot be a matter of indifference whether 50,000 strangers shall be fed out of the public store, or whether their labour should contribute to fill it.'[22]

It was not merely 'the difference of dress and language, and the insular situation of the country' that appeared to make escape by prisoners of war very difficult but, specifically for those confined in Edinburgh Castle, the apparently formidable character of the fortress itself, situated as it was on a high and precipitous rock, and garrisoned by large numbers of troops.

On 12 April 1811, however, the unlikely, even the apparently impossible, happened at the Castle. 'Last night,' the *Caledonian Mercury* reported next day, 'about eleven o'clock, 49 French prisoners, among whom was a Captain (who also contrived to get away his baggage), escaped from the south-west corner of their prison in the Castle. They had cut a hole through the bottom of the parapet wall, below the place commonly called the *Devil's Elbow*, and let themselves down by a rope. One of the prisoners, losing his hold, fell from a considerable height, and was so dreadfully bruised that he is not expected to live. Five of them were retaken this morning and fourteen of them were seen on the road to Glasgow. The night being dark, the operations of the prisoners were not observable; but the sentinel, on hearing some noise, became suspicious of the cause and, firing immediately, gave the alarm to the guard; otherwise it is probable the whole might have effected their escape.'

It was the greatest mass escape from any depot in Scotland during the Napoleonic Wars.

Malcolm Wright, Transport Board agent at the Castle, placed an advertisement that filled three quarters of a column in the next issue of the *Edinburgh Evening Courant*, listing the names and physical descriptions of 44 of the escapers still at large, and offering the 'usual Reward together with all necessary expenses' for their recapture.[23] For some weeks afterward the press carried reports of sightings or recaptures of the 44 prisoners who had succeeded in getting away from Edinburgh.

All the escapers from the Castle appear to have been recaptured within six weeks. Given the absence of names and some contradictions in the press reports about numbers, and the lack of information in the Castle General Entry Book, it has not proved possible, except in a few cases, to establish the date and place of each individual's recapture. Thus the identities of the five said by the *Caledonian Mercury* to have been recaptured within a few hours and who were not included in Malcolm Wright's advertisement on 15 April, are unknown. Nor is it clear whether the escaper who suffered apparently fatal injuries in his fall down the Castle rock was one of those five. If he was not then there must have been 50 escapers, not 49. If he died from his injuries, as the *Mercury* implied, then it appears virtually certain that he was Pierre Woemeseuil or Wormeseul, a midshipman aged 20, captured on the naval brig *Requin* in July 1808, and whose death was entered in the General Entry Book on 14 April.[24]

The fourteen or so escapers who were 'seen on the road to Glasgow' were recaptured on 14 April at Linlithgow. Their statements indicated the escape had been planned for a month beforehand. '... no sooner were they lodged in the Castle [from Esk Mills, in early March] than plans were formed for effecting their escape and, it would seem, carried into execution with the greatest secrecy. They had procured information of the nearest place of embarkation, and being furnished with maps and that part of the almanack containing the principal roads through the country, they bent their way to Grangemouth, where they were to have gone on board some foreign vessels lying there. At Linlithgow, where they stopped at night to get some refreshment, they were challenged as prisoners who had made their escape, when they took to their heels and were found next morning, after a diligent search by the local militia, in the plantations near Polmont, quite exhausted with hunger.'[25]

Four more of the escapers were recaptured on 18 or 20 April in Dundee and, escorted by dragoons, immediately marched off to Perth gaol. Ten others, who had been 'lurking for several days' near St Andrews were caught 'cutting out a small sloop', and were sent back to Leith on 23 April. By then a further half dozen were reported in custody at Perth and Montrose and four at Greenock and Glasgow. On 11 May the press reported the recapture of another four of the escapers at Banff—but these were apparently the four who had escaped from custody at Perth after their first recapture at Dundee. Though the numbers of reported recaptures seem somewhat contradictory what appear to have been the last four escapers still on the run were recaptured on 27 May at Tynemouth, five miles east of Newcastle. The four 'were apprehended in the act of going on board an American ship off Cullercoats, and lodged in the house of correction at Tynemouth.'[26]

Even before all the escapers of 12 April had been recaptured, however, there was a further considerable escape from Edinburgh Castle—this time by a dozen prisoners. 'Last night,' reported the *Caledonian Mercury* on 27 April, 'the prisoners in the Castle made another effort to escape, by cutting a hole through the wall near the place where they last made their exit. About twelve of them got out but were soon after retaken by the soldiers on guard.' Thus, although all of them appear to have been recaptured, more than sixty prisoners had escaped from the Castle within a fortnight.[27]

The mass escape of 12 April from the Castle inevitably aroused alarm in official circles and some sections of the press. After the first recaptures a couple of days later of escapers at Linlithgow the *Glasgow Herald*, for example, commented: 'We trust, therefore, they will now be more strictly guarded, as the circumstance of such a set of desperadoes being loose in the country may be attended with the worst consequences.'[28]

How had so many prisoners been able to get out of the Castle and how had they been able to get a rope or ropes long enough to enable them to descend the precipitous 150 feet high Castle rock on the south or West Port side? On 17 April the Transport Board opened fire on Malcolm Wright, its agent at the Castle. 'Rear Admiral Otway [at Leith] having reported that you had not complied with his directions to take from the prisoners every evening their fencing foils, the various tools they are allowed to use, and the lines for drying their clothes, in consequence of which the escape of the prisoners who lately broke out from Edinburgh Castle was facilitated, we desire that you will account for your not attending to the orders of the Rear Admiral on this subject.'[29]

The Board's opening shot was swiftly followed by what was intended to be the coup de grâce for Wright. 'The Lords Commissioner of the Admiralty,' the Board informed Wright next day, 'having been pleased by their Order dated 17th April to direct us to dismiss you immediately in consequence of Rear Admiral Otway's report that the late escape of 49 French prisoners from Edinburgh Castle was attributable to your neglect in discharging an order he has given to you for the better security of the prisoners there, and to appoint Captain Thomas Heddington in your room, we acquaint you that we have appointed Captain Heddington accordingly, and we direct you to deliver over to him the charge of your Department, the prisoners by muster and the stores by inventory with all public papers in your possession not necessary to the final settlement of your accounts, taking his receipt for the same.' The Board wrote simultaneously to Admiral Otway, who had asked the Admiralty to appoint Heddington agent at the Castle in place of Wright, as well as to Captain Pellowe, agent at Valleyfield, and to Heddington, who had been acting as Pellowe's assistant at Valleyfield since the closure of Esk Mills depot in March, informing them of the decision.

But Wright did not give up without a struggle. On 26 April he wrote to the Transport Board, enclosing a copy of a memorial he had submitted to the Lords Commissioner of the Admiralty about his supersession as agent at the Castle. The Board's formal acknowledgement of receipt was followed by its peremptory demand that Wright should send his final accounts for his time as agent at Greenlaw depot (which had ended the previous January) 'without delay'.[30] Meantime a court of enquiry into the escapes from the Castle had been at work. 'Pray,' wrote Commissioner Bowen of the Transport Board from Edinburgh on 12 May to Alexander McLeay, the Board's secretary in London, 'what is to be done with Mr Wright? The Court of Enquiry I understand sat two days. All is secret and kept completely so from me. I understand the report went away two or three days ago and I believe the only crime imputable to him is being too kind and too indulgent to the prisoners. There might have been some neglect and disobedience of orders. Not understanding the nature of military service I believe was the real cause, not out of disrespect or want of attention.' As Wright had been agent for prisoners of war at Edinburgh and Greenlaw for well over a decade since his original appointment during the French Revolutionary Wars others might have concluded that by 1811 he had had time enough to reach some understanding of 'the nature of military service'.[31]

Wright had, however, as already observed, influential friends or patrons. They must again have gone to work on his behalf. For on 6 June the Transport Board informed him that 'The Lords Commissioner of the Admiralty having been pleased to authorise us to employ you as our agent in receiving such parole and other prisoners as may be sent to Leith, and for passing them and their baggage to their different destinations, we acquaint you therewith, and direct you to attend this service accordingly.' Once again Wright, placed metaphorically in front of a firing squad, the smoke and din from the discharge of whose muskets proved, however, to be merely from blanks, had emerged bearing another official appointment in the care and custody of prisoners of war.[32]

In mid July, a month after Wright's new appointment and a month also after Captain Heddington, who had been on extended leave in England, had succeeded him as agent at Edinburgh Castle, the Castle suffered a third mass escape of prisoners of war. Perhaps they intended the timing of their escape as a celebration of Bastille Day, for both took place on Sunday, 14 July 1811. 'Last night,' reported the *Caledonian Mercury* next day, '18 French prisoners contrived to make their escape from the depot in the Castle, but we hear were all retaken except one.'[33] Such a series of escapes, however, even though recaptures were almost complete, inevitably undermined the belief that the Castle was an especially secure depot.

Though evidence is once more lacking to prove these frequent escapes between April and July were the reason, what other explanation is more likely for the removal on 14 August from the Castle to Greenlaw depot of 321 prisoners of war, followed within three weeks by a further 44?[34] Thus by August 1811, after only a few months of employment as a depot, Edinburgh Castle was being almost emptied of prisoners of war, so vulnerable had its security proven. A Transport Office return on 11 June that year had shown 288 prisoners of war confined in the Castle; on 26 August the number was only 13. Edinburgh Castle, as the Transport Board commissioners admitted in a letter to the Admiralty in February 1812, they knew from experience '... is not sufficiently secure for the confinement of French prisoners.'[35]

A lesser contribution to the decision to remove all but a handful of prisoners from the Castle may have been the bad relations between two of the three depot agents in Scotland and the promotion of one of them to a more senior position in the south of England. In the first half of August Captain Pellowe, agent at Valleyfield depot, had been appointed by the Admiralty to become agent for prisoners of war at Plymouth, a major centre of the work of the Transport Board. Captain Heddington, earlier transferred to Edinburgh Castle from Valleyfield, where he had been assistant to Pellowe, was directed by the Transport Board, in accordance with the Admiralty's instructions, to become agent at Valleyfield. His bad relations with Pellowe had already prompted the

Transport Board to suggest to the Admiralty on 2 August that 'the service cannot be benefitted [sic] from their being both continued in their present situations.' By 19 August therefore the Board had ordered Malcolm Wright to relieve Captain Heddington at Edinburgh Castle, so that Heddington could take up his appointment at Valleyfield. But Heddington declined to take it up. Thus Heddington left Scotland and the service of the Transport Board, Pellowe went to Plymouth, Captain E. J. Moriarty, RN, became agent at Valleyfield, and Malcolm Wright reappeared as agent at the Castle.[36]

After the transfer, therefore, in August of virtually all its prisoners to Greenlaw the Castle was rapidly run down as a depot. In mid-September all the medicines and other medical stores were sent to Greenlaw, only enough being retained 'for the use of the sick among such prisoners as may be sent to Edinburgh Castle.' A few days later Wright was instructed by the Transport Board to terminate the services of the surgeon and the interpreter at the Castle, retaining only one clerk and one turnkey. If medicines were needed for prisoners of war at the Castle, 'though it is unlikely', they were to be got from Greenlaw depot. From that depot on 16 November Lieutenant Priest, its agent, was instructed by the Board to send to the Castle 'the whole of the prisoners in the Black Hole, unless there should be one or two of them you may think sufficiently punished.' The Castle General Entry Book shows eight seamen—presumably till then occupants of Greenlaw's black hole—arrived at the Castle on 20 November. And on 12 December Priest was told to send some prisoners he had reported presumably for bad conduct, 'for better security to Edinburgh Castle, to be confined in the cachot there.' The Castle General Entry Book shows five prisoners, one of them that irrepressible mariner Lieutenant Jacques Adam, arrived from Greenlaw on 17 December. Thus in the second half of 1811 the Castle continued to be used as a place of punishment for *mauvais sujets* among prisoners at Penicuik, as well as for a few prisoners from Scots parole towns.[37] But in the four and a half months between 15 August and 30 December inclusive that year the Entry Book shows a total of only 15 prisoners arrived at the Castle.

'For better security to Edinburgh Castle ...' The phrase once more rang ironically when on the night of 18-19 December 14 prisoners of war escaped from the Castle 'by means of a rope thrown over the wall at the place called the Devil's Elbow. The rope reached almost to the public road.'[38] The escape appears to have been from the same spot in the vaults or sub-vaults as the earlier substantial escapes on 12 and 26 April—and by the same means. Eleven of the prisoners were recaptured on 22 December, and two others on 12 January 1812. The remaining one of the 14, Jean Baptiste Zoutin, a privateer seaman, appears to have got clean away.

This further sizeable escape proved the last straw—at least for the time being—for the Castle as a depot for prisoners of war. 'The Lords Commissioner of the Admiralty,' wrote the Transport Board on 28 December to Lieutenant General Lord Cathcart, army commander in Scotland, 'having in consequence of the facility with which French prisoners can escape from Edinburgh Castle been pleased to direct that this Depot be entirely abolished, we acquaint you therewith.' The Board added that Lieutenant Richard Glinn, RN, agent for transports at Leith, was to carry on the work of dealing with prisoners, including parole prisoners, landed at or sailing from Leith which had until then been the responsibility of Malcolm Wright. Wright was simultaneously ordered to send the few prisoners still in Edinburgh Castle to Valleyfield at once, 'excepting such as have been sent from thence or Greenlaw in consequence of important information, who are to be put on board the [HMS] *Regulus*.'[39]

It was also the end of the road at last as a Transport Board agent for Malcolm Wright. That same day the Board informed him of the decision to close down the Castle as a depot 'and that your pay as well as that of your clerk and turnkey is to cease on the 31st of this month.'[40]

Thus by the end of 1811, the year of 'new arrangements', two of the four depots for prisoners of war in Scotland—Esk Mills and Edinburgh Castle—had had to be closed. To the two that remained—Greenlaw and Valleyfield, building work was, however, proceeding speedily that winter for the addition of a third: Perth.

7

Perth Depot

The building of a depot at Perth, suggested by General Lord Cathcart in October 1810 and enthuastically supported by Commissioner Bowen of the Transport Board, had begun on 2 September 1811, when several hundred building workers were set on to the task. It was to become both the first purpose-built and the largest depot for prisoners of war in Scotland.

All that autumn and winter and on through the spring and summer of 1812 the building work was pressed ahead as the flow of prisoners into Britain, particularly from the war in Spain and Portugal, continued unabated.[1] Under the general direction, and from the plans and designs, of Robert Reid, government or crown architect in Scotland, those contracted by the Transport Board to build the depot were the firms of J. Thin and others in Edinburgh.[2] The depot was 'completed very much to our satisfaction, although not within the time limited by the contract,' the Board afterwards wrote, adding that the contractors 'have repeatedly stated to us that they have been losers by the contract ...'[3]

Under pressure to complete the depot speedily, the builders faced several problems. One was the extreme cold during the winter of 1811-12. The *Caledonian Mercury* reported on 14 December, for example, that '... last week the cold was so intense in Perth that ice was found of an inch and half in thickness after only 12 hours' frost. A number of fine stones from Kingoody quarry were split at the depot, and the contractors are said to have sustained a very serious loss.' George Penny, a contemporary historian of Perth, wrote that 'fires were used to thaw the lime, and large coverings of straw to preserve the hewn stones from the frost.'[4] Another problem appears to have been a shortage of building workers, particularly of stone masons. On 22 August and again on the 24th, a week before building work began, an advertisement in the *Caledonian Mercury* had been addressed 'TO MASONS, QUARRIERS, AND DIGGERS. WANTED, a great number of MASONS, QUARRIERS and DIGGERS, at Perth, for erecting the Depot for Prisoners of War, to be built immediately there, where good encouragement will be given; and as the works are so late in the season in beginning, there will be winter's employment when weather permits.' Three days after work had begun, when the paper reported 'Several hundreds of people are already employed and it is said that in a few weeks employment could be given to upwards of 800', a further advertisement in the *Perth Courier* announced 'A considerable number of whin-stone Quarrymen and Carters are immediately wanted for the depot now building at Perth. Such as wish employment will apply at the Work, where the most liberal encouragement will be given.'[5] On 23 November another advertisement in the *Edinburgh Evening Courant* announced: 'MASONS WANTED For the Depot building at Perth. Stone cutters or hewers will meet with good encouragement, by applying to the foreman at the works.' And the same paper on 12 December carried a further advertisement, repeated two days later, this time implying in its appeal that the building work was characterised by altruistic concern for the workers on the part of the contractors: 'TO MASONS. The Contractors for building the DEPOT for prisoners-of-war at PERTH, being resolved to exert themselves in giving employment to MASONS during the winter, Intimation therefore is hereby given to all masons who may want employment to apply to any of the contractors, or John Hogarth, foreman at the depot, where they will find work every day that weather permits. Information may be had from any of the contractors who may be in Edinburgh at the time.'[6] The services of the masons were, however, lost to the depot for a day in March when they went on strike against a refusal by the contractors to be sufficiently altruistic as to increase their wages. On the forenoon of Monday, 2 March, the masons 'assembled on the North Inch, where, though perfectly peaceable, they appeared very formidable by their number. To prevent bad consequences, the Provost and Sheriff judiciously warned them of the laws against combinations and unauthorised meetings, which they might through ignorance infringe, and the warning was civilly and gratefully received. After some conferences with the Contractors, the disagreement was satisfactorily adjusted and the Masons returned to their work on Tuesday afternoon.'[7]

The building of the depot was obviously a major undertaking that necessitated the employment of large numbers of workers and incurred great expense. The cost was said to be £130,000—almost twice that of building Dartmoor depot.[8] According to George Penny, 'upwards of 1,500 hands were employed about the work, besides an immense number of horses and carts ... Stone quarries were opened in several quarters, and roads made from them at vast expense ...'[9] Nor was the building work completed without at least one serious accident to workers engaged on it. 'On Friday last,' reported the *Perth Courier* on 9 April, 'two workmen employed at the depot were precipitated from the roof of one of the buildings, in consequence of the yielding of the scaffold on which they stood. They were both severely hurt by the fall but none of their bones were broken, though they fell from a height of at least thirty feet. A third, who was on the scaffold at the time, luckily escaped the

All Men Are Brethren

fate of his companions by clinging to a ladder. The two men who were hurt are in a fair way to recovery.'

By early July 1812, nine months after building work had begun, the new depot at Perth was reported to be 'nearly completed.' 'These extensive buildings,' the *Perth Courier* reported, 'are, we understand, to contain 7,000 prisoners, with the troops on guard over them, as also accommodation for the sick and lodgings for the several officers of the establishment, forming altogether the greatest establishment of the kind in Britain ... Whether we consider the general arrangements of the plan of the Depot, in giving all its parts the fullest command inspection to the Military on duty, the ingenious and unusual mode adopted for ventilating and introducing fresh air into the different prison buildings, and other means for ensuring the health and cleanliness of the prisoners, or the secure manner in which every part of it is constructed, it is certainly the most complete depot or place of confinement which has been erected.[10] The work has been performed under contract by a company of respectable builders from Edinburgh with a dispatch wholly unprecedented and in a manner very creditable to them, and will we understand be completed at an expense comparatively much less than any similar establishment in England. This extensive work has given employment to a great number of people during its progress, not less we are informed than from 1,000 to 1,200 having been daily at work since the commencement. The whole of this great concern is executing under the direction and from the plans and designs of Robert Reid, Edinburgh, H.M.'s Architect for Scotland, and while it is to be deplored that the necessity of [sic] such establishments exists, it is at the same time satisfactory and creditable to the country also that such accommodation is provided for our prisoners as admits of their enjoying every comfort and convenience consistent with their unfortunate situation.'[11]

The new depot had certainly been built in a remarkably short time. Whether, unlike Esk Mills and Edinburgh Castle, it would ensure the secure confinement of its inmates only time would tell. But the Transport Board appeared confident it would do so. Writing on 24 September to the Admiralty about Dartmoor depot the Board declared: '... that Prison is considered the most secure Depot in the Country, excepting the new Depot at Perth, which is built upon nearly the same Plan.'[12] The description of Perth depot as 'the greatest establishment of the kind in Britain' and as 'the most complete depot or place of confinement which has been erected' may have seemed to diminish the importance of other purpose-built depots but on the whole the description appeared justified. Dartmoor, which took three years to build between 1806 and 1809 at a cost of £74,000, covered thirty acres and was therefore more extensive than Perth, which covered about eight or nine acres; but Dartmoor was intended to hold only 5,000 prisoners of war, although later alterations to the depot increased the number to about 9,000. The depot at Portchester Castle near Portsmouth, which like Perth held about 7,000 prisoners, was not purpose built—indeed, the castle, Roman in origin, had also been a Norman fortress—though it had undergone extensive reconstruction early in the Napoleonic Wars. Norman Cross depot in Huntingdonshire occupied 22 acres, had been purpose built in only four months in 1796-7 at a cost of £34,500, and held 'in the most crowded period of its occupation' at least 7,000 prisoners although normally between 5,500 and 6,300. But Norman Cross, unlike Perth and the other purpose-built depots, was built of wood. Stapleton depot, at Bristol, originally purpose built in 1782, was later extended to hold 8,000 prisoners, although it appears to have held a thousand fewer than that in 1810 and an average between 1805 and 1814 of about 5,500.[13]

A fuller description of the features of the new depot that explains some of the references in that contemporary report by the *Perth Courier* was provided in 1849 by the Perth historian David Peacock. The depot, he wrote, 'was considered the finest of this species of architecture in Scotland. It consisted of a range of massive and very commodious buildings … The space occupied [immediately beyond the South Inch] is about 600 feet along the Great North Road, by about 700 feet from that eastward to the bank of the Tay. The eastern portion formed five octagonal sides; while of the western portion nearly the half was a continuation of one of these on either side of the road, forming a square area of about one-half the entire space. On the octagonal portion there were five prisons, parallel to the five sides above mentioned. Each of these consisted of three storeys, each flat constituting a ward. Each of these was 130 feet long, with outside stairs at both ends. The inside width was 30 feet, and each of the five buildings accommodated 1,140 men. Each had an airing yard converging upon a common centre, or rather upon what was called the "Market Place", from which they were separated by a high iron palisade which surrounded it. The same sort of barrier separated them from one another. In the centre of the Market Place was a high embattled tower for observation, on which was the flag-staff. On the south side of the square, extending westwards, was the prison for "petty officers" (the better class being on parole), and contained 1,100 inmates. This erection, still standing, is two storeys high; and on the north side of the square is yet to be seen what was the Hospital, also of two storeys, that contained 150 invalids. All these were included within the range of defences, or rather of security against escape. These were first—reckoning from the inside—a canal or moat, ten feet wide all round. On the outside brink of this was a strong high palisade of iron, similar to those separating the airing-grounds of each prison. Beyond that there were the high walls yet standing, with triangular indentations from the outside; and in the recesses thus created flights of steps were erected, rising both ways, from the low "military walk", with level platforms on the top, nearly as high as the walls, on which sentinels were continually posted. Outside this again was the "military way" just mentioned, about fifteen feet wide. This extended round the whole, and was divided from the open field by a low retaining wall and parapet. The kitchens stood on either side of the Market Place, and within the inner gate. Excluded by the canal and palisade, there was a square immediately within the outer entrance gate, where were the Agent's house on the right, and the Surgeon's on the left, each of two storeys, yet standing, and now converted into residences for the Governor and the Chaplain of the General Prison. Further inwards, but without the inner gate, were four buildings, of one storey high, for officers of the establishment. There were guard-rooms with verandahs beyond these on either side, just within the west wall; and there stood a third guard-room on the military way, at the extreme opposite end. The whole plan was one of the most minute regularity. ... a guard of 300 men mounted every day, and this required the appointment of three regiments of foot in Perth, partly stationed at the Barracks, partly quartered in the town.'[14]

A few further details concerning the buildings were added almost half a century after Peacock's description by another Perth historian, William Sievewright. 'The stone is dark whin-stone, hard and flinty looking in the grain ...' In the basement and on the second floor of the high tower at the Market Place, at the latter of which Sievewright said he believed 'articles manufactured by the prisoners were sold', there were 'a reservoir for water, some strong dark cells, and other apartments.' Sievewright went on to describe what he considered was the way in which each ward in the depot would have had to accommodate 380 prisoners of war. 'With four tiers of sleepers there would thus be nearly 100 in each, at all events 95 or 96, rather more than 16 inches to each. This arrangement would have left one centre passage of six feet, or three narrow passages of two feet each along the ward.' If Sievewright's view was correct then the prisoners at Perth must have been packed in their hammocks at night like herrings in a barrel.[15]

A description of the depot, although exaggerating the number of prisoners it could hold and probably some other details, as well as contradicting some aspects of the descriptions given in other sources, was recorded almost thirty years after it opened by a prisoner of war who had arrived in it from Valleyfield on 2 September 1812, within a month of its opening: Marote-Carrier, privateer lieutenant, whose recollections of his captivity at Esk Mills and Valleyfield have already been so often quoted. Since Marote-Carrier, unlike contemporary or later historians, was for almost eighteen months actually an inmate of Perth depot his recollections of its buildings and its apparent security, although recorded many years later, deserve attention.[16] Upon the new depot, he recalled, 'workers were still working when we entered it. Situated in the great plain of Perth, a circular wall ran round all the buildings. Many villages were not as extensive. This surrounding wall was twelve to fifteen feet high and five to six in thickness. From point to point sentries marched on it watching simultaneously inward and outward. A ditch of ten to twelve feet wide and filled with running water flowed at the foot of the wall, and ran round all the inside of the prison. We crossed this ditch on a drawbridge. The prisoners were shut up in ten groups of separate blocks. Each of these particular buildings contained two rooms, one on the ground floor, the other above it. Each of these rooms could hold 500 prisoners. The whole could contain up to 10,000 men. Each prison was numbered—from one to six. The inside edge of the ditch was strengthened with strong iron palisades six feet in height and very close. A wall the height of a man encircled each prison and formed a little yard connecting with the central yard. In the middle of this last stood a kind of big fortified barracks surrounded with iron palings like the ditch. It housed a garrison of artillery men, and ten 18lb guns in it were aimed at each of the ten gates set in the surrounding wall. These guns were always loaded, and an artilleryman on guard stood watching there with match ready lit. Sentries were posted on the outside wall … they had their guard-house near each gate, and in the evening a lantern quite high up was lit in front and shone all night, lighting up both sides of the wall.

'The hospital was in the central yard, near the fortress. It was well laid out, very big, and surrounded also with iron palisades. The commandant's [agent's] residence was situated to the left of the hospital not far from the gate giving on to the main road and by which we had entered. Ten jailers [turnkeys] were responsible for watching over the entrances and exits, and each of them had his lodging at one of the ten gates.

'The building contractor for the prison had committed himself to constructing it in such a way that neither a rat nor a mouse could escape from it. Add to … that all the large buildings were in very hard ashlar, joined by cement made from powdered stone, and you will see like us that the assertion of the contractor would have been difficult to contest. A very thick wall, a wide ditch, deep and full of water, a row of iron palisades, a further wall encircling each prison, the prison wall itself—what obstacles to overcome! Then the most meticulous surveillance, day and night cannons aimed and matches lit, sentries along the whole length of the surrounding wall, jailers at all the gates, patrols at all hours of the night inside and outside the walls—how many spies there were to take in and thwart! All that was to make us despair of ever regaining our liberty.'[17]

Part of the Transport Board's necessary preparations for the arrival of the first prisoners at Perth was to secure the appointment of an agent, a surgeon, and a supporting staff of clerks, turnkeys, matron, and others. At the beginning of June 1812, when it described the depot as being 'in a sufficient state of forwardness to require the Appointment of an Officer to superintend the same', the Board asked the Admiralty to appoint an agent and also asked whether James Gillies, surgeon at Valleyfield, should be appointed as such at Perth.[18] The Admiralty acted swiftly: four days later Captain E.J. Moriarty, RN, who had been agent at Valleyfield since the previous August, was appointed agent at Perth. Moriarty was told that 'The Depot at Perth is intended to receive Prisoners about the 1st of next Month.' Gillies's appointment as surgeon was confirmed to him the same day.[19] By 20 June the Board had itself appointed Andrew Johnston as first clerk, two assistant clerks, a dispenser, a hospital clerk cum interpreter, a matron, a steward, a hospital steward, two turnkeys and a seamstress. Three more turnkeys were appointed within the following three weeks.[20]

As early as the end of April the Transport Board had advertised in the press for tenders, to be submitted by 26 May, for victualling prisoners of war at Perth for six months from 1 July.[21] But as had happened with Esk Mills and Valleyfield, the date of opening of the new depot crept backward. On 10 July Moriarty, then still at Valleyfield, was told by the Board, 'You are immediately on your arrival at Perth to report the state of the prison and at what period prisoners may be sent thither.' Three days later all the others appointed to the depot staff were told to go immediately to Perth.[22]

Still, however, building work at the depot was not completed. Then another problem arose concerning the navigable depths of the Tay. On 21 July Moriarty, who appears to have arrived at Perth that day or the next, was instructed by the Board that, 'The *Mathilda* Transport being about to proceed from Plymouth to the Tay with the prisoners for the depot at Perth, make enquiry and report to us how far up the Tay this vessel can proceed, her draft of water being 16 feet. The master of the *Mathilda* will be directed to report himself to you on his arrival and you will make arrangements for engaging craft to take the prisoners from the *Mathilda* to Perth with their baggage, and for a guard.'[23]

The Board's instruction to Moriarty crossed with an undated letter, not preserved, from him in which he must have asked for more time to prepare the depot for receiving its first intake of prisoners. '... the Board,' said its reply of 22 July, 'cannot now stop the *Mathilda* from proceeding, the Lords Commissioner of the Admiralty having ordered a convoy for her from Plymouth to the Downs and from thence to the river Tay with about 300 French prisoners, and the Board trust that you will be prepared to receive them on their arrival. There will probably be about 1,000 more prisoners sent to Perth in the course of a month and by that time the Board expect that the whole depot will be finished. It is considered that the prisoners now sent will be found useful in accelerating the completion of the workings by assisting in levelling the ground, removing rubbish, etc.'[24]

The *Mathilda* had arrived at Plymouth from the Peninsula with prisoners of war earlier that month. Many such prisoners were in poor health and wretchedly clothed, some of them more or less naked, after weeks or months of captivity in Spain or Portugal. The Transport Board was anxious that all prisoners sent to the new depot at Perth 'should be such as are in good health and are well clothed,' and had asked the Admiralty to postpone the departure of the *Mathilda* to the Tay for a few days 'in order to afford time for making arrangements for the prisoners now on board her and cleansing her should it be necessary.' On 28 July the Board asked the Admiralty to send a second ship, the frigate HMS *Regulus*, from Portsmouth to the Tay with more prisoners for Perth, 'as we are informed the *Regulus* can go up the Tay as far as Dundee', and that strict instructions should be given its captain to give notice of his arrival there to Captain Moriarty.[25]

Meantime Captain Moriarty was told by the Transport Board that 400 French prisoners had been embarked at Plymouth on the *Mathilda* on 24 July for the Tay, and that 'you will therefore lose no time in getting all things in readiness for the reception of ... them. Each of the prisoners embarked was supplied with a hammock, a bed and a blanket, which you are to receive from the master [of the *Mathilda*], as also the list of the prisoners. We wish you to proceed to Dundee in order to make arrangements for conveying the prisoners from the *Mathilda* (which draws 16 feet of water) to Perth; or if the wind should not be fair, to Newburgh, from which place they are in that case to be marched.'[26] *Mathilda's* arrival in the Tay proved not only the first but also the last occasion on which prisoners of war were landed there for Perth depot. The Board had evidently underestimated the problems of the depth of the river and of the estuarial tides. On 1 August it wrote again to Moriarty: 'Reference yours of 27th ult., stating that on the bar of the Tay there is about 17 feet at low water, subject to a very heavy swell on it with any wind and no safe anchorage without, and that the tide was from *16 to 20 inches* ... you will explain whether instead of *Inches* you did intend to have written *Feet*.' When the next batch of prisoners arrived for Perth a fortnight later on HMS *Regulus* they were landed not at Dundee or Newburgh but at Kirkcaldy in the Firth of Forth and marched from there to Perth.[27]

The *Mathilda* with its 400 prisoners arrived at Dundee on Monday, 3 August. Next day a prisoner who had died during the voyage was brought ashore for burial. On Wednesday, in the presence of Captain Moriarty, all the prisoners were disembarked and at once marched off on the twenty or so miles to the depot at Perth, escorted by a detachment of militia. 'The crowd of spectators assembled at the Shore and in the streets of Dundee was immense, the boys huzzaing at the sight of so many captive foes, and the men and women, influenced by more philanthropy though not less nationality, distributing bread and other presents among the unfortunate victims of war.'

Those prisoners 'who might be unable to proceed further than Inchture (a distance of about 8 miles from Dundee) were to be accommodated for the night in the church of that parish.'[28]

There is some uncertainty whether all the prisoners or, as indicated by the *Dundee Advertiser*, only those too weak or debilitated to march further on the first day, were lodged that night in Inchture parish church. It seems unlikely that all 400 could have been packed into the church: perhaps if they were all halted there overnight some spent the night in the open outside the church, closely guarded by the militia. What is certain is that all 400 were recorded in its General Entry Book as having arrived at the depot on 6 August. If some had arrived directly from Dundee on 5 August and others not until the 6th that fact presumably would have been recorded in the Entry Book. The *Perth Courier* reported that all the prisoners marched from Dundee to Inchture, 'where they lay all night. They again marched at four in the morning, and after passing through the town [Perth] reached the depot about 9. They were escorted by parties of the Durham and Fifeshire militia [the *Dundee Advertiser* said the escort was provided by the Renfrewshire militia]. One prison had been completely prepared for them, though the whole of the Depot was not then finished.' The contemporary Perth local historian Penny added that the prisoners 'were in pretty good condition, and had some women with them.' The arrival of the prisoners at Perth was considered sufficiently significant to merit a three-sentence report in *The Times*—another of the few occasions on which prisoners of war in Scotland attracted its august notice.[29]

What immediately became clear, however, was that the choice of Inchture parish church as an overnight lodging proved, hardly surprisingly, ill-advised. These prisoners of war were men who in many or most cases must have long been accustomed to 'marching on their stomachs' in Spain or Portugal, and not only filling their stomachs as best they could at the expense of the crops and livestock of the peasantry there but at least some of them also their pockets and knapsacks from looted houses and churches.[30] Yet the great majority of the prisoners in that first batch entering the depot were evidently aghast at the vandalism and theft committed in the church by a few of their number. A letter from 'A Citizen' in the *Perth Courier* a week later seems to give the fullest account of what had happened en route at Inchture: 'The French prisoners who were brought to the Depot here on Thursday morning last from Dundee were lodged the preceding night in the church of Inchture, where it is said they contrived to draw many of the nails from the seats and break a number of the panes of the windows; and one of their number stole the two mortcloths belonging to the church. The Beadle being sent after them to the Depot the theft was instantly discovered, which so incensed the prisoners against the thief that they called out to have him punished, and asked permission to do so, by a Court Martial. Having held this Court they ordered him a naval flogging of two dozen [lashes] with the end of a hard rope. The culprit was tied to a lamp post and with the first lash the blood sprung. The punishment went to 17 lashes when the poor creature fainted away, but has seven more lashes yet to receive when he is able to bear them.' Captain Moriarty, having reported the incident at Inchture at once to the Transport Board, was instructed by it on 11 August 'to cause the glass and other damage done to be repaired and the church to be cleaned, putting the prisoners on short allowance [of rations] to make good the amount.'[31]

The first prisoner to be enrolled in the General Entry Book of the new depot was Jean Chaseau, a soldier from the 2nd battalion of the 64th line or infantry regiment. Chaseau had been captured in May 1811 at Madra (or Madre) Lego. Born at Nollet, he was aged 24, and was described as 5 feet 5¼ inches tall, of medium build, with an oval face, fresh complexion, brown hair, grey eyes, and had been wounded in the left leg.[32]

Two further intakes of prisoners arrived at Perth before the end of August. Some 388 arrived on the 20th and 21st from Portsmouth aboard HMS *Regulus*, having been landed at Kirkcaldy and marched the 24 or so miles to the depot via Falkland, where they appear to have been lodged overnight in the dungeons of the Palace. A further 306 arrived on 29 August from Portsmouth on the frigate HMS *Freya* and were likewise landed at Kirkcaldy and marched via Falkland to Perth. They included four women and two young children.

A Falkland correspondent (whose name appears to have been Charles Holland) of the banker-historian J. Macbeth Forbes, writing to him from there in 1893, eighty years after the scenes he described, said the prisoners passed through Falkland 'in considerable numbers' on their way to Perth. '... they were sent across from Leith to Pettycur, Parish of Kinghorn, the then Harbour for Fife and they were walked on to Falkland en route for ... Perth. The old folks here have often told me about them and how, when word came that another batch of prisoners was on the road, they ran to the Eastern slope of the Lomond Hill, to meet and escort them to Falkland Palace. They were imprisoned in ... what was called the dungeons, which were barely light, on nothing but some filthy straw. On one occasion the prisoners refused to enter, but were driven in at the point of the bayonet. There were ... one or two officers with them, and they were lodged in the Palace Inn adjoining—now the Gardeners' Bothy. There were also some buildings between the Palace and "The Sketchpool" (Tennis or Racquet Court) and when the dungeons were full, the prisoners were lodged in these buildings and in the Racket Court, which, however, is open above. The street in those days extended right in to the Palace, and the Townspeople often looked in through the barred windows at the Prisoners, several of whom were employed in carving nic-nacs [sic] out of bones, and they plaited baskets and other articles out of straw, which they sold among the Townsfolks. ... They were only a short time here, and were moved on to Perth, to make way for another bevy.'[33]

Then on 2 September 207 prisoners arrived from Penicuik—140 from Greenlaw and 67 from Valleyfield. Those from Greenlaw were part of the removal of all 640 French prisoners from that depot who, as the Transport Board had explained to Captain Moriarty on 18 August, were being transferred 'in order that the prison at that place may be cleaned and prepared for the reception of American prisoners ... such of those prisoners as cannot conveniently be removed to Valleyfield are under orders to be forthwith sent to Perth.' War on Britain had been formally declared by the United States on 19 June. Among these prisoners from Greenlaw were several familiar figures, including the privateer Lieutenant David Fourneau, who had escaped from Esk Mills in the mass escape of 19 February the previous year, the naval ensign Valerian Feraud or Ferand and the privateer prize master Jean Baptiste Callop, both of whom had been among the mass escapers from Edinburgh Castle on 12 April 1811. The prisoners who arrived the same day from Valleyfield included the equally familiar figures of Marote-Carrier, the two De Kuypers (L.J. or L.I.. of Ghent, and Charles) and Jacques Adam.[34]

By another later in September and in 23 successive intakes between October and 14 January 1813 Perth received a further 5,691 prisoners. By the latter date a total of 6,891 had entered the depot. Of these 1,099 had come from the hulks at Plymouth, 50 from one at Chatham, 207 from the two depots at Penicuik, 227 evidently direct from Lisbon, and all the remaining 5,308 from the hulks at Portsmouth.[35]

Thus in the five months between its opening at the beginning of August 1812 and mid-January 1813 the new depot at Perth had become virtually filled to its capacity. The Transport Board wrote to the Admiralty on 11 January to ask that as 'there are as many prisoners now sent to the prison at Perth as it can at present properly accommodate ... those intended to be sent in HMS *Regulus* from Portsmouth may not be sent at present.' Three days later the press reported that on 12 January '350 French prisoners, under an escort of the Perth and Ayrshire militia, marched from Leith for Greenlaw, the depot at Perth being full.'[36] No more intakes of prisoners came to the Perth depot from England or direct from the Peninsula. So great was the inflow of prisoners of war into Britain in those years that at Perth, as at Dartmoor, too, during its building in 1805-09, every bed- or hammock-space was filled as it were even before the depot was opened.[37]

Its four General Entry Books show Perth took in an aggregate of 7,761 prisoners in 1812-14. Apart from a few recaptured escapers, who were re-entered in the routine manner in the General Entry Books with a new and later or higher number, all those between No. 6,891 and No. 7,761 came in several separate intakes between June and August 1813 to Perth from Valleyfield.

Conversely, over 1,200 prisoners ceased to be confined in Perth depot before the end of the war: a handful sent away on parole, a couple of dozen sent to Edinburgh Castle, about 80 either invalided or for other reasons repatriated, some 200 who died in captivity and were buried at the depot, around 175 sent to join the armies of Britain's allies, and over 850 transferred in July-August 1813 to Valleyfield depot. Thus the total number confined at Perth between January 1813 and the end of the war was always around 7,000.[38]

In the two years between February 1811, when Esk Mills opened as a depot, and January 1813, when Perth received its last intake from England or the Peninsula, the number of prisoners of war in close confinement depots in Scotland had thus increased from the 500 or 600 at most held at any time at Greenlaw before 1811 to around 12,000 or 13,000 held in aggregate at Perth, Valleyfield, Greenlaw, and (although from the end of 1811 only a handful and mainly for disciplinary reasons) Edinburgh Castle.

A closer look ought now to be taken at some of the experiences, characteristics, and activities of those thousands of prisoners who languished in the close confinement depots in Scotland during the Napoleonic Wars.

8

Places, Dates and Circumstances of Capture, Recaptures, and Length of Captivity

One Sunday in the later years of the Napoleonic Wars, William Chambers, then a boy of twelve or so, and his father visited Penicuik, and from the edge of the parish churchyard in the centre of the village looked down on Valleyfield depot in the natural bowl below. Chambers (1800-1883), future publisher, lord provost of Edinburgh in 1865-9, was born, and until 1813 grew up, in Peebles. It was in that year his father was forced to leave Peebles with his family and move to Edinburgh because of the failure by parole prisoners to repay their debts to his draper's business. Writing more than sixty years later, William Chambers vividly recalled what he had seen that day on his visit to Valleyfield:

'Here, on a level space in the depth of a valley, was a group of barracks, surrounded by tall palisades, for the accommodation of some hundreds of prisoners, who, night and day, were strictly watched by armed sentries, ready to fire on them in the event of outbreak.

'The day on which we happened to make our visit was a Sunday, and the scene presented was accordingly the more startling. Standing in the church-yard on the brink of the hollow, all the immediate surroundings betokened the solemnity of a Scottish Sabbath. The shops in the village were shut. From the church was heard the voice of the preacher. Looking down from the height on the hive of living beings, there was not among them a vestige of the ordinary calm of Sunday—only *Dimanche*! Dressed in coarse woollen clothing of a yellow colour, and most of them wearing red or blue cloth caps, or partly-coloured cowls, the prisoners were engaged in a variety of amuse-ments and occupations. Prominently, and forming the centre of attraction, were a considerable number ranked up in two rows, joyously dancing to the sound of a fiddle, which was briskly played by a man who stood on the top of a barrel. Others were superintending cookery in big pots over open fires, which they fanned by the flapping of cocked-hats. Others were fencing with sticks amidst a circle of eager onlookers. A few were seated meditatively on benches, perhaps thinking of far-distant homes, or the fortune of war, which had brought them into this painful predicament. In twos or threes, some were walking apart to and fro, and I conjectured they were of a slightly superior class. Near one corner was a booth—a rickety concern of boards—seemingly a kind of restaurant, with the pretentious inscription *CAFE DE PARIS* over the door, and a small tricolor flag was fluttering from a slender pole on the roof. To complete the picture, fancy several of the prisoners, no doubt the more ingenious among them, stationed at small wickets opening with hinges in the tall palisades, offering for sale articles, such as snuff-boxes of bone, that they had been allowed to manufacture, and the money got by which sales procured them a few luxuries.

'Altogether, the spectacle to me, as a boy, was very extraordinary, and has left an indelible impression on my memory. What has since struck me as the drollest thing about the scene was that the multitudinous diversions and occupations should have been going on at full blast in the hollow of a pretty Scottish dell on a Sunday forenoon, almost within the sound of psalm-singing in the parish kirk.'[1]

The scene at Valleyfield was no doubt similar to those that other spectators might have observed in those years at any of the other close confinement depots in Scotland. Chambers's account raises many questions. What, for instance, had been the experiences of the prisoners before their capture? Where had they been captured? How long had they been in captivity? Were they able to keep in touch with their families at home? What were the relations, friendships, quarrels, among them? How good or bad was their food at the depots? How well or badly were they clothed? Were they put to obligatory labour? What medical and hospital provision was available to them? How were they treated by their guards? Did they have any contact with local inhabitants? How frequent were escapes and were there organised escape committees among the prisoners? What contacts, if any, did they have with prisoners of war at other depots in Scotland or England? How did they pass the wearisome years of captivity? An attempt will be made in the chapters that follow to offer answers to these and many other questions about the prisoners.

The information that survives about the prisoners in Scotland as individuals is contained mainly in the General Entry Books of the depots where they were confined. Although every prisoner was listed in those Books the bare information there given about them was, of course, compiled for administrative purposes, not to provide answers to questions that interested readers might want to ask two centuries later. But some further information about individual prisoners is sometimes available in other official archives or in the contemporary press, or in memoirs, correspondence, or other sources—particularly about those prisoners, including escapers, who got into trouble of one sort or another with the authorities, or who applied for permission to do this or that, or otherwise left some footprint, however faint, in the sands of time. Unfortunately, though unsurprisingly, in an age of illiteracy among so many ordinary people, very few of the prisoners of war in Scotland ever wrote about their captivity: Sergeant Major Philippe Beaudoin and Captain Paul Andreas Kaald, both at Greenlaw, and, through his later recorded oral recollections, Lieutenant Henri-Ferdinand Marote, alias Jean Baptiste Carrier, at Esk Mills, Valleyfield and Perth, were important exceptions. Without their diaries or recollections it would be even more difficult to develop a fuller understanding of what it was like to be a captive in Scotland during the Napoleonic Wars.

The places of capture of the French and other prisoners in Scotland illustrate the almost worldwide character of those wars, above all in the struggle between Britain and France. Although depot General Entry Books had a column for entering the place of capture of each prisoner, it was sometimes left blank (especially at Esk Mills) or the entry was vague: 'At sea', 'Off Africa', etc. Sometimes also places of capture, such as 'West Indies' or 'St Domingo', given in the Entry Books leave it uncertain whether capture took place on land, in harbour, off the coast, or miles out at sea. Occasionally, too, the place of capture given in one official source was contradicted by that given in another. Despite these difficulties some picture, though not a wholly comprehensive or accurate one, can be formed of the wide range of places of capture of the prisoners of war held in Scotland.

Many were captured at sea or arrested on ships in port as their native countries were drawn into the war against Britain. Of such prisoners Greenlaw, among the depots in Scotland, held a particularly high proportion. Without exception all 1,000 prisoners listed in the two Greenlaw General Entry Books for Danes were seamen taken at sea or, in a handful of cases, in port. Those two Greenlaw Entry Books cover the period between November 1807, shortly after the outbreak of war between Denmark and Britain, and May 1811. Of the 1,000 prisoners listed in them, the vast majority were captured, as might be expected, in the North Sea or around its shores. Thus 470 were made prisoner 'off Norway', a further 36 'off Drontheim' [Trondheim], 260 or more in 'North Sea', over 160 'off Jutland', 67 'off Scotland', 27 'off Aberdeen'. In the Skagerrak three were taken 'off Christiansand', and in the Kattegat over 50 'off Gottenburg'. A handful among the 1,000 were taken prisoner in further-flung places: four, for instance, on a merchant vessel within the Arctic Circle, at or off the North Cape in Norway; two others 'off Iceland', and 2,500 miles south of there three on a merchant vessel 'off Madeira'. Of those few arrested in port, ten were marched off to Greenlaw in August 1807 from the merchant vessel *Magnus* at Stranraer; three sent from Stornoway from the merchant ship *Five Broders* (including a merchant named A.C. Knudsen, who was transferred immediately on parole to Peebles) arrived at Greenlaw in October that year. Four others of those 1,000 Danes at Greenlaw were taken prisoner at places unstated in the Entry Books. A particularly interesting tale might have been that of two captive seamen said to have been 'Pressed' from two separate merchant ships at Limerick, one on Christmas Day 1807, the other on New Year's Day 1808. When the press gang discovered they were enemy aliens it appears to have passed them on promptly to Greenlaw, where they arrived respectively on 10 January and 4 February.[2]

The North Sea was also the place of capture of all but one of the 97 Dutch prisoners of war held in 1803-4 at Greenlaw or earlier in the Edinburgh Bridewell. The single exception was Captain Sjourd Tetmans of the merchant vessel *Nortstaar*, captured in December 1803 in Aberlady Bay in the Firth of Forth.[3] An Orkney shore of the North Sea was where a further 150 or so Dutch prisoners at Greenlaw during March and April 1807 had been captured: they were the crew of the frigate *Utrecht*, shipwrecked there on 26 February.[4]

The Atlantic and the West Indies, on the other hand, were where all 48 Spanish seamen listed in the Spanish General Entry Book for Greenlaw had been captured. A dozen of them were taken prisoner off Newfoundland, the remainder elsewhere in the Atlantic or in the West Indies, where almost all 48 of them had already been confined on prison ships at Jamaica before they arrived at Greenlaw between July 1805 and March the following year.[5] The further 68 Spanish prisoners at Greenlaw listed in the hybrid General Entry Book ADM 103/115 were captured in or off the West Indies (26), Newfoundland (37), 'Spanish coast' (one), St Helena (one), and 'Uncertain' (three).

A much greater variety of places of capture at sea is, hardly surprisingly, shown for those far more numerous Greenlaw prisoners listed for the years 1803-12 in the three 'French' General Entry Books for the depot. The Book for 1803-4 to 1809 lists 444 prisoners of whom all were seamen except 14 soldiers and a similar number of passengers.[6] The largest single group were captured 'off Scotland'. They were the 64 members of the crew of the privateer *Passe Partout*, made prisoner in May 1808. Places of capture of others among the 444 included: 'North Sea' (45), 'On coast of Scotland' (six), 'Off Coast of Forth' (five), 'Off Norway' (two), 'West Indies' (50), 'St Domingo' (i.e., Haiti) (28), 'Off St Domingo' (14), 'From prison ship in Jamaica' (20), 'From Jamaica' (13), 'Off Jamaica' (two), 'Cuba' (15), and from 'Havannah' (seven). These last seven included the diarist Sergeant Major Philippe Beaudoin and five other soldiers, captured off that port in April 1804 on board the transport ship *Mary Ann*. From the seas around, or from other harbours in, the West Indies and Central America, including Puerto Rico, St Thomas, Bermuda, Barbados, Dominique, Surinam, Guadeloupe, and Demerara, came in ones or twos at least a further score of prisoners. The remainder of the 444 came to Greenlaw mainly in groups of less than ten from a wide range of other places of capture, including 'In Ireland', Halifax (Nova Scotia), Cartagena (whether in Spain or Colombia is unstated), 'Off Toley Bridge',

'Coast of Spain', 'Off Brest', and the Azores. Two seamen, among the earliest prisoners in the war, had been 'Captured on a fishing boat' at St Pierre (Newfoundland?) in July 1803. There were still other places which were distinctive. Two seamen, one of them No. 156 Jean Gillevere, whose alias or *nom de guerre* was Pierre A. Coulon, were 'Taken on Board the American ship *George* of New York in South Shields, 5 November 1804, and sent from thence to Newcastle and from Newcastle to Leith.' Two other seamen had been 'Released from Prison at Quebec for Navigating the *Mary* Merchant Brig from thence to Hull and from Hull to Leith in the Edinburgh Packet *Captain Dunbar*,' en route to Greenlaw. Another five seamen appear to have had a particularly eventful time before arriving at the depot in spring 1805, having been 'Taken by a British merchant vessel off Leith in another British vessel, name unknown, retaken from *L'Alerte* privateer off Dunkirk.' Hardly less interesting a tale could perhaps have been told by a merchant seaman 'captured at Glasgow, 6 April 1808, by presser.' Into its nets the press gang appears thus occasionally to have swept up enemy aliens in British ports.

After excluding, to avoid duplication, those of the 904 French prisoners at Greenlaw in 1811-12 listed in the 'French' General Entry Book ADM 103/157 who had been captured at sea but who came to that depot from Edinburgh Castle or Valleyfield, 199 remain. No less than 161 of those 199 had been captured at the battle of Trafalgar in October 1805. All but six of the remainder had been taken at the Cape of Good Hope (12), the French naval base at Rochefort (11), or on ships in the West Indies (5), the English Channel (1), or 'At sea' (3).

Those remaining six prisoners were captured only fifteen miles from Greenlaw. When the very small Grangemouth merchant sloop *Fame*, sailing from London to Arbroath with a cargo of hemp and flax, was seized off South Shields at one o'clock in the morning on 25 October 1811 by the French privateer *Grandfury*, the *Fame*'s master Thomas Johnstone, one of his crew of three, and a passenger were taken off her by the privateers. They put their own prizemaster and five Dutch seamen aboard *Fame* to sail her to France. An old man and a boy of 13, who were the remaining members of the *Fame*'s own crew and were unlikely to prove a threat to the security of the privateers, were left aboard to help sail her. Thereafter they were destined, it seemed, like their two shipmates and the passenger, to become prisoners of war in France. A gale, however, began to blow from the south-east. The *Fame*, with the prize crew, the old man and the boy aboard, was driven back northward and eventually, as the gale shifted to the north-east, into the mouth of the Firth of Forth. Neither the prize crew nor the old man were familiar with the navigational hazards of the Firth. In the blackness of the night, without candles to see by, the compass could not be read. The ship was at the mercy of the gale. The boy, however, recognising a light on Inchkeith island, took the helm of the *Fame* and steered her safely up the Firth of Forth. At St Margaret's Hope, west of North Queensferry, the boy hailed a ship, the *Rebecca*, lying close by at anchor, and announced 'he had six French prisoners on board, demanding assistance to get them secured.' As soon as a boat sent from *Rebecca* came alongside *Fame* the boy seized the privateersmen's pistols, 'as his right by conquest', and refused to give them up to the *Rebecca*'s boatmen. 'The prisoners acknowledged the skill of the boy in navigating the vessel, to which their own safety and that of the ship and cargo was altogether owing.' The privateersmen—Jan Peters, prizemaster, from Hamburg, himself in that era quite elderly at the age of 66, and the five Dutch seamen, all belonging to Amsterdam and aged respectively 20, 22, 26, 30 and 45—were held in the custody of the militiamen on Inchgarvie island in the Forth until they were sent as prisoners to Greenlaw on 6 November. Of the 13-year old boy, the *Caledonian Mercury* declared: 'The determined spirit and gallantry of this boy ... claims universal admiration, and such an early promise of prominence in the line of his profession deserves every mark of favour and encouragement. A statement of the whole affair has, we understand, been accordingly sent to the Admiralty and to the Committee of the Patriotic Fund at Lloyd's, for the purpose of procuring to the boy some token of public approbation.'[7]

Finally, in a separate section of this Greenlaw 'French' General Entry Book there are listed 48 American merchant seamen who, soon after the declaration of the War of 1812 by the United States on Britain on 18 June that year, found themselves arrested on their vessels by the Royal Navy and sent as prisoners of war to Greenlaw. They came there from Leith (9), the Faroe Islands (24), the Little Belt (Lillebaelt, in the Baltic, between the Danish provinces of Sonderjylland and Fyn) (14), and 'Off Teneriffe' (1).

At Esk Mills the places and dates of capture of only the first 1,591 of the aggregate of 2,817 prisoners held during the five weeks of its existence as a depot in February and March 1811 were recorded in its General Entry Book. Of those 2,817 exactly 194 had come from Greenlaw, so places of capture of some of these latter have already been outlined above. Upon its sudden closure some 2,250 of the Esk Mills prisoners, as already seen, were or appear to have been transferred on 11 March 1811 to Valleyfield (and a further 100 or so by the end of April). Of the other prisoners at Esk Mills 11 were sent to Edinburgh Castle between 4 and 9 March and 450 on 11 March. Keeping track of all these prisoners, some of whom were moved from one depot to another in Scotland between 1811 and 1814 or in other cases were discharged for a variety of reasons to a variety of other places, would be a formidable task, as would identifying, and avoiding duplication in listing, their respective places of capture.[8] What is attempted here therefore for Esk Mills (based on the information in the first three Valleyfield General Entry Books and in the Edinburgh Castle Entry Book where respectively the transferred former Esk Mills prisoners are listed), as well as for Edinburgh Castle, Valleyfield and Perth (the last two of which interchanged several hundred prisoners in 1812-13) is the sketching of as clear, although inevitably not comprehensive and detailed, a picture as the sources permit of where their inmates had been captured.

Analysing the places of capture of those at Esk Mills who had been made prisoner at sea or on board vessels in port, is helped by the comprehensive listing by the depot Entry Book, despite its other shortcomings, of the ranks of the inmates. Their ranks show that of the aggregate of 2,817 held in the depot during February-March 1811 about 1,535, or 54.5 per cent, were sea-going (mainly seamen in rank, but including some officers, warrant and petty officers, et. al.) and not soldiers. Ten passengers captured on board ships are included in the 1,535. Of those of the 2,486 prisoners sent from Esk Mills to Valleyfield in March and April 1811, as shown in the first three General Entry Books of the latter and who were or appear to have been captured at sea, the largest single group, totalling 450, were made captive in places that the Entry Books leave either unstated or as vague as 'Off Africa', 'Off the passage'.[9]

The next largest group of 367 had been captured in the English Channel. They included 18 captured 'Off Dover', 10 'Cape Lizard' (Lizard Point, Cornwall), three 'Isle of Wight', and one 'Off Barfleur'.

Some 194 others had been taken prisoner in the North Sea, including eight in 'Yarmouth Roads', six 'Doggerbank', and three 'Off Norway'.

A further 204 were captured in the Atlantic. They included 124 taken at the battle of Trafalgar or in its immediate aftermath in the Franco-British naval encounter off Cape Ortegal on 4 November 1805, 33 'Off Ireland' or 'Coast of Ireland', 25 the Bay of Biscay (13 'Off Rochefort', 12 'Off Brest'), 8 'Azores' or 'Off Azores', 3 'Cadiz' or 'Off Cadiz', 2 'Off Ferroles' (Ferrol), and half a dozen individuals captured respectively 'Off Maderia', 'Off Cape Clear' (south-west Ireland), 'Off Charleston' (South Carolina), 'Off Cape Finisterre', 'Off Malian' (Malin Head?), and 'Off St Peters' (presumably Newfoundland).[10]

The next largest group of 141 had been captured in the Mediterranean, including 63 'Isle of Corfu', or 'Off Corfu', 13 'Gulf of Otranto', 7 'Gulph of Venice', 4 'Port Mahon' (Minorca), 3 'Levant', 3 'Isle of Sefaleoni' (Cephalonia), and 1 each 'Cypress', 'Off Marseilles', 'Corsica', 'Off Malta', and 'Coast of Barbary' (Morocco, Algeria, Tunisia). The remaining 43 were recorded simply as made captive in 'Mediterranean'.

From the West Indies and the Caribbean 131 prisoners had come first to Esk Mills then to Valleyfield: 34 from 'St Domingo' (Haiti), 'Off St Domingo',

'Capitulation of St Domingo', 'Cap François' and 'Port au Prince', 22 from 'Saintes' or 'Off Saintes', 11 'Martinique' or 'Capitulation of Martinique', seven from the frigate *La Félicité* captured in June 1809 off Guadeloupe, 6 'Off Barbadoes', 5 'Off Cuba', 3 'Ile du Vent' (Windward Islands), 2 each from 'Porto Rico', 'Off Cayenne', and 'Off Antigua', 1 each from 'Off Bermuda', 'Marie Galante', 'Off St Thomas', and 'Coast of New Spain' (Mexico), and the remaining 33 simply from 'West Indies'.

Some 42 others had been captured either in 'East Indies' (36) and the Indian Ocean (2—of whom 1 was taken 'Off Bourbon' (Réunion), and the other 'Off Ile de France' (Mauritius), or 'Cape of Good Hope' (4).

Of two remaining prisoners taken at sea or in port, one was Antoine Muchet, a seaman, 'Pressed out of an English Privateer', who had been made captive in August 1804, apparently another unexpected catch in the nets of the press-gang. The other was made prisoner within ten miles of the Penicuik depots. He was Martin Lewis, a seaman, captured 'on an American ship' at Leith in February 1811.[11]

None at all, perhaps surprisingly, among those 1,535 appears to have been taken prisoner in the Baltic, Skagerrak or Kattegat, and none either in the Pacific, Persian Gulf or Red Sea.

Of the 461 prisoners transferred in March 1811 from Esk Mills to Edinburgh Castle 342 (74.2 per cent) were sea-going.[12] Accuracy is more difficult to achieve in presenting the places of capture of those evidently made prisoner at sea, but many seas were involved. Perhaps surprisingly only one appears to have been taken prisoner in the North Sea (at Doggerbank). Two were said to have been captured in the East Indies; 8 in the Mediterranean; 23 in the Caribbean or West Indies ('Off Cuba', 'Off Barbadoes', and elsewhere); 54 in the Atlantic (13, for instance, at Trafalgar, nine 'Bay of Biscay', 11 'Rochefort' or 'Off Rochefort', 5 'Cape of Good Hope', etc.); 88 in the English Channel (9 'Off Cherbourg', 2 'Off Dover', etc., but no fewer than 72 simply 'Channel'). For no fewer than 160, place of capture was simply given as 'At Sea', and for a further 28 no place of capture at all was stated.

Among the almost 5,000 other prisoners at Valleyfield who arrived there during the three years after the intakes from Esk Mills of March-April 1811, some 843 (or almost 17 per cent) were, or appear to have been, taken at sea or in port. The largest single group of them (251) were captured in the Atlantic. No fewer than 169 of these, of whom 152 were soldiers, had been taken prisoner at the battle of Trafalgar or in the naval encounter a fortnight later off Cape Ortegal.[13] Another 31 of those captured in the Atlantic had been taken 'Coast of Ireland' or 'Off Ireland'—and all but two of these also were soldiers, in their case from the 66th or Basque infantry regiment, captured in

November 1809. From 'Cadiz', 'Bay of Cadiz' or 'Cadiz Roads' came a further 19 prisoners, from 'Off Brest' 15 more, 5 each 'Off Lorient' and 'Azores' or 'Off Azores', and 1 each from 'Off Cape Finisterre', 'Off Quiberon', 'Off Ushant', 'Off Madeira', 'Belleisle', and 'Scilly Islands'. The remaining 4 taken prisoner in the Atlantic had been 'Off Lisbon, in a Boat'.

Almost as many (245) had either no, or only a vaguely stated, place of capture (e.g., 'Coast of France', 'Coast of Spain', or 'At Sea') entered in the Valleyfield General Entry Books. One prisoner was said to have been captured 'Off Constanton': if this was intended to be Constanta then he appears to have been the only prisoner at Valleyfield taken in the Black Sea.[14]

From the Mediterranean came a further 107 of these Valleyfield prisoners: 45 taken 'Off Corfu', three each 'Reggio Channel' (Straits of Messina), 'Off Toulon' and 'Port Mahon' (Minorca), one 'Off Naples', and the remaining 52 simply 'Mediterranean'.

Of 95 captured in the North Sea, 89 were the crews of three privateers, *Petit Edouard*, *Le Figaro* and *Ravisseur*, taken 'Off Coast of Norway'. Two others were taken prisoner at 'Doggerbank' and the remainder simply 'North Sea'.

Almost equal numbers were made prisoner in 'English Channel' (43) and the Bay of Biscay (48). In the latter, 31 were taken 'Rochefort' or 'Off Rochefort', 5 'Near Bordeaux' or 'Off Bordeaux', 1 each 'Off La Rochelle' and 'Bilboa', and the remaining 10 simply 'Bay of Biscay'.

From the West Indies and Caribbean some 28 of these prisoners arrived at Valleyfield: nine 'St Domingo', 'St Domingo Bay' or 'Off Cap Francois', four 'Off Bermuda', two 'Off Antigua' and two more 'Martinique' and 'Off Martinique', and one each from 'Porto Rico', 'Off Jamaica', 'Off Curacoa', 'Off Cuba' and 'Off Guadeloupe'. The other six prisoners were entered as 'West Indies'.[15]

Of the remaining 25 prisoners from the total of 843 captured at sea or in port, 11 were taken 'Cape of Good Hope', 10 'East Indies', 2 'Gulph of Persia', 1 'Off Madras', and 1, a seaman on the *Pilotin* privateer, in the Baltic.[16]

The only notable ocean or sea from which prisoners appear not to have come to Valleyfield was the Pacific. There is a striking contrast between the larger number of prisoners captured at sea or in port among the 2,486 who came in March and April 1811 from Esk Mills to Valleyfield and those so captured among the 5,000 or so who entered the depot between then and the end of the war in 1814. That fact reflected the growth in the number of prisoners taken on land, particularly in Spain and Portugal, as the war continued.

❖

At Edinburgh Castle the principal Entry Book covered the months from March 1811 (when, as has been seen above, 461 prisoners arrived from Esk Mills) to December that year, when the Castle, from which frequent escapes had demonstrated its lack of security, ceased to be used by the Transport Board except as an occasional staging post for prisoners in transit or as a place of punishment for *mauvais sujets*. After the large intake from Esk Mills only 83 more prisoners arrived at the Castle between April and December 1811. As almost half of those 83 had come from Greenlaw or Valleyfield, or were recaptured escapers from the Castle itself, their places of capture have already been indicated above (or will be below, in the case of those captured on land). The other half, 44 members of the crew of the privateer *Le Figaro*, who arrived at the Castle in mid-July a few days after the capture of their ship by HMS *Plover*, which landed them at Leith, had all been captured in the North Sea. So the latter sea alone needs adding to the picture already drawn of the places of capture at sea for the aggregate of the 544 prisoners held at the Castle as a depot in 1811.[17]

At Perth depot, in contrast to Greenlaw, Esk Mills, Valleyfield and Edinburgh Castle, relatively few of the prisoners had been, or appear to have been, taken at sea. Of the aggregate of 7,761 prisoners listed in the four Perth General Entry Books, only about 300 seem to have been captured at sea. Of those 300 some 117, or 39 per cent, were prisoners transferred to the new depot on 2 September 1812 from Greenlaw and Valleyfield and whose places of capture have therefore already been indicated above.

Of the other 180 or so prisoners at Perth captured at sea but who did not arrive at the depot from Greenlaw or Valleyfield (or via them from Esk Mills), the largest single group (74) were taken in places unspecified—71 of them simply 'At Sea'. A further 35 were 'English Channel', 26 'Mediterranean' (and in addition three 'Off Corfu' and one 'Gulf of Venice'), 12 in 'North Sea' (plus one 'Zealand'), and the others in single figures in 'Atlantic' (including five 'Off Brest'), a dozen from the West Indies, including one 'Surinam', and one from 'East Indies'. Of those taken simply 'At sea' 54 were soldiers captured by HMS *Active* in February 1808. Sixteen other prisoners at Perth had been captured on the French warships *Formidable*, *Duguay-Trouin*, and *Scipion* on 4 November 1805 in the aftermath of the battle of Trafalgar. One prisoner, Fiacre Massé, First Lieutenant of the privateer *Incomparable*, had been captured in June 1812 when 'Driven ashore in a boat' from his ship. Massé, born at Lyons and aged 24, arrived at Perth from Plymouth on 6 August that year.[18]

In summary, therefore, it may be said that of the aggregate of some 12,000 or 13,000 prisoners of war held captive in the close confinement depots in Scotland between 1803 and 1814, a substantial minority of between 4,500 and 5,000 had been, or appear to have been, captured at sea. Most of them were in rank seamen (as distinct from officers, warrant or petty officers) from the warships of France and some of its allied or subject states or from their privateering or merchant vessels. The others were soldiers captured on board French warships or transport ships or even, in a few cases, on privateer ships. There were also among the prisoners in the Scots depots a very small number of civilian passengers who had been captured at sea.

Captives were taken at sea especially in the earlier years of the Napoleonic Wars. Hence Greenlaw, the first and for many years the only close confinement depot in Scotland, had a particularly large ratio of seamen among its inmates—more or less exclusively so in the case of its Danish (or Scandinavian), Dutch, Spanish, Prussian and American prisoners. Half of the prisoners at Esk Mills during the few weeks it was a depot were seamen. At Valleyfield (including those who came there in March-April 1811 from Esk Mills) seamen formed almost a third of all its aggregate of 7,500 prisoners. At Edinburgh Castle, of the 544 prisoners listed in the main Entry Book in 1811, no fewer than 420 or 77 per cent were seamen. At Perth, on the other hand, seamen and soldiers captured at sea were in a small minority—only about 300 out of the aggregate of some 7,700 prisoners. The prisoners in the depots in Scotland who had been captured at sea were, or appear to have been, taken in one or other of most of the oceans or seas of the world, with the major exception of the Pacific.

Accounts of naval battles or other actions at sea, including the capture of privateers and merchant ships, sometimes contain graphic descriptions of the circumstances in which prisoners were taken there. The murderous carnage of war, similar experiences of which must have haunted many survivors among the prisoners of war in Scotland, is illustrated in an account, for example, of the firing from the port bow of Nelson's flagship HMS *Victory* near the beginning of the battle of Trafalgar of a 68-pounder carronade (a short cannon with a large bore, first manufactured at the Carron ironworks at Falkirk), 'containing its customary charge of one round shot and a keg filled with 500 musket-balls ... right into the cabin windows of the *Bucentaure*' (the flagship of the French fleet). And 'As the *Victory* slowly moved ahead, every gun of the remaining 50 upon her broadside, all double, and some of them treble shotted, was deliberately discharged in the same raking manner ... While listening, with characteristic avidity, to the deafening crash made by their shot in the French ship's hull, the British crew were nearly suffocated with the clouds of black smoke that entered the *Victory*'s port-holes ...' These murderous discharges alone killed or wounded nearly 400 of the *Bucentaure*'s crew, dismounted 20 of its cannons, and reduced the ship 'to a comparatively defenceless state.' Severe losses were also suffered at Trafalgar by the French man-of-war *Redoutable*, some of the surviving members of whose crew (unlike, it appears, those of the *Bucentaure*) passed eventually into captivity in Scotland: out of a crew of 643 the *Redoutable* lost 300 killed and 222 wounded, including almost all her officers. Her fellow man-of-war *Achille*, a few members of whose crew also became prisoners in Scotland, had already suffered heavy losses in the fighting at Trafalgar when she caught fire and blew up at the end of the battle, 'and with her perished her then commanding officer ... and a great portion of her crew.'[19]

The personal experiences, however, of prisoners in the Scots depots at the time of their capture at sea are not known to have been recorded except in the diaries or later recollections of Sergeant Major Beaudoin and Captain Paul Andreas Kaald, both at Greenlaw, and Henri-Ferdinand Marote, alias Jean Baptiste Carrier, who was successively at Esk Mills, Valleyfield and Perth. Beaudoin succinctly describes in his diary his capture by a British naval vessel off Havana, Cuba, in April 1804 when he and other veterans who had escaped from the defeat of French forces on St Domingo (Haiti) were sailing homeward to France on board a French ship. He and his fellow captives were sent on board the British corvette *Scotland*, 'accompanied by heavy blows from the flat of sabres' and were denied 'for twenty-four hours anything to drink or eat'. Later he and five other prisoners were sent aboard the *Gassie*, a merchant vessel, which took them first to Belfast then to Greenock, which Beaudoin reached on 30 May.[20]

Marote-Carrier, first lieutenant of the privateer *L'Aventurier*, gives a more detailed account of his capture than Sergeant Major Beaudoin does of his. In mid-November 1810 *L'Aventurier* had set sail from her base at Calais on a privateering cruise into the English Channel, under the command of her second captain Orey, the captain himself having had to go ashore with 'a serious illness'. The crew were overjoyed at setting sail 'for hardly ever had we been at sea without taking an important ship as prize. We normally cruised for 10 or 12 days before returning to port,' recalled Marote-Carrier long afterwards, 'except when we captured some merchant ship. In that case we came back to Calais. Two-thirds of the value of the cargo and of the prize ship were distributed according to rank to each of our men, to whom some days' shore leave was granted so they could see their families again and rest from their labour. Most of them were from the French coast. We also had several Flemings and Dutchmen on board who had settled their family at Calais, Dieppe or another Channel port. I was one of that number. Since we had begun cruising my wife and her parents had come to live at Calais [from Ostend, to which Marote-Carrier belonged], where the share I as lieutenant received from the prizes we took enabled them to live comfortably.'[21]

The crew of *L'Aventurier*, Marote-Carrier recalled, numbered about 125 men, including the second captain, eleven other officers, and 'a sizeable number of old soldiers who, wearying after their discharge [from the army], had signed on board as volunteers. Almost all of them, grognards [veterans, literally 'grumblers'] with grey moustaches and slashed with scars, had been through most of the wars of the Republic and the Empire. All their lives had been passed in marching and counter-marching, amidst clouds of gunpowder, hails of bullets, and the clamour of combat. They were bored with the enforced idleness to which they were condemned by a war that had ceased to be general.' Orey, the second captain, then in his forties, had sailed on *L'Aventurier* since he was fifteen years old.

L'Aventurier was, however, out of luck. She was found and pursued in the Channel by a British frigate, HMS *Royalist*. In an attempt to escape capture by lightening his ship second captain Orey ordered that nine of the *L'Aventurier*'s 20 cannons be thrown overboard. 'So also were barrels of wine, barrels of biscuit, food, and various other expendable objects.' But after considerable exchanges of cannon and musket shots British sailors from HMS *Royalist* boarded *L'Aventurier* and the privateer was forced to surrender. 'I went down to the wardroom,' recalled Marote-Carrier, 'and as I was not fully dressed, my first care was to pull out my trunk and open it. I was afraid of looting and wanted to save at least some of my stuff. Almost all the officers were there with me. We barricaded the door as a frightful din resounded above us. Then I hurriedly put on on top of my clothes a brown topcoat with three collars that was almost new. I seized a pair of very strong boots but hardly had I put one on when I heard the door of the wardroom shudder as it was assailed. I took some money I had and slid it into my boot. When I turned round the door was broken in and the English hurled themselves on us. Two of them put their pistols to my forehead and threatened me with their boarding axes. My companions were in the same position. We surrendered of necessity a second time. The second captain had been attacked in his cabin and made prisoner like us.[22]

'The English lost no time in transferring us on to the frigate. We were pushed roughly along, helter skelter, struck by musket butts and even sabres, on to the bridge [of *L'Aventurier*] from which we were thrown—that's the correct word—into a longboat that the frigate had lowered on to the sea. A rope had been tied to this longboat, and when it was full the men of the frigate pulled it towards it. Then we had to climb up the vessel by the hatchways. The crew [of the *Royalist*] numbered about 600 men. Once we were aboard the English ship we could see the ravages caused by our cannons and sharpshooters. The sails and masts and spars were in a really bad state. The bridge, covered in debris, was stained with blood. We saw 19 bodies thrown into the sea, while a chorus of wailing and cries of grief told us of the large number of wounded. There were in fact 37, as we learned afterwards. We had nine dead and 13 wounded.

'When our transfer on board the frigate was completed, a midshipman of the *Royalist* crossed on to our poor lugger [*L'Aventurier*] to count the number of guns it had. That was soon done. "Twelve pieces!" he cried. "Poor people!" said the captain of the *Royalist* as he turned towards Orey, me and some officers who stood around him, "You can't be parole prisoners."'[23]

Marote-Carrier then recounted how the officers of *L'Aventurier* were all interrogated by the captain of HMS *Royalist*, had their names taken and asked whether they had taken any steps toward scuttling their ship. Their statements were confirmed once its British captors had examined *L'Aventurier*, and a prize crew of 100 British sailors was put aboard her to sail her to Portsmouth, while HMS *Royalist* with its prisoners of war headed up the Channel, first toward Dover and then to the hulks at Chatham. 'The English habit,' Marote-Carrier recalled, 'is not to make use of a privateer vessel that falls into their hands, but beach it, remove its guns, provisions, etc., then saw up the hull and sell it as firewood. That was no doubt the fate of our poor *L'Aventurier*...'

As HMS *Royalist* headed toward Dover Marote-Carrier discovered that in his haste to get dressed on board *L'Aventurier* he was wearing one light boot and one big sea-boot.[24]

It was, however, on land, not at sea, that most prisoners of war in close confinement depots in Scotland between 1803 and 1814 had been captured.

The exception was at Greenlaw. There the aggregate of 3,000 or so prisoners held during those years consisted, as already observed, predominantly of seamen captured on one or other of the seas of the world or while in port. Those captured on board ships did include numbers of soldiers, of whom Sergeant Major Beaudoin was one. But in the seven surviving General Entry Books kept separately at Greenlaw for 'Danes', Dutch, French, and Spanish prisoners it appears that from that aggregate of 3,000 only about 570 were soldiers captured on land.

Except for 36 (of whom 20 were captured in 1809 at Flushing in Holland during the major British landing then on Walcheren island intended to open a second front against Napoleon in western Europe while the Austrian Empire re-entered the war against him further east, nine others in the West Indies on Martinique and St Domingo, and seven in Calabria in Italy in 1806), all those 570 at Greenlaw were captured in Spain or Portugal between 1808 and 1812.

Many of the 570 were taken prisoner at major battles such as Salamanca (37) in July 1812, at the capture of Badajoz (23) in April that year, or of Oporto (34) and Vigo (64) in 1809. At least 135 became captives while serving with General Dupont's ill-fated army in Spain in the summer of 1808. A further

144 were or appear to have been taken prisoner from the army of Marshal Masséna in Spain and Portugal in 1810-11.[25]

For Esk Mills the places of capture of those made prisoner on land are to be found in the first three Entry Books of Valleyfield depot and in the main Entry Book for Edinburgh Castle, to which in March 1811 2,486 (88 per cent) and 461 respectively of the Esk Mills prisoners were transferred. Of the 2,486 transferred to Valleyfield, almost 1,000 were or appear to have been captured on land. The largest single group was captured in the West Indies (352: 295 on Martinique, 54 on St Domingo, and three on Guadeloupe). Spain and Portgual were the places of capture of a further 256 (151 in Spain, 105 in Portugal), Flushing and Zealand of 219 (209 at Flushing, 10 Zealand), and Italy or islands in the Ionian Sea of a further 51 (34 on Corfu, 15 on Zante, two in Calabria). No place of capture was recorded for another 26.[26] Of the 461 prisoners marched from Esk Mills to Edinburgh Castle, approximately 25 per cent had been captured on land. The largest number of them appear to have been taken prisoner in Spain or Portugal (50: 34, for example, 'Portugal', five, including three chief apothecaries, at Coimbra, three others at Vigo, etc.). A further 27 had been captured at Walcheren or Flushing, and smaller numbers at a variety of places, including Sicily, Calabria, Corfu and the West Indies.[27]

At Edinburgh Castle the prisoners listed in the main Entry Book for the months between March and December 1811, when the Castle was functioning as a depot like the others in Scotland, consisted of the 461 from Esk Mills and a further 83 who arrived by the end of the year. Of those 83 half, as has already been seen, were seamen captured in the North Sea in July 1811. The remaining 39 were all either transferred to the Castle from Greenlaw or Valleyfield, or were recaptured escapers from the Castle itself. So their places of capture have already been indicated.[28]

At Valleyfield, of the almost 5,000 other prisoners who entered the depot in the three years after those from Esk Mills and of whom almost 4,000 had been captured on land, the largest single group—about 1,800—had been captured in Spain or Portugal. Of these about 30 had been captured at Baylen, at least 176 at Vigo, around 600 at the fall of Badajoz in April 1812, 283 others at Le Quito, at least 115 at Salamanca, and hundreds of others at innumerable other places in the peninsula.

At least 1,400 others had been taken prisoner in the West Indies—about 1,250 of them at the capitulation of Martinique. A further 370 or so had been captured at Flushing or elsewhere on Walcheren, 55 in Calabria or Sicily, eight in Dalmatia, and over 100 in places unspecified.[29]

If the presence at Valleyfield of a much higher proportion (compared with Greenlaw or even Esk Mills) of prisoners captured on land was a result of the opening of new campaigns by the British army from 1808 onward, particularly in the West Indies, on Walcheren, and above all in Spain and Portugal, that result was even more obvious at Perth depot. There, as already observed, out of all the 7,700 or so prisoners only about 300 had not been captured on land.

It was in Spain and Portugal that a huge majority of the prisoners at Perth had been taken. Many hundreds of them were indeed described simply in the depot's four General Entry Books as having been captured 'In Spain' or 'In Portugal'. Many hundreds of others had their places of capture specified as one or other of a lengthy list of towns, villages, sieges, and battles in the Peninsular War. About 4,450 of them out of the aggregate total of 7,700 had been captured at respectively Albuera (84), Badajoz (1,556), Baylen (46), Busaco (10), Ciudad Rodrigo (400), Coimbra (480), Madrid (677), Rio Del Molino (282), and Salamanca (914)—all places that among many others symbolised the protracted and bloody struggles of that war.[30]

Much smaller numbers of the prisoners at Perth had been captured at Flushing or elsewhere on Walcheren island (466), in the West Indies (393—all but a score of them on Martinique), Calabria (59), Corfu (28), and Ile de Bourbon (Réunion) in the Indian Ocean (11).

Not only places but also dates of capture are generally given (except at Esk Mills) in the General Entry Books of the depots in Scotland. These dates indicate the lengths of captivity endured by prisoners. Apart from many or most Dutch, Spanish and Prussian prisoners, others who could prove they were citizens of neutral states or who were able to establish their claim to belong to certain other nationalities or territories (some of them his former allies, such as Spain until 1808, or subject or satellite states of Napoleon which the fortunes of war had converted into allies of Britain), as well as those repatriated during the war because of their age or wounds or for other reasons, and those who succeeded in escaping back home, the vast majority of the prisoners of war in Scotland remained in captivity until the early summer of 1814, following Bonaparte's first abdication in April that year, the speedy ending then of the war, and the signing with France at the end of May of the peace Treaty of Paris.[31]

In establishing accurately the years in which the prisoners in Scotland were captured much the same difficulties apply that beset the drawing of a comprehensive and accurate picture of their respective places of capture. Nonetheless an analysis, perhaps at least 95 per cent accurate, of respective years of capture can be presented from an examination of the appropriate column ('Time When') in the depot General Entry Books.

Greenlaw, as already noticed, was distinct from the other depots in Scotland in having ostensibly separate General Entry Books for at least the most numerous of the several nationalities among its prisoners. Thus the two Greenlaw Entry Books listing 1,000 'Danish' prisoners there between 1807 and 1811 show their respective years of capture thus:

1807	1808	1809	1810	1811
105	360	296	159	80
TOTAL: 1,000[32]				

Of the 97 Dutch prisoners listed in the Edinburgh bridewell and Greenlaw Entry Book for 1803-04—all of them captured between July 1803 and August 1804, and all of them seamen, apart from five marines and seven soldiers—41 had been repatriated by the end of 1804, a further 51 had joined the British navy, army or militia, one (No.53 Alexander Linde, a seaman from the warship *L'Union*) had died in June 1804, six weeks after his capture and a month after his arrival at Greenlaw, and the fate of the remaining four is not clear.[33]

In the 'Spanish' General Entry Book for Greenlaw, which lists 48 prisoners, all of them seamen, it is said that the 'Particulars' of the first seven prisoners 'cannot in any degree be relied on'. The first five of the seven arrived at Greenlaw in July 1805, the other two in September that same year. As Spain had declared war on Britain in December 1804 the seven (unless captured aboard French vessels) must have been taken prisoner either that month or in 1805. So must the following 29 Spanish prisoners, who arrived at Greenlaw during 1805. The remaining twelve, who arrived in March 1806, may have been taken prisoner in 1804, 1805 or 1806. Thirty-four of the prisoners were sent on 2 January 1806 to Portsmouth—presumably to the hulks there. Of the remaining 14, two joined the British navy, two the band of His Britannic Majesty's 27th regiment of foot, one (No. 40, François Couvertier) died at Greenlaw on 20 May 1806, but about the fate of the other nine the General Entry Book is silent, although by implication they may have remained for some time longer in captivity at Greenlaw.[34]

Of the 1,537 prisoners listed in the three Greenlaw 'French' General Entry Books covering the years 1803-12, the years of capture appear to be as follows:

1803	1804	1805	1806	1807	1808	1809	1810	1811	1812	*No date*
119	93	219	144	86	255	221	85	94	174	47
TOTAL: 1,537[35]										

At Esk Mills, out of the total of 2,817 prisoners listed in the General Entry Book, date of capture is shown for only the first 1,591. But, as for places of capture, dates are given in the first three General Entry Books for

Valleyfield for the 2,486 Esk Mills prisoners transferred there in March and April 1811, thus:

1803	1804	1805	1806	1807	1808	1809	1810	1811	No date
62	15	159	264	161	327	881	503	22	92
TOTAL: 2,486[36]									

Of the 461 transferred in early March 1811 from Esk Mills to Edinburgh Castle, the years of capture were these:

1803	1804	1805	1806	1807	1808	1809	1810	1811	No date
9	6	26	99	47	112	89	35	8	30
TOTAL: 461[37]									

At Edinburgh Castle, as has already been observed, only a further 83 prisoners arrived between April and December 1811, when it ceased to be a depot except for prisoners of war in transit or for punishment of *mauvais sujets*. As almost half of those 83 came from Greenlaw or Valleyfield or were recaptured escapers from the Castle itself they have already been included in relevant statistics above. The remaining 44 of the 83 were members of the crew of the privateer *Le Figaro*, captured in the North Sea in July 1811. If those 44 are added to the eight already shown in the table immediately above as captured in 1811, that amended table then becomes the breakdown of the years of capture of those 505 prisoners at Edinburgh Castle.

Of the 5,164 prisoners who entered Valleyfield in 1811-13, later than those from Esk Mills, the years of capture were, or appear to have been, these:

1803	1804	1805	1806	1807	1808	1809	1810	1811	1812	1813	No date
15	3	190	136	130	179	2,217	389	445	1,170	35	255
TOTAL: 5,164[38]											

At Perth depot the years of capture of the 7,761 prisoners were, or appear to have been, these:

1803	1804	1805	1806	1807	1808	1809	1810	1811	1812	No date
10	8	43	126	76	224	1,162	803	1,267	4,030	4
TOTAL: 7,753[39]										

❖

'I have sent over the officers taken,' Marshal of the Portuguese army William Carr Beresford wrote to Wellington on 17 January 1814 from Ustaritz concerning some French prisoners of war, 'and the sea officer is of St Jean de Luz, who, I understand, has had the pleasure of being nine times a prisoner to the English.'[40] There was no one, so far as is known, among the prisoners in depots in Scotland who had fallen as often as that into the hands of the enemy. But, apart from recaptured escapers from the depots themselves, a few prisoners—probably a very few out of all the thousands—had certainly been captured more than once. 'I have heard of an East India captain,' Louis Simond, the Franco-American visitor to Edinburgh Castle early in 1811, has already been observed recording, 'who was taken in 1793, liberated in 1802; taken again the following year, and [is] now a prisoner with a wife and family in France.'[41] From Greenlaw depot J.B. Paulon or Pauron, a merchant who had been captured on the privateer *General St Simon*, was transferred early in 1811 to Esk Mills. From both depots he applied to the Transport Board for the restoration of his parole. 'It seems that he has once broke his parole and got to France, but has been taken a second time ... He is a merchant and never bore arms; was on his passage from Isle of France when taken; is in a bad state of health, etc.'[42]

At Valleyfield, too, there appears to have been at least one prisoner who had been captured twice. But the entry in the General Entry Book concerning him is full of contradictions. No. 3344 Guillaume Hermann, a soldier in the 1st infantry regiment, who arrived at Valleyfield in September 1811, is said to have been captured at Campveer (Veere) on Walcheren on 31 July 1809. Born at Neissar, he is described as aged 26, 5 feet 4 inches tall, of stout build, round face, brown complexion, brown hair, hazel eyes, and with no marks or wounds. The General Entry Book says Hermann had an alias, Jean Bapstiste Caryman Traut, under which he had earlier been captured as a soldier in the 4th artillery regiment on 24 February 1809 in Martinique. But Traut's physical description is hardly that of Hermann: 5 feet 10½ inches tall, slender build, long face, fresh complexion, dark brown hair, grey eyes, smallpox marks, and blind in his right eye. Hermann was released in June 1814 in the general repatriation of prisoners of war.[43]

At Perth depot there were at least five prisoners who had been captured more than once. One was Charles Fonquet, a corporal, regiment not stated, who was at Perth from August 1812 until the general release in June 1814. Captured on 25 July 1809 at Fort Carole, he had earlier been captured under the name (which was probably his correct one) Charles Dutilleul, as a seaman aboard the warship *Marengo*, at the Cape of Good Hope on 13 March 1806.[44] A second was Pierre Neveaux, a soldier in the 2nd regiment of light infantry, captured at Salamanca on 22 July 1812. Under his alias Firman Lapine he had earlier been captured as a carpenter on the privateer *Rabrocheus* off Plymouth on 10 December 1804. Born at Dieppe and aged 25, Neveaux-Lapine arrived at Perth in December 1812; he was released in June 1814.[45] A third was Pierre Vincent Fournier, a soldier in the 4th battalion, Colonial Infantry, captured at Flushing on 15 August 1809. As a seaman on the merchant ship *David*, Fournier had earlier been captured, no date given, under his alias Alexandre Gasteboit. Born at Paris and aged 23 Fournier-Gasteboit, a prisoner at Perth from January 1813, was released from captivity on 2 June 1814.[46] A fourth was Pierre Louis Thomas, a sergeant in the 39th infantry regiment, captured on 11 May 1811 at St Felix Bridge, near Almeida in Portugal, and who arrived at Perth in early January 1813. Under his alias Jean Baptiste Legrand, then a seaman on *L'Ami* privateer, he had been earlier captured on 10 March 1810, no place given in the Entry Book. Thomas-Legrand, born at Combe and aged 27, was released to France on 10 June 1814.[47] The last of these five is mentioned by Marote-Carrier as a depot hospital nurse who was released with him from Perth early in 1814, both men being ostensibly citizens of the neutral state of Oldenburg. 'This travelling companion,' says Marote-Carrier, 'displeased me. I knew his background too well for it to be agreeable to me to have to be with him. Originally from Dunkirk, he had a wife and children. Twice he had armed and commanded a privateer ship. Taken by the English, he had preferred, rather than remain in the prisons, to take service against his own country. But disheartened by the mistrust and flagrant insults that the English lavished on a turncoat, he had twice deserted. Made prisoner a third time, he was recognised ... and he was going to be thrown on board the hulks when, to inspire confidence, he profaned one of the most sacred things in the world and married a poor young girl and thus became guilty of bigamy. The next day he obtained permission to go ashore with his new wife. Hardly had he disembarked than he slipped away and abandoned her, leaving her alone and dishonoured. The most minute search was made but he could not be found: he had passed back to France. All that was known was that he was from Dunkirk and it was learned later that he had been married there a long time. From that time he brought on himself the punishment of bigamy, a very severe punishment in England. So our man trembled when he was retaken a fourth time. Fortunately, he was not recognised, and fearful of giving exact information about himself which could have led to his downfall, he said he was from Oldenburg and took a false name. Only the prisoners knew his history and among themselves they called him the man from Dunkirk.'[48] The Perth General Entry Book shows that Marote-Carrier's travelling companion was Frederik Haultz, lieutenant on *Le Vengeur* privateer, who, having been captured on 17 October 1810 in the English Channel, had arrived at Perth on 2 September 1812 from Greenlaw. Haultz's place of birth is entered as Oldenburg. He was aged 32, and was described as 5 feet 4 inches tall, of stout build, with a round face, sallow complexion, brown hair, grey eyes, and no marks or wounds. Haultz and Marote-Carrier, sent that day to Leith on the first stage of their journey home, were the only prisoners liberated from Perth on 17 February 1814.[49]

One prisoner who refused to become again a captive was the captain of the Danish privateer *Arbrewbraker*, which was captured in November 1811 by the sloop HMS *Cherokee* and sent into Methil harbour in Fife. The *Arbrewbraker* '... carried two guns and twenty men, had been out fourteen days from Norway but had made no capture this cruise. The captain of the privateer leaped overboard and was drowned when his vessel was on the eve of being captured by the *Cherokee*. The reason assigned for this suicide is that he had been many years a prisoner in Britain and had only lately returned to his native country.' In those long wars it was likely there were at least a few others who did as he did.[50]

It was even more likely, too, that confined in the depots in Scotland there were more than the mere handful of examples shown here of prisoners who had been captured more than once but who concealed their earlier captivity and it went unrecorded in the General Entry Books or other official records.

From this account of places, dates and circumstances of capture some impression may be formed of the great variety of experiences undergone by the prisoners of war in Scotland. Only relatively small numbers of the inmates of the depots had been captured in the first two or three years of the Napoleonic Wars. Nonetheless, like Lieutenant Nicolas Aucamp, who gazed outward successively from Greenlaw, Esk Mills and Valleyfield between his capture in 1803 and his repatriation at the peace in 1814, there were some who had to endure ten or eleven years of captivity. On the other hand more than half the 7,700 prisoners at Perth were captured in 1812 and, like the much smaller numbers of those at Valleyfield and Greenlaw captured that year, endured a relatively short period of captivity before their release in early summer 1814 or, in some cases, earlier. Of all the thousands of prisoners held captive in Scotland only 35 appear to have been captured as late as 1813.[51]

Some impression of the respective lengths of captivity endured by the prisoners in the depots in Scotland can be formed from their year of capture. The conversion of that impression into an entirely accurate and comprehensive picture would demand an amount of computation in the General Entry Books of the depots that lies beyond the scope of the present work. Yet it is hoped even the outline so far sketched is enough to show that, taking Greenlaw, Esk Mills, Valleyfield, Edinburgh Castle and Perth together, and after making adequate allowance for factors such as duplication of entries in the depot registers, there were at least 2,000 prisoners who had been captured between 1803 and 1807 inclusive and who by the end of the war in 1814 had therefore spent between six and eleven years in captivity. Those in the latter case were prisoners for almost twice as long as even the most long confined among prisoners of war liberated in 1945 at the end of the Second World War.

To what extent their length of captivity affected the attitudes and behaviour of prisoners in the Napoleonic Wars is a leading question, some answers to which are offered in several of the chapters below. But the prolongation of privations that included a diet that was usually at best inadequate, overcrowding, bad (or lack of any) news from home, and what must have seemed the permanence of the war to those captured in its earlier years, were daily causes of suffering among the prisoners. The unfortunate captive at Perth recalled many years later by Marote-Carrier can hardly have been unique in his misery. 'Among the prisoners in our room,' said Marote-Carrier, 'I noticed one, four hammocks away from mine, who was always lying down at the window busy making things with straw. A deep sadness was always imprinted on his face and I had never seen him smile. This man had suffered. I believed he underwent some secret suffering and I wanted to console him ... He was a Nantes man and had embarked ... after the Treaty of Amiens [by which an uneasy peace existed between Britain and France from March 1802 until May 1803] on board an American vessel with his wife and seven children. They were going to the United States. The weather was magnificent, the sea was calm, the sun shone, everything foretold a happy crossing. Suddenly a sail appeared on the horizon. It was a cruiser under the English flag ... It sent alongside the American ship a longboat whose lieutenant proceeded to inspect it. He learned of the French origins of the man from Nantes and immediately declared he was a prisoner. In vain the unfortunate man claimed the protection of the treaties signed by France and England at the time of his departure from Nantes. In vain he declared that it was only on the basis of that guarantee that he had embarked and was taking all his family aboard. The English lieutenant pointed out that the Treaty of Amiens was ended and ordered the American captain to send the man from Nantes on board the English ship. As for his wife and children he let them go free. These unfortunates begged on their knees for permission to accompany their father and husband. All these entreaties were in vain, and once the man from Nantes was taken off the English cruiser sailed away and the American ship resumed its course for the United States, carrying with it the unfortunate family, henceforth without its head and its support. When I arrived at Perth [in September 1812] this unfortunate man had languished for ... years in the prisons. Racked with terrible anxiety about the fate of his loved ones, having written to Nantes, to the United States, everywhere, and having received no reply from anywhere ... he found himself in this cruel uncertainty. That was the cause of the sadness and of the deep depression by which I saw him always overwhelmed. I do not know if he ever recovered his liberty, if he ever found his family again. For when I left Perth [early in 1814] he was still there.'[52]

At Valleyfield also, Marote-Carrier, reflecting that '… if I were unfortunate I was not the worst off,' recalled another civilian fellow-prisoner who had already been in captivity for almost two years: '… a poor Fleming who … came from the island of Cassant, near l'Ecluse. Each year it was his custom to go and mow for several farmers on the island of Walcheren. He was there in 1809 as usual when the English descended on it after the capture of Flushing. The man of whom I am speaking was peacefully mowing, his knees bare, in his shirt and his linen underpants. The English approached him and by an unfortunate chance found at his neck a button inscribed with the pike and cap of liberty. That was enough. That trifling circumstance cost him his liberty. The English led him away with them. Father of a large family whom he supported by his labour, the unfortunate man was thrown into the hold of a warship and taken to the hulks at Plymouth then to Valleyfield, where I came to know him. A miserable button had deprived him of … years of liberty, and God knew how many more he had still to undergo in prison. Add, moreover, to that that he was in a horrible state of destitution. Since 1809 he had not only not received any support, but not even news of his abandoned family; and he had lived from day to day, covered in rags, torn with cruel anxieties about the fate of his loved ones, and kept going by the wretched alms given by some of the prisoners, generous in his time of need. The unfortunate man knew that I came from Ostend. He implored me when I wrote to my wife to ask her if she knew anything of his family and to pass to him through me any news which would end his terrible uncertainty about them. The poor man did not dare ask for any support. I wrote to my wife as he asked. But as I left Valleyfield [for Perth] soon afterwards I lost touch with this poor prisoner, and I did not know if he had received some message from his family, whom my wife had hastened to contact at Breskens—as I learned later.'[53]

Confined in the depots in Scotland (as in those, and on the hulks, in England), there were therefore, as the boy William Chambers had observed on his Sunday visit to Valleyfield, all sorts and conditions of men. The prisoners were not only from the armed forces, and even in some cases from among the civilian populations, of Napoleon's empire and its allied or satellite states, but also from several other countries, including the United States of America.

9

Seamen, Soldiers, Civilians, Ships, Regiments, Corps, and Ranks

However motley the crowds of captives observed at Valleyfield by William Chambers they were nonetheless, like all other captives in depots in Scotland (as in those, and on the hulks, in England), classifiable into three broad categories: seamen, soldiers, and civilians.

The civilians, mainly passengers captured aboard ships, or fishermen, were very few, their numbers in the depots having been further reduced in some cases by repatriation, in others by the grant of parole.

Among the overwhelming mass of prisoners who were either seamen or soldiers, the seamen were themselves classifiable into three groups: naval, privateer, and merchant seamen.[1] Analysis of the General Entry Books or registers of depots in Scotland indicates that, with the usual reservations, the respective aggregate groups of seamen of all ranks among the prisoners were approximately these:

	Naval	Privateersmen	Merchant Seamen	Uncertain
At Greenlaw: 'Danes':[2]	107	464	418	11
'Dutch':[3]	77	1	19	
'Spanish':[4]	4	49	26	37
'Prussian':[5]			131	
'French':[6]	57	150	103	110
'French':[7]	106	201	8	6
American:[8]			48	
Total:	*351*	*865*	*753*	*164*
At Esk Mills:[9]	655	972	93	5
At Edinburgh Castle:[10]	155	232	9	24
At Valleyfield:[11]	794	1,097	79	48
At Perth:[12]	90	173	10	9

Privateersmen were thus by far the largest single category among the seamen in captivity in Scotland, and (discounting some 250 prisoners whose ships were 'uncertain') at every depot except Greenlaw they were in aggregate (i.e., approximately 3,300) more numerous than naval and merchant seamen combined. Even at Greenlaw, however, where in aggregate soldiers were substantially outnumbered by seamen, the largest single group of the latter were or appear to have been privateersmen (about 865 of them), followed by merchant seamen (753), and navy men (351), with a further 164 from ships 'uncertain'. At Perth, on the other hand, where seamen were in a very small minority compared with soldiers, there were only 10 from merchant ships, 90 from naval, and 173 from privateer, with a further nine 'uncertain'. At Esk Mills, seamen (some 1,725 of them) formed a distinct majority of the prisoners (though not such a substantial one as at Greenlaw), with the largest group among them privateersmen (972), followed by navy men (655), but far fewer merchant seamen (93), plus five 'uncertain'. At Edinburgh Castle, too, where most of the prisoners listed in the main register had come from Esk Mills upon its sudden closure in March 1811, privateersmen (232) were the largest group there among the seamen, followed by naval (155) and merchant (9) seamen, plus 24 from ships 'uncertain'. At Valleyfield, where seamen were in a minority, even if it was a substantial one, the largest group of them (1,097) were privateersmen, followed by navy men (794), and merchant seamen (79), with another 48 'uncertain'. Of naval prisoners, by far the largest numbers were at Valleyfield (794) and Esk Mills (655); and of merchant seamen, Greenlaw with 753, of whom no fewer than 418 were 'Danes', held far more than did all the other depots in Scotland put together.

The naval prisoners, the aggregate number of whom was more than 2,000, formed the second-largest group among sea-going captives in the Scots depots. They came from more than 230 ships in the fleets of Napoleon and his allies.[13] Some among them had been captured, as has been seen, in the awesome battle at Trafalgar in 1805. But most of them were taken in one or other of a host of much smaller and less well known encounters fought out on one or other of many of the seas and oceans of the world.

Some of the vessels on which these navymen had been captured were large and formidable men-of-war. An outstanding example was the *Impérial*. 'The strongest and most beautiful vessel ever built in any country in the world', the *Impérial*, a three-deck man-of-war armed with between 120 and 130 cannons, had a crew of about 1,200 but also carried two or three hundred soldiers at the time of her destruction in an encounter with a British naval squadron near St Domingo (Haiti) early in February 1806. Accompanied by five other line-of-battle ships and three frigates, the *Impérial*, dismasted by the exchanges of massive broadsides directly the battle began, was driven on shore, and her crew 'flocked to the upper part of the ship in the utmost apparent distress.' Almost half the crew were killed or wounded, but 'scarcely half a dozen persons, and none above a forecastle man' (i.e., rank and file seamen) were taken prisoner. In the Scots depots there was a handful of prisoners from the *Impérial*. Two of its crew who found themselves at Valleyfield, for example, were Jean David and Emmanuel Hervé Gauvin.[14]

All other naval vessels on which prisoners in the Scots depots had been captured were, however, much or very much smaller than the *Impérial*. Many of these prisoners had been members of the crews not of line-of-battle ships but of frigates armed with up to 44 cannons, or of sloops with between 14 and 18, or of gun-boats or gun-brigs that had 14 or fewer. Others again had been taken prisoner on craft that were even smaller than those and with fewer cannons or none at all. Adolphe Douzon, for example, a midshipman on *La Mouche* (The Fly), which was variously described as a naval packet, sloop or schooner, was captured aboard it 'at sea' in March 1809. Douzon was an inmate successively at Esk Mills, Edinburgh Castle and Greenlaw. Desiré Molinière, a seaman aged 26 and born at l'Ouant, had been captured 'in a small boat at Cadiz' in June 1808. Molinière escaped from Greenlaw in November 1811, but it is not known whether from some shore or harbour such as Leith he consequently returned home, perhaps once more in a small boat. Another naval prisoner taken in a humbler craft than the mighty *Impérial*, was the Danish lieutenant Holten Soberg, captured in July 1811 in the North Sea 'in a row boat belonging to a sloop of war'. Soberg made only a brief sojourn at Greenlaw before he was sent on parole in September that year to Peebles.[15]

Privateersmen were generally regarded by the depot authorities as particularly difficult prisoners. Francis Abell, a pioneering historian of prisoners of war in Britain during both the later 18th century and the Napoleonic Wars, wrote of the privateer captains who formed the majority of the prisoners confined on the *Bahama* hulk at Chatham about 1806, as 'the most restless and desperate of all the prisoners of war, men who were socially above the common herd, yet who had not the *cachet* of the regular officers of the navy, who regarded themselves as independent of such laws and regulations as bound the latter, and who were also independent in the sense of being sometimes well-to-do and even rich men.'[16] Partly the reputation of privateersmen, whatever their rank, as troublemakers actual or potential in the depots arose from the fact that many of them, like Captain Paul Andreas Kaald at Greenlaw and Lieutenant Marote-Carrier of Esk Mills, Valleyfield and Perth, had previously been merchant seamen. But, their livelihoods disrupted by the war, they had voluntarily taken up arms by sailing in vessels licensed by Napoleon's government or those of his allies to attack British and British-allied shipping. Although there proved to be, from the authorities' point of view, no lack of *mauvais sujets* or troublemakers among naval and army prisoners too in the depots in Scotland, yet these latter prisoners, as Abell pointed out, were at least accustomed to conforming to naval or military discipline. Privateersmen, while subject to a measure of discipline aboard their own ships, were accustomed to enjoying more personal freedom than men in the navy or the army. Being a prisoner of war was hardly an agreeable experience (although less disagreeable than being killed), no matter whether he who had to endure captivity was a soldier or a naval, merchant, or privateer seaman. For many privateersmen, however, captivity may have been particularly difficult to thole.

Privateer officers, moreover, however much they might be accustomed to leadership and responsibility, were not necessarily entitled to the benefit of parole. Commissioned officers of the navy and army (as well as midshipmen or aspirants, even though they did not, or did not yet, hold commissions), and also the two most senior officers of any captured merchant vessel, might expect, provided they formally undertook to observe the regulations governing parole, more or less automatically to be granted it.[17] There were, of course, a few officers eligible for parole who chose not to accept it since parole made them honour bound not to attempt escape. On the other hand, the grant of parole to privateer officers was not only conditional on the number of mounted guns or cannons their ships carried at the time of capture, but even if that condition were met parole was restricted to the captain, second captain, and surgeon, and thereafter to one lieutenant for every hundred men in the crew. Many, perhaps most, privateering ships failed to meet the first or last criterion.[18] A Transport Board list, dated 20 September 1813, of French prisoners of war on parole in Britain, shows: 672 naval officers, 1,671 army officers, 145 chief surgeons and 90 assistant surgeons of the navy and army, 152 masters and mates of merchant vessels, at least 401 others (civilians), but only 72 captains and lieutenants of privateers.[19]

Privateersmen presented difficulties to the depot authorities partly also because sizeable sections of the officers and crews of particular privateer ships were sometimes confined together in the same depot. Thus of the crew of 125 or so of the privateer *L'Aventurier*, on which Marote-Carrier was first lieutenant, at least 34 were together in captivity at Valleyfield in 1811.[20] There, too, among the privateersmen were 40 members of the crew of the *Héro du Nord*. At least 54 of the officers and crew of *Le Vengeur*, captured in October 1810, likewise shared their captivity early in 1811 at Esk Mills.[21] There were similar clusters of privateer crews at Greenlaw: 45 of the crew of *Le Figaro*, for example, in 1811-12, and in 1808-09 the captain, 2nd captain, 1st lieutenant, surgeon, ensign, clerk, two gunners, four boys, and 32 seamen of the *Passe Partout*.[22]

The presence in each depot of such sizeable groups of shipmates appears to have endowed some privateersmen, more so than many other prisoners, with a degree of cohesion, camaraderie, and higher morale—and consequently greater determination to escape from their captivity.[23] Because of such factors privateersmen, particularly privateer officers in the first of these events, played a major part in, for example, the mass escapes from Esk Mills and Edinburgh Castle in 1811. Of the 23 escapers from Esk Mills on 19 February that year all but one or at most two were privateersmen—five or six of them shipmates from *Le Vengeur*; and of the 44 escapers from Edinburgh Castle on 12 April four were soldiers, two merchant seamen, 12 (and possibly a further four) navy, and no fewer than 21 (and possibly a further four) were privateersmen.[24]

Where they were confined together in depots, as was the case at one time or another in Scotland, privateersmen and also commissioned naval or army officers sent there from the parole towns as punishment for breach of their parole, the mixture could prove especially troublesome to the authorities. 'Herewith copies of a letter and its inclosures from Lieutenant General Henry Wynyard,' wrote the Transport Board on 5 October 1813 to Vice Admiral Otway at Leith, 'representing the inconveniences arising from the confinement at Perth of French prisoners who have broken their parole and prisoners taken in privateers and suggesting certain alterations for the better security of the prison. We also inclose a list of parole breakers now confined at that depot, and we request to be informed whether you consider the removal of those prisoners to Edinburgh Castle likely to answer the desired effect ...'[25]

That troublesome mixture of privateersmen with commissioned officers confined together in close depots appears to have contributed, for example, to the transfer from Valleyfield to the hulks at Portsmouth in October 1811 of ten 'Dangerous and refractory characters'. One of these, Charles Laurent Faures, who had been recaptured after escaping from the parole town of Jedburgh, was captain of the privateer *Le Loup Garou*, taken a year earlier in the English Channel. 'Faures is particularly reported to be a desperate fellow without principle or honour.'[26] Faures is described as aged 45, 5ft 5in in height, 'born in France' (a grudging admission on Faures' part that indicates his non-cooperation with the Transport Board and depot authorities), of straight (sic) stature, round face, swarthy complexion, black hair, hazel eyes, and no marks or wounds. The other nine 'dangerous and refractory characters' sent to the hulks with him included: (1) J.B. Mutel, aged 25, a surgeon, Medical Staff, captured with general Dupont's army at Baylen in Spain in 1808, and who had been recaptured at North Shields after escaping from his parole at Selkirk; (2) Louis Marie Antoine Gérard de Riviers, aged 25, captain, 70th infantry regiment, captured in July 1811 in Estremadura, Spain, and recaptured like J.B. Mutel at North Shields after escaping from parole at Selkirk; (3) Pierre Boulle, aged 33, surgeon, *Milan* privateer, captured in the English Channel in October 1810, recaptured after escaping from parole at Jedburgh; (4) D.

Revol or Ruval, aged 30, surgeon, *Brocanteur* privateer, captured in the English Channel in February 1810, recaptured, like Pierre Boulle, after escaping from parole at Jedburgh.[27] Details of the other five prisoners sent with them to the Portsmouth hulks have proved more elusive, but according to the Register of Prisoners' Applications, dated 27 October 1811, they were all privateers-men: F. Formantin, captain, *Revenge*; Hyacinthe Amard, lieutenant, *Barbier de Seville*; L.F. Beheut (or Behut), seaman, *Brocanteur* (or *Barbier de Seville*); F. Giotin, seaman, *Le Vengeur*; and Isidore Franchard, seaman, said to be from two privateers, *Hypolite* and *Requin*. Precisely what (apart from attempting escape) was the nature of the 'dangerous and refractory' activities of these ten prisoners is not mentioned in the surviving archives.

There were thus in all the depots in Scotland prisoners who had been captured on privateer ships. Not all such prisoners were themselves priva-teersmen: some, as has been seen, were soldiers, and a handful were civilian passengers.[28] Contradictions and discrepancies in the depot registers concern-ing places and dates of capture of these privateer ships make it impossible to arrive at a completely accurate total of them. But a conservative reckoning based on a comparison of those sources indicates that prisoners came to the Scots depots from at least 450 captured privateer ships or recaptured British or other vessels with privateer prize crews aboard them. Prisoners at Greenlaw, for example, included many 'Danes' (of whom the diarist Captain Paul An-dreas Kaald was one) who had been captured on one or other of 25 privateer ships entered in the depot register as belonging to that kingdom.[29]

Merchant seamen were the least numerous of the three categories of cap-tured seamen in the depots in Scotland—except at Greenlaw Among the 1,000 or so 'Danes' there, merchant seamen were almost as numerous as privateersmen, and each of these two groups far exceeded the number of their captured compatriots from the navy. Moreover, the 131 'Prussian' sea-men marched out from Leith beween June and November 1806 to captivity at Greenlaw, were all from merchant vessels. So also were the 48 Americans sent into brief captivity there following the outbreak of the War of 1812, although there was also a handful of Americans at Greenlaw and other Scots depots who had become prisoners before 1812 while serving on board French or French-allied privateers.[30]

Merchant seamen were indeed the first prisoners in the Napoleonic Wars to find themselves in captivity in Scotland. Members of the crews of merchant vessels such as *Neptunis*, *Elizabeth*, *La Flore*, *Droiture* and *Prudence*, all captured in the North Sea in July or August 1803 within a few weeks of the outbreak of war, were confined from early that autumn in the Edinburgh bridewell, then from the spring of 1804 at Greenlaw. Nicolas Bokman, for example, a seaman on the *Neptunis*, was No.1 in the General Entry Book of 'Dutch' prisoners at both depots. Nothing more is known about him except that after nine months of captivity he trod the road out of Greenlaw that so many others were to follow, by volunteering into His Britannic Majesty's forces—in Bokman's case, the Royal Navy. His shipmate Aarnold Volner was more, or perhaps less, fortunate in that 'being an Invalid [he was] embarked at Leith for Embden' in July 1804. Another crew member, Hendrik Smit, was exchanged and repatriated to Holland in December 1804. Smit was the last of the crew to leave Greenlaw, for by the summer of that year all ten other captive seamen from the *Neptunis* had enlisted, like Bokman, in Britain's armed forces.[31]

The number of merchant vessels from which prisoners came to the depots in Scotland totalled (with the familiar reservations) approximately 246. Of these ships no less than 111, or 45 per cent, were 'Danish'—that is, Danish or Norwegian. The severe loss of merchant seamen and shipping suffered in the war by the kingdom of Denmark, whose king remained a loyal ally of Napoleon from 1807 until 1814, was clearly exemplified by the number of Danish subjects confined at Greenlaw. 'The Danish colonies passed into British hands;' an historian of Scandinavia has written of those years, 'the lucrative carrying trade in colonial wares likewise came abruptly to an end; some 1,400 ships were confiscated; and about 7,000 Norwegian and Danish seamen were confined in the hulks at Chatham and other British ports.' Greenlaw was not a port nor did it have any hulks, but it was at any rate within easy marching distance of the port of Leith.[32]

While merchant seamen trudged into captivity at Greenlaw or other depots in Scotland, some of the vessels on which they had been captured, including considerable numbers of Danish and Norwegian ones forming part of that severe wartime loss of 1,400, were sent into Aberdeen, Peterhead, Lerwick, Arbroath, Berwick, Dundee, Greenock, even MacDuff, but above all into Leith, by their British naval, or occasionally British privateer, captors. As early in the war as 4 August 1803, the *Caledonian Mercury* published a letter from Lerwick written a fortnight previously which reported that: 'The *Ethalion* frigate has sent in here a French vessel from St Domingo which Captain Stewart captured just as she was getting into Bergen. Her cargo is sugar, tobacco, cotton and wool, valued at £12,000 sterling. ... The *Cruizer* brig, Captain Hancock, has sent in here this morning the *Neptune* [i.e., *Neptunis*], a Dutch ship, 400 tons burden, from Surinam for Amsterdam, laden with sugar, coffee, cotton and wool, a very valuable prize.' The same paper reported on 29 April 1809: 'Arrived in Leith Roads the following [captured] Danish sloops and galliots, etc., *Johanna Margaretta*, *Frau Anna*, *Emanuel*, *Express*, *Hoffnung*, *Frau Anna Margaretta*, and *Thagen*. These prizes have been sent in by His Majesty's *Nymphen*, *Rover*, *Childers*, *Leveret*, and *Melpomene*.' Like captured privateer ships, merchant vessels and their assorted cargoes were put up for public auction following advertisement in local newspapers.[33] To the victor belong the spoils of the enemy. While the captains and officers, and to an appropriately regulated lesser extent the other ranks of the crews, of these Royal Navy warships enjoyed their share of the subsequent prize money, members of the crews of these captured merchant vessels were having to learn the ropes of their changed lives at Greenlaw or other depots.[34]

Merchant ships were where had been taken prisoner many among the few score of civilians who found themselves confined in the depots in Scotland. Most of them had been passengers. A few other civilians had been captured on land while employed as administrators attached to Napoleon's armies. A further handful were fishermen.[35]

The 'Danes' at Greenlaw included the largest number of civilian prisoners in any depot in Scotland—32 altogether. But several of them did not remain there for more than a few days. One such was Anders Iversensand, captured in October 1807 off Norway on the merchant vessel *Else Kierstine* on which he was sailing as both owner of the vessel and passenger. Iversensand was sent on parole to Peebles. There, too, after an even shorter sojourn at Greenlaw was sent A.C. Knudsen, the merchant who had been taken prisoner in October that year on the *Five Broders* merchant vessel at Stornoway. Two boys, Christian Enevold Ritmer and Wilhelm Eikard, who had been captured off Norway in mid-December 1808 as passengers on the merchant vessel *Scarvan*, were similarly confined at Greenlaw for less than a week before being sent to Peebles on parole. Another boy, Bernt Mortensen, was in the short term less fortunate. Captured on a transport ship in September 1809 off Jutland, Bernt, who was the son of the master of the vessel, spent a year in captivity at Greenlaw before he was repatriated as 'a boy under age'—i.e., under the age of 12. That was the age at which boys were officially considered old enough to fight for king (or emperor) and country. As the Transport Board told its agent at Valleyfield: '... no Boys can be released whose age exceeds 12 years on any Account whatever ...'[36]

Three other captured civilian passengers who arrived at Greenlaw from Greenock as early as July 1804 were French: Jean Bouchu (or Bochu), Pierre Baille and Pierre Baille junior, all of whom had been 'Taken in Ireland and sent from thence to Greenock.' Difficulties in following the footprints of some prisoners in the Scots depots are illustrated by the later history of those three. Bouchu (then described as a merchant seaman captured on *La Flore* in July 1803) was among the 192 French prisoners transferred from Greenlaw on 4 February 1811 to become the first inmates of Esk Mills. But he did not remain long at Esk Mills: on 26 March 1811 he was sent on parole to Kelso as servant to Adjutant General Charles Prévost De Boissi. Bouchu (the Kelso Entry Book spells his name Bouchut, and says he was a seaman captured in 1803 on the merchant vessel *Thenasa*) appears, however, to have escaped from Kelso on 3 November that year.[37] The two Bailles (both by this time described as seamen captured in July 1804) were apparently discharged from Greenlaw to the Nore, no doubt as part of the general transfer at that period of French prisoners from there to the hulks at Chatham, Baille senior on 11 July 1809, Baille junior on 31 October that year.[38]

One whose later experience was very unusual, although not unique, among civilian captives in Scots depots was Pierre Digurt, a steerage passenger on the merchant vessel *La Flore* when it was captured in the North Sea in August 1803. After ten months' captivity at Greenlaw Digurt was released, having volunteered himself into the Royal Navy.[39] Another with an unusual, though also not unique, distinction was Constant Yvert, captured as a passenger on the merchant vessel *La Franchise* at St Domingo in May 1803. Born in L'Aigle and aged 28, described as 5 feet 7½ in tall, of stout build, with an oval face, fresh complexion, dark brown hair, hazel eyes, and no marks and wounds, Yvert appears to have been one of only two or three civilian prisoners in any close confinement depot in Scotland to escape—which he did from Valleyfield in July 1812.[40]

A civilian prisoner who had not been a sea-going passenger but a customs officer 'captured on shore at Waren by English boats' in August 1810 was R. Colignon, who arrived at Esk Mills in February 1811 after a brief sojourn in Edinburgh Castle.[41] Brief sojourns in captivity were not the fate of two civilians at Perth depot, Pierre La Coste, born at Libourne and aged 25, and Pierre La Borde, born at Bordeaux and aged 21. On the contrary, both of them languished as prisoners of war for ten years. Both had been passengers on troopships captured in 1804, La Coste in the North Sea, La Borde in the Mediterranean; both had earlier been confined successively at Esk Mills and Valleyfield before being transferred in September 1812 to Perth, and both were released only at the end of the war in June 1814.[42]

Fishermen, although civilians and non-combatants, were also among the prisoners in the Scots depots. Their capture was contrary to an agreement concerning immunity for fishermen made in 1758 during the Seven Years' War, but which agreement was subsequently not always observed. In June 1804 the Transport Board, in response to an attempt to secure the release of Dutch fishermen, whose situation had earlier been described by the London-based agent for Dutch prisoners of war in Britain as 'most distressful', informed the Admiralty that there were then 158 held prisoner in Britain. The Board's recommendation was that 'as all these men are fit for service, and [are] good pilots, it would not be adviseable to allow them to return to

Holland, upon [any] condition whatever, as it is known by experience that such persons being on parole would not prevent the French Government from employing them whenever it should think their services necessary.'[43] Six years later, when the Board circularised its agents at the depots and hulks, it found that no fewer than 411 French fishermen were held captive in them—the return from Greenlaw, then the only depot in Scotland, was shown as '( )'.[44] Fishermen were, however, occasionally sent to Greenlaw. For example, a large Dutch fishing dogger with a crew of 14 was captured some miles off Aberdeen on 8 May 1809, and five captured Dutch doggers were sent into Leith by Royal Navy warships on 19 July 1810.[45] The issue of whether fishermen, at any rate non-French fishermen belonging to states hostile to Britain, should be regarded as non-combatant civilians or legitimate prisoners of war was raised again with the Transport Board as late as July 1813 by Vice Admiral William Otway at Leith. 'Gentlemen,' he wrote on the 23rd of that month to the Commissioners, 'His Majesty's hired brig *Charles* having captured off the Orkneys three Schevelling fishing vessels and sent in their crew, amounting to between 30 and 40 men, I beg to be informed whether they be considered as of the character of Dutch fishermen or as French prisoners from the ci-devant Holland, now forming a part of the French Empire.' The captured fishermen, who included Danes as well as Dutch, had been landed at Peterhead then sent on by sea to Leith. When the Transport Board Commissioners duly sent on a copy of Admiral Otway's letter to the Admiralty for its instructions to them on the issue, J.W. Croker, secretary to the Admiralty, wrote on the bottom of it: 'Their Lordships are not aware what he means by the restriction [? distinction] as between Dutch fishermen and French prisoners of war.' The Board politely replied that the Admiral was asking whether the captives were to be released as fishermen or confined as French prisoners of war. Apart from an Admiralty directive quoted in a letter from the Transport Board in September that year, that only fishermen who fished daily off their own coasts could be immune from being taken prisoner, the official archives appear to shed no further light on the issue.[46]

Two captured 'Foreign Fishermen' at Leith who had, however, been granted passports by the appropriate official at Edinburgh Council Chambers allowing them in January 1813 to return home, presumably to Holland if their names are a guide, were Pieter van den Berg and Philip Schop.[47] There appear not to have been any fishermen held in captivity at Perth, but there were apparently two or three at Esk Mills and Valleyfield. P. J. Bernard, described as a clerk on a fishing boat, found himself at Esk Mills after being captured in July 1808 at Guadeloupe; and of the handful at Valleyfield Captain Peter Walinck, aged 60, from Ostend, was one. He had been captured on his fishing vessel *Droiteur* or *Droiture* in the North Sea as early as August 1803 and remained a prisoner of war for eight years until he was released from Valleyfield in October 1811. A few months earlier Claude Briant, aged 30 and born at St Malo, 'Fisherman, Boat No. 3', who had been captured on the fishing vessel *Sauvage* in the North Sea, date unstated, also applied to the authorities to be released, according to a cryptic entry in the Register of Prisoners' Applications, and 'As a fisherman Captain Pillius [? Pellowe] says that he believes his statement to be true.' True or not, Briant's statement did not secure his repatriation and he remained a prisoner at Valleyfield until 1814.[48]

Certain other fishermen among the prisoners in the Scots depots were more fortunate. In December 1813 Hyndhert Davus, described as a seaman but in fact a Dutch fisherman, was released from Valleyfield 'in order to assist Mr Dugald Fergusson of the Cod and Herring Fishery at Greenock.' More or less as Davus passed out of the gates of the depot the Transport Board was seeking a copy of 'the bond given by Mr James Henderson of Clyth and Wick, in the county of Caithness, Fish Curer, on the 4th July 1812, for the security of certain Dutch fishermen, prisoners of war, who were delivered to him for the purpose of instructing the inhabitants in the Dutch mode of gripping and curing picked [pickled?] herrings.'[49]

But it was soldiers, not seamen or civilians, who formed the majority of the prisoners in the depots in Scotland. The depot General Entry Books indicate that the aggregate numbers of prisoners belonging to the armies of Napoleon or his allies were, with the usual reservations, approximately these:[50]

At Greenlaw: 'Danes':	None[51]
'Dutch':	12[52]
'Prussian':	None[53]
'Spanish':	None[54]
'American':	None[55]
'French':	801[56]
Total:	813
At Esk Mills:	1,059[57]
At Edinburgh Castle:	125[58]
At Valleyfield:	5,677[59]
At Perth:	7,449[60]

These army prisoners came to the depots in Scotland from virtually every arm of Napoleon's land forces: infantry above all, but also cavalry, artillery, and other corps or units such as medical and hospital staffs, supply

149

and transport troops (who included bakers, waggoners, and muletiers), engineers, miners, sappers, pioneers, artificers, gendarmes, and servants or batmen.

In addition to prisoners taken from most of the Line (or *Ligne*) and Light (or *Léger*) infantry regiments, with 90 and 26 respectively of which the French army began the war in 1803 and which by 1813 had increased to 203 Line and 40 Light, each with four or occasionally five and even six field or fighting battalions, plus a depot or training battalion,[61] there were other prisoners who had fought on horseback in their dragoon, hussar, lancer, cuirassier, or other cavalry regiments, of which by 1808 Napoleon had a total of about 80, each consisting of between about 600 and 800 men.[62] There were also some regiments of *chevau-légers* or lancers but from which almost none of the prisoners in Scotland came.

From that elite corps of Napoleon's army, the Imperial Guard, came a small group of the prisoners in Scots depots, and there were also two soldiers there from the Guard of Napoleon's elder brother, King Joseph of Spain.[63]

While the other Scots depots each held one or two of them, the largest group of prisoners from Napoleon's Imperial Guard was at Valleyfield—more than 30 of them. All of these latter were captured in Spain between 1808 and 1812—no fewer than 23 of them as cavalry of the Guard in December 1808 at Benavente, during the retreat by Sir John Moore's army to Corunna.[64] One of the Imperial Guard captured at Benavente was J.P. (or Pierre François) Giscard. Giscard, born at Nesse and aged 22, described as 5 feet 9 inches tall, of 'stoutish' build, long visage, fair complexion, light brown hair, hazel eyes, and with no marks or wounds, escaped from Valleyfield almost exactly four years afterward but was recaptured a fortnight later and transferred in July 1813 to Perth depot, from which also he escaped.[65]

The two soldiers who came from that other elite corps, King Joseph's Guard (also referred to as the Garde Roi and Garde de Corps), were Louis Denis, captured on 26 February 1811 at Salamanca, and who was a prisoner at Valleyfield for at least several months until the end of the war; and Barthelemy Bellus, who began his captivity in Scotland at Perth, where he arrived in December 1812. He had been captured by Wellington's troops on 14 August that year at Madrid. Born at Gropo, Genoa, Bellus was aged 29. The Perth Entry Book indicates he was released from there at the end of the war in July 1814, but a contradictory entry in the Valleyfield register shows Bellus to have been a prisoner there from (probably) August 1813 until he was released in March 1814.[66]

From almost 90 of the French Line infantry and more than 30 of the Light infantry regiments prisoners came to the depots in Scotland. By far the largest number from any of these 120 or so regiments belonged to the 82nd Line. There were in aggregate 1,047 of its soldiers at Valleyfield, 289 at Perth, 153 at Esk Mills, 10 at Greenlaw, and six at Edinburgh Castle. Some of them had been captured in the Peninsular War, others at the capitulation of French forces in February 1809 on Martinique. One among the many made prisoner from the regiment then on Martinique was Bernard Gassione, born at Lyons and aged 28, who became one of the outstanding escapers from depots in Scotland and about whom more will be said in a chapter below.

Among the many other infantry regiments from which, on the other hand, only a very few prisoners found themselves in depots in Scotland were two soldiers at Esk Mills, Pierre Crokel and Jean Levergue, who had been captured at Flushing in August 1809 and were said to belong to the 'Russian Carabiniers'. It has not proved possible to identify this regiment.[67]

The Colonial battalions, so titled, provided the depots in Scotland with prisoners, some at least of whom may have had distinctive experiences before their capture. For the Colonial battalions were punishment units. Known as *insoumis* and *réfractaires*, evaders of conscription to and deserters from Napoleon's forces were extremely numerous. One historian of the subject has written that 'The Revolution and Empire drove hundreds of thousands of Frenchmen to seek their salvation from the armies in either desertion or *insoumission*.'[68] Some of these dissidents who had voted with their feet against an enforced military career were on their capture or re-capture by Napoleon's agents sent to the Colonial battalions. The Chasseurs Rentrés, from which also there were some prisoners at Valleyfield and Perth, was similarly a regiment formed originally in 1802-3 from French deserters retrieved from the Austrian army and which from 1808 recruited also into its ranks foreign prisoners of war.[69] But nothing is recorded in the Entry Books or other Transport Board archives of the earlier individual experiences of men from those units in the Scots depots, most of whom were captured by British forces at Flushing or elsewhere on Walcheren in August 1809.

Among prisoners from the cavalry regiments the only notable absentees were any from either of the two regiments of French carabiniers or heavy cavalry.[70] There appear to have been only two from those other elite French heavy cavalry regiments, the Cuirassiers. One of them, confined at Greenlaw in November 1810 for a few days only until sent on parole to Peebles, was 2nd lieutenant J. P. Navetier of the 2nd Cuirassiers, captured in September that year while serving with Marshal Masséna's army in Spain and Portugal. The other was among the first prisoners to arrive at Perth depot on its opening in August 1812. He was François Meunier, a cuirassier from the 10th Regiment, who had been captured by Spanish forces at Baylen on 19 July 1808. Born at Bove or Bowe, Meunier was aged 28. He remained in captivity at Perth until the end of the war.[71]

From the Chasseurs à Cheval, Dragoons, Hussars and several otherwise unspecified regiments of French cavalry there were certainly numerous other captives in the depots in Scotland. Though the evidence is ambiguous it may mean that uniquely at Perth there was one prisoner from a French (as distinct from Polish or other) regiment of lancers. He was M. Spechoc, said simply to be a soldier in the 1st Regiment of Lancers, who had been captured in January 1812 at Decuan, and who arrived at Perth on 6 August that year. Born at Hurey (or Strey?), aged 27 and 5 ft 7 inches tall, he was of medium build, with an oval face, sallow complexion, dark hair, hazel eyes, and with 'Cut of the Left Hand'. He remained in captivity at Perth until the end of the war in 1814.[72]

Artillerymen were also present among the prisoners in Scots depots, the largest number of them at Perth—122 from the 1st Regiment alone, many of them captured at the fall of Badajoz to Wellington's army in April 1812. Among other troops belonging to the French artillery, such as armourers, artificers, workmen or labourers, and waggon drivers, were *pontonniers* or pontoon bridge builders, of whom six from the 1st Battalion were prisoners at Perth, all six captured at Madrid in August 1812.[73]

Perth depot also was where most, or in some cases even all, prisoners in Scotland from other French regiments or corps were held captive: engineers, miners, sappers, transport and supply troops, pioneers, medical personnel, gendarmes, Veterans, and some others, including at least some naval troops (from battalions of *marins* or 'marines' as they were often incorrectly referred to in the General Entry Books of the depots).

That Perth had around a hundred miners and sappers among its inmates may have been particularly helpful to those prisoners planning or preparing escapes, especially when tunnelling was involved. There were also miners among the prisoners at Edinburgh Castle and Valleyfield, and sappers at both those depots and at Greenlaw. Among 26 prisoners at Perth from the 2nd Battalion of miners was Nicolas Dausseur, captured with a dozen others of his battalion at Ciudad Rodrigo in Spain in January 1812. Aged 30, born at Lifolepty (or Lipolepty), and described as well made, with an oval face, swarthy complexion, dark brown hair, blue eyes, and with no marks or wounds, Dausseur is said by the Entry Book to have been 3 feet 6 inches tall. He remained in captivity at Perth until the end of the war.[74]

Captured army medical personnel in Scots depots very briefly included at Valleyfield a Director of Hospitals. He was Dominique Andry, captured in Spain or Portugal, probably in 1809. Formerly on parole at Cupar before his transfer in January 1812 to Lanark, he arrived at Valleyfield depot hospital at the end of the following month for medical treatment himself. But he died there five days later from phthisis and was buried in the depot cemetery.[75]

All but two of the score of gendarmes or military police in captivity in Scots depots were at Perth. The two exceptions were at Greenlaw (but only very briefly as they were sent within a few days of their arrival there in November 1810 on parole to Peebles). A gendarme who died in captivity at Perth was Joseph Coilit (or Coury), alias Koehly, aged 27, born at Dol (or Marcolsem), and captured at Madrid in August 1812, four months before his death.[76]

At Perth, too, were to be found all three prisoners in Scotland from regiments of Veterans; and there also were all but one of several other prisoners of more miscellaneous provenance, including four 'Followers of the Army' and five servants or batmen—the exception was one courier, confined at Valleyfield. The four 'Followers of the Army' at Perth included two men further described in the Entry Book as 'hospital nurse', plus a storekeeper, and perhaps more surprisingly a sergeant whose regiment is not given (it seems likely his inclusion among these four was a clerical error). One of the two hospital nurses was Amand Gabio ('German' is pencilled in on the Entry Book after his name). Said to have been born in Flanders, he was aged 29 and remained in captivity at Perth until the end of the war.[77]

Most of the naval troops in captivity in Scotland were, on the other hand, at Valleyfield—22 of them, for example, from the 44th Battalion. Described in the Entry Book as 'Marines' they were in fact *marins*, i.e., seamen. Two of their number were Yves Torreau and Louis Panneau, the latter a Swiss, the former born at Angers. Both men were transferred to Perth in the summer of 1812. Battalions of seamen had first been formed by Napoleon in 1808, to cope with the problems of manning French warships. Each battalion was intended to form the major part of the crew of a middle-sized warship. But two at least of the battalions of *marins*—the 43rd and 44th—were attached by Napoleon to his army and entered Spain with it in 1810. That autumn a company of the 44th was made responsible for guarding some 4,000 French wounded and sick troops in a convent hospital at Coimbra during Marshal Masséna's advance into Portugal, but the 44th's company was forced to surrender to Portuguese militia under the command of the British colonel Nicholas Trant. Many of the prisoners from the 44th Battalion at Valleyfield and Perth had been captured then at Coimbra.[78]

Hundreds of soldiers belonging to regiments of Napoleon's foreign allies or subject states were among the prisoners in the depots in Scotland. The largest single group of them were Germans from the Hesse-Darmstadt regiment, over 200 of whom were held first at Perth then at Valleyfield. It was hardly surprising that many non-Frenchmen should be among the prisoners: 'After 1806 approximately one-third of the Grande Armée was foreign; in

1812, more than half.'[79] The wide range of nationalities among the prisoners will be discussed in a following chapter.

The overwhelming mass of the prisoners of war in the depots in Scotland were thus, unsurprisingly, rank and file soldiers and seamen. Many non-commissioned, petty, and warrant officers were there, too. The number of prisoners in the depots who were commissioned army or navy officers or officers of equivalent rank from merchant and privateer ships was, however, relatively small. The presence in the depots of these commissioned officers and officers of equivalent rank was due to one or more of six reasons. They had not been eligible for parole, or had declined to apply for it, or they were awaiting a decision on their application for it, or they had applied unsuccessfully for it, or they had lost their parole through breach of its rules, or (in the case especially of the hospital at Valleyfield) they were in the depot only temporarily for medical treatment, having been granted for that purpose leave of absence from their parole towns in the Borders or elsewhere in Scotland.

The individual ranks (or 'Quality', as the appropriate column in the depot General Entry Books was headed) of the prisoners in the depots therefore ascended pyramid-like from the masses of ordinary soldiers and seamen through the various layers of tradesmen or specialists and non-commissioned, petty, and warrant officers, to the relatively small apex of commissioned officers and merchant or privateer ship officers of equivalent rank. The table in Appendix 5 below offers, subject to all the usual reservations, an indication of the ranks of the prisoners in the Scots depots.

Along with Brigadier General Edouard-François Simon, who was confined alone with his servant in 1812-14 in Dumbarton Castle,[80] the most senior prisoner in any of the Scots depots appears to have been Adjutant General Charles Prévost De Boissi. An ambiguous, even mysterious, character, De Boissi had been captured on board a privateer, the *Lucien Charles*, in June 1809. He had been on parole first at Wantage in Berkshire, then at Thame in Oxfordshire. There he lost his parole and was sent into confinement at Portsmouth. Transferred to Scotland, he landed from HMS *Dictator* at Leith and arrived at Esk Mills on 6 March 1811. From there De Boissi immediately appealed to the Transport Board for readmission to parole, enclosing 'two certificates from English surgeons of the very bad state of his health, also a letter from Mr Stopford to Admiral Stopford, by which it appears that he really is Adjutant General and has behaved well to British prisoners, etc., etc.' The Board's or Transport Office's remarks on De Boissi's application were: 'This is the same Gent who wrote a letter to Lucien Bonaparte which was not sent, by the Board's order.' De Boissi's application, however, was granted and he was sent on parole from Esk Mills on 26 March to Kelso, where he appears to have remained until the end of the war.[81]

Lack of explicit evidence makes it difficult to be sure how far the military, naval or shipboard discipline to which the prisoners, apart from the handful of civilians among them, had been accustomed and in which rank had played so important a part, still applied or was observed amid the conditions of captivity in the depots. Marote-Carrier long afterwards recalled that at Valleyfield 'The officers were separated from the crowd [of ordinary rank and file prisoners] and given a separate quarter.'[82] As the only purpose-built depot in Scotland, Perth had a separate 'prison for "petty officers" (the better class [i.e., commissioned officers] being on parole), and contained 1,100 inmates'.[83] As discussion in chapters below of some other aspects of the prisoners and the depots will indicate, there was certainly organisation and discipline among the prisoners, at least for certain purposes. One illustration of that discipline already observed was the holding of their own court martial and the punishment it meted out to one of their number found guilty of vandalism and theft at Inchture parish church during the march in August 1812 of the first batch of prisoners from Dundee to Perth depot.[84] But how far such action was the result of the exercise of residual and accepted prerogatives of rank among the prisoners, or rather of a general acceptance among them of the need to maintain certain standards of discipline or behaviour despite the daily depressing regime in captivity, is not clear. It was virtually axiomatic that within the depots conventional military or naval rank was of distinctly less importance among the prisoners than before their capture. Consequently, force of character, the exercise of distinctly personal powers of persuasion, organisation and leadership, and personal, group, or national loyalties became correspondingly more important. These personal qualities and loyalties, rather than the continued exercise of and obedience to the prerogatives of conventional and pre-capture military or maritime rank, appear likely to have been the factors that established or maintained innumerable and diverse groups, large and small, of friends, shipmates, regimental comrades, roommates, fellow countrymen, fellow townsmen or fellow villagers. These were groups to which the great majority of the prisoners may have gravitated as a means by which they could better cope with their captivity.

'In the Napoleonic Wars both sides separated the officers from the men in captivity,' wrote the distinguished naval historian Michael Lewis in his study of British prisoners of war then in France.[85] Professor Lewis added: '... except, oddly enough, in punishment depots, where the officer-prisoners were held to have forfeited officer rights.' Whatever may have been the position of British prisoners in France it was not the case that there were no officer-prisoners among the French and other inmates of the depots in Scotland. Nor, as has been seen, was it necessarily the case that all officer-prisoners in those depots were there because of breach of parole on their part. The problem is to establish what the influence of officers among the prisoners in the Scots depots actually was, and how far that influence was based only or mainly on obedience to conventional military or naval rank.

10

Women and Children; Ages

'This morning,' reported the *Edinburgh Evening Courant* on 26 August 1811, 'a number of prisoners of war were brought from Leith and marched to Penicuik. There were four women with them.' Although the evidence is limited it does confirm that a few wives or partners accompanied their menfolk among the prisoners to the close confinement depots in Scotland. Whether these devoted women actually passed through the gates into the depots and shared the captivity of husband or partner within is less clear—but in at least one case (and possibly in several others) even that appears to have been so. Marote-Carrier, who is such an invaluable source of information about some of the inner history of Esk Mills, Valleyfield and Perth depots that never percolated into the official records of the Transport Board, asserts that first at Valleyfield then at Perth there was a woman living among the prisoners.[1]

The Transport Board's policy toward non-combatants, including women and children, numbers of whom had already been captured while voyaging as passengers aboard enemy ships, had been made clear as early as 5 October 1803. In a circular then to all its parole agents, but which by implication applied also to any women accompanying prisoners at the close confinement depots, the Board directed that 'you will inform all the French prisoners under your care who are not connected with the naval or military service of the enemy, nor seafaring persons, that the British Government, not carrying on hostilities like barbarians, nor willing to distress persons of that description by any strictness which it may be necessary to exercise towards those of a military character, have resolved to permit them to return to their own country immediately, and that the necessary orders will be sent to you in the course of a day or two for their release accordingly. It is proper that you should apprize them that they must leave the country at their own expense.'[2]

In the Napoleonic Wars, as in earlier wars, it was the practice for some women, sometimes with their children, to accompany their husbands on campaign.[3]

The press report on 26 August 1811 of four women accompanying prisoners of war from Leith out to Penicuik (or Edinburgh Castle) appears to be the earliest mention of that aspect of captivity at the close confinement depots in Scotland. Almost certainly those four women were Dutch, for four days after the press report, the Transport Board wrote to Vice-Admiral Otway at Leith: 'Lieutenant Priest, our Agent at Greenlaw, having informed us that he has received into his Charge 4 Dutch women, who were taken with their husbands out of French gun boats captured by the Heligoland Squadron, we request that if it be possible you will cause the Women in question to be sent Home, as we have no means of accommodating them in the Prison, and they must if they remain become a useless Burthen upon the Public.' On the same day Lieutenant Priest was told by the Board: '... you are in the mean Time to subsist and lodge them in the best way you can.' On 10 September the Board wrote again to Vice-Admiral Otway: '... until an opportunity shall offer for the four Dutch women ... to be returned home they will be permitted to remain in the neighbourhood of Greenlaw Prison and be allowed one shilling each per diem for subsistence.' And six days later the Board told Lieutenant Priest: 'The four Dutch women are to be sent home by the first opportunity in order to get rid of the great expense of maintaining them.' It appears, however, that Lieutenant Priest was sympathetic to the women's case: '... the four Dutch women,' the Board told him on 19 September, 'may be allowed to remain in the neighbourhood of Greenlaw prison upon the conditions stated by you, and we direct you to discontinue the allowance made to them of one shilling per diem for their subsistence.' No later reference to these four women has been found.[4]

Four months later, at Valleyfield, another woman became the subject of correspondence between the agent there, Captain Moriarty, RN, and the Transport Board. 'We have received your letter of the 11th Instant,' the Board told Moriarty on 16 January 1812, 'and direct you to state who the Woman is you mention to have accompanied the prisoners landed from the *Zealous* [at Leith on 10 January], and to which of the Prisoners she belongs.' After receiving a prompt reply from Moriarty, the Board told him: '... the Woman thereinmentioned is to be Victualled while she remains; but she may proceed when she pleases to France.' Three months later almost certainly the same woman was the subject of further correspondence between the Board and its agent at Valleyfield: '... the Agent for Parole prisoners at Biggar having stated that Catherine Didon, wife of a Prisoner named Louis Didon at Valleyfield, intends to reside at Biggar ... you will state whether this Woman be a Frenchwoman and if so by what Authority she resides in Scotland.' Moriarty's reply of 30 April has not survived, but on 4 May the Board directed him '... to send the Woman Catherine Diedont [sic] to Portsmouth by the return of the [HMS] *Regulus*, to be delivered into the charge of Captain Woodriff, the Agent for Prisoners of War at that port.'[5]

At Valleyfield, according to the Scots banker-historian Macbeth Forbes, 'Several women, the wives of prisoners, arrived from time to time ... and they used to go to Edinburgh and offer the nick-nacks made by their husbands to likely buyers.'[6] Marote-Carrier, himself a prisoner there from spring 1811 until his transfer on 2 September 1812 to Perth, testifies, as mentioned above, that there was a Spanish woman actually living in Valleyfield depot, and according to him she was the first woman to do so. Like Marote-Carrier she also was transferred to Perth. 'In the second convoy that came from Valleyfield,' he recalled, 'there were an artilleryman and a young hussar who had arrived together from Spain several months earlier. They both lived in the same room as me; but shortly afterwards it was discovered that the so-called hussar was no other than a woman in disguise. The severity of the English was marked in this matter. No woman had until then been allowed to live in the prison. So hardly was the deputy commandant [i.e., the chief or first clerk, Andrew Johnston] informed of the fact than he brought the artilleryman and his woman companion before him and angrily told them that the latter must immediately leave for London from which she would be transported to Spain. Then there were torrents of tears and earnest supplications.

'They were a married couple and their story was one of the most moving. He was from Provence, she was from around Cadiz, an Andalusian. The artilleryman, after leaving his native village, had gone to the war in Spain. In 1811 he had been cut off from his comrades, pursued by guerrillas, and had taken refuge in a cottage half screened by orange and pomegranate trees. It was there that he saw for the first time the young girl who had become his companion. She was alone and had the courage to hide him and to receive with such self-possession the enemies who pursued him that they became convinced he had given them the slip. He spent eight days in that hospitable cabin, protected from the searches that went on for him, awaiting a French party that might pass... But he was handsome and his heart was ardent and noble. He fell in love with the young Andalusian, who loved him in return and said to him simply and frankly on the eve of his departure: "I love you. Will you marry me?" He spoke about the dangers presented by the war; she replied that she would share them with him, that she would follow him everywhere whether as conqueror or conquered ... He loved her! He agreed to the proposal of the young girl. The next day the village priest united them in marriage.

'The day after that, despite the tears and entreaties of her parents, the young girl, disguised as a man, departed with her husband. At that time many young people, still almost children, fought in the ranks of the French army. No one saw her for what she was, and in the clamour of the fighting no one enquired where she came from nor where she was born. For a year all went well. Never did the brave young woman flinch before the fire of the enemy; love gave her strength. In the greatest of dangers she was at the side of her spouse, who was as brave and fearless as she was. About the middle of 1812 a desperate struggle took place between the French and the English. The two spouses were among the former. The artilleryman saw all his comrades fall at his side. He remained alone with his wife to man the battery. The English mounted an attack, the two spouses impassively aimed the cannons and blew a horrible hole in the enemy ranks. They were, however, taken prisoner; and without anyone realising the sex of the young Spanish woman, she was sent with her husband to the prisons in Scotland. It was only at Perth that the truth came out.

'The deputy commandant Johnson [sic] was not moved by this touching story. He remained deaf to the sobs and prayers of the young woman and brusquely ordered her to prepare to leave Perth the next day. At those words she fell backwards—cold, blue, as if she had been struck by lightning. Alarmed, Johnson had her taken to hospital. The doctors declared it was an epileptic attack. Eight days later, when she had fully recovered, Johnson returned to present her with the same order. She immediately fainted and showed all the same symptoms as before. The attacks recurred on three separate occasions. Johnson at last was moved and allowed her to remain with her husband on condition she would be willing to accept half-rations. The young girl accepted with gratitude and stayed on in our room where she still was when I left Perth [in February 1814]. This admirable act of devotion of a woman who sacrificed her liberty to share the captivity of her spouse and who had recourse to a ruse to stay in the prison (for once she was allowed to remain at Perth she experienced no more attacks of the ailment which had enabled her to attain her objective) found few imitators.'[7]

The Andalusian hussar was not the only woman at, or at least accompanying prisoners to, Perth depot. The contemporary Perth historian George Penny, describing, as already mentioned, the arrival there of the first intake or division of prisoners on 6 August 1812, wrote: 'This division were in pretty good condition, and had some women with them.'[8] If Penny's reference to women is accurate then they could not have been among the seven women who, uniquely at any depot in Scotland, were actually listed in the General Entry Books for Perth. Four of these seven women did not arrive at the depot until 29 August, another not until 14 October, and the two others not until respectively 2 December 1812 and 9 January 1813. One of the seven women had her two infant girls with her. These seven women are each described in the Entry Books simply as 'Woman'. But some further information about them and their husbands, as well as the two infants, is contained in a large bundle of printed proformas, arranged in groups according to the dates of arrival of prisoners at Perth, which was an almost duplicate version of the information written into the General Entry Books.[9] The seven women and two infants were:

Charlotte Kaiserlich, No. 931 in the Entry Book, which shows she was born at Arras, was aged 29, and is described as 5 feet 2 inches tall, stout person, oval face, fresh complexion, black hair, hazel eyes, and with no marks or wounds. Charlotte had been 'captured by Lord Wellington's Army', but with no place or date of capture given in the Entry Book. It may have been at the fall of Badajoz on 7 April 1812, as prisoners listed immediately before and after her in the Entry Book were captured there. It is perhaps more likely, however, that she was captured with her husband, about whom the Entry Book says nothing but whom the printed proformas identify as No. 813, Christian Vanherff, a sergeant, 1st Battalion, Dutch Mineurs, captured at Almeida in Portugal on 11 or 18 May 1811. Vanherff, born at Maastricht ('Mastrick'), was aged 30. Charlotte and her husband arrived at Perth on 29 August 1812, evidently having marched there after being landed from HMS *Freya* at Kirkcaldy among 300 or so prisoners of war. Vanherff remained at Perth until he was discharged to Leith on 1 December 1813 for reasons and destination not stated. But he appears likely to have been one of twenty Dutchmen who that day, according to the *Edinburgh Evening Courant*, 'were marched off from the depot at Perth to join the large brigade of their countrymen presently forming in England, for the glorious purpose of assisting the independence of Holland.'[10]

Maria Roulette, No. 932 in the Entry Book, had no date or place of capture entered against her name there, nor is her husband identified. But the proforma listings show him to have been No. 814 Etienne Lantigny, a soldier, no regiment stated, who was captured at Coimbra in Portugal on 7 October 1810. So it seems likely those were also Maria's place and date of capture. Maria was born at Turin, was aged 21, and was said to be 5 feet 3 inches in height, of stout build, oval face, fresh complexion, black hair, hazel eyes, and with no marks or wounds. Her husband, aged 36, was born in Paris. Like Charlotte Kaiserlich and her husband they both arrived at Perth on 29 August 1812 and by the same means. Etienne Lantigny remained at Perth until he was released in June 1814 after the end of war.

Maria Lantigny, No. 935, is described in the Entry Book simply as 'Child', place of birth 'Unknown', age (blank). Some zealous official, apparently anxious to set down her description lest she might escape, had duly ascertained Maria's height to be 2 feet 1 inch, and that she was of stout person, oval face, fresh complexion, light hair, blue eyes, and with no marks. Her mother's name is not indicated in the Entry Book. Curiously, the child and her sister Anne (also referred to as Marie Ann) are not listed in the Entry Book directly after or before their mother, Maria Roulette, but after two other women, Rosa Maria and Maria Martin. But for the additional information provided in the printed proforma it might have been concluded they were daughters of Maria Martin.

Anne (or Marie Ann) Lantigny, No. 936, is likewise described as 'Child' and also of unknown place and date of birth. At precisely 2 feet she was an inch shorter than her sister, and was said to be of stout build, oval face, fresh complexion, light hair, hazel (or blue) eyes, and with no marks or wounds.

The two other women, Rosa Maria and Maria Martin, who like Charlotte Kaiserlich and Maria Roulette and her two children arrived at Perth depot on 29 August 1812 and by the same means, were respectively Nos 933 and 934 in the General Entry Book. Their place and date of capture are not entered there nor are the names of their husbands. The proformas, however, show they were the wives respectively of Joseph Hilene, soldier, 17th Regiment, and Etienne Le Brun or Lebrun, soldier, 13th Chasseurs.[11] Rosa Maria was born at Paris, was aged 30, and was described as 5 feet 2 inches tall, of slender build, long visage, fair complexion, black hair, blue eyes, and with no marks or wounds. Maria Martin, against whose name was pencilled 'Spanish Woman', and for whom no place of birth or age is entered, was also 5 feet 2 inches tall, of stout build, long visage, fair complexion, black hair, blue eyes, and with no marks or wounds.

Rosalie Millet, No. 2105, and described in the Entry Book like the preceding four simply as 'Woman', had been captured 'with the 28th Light Regiment' by Wellington's army at Badajoz on 7 April 1812. In the proformas (but not in the Entry Book) she is said to be the wife of André Millet, a sergeant 'in the 28th Regiment'.[12] Rosalie arrived at Perth on 14 October 1812 having evidently marched there with her husband, among more than 500 prisoners of war landed at Burntisland from the *Golden Fleece*. She was born in Paris, was aged 27, and was said to be 5 feet 2½ inches tall, well made, oval face, fresh complexion, black hair, blue eyes, and with no marks or wounds.

Neither Rosa Maria nor Maria Martin nor Rosalie Millet are shown in the Entry Book to have been issued with any bedding or clothing at Perth depot. But was the second hammock given her husband Etienne Le Brun three weeks after the one he had already received intended for use by Maria Martin?

Catherine Latyce (or Catherine Leliot, as she is named in the proformas), was captured by British forces at Madrid on 14 August 1812. Not the Entry Book, where she is No. 4520, but the proformas give her husband as Pierre Dervi, soldier, 15th Regiment (though in another column in the proformas he is said to have been in the 50th Regiment).[13] Catherine arrived at Perth on 2 December 1812, with her husband, having been landed at Burntisland and marched overland from there to the depot. Born at Arras, she was aged

30, and was described as 5 feet 6 inches tall, of stout build, oval face, dark complexion, black hair, hazel eyes, and with no marks or wounds.

Marie Manuel, also captured by British forces at Madrid on 14 August 1812, was said in the Entry Book, where she is No. 5611, to be in the 3rd Regiment of Artillery. Pencilled against her name is: 'Wife of Blaise Peuxe, No. 5668'. He was a *cannonier auxiliare* (auxiliary artilleryman) in the 75th Line infantry regiment and was also captured at Madrid on 14 August 1812.[14] Marie Manuel was born in Paris and was aged 25. She was exactly 5 feet tall, of stout build, long face, sallow complexion, brown hair, grey eyes, and had no marks or wounds. Her husband and she both arrived at Perth on 9 January 1813, having been landed at Burntisland from the frigate HMS *Freya*, evidently from Lisbon, and marched to the depot with other prisoners. Significantly, and unlike any of the other six women listed in the Entry Books at Perth, Marie Manuel is shown to have been issued with bedding, clothing and footwear: a hammock on her arrival at the depot on 9 January 1813, a jacket, waistcoat, trowsers (sic), and shirt a month later, another shirt on 16 November, and a pair of shoes on 3 December that year.[15]

If Marote-Carrier were not so positive that his Spanish woman hussar and her French artilleryman husband had already been at Valleyfield before being sent to Perth in September 1812, and that the husband was a Provençal (Blaise Peuxe's birthplace of Meulon given in the Entry Book has not been identified), and were it not that Marie herself according to the Entry Book was born in Paris (though it is possible, if unlikely, she was born there of Spanish parents), then it would be tempting to conclude the couple were in fact Marie Manuel and Blaise Peuxe.

No correspondence between the Transport Board and Captain Moriarty, RN, its agent at the depot, about the presence of these women at Perth has been found before the end of November 1812, almost four months after the earliest of them had arrived there. Replying in its letter of 1 December to Moriarty's of 26 November, the Transport Board told him: "Unless the Women mentioned by you be content to live with their Husbands in the Prison they must be sent by the return of the first Transport to Portsmouth in Order that they may be sent to France.' A letter that same day from the Board to Lieutenant Richard Glinn, RN, their agent for transport at Leith, informed him there were five women and two children at Perth depot, and asked Glinn to send them to Portsmouth 'by the first opportunity of a Transport proceeding thither', directly Moriarty applied to him for it.[16] There is an ambiguity in the correspondence which leaves it uncertain whether the women were already living within the depot with their husbands (and the two children with their father).

But there was no ambiguity about the Transport Board's order dated 1 December that the two children Lantigny and five of the seven women—

Charlotte Kaiserlich, Maria Roulette, Rosa Maria, Rosalie Millet, and Catherine Latyce or Leliot (who according to the Entry Book had arrived at Perth the day after the Board's order was signed)—were to be sent back to France via Portsmouth. All of them were accordingly sent away from Perth on 8 January 1813—except Catherine Latyce or Leliot, who was given a day's grace. 'This Woman,' says the proforma concerning her, 'was in such Fits that the Surgeon judged it improper to send her this day [the 8th]. Victualled for this day and tomorrow the 9th instant.' Charlotte Kaiserlich may, however, have been reunited with her husband at the end of that year, when he was released from Perth in order, it would appear, to return to Holland to fight for the Prince of Orange against Napoleon.[17]

What is not clear is why, at least according to the Entry Book, the two other women at Perth—Maria Martin and Marie Manuel—were able to remain at the depot until, with their husbands, they were released to France after the end of the war, on 1 June 1814. Is there a clue to an explanation for the different official view taken of their presence at the depot contained either in the recollection of Marote-Carrier about the Spanish woman 'hussar', or in the fact that alone of these seven women Marie Manuel was issued, according to the General Entry Book, with bedding, clothing and footwear? Even if those may suggest some explanation in Marie Manuel's case, what grounds were there for Maria Martin also being allowed to remain with her husband until the end of the war? These are merely a few among many other unanswered and apparently unanswerable questions concerning the prisoners in the depots in Scotland.[18]

The two little girls Lantigny at Perth, even if not themselves prisoners and if indeed they were actually living within the depot, appear to have been the youngest inmates of any depot north of the Border. Yet a few of the prisoners were themselves only half a dozen years older than those two girls. There were certainly some prisoners who, had they been living in the present century, would still have been attending primary, let alone secondary, school. The Napoleonic Wars were fought in an era when it was by no means uncommon for such very young boys and youths to serve in their country's armed forces and merchant navies.[19] Nor, of course, should it be forgotten that prisoners of war trudging out to Penicuik were passing more or less within sight of coal pits in Midlothian where even younger boys, and also girls, were then employed underground by coalmasters such as the Marquis of Lothian, the Duke of Buccleuch, Dundas of Arniston, and Clerk of Penicuik.

While conscription was applied in France and some other parts, such as Italy, of Napoleon's empire to young men aged between 20 and 25, that was one factor that ensured the great majority of the prisoners in the depots in Scotland were, as might be expected, between the ages of 20 and 40. There was, however, a not inconsiderable minority among them who were either younger than 20 or older than 40. What the proportions were of conscripts and of volunteers or regulars among the prisoners it is impossible to say. Privateersmen and merchant seamen were not conscripts (though some among them may have been deserters from the army or navy, or have gone to sea to escape conscription to them), and neither of course were all navy men or soldiers conscripts. Sergeant Major Beaudoin, the diarist at Greenlaw, for example, was as a volunteer far from being unique. Born in 1775 in the village of Batilly-en-Gatinais, the son of a wine grower, Beaudoin had volunteered at the age of 17 during the critical days of the French Revolution in September 1792, into the 3rd Battalion of the Département of the Loiret, which later formed part of the 31st demi-brigade of infantry of the Line and which in turn in 1804 became the 7th regiment of the Line. 'I enlisted at the age of 17,' Beaudoin recalled a few years before his death in 1864. 'At that time volunteers were asked to serve for six months—I did 22 years! The mayor had the job of arranging the enlistments. He put all the young people in one line on the [village] square and told them the rules of engagements. He then said, "I'll give my *bonnet rouge* to the first man who steps forward to enlist." A man named Champion was first; I and several others followed him. When I went home my mother said to me, "*Chacré chien*, you want to enlist, but you will have a hard time of it!". I saw later on she'd told me the truth.' There must have been many other prisoners in the Scots depots with experience of volunteering similar to Beaudoin's.[20]

Much the same difficulties in presenting so many other aspects of their lives arise also in tabulating the ages of the prisoners in Scotland. At Esk Mills, only the first 25 of all the 2,817 prisoners who entered its gates in February and March 1811 had their ages entered in its General Entry Book. It is, however, possible to find in the first three Entry Books for Valleyfield the ages of the great majority of the Esk Mills prisoners who were transferred there after the crisis of early March 1811, and in the Entry Book at Edinburgh Castle the ages of the other 461 simultaneously sent there. At Greenlaw, where separate Entry Books were devoted to each of what were ostensibly the several main nationalities among the prisoners, ages were in many cases not entered. Few of the 'Danes', none of the 'Dutch', 'Spanish' or 'Prussians', and far from all of the 'French' there had their ages recorded. Nonetheless the evidence in the Entry Books indicates at least the wide range of ages among the prisoners at Greenlaw, while for Edinburgh Castle, Valleyfield and Perth a fairly comprehensive picture of ages can be drawn.[21]

At Greenlaw, ages recorded for a small minority of 126 among the 'Danes' show:[22]

Age	Number of prisoners
10-14:	1
15-19:	9
20-24:	39
25-29:	34
30-34:	16
35-39:	11
40-44:	6
45-49:	5
50-54:	3
55-59:	1
60-64:	1
Total:	126

The youngest of those 126 'Danes' was Jan Stolls, aged 14, born at Memel (now Klaipeda in Lithuania). When the privateer *Prince Christian* was captured off Norway on 9 May 1811 Jan's position in her crew was Boy. When he arrived at Greenlaw a week later Jan was described as exactly 4 feet tall, of stout build, with an oval face, fresh complexion, light brown hair, hazel eyes, and with no marks or wounds. Of the nine other 'Danes' aged between 15 and 19, one was 16, one 17, three 18, and four 19. Hardly surprisingly, no fewer than 100 (79 per cent) were aged between 20 and 39. The oldest among the 126 was Claus Stevensen, aged 62, a seaman from *Albion* man-of-war, captured in May 1811 off Norway. Claus was a Norwegian, born at Bergen, 5 feet 3 inches tall, stout build, oval face, fresh complexion, grey hair, hazel eyes, and with no marks or wounds. He trudged into Greenlaw on the same day as the boy Jan Stolls, 48 years younger than him.[23]

An even smaller group at Greenlaw, all of whose ages, however, were entered in one of the 'French' Entry Books were the 48 American merchant seamen made captive after the outbreak of the War of 1812:[24]

Age	Number of prisoners
15-19:	5
20-24:	15
25-29:	10
30-34:	9
35-39:	3
40-44:	3
45-49:	3
Total:	48

Of the five aged 15-19, two were only 16. One was Pardon Cook, a seaman from the *Francis Ann* merchant ship, detained with the rest of the crew at Leith on 4 August 1812 and marched into Greenlaw with them on 19 October. Born at Dartmouth (whether Nova Scotia, Quebec, or Devon is unstated), Pardon was 5 feet 3½ inches tall, stout build, round face, black complexion, black hair, and black eyes, and in the prevailing attitudes of the era was described as 'A Black' in the Entry Book column headed Marks or Wounds. He was sent with most of the other American prisoners from Greenlaw to Leith on 3 December 1812, the first stage of their journey to a hulk or land depot in the south of England. The other 16-year old American was James Smith, a seaman from the merchant vessel *America*, detained in August 1812 at the Faroe Islands, and who also arrived, as did all these 48 Americans bar one, at Greenlaw on 19 October. James, born at Marblehead, Massachusetts, was 5 feet 1 inch in height, of 'stoutish' build, long face, fresh complexion, black hair, hazel eyes, and with smallpox scars. He, too, left Greenlaw for Leith on 3 December that year. All three of the oldest Americans were aged 47. One of them was Pelig Clark, a seaman from the merchant ship *Joseph Ricketson*, detained in the Faroes on 23 August. He, too, entered Greenlaw on 19 October and left it on 3 December for Leith. Born in Rhode Island, he was 5 feet 8½ inches tall, stout build, long face, fresh complexion, fair hair, grey eyes, and with a 'Speckle in Right Eye'.[25]

An analysis of the ages of the 905 prisoners in the only one of the three Greenlaw 'French' Entry Books where that information is given (at any rate for nine-tenths of those listed in it) shows:[26]

Age	Number of prisoners
10-14:	2
15-19:	21
20-24:	175
25-29:	226
30-34:	169
35-39:	130
40-44:	51
45-49:	21
50-54:	5
55-59:	6
60-64:	2
65-69:	4
No age given:	93
Total:	905

Of these prisoners no fewer than 700 (86 per cent of the 812 whose ages were stated) were, as might be expected, between the ages of 20 and 39. Of the four prisoners aged 65-69 two were 65, one 66, and the oldest, Armand Kreyer, 2nd captain of the privateer *Le Petit Edouard*, was 68. Captured on his ship in the North Sea in October 1811, he arrived at Greenlaw a month later. Born in Friesland in northern Holland, Kreyer was 5 feet 4½ inches tall, stout, with a round face, fresh complexion, bald, hazel eyes, and with no marks or wounds. He was sent off to Portsmouth in August 1812 for repatriation as an invalid. Since the average expectation of life for men in Western Europe in the early 21st century, 200 years after Armand Kreyer entered Greenlaw, has increased to 74 years, his age at 68 in 1811 would be equivalent nowadays to that of a much older man.[27]

At the other end of the spectrum of ages among those 'French' prisoners at Greenlaw were two ships' boys. One was Sven Larsen, who was 14. Born in Copenhagen, Sven was captured with the rest of the crew of the privateer *Le Figaro* in the North Sea in July 1811 and arrived at Greenlaw from Edinburgh Castle the following month. (His age had been entered in the Castle Entry Book as 'not quite 12').[28] Of slight build, he was 5 feet 1 inch tall, with an oval face, fair complexion, fair hair, and blue eyes. He was at Greenlaw only a month when he was released in order to join His Britannic Majesty's Navy. The other boy, and the youngest, so far as the Entry Book indicates, of all these 905 prisoners, was Michel or Martial Champagne or Champaigne, aged 12. Captured in the Bay of Biscay on the privateer *Comtesse Laure* on 1 November 1809, evidently when he was 9 or 10 years old, Michel was among the several hundred prisoners transferred from Esk Mills in March 1811 to Edinburgh Castle. From the Castle he was sent in mid-August that year to Greenlaw. Born at Blaye, Michel was 4 feet 11 inches tall, and said to be of stout build, with a round face, fresh complexion, dark brown hair, hazel eyes, and with no marks or wounds. Transferred to Valleyfield on 1 September 1812 he remained there less than three weeks before, according to the Entry Book, being sent to 'Leith for a passage to Plymouth'. That entry was, however, incorrect: he was in fact sent then as a servant to General De Boissi, on parole at Kelso.

Some ages do appear sometimes to have been brought up to date in the Entry Books with the passing of years of captivity. That Michel Champagne's age was said to be 12 in both the Greenlaw and Valleyfield registers almost three years after his capture indicates he had indeed been only 9 or 10 when he was captured—an indication apparently confirmed by his age being given in the Edinburgh Castle Entry Book in or around March 1811 as 10½. Thus in the year and a half between February 1811 and September 1812 this young boy endured captivity in Scotland in four successive confined depots and one parole town.[29]

❖

At Esk Mills, as already indicated, the ages of only the first 25 of the 2,817 prisoners confined there between the opening of the depot in February 1811 and its closure five weeks later were recorded in the depot Entry Book. But their ages can be gathered from the main Edinburgh Castle Entry Book and the first three Entry Books at Valleyfield. This collated information for Esk Mills indicates:[30]

Ages of the 461 sent in March 1811 to Edinburgh Castle and of the 2,486 sent in March-April 1811 to Valleyfield:

Age	Number of prisoners sent to Edinburgh Castle	Number of prisoners sent to Valleyfield
9:	Nil	3
10-14:	16	24
15-19:	51	144
20-24:	139	655
25-29:	106	594
30-34:	63	441
35-39:	26	200
40-44:	18	149
45-49:	9	84
50-54:	2	74
55-59:	Nil	54
60-64:	Nil	31
65-69:	Nil	5
70 +:	Nil	1
No age given:	31	35
Total:	461	2,494

Among the six oldest prisoners at Esk Mills was Pierre Marie Baladier, born at Calais and aged 65, lieutenant on *Le Renard* privateer, captured in November 1807. He was repatriated from Valleyfield to France in October 1811. Another of advanced years was Philippe Brasse, born at Havre de Grace and aged 67. He had been captured on the merchant vessel *Bergère* in the Mediterranean in April 1806. He, too, was repatriated from Valleyfield to France in October 1811.[31]

But the oldest prisoner at Esk Mills, and later at Valleyfield, appears to have been Joseph Jamesee (or Jamesse). He was aged 70. Born at Le Havre, he was a seaman on the privateer *Le Vengeur*, captured in October 1810 in the English Channel. He was 5 feet 2 inches tall, of stout build, with an oval face, fresh complexion, grey hair, hazel eyes, and with no marks or wounds. Joseph spent eight months in captivity at Penicuik, first at Esk Mills then at Valleyfield, before being repatriated to France in October 1811.[32]

At the other end of the age range, there were at Esk Mills before their transfer either to Edinburgh Castle or Valleyfield in March 1811 no fewer than 43 prisoners aged between 9 and 14 years. The three aged nine were all sent to Valleyfield. One was Michael Floriot, captured as a ship's boy aboard the privateer *Somnambule* in the English Channel in October 1810. Michael, born in Le Havre, was 4 feet 7 inches tall, with a round face, brown hair and grey eyes. After spending 18 months in captivity successively at the two Penicuik depots Michael was sent home to France in September 1812. So was another nine-year-old prisoner, Pierre Decrock, described as a seaman on the privateer *Comtesse d'Hambourg*, captured in October 1810 in the North Sea. Born at Dunkirk, Pierre was 4 feet 6½ inches tall, of stout build, with a round face, fresh complexion, light brown hair, hazel eyes, and with no marks or wounds. The third nine-year-old was Jean Renault Fleurette, described as a seaman, captured on *Le Temperaire* [? *Le Téméraire*] privateer in the English Channel in October 1810. Born at Brest, Jean was 4 feet 4 inches in height, of stout build (many of His Britannic Majesty's foes, even such youthful ones as these, had apparently developed their physiques well for the struggle), oval face, fresh complexion, light brown hair, hazel eyes, and with no marks or wounds. Jean was released from Valleyfield and sent home to France at the same time as his two fellow nine-year-olds.[33]

Of the 40 Esk Mills prisoners aged between 10 and 14, eight were 10-year-olds, 10 were aged 11, 11 were aged 12, three were aged 13, and eight 14. One of the 10-year-olds was Vincent Failés, born at Bordeaux and 5 feet tall, well made, with an oval face, sallow complexion, light brown hair, grey eyes, and no marks or wounds. Described as a seaman, captured at Finisterre three days after the battle of Trafalgar in October 1805 on the sloop of war *Hebe*, Vincent, transferred to Edinburgh Castle in March 1811 from Esk Mills, was issued the following month with a blanket and early in August with a pair of shoes. On what happened to him thereafter the Castle Entry Book is silent.[34]

But, as in all the depots in Scotland, the great majority of the prisoners at Esk Mills—2,224, or 77 per cent of all those whose ages were stated—were aged between 20 and 39.

At Edinburgh Castle the main Entry Book lists a total of 544 prisoners, of whom 461 came from Esk Mills in March 1811, and 83 from several other places between April and December that year. Of the 83, nine were recaptured escapers from the Castle itself. Excluding those nine, the ages of the remaining 74 when added to the table already presented above of the ages of the entrants from Esk Mills provide the following portrait of the ages of those 535 prisoners at the Castle during 1811, after which it ceased to be an ordinary depot:[35]

Age	Number of prisoners
9 or under:	Nil
10-14:	18
15-19:	61
20-24:	156
25-29:	124
30-34:	68
35-39:	30
40-44:	21
45-49:	11
50-54:	3
55-59:	Nil
60-64:	1
65 +:	Nil
No age given:	42
Total:	535

Some 3.6 per cent of the prisoners whose ages were stated were aged between 10 and 14: four were aged 10, two 11, four 12, four 13, and four 14. A further 12 per cent were aged between 15 and 19: four were 15, seven 16, seven 17, 16 were 18, and 27 were 19. One of those aged 10 was Jean Marie Harve (or Harvé), captured two years earlier as a ship's boy on the privateer *Point du Jour* in the English Channel in December 1808 (was he aged 10 then or perhaps only seven or eight?), and who arrived at the Castle from Esk Mills in March 1811. Born in Isle de Bas, Jean Marie was 4 feet 6 inches tall, with a round face, fresh complexion, light brown hair, brown eyes, and he was slightly pockmarked. He was issued with a blanket on 1 May and with shoes on 10 June 1811. The Entry Book provides no more information about him.[36]

At the other end of the spectrum, only one prisoner was aged 60 or more. He was Etienne Castel, aged 60, a seaman captured on the privateer *Le Figaro* in the North Sea in July 1811 and who with his shipmates arrived unusually speedily at Edinburgh Castle that month within four days of capture. Born in Sardinia, Castel was of stout build, with a round face, fresh complexion, grey hair, hazel eyes, and 'Lame third finger left hand & ruptured'. The issue to him of a hammock and a blanket on his arrival at the Castle is the only other information about him that the Entry Book gives.[37]

The great bulk of the prisoners were, however, aged between 20 and 39: 378 out of the total of 535 (or 76.6 per cent of all those 493 whose ages were stated).

At Valleyfield, where of the aggregate total of 7,650 prisoners some 5,165 arrived during the three and a quarter years after the intake in March and April 1811 of those from Esk Mills, the range of ages appears to have been:[38]

Age	Number of prisoners sent to Valleyfield from Esk Mills in March–April 1811	Number of prisoners entering Valleyfield after April 1811	Total
9:	3	4	7
10-14:	24	6	30
15-19:	144	202	346
20-24:	655	1,813	2,468
25-29:	594	1,328	1,922
30-34:	441	805	1,246
35-39:	200	400	600
40-44:	149	175	324
45-49:	84	74	158
50-54:	74	41	115
55-59:	54	20	74
60-64:	31	16	47
65-69:	5	4	9
70 +:	1	Nil	1
No age given:	35	281	316
Total:	2,494	5,169	7,663

Some 6,236 of the aggregate total of 7,650 prisoners (or 85 per cent of those whose ages were stated) at Valleyfield were aged between 20 and 39. But as in all the other Scots depots there were at opposite ends of the range of ages some old men and some very young boys. Of the seven prisoners aged 9 at Valleyfield, Michael Floriot, Pierre Decrock and Jean Fleurette have already been mentioned among those who came there from Esk Mills in March 1811. Three others of the seven were also captured on privateer ships. One was Jean Alvaretz, ship's boy on *Le Petit Edouard*, captured off Norway on 22 October 1811. Jean arrived at Valleyfield a week later. Born at Dunkirk, said to be 9½ years old, 4 feet 7 inches tall, of stout build, oval face, fresh complexion, brown hair, hazel eyes, and no marks or wounds, he was 'Discharged' from the depot, no date or destination given. Jean's shipmate from *Le Petit Edouard*, Henry Fockeday, also born at Dunkirk and also said to be 9½ years old, arrived with him at Valleyfield and was likewise 'Discharged', no details given. Henry was an inch shorter than Jean Alvaretz, of stout build, oval face, fresh complexion, light (? brown) hair, hazel eyes, and he had a few smallpox scars. The third privateer ship's boy was René (or Pierre) Vasseur, captured aboard the *Ravisseur* off the coast of Norway in February 1813 and who came to Valleyfield from Greenlaw in July that year. René, also born in Dunkirk, was said to be aged 9, 4 feet 4 inches tall, 'stoutish', with a round face, fresh complexion, light brown hair, light hazel eyes, and with some slight smallpox scars. He was repatriated to France at the end of August 1813 via HMS *Adamant* at Leith. The seventh 9-year old prisoner at Valleyfield, unlike the other six, was not a seaman or ship's boy but a soldier. He was François Vanderboom, described as a soldier in the 5th Regiment, captured in July 1809 at Campveere during the British landing on Walcheren. Born at Harlingen, François was 4 feet 8 inches tall, of stout build, with an oval face, fair complexion, brown hair, grey eyes, and no marks or wounds. Arrived at Valleyfield in September 1811 via the frigate HMS *Brune* along with 400 other prisoners from Plymouth, François was repatriated to France exactly a year later.[39]

Of the 30 other prisoners at Valleyfield who were aged between 10 and 14, five were aged 10, 12 were aged 11, nine 12, and four 14.[40]

Although aged 12 on his arrival at Valleyfield in October 1811 with over 100 other prisoners via HMS *Venus* from the Nore (and therefore probably from the hulks at Chatham), Jean Perrine, a boy captured in January 1807 on shore at 'Caracoa' (presumably Curaçoa in the Dutch West Indies), had possibly been at the time of capture younger than any other prisoner brought to Scotland. Assuming his age was amended in the Entry Books from time to time as the years of his captivity passed, Jean had presumably been only seven or eight years old when captured. Born at 'Dinand' [? Dinan in Brittany, or Dinant in Belgium?], Jean was 4 feet 8 inches tall, stout build, with a round face, fair complexion, light [sic] hair, dark brown eyes, with no marks or wounds. He remained in captivity at Valleyfield until after the end of the war and the general release of prisoners in June 1814. By then still only 14 years old, he had apparently spent half his life as a prisoner of war.[41]

The oldest prisoner at Valleyfield, as he had been at Esk Mills, was Joseph Jamesee (or Jamesse, as his name was spelled in the Valleyfield Entry Book), aged 70.[42] Of the nine who were aged between 65 and 69, four were aged 65, three 66, one 67, and one 68.[43]

Two examples at Valleyfield of the presence among the prisoners in the depots in Scotland of both some relatively old men and some boys of primary school age were provided in the case of the crews of two privateers, *Le Petit Edouard*, captured off the coast of Norway in October 1811, and *Ravisseur*, captured there in February 1813. *Le Petit Edouard* was said to have had five carriage guns or cannons and a crew of 35 men. Of the 35 at least 31 were together at Valleyfield: the ship's lieutenant, Benoit Saunier, 28 seamen, and the two 9-year-old boys, Jean Alvaretz and Henry Fockeday, already mentioned. Of the 28 seamen, the ages of two were not given in the Entry Book. Of the remainder, one was 17, two were in their twenties (respectively 23 and 26), two were in their thirties (30 and 36), five were in their forties (40, 42, 46, 48, and 49), six were in their fifties (two 56, three 58, and one 59), and no fewer than ten were in their sixties (one 61, three 62, two 64, two 65, one 66, and one, Jacob Kesamere from Strasbourg, aged 68). Given the great increase in average expectation of life in western Europe since those early years of the 19th century, a voyage by *Le Petit Edouard* must have borne some resemblance to a present day pensioners' outing, but with some of the places occupied by accompanying sons, grandsons, even great-grandsons. The crew of the *Ravisseur*, 35 of whom also found themselves at Valleyfield, had a not dissimilar range of youth and age. Their lieutenant, J.H. Dennis of Dunkirk, was 62, the 24 seamen included one aged 61, another 64, and four in their fifties; the steward was 62, the bosun 63, and the surgeon 64. On the other hand, there were four ships' boys (all of them belonging to Dunkirk) aged respectively nine (he was René Vasseur, already mentioned above), 10 (Joseph Olivier), and two who were 11 (Antoine Ghemar and C.J. Bomont).[44]

If at Valleyfield the presence of a sizeable proportion of seamen among the prisoners resulted in a widening of the range of ages, conversely the relatively small number of seamen at Perth reduced the range there. Ages at Perth (with the familiar reservations) appear to have been:

Age	Number of prisoners
9:	Nil
10-14:	5
15-19:	214
20-24:	2,418
25-29:	2,964
30-34:	1,301
35-39:	472
40-44:	216
45-49:	80
50-54:	25
55-59:	11
60-64:	4
65-69:	1
70 or over:	Nil
No age given:	28
Total:	7,739[45]

No fewer than 7,155 of the prisoners at Perth (or 92.7 per cent of all those whose ages were stated) were aged between 20 and 39. That was a distinctly higher percentage of that age group than at any of the other depots in Scotland. Conversely, the number and percentage of boys and youths at Perth was lower than at the other depots. At Perth there appear to have been 219 prisoners aged between 10 and 19, whereas of those aged from nine to 19 Valleyfield (which had virtually the same aggregate total of prisoners) had 383, and even Esk Mills (which held just over a third of the prisoners that either Perth or Valleyfield did) had 238. Similarly, Perth appears to have held only 41 prisoners aged between 50 and 70, whereas Valleyfield had 246 and Esk Mills 168. The explanation for these differences in the sizes of the various age groups was the presence at Perth of far more soldiers and far fewer seamen than was the case at either Valleyfield or Esk Mills.

At Perth, of the five prisoners aged between 10 and 14 years, one was said to be 10, two were 11, one was 12, and one was 14. The 10-year-old was Nicolas Le Roy, junior, a passenger on the privateer *Hirondelle*, of which his father was captain, when it was captured in September 1810 in the English Channel. Nicolas arrived at Perth in September 1812 from Valleyfield, which he had entered 18 months earlier from Esk Mills. He was 4 feet 11 inches tall, of stout build, with a round face, fresh complexion, brown hair, hazel eyes, and with some smallpox marks. The Perth Entry Book shows he was issued a month after his arrival there with a hammock and a bed, and in the following year with a shirt, a hat, a jacket, a waistcoat, trousers, another hammock, and a pair of shoes. But he remained a prisoner of war at Perth until after Napoleon's first abdication and the general repatriation of prisoners to France in June 1814. The accuracy of the entry for Nicolas's age raises yet again the question of the reliability of statistics drawn from the Entry Books. Clearly, Nicolas could not have been 10 when he entered Perth if he had been 10 when he had entered Valleyfield in March 1811. Had he in fact been 10 at the time of his capture in September 1810? At any rate, not unlike the boy Jean Perrine at Valleyfield, Nicolas was presumably 13 or 14 when at last he was released from a captivity in which he had passed almost four years of his young life.[46]

If Nicolas Le Roy was the youngest prisoner at Perth, the oldest was Jean Baptiste Ritkembourg, a seaman aged 69. Captured on the privateer *Le Pilotin* at 'Isle a La Land Baltic' (the Aland Islands in the Baltic) in October 1812, Ritkembourg arrived at Perth the following month. He was born at Ostend, was 5 feet 6 inches tall, of stout build, with an oval face, dark complexion, brown hair, hazel eyes, and with no marks or wounds. He remained at Perth until the end of the war and the general release of prisoners in June 1814, by which time he may have been 70 or 71 years old.[47]

A distinctive group of 21 mainly older men among the Perth prisoners were from the 1st Polish Infantry regiment. Captured in Calabria in Italy in July 1806, they arrived together from Portsmouth on 20 and 21 August 1812, in the second intake of captives at the depot. The ages of these Polish veterans in Napoleon's army were: five in their 20s (one 25, three 28, and one 29), one aged 35, 12 in their 40s (two aged 40, one 41, one 42, one 44, four 45, one 46, one 48, and one 49), and three aged 50. The older men among them may well have been fighting, and were almost certainly exiles from their homeland, for almost two decades following the final partition and extinction of Poland as an independent state in 1795.[48]

The presence among the prisoners of some very young boys had led to a decision on the subject by the Transport Board early in the war. 'It being particularly desirable from motives of humanity,' the Board declared in a letter of 4 December 1805 to Lieutenant General Hewitt of the Barrack Office, 'that the boys among the French prisoners of war ... should be kept in a building by themselves, separate from the men; and as from the great increase of prisoners of war in this country it will be necessary to erect an additional building for the boys in question, we have to request that you will be pleased to give the necessary directions for a sufficient spot of ground being allotted for this purpose ...'[49] This letter referred, however, not to boys in any depot in Scotland but to those in the one at Norman Cross in Huntingdonshire. Separate accommodation there for boys appears to have been duly built and occupied by 1807, as a description of the depot in June that year by a visiting vicar, the Rev. Robert Forby, stated: 'In particular the boys are kept apart and taught, so that in all probability their captivity is a benefit to them.'[50] Among British prisoners in France, too, boys appear, at least at Verdun, to have been kept in separate accommodation and were obliged to attend a school in that depot that was funded by contributions raised by officers 'and a few other benevolent men' among the prisoners.[51] But no evidence has been found of any provision of separate accommodation for boy prisoners at any of the depots in Scotland. Paul Andreas Kaald, the Norwegian privateer sea captain and diarist at Greenlaw, makes several comments about boys there but in no case is there any reference to their being in accommodation separate from the adult prisoners. On 21 July 1809, for instance, Kaald noted that 'a little French boy came here as prisoner. He had just come from Jamaica.' Kaald implies, however, that there was some schooling provided for boy prisoners at Greenlaw: 'Mr Wright [agent for the depot] and Mr Fraser [chief clerk] were up here today [16 September 1809] and [said] that the two small boys [are] to go to school in future.' Kaald himself seems to have taken a protective interest in the welfare of a boy who had been captured in 1808 with the rest of the crew while serving on board Kaald's own former ship *Den Kjaekke*, and who, along with 200 other Danish captives was sent away from Greenlaw on 22 May 1809: '... among whom was also the boy Sivert Wiggen, whom I took good care of; all that trouble I went to just to keep him with me, but it was really quite impossible.'[52]

Concerning boys as well as older men among the prisoners the Transport Board did, however, follow a policy that was applied, even if not always consistently, to those in depots in Scotland as well as elsewhere in Britain. As Kaald noted in his diary at Greenlaw on 27 September 1809: 'Mr Fraser [the depot clerk] was up here and wrote down all the boys' ages—those under 12 years of age and all the old over 50.' Fraser's list was part of the Transport Board's routine surveys of prisoners of those ages so that it might decide whether they could be released from captivity and repatriated. For in a circular eleven days earlier to all its depot agents, the Board had instructed them to 'transmit as soon as possible a list of all the Danish Boys under 12 years of age.' And indeed on 9 October the Greenlaw agent Malcolm Wright was ordered by the Board to release 28 Danish prisoners over 50 years of age and eight boys under the age of 12.[53] That was why and how young boys in the depots in Scotland, such as Michael Floriot, Pierre Decrock, Jean Fleurette, René Vasseur and François Vanderboom, all aged nine, and some old men, such as Joseph Jamesee, aged 70, whose case has also been mentioned above, came to be repatriated. There were, of course, exceptions. Explanations for these exceptions can only be surmised. Jean Perrine, for example, captured in 1807, probably at the age of only seven or eight, had to endure seven years in captivity before he was released at the end of the war, apparently still aged only 14. It may be that bureaucratic failures and delays in the early years of his captivity deprived him of repatriation. Once he reached his 12th birthday he ceased even to be eligible for possible release on grounds of age.

11

Race and Nationality

Pardon Cook, the seaman aged 16 detained at Leith with his shipmates from the American merchant vessel *Francis Ann* in the opening weeks of the War of 1812 between the United States and Britain, was one of an evidently small number of black prisoners in the depots in Scotland. Of the other 47 American merchant seamen detained in port or captured at sea and marched like Pardon Cook into Greenlaw depot in the autumn of that year, six were black. All were seamen in rank. All seven, including Pardon Cook, were entered in the Entry Book under the heading Marks or Wounds, as 'Black' or 'a Black'.[1]

At Greenlaw there were at least three other black prisoners. One was Jacob Smatt, a seaman captured on the privateer *Roland* off Norway in August 1809, and who appears to have come exactly two years later from Edinburgh Castle to Greenlaw, where he was described in the Entry Book in the language of the era as 'a Negro'. Two others were similarly described: Ferdinand Antonia, a seaman captured on the privateer *Le Vengeur* in the English Channel in October 1810, and Charles Gittet, a seaman from an 'uncertain' vessel, captured in September 1810. Both these men were transferred on 4 February 1811 from Greenlaw to Esk Mills.[2]

A few other black prisoners were confined at Edinburgh Castle, Valleyfield or Perth. At the Castle, in addition to Jacob Smatt, there was Abraham Daniel Levie, described in the Entry Book as 'Man of Colour'. He was a seaman, captured on the privateer *Le Ravisseur* off the coast of Norway in February 1813, and, via HMS *Adamant*, arrived the following month at the Castle. He left it a month later, having volunteered into His Britannic Majesty's Royal Navy.[3]

At Valleyfield there appear to have been seven black prisoners, of whom six had previously been in captivity at Esk Mills. Described, under Marks or Wounds, as 'Negro' were two American seamen, Isac (sic) Richard, captured on the privateer *Roy de Naples* in December 1810, and Charles Fille, taken prisoner on the privateer *La Tillise* in September that same year. Described as 'Mulato' was another privateersman, Jean Baptiste Moreau, captured in the West Indies in October 1810 on *La Caroline*. Likewise described was Dominique Chartran, a soldier in the 82nd Regiment, who had become a prisoner of war in February 1809 with the capitulation of French forces on Martinique. The last two of the six who came to Valleyfield from Esk Mills in spring 1811 were both seamen described as 'Negro'. One was Charles Soil, captured on the privateer *L'Aventurier* (on which Marote-Carrier was lieutenant) in December 1810 in the English Channel. The other was François Julien, taken prisoner on the merchant vessel *La Félicité*, no place or date given.[4]

The last prisoner described as Mulato found in the Entry Books at Valleyfield was Antoine Figaro, a young seaman, born in Mauritius and aged 18—which, if so, meant he could have been only 11 or 12 at the time of his capture on the man-of-war *Atalante* at the Cape of Good Hope in January 1806. Antoine Figaro's experiences as a prisoner of war were somewhat different from those of the other black prisoners at Valleyfield. He appears to have been landed at Leith in April 1812, one among the large number of parole prisoners transferred at that period from the south of England (in his case, from Launceston in Cornwall) to Scotland. He was sent from Leith to Hawick. Not himself entitled to parole as a mere rank and file seaman, Antoine Figaro was one of those fortunate few who were, however, granted parole because of their employment in captivity as servants to commissioned officers—in his case to Enseigne de Vaisseau Louis Préfort of the *Atalante*. What breach of parole was committed by Antoine Figaro at Hawick is not specifically recounted in the Transport Board archives but it seems likely to have been an attempt to escape. On 19 March 1813 the Board instructed William Nixon, its agent at Hawick, 'to send M. Figaro in proper custody to Valleyfield prison', and on 6 April Captain Andrew Brown, agent there, was instructed that Antoine Figaro was 'to be kept on short allowance to make good the sum of £3.6.0., the amount of expenses incurred in apprehending him and conveying him to Valleyfield.' Arrived there on 29 March, he is described in its Entry Book as 5 feet 5 inches tall, of slender build, with an oval face, sallow complexion, black hair and black eyes. On 8 November that year, by order of Admiral Otway at Leith, Antoine Figaro was sent to Portsmouth (presumably to the hulks) for breach of parole. If he remained there on the hulks until the end of the war several months later then his was another case of a youthful prisoner of war who by the time of his release had spent almost half his life in captivity.[5]

At Perth there appears to have been only one black prisoner. He was Charles Scharle, described in the Entry Book not even as a soldier but simply as 'Negro' in the 59th Regiment of the Line. Born in Jamaica and aged 38, Charles Scharle had been captured at Madrid upon its fall to Wellington's army in August 1812. He was 5 feet 2 inches tall, described as of 'thick' person, and with some smallpox scars. He remained in captivity at Perth from his arrival there on 3 December 1812 until the general release of prisoners in July 1814.[6]

In a war fought out in so many parts of the world between the rival imperialisms of Napoleon and of the successive Coalitions formed against him by Britain and other Powers between 1803 and 1814, the presence in the Scots depots of some prisoners from continents other than Europe who had been drawn willy-nilly into the conflict was hardly surprising. At Edinburgh Castle and Greenlaw successively there was a prisoner said (as usual, under the heading Marks or Wounds) to be 'an Indian' from South America. He was Manuel Roderique, a seaman captured on the privateer *Le Figaro* in the North Sea in July 1811 and who, landed at Leith with other prisoners from HMS *Plover*, arrived at the Castle only four days after his capture. Said to be aged 40, Manuel Roderique had been born at Pernambuco on the Atlantic coast of north-east Brazil. He was described as of stout build, oval face, very dark complexion, dark curled hair, and 'In appearance an Indian'. Transferred a month after his arrival at the Castle to Greenlaw (whose Entry Book described him as 5 feet 2¾ inches tall and aged not 40 but 58), he was discharged in October that year to Portsmouth, and thence presumably to France, as an invalid.[7]

Of racial discrimination there was abundant evidence at some of the depots or hulks in England, as well as in attitudes of the Transport Board and the Admiralty (and likewise of Napoleon's government) toward black prisoners. 'Being informed,' the Board wrote on 16 November 1803 to Sir Evan Nepean, then secretary of the Admiralty, 'that the French government have forced into their service all negroes found on board the British vessels which have been carried into the ports of that country, we think it proper to acquaint you for the information of the Right Honourable Lords Commissioner of the Admiralty that there are now confined at the several depots for prisoners of war in this country 65 negroes, who are chiefly seamen and fit for service; and we request you will signify their Lordships' directions for the disposal of them.' Nepean wrote on the bottom of the Board's letter: 'Orders to send them to the nearest King's ports to be put on to the flagships to be disposed of as the Admiral may desire.'[8] No such evidence of racial discrimination, apart from the entries 'Black', 'Man of Colour' and 'Mulatto' under the heading Marks or Wounds in the Entry Books, has been found at the depots in Scotland. But it would be naive to assume discrimination against black prisoners somehow never advanced north of the Border and that absence of evidence meant it was never practised in the Scots depots either by the depot authorities or among the prisoners themselves.

One prisoner who might perhaps have been expected to comment on black fellow prisoners, but who in fact did not commit to writing whatever thoughts on the subject he might have had, was the Greenlaw diarist Sergeant Major Philippe Beaudoin. Beaudoin had been one among the thousands of troops, many of them doomed to die there of yellow fever, sent in 1801-2 by

Napoleon to reconquer the French colony of St Domingo (Haiti) and reimpose slavery on its black population. Stationed at Brest, Beaudoin had watched the first expeditionary fleet sail away to St Domingo in December 1801. 'I saw them go,' he wrote, 'and as soon as the last one was gone I drank a bottle to celebrate that I hadn't been sent on the expedition.' But he was among the reinforcements sent six months later and he remained on St Domingo and took part in the fighting until the evacuation of the island by French forces and the capitulation of most of them to the British fleet at Cap St François in August 1803. Many of those who capitulated found themselves later in captivity in Scotland.[9]

Beaudoin himself had become seriously ill on St Domingo and like so many thousands of his fellow soldiers he almost certainly would have died there. But he was fortunate to receive the devoted care of a young woman named Sophie, whom Beaudoin describes as a Mulatto, and who saved his life. They fell in love and lived together. When evacuation of the French troops became essential Beaudoin arranged to take Sophie, disguised as a soldier, with him on board the transport ship but the plan miscarried and as a woman she was forbidden at the quayside to embark with the troops. Beaudoin fainted with shock. On his recovery he tried in vain to return ashore. 'At that moment,' he wrote in his diary afterwards of the setting sail of his ship amid shots fired at it by the advancing black troops, and of his grief at the certainty that he would never again see Sophie, 'I was more dead than alive.'[10]

It was no doubt the very small number of black prisoners in the depots in Scotland that helps explain the paucity of information about them, no less so since none of them is known to have left any account of his captivity there.

If there were confined in the depots in Scotland prisoners from several of the races of mankind, far more numerous were the nations, states or territories to which they belonged. It will already be plain as a pikestaff that by no means were all the prisoners French. How many or what percentage were French can be only a guesstimate. Taking all five depots in Scotland together, it is probable that between two-thirds and three-quarters of the prisoners in them were French. An exception, at least at times, was Greenlaw, given the presence of 1,000 or more 'Danes' among the net total of some 3,000 prisoners there during the decade to 1814, and the presence also as has been seen of 'Dutch', 'Prussian', 'Spanish', American, and other non-French prisoners. The proportion of Frenchmen at Greenlaw was at times less, even much less, than two-thirds. Whatever the exact number or proportion, there can at least be no doubt that the majority of the prisoners in Scotland were French, even at Greenlaw if its whole decade 1804-14 as a depot is taken into account, and even if at times within its walls 'Danes' were more numerous than French.[11]

A handful of prisoners, for reasons best known to themselves, refused to say where they had been born. One such at Perth, for instance, was Jean Norvant, a soldier from the 28th Light Infantry regiment, who was captured at Badajoz in April 1812 and arrived at Perth in September that year. He, according to the depot Entry Book, 'Will not inform of his nativity.'[12]

For much larger numbers of others no place of birth was recorded in the Entry Books because either it was not known or could not be established or, above all at Esk Mills, the depot clerks were so overwhelmed with intakes of prisoners that they could not find time to record such details.

The basis for any attempt to calculate the numbers of the different nationalities among the prisoners is the column in most depot Entry Books headed Place of Nativity. The usual difficulties confront attempts to calculate those numbers at Greenlaw, where that and some other information was not included in most Entry Books as they were of smaller format. At Esk Mills, although its Entry Book was large format, out of the 2,817 prisoners Place of Nativity was entered for only two (both born in Dunkirk). Even where, as in the large format Entry Books for prisoners at Valleyfield, Edinburgh Castle and Perth, the place of nativity or birth is almost always given, that place might not necessarily, however, determine nationality. It is no doubt regrettable, from the point of view of readers in the 21st century, that in none of the depot Entry Books was there a column headed Nationality. One among many illustrations of the consequent difficulty in establishing certainty about the nationality of at least some of the thousands of prisoners in the Scots depots will be seen in a page below, where at least 15 of those at Greenlaw described as 'Danes' are shown actually to have been born in Britain—at Lerwick in the Shetlands, but presumably of Danish or Norwegian parents or at any rate fathers. It was equally certain that some prisoners, even if their place of nativity was in, say, Germany, Italy, Spain or the Low Countries, were actually French and not Germans, Italians, Spanish, Dutch or Belgians (and no doubt in the case of some other prisoners, the converse was true). The numerous and extensive redrawings of parts at least of the political map of Europe since the Napoleonic era, and also the awakening then of national consciousness among some of the peoples of the continent, partly through the influence of the French Revolution but not least in, for instance, Spain, Germany, and Russia as a reaction against Napoleon's imperialism, moreover make attempts to establish the nationalities of at least some of the prisoners in the Scots depots fraught with dangers of anachronism. Germany and Italy, for example, in the early years of the 19th century were far from being unified states each with a single national government. In fact, Germany and Italy were still largely, as the Austrian chancellor Metternich was later to remark of Italy, each a 'geographical expression'. Napoleon markedly reduced the number of separate states in Germany and Italy in bringing as he did large parts of both areas under direct or indirect French control.

Nationalism in many areas of Europe was still then dormant or just beginning to stir. Until 1815, for example, the kingdom of Denmark included Norway and Iceland. Sweden still held western Pomerania across the Baltic on the German shore, and until 1809, when it lost it to Russia, possessed Finland, too. Belgium (or the Austrian Netherlands as it had been since 1715) from the 1790s was part of the French state, as was, if to a lesser degree, Holland. Most of the eastern littoral of the Adriatic had likewise become part of Napoleon's empire. Poland had altogether disappeared as a state in the 1790s, partitioned and swallowed up by its expansionist neighbours Russia, Prussia and Austria. In south-eastern Europe the Ottoman or Turkish empire continued to embrace all, or almost all, the territory that lay between the Black Sea and the Adriatic, and between Belgrade and Crete. Spain still possessed almost all central and south America, and Portugal Brazil, although historic changes in the political map of that vast sub-continent were beginning to develop as a result of Napoleon's invasion and occupation in 1808-13 of so much of the Iberian Peninsula.

With these among the more obvious reservations, the range of nationalities represented among the prisoners in the depots in Scotland nonetheless appears to have been extensive. Yet that range was hardly surprising. From the early years of the war, as already indicated, non-French troops were increasingly numerous in the Grande Armée and by 1812 formed more than half its strength. Captured ships' crews, too, were often by no means composed only of Frenchmen or 'Danes' or Dutchmen or indeed of men, youths and boys of any other single nationality.[13] The crew of *L'Aventurier*, for example, the privateer on which Marote-Carrier was lieutenant, included at least two Swedes, a black American, and a Norwegian. Random selections of at least some of the better known places in Europe and elsewhere in the world where prisoners had been born are presented in Appendix 6 below and illustrate the apparent range of nationalities.

After the French the next largest group of prisoners in the Scots depots appears to have been 'Danes'. The 'Danes' were mainly Danes and Norwegians.[14] But the Entry Books show the Scots depots (as no doubt those, and the hulks, in England) also included some prisoners taken from among the other Scandinavian peoples. Between 1807, when Denmark entered the war as an ally of Napoleon against Britain, and 1810-11, when it appears that successively in May 1810 and April 1811 about 500 'Danes' were transferred from Greenlaw to Chatham and Portsmouth, a sizeable proportion of all the 'Danish' prisoners in Britain were confined at that Scots depot.[15] Indeed, as already indicated, Greenlaw's two Entry Books for 'Danes' show 869 had passed by the end of 1810 into captivity there.[16] In addition a few prisoners entered in the 'French' and 'Dutch' Entry Books for Greenlaw, as well as a few among the 'Prussian' prisoners confined there in 1806, were in fact 'Danes' or other Scandinavians. Thus, for example, some 'Danes' were among the crew of the Dutch frigate *Utrecht* who were confined for a short time at Greenlaw after the vessel was wrecked in February 1807 on the shores of Orkney.[17]

At the other depots in Scotland, too, the Entry Books indicate there were prisoners who were Danes, Norwegians, or other Scandinavians. Jean Talise Simonsen, for example, born at Christiansand in Norway and aged 23, who was captured as a seaman (or bosun) in December 1810 on the *Mameluke* privateer off Dover, was one of the *mauvais sujets* sent on 4 March 1811 from Esk Mills to Edinburgh Castle. At Valleyfield, Sylvanus Peters was a Norwegian seaman captured off the coast of his homeland in October 1811 on the privateer *Le Petit Edouard*. He was released home in August 1812, presumably on grounds of age as he was 65.[18] And at Perth, where there were relatively few prisoners from any of the Scandinavian countries, a Norwegian transferred there in September 1812 from Valleyfield (to which he had come from Esk Mills) was Suven, Suren or Sven Jacobsen. Aged 28 and 6 feet and half an inch tall, he was a lieutenant on the privateer *Héro du Nord*, captured in December 1810 in the North Sea. He was discharged in December 1813 to Leith.[19]

If Danes and Norwegians were easily the most numerous of the Scandinavian prisoners in the Scots depots, there were certainly a few Swedes, Finns, Icelanders, Faroese and Greenlanders there, too. Iceland, like Norway, the Faroes and Greenland, was part of the kingdom of Denmark but was cut off from the latter in 1807-14 through the mastery of the seas by Britain, which, however, allowed Iceland full self-government in the latter years of the war.[20] Of 27 Icelanders, Faroese and Greenlanders who were prisoners of war in Britain in April 1810, several were confined at Greenlaw. One was Marius Christian, a seaman captured on the merchant vessel *Fryhling* off Norway in September 1807, who remained at Greenlaw from shortly after his capture until his release 'as native of Iceland' early in April 1810. Two others, Jens Linden Gero, a carpenter on the *Fryling*, and Jacob Johanesen from the *Jonge Jacob*, were released from Greenlaw for the same reason on the same day as Marius Christian.[21] A further 14 Icelanders were released from Greenlaw in March 1811 'to assist in navigating the Iceland vessels *Regina* and *Orion*, but no prisoners of any other description are to be released for this purpose.'[22] As for Greenlanders, Captain Paul Andreas Kaald, the Norwegian diarist at Greenlaw in 1808-10, recorded on 29 November 1809 that '14 prisoners of war, all from Greenland, came here. They were bound for Kristiansund, but about 5 or 6 miles from the island were taken by the English brig *Fancy*.'[23] Some thirty other Greenlanders were the subject of an act of humanity by the Admiralty and Admiral Otway, Royal Navy commander based at Leith, in the midst of the war in October 1811. 'Rear Admiral Otway ... having by his letter of 30th ult. transmitted to my Lords Commissioner of the Admiralty a list of persons, passengers, found on board a Danish brig which had been detained and sent into the port by HM's sloop *Rifleman*, who state themselves to have been inhabitants of Greenland and obliged at any risk to quit that country in consequence of the great scarcity prevailing of every article of provision, which had reduced them nearly to a state of starvation; I ... acquaint you that the Rear Admiral has been directed to send them in a flag of truce to Tonningen by way of Heligoland.' The group of thirty included four men each described as 'chief of a factory', the wives of two of these men, and their five children.[24]

At least 15 of the 'Danes' at Greenlaw had been born in Scotland, presumably of Danish or Norwegian parents or at any rate fathers, in Shetland at Lerwick. One of them was Hendrick Beeken, master of the merchant ship *Havneren*, captured in the North Sea on 30 September 1808 and who arrived five weeks later at Greenlaw. Another was Anders Andersen, 2nd captain of the privateer *Mars*, captured in the North Sea on 3 May 1808, and who arrived three days later at Greenlaw. The other 13 were seamen: three captured on the *Mars*, two on the merchant ship *Scarvan* in the North Sea in December 1808 and who came to Greenlaw in February 1809, one captured on the privateer *Einighiden* off Iceland in April 1808, who arrived in Greenlaw the following month, and the other seven on the man-of-war *Albion*, captured in the North Sea in May 1811 and who entered Greenlaw that month.[25]

Sweden, though an ally of Britain from 1805 until the end of the war (apart from a period of some 18 months in 1810-12, when the French marshal Bernadotte had been newly elected its crown prince and before he had re-allied Sweden with Britain and Russia), nonetheless had a few of its subjects held captive in Scotland. They had been taken prisoner by the British navy while serving as seamen on board 'Danish', Dutch, or other enemy ships. As early as July 1803 an unnamed seaman (or possibly passenger) 'From the King of Sweden's dominions' who had been on board one of three Dutch ships captured by the British privateer *St Joseph*, was landed at Ullapool with 86 other prisoners and marched across country to Fort George from which, it appears, he was soon afterward repatriated.[26] At Greenlaw seven prisoners entered in one of the two registers of 'Danes', nine entered in the list of 131 'Prussians' marched there between June and November 1806, and a further seven entered in one of those purporting to be of French prisoners, proved to be Swedish subjects and were repatriated, as also were, it appears, seven or eight at Valleyfield.[27] An active part in securing their release from the depots was played by the Swedish consul-general in London, Claes Grill.[28]

There appear also to have been a few Finns among the prisoners in the Scots depots. At Greenlaw, where the evidence is contradictory, there were apparently six—of whom four were, or may have been, repatriated in 1810-11 but the other two appear to have been transferred then to Chatham, presumably to the hulks there.[29]

Germans formed another sizeable group among non-French prisoners in the depots in Scotland. Within three months of the resumption of war, more than half the 87 prisoners taken by the British privateer *St Joseph* on board 'three Dutch Greenland ships' who were landed at Ullapool and marched overland into captivity at Fort George proved to be Germans—24 of them from 'the King of Prussia's dominions', and a further 27 from the smaller German states of Oldenburg, Osnaburg (Osnabruck), Hamburg and Bremen.[30]

At Greenlaw, 32 prisoners sent to Leith early in July 1804 as volunteers into the Royal Navy were said to include Prussians.[31] The 131 'Prussian' seamen sent from Leith into captivity at Greenlaw between June 1806 and February 1807 as a result of the war declared by Britain on Prussia during those months proved, as has been seen above, to include nine Swedes and, it seems, three from the neutral German state of Oldenburg; and it would be surprising if there were not also included among them a few Danes, Norwegians, and Dutch. But the great majority of the 131 were at any rate Germans, if not for certain all Prussians.[32] Among the prisoners listed in the depot's two 'Danish' Entry Books were at least thirty whose places of birth indicate they, too, were German. On 9 May 1809 Captain Paul Andreas Kaald recorded in his diary that 'Today 21 Danish, Norwegian and German prisoners came here.' A few days later, Kaald wrote: 'Today, 15th, when the prisoners were out to collect water a Prussian deserted. He was immediately pursued. After half an hour and a quarter of a mile from here, he came so near to them that they shot him. The bullet went in the back and came out again under the breast. With this shot he fell. The poor man was to be pitied that he met his death in such a way, instead of his freedom.'[33] Some Germans appear to have been among the prisoners at Greenlaw until virtually the end of the war. One fortunate to be confined there only for a couple of months in 1811 was Frederik Smitt, aged 58 and born in Konigsberg in East Prussia, who was captured on the privateer *Klempa* off Norway in May that year, arrived a few days later at Greenlaw, spent most of June in the depot hospital, but in mid-July was released 'To assist in Navigating a Lobster Vessel, per Order of Commissioner Bowen' of the Transport Board.[34]

There were also Germans among the prisoners at Edinburgh Castle, at least during 1811, as was indicated by such places of birth in the Entry Book as Hamburg, Cologne, Franconia, Konigsberg, Oldenburg, Lübeck, Hanover and Pappenburg. One, for example, who came in November that year to the Castle from Greenlaw along with seven other seamen was Jean Baptiste

Zoutin (or Soutin), aged 21, born in Oldenburg. Zoutin was one of the 14 prisoners who escaped from the Castle on the night of 18-19 December 1811 by means of a rope over the Devil's Elbow. The other 13 were recaptured, but Zoutin appears to have got away successfully. It was this escape which proved the last straw for the Admiralty, which a few days afterward ordered the Castle 'entirely abolished' as a depot for prisoners of war.[35]

Despite the virtually complete absence of places of birth in the Esk Mills Entry Book, it is certain there were some German prisoners there, given relevant entries in the Books for Edinburgh Castle and Valleyfield, to one or other of which all the Esk Mills prisoners were transferred in March-April 1811. At Valleyfield, birthplaces of some of the approximately 2,400 prisoners who came then from Esk Mills included Konigsberg, Hamburg, Oldenburg, Mayence (Mainz), Prussia, Berlin, Danzig, Bremen, Emden, Hanover, Leipzig, and Stettin. One German seaman from Esk Mills who was repatriated, presumably on medical grounds, after only six or seven months' captivity at Valleyfield was Frederick Sprenger, aged 27, born in Oldenburg, who had been captured in 1810 on the privateer *La Pomme Rouge*. Whether before, at the time of or since his capture is unstated, but Sprenger had lost his right hand. Another German seaman, also born at Oldenburg, who like Frederick Sprenger came from Esk Mills but unlike him remained for ever at Valleyfield, was Johann Vandenberg, captured on Marote-Carrier's privateer *L'Aventurier* in the English Channel in December 1810. Vandenberg died at Valleyfield on 22 April 1812 and was buried there.[36] Of Germans who arrived at Valleyfield after the intakes from Esk Mills, birthplaces entered in the depot registers included Prussia, Westphalia, Hamburg, Kozenau, Stettin, Hanover, and, logically enough, 'Germany'. But it was of Hesse-Darmstadt that by far the largest group of Germans at Valleyfield were natives. They were the 200 soldiers of the Hesse-Darmstadt regiment transferred in July 1813 from Perth depot.[37] Notable among the German and several thousands of other prisoners of various nationalities at Valleyfield, almost all of whom were drawn from those lower social classes which twenty years earlier Edmund Burke, in his *Reflections on the French Revolution*, had been pleased to refer to as a swinish multitude, there appeared briefly in the summer of 1812 a Prussian aristocrat. Baron Frederick de Lynkersdorft, a captain in the 1st Prussian Regiment, who had been captured at Flushing in August 1809, arrived at the depot in mid-June 1812 from Selkirk, where he had been on parole. Aged 40, 6 feet tall, said to be of stout build, with an oval face, fresh complexion, brown hair, grey eyes, and, perhaps appropriately for a Prussian officer, a scar over his left eye and on his left cheek, the Baron for reasons unstated was repatriated on 31 August.[38]

By the spring of 1813, with the disastrous defeat of the Grande Armée in Russia, the formation at Kalisch on 28 February of an alliance between

Prussia and Russia, and the declaration of war and mobilisation by Prussia against France, the British government through the Admiralty and the Transport Board was preparing to recruit sizeable numbers of Prussian and other German prisoners of war in the depots to the allied cause against Napoleon. On 12 March the Transport Board sent a confidential circular to all its depot agents instructing them to 'report with the least possible delay for the information of the Lords Commissioner of the Admiralty the number of Germans and Italians respectively among the prisoners in your custody.' On 10 July, the Transport Board reported to the Admiralty there were 238 German prisoners at Valleyfield. A month afterward, in reply to questions by the War Office, the Board reported that 627 German prisoners of war had been assembled at Valleyfield, though it was unable to say how many of them were 'fit for service'. No fewer than 389 Germans, including the 200 soldiers of the Hesse-Darmstadt Regiment, had thus by August been transferred from Perth to Valleyfield.[39]

At Perth, almost exactly half of the first batch of 399 prisoners to arrive at the depot on 6 August 1812 were German soldiers from the Hesse-Darmstadt regiment, captured at the fall of Badajoz by Wellington's forces in April that year.[40] It was they, along with a further 200 or so Germans who followed them during the succeeding twelve months into captivity at Perth, who were transferred in July 1813 to Valleyfield. It was probably in the spring of 1813 that the depot clerks at Perth, instructed to list all German prisoners there, pencilled here and there against names in the four Entry Books the word 'German'. A glance at Appendix 6 below will show a few of the places in Germany to which these prisoners belonged (or at least where they had been born), including Oldenburg, Hamburg, 'Ex la Chapel' (Aix la Chapelle), Berlin, Speier, Diens, Cologne, Coblentz, Düsseldorf, Hanover, Hesse, Baden, Treves (Trier), and Kaiserslautern. A German who remained less than a year at Perth before being invalided home in August 1813, was Jean Keller, aged 39 and born at Dockbac, of the Hesse-Darmstadt regiment, captured in April 1812 at Badajoz.[41] A German soldier from the same regiment who died at Perth on 28 October 1812 only two weeks after his arrival and was buried there, was Gaspard Potpaune, aged 23, born at Ampt Asfeld, and captured, too, at Badajoz in April 1812.[42] A few of the Germans at Perth were seamen. Frederik Boelard, for example, 1st lieutenant of the privateer *Barbier de Seville*, captured in November 1810 in the English Channel, who came to Perth in September 1812 from Valleyfield, was aged 29 and was said to have been born at 'Rotterdam proper place of Nativity Altona', near Hamburg. He was discharged to Leith in December 1813.[43]

Italians were at least as numerous as Germans among the prisoners in the depots in Scotland. As 142,000 young Italians were conscripted, and a further 44,000 volunteered, into the army of Napoleon's satellite kingdom of Italy (which embraced the entire north-east of that country) between 1805 and 1814, and there were also numerous soldiers and seamen in the French imperial forces who were drawn from other Italian states, it was hardly surprising that several hundreds of them should find themselves in captivity in Scotland.[44]

At Greenlaw, although as usual the evidence is less clear than for most of the other depots, there were some Italians in captivity. One born in Piedmont was Pierre Savasse (or Philippe Lavasse), a soldier aged 35, who had been captured aboard a warship at the battle of Trafalgar in October 1805. He arrived at Greenlaw in September 1811, spent a month soon afterward in hospital at Valleyfield but died at Greenlaw on 26 May 1812 and was buried there. Another soldier, also, it seems, an Italian as he was born at 'Salust' (presumably Saluzza, in Piedmont) but who did not remain long at Greenlaw, was Anton Ansalde of the 82nd regiment. He had been captured at Vigo in March 1809 and arrived at the depot in September 1811. He escaped on 29 November, two months after his arrival. Another Italian who remained in the depot only a couple of months was Etienne Castel, a seaman born in Sardinia, aged 60, captured on the privateer *Le Figaro* in July 1811, who came to Greenlaw in August that year after a month at Edinburgh Castle, but who presumably because of his age, rupture and other disabilities was discharged in October to Portsmouth, for a passage home as an invalid. In at least one of the 'French' Entry Books for Greenlaw places of nativity are given which, including as they do Naples, Tuscany, Venice, Turin, and Milan, as well as Sardinia and Piedmont, indicate the presence at the depot of numbers of other Italian prisoners.[45]

From Esk Mills to Edinburgh Castle in March 1811, and later that year from the Castle to Greenlaw or Valleyfield and in some cases eventually to Perth depot, trudged some other Italian prisoners. In 1813 still others arrived at the Castle from Valleyfield, Perth, and the south of England. The places of birth of men in these two inflows to the Castle included Naples, Toscane (Tuscany), Turin, Venise (Venice), Rome, Sardinia, Genoa, Piedmont, and Ancona. Among Italians who passed via the Castle to Valleyfield was Frederick (or Ferdinand) Periano or Pejrano or Peyreano, born in Genoa and aged 28, a surgeon on the privateer *Sans Peur* when captured in the Mediterranean in June 1810. He arrived at the Castle from Perth in July 1813, passed on after a few days to Valleyfield and remained there until his release at the end of the war in the following March.[46] From Perth to the Castle also briefly in November 1813 came Sergeant Major François Le Prince, born at Turin and aged 39. Le Prince, whose regiment or corps is entered simply as 'French army' but is elsewhere said to have been the Calabrian Guards, had been captured in July 1806 in Calabria. He was 5 feet 6 inches tall, of stout build, with a long face, sallow complexion, brown hair, grey eyes, and a scar on the right side of his mouth. By order of Admiral Otway at Leith Le Prince was sent from the Castle three weeks after he had entered it, to Portsmouth—presumably to the hulks there, as he had committed a 'breach of parole'.[47]

Valleyfield and Perth together in mid-1813 apparently held 644 Italian prisoners. That total was established as a result of the Transport Board's confidential circular of 12 March 1813 to all its depot agents which sought the number of Italians and Germans in their custody. By 10 July the Board was able to inform the Admiralty that at Perth there were 463 Italians and at Valleyfield 181.[48] Among Italians at Valleyfield who had come there from Esk Mills in March 1811 places of birth included Venice, Genoa, Savoy, Leghorn, Sardinia, Messina, Milan, Modena, Ancona, Pavia, Rome, Florence, Parma, Naples, Bergamo, Asti, Brescia, Piedmont, and Turin; and birthplaces of those who came to Valleyfield after the intakes from Esk Mills included also Montebello, Verona, 'Carawaga' (? Caravaggio), Marengo, and Sicily.[49] Among Italians at Valleyfield who had come there from Esk Mills, was Diego Maglione, captain of the privateer *L'Anonciade*, captured in the Sicilian Channel (Straits of Messina) in September 1809. Born in Naples, he was aged 45. He was among the 66 prisoners, almost all privateersmen, transferred to Perth in September 1812.[50] An Italian with a relatively unusual function or rank among the prisoners in Scotland was Jean Tépateau, aged 36 and born in Piedmont, described as a waggoner in the 6th Regiment, who had been captured, no date given, in Portugal, and who in September 1811 arrived at Valleyfield, where he remained until the end of the war. Three Italians were among the oldest and youngest prisoners at Valleyfield. One was Joseph Guariano, born at Genoa and aged 62, a seaman captured on *La Dorade* privateer in March 1808. He was repatriated, no doubt on grounds of age, in October 1811. The second was Antonio Signori, aged 61 and born in Bergamo, a soldier in the 2nd Italian Regiment, who had been captured off Corfu in October 1809. He, too, was repatriated, also presumably on grounds of age, in August 1812. Thirdly, there was Martin Robiche, aged only 11 and born in Venice, who was serving as a boy on board the man-of-war *Friedland* when captured in December 1807. If Martin was 11 when he came to Valleyfield from Esk Mills in 1811 then he had been only seven or eight at the time of his capture. Said to be of stout build, 4 feet 11 inches in height, with an oval face, fresh complexion, dark brown hair, grey eyes, and with no marks or wounds, he was one of those boys under the age of 12 who nonetheless failed to win release on grounds of age, for he remained a prisoner at Valleyfield until the end of the war in March 1814.[51] Several other Italians never did leave Valleyfield: they died and were buried there. One was Giovanni Boldrini, aged 20 and born in Verona, a soldier in the 3rd Italian regiment who had been captured in 1809 in the Gulf of Venice and who came in March 1811 from Esk Mills to Valleyfield, where he died six months later.[52]

The largest group of Italian prisoners in Scotland—some 463 of them—was, as has been seen, at Perth. Their places of birth, besides many less well known ones, included Milan, Pavia, Vicenza, Modena, Turin, Piedmont, Parma, Asti, Pisa, Genoa, Florence, Marengo, Sicily, Rome, Naples, Tuscany, Leghorn, Romagna, Como, Fori, Padua, Verona, Montebello, Siena, Tivoli, Legnano, Pistoia, and Alessandria.[53] In some cases place of birth may have denoted a kingdom (such as Naples or Sardinia), rather than the city or island of the same name. The Romans among those prisoners included Jacques Paccini, lieutenant, 1st Italian Horse, who had been captured in Catalonia in January 1811. Arrived at Perth in September 1812 from Valleyfield, where he had been sent three months earlier for a breach of his parole at Biggar, Paccini, aged 26, was transferred in November 1813 to Edinburgh Castle, and from there that same month to the hulks at Portsmouth.[54] One of the tallest prisoners at Perth was an Italian from Vicenza: Ambrose Bellrose, 6 feet 2 inches, of stout build, oval face, fresh complexion, light hair, blue eyes, and with no marks or wounds, a soldier aged 27 who had been captured on board an unnamed transport vessel in the Mediterranean in April 1809, who arrived at Perth in the second batch of prisoners to enter the depot in August 1812, and who was sent a year later to Valleyfield.[55] Another Italian among the second batch of prisoners to arrive at Perth in August 1812 but who was one among several of his fellow countrymen whose last resting place the depot proved, was Joseph Rouvsere (or Rouvière), aged 27, a soldier captured on the naval sloop *La Créole* at Dominica in January 1807. Rouvsere died at the depot on 25 May 1814, after the war had ended, and was buried there.[56] An Italian soldier at Perth who was one of 'King Joseph's Guard' captured at the fall of Madrid to Wellington's army in August 1812, and who arrived, as has been seen, at the depot in December that year was Barthelemy Bellus, born in 'Gropo Genoa'.[57] Whether Ignacia de Simone remained until then too is not certain: a sergeant major captured at Ischia Castle (no date given but probably some time between 1806 and 1809), he appealed to the Transport Board in March 1813 to be released 'By virtue of a capitulation entered into between General Stuart and Prince Stigliano that all Neapolitans should be exchanged and sent home. States he is the only one remaining in this country.'[58] One of the seven women who accompanied their menfolk among the prisoners to Perth depot, was, or appears to have been, Italian: Maria Roulette.[59]

Dutch prisoners were also numerous in the depots in Scotland and some, as has been seen, were among the earliest to be made captive at the resumption of war in 1803. They found themselves confined at first in the Edinburgh bridewell until Greenlaw was opened as a depot on 31 March 1804. Greenlaw's separate Entry Book for Dutch prisoners listed 97 captured between July 1803 and August 1804, all of them seamen except for

a dozen marines and soldiers.[60] Several of the 97 were almost certainly not
Dutch but Scandinavian, Belgian or German. On the other hand, there were
among the depot's five separate Entry Books for 'Danes' and 'French' some
prisoners who were, or appear to have been, Dutch.[61] Other Dutch prisoners
found themselves in later years at Greenlaw. Among them was Jan Bernick,
an elderly seaman aged 65, born in Amsterdam, who was captured in August
1811 off the coast of Holland on 'French Gun boats'. Of stout build, 5 feet 4¼
inches tall, with an oval face, good complexion, hazel eyes, light brown hair
(but also described as bald), he was transferred to Valleyfield in September
1812. Another even older Dutch seaman already encountered at Greenlaw
was Armand Kreyer, aged 68 and born in Friesland.[62] A Dutch seaman who
died from consumption in December 1810 and was buried at Greenlaw was
Volkert Ares, born in Amsterdam and aged 54, captured on an unspecified
ship in the North Sea two months before his death.[63]

There were also Dutch prisoners at Esk Mills and Edinburgh Castle. At the
latter a seaman named Gesima, a 'native of Holland', volunteered in August
1811 to join the British navy and was released from captivity to become a
member of the crew of HM's sloop *Nightingale*.[64] Fellow countrymen confined
in the Castle who followed Gesima's example in joining the British navy included in April 1813 some 13 members of the crew of the privateer *Ravisseur*,
captured in February that year off the coast of Norway. Two of the 13 were
B. Bontaus, prizemaster, born in Friesland and aged 32, and Jan Latx, bosun's
mate, born in Amsterdam and aged 27. Daniel H. Hoft, a seaman aged 30
and born in Leiden, another Dutch member of the *Ravisseur*'s crew, gave the
depot authorities a run for their money before he, too, volunteered into the
British navy. He escaped from the Castle on 2 April 1813 but was recaptured
and brought back next day, and three days later was released from captivity at
the Castle to join the navy.[65] At Esk Mills there were Dutch prisoners whose
places of birth included Amsterdam, The Hague, Rotterdam, Utrecht, Breda,
Delft, Maastricht, Middleburg, Friesland and, appropriately, 'Holland'.[66] One
of the natives of Amsterdam was Gilus Gronewoud (or Gilles Gronwoud),
described as a seaman, who was aged 11, and who had been captured on the
privateer *Héro du Nord* in October 1810 in the North Sea. Said (almost inevitably) to be of stout build, 4 feet 10½ inches in height, with an oval face,
fresh complexion, light hair, blue eyes and with no marks or wounds, this
youthful warrior was transferred with the great majority of other Esk Mills
prisoners in March 1811 to Valleyfield. Another Dutch boy in captivity first
at Esk Mills then at Valleyfield was also a native of Amsterdam: Roelf Van
Weltingen, also aged 11, captured in October 1810 in the North Sea while
serving as a ship's boy on the privateer *Sans Souci*. Of slender build, 4 feet
9 inches tall, with an oval face, fresh complexion, light hair, blue eyes, and
with no marks or wounds, Roelf was released and repatriated in September

1812, presumably as a boy under age. Another Dutch seaman at Esk Mills was Daniel Vilser, alias David Fisher, born in Amsterdam and aged 53, who had been captured in the English Channel, no date given, on a prize to the privateer *Le Parla*. In May 1812, rather more than a year after his transfer to Valleyfield, he joined the British navy. But that not all the Dutch prisoners at Esk Mills were seamen was illustrated by the presence there of, for example, Lambert Happers, a soldier from the 1st Dutch Regiment, a native of Utrecht aged 39, who had been captured in August 1809 at Flushing and who, no date given, was invalided home after his transfer to Valleyfield.[67]

At Valleyfield, in addition to all the Dutch prisoners who came to it on the closure of Esk Mills, there were numerous others who entered its gates after the spring of 1811. One was that youthful soldier from the 5th Regiment, François Vanderboom, born in Harlingen and aged nine.[68] A fellow prisoner from the 5th Regiment was one of its drummers, Pierre Press, born at Middleburg and aged 15, who had been captured in July 1809 at Campveer, and who spent just over two years in captivity at Valleyfield until he was released in November 1813, evidently to go off and fight then for the Prince of Orange against the forces of Napoleon. The case of yet another prisoner from the 5th Regiment was remarkable, though not unique: Barthelemy Schmidt, aged 17, born at Breda, 4 feet 7 inches in height, and captured likewise at Campveer in July 1809, who arrived at Valleyfield in September 1811 but was repatriated, no reasons given, a year later. He shared his captivity at Valleyfield with his father, Jan Schmidt, born at Harnhem (? Arnhem) and aged 48, a sergeant in the same regiment and captured at the same time and place, who was a prisoner at Valleyfield until released in November 1813, no doubt as in the case then of so many other Dutch prisoners in order to fight for the Prince of Orange.[69] Described as 'Workman' Charles Jansens, born at Flushing and aged 18, who had been captured at his native place in August 1809, was a prisoner at Valleyfield from October 1811 until his transfer in 1813 to Perth. An example of the presence, too, at Valleyfield of Dutch seamen was Jan Vanderham, born in Alkmarck (Alkmaar) and aged 32, captured off the coast of Norway in February 1813 when prizemaster on the privateer *Ravisseur*, who came from Greenlaw to Valleyfield in July that year and remained there, perhaps suffering from a wound in his left leg, until he was released four months later. Finally, among a dozen or more Dutch prisoners who died and were buried at Valleyfield was Gerrit Gosling, a seaman born in Rotterdam (or Amsterdam) and aged 45 (or 62), who had been captured on the privateer *Le Petit Edouard* in October 1811 off the coast of Norway, and who died on 22 March 1812.[70]

At Perth, where a guesstimate of the number of Dutch may be based on the release of no fewer than 149 prisoners between December 1813 and 19 February 1814 as volunteers to fight for the Prince of Orange[71], there was

the usual further indication of nationality in the places of birth listed in
the Entry Books, including Flushing, Amsterdam, Breda, Rotterdam, The
Hague, Maastricht, Holland, Friesland, and Groningar (Groningen). Christian
Vanherff, for example, born at Maastricht, was, as has already been seen, accompanied in August 1812 by his wife Charlotte Kaiserlich to his captivity at
the depot. Her departure home in January 1813 was not, however, followed
by his until December that year, when he went off from Perth, it seems to
fight for the Prince of Orange.[72] Another Dutch prisoner who left Perth the
same day and for the same reason as Vanherff was André Prucenar, born in
Rotterdam and aged 50, 1st lieutenant of the privateer *Roy de Naples*, captured
in the English Channel in October 1810, and who had come from Valleyfield
to Perth in September 1812. Phelix Volbracht, born at Maastricht and aged
23, had been clerk on the privateer *Friedland* when captured in the North
Sea in October 1807, and came from Valleyfield to Perth at the same time
as André Prucenar. Volbracht volunteered into the 1st Dutch Regiment and
was released from captivity in February 1814. So was H. Amand, alias Amand
Hams, born in Dortrigt (Dordrecht) and aged 17, who had been a passenger
on the privateer *L'Adolphe* when captured in the North Sea in January 1807.
Like his two preceding fellow countrymen, Amand-Hams had come to Perth
from Valleyfield in September 1812. He was one of the very few civilian
prisoners in any depot in Scotland who gained release from captivity by volunteering into the armed forces of a Coalition state.[73] A Dutch prisoner who
regained his freedom by escaping was the same Charles Jansens, although
now described as a seaman rather than 'Workman' and captured in August
1809 on 'French Boats' at his native town, who had come in July 1813 from
Valleyfield to Perth, from which he escaped less than a month later.[74] Given
the obscurity and ambiguity of many places of birth in depot Entry Books it
may be rash to assert that no Dutch prisoners died in captivity at Perth, but
at least it appears that none did.

As Belgium did not emerge as an independent state with that name
until a decade and a half after the Napoleonic Wars, it is admittedly anach-
ronistic to report the presence in the Scots depots of Belgian prisoners.
From within the frontiers of the territory, however, which as a result of the
revolutions of 1830 became Belgium, belonged quite a few of the prisoners in the depots. The first escapers indeed from any depot in Scotland
were five Belgian seamen who in October 1803 broke out of the Edinburgh
bridewell.[75] Marote-Carrier, that significant source of information about
Esk Mills, Valleyfield and Perth during his successive sojourns in each, was
himself a Belgian from Ostend. Among the better-known places of birth
in the Entry Books which point to the presence of appreciable numbers
of Belgians among the prisoners in the Scots depots were Brussels, Liège,
Flanders, Gand (Ghent), Brabant, Tournai, Anvers (Antwerp), Ostend,

Namur, Bruges, Menin, Dinant, Courtray (Courtrai), Blankenberge, Mons, Nivelles, Louvain, Malines, Charleroi, Dixmude, and Jemappes. Another rough indication of numbers may be suggested by entries in the Entry Books at Valleyfield recording the deaths there of nine Belgian prisoners, and at Perth ten. To Belgians, or at least Flemings, at Greenlaw there was a reference in the press as early as 12 July 1804, when the *Caledonian Mercury* reported that two days earlier, '32 prisoners of war were brought to Leith from Greenlaw and entered as volunteers in the British Service on board HMS Roebuck. They are mostly Flemings, Prussians, etc.' Among later evidently Belgian prisoners at Greenlaw at least one had a distinctly un-Belgian name: Frank Brown, born in Brussels and aged 36, lieutenant of the privateer *Le Petit Edouard* when captured in October 1811 off the coast of Norway, and who escaped from Greenlaw in January 1812 along with the captain of his ship, Pierre Jean Colas, aged 52 and known also, it seems, as 'Landau'.[76] At Edinburgh Castle another prisoner born in Brussels, and a namesake of Pierre Jean, was sergeant Michel Colas, aged 28, regiment unstated, who had been captured on a transport vessel in March 1809 at 'W. Islands'. He arrived at the Castle in September 1813 having been 'taken in Edinburgh. Supposed to have escaped from Perth Depot'—as indeed he had four days earlier. He was transferred a month later to Valleyfield, from which he had been transferred to Perth as recently as August.[77]

That Esk Mills held some Belgian prisoners, too, during its short existence as a depot is evident from the places of birth shown in the Entry Books for Valleyfield of the 2,400 or so prisoners who came to it from there. One was Jean Baptiste De Mausure, born in Brabant and aged 23, a soldier in the 2nd light infantry regiment when he was captured in Portugal in August 1808. After enduring five and a half years of captivity he died at Valleyfield on 28 April 1814, three weeks after Napoleon's first abdication and the ending of the war.[78] Two other Belgians at Valleyfield, but who arrived there in October 1811 after the intakes from Esk Mills, were each described as 'Workman'. Jean Destroop, born at Courtrai and aged 23, and Jacob Rottiers of Anvers (Antwerp), aged 35 and who had a finger missing from his left hand, had both been captured in August 1809 at Flushing. Rottiers was released from captivity in November 1813, having volunteered into the King's German Legion in the British army, and Destroop left Valleyfield two months later, as a volunteer into the 1st Dutch Regiment.[79]

At Perth, of the aggregate of 7,761 prisoners the oldest was the Belgian seaman Jean Baptiste Ritkembourg, aged 69 and born at Ostend.[80] Of the 10 Belgians who died in captivity at Perth one was Armand Varraguier, a soldier in the 59th infantry regiment, aged 35 and born at Antwerp, who had been captured in July 1812 at the battle of Salamanca. He reached Perth on 3 December that year and died five days later.[81]

Belgian, or Flemish and Walloon, prisoners were not accorded a separate Entry Book at Greenlaw but there was one there for Spanish prisoners. It showed 48 men, all of them seamen, who arrived at the depot, mainly from prison ships in the West Indies, in small groups between July 1805 and March 1806. All but about fourteen of them were sent to Portsmouth, presumably to the hulks there, in January 1806. Four gained their release from Greenlaw by volunteering to serve in His Britannic Majesty's forces: Pedro Gomes and Jean Crevis, in the navy, and Joseph Costes and Joaquin Detarre, in the band of the 27th infantry regiment. Concerning what befell the remaining ten the Entry Book is silent.[82] One Spanish prisoner at Greenlaw who never returned home was Jean Flouret, born at Barcelona, a seaman captured on the privateer *Félicité* in the West Indies, and who died at the depot in October 1805 from tuberculosis.[83] Not all Spanish prisoners at Greenlaw, however, were included in the 'Spanish' Entry Book. Four who appeared in one of the 'French' Entry Books and were described as 'Spaniards ... discharged as allies' in August 1808, were Salvator Bages, Manuel Rodriguez, Antoine Issou, and Antoine Delavrou.[84] In another 'French' Entry Book at that depot Ferrol and Cartagena (assuming the latter was the Spanish, not the Colombian, city) were among prisoners' birthplaces.[85] In yet another Entry Book, headed 'Edinburgh', but which appears to be of prisoners at Greenlaw, some 68, many of whom at least seem by their names to have been Spanish, are shown to have arrived there between July 1805 and October 1808. Against some of them is written from July of the latter year, when Spain ceased to be an ally of Napoleon and became instead one of Britain: 'To go home'.[86]

At Edinburgh Castle itself places of birth in the main Entry Book that include Barcelona and San Sebastian indicate at least a few Spanish inmates. Some had come there from Esk Mills in March 1811; others, whose birthplaces included Ferrol and Cartagena (again assuming Spain, not Colombia) arrived at the Castle after the intakes from Esk Mills.[87]

At Valleyfield, evidence of the presence of Spanish prisoners is more plentiful, with birthplaces listed that included Figueras, Asturias, Castille, Minorca (a British possession for almost a century until the Peace of Amiens in 1802 restored it to Spain), Vigo, Barcelona, Tarragona, Cartagena, Cadiz, Leon, and, appropriately, 'Spain'.[88] Cadiz was the birthplace of, for example, Jean Porter, lieutenant on the privateer *Le Vengeur* captured in the English Channel in October 1810, who arrived from Esk Mills at Valleyfield in March 1811 and who was released six months later to join the British navy.[89] Barcelona was the birthplace of two other Spanish seaman at Valleyfield: Pierre Fourcholle and François Columba. Fourcholle, captured on the merchant vessel *La Concession* in May 1808, was aged 20 and he, too, had come to Valleyfield from Esk Mills. He was transferred to Greenlaw in May 1811. Columba, aged 30 and from the privateer *Bannette*, no details of capture, arrived at Valleyfield from Greenlaw in September 1812.[90] A Spanish prisoner who never saw his homeland again was Sebastien Surina, born in Minorca and aged 56, a seaman captured on the privateer *Somnambule* in October 1810 in the English Channel. Transferred from Esk Mills in March 1811 to Valleyfield he died a few days later and was buried at the latter depot.[91]

At Perth, evidence of the presence of Spanish prisoners is not so obvious as at the other Scots depots. A seaman there who appears to have been Spanish was J. L. Guilmin, born at Burgos and aged 17, who was captured 'at sea' in February 1809 on the sloop *Thebée*, and who arrived from Portsmouth in August 1812 among the first intakes of prisoners. He remained at Perth until the general repatriation in June 1814.[92] One not actually a prisoner but who accompanied her husband to his captivity at Perth and may have remained there with him until the end of the war, was Maria Martin, 'Spanish Woman'. Marie Manuel, that other devoted wife at Perth, although born in Paris possibly had Spanish parents.[93]

The remaining most sizeable groups of prisoners belonging to European countries and confined in the depots in Scotland were Swiss and Poles—but they were much fewer than the nationalities already mentioned.

The main hope of reversing the successive Partitions of the late 18th century which had removed Poland from the map of Europe appeared to most Poles to lie in victory by France in war against Russia, Prussia and Austria, the Partitioning Powers. Tens of thousands of Poles therefore fought in the French forces during the 20 or so years before 1814, at first as volunteers but later, with the establishment in 1807 by Napoleon of the Duchy of Warsaw, in many cases as conscripts to his armies. Fighting as they did in Italy, Spain, Portugal, and in some other campaigns where British troops were among their opponents, it was not surprising that some Poles should find themselves prisoners of war in one or other of the depots in Scotland. How many did so might be guesstimated at about a hundred. At Greenlaw, although only for a few days in November 1810 before they were sent on parole to Peebles along with 120 or so other officers taken prisoner at the surrender in July 1808 of General Dupont's army at Baylen, were nine Polish officers—seven of them from the 2nd Polish infantry regiment, the other two from the 1st Polish Lancers. The two latter were Captain Kajetan Stokowski and Lieutenant Joseph Starviaski. Of the seven infantry officers (two captains and five lieutenants), one was Captain F. Lascuiski, another Lieutenant Ignace Regulski.[94] It is difficult to believe there were no other Poles, especially rank and file soldiers and seamen, at Greenlaw between 1804 and 1814 but the absence of prisoners' places of birth in most of the depot's Entry Books makes it difficult to prove the presence of Poles, for whom no separate Book was kept.

At Edinburgh Castle 'Pologne' as place of birth occurs very rarely. At Valleyfield and Perth, however, there is more evidence of the presence of Poles, not only in the incidence among birthplaces of Varseau or Varsovie (Warsaw) and 'Poland' (as well as of far less generally known places in that country) but also from other evidence. Among prisoners born in Varsovie, for example, was Berth Libare, a seaman captured on the privateer *Comtesse de Hambourg* in the North Sea in October 1810. Aged 30, he came to Valleyfield in the intakes in March 1811 from Esk Mills. Berth Libare was released from captivity at Valleyfield in May 1812 as a volunteer into the British navy. Another entrant from Esk Mills was Joseph Showwisky, born at Beto, a soldier in the 53rd French infantry regiment, captured at Flushing in August 1809, who was aged 53, and who was released from Valleyfield in February 1814. Among post-Esk Mills Polish arrivals at Valleyfield was Albert Pooloski, born at Poilzen [? Posen] and aged 29, a soldier in the Irish Battalion, who had been captured in August 1809 at Flushing. He, like Joseph Showwisky, was released from the depot in February 1814.[95] Another of several Polish prisoners at Valleyfield who had been serving in the Irish Battalion or Regiment when captured (no place or date is given for his capture) was Mathew Kitzlerost, born in Lemberg and aged 29. He never returned to Poland, for he died and was buried at the depot in January 1813.[96] For five months in 1813 Valleyfield also held a captain in the 1st Polish Lancers: Jean Schultz, born 'Poland', aged 40 and 6 feet 3 inches tall. He had been captured in March 1809 at Govannes and arrived at the depot exactly four years later from Kelso, where he had been on parole. Captain Schultz was released from Valleyfield and from captivity, presumably on medical grounds, in August 1813.[97] And from the 1st Polish Regiment to the depot came thirty or more soldiers captured in Calabria by British forces in July 1806. One of them was Martin Foutz, born Varseau, aged 46 and 6 feet tall, who arrived at Valleyfield on 2 October 1811 but seems not to have remained long there as he volunteered on 17 November (year not given but presumably 1811) into the King's German Legion.[98] Apart from Foutz and a couple of others who left Valleyfield earlier, these Poles proved to be the last prisoners to leave Valleyfield, in September 1814.

At Perth, where the evidence of places of birth in the Entry Books is similar, there appears to have been at least the same number of Poles as at Valleyfield. Among the second intake at Perth in August 1812 were 21 soldiers of the 1st Polish Regiment, captured by General Sir John Stuart's expeditionary force in July 1806 in Calabria, and who remained in captivity at the depot until the end of the war.[99] Other Poles at Perth included several soldiers taken prisoner at Flushing in August 1809 or at Coimbra in October 1810. One taken at the former place as a soldier, possibly a sergeant, in the Irish Legion was Frantz Cowalsky, born at Warsaw and aged 41, and who reached Perth in the third week of August 1812 and remained there until the end of the war. Another, made prisoner at Coimbra as a soldier in the French 69th infantry regiment, who arrived the same day at Perth as Cowalsky, was

Simon Patersky, born 'Poland', aged 23, and who also remained at the depot until the end of the war.[100]

Swiss prisoners are even more subject than Poles to mere guesstimate of their numbers in the depots in Scotland.[101] But that places of birth given in the Entry Books included such well known ones as Lucerne, Lausanne, Geneva, Berne, Neufchatel, the canton of Vaud, and Basle (plus, inevitably, 'Switzerland'), as well as, no doubt, others which were relatively obscure villages or hamlets, confirms the presence of Swiss among the prisoners. There may have been about 50 or 60 altogether.[102]

At Greenlaw, there is less obvious evidence than at the other Scots depots of Swiss prisoners. One, however, sent there from Valleyfield in May 1811 was Louis F. Guariant, born at Neufchatel, a seaman captured on the man-of-war *Scipion* in November 1805 in an aftermath of the battle of Trafalgar.[103] A score of officers from the 3rd and 4th Swiss Regiments were briefly confined at Greenlaw in November 1810 before they were sent on parole to Peebles. All of them had been captured at the surrender in July 1808 of General Dupont's army at Baylen. From the 3rd Regiment there were nine lieutenants and a surgeon; from the 4th, a captain, eight lieutenants and a 2nd lieutenant. Of Rodolf Blatter, a lieutenant in the 3rd, and Charles Scheurmann, a lieutenant in the 4th, more will be said below.[104] At Greenlaw briefly, in August-September 1811, was also Louis Paneau, aged 28, born 'Switzerland', captured serving with a battalion of seamen at Flushing in 1809, and who arrived at Esk Mills from Portsmouth via HMS *Gorgon* on 5 March 1811. Sent six days later to Edinburgh Castle, Paneau was transferred from there to Greenlaw, from there in September to Valleyfield, and from there in July 1813 to Perth, from which in February 1814 he was discharged to Leith, presumably for repatriation.[105]

At Esk Mills and Edinburgh Castle evidence of the presence of other Swiss prisoners is slighter.

Captain Peter Martys of the 4th Swiss Regiment, aged 27, captured at Baylen in 1808, escaped with two other officers in April 1813 from the parole town of Lanark. Recaptured with them a few days later in Edinburgh, he spent some months successively at Valleyfield and Perth before he was sent in August to the Castle and at the end of November from there to the hulks at Portsmouth.[106] But whether Martys actually was Swiss is perhaps doubtful: he was born in Alsace. At both Valleyfield and Perth, however, evidence of the presence of Swiss is unambiguous and relatively plentiful. Alexis L'Amy, for example, born at Geneva and aged 24, a cook in the 8th Dragoons, was among the first prisoners to enter Valleyfield from Esk Mills in March 1811. He was repatriated in June 1814 at the end of the war. Among recaptured escapers from Valleyfield were two Swiss, Jean Choulie and Jean Elie. Choulie, born in Berne and aged 25, a soldier in the 1st French infantry regiment, had been captured in Spain (in 1806, according to a misdated reference in the Entry Book) and reached Valleyfield from Esk Mills in March 1811. He escaped a year later but was recaptured. Jean Elie, born in Lausanne, a seaman on the privateer *L'Henriette* when captured in June 1806, was aged 26. He, too, came from Esk Mills to Valleyfield, from which he escaped in November 1813, but he, too, was recaptured and remained at Valleyfield until released in May 1814.[107] A Swiss who never returned home from Valleyfield was Jean Louis Caron (or Carron), born at Berne and aged 21, a soldier in the 75th French infantry regiment and captured in Spain in June 1810. He died and was buried at the depot in June 1812.[108]

At Perth likewise, there were numbers of Swiss prisoners. One was Eugene Guchant, born at 'Bazle in Switzerland', a soldier whose regiment was not given in the Entry Book, but who was captured on the sloop of war *Hebe* in February 1809, and who arrived at Perth among the first intakes of prisoners in August 1812. Aged 18, he remained a captive there until released in February 1814.[109] Then also released from Perth was Pierre Joseph Mudri, born at Geneva, though described in the Entry Book as 'a German'—by which may have been meant a German-speaking Swiss. Mudri, a sergeant major in the French 6th Light infantry regiment, captured in October 1810 at Coimbra, was aged 29. Among several Swiss who died and were buried at Perth depot was Jean Baptiste Ridon or Redon, born at Berne and aged 31, who was a cannonier in the French 1st Artillery regiment. Captured at Badajoz in April 1812, he arrived at Perth on 15 October that year and died almost exactly a year later from tuberculosis.[110]

If then a massive majority of the prisoners in the depots in Scotland were certainly French there were nonetheless also confined there at one time or another between 1803 and 1814 hundreds of Danes and Norwegians, Germans, Italians, Dutch and Belgians, as well as smaller numbers of perhaps a hundred or more each of Spanish, Poles and Swiss. In addition there were a few prisoners from other European peoples and even from outside Europe, although they appear respectively to have numbered only (except in the case of those from the United States of America) between one or two and at most a score or so. From among these other European peoples were, or at least appear to have been, Austrians, Greeks, Dalmatians (who in the 21st century might be Croats or Bosnians), Hungarians, Luxembourgers, Maltese, Portuguese, Russians, and at least one Czech. Given the cosmopolitan and polyglot character of Napoleon's armed forces, the misfortune of some citizens of neutral states in finding themselves detained on land or sea by British or allied forces in the course of the war, and the obscurity of many of the places of birth given in the Entry Books, it is not impossible, despite the apparent lack of specific evidence, that among the prisoners in the depots in Scotland there were also one or two from south-eastern or eastern Europe, such as Turks, Serbs, Slovenes, Slovaks, Albanians, Rumanians, Bulgarians, and Ukrainians.

Among these smaller groups from Europe the presence of Austrians is suggested by the recurrence of Vienna as birthplace of a few prisoners at Valleyfield and Perth.[111]

Austerlitz, that historic battlefield of 1805 in what is now the Czech Republic, was the birthplace of Pierre Ocford, a soldier captured on the frigate *Minerve* off Rochefort in September 1806. So was he a Czech or an Austrian, or perhaps some other nationality? Aged 22, he remained in captivity at Perth from October 1812 until the end of the war.[112]

Dalmatia, control of which passed successively during the decade 1797-1805 from the Venetian republic to the Austrian empire and then to Napoleon's empire—was where at least a couple of prisoners had been born. Matu Bronzan, alias Baptiste Hidgy, a seaman captured in February 1810 in the English Channel on the privateer *Auguste*, was born there in Ragusa (Dubrovnik). Aged 28, of stout build, 5 feet 10 inches tall, with an oval face, sallow complexion, dark brown hair and grey eyes, he was first at Esk Mills, then Valleyfield, from the latter of which he escaped in February 1812. His fellow Dalmatian, Philipe Vocowihi, a seaman born at 'Spalatio' (Spalato, now Split) and aged 32, who had been captured, no date given, at Corfu on the transport vessel *Neptune*, was also of stout build and was 6 feet tall. He, too, like Matu Bronzan, was transferred in March 1811 from Esk Mills to Valleyfield but, unlike Bronzan, remained at the latter until his release three years later.[113]

Greeks at Valleyfield are mentioned in the Register of Prisoners' Applications in August 1811: 'Dematre Pearre, Trasmagarker, Spero Selencio—Seamen, Greeks. Turkish transport. Request to be permitted to enter into a battalion in the Islands. Have been ordered to be released by request of Admiral Otway for HMS [blank], 18 Aug.'[114] There was also, first at Esk Mills then at Valleyfield, until the general repatriation in June 1814, Dominique Mondine or Mondini, a soldier from the 2nd Grecian Regiment. Aged 37, he had been captured in September 1809 on Corfu. But was he Greek or, much more likely, Italian? His birthplace was given as Crima—which may have been a misspelling for Crema, near Milan. He shared his captivity at both depots with ten other soldiers from his regiment.[115] Rhodes was the birthplace of a prisoner at Edinburgh Castle. He was Pierre Julian, a soldier in the 50th Line regiment, who had been captured at Pontebello on 12 March (no year given, but probably 1811), and who arrived at Edinburgh Castle on 12 January 1813 via the transport ship *Malabar*. Aged 25 and 5ft 5½ins tall, Pierre Julian was well made, with an oval face, swarthy complexion, dark hair, hazel eyes, and with no marks or wounds. Apart from the issue to him in February 1813 of a jacket, shirt and shoes, there is no other information in the Entry Book about him.[116] Corfu and the Morea were birthplaces of other prisoners at Valleyfield. One was a seaman with the apparently Greek name Demetrio Pereri, born in Corfu and aged 23, who had been captured in October 1811 on the merchant vessel *Bondieus* (sic) in the Mediterranean, and who also had first been at Esk Mills but who was released from captivity as a volunteer into the British navy in May 1812. Two others born in Corfu and another in the Morea illustrate the difficulty of identifying nationality, as they were soldiers with apparently Italian names who had been captured while serving in the 2nd Italian Regiment. Of these three, Gregorio Antonio, born in the Morea, and Andria Bastianela, born in Corfu, were discharged from Valleyfield to France, presumably as invalids, in October 1811. The third, Espira Selencia, remained a prisoner at Valleyfield until the general release in June 1814.[117]

First at Perth from August 1812 then a year later transferred to Valleyfield was a prisoner born in Hungary: François Pavien, Pavren or Parren, aged 21, a soldier in the 9th French infantry regiment, who had been captured at Badajoz in April 1812, and who was released in November 1813 as a volunteer into the King's German Legion of the British army. Was he Hungarian or was he French? Had he perhaps been captured while serving with the Austrian army and likewise volunteered, or been volunteered, into Napoleon's infantry? As so often with questions that seek to pass beyond the bare information provided in the official sources, answers are lacking.[118]

There is less uncertainty about Luxembourgers in captivity at Edinburgh Castle, Valleyfield and Perth. At Perth, for example, Jean Filiare, aged 30, a soldier in the 1st Regiment of artillery, captured in January 1812 at Ciudad Rodrigo, spent only seventeen months in the depot before he was released in the general repatriation in June 1814. His fellow countryman, Sergeant Nicolas Brasseur, aged 32, of the 5th Regiment of artillery, who had been captured in April 1812 at Badajoz was, however, less fortunate. Wounded in the breast and left arm, he died at Perth in November 1813 from tuberculosis.[119]

Of Maltese in the Scots depots one, Thomas J. Samson, clerk on the privateer *Le Surcouff*, captured in the English Channel in November 1810, and who had arrived at Edinburgh Castle from Esk Mills in March 1811, escaped from the Castle the following month in the mass break-out of 12 April.[120] Another Maltese first confined at Esk Mills was Carlo Riccardo, a seaman aged 33, who had been captured on the man-of-war *Pluton* off Cadiz in June 1808, and who in March 1811 was transferred to Valleyfield, where he remained until his release in March 1814, virtually at the end of the war.[121] A fellow seaman born in Malta who had been captured on the man-of-war *L'Aigle* at the battle of Trafalgar in October 1805 and who, like Carlo Riccardo, later found himself first at Esk Mills, then at Valleyfield until his release in 1814, was Pierre Leblanc, aged 22.[122]

'Antonio and 8 other Portuguese seamen. Privateers. Request their Liberty. Were forced to serve, etc.', is the comment in a Register of Prisoners' Applications from Valleyfield in July 1811; and the same register the following month contains a reference to another Portuguese seaman at Valleyfield: 'Gaitana Lega. *Aventurier* privateer. Request to be admitted into His Majesty's Service. To be released by request of Admiral Otway, 18th Aug.'[123] Although a Transport Board instruction in May 1812 to transmit names of Portuguese prisoners received a nil return from Greenlaw, Valleyfield reported the presence there of 13 (out of a total of 91 then in depots and hulks in Britain). But one of the Greenlaw 'French' Entry Books covering the period August 1811 to December 1812 includes Lisbon as a birthplace, so there may well have been at least one Portuguese prisoner there who had either departed before or had arrived after the Board's instruction was received.[124] As late as October 1813 Valleyfield still held in captivity seven Portuguese soldiers, out of a total of 22 Portuguese prisoners in Britain.[125] A Portuguese seaman who died and was buried at Valleyfield in April 1812 was Antoine Sangreti, born in Lisbon and aged 49, captured on the privateer *La Désirée* in 1809 in the English Channel, and who had come to the depot a year earlier from Esk Mills.[126] There appears to have been at least one Portuguese prisoner at Perth: 'Report the case,' the Transport Board ordered Captain Moriarty, RN, its agent there, on 13 November 1813, 'of Manuel Antonio Correa, said to be a Portuguese subject, in your custody.'[127]

'… the Russian vessel *Speedy Reconciliation* now at Leith has been released,' wrote the Transport Board on 22 June 1809 to Malcolm Wright, their agent at Greenlaw, 'and the six men named … who belonged to her, and are now in your custody, may be liberated in order to join her …' The six men were Pette Demush, Thomas Havre, Simon Falkin, Matheu Parkmloff, Gregorio Gaventa and Ivan Dewerky.[128] Reference to another Russian prisoner at Greenlaw was made in his memoirs by Andrew Johnston, later chief clerk at Perth: 'Early in a morning (sic) of June 1810 about 30 prisoners got out by a mine from Greenlaw. The Pennycuick Volunteers were beat to arms to assist the military. They were all retaken in the course of the day. Three were severely wounded, one a Russian by a bayonet in the breast, and two shot by an Aberdeen soldier while secreting themselves sitting under a tree … They all recovered from their wounds.'[129] Yet more Russians at Greenlaw were revealed when on 28 February 1811 the Register of Prisoners' Applications succinctly recorded: 'Alexey and others. Russians. Seamen. Request: their Liberty. They belonged to a merchant ship bound from Archangel to Drontheim [Trondheim] and never having fought hope to be released.' It appears, however, that Alexey and his fellow Russians had to endure a delay of 18 months or more before a decision in their case was reached, if the date on a postcript in the Register was accurate: 'Memorandum: Wrote to the agent for information, 13 July 1812.'[130]

Among those in the Scots depots whose homelands were, or appear to have been, outside Europe were, as already observed, some from the Americas: the United States, and such European colonies in South America as Brazil, Montevideo and Demerara, a few apparently French Canadians from Quebec and Montreal, as well as other prisoners born on islands in the Caribbean or West Indies such as Cuba, Guadeloupe, Martinique, Grenada, Jamaica, Marie Galante, and St Domingo. There were also some prisoners whose homelands lay in the Indian Ocean, on Ile de France (Mauritius) or Ile de Bourbon (Réunion), or, in the Atlantic, on the Azores, or, in the Pacific, on the Philippines—all of those islands at that period being colonies of western European states. There appear to have been one or two prisoners, too, whose place of birth was North Africa, specifically Barbary, Morocco, Ceuta. Depot Entry Books, and some other sources, provide examples that confirm or at least suggest that even these wider ranges of peoples or nationalities were represented among the prisoners.

Of these non-Europeans among the prisoners in the depots in Scotland, the largest group appears to have been Americans from the United States. The 48 who were marched into captivity at Greenlaw soon after the outbreak of the War of 1812, and several other individual American captives taken before then on French or other enemy ships, have already been mentioned.[131] As there were, of course, some others in the latter category the total number of captive Americans appears to have been about 60 or 70. They were born in, for example, New Orleans, Norfolk, Portsmouth, Florida, Philadelphia, Virginia, and New York. There appear not to have been any Americans at Perth but at one time or another some were in captivity at the other Scots depots. Neil Nicolson, for instance, a seaman captured on the merchant vssel *Fontaine*, no date or place given, was born in 'Portsmouth, North America.' Aged 24, 5 feet 10½ inches tall, and said to be of stout build, long face, fresh complexion, dark brown hair, grey eyes, and no marks or wounds, he was sent from Esk Mills to Valleyfield in March 1811 and released from the latter in August that year into His Britannic Majesty's navy. His fellow American and merchant seaman Abram Bays, born in New York and aged 26, who had been captured on *Le Phantome*, no place or date given, was also successively at Esk Mills and Valleyfield before he left the latter on the same day as Neil Nicolson to join the Royal Navy.[132] One or two other captives born in the United States (or at least in territories that as a result of the Louisiana Purchase in 1803 had then become part of the United States) were marched from Esk Mills in March 1811 to Edinburgh Castle. One who came to Greenlaw from the Castle was Santiago Ivon, born in Florida and aged 26, a seaman on the privateer *La*

Pronta, captured in the Mediterranean in June 1805. In November 1811 he, too, joined the Royal Navy.[133]

From Canada came to the Scots depots a few prisoners who had been born in Quebec or Montreal. Two, for example, both seamen, who were first at Esk Mills then at Valleyfield were Pierre Lerouge of Quebec, who had been captured in a small boat at St Domingo in 1809, and Louis Jongh of Montreal, who had been captured at the capitulation of Martinique in 1809. Lerouge, aged 35, 5 feet 1 inch tall, of stout build, oval face, sallow complexion, brown hair, grey eyes and no marks or wounds, was released from captivity in May 1812 on joining the Royal Navy; Jongh, aged 25, was at Valleyfield less than a month before he, too, joined the navy.[134]

A few prisoners also there were whose birthplaces were in Latin America: Santa Caterina (whether Mexico or Brazil is uncertain), Brazil, Demerera, and Montevideo. It was, for instance, 'Santa Caterina, South America', where Francis Jozé, a seaman on the privateer *Figaro*, had been born. He entered Edinburgh Castle in July 1811, a young man aged 26, of 'middling' person, with a long thin face, pale complexion, dark hair, dark eyes, and 'Squints a little and a little marked with smallpox.' At the Castle, too, although for barely a month in March-April 1813 until he entered the Royal Navy, was Abraham Daniel Levie, born in Demerera (Georgetown).[135] Montevideo was the birthplace of at least half-a-dozen prisoners, including Carlos Gonsalvez at Greenlaw, a seaman captured 'at sea' in May 1806 on the privateer *La Dolores* or, according to another source, on the frigate *L'Atalante* at the Cape of Good Hope.[136] Rio de Janeiro was where Louis Manga had been born, a carpenter captured 'at sea' in July 1811 on the privateer *Le Figaro*, and who came that month to Edinburgh Castle aged 28, of stout build, with a long face, very dark complexion, 'black dyed' hair, dark eyes, and a scar on his left wrist.[137]

Among numbers of prisoners whose birthplaces were Caribbean or West Indian islands that were, or had been, French colonies was, for example, Jean Boulogne, born on Marie Galante, a soldier captured 'at sea' in October 1808, on the schooner *La Mouche*. Aged 23, he was in the first batches of prisoners to arrive in August 1812 at Perth and there he remained until the general repatriation in June 1814.[138] At Valleyfield Charles Peters, 'a creole of Martinique', which island had been captured three years earlier by British forces, applied in summer 1812 'to be admitted into His Majesty's Service.'[139] Guadeloupe, likewise captured from the French by British forces in 1810, was where several prisoners had been born. One was Jacque (sic) Marie Jofroi, a seaman captured off Cape Finisterre in April 1806 on the privateer *Finisterre*, who presumably afterward had escaped or been exchanged or released as, under the alias Jacques Godfroy, and as a soldier in the 1st Colonial Battalion, he appears to have been captured again (no date or place given) and arrived first at Esk Mills early in 1811 and was then transferred to Valleyfield, from which in August 1813 he was sent to Perth. Aged 24, he was 4 feet 9 inches tall, of slender build, oval face, fresh complexion, dark brown hair, grey eyes, and with no marks or wounds.[140] Cuba, specifically Havana, was where John Antonio was said to have been born, a seaman aged 35 captured in July 1811 in the North Sea on the privateer *Le Figaro*, who found himself a few days afterward in captivity in Edinburgh Castle, a 'Very dark man', of middling stature, full face, dark complexion, black hair, and dark eyes and with 'Scar under right eye'. When, however, he was transferred in August that year to Greenlaw his birthplace, as well as his age, were said to be quite different, as will presently be shown.[141] Among the prisoners born in the West Indies was, as already observed, at least one who had been born on the British colony of Jamaica: Charles Scharle. How he had come to be captured at Madrid in August 1812 as a soldier in the French 59th infantry regiment must remain one of many thousands of what might have been fascinating accounts of the individual experiences of prisoners but which cannot be told because of the virtually complete absence of such other information about them.[142]

On the Indian Ocean island colonies of France of Ile de France (Mauritius) and Ile de Bourbon (Réunion), both of which were seized in 1810 by British forces, had been born some other prisoners. One from the Ile de France was Alexis Pissaro, no rank given, who had been captured on the man-of-war *Marengo* in the south Atlantic in March 1806.[143]

A birthplace even further away from Scotland was, or ostensibly was, that of John or Jean Antonio, seaman captured in the North Sea in July 1811 on the privateer *Le Figaro*. When the following month he was transferred from Edinburgh Castle to Greenlaw two radical changes appeared in his description in the latter's Entry Book. Whereas at the Castle he was said to be 35, at Greenlaw he became 65—but also his place of birth, which at the Castle had been Havana, became Manila. Were these merely clerical errors and, if so, were they errors made at the Castle or at Greenlaw? Both Cuba and the Philippines were Spanish colonies but whether Jean Antonio was Cuban or Filipino remains an unanswerable question and thus another illustration of the difficulties in identifying the nationality or peoples that some of the prisoners belonged to.[144]

Africa and, although less certainly, the Middle East appear to have been the birthplaces of two or three of the prisoners. The same difficulties arise in trying to establish their nationality or ethnicity. François Toussaint Benet, for example, a seaman aged 27, captured on the man-of-war *Scipion* in November 1805 in an aftermath to the battle of Trafalgar, had been born at Ceuta in Spanish Morocco. Arrived at Valleyfield in March 1811 among the intakes then from Esk Mills, Benet, described as 5 feet 8 inches tall, of stout build, oval face, fresh complexion, black hair, hazel eyes and with no marks or wounds, was sent to Stonedykehead in January 1814.[145] It appears more likely, especially given his name, that it was not the Levant—that part of the Middle East where lie in the early 21st century Lebanon, Syria, Israel and the Gaza strip, but Levante near Genoa which was the birthplace of Giovanni Brugnoli, aged 40, a soldier in the 2nd Greek Regiment, who was captured in September 1809 on Corfu. He came from Esk Mills to Valleyfield and remained there until he was released from captivity three years later in March 1814.[146] But excluding the six towns or cities of that name in the United States of America, Canada or South Africa (not to mention Dunbartonshire), which Alexandria was the birthplace (and what was the nationality) of Louis Tourlasky, aged 34, a soldier in the Chasseurs Rentrés regiment, captured in August 1809 at Flushing, and who came in March 1811 from Esk Mills to Valleyfield? Was it Alexandria in Italy, in Bulgaria—or in Egypt? Whichever it was, Tourlasky passed three years at Valleyfield before his release in March 1814.[147] At Perth there were at least two prisoners whose places of birth were said to be respectively Barbary (the north coast of Africa) and, more specifically, Morocco.[148]

Finally, one other nationality, or group of nationalities, a few members of which might perhaps have been expected to appear among the captives in the Scots depots, were Britons—English, Irish, Scots, or Welsh, enrolled in the forces of Napoleon or his allies when taken prisoner by British or British allied forces. Frank Brown, Martin Lewis, James Smith, George Miller, Joseph Gerard, Charles Simon, Benjamin Martin, Neil Nicolson, Gilbert Folly, Archibald Williams—names such as these that strike the eye in even a cursory glance through the lengthy lists of prisoners in the Scots depot Entry Books may indeed suggest the presence of at least some Britons. Closer scrutiny, however, indicates that even if such names might appear to be British, their possessors in fact were not (or, given the absence of more detailed information, at least seem not to have been) subjects of His Britannic Majesty. Lieutenant Frank Brown, for example, captured on the privateer *Le Petit Edouard*, was born in Brussels (although perhaps of British parents or at least a British father?) and was scarcely able to speak English. Martin Lewis, captured when bosun on the merchant vessel *L'Aurore* in 1808 (or when a seaman on 'an American ship' at Leith in 1811) and who came from Esk Mills in March 1811 to Valleyfield, was born at Konigsberg, East Prussia: perhaps his was an alias and, if so, his own name might have been more recognisably Germanic. Charles Simon, a corporal captured on the man-of-war *Duquesne* at St Domingo in 1803, was a name which could have been that of a subject or citizen of any one of several European nations or of the USA—but in his case it was France, where he had been born at Vesoul. Neil Nicolson, a captured merchant seaman, was certainly born at Portsmouth—not Portsmouth, England, but at an unspecified one of the three American Portsmouths (in New Hampshire, Ohio, or Virginia). Thus prisoners in the Scots depots who at first sight might appear to have been English, Irish, Scots or Welsh have proven, without exception so far found, to have been (or claimed to have been) either Americans, or citizens or subjects of other European states, but who had, or may have had, British fathers or forebears, or had adopted British-sounding aliases, or in some cases perhaps had had their names written in Anglicised form by the depot clerks. The British authorities were certainly watchful for Britons who might have volunteered themselves, or might claim to have been forcibly enrolled, into the forces of Napoleon. As early in the war as May-June 1804, correspondence between the Admiralty, the Transport Board and Malcolm Wright, its agent at Greenlaw depot, provided an illustration of unfounded official suspicion that 13 members of the crew of the Dutch privateer *Union*, captured by HMS *Ethalion* and brought into Leith, were in fact British. 'Their Lordships will observe,' wrote the Transport Board commissioners consequently to the Admiralty, after investigations by Wright, 'that there is not an individual among the prisoners [from the *Union*] ... who can on any likely ground be suspected to be a British subject; ... [the] 13 men ... state themselves to be Americans.' On the other hand, that there were indeed some English and Irish, and perhaps also some Scots and Welsh, serving in the forces of Napoleon or those of his allies, is also attested in a chapter below. Apart from some such individual Britons, most of whom appear to have been prisoners of war in French hands and who had enlisted in Napoleon's forces either out of despair at the prospect of their continuing captivity or in the hope that, once on campaign or the high seas, they would be able to escape from the French forces back into those of Britain or its allies, there was also in Napoleon's army from 1803 an Irish Legion (later retitled the Irish Regiment or Battalion) which was at least partly composed of members of the revolutionary Society of United Irishmen in exile after the failure of the Irish rebellion of 1798. From that legion, regiment or battalion there were indeed a few captives in the Scots depots. At Valleyfield, for instance, there were a dozen from the Irish Battalion who had been captured in November 1810 in Portugal. But none of them had Irish names, and the dozen appear to have consisted in fact of Frenchmen, Italians, Germans, and Poles. Although there is evidence of Irishmen and Englishmen among prisoners of war held in England, no such evidence has been found, so far at least, of any Irish, Welsh, English or Scots among prisoners in the Scots depots.[149]

If the boy William Chambers, later publisher and lord provost of Edinburgh, in observing the prisoners at Valleyfield during his visit to Penicuik that Sunday in 1811 or 1812 had also, from his vantage point at the top of the steep slope high above the depot, been able to hear them conversing among themselves, he might have been reminded of the Tower of Babel. Whatever the difficulties in establishing the full range and numbers of nationalities or ethnic groups in the Scots depots there can be no doubt the prisoners in them were drawn from many, indeed most, of the peoples of Europe and even from a few of those beyond Europe.

12

Marks or Wounds; Heights, and Aliases

Although their purpose was to facilitate recapture in the event of escape, the descriptions in the depot Entry Books of the prisoners' physical appearances include at least two items of some historical, demographic, and perhaps medical significance: marks and wounds, and heights. In examining these items all the familiar difficulties about the reliability of entries, as well as about the absence of any such entries for some prisoners, arise. For most of the prisoners at Greenlaw, and for all but the first 192 who entered Esk Mills, for example, no information about heights or marks and wounds was recorded (or at least, in the case of Greenlaw, appears not to have survived). For those transferred from Esk Mills to Edinburgh Castle and Valleyfield information is, however, generally available in the Entry Books of the two latter depots. Where they were recorded, as they were for the overwhelming majority of prisoners at Valleyfield and Perth, for instance, heights (which were taken usually to the nearest quarter inch) were probably generally accurate and reliable. Whether the recording of marks and wounds, where there was greater scope for more subjective and less systematic coverage, was equally reliable is more doubtful. But at least what the Entry Books do provide is an indication of wounds or injuries suffered by some of the prisoners, as well as of the almost obsessive care sometimes taken by the depot authorities to record physical characteristics that might make identification of an escaped prisoner easier. Random examples of descriptions of marks or wounds recorded in Entry Books of all five depots in Scotland are presented in Appendix 8.

The marks and wounds recorded are separable into three main categories. The first and largest category consists of those physical features, such as 'Scar under Chin', 'lisps', 'freckles', 'Red Whiskers', 'sore Eyes', 'roundshouldered', 'Dimples Cheek', 'Anchor on right Hand', 'Moles under Lip', and many others, whose recording in the Entry Books appears to have had little or no purpose other than to facilitate recognition in the event of the prisoner's escape. The second category, which no doubt would also make it easier or even easier to recognise escaped prisoners, appears at least to have more historical or medical significance than those in the first category and consists of what are, or appear to be, wounds or injuries. Not all of these, of course, might have been suffered from fighting in the Napoleonic or earlier wars. 'Wants Parts of both Fore Fingers', 'Wound left Leg', 'Wound in Breast', 'right Leg amputated', 'blind left eye, diff. Wos Body' (sic—different wounds on the body), 'lost right Hand', 'Gunpowder Marks in Face', 'Wounded Ears', are among many examples. Whether some wounds—such as a missing right index finger or missing front teeth—had been self-inflicted it is not possible to be sure. French conscripts were required by law to be strong and healthy: those (and there were many) reluctant to serve in Napoleon's forces might hope to escape service by cutting off their right, or trigger, forefinger or knocking out their front teeth, essential items in loading or reloading a musket. Such acts of self-mutilation were by no means uncommon among those dreading their call-up.[1] The third category, which may offer some demographic and medical interest and even significance, is the incidence recorded among the prisoners of smallpox scars. Whether, and if so what percentages of, these scars were the result of smallpox contracted before, or actually while serving on campaigns in, the Napoleonic Wars, it is impossible to say.

Apart from mentions of smallpox scars, the entries for marks and wounds contain, logically enough, very few references to illnesses, diseases or other medical conditions, including tuberculosis, pneumonia, and fevers, some of which proved fatal to several hundred prisoners in the depots in Scotland. These illnesses or conditions will be discussed in Chapter 19. But among the occasional such references (apart from smallpox scars) that were made in the marks and wounds columns are some to ruptures and hernias, deafness, blindness in one eye, and scrofula (tuberculosis, especially of the lymphatic glands).

Of several prisoners at Perth said to be suffering from scrofula, for instance, one was Sergeant François Berland of the 50th infantry regiment, captured (no place given) in January 1812, who arrived at the depot in January 1813. Born at Petosse and aged 41, he also had 'mark on chin'. He was released home after the end of the war, in July 1814.[2] One who was 'Very deaf' was François Sabatier, a soldier in the 82nd infantry regiment, who had been captured on Martinique in February 1809. Born at St Marin and aged 35, he arrived at Valleyfield in September 1811 and a year later was transferred to Perth, from which he was sent home only after the end of the war.[3] One of a number of prisoners in the Scots depots who were blind in one eye (though whether as a result of action in the war is unstated) was Pierre Nolle, a soldier in the 5th infantry regiment, captured at Campveer in July 1809. Born at Graff and aged 50, he arrived at Valleyfield in September 1811 and was released in November 1813; whether as a result of his blindness (in his case in his right eye) is unstated but that would seem probable.[4] A prisoner at Greenlaw said to be 'Very hoarse in speech' was Hendrick Lieven, a seaman captured on the frigate *La Gloire* off Rochefort in September 1806, and who entered that depot in August 1811 from Edinburgh Castle. Aged 28 and born at Dunkirk, Lieven's problems with his speech or throat did not prevent him from joining His Britannic Majesty's navy three months after his arrival at Greenlaw.[5]

Some of the wounds or injuries and medical conditions suffered by some of the prisoners were considered by the depot authorities and the Transport Board to be sufficiently, and more or less so permanently, incapacitating as to justify repatriation—and examples of such cases are given in Chapters 19 and 20. Provision for hospital treatment of sick or injured prisoners was made at the depots (Valleyfield depot hospital in particular dealt with numbers even of parole prisoners sent for medical treatment from the parole towns in Scotland), and this subject is also discussed in Chapter 19.

It may be surprising that only a few references, such as 'Anchor on right Hand', appear to have been made under marks and wounds to tattoos, an ancient practice, interest in which in Europe had re-emerged from the 16th century onward as a result of the voyages of discovery and exploration to America and the Pacific. One prisoner, who figures more prominently in Chapter 22 in another connection, and who was one of the few noted as having tattoos, was François Petit, a seaman aged 22, captured on the privateer *Le Vengeur* in the English Channel in October 1810, and who was successively at Greenlaw and (though not always continuously) Esk Mills and Valleyfield between November 1810 and April 1813. Whether his tattoo was acquired during one of his absences without leave from the two latter depots, or the depot authorities at Greenlaw and Esk Mills had simply failed to notice or record it, is uncertain. But his description in the Valleyfield Entry Book includes a 'Variety of marks on Breast and Arms under which are the words [sic] Mariette and Strongly marked on Nose with smallpox and Particularly on the left Arm'.[6]

Smallpox scars were far from uncommon among the prisoners in the depots in Scotland. The discovery as recently as 1796 by Edward Jenner (1749-1823), the English physician and surgeon who pioneered vaccination, that inoculation with cowpox gave immunity to smallpox was an historic turning point in the struggle against that acutely infectious and deadly disease. Until then smallpox had been endemic in Europe and a major cause of death, and it remained so in some other parts of the world until the later 20th century when it was considered to have become eradicated. The award in 1804 to Jenner of the Freedom of the City of Edinburgh happened to take place later in the same year that Greenlaw became a depot for prisoners of war.[7] In France, vaccination inspired by Jenner's discovery had begun in 1799 and 'was rapidly diffused by the diligence of the prefects, with noticable effects on infant and child mortality.'[8] In 1805 Napoleon, who had a keen interest in new medical developments, ordered the vaccination of all recruits except, it seems, those who had already had smallpox, with the result that that disease greatly diminished in the Grande Armée.[9]

Among prisoners of war there were outbreaks of smallpox on the *Crown Prince* hulk at Chatham and, more seriously, at Dartmoor early in 1815 among American prisoners there, when 70 died from the disease. No such outbreaks of smallpox occurred in any of the depots in Scotland during the Napoleonic Wars. But it has been argued that generally the smallpox virus contributed to many deaths ostensibly occurring from other causes, including the 'bloody flux' and perhaps diarrhoea; and because many prisoners of war had suffered from childhood infection by it in a form which, however, left no distinguishing pock marks on the face, 'men lost their early resistance to other diseases, especially bronchitis and broncho-pneumonia and smallpox could also release latent tuberculosis bacillus.'[10] At Greenlaw, for instance, out of 47 American prisoners from merchant ships sent there in October 1812, five had smallpox scars. Out of 80 'Danes' in another Entry Book, 20 were said to have the scars; and in one of the 'French' Entry Books, 162 out of some 904 prisoners.[11] Among the first 192 prisoners who entered Esk Mills on 4 February 1811 from Greenlaw, 31 were recorded as marked by smallpox.[12] At Edinburgh Castle, 89 of those 461 transferred from Esk Mills in March 1811 had smallpox scars.[13] Among a further 466 prisoners who arrived at, or at least passed in transit through, the Castle in the year between December 1812 and December 1813, 120 were recorded as scarred by smallpox.[14] At Valleyfield, out of the aggregate total of some 7,650 prisoners it appears that approximately 200 had no information about marks or wounds entered against their names. Of the remaining 7,450 some 978 were recorded as having smallpox scars. Of those 978, 394 had entered Valleyfield in March 1811 from Esk Mills. The relevant total at Esk Mills, therefore, must have been at least 483 of the 2,817 prisoners confined there. At Perth, out of an aggregate total of 7,761 prisoners some 1,211 were said to have smallpox scars.[15]

The information available in the Entry Books therefore suggests that the percentages of prisoners at the depots in Scotland who bore smallpox scars to one extent or another were approximately these: at Greenlaw (but only among those 'French', 'Danes' and Americans mentioned, who totalled 1,031 men) 18.1 per cent, at Esk Mills 17.1 per cent, at Edinburgh Castle 22.5 per cent, at Valleyfield at the very least 12.8 per cent, and at Perth 15.6 per cent. Taking all five depots together the average on the basis of those figures was therefore about 17.2 per cent, or approximately one prisoner in every six. But these are almost certainly underestimates.

❖

The heights of the prisoners as recorded in the depot Entry Books indicate that, at least by 21st-century standards, Napoleon's forces were certainly not tall men. Conscripts in the French army had to be at least 5 feet 1 inch, the elite grenadiers in infantry regiments at least 5 feet 5 inches, grenadiers of the Imperial Guard at least an inch taller still. On the other hand, for *voltigeurs*, the elite shorter troops forming the left company of an infantry battalion, the *maximum* height was 4 feet 11 inches.[16]

Of 760 prisoners in one of the 'French' Entry Books at Greenlaw whose heights, measured to the nearest quarter of an inch, are given, analysis shows:[17]

6 ft 1 in:	1	5 ft 8½ ins:	16	5 ft 5 ¼ ins:	21	5 ft 2 ins:	14
6 ft:	2	5 ft 8¼ ins:	5	5 ft 5 ins:	56	5 ft 1¾ ins:	1
5 ft 11½ ins:	1	5 ft 8 ins:	20	5 ft 4¾ ins:	25	5 ft 1½ ins:	8
5 ft 11¼ ins:	1	5 ft 7¾ins:	7	5 ft 4½ ins:	49	5 ft 1¼ ins:	1
5 ft 11 ins:	5	5 ft 7½ ins:	23	5 ft 4¼ ins:	19	5 ft 1 in:	6
5 ft 10¾ ins:	1	5 ft 7¼ ins:	12	5 ft 4 ins:	57	5 ft 0¾ ins:	5
5 ft 10½ ins:	3	5 ft 7 ins:	38	5 ft 3¾ ins:	17	5 ft 0½ in:	3
5 ft 10 ins:	4	5 ft 6¾ ins:	18	5 ft 3½ ins:	26	5 ft:	4
5 ft 9¾ ins:	3	5 ft 6½ ins:	45	5 ft 3¼ ins:	12	4 ft 11½ ins:	2
5 ft 9½ ins:	10	5 ft 6¼ ins:	11	5 ft 3 ins:	32	4 ft 11 ins:	2
5 ft 9¼ ins:	6	5 ft 6 ins:	50	5 ft 2¾ ins:	11		
5 ft 9 ins:	8	5 ft 5¾ ins:	16	5 ft 2½ ins:	22		
5 ft 8¾ ins:	7	5 ft 5½ ins:	46	5 ft 2¼:	8	*Total:*	**760**

Of those 760 prisoners only three (0.39 per cent) were 6 feet or more, 45 (5.9 per cent) were 5 feet 9 inches or more, 297 (39 per cent) were 5 feet 6 inches or more, 416 (54.7 per cent) were from 5 feet to 5 feet 6 inches inclusive, and four (0.5 per cent) were under 5 feet.

Of 346 'Danes' at Greenlaw whose heights are given, the profile that emerges is:[18]

6 ft:	1	5 ft 6¾ ins:	4	5 ft 3½ ins:	17
5 ft 11¼ ins:	1	5 ft 6½ ins:	15	5 ft 3¼ ins:	4
5 ft 11 ins:	3	5 ft 6¼ ins:	1	5 ft 3 ins:	25
5 ft 10½ ins:	1	5 ft 6 ins:	36	5 ft 2¾ ins:	1
5 ft 10 ins:	4	5 ft 5¾ ins:	1	5 ft 2½ ins:	15
5 ft 9½ ins:	5	5 ft 5½ ins:	24	5 ft 2 ins:	6
5 ft 9 ins:	9	5 ft 5 ¼ ins:	3	5 ft 1½ ins:	7
5 ft 8½ ins:	14	5 ft 5 ins:	21	5 ft 1 in:	2
5 ft 8¼ ins:	1	5 ft 4¾ ins:	5	5 ft 0½ in:	3
5 ft 8 ins:	17	5 ft 4½ ins:	22	5 ft:	2
5 ft 7½ ins:	17	5 ft 4¼ ins:	8	4 ft 11 ins:	2
5 ft 7¼ ins:	1	5 ft 4 ins:	30	4 ft 10 ins:	1
5 ft 7 ins:	13	5 ft 3¾ ins:	4	*Total:*	346

The only prisoner among those 346 'Danes' who was six feet or more tall was Christian Larsen, a seaman captured on the merchant ship *Scarven* off Norway in December 1808. Aged 48, he was exactly six feet. Of the three among those prisoners who were less than five feet tall, the shortest was Ole Olsen, another seaman, captured on the transport ship *Carina Maria* in the North Sea in December 1810. Aged 35, he was exactly 4 feet 10 inches in height.[19]

At Valleyfield, where there were in aggregate some 7,650 prisoners between 1811 and 1814, the heights of all except some 328 were entered in the Entry Books. The fairly comprehensive profile of heights that can therefore be drawn for that depot is presented in Appendix 9. What it shows is that out of those 7,322 prisoners only 43 (0.58 per cent) were 6 feet or more in height. Half of the 43 were exactly 6 feet, and the heights of the other 21 ranged from 6 feet ¼ inch up to 6 feet 4 inches. The tallest prisoner at Valleyfield (unless there was one, or more than one, taller among the 328 whose heights went unrecorded) thus appears to have been Charle (sic) G. Conetable, a soldier in the 1st West Indian regiment when he was captured at Flushing in August 1809, and who was 6 feet 4 inches. Born at Paris and aged 21, he arrived at Valleyfield in October 1811 and remained there until the general release in June 1814.[20]

On the other hand, out of those 7,322 prisoners there were 62 (0.84 per cent) who were less than 5 feet tall. Many of them were young boys some of whom have already been mentioned, such as the seven who were only nine years old and who included Michael Floriot, 4 feet 7 inches tall, Pierre Decrock, 4 feet 6½ inches, and Jean Renault Fleurette, 4 feet 4 inches; and others were among the other 30 prisoners at Valleyfield who were aged between 10 and 14.[21] But some of those 62 prisoners under 5 feet were adults. François Giraux, for example, born in Paris, was aged 20, a soldier in the Basque 66th Regiment, who had been captured off Ireland in November 1809, who entered Valleyfield in September 1811 and remained there till the general repatriation in June 1814. Giraux was 4 feet 6 inches tall. The shortest prisoner at Valleyfield was also an adult, not a boy: Noel Hubert Landria, a sergeant, regiment unstated, who had been 'Taken at the Capitulation of the Saints', and who arrived at and left Valleyfield at the same time as François Giraux. Sergeant Landria, born at La Haree [? Le Havre] and aged 33, was 4 feet 3½ inches tall.[22]

At Perth, out of the aggregate total of 7,761 prisoners confined between August 1812 and the general release in June and July 1814 only a couple of dozen appear not to have had their heights recorded. The number who were 6 feet or more in height out of all that mass of 7,735 or so prisoners was only 24 (0.32 per cent)—19 fewer even than at Valleyfield. On the other hand, there were, or appear to have been, fewer prisoners under 5 feet in height at Perth than at Valleyfield: 21 (0.27 per cent) at the former, 62 at the latter. Doubtless among the reasons for this latter difference were that at Perth there were fewer seamen and boys, only five prisoners there being aged between 9 and 14, whereas at Valleyfield there were 37.[23]

Of those 24 prisoners at Perth who were 6 feet or over, nine were exactly 6 feet, three were 6 ft 0½ in, one 6 ft 0¾ in, six 6 ft 1 in, one 6 feet 1½ ins, one 6 ft 2 ins, one 6 ft 6 ins, one 6 ft 6½ ins, and one 6 ft 7 ins. It was David Lamourouse, born at Lunet and aged 27, a soldier in the 82nd infantry regiment, captured on Martinique in March 1809, who at 6 ft 7 ins was the tallest prisoner recorded at Perth. Lamoureuse arrived at the depot in October 1812 and remained there until the general release in June 1814.[24]

Of the 21 at Perth who were under 5 feet in height, four were 4 ft 11½ ins, seven 4 ft 11 ins, one 4 ft 10½ ins, two 4 ft 10 ins, three 4 ft 9 ins, three 4 ft 6 ins, and one 3 ft 6 ins. Two or three of these prisoners were young boys such as Nicholas Le Roy, aged 10 and 4 ft 11 ins tall, a passenger on the privateer *Hirondelle* when captured in 1810; and Gabriel Legrand, born at Bayonne, aged 11 and 4 ft 6 ins tall, of the 11th Mineurs, captured at Madrid in August 1812, who arrived at Perth in December 1812 and was repatriated in July 1814. But most of the 21 were adult men, many of them in their thirties, and one, August Devot, born at Charrey, a soldier 4 ft 9ins tall from the 36th Light infantry regiment, was aged 45. Captured at Madrid in August 1812, he arrived at Perth in November that year and was released after the war ended, in July 1814. The shortest prisoner at Perth was, or may have been, significantly, like the boy Gabriel Legrand, a soldier from the Mineurs, in his case the 2nd battalion, but unlike Gabriel Legrand, an adult: Nicolas Dausseur, who, as already observed, was 3 ft 6 ins in height.[25]

Aliases or *noms de guerre* were used by several hundred of the prisoners in the depots in Scotland. In addition to those aliases (at least 127 at Valleyfield and 194 at Perth, for instance) which were noted in the Entry Books or other official documents, it is highly probable that many others were not known to or not noted by the depot authorities. One among what may well have been many such examples of a prisoner using an alias and not being known by his real name was, of course, that invaluable informant about aspects of the internal histories of three of the Scots depots, Lieutenant Marote-Carrier. There is no reference whatever in any depot or other official document to Henri-Ferdinand Marote, his real name, but only to Jean Baptiste Carrier, his alias or *nom de guerre*. Even in his published recollections, gathered and edited by the Belgian historian Léon Wocquier thirty years after the Napoleonic Wars, Marote nowhere mentions that as a prisoner of war successively at Esk Mills, Valleyfield and Perth he was known by his alias, never by his real name.

If aliases or *noms de guerre* by definition meant concealment, or attempted concealment, of identity why was such concealment felt necessary by so many of those who were prisoners in the depots in Scotland? Needless to say, no explanations are provided in the surviving documentation. But reasonable surmise might point perhaps to a need in some cases to escape the consequences of some military, naval, civil or criminal offence (such as desertion from Napoleon's armies into his sea-going forces, or the converse, or attempting to avoid conscription by joining the crew of a privateer ship), or to conceal the fact (illustrated certainly by a few of the aliases used by prisoners in the Scots depots) that they had already been prisoners of war in earlier stages of the conflict but had either escaped or been exchanged or released on medical grounds or (much less likely, although it did happen in the case of that other invaluable informant Captain Paul Andreas Kaald at Greenlaw, who, however, appears never himself to have used an alias and was only once taken prisoner) granted parole to return home. Other aliases may have been adopted because of domestic or family or financial problems, and others again for a variety of perhaps less pressing reasons.

At Greenlaw, very few aliases appear to have been recorded. But two seamen there each with an alias were Jean Gillevere and Pierre Gerrin (or Serrin). Jean Gillevere, alias Pierre A. Coulon, had, as has been observed in an earlier chapter above, been 'Taken on Board the American ship *George* of New York at South Shields' in November 1804 and sent from there first to Newcastle then to Leith and then into captivity the following month at Greenlaw. Pierre Gerrin, alias Jean Brilbord, had been 'Taken in the North Sea on Board a British Coals Vessel Captured by a Privateer of Flushing and sent to Leith', and from there he, too, entered Greenlaw in December 1804.[26]

Aliases were more conspicuous among the prisoners at Esk Mills. There ten men—all but one of them seamen—had their aliases recorded in the Entry Book, although for many others it was only after their transfer in March 1811 to Valleyfield that such information about them was recorded. Three of the ten had served aboard men of war of the French navy, another on one of its sloops, two others aboard merchant or transport ships, a further three aboard privateers, and the remaining one was a soldier who had been captured aboard a privateer. The soldier was Pierre Sepinetly, alias Joseph Ferrard, captured on the privateer *Finisterre*, no date or place given. The three seamen who had served on men of war were, from the *Alexandre*, captured in February 1806 at St Domingo, Pierre Denis Billiard, alias Amand Le Clerc; from the *Brave*, captured at the same time and place, Jean Lecheneau, alias Jean Lechevre; and from the *Achille*, captured in October 1805 at Trafalgar, J. P. Mascara, alias Martinet. Of the two seamen taken on board a merchant or transport vessel, one was François Scagliano, alias François Leonaro, from the *Providence*, no date or place of capture given. Pierre Petit was the uncharacteristically unimaginative alias of François Petit, privateersman, who escaped, as already observed, from Esk Mills on 7 March 1811. Why Benjamin Barbel, surgeon, captured on the privateer *Gustave*, no date or place given, should have adopted an alias as José Palucio is no more obvious than was theirs for those other nine at Esk Mills.[27]

At Edinburgh Castle, to Julien Verté, drummer, 47th infantry regiment, born at Rennes and aged 22, captured at Coimbra in October 1810, may have been attached a nickname rather than an alias, for he was recorded as 'dit Bataille'. Transferred from the Castle in October 1813 to Valleyfield, however, he was entered there as 'alias Battail'.[28]

Verté was one of some 104 prisoners at Valleyfield whose aliases were recorded in the Entry Books. One already encountered was the privateer seaman Matu Bronzan, alias Baptiste Hidgy, who escaped from Valleyfield in February 1812.[29] Pierre Chuchère, another privateer seaman, in his case captured on the *Somnambule* in the English Channel in October 1810, was less fortunate: 'Shott 24 May 1813 Attempting to escape' from the depot. But under *Somnambule* in the Entry Book at the entry for Chuchère was also written in ink the name of another privateer vessel, *Grand Napoléon*, and 'Jean David Dominique Jance'. Had Pierre Chuchère therefore been captured twice, the first time under the latter name? A Dutch prisoner, already observed, at Valleyfield whose alias seems apt for a volunteer, as he became, into the British navy in May 1812 was Daniel Vilser, alias David Fisher, a seaman. Jean Baptiste Destrais, the last prisoner entered in the Valleyfield Entry Books, variously described there as a soldier captured at the 'Capitulation of the Saints' but also as a seaman on the frigate *L'Amphitrite* when captured in February 1809 at Martinique, and who will be encountered again later, was alias Pierre Calmain.[30]

Some prisoners' aliases, if indeed intended to conceal identity, appear (like that of François Petit, alias Pierre Petit) to have offered distinctly inadequate cover. Thus at Valleyfield, Roussel Mathieu, aged 27 and born at Rouen, a soldier in the 4th infantry regiment, who had been captured in March 1809 in Portugal, had his alias solemnly set down as Mathieu Roussel; and Jacque (sic) Marie Jofroi, a privateer seaman, captured in 1806, evidently had as his alias Jacques Godfroy, under which he seems later to have been captured, no date or place given, as a soldier in the 1st Colonial Battalion.[31]

At Perth at least two prisoners had each three names or aliases. One of these two was Lazar Cairel, aged 38, 5 ft 4½ins tall, with an oval face, fresh complexion, light brown hair, grey eyes, and with no marks or wounds. As Lazar Cairel he was evidently captain of the privateer *Marie Louise*. As Louis Etienne Blanc he was a soldier in the 26th line regiment. As Aimé Julien, he was quartermaster on the frigate *Rhin*. Captured on 9 February 1809 at Martinique, it is not known in or under which of these three capacities or aliases he had become a prisoner. Born at Samel, Cairel-Blanc-Julien arrived from Valleyfield in September 1812 at Perth and remained there until the general release in June 1814. The other prisoner who had three names or aliases was Mathieu Lavy. Described as a soldier in the 66th regiment of the Line he had been captured at Guadeloupe in February 1810. He was said to be known also as both Canuet and Galabert, the latter 'his proper name'. Born at Nantes and aged 20, Lavy, like Cairel, was released from Perth in the general repatriation in June 1814. That Mathieu Lavy had already borne three names or aliases by the age of 20 illustrates that the use of aliases was not by any means monoplised by more mature prisoners of war. Another slightly younger prisoner than Mathieu Lavy was Pierre Mouszin, aged 19, a drummer in 'French Army', who had been captured at sea in February 1811 and was transferred in August 1813 from Valleyfield to Perth. Mouszin, born at Nancy, 5 feet 4 inches tall, of thin build, oval face, fair complexion, white (sic) hair, grey eyes, and with a mark on his forehead, was alias 'Jacques Delcour *dit* Le Blon'. One at Perth even younger than Mathieu Lavy or Pierre Mouszin was Jean Vigneron, born at Lyons and aged 15. His alias was Durand. He had been a musician in the 1st Garde de Paris when captured at Baylen in Spain in July 1808. Whatever horrors this young boy may have witnessed or indeed himself suffered after his capture at Baylen are not recorded.[32]

Among numbers of prisoners at Perth, as at Valleyfield, with aliases and who had evidently served successively as soldiers and seamen, and who were or appear to have been among those who became prisoners of war more than once, was J.C. Le Breton, a soldier in the 1st Regiment of Artillery, captured on Martinique in February 1809, but who was alias Alex Toussaint, sailor on the *Amphitrite* (presumably either the man-of-war of that name, or a privateer vessel of the same name), no place or date of capture given. Born at Falaise in Normandy, he was aged 27. He was transferred from Valleyfield to Perth in August 1813 and remained there until his release in June 1814.[33]

Many among the hundreds of prisoners in the depots in Scotland who had aliases may well therefore have had particularly interesting personal experiences. Those experiences were not, however, except in rare cases such as that of Marote-Carrier, recorded or preserved for posterity. The cloak of concealment, at least from the eyes of later generations, thus descended eventually on virtually all those prisoners who had adopted aliases, just as it did on the overwhelming mass of all the thousands of rank and file prisoners in the depots north of the Border. Apart from their physical descriptions, and some limited account of the experiences of those who attracted the attention of the authorities, whether by applying or appealing, by breaching depot rules, by volunteering into His Britannic Majesty's services, by falling sufficiently ill to merit being sent into a depot hospital, by being exchanged (a rare occurrence), by being repatriated on grounds of old age or physical incapacity, by escaping, or by dying, relatively little is known about the prisoners as people, even less about their lives before and after their years of captivity.

13

Beds and Bedding, and Clothing

Sleeping space allowed to ratings in the British navy in the era of the Napoleonic Wars was a standard width of 14 inches per man. In practice, however, each rating usually had double that width, since the starboard and larboard watches into which ships' crews were divided worked alternate watches and thus were not all below in their quarters at the same time.[1] But even a double width of 2 feet 4 inches per man hardly provided spacious sleeping conditions.

Such regulations, prescribed for British sailors by the Admiralty, of which the Transport Board was a section, were unlikely to be made more generous in the provision of sleeping conditions for prisoners of war. The latters' generally overcrowded conditions were made worse as the war continued by the growing number of captives and the difficulties in finding secure 'receptacles' for them. At Greenlaw, for example, according to the banker-historian Macbeth Forbes (who does not give his sources): 'The prisoners were shut up in apartments each about 20 feet square with 30 hammocks placed in two tiers one above the other. The rooms had windows and shutters and strong thick doors with iron bolts. A turnkey locked the prisoners up each night at sunset and lights had to be extinguished when the drum beat, and noises had then to cease. There were two sentinels nightly pacing the passage within the House.'[2]

That invaluable witness among the prisoners at Greenlaw, Paul Andreas Kaald, noted in his diary on Friday, 11 November 1808: 'In this room are 12 Danes altogether and 16 French, which is far too many since it is so dreadfully cramped here. I have my place right beside the door where the night tub [i.e., communal chamber pot] lies. I have to eat and drink here and keep all my household belongings in the chest next to the above mentioned night tub.' Two days later Kaald wrote: 'At 3.30 or 4 p.m ... we will now be locked up for 17 hours in the same room with many other people. Some are people who have had little upbringing, others again are extreme (pardon me for saying so) pigs. But we are forced to be living on top of each other since through the time spent there the room becomes tightly packed, so full of moisture and unhealthy air that you can soon become sick. There are some who stay in bed all the time… The room is furnished with timber framework and pillars so that each man lies in a hammock right next to others … a room is never cleaned out or washed, only the rough is brushed out in between times. So you can imagine how healthy and pleasant it is here.'[3]

At Esk Mills the crisis in early March 1811, marked by the stampede among the prisoners, the consequent crushing to death of two of their number, the immediate transfer of all the prisoners to Valleyfield or Edinburgh Castle, and the closure of the depot itself, was reported in at least one newspaper to have been the result of 'the want of sufficient accommodation for so great a number of people in the place where they are confined.'[4] And at Perth the five three-storey buildings, the interior of each storey of which was 130 feet long by 30 feet broad, each held 1,140 prisoners—indicative of how closely they were packed in. 'I have tried,' wrote the local historian William Sievewright, 'to picture the prisoners asleep in their wards, and have wondered how much they did when they felt a desire to change their position… When the full complement was in the prison each ward [or storey] would have to provide room for 380 men. With four tiers of sleepers there would thus be nearly 100 in each, at all events 95 or 96, rather more than 16 inches to each. This arrangement would have left one centre passage of six feet, or three narrow passages of two feet each along the ward. I fancy there must have been some resemblance between their condition overnight and that of the American prisoners at Libby. They had been obliged "to lie spoon fashion", and when the one side got uneasy on the hard hammocks, they had possibly got the word of command as at Libby, "Attention, squad number four! Prepare to spoon! One-two-spoon!" The whole squad flopping over on the other side.'[5]

It appears not unlikely that, generally, living and sleeping conditions in the depots in Scotland during the winter months and in early spring and late autumn were 'terribly cold, there were no windows, no warmth', as Mr John Cowan of Beeslack, Penicuik, during his visit to the Invalides in Paris in 1845, was told by the old soldier Marcher when recalling his captivity at Valleyfield. Charles Cowan, another member of the family of the papermill owners at Valleyfield during the Napoleonic Wars, recalled long afterwards, as already observed, that at that depot the new prison blocks, three storeys high and built chiefly of wood, 'had no glass in the openings for light and air, which were closed at night by very strong wooden shutters, and secured by strong iron stanchions, nor were there any fireplaces or artifical heat, for it was expected that the animal heat would suffice for their comfort, the prisoners having been stowed away as close almost as herrings in a barrel…'[6] The analogy seems apt. For it is not unlikely that a purpose the Transport Board had in packing in the prisoners was to save government expenditure on heating their accommodation.[7] Perhaps a reasonable conclusion may be that, depending partly on the season of the year, the prisoners' sleeping accommodation was either cold or stuffy.

At Greenlaw depot, where the small format of almost all the General Entry Books did not include columns of information about the issue to prisoners of beds or hammocks and bedding, there is little surviving evidence of that provision. But the larger format Entry Books used at the other depots in Scotland do offer at least some indication of what prisoners had. The wording of the relevant entries in the large format Entry Books was: Date of Supply: Hammock, Bed, Palliasse, Bolster, Blanket. From the evidence of the entries marked in those columns there seems little doubt that it was in hammocks, not beds, that prisoners in the depots in Scotland slept. Such references as there are to beds appear ambiguous. What seems to be meant when they are mentioned is a hammock plus either a palliasse that could be filled with straw or flock (wool or cloth waste) or a light hair mattress. That appears to be confirmed by a list of bedding contained in a letter of December 1810 from the Transport Board to the Admiralty (which had asked the Board to 'report precisely' what the provision for prisoners of war was) and which says prisoners 'If on shore' [i.e., in land depots] were issued with a hammock, a palliasse, a bolster and one blanket. Those on board ship were said to be provided with a hammock, a flock bed—a bed, or really a palliasse or mattress, stuffed with wool, and a blanket.[8] In addition to the invaluable written evidence he provided in his diary at Greenlaw about the prisoners and their conditions and the events there, Captain Paul Andreas Kaald sketched the interior of his own room in the old mansion. The foreground of his sketch presents an example, unique for any depot in Scotland, of hammocks hanging about six feet above the floor from the crossbars of four tall posts reaching from floor to ceiling, and upon the wall to the left are two other hammocks, one end of each of which hangs from a similar crossbar and their other ends no doubt await being fixed at night to the opposite crossbar. There is also some cross-strapping underneath each hammock which suggests some kind of mattress, no doubt either of straw, flock or hair.[9]

Another difficulty that arises in any attempt to paint a picture other than an impressionistic one of the provision of beds and bedding among the prisoners in the Scots depots is that even where no issue of these items was recorded or no record of such was preserved, it did not necessarily mean the prisoners concerned had to sleep on the floor without bedding of any kind. For on the transports that conveyed them up the North Sea from the hulks or depots in the south of England to Leith many prisoners appear to have been embarked along with their hammocks and bedding. On 12 February 1811, for example, in the midst of the cascade of landings at Leith of prisoners for

Esk Mills depot, the Transport Board informed Malcolm Wright, its agent at Edinburgh, that Captain Pellowe, agent at Esk Mills, had suggested no prisoners should be landed in future without their baggage being sent ashore with them, 'as many of the Prisoners lately sent to Esk Mills are very much distressed from the Number of Beds and other Things lost to them.'[10]

Throughout the war there were numerous letters exchanged between the Transport Board and its depot agents in Scotland about the provision, or absence, of hammocks and bedding for prisoners. Thus on 24 September 1808 the Board told Wright, then its agent at Greenlaw, that '... 300 sets of bedding will be sent to you without delay. You will purchase a supply of old rope for the prisoners to make clews to their hammocks with, as is done at the other depots, and thimbles are not necessary.'[11] Three days earlier the Board, in a circular to all depots that reflected its concern both for economy and for distribution of such supplies being duly accounted for, had instructed that there should be sent to its office in London 'all the old samples of bedding ... now in your possession, excepting such as are actually in use, and you will in future always return old samples upon our furnishing you with new ones of the same nature.'[12] The Board's concerns were demonstrated in another circular to all depots on 27 March 1811, in which it instructed its agents to warn inmates 'that if any prisoner, upon orders being given for his release, should be found deficient in any of the articles of bedding delivered to him, he will be detained.'[13] In one of a number of similar such instructions issued by the Board to its agents, Captain C. Patton, RN, at Portsmouth, was directed on 20 August 1812 'to put on board of each vessel proceeding to Scotland with prisoners direct from Portugal a number of good washed beds and blankets equal to the number of prisoners on board.'[14] From some of the correspondence arise implications of pilfering of hammocks and bedding en route to or after their delivery in Scotland, or incompetence and irresponsibility on the part of at least one agent of the Board. Thus on 12 December 1811, the Board replied to a recent letter from Captain E.J. Moriarty, its agent at Valleyfield: '... we inclose Extracts of Letters from Agents for Prisoners of War at Portsmouth, Plymouth and Chatham, containing their Reports on the Subject of the Bedding supplied to the Prisoners sent from their respective Depots to Scotland, but which the prisoners deny to have received.'[15] And the following year, on 17 July 1812, the Board expressed its urgent concern to Malcolm Wright, formerly its agent at Edinburgh until his dismissal the previous December, that: 'The purser of HMS *Ardent*, which conveyed prisoners and stores from Portsmouth to Leith in the month of February 1811, having applied for a remuneration for taking care of the articles stated below [including 500 beds and 500 blankets], and he having been called upon to state how the said stores were disposed of, we inclose a copy of his report together with an extract of a letter from the commander of the *Ardent* on this subject, by which it appears that the whole of the said stores, with the exception of a few articles which had been issued to the prisoners during the passage, were delivered into your charge. Report to us with the least possible delay the number of each article actually received by you and how they were afterwards disposed of.' The Board's letter went on to tell Wright that, 'An account of the receipt and expenditure of all the stores supplied for the service of prisoners lately confined in Edinburgh Castle during the time of your Agency is much wanted, as is also an account of all the stores delivered into your charge as our Agent for prisoners of war at Leith, distinguishing in said account how the stores were disposed of. The want of this account has been long felt at this office, it being impossible without it to charge the several stores against the Agents to whom they were forwarded.'[16]

Sometimes the quantities of beds or hammocks and bedding sent by sea to Scotland were large: on 20 August 1812, for example, the Board informed Lieutenant Glinn, RN, its transport agent at Leith, that '5,000 new hammocks will be forwarded from London.' Glinn himself, however, was reproved by the Board three months later for failing to 'apply to the Admiral for the use of tarpaulins for the prisoners' bedding, which was entirely wet on arrival at Perth.'[17]

Whatever or whoever was responsible for failures in distribution or for pilfering or purloining of supplies of beds and bedding, it was the prisoners who were the sufferers. At any time in all of the Scots depots it seems likely that at least some prisoners had no hammocks or blankets and had to sleep on the floor with whatever covering they could find. That was certainly the experience, for example, of 240 prisoners who entered Esk Mills on 7 February 1811, having 'remained all the preceding night at Edinburgh Castle, without beds or anything to sleep on, and that their bedding had not yet been landed [at Leith].'[18]

At Greenlaw, among the limited information available about the issue of beds and bedding is that concerning the 48 American merchant seamen confined there between October 1812 and February 1813. To the 48 were distributed 44 hammocks, 18 beds, and 39 blankets. So 14 each received a hammock, a bed and a blanket, 23 a hammock and a blanket, four a hammock and a bed, three a hammock only, two a blanket only, and the remaining two nothing at all.[19]

At Esk Mills, where the rapid succession of intakes of prisoners in February and early March 1811 overwhelmed the clerks' efforts to complete details that should have been recorded in the Entry Book, fewer than 100 of the total of 2,817 prisoners had their issue of beds and bedding recorded. The most that was issued to any among that handful of prisoners was a hammock and one blanket—in the other cases it was only a blanket.[20]

At Edinburgh Castle, among the eleven 'ringleaders' marched there following the troubles at Esk Mills early in March 1811 two (Antoine Morel or Morete and Louis Jean Lepine or Lepin) were each issued two months later with a blanket, and two others (Grandjean Duhenot and Hipolyte Decreuze) each on 6 April with a bed and blanket. Those among the other 530 or so prisoners listed in what was the main General Entry Book for the Castle who were recorded as receiving items of bedding appear to have been issued at most with a bed and blanket or a hammock and blanket, some among them, such as No. 476 Adolphe Douzon, midshipman, receiving only the one or the other.[21]

Issues at Valleyfield appear to have been not dissimilar, although there were exceptions, as in the case, for example, of that remarkable escaper François Petit, privateersman, who a month after his recapture at Glasgow in November 1811 received a hammock, bed and blanket; and of another privateersman, François Armand, who also found himself at Valleyfield following his recapture in October 1813 after escaping from Perth, and who received a hammock, palliasse and bolster—before escaping briefly from Valleyfield, too, shortly afterwards.[22]

A hammock and a blanket were issues commonly made also to prisoners at Perth. Johan Walle of the Hanoverian Legion, who had been captured at Oporto in May 1809 and who arrived at Perth in August 1812, was among those more fortunate in receiving at the depot a month later a hammock, bed and blanket.[23] An unusual case was that of Nicolas Le Roy, the boy passenger aged 10 captured in September 1810 on the privateer *Hirondelle*, of which his father, also taken prisoner, was captain, and who were among those transferred at the beginning of September 1812 from Valleyfield to Perth. A month after his transfer the boy was issued with a hammock and a bed—and then a year later with another hammock. Whether his first had by then become unusable or perhaps had been purloined by a fellow prisoner, is not stated.[24] Another passenger, Pierre La Coste, captured much earlier in the war, in March 1804, and transferred also in September 1812 from Valleyfield to Perth, was issued at the latter a year later with a hammock and a blanket—then within a further seven weeks with another blanket—presumably, too, because his first blanket had become too thin or torn or otherwise unusable or had been stolen.[25] The issue on 12 October 1813 of a hammock and a blanket to Beniot [? Benoit] Pairin (or Perine), a soldier captured on the *Varsovie* man-of-war at Rochefort in April 1809 and who arrived at Perth almost four years later, came too late to be of any comfort to him: he died the same day.[26] A prisoner at Perth who appears to have received every item possible of the bedding issuable was Nicolas E. Jennat, a soldier captured at sea on board the privateer *Renoir* in March 1808 and who arrived at Perth in August 1812. He was issued with a hammock, bed, palliasse, bolster and blanket. That unusually extensive provision appears to have done little to reconcile him to his captivity: he escaped on 4 June 1814, two months after the end of the war, though he was recaptured the same day.[27] As already observed, only one of the seven women entered in the Perth Entry Books is recorded as receiving any bedding: Marie Manuel received a hammock on 9 January 1813, the day she arrived at the depot via HMS *Freya* from Lisbon with her husband Blaise Peuxe.[28]

Amid the general overcrowding, cold or stuffiness, in the prisoners' sleeping accommodation in the depots in Scotland, there were no doubt some who, because either they could by their manual or other skills secure themselves some income or their family or friends were able to send them some money from home, were able to make themselves more comfortable by night as by day. One example was that other invaluable witness Marote-Carrier. He has already been observed providing himself with what he described as a *cadre*, 'a kind of wooden hammock or bed without feet, suspended by cords above the floor', for which he was also able to obtain a mattress and two covers.[29]

Beds and bedding, or at any rate the airing of them, appear on at least one occasion to have become a fulcrum for prisoners' frustrations and complaints. 'I enclose for the [Transport] Board's consideration and reply,' wrote James Bowen, one of its Commissioners, from Edinburgh on 5 May 1811, 'a packet of grievances I received yesterday from prisoners at Valleyfield, and will thank you to get their cases considered as soon as possible. There was a demur to bringing out the hammocks yesterday, the weather being fine, and nothing but a determined spirit of insubordination could induce them to disobey the orders.' Bowen had told the prisoners that 'if they did not obey all orders and regulations that were adopted for the benefit of their health and comforts I would tomorrow take all their hammocks from them and then they should have nothing but the boards and floors to sleep on, and that the prisons should be cleared and aired every fine day. Notwithstanding this they held out until near 4 o'clock, when they put out their hammocks ... I left them peaceable and ... I hope the resistance made to their breach of duty will have a good effect.'[30]

'Today,' noted Captain Paul Andreas Kaald in his diary on 31 December 1808 at Greenlaw, 'clothes were given to all the prisoners—something we had long wished for. Clothing was one pair of yellow trousers, underpants, a vest, a blue and white shirt, a pair of socks, a pair of shoes, all marked with the emblem of King George: T.O.' The initials of the Transport Office were marked on all clothing issued to prisoners for two obvious reasons: to deter their illicit sale and to ensure escaped prisoners still wearing those clothes were conspicuous and easily identifiable. 'All articles of bedding and clothing supplied to Prisoners of War,' the Transport Board instructed, for example, Lieutenant Priest, RN, its agent at Greenlaw in August 1811, 'should be properly marked before delivery.'[31]

'Today,' Kaald again began his diary entry at Greenlaw the following day, 1 January 1809, 'we had the pleasure of seeing the biggest part of the prisoners in their new uniforms, which everybody is pleased about, since it has very striking colours.' Kaald may have overestimated the degree of pleasure among some of the prisoners. Those who nourished hopes of escape from the depot must have seen immediately that the 'striking colours' confronted their hopes with yet another obstacle to their realisation.[32]

There is abundant evidence that clothes issued to the prisoners were certainly deliberately colourful. 'Inform you,' announced a Transport Board letter in October 1811 to an official correspondent, 'that Mr John Maberley, the contractor for supplying yellow clothing for prisoners of war, has stated that between 4,000 and 5,000 suits are nearly ready for delivery; and that the supply of the remainder will be forwarded.'[33] At Greenlaw depot, the agent was told by the Board in April 1809 that 'Samples of clothing for prisoners of war have been sent: three suits of yellow clothing, numbered 2, 3 and 4 … One suit of green clothing, one pair of linen drawers.' Whether the linen drawers were yellow or green or of some other hue went unmentioned, but the omission was hardly significant as they were garments less likely to be immediately visible to public gaze and identification should their wearers escape.[34]

The comments on clothing made by that other diarist among the prisoners at Greenlaw, Sergeant Major Philippe Beaudoin, were, unlike those of Captain Kaald, decidedly bitter: 'The clothing received is yellow. With this costume one looks like a savage. This colour has been adopted by the English government to prevent the prisoners selling their belongings. In a word, the English are all brigands.'[35]

When Louis Simond, the French-born traveller who had lived for over twenty years in the United States of America, visited Edinburgh Castle in February 1811 during his tour of Britain, he found the prisoners of war there 'walking to and fro in their narrow inclosure, most of them talking merrily enough, poorly clad, though not in rags. Those who have no clothes of their own receive certain yellow jackets which, by their remarkable appearance, render their escape more difficult; instead of shoes they had most of them a sort of galoches, the sole of wood and the top of list. I understood that many had lost their shoes in the muddy road, and that 150 of them were really in great want of that important article, which Colonel Maghee assured me was to be supplied before they left the Castle to go to the depot [at Penicuik].'[36] If that was really the reason for so many barefoot prisoners, then searching for shoes sucked into the muddy streets of Scotland's capital city must surely have provided a hitherto unrecorded but animated occupation for some of its more needy but enterprising citizens—a variation on legendary streets paved with gold.

William Chambers's vivid recollection of looking down as a boy about 1811-12 from the slopes above Valleyfield upon the prisoners below included his description of them as 'Dressed in coarse woollen clothing of a yellow colour, and most of them wearing red or blue cloth caps, or partly coloured cowls ...', while some among them tended cooking pots over open fires, 'which they fanned by the flapping of cocked-hats.'[37] Chambers also recalled how at his native Peebles about that same period, 'One afternoon on coming out of school, and emerging on the main street, my companions and I were startled with the spectacle of a party of French prisoners of war under a military escort. Even to boys, who are not very sensitive, it was an appalling scene; something at least which I can never forget.' The prisoners were recaptured escapers from Penicuik and 'All were dressed in the yellow prison garb, which would everywhere reveal their character.'[38] Even prisoners who were patients in the Valleyfield depot hospital appear to have worn distinctive yellow clothing, as Charles Cowan of the mill-owning family there, whose mansion house was converted into the hospital, long afterward recalled. 'Well do I remember their grotesque appearance, enveloped as they were in long capacious bright yellow dressing-gowns, with caps to match.'[39] It may have been Cowan's *Reminiscences*, privately published in Edinburgh in 1878, rather than the recollections of William Chambers, which prompted Robert Louis Stevenson to exclaim, when writing in Samoa in 1893-4 his adventure story *St Ives*, about a French prisoner of war who escaped from Edinburgh Castle: 'I had miserable luck with *St Ives*; being already half-way through it, a book I had ordered six months ago arrives at last, and I have to change the first half of it from top to bottom! How could I have dreamed the French prisoners were watched over like a female charity school, kept in a grotesque livery, and shaved twice a week? And I had made all my points on the idea that they were unshaved and clothed anyhow.'[40]

A prisoner at Esk Mills who clearly recalled donning distinctive hospital garb there was Marote-Carrier. 'It was,' he said, 'a sort of wide dirty yellow underpants; a green overcoat that was quite long and on the back of which were embroidered two big yellow letters T.O. The white metal buttons likewise bore these two letters. We were ... given lisle stockings, a cotton cap and a shirt. We put these things on and we laid aside our own things, so that we could pick them up again when we left hospital. This peculiar combination of green and yellow in the hospital uniform led the soldiers of the guard to give us the name French parrots.'[41]

François Petit, that remarkable escaper from both Esk Mills and Valleyfield, as well as from several towns in Scotland, en route back to the latter depot after his successive recaptures, was said by two women witnesses at Falkirk of one of his escapes in December 1811 to have worn 'coloured clothes'. But given Petit's resourcefulness they seem unlikely to have been those issued to the prisoners.[42]

Transferred with other prisoners at the beginning of September 1812 from Valleyfield to Perth, Marote-Carrier long afterward recalled in his discussions with the Belgian historian Léon Wocquier that: 'At the time of our entry to Perth, a distribution had been made to us of a uniform clothing: this was two shirts of coarse linen waste, a pair of trousers, a shortened jacket, and a waistcoat, all coloured yellow so that the thing might be more extraordinary and that it might be easier to spot us in case of escape. Each piece of clothing bore, imprinted in oil [i.e., ink?], the two ritual letters TO. We were told that these issues of clothing would be renewed every 18 months.'[43]

The soldiers among the thousands of prisoners of war in the depots in Scotland had worn the handsome uniforms of Napoleon's armies or those of his allies and had taken part in what for some years from 1803 onward appeared to be their invincible advances through huge areas of Europe. Wearing the distinctive clothing issued to them as prisoners of war by the Transport Board and its agents must therefore have been felt by many of them to be a daily humiliation. Unless they possessed equanimity, an unshakeable sense of humour, or little or no vanity about their appearance, that distinctive clothing seems likely to have placed additional strain on their morale.

The actual items of clothing issued or issuable to the prisoners were detailed in a letter of December 1810 from the Transport Board to the Admiralty. Prisoners were said to receive: 'for 18 months 1 cloth jacket, 1 cloth waistcoat, 1 cloth trowsers, 2 cotton shirts, 2 pairs stockings, shoes as often as necessary, 1 hat.'[44] But also, of course, actual issues to individual prisoners were, or appear to have been, entered in the large format General Entry Books of the depots. A series of narrow columns in those Books, headed respectively hat, jacket, waistcoat, trowsers [sic], shirt, shoes, stockings, handkerchief, and the date of issue, had appropriate ticks entered in them. The first prisoner listed in the first Valleyfield Entry Book, for example, was Thomas Paumier. Paumier arrived at the depot with all those 2,400 or so other prisoners from Esk Mills on 11 March 1811. A month later, according to the Entry Book, he was issued with a pair of shoes. On 1 November that year he received a hat, a jacket, a waistcoat, trousers, and a shirt; a month later another shirt and another pair of shoes; and in February 1814 another hat, jacket, waistcoat, trousers, shirt and pair of shoes. That was about as generous an issue of clothing in three years as any other prisoners in the depots in Scotland received.

Sergeant Major Beaudoin at Greenlaw appears to have been much less fortunate than Paumier at Valleyfield. Beaudoin's case further illustrates the variety of experience of many of the prisoners in particular matters such as clothing. No doubt that variety of experience was an outcome of a range of factors which included the amount of supplies sent by the Transport Office to the depots, stocks held there, and the sympathetic care and diligence or otherwise of the depot agents and their staffs. 'When I arrived in prison my shirt had rotted on my back and I had no other to change into,' Beaudoin recorded. 'Besides I hadn't a penny to bless myself with and I was crawling with vermin. Fortunately for me I found a humane man who loaned me a change of clothes so that I could wash thoroughly those I was wearing, which helped me a lot ... clothing was supposed to be renewed every year. Well, I was there [at Greenlaw] five and a half years [from 1804 to 1809] and I received only one new set of clothing.'[45]

Some prisoners fared, at least for a time, even more badly than Beaudoin with clothing. 'From 400 to 500 prisoners have arrived at the [Perth] Depot since this day week,' reported the *Perth Courier* on 19 November 1812. 'They were quite destitute of clothing but upon their arrival here were supplied with all these necessaries and made as comfortable as their situation could admit of.' Two weeks later the paper told its readers that: 'During the last few days a great number of French prisoners have passed through Kirkcaldy on their way to the Depot at Perth. They are in general wretched looking creatures, very dirty, and very ill clad, having been on their march through Portugal, as they themselves declare, stripped of almost all their clothing by the Portuguese. A striking contrast to this barbarity was exhibited by two amiable young ladies of Kirkcaldy, who took the mantles from their shoulders, and the blankets from their beds, to bestow upon the prisoners. Many others of the inhabitants, influenced by similar philanthropy, contributed provisions and such articles of clothing as they could spare.'[46] There was almost simultaneously a similar scene at Leith, where, as the *Caledonian Mercury* reported on 14 November 1812, 'About 25 sick prisoners of war were landed yesterday morning from the *Latona* transport and conveyed in carts to the Royal Infirmary. They appeared to be in a very languid and debilitated state and seem to have had no other covering but a blanket to defend them from the cold. Every attention was paid to them which their unfortunate situation would allow; and one instance of humanity in a seaman belonging to a passage boat deserves to be noticed—on observing a prisoner who had little or no clothing on and who was in a very feeble state, and shivering with cold, he immediately pulled off his waistcoat and gave it to the unfortunate stranger.'[47]

That many prisoners were indeed stripped of their clothes by hostile peasants or others when they were captured in Spain or Portugal or as they passed through those countries on their way to the next stage of their captivity in depots or hulks in Britain, is attested in contemporary memoirs.[48] Some, perhaps many, prisoners in the depots in Scotland had lost clothing, not to

Spanish or Portuguese but to British hands. Sergeant Major Beaudoin, for example, who was captured not in Spain or Portugal but in the West Indies, noted in his diary at Greenlaw in the summer of 1809: 'Until the present I had increased the amount of linen I have, for when I arrived in prison my bag was light; in taking me prisoner, the English left me only with what I had on my back.'[49] But that some such prisoners should arrive weeks or months later in Scotland still with little or no clothing reflected badly on the humanity and efficiency of the Transport Board or those of its agents through whose hands the prisoners passed en route to their landings at Leith, Kirkcaldy or Burntisland and then toward their confinement in the depots at Penicuik, Edinburgh Castle or Perth.

The scenes described in Fife en route to Perth in November 1812 indeed aroused severe criticism from two senior officers in Scotland. Their criticisms were concerned, however, not merely with the lack of clothing but also with brutal treatment evidently suffered by some of the prisoners said to be mortally ill. '... yours of the 17th instant received,' wrote the Transport Board on 20 November 1812 to Vice-Admiral Otway at Leith, 'with the copy of the letter therein referred to from Major General Fergusson [sic], stating the wretched condition of the prisoners landed at Burntisland from the transports lately arrived; and in return we inform you that the prisoners in question were embarked at Lisbon in the most wretched and exhausted condition, and the greater part in a state of absolute nakedness. Anticipating from experience the destitute condition of prisoners arriving from Portugal, the most strict orders were given by us for removing all the sick from among them and making up their number by healthy prisoners and for clothing the whole completely, previously to their sailing for Scotland. It is feared that many of these prisoners may after attaining a state of convalescence have again relapsed or fallen sick, from the change of climate and other causes naturally belonging to the situation and circumstances under which they have been unavoidably placed, so little according with their former habits and mode of life. With respect to the alleged want of clothing among these prisoners, we are totally at a loss to account, our orders having been, as before observed, most positive and express for causing the whole of the prisoners to be removed being comfortably clothed, previously to their sailing. ... we ... have further to inform you that in order to prevent, in future, any of the very unpleasant circumstances which have lately occurred, we have given directions for all prisoners arriving from Portugal being removed immediately upon their arrival in this country and fresh prisoners in health and well clothed, being embarked in their stead after the ships shall have been properly cleaned. We have further to observe that it was with the utmost regret we learnt that any prisoners in a state of sickness or destitute of clothing should have been removed in *open carts* as represented by General Ferguson, and we have called upon Lieutenant Glinn to account for so extraordinary a circumstance, at the same time admonishing him against any similar event in future.'[50]

That same day Alexander McLeay, secretary to the Board, wrote the first of two letters within two days to Lieutenant Glinn concerning these very serious complaints: 'It having been represented to the Board by Vice Admiral Otway that some of the prisoners landed from the *Latona* were put into open carts in a dying state without clothing, medical aid, or any comfort or assistance, I am directed to express to you the Board's great regret and surprize that any sick prisoners should have been so removed and to desire you will report to them on the subject. I am at the same time to acquaint you that, in future, you are on no account to remove any prisoners under similar circumstances. Orders have been given for all prisoners arriving from Spain or Portugal being landed at the port of their arrival, and fresh prisoners in health and well clothed being embarked for Scotland, so that it is trusted few, if any, cases will occur of sick prisoners arriving in Scotland.'[51]

That Lieutenant Glinn survived in his appointment as transport officer based at Leith despite the severe criticisms of the brutal treatment of those prisoners on the way to Perth seems even more surprising than the Transport Board's 'great regret and surprize' at his actions or failures. According to George Penny in his *Traditions of Perth*, published twenty years after the Napoleonic Wars, prisoners marched through Fife to the depot at Perth in the winter of 1812-13, when 'the weather was dreadfully wet, and the roads bad', were '... poor creatures, many of them half naked, ... in a miserable plight; many of them gave up on the way, and were flung into carts one above the other; and when the carts were capable of holding no more, others were tied to the back of the carts with ropes, and dragged along.' Penny gives no source for his comments, but since he was writing of events well within living memory it appears likely that his source was either his own recollection or that of eye-witnesses in Fife or Perth.[52] It is not clear whether it was the appalling treatment of those prisoners en route through Fife to Perth that was the actual source several months later of a complaint to the Transport Board by the French government, or whether its complaint did arise from a further case of maltreatment of prisoners who were said to have been invalided home around that same period to France from either Valleyfield or Perth or both. But on 28 May 1813 the Board ordered its agents at the two depots, and also Lieutenant Glinn at Leith, to 'report fully what were the means used in the conveyance of those [invalids] sent ... and what was their actual condition at the time of their removal.' The French government declared that the repatriated invalids had complained 'that many of them were removed in a dying state in carts to which they were bound and that some of them died on the journey.' The agents' reports appear not to have survived. Such maltreatment, once proven, could well have resulted in retaliation upon British prisoners of war held in France.[53]

Among other aspects of the subject of the clothing of the prisoners in the depots in Scotland, a subject clearly important to their well-being, there were several which justify some further discussion. Of overcoats, for example, there appears to have been no issue—a significant lack in a climate like that of Scotland between October and April. The evidence is very scrappy indeed but some, perhaps many, prisoners had no doubt been able, like Marote-Carrier, to fetch a top coat with them into captivity: 'I hurriedly put on,' he recalled, 'a brown carrick [overcoat] with three collars [layers of shoulder coverings] that was almost new on top of my clothes', as the boarding party from the British frigate *Royalist* had clambered aboard his privateer ship to make him and his shipmates prisoners. And in the sketch dated July 1813 by Robert Reid, crown architect in Scotland, of prisoners at Greenlaw at least a quarter of the two dozen small figures depicted appear to be wearing knee-length top coats. If this sketch was a reasonably accurate depiction at that season it surely also suggested the need for topcoats between autumn and spring.[54]

Hats issued appear to have been of several types. Whether all the cowls and red or blue cloth caps observed by William Chambers being worn by most prisoners at Valleyfield were one of those types, or were headgear the prisoners had themselves fetched into their captivity, is uncertain.[55] Whatever cocked hats they had—such as Chambers saw being used to fan cooking fires at Valleyfield—must have been the prisoners' own. But there were also the 'Dutch caps', 1,000 of which were sent in February 1811 by the Transport Board to, for example, its agent at Esk Mills.[56] There were also what appear to have been hats with a high rounded crown and a broad brim to which Captain Paul Andreas Kaald referred when he wrote in his diary at Greenlaw on 6 February 1809: 'Today all the prisoners were given a hat, which had been promised to them since they received clothes. All the hats are of a black quaker type.'[57] In two of the detailed sketches he made that year of Greenlaw and its inmates Kaald depicts in one a dozen prisoners at work on various tasks in the airing ground in front of the old mansion house, and in the other six prisoners, including himself, inside their room in the prison. In the first sketch virtually all the prisoners seem to be wearing the 'black quaker type' hat; and in the second, what appear to be three such hats are hanging on nails or hooks on the walls of the room. A conclusion to be drawn about the prisoners' hats, therefore, is perhaps that they were about as motley as the rest of their clothing appears to have been.

In the prisoners' footwear there appears also to have been variety. Some, again perhaps many, arrived in the depots in Scotland still wearing whatever boots or shoes they had been captured in. Others, as already noticed, were, at least for a time, barefoot. But many, perhaps most, were issued with shoes

Fort George, on the Moray Firth near Inverness, held 87 prisoners of war for a time in 1803, but none thereafter during the Napoleonic Wars. Crown copyright, 2007, Historic Scotland Images, Ref. 7602.2.

The Edinburgh bridewell at Calton, with Salisbury Crags and Arthur's Seat in the background. The bridewell held the non-parole prisoners of war in Scotland from September 1803 to March 1804. Courtesy of Edinburgh City Libraries, Ref. (12)p YDA 2327 [681].

A sketch, 1809, of Greenlaw depot by Captain Paul Andreas Kaald, Norwegian privateersman, and himself a prisoner of war there, 1808– 10. Prisoners are shown at various tasks in the airing ground in front of the old mansion house, others at the heavily barred windows. By the door at left is what seems a pile of coal. The tables and trestles to the right were probably for use in the prisoners' market stalls. Clothes dry on the line at left. Courtesy of Trøndelag Folkemuseum, Trondheim, Norway.

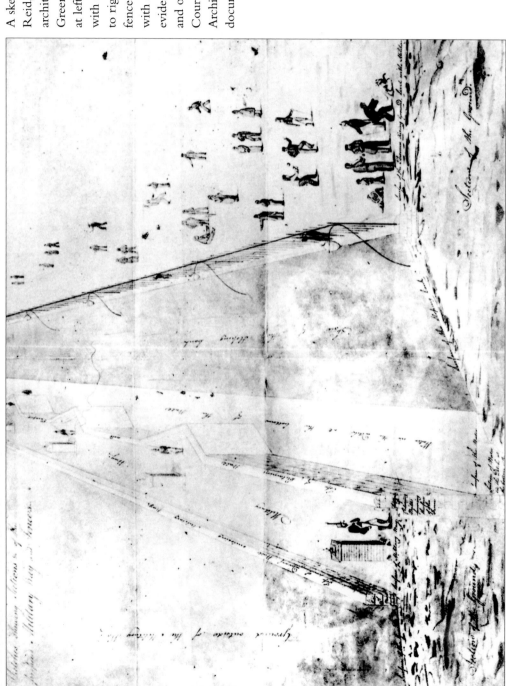

A sketch, 1813, by Robert Reid, government architect, of part of Greenlaw depot, including at left the military way, with soldiers on guard, and to right of the high metal fence prisoners of war, one with a dog, a group of five evidently playing cricket, and others dancing. Courtesy of The National Archives, Admiralty document.

A contemporary sketch of Greenlaw depot, showing prisoners of war within the palisades surrounding the airing ground or exercise yard in front of the old mansion house, sentries on guard, and militia or depot officers in the foreground. Courtesy of National Archives of Scotland, Ref. GD1/405/4/1.

Leith harbour, where thousands of prisoners of war were landed, or sailed from, during the Napoleonic Wars. Across the Firth of Forth, on the coast of Fife visible in the background, thousands of prisoners were also landed at Burntisland and Kirkcaldy harbours on their way to Perth depot.

The stone guard tower at what was the Greenlaw prisoner of war depot during the Napoleonic Wars. Greenlaw, which was also then renamed Glencorse, became in the later nineteenth century what it has since remained – an army depot and barracks. The guard tower probably dates from the huge extension of the prisoner of war depot in 1812–14. Courtesy of the Ministry of Defence.

Esk Mills as they looked in the twentieth century. Some 2,800 prisoners of war were held in captivity at the Mills for several weeks in 1811. The North Esk river can be seen in the upper right hand corner of the picture, with the railway running close beside it.

Captain Paul Andreas Kaald, Norwegian privateersman, a prisoner, 1808–10, at Greenlaw depot. Kaald's diary of his captivity there provides a uniquely detailed account of daily life at the depot. Courtesy Trondelag Folkemuseum, Trondheim, Norway.

A unique sketch, 1809, by Captain Paul Andreas Kaald, Norwegian privateersman, of himself and other Norwegian or Danish prisoners of war in their quarters at Greenlaw depot. The prisoners are, from left: No. 1, Capt. Sigismund Richelieu; No. 3 (facing Richelieu), 2nd Capt. Hans Locke; No. 2, seated at the heavily barred window, his back to the room, Capt. Kaald himself; No. 4, centre front, seated on a chest, Drengen S. Wiggen; No. 5, seated at window to right, Capt. Egelin; No. 6, seated at the fire, Capt. Bugge. The prisoners' hammocks (the two at left with their mattresses or palliasses), the frames from which they hung, items of clothing, and various utensils, are also depicted. Courtesy of Trondelag Folkemuseum, Trondheim, Norway.

Above. Edinburgh Castle from the south-east, n.d., but c.1740, by the Hon. John Elphinstone (1706-53), engineer. The 49 prisoners of war who escaped from the Castle one night in April 1811 did so by sliding on a rope down the rock from their quarters at the base of the buildings at the left. Courtesy of the National Archives of Scotland, Ref. GD1/405/4/1.

Left. The heavily barred gate into the vaults where the prisoners of war were held at Edinburgh Castle. Crown copyright, 2007, Historic Scotland Images, Ref. DSC 1899.

The steps leading down to the vaults where the prisoners of war were held at Edinburgh Castle. Crown copyright, 2007, Historic Scotland Images, Ref. DSC 1794.

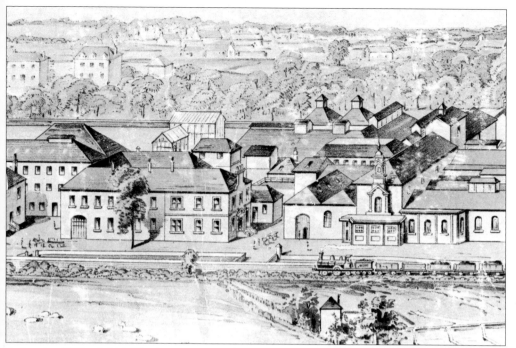

A sketch of Valleyfield Mills about 1860, with Penicuik in the background. In some of these buildings 7,600 prisoners of war were held during the years 1811-14. Courtesy of Midlothian Libraries, Black Coll.

Valleyfield after the demolition and complete removal post-1975 of the paper mill buildings. The monument to the 300 or so prisoners of war who died at Valleyfield in 1811–14 is at bottom left. The view, looking down from the slope at the top of which is St Mungo's parish churchyard, was the one the boy William Chambers had when he observed the prisoners there one Sunday about 1811–12.

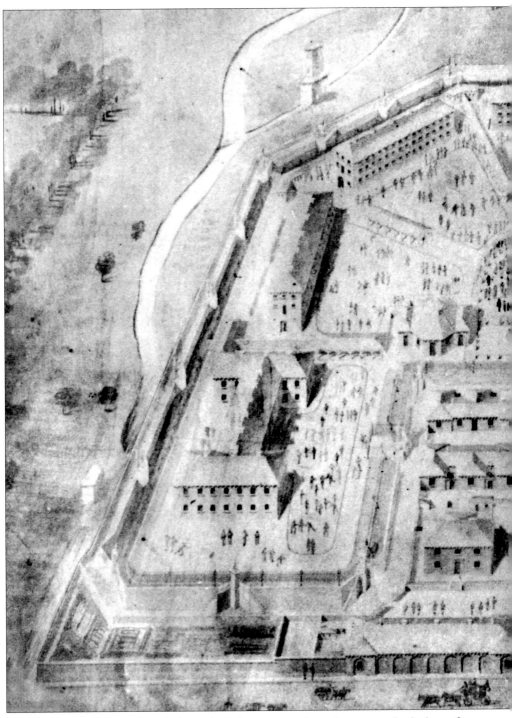

A contemporary sketch of Perth depot, built in 1811–12, the only purpose-built depot for prisoners of war in Scotland during the Napoleonic Wars. Prisoners are shown in the airing grounds or exercise yards in front of each two- or three-storey block, which housed altogether 7,000 prisoners. The depot market place, with the high tower from which prisoners could be watched, is in the centre. The two-storey block at the front, extreme right, housed 1,000 or so non-commissioned and warrant officers and the relatively few commissioned officers and their

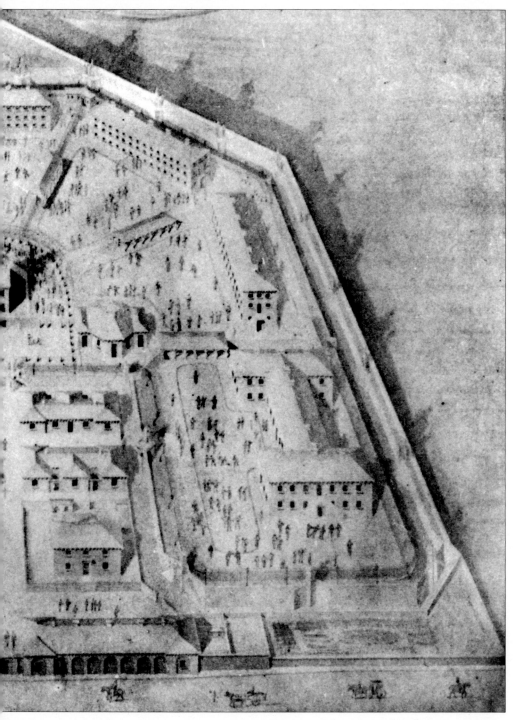

equivalents among the merchant seamen and privateersmen; the three-storey blocks the other ranks. The two-storey building at the front, extreme left, was the hospital, with beds for 150 sick prisoners. In the front centre were (at right) the house of the agent and (at left) of the depot surgeon; behind them, four one-storey buildings for officers of the depot. A 10-feet wide moat or canal, a high iron palisade, and high outer stone walls surrounded the prisoners' blocks. Courtesy of National Archives of Scotland, Ref. GD1/405/6A.

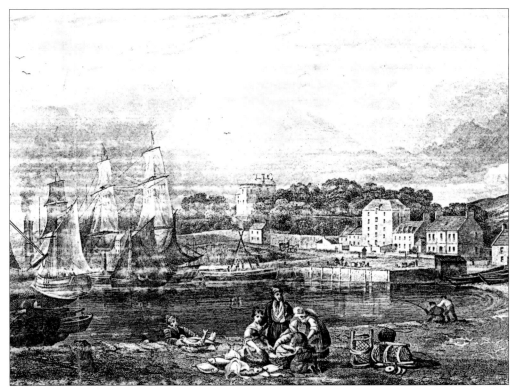

Burntisland harbour, where thousands of prisoners of war were landed in 1812–13 before being marched through Fife to Perth depot. The illustration is from John Leighton, *History of the County of Fife* (Glasgow, 1840). Courtesy of Fife Council, Central Area Libraries.

This painting of Kirkcaldy from the east in 1838 shows in the foreground the harbour at which many prisoners of war were landed before being marched through Fife to their captivity in Perth depot. In the background are discernible to the left Edinburgh Castle, Salisbury Crags and Arthur's Seat. Courtesy of Kirkcaldy Museum & Art Gallery.

at the depots during their captivity. The seaman Thomas Paumier, as also already seen, was among the more fortunate in receiving successively three pairs of shoes at Valleyfield between April 1811 and February 1814. Shoes issued appear sometimes to have been made of leather, sometimes, as Louis Simond observed at Edinburgh Castle in February 1811, 'a sort of galoches, the sole of wood and top of list.'

Large supplies of both leather shoes and list were sent by the Transport Board to Scotland for the various depots. Thus Malcolm Wright, for example, then agent at Edinburgh and Greenlaw, was told by the Board on 23 October 1810 that, among other supplies, 500 pairs of shoes were being sent to him immediately; and on 18 February 1811 Captain Pellowe, RN, agent at Esk Mills, that 1,000 pairs of shoes were being sent there.[58] At Perth, Captain Moriarty, RN, the agent, was informed by the Board on 11 November 1813 that, among other items of clothing, 1,500 pairs of leather shoes were on their way to that depot. A few days even after the war had ended, Captain Andrew Brown, RN, agent at Valleyfield, was told by the Board on 27 April 1814 that in response to his letter a week earlier 3,000 pairs of leather shoes were being sent to him—presumably to forestall any criticism at the coming repatriation of prisoners that they were not well shod when embarked for home.[59]

A significant instruction in the Board's letter to Pellowe at Esk Mills in February 1811 was that 'the Shoes and Stockings [of the latter of which a supply of 1,000 pairs was also being sent] are only to be used on particular Occasions.' Those occasions were specified by the Board in a letter of 19 November 1813 to Captain Moriarty at Perth, as 'when prisoners are ordered to be discharged or removed to another depot'—in other words, when prisoners were exposed en route to the public gaze. On all other occasions, or so it would appear, the prisoners had to wear their other footwear, in effect clogs made of wood and list, or go barefoot, unless they possessed footwear of their own.[60]

List or selvage, strips or edgings of cloth, was also sent in large quantities by the Transport Board to the depots in Scotland. Thus Captain Brown at Valleyfield was told by the Board in November 1812 that, as well as '1,000 sets of leather', five hundredweight of list was being sent to his depot; and in April 1813 Captain Moriarty at Perth was sent no less than '20 hundredweight of list and 3,000 setts of leather' by the Board.[61] Clogs are mentioned specifically in a letter of 2 November 1812 from the Board to Captain Brown at Valleyfield, which said their issue there was left to his discretion.[62] Costs were, of course, of constant concern to the Transport Board, and Malcolm Wright was instructed in a postcript to a letter it sent him on 27 February 1811 that 'You will inform us whether list or leather can be procured at a lower rate at or near Edinburgh.'[63] But that same day the Board directed its agents at Esk Mills and Valleyfield 'to cause list clogs, of which a sample will be forwarded to you together with a supply of list and leather, to be made by the prisoners of war in your custody, and for your information we enclose a statement of the expense of the materials and labour for making 1,000 pairs of such shoes at the depots in England. Some prisoners acquainted with this manufacture will be sent to Esk Mills and Valleyfield. A supply of list and leather will be sent to you. The other materials are to be procured by you on the spot.'[64] The information sent about costs at English depots has not survived, but some relevant notes are preserved in the Andrew Johnston Collection in the National Library of Scotland. These notes probably concern costs at Perth, where Johnston was chief clerk, though he had been employed earlier as a clerk, first at Esk Mills then, until Perth depot opened in summer 1812, as clerk or chief clerk at Valleyfield. What the notes indicate is that prisoners could make 1,000 pairs of what were described as list slippers for as little as 1½d each, excluding the cost and transport of the list from England; and they could make 1,000 pairs of wooden clogs for 1d. a pair, excluding the cost of materials, and likewise could nail the slippers to the clogs for 8s. per hundred pairs. So that the cost of a pair of list clogs appears to have been 1s.9¾d.[65] Thus the making of list clogs at the depots from materials provided by the Transport Board was one of the tasks carried out by some of the prisoners themselves. 'Two thousand pairs of shoes and 3,000 pairs of stockings,' the agent at Perth was told by the Board in October 1812, 'will be forwarded for the use of such of the prisoners as may stand in absolute need of those articles until a place shall have been erected [at the depot] for making list clogs. A supply of list and leather for this purpose has been ordered.' And two months later the same agent was told: '... you are to appropriate some part of the present buildings as a shop for the manufacture of clog shoes by the prisoners.'[66] A further attraction for the Board of the use of list was shown in a letter it sent to its agent at Valleyfield at New Year 1812: '... we acquaint you that no Stockings will be supplied with the Clothing ordered to be sent to you, as the List Shoes are so made as to render Stockings unnecessary.'[67]

What was rendered necessary for prisoners at Greenlaw, because of the 'extremely unclean' or muddy mess in the restricted airing ground, enclosed as it was 'with high and strong picket fencing', as Captain Paul Andreas Kaald there noted in his diary on 13 November 1808, was the wearing under their shoes of wooden blocks between 4½ and 6 inches thick.[68]

Clothing, as well as food and apparently bedding, were subjects of complaint concerning prisoners at Edinburgh Castle almost as soon as it became a depot early in 1811. 'We enclose a statement of complaints made to us on the subject of the badness of the provisions issued to the prisoners at Edinburgh Castle, their deficiency of clothing, etc., and the General Want of Arrangement and Accommodation at that Depot; and we direct you to take Measures for rendering the Situation of the Prisoners confined there as comfortable as possible.' These instructions by the Transport Board to Malcolm Wright, its agent at the Castle, in March 1811, appear to have been the result of criticisms expressed to the Board not by prisoners themselves but by the much more influential pen of Rear Admiral Otway at Leith. A few days later, Otway was appointed by the Admiralty to 'exercise a general superintendence of the depots for prisoners of war in the vicinity of Leith', and the agents at the Scots depots, informed accordingly, were told by the Transport Board to apply to the Admiral 'for orders in all cases of emergency wherein it may be inconvenient to wait for directions from us.'[69] Thus prisoners' clothing, or the inadequacy or lack of it, was evidently a factor that led to this change in the official responsibility for the prisoners in the depots in Scotland.

Of other complaints about clothing by prisoners themselves there is surprisingly little evidence—apart from comments already quoted from Sergeant Major Beaudoin and Lieutenant Marote-Carrier. That, of course, is not to conclude that prisoners had no complaints on the subject. Some of those at Greenlaw early in 1810, for instance, may well have been both bemused and angry when, as Captain Paul Andreas Kaald noted in his diary on 14 February that year, '… every one of the prisoners who had come here in the years 1807 and 1808 were given a shirt and a pair of stockings, but all those who had come here in the years 1809 and 1810 received a whole new outfit of the usual prison clothes.'[70]

Complaints against some prisoners for abuse of issued clothing were, on the other hand, made by the Transport Board and its agents. Most of these complaints concerned that particular group of prisoners who were to be found in every depot and who were described as *miserables* or *raffalés* and who will be discussed in Chapter 17. It appears not, however, to have been only to some of the latter that a letter to the Board's agents at Valleyfield and Perth in December 1813 referred: '… in future discharged prisoners are not to be supplied with clothing until they shall arrive at the gates upon their departure, and then to direct the conductor and request of the commanding officer, if they should proceed under one, to use every practicable means in order to prevent the prisoners selling or otherwise making away with their clothing on the march.'[71]

Of three other aspects referred to in extant sources concerning the provision and care of clothing for the prisoners one aspect is obscure and for the other two there appears to be little or no evidence concerning depots in Scotland—except, in one case, at Greenlaw. First, there is an unexplained reference in the Transport Board's correspondence in August and September 1812 with Captain Moriarty, RN, its agent at Perth depot, to tickets: 'By the coach of yesterday we forwarded to you 150 tickets belonging to the prisoners embarked at Portsmouth on board the *Freya* for Perth.' A month later the Board instructed Moriarty to 'pay the sum of £16.16.8, which has been charged for the carriage of the clothing tickets.'[72]

Second, the washing of prisoners' clothes is mentioned by Captain Kaald at Greenlaw, and one of his own sketches of the depot shows prisoners evidently at work at large washing boards in the airing ground in front of the old mansion house. The same 'uncleanliness' or deep mud that made it necessary for prisoners there to wear wooden soles up to six inches thick on their footwear also made their 'socks and clothes ... exceedingly smelly ... To the right of the courtyard are the washmen, numbering between 6 and 8 altogether, and clothes poles and washing lines, to hang the clean clothes up to dry. These men wash for all the prisoners, and are paid 1d. for a shirt, a towel, a pair of underpants, and for small items ½d., and for one sheet, trowsers, etc., 1½d.'[73]

Third, since clothing for prisoners in the depots in Scotland appears, with the exception of list shoes that were made by the prisoners themselves, to have been sent up from England by the Transport Board, there appears to have been little or no scope in that aspect of provision for private contractors in Scotland to flourish in the corrupt practices of their confrères in England. 'We read,' wrote Francis Abell a century ago in his pioneering history of the prisoners of war concerning conditions south of the Border, '... of hundreds of suits of clothing sent of one size, of boots supposed to last eighteen months which fell to pieces during the first wet weather... Out of 1,200 suits of clothes ordered to be at Plymouth by October 1807, as provision for the winter, by March 1808 only 300 had been delivered! [The latter fact] ... meant, firstly, that the contractor had never the smallest intention of delivering the full number of suits. Secondly, that he had, by means best known to himself and the officials, received payment for the whole. Thirdly, that hundreds of poor wretches had been compelled to face the rigour of an English winter on the hulks in a half naked condition, to relieve which very many of them had been driven to gambling and even worse crimes ... the war-prison contract business was a festering mass of jobbery and corruption, ... large fortunes were made by contractors, ... a whole army of small officials and not a few big ones throve on the "pickings" to be had.'[74]

If there is little clear evidence, so far as clothing and bedding were concerned, of such corruption at the depots in Scotland there does appear to be evidence of at least sporadic corruption in the provision of food for the prisoners.

14

Food and Drink

'I hereby beg leave to tender to supply the Prisoners of War in health at Greenlaw near Edinburgh for Six months from the first day of December next and until three months' notice shall be given—with provisions—on terms of a Schedule of a contract thereanent—exhibited by your Agent for that Depot—at the rate of Seven Pence and Ten Thirty Seconds of a penny each man per day.'

This tender, dated 11 November 1808, and evidently submitted by the contractor James Miller, Leith, to the Commissioners of the Transport Board, appears to be one of the few and also one of the earliest known to survive for victualling prisoners in any of the depots in Scotland during the Napoleonic Wars.[1] It appears to have been submitted by Miller in response to an advertisement placed by the Transport Board in local newspapers, including the *Edinburgh Evening Courant*, inviting sealed tenders by 15 November at its Edinburgh office, 'for victualling prisoners-of-war in health at Greenlaw for six months certain from 1 December 1808.' The advertisement was composed in the standard form: the tenderer or his agent had personally to attend at the office then, and 'Each letter must be accompanied by a letter from two respectable persons engaging to become bound with the person tendering in the sum of £2,000 for the due performance of the contract.'[2]

An immediate question Miller's tender (assuming it is authentic) raises is how much (or how little), and what kinds of, food might a prisoner enjoy in 1808-9 for a little less than 7½d. [three pence] per day?

At the beginning of the Napoleonic Wars, in May 1803, the Transport Board had written to the Admiralty about amounts and items of food and drink that should be provided to prisoners of war. Given 'many reports', said the Board's letter, 'of the insufficiency of the daily ration' during the previous French Revolutionary Wars their Lordships of the Admiralty might wish to consider 'how far it may be proper to continue the ration which has been the subject of so much complaint.' The letter enclosed a table of rations that had been issued to prisoners of war until 1 December 1797 and another table of reduced rations that had been issued after that date and until the end of the war in 1802 to French and Dutch (though not to Spanish) prisoners. 'Although the reduced ration has been, and, we believe, justly, considered sufficient for the maintenance of persons in good health,' declared the Board, 'yet it must be admitted that it has been found to be inadequate to the re-establishment of health in cases of convalescence; and from this cause, there is reason to believe, that considerable additional expense for such prisoners was incurred by the public during the later years of the last war for medicine as well as a breakfast of gruel.' The Board then recommended to the Admiralty that, 'To avoid such expense on the present occasion, as well as to prevent any cause of complaint of the ration … an addition of half a pound of bread be made to the ration as it now stands, so that the daily allowance to each prisoner in health may be One Pound and a half of bread, half a pound of beef, a quarter of a pint of pease, and one-third of an ounce of salt. We are the more inclined to propose this addition, because the French are great consumers of bread, and the scarcity of corn, which prevailed during a great part of the late war, happily no longer exists.' The Board's recommendation appears to have been accepted by the Admiralty, at least so far as the ration of bread, beef and salt was concerned.[3]

The tables of rations enclosed with the letter showed that before 1 December 1797 the daily ration for prisoners in health had been one and a half lbs of bread, three-quarters lb of beef (except on Saturdays, when no ration of it was issued), 4 oz. of butter on Saturdays only, half a pint of pease on Sundays, Tuesdays, Thursdays and Saturdays, one-third of an oz. of salt, and a quart of beer. From 1 December 1797 until the end of the Revolutionary Wars in 1802, French and Dutch prisoners of war in health were said to have had a daily ration of one lb of bread, half a lb of beef, a quarter pint of pease, and one-third of an oz. of salt; Spanish prisoners continued to receive the pre-December 1797 scale of rations.

The relief expressed in the Transport Board's comment about the ending of the previous scarcity of corn proved temporary, however: bad harvests in Britain in 1809 and 1811 were accompanied by a rise in annual average wheat prices in 1812 to 126s.6d. per quarter—the highest in the 19th century. Five-year average wheat prices rose sharply between the beginning of the French Revolutionary Wars in 1792-3 and the end of the Napoleonic Wars in 1814-15, thus: 1790-5—53s.8d., 1796-1800—73s.5d., 1801-5—80s., 1806-10—87s.11d., 1811-15—94s.3d. Annual average wheat prices per imperial quarter in the United Kingdom during the Napoleonic Wars were: 1803—58s.10d., 1804—62s.3d., 1805—89s.9d., 1806—79s.1d., 1807—75s. 4d., 1808—81s.4d., 1809—97s.4d., 1810—106s.5d., 1811—95s.3d., 1812— 126s.6d., 1813—109s.9d., 1814—74s.4d., 1815—65s.7d.[4]

A more detailed list of rations provided to prisoners in the depots is contained in a letter of December 1810 from the Transport Board to the Admiralty, which had asked the Board 'to report precisely all the particulars of the treatment and allowance of English [by which their Lordships meant British] prisoners of war … in France, compared with the treatment and allowances of French prisoners in England [by which their Lordships meant Britain]. The Board listed the latter for the seven days of each week thus:

Daily Ration:

5 Days in each Week: 1½ lb of Bread, ½ lb of fresh Beef, 1 oz. Barley, ¼ oz. Onions, ½ lb Cabbage or Turnips, one-third oz. Salt

1 Day: 1½ lb of Bread, 1 lb of good sound Herrings *, 1 lb of good sound Potatoes

1 Day: 1½ lb of Bread, 1 lb of good sound Codfish, 1 lb of good sound Potatoes

* Red and White Pickled Herrings are issued alternately.

N.B. The Provisions are cooked and Mess Utensils provided at the Expense of the British Government.[5]

Adjectives such as 'fresh' and 'good sound' to describe some of the rations at times received by prisoners in depots in Scotland might have raised among them wry grins or wrathful expostulations, given some of the experiences recounted below by such consumers of those rations as Captain Kaald, Lieutenant Marote-Carrier, or Sergeant Major Beaudoin. That those were indeed at least some of the kinds and amounts that figured mainly in the prisoners' rations was suggested, however, by comments (including statements of prices, the totals of which appeared to come to distinctly more than those in James Miller's presumed tender for Greenlaw in 1808) made by Louis Simond, the expatriate Frenchman from the United States of America, when early in 1811 he visited Edinburgh Castle and observed and enquired about the prisoners there. 'The daily ration,' Simond wrote, 'is 1½ lb of bread, at 3d.; ½ lb of meat, at 6¾d. per lb; once or twice a week they have fish instead of meat.'[6] It was significant that the Transport Board itself described in 1811 the daily scale of rations for prisoners in health as one 'which we are by experience convinced is on as low a scale as is consistent with the health of the prisoners.'[7]

While the surviving evidence about the prisoners' rations in the Scots depots is not comprehensive or entirely clear, it appears that at least officially it included week by week (though daily only in the case of bread) bread, beef, pease, cabbage, onions or turnips, potatoes, barley, salt, herrings, cod. Items that appear not to have figured in their rations included perhaps most obviously to the reader in the early 21st century: cheese, milk, tea or coffee, sugar and, at least in the summer or early autumn, fresh fruit. Of course, prisoners who possessed some money were, or might be, able to buy at the depots some of those foods that were additional to or different from those constituting their rations; and, under the regulatory eye of the Transport Office, they were also permitted to buy small, that is, weak or inferior, beer. If men leading moderately active lives need between about 2,000 and 3,800 calories a day or between 14,000 and 26,600 per week, allowing for varying rates of metabolism, then the official rations provided to depot prisoners in Scotland appear barely adequate.[8]

The absence of fresh fruit and milk from the standard rations of the prisoners was no doubt due, as with other absent items, to their cost but also in their particular case to the problem in an age of slow transport of ensuring they were fresh when they reached the depots. To butter, four ounces of which were said to have been issued on Saturdays only to prisoners during the French Revolutionary Wars, no reference has been found in rations or ration scales at the depots in Scotland during the Napeolonic Wars.[9]

As for coffee, it was almost inconceivable it would have been included in prisoners' rations since it was a beverage, drinking of which, despite an almost ninefold increase in public consumption between 1801 and 1811, was still largely confined in Britain to the middle and upper classes.[10] On the other hand, an attempt in autumn 1811 to dump surplus stocks of coffee on the prisoners of war as a substitute for other rations was successfully resisted by the Transport Board, and also showed that prisoners were not already receiving coffee as part of their rations. When HM Treasury asked the Board for its view on a memorial from the 'coffee planters, merchants and others concerned in that trade, requesting that measures may be adopted for relieving them from their present accumulation of coffee' and proposing 'introducing coffee into use among the prisoners of war', the Board replied that if, as proposed, coffee were substituted for the 2½ lbs per week of beef (including bone) the removal of the beef from the prisoners' rations would be 'also to deprive them of the soup with which it is cooked, and made by them, which is the most nutritious part of their diet.' The memorialists appear also to have proposed reductions in the prisoners' rations of fish and bread to make way for coffee. Any such reductions, the Board declared, would result in 'the greatest complaints', especially as 'The ration of bread is so essential to a Frenchman.' 'That the issue of coffee to the prisoners would be very acceptable to them there can be no doubt,' concluded the Board in an argument sure to appeal to the Treasury, 'but if it were served in addition and as a boon to the present allowances it would create an increase of expense of not less than £500 per diem for coffee only, exclusive of sugar, which must of course be used with it. This is consequently a measure we can by no means recommend to their Lordships [of the Treasury]. It would be proper to observe that a reduction of their [the prisoners'] present nutritious diet might occasion disease which would require hospital care, and consequently be attended with a quadruple expense to the public.'[11]

Tea, on the other hand, whose average consumption per annum in the United Kingdom between 1801 and 1810 was almost 24 million lbs (much greater than that of coffee), may perhaps appear a more surprising omission from prisoners' rations.[12] Some prisoners did drink tea: Lieutenant Marote-Carrier's 'tea captain' at Esk Mills was a supplier.[13] An inventory, compiled at the end of the war, of stores at Greenlaw depot included not only '7 Large Cook House Tubs, 754 Tin Mess Basins' but also '898 Tin Tea Quart Cans'.[14] But had the tea cans actually been used for tea, rather than some of them for other liquids such as soup or water or even for foodstuffs? In short, was tea a basic item in the prisoners' rations? It may have been, but there is a lack of clear evidence.

What is sure is that the standard depot rations issued to the mass of the prisoners did not include beer. Small or weak beer, on the other hand, could be bought by the prisoners if they had money for it. In the summer of 1808, for instance, when Greenlaw was still the only depot in Scotland, a circular from the Transport Board to all depot agents in Britain directed them 'to transmit to us an account in the annexed form, of the sale of small beer, and the profits thereon, since the last settlement authorised by us, up to the end of the last quarter.'[15] Nine months later agents were told by the Board 'to distribute the profits of the small beer sold to the prisoners up to 30th June last, in the proportions directed, to the several persons concerned.' They were also instructed that only 'Sixpenny beer or beer the nearest to that price that is made in your neighbourhood is to be sold to the prisoners, and be careful that the retail price do not in any case exceed eight pence [8d.] per gallon. You are also from time to time to examine the beer and to satisfy yourself as to its quality and price.'[16] By the end of the following year, when the subject of the small beer was proving increasingly controversial, the Board appeared uncertain about how best to handle matters and most unusually it invited suggestions not only from the depot agents but even from some of the prisoners themselves: 'Having received many complaints respecting the present mode of supplying prisoners of war at the several Depots with small beer, we desire you to consider this subject attentively and to report to us your opinion as to the mode you consider the best adapted for supplying the prisoners with beer on the cheapest terms possible, and so as most effectually to exclude the introduction of strong beer or spirituous liquors. We think it advisable that in the consideration of this business you should consult with some of the most respectable of the prisoners, in order to obtain their sentiments on the subject, and you are to transmit their opinion in writing with your own report.'[17] Although the agents' and prisoners' suggestions have not survived, they seem likely to have been reflected in a circular issued in June 1811 by the Board to its depot agents: '... we direct you in future to regulate the sale of small beer ... in the following manner. The profits on the sale of small beer shall be in future divided amongst the prisoners, without any clerk, steward, or other person employed under this Department having any advantage or emolument thereupon whatever. The prisoners in each prison building (and on board each prison ship) are to be divided into a certain number of companies, according to their numbers, who are to appoint two prisoners from among themselves to sell the beer, and to be accountable for the prime cost of it, and the profits thereon. The beer authorised to be sold shall be purchased at the rate of sixpence [6d.] per gallon, and be retailed at the rate not exceeding sevenpence [7d.] per gallon; and each company shall continue to enjoy the privilege and emoluments attending upon the sale for fourteen days, at the end of which time the profits shall be equally divided among the members of such company and a new company shall then in like manner be appointed and so proceed, alternating until the whole of the prisoners shall have received an equal share of the said profits, when the same system is to be again repeated. You will use the utmost care and cause the several officers employed under you to do the same to prevent the prisoners from being imposed upon in the price of the beer they may be supplied with for sale, as also to prevent any imposition on the part of the companies having the benefit of the sale for the time being; distinctly apprizing them that should any company be found guilty of imposition, or other irregularity, the benefit thus granted will be taken from them, and they will subject themselves to severe punishments, the present regulation being wholly intended for their advantage and comfort.'[18] By the end of that year, however, the new scheme appears to have run into difficulties which were indicated in a circular the Board sent the agents at Valleyfield, Greenlaw, and six depots in England. The Board announced that it intended 'in order to prevent abuses by the introduction of strong liquors at the several Depots for prisoners of war, to appoint a person at each Depot to superintend and be accountable for a canteen, through whom the sale of small beer shall be conducted, the profits of which are to be divided among the several clerks, as an increase to the present salaries.' The person appointed at each depot was to be a depot clerk, the profit on sales was to remain 1d. per gallon, the clerk was to make a weekly return to the depot agent of supplies of small beer received and sold, and the agent a quarterly return to the Transport Board.[19] This system, too, however, proved unsuccessful and 'occasioned considerable discontent without fully answering the objects which we had in view in proposing them,' the Board told depot agents in September 1813. From the end of that month, therefore, the system established in June 1811 was restored, by which the prisoners themselves again managed the sales of small beer.[20]

The Board's correspondence with individual depot agents in Scotland sheds light on these and other aspects of the subject of beer but also of spirits (which needless to say did not figure in the standard rations) and their consumption by prisoners. First, repeated reminders were sent by the Board to the agents that both strong beer and spirits were forbidden to prisoners.[21] Despite that prohibition, Captain Paul Andreas Kaald, for example, recorded several occasions during his captivity at Greenlaw in 1808-10 when he or some of his fellow prisoners there were 'tipsy' or 'in Paradise, and enjoying some products', which included 'a few bowls of toddy'.[22] Second, profits from the sales of small beer were not inconsiderable, and the beneficiaries among the staff, at Valleyfield, for example, in September 1812, who shared £126 in varying amounts according to seniority, were: Andrew Johnston, 1st clerk, and A. Munro, Superintendent Clerk, £20 each, John Macfarlane and James White, extra clerks, £15 each, James Lewis, hospital clerk, and Robert Aitken, prison steward, £15 each, and William Doig, hospital steward, and James Rushmore, superintendent steward, £13 each. Two months later a further £52.1.9 profit had been made and there was a similar distribution of it among ten members of the staff, most of them the previous beneficiaries. Mainly the same staff benefited again from another distribution of profits of almost £200 in October 1813. Some £100 of profit from the sale of small beer at Perth between April and September 1813 was likewise distributed among seven clerks and stewards of the depot staff.[23] Third, the retail price of small beer to be sold to the prisoners was stated in another Board letter in 1812 to the agent at Valleyfield as: '... Pint 1d., Quart 2d., Half Gallon 3½d., Gallon 7d.'[24] Finally, a note by Andrew Johnston, chief clerk at Perth, shows that in the week 11-18 January 1813, 22 casks of small beer were sold there to the prisoners, the income was £19.16.0, of which the Perth Brewery Company was paid £16.10.0, and the balance of £3.6.0 paid into the depot office.[25]

The kinds and the amounts of rations provided to the prisoners were determined chiefly by what was considered by the Transport Board and the Admiralty to be the minimum cost of keeping them alive and healthy enough to avoid their becoming an additional burden on government funds through contracting ailments arising from malnutrition and which would demand hospital or at least medical treatment. Decisions by the Board, or ultimately by the Admiralty, concerning prisoners' rations had also to take some account of the French government's provision for British prisoners of war in France. If the Board's provision was shown to be less, or even less, than that for British prisoners in France, then not only might the latter suffer a reduction in their rations but also Napoleon's government could be expected to exploit to the maximum the propaganda value of such a difference in provision. The Board, for the information of the Admiralty, listed in December 1810 the daily rations given by the French government to British prisoners of war as being 1 lb of bread, ½ lb of meat, 2 oz. peas, 1/30th oz. of salt, and 7½ centimes in money—equal to three farthings or three-quarters of 1d., plus 'Firing, lights & cooking utensils'.[26]

Since the Board was a section of the Admiralty it seems likely that a glance by both at the level of provision for seamen in the British navy guided to some extent their decisions about the amounts and kinds of rations for prisoners of war in the depots in Scotland and elsewhere in Britain.[27] An official table issued in 1808 of their provisions showed that navy men were entitled to receive every week, in daily or twice or thrice weekly amounts, 7 lbs of biscuit [bread baked hard], 7 gallons of beer, 4 lbs of beef, 2 lbs of pork, 2 pints of pease, 1½ pints of oatmeal, 6 oz. sugar, 6 oz. butter, 12 oz. cheese, and up to half a pint of vinegar.[28] Those rations compared with the weekly scale in 1810 for prisoners of war in Britain of 10½ lbs of bread, 2½ lbs of beef, 2 lbs of fish, 2½ lbs of cabbage or turnip, 2 lbs of potatoes, 5 oz. of barley, 1¼ oz. onions, and 1 2/3 oz. of salt. At least on the face of it, the prisoners' rations included more vegetables, fresh bread instead of biscuit, and fish, but much less meat and none of the oatmeal, sugar, butter and cheese that the seamen were entitled to. Nor had the prisoners anything like the seamen's evidently huge allotment of beer. For navymen on southern voyages 'a pint of wine or half pint of brandy was substituted for the beer, which never remained fresh for long at sea. Rice was issued instead of oatmeal, olive oil for butter. When in port fresh meat was usually obtainable, but fresh vegetables did not become the rule until the end of the [19th] century.'[29]

Another comparison that may be made, or attempted, is between the food and drink of prisoners in the depots in Scotland and of those on the hulks in the south of England. Amounts and kinds of rations were no doubt much the same. Execrable, however, was how the quality of the provisions on the hulks was described by the French general René-Martin Pillet, a prisoner from 1808, first on parole then after a failed attempt at escape, on the hulk *Brunswick* at Chatham. Pillet added that to any complaints by the prisoners the answer given was 'any food was good enough for French dogs.'[30] Similar comments were made by Sergeant Major Beaudoin, who after five years' captivity at Greenlaw, was transferred in autumn 1809 successively to the hulks *Bristol* and *Fyen* at Chatham, where, he complained, 'Half the time they give us provisions which the very dogs refuse. Half the time the bread is not properly baked, and is only good to bang against a wall; the meat looks as if it had been dragged in the mud for miles. Twice a week we get putrid salt food, that is to say, herrings on Wednesday, cod-fish on Saturday. We have several times refused to eat it, and as a result got nothing in its place, and at the same time are told that anything is good enough for a Frenchman.'[31] Nor were the recollections of Lieutenant Marote-Carrier, who spent the first part of his captivity in the winter of 1810-11 on the hulk *Glory* at Chatham, any more flattering about the food and drink provided there: 'The food, far from being appetising, had all the opposite qualities. It was most often salty herrings and spoiled cod that was distributed to us with the most squalid economy. Thus we received four ounces of bread per man every 24 hours. Fresh water being rare on the hulks, this bread was made with sea water, a double blessing for the baker who had no need to season it with salt. It was hardly baked when we were given it, so it was sometimes moist to the extent that if it was thrown against the partitions, it stuck to them. Such was, along with unseasoned potatoes and soup that perfectly resembled lukewarm greasy water, the staple of our meals ... Five days a week we were given a half-pound of bad meat per man ... Our drink was of pure water, except for those who wished or could afford the expense of procuring for themselves other liquids that the English women sold at an exorbitant price ... [Even the water given the prisoners was] only a litre a day, a ration that was quite insufficient when the salty food caused a tremendous thirst.'[32] It may be, therefore, that many, even most, of those thousands of prisoners who, like Marote-Carrier, were transferred from the hulks at Chatham, Plymouth or Portsmouth to the depots in Scotland found the food at the latter at least less bad than it had been on the hulks.

A comparison made in September 1807 by the Transport Board itself may illuminate from another angle the provision for the French and other prisoners of war in the depots in Scotland and England. The comparison was contained in the Board's assertion, or admission, in its correspondence then with the Admiralty that the prisoners '... are already fed and clothed by Government much better than the labouring poor of this country.'[33]

A final comparison which may be made is with the rations allotted the soldiers in Napoleon's armies, at least when they were in barracks, camp or billets and not on campaign when they had to find food as best they could by foraging. An order by Napoleon himself in May 1809 laid down that: 'The NCOs and soldiers will receive, independently of their bread ration (of seven and a half hectogrammes or twenty-four ounces): For breakfast: soup and brandy (a sixteenth part of a pint). For dinner: soup, ten ounces of meat, vegetables, and half a pot of beer or wine. For supper: some vegetables and half a pot of beer or wine. Thus the soldier's ration will consist of twenty-four ounces of bread [*pain de munition*—ration bread, made from three parts wheat flour to one part rye], four ounces of soup bread [a finer bread which readily dissolved in soup], sixteen ounces of meat, two ounces of rice or four ounces of dried vegetables, a sixteenth of a pint of brandy, a pint of beer or a bottle of wine, depending on the [produce of the] country.'[34] On the face of it, these rations, the wine, brandy and vinegar apart, appear to have been not radically different from those officially provided by the Transport Board to prisoners of war in the depots in Scotland.[35]

It would appear on the whole, therefore, that significant complaints (which were not infrequent and were sometimes a source of disturbances among them) by the prisoners of war in the depots in Scotland about their food and drink arose not from any drastic difference (wine and spirits apart) in the amounts or kinds they were provided with by the Transport Board compared with what they had been accustomed to before their capture, at least when in camp, barracks or billets or on shipboard, but from the quality of it and also sometimes perhaps by the way their food was cooked.

Complaints about their food and drink were no doubt inevitable among many of the prisoners, given the circumstances of their captivity. Confined in a foreign country, far from home, enduring a climate different from that of their homelands, deprived in many cases by their illiteracy of news from their families, living in generally overcrowded conditions, dressed in captives' clothing many of them found humiliating, undergoing lengthening years of captivity in a war to which there seemed to be no end, depressed, in the case of those many among them who remained devoted to Napoleon, during what proved to be the last couple of years of the war by the turning of the tide against him, the prisoners were sure to express some of their frustrations and anxieties by complaining about their food.

But such general complaints or grousing apart, what were, or appear to have been, the justified and significant complaints they made about their food and drink? Those complaints appear usually to have fallen into one or other of two main categories. The first was whether the scales of rations formally prescribed for prisoners by the Transport Board were actually what the prisoners received. The second concerned the quality of the provision.

In dealing with complaints the Transport Board was aware of the propaganda Napoleon's government could work up if the mass of prisoners of war in Scotland and elsewhere in Britain were shown to be kept seriously short of food or as a matter of course given food that was inedible. The Board was equally aware that such an indictment could lead to serious repercussions for British prisoners in French hands. Prisoners of war were in effect hostages for the good behaviour of their own governments toward enemy prisoners—and not only in the matter of food. Some of the Transport Board's substantial correspondence with the Admiralty, but especially with its own agents at the depots in Scotland and elsewhere in Britain, was therefore often concerned with questions arising from the provision of the prescribed scales of food and drink for the prisoners. The Board appears on the whole to have sought to ensure that they received their entitlement or, when particular items were in short supply or unavailable, that substitutes of some kind were provided instead. But prescribed quantities were one thing, the quality of the food actually provided by the contractors could be, and not seldom was, quite another.

Bread, a particularly important item in the prisoners' rations, was a frequent subject of complaints. A general circular issued regularly from 1804 onwards by the Transport Board to depots directed agents to send to the Transport Office in London by the next coach 'a loaf taken indiscriminately from that [sic] issued to the prisoners in your custody' on the day the circular was received. A week after such a circular had been issued on 9 July 1808, for example, the Board informed agents that, 'Frequent complaints having been recently made respecting the quality of the provisions supplied at some of the Depots ... we direct you to be particularly attentive to the quality of all the provisions which may be furnished by the contractors, and especially of that of the bread, which has been most complained of, by which there is reason to believe it has been latterly very much inferior to contract. You will apply immediately to two respectable bakers in your neighbourhood, and obtain from each of them a loaf of bread, made of wheaten meal, as described in the contract, in such a way as of necessary [sic] they can swear to the bread being of that precise quality. These two loaves are to be sent to this office without delay, packed in a box.'[36] Given that it took several days by road or by sea, for goods or persons sent from Greenlaw depot to reach London, the state of such sample loaves when they eventually reached the Transport Office there may be easily imagined. That was a practical difficulty which beset all the subsequent similar instructions by the Transport Board to depot agents in Scotland about sending sample foodstuffs.[37]

That the Board attempted at least from time to time to check the quality of bread issued to the prisoners in the depots by asking that sample loaves be sent it, as well as by instructing agents in January 1811 regularly to obtain loaves made of wheaten meal from 'each of two respectable bakers in the neighbourhood of the prison' who could swear to the bread being of the precise quality specified in the contract with the depot contractor, is shown by similar circulars it sent to its agents on the question in August 1810 and December 1811.[38] But that its efforts, at least so far as some depots were concerned, remained ineffectual and the quality of the bread distinctly dubious, was indicated by its issue in September 1813 of yet another circular, this time marked 'Secret and Confidential', to its agents at Greenlaw, Valleyfield and Perth (as well as to five in England). 'Having occasion to believe from information which we have received,' the circular declared, 'that the bakers who are employed by the contractors to furnish bread for the prisoners of war at the several Depots are in the habit of using other ingredients in the manufacture of the bread than pure wheaten flour we direct you to take particular care that the bread supplied to the prisoners be fully equal to contract and you are to visit the bakehouses from time to time at uncertain periods for the purpose of examining the materials from which the bread is made, reporting the result to us.'[39]

When fresh or soft bread for whatever reason was not supplied or not available, the substitute provided was normally biscuit, hard baked bread. The supplementary standing orders and regulations issued to its agents by the Board in January 1811 directed that 'Two days' supply of biscuit is to be kept constantly in store, to be issued weight for weight, in case of the failure of the contractors to supply bread in proper time, or of his furnishing bread of an inferior quality.'[40] But issues of biscuit to the prisoners also encountered difficulties, for in September 1812 the Transport Board in another circular to depot agents directed them, '… in future to issue in no case, whether by default of the contractor or otherwise, more than one pound of biscuit, in lieu of the ration of soft bread, but you will report to us the particulars of any such default, in order that we may be enabled to mulct the contractor accordingly. And you will not fail to supply one pound of biscuit in lieu of soft bread, whenever the contractor shall fail to provide the latter or not supply it in proper time, agreeably to the terms of his contract.'[41] New instructions about the issue of biscuit were circularised by the Board to its depot agents in July 1813: '… in future when biscuit is issued … in lieu of bad bread one pound and a half is to be distributed to each prisoner as heretofore; but if from bad weather or any unavoidable accident the contractor should be prevented from issuing soft bread then no more than one pound of biscuit is to be given to each prisoner; and you are to cause this regulation to be made known to the prisoners.'[42]

At all the depots in Scotland, except apparently at Perth, complaints by the prisoners were made, sometimes vociferously and at least once to the point of uprising, about the bread and the biscuit issued. The latter were no doubt included with complaints made in March 1811 at Edinburgh Castle, for example, 'on the subject of the badness of the provisions issued.'[43] At Greenlaw, Captain Paul Andreas Kaald refers in his diary in November 1808 to the prisoners receiving 'soft and for the most part doughy (half raw) bread.'[44] Seven months later, on Sunday, 25 June 1809, Kaald records that he, and it appears the other prisoners, received 'a piece of blue-moulded bread'.[45] The following year, the depot agent's action in 'returning the inferior bread' was approved by the Transport Board.[46] It was likely that complaints by prisoners led the Board early in 1813 to instruct the agent, and also the naval transport officer at Leith, that in pending local press advertisements for tenders for supplying victuals at that depot it should be made clear that 'quality of bread required is to be different from existing contract.'[47] Two months later the Board told the depot agent to 'pay particular attention to the quality of the bread' and to procure 'as a sample for his guidance' from his colleague at Valleyfield 'a loaf of good and well baked bread'.[48] At Esk Mills, despite its short existence in February-March 1811, complaints against the bread issued to them appear to have been among the reasons for unrest and insubordination among prisoners and to the transfer on 4 and 5 March to cells in Edinburgh Castle of some of those 48 of 'bad character'.[49] 'You will send a sample loaf of the bread now issuing to the prisoners,' Captain Pellowe, RN, agent at the depot, was instructed by the Transport Board on 4 March.

At Valleyfield, too, prisoners complained about the bread and sometimes refused to eat it: 'The Bread rejected by the Prisoners as mentioned by you,' the Board told the agent there in March 1811, 'is to be sold ...'[50] A month later the agent sent the Board a loaf 'which we [the Board] do not consider to be objectionable.' But the Board in its reply told the agent that 'no bread, improperly baked, is to be received [at the depot], nor,' as the exercise of some common sense might have concluded much earlier, 'is there any necessity for your sending Samples hither, as the Distance renders it impossible to judge of the Quality.'[51] The subject continued to concern both the Valleyfield agent and the Board, which replied on 12 August that year to a letter from him: 'With respect to the Quality of the Bread to be issued to the Prisoners, we refer you to the Contract and direct you to cause a sample Loaf to be made according to it, transmitting to this Office a Sample of the Meal of which it is made.'[52] A few months later, however, the Board appeared either to have forgotten earlier experience or to have changed its mind, for it informed its agent at Valleyfield that 'by the Coach of this Day will be furnished to you a Loaf of the Bread issued to the Ordinary [Seamen] of the Navy at Chatham which [is] a Sample of the Quality of the Bread to be supplied to Prisoners of War at Valleyfield under the new Contract to be entered into.'[53] That summer, informing Capt. Andrew Brown, who by then had succeeded as agent at Valleyfield, that a sample loaf of the quality the contractor should provide for the prisoners was being sent by coach, the Board did at least warn him that 'Allowance will of course be made by you for the Distance this Bread has been removed, being from Chatham to Town [i.e., London] and from thence to Valleyfield, in consequence of which it may be reasonably supposed that at this Season of the Year it will be somewhat deteriorated.'[54]

By early 1813 complaints by prisoners at Valleyfield about the provision of bread and its substitute biscuit had become more pressing and even threatening. The Board told the agent to lay in two days' supply of biscuit and charge it to the contractor, since the latter had failed to supply any. A two days' supply of biscuit in fact was to be kept constantly in the depot store. In a separate though simultaneous reply to an enquiry from the agent the Board told him that it 'can by no means sanction supply of ½ lb of biscuit [to prisoners at Valleyfield] as we know by experience that it would lead to Tumult and Disorder, besides One Pound of Biscuit is as much as is allowed to a British Seaman and one third more than to a Soldier.' The Board added: 'As to the Menaces of the Prisoners you will of course not heed them, but act firmly up to your Duty, and if necessary call in the Aid of the Military.' A few days later, in response to another letter from the agent the Board told him that Lieutenant Glinn, Transport Officer at Leith, would arrange the baking and sending of biscuit to Valleyfield if difficulty arose again. The Board also expressed approval of the agent's 'allowing the Baker of the 82nd [French infantry] Regiment to be employed in the Bakehouse as stated by you.' Almost needless to add, the Board had also sent by coach to the depot from London a sample loaf.[55]

The complaints of the Valleyfield prisoners had become loud enough to reach the ears of Vice Admiral Otway at Leith. He wrote the Board on 19 January concerning the 'Discontent of the Prisoners at Valleyfield respecting the Bread supplied to them.' The Board in reply explained that '… for a considerable time and until very lately the Prisoners have been allowed to benefit by any Defalcation of the Contractors in the Supply of Bread, by being supplied with One Pound and a Half of Biscuit in lieu of the like Weight of soft Bread, but only in such cases of Default. As, however, this practice has latterly been found to lead to Tumult and Disorder, by the Prisoners riotously demanding the full Ration of Biscuit when the Contractors have not been in fault, and particularly in a recent instance at Dartmoor Prison, where the Bakehouses were destroyed by Fire—it was found to be absolutely necessary to discontinue a Practice which was attended with these Inconveniences, and by which the Prisoners so demanded as a Right what was humanely granted to them as a Favor [sic]. The Contractors will not by this Alteration escape an adequate Mulct upon any Failure, the Amount of which it is our Intention shall be disposed of in procuring some additional Comforts for the Prisoners should they by their Orderly and proper Conduct be judged to merit the same.'[56]

The complaints about bread at Valleyfield, however, persisted into the following month. The action of the agent in issuing 'One Pound of good Biscuit' to the prisoners for every ration of soft bread rejected', was approved by the Transport Board, which assured him that 'The contractors will be mulcted the price of half a pound of biscuit for each rejected ration of bread over and above the supply of one pound of biscuit.'[57] Echoes of these complaints continued in the Board's correspondence with the agent at Valleyfield for several weeks afterward.[58]

Adulteration, potentially or actually fatal, of the prisoners' bread rations at Valleyfield was alleged by Lieutenant Marote-Carrier, himself a prisoner there between March 1811 and September 1812. 'One day,' he long afterward recalled, 'we had been distributed with our ration of a pound and half of bread. This bread, less moist than that of the hulks [at Chatham, where Marote-Carrier had spent the first couple of months of his captivity], had always seemed preferable to us. However, it sometimes grated between our teeth, and we did not know the reason. That day when the bread was dissolved and broken up in the soup we found at the bottom of the mess kettle some glass ground to powder. That was the unknown seasoning! The first thought that struck us was that England, tired of feeding at its expense and lodging so many prisoners, had decided to reduce the number of them, but to do so clandestinely and in a cowardly way: it would tear their insides to bits while affecting to treat them humanely. We complained to the contractor who provided the food. Beating about the bush and with an embarrassed air he told us that he did not know anything about it, that it was due to the negligence of the baker, that he could not watch over everything ... This evasive reply in a way justified our suspicions. So from then onwards I no longer ate the bread provided, and I bought from Scots people some bread rolls that they came to sell every day and which cost a few pence. At least those were not adulterated ... [But] the bread kneaded with glass ploughed new wounds each day in the unfortunate men who could not buy other food.'[59]

Perth seems to have been the only depot in Scotland where collective complaints by prisoners about their bread or biscuit were either not made or not made vehemently enough to have left traces in the archives.

Fish, on the other hand, was a source of 'tumult' by prisoners at Perth depot in March 1813. 'Hard fish had formerly been served out to them every Friday,' the *Perth Courier* reported on 25 March, 'but on Friday last [19 March] soft fish (the quality of which we are told was excellent) had been substituted in its place. This change they did not like and made their remonstrances in a manner which was rather disorderly. But by the interference of Captain Moriarty [the agent], who enquired with the greatest impartiality into the cause of their complaint, and who was assisted by officers of the regiments [of militia] on duty, the disturbance was immediately suppressed.' The *Dundee Advertiser* reported that the prisoners had been 'in a state of mutiny' on 17 March 'on account of some of their provisions not being exactly what they wanted', although 'Every person acquainted with the quality and quantity of their rations admits them to be abundantly sufficient.'[60] Little further light is thrown on the incident by surviving correspondence between the Transport Board and Moriarty. When the latter, according to Messrs James Lindsay & Co., contractors for victualling the prisoners at Perth, had declined a fortnight or so before the incident to receive 'Wet Salt Fish,' the Board had written on 13 March to Moriarty to 'acquaint you that 1 lb 3 oz. of good wet salt Cod is to be received instead of one pound of dry Cod, but no fish excepting [it] is to be received.' A letter written on 25 March from Moriarty to the Board has not survived, but four days later the Board told him to 'report if the fish tendered by the contractor was of unexceptionable quality and also if 1 lb 3 oz. per ration were offered, and further whether dry cod fish be procurable.

The issue of 1 lb 3 oz. of good wet cod fish was considered by us to be an advantage to the prisoners.'[61]

Fish had been indeed the subject of several general circulars to depots, including those in Scotland, issued by the Transport Board during the three years to November 1812. Agents were asked in November 1809, for example, if herrings were issued to the prisoners and, if not, they were to insist on a regular supply and 'to take care that they be of a proper quality.'[62] Two similar instructions within ten days were sent to depot agents in September 1810 about contractors issuing herrings.[63] 'In order that the prisoners may be enabled to soak the Salt Fish supplied to them, previously to its being dressed,' a Board circular to its agents in May 1811 declared, 'we direct you in future to cause the Salt Fish to be issued the evening before it is due, if the prisoners should choose to receive it then for that purpose.'[64] And a circular from the Board on 11 November 1812 which was directly relevant to the 'tumult' that broke out four months later at Perth depot, directed its agents that 'Whenever it may be necessary to allow the contractor to issue Wet Cod Fish in consequence of his being unable to procure dry Cod the prisoners are to be supplied with 1 lb 3 oz. of wet fish in lieu of 1 lb of dry fish.'[65]

Pilchards, along with herrings, may have been an earlier source of controversy at Greenlaw depot. 'In pursuance of an order of the Right Honourable Lords Commissioner of the Admiralty dated 17 January last,' the Transport Board wrote to the secretary of that department in May 1807, 'we gave the necessary directions for issuing herrings or pilchards to all prisoners of war in this country for their food on two days in each week … But as it appears in the reports made to us by the Agents at the several depots that the prisoners generally refuse to receive pilchards, and many of them herrings also, choosing rather to receive a bread ration only on the days on which fish is only issued, we request you will give this information to their Lordships, and signify to us their direction, whether, under these circumstances, we are to continue to supply prisoners of war with fish, and particularly with pilchards. We also request their Lordships' directions respecting the disposal of fish and potatoes now on hand in consequence of the refusal of the prisoners to receive them, there being at present above 143 hogsheads of pilchards weighing about 63,000 lbs, and about 37,000 lbs of potatoes which have been so rejected and which, unless they may be disposed of, will be spoiled and totally lost to the public whose property they now are.'[66] In one of the earliest entries in his diary at Greenlaw Captain Paul Andreas Kaald noted on 12 November 1808 that 'Every 14 days on a Wednesday every man gets 2 small pieces of salted herring and 3 or 4 potatoes.'[67] Seven months later, on Sunday, 25 June 1809, Kaald noted that that entire day's food consisted of a piece of blue-moulded bread, and 'a piece of rotten and uncooked dried cod, as well as 4 uncooked potatoes and water.'[68] Then a year afterward, on 3 July 1810, Kaald recorded that all 23 Danish captains in captivity at Greenlaw were called down to the office of the agent, still then Malcolm Wright. Fish was no doubt mentioned in their submissions when, for quarter of an hour, the captains told Wright and Alexander Fraser, his chief clerk, who was also present, 'about the poor provisions we recently had complained about.' Wright promised better provisions in future. Two days later the Danish captains were all called down again to Wright's office, where, says Kaald, 'we signed a complaint against the provisions manager [i.e., contractor] Mr Stone (who is the strictest of all those that govern or command here), and this complaint [they were told] would be sent to the Transport Board.'[69] Kaald himself was released from captivity and repatriated in October 1810, so his detailed daily account of life at Greenlaw ends then. But since his experiences with and opinion of the fish ration at that depot must have been those of many or most other prisoners there, it may be that discontent grew to a point where in August 1811 some kind of remonstrance or confrontation by the prisoners with the depot authorities occurred. Whether pilchards, herrings or cod or indeed fish of any sort were the subject, or part of the subject, of the Board's reply that month to a letter from Lieutenant Priest, RN, by then agent at Greenlaw, is not certain. But Priest was instructed that if any of his inmates refused 'good provisions' they were not to be given any other. 'You are not to enter into any discussions with the prisoners and if they should be refractory we direct you to call in the aid of the military.'[70]

Herrings appear certainly to have played some part in the 'very insolent and refractory' behaviour of prisoners at Esk Mills in the first week of March 1811 which, preceded by the mass escape on 19 February and a further attempt at escape on 9 March, culminated two days later in the panic as one of the depot buildings appeared to be collapsing, the consequent crushing to death of two prisoners, and the closure of the depot and the transfer of its inmates to Edinburgh Castle and Valleyfield.[71] The depot agent, Captain Pellowe, RN, was instructed by the Transport Board on 4 March 'to cause the Herrings refused by the prisoners put on short allowance to be sold, and to give credit for the proceeds in your accounts with this office.'[72]

At Edinburgh Castle, where the French expatriate visitor Louis Simond noted that the prisoners 'once or twice a week ... have fish instead of meat', there is no specific evidence that the rations of fish were a source of tumult or disorder among them. It seems probable, however, that the complaints passed by Rear Admiral Otway at Leith to the Transport Board on 18 March 1811 about 'the badness of the provisions issued to the prisoners at Edinburgh Castle' included some reference to fish.[73]

At Valleyfield the prisoners rejected their ration of herrings (as well as bread) within a fortnight of the opening of the depot in March 1811, and the fish (and the bread) had to be sold off.[74] The subject of the fish ration at the depot may have become somewhat odorous even before the depot opened, for as early as 2 February that year the Transport Board wrote to Captain Heddington, then its agent at Valleyfield, that 'Notwithstanding the stipulation in the contract, we acquaint you that it is not intended that the cod-fish to be supplied to the Prisoners in your Custody should be of the Newfoundland Fishery.'[75] Cryptic though the statement is its implication may have been that the fish supplied by the contractor would be of inferior quality to that stated in the contract. At any rate fish appears to have remained a source of controversy at Valleyfield. 'Approve of your allowing Beef to be issued instead of Fish until the New Potatoes are fit for Use, if Commissioner Bowen [of the Transport Board] should see no objection,' the Board informed the depot agent in July 1811.[76] '... if the Prisoners will not receive unobjectionable fish, you are to cause it to be sold,' the Board told the agent four months later, 'and the Prisoners are not to be supplied with anything in lieu.'[77] In 1813, after instructing the agent in February that the prisoners should be given 1 lb 3 oz. of wet fish whenever the contractor was unable to provide them with 1 lb of dry fish, the Board emphasised in mid-September in reply to a report from the agent, that 'if the fish be good the prisoners must receive it or have nothing in lieu.'[78]

Other items in the prisoners' rations appear not to have aroused their complaints as often or sometimes as heatedly as did the bread and fish. But that is not to say that the vegetables, the meat, the soup, the barley, the oatmeal, and the salt included also in their rations were invariably of good quality, popular, and provided in adequate amounts. Even a witness as generally good humoured as the diarist Captain Paul Andreas Kaald at Greenlaw passed scathing comments occasionally on some of those items. Writing on Boxing Day 1808, for example, Kaald said: '... the soup we had yesterday and today is just clear boiled water. Before there has only been a bit of grain and onion peel ... But now there is at least 10 to 12 grains to each person and not an onion peel in sight. One can see what a pleasant diet we have had during these holy days.' On another occasion a few weeks earlier Kaald described the food at the depot as 'very repulsive, reminding me of the smell of my neighbour.'[79]

The importance of vegetables in the prisoners' diets at Greenlaw appeared to have been given a nod of recognition as early as the summer of 1804, a few months after the depot opened. The Transport Board was told then by the Commissioners for Sick and Wounded Seamen that Mr Kellie, the surgeon at Greenlaw, had reported 'several of the prisoners at that depot are afflicted with the scurvy, and recommending that they should be supplied daily with one pound of vegetables.' The Board replied that directions had already been given on the subject to Malcolm Wright, agent at the depot, as well as to all depot agents in England.[80] The belief, however, that, at least at Valleyfield, prisoners had a plot or plots on which to grow their own vegetables appears to be based on very sketchy evidence and is almost certainly fallacious.[81] To allow prisoners to grow their own vegetables within the walls of the depots in Scotland would have been difficult not only because of lack of space, but also because to do so would have been likely to have aroused strong opposition from the provisions contractors. Vegetable plots outside the depot walls would have raised the likelihood of escapes or attempted escapes and would have demanded the deployment of additional guards. There is, however, incontrovertible evidence that the presence at both Valleyfield and Perth of thousands of prisoners of war led to much vegetable growing by local farmers and landowners, in some cases by arrangement with the provisions contractors. Such vegetable plots appear to have included Penicuik public park and Cornbank farm, the latter of which was said to have been leased from Sir George Clerk so that vegetables could be grown for Valleyfield (and perhaps for Greenlaw, too) and where according to a local (and perhaps erroneous) tradition prisoners were said to have worked in manacles.[82] The Cowan brothers, paper makers, who had sold Valleyfield mill to the government in December 1810 for use as a depot but who remained lessees of some local farm and other land, themselves became involved in providing cabbages, turnips and potatoes for contractors at Valleyfield and Esk Mills.[83] At Perth, too, there is no evidence of vegetables being grown in plots by the prisoners themselves, although 'Many acres of potatoes were planted in the neighbourhood for the supply of the Depot and the greatly increased military strength of the garrison.'[84] Turnips were also in great demand there: 'About five acres of Swedish turnip were sold on the 9th instant by the public roup off the farm of Newton of Huntingtower at 3/11¾d. per fall, equal to £31.16.8 per acre, and the expense of carriage to be paid by the purchaser. We understand this very high price was given by the contractor for the Depot of French prisoners.'[85]

When vegetables were not available, not provided or not of good enough quality, substitutes were sometimes issued. At Valleyfield, for example, the Transport Board told the agent in May 1811 to make barley a substitute if good turnips could not be provided, and in January 1814 approved the agent's allowing the contractor to substitute 'two ounces of barley until vegetables can be procured.'[86] In July 1811 the agent was told that 'If the Potatoes that are to be procured be good and wholesome they are to be issued, and nothing in lieu. But if not good the Beef Ration must be supplied until good Potatoes can be got.'[87]

Obviously, the quality and sufficiency of the prisoners' food and drink depended very largely on the ration scales laid down by the Transport Board or ultimately the Admiralty, the degree of concern and vigilance exercised by the Board and its agents at the depots in ensuring the scales and qualities were implemented, and by the honesty and diligence of the private contractors who tendered competitively every six months or so to provide those rations. Unfortunately for the prisoners, any expectation of honesty and diligence on the part of contractors often proved short-lived, not to say illusory. Examples of contractors' rascality, including complaints of adulteration of bread, have already been observed above. Few, if any, of those contractors were altruists concerned for the welfare of the prisoners; on the contrary, maximum profit and minimum concern appeared all too often to be their guiding lights.[88]

At the beginning of the war in May 1803 the Transport Board had replied to an enquiry from their Lordships of the Admiralty 'whether in our opinion any better mode can be adopted for victualling the prisoners of war than what was practised during the late [French Revolutionary] war; and in answer … it appears to us that the prisoners in health can only be properly victualled either by contract, at a certain rate per head, as was done during the late war, or with provisions to be supplied by the Commissioners for Victualling His Majesty's Navy; and we are of opinion that the former mode would be the least expensive to the public, and certainly not less advantageous to the prisoners, provided the agents at the several depots be fit persons and attend to their duty.' The Admiralty accepted the Board's recommendation that subsistence for the prisoners be contracted in the usual way.[89]

Separate contracts were sought by the Transport Board for prisoners in health and for those who were sick, since separate diets were provided for the two categories. A list of contractors at Scots depots which survives for the last months of the war shows James Miller as contractor for prisoners in health at Greenlaw, Lyall & Stone at Valleyfield, and James Lindsay & Co. at Perth, with W. Smith as contractor for prisoners in sickness at Valleyfield, Lyall & Stone at Perth, and no such contract at that time at Greenlaw. Earlier, in November 1811, at Edinburgh Castle, the contractor for prisoners in health was Durie, for those who were sick Lyall & Stone, and the latter then had contracts for prisoners in health and in sickness at Greenlaw and Valleyfield. These are the contractors whose names recur throughout the war in connection with the depots in Scotland.[90]

Supplying hundreds and then, as their numbers hugely and swiftly increased from early in 1811, thousands of daily rations to the prisoners in the depots in Scotland was a major undertaking, especially given rising wartime prices, particularly of grain, especially wheat, and such other obvious difficulties as transport and bad weather.[91] The Transport Board itself, which constantly sought to exert detailed control over depots and their agents, even in such trivial matters as agents' purchases of broom handles and wheelbarrows, was far away in London.[92] Once a contract was signed it was difficult for the Board or its agents at the depots to keep a tight grip on dishonest and slippery contractors (many contemporaries might have claimed there were no others). It was significant, for example, that Admiral Otway at Leith asked the Transport Board in March 1811 to send him 'the respective contracts in force for victualling the prisoners' at the depots in Scotland.[93] In November that year the Board felt obliged to send a circular to all depot contractors informing them that 'in future you will be required to make affidavit quarterly that the contract in all its articles has been strictly and bona fide executed.'[94] On the other hand, it was true that in tendering the contractor had to name 'two respectable persons' who would stand surety for £2,000 for the due performance of the contract. References to defalcations by contractors and their mulcting or fining by the Transport Board occur from time to time in the Board's correspondence with its agents at the depots in Scotland (and are also mentioned, for example, in the Board's correspondence in January 1813 with Admiral Otway about the provision of bread and biscuit at Valleyfield).[95] But the only evidence found of such mulcts or fines actually being imposed by the Board on contractors at work north of the Border is in a letter in July 1813 from the Board to its agent at Valleyfield, instructing him to buy and distribute to the prisoners there 'potatoes to the amount of £12.18.6., being the stoppages from the contractor on account of biscuit issue.'[96] Let the last words on contractors at Scots depots rest with the equable Captain Paul Andreas Kaald, diarist at Greenlaw. 'A new contractor has come here at this time to the prison in Mr Durie's place,' Kaald noted on 2 December 1808. 'He also treats us badly.' And when in July 1810 all the Danish sea captains in the depot, including Kaald, signed a complaint against the contractor Stone, Kaald described him as 'the biggest scoundrel of all.'[97]

'… he who has only basic rations to live on is unfortunate, the rations being less good than those of France,' Sergeant Major Beaudoin remarked in his diary of his captivity at Greenlaw during the years 1804-9.[98] There were several means by which prisoners could, or could try to, supplement their rations. The most obvious of these was by acquiring some money, or adding to or deploying whatever sums they already possessed, to buy extra food and drink. The acquisition of money (and not merely for buying extra food) could be pursued in a variety of ways, several of which will be more fully discussed in the next three chapters.

Gambling was one of these ways. Whether, for example, the prisoners observed by Andrew Johnston, extra clerk at Esk Mills, to be playing pitch and toss beside the dead body of an attempted escaper from there on 19-20 February 1811 were hoping to buy extra food with their winnings is not known.[99] But Marote-Carrier, transferred from Valleyfield to Perth in September

1812, recalled that at the former depot 'Several of us, despite the outcome or the trouble in which they found themselves, were consumed with an unbridled passion for gambling. Three or four hundred unfortunates were thus despoiled not only of their clothes but even of their blankets which they had played for and lost after dyeing them and converting them into pieces of clothing. At the time of our entry to Perth a distribution had been made to us of a uniform clothing. ... These unfortunate men had not, however, given up their sad passion, and having nothing more to gamble with they came to the point of risking their daily ration of food on a throw of the dice, or on the chance combination of a game of cards.'[100] If gambling might sometimes result in wins with which more food could be bought, it could thus also, and sometimes did, result in a complete loss of rations.

Nor was it unknown for prisoners to sell their rations, possibly in some cases in order to buy food more agreeable to their tastes. Had that been the intention of an unnamed ship's boy at Greenlaw who was the subject of a letter in April 1809 from the Transport Board to their parole agent at Peebles? 'You will inform M. Jensen,' wrote the Board, 'that his Boy cannot be allowed parole, having conducted himself improperly at Greenlaw in selling his rations of provisions.'[101]

But there were many other less risky, dangerous or reprehensible ways of acquiring or increasing money for extra food. Marote-Carrier, who himself already had some wherewithal, describes the method he and a Dutch one-eyed fellow prisoner and privateer officer named Van Gruthem followed at Perth: 'It was necessary to find a resource that protected us from need ... There was held near the barrier at the main gate a sort of market where the English [i.e., people of Perth and district] came to buy the things made by the prisoners, and where the prisoners themselves came to procure all sorts of supplies. I resolved to try this means of existence... To ensure the success of our commercial speculation we [he and Van Gruthem] resolved to set up a shop where there would be available things that were most needed by the prisoners and which they used most. After mature reflection we chose tobacco as the basis of commerce, then sugar, coffee, snuff boxes, pipes, etc. We devoted to the first purchases about thirty louis [gold coins, replaced by napoléons, and each worth about 24 francs]. Then we began business, he in the room, I at the barrier where there were at least 300 tables loaded with boxes, straw, knick-knacks in bone, watch chains, etc. We sold pipe tobacco for a penny, with the pipe thrown in, for the tobacco was very dear and we hardly made a profit of a shilling on every pound sterling's worth we sold. However, with this meagre profit we could if we lived economically make something out of it. In the evening our merchandises were put into an iron box that was double locked and placed near our hammock. Such was the miserable trading that we followed all the time I stayed at Perth.'[102]

At Perth, too, 'among the thousand forms of trade the prisoners carried on' was one where 'several of them ran about the rooms and the yards, carrying and selling cooked potatoes enclosed in a sort of tin boiler that was quite sizeable and had a lid.'[103]

At Greenlaw, Captain Paul Andreas Kaald noted, there were on one side of the courtyard or airing ground '6 ovens built where some of the French cook potatoes and sell them. They cook [these potatoes] for the rest of us for ½d. [each] in 4 small ovens. These French have to build the ovens themselves and buy raw potatoes and pit coal.'[104] When James Anton served with the militia guarding the prisoners at Greenlaw he found that 'Some of them were occupied in culinary avocations, and as the guard had no regular mess, the men on duty became ready purchasers of their [the prisoners'] *labscusse*', which was described as 'a thick soup, consisting of very little mixed meat, a good seasoning of pepper, and plenty of potatoes. It may be said to be a dish between potato soup and Irish stew.'[105] At Greenlaw also, much as at Perth, there were 'At the edge of the courtyard nearest to the prison ... numerous small tables which belong to some of the prisoners, who purchase cigarettes and tobacco, butter, meat, bread, pepper, salt, onions, small clay-pipes and candles, and sell them to the others in pennyworths and half-pennyworths, just as much as we can afford to buy.'[106] Kaald himself, along with all the other Danish prisoners at the depot, received 4s.6d. at Christmas 1808, and noted that 'From now on every Danish prisoner will get 14d. per week ... which is a little help, thank God.' On one occasion he records that he used his money to provide himself with 'a good lunch, consisting of a small cup of coffee with egg in it, and two boiled eggs with butter and bread.'[107]

No prisoners in any of the other depots in Scotland enjoyed the liberty granted at Greenlaw to Kaald and some of his fellow officer captives during the distinctive regime of Malcolm Wright, agent there in 1804-10, thanks to which they were able often to visit nearby hostelries or private homes (including, at least in Kaald's case, that of one of the depot turnkeys) in order to partake there of food and drink.[108]

The cooking and distribution of food to the prisoners are touched on in both official and non-official sources. 'Cooking houses ... and cooking utensils,' the Transport Board reminded one of its own members, Commissioner Bowen, concerning the new depot about to be opened at Esk Mills early in 1811, 'must be provided by Government, as at all other depots. The ovens, slaughtering houses and store houses for the provisions are, of course, to be provided by the contractors as usual.'[109]

No evidence appears to survive of how prisoners at Edinburgh Castle received their rations or meals, but it seems unlikely the system there was much different from that at other depots in Scotland. At Greenlaw, according to Kaald, the prisoners were grouped in messes each of six men who shared two loaves of bread for breakfast and similarly shared whatever was on the menu for the midday meal. 'For supper we never get anything, unless you yourself fetch a jug of water to drink and have saved something from dinner. It is good to have something to eat in the evening. If not, you have to go hungry until after 9.30 next morning, when you get some bread again.'[110] Enlargement of the cookhouse at Greenlaw was the subject of an instruction by the Transport Board to Robert Reid, crown architect in Scotland, in February 1812.[111]

William Chambers' recollection of looking down from the Penicuik parish churchyard when he was a boy, at the prisoners in Valleyfield 'superintending cookery in big pots over open fires, which they fanned by the flapping of cocked hats', was really a description of their efforts to supplement the food (described by Lieutenant Marote-Carrier, one of its consumers in 1811-12, as 'spoiled and disgusting') they received from the depot cookhouse. There appears to be no evidence that any other depot in Scotland possessed anything resembling what Chambers recalled seeing at Valleyfield: 'a booth—a rickety concern of boards—seemingly a kind of restaurant, with the pretentious inscription *'Café de Paris'* over the door, and a small tricolor flag ... fluttering from a slender pole on the roof.'[112]

Of the food and its distribution at Perth depot, Marote-Carrier, an inmate there in 1812-14, recalled that 'it was prepared in a less disgusting manner than on the hulks [where he had languished during the first few weeks of his captivity], and of better quality than that of Valleyfield. In the kitchen big plates were suspended that bore a serial number. Two drums or tins bore the same number and were used to carry the soup. Each drum contained six litres. The two drums and the plate constituted the share of the soup and vegetables of a dozen men who came together at each meal. Each day one of them took his turn at serving, that is to say, he had to go to the kitchen, his numbered meat-skewer in his hand, a tinplate sheet at his neck, to claim the share of the meat for his companions, as well as the rest of the meal. The cook called them out in order, and gave each the plate and the drums with his number on them. The meat was shared out in equal portions in the room, and these portions were distributed as on the hulks, but more hygienically. As a Catholic, Captain Moriarty [depot agent at Perth] slimmed us down three times a week, on Wednesdays, Fridays and Saturdays. On those days potatoes formed the basis of the meal. It was also an economical system, for they were very common in Scotland and of such a size that often three were enough for two men. Some poor devils traded the bones in the meat portions and gave pepper in exchange. They ran through all the rooms crying, "Who wants pepper for bones?!" These bones, picked clean and quite dry, were resold to the prisoners who made from them delicate little nick-nacks, such as [model] ships, little houses, handles of carving knives, etc.'[113]

Depot cooks appear to have been appointed from among the prisoners. According to an instruction from the Transport Board to the agent at Esk Mills in February 1811, those prisoners employed as cooks at the depot hospital were, along with other prisoners employed there on other tasks, 'to be paid by the contractor 6d. each per diem.' Whether the non-hospital cooks were similarly paid is not known.[114] A horrifying accident which occurred in the cookhouse at Perth depot in June 1813 caused the death of one of the prisoners employed as a cook. Julien Foret (or Foiret), a soldier, born at Ferici or Fevici and aged 26, of the 88th regiment of infantry, had been captured at Badajoz in April the previous year and had arrived at Perth in August. On 11 June 1813 Foret 'fell into the large boiler and was so dreadfully scalded that he died in the depot hospital a few hours later.' He was interred at the depot.[115] Surviving lists of prisoners employed at Greenlaw depot hospital include as cooks Jean Fauché, there in the summer of 1812, Michel Tastillon or Dastillon between November 1812 and January 1813, and Louis Boisdefray (assistant cook) in December 1812. Tastillon or Dastillon was similarly employed in July-August 1813 at the hospital at Edinburgh Castle.[116]

'Today,' Captain Paul Andreas Kaald wrote in his diary at Greenlaw on 14 January 1810, 'Locke [a fellow prisoner and friend] and I were the supervisors in the cookhouse.'[117] They were carrying out that duty in accordance with Transport Board regulations for all depots, No. 8 of which declared: 'The prisoners in each prison are to appoint three or five, from among their own number, as a Committee for examining the quality of the provisions supplied by the contractor; for seeing that their full rations, as to weight and measure, are conformable to the Scheme of Victualling ...; and if there should be any cause of complaint they are to inform the agent thereof; and should he find the complaint well-founded, he is immediately to remedy the same. If the agent should neglect this part of his duty, the prisoners are to give information thereof to the Commissioners [of the Transport Board], who will not fail to do them justice in every respect.'[118]

About these inspectors and the carrying out of their duties at the depots in Scotland little information is known to survive. Bare lists give the names of five inspectors at Edinburgh Castle depot in July 1813. Four of those five re-appear in a similar list of six inspectors which seems to be for Greenlaw depot for the months between January and July 1813 in the case of five, and for the sixth, from April to July 1813.[119] The only other references found to inspectors were to those at Valleyfield early in 1813. There the prisoners, as already observed,[120] had been complaining strongly about their bread ration in particular. On 2 January the Board wrote to the Valleyfield agent, Captain Andrew Brown, RN, enclosing 'letter which has been addressed to the

Board by certain prisoners in your custody and to desire that you will report thereupon, especially with regard to the confinement of one of the Inspectors …'[121] The Board's letter crossed with one from Brown written the same day in which he proposed the employment of three additional inspectors, which the Board approved on 6 January. A month later, after receiving another letter from Brown, the Board replied on 15 February: '… the contractor has no right whatever to object to any of the prisoners appointed to inspect the provisions … The contractor will be severely mulcted for his repeated attempts to issue inferior provisions and in the meantime you are to procure good provisions in lieu of all articles that the contractor may send in inferior to the contract.'[122]

Rations for the sick and for convicted sinners against depot rules were different from the standard provision. Those prisoners guilty of any of the more serious breaches of the rules and regulations, such as violent behaviour toward turnkeys or other depot staff, damage to depot buildings, or attempted escapes, were (if not transferred in particularly serious cases to the hulks in the south of England or to the more punitive quarters at Edinburgh Castle) sentenced by the agent to a period in the depot's cachot or cells and also put on short allowance of food and drink.

Sometimes, depending on the nature of the offence, the imposition of short allowance—usually two thirds or one half of the standard provision—fell as a collective punishment on all the prisoners at the depot, or on sizeable groups of them. 'During these days,' Captain Kaald wrote in his diary at Greenlaw on 23 November 1808, only a fortnight after he had arrived there, 'there is talk that all the prisoners will be put on half rations. I think there is little enough to live on to keep a healthy body.' Five days later Kaald added: 'It has just happened that we now only get two thirds of the ration which we previously received. Everyone thinks it is far too little to live off. One gets far too little. The reason for this [reduction] is that here in the prison a number of prisoners have been very badly behaved and now all shall suffer, since nobody knows who the culprits are.' 'One day we get our half ration, the next day absolutely nothing to talk about—so it now looks bad,' Kaald recorded on 2 December. 'It is good if you have a halfpenny to help with things; if not, you must go hungry, which is one of the most unpleasant experiences, as well as when you have lost your freedom.' Three days later he noted: 'The half ration still lasts, and it is said that it will continue for 14 days yet.' Whether as a result of the reduction in rations or from other causes, Kaald himself fell ill for a week in mid-December, and his diary does not record the ending of the short allowance of food.[123]

Nor did the prisoners always know the reason for collective punishment of that kind. 'Today,' Kaald wrote at Greenlaw on 13 May 1810, 'we were all put on half rations, except those who came in [to the depot] last. What for and for how long this will last, we don't yet know.' 'On the 4th [of June],' he wrote that week, 'we finally got whole rations again after having been on half rations for three weeks (really a long time to starve).'[124]

Transport Board correspondence with the depot agent at Greenlaw provides other instances of the imposition of short allowances. Thus in January 1809 the Board approved of putting the 'Prisoners on short allowance to make good the amount of the expence necessary for the repair of the damage done by them.' Similarly in August that year the Board approved of '… your having ordered 367 of the prisoners in your custody to be put on short allowance for five days, to make good the expence attending the damage done by them in attempting to escape.' In May 1810, on what appears to have been one of the occasions noted by Captain Kaald (although in that case it looks as if the agent exceeded his instructions and reduced the allowance by half), the Board told the agent that damage done by the prisoners should be immediately repaired, '… keeping them on two thirds allowance until the expence is made good … You will also do the same daily in future whenever any damage may be done. The most refractory of the prisoners are to be the first among them to be removed to [the hulks at] Chatham.' What was normally an automatic case of short allowance was exemplified by an instruction by the Board to the agent in March 1811: '… approve of your paying the usual reward of one guinea for recapture of the escaped prisoner mentioned … he is to be kept on short allowance until the same is made good.' And in February 1812 approval was given by the Board to action by the agent '… in having put the prisoners in the ward, the ceiling of which had been cut through, on short allowance to make good the damage done.'[125]

There were at all the other depots in Scotland many similar cases of short allowance being imposed on prisoners. Those, including four French officers regarded as ringleaders, transferred to Edinburgh Castle early in March 1811 for being concerned in 'outrageous proceedings' at Esk Mills, were ordered by the Transport Board to be put at the Castle in 'solitary cells on short allowance of provisions'.[126] And five of the prisoners recaptured after the mass escape from Edinburgh Castle on 12 April 1811 were ordered by the Board to be put on short allowance 'to make good among them the sum of £13.1.6.' incurred in their recapture.[127]

At Esk Mills, in the aftermath of the mass escape of 19 February 1811, all 1,600 or so prisoners then at the depot were put on short allowance for three days.[128] It was in connection with those events, too, that the Transport Board informed the agent that 'The amount considered to be made good by the stoppage of one third of a prisoner's rations is 2d. per diem.'[129] Prisoners already on short allowance at Esk Mills soon afterwards refused to eat her-rings they were given as part of their rations.[130]

When at Valleyfield early in April 1811 a prisoner named Jacques Perrot had his face marked, apparently by some fellow prisoners, in a manner and for reasons unstated, the agent was instructed '... to keep all the prisoners at Valleyfield on short allowance until they give up the perpetrators of the inhuman act.' There were then more than 2,400 prisoners in the depot.[131] Whenever projected occasional visits to Valleyfield and Perth depots by Robert Reid, crown architect in Scotland, revealed wilful damage to the buildings, the depot agents were ordered by the Transport Board in September 1813 'from time to time [to] put the prisoners on short allowance to make good the amount of the damage as done by them.'[132] A parole prisoner sent from Hawick for breach of his parole was kept on short allowance 'to make good the sum of £3.6.0., the amount of expenses incurred in apprehending him and conveying him to Valleyfield.'[133] And at Perth, even after the war had ended in the spring of 1814 but before the general repatriation of prisoners had taken place, the Board wrote to the agent to '... approve of the system which you propose to adopt with respect to the prisoners on short allowance for damaging the prison buildings.'[134]

Reduction of prisoners' rations to a half or even two-thirds could obviously affect their health if the reduction was prolonged for more than a limited period. If prisoners died as a result of prolonged under-feeding retaliation might well follow against British prisoners in French hands. At the least, the French authorities could be expected to make much propaganda out of such deaths. The Transport Board appears to have calculated that two months of reduced rations would place the health, or even the lives, of prisoners at risk. '... in future,' the Board directed its agents at all depots in May 1809, 'all prisoners who may have been on short allowance more than two months are to be reported by name regularly every week, with a statement of how long they may have been on that allowance and the sums remaining to be made good by them respectively.'[135] Less than a year later, some anxiety on the issue was again expressed by the Board in another circular sent by its secretary to depot agents, though the Board's anxiety arose at least partly from its perennial concern to keep down expense: 'As several prisoners have been long confined on short allowance, I am directed to signify to you the Board's desire to be informed if they have other means of procuring any food in addition to the reduced ration; also whether the health of any of them be materially impaired by the confinement, in order that, with a view of saving the expense which would attend them if sent to the hospital, the Board may, if they should judge proper, direct their close confinement to be terminated. A note to this effect is to be put to every Weekly Black Hole [i.e., cachot or depot cells] Return.'[136] The agent at Valleyfield was told in May 1812 that,

'[The Board] desire to be informed if the Health of the Prisoners in the Black Hole be impaired in consequence of their Confinement.'[137] Agents must presumably have kept some record of their sentences on prisoners to periods of short allowance of rations, but, if so, no such records are known to survive for depots in Scotland, other than the references in correspondence with the Board of the nature quoted above. Nor have any black hole or cachot official returns been preserved.[138]

A Valleyfield prisoner who provided some account of the food and drink he said he obtained during several days he spent in the cachot or black hole there was that almost ubiquitous witness Lieutenant Marote-Carrier. Sentenced along with a fellow prisoner to the black hole after an unsuccessful attempt at escape from the depot, Marote-Carrier long afterward recalled: 'The next day we were brought the same food as in the prison.' The sergeant of the guard proved to be sympathetic and Marote-Carrier gave him some money he had successfully concealed in his clothing, 'begging him to bring us a bottle of rum with the midday meal. At one o'clock he came in with the dinner and the bottle and gave me back the rest of the money. I offered him a glass of rum, he accepted it and began to speak to us for a few minutes. He ended by telling us that we were mad to remain in the black hole, and advised us to declare ourselves ill and to ask to be taken to the hospital.' The stratagem succeeded.[139]

What Marote-Carrier found in the way of food and drink in Valleyfield hospital after he had succeeded in enlisting the sympathy of the depot surgeon and being transferred there from the black hole, illustrated the distinct contrast between the prisoners' standard rations and those they might expect to enjoy as patients in the hospital. Though again no record of such pressures appears to have survived, there must have been many prisoners in all the depots in Scotland during the Napoleonic Wars who often pondered how they could feign illness successfully, as on that occasion Marote-Carrier did.

Marote-Carrier had, of course, already been a genuine patient in February-March 1811 in the hospital at Esk Mills. There, suffering from a severe fever, he had found the food was good, although at first he had been put on a strict diet of a quarter ration: '... about ten o'clock there was a plate of excellent *bouillon* [beef and vegetable tea] and two eggs; in the evening another plate of *bouillon*.' Once he was feeling much better Marote-Carrier had understandably tried to remain in the Esk Mills hospital as long as he could. 'A good fire, excellent food in abundance, fine wines that were handed round us quite liberally ... how many reasons to be ill a little longer! But alas!' Marote-Carrier had been turned out from the hospital and sent back to the grey world and standard rations of the depot—this time, however, at Valleyfield, since Esk Mills had ceased to be a depot while he had been in its hospital.[140] A year or so later, miraculously translated from Valleyfield's black hole to its hospital, he recalled, 'It was the same distribution, the same order as that of [Esk Mills]. On entering we received the regulation clothing, the parrot's uniform. Then we were taken into a well heated place where we were each given good soup, white bread, excellent meat and about half a litre of fine wine. It was a delicious meal, compared with the wretched ordinary food of the prison.' When, however, the depot agent, Captain Moriarty, appeared at the hospital he and the surgeon had a heated altercation about the presence there of Marote-Carrier and his colleague who, Moriarty quite accurately declared, had nothing wrong with them. The surgeon, however, insisted he and not Moriarty was in charge of the hospital and, according to Marote-Carrier, added: 'If the hospital is overcrowded, how many of the prisoners there have come into it exhausted and half-consumptive by their stay in that damp Black Hole where you throw them in for mere trifles? Each year you burden the government with big expenses that would be easy to remove. For I like to believe that you know as well as me that the treatment of a sick man costs more than double that of an able-bodied prisoner.' There indeed was an argument likely to appeal to the Transport Office, to which, Moriarty remarked as he left the hospital, 'his face suffused with anger', the surgeon would have to justify himself. The surgeon then told Marote-Carrier and his colleague they could remain in the hospital 'until you no longer feel the slightest indisposition. And he ordered that we should be served the whole ration as on the preceding day when we were taken in.' Soon afterwards, however, when the surgeon had been called before the Transport Board in London, his deputy took Marote-Carrier's feigned illness seriously and insisted on applying a drastic remedy for it that speedily drove him out of the hospital and back to the inferior rations and overcrowded rooms of the depot.[141]

Although no tenders by contractors, and only one other relevant document, are known to survive for depots in Scotland detailing the provision of rations for prisoners in sickness, i.e., in hospital, a reasonably accurate impression of those rations may be formed from information available for depot hospitals in England. 'The full diet for hospital patients was on a generous scale,' says an historian of Dartmoor depot. '1 pint of tea, morning and evening, 16 oz. of white bread, 16 oz. of beef or mutton, 1 pint of broth, 16 oz. of greens or good sound potatoes, and 2 quarts of small beer, besides barley water acidulated with lemon juice. For patients suffering from debility, or capricious in appetite, the surgeon had licence to substitute for the beef fish, fowl, veal, lamb or eggs.'[142]

The one known surviving document indicating actual rations of food and drink provided to prisoners in hospital at any Scots depot concerns Valleyfield. It is a note by Andrew Johnston, clerk or chief clerk there in 1811-12 before he became chief clerk at Perth, and is headed 'Note of one day's expense and profit on the victualling of the Hospital at Valleyfield, 1810' [sic—an error for 1811 or 1812, as Valleyfield opened as a depot only from March 1811]:

19 @ 1/10d.	£1. 15. 7½d.
92 @ 1/7½d.	£7. 9. 6
5 @ 8d.	3. 4
20 @ 1/10d.—cooks, nurses, etc.:	£1. 17. 6
	£11. 5. 11½d.

	£	s	d
Say 39 lbs beef @ 6d.		19	6
46 lbs mutton @ 6d.	1	3	-
132½ bread @ 4d.	2	4	-
8½ barley @ 3d.		2	1½
85 quarts beer 1½d.		11	½
Cooks and Washermen		2	6
35 pints milk @ [sic]		6	0
85 Greens @ [sic]		7	0
8 lbs sugar @ 9d.		6	0
2 lbs tea @ 10/-	1	0	0
10 cwt coals @ 9d.		8	0
Agent		6	0
5 lbs Amons [sic] @ 2d.			10
Parsley 2d.			2
	£7	16	2
Gain:	£3	9	9½[143]

The first four lines of Johnston's note appear to give the total numbers victualled that day, the varying grades or rates of rations they received, and the cost per head. The details and costs of the kinds of food and drink provided in the rations, as well as what appear to be payments to the agent and to the cooks and washermen, leave a profit—to the contractor presumably—of £3.9.9½ or almost 31 per cent. If that was an accurate and an average daily profit for the contractor, then providing rations for prisoners at the depots in Scotland must indeed have been a profitable business.

Prisoners, as at Esk Mills and Valleyfield, fortunate enough to be employed at the depot hospitals in Scotland as assistant surgeons, surgeons' clerks, nurses or washermen enjoyed the full hospital diet.[144] On the other hand, convalescent prisoners in depot hospitals received, or were supposed to receive, only the standard prison rations. When the Valleyfield agent sent the Transport Board a recommendation from Dr John Macansh, the depot surgeon, shortly before Christmas, 1812, recommending that convalescent prisoners 'should be allowed firing, candles and soap to enable them to keep themselves clean', the Board replied that such prisoners 'are to receive only the prison rations, but they may be supplied with a weekly allowance of coals and candles and soap for washing their linen, etc., as suggested by Mr Macansh. They are also to be allowed a barber, a nurse and a washerwoman at 3d. per day each.'[145]

For all the depot hospitals, except for the short-lived depot at Esk Mills, there are numerous references in Transport Board correspondence with the depot agents about the provision of wine, including port wine. Porter or dark sweet malt ale, as well as red wine, was to be 'procured when wanted for the use of the hospital', for instance, at Valleyfield in May 1811; and the agent at the latter was told by the Board shortly before then that he was to send five bottles of port from Valleyfield to the hospital at Greenlaw.[146] One question asked by the Board of the agent at Perth in December 1812, but to which no answer has survived, was why '80 bottles of white wine had been issued to Mr John Lewis, the Hospital Clerk'?[147]

Finally, another statistical table compiled by Andrew Johnston, first or chief clerk there, records 'Numbers victualled in the Hospital at Perth Depot from 1st April 1813 to 1st April 1814: April 4760, May 4498, June 3640, July 1310, August 880, September 792, October 819, November 799, December 704, January 699, February 766, March 877.'[148] These totals may well appear astonishing, given that Perth held an aggregate total of 7,761 prisoners from its opening in August 1812 until its closure at the end of the war. Perth depot hospital contained only 150 beds.[149] Johnston's monthly totals therefore, contrary to the implication of the heading on his note, cannot be of the number of individual prisoners victualled per month in the hospital. They must represent instead the aggregate number of rations provided. Hospital rations were provided three times a day, and, as Johnston indicated, the numbers victualled included 'French Surgeons, Nurses, Washermen, etc.', of whom at any given time there were probably between half a dozen and a dozen. To attempt even to begin to arrive at monthly totals of the number of prisoners receiving hospital rations Johnston's monthly totals must therefore be divided by three. The outcome of that division would then have to be divided by the number of days in each respective month. The sharp fall from mid-summer 1813 in the number of prisoners in hospital, and hence of the number of hospital rations provided, appears to be borne out by newspaper reports. 'For two months back,' the *Perth Courier* reported, for example, on 26 August 1813, 'the sick list [at Perth depot] has fluctuated between 30 and 14', and that day there were 'only 16 in the hospital.' Two months later there were apparently only 10 prisoners in hospital out of a total of more than 6,800 in the depot.[150]

If, as Napoleon is supposed to have said, an army marches on its stomach, food and drink were certainly no less important to those thousands of soldiers—and seamen—from his forces who found themselves in captivity in the depots in Scotland between 1803 and 1814.

15

The Slow March of Time: Boredom, Activity, Letters to and from Home

'Nothing happened.' That, or some other but synonymous comment, was the entry Captain Paul Andreas Kaald made in his diary on no fewer than 271 of the 660 days he passed in captivity at Greenlaw between 10 November 1808 and his repatriation to Norway on 22 August 1810. Except for two—3 March and 19 April 1809, Kaald wrote in his diary every day he spent at Greenlaw. So far as he was concerned, therefore, nothing happened on 41 per cent of all the days he was in captivity. No other prisoner in any depot in Scotland kept, so far as is known, such a punctilious daily note as did Kaald. But even if other prisoners had done so, it is doubtful whether their recording of uneventful, empty days would have varied much from his. Yet Kaald was fortunate. He was a prisoner of war for rather less than two years. Thousands of fellow prisoners in the depots in Scotland were confined for more years than was Kaald—at least 300 of them for up to ten or eleven years.[1]

So how did the prisoners in the Scots depots cope with the slow and, in so many of their cases, prolonged passage of time? No doubt time moved the more slowly for them because, unlike convicted criminals sentenced to a stated term of imprisonment, none of those thousands of prisoners of war knew when the war would end and their repatriation take place. Finding things to do therefore was of cardinal importance in keeping themselves as physically and mentally fit as the circumstances of their captivity allowed.

It was all the more important that they create or follow their own interests and activities because the Transport Board and depot authorities did not compel the prisoners to work on the land or the forests or in mines or at building or other tasks, contrary to the experience of prisoners in many other wars. Work, in fact, was provided in or about the depots in Scotland for very few of them.

Among the 'variety of amusements and occupations' at Valleyfield, for example, that prisoners were occupying themselves with when about 1811-12 the boy William Chambers gazed down on them from his vantage point at the edge of the parish churchyard above the depot, he observed 'several ... no doubt the more ingenious among them, stationed at small wickets opening with hinges in the tall palisades, offering for sale articles, such as snuff-boxes of bone, that they had been allowed to manufacture, and the money got by which sales procured them a few luxuries.'² Scenes similar to that at Valleyfield were regularly visible at the other depots, too, in Scotland. What the boy Chambers did not see, or did not describe seeing, were prisoners actually at work making the kinds of articles he watched them selling at the depot market.

Those articles were made not only of bone but also of wood, paper, straw, hair, cloth, clay, or indeed any other materials which the prisoners could employ in their handicrafts. 'Seven or eight days after I arrived,' Sergeant Major Beaudoin noted in his diary for mid-summer 1804 at Greenlaw, 'I saw several prisoners were working away at different tasks. One was to make a straw plait for women's coiffures, which is the great fashion in this country. Others were making horned plaits for baskets and hats; others again were making domino boxes and a lot of other kinds of little tasks. Others were working with hair, making watch-chains out of it; others, horsehair rings in all sorts of colours; others again books made of wood and embellished with coloured straw. All that was sold at the barrier gate. It was like a factory.'³

Straw but also hair, both horse and human, were the materials worked on a few years later at Greenlaw by Captain Paul Andreas Kaald together with his two privateersmen friends Captain Richelieu and 2nd Captain Locke.⁴ Some other Danish seamen prisoners at Greenlaw in the spring of 1810 'had recently sent to their sovereign a small [model] vessel made of bones, and the sails and ropes of which are made of their own hair. His Majesty, considering this present was a proof of their attachment to their profession, has ordered it to be exhibited at Copenhagen, and the profit transmitted to them.'⁵ At Greenlaw, too, the militiaman James Anton, on guard over the prisoners, in commenting that 'no work was required at their hands, yet few of them were idle', observed that besides those engaged in cooking *labscuse*, etc., 'Others were employed in preparing straw for plaiting; some were manufacturing the cast-away bones into dice, dominoes, paper-cutters, and a hundred articles of toy-work; while a considerable number were employed in vending these articles and by this means realised considerable sums of money.'⁶

When Louis Simond visited Edinburgh Castle in February 1811 and saw the prisoners of war there, he found among them that 'Many supplicating hands offered for sale the produce of their industry: watch-chains made of hair, and other trifling articles, most of them very ingeniously manufactured. A young man, his countenance all radiant with good humour, informed me he had been seven years thus engaged, having been one of the first taken at the renewal of the war.'⁷

At Esk Mills some such handicraft work was no doubt begun by some of the prisoners but no evidence of it has been found, so briefly did that depot exist in early 1811. At Valleyfield, appropriately enough, where for a century before their confinement there paper had been produced at the mills, prisoners used compressed paper among other materials in making items for sale.[8] Among other items made there from bones, horse hair, straw, etc., were 'flutes, whistles, watch-guards, boats, toys, etc.'[9] An order for almost 160 items, including 25 pairs of bracelets and 30 or more large chains all made of hair, as well as one small and two large straw boxes and six rackets [for use perhaps as alarms by turnkeys, rather than for tennis], by Andrew Johnston, depot clerk or chief clerk at Valleyfield until his appointment from summer 1812 as chief clerk at Perth, was fulfilled for him at the former by a prisoner named Jean Faussié (or Fourtrie), who in October that year sent Johnston an invoice for £6.10.12. (sic) for these goods, with an apology for his inability to acquire also for Johnston some boxes of dominoes. Unusually large items made of wood by another prisoner either at Valleyfield or Perth were apparently desks. They were ordered also, it appears, by Andrew Johnston and were made for him by one Lelade, a sergeant fourier.[10] It is not clear if the order for desks was a purely personal one by Johnston or an official one placed by him on behalf of the depot. At any rate a quid pro quo was sought for their making. In his letter to Johnston Lelade says: 'I have the honour to inform you that the desks that you have requested me to make are finished and as I have nowhere safe to keep them you will no doubt want to fetch them as soon as possible. Monsieur, I have a favour to ask of you, if it is in your power to grant it. On the list opposite [which has not survived] you will find ten of us who are in the same Company. The favour I ask is to arrange that we would be in the first batch to leave for France. On that condition I make you a gift of the making of the said desks. Please reply at once, Monsieur, so that I may take steps in that matter ... Your very humble and obedient servant, Lelade, Sergent Fourier.' Whether the favour sought was granted is not known.

At Perth, where the Transport Board instructed the agent two months after the depot opened in August 1812 to submit an estimate for the cost of building 'six small shops within the yard of the engine house for the prisoners who sell toys', items made by the prisoners included some which may have been unusual. One was a remarkably detailed model in bone of a woman at work at a spinning machine; another a beautifully carved box containing a set of dominoes, all in bone.[11] Bones traded for pepper were, of course, what Lieutenant Marote-Carrier, himself a prisoner at Perth in 1812-14, observed 'some poor devils' among his fellow captives actively engaged in, the outcome of which trading was the making of 'delicate little nick-nacks, such as ships, little houses, handles of carving knives, etc.'[12] Others 'dug clay out of their courtyards and modelled figures of smugglers, soldiers, sailors, and women.'[13] The making of straw-plait, 'a manufacture then in its infancy in this country', was another occupation followed by some of the prisoners at Perth, as at other depots in Scotland: 'It is possible that their hammocks may have to some extent yielded straw for the plait'; and 'numbers made shoes out of bits of cloth, their clothes being cut up for this purpose.'[14] The prisoners, a newspaper circulating in the region reported, 'are not only ingenious, but exceedingly industrious, and anxious to dispose of their innumerable toys among the strangers and townspeople who flock every day to visit them.'[15]

Among the prisoners so engaged there were clearly some who were skilled craftsmen. Nor was that surprising since the recruitment of Napoleon's forces was so extensively by conscription. But many others, perhaps most, of the prisoners in the depots in Scotland who busied themselves making things from those various raw materials were, at least to begin with, not skilled or experienced in craft work. Captain Kaald and his two friends Richelieu and Locke, for instance, were not, and neither was Sergeant Major Beaudoin.

Nor were all the prisoners who were occupied in making things self-employed. Although the evidence for Scotland is limited, Beaudoin's recollections at Greenlaw suggest that there and perhaps in the other depots north of the Border there were prisoners who organised and employed others to prepare and process materials that could either be sold or made into items such as hats or baskets or decorated boxes. 'To try to lighten my unhappy fate a little,' Beaudoin wrote, 'I attempted to make some straw plait. It seemed at first very difficult, I had fingers that were too fat, but after some days I managed to make it well, and I went to ask for work. There was a prisoner in the prison who was an entrepreneur and who made bonnets and hats for the townspeople. He took the straw on his account and gave it out to those who knew how to work it up. That work was done for him, he paid three sous per *brasse* [fathom, six feet]. There were some who could make up to a dozen *brasses* per day. I asked him if he would give me some work, showing him what I had done myself. He told me that he wanted to have forty more. I set to work. At the end of two months I became one of the good workers in the prison in this art. I made six or seven *brasses* a day—and they were well done. My first care was to obtain shirts [to wear] as I made money, afterwards other things. As soon as I made a few sous, I obtained straw and worked on my own account. This work lasted four years.' Complaints by British makers of straw-plait goods led to the prisoners being forbidden to make them. Beaudoin, like many other prisoners, found himself obliged to change his work. 'I then learned to make rings from [human] hair, with people's names inscribed on them, that I sold for 6d. or eight sous each, and those in horsehair a shilling. During five and a half years I passed in this prison [Greenlaw] that was the occupation I followed and which greatly affected my sight, but there is no easy way. That work safeguarded my existence ...'[16]

As well as their raw materials of bone, paper, straw, wood, etc., the prisoners who made items for sale had to equip themselves with tools and usually to present their products for sale at the depot markets. About tools they used at any of the Scots depots very little information is available. If a few prisoners, despite searches by their captors, had perhaps been able to fetch one or two very small tools along with them into their captivity, it is probable that most of those who made things for sale had either to improvise tools as best they could from whatever materials they might be able to salvage at the depot, or to try, perhaps with the help of sympathetic or bribeable depot staff or guards, to buy more adequate tools with money from sales of their craft work. The only specific references found to tools at any of the Scots depots are two or three in Kaald's diary at Greenlaw for December 1808, and in the recollections of Marote-Carrier at Valleyfield and Perth. A month after he himself had arrived there Kaald noted, for example, that Alexander Fraser, chief clerk at the depot, informed the French prisoners they must be ready to leave Greenlaw three days later. Consequently, Kaald wrote, '... the French are selling all their tools and other things such as clothes for next to nothing.' On the appointed day, however, when the Frenchmen were all ready to depart, they were told 'that they should wait some more days.' Three weeks after his original announcement, Alexander Fraser '... told us ... that none of the French prisoners will be moving.' And the following day Kaald noted that, 'There is a great noise now with the French and the Danes, since the former want back that which they sold to the latter.' At Valleyfield, Marote-Carrier describes a distinctive prisoner known as the Galérien, and to whom fuller reference will be made below as well as in a later chapter, who 'went rummaging in all the corners, picking up scrap iron, anything metallic that he found' later 'heating and fashioning his iron to which he gave strange forms without explaining the use he wished to make of them.' The Galérien's metal work proved in fact to be more relevant to escape than to making goods for sale at the depot markets. In another passage in his recollections Marote-Carrier mentions the sawing of planks by prisoners at Valleyfield—but again this was in the context of a projected escape, not of the making of items for sale. At Perth, he mentions how the tools of workmen still engaged there in completing the new depot were stolen by prisoners—but there, too, for the purpose of preparing an escape.[17]

Markets, though not exclusively devoted to the sale of items made by the prisoners, were held at all the depots in Scotland regularly and often. Orders for the guard on duty over the prisoners at Greenlaw laid down as early as September 1805 that: 'A serjeant of the Guard attended by one of the Turnkeys is to attend the markets usually allowed and follow such regulations as the agent for the Prisoners will give.'[18] The market there, described by Kaald as composed of 'numerous small tables which belong to some of the prisoners' and situated 'At the edge of the courtyard nearest to the prison', and by Sergeant Major Beaudoin as 'at the barrier gate', has already been mentioned.[19] Elsewhere in his diary Kaald indicates that the market at the depot was open each day for two hours from 9 a.m. to 11 a.m.[20]

At Edinburgh Castle, the engineer James Nasmyth recalled from his boyhood in the city the cramped conditions at the prisoners' markets for the sale of their handicrafts. 'These poor prisoners of war were allowed to work at their tasteful handicrafts in small sheds or temporary workshops at the Castle, behind the palisades which separated them from their free customers outside. There was just room between the bars of the palisades to hand through their exquisite works, and to receive in turn the modest prices which they charged. The front of these palisades became a favourite resort for the inhabitants of Edinburgh; and especially for the young folks. I well remember being impressed with the contrast between the almost savage aspect of these dark-haired foreigners, and the neat and delicate produce of their skilful fingers ... The articles were to be had for a mere trifle, although fit to be placed along with the most choice objects of artistic skill.'[21]

At Valleyfield, according to Macbeth Forbes (who, however, does not give sources for this information), 'Very many citizens went from Edinburgh especially at the week-end to see the prisoners grinning through their gratings and offering for sale articles of their own making. The charitably disposed who ... took the larger view, bought from the Frenchmen on principle, with the purpose of alleviating their suffering.' Precisely how often the markets were held at Valleyfield is uncertain. Abell, also without giving his source, refers to 'the daily market'; Charles Cowan of the mill-owning family, to its being 'once or twice a week', and the Penicuik historian J.L. Black, to 'a weekly market'.[22] Black adds, but again without giving any source, that besides the weekly market, 'the prisoners at the half-yearly market had a stall on the High Street [of Penicuik], near to what is now the entrance to Valleyfield House, while soldiers acted as guard over them and their goods.'[23]

At Perth, where the prisoners 'are allowed to hold a market every day for the purchase of such little luxuries as their private funds may afford and also for the purpose of selling the works of their own ingenuity', the market was open for four hours per day.[24] It was at the market held 'near the barrier at the main gate ... where there were at least 300 tables loaded with boxes, straw, knick-knacks in bone, watch chains, etc.', that Lieutenant Marote-Carrier and his Dutch fellow privateer officer Van Gruthem, along with many other prisoners, sold most of their wares.[25] Penny, the contemporary historian of Perth, declared that 'To the daily market of the prisoners all [members of the public] were admitted, provided they carried no contraband articles ... Vast multitudes went daily to view the market, and buy from the prisoners their toys, of which they had a great variety—many of them made from the bones of their beef. They had stands set out all round the railings of the yards, on which their wares were placed, and a great number of purchases were made every day by the numerous visitors, for which they paid high prices.'[26]

Honest trading no doubt prevailed at all the depot markets in Scotland, but an example of the kinds of fraud that also were sometimes perpetrated by some prisoners on unsuspecting customers was provided by Penny concerning the market at Perth. It involved straw plait, trade in which was prohibited by the authorities. 'As much straw plait as made a bonnet was sold for four shillings,' explained Penny, 'and being exceedingly neat, it was much inquired after. In this trade many a one got a bite; for the straw was all made up in parcels, and smuggled into their pockets for fear of detection ... An unsuspecting man having been induced by his wife to purchase a quantity of straw plait for a bonnet, he attended the market and soon found a merchant. He paid the money, but, lest he should be observed, he turned about his back to the seller and got the thing slipped into his hand, and then into his pocket. Away he went with his parcel, well pleased that he had escaped detection. On his way he thought he would examine his purchase, when to his astonishment he found, instead of straw plait, a bundle of shavings very neatly tied up. The man instantly returned and charged the prisoners with the deception, and insisted on getting back his money; but the man could not be seen from whom the purchase was made. Whilst hanging on to catch a glimpse of him he was told that if he did not get away they would inform the turnkey, and get him fined for buying the article. Seeing there was no chance of getting amends, he was retiring, when one came forward and said that he would find the man, and make him take the shavings back, and get the money. Pretending deep commiseration, he [the prisoner] said he had no change, but if he [the dupe] would give him sixteen shillings he would give him a note, and take his chance of the man. The dupe was simple enough to give the money and take the note, thinking himself well off to get quit of his purchase—but to his mortification he found the note to be a well executed forgery on the Perth bank. Enraged at his own simplicity, he again returned in the hope of finding the fellow who deceived him, but in vain. He was advised to apply to the governor [i.e., depot agent] ... but the dread of being informed on for buying the plait prevented him, and he lost both money and straw.'[27]

Straw and straw-plaiting and the uses to which they were put by prisoners of war in Britain had in fact long been a source of complaint and controversy that had prompted prohibitions by the Transport Board. A letter in September 1807 from the Board to the Hon. W.W. Pole, first secretary to the Admiralty, explained that, '... in consequence of a communication from Mr Rose in the year 1799,[28] stating that very great injury was sustained by the Revenue and manufacturers of this country from the manufacture of straw hats and bonnets having been carried on by the French prisoners at all the Depots, to such an extent as not only precluded the use of those articles of any other manufacture in the respective neighbourhoods but also very much interfered with the general consumption of them throughout the kingdom, this Board issued an order for prohibiting the sale or manufacture of straw hats or bonnets at all the depots, and printed notices to that effect have since been stuck up both within and without the walls of the several prisons. Finding, however, from representations made to us by several persons and particularly by Mr Rose to our chairman in the month of October 1805, that our orders on this subject were not attended with the desired effect as hats and bonnets, or at least plait to be formed into those articles, continued to be privately made by the prisoners from straw, which they were allowed to have under the pretence of its being intended for boxes and toys, we felt it our duty to prohibit entirely the use of straw to the prisoners, as the only effectual means of stopping the trade, so much and in our opinion so justly complained of. This prohibition having in the end proved to be in vain and notwithstanding the utmost vigilance of the officers of this Department, the soldiers on guard at the several prisons and particularly at Stapleton near Bristol, carried on a traffick with the prisoners in straw and straw plait to a considerable extent. We submitted the case to the Commander in Chief [the Duke of York] on the 2nd of June last, requesting that His Royal Highness would be pleased to give the necessary orders for preventing the guards doing duty at the several depots from assisting the prisoners in any way in the sale of straw hats or in any other article made of straw; and we now inclose for their Lordships' [of the Admiralty] information copies of a letter which we have received from Lieutenant Colonel Gordon and of its inclosure from Lieut-General Tarleton on the subject; and we request you will move their Lordships to signify to us their direction thereon. With respect to the reasons which Lieut-General Tarleton gives for recommending that the prisoners should be allowed to manufacture hats and bonnets as well as all other articles of straw, we request you will submit our opinion that, as this is a manufacture known to British subjects as well as Frenchmen, the practice of it in the prisons cannot fail to be injurious to our own poor people; and as a further proof, that it is considered so by those who are best acquainted with the nature of the manufacture, we inclose for their Lordships' information a copy of a letter which we have received from Mr S. Dight, a manufacturer of Bristol, stating that his trade is very much reduced in consequence of the manufacture of the prisoners. We shall only add with respect to General Tarleton's recommendation of the privilege in question, on the score of humanity, that it appears to us to be consistent neither with justice nor good policy that prisoners of war, who are already fed and clothed by Government much better than the labouring poor of this country, and who have no taxes or duties of any kind to pay, should be allowed to avail themselves of any branch of manufacture to the detriment of His Majesty's subjects, whose sole dependence is on the encouragement given to the particular branch of manufacture in which they are engaged.'[29] Although the letters from Lt Col. Gordon, General Tarleton and Mr Dight appear not to have survived, the Board's own letter certainly expresses the strength of its feeling against the prisoners being allowed to use straw or straw-plaiting in making hats or bonnets. The Admiralty seems to have endorsed the view of the Transport Board, for in September 1808 the Board sent a circular to all depots concerning '... very serious injury ... sustained by the industrious poor of this country who exclusively depend upon the produce of their labour for the subsistence of themselves and families, in the manufacture of certain articles, and particularly in straw hats, clothes, boots, and shoes, which the prisoners of war in this country have also been allowed to manufacture while they are amply supplied with food and clothing at the public expense, we have, in pursuance of instructions from the Lords Commissioner of the Admiralty, to signify to you our particular directions to take especial care in future that no prisoner of war who may be placed in your custody be suffered to manufacture any of the articles abovementioned, or any other article whatever interfering with the employment of the labouring poor of Great Britain.'[30] In January 1811 Standing Orders supplementary to the printed instructions for every agent were sent by the Board to all depots in Scotland. Article 9 of the Standing Orders laid down that 'No straw, hats, clothes, boots and shoes, or any other article whatever, interfering with the employment of the labouring poor of Great Britain, to be suffered to be manufactured by the prisoners.'[31] By summer 1812 the government had apparently decided to undertake a 'difficult enquiry' into the manufacture of straw by prisoners of war in the depots.[32] Almost a year later, the following official advertisement appeared in the *Edinburgh Evening Courant*: 'TO THE PUBLIC And to Straw Hat Manufacturers in particular. It having been the practice of a number of persons to buy from the French prisoners *straw plait* at the different depots in England, Scotland, etc., etc., and as those persons have been in the habit of retailing it in Edinburgh and Glasgow, etc., this is to inform those who may purchase that article, that a fine of *ten pounds sterling* is exigible from any person buying a single packet of *straw plait* made at any of the prisons, and also from any person having it in their possession to make up for use, as the encouraging of this illicit trade may be the means of ruining the families of many thousands in England, Scotland, etc., who are entirely supported by the manufacturing of this article. May 1.'[33]

The references to straw-plaiting and items made of straw at Greenlaw already quoted from Sergeant Major Beaudoin, Captain Kaald, and the militiaman James Anton, as well as those at Valleyfield,[34] show that such work by prisoners was taking place in Scots depots from early in the war. But it appears to have been in 1812 that the first specific case concerning straw and its use in any depot north of the Border became the subject of correspondence by the Transport Board. 'We do not consider that we have any right to seize Pipe Straw out of the Prison,' the Board wrote in September that year to its agent at Valleyfield, 'but if any should be seized within the Prison we direct you to destroy it.'[35] The issue of straw and straw plait recurred several times at the depot in the 18 months before the end of the war. Thus orders for the destruction of all straw plait seized at Valleyfield were requested by the Board from the Commander of the Forces in North Britain in December 1812.[36] On 4 June 1813, the Board told the depot agent that they '... cannot recommend the sharing of the straw plait among the military as suggested by the Commanding Officer, and that they are not aware of any law which authorises the seizing of the straw plait out of the prison.'[37] A fortnight later, in a clarification of their views, the Board told the agent that '... the sentries did their duty in seizing the straw discovered by them, the traffic in which we are of opinion might be prevented, but we do not think fit to prevent the total admission of straw into the prison, as it would operate as a punishment on those prisoners who are only employed in making boxes and other authorised articles.'[38] A few days later the Board replied to an enquiry from the depot agent that Alexander Greig, the Admiralty solicitor in Edinburgh, 'has been directed to defend any action that may be brought against John Crank [?], the soldier, on account of his having seized the straw plait thereinmentioned.'[39] A few weeks before the war ended, when the agent again reported straw seized at the depot, he was told by the Board that the straw must be destroyed but that he should 'pay one third of the value as a reward to the person who seized it.'[40] Finally, at the end of January 1814 the agent was told by the Board: 'You are to take particular care that Wingrave be on no account whatever admitted into the prison.'[41] Matthew Wingrave, a Bedfordshire dealer in straw goods made by the prisoners of war, found the trade so profitable that he had bought land near Valleyfield on which to grow wheat and barley for straw as raw material for his business. Wingrave was put on trial in 1813 for trading in straw-plait with the prisoners at Valleyfield. 'The evidence showed that he was in the habit of bribing the soldiers to keep their eyes shut, and that not a few people of character and position were associated with him in the business.'[42] Thomas Gray, a militiaman on guard at Penicuik over prisoners of war, was another during whose trial at the High Court in Edinburgh in July 1814 on much more serious charges evidence was incidentally given that 'he had had some dealings with the prisoners in articles of plaited straw—which was contrary to orders.'[43]

For Perth, although there is less official evidence than for Valleyfield of the struggle over straw, there does survive a note in French, signed by Captain Moriarty, the depot agent, and dated 11 [? 15] May 1813, which declares: 'Every merchant who brings straw into this market will not only be punished for the abuse of the privilege I have granted him but will also be expelled from the market for having so grossly flouted the firm orders of the government.'[44]

At Perth and at the other Scots depots, sales of items made by the prisoners were not confined to the depot markets. The orders, although perhaps unusually substantial, placed at Valleyfield by Andrew Johnston, depot clerk there and at Perth, doubtless exemplified many others placed at depots by members of their staffs and by militia guards. But also the following advertisement, placed by a Glasgow merchant in a city newspaper on Christmas eve, 1811, suggests that at least some of the items made by the prisoners may have found distinctly commercial outlets as well: 'D. Burton, Perfumer, 58 Glassford Street, Glasgow, Most respectfully begs leave to inform the Ladies and Gentlemen of Glasgow and the Public in general, that he has just recived a LARGE and ELEGANT assortment of the following articles, which he is determined to sell on moderate terms. A few FINE TOYS and LADIES' WORK BOXES made by the *French prisoners.*'[45]

Their handiwork thus not only employed the skills and filled constructively the otherwise empty and bleak days of some, perhaps even many, of the prisoners in the depots in Scotland but also provided them with money from their sales. At Valleyfield, for example, it was said that total sales amounted at times to £200 a week.[46] While no information is known to survive about amounts earned by individual prisoners, apart from what may be conjectured from the sums, for example, paid by Andrew Johnston for items of their work which he ordered,[47] James Anton, a militia guard at Greenlaw, referred to some of the inmates there as 'hoarding up money', some of which he implied came from the sale of their handicrafts; and the *Perth Courier* reported in September 1813 that 'The eagerness of the prisoners [at Perth depot] to obtain cash is very great, and as they retain all they procure, they have drained this place almost entirely of silver, so that it has become a matter of difficulty to get change of a note.'[48] It was probably partly arising from the question of income from such sales that in December 1810 a Transport Board circular to depot and parole agents instructed them to inform '... all the prisoners in your care who may in future be sent to France that they will not be allowed to take with them any of the current coin of this realm, and that a strict search will be made previously to their embarkation to prevent their doing so.'[49] And again, at the end of the war, the Transport Board having, as it said, '... reason to believe that the French prisoners in this country have in their possession guineas and other gold coin of the realm to a very considerable amount,' sought the instructions of the Admiralty whether 'we should take measures for preventing such coin from being carried out of the country by giving the prisoners foreign coin in lieu thereof, or otherwise.'[50] Whether prisoners in any of the Scots depots profited so greatly from the sales of their handicrafts as to be able, as were apparently some at Norman Cross depot in Huntingdonshire, 'to carry off upon their release more than 100 guineas each' is not known; but certainly numbers of them must have returned home from Scotland in 1814 not only in better mental and physical health as a result of employing their skills than would have been the case had they remained idle in their captivity, but also with some useful savings from their labours.[51]

But by no means all the prisoners in the depots in Scotland occupied themselves in making things for sale. Some prisoners (including no doubt at least some of those who also busied themselves with their handicrafts) took part in physical recreation, sport or games. Among 'the variety of amusements and occupations' observed, for example, at Valleyfield by the boy William Chambers, were 'Prominently, and forming the centre of attraction ... a considerable number' of prisoners 'ranked up in two rows, joyously dancing to the sound of a fiddle, which was briskly played by a man who stood on the top of a barrel ... Others were fencing with sticks amidst a circle of eager onlookers.'[52] Chambers's is one of only four references found to dancing by the prisoners. A second is a sketch in 1813 by Robert Reid, crown architect in Scotland. His sketch, depicting some thirty prisoners in the airing ground at Greenlaw, shows one in the foreground who appears to be dancing a jig by himself. But if at Valleyfield prisoners, as Chambers testified, were dancing in sizeable formations it seems likely that similar recreation took place among those at the other Scots depots, too. That assumption is strengthened by the third reference, which appears in Captain Paul Andreas Kaald's diary at Greenlaw. On Christmas Day, 1809, Kaald noted: 'In Sande's room (which is the largest) is a skipper Romer from Kragero, who played the violin and there was dancing there until 1 a.m. We were 60 officers gathered there and had a right good time.'[53] Kaald's diary is likewise the source for the final reference found to dancing. 'Since it is our gracious King Frederick VI's birthday,' he wrote on 28 January 1810 at Greenlaw, 'we have illuminations this evening of 6 candles in every window throughout the entire prison. Then [2nd Captain] Locke and I were in another officer's room, where we danced, sang and drank the King and Queen's health with many hurrahs, numerous times, though only with beer (for we didn't have anything else) to midnight ...'[54]

For fencing there is rather more evidence. At least one, and possibly two, of the figures depicted in Robert Reid's sketch at Greenlaw look as if they are holding fencing sticks or foils. At Edinburgh Castle, some prisoners certainly had fencing foils and had been allowed to practise with them at least until the mass escape on 12 April 1811. Malcolm Wright, agent at the Castle, was then found to have failed to carry out instructions from Rear Admiral Otway at Leith 'to take from the prisoners every evening their fencing foils'.[55] Soon afterward, in July that year, a Transport Board circular to all depot agents reported the recent deaths of two prisoners through the use of fencing foils at different (unnamed) depots, and ordered the agents 'in future strictly to prohibit the use of all metal foils by the prisoners in your custody, taking care also to destroy all those now in possession of the prisoners.'[56] One of those two deaths had taken place at Edinburgh Castle. Lieutenant Auguste Belisaire Bourignons of the 65th Infantry regiment, who was aged 20 and had been captured at Flushing in 1809, died on 25 July 'betwixt the hours of 6 & 7 in the Morning by a wound from a fencing foil, which entered the right side of the thorax between the 3rd and 4th rib wounding the right lung [two or three words are then illegible] … near its entrance into the right branch of the heart, thereby occasioning his death in about half an hour after the wound was received.'[57] The very early hour and other circumstances of his death suggest that Bourignons died as the result not of mere recreational fencing but of a duel with a fellow prisoner. That the Board's order prohibiting metal foils was not strictly enforced at all depots was indicated by its further circular to agents in January 1814 following the death of a prisoner at Dartmoor in a duel with a fellow prisoner in which foils had been used 'from which the buttons had been previously taken off.' All the agents were ordered to 'immediately seize and send to this Office all foils which may be found in the possession of the prisoners in your custody and that you will not on any account allow any to be introduced in future.'[58] At Perth depot, at least one of the prisoners gave lessons in fencing and his pupils included the father of Thomas Walker, later historian of Norman Cross depot in Huntingdonshire. Whether these lessons were given using metal foils or only wooden sticks is not clear.[59] Despite the Transport Board's prohibitions, sharpened foils were used by two prisoners at Perth in May 1813—although not for recreational purposes but in a duel in which one was wounded, apparently not fatally.[60]

Ice-skating seemed unlikely to be a recreation enjoyed by any prisoner in the Scots, or indeed any other, depots. Yet at Greenlaw, during the idiosyncratic regime of the then agent Malcolm Wright, Captain Paul Andreas Kaald on 20 February 1810 was 'so lucky to get permission to go to Penicuik, albeit under the guard of 2 big Grenadier soldiers. I nevertheless had the pleasure of skating for an hour on lovely ice, under the baronet's [i.e., Clerk of Penicuik's] manor house.'[61] Kaald's was perhaps not a unique case among some at least of the officer prisoners at Greenlaw, but there is no evidence that prisoners at any of the other Scots depots were ever able to enjoy ice-skating.

Cricket seemed perhaps even less likely a sport that would be played in their captivity by men of Napoleon's armed forces. Yet Macbeth Forbes, pioneering historian of the prisoners in the Scots depots, wrote (again, however, without identifying his sources) that at Valleyfield 'The open air pastimes of the prisoners were mostly hand sports which included a form of cricket.'[62] And Robert Reid's sketch in 1813 of prisoners at Greenlaw depicts indeed what seem to be five prisoners playing that game: a bowler (underarm, it appears), a batsman, a wicket-keeper (seated on the ground), and two fielders.

If fencing, ice-skating and cricket were outdoor activities engaged in by at least some of the prisoners, indoors some played draughts and billiards. At Edinburgh Castle, in one of the larger vaults that housed the prisoners, there was 'a most ingenious imitation of a draft-board' cut into the floor.[63] Since they made dominoes for sale, it seems likely some prisoners must have played that game themselves at the depots in Scotland: certainly at Greenlaw the militia guard James Anton referred to some prisoners there who 'took to the cards, dice or dominoes.' At Valleyfield, in 1811-12, as Marote-Carrier recalled, with the permission of Captain Moriarty, the agent, '... seven of us came together to buy a billiard table that cost us 63 louis. We had had a shed built in the yard to protect the game against the inclemencies of the weather, and we had begun to use it. We had fixed at a penny the price for the game of 24 points, and we had chosen as scorer a prisoner to whom we gave six sous a day and a ration of bread. The success of the enterprise was immense, above all at the beginning. The billiard table was in constant use. It was a raging passion with some individuals, who went so far as to sell their daily ration [of food] in order to play some games. Within several weeks each of the shareholders in the billiard table received a dozen and even fifteen francs profit. ... I made billiards my favourite pastime and I didn't give it up until my departure from Valleyfield [in September 1812], when I sold my share to a Provençal officer for seven louis.'[64]

As for chess, the only mention of it found occurs in the diary of Captain Kaald at Greenlaw, on Good Friday, 20 April 1810, when he and his friend, shipmate and fellow prisoner 2nd Captain Hans Locke, were permitted, thanks to the idiosyncratic practices of the depot agent Malcolm Wright, to visit the nearby home of the owner of Esk Mill papermill, where Locke, their host, another prisoner and the depot clerk Francis Wharton 'played a game called chess', in which Kaald himself, however, 'Since I had the worst toothache ever', could not take part.[65]

Music, as already suggested in William Chambers's recollection of the prisoner at Valleyfield playing his fiddle from atop a barrel, no doubt for some captives in the Scots depots had charms to soothe, if not their savage, then their homesick, anxious, sad, even melancholic, breast. Among the prisoners in all the Scots depots (except Greenlaw, which evidently held fewer than half a dozen) there were numbers of regimental and other musicians, particularly drummers and trumpeters. How many, if any, of these musicians had been able to carry their instruments into captivity is unknown, but drums and trumpets seem unlikely to have been among them. It appears, however, such small instruments as flutes or fifes were carried in or otherwise acquired by a few of the prisoners; and others may have been able in due course to save enough from their income from the sale of handicrafts, etc., to buy instruments. A fiddle or violin is mentioned not only at Valleyfield but also at Greenlaw, where Kaald noted in his diary how on Christmas Day, 1809, one of his fellow sea-going officer captives played his violin there for a large and appreciative audience.[66] Though it would be surprising if none did, there is no evidence of prisoners forming choirs or singing in smaller groups or even solo (apart from such special occasions, mentioned below, as creating 'an appalling uproar' during an attempt at escape, or, as mentioned above, of Captain Kaald and his friends celebrating the king of Denmark's birthday). At Valleyfield, according to Lieutenant Marote-Carrier, officers like him, who were less overcrowded in their separate quarters than the rank and file prisoners in theirs, did not go outside if the weather was bad 'and each busied himself according to his tastes. Music was the most general pastime in those days of confinement. Some played, others listened.'[67] There, too, it appears there was at least one prisoner engaged in setting to music verse written by a fellow prisoner.[68] At Perth, when Marote-Carrier arrived there from Valleyfield in September 1812, he soon found that 'Many of us were musicians. One named Laurencini had a quite remarkable talent on the flute. The poor devil was sunk in misery and aroused deep pity in me. But as on account of his sensitivity he had not wanted to accept any help except as payment for some service, I offered to take lessons on the flute from him and to pay him in tobacco and, over and above that, a penny a day. He gladly accepted, began to give me lessons right away, and I took them for about six months.'[69] Another reference to music at Perth occurs in Marote-Carrier's recollections, when, describing a critical point in preparations by him and other prisoners to escape from that depot, he says: 'So that the English [guards] might not be suspicious of us, we brought together all the musicians in our room. They began to play, and we to sing and dance, in order to create an appalling uproar.'[70] It would be interesting to know how many musicians were then present and which instruments they played. Their playing on that occasion, however, had little to do with creativity or recreation. At the depot markets at Perth, according to the contemporary local historian George Penny, '... some [of the prisoners] were playing on the fiddle, flute, and other instruments, for halfpence.'[71]

Of drawing or painting by prisoners in the depots in Scotland the only examples found concern Captain Paul Andreas Kaald at Greenlaw. Not only did he illustrate his invaluable diary with two sketches of the depot, including one of the interior of his own room there, but also (presumably during one of his visits to the village that were authorised by the depot agent Malcolm

Wright) he executed what appears to be one of the earliest known sketches of Penicuik. Clearly, Kaald was a talented non-professional sketcher, and he again put his talent to good use when on the 24th birthday in April 1810 of his friend and fellow prisoner at Greenlaw 2nd Captain Locke, he presented him with a small portrait. Although it is difficult to believe there were no other prisoners, even if perhaps without Kaald's skill, working with brush or pencil at any other of the close confinement depots in Scotland as a means of passing their time and developing new or practising existing skills, no evidence concerning them appears to survive.

'Having understood that Theatrical Representations have been exhibited by the French officers at many of the parole towns where they are detained,' a Transport Board circular to its agents at all the parole towns in Scotland, England and Wales declared in October 1811, 'it is our duty to inform you that we have never approved of or allowed theatrical Representations at any of the Depots under our charge, nor is it consonant with the Laws of this Realm, that any Foreigners should institute such unauthorised Exhibitions, whose Tendency may be Dangerous in political or licentious Principle, and may occasionally and improperly draw together some of His Majesty's Subjects to attend them. If, therefore, these Theatrical Representations are not immediately put a Stop to, we shall be under the Necessity of removing the Prisoners at … [blank] to some other Depot without Delay.'[72] But were there attempts by the rank and file prisoners confined in the *closed* depots in Scotland to enliven their dreary days through theatre? Apart from 'Punch's opera and other puppet shows [which] were got up in fine style' at Perth,[73] only one reference has been found to what might be described, however loosely, as theatrical activity on their part. 'I acted,' Captain Paul Andreas Kaald wrote in his diary at Greenlaw about the 'right good time' he and 60 other officers had there on Christmas Day, 1809, 'I acted as a fashionable young woman, very well dressed in patterned clothes. The 2 others, namely, the Mate Reick and the Mate Kook, acted as quite ordinary servant hussies.'[74]

Story telling and reminiscing helped fill part of the days or evenings of many of the prisoners. At Valleyfield, says Marote-Carrier, 'When the air was calm and the cold not too biting we went into one of the yards, where we mingled with the other inhabitants of our building. There we walked about (and that was generally the case) or sat on the wooden benches that we had had made up at the common expense. Then we went over past deeds, one of us recounted either the combats in which he had taken part or the adventures that had befallen him. But most often our memories turned back toward home. That was either the rich countryside of Flanders or the sandy coasts of Brittany which we liked to converse about. We saw ourselves ploughing for the first time through the blue waves of the North Sea on the little boat sailed by our fathers, or taking part in the gentle and simple joys of a village fair, or leaving for a distant expedition, such as that which had proven so fatal to us. Thus our memory revived, became fertile, and the reminiscences poured out from the heart and the lips. We reminded ourselves of the preparations for leaving home, our last adieu… We reconstructed our past in a way different from what it had actually been… Sometimes it was a prisoner from Spain whose turn it was to speak. Then he told us of the gigantic struggles of France against Europe. Most often it was an old soldier who had taken part in all the battles of Napoleon. He became enthusiastic at the memory of Marengo, Austerlitz, Wagram. He told us in his picturesque and animated words of the prodigies of valour which characterised the French armies, and became indignant at being a captive and not being able to follow his old companions in their noble and glorious career… Then suddenly the harsh voice of the gaoler ordering us to go back into our prison recalled us to the sad reality and without pity shattered the artificial happiness we had created. We went back, silent and saddened, into our room. The walls seemed more sombre than ever, the windows narrower, the bars thicker. A feeling of sadness seized us and often a furtive tear slipped under an eyelid to wet a cheek that for a long time had not felt one run down. Those nights I did not sleep, and I thought of liberty and happiness.'[75]

One prisoner in particular at Valleyfield appears to have excelled at story-telling. 'If you had entered our prison at Valleyfield,' Marote-Carrier recalled, '(God forbid you do so in the same circumstances as we did), if you entered it at the hour when we were permitted to go out into the three courtyards to which all our promenades were restricted, no doubt you might have noticed right away quite a small man shouting with all the force of his lungs, gesticulating with all his might in the middle of a circle of attentive listeners, hanging on his every word, now listening to him with marked seriousness and as if captivated by the interest of his stories, now guffawing at his displays of buffoonery, at the mad things that the story-teller recited. It was not the lowest ranking prisoners who came thus to lend an ear to his narratives: often the officers did not disdain to line up in the audience. Indeed even a sentry who was not too surly would let himself be tempted by the high spirits of the narrator, and would transgress his instructions a little in order to come and hear some bits of a story that he hardly understood and most often did not understand at all … If you had approached a prisoner and asked who that man the story-teller was, you would have inevitably have been told, "He's the *galérien*." In fact, whoever you had asked all would have said, "He's the *galérien*."'[76] Of the *galérien*, or convict who had been condemned in France to the galleys but who helped pass the time for numbers of his fellow prisoners at Valleyfield by his story-telling, more will be heard in a later chapter.

New arrivals at the Scots depots, whether they had been recently captured or were transferees from another depot or a hulk, might also prove sources of information and news the telling of which could help other inmates, old or new, pass the weary hours. At Greenlaw, for instance, Captain Kaald recorded that: '45 Danish prisoners came here in the afternoon. Among these were a number of merchant navy people, and some privateersmen. Among these was Captain Griff, who sailed quite a new brig from Bergen, cunningly captured by the [British] frigate *Ariadne* [the previous month] on its voyage to Denmark ... [One of the new prisoners] told me that my own prize master H. Thomsen, along with his second in command and one of his boys, had gone ashore in Kristiansand about 9 weeks ago. He brought 2 small Danish books to me from Thomsen.'[77] In another entry, typical of so many others in his diary during the two following years, Kaald wrote soon after his own arrival at Greenlaw in November 1808, but without mentioning his source: 'Today I heard that the truce between the Russians and the Swedes is broken. The best news was that the Swedes got their hides well-tanned. Well done!'[78]

Reading newspapers, if they were available, could obviously help prisoners pass their days. But whether and, if so, how extensively and regularly newspapers circulated among the prisoners in the depots in Scotland is uncertain. Greenlaw apart, there are almost no references to that subject. At Valleyfield, for instance, Marote-Carrier says only that, '... if the gaoler was not too bad tempered..., if the sentries were not too surly, we asked them for news of France and of the war. But always they tried to deflate us, giving us partial and inaccurate accounts of disasters suffered by the Emperor in Spain and the glaring advantages that England had over France. But we refused to believe these stories which undermined the idea we held of the power of Napoleon, who till then had always been victorious; and we slipped away from these biased and partial informants, who missed no chance to abase us in judging our compatriots, whenever they did not make us feel their power by their tyrannous vexations.'[79] Newspapers do, however, according to Captain Kaald, appear to have been often available at Greenlaw. But because of the distinctive regime at Greenlaw conducted by Malcolm Wright as agent in the period from 1804 to the end of 1810, during the latter two years of which Kaald was a captive there, the availability of newspapers to prisoners at that depot may well not have been typical of the position at the others. 'Nothing new to be heard here, and no newspapers where you could get some news are coming here either,' Kaald wrote in one of the earliest entries in his diary at Greenlaw in November 1808. Only five days later he wrote: 'Yesterday I heard that it was reported in the newspapers that the Spanish were completely slaughtered by the French ...' Had he been told that by a fellow prisoner who had himself read it in a newspaper, or was it perhaps a member of the depot staff or one of the guards who had read it and passed the news on to the prisoners? At least at times, guards certainly did pass on news to the prisoners, and there was some expectation on the part of the latter that they would do so: 'Nothing new is heard today with the arrival of the guard, so we don't know how things are in Spain or anywhere else,' Kaald wrote early in December 1808.[80] In the middle of that month, however, Captain Beck, a fellow prisoner at Greenlaw, was given official permission to go into Edinburgh 'and came back in the evening bringing with him an *Edinburgh Star* newspaper from the 12th of the month.'[81] Not seldom the 'news' the prisoners received, whatever its source, was distorted: 'They say that 30,000 men from the Highland Regiment have marched off to help Spain.'[82] Some of the references to newspapers in Kaald's diary are ambiguous and suggest that much of whatever information reached the prisoners from the press indeed came to them via readers among depot staff or guards who passed it on to them—sometimes, it seems, with the kind of malicious intent complained of by Marote-Carrier at Valleyfield. But most of the numerous relevant entries made by Kaald clearly indicate that he and other prisoners at Greenlaw were often able to read newspapers. 'We saw in the newspaper with today's date,' he wrote for instance on 5 May 1809, 'that the English with some warships attacked Bornholm and Kristiansoy ... last month ...'; 'I read in the paper today,' he wrote on 27 November that year, 'that the French fleet in Tulong [Toulon] ... hadn't sailed from there ...'; and 'Today,' he recorded six months later, on 8 May 1810, 'we read in the paper that a revolution had just broken out in Sweden.'[83] Perhaps reading newspapers was a privilege enjoyed mainly or only by those prisoners at Greenlaw who, like Kaald, were officers.

To every prisoner, whatever his rank, who could read an obvious way of absorbing time lay in reading books. But were books available to or obtainable by them at the depots in Scotland? Only a couple of references to books there have been found. One, already noticed above, was by Captain Kaald to the two volumes sent him at Greenlaw by a former shipmate. The other, and fuller, was in a letter written in English by a French prisoner on 12 September 1811 and addressed to Charles Stewart, a printer in the Lawnmarket, Edinburgh: 'Dear Sir, I am frequently at a loss for Books here. Our friend Mr Walker used to supply me ... but of late I have not been able to procure any from him. Having no Collection of my own, it is great Charity to give me Books to read during my Captivity, and as I think you have many which would both afford Amusement and Instruction, I should esteem it as a great favour would you be so good as send me a Volume or two of any Book you can conveniently spare upon any Subject. I am fond of a Magazine or a Review when I can lay my hands upon either by means of a Friend. But any Book you may happen to have by you upon any Subject will be acceptable, and you may depend upon the greatest care being taken of such Books as you may have the goodness to favour me with and upon their being most faithfully returned to you. I own, I use great freedom upon all occasions, but I hope you will pardon me. With best Compliments to Mrs Stewart, believe me, I remain with great Respect, Dear Sir, Your very obedient humble servant. [Signed] C. Scheurman.'[84] Charles Scheurman or Scheurmann, a lieutenant in the 4th Swiss Regiment, arrived at Greenlaw in November 1810 along with other captives from Dupont's army in Spain. That same month he was sent, with those others, on parole to Peebles. A year later, along with all the other parole prisoners at Peebles, Scheurman was transferred to Dumfries. From there he escaped on 5 March 1812 but was recaptured and sent first to Valleyfield, then in September that year to Perth, from which he was transferred in November 1813 to Edinburgh Castle. Toward the end of that month he was sent off from the Castle to Portsmouth, presumably to the hulks there. The description issued at the time of his escape says Scheurman was aged 24, 5 feet 10 inches tall, of stout build, with fair hair, an oval face, good complexion, hazel eyes, and no marks or wounds. The Edinburgh Castle Entry Book gave his age as 25, and said his face was long, his hair brown, his eyes grey, and that he was marked by smallpox. Had Mr Walker supplied books to Scheurman when he was at Greenlaw briefly in November 1810? It is possible although perhaps unlikely, given the shortness of his stay there. Certainly, the date of Scheurman's letter to Charles Stewart shows that it was not from Greenlaw he wrote it—but months later when he was a parole prisoner at Peebles.[85]

Writing, for those prisoners who were literate, was another way of passing time. The most obvious forms were letter-writing, creative writing, and diary keeping. If, as seems probable, there were in the Scots depots prisoners other than Sergeant Major Beaudoin and Captain Kaald who kept diaries their work is not known to have survived. Some of the entries in Beaudoin's diary show signs of having been written or re-written after his captivity at Greenlaw between 1804 and 1809. But Kaald's was written day by day during his sojourn there in 1808-10; and as well as providing later readers with a uniquely contemporaneous account of the daily routines and the sometimes unusual events at that depot, it helped him fill his day with a task he clearly enjoyed.

Creative writing, especially perhaps verse, appears likely to have been undertaken by at least a handful of prisoners. Yet the work of only two prisoners in the Scots depots is known to survive. One was an inmate of Perth named Canette, at least some of whose verses were inspired by the ending of the war in the spring of 1814.[86] The second was François Diot or Dioz, a prisoner at Valleyfield where, in the winter of 1813-14, he presented the depot agent, Captain Andrew Brown, with two successive works in verse. The first, presented on 3 December 1813, was dedicated to the agent's 'Aimable Enfant', apparently a boy; and in an accompanying letter Diot expressed the hope that the child's innocent caresses of his father would remind the latter of 'a hapless wretch who solicits your benevolence.' Diot's poem was therefore not an example of art for art's sake. His letter added that, following kindly promises by 'Mr Maners' [? Alexander Munro, the depot chief clerk], he had been long awaiting an alleviation of his sorrows either by being given any employment at the depot that it would please the agent to grant him or by obtaining such for him with Mr Macansh, the depot surgeon, or with the contractor. Of the ten verses in this work, the first read:

> Dans les fers d'Albion, l'amour de ma Patrie,
> de mes esprits glacés Réchauffe le Génie,
> Mon coeur, longtems [sic] fletré par la Captivité,
> Sur l'appui des Vertus, Brave l'adversité.
> O! Vous, qui Commandez ce sejour de Souffrance,
> Vous, qui devez genies d'une triste Puissance,
> De la Paternité, Vous goutez le Bonheur,
> Au nom de Votre fils soyez mon Protecteur.

Whether these verses moved Captain Brown into granting Diot's wish for employment is not known. Diot's submission on 1 January 1814 to Brown of a further work in verse, titled *Romance of the Valleyfield Prisoner*, may be seen as either a renewed attempt to gain employment or an expression of gratitude for that favour granted. These verses, too, were accompanied by a letter from the author to the agent, in which he explained that, to mark his respectful esteem, he was presenting Captain Brown with the poem as a New Year gift. The work, in which again there was some poetic licence with spelling, this time ran to three verses. Whatever the intended objective of Diot's poem, its last five words were hardly likely to please Brown, the Transport Board, or the British government:

> *Rommance du prisonnier de Valleyfield*
>
> Dans ma sombre Retraite
> j'ose interoger l'avenir
> Et mon âme inquiètte
> ne cesse de gémir
> Beaux lieux, terre cherie,
> Adieux, riants objets
> O, Ma Chère Patrie
> recevez mes regrets.
>
> Aussi-tot que l'Aurore
> du jour, précède la Clarté
> Mon Coeur repete encore
> le Cri de Liberté.

Liberté Descrée
　　premier bien des Mortels,
Déja, dans ma Pensée
　　j'Encence les Autels.

Reviens douce Espérance
　　alléger les poids de mes fers
je calme ma Souffrance
　　en repetant ces Vers,
qu'au Temple de la Gloire,
　　au giè de mes souhaits
La Paix et la Victoire,
Couronnent les Français.

To his poem Diot added a postcript for Captain Brown, that 'one of my companions in misfortune is going to busy himself writing down the air on which I have based my verses, so I shall have it set to music in a few days.'[87]

Writing, as well of course as receiving, letters was another means—not always an agreeable one if news from or for home was bad—by which prisoners, at least those who were literate, or who could enlist the services of a fellow prisoner who was so, could pass some of their time. It was an activity that many more prisoners took part in than diary-keeping or creative writing. Paradoxically perhaps, the diary Sergeant Major Beaudoin kept during his five years at Greenlaw makes no mention of his ever writing or receiving any letters there. The only two letters he does mention are one that 'one of our companions in misfortune' at the depot received from the hulks at Chatham, and another written by 'a capable man among us' on behalf of all the other prisoners, complaining of their treatment and begging 'the government' (by which Beaudoin no doubt meant the Transport Board) 'to have regard for our unhappy fate.' This was the letter, already noticed, which enraged the Greenlaw agent Malcolm Wright and which led, Beaudoin says, to Wright's receiving a severe reprimand.[88]

On the other hand, Captain Kaald, the other Greenlaw diarist, makes many references to letters he and other prisoners there wrote or received. On nine separate occasions between April 1809 and August 1810 Kaald notes the arrival of letters from Norway or England for numbers of prisoners at the depot. There may have been other occasions, too, he did not record when mail for his fellow prisoners arrived. But it was only on 26 March 1810, fourteen months after his arrival at Greenlaw, that Kaald himself received his first letter from his home in Trondheim. It had taken two and a half months to reach him. 'Poor darling mother,' Kaald, who was then unmarried, had written in his diary several weeks earlier. 'Good God in heaven keep her in good health. I long for a letter from her.'[89] Such a prolonged period without letters or news from their families at home was not an uncommon experience for prisoners, even such highly literate ones as was Kaald, in the depots in Scotland. Kaald had, however, at least learned the previous month in a letter to his friend and shipmate 2nd Captain Hans Locke from the latter's father in Trondheim, that his own mother and other members of his family there were well.[90] Kaald's diary indicates that he received a total of 33 letters at Greenlaw during his 22 months of captivity there. The letters came to him from friends, relatives, shipmates, his former landlady in Norway, or other people, at Gothenburg, Bergen, Trondheim, Kristiansand, Galway, Aberdeen, Glasgow, Leith, Peebles, and the hulks at Chatham. It seems unlikely that many prisoners in the Scots depots received as many letters as did Kaald, or from so many different places. As for letters he wrote himself, the total appears to be 37, although three of them were evidently not sent as the intended bearer did not arrive at Greenlaw to collect them. The places they were addressed to are not always stated but appear to have been the same as those from which Kaald received letters, except that Gothenburg, Galway, and Aberdeen are not specifically mentioned, and Kaald, jointly with his friend 2nd Captain Locke, sent one of the 37 letters to the officer commanding the guard at Greenlaw, seeking 'permission to take a walk in the neighbourhood of the prison', which permission, however, was not granted.[91] Again it seems unlikely that many of his fellow prisoners in the depots in Scotland would have written as many letters as he did in less than two years.[92]

As well as illustrating the delays in delivery encountered by letters from or to the prisoners, Kaald's diary indicates that the cost of postages must have made it difficult for the great mass of prisoners in the Scots depots or their families to be able to afford to correspond. Thus Kaald notes on 19 and 21 October 1809 that two successive letters he had received then from Gothenburg from his former ship's master and escaped fellow prisoner from Greenlaw, Captain Sigismund Richelieu, had each cost 2s.6d. [12½ pence].[93]

On letters written or received by prisoners some further light is thrown by Lieutenant Marote-Carrier from his experience at Valleyfield and Perth depots. One aspect he recalled at Valleyfield but which applied to prisoners' letters at every depot was censorship by the agent: 'All letters, either leaving or arriving were opened by ... Moriarty [the depot agent], who had them explained to him by [one of] four interpreters ... It was therefore extremely imprudent to speak badly either of the English, or the accommodation, or the food. No sign of discontent ought to be shown.'[94] A Perth prisoner's letter preserved in the National Library of Scotland appears likely to have been confiscated by the depot agent for the reasons Marote-Carrier indicates. Written from that depot in June 1813 by a prisoner named Pirratz or Pissarts to a naval lieutenant at Antwerp, the letter says the writer, by then a prisoner for four years, had hoped for some time 'to get away from this country of brigands and see my friends again but any such illusion has been shattered ... All that is left to us is an impotent hatred ... In this country among a nation a thousand times more barbarous than the savages of the north [i.e., the Russians], our fate is to languish in misery, deprived of all the consolations of society ... For ten years this frightful and inhumane Government has held its prisoners shut up or rather caged in these depots ... My only desire is to avenge myself on this barbarous people ...'[95] At Perth, Marote-Carrier recalled, 'There was a box at the barrier in which the prisoners deposited their letters, which were picked up by a gaoler.'[96] Once they had been read, and if necessary censored, by the depot agent, the prisoners' letters were sent on by him to the Transport Office in London, along with the postages paid by the prisoners who wrote them.[97] '... return to you herewith,' the Transport Board wrote on 27 July 1812 to Francis Freeling, secretary of the Post Office, 'a box which has this day been received at this office by the mail from Valleyfield, containing letters for prisoners of war, and ... request that you will cause the amount of what has been charged for the weight of the box to be repaid to this Department.'[98] Letters could of course escape censorship by the agent if they could be carried out of the depots by, for example, escapers, or transferred or released prisoners. Thus Sergeant Major Beaudoin, having secured his repatriation from the hulks at Chatham in 1812, three years after his transfer there from Greenlaw, carried home clandestinely with him, some concealed in the soles of his shoes and most others in a box with a false bottom, no fewer than 260 letters from fellow prisoners.[99] Marote-Carrier himself received his first letter from his wife some five months after he had been captured and about two months after his arrival at Valleyfield. Another year passed after that before he received another letter from his wife, who had moved from Calais to Ostend with their children soon after his capture in December 1810. The delay, as he learned later, was because his transfer from the hulks at Chatham to Esk Mills in February 1811 and then a few weeks later to Valleyfield, had not been notified by the authorities to his wife, who had great difficulty in finding where he was being held captive. Her difficulty was compounded by the rascality of an English merchant who had undertaken to pass on a large sum of money from her to Marote-Carrier but instead pocketed it himself and was never heard of again.[100]

Three other references made by Marote-Carrier to letters he wrote or received involved escapes or attempted escapes. First, in May 1811 at Valleyfield he received a letter from a Dutch seaman named Hummel, of whom more will be said in a later chapter.[101] Second, Marote-Carrier himself asked a fellow prisoner preparing to escape from Esk Mills in February 1811 to visit his wife and ask her if she had received letters he had sent her. Third, much later, when Marote-Carrier himself was on the eve of attempting to escape from Perth depot, he 'met with all the men from Ostend [his own home town] and I had taken their messages and their letters and promised to speak of them to their families.'[102] In addition, Marote-Carrier recalled two particularly sad cases among his fellow prisoners, one at Valleyfield, the other at Perth, in attempts to resolve whose problems the writing of letters played a part. Marote-Carrier himself wrote to his wife from Valleyfield to ask her to enquire about the family of the poor Flemish peasant taken prisoner at Walcheren for wearing a button inscribed with a pike and cap of liberty and who had languished in captivity for two or three years without news of his wife and children.[103] The other case, of the prisoner at Perth with 'a deep sadness always imprinted on his face' who had been arrested by a boarding party from a British warship and separated from his wife and seven children while he was sailing with them to the United States of America at the beginning of the war in 1803, and who had 'written to Nantes, to the United States, everywhere', but had received 'no reply from anywhere for a dozen years', has also already been noticed above.[104]

Letters to or from home were sometimes subject to hazards that did not affect most other ways prisoners passed their time. Occasionally there were delays, and more than once even the prospect of a complete breakdown in the arrangements for exchanging letters between prisoners and their families or friends in France or elsewhere on the continent. Letters were carried in each direction across the English Channel on board a cartel ship which, under a flag of truce, was normally allowed to sail between Plymouth and Morlaix in Brittany with invalided or other repatriated prisoners of war, and which also ferried official negotiators on the few occasions formal discussions between the two governments took place concerning exchanges of prisoners. An implied threat of retaliation, however, for what the Transport Board considered was a prohibition at that time by the French authorities on 'all communication whatever with this country' by British prisoners in France and non-delivery for many months past of letters to them from their families in Britain, despite the inflow of 'many packets containing letters for French prisoners in this country', was contained, for example, in a letter from the Board to the Admiralty in February 1808.[105] A few months later, in May, the British cartel vessel was fired on by the French authorities when it arrived at Morlaix, and had to sail back again to Plymouth, having been unable to unload 'Two packets containing several thousand letters from French prisoners to their friends in France'.[106] When a situation similar to that in February 1808 recurred two years later in January 1810, the Board asked the Admiralty 'whether the letters received for French prisoners should at present be forwarded to them, and whether any more French prisoners' letters should be sent to France, until the French Government again open the communication between our people detained there and their Friends in this country.'[107] Even within a depot there might sometimes be delay in sending on letters: '... among the letters last transmitted by you to this office from prisoners under your care,' the Transport Board complained in January 1814 to Captain Moriarty, agent at Perth, 'many were of very old dates ... You will explain the cause of the unusual and improper delay.' Moriarty's reply has not survived.[108] Some of the problems confronting prisoners' correspondence, and a rough and ready indication of its volume at that depot, were illustrated at the end of the war in a report in the *Dundee Advertiser* about the position at Perth: 'It is reported that in consequence of the repeal of Bonaparte's post office restrictions, the postages on letters to prisoners of war at Perth, which had till now been detained, amounted on one day lately to £30; but so many of the prisoners to whom these letters were addressed are now dead or returned to the continent that only £1 of the £30 was paid to the post office.'[109]

If writing and receiving letters might at least help break the monotony of the prisoners' existence in the depots, the few known surviving letters which were sent to or from those in Scots depots exemplify the gamut of anxieties, hopes, disappointments, and occasional elation but more frequently depression or even despondency to which the captives and their families were subjected, in some cases for a decade or more. One which, as in any war, illustrates the anxieties which many prisoners in Scotland and their families at home suffered between 1803 and 1814, was written from Roscoff in Brittany on 30 December 1812 to 'Monsieur Rene Jezequel, Prisoner of War, frigate [name difficult to read but probably the *Guerrière*, captured in July 1806], coming from the Isle de France—at new Mill Bay Prison, Scotland [i.e., a confusion between Mill Bay depot at Plymouth and Esk Mill at Penicuik]' by 'Pour le momen [sic] your mother La Jezequel.' The letter is very difficult to read but appears to begin by saying: 'Dear Son, I've already written but have not received a single detail ...'[110]

Another letter, which, conversely, illustrates the possibly even more frequent lack of any news from home reaching prisoners in Scots depots was never in fact posted. It was found in 1881, almost three-quarters of a century after the end of the war, under floorboards at Valleyfield. The letter, dated 16 March 1812, and addressed from 'Prison Valleyfiel' to 'Mon Chere Perre et ma cher Mere', had been written by their son, M.J. Silas Priere, a seaman on the frigate *L'Amphitrite*, which was destroyed on 4 February 1809 during the British attack on Martinique, but who was said in the depot General Entry Book to have been 'captured General provosts' army' on 24 February that year. Born at Havre and aged 26, Priere was described as 5 feet 6½ inches tall, of stout build, with oval face, sallow complexion, dark brown hair, grey eyes, and with smallpox scars. He had come to Valleyfield in March 1811 with the other 2,400 or so prisoners from Esk Mills. He had, he said in his letter to his parents, written them several times since he had come to Britain, but without receiving any reply. He could not understand the reason for this, remained eager to hear from them, and hoped they and his brothers, sister, and friends were in good health. Whether Priere ever did hear from his family is unknown. He died at Valleyfield on 27 May 1814, soon after the end of the war, when all the other prisoners were preparing to be sent home.[111]

Among the few known surviving letters to or from prisoners in the Scots depots are eleven in a collection of 1,183 which, more than a century after the end of the Napoleonic Wars, were discovered in the Belgian state archives at Liège. All those 1,183 letters had been written by Belgian, mainly Walloon, conscripts in Napoleon's forces who came from the département of L'Ourte. From prisoners in the hulks or depots in Britain some 52 of the letters had come, ten of them from Valleyfield and one from Esk Mills. The latter was written by Henri-Joseph Hankar, conscripted in 1807 and employed at first as a stonemason at the harbour at Boulogne, who later became a seaman or, as he claimed, a master of arms, on the privateer *Le Roi de Naples*, from which he passed into captivity, first on the hulks at Chatham, then at Esk Mills, where he arrived in February 1811. In a letter written on the 26th of that month, Hankar told his brother at home that a land depot was better than the hulks 'for food, for [the avoidance of] illness and for everything.' That, he said, was the third letter he had written his brother; he had had no reply to the previous two.[112] From Valleyfield, in a letter dated 1 February 1813, Albert Xhignesse, a grenadier in the 26th infantry regiment, wrote home to Flémalle near Liège and poured out his heart as so many of his fellow prisoners must have done in their letters: 'How agreeable and reassuring it would be for me to spend even a moment with you. I feel the need to open my heart to you and tell you a little of my sufferings. Nothing is harder than being so far from you, being separated from those who for me are the dearest people in the world, and being deprived of your news. There isn't an hour in the day that I don't long to be with you.'[113]

Those Belgian conscripts' letters also illustrate the fact that even the ill winds of captivity might occasionally blow somebody some good. 'I urge my brother to practise writing if he can,' Laurent Maquet, a soldier captured while serving with the 58th infantry regiment in Portugal in August 1808, wrote home in March 1813 from Valleyfield to his parents in the village of Jupille near Liège. 'For when I left home I didn't know any more about it than he does, and now he's reading my letters which are written in my own hand!' A similar pride in new-found literacy was expressed by Nicolas Terwagne, a soldier in the 26th infantry regiment who was another Belgian prisoner at Valleyfield when, writing home in September 1812 to Amay, half-way between Liège and Namur, he added in a postscript: 'You see that this letter is written by me in my own hand.'[114]

Learning to read and write thus became, at least for some prisoners in the Scots depots, an activity on which time was particularly well spent. Illiteracy among the armed forces of Napoleon and in their recruiting grounds was widespread. In Belgium itself, for instance, 'at least half of the men were illiterate and among the female population the proportion was probably much higher.'[115] Italians, of whom there were sizeable numbers in captivity in the Scots depots, suffered likewise from a 'high degree of illiteracy' among the 'lower classes and minor gentry'.[116] But the vast majority (between two thirds and three quarters) of the prisoners in the Scots depots were French—and most of the soldiers among them were illiterate.[117] Adelbert J. Doisy de Villargennes, a *sous* or 2nd lieutenant in the 26th infantry regiment, who was captured in Spain in May 1811 and passed, via a very brief sojourn at Valleyfield, into captivity on parole at Selkirk in October that year, emphasised long afterwards in his memoirs how extensive that illiteracy was. '... incredible as it may seem,' he wrote, 'in a company of one hundred and twenty-one men, I have, excluding sergeants and corporals, counted only eight men capable of reading or writing.' Doisy de Villargennes throws further light on the problem of communication between prisoners of war and home, and on letter-writing and letter-reading at the depots in Scotland: 'From this strange state of ignorance arose a curious result, peculiar, I believe, to the French army, and pregnant with remarkable consequences. The young men in the ranks had, when leaving home, left earnest requests for news to be forwarded to them by letters written by the priest or the school-master of their respective villages. Such letters, after reaching the regiment had to be read and answered, but by whom? For they sometimes contained information either ludicrous or susceptible of bringing a blush to the cheek of the recipient. To communicate such correspondence to those of their comrades learned in the alphabet might have exposed them to the jeers and perhaps the contempt of their fellow soldiers; to apply to field officers, or even to captains, would have been too wide a leap over the chasm separating the ranks. There remained one resource—the *sous-lieutenants*. These were nearly of an age with the recruits, and sufficiently superior in rank to remove the fear of indiscretion among the soldiers. Hence, the *sous-lieutenant*, or sometimes the first lieutenant of each company, became the amanuensis, and necessarily the intimate confidant of the great majority of his men. It was thus, that before I was twenty years of age, I had become acquainted with the special and family affairs of upwards of fifty men, and had written for them several wills, powers of attorney to their relatives, or vows of eternal love to their sweethearts. The consequences may be anticipated. The young officers became seriously interested in the welfare of their men; the latter could hardly find opportunities enough to evince their ardent attachment for their youthful protectors.'[118]

During the Napoleonic Wars captive commissioned officers (unless they were convicted of some offence against Transport Board regulations, or declined to accept parole, which involved undertaking not to attempt escape) were separated from the other ranks confined in the depots or hulks, and were allowed parole at one or other of the towns in Scotland, England or Wales officially approved for that purpose. The letter-reading and letter-writing role of the junior officers described by Doisy de Villargennes then virtually ceased. Illiterate prisoners who wished to keep in contact with their families or friends at home had therefore either to find literate fellow prisoners to read and write for them, or themselves learn to do so. Whichever choice they made they almost certainly had also to find the wherewithal to pay fellow prisoners for their services as readers or writers or as teachers of literacy. That in turn must have acted as an incentive for some, perhaps many, prisoners at the depots in Scotland to find paying tasks, which also helped keep them occupied. It provided some income, too, for those who provided such literacy services.

Literacy was not the only subject in which educational classes were held or attended by prisoners at the depots in Scotland. 'Longitude direction' or trigonometry, for instance, was a subject on which in October 1809 Captain Kaald at Greenlaw began to take instruction from Mr Oxholm, a newly arrived fellow prisoner, who had been first mate on the privateer *Roland*.[119] Whether Sergeant Major Beaudoin's attempt to improve his education during his captivity there by studying arithmetic was buttressed by attendance at a class is not certain, but what is certain is that his notebook, filled at the depot on that subject, was preserved by his family after his death in 1864 at the advanced aged of 89.[120] At Perth, Marote-Carrier refers to 'Leroi, a scholarly mathematician, who had more than sixty pupils in the prison'.[121] Apart from the lessons in French given the historian Thomas Walker's father at Perth by a prisoner there,[122] little or no evidence appears to survive that classes, or at least tuition, in languages or science, for example, were held in any of the Scots depots, although it seems very probable that some prisoners would help others learn, for instance, a little English.[123] A cryptic entry in Kaald's diary at Greenlaw suggests there was some provision there of educational classes for those of the prisoners who were young boys: 'They [the depot agent and his chief clerk] forbade … the 2 small boys to go to school in the future.' The context of Kaald's note further suggests that the small boys' 'school' may have been extramural rather than within Greenlaw's palisades.[124]

On a less cerebral plane, some of the prisoners helped pass the time by keeping pets. In his sketch in 1813 of prisoners in the airing ground or courtyard at Greenlaw, Robert Reid, crown architect in Scotland, depicts in the foreground a prisoner playing with a dog. Kaald describes how the prisoners at that depot were once awakened at 2 o'clock in the morning by a loud cry from one of the sentries on guard. 'We jumped up from our beds and could see, by peering through the damned iron bars, that all the sentries were at their posts with their hands gripping their guns. The entire guard and the officer, too, searched round the entire prison but they saw and found nothing … In the morning the reason for the redcoat's cry was investigated and was as follows: a big cat had run through the window of Mr Hees's [a prisoner's] room. The sentry who has his post just outside was greatly alarmed, and in a loud voice demanded to know 'Who goes there?!' But the cat, in spite of being Scottish, never answered him, neither the first nor the second time. However, the third time the sentry shouted, the cat became somewhat frightened and ran rather carelessly out of the window. The cat ran away so hastily that the sentry couldn't see it to shoot it so he'd bellowed, "Sergeant of the Guard! Sergeant of the Guard!" … We had great pleasure from this.' Whether the big cat, despite its nationality, was nonetheless the pet of one of the prisoners is not known.[125] What is known, however, is that several of the prisoners at Valleyfield kept tame rats and other animals and birds. 'One man had a large cage with two tame rats he had trained to play tricks.'[126] Many decades after the war Macbeth Forbes was told by 'An old female residenter at Penicuik … that when the French were leaving [Valleyfield] they carried home with them parrots, geese, rabbits, rats, and pets of all sorts.'[127]

'Tobacco was in great request,' Rifleman Edward Costello recalled of the French troops with whom he and others in the Rifle Brigade frequently fraternised in 1810-11 during the Peninsular War. 'We used to carry some of ours to them, while they in return would bring us a little brandy.'[128] There may have been no such barter in the depots in Scotland into which almost certainly some of those same French troops later passed as captives, but the demand for tobacco by many, perhaps most, prisoners in those depots appears to have remained strong. Smoking no doubt helped console them during their dreary days at Greenlaw, Esk Mills, Edinburgh Castle, Valleyfield or Perth. Kaald's sketch of the interior of his room at Greenlaw shows his old shipmate and fellow prisoner Captain Richelieu puffing on a long stemmed pipe, and in his diary Kaald makes several references to tobacco. It was in his first week at Greenlaw in November 1808 he noted in the courtyard the 'numerous small tables, which belong to some of the prisoners, who purchase cigarettes and tobacco' and other items, and which they sold to others in halfpenny and penny amounts, 'just as much as we can afford to buy.' On two later occasions he mentioned that he and two of his shipmates had 'enjoyed pipe tobacco'; and shortly before his own release and repatriation in August 1810, he noted that every Danish prisoner at Greenlaw was sent three shillings by their fellow countryman in London, Pastor Ulrik Frederik Rosing ('this clergyman has done great things for the prisoners'), who promised to send also 'two shillings' worth of tobacco to every man.'[129] Sergeant Major

Beaudoin does not mention tobacco or smoking during his five and a half years at Greenlaw. But at Perth it was tobacco that was chosen by Lieutenant Marote-Carrier and his Dutch fellow sea-going officer Van Gruthem as the basis of their trading at the depot market. 'We sold pipe tobacco for a penny, with the pipe thrown in, for the tobacco was very dear and we hardly made a profit of a shilling on every pound sterling's worth we sold. However, with this meagre profit we could if we lived economically make something out of it.'[130] It was partly in tobacco that Marote-Carrier paid his fellow prisoner Laurencini for lessons on the flute.[131] Tobacco and smoking were thus, like so many other activities of the prisoners, not only a means of passing time but also for some of them a source of income.

Fortuitous or occasional organised events at the depots also helped pass the time for prisoners. An annual event, about which more will be said later, that gave many or most of the prisoners something to celebrate as best they could, was Napoleon's birthday on 15 August. Their celebration at Perth depot in August 1813 proved especially ambitious. Publicity for the event, to be held not on Sunday, 15 August but the preceding day, began to be issued well in advance to press and public by or with the approval of the depot authorities. The loyalty of the prisoners to their emperor, declared the weekly *Perth Courier*, on 5 August, 'no person can be disposed to condemn, though they might wish that so laudable a feeling were directed to a better object. A large and elegant balloon will be sent up from one of the [depot] yards in honour of the occasion, but though Sunday is universally preferred in France for popular spectacles, the prisoners, at whose expense and by whose ingenuity the balloon has been prepared, have resolved to show respect for the principles, even for what they regard as the prejudices, of a country in which they are forcibly detained, by commencing their rejoicings with this exhibition on Saturday 14th August, and by forbearing to attract the public attention on a day which is here exclusively devoted to religious duty.' A further brief puff for the forthcoming celebration appeared in the *Courier* on 12 August, followed by a full report on the 19th of the event itself: 'About three in the afternoon a numerous crowd of people assembled in the South Inch to see the balloon ascend but were disappointed by an unlucky accident. The balloon, which was large and elegant, had been constructed with much taste and ingenuity by Monsieur de Cuyper, a meritorious young gentleman of Ghent. After its inflation by air, which had been rarified by straw burnt underneath it, Monsieur de Cuyper having stepped aside to prepare the car, flags, and other ornaments, its ascending force became so powerful from a hasty increase of the fire with a view to preserve its upright position against the force of the wind, that it burst the strings which fastened it to the hoop, and rising without ballast for giving it steadiness, or the necessary apparatus for continuing the rarification of the air, it soon descended and was torn against a tree. We regretted this accident, both on our own account, as we saw that the ascent of the balloon would have otherwise been extremely splendid, and on account of its ingenious artist, whose acquaintance we have the pleasure to boast, as without any error of his own he was disappointed in the result of his labour, after repeated and uniform success in similar experiments. At night all the prisons ... were brilliantly illuminated. In some of the windows were transparencies which produced a fine effect, and which appear to have been executed with much taste.'[132] The depot authorities, the *Perth Courier*, and the douce citizens of Perth who turned out to see the balloon might have been less sympathetic to Monsieur de Cuyper had they realised his ingenious activities may have been intended also to help mask a major attempt at escape by prisoners from the depot ten days later.[133] Although no reports appear to have survived about celebrations of Napoleon's birthday at other Scots depots, except for one at Edinburgh Castle, it is difficult to believe none ever took place at Greenlaw or Valleyfield. At Edinburgh Castle the only such celebration of which a report has been found took place also in August 1813. The prisoners at the Castle, however, unlike those at Perth, evidently made no concession to the religious sensibilities of the citizens, and held their celebration on the due day, Sunday, 15th. 'They paraded their airing ground, carrying portraits of the Emperor and Empress, singing national songs, and shouting "*Vive l'Empereur et Marie Louise!*"'[134]

At Greenlaw Danish prisoners, including Captain Kaald, similarly celebrated the birthday on 28 January 1810 of 'our gracious King Frederik VI', in whose honour '... we have illuminations this evening of 6 candles in every window throughout the entire prison. Then Locke and I were in another officer's room where we danced, sang and drank the King and Queen's health with many hurrahs, numerous times, though only with beer (for we didn't have anything else) to midnight when we went back to our rooms, sometimes through the secret passages since the doors were locked.'[135]

A fortuitous and trivial daily event at Valleyfield, no doubt typical of many others there and at the other depots, which nonetheless created considerable interest for a time for Lieutenant Marote-Carrier and other prisoners who watched her, were the twice daily appearances of a very old woman who filled her pitcher with spring water 'renowned for freshness and cleanness' on the hill overlooking the depot. 'Every day,' Marote-Carrier later recalled, 'numerous inhabitants [of Penicuik], men and women, came there to fill earthenware pitchers that were of distinctive shape and very common in Scotland. From the first days of our stay at Valleyfield we noticed a very old woman who came, with punctilious punctuality, to fill her pitcher at the fountain once in the morning and once in the evening. She never failed to do so and no day ever passed that we did not see her come down from the cottage. With bent back she walked only with some difficulty, leaning on a stick. One morning she came close to the palisades and we could see her at last closer up. Her face was so wrinkled and drawn it was hardly possible to see her deeply sunken eyes, quite limited in their sweep. Her hand was so emaciated that all the bones could be seen like those of a skeleton. Her feet were bare, despite the rigour of the season, and her tattered clothes showed her poverty. She held between her lips an ancient clay pipe from which she puffed out big clouds of smoke, all the time looking at us with her dull, expressionless eyes. We approached her and looked at her from our side [of the palisades]. After a few seconds she turned aside with a certain disdain and murmured: "These are Frenchmen there?" Perhaps she expected to find us walking on all fours or with faces and tails like monkeys. We asked the gaoler who this woman was. She was the oldest person at Valleyfield and in the country ... born in 1688.' There may have been a little exaggeration of her age, which, if accurately reported, would have meant Marote-Carrier and his fellows prisoners were passing some of their time gazing at a woman some 123 years old. From as long as people could remember, however, she had come to fill her pitcher at the source on the hill, 'and age and its infirmities had not so weakened her that she had lost any of her faculties. Her eyesight was no longer so piercing as in the time of her youth, her bearing was no longer so sure, her sense of taste was more or less limited to strong liquor and smoking the strongest tobacco, and yet she had still wanted to see us. She was a prodigy of longevity and of the eternal inquisitiveness of women! However, as if that curiosity had been disappointed in its expectations, the old woman never came back to visit us, but we did see her come regularly to the fountain, and each time she appeared we said to ourselves, "There's the old lady of Valleyfield!" One day, at the end of autumn 1812 [Marote-Carrier means 1811, since he was transferred at the beginning of September 1812 to Perth], she failed to make her daily journey ... We learned in the evening that the old woman was dead, without pain, without illness, dead without having had presentiment of her end. She had just drunk her glass of brandy and lit her pipe, and went to take her pitcher when she suddenly fell backwards ... She was found stretched out on the floor of her cabin, her eyes open and fixed, her heart no longer beating ... That death left a gap in our monotonous existence, in which all events succeeded each other and periodically recurred, and in which the coming of the old woman to the spring of water was not the least outstanding.'[136]

The old woman of Valleyfield was among the relatively few women of any age ever visible (and even then often at some distance) to the prisoners confined within any of the depots in Scotland.

16

Boredom and Activity: Philandering, Praying, Gambling, Forging, Working

A return to Parliament made by the Transport Board at the end of June 1812, a few weeks before the opening of Perth depot, showed there were then, as accompanying dependants of prisoners of war at the confined depots in Britain, 37 women and children.[1] No separate figures for women and for children were given, nor were the depots named. How many of those women may have been at depots in Scotland is therefore not known. But as already observed in an earlier chapter, the number appears unlikely at that time to have been more than half a dozen—possibly four Dutch women at, or at least living in the vicinity of, Greenlaw, the Andalusian wife of the French artilleryman who, according to Marote-Carrier, had been together within Valleyfield until September 1812 when, like him, they were transferred to Perth; and at or near Valleyfield briefly but perhaps just long enough to be included in the Parliamentary return, Catherine Didon or Diédont, wife of a prisoner there. Within five months of its opening at the beginning of August 1812, at least seven women (and two infant girls) accompanied prisoners to, and lived for a time either within or in the vicinity of Perth depot.[2] These dozen or so women apart, the only other women whom prisoners in Scots depots saw, or were likely to have seen, or had any contact with, even at a distance, during their captivity were those encountered in one or more of the following circumstances.

First, there were half a dozen women employed at any one time at three of the five depots as matron or sempstress—two each on the staffs of Esk Mills, Valleyfield and Perth.[3] At Esk Mills there seem in addition, at least for a time, to have been some other women employed. 'We approve of your having employed some women in picking hair,' the Transport Board told the agent at that depot in January 1811, a fortnight before it opened. But whether these women were still employed on that or other work at Esk Mills after the prisoners began to arrive there the following month is not known.[4]

Second, there were women, of course, among the visitors and buyers who came to the regular and frequent markets held at the depots for the sale of the range of items the prisoners made in bone, paper, wood, hair, etc. According to the banker-historian Macbeth Forbes, again without naming his sources, 'The offering of the prisoners' wares for sale at the markets furnished an occasion which was utilised as only a lover can do with limited time at his disposal. Making love through the grille was a common distraction at Valleyfield.'[5] For example, too, the Transport Board, in reply to a recent letter from him, directed the agent at Valleyfield in November 1813 'not to allow the woman therein mentioned to go near the market in future.'[6] Two months earlier at Perth '... a woman coming from the market at the Depot was searched by order of Captain Moriarty [the agent],' and, when counterfeited bank tokens were found 'about her person', she was arrested.[7]

Third, there were women among those inhabitants of Edinburgh, Penicuik, Perth, and adjoining neighbourhoods who, like the boy William Chambers and his father at Valleyfield and the boy James Nasmyth at Edinburgh Castle, were moved by curiosity or other motives to come to the walls or palisades of the depots to gaze on the prisoners. At Greenlaw, for example, Captain Kaald noted on two or three occasions in his diary the presence of women at the gates or palisades of that depot. On 18 March 1810, for instance, he wrote: 'There were ... a number of Ladies and Gentlemen up here, but none of them was allowed to come near the prison's stockade in order to touch a few of the prisoners.' A month later, he observed: 'Nothing happened [today], except that there were a number of the fairer sex outside the prison.' Was there some more serious purpose than idle curiosity, however, on the part of those Kaald noted on 6 May that year: '... a gentleman as well as ladies [who] were here in the prison to visit us poor prisoners'?[8]

Fourth, there were some women whom Kaald and some of his fellow officer prisoners at Greenlaw encountered when, thanks to the privilege granted them, contrary to Transport Board regulations, by the then agent Malcolm Wright, they made brief outings to Penicuik and neighbourhood and even to Edinburgh or Leith. On these jaunts Kaald and the relatively few other prisoners so privileged met and enjoyed the company of women some of whom were the wives or daughters of local millowners, shopkeepers, or others.[9]

Fifth, the arrest of a woman on suspicion of being involved in the escape in January 1813 of three prisoners from Perth who sailed away in a stolen smack from Broughty Ferry, raises the question how far, if at all, other escapes from the depots also involved women and, if so, why and how they became involved. These questions are touched on in later chapters below.[10]

Sixth, at least one prisoner may while in captivity have married a Scots girl, possibly in or near Edinburgh, although the facts are far from certain. When Lieutenant Marote-Carrier found himself released from Perth depot in February 1814 he was accompanied on the first stages of his way home by another released prisoner, a privateer officer from Dunkirk, who had a wife and children there. When Marote-Carrier and he reached Edinburgh on their way home, they were exploring the city streets 'when suddenly a pretty young woman, stopping in front of my companion, cried indignantly with tears in her eyes—"What! You are here?"' She was the Dunkirk officer's bigamous wife. The Dunkirk man immediately slipped away, disappeared into the crowd in the street and, after a brief conversation soon afterward with Marote-Carrier, was never seen by the latter again. The evidence is slender indeed but does it at least suggest that the bigamous wife belonged to Edinburgh or its hinterland and, if that were so, that the Dunkirk man had married her there or at least somewhere in Scotland? If he did, then it appears to have been a unique case (apart possibly from that of François Petit, the pre-eminent escaper) of marriage in Scotland between a prisoner of war (other than a parole prisoner) during his captivity and a Scotswoman.[11]

Seventh, at least at Valleyfield the agent or his wife employed a young woman as a maid. This young woman appears to have attracted the eye of one of the prisoners there named François Hugue. Whether the maid responded to Hugue's interest in her is unknown, but it appears that he did not even know her name. At any rate Cupid, possibly with assistance from some other gods, though there is no evidence they included Bacchus, prompted Hugue in April 1814, as the war was ending, to write not only to the maid herself but also to the depot agent, Captain Andrew Brown, and his wife. 'Not being far advanced in English pronunciation', Hugue may well have employed a fellow prisoner to translate into distinctly flowery English his letters, which he had written in imperfect French. Captain Brown's reply (in the unlikely event he made any) to Hugue's invitation to put in a good word for him with the maid, has not survived.[12]

Finally, it was only at Perth that there is evidence of what appears to have been an attempt to provide within the depot the services of a member of the oldest profession in the world. 'An under clerk at the Depot,' the *Perth Courier* reported in July 1813, 'has been very properly suspended from his office for attempting to introduce a profligate woman into one of the prisons.' The woman had been 'disguised in Sailors' Clothes.'[13]

It was therefore axiomatic, taking all those circumstances into account, that philandering was an activity scarcely available to prisoners confined in the depots in Scotland. That was one of the contrasts between their conditions of captivity and those enjoyed by officers in parole towns such as Peebles, Kelso, Hawick, Lanark, Cupar Fife, and Dumfries. The prisoners in the depots were men essentially deprived of the company of women for the duration of their captivity—which in most cases was for between two and nine years, but in some three hundred others for as long as ten or eleven years.

Yet there is no evidence that, deprived of the company of women as they were, and living for years in generally overcrowded conditions, homosexuality was practised among prisoners in the Scots depots. The absence of evidence might make it naive consequently to assume that homosexuality did not exist among them. But certainly none of the witnesses so often already quoted, such as Captain Kaald and Sergeant Major Beaudoin at Greenlaw and Lieutenant Marote-Carrier at Valleyfield and Perth, refer to, or even infer there were, homosexual relations among any of their fellow prisoners. Nor do Abell and Macbeth Forbes or such other pioneering historians of the Scots depots, as for Perth, Penny, Peacock or Sievewright, mention or imply homosexual practices there. Although during the Napoleonic Wars courts martial of seamen in the British navy showed 'a good many cases of sodomy', for which those found guilty were executed,[14] and it was the Admiralty of which the Transport Board and its Office was a section, no reference to homosexuality has been found in the substantial surviving correspondence between the Board and depot agents in Scotland between 1803 and 1814.[15]

If sexual activity by prisoners in the Scots depots was thus indeed distinctly limited, did they find any consolation, and another means of passing some of their time, in a very different activity—the practice of religion? Early in the war the policy of the Transport Board toward religious observance among the prisoners was explained by its chairman, Sir Rupert George, in a letter to a Home Office official. Sir Rupert wrote that the Board had been directed by the Admiralty 'to permit the French Ecclesiastics to visit "such French prisoners of war as are supposed to be in a dying state"; and, in conformity thereto, the Board gave orders to their agents at the different depots. The order therefore to admit the French priests to visit the prisoners *in general*, they are not competent to issue, and, if they were, they would do it with very great reluctance, as they know from the experience of the last war that the priests visited the prisons with views very different from those held out by the Bishop of St Pol de Léon [in Brittany], who, notwithstanding the confidence with which he spoke of the characters of the French priests whom he recommended, was the instrument of introducing men who entertained principles hostile to the police of the prisons, and probably to the British Government.'[16] Exactly eight years later, the Transport Board's reluctance to allow clergy entry to the depots was re-emphasised to Robert Peel, then under-secretary for War and the Colonies. Peel had sent the Board an extract of a letter received by his departmental minister Lord Liverpool from Dr Thomas Coke, a leading Methodist clegyman, 'requesting that permission may be given for Mr Poare, Mr de Kerpexdron and Mr le Sueur to preach to the French prisoners in the different prisons in this country and signifying his Lordship's desire that the permission solicited by Dr Coke may be granted, provided this Board do not see any objection ... [The Board] acquaint you, for the Earl of Liverpool's information, that although such permission being partially granted (as on board prison ships)

may be attended with beneficial effects yet as a general measure to be adopted at the larger depots on shore, they do not consider the measure to be advisable, particularly as, in consequence of a similar permission being given lately at Norman Cross [depot] at the request of several gentlemen of high respectability, very great disorder and confusion took place in the suppression of which the commanding officer of the troops refused to give his assistance. If therefore his Lordship should think proper that the permission required by Dr Coke should be given to the extent required by that gentleman, the Board submit that orders should be given to the officers commanding the guards at the several depots to be in readiness to preserve order and repress any tumult which may happen, similar to that complained of at Norman Cross.'[17]

That reluctance by the Board was, however, evidently set aside the following year by an order from the Admiralty 'signifying to us their Lordships' Direction to give Orders for clerygmen of the Established Church to visit French prisoners of war for the purpose of preaching to them in their own language and instructing them in the doctrines of the Christian Religion, the said clergymen to be appointed by a Committee of Gentlemen for that Purpose.'[18] When, more or less simultaneously with the Admiralty's order, the depot agent at Valleyfield submitted a request from the prisoners there 'to have a Priest admitted within the Prison' it was rejected by the Board.[19] Presumably the rejection was because the clergyman sought by the prisoners was a Roman Catholic, whereas the Admiralty had laid down visiting clergymen must be Established Church, i.e., Church of England in depots south of the Border and Church of Scotland in those north of it.

Hence four months later, the Board wrote to its agents at Valleyfield and Greenlaw: 'We direct you to permit the Revd Mr Aikin of Edinburgh to enter the Prison for the purpose of conveying Religious Instruction to the Prisoners in your Custody under the usual Regulation.'[20] How many, if any, of the prisoners at either depot were attracted to the ministrations there of Rev. Aikin is not known as no further reference to him has been found. But his impact on the prisoners is unlikely to have been profound, not least since the war ended within a couple of months of his arrival there but also because in so far as the prisoners professed any religion it was not Protestantism (except for numbers of the minority of Germans, Dutch or Scandinavians among them) but Catholicism.

Rev. Aikin's was perhaps not the only clerical voice, however, that some prisoners in the two Penicuik depots may have passed some of their time listening to in what proved to be the closing months of the war. A cryptic reference by Macbeth Forbes (again without giving his sources), suggests that Rev. Coulson, the Penicuik parish minister, may also have ministered in that period at least to Protestant prisoners at Greenlaw and Valleyfield.[21]

Earlier in the war, however, in 1809, there had apparently been some penetration at Greenlaw among the Danish (and later the Dutch and even French) prisoners by religious activists. This was during the regime of Malcolm Wright as agent there and may well have been another example of his diverging from Transport Board policy. During a visit in September 1809 to the prisoners at the depot by 'a few gentlemen on behalf of the Edinburgh Bible Society ... [a] distribution of the New Testament in Danish was made among them, one copy being presented to each of the officers, and the rest granted to the men in general. They were accepted with gladness as fit companion to a solitary *Old Testament* in this language, which was produced as belonging to one of the officers. It had been preserved, he said, out of many things which he had lost. This gift of the Society was received by the prisoners with evident marks of gratitude and esteem. The gentlemen are happy to assure the friends of this Institution, and the public in general, that they have every reason to expect the Testaments will be perused with attention; they on this account promised a further distribution if necessary upon application from the officers.' Sure enough, a month later at the general meeting of the Bible Society in Edinburgh 'an additional supply of New Testaments in Danish were granted to the prisoners of war at Greenlaw'; and in January 1810 the directors of the Society 'voted supplies of the Scriptures to the French and Dutch prisoners at Greenlaw.' Presumably therefore at least some of the prisoners there devoted some of their time to reading the scriptures.[22]

The only comment about religion or clergymen made by Sergeant Major Beaudoin, a prisoner at Greenlaw in 1804-9, he made on 4 June 1804, when he was newly landed at Greenock and had not yet set off with his escort to march to his captivity at Penicuik. The 4th of June was the birthday of King George III, and Beaudoin noted that 'A refractory French priest came to look for me on the Roads to show me the fête, celebrated by the militia of the place by volleys by platoon and battalion, accompanied by cannon.'[23]

Captain Kaald, on the other hand, confined at Greenlaw in 1808-10, was, without being pious, clearly a man of stronger religious belief than Beaudoin appears to have been. When he took ill a month after his arrival at the depot, Kaald wrote in his diary: 'God, take care of the sick in this unhealthy prison ... I ... now pray to God that he will with his good means help me, as I strongly fear for my life ...' The Deity was invoked several times in succeeding days as Kaald regained his health, and at Christmas that year, 1808, Kaald wrote: 'We Norwegians rejoice over this joyful and holy feast.' Christmas Day was marked by some religious observance in the morning by him and some others, but the apparent indifference of the great mass of the prisoners at Greenlaw to observing that holy day was shown in Kaald's note: '... every day is holy for us and ought to be praised by us. But it has hardly been so—only 10 out of 500 people.' At Easter 1809 Kaald observed: 'We now have this great solemn festival. We keep it as holy as we can ... May the Almighty be praised for our health and our living.' When, the following month there was some prospect of prisoners being repatriated as a result of negotiations between belligerent governments, Kaald exclaimed: 'God in heaven dispense some solution to us soon.' When he was released at last after a further 18 months of captivity at Greenlaw and was reunited with his mother, brothers and sisters in Trondheim in October 1810, Kaald wrote in his diary: 'God the Almighty be praised for my good health and that He with grace had led me to my good home again.'[24] Kaald, then, although a man of religious belief, could hardly be said to have occupied much of his time during his captivity at Greenlaw in religious devotions.

At Perth, as at Valleyfield, Lieutenant Marote-Carrier, like Sergeant Major Beaudoin at Greenlaw, made no comment about religion. But at Perth those prisoners concerned in the celebration of Bonaparte's birthday in August 1813 brought forward the event, as has been observed, from Sunday to Saturday 'to show respect for the principles, even for what they regard as the prejudices, of a country in which they are forcibly detained.' When in June and July 1814 they ceased to be forcibly detained at Perth or anywhere else in Britain and were repatriated, prisoners at Perth promptly sold almost all the Testaments in French presented to them from a donor in Edinburgh, as they made their way to the vessels taking them home to France.[25] The prisoners' action was hardly that of men likely to have devoted much time in captivity to the consolations of religion.

In the rites and observances of freemasonry, however, some prisoners did occupy some of their time in at least one Scots depot—Valleyfield. There freemasons among the prisoners established their own lodge, aptly titled *De l'Infortune* (Misfortune). The Valleyfield lodge was one of seven established by prisoners of war in Scotland—the other six were formed by those in parole towns. Many other lodges were established by prisoners south of the Border. 'At that time,' wrote the historian of these French prisoners' lodges, 'Freemasonry was exceedingly popular in the French army, many regiments having lodges attached to them. It was therefore only natural that, during their enforced idleness, the Freemasons amongst the prisoners should seek to relieve the monotony of their existence by devoting some portion of their time to the working of the Masonic ceremonies in Lodges established by themselves.'[26]

A certificate issued in October 1813 to Sergeant Martin Meric, of the 4th regiment of light infantry, a member of the Valleyfield lodge, declared: 'We, Worshipful Master, Officers, and Members of the W. Lodge of St John, regularly constituted under the name of "Misfortune" at Valleyfield, Scotland, and assembled by the Masonic Numbers known only to true Masons, declare, certify and attest, that the very dear brother Martin Meric ..., a member of the legion of honour, age 37 years, native of Castanet in the Département of the Haute Garonne, is a member of our W. Lodge in the third degree of symbolic Masonry. That the regularity of his conduct and his good manners during our labours have made him dear to us and worthy of recommendation. We therefore pray all regular Masons, both of French and foreign Lodges to receive the said Brother Meric in the said degrees, to give him all the consideration that is due to him, and to render him all the assistance which he may need, as we should be pleased to do for them. Done and delivered in our Lodge at Valleyfield, Scotland, the second day of the ninth month of the year of True Light 5813. Signed by us ... this second day of October 1813.'[27] How many prisoners were members of the Valleyfield lodge is not known. Nor is there is any evidence of lodges at any of the other depots in Scotland, but if they did exist the two most likely depots where freemasons among the prisoners might have been able thus to organise themselves were Greenlaw and Perth. Equally obscure is what, if any, contacts existed between those freemasons who were prisoners and those who may have been members of depot staffs or militia guards at the Scots depots or civilian visitors to the depot markets. Thorp's reference to British freemasons doing 'their utmost to alleviate the distress of these French Brethren' appears to be to parole prisoners among the latter, not to those confined in the depots. But he does say that 'Bro. Burnes, a Magistrate and Master of a Lodge at Montrose, took the responsibility of removing some French prisoners from the local jail to his own house, because they were Masons.'[28] Whether Brother Burnes was dealing with recaptured prisoners who had escaped from Perth, Penicuik or Edinburgh Castle is not known, nor is it certain it was during the Napoleonic Wars, not one of the earlier wars with France between 1756 and 1802, that his sympathy for them at Montrose was thus shown.

Far more widespread than freemasonry as an activity undertaken by the prisoners was gambling. 'The passion for gambling,' as the historian Abell wrote, again confusing England with Britain, 'fomented by long, weary hours of enforced idleness, wrought far more mischief among the foreign prisoners in England than did the corresponding northern passion for drink among the British prisoners abroad, if only from the fact that whereas the former, ashore and afloat, could gamble when and where they chose, drink was not readily procurable by the latter.'[29] At Esk Mills the depot clerk Andrew Johnston had noted how that passion for gambling had preoccupied prisoners whom he observed 'playing pitch and toss with the Gog within an inch ...' of the head of a fellow prisoner newly shot dead during the mass escape there on 19 February 1811.[30] At Perth in 1812-14, declared Lieutenant Marote-Carrier, 'Several of us, despite the outcome or the trouble in which they found themselves, were consumed with an unbridled passion for gambling ... a deplorable failing that ended by creating such grave excesses that it was necessary to put it right by rigorous measures.'[31] James Anton, the militia-man on guard duties at Greenlaw for a couple of years from about 1806, was critical of some of the prisoners there who, he wrote, 'took to the cards, dice or dominoes'.[32] At Greenlaw, too, an entry, though in part cryptic and ambiguous, by Captain Kaald in his diary on 7 April 1810 describes a fracas which may have erupted from gambling among the prisoners and in which even some of the militia guards may have been participants with them: 'Today there is a whole revolution in the prison ... all the work benches and tables are smashed to pieces, and when beer was driven in from the brewery to the beer cellar some of these crazy people smashed some of the beer barrels to bits, so the blessed beer ran all over the floor. What is left over, they are now drinking with all their might. So here there is fighting, noise and snarling everywhere. Bloody faces swarm everywhere, but what's more is that the guards are drinking with them and the greatest number of them are just as full. There is also fighting among the guards.'[33]

If gambling had indeed thus led to a bloody fracas at Greenlaw, it became such an addiction for a young Dutch seaman at Valleyfield recalled by Andrew Johnston, depot clerk there, that it caused his death. The young seaman 'was well dressed in blue Jacket and trousers when received at Esk Mills Depot [in February or early March 1811],' Johnston wrote. 'Three months afterward I was informed at Valleyfield [to which the seaman had meantime been transferred] of a prisoner in rags and in the last stage of debility. I found him to be the young man who had gambled away his clothing and all he had—and lastly his rations for a fortnight. He was taken into the Hospital ... given some broth, laid his head back upon the chair, and expired.'[34] That young Dutchman was, however, far from being the only prisoner in the Scots depots who died from debility or other ailments which were or appeared to have been caused by excessive addiction to gambling, as will be seen in the next chapter, part of which discusses those prisoners known as *rafalés* (down and outs) or miserables. Gambling was therefore a pastime which could, and for numbers of prisoners did, prove dangerous and even fatal.

No less risky (and even fatal, for about half a dozen of those in hulks or depots in England, although none in any of the Scots depots), a pursuit in which a few of the prisoners busied themselves was the forging of banknotes. Unlike gambling, forgery by nibbling at the enemy's currency could appear a respectably destructive and hence patriotic activity which might contribute, on however small a scale, to winning the war. Moreover, if prisoners could make personal profits out of such a patriotic activity, so much the better for them. This activity for the probably quite small number of prisoners engaged in it also created useful contacts for them with some of their guards at the depots and some local civilians willing to dabble in forgers' ink. These forgeries inevitably aroused the concern, not to say alarm, not only of the banks whose notes were being forged but also of the legal authorities (or Civil Power, as the Transport Board and depot agents usually referred to them). Consequently, more information is available about both the activity of those relatively few prisoners engaged in that branch of penmanship and its tentacles among those militiamen and civilians concerned in uttering and vending its products than about many other activities in which the prisoners passed their time.[35]

The earliest case of a banknote believed to have been forged by the prisoners in any Scots depot was discovered, according to Macbeth Forbes, on 30 July 1811 at Edinburgh Castle. It purported to be a Bank of Scotland one guinea note dated 11 October 1808, was three-quarters of an inch larger than a genuine note, the names on it were 'ill imitated', having been done with a pen and printing ink and not engraved, and the seals were faint. 'There were many forgeries at this time, but the banking experts soon got to know what was French work and what was not: French handwriting and workmanship told their own tale.'[36] No correspondence between the Transport Board and its agent at the Castle concerning this forged note has been found. But the alarm felt by the Bank of Scotland about forged notes had been illustrated almost two years earlier by the following advertisement which it placed in the *Edinburgh Evening Courant* on 11 September 1809 and repeated in three issues of the paper within a fortnight: 'FIVE HUNDRED POUNDS REWARD. A forgery of the guinea notes of the Governor and Company of the Bank of Scotland, having recently appeared, the Directors hereby promise a Reward of FIVE HUNDRED POUNDS Sterling, to anyone who shall within three months of the date hereof, give such information as may lead to a conviction of any person or persons concerned in forging the said notes, or in uttering them, knowing them to be forged. The reward to be paid on conviction. The engraving, the paper and the seals of the forged notes are much coarser than those of the true. In the forged notes, the ink is browner, and the words "One Pound One Shilling" fainter, and less distinct, than in the real notes. The forged notes may thus be easily distinguished from the real ones. There are more minute differences, which the Bank Officers and Agents will point out.' Was this forgery an even earlier example of the work of French prisoners than that of July 1811? If it was then it had been produced presumably at Greenlaw, the only depot in 1809 in Scotland.

Other notes of the same set as discovered on 30 July 1811 turned up daily for some time afterward. 'The theory that this forged note was not engraved was formed from the sample submitted to the banking authorities,' wrote Macbeth Forbes, 'but events showed that an engraver had also been at work.' Three weeks later the plate used in this latter or 'foreign' forgery was handed in to the Bank of Scotland, having been found by a miller and his men when they were cleaning the mill lade at Stockbridge in Edinburgh.[37]

That discovery suggested that if the forgers were indeed prisoners of war they must have had one or more native accomplices.

The next two incidents in the chain of forgeries came within a few days of each other, in September 1811. First, on the evening of the 18th 'several French prisoners from Greenlaw were brought to town [Edinburgh] and lodged in the gaol [the Tolbooth], suspected of having committed forgeries upon some of the banks here.' Second, when on the 26th some 300 prisoners from Plymouth were landed at Leith from HMS *Mermaid* for confinement at Greenlaw, one was 'brought on shore in custody of two Sheriff officers and was lodged in the [Edinburgh] jail here, charged with having several forged Bank of England notes in his possession.' His arrest was the result of investigations by solicitors to the Bank of England, the results of which they had passed earlier that month to the Transport Board.[38]

There were in fact five prisoners 'delivered over to the Civil Power', i.e., sent to the Edinburgh Tolbooth, on 18 September from Greenlaw. They were: Grandjean Duhenot (or Benoit P. Grandjean), a lieutenant in the 65th infantry regiment, who had been captured at Flushing in 1809; Germain Nivelet, aged 25, born at Le Havre, ensign on the *Surcouf* privateer, captured in the English Channel in 1810; Pierre Caron, aged 20, born at Dieppe, a seaman on the privateer *Général Canclaux*, captured in the English Channel in 1806; Philippe Plantaut (or Plantant), aged 34, born at Casalan, a captain in the 12th light infantry regiment, captured at Coimbra in 1808; and Carlos Gonsalvez, aged 22, born at Montevideo, a seaman, captured in 1806. Nivelet, Caron and Gonsalvez were sent back from the Tolbooth to Greenlaw on 31 October, but the two latter were returned to the Civil Power and the Tolbooth on 12 February 1812. Duhenot and Plantaut appear to have been cleared of any accusations of forgery—or was it that the reason for their arrest had been rather to place them in protective custody as witnesses against suspected fellow prisoners at the depot? For on 25 September, after it had received a report on the case from the depot agent at Greenlaw and the sheriff at Edinburgh, the Transport Board instructed the former, in terms that made it seem a reward was being conferred on the two men, 'to send them again on parole, to any parole town they may prefer in North Britain.'[39] Plantaut had been a parole prisoner at Kelso until in May 1811 he was sent to Edinburgh Castle for 'improper conduct'. From the Castle he had been transferred on 14 August that year to Greenlaw, one of 365 prisoners who trod the same path between then and 7 September. Duhenot had been one of the eleven 'ring-leaders' sent from Esk Mills on 9 March 1811 to the Castle. Then, like Plantaut, he had been transferred from there on 14 August to Greenlaw. Both Plantaut and Duhenot were therefore released from the Edinburgh Tolbooth and sent on 4 October on parole to Cupar Fife and from there they were sent, with all the other prisoners, to Lanark in November 1811, where they both remained until released to France at the end of the war, in June 1814.[40] The prisoner arrested as he landed from the *Mermaid* at Leith was Jean Pierre L'Ami or Lami, aged 31, born at Carrba (? or Cassaba), a soldier captured in 1805 on the man-of-war *Mont Blanc* a few days after the battle of Trafalgar.[41]

According to Macbeth Forbes, 'The total of forged notes of the Bank of England of which payment was refused at the Bank from 1st January 1801 to 31st December 1811—in all, eleven years—was £101,661. This return included fabrications of all kinds abroad and at home.'[42] However industrious the forgers among the prisoners of war, they were not solely responsible for that impressive output: apart from the contribution by forgers other than they, the war itself had not been begun or resumed until May 1803. How much of that total circulated as a result of forgeries carried out by prisoners in Scots depots is unknown but seems likely to have been extremely small. Prisoners there appear to have preferred to concentrate their efforts on simulating notes of the Bank of Scotland and the Commercial Banking Company of Scotland. 'The reason for this,' Macbeth Forbes wrote, 'is said to have been the greater ease in dealing with these notes, which had little or no pictorial delineation, and consisted almost entirely of engraved penmanship. Of course they had to get suitable paper, if that could be got; and, as there were no steel pens in those days, a few crow quills served their purpose; and then they went ahead in a secret corner with their imitation. They used to have confederates who watched the ins and outs of the turnkey; and, in addition to imitating the lettering on the face of the note, they had to forge the watermark, the seals of the bank, and the Government stamp.'[43] It was no doubt helpful to their enterprise that both Esk Mills and Valleyfield until acquired by the government in late 1810 as depots had been paper mills. As well as Valleyfield, the Cowans owned a nearby former cornmill on the river Esk which they had converted into a paper mill known as Bank Mill because there 'they manufactured the paper for making bank-notes'. It was a manufacture which, according to another Penicuik historian, continued throughout the Napoleonic Wars and 'many of the [depot] guards had part-time jobs there and they no doubt stole paper for the prisoners.'[44]

As for Jean Pierre L'Ami, the soldier arrested for having what seemed to be forged Bank of England notes in his possession when he disembarked from the *Mermaid* at Leith, it had been Messrs Kaye and Freshfield, solicitors to the Bank of England, who had alerted the Transport Board to an outcome of their investigations. '... it appears that Pierre Laroche, a French prisoner on board the the *San Isadoro* prison ship at Plymouth, who is charged with the forgery of bank notes, gave a forged bank note for £5, No. 20,428, and also a forged bank note for £2, to Jean Pierre L'Ami who some time ago was confined in the same cachot on board the *San Isadoro* but has since been removed in HMS *Mermaid* to Leith.' The Board on 9 September ordered Malcolm Wright, its agent at Edinburgh, to have L'Ami very carefully searched immediately he landed at Leith. '... if these forged notes should be found upon him ... mark them so that they can be identified, and then transmit them to this office; and also ... examine L'Ami as to his knowledge of Laroche's proceedings ... reporting the result to us without delay.'[45] But the suspicions raised against L'Ami appear to have proved unjustified. On 30 September the Transport Board instructed Malcolm Wright that 'The Bank Notes found upon the prisoner L'Ami are to be taken from him, notwithstanding they should prove to be genuine, and they are to be issued to him in the proportion provided by the [standing] instructions, viz., two guineas per week.' L'Ami was released from the Tolbooth on 21 October and sent to Greenlaw, and from there he was transferred almost a year later to Valleyfield.[46]

It was at Valleyfield, toward the end of September 1811, more or less simultaneously with the arrest of the five prisoners at Greenlaw and of L'Ami at Leith, that the agent reported the discovery of forged notes. The Transport Board ordered him on 26 September 'to discover from which prisoners the forged notes ... were received; and to cause vigilance to be used to prevent the Manufacture and Circulation of Forged Notes by the prisoners.' When a few days later the agent made a further report the Board instructed him that 'The prisoners named by you as having passed forged notes are to be kept in the Black Hole until they discover [i.e., name] the forgers of the notes.' Another scrap of information was added soon afterwards: 'The two prisoners who passed the forged notes mentioned by you must declare the names of the prisoners from whom they received the notes at Plymouth, as alleged by them.'[47] A dramatic development, as it seemed, took place three weeks later: 'Captain Moriarty, the agent for prisoners of war at Valleyfield, having stated to us,' the Transport Board informed Vice Admiral Otway on 1 November on his flagship HMS *Adamant* at Leith, 'that a Dutch boy received by H.M.S. *Brune* from Plymouth had given him information by which he was enabled to detect a French prisoner concerned in the fabrication of forged bank notes, and that the life of this boy is in danger among the prisoners on account of this and other information he has given, we request the favour of you as an accommodation to this Department to keep the said boy on board your ship, until it be seen whether his evidence will be wanted. We have referred the subject of the forgeries in question to the solicitors of the Bank of England.'[48] It soon appeared, however, that Captain Moriarty had caught not a forger but a crab: 'We inclose for your information,' the Transport Board told him on 4 November, 'an extract from a letter from Captain Pellowe, stating the result of the measures which he had adopted in conjunction with Captain Hawkins, the Superintendent of Prison Ships at Plymouth, for the detection of the prisoners at Plymouth stated to be concerned in forgeries, by which it appears that nothing has been discovered to implicate the three prisoners pointed out to you. We think it proper on this occasion to caution you against giving too much credit to the plausiable [sic] statements of French prisoners.'[49]

A new phase in forgery by the prisoners appears to have begun in the winter of 1811-12. A Transport Board circular to all depots and hulks, except Dartmoor, on 22 January 1812, warned that: 'It having been reported to us that the implements, etc., used by the prisoners in forging bank notes are conveyed to the prisons in small casks, fixed in the casks in which the small beer is supplied to the prisoners, we desire that you will cause any such cask to be strictly examined when received and also when sent out of the prison or prison ship.' The circular added: 'We desire that you will immediately discontinue the employment of French clerks, it appearing that they are instrumental in forwarding improper communications to and from the prisoners; and particularly in procuring for them the materials and implements necessary for forging bank notes.'[50]

Whether either or both of these problems for the authorities had emerged in any of the Scots depots is not known. But three weeks after it had sent out its circular the Board informed its agent at Greenlaw it approved 'of your having delivered over to the Civil Power the Five Prisoners ... who appear to be concerned in fabricating Forged Bank Notes.'[51] The five prisoners were all seamen, of whom, as already observed, two, Pierre Caron and Carlos Gonsalvez, had been sent as suspected forgers the previous September from Greenlaw into the Edinburgh Tolbooth and the hands of the Civil Power but had been returned the following month to the depot. The other three seamen were Jean Bouyer, aged 28, born at Bordeaux, who had been captured on a retaken unidentified vessel in the English Channel in 1809; François Guillemard, aged 19, born at St Malo, captured on the *Prince Murat* privateer in 1806 at a place unstated in the General Entry Book; and Jean Raymot, purser's clerk, who had escaped from Edinburgh Castle in July 1811 but had been recaptured a couple of days later at Queensferry.[52]

As these five suspected forgers were adjusting (or readjusting, in the case of Caron and Gonsalvez) themselves to their quarters in the Tolbooth (whose peculiarity, as a later historian of Edinburgh put it, was that 'nearly every criminal of rank [confined] in it achieved an escape'),[53] the Bank of Scotland was simultaneously inserting the following advertisement in the press throughout Scotland: 'FORGERY. Several forged notes in imitation of the notes of the Governor and Company of the Bank of Scotland having appeared, chiefly in the neighbourhood of the depots of prisoners of war, a caution is hereby, on the part of the said Governor and Company, given against receiving such forged notes in payment. And whosoever shall within three months hereof give such information as shall be found sufficient, on lawful trial, for the conviction of any persons, concerned in the fabrication or not, in feloniously uttering or otherwise feloniously using any of the said forged notes shall receive from the said Governor and Company a reward of one hundred pounds sterling.

'These forged notes being executed by the hand with a pen or pencil, without any engraving, further description applicable to all of them cannot be given. In most of them the body of the notes has the appearance of foreign handwriting. The names of the Bank officers, though common and well known in this country, are in the forged notes most illegible or wrong [sic] spelled. The ornamented characters and the figures, are in forged notes generally ill executed. In the forged notes the seals are very ill imitated. In the genuine notes the seals have a firmness and distinctiveness far superior to the counterfeit seals. To this mark particular attention is requested. By order of the Court of Directors. (Signed) Geo. Sandy, Secretary, 10th February 1812.'[54] Within a fortnight of the advertisement's first insertion more than 50 forged banknotes had been handed in to the Bank of Scotland.[55]

Nor, if a report in the *Kelso Mail* was accurate, were the forgeries confined to notes of the Bank of Scotland: forged one-pound notes of the Commercial Bank of Scotland and other banks had also been discovered. 'We now understand,' that paper told its readers on 13 February, 'that this species of forgery has been practised for some time by the French prisoners in the neighbourhood of Edinburgh, also on the British Linen Company, Sir William Forbes and Company, and the Leith Bank. The matter ... is now in a regular train of investigation before the Sheriff of Edinburgh.' The *Glasgow Courier* added that the forgeries, clumsily executed, 'seem to be done with a pen, or camel's hair pencil, and consequently cannot proceed to any alarming extent.'[56]

Nonetheless the banks—or several of them—in Scotland had become increasingly concerned at these forgeries by the prisoners or others. The advertisements in the press were an expression of their concern. The five banks mentioned in the *Kelso Mail* report, plus the Aberdeen Banking Company and the Falkirk Banking Company, had already entered into an agreement along with the government Stamp Office (whose stamp appeared on all banknotes, forgeries of which were thus also a fraud on government revenues). What they agreed was to bear equally among themselves the cost of any joint inquiry that might be held into the forgeries, and of prosecuting the forgers and utterers or venders of those notes. As early as August 1811 it had been agreed by these bodies that, to avoid duplication of effort and keep down costs, only one of them acting on behalf of all should investigate and take evidence or precognitions from witnesses. The depute solicitor of Stamps was asked to conduct the actual investigation. Concerning the next stage, of indictments and trials of suspects, each bank was left to decide its own action. The investigation then got under way, a good deal of evidence was taken about some of the forgeries in connection with which numbers of those arrested were or appeared implicated. The Lord Advocate's advice was that the Stamp Officer in charge of the case should bring it to court. On the ground, however, that there was no legal evidence of forgery the banks refused to proceed further. They then gave in January 1812 the due six months' notice to terminate the joint agreement made the previous August, which thus ended on 23 July 1812. Their campaign of press advertisements in February and March, however, as already seen, demonstrated the banks' distinct concern about the forgeries. 'This advertisement,' according to Macbeth Forbes, 'was to be printed and put outside the walls for the militia on guard at the depots, and a French translation within for the prisoners, and both to be transmitted to agencies where [as, for example, in the Scottish Borders towns] there were prisoners on parole. In addition, the military authorities were eternally on the *qui vive* for forgers. The governors of the different depots ordered the turnkeys to examine narrowly notes coming in and out of prison. Lord Ross-lyn, deputy-governor of the [Edinburgh] castle in 1811, gave strict orders to this effect, and said that "the turnkey of the prison there, John Campbell, who is a brother of one of the Bank of Scotland's servants, has been warned to observe strictly all transactions by the prisoners during the market hours, with the view of seeing if they try to pass notes." The militiamen had also to be watched, as they acted so frequently as intermediaries.'[57]

It was, however, the banks which had to meet at least in part the costs of the board and lodging of the suspected banknote forgers in the Edinburgh Tolbooth, or, according to Macbeth Forbes, 'they would not have been clapped in jail at all.' In fact, the banks, he says, 'had to pay dearly for the forgeries, besides paying, as a rule, the notes so forged, which were, however, almost always of the denomination of one pound.' When in June 1812 the solicitor of one of the banks was instructed to report on the suspects then confined in the Tolbooth and the likely cost of their board and lodging he found 'there were nine prisoners in jail—seven culprits and two witnesses—for uttering forged notes.'[58]

The escape of the 'seven culprits' early on a Sunday morning a month later, and the expenses incurred in their recapture, added further to the costs the banks had to meet. 'Very early yesterday morning,' the *Caledonian Mercury* reported on 20 July, 'seven Frenchmen who were committed to the Tolbooth of this city on suspicion of forgery effected their escape. They were confined in the north-west room on the third storey, and they had penetrated the wall, though very thick, till they got into the vent of Mr Gilmour's shop, into which they descended by means of ropes. When they had got into the shop they ascended a small stair, and having taken out half the window, they descended one by one into the street and got clear off. In the course of the morning, one of them was retaken.' Some further details were provided by the *Edinburgh Evening Courant* that same day: the seven had dug through the thick wall with the handle of an old frying pan and a small poker; after they had dreeped from the window to the street 'they were tracked by the sooty marks on their feet to the Grassmarket, where one of them was taken again'; except, it seemed, for one, 'they all speak English'. Three of the remaining six were recaptured wthin a week at Glasgow. According to Macbeth Forbes, though he did not give his source, the seven escapers had 'left a note on the table of [Mr Gilmour's] shop, saying they had taken nothing away.' The names and descriptions of the other three were given in a press advertisement by Edinburgh Town Council a week after their escape: 'PRISONERS ESCAPED FROM EDINBURGH TOLBOOTH: CARLOS GONSALVEZ, about 6 feet 2 inches high, slender made, stoops a little in walking, dark complexion, dark brown eyes, large wiskers [sic], was formerly a prisoner at Greenlaw; speaks broken English; was seen dressed in black clothes after his escape. FERDINAND LEFEBVRE, upwards of 5 feet 8 inches high, stout made, dark complexion, marks on his breast and arms by gunpowder, inserted under the skin; speaks broken English. L'IMBERT ALTIER, about 5 feet 9 inches, stout made, dark brown complexion, speaks very hoarse, long nose; wants part of the fore and middle fingers in his left hand. Any person apprehending any of the above prisoners and bringing him to this office, will be handsomely rewarded, over and above the reward by Government, and those found concealing them after this notice will be proceeded against as the law directs.'[59] Within a week of the publication of the advertisement Altier was 'apprehended in Dublin, and committed to Kilmainham Jail.' He remained there for a couple of weeks and then was shipped off to Plymouth, no doubt to the hulks. From Glasgow the three other recaptured prisoners were brought back to the Edinburgh Tolbooth at the expense of the banks. Carlos Gonsalvez and Ferdinand Lefebvre appear not to have been recaptured.[60]

Of the seven 'culprits' who had escaped from the Tolbooth, five, as already observed, had arrived there in February from Greenlaw. The other two, L'Imbert Altier and Lefebvre, and also the two witnesses held at the Tolbooth, had come on 1 April from Valleyfield. It was at Valleyfield, according to Macbeth Forbes, who does not give his source, that the agent, Captain Moriarty, on 19 March 1812 had 'discovered a prisoner called Rosier in the act of forging bank notes, and he reported the matter to the authorities. Though he had two witnesses to the deed, there is no record of the forger suffering any punishment.'[61] There is some confusion of identities here that is difficult to resolve since of the nine prisoners, including the two witnesses, in the Tolbooth only three (Gonsalvez, Lefebvre and Altier) of the seven escapers were named in the press advertisement. Assuming neither of the two witnesses held in the Tolbooth were indeed among the seven escapers, then (despite Macbeth Forbes naming him as a forger) Rosier (Roset) may not in fact have been suspected of or charged with forgery but was instead a witness to forgery by Lefebvre and/or Altier; and the second witness in the Tolbooth appears to have been Augustin Flour. If that were so then of the other four prisoners in the Tolbooth (Caron, Bouyer, Guillemard and Raymot) it is not clear which one had been recaptured in the Grassmarket or which three at Glasgow.

A new phase in forging, however, appears to have opened at Valleyfield in the autumn and early winter of 1812 and may have been due largely to an influx of prisoners from Greenlaw. The Valleyfield General Entry Books show that between 9 October and 11 December inclusive eleven prisoners were discharged to the sheriff of Edinburgh. Beyond that, the reasons for their going were not stated in the Entry Books. But it may be reasonably inferred from an acknowledgement by the Transport Board to a letter of 3 December from the depot agent concerning the seven handed over to the sheriff the previous day, that the other four cases were similar: '... approve of your having discharged the prisoners concerned in the forgery of bank notes into the custody of Mr Bruce upon the warrant of the sheriff.'[62] It was probably significant that of the eleven nine had come to Valleyfield on 1 September that year from Greenlaw.[63]

Even these arrests and transfers to the custody of the sheriff in Edinburgh did not, however, bring to an end the forging of banknotes at Valleyfield. In July 1813 the depot clerk sent to the banks 26 forged guinea notes 'which were about to be sold but were detected by the turnkey'.[64] In October that year 'Mr Aitken of the Canongate jail lately detected and took from the person of a private soldier in a militia regiment stationed at Pennycuick, and who had come into the Canongate prison to see a friend, forged guinea and twenty shilling notes, on two different banks in this city and two others in the country, amounting to nearly £70. The soldier was immediately given over to the civil power, and from thence to the regiment to which he belongs until the matter is further investigated. The two banking houses in Edinburgh have liberally given to Mr Aitken, and the prisoners under his charge, four guineas, in appreciation of their conduct.'[65] The soldier was Private Thomas Gray of the Kirkcudbright Militia, of whose case more will presently be said. In mid-December 1813 the press reported that 'Counterfeit notes, the greater part on the Bank of Scotland and the Perth Bank, are at present very prevalent in the south of Scotland.'[66] In the last days of the war, on 23 March 1814, William Scott, procurator fiscal at Edinburgh, was asked by the Valleyfield agent 'what is intended to be done with Joseph Villette, who is under close confinement for passing forged notes.'[67] Even as late as the middle of May the *Evening Courant* warned its readers that 'A number of forged notes are at present in circulation, against which the public ought to be on their guard.'[68]

In the summer of the previous year forged money had appeared at Perth depot. The earliest reference appears to be in the *Perth Courier* in August

1813: 'On Monday a man was apprehended and after examination committed to prison, for circulating base money at the depot.'[69] The *Courier* commented a fortnight later: 'We are sorry to learn that the forgery of notes of various banks is carried on by the prisoners at the Depot, and that they find means to throw them into circulation by the assistance of profligate people who frequent the market. The eagerness of the prisoners to obtain cash is very great, and as they retain all they procure, they have drained this place almost entirely of silver, so that it has become a matter of difficulty to get change of a note.'[70] Complaints voiced in October 1813 against the prisoners at Perth by a meeting of the county's freeholders, presided over by the Duke of Atholl, lord lieutenant of Perthshire, included a reference to 'the evils which resulted from the too easy intercourse between the prisoners and the public, such as throwing forged bank notes into circulation'. But a proposal that the meeting should seek the intervention of the secretary of state (in that era the Home Secretary) was turned down in favour of asking the lord lieutenant and his deputies to deal with the problem.[71]

If forging banknotes thus provided a creative, and in some cases no doubt a profitable, pastime for some of the prisoners, it provided the depot authorities, the Transport Board, banks, and the legal and administrative authorities with a distinct problem. One means of grappling with it, as already observed in the evidently spurious case of the young Dutch boy in autumn 1811 at Valleyfield, was for depot agents to make use of informers among the prisoners. A question which inevitably arose was how to protect informers from the wrath of their fellow inmates. This question was taken up with the Admiralty in June 1812 by the Transport Board: 'There being at the Depots several French Prisoners who have given Information of their Fellow Prisoners concerned in Forgery, or in committing Depredations at the Prisons and on board the Prison ships; and as the Lives of these Prisoners would be endangered if they were not kept separate from the others, or even if they were sent to France, to which they strongly object; we submit to the Right Honourable the Lords Commissioner of the Admiralty whether it may not be adviseable [sic] to allow these Informers to be released to serve on board Merchant Vessels, not more than one of them being sent to any one Vessel.'[72] The Admiralty's reply has not been found but its substance may be inferred from the following circular sent two days later by the Transport Board to depot agents: '… you will transmit for the information of the … Admiralty a list of the prisoners who are in danger of ill-treatment in consequence of having given information of their fellow prisoners concerned in forging or in committing depredations at the prisons or on board the prison ships.'[73]

So far as prisoners in the Scots depots were concerned it was obvious from the earliest stage of their forgeries that in circulating them, as well as in acquiring some of the necessary paper and tools for their work, they had accomplices among the militiamen on guard duty at the depots and among some of the civilians who frequented depot markets. 'In Edinburgh of late the issuing of forged notes among the lower orders of society has become a branch of traffic to a considerable extent, and men and women frequently convicted. On Tuesday last [6 April], Mrs Stewart, a broker in St Mary's Wynd [Edinburgh], and a vender of those articles, was convicted by the sitting Magistrate in the Police Court of issuing two of these notes, and committed to Bridewell for sixty days, and thereafter bound over for her good behaviour under a heavy penalty. On Wednesday, Susan Burn, convicted of a similar crime, was also committed for sixty days, and banished the bounds of police.'[74]

Seven months earlier, the first notable trial involving prisoners' militia or civilian accomplices had taken place in the High Court in Edinburgh. Private Alexander Thomson, alias John Laurie, of the Aberdeenshire Militia, pleaded not guilty to uttering forged notes, knowing them to be forged. Bank officials, clerks and other witnesses testified they had seen a pocketbook taken out from between Thomson's shoe and stocking which contained six Bank of Scotland and four Commercial Bank notes—all forgeries, with no watermark, and apparently all made with a pen. A lieutenant in the Aberdeenshire militia, in which Thomson was one of the soldiers on guard at 'the depot' at Penicuik (i.e., Valleyfield), said he had 'heard that the French prisoners were in the habit of forging notes, and frequently has himself warned the soldiers against having anything to do with them.' A private in the same regiment said he had 'seen the French prisoners offering things like notes, which they called pictures, for sale, but never was near enough to see them distinctly.' Other witnesses testified to being paid for goods or services with forged notes, some of them passed to them by Thomson himself. Thomson's declarations, 'of a most contradictory nature', were first that he was a drover and had received the notes in change at Berwick and elsewhere, second that he was a soldier. Witnesses in his defence 'gave him an excellent character', as a good soldier and of hitherto unblemished integrity. By a majority the jury found the charges against Thomson not proven. 'The Court, on receiving the verdict, remarked that had they had the honour to have been on the jury they should have considered it as their duty to have voted with the minority.'[75] Since forgery was a capital offence, Thomson was indeed fortunate to escape the gallows or at the least a sentence of several years' transportation to the penal colonies in Australia. In a confession he made to someone when he was set free after the trial, Thomson, according to Macbeth Forbes, 'admitted having received the notes from a soldier in the Cambridge Militia, under the name of "pictures", within the house of a grocer and change-keeper of Penicuik (beside Valleyfield depot), and that the soldier had, by Thomson's desire, purchased them for 2s. each from the prisoners at the depot.'[76]

During the following two years there were several arrests of militia guards and civilians, precognitions taken, and High or Circuit Court trials held of alleged accomplices in the uttering of the depot prisoners' forged banknotes. The Lord Advocate's papers show, for example, that John Shaw was arrested at Edmonstone in Midlothian for having two 'very badly done—not engraved, but with a pen or pencil' forged £1 notes of the Bank of Scotland in his possession, 'part obviously of those fabricated by the French prisoners at the depot.' There was no evidence, however, that Shaw had been concerned in the forgery 'though he must have known they were so'. The same papers indicate that the Lord Advocate left the decision whether to prosecute in such cases to the banks.[77] Following the arrest of William Crombie, another private in the Aberdeenshire Militia stationed at Penicuik, a precognition in August 1812 by William Dowie of West Linton in Peeblesshire, formerly a limeworks tacksman and latterly a farm worker in East Lothian, indicates how forged notes made by the prisoners were circulated. As he was walking from East Lothian to West Linton, Dowie 'fell in with William Crombie upon the road between Dalkeith and Greenlaw, when some conversation took place between them about the French prisoners, in the course of which Crombie said to Dowie that if he had been at Dalkeith he had four pound notes of the Commercial Bank of Scotland which he would give Dowie for very little money. Crombie then said that if Dowie would go with him towards Greenlaw he would get more notes there. Dowie accordingly went with Crombie to the prison, and after going round and looking at the prisoners he came out again and Crombie afterwards joined him, bringing with him some rings upon a painted stick, saying that this was necessary to make the Guard believe he was purchasing something for Dowie. Crombie … then delivered to Dowie four one pound notes of the Governor and Company of the Bank of Scotland, also two guinea notes of the Falkirk Bank and Company, for which notes the Declarant paid Crombie twelve shillings and six pence in silver.' Dowie said he met Crombie again after that and got further notes from him, some of which he passed on to members of his family or paid to shopkeepers and others for goods. In a later meeting at a public house at Auchendinny, near Greenlaw, Crombie told Dowie that 'he had easily put off one of the Commercial Bank notes at Kirkhill [at Penicuik] by putting on Coloured Cloaths,' and that he [Crombie] had sent away seven of these notes to a friend and that he expected to procure as many as would purchase his discharge besides some to take home with him. Crombie had also told Dowie that a sergeant of an English militia regiment quartered at Greenlaw was very active in circulating some of these notes.[78]

A militiaman who suffered, though very temporarily, the full rigours of the law for possessing forged banknotes knowing them to be forged, was Private Thomas Gray, Kirkcudbrightshire Militia, stationed at Penicuik, whose trial took place in the High Court in Edinburgh soon after the end of the war, in July 1814. Gray's was said by the *Edinburgh Evening Courant* to be 'a case of the greatest importance to the public and ought to be universally known throughout the Kingdom'. During a search by his battalion adjutant of his barrack room at Penicuik the previous December some 33 forged notes of half a dozen banks had been found below his bed in a box belonging to Gray. Gray said he had found the notes near the palisades, wrapped in paper and cloth. He had examined them in his barrack room, became convinced they were forged, wrapped them again in their parcel, put it in his box, never mentioned the business to anyone else, and had not passed or attempted to pass any of the notes. Several of his regimental officers who had known Gray for ten years 'gave him a good character, as an honest well behaved man'. Despite 'a very able and ingenious' defence by his counsel, the redoubtable Henry Cockburn, the jury by a majority found Gray guilty of having in his possession two forged notes of the Bank of England and two of the Bank of Scotland knowing them to be forged, but 'unanimously and most earnestly recommended him to mercy.' He was sentenced to 14 years' transportation. Two months later, however, the Prince Regent commuted his sentence to six months' imprisonment from the date of his conviction.[79]

Most of the civilians who were charged with uttering or vending banknotes forged by the prisoners in the Scots depots were less fortunate in their verdicts and sentences than was Gray or his fellow private in the Aberdeenshire militia, Alexander Thomson or Laurie. The first to be brought to trial was Nathaniel Blair, alias Sawers, an Edinburgh hackney carriage and cart- and horse-keeper, who was arrested and confined in the Tolbooth at Inveraray in November 1813, charged with forging or causing to be forged banknotes at Greenlaw or Valleyfield in 1812-13, and, knowing them to be forged, uttering and vending them in autumn 1813 in Argyll. The forgeries were on notes of the Bank of Scotland, the British Linen Co., the Commercial Bank of Scotland, and the Falkirk Banking Co. A young woman accompanying Blair in Argyll had also been attempting to vend counterfeit notes. Blair, 'a good looking man about 34 years of age', was found guilty unanimously by the jury at the High Court in Edinburgh on 31 January 1814 on four out of five indictments of uttering banknotes forged by prisoners at Penicuik, and was sentenced to be hanged. But on 4 February in the condemned cell while awaiting execution he hanged himself.[80]

Blair's conviction and suicide were followed on 15-16 March by the trial, at the High Court for uttering forged banknotes, of two Glasgow stonemasons, William Beattie, alias Beaton, and Alexander Tolmie—or at least in Beattie's case trial would have taken place had he not failed to appear in court. He was outlawed; on Tolmie the jury returned a majority verdict of not proven.[81] In July came on two further trials at the High Court. The first was that on 4 July of James McDougall, an Edinburgh cattle dealer, who was unanimously found guilty of uttering and vending at Edinburgh and at Saltoun and Belhaven in East Lothian, forged notes of the Bank of Scotland. McDougall was sentenced to death and was hanged on 10 August.[82] The second trial, on 15 July, again for vending and uttering forged notes, was that of John Horn (and would have been also of William Veitch had he not failed to appear: Veitch was outlawed). Horn admitted uttering forged notes, but not to uttering them as genuine notes. He was found guilty and sentenced to five years' transportation.[83] Another trial, this time at Perth, took place in April 1814. There at the end of August or beginning of September 1813, as already observed above,[84] a woman coming from the depot market had been searched by order of the agent, 'when there were found about her person pieces of base money in imitation of Bank tokens (of which the prisoners are suspected to have been the fabricators) to the amount of £5.17.0.' She was arrested and put in gaol.[85] She was Margaret Baxter, alias Reekie, whose trial at the Circuit Court at Perth took place on 21 April 1814, when two charges against her of passing forged notes were found not proven, but she was found guilty on a third similar charge and was sentenced to seven years' transportation.[86]

Yet another trial, recounted by William Chambers but about which no reference has been found in official papers or in the press, concerned Will Broun, a bonnet laird or small landowner, who lived with his widowed mother and sister in a thatched cottage near Chambers's boyhood home in Peebles. According to Chambers, the Brouns, although well off with six acres of land, potatoes, and a cow, lived frugally. Will Broun, who, says Chambers, had had a good education and translated Latin inscriptions on tombstones, became acquainted with an Irishman who came to Scotland 'to pick up bounties for substitutes in the militia before returning to Ireland with the cash.' Broun, influenced by this Irishman, himself visited Ireland and from then on 'may be said never to have done any good ... According to his notions, all that was estimable belonged to the poor and struggling classes; all who moved in a dignified or simply respectable position were worthless oppressors.' Broun married a Peebles girl handloom weaver named Tilly Tait, sold all his land, house and cow, and moved to Penicuik to set himself up as a merchant with a grocer's shop and selling whisky. When Chambers and his father visited Valleyfield to observe the prisoners of war that Sunday about 1811-12, they also called on Will Broun at his shop in Penicuik. There William Chambers himself saw a prisoner 'in his yellow garb' and escorted by a soldier carrying a drawn bayonet, come to Broun's door. Chambers learned that 'Will had dealings with the prisoners, by disposing of some of their articles of manufacture on commission besides helping them to purchase raw materials as a matter of trade.' When, Chambers says, early in 1812 newspapers began to report that prisoners of war in Scotland were making and trying to distribute forged banknotes, and it became clear that the forged notes were passed to someone in a village or town adjoining the depot, at Penicuik 'a suspicious connection with these transactions ... fell upon Will [Broun]... Summarily, by a warrant of the Sheriff ... he was captured and lodged in the Old Tolbooth of Edinburgh. ... At his judicial examinations Will professed to know nothing about forged notes. He was a dealer in "yarn", on commission. The prisoners made the yarn and sent him neatly sealed packets of it for disposal.' Will Broun understood that by 'yarn' was meant pictures to amuse children. 'Packets containing five of these imaginary pictures were, when he received them, marked "Small Yarn"; and packets of larger dimensions bore the inscription "Large Yarn". He had been in the habit of executing orders for these packages, knowing absolutely nothing of their contents. Will said his customers for "yarn" were "respectable" dealers in sheep and cattle, etc., in Roxburghshire. The explanations,' said Chambers, 'were ingenious. Will was set down as a sort of simpleton. He could not, with a chance of conviction, be charged with a knowledge of "felonious utterance". With a strong admonition, he was dismissed. Thankfully, he quitted the Tolbooth after having, in a sense, "rubbed shoulders wi' the gallows". What was done with his customers for "yarn" in Roxburghshire, I never heard with any precision.'[87]

A striking fact about these banknote forgeries was that no prisoner at any depot in Scotland was ever prosecuted for them. That fact contrasted with the fate of several prisoners on hulks or in depots in England, where at least six were tried, convicted and executed in March-April 1812 for forging banknotes, and two other prisoners languished in gaol nine years from 1805 to 1814 for the same crime.[88] What appears to explain the difference in the treatment of these prisoners in Scotland and England was that in the latter the Bank of England, unlike the banks in Scotland, was sufficiently influential and determined to secure the trials and hence the convictions and executions that took place.[89]

What happened to the sixteen prisoners from Greenlaw and Valleyfield held in the Edinburgh Tolbooth on charges, or at least suspicion, of forging banknotes? From the Tolbooth 'they were sent down under a strong escort ... [and] put on board the *Adamant* flagship' of Vice Admiral Otway at Leith on 3 December 1812, the Transport Board having recommended the Admiralty to direct him to 'send them to [the hulks at] Chatham by the first opportunity.'[90] Their fate was therefore not the gallows but confinement on the hulks for the remaining 18 months the war lasted, at the end of which time they, like all the other prisoners of war in Britain, were released and repatriated. The last words on the prisoners' activities in forgery may be left with William Chambers, on whose memory from his boyhood visit to Valleyfield they had left such an indelible impression. 'What was truly revolting to every sense of propriety,' Chambers wrote, 'was the spectacle of vast groups of prisoners ... at Penicuik, ... at Perth ... and so on—confined like wild beasts for years within palisaded enclosures, and in a state of that utter idleness which led ... to criminal acts—forging bank notes, as it were, to relieve the tedium of their dismal incarceration.'[91]

Utter idleness was, however, avoided by a number, admittedly small, of the prisoners in Scotland who did succeed in obtaining some employment (usually paid, however meagrely) within the depots. There were even a score or more of non-French prisoners who found themselves employed not only outside but far away from the depots. In August 1809, for example, the Transport Board instructed its agent at Greenlaw to release three Danish prisoners and deliver them 'to Mr John Scott, St Mildred's Court, London, ... for the purpose of instructing certain Highlanders in the manufacture of Tar, Mr Scott having engaged for their good conduct on going to, staying at, and returning from, the Highlands.'[92] From Greenlaw also, on the personal orders of James Bowen, a Transport Board commissioner, three other prisoners were sent in July 1811 'to assist in navigating a Lobster Vessel.'[93] It is not certain (although it seems likely) whether the following year 'certain Dutch fishermen, prisoners of war,' were in a Scots depot or depots when, as already observed, in July they were 'delivered over' to 'Mr James Henderson of Clyth and Wick, in the county of Caithness, Fish Curer, ... for the purpose of instructing the inhabitants in the Dutch mode of gripping and curing picked [sic—pickled?] herrings.'[94] Hyndhert Davus, a Dutch fisherman confined at Valleyfield, was released from there, as also already seen, in December 1813 on the orders of the Admiralty, 'to assist Mr Dugald Fergusson of the Cod and Herring Fishery at Greenock.'[95] To help sail merchant vessels eight Danish and 14 Icelandic seamen were released from Greenlaw during the year 1810-11.[96] Several other prisoners were sent from the depots to work as servants or batmen for officers in captivity in the parole towns. Among these fortunate few was Charles Chalet or Chatet, aged 24, born in Vigneux, a soldier captured in Spain in 1808 when he was 'Secretary, 1st Regiment Horse', and who had been at Valleyfield less than three months after his arrival from Esk Mills when he was sent in June 1811 to Northampton 'as Servant to Captain Berar.' In January 1813 Lieutenant Colonel Antignac, on parole at Kelso, was 'allowed Klintz Chasson of the 22nd Regiment now confined at Valleyfield, for his servant'; and in November that year the agent at Perth was told by the Transport Board to send a prisoner named Steiner to Oswestry in Shropshire as a servant to General Nielund.[97]

One proposed source of employment for prisoners, at least at Esk Mills depot, was promptly and emphatically prohibited, however, by the Transport

Board in February 1811: 'We cannot sanction the prisoners being employed in working in any manner for the persons belonging to the establishment of the depot.'[98]

Otherwise, those relatively few prisoners who were given employment were given it within the depots. Some of them were employed by their fellow prisoners—as was, for example, the master of arms employed at Valleyfield by Marote-Carrier and his fellow officers to act as doorkeeper of their separate quarters, 'to turn away anyone who sought to enter without authorisation', and whose salary was 'a ration of bread and wine that we raised ... from among a certain number of us.' To the prisoner who acted as scorer for the games of billiards Marote-Carrier and several of his fellow officers played on the table they had bought themselves at Valleyfield they paid 'six sous a day and a ration of bread.' At Perth there were 'four strong soldiers, all *batonnistes* [cudgel players] and masters of arms' who were elected by their fellow prisoners to distribute rations of food to the *rafalés* and force them to eat, in return for which service the four were paid 'a remuneration raised from the mass of the prisoners.'[99] Most of the officers in captivity at Perth, according to Marote-Carrier, employed servants, as he himself did. His own servant was 'a young man from a poor family of Ostend. He had served as an artilleryman until he had his arm broken at Burgos ... I took him into the room I inhabited and replaced his clothes, which were in complete disrepair ...'[100]

But probably the majority of those prisoners given employment within the depots were given it by the depot authorities. At all the Scots depots, except perhaps Esk Mills, some prisoners were, or appear to have been, set on at least for a time to labouring work. Thus the agent at Valleyfield was told by the Transport Board on the day that depot opened in March 1811: '... approve of your employing prisoners to level the airing ground', then a fortnight later he was instructed that: 'The airing ground is to be levelled and coated over with gravel by the prisoners.'[101] '... approve,' the Board told the agent there a few months afterward, 'of your having employed some of the prisoners for cutting the airing ground for a Run of Water.' Whitewashing depot buildings, including its hospital, was another task that in May 1813 prisoners there were set on to.[102] At Greenlaw, the agent was given permission by the Board in January 1813 'to employ a prisoner as a labourer.'[103] Five months later, after it had asked the agent to report 'if graves cannot be dug by the prisoners', the Board approved '... of your employing a prisoner as a labourer at 3d. per diem who is to dig graves when wanted.'[104] A change in the Transport Board's policy on grave-digging appears to have taken place by then, since the Board had told the agent at Esk Mills in March 1811 that at the depots in England 'No charge is made ... for digging the graves, this being done by the prisoners.'[105] At Edinburgh Castle Pierre Ballizote was employed as a labourer for several weeks in the summer of 1813, but exactly what work he did is not stated.[106] At Perth, as at Valleyfield, the first prisoners to arrive at the newly opened depot in summer 1812 would, the Transport Board told the agent, '... be found useful in accelerating the completion of the workings by assisting in levelling the ground, removing rubbish, etc.'[107] Four months after the depot opened the agent was instructed by the Board 'to employ two or three labourers from among the prisoners for the present.'[108] It seems more likely to have been outside contractors than prisoners who were the subject of a reply by the Board to a letter (which has not survived) from the agent at the end of 1813 concerning what appears to have been 'damages repaired in the privy pit of Prison No.2: ... the price of the whisky cannot be allowed but extra wages will be allowed as an equivalent for the particularly unpleasant service therein referred to.'[109]

There were diverse other employments given to a few prisoners in all the Scots depots. They included baking, cooking, repairing hammocks, picking hair, making clogs, repairing tin cans and wooden kids or tubs, slaughtering cattle, repairing shoes, and work as inspectors, turners, coopers, tailors, clerks, barbers, nurses, and surgeons.

'The contractors having applied to us,' the Transport Board told the agent at Valleyfield, for example, in October 1811, 'to be allowed to employ prisoners to assist at baking the bread and slaughtering the cattle, we direct you to permit them to employ prisoners for this purpose, upon their being accountable for the security of the prisoners who may be so employed.' Difficulties, however, appear to have arisen at the depot more or less immediately over the baking. 'We have received your letter of the 12th instant,' the Board told the agent a month later. '... allowing the three prisoners therein mentioned to bake was entirely for the public good, and for the prevention of complaints of the bread, and by no means for the private convenience of any individual whatever. But as this permission has been granted by you, we think it proper that it should be withdrawn; and we direct you to discontinue the permission accordingly.' Whatever the difficulty it seems to have been overcome: 'We have received your letter of the 19th instant,' the Board told the agent a few days later, 'and ... we have no objection to the prisoners thereinmentioned continuing to be employed by the contractor to bake the bread for the prisoners.'[110] When in January 1813 there were problems at the depot over the contractor's supply of biscuit (bread baked hard) to the prisoners the Board told the agent: 'We approve of your allowing the baker of the 82nd [French infantry] regiment to be employed in the bakehouse ...' This arrangement seems to have worked well and two months later the agent was instructed by the Board to 'allow the contractor to employ another French baker in baking the prisoners' bread.'[111] As for the slaughterman or butcher, 'We approve,' the Board told the agent in December 1813, 'of the French butcher being again employed in the contractor's slaughterhouse provided you see no objection thereto.'[112] At Perth, too, the Board granted permission for 'a prisoner to assist in slaughtering the beasts, care being taken that he do not escape.'[113]

Picking hair seems likely because of the wages paid for it to have been a job given in December 1812 at Greenlaw to prisoners rather than to civilian workers. But there is no doubt that a sailmaker among the former was employed in February that year to repair their hammocks 'and he is to be paid at the rate of three pence per diem while he may be so employed.'[114] A sailmaker from among the prisoners at Edinburgh Castle was employed there also and presumably for the same purpose as at Greenlaw.[115] The employment of inspectors from among the prisoners at presumably all the Scots depots has already been observed in an earlier chapter.[116]

Uniquely at Edinburgh Castle it might seem a chimney sweep was employed from among the prisoners.[117] Although perhaps an apt appointment in the fortress of a city popularly known as Auld Reekie, it may be that 'sweep' meant not of chimneys but a sweeper of dirt and litter from the depot floors. On the other hand, in all the depots prisoner-cooks were employed and, as already observed, one of them, Julien Foret (or Foiret), from the 88th infantry regiment, was scalded to death at Perth in June 1813 when he fell into a large boiler in the depot kitchens. Prisoners who presumably had some skill and experience in cutting hair and shaving others appear likewise to have been employed in the Scots depots. There were certainly two at Edinburgh Castle, three at Greenlaw, and one at Esk Mills, although most if not all of them were or may have been employed in the hospitals at these depots rather than that their services were available to all the prisoners. At Valleyfield as well as clogmakers there were employed 'a Tinman and cooper from among the prisoners to repair the Tin Cans and Wood Kids [tubs]'.[118] At Perth, too, prisoners were said to be employed as tinmen and coopers, as well as clogmakers and turners, and there were two shoe repairers.[119] Employment was also given there to several prisoners who were tailors: 'We direct you,' the Board told the agent in November 1812, 'to employ the sempstresses with some of the prisoners who are taylors [sic] in making up the 1,500 palliases received from the military depot at Leith into proper sizes. The prisoners while so employed are to be allowed 6d. each per diem.'[120] It is not known whether there was any positive response from agents at any of the Scots depots to an instruction sent out by the Transport Board in May 1811: '... you will state if there be any prisoners in your custody from Alsace or Lorraine who are acquainted with the art of making plate glass.'[121]

A handful of prisoners worked as clerks in the depot offices or hospitals. Perhaps it was a proposal to employ a clerk that was, however, rejected by the Transport Board in its response in January 1812 to its agent at Greenlaw: '... you cannot be allowed to employ a French prisoner in your office for the purpose mentioned by you.'[122] A prisoner at Valleyfield was more fortunate: there the agent was told by the Board in December 1811 that '... the French clerk employed by you to make out the lists for the French Government is to be paid at the rate of 6d. per diem.'[123] At Valleyfield, too, the extra administrative work involved at the end of the war in preparing for the repatriation of all the prisoners may have resulted in some of them being taken on as clerks after the Board directed the agent '... to employ additional assistance to make out the Embarkation Lists.' Shortly before the opening of Esk Mills depot the Board had instructed the agent that 'If a clerk be necessary for the Hospital a French prisoner is to be employed and paid at the rate of 6d. per diem.'[124] At Perth it may be it was prisoners rather than depot clerical staff who were the subject of a decision by the Board in November 1812: 'No more than 6d. per hundred can be allowed for copying of the alphabetical list.'[125] In general, the employment of some prisoners as clerks at the depots appeared confirmed by one of the Standing Orders and Regulations which the Transport Board sent to all its depot and parole agents (except, for reasons not explained, Malcolm Wright at Greenlaw and the parole agent at Peebles) in January 1811: 'Quarterly lists are to be transmitted to this Office regularly, of the prisoners received and of those who have died at the depot, which lists must be made out by an intelligent French prisoner who can write well, being required for the information of the French Government.'[126] On the other hand, in what appears to have proved only a temporary prohibition, the Transport Board ordered all depot agents in January 1812 no longer to employ French clerks, as they appeared to be abusing their position by passing 'improper communications' among prisoners and helping in the forging of banknotes.[127]

The largest source of employment for prisoners at the Scots depots appears to have been in their hospitals. At Esk Mills hospital, for example, three prisoner-nurses, two washermen, a cook and a barber were employed.[128] In an ambiguous entry in the same source which leaves it unclear whether the hospital concerned was at Edinburgh Castle or, much more likely, Greenlaw or perhaps even Valleyfield, there are listed in January 1813 some 21 prisoners employed: eight nurses, six washermen, three barbers, one cook, and three assistant surgeons. In another entry, but for which no date is given, there are said to have been one surgeon, one assistant surgeon, one cook, and one washerman. In yet another, this time clearly headed 'List of American prisoners of war employed in the hospital at Greenlaw Depot', three prisoners are listed, all nurses, one employed at the hospital for a week in November 1812, the two others that month for only three days each. In a final entry, 16 'French prisoners of war employed in the Hospital at Greenlaw Depot' are listed who were employed there for varying periods from November 1812 onwards: nine nurses, two washermen, one cook, one assistant cook, one steward, one barber, and one assistant surgeon.[129] Over-manning by prisoners employed as nurses at Perth depot was detected in November 1813 by the Transport Board: 'It appearing by your accounts for the last week that although there are only 13 patients in the hospital there are 7 nurses employed, we direct you to cause the number of nurses to be immediately reduced and to take care that they may be regulated in future by the number of patients in the usual proportion, viz., 1 nurse to every 10 patients.'[130]

Surgeons, hardly surprisingly, had their work more highly valued by the Transport Board than that of other employed prisoners. Yet in March 1811 the Transport Board specified at Greenlaw a payment equal to that usually made to clerks or craftsmen among the prisoners: '... when necessary,' the Board told the Greenlaw agent then, the depot surgeon (at that time William Hill, who had himself been a prisoner of war at Verdun from 1804 to 1809) '... is to employ a French assistant who will be allowed 6d. per day.'[131] When, however, in the winter of 1810-11 Esk Mills and Valleyfield were being hastily prepared for opening, the Transport Board had declared that there should be employed at Esk Mills 'As many French Assistant Surgeons as may be absolutely necessary—to be paid at the rate of 1s. each per diem.'[132] And John Macansh, the depot surgeon at Esk Mills, evidently nominated six French surgeons for employment there, of whom one was to work as a hospital mate but also at 1s. per day.[133] At Valleyfield at least one assistant surgeon among the prisoners appears to have sought a quid pro quo in May 1813 in return for his professional services in the depot hospital: '...the French assistant surgeon ... mentioned cannot possibly be allowed to go in and out of the prison,' the Board told the agent.[134]

The available evidence indicates that some, perhaps many or even most, of the prisoners who were given employment by the depot authorities in Scotland were employed for limited periods, sometimes for a few days only. Payment, where it was made, as appears usually to have been the case, varied between 3d. (1¼ pence) a day for labourers, 6d. (2½ pence) a day for clerks and craftsmen such as tailors or sailmakers, and normally a shilling (5 pence) a day for assistant surgeons.[135]

A distinct advantage for prisoners employed in the depot hospitals was that they enjoyed also the better rations which were provided for the patients. 'The French assistant surgeon and the surgeon's clerk, as well as all other prisoners who may be employed in the hospital, are to be entitled to the full hospital diet,' the Transport Board instructed the agent at Esk Mills soon after that depot opened in February 1811.[136] In fact, there was an official departmental form concerning this provision that had to be completed regularly and returned to the Transport Office by depot agents: 'Transmit immediately,' the Board ordered the agent at that depot, for example, in October 1813, 'the quarterly list of the French servants victualled in the hospital at Perth agreeably to the enclosed form, signed by yourself and the surgeon, from the 1st October 1812 to the 30th September 1813. This list ought to have accompanied the quarterly account of patients victualled in the hospital.'[137]

Some prisoners did not wait to be asked or directed by the depot authorities to work. From among what seem likely to have been numerous written appeals from prisoners for employment at the Scots depots, only a few survive. They indicate the eagerness, even desperation, which impelled their writers to seek work. Yet those written appeals may well have been fewer, even far fewer, than others made to the depot authorities by prisoners by word of mouth: illiterate prisoners could speak. Of the few surviving written applications one, perhaps characteristic of many others, was sent on 29 August 1812 to 'The Honourable Commanding Agent' at Perth by Eugene Guchant, a soldier, confined at 'Edinburgh Prison', who has already been encountered above. Guchant's letter, written in English, is preserved in the Andrew Johnston Collection in the National Library of Scotland. 'I beg you [sic] pardon,' he wrote, 'for the liberty which I, your most humble and most obedient servant, do take to address you with these lines to implore a favour of you which I hope you will do me when you know my motive for so doing.' Guchant explained he had experience as a nurse on board ship but was also willing to take other employment, too. '… as I can speak, write and read the English tongue well enough, I most humbly beg of you, Sir, for the kindness to be so good as to give me an employ in the hospital as a Nurse-major if there be any such employ unfilled, or when there shall be any, or an employ of storekepeer. You may be well persuaded, Sir, that if you were pleased to indulge me so far, I will do all my endeavour to deserve such a kindness by all the faithfulness and activity I am capable of, or else, if you or any of your acquaintance had any occasion for a servant, I may assure you I would perform that employ very well. Seeing I have been in the service of a gentleman in France and as I have no relations, nor anything that can attract me to France, I would willingly remain in England all my days, Sir, if I was so happy as to receive so great a kindness from you. I would endeavour to show all my thankful for it.' Whether Guchant's application was granted is not known.[138] On the same day as Guchant wrote, so did a prisoner at Valleyfield, M.J.S. Priere, a seaman aged 26, captured on the frigate *Amphitrite* in 1809. Four of Priere's letters have survived, as has already been observed. Priere in his letter of 29 August 1812, addressed to Andrew Johnston at Perth, to which a couple of months earlier Captain Moriarty had been transferred from Valleyfield as agent, offered himself as an interpreter or translator: 'I beg leave to offer you my services at Perth, if you can obtain me, a word from you to Captn M[oriarty] will do much. You may be perhaps at a loss, especially about the Italian, Spanish and Portuguese languages. I have wrote to Captain M. through the same bearer, but I don't much depend on Captn M.'s memory.'[139] Priere was unsuccessful. The bitterness he had expressed in his earlier letter to a clerk on the hulk *San Antonio* at Portsmouth in June 1811 from Valleyfield, where Priere had written of his failure to find employment as a clerk at the depot as 'our agent doesn't employ any French clerks at present', was unlikely to have been diminished by his further failure to secure a transfer to and employment at Perth.

Not to Andrew Johnston but to the agent Captain Moriarty himself at Perth was addressed a letter in January 1813 from Jean Dals. A soldier in the 14th line regiment, who had been captured at sea four and a half years earlier, Dals had arrived from Portsmouth in August 1812 at the depot. His letter, he explained, was the second he had written to the agent in his attempt to secure appointment as a barber at the depot—to the first he had received no reply. 'I shall discharge my duty with complete integrity: my actual job is that of barber.' Whether Dals' qualifications, experience, and perseverance secured him a job at Perth shaving his fellow prisoners and cutting their hair is not known. Dals, born at Darsc (or Darx?), and aged 21 when he wrote, remained at Perth until the general repatriation in June 1814.[140] Finally, a letter pleading for a job not for the writer himself but for a fellow prisoner, was sent from Valleyfield in August 1812 by a prisoner named de Maillier to Andrew Johnston at Perth depot. The fellow prisoner on whose behalf de Maillier made his plea was named Grouet. Grouet, about to be transferred from Valleyfield to Perth, had already been a prisoner for seven years. 'At present,' wrote de Maillier, 'he is without any ressources at all. You would render him a very great service if you were to give him a job as a supervisor. No one deserves more than he does. He's an honest man who enjoys general esteem.' Whether de Maillier's plea on behalf of Grouet proved successful is also not known.[141]

Employment in the depots in Scotland must therefore have been for those few prisoners who were given it a godsend for their physical and mental welfare, especially for those who languished in captivity for many years. Moreover, so far as the available evidence indicates, it was usually paid employment, even if the payments were as meagre as 3d. or 6d. a day for most of those given work by the depot authorities or, in a few cases, by the contractors who supplied the prisoners with their rations of food, or even in those other cases where, as recalled by Marote-Carrier at Valleyfield, prisoners employed by their fellow prisoners were paid partly or wholly in kind. Although some, perhaps many, even most, of those employments were not for extended periods of years or months but for only a few days, they helped at least for a time to keep the wolf from the door. The wolf could appear in many forms, among them boredom, penury, lassitude, demoralisation, as well as depression and other illnesses.

17

Money; Miserables; Disobedience and Discipline

Money could not buy the release and repatriation of a prisoner but it could obviously make a crucial contribution to his well-being within the depot. Some prisoners, like Marote-Carrier with his thirteen louis, no doubt entered on their captivity with some money, if not in their pockets then, like him, hidden in their boots or elsewhere about their person or their clothing.[1] Money, as has been seen, might also be acquired in the depots through paid employment by the authorities or fellow prisoners, by making things and selling them at the depot markets, by successful gambling, or even by forging and uttering banknotes. But money was also received by some prisoners from their families or friends at home, in at least one case from their government or prince through their former regiment, and in at least one other from bystanders watching them trudge up from Leith to Edinburgh and on to the Penicuik depots. Danish prisoners in the Scots depots, as those two inmates of Greenlaw, Sergeant Major Beaudoin and Captain Paul Andreas Kaald testify, received regular payments from their government; and it is possible, though unlikely, that the American merchant seamen who found themselves briefly confined at Greenlaw after the outbreak of the War of 1812 received while they were there some financial support from the United States government.[2]

Seven weeks after he arrived as a prisoner at Greenlaw in November 1808, the Norwegian 'Dane' Captain Kaald noted in his diary: 'Mr Fraser [the depot clerk] was here today and gave 4 shillings and 6 pence to each Danish prisoner. From now on every Danish prisoner will get 14 pence per week as decided—which is a little help, thank God.' Ten days later Kaald wrote: 'Today is one of the best days we have had in the prison, since all the Danish Captains and Officers received 3 shillings and 6 pence weekly from 5th December. This was a great help.'[3] Another entry in his diary on 18 January said: 'Today we got the money granted to us by the Consul in London.' Between then and the end of his captivity in August 1810 Kaald noted on a further fifteen occasions payments, at monthly, fortnightly or three weekly intervals, made through the depot authorities to the Danish prisoners at Greenlaw. It is possible, even likely, that on several occasions other such payments were made but Kaald did not trouble to note them because they had by then become so routine. In addition there were several windfalls for the Danes at Greenlaw. In May 1809, Captain Moller who, having apparently been released from captivity, was about to sail in command of an Icelandic ship to Denmark, visited Greenlaw before his departure and 'brought £5 to be divided among the Danish prisoners. All received 3 pence.'[4] Five weeks later, in addition to their regular payments, there were gifted to them '3 shillings per man as a treat from Denmark and Norway.'[5] The distribution in September 1809 of another donation led, however, to a rumpus among the Danish prisoners. When, in the presence of Kaald and two other sea captains, £30 was being distributed 'among those most in need ... all the others who didn't receive anything were angry about it and took the money forcibly from those who had received it, and dealt it out evenly among all, except the Captains. So they all received 14 pence each.'[6] Shortly before Christmas that year 'every Danish and Norwegian prisoner of war accepted 18 pence each, which will be a treat from Denmark, sent through Messrs Wolff and Dorville in London to our commissioner, to be shared among us sinners at the Christmas Feast. Thanks to whoever they are,' wrote Kaald.[7] A month later a further 1s.4d. was sent from Denmark for every Danish prisoner. Then three shillings were sent in May; and, as already observed, a further 3s each in July 1810 to his fellow countrymen who were prisoners were sent by the Danish pastor in London, Ulrik Frederik Rosing, a clergyman who 'has done great things for the prisoners', and who also promised to send 2s. worth of tobacco to every man.[8] Kaald himself was sent three guineas in a letter from a friend and fellow captain in Bergen in July, but when he received the letter the money had been removed from it and, Kaald supposed, slipped into the pocket of the depot clerk.[9]

When Danish seamen in captivity at Greenlaw (rather than at Edinburgh Castle, as was reported in the press), had, as already observed, sent to their king in Denmark in 1810 a model ship made with bones but whose sails and ropes were made from their own hair, the king ordered the ship to be exhibited at Copenhagen and the profit from the exhibition to be sent to the prisoners who had made it.[10]

For the Danish and Norwegian prisoners at Greenlaw or other Scots depots, therefore, receiving monies from their government or other sources mentioned made to their well-being a contribution perhaps comparable with that made by Red Cross parcels to the welfare and morale of British and Commonwealth prisoners in German or Italian hands in the Second World War.[11]

The extent of support from Denmark for its subjects in captivity in Britain during the Napoleonic Wars was suggested in an entry in Kaald's diary in June 1809: 'It is reported from Copenhagen that in May there were 3,547 Danish prisoners in England [i.e., Britain] and the weekly assistance amounts to £360 sterling.'[12]

It was such financial support for his Danish fellow prisoners, contrasting as it did so sharply with the absence of any similar support from the French government for members of its own forces in captivity, that prompted bitter reflections by Sergeant Major Beaudoin at Greenlaw. 'The Danes,' he noted in his diary, 'belonged to a poor nation which, however, safeguarded the existence of these prisoners. They received four sols daily, privateer captains and merchants received six pence, and a nation like France gave [us] no help; and as the price of our recompense we might be a dozen years in prison!'[13]

More fortunate than their French comrades in arms were those German prisoners from the Hesse-Darmstadt regiment who, captured in April 1812 while fighting as part of Napoleon's forces at the siege of Badajoz, found themselves a few months later confined in Perth depot.[14] In October that year Captain Moriarty, agent at Perth, received the following letter from Colonel Rechler, commanding officer of the Hesse-Darmstadt regiment, who was himself then a parole prisoner at Llonry Uyn [or Llanuyllyn or Llanogllyn?] in Montgomeryshire: 'Sir, Being informed that some hundred soldiers of the German Regiment Hesse Darmstadt—prisoners of war since the taking of Badajoz—have been moved from Dartmoor and Plymouth to the Depot in Scotland, I address to you this letter on purpose to beg you to send me a namely [sic] and accurate list of all the prisoners of the mentioned Regiment who are now in Scotland. Having received money from my Government two months ago for distributing them [sic] among all the individuals of this Regiment I can not do anything for those who are in Scotland before I am in possession of the namely list which I desire to receive as soon as possible. Whereas it would be too much trouble for you to make the list, I have written few lines [sic] to one of the Corporals, giving him an order to write it and to remit it to you. I hope you will permit him to do so. I expect your answer with impatience and have the honour to be [Signed] Rechler.' The 'few lines' addressed 'to one of the Corporals of the german [sic] Regt of Hesse Darmstadt, prisoners of war in Scotland,' and signed by Col. Rechler on 24 October, then followed thus: 'I the undersigned Colonel of the German Regiment Hesse Darmstadt, prisoner on parole in this town, hereby charge one of the Corporals who is among the prisoners of war of that Regiment in Scotland, to draw up a namely and accurate list of all the individuals of the mentioned Regiment who are with him there. It is very necessary to observe by every one of the Soldiers to which Bataillon and Company he belonged to. The List will you remit to your Agent. As soon as I am in possession of it, I will send you through the hand of your Agent the money which I received from our Government for the individuals of the Regiment.' The outcome was a foolscap sheet headed 'The prince of Hesse Darmstadt Regiment. A nominated list of every man who are present and are to receive the money which has been sent by their Sovereign'. The list, written on both sides of the sheet, gives the names of 95 men, all of whom are said to be in the '1st Bataillon': 34 in the Grenadier Company (including two corporals), 17 in the 1st Company (including three corporals), 21 in the 2nd, 16 in the 3rd (including one corporal), and seven in the 4th. One man in the 4th Company was said to be dead and no payment was made in his case. The corporals, of whom there were six, apparently received £2 each, all the ordinary soldiers, including the Grenadiers, £1 each—except that one Grenadier received £1.10s., a soldier in the 1st Company £1.6s., and another in the 2nd Company £3. The total sum distributed was £104.16.0. All the men signed their names—or put their mark—against the amount they received: 57 signed their names, 38 put their mark. A note written on the list by Andrew Johnston, the depot chief clerk, says: 'This is the list required by Colonel Rechler—only part of it. There is [sic] about Six Hundred and Fifty of them in the Depot, Perth. The entire regiment of Hesse Darmstadt were taken prisoners. They were the quietest men in the prison.'[15]

Another source of a little money for some of the prisoners was indicated by the privateer lieutenant Marote-Carrier.[16] When he and other prisoners destined for confinement at Esk Mills were landed early in February 1811 from HMS *Vanguard* at Leith, some among the great number of spectators, who 'appeared to us more sympathetic than in England', watching the prisoners march under an escort of troops through Leith 'threw over the top of the line of soldiers pieces of money of all kinds.' The column of prisoners and its escorts marched quickly from Leith to Edinburgh, where in Parliament Square, beside St Giles' Cathedral, they halted for a respite before continuing their march out to Esk Mills at Penicuik. 'We were enclosed within a triple ring of troops, the last line was made up of cavalry,' said Marote-Carrier. 'The crowd was all around, it packed the square in which we were placed. At the windows of the prosperous looking buildings that circled the square we saw ladies in full finery who looked at us from afar ... We asked [the guards] for something to drink, pleading a raging thirst caused by the long march we had made, but we were bluntly refused. We were obliged to take the dirty trampled snow to slake our thirst. The exclamations of pity from the crowd redoubled on all sides, and pieces of money, sixpences and shillings, fell in greater abundance than during the march.'[17]

There is no reason to doubt the accuracy of Marote-Carrier's recollection that money was thrown to the prisoners by townspeople lining the streets of their march through Leith and Edinburgh. No other evidence is known to survive of similar 'pour-oots' of money for any of those many other columns of prisoners marched during the war from Leith to confinement in the depots at Penicuik or Edinburgh Castle, or from Dundee, Kirkcaldy or Burntisland to Perth. But it is difficult to believe that in receiving such windfalls of copper and silver Marote-Carrier's column was uniquely fortunate. How much was thrown and how much of it individual prisoners were able to pick up for themselves it is impossible to say, but even a copper or two could help ease the privations endured by the captives.

For most prisoners, however, other than perhaps the Danes and Norwegians and the men of the Hesse-Darmstadt regiment, whatever money they received as gifts during their captivity came from their own families or friends (or, for those relatively few prisoners wealthy enough to have such, their own bank accounts) at home. At Valleyfield, for example, two Belgian soldiers, Henri Mossoux from Warzée and Laurent Maquet from Jupille, villages respectively 22 kilometres south-west and 5 east of Liège, were among prisoners who received money from home. Mossoux received from his parents at the turn of the year 1811-12 the sum of 27 livres 12 sous (roughly £1.2.8d. or £1.14). Writing from Valleyfield on 15 January 1812 to thank his parents, Mossoux said the money had relieved him from poverty and also enabled him to continue his education in which he was busying himself as much as possible. The money, although a small amount, which Maquet had received from his parents had, he said in his letter of thanks on 25 March 1813, nonetheless been able to last him six months and had contributed to enabling him to learn to write.[18]

The uniquely surviving ledger of monies received by prisoners at Perth, however, provides the most detailed picture for any Scots depot. Each page of the ledger has five columns headed thus: From Whence for Whom, Number on General Entry Book, Amount Received, Amount Paid—Date and Sum, Signature. The ledger, which has 230 pages, lists 4,602 separate payments made to prisoners between 2 September 1812 and 26 May 1814, within a few weeks after which latter date all the prisoners had been released and repatriated. Some prisoners received more than one payment. But even after making a generous allowance for them what the ledger indicates is that at least half of the aggregate of 7,761 (or, after deducting recaptured escapees, the approximate net total of 7,700) prisoners received money from home during their captivity at Perth.[19]

Some of the amounts received were quite small—a few shillings only. Thus several prisoners each received from their families at home five shillings in May 1814, no doubt to help them make their way home on their release from captivity in the following few weeks. No. 1988 Prosper Le Clerc or Leclaire and No. 7694 Jean le Soeuf or Soiffe, who each received his five shillings on 11 May 1814, were among those prisoners.[20] Several others received six shillings each. Behind the gathering and sending of such small amounts there doubtless lay much scraping and saving and many anxieties on the part of those prisoners' families and friends at home.

At the other extreme a few prisoners at Perth, mainly officers confined there for breaking their parole, received large amounts of money from home. The outstanding example was Auguste Petry, a lieutenant in the 3rd Hussars. Captured in early autumn 1810 while serving in the Peninsula with Marshal Masséna's army, Petry had arrived at Perth in September 1812 from Valleyfield, where he had been sent after breaking his parole and escaping from Dumfries.[21] In the thirteen months between September 1812 and October 1813 during which he was confined at Perth, Petry received from home in six successive payments a total of no less than £134.9.4. His regimental comrade, friend and fellow parole-breaker Lieutenant Charles Hivert, born at Montelbar and aged 29, received in three successive payments during that same period almost as much as Petry: £126.0.1.[22] Even so, it was not Petry or Hivert but two other prisoners to whom the largest single sums were sent, although unlike Petry and Hivert neither appears to have received any others: Barthelemy Pascal received £60 in March 1813, and J. J. Dormier £66 in December that year.[23] Including Petry, Hivert, Pascal and Dormier, there were at Perth fourteen prisoners who received from home large sums in a single payment ranging from £25 upwards to Dormier's £66.

To put into some perspective these large sums of money received by a few prisoners at Perth (and also, it may reasonably be assumed, by a few at the other Scots depots for which, however, no payments ledgers are known to survive) it is worth recalling that in Scotland at that time the earnings of coalminers, 'a well-paid group', were between four and five shillings (20 to 25 pence) a day, the weekly earnings of cotton spinners (described as 'among the better off' workers) were probably rather more than £1, and in 1812 weekly average wages in ten trades other than handloom weaving were 18s.4½d. (92 pence).[24] Thus Petry, Hivert, Pascal, Dormier and the other ten prisoners at Perth who received the largest amounts of money acquired thereby sums equal to between half and two and a half times the annual earnings of the best paid workers in Scotland.

The overwhelming majority of the amounts received from home by prisoners at Perth were of course much less than those sent to the fourteen there who enjoyed such large sums. Of 145 individual payments recorded in the ledger's first twelve pages alone, for example, covering the fifteen weeks from 2 September to 14 December 1812, the amounts received were:

Between £50 and £60:	1 (Hivert – £53)
Between £40 and £50:	Nil
Between £30 and £40:	1
Between £20 and £30:	1
Between £15 and £20:	5
Between £10.1.0 and £15:	3
Between £5.1.0 and £10:	13
Between £2.1.0 and £5:	49
Between £1 and £2:	48
Less than £1:	24

Thus in the first four months Perth depot was open those prisoners receiving £20 or more represented only 2 per cent of the 145 recipients, those receiving £5.1.0 or more represented 16.5 per cent, and those receiving between 5 shillings and £5 represented 83.4 per cent.

The incidence of payments recorded in the ledger indicates it was only from May 1813, nine months after the depot had opened, by which time no doubt the whereabouts of many of the prisoners had become known to their families and friends at home and the arrangements for sending money to them completed, that the number of prisoners receiving money began to increase. Thus in September 1812, the first month the ledger recorded payments, only a dozen were made, but in December more than 30, in March 1813 about 140, in May almost 240, and thereafter they remained at a high level. Between the beginning of March 1814, when it was obvious the war was at last ending, and the end of May, when the general release and repatriation of prisoners was imminent (and had even begun in the cases of a few specially favoured prisoners), there was a torrent of some 919 payments.

Of all the prisoners at Perth who received such sums of money in 1812-14 no fewer than 1,322 were illiterate, as was shown by their signing their receipt in the payments ledger with their mark, a cross. The overwhelming majority of those 1,322 prisoners received only one payment, but 215 of them received two, 39 three, and seven four.

The total sums received from home by prisoners at Perth during the 23 months the depot existed amounted, according to the payments ledger, to £9,002.5.3. What the prisoners spent the money on is of course not recorded in the payments ledger, but it may be safely assumed that food, drink and tobacco absorbed much or most of at least the smaller sums sent. A total of that magnitude must have made some contribution to the economy of the city of Perth and its hinterland.

Some of the money they received from home was almost certainly husbanded by some prisoners for use in escapes. The ledger provides several examples of money taken from prisoners after they had made unsuccessful attempts to shake the dust of the depot from their feet. Lieutenant Dominique Dewatre (or Delvatre) of the privateer *Le Figaro* was one. Born at Calais and aged 22, Dewatre was captured in the North Sea in 1811 and arrived at Perth little more than a year later, in September 1812, from Greenlaw. Dewatre hardly waited to acquire dusty feet at Perth. A fortnight after his arrival he 'escaped over the wall ... retaken in the adjoining field'. From his pockets the depot authorities then removed '£4.9.6, in silver.' But it was paid back to him by the end of that month in two instalments of £2.4.0 and £2.5.6.[25] There was an interesting collection of gold and silver coins likewise removed by the depot authorities 'from the following Prisoners attempting Escape 22 February 1813: Captain Croesec, 2 double Napoleons, 8 single louis, 1 English guinea, 1 Portuguese [sic] in Silver; D. Fleury, 4 double louis, 13 single ditto; Victor Cretien, 5 single louis, 1 Spanish pure [sic] same size in Silver; Raquiet [or Raquet], 19s. in silver.'[26] How much of that haul had reached those prisoners from home since their arrival at Perth it is impossible to say but it seems hardly likely that all of it had done so.

It was not only money returned later to unsuccessful escapers but also all money received from home in sums greater than two or three pounds that was doled out to prisoners in instalments. 'With respect to the Weekly Sum to be paid to the Prisoners out of the Money belonging to them,' the Transport Board told, for example, its agent at Valleyfield in April 1812, 'we refer you to the 31st Article of your Instructions.'[27] It was at Valleyfield, where he was confined for 18 months until his transfer in September 1812 to Perth, that Marote-Carrier himself encountered that administrative instruction or regulation. Told by his wife in her letter to him that she was sending him 50 napoleons (equal to about 1,000 francs or roughly £50), Marote-Carrier was aggrieved to find that the depot authorities passed to him only £2 sterling in paper money. He sought an interview with the agent, Captain Moriarty. 'The hour for the interview,' Marote-Carrier long afterward recalled, '… came at last. I hurried into the poky little shack which served as … reception room. It was only after several formalities that I appeared in front of the agent. It was the first time that I had recourse to him, so the wrinkling of eyebrows habitual to him and the air of severity imprinted on his face intimidated me a little. However, full of confidence in the justice of my complaint I screwed up my courage and … awaited the pleasure of the agent in questioning me. Some minutes passed without his addressing a word to me. After eyeing me up and down with a haughty air, he turned back towards his table where he leafed through some papers, muttering to himself. At last he said to me in a rather gruff voice: "What do you want of me?" "Commandant, I have a complaint to make to you." "A complaint. Let's hear it! Quickly! And first, what's your name?" I gave him my name. He looked at me in such a peculiar way that I thought he was sceptical about the subject of my request. "Well!" he said, "speak quickly and no beating about the bush. I have little time to waste." I began to speak to him about my 50 napoleons and did so with the utmost brevity I could manage. He appeared little impressed with the presentation I made to him about my unfortunate situation, and after some minutes of reflection he said: "I have received the sum of which you speak but it is not in napoleons nor other coin but in paper pounds sterling." "Dare I beg you, commandant, to pass it to me?" "Ah!" he said, "that's something else! The government prohibits sizeable distributions of money to the prisoners." "But," I replied, "that money belongs to me!" That objection seemed to annoy him. "Agreed," he said, "but I can only conform to my instructions and they prohibit me from passing it to you." "So you are going to keep it!" I replied in a voice sufficiently clear and sharp that he understood the accusation I was levelling against him. "Keep it? Yes! In part, at least. The needs you have here are not so extraordinary that you will not have a sufficient sum to meet them. And who knows if sometimes you would not misuse it if you held it freely?"' Marote-Carrier lost his temper, exclaimed, "'Oh, well, keep it!"', and made for the door, but Moriarty, his voice distinctly softer, called him back. "'What the devil," he said to me with a smile, "you take offence over nothing! You haven't understood. I have no intention of keeping your money. No," he said, "only I will pass it to you in a series of sums … Each week you will receive something to meet your needs, and it will be a reasonable sum. I will pass to you each time two pounds sterling. That's enough, isn't it?"'[28]

Marote-Carrier's experience at Valleyfield was exemplified by some of the entries in the Perth payments ledger. Thus when £12.8.0 was sent there on 2 September 1812 for Auguste Petry it was paid to him not in a single sum but in six weekly instalments: one of £2, three of £2.2.0 each, and two of £2.1.0 each. When a further sum of £13.11.1 was sent to Petry on 15 October it, too, was paid him in seven weekly instalments beginning that day. Was it, however, because he had run up pressing debts to that amount that Petry's regimental comrade and friend Lieutenant Charles Hivert was promptly paid £25 from a sum of £53.15.0 sent to him on 2 October 1812, although the remainder was only paid him in thirteen weekly instalments of £2.2.0 and one (the last, on 14 January 1813) of £1.9.0?

Concern about the possible misuse of such sums received by prisoners was expressed in the prohibition by 'the government' or Transport Board of 'sizeable distributions' to them, to which Captain Moriarty had referred in Marote-Carrier's interview with him. That concern arose mainly from the prospect of escapes being thus funded, with bribing of guards conceivably included as items in the expenditure columns of escapers' budgets. Determined as they were to prevent or at least to deter attempts at escape the Transport Board and the depot authorities were faced with a dilemma over the arrival of these sums of money for prisoners. Part of the solution appeared to be to hand over the money to the prisoners in limited instalments. That might be effectual so far as the great majority of prisoners were concerned. But, short either of impounding for the duration of the war or paying in very much smaller instalments over a far longer period the large amounts sent to such a relatively wealthy prisoner at Perth in 1812-13 as Auguste Petry, how could the authorities prevent him from rapidly accumulating sizeable funds that might be used in attempts at escape, in which indeed, according to Marote-Carrier, Petry certainly was deeply involved?

Not all transfers of money from home to prisoners in the depots in Scotland were smoothly implemented, as Marote-Carrier and his wife found when she, and other wives of prisoners, entrusted such money to an English merchant at Calais named Knighton who proved a thoroughly unscrupulous embezzler of their funds and was never heard of again.[29] A surviving letter of 5 September 1813 from the brother in France of Jean Baptiste Didiot, a soldier in the 26th regiment of Horse Artillery, prisoner No. 3,835 at Perth, indicates that there were no doubt in every Scots depot prisoners who did not receive monies sent them from home or who had to endure unexplained delays in their safe arrival. 'We have just received your letter dated from Perth 20 July last,' Didiot's brother wrote him. 'We are all five of us saddened to see you have not received your money, but we hope you will receive it ...' Didiot's family, however, did not sit idly by. They enlisted the help of Thomas Innes, 'bien aimable homme', a British prisoner of war confined at Verdun. Innes wrote on 24 September 1813 to his brother William at Tweed Place, Stockbridge, Edinburgh, pointing out that he had already asked him to pay Didiot at Perth 50 francs (which he says was £2.1.8 in sterling). But if he has not yet done so he is to send Didiot the money at once, get a receipt from him for it and send the receipt to him, Thomas, at Verdun. Whether Didiot duly received his money is not known.[30]

There were perhaps inevitably some cases, too, where sums of money from home were wrongly delivered to some other prisoner with the same or a similar name. 'Sir, I your most humble and obedient servant,' wrote Gaspard Foux, a soldier in captivity at Perth, to the agent there on 19 January 1814, in English that was not quite perfect, 'do take this liberty to implore your sensibility and Justice and to beg a favour of you which I hope you will be so good as to do me when you know my motives for so doing, sir. I am informed by my friend he has see my name on the last list what his came and that Depot. I have been called for a letter from my family by which I am informed they have sent to me the sum of £120 first sum, the last sum £140. But, Sir, finding By my letter what I have writing to my father I was to receive that sum before the month of October. But, sir, I am informed by my friend during the elapse of six months, as it may be certified by the man or men what he has received my first sum £120 more a letter whom these sum here directed to Gaspard Foux, soldier of the 27th Regiment of Line, the man what he has received my first sum he his same Nicolas Naws these one he has Received the sum of £120 more my letter. one another he has Received the sum of 1240 £. Those on he his name Jame Omleur, sir. I therefore most humbly beg of you sir to be so good as to order me to be brought before you and I hope if you will be pleased to do me this kindness that I will be able to justify myself ... Gaspard Foux, Soldier of the 27th Regiment Line, No.6 of Prison, No. 4082.' The outcome of Foux's plea is unknown. If indeed he had been sent £260 in two lots by his family it must have been the largest payment made to any prisoner at Perth.[31] Another apparently similar case was that of a prisoner at Portsmouth named C. Dufour, for whom a sum of £27.1.0 was misdelivered in January 1814 to Michel Dufour, a prisoner at Perth. 'The four pounds paid Michel Dufour by instalments he is to repay me from the first money coming to him, and he has given me an acknowledgement to that purpose. [Signed] A. Johnston [depot chief clerk].'[32]

'To send me money,' Laurent Maquet, a prisoner at Valleyfield, wrote to his family at Jupille, near Liège, 'you must go to some merchant who has correspondents in England.'[33] Many, perhaps most, of the transfers of money from home to prisoners in the Scots depots, as well as those in England, were handled by the bankers Perregaux, Lafitte & Co. in Paris and by Messrs Coutts & Co. in London. But the Perth payments ledger, as well as the recollections of Marote-Carrier, show that other bankers, merchants or lawyers were also engaged in the transfers.[34] A letter in November 1811 from the Transport Board to J.W. Croker, secretary of the Admiralty, explained the mechanics and extent of the transfers: '... we have for some time past been in the practice of forwarding monies received by Messrs Coutts & Co., Bankers, for the use of prisoners of war at the several places of parole and depots in this country; but ... as these payments are now become very considerable, amounting to a sum not less than between £20,000 and £30,000 per annun, we thought it proper to inform Messrs Coutts & Co. that we did not consider it adviseable to take upon ourselves the responsibility attached to the disbursement of so large a sum of money, and suggested that they would therefore adopt some other mode of making their remittances to French prisoners, offering to them at the same time assistance in our power on the occasion. Those gentlemen, however, have signified to us that as they have no profit in the business they cannot continue to conduct it without the assistance of the agents of this Department, and under our guarantee. We therefore submit the same to their Lordships' [of the Admiralty] consideration and request you to signify to us their Lordships' direction upon the subject ...'[35] Less than a month later the Transport Board sent out this circular to all its depot and parole agents, including those in Scotland: 'It not being intended that any money remitted from France for the prisoners in this country shall in future be paid to them through the medium of this Office, we direct you to cause such payments to be made as you shall be requested by Messrs Coutts & Co. to make from time to time to the prisoners of war in your charge, returning to those gentlemen the receipts, which they will transmit to you in blank, properly signed by the respective prisoners, as expeditiously as possible, under a cover addressed to this Office, and the bill drawn by you on Messrs Coutts & Co. for the amount after you shall have so done will of course be paid on presentation. You will further conform to such other regulations as Messrs Coutts & Co. may think fit to adopt respecting such payments, provided they do not militate against any directions which have already been given to you by this Office. You will further observe that all your correspondence with Messrs

Coutts & Co., as also the signed rceipts, are to be sent to this Office by post, under a cover separate from your letters to us. The business regarding the remittances of merchants and others for the prisoners is notwithstanding the above regulation to be conducted as heretofore.'[36] Three months afterward the Transport Board, through which some relief monies were also forwarded to British prisoners of war in France, acknowledged receiving from Croker his letter dated 25 February, 'transmitting to us, by direction of the ... Lords Commissioner of the Admiralty, a copy of a letter from Messrs Coutts & Co. containing a plan for regulating the remittances made through their House to French prisoners of war, and expressing their Lordships' desire that the payments in future should be made on the principle agreed upon between their Secretary, the Chairman of this Board, and Mr Coutts ... as stated in the above mentioned letter of Messrs Coutts & Co.; also acquainting us that their Lordships are pleased to authorize us to employ an additional clerk to compensate [for] the trouble which may be imposed on this office by the present arrangement. ... we shall immediately make the necessary arrangement for carrying on this service agreeably to their Lordships' direction; but as the French prisoners in this country actually derive an advantage of at least 30 per cent by the rate of exchange on all money remitted to them, and the British prisoners in France suffer a loss to the same extent on the sums sent to them from hence, we submit ... whether it be not reasonable that all expenses attending the proposed arrangement should be defrayed by the French prisoners themselves; and if their Lordships should approve of this suggestion we propose to make a deduction of two per cent from all sums remitted through this office for the use of French prisoners for the purpose not only of paying the additional expense that this arrangement will occasion in our Office but also of making some allowance to the several agents who are to have the trouble and responsibility of paying the money to the prisoners. We think it proper to add that there is no reason to believe that the French Government will have any objection to such a deduction being made, because in the last War they made an allowance of 5 per cent to our agents for all the money which passed through their hands.'[37] The Transport Board circularised all its agents a few days later, informing them of the Admiralty's instructions that the monies sent through Coutts & Co. for French prisoners in Britain should be made through the medium of the Transport Office, and adding: '... we desire that you will pay to the prisoners in your charge such sums of money as you shall from time to time be informed by Mr Christie, the clerk whom we have ordered to attend to this business, are intended for them respectively, drawing bills upon him for your reimbursement and corresponding with him relative to these remittances.'[38]

Gold sent to prisoners in Scots depots (or at least at Valleyfield and Perth) was or might be changed into paper money by Jews, according to Lieutenant

347

Marote-Carrier. Marote-Carrier himself complained that at Valleyfield when he had received nine louis in paper money sent by his wife through a London banker, 'I lost a good deal in the processing of the paper, which produced for me only 22 francs per pound sterling, whereas gold was exchanged at an extremely advantageous rate. Thus a guinea [£1.1.0] was exchanged for 27 or 28 francs by the Jews who came to the prison and who argued covetously among themselves when they could procure some.'[39] After Marote-Carrier and some 66 other prisoners, almost all like him privateersmen, were transferred in early September 1812 from Valleyfield to Perth, he found that at the latter depot 'As at Valleyfield Jews came to change the prisoners' gold for paper notes. They gave up to 28 and 30 shillings per louis.'[40]

Money-changing also attracted at Perth, however, the intervention of an unnamed prisoner who had been a shipmate of Marote-Carrier on the privateer *Aventurier*. 'He offered 26 shillings per louis to those who wished to do business with him,' recalled Marote-Carrier. 'For some time he managed quite well and fulfilled his engagements scrupulously. The day before the visit of a Jew whose probity was well known and who never missed coming on his rounds on certain days, the money-changer gathered the gold and the next day reimbursed his trustees in full. He won the confidence of a large number of prisoners to such an extent that one day he received on the security of his word between eighty and a hundred louis. He approached me, too. I was too cautious and prudent to risk the little money I had or that I had gathered amid so many difficulties by my own hard work. So I emphatically declined to confide anything to him. It was a lucky inspiration. Eight days passed after the visit of the Jew without any of the creditors of the so-called money-changer being paid. There was a general uprising against him. The deputy commandant [i.e., chief clerk] Johnston, once informed of the facts, made the Jew come and confronted him with the accused, who did not dare maintain that he had remitted the gold to him. Mr Johnston, convinced of his guilt, handed him over to the prisoners to deal with. A sort of tribunal was formed by his victims before which he was led bound at his feet and hands. He shamelessly refused to say what had become of the funds entrusted to him and kept protesting that they were no longer in his possession. His judges, angered by his deceit, condemned him to receive 200 strokes of the cane. The punishment was inflicted on him in the yard. Tied to a post, he suffered the 200 strokes without his protests and cries reducing the fatal number by a single one. The poor devil almost died and endured three months of suffering in hospital.'[41]

If the sending by French families of money to their fathers, sons and brothers in captivity in Scotland might be construed as giving help, however unintentionally, to Britain by contributing in effect to its economy, other consequences might on the other hand include those suggested in a report in a Scots newspaper concerning similar help sent to British prisoners of war in France. Reporting a collection for the latter of £26.8.10d. at a church in Dumfries, the paper added that, '£13,000, collected from different quarters of the United Kingdom, were last year sent over to the prisoners of rank, and by them distributed among their more indigent brethren, when 6,000 received occasional relief. Of these several were snatched from the jaws of the grave, and others were saved from the unnatural alternative of engaging in the service of the enemy.'[42]

One particular group of prisoners in the Scots and other depots among whom few if any did choose 'the unnatural alternative of engaging in the service of the enemy,' but several of whom, alas, could not be snatched 'from the jaws of the grave', were those described as miserables or *rafalés*. These were men, some of whom had been demoralised by their experience of war, in some cases perhaps even before they had become prisoners, but particularly by their experience of captivity, or who in many, perhaps most, cases had become victims of their addiction to gambling. It is not certain that any of the miserables in the Scots depots had actually been members of those freebooting bands of French troops in Spain and Portugal whose military discipline had broken down and who, composed as they were of men alienated by the character of the war in the Peninsula, and others otherwise disillusioned or severely homesick or simply stragglers from their units, were known as the *démoralisés*.[43] But it is at least possible that a few had been *démoralisés* before they became, at Greenlaw, Valleyfield or Perth, *rafalés* or miserables.

More or less a universal phenomenon among the prisoners of war in the depots and on the hulks in Britain, the miserables or *rafalés* were distinguished by their visible demoralisation. They were men who had gambled away or otherwise sold off their clothing, their bedding, and often even their rations of food. For the benefit of the agent at Valleyfield who, along with his depot surgeon, had expressed concern about the miserables there, the Transport Board summed up in May 1813 its view of the nature of the problem. '... in reply to your and Mr Macansh's observations on the miserable state of the prisoners called "Raffallées" in consequence of their disposing of their Food and Clothing,' the Board declared, 'we acquaint you that this is an evil of many years' standing and unfortunately prevails at all the Depots without our having yet been able to find an effectual remedy for it. Nor were the French Agents more successful in their endeavours when [for a time during the French Revolutionary Wars] they victualled and clothed the prisoners in this country. If, however, the purchasers of the clothing and rations were discovered and punished it might check the evil in some degree, and we desire to be informed whether any and what measures are taken for this purpose, and also what further practicable measures you would propose to put a stop to this pernicious affair.'[44]

At Greenlaw the earliest reference found to what may have been the action of a miserable in selling his ration of food occurred in 1809. It was unlikely no such problem had arisen at the depot before then. But, as has been seen, it was in April that year the Board told its agent at Peebles to inform M. Jensen, a parole prisoner there, 'that his [ship's] Boy cannot be allowed parole, having conducted himself improperly at Greenlaw in selling his rations of provisions.'[45] It was certainly in the middle years of the Napoleonic Wars, even if he does not provide precise dates, when James Anton, as a militiaman doing guard duty over the prisoners at Greenlaw, observed miserables among them. 'I shall leave it to a political economist,' Anton afterward wrote, 'to determine whether there was justice done to the country, or kindness shown to the prisoners, in keeping them thus shut up unemployed to public advantage. Those prisoners were well provided for in every respect; and treated with the greatest humanity; yet to the eye of a stranger they presented a miserable picture of distress, while some of them were actually hoarding up money by the most unjustifiable means, evading taxes to which our industrious artisans had to submit, and even forging our paper currency without being arraigned. Others were actually naked, with the exception of a dirty rag as an apron—some even destitute of this; and the strangers who visited the prison commiserated [sic] the apparent distress of this miserable class, and charity was frequently bestowed on purpose to clothe their nakedness; but no sooner would this set of despicables obtain such relief than they took to the cards, dice or dominoes, and in a few hours were as poor and naked as ever. From the wretched appearance of those gamesters, casual visitors and philanthropists concluded that the fault lay in the management; but a Howard could not have made these wretches more comfortable, without having recourse to strong coercive measures; for, strange as it may appear, when they were indulged with permission to remain in their hammocks when the weather was cold, they drew the worsted out of the rugs that covered them, wound it up in balls, and sold it to the industrious knitters of mitts and left themselves without a covering by night.'[46] The only other reference found to miserables at Greenlaw occurred in a letter of May 1813 from the Transport Board to the agent at the nearby depot of Valleyfield, who was told that his 'suggestion for a detached situation from the main prison being appropriate for the confinement of prisoners in the habit of disposing of their Clothing, Provisions, etc., will be attended to in the construction of the new prison at Greenlaw.'[47] If in fact separate quarters for miserables were constructed as part of the huge new extension to Greenlaw in 1812-14 they never occupied them, for just as the new buildings were nearing completion the war ended.

No reference has been found to miserables at Edinburgh Castle, though it would be incautious to assume there were none among the prisoners there. As Esk Mills functioned as a depot for only a few weeks in February-March 1811 there was hardly time for any miserables to be identified or mentioned there; even so, at least one of its inmates, a young Dutch seaman, was, as already observed, on the edge of the slippery slope that ended three months later with his death from debility at Valleyfield.[48]

For both Valleyfield and Perth depots, however, there is much more information available about the miserables or *rafalés*. When, 18 months after the opening of Valleyfield, Commissioner Douglas of the Transport Board visited the depot early in September 1812 he reported that the agent, Captain Andrew Brown, 'is very desirous of having a part of the south west prison and a small part of the yard divided for the prisoners who are in the habit of selling their clothing. There are about 150 of that description. I saw several with only a small piece of blanket round their waists. I think it might be done at a small expense, and if the stockade be made quite close, they could not be seen by the persons walking round the prison. At present they are exposed to public view.'[49]

Partitioning one of the depot buildings at Valleyfield in order to house miserables was a theme first heard the previous spring. The agent, then Captain Moriarty, had been instructed by the Transport Board in April to that effect, and a reference in their correspondence a month later indicates partition had been duly carried out.[50] As soon as the Board received Commissioner Douglas's report on Valleyfield in early September it ordered the new agent to carry out without delay the commissioner's recommendations about partitioning.[51] When the agent suggested in May 1813 the advantages of accommodation for miserables separate from the main depot buildings, the Board, as already observed, told him provision for that would be made in the new extension then being built a mile or so down the road at Greenlaw.

Their selling of their rations of food, as well as their clothing and bedding, as a result of which at least 14 of these prisoners died there from debility or hypothermia, was a characteristic of the miserables with which the depot authorities often sought to grapple at Valleyfield.[52] The agent's buying of straw in May 1812, for example, to use in the building specially partitioned to house the miserables who were 'in the habit of making away with their Bedding', was approved by the Transport Board.[53] In what appears to be a further reference two months later to the miserables a decision by the newly appointed agent Captain Andrew Brown, in 'causing the worn Bedding to be repaired and distributed among the destitute Prisoners' was also approved by the Board.[54] Similar decisions were taken in the matter of providing the miserables with clothing. '... desire,' the Board told the agent in December 1811 after he had written naming certain prisoners, 'you will furnish the destitute Prisoners thereinmentioned with any <u>old</u> [sic] Clothes you may have in Store.' Again in August the following year the agent was instructed to provide them 'with any Clothing that may be in Store.'[55] Only a week later the agent was directed 'to supply new Clothing to a sufficient Number of Prisoners of good Character whose Clothing is worn and to give their old Clothing to the miserable Objects mentioned by you, but you are distinctly to apprize the latter that if they should dispose of these they shall not be allowed any others in lieu.'[56] The warning was repeated two months later: '… we direct you,' the Board told the agent in reply to another letter from him on the subject, 'to supply the destitute persons therein mentioned with such Clothing and Bedding as they may stand in need of to furnish them completely for the Winter but not until they shall have been separated from the other Prisoners and removed into the Place which has been prepared for their reception; after which they are not on any account whatever to be allowed to mix with the Body of the Prisoners. Whenever you may be about to supply them as above directed you will assemble them and cause an intelligent Prisoner to explain to them distinctly in their own language that they will not be furnished with any more if they should again make away with their Clothing or Bedding and thereby expose themselves to the rigours of a Winter in Scotland. They must abide the consequences of their own imprudence, however severe their sufferings may be.'[57] The miserables were the subject of a further exchange of letters a week later, in which the Board approved the agent's 'shutting up the Windows entirely in the Manner you propose and of your deferring the supply of Clothing to these Prisoners.'[58] It was again the miserables who appear to have been the subject of correspondence between Board and agent several weeks later: 'The prisoners mentioned by you cannot be new clothed, but you may supply them with old clothing or bedding.'[59] In March 1813 there were two instructions on the subject within a week from the Board to the agent. First, he was told to 'again supply the destitute prisoners with such old bedding as may be in store.' Then a few days later he was told in the sentence immediately after one dealing with clothing the destitutes (although it is possible this second sentence was intended to refer to the prisoners in general and not to the miserables only): '… you will on no account suffer yourself to be deterred by the threats or riotous conduct of the prisoners but not lose a moment in calling in the aid of the Military if necessary.'[60] At the beginning of autumn that year the agent was instructed to 'make a general issue of clothing to the "Miserables", distinctly apprizing them that if they should make away with the Articles now supplied they will not be furnished with any more until clothing shall again be due to them.'[61] In January 1814 the Board approved the agent's action in 'having supplied the miserables with an extra allowance of straw in consequence of the severity of the weather.'[62] Resort to violence by the miserables appears to have been rare, but that same month the agent was instructed that 'The miserable who threw the Stone at Player the Turnkey is ... to be confined in the Black Hole until further orders.'[63] The concern that Captain Andrew Brown, as agent at Valleyfield from the summer of 1812, repeatedly showed for the welfare of the miserables at the depot was exemplified not least in October that year when the Transport Board approved 'of your employing an additional Barber for the "Miserables" while it may be necessary ...'[64] But the correspondence of Brown and of Moriarty, his predecessor there as agent, with the Board also demonstrated the intractability of the problem which the miserables presented to the authorities.[65]

At Perth the General Entry Books identify no fewer than 168 miserables or *rafalés* among the 7,700 prisoners there. Whether identification by having the one word or the other scribbled in pencil under certain prisoners' names was systematic and comprehensive is not known: there may have been more than the 168 so marked. The first to be so described was Joseph Levalle, aged 24, born at Valdajou, a soldier in the 24th infantry regiment, who had been captured at Cadiz in November 1811, and was in the second batch of prisoners to enter Perth, arriving there on 20-21 August 1812 from Portsmouth. He remained at Perth until he was repatriated to France in the general release of the prisoners in June 1814. Four of the 168 identified miserables did not, however, ever return home: they died and were buried at Perth. One of the four was François Le Couste, aged 24 and born at Calais, a soldier in the 34th infantry regiment when he was captured at Arroyo de los Molinos in Spain in October 1811, and who two years later, having been confined there eleven months, died at Perth.[66]

The comparative lack of correspondence between the agent at Perth and the Transport Board about the miserables or *rafalés* there may suggest that Captain Moriarty was less sympathetic to their condition than was Captain Brown at Valleyfield, or that the problem at the latter was greater or more pressing than at Perth, even if there appears not to have been a marked difference in the number of miserables at the two depots. The only ostensible reference found in the official correspondence occurred in a letter in May 1813 from the Board to Moriarty, when he was told to 'supply the destitute prisoners with straw as proposed by you'.[67] The contemporary Perth historian Penny, however, may well himself have seen the miserables among the prisoners about whom he wrote: '... there was another class who gambled away every thing, even the clothes from their bodies; and some of them were to be seen wandering about with a bit of blanket round them, without any other covering.'[68]

Penny's observation was confirmed and amplified by that articulate privateersman, himself a prisoner in 1812-14 at Perth, Lieutenant Marote-Carrier. If his recollection thirty years later was accurate then there were twice as many miserables or *rafalés* at Perth than had one or other of those words pencilled at their names in the Entry Books. Marote-Carrier also added to what was known about action by the agent, Captain Moriarty, concerning the miserables. 'Several of us,' Marote-Carrier recalled, 'despite the trouble in which they found themselves, were consumed with an unbridled passion for gambling. Three or four hundred unfortunates were thus despoiled not only of their clothes but even of their blankets that they had played for and lost after dyeing them and converting them into pieces of clothing ... [They] had been so badly affected by gambling that all that covered their bodies were shreds of material, and they shivered terribly even at the height of summer ... These unfortunate men had not, however, given up their sad passion, and having nothing more to gamble with they came to the point of risking their daily ration of food on a throw of the dice or on the chance combination of a game of cards. The commandant [Captain Moriarty] having learnt of these excesses resolved to put an end to them and had all the card games, dice, etc., seized. He did not make a new distribution of clothing to them as he feared he would not be compensated for the loss, but docked something from their daily ration and applied it to their payment of their clothing. He brought all of them together afterwards in the lower room of prison No. 2 which he assigned to them as their accommodation and which from then on was known as the *Salle des Raffalés* [The *Rafalés'* Room]. Despite everything they continued to gamble away their food, so much so that they grew thin and wasted away, most of them in an appalling manner. One morning one of them was found dead. The corpse was transported to the hospital, an autopsy carried out, and the doctors declared him dead from starvation. They had found in his stomach only a herring head scarcely chewed.

'It was necessary to take effective measures to bring this horrible state of things to an end. We elected four strong soldiers, all expert cudgel players and masters of arms; and in return for a remuneration raised from the mass of the prisoners we made them responsible for distributing the ration of food to the *rafalés* and forcing them to eat it. In co-operation with the English two big tubs were taken into their room. Immediately the food was distributed those who did not eat it lost their right to it and received only a quarter. Care was taken to prevent them selling or gambling away their bread by cutting it into tiny pieces. The same was done with the meat that was afterwards thrown into the tubs from which the prisoners ate and that the *rafalés* had to empty without delay in the presence of the inspectors paid by us. Despite everything these unfortunate men continued to wallow in abject filth, sleeping on bundles of straw that replaced what they had lost or gambled away, eaten away by vermin and a prey to horrible and disgusting ailments.'[69]

About those prisoners in the depots in Scotland whom the Transport Board held partly responsible for the presence of miserables there and in its other depots, and whom the historian of Norman Cross depot in Huntingdonshire denounced as 'the curse of the prison, those illicit traders and usurers who bought the rations and clothes of their fellow prisoners and reduced them to starvation, the unfortunate victims being as a rule the slaves to the vice of gambling', nothing more is known.[70]

When soldiers and seamen of Napoleon or of his allies found themselves prisoners in the depots in Scotland or England the depot regulations, discipline and routines to which they then became subject were not completely unlike some of those to which they had been accustomed in their regiments or barracks or on shipboard. But whatever the similarities or differences, the prisoners' daily lives were affected to some extent by the army orders for the militiamen (or occasionally regular soldiers) who guarded them, but much more so by the rules and regulations laid down by the Transport Board and implemented, no doubt at some times and in some depots more systematically and rigorously than at others, by the depot agents and their staffs. The idiosyncratic implementation, or non-implementation, of some Transport Board rules and regulations at Greenlaw, for example, during the years 1804-11 when Malcolm Wright was agent there, has already been observed.[71]

It was hardly likely that all the prisoners in the Scots or other depots would behave there at all times like obedient sheep, meekly and submissively enduring their captivity until the war ended and they were at last repatriated. Even if their personal experiences in the war are known in some detail in only a handful of cases, such as those of Sergeant Major Beaudoin, Captain Kaald, and Lieutenant Marote-Carrier, it was surely the case that some of the prisoners in the Scots depots had passed through especially traumatic events. These might have included, for example, witnessing atrocities perpetrated during the Pensinular War by French, Spanish or Portuguese elements, or even themselves taking part in some atrocity perpetrated by French or French allied troops. It is also virtually certain that among the prisoners in the Scots depots were some Frenchmen who, even before being hauled into Napoleon's forces, had endured weeks, months, even years as *insoumis* or conscription dodgers, hiding out in the woods, hills or villages of France; and that there were some others who, after serving for a longer or shorter period, had deserted from the emperor's armies. Numbers of other prisoners, whether intensely patriotic, unshakeably loyal to Napoleon, determined to escape from captivity or otherwise to cause as much difficulty as they could for the enemy authorities, were hardly likely to prove meek and submissive inmates at the depots. Several hundred others, miserables or *rafalés* as they were, presented, as has been seen, certain other disciplinary problems for the depot authorities.[72] Disciplinary regiments, including Colonial battalions, were formed by Napoleon to deal with *insoumis* or refractories and other *mauvais sujets*—and there were some prisoners in Scots depots who had come from the Colonial battalions. Baylen marked not only a signal defeat by Spanish forces of a French army in the Peninsula but also the beginning of appalling atrocities perpetrated on the French prisoners taken there, thousands of whom died in captivity in shocking conditions, in some cases on the prison hulks at Cadiz but particularly on the island of Cabrera in the Mediterranean. There were numbers of prisoners in all the Scots depots who had been captured at Baylen.[73] All prisoners in the depots, but especially those who, whatever their motives, aspirations, or state of demoralisation, were unwilling or unable to conform to the rules and routines that were intended to regulate their daily lives in captivity, were consequently subject to a range of sanctions or punishments that it lay within the power of the Transport Board and its agents to impose upon them.

One of these sanctions which was quite often imposed by the authorities at the depots was a reduction in prisoners' rations of food by a third—or occasionally even by a half. Examples of the range of circumstances or of infringements of depot rules that resulted in the imposition of this sanction have already been observed.[74] Reduction of rations was a punishment imposed often enough on some offending individual but also it could sometimes be collective—intended to put such pressure on a larger group of prisoners as to make them, for example, identify an offender or offenders among them, as in a case mentioned by Captain Kaald at Greenlaw.[75]

It was, of course, always open to the authorities to impose more than one sanction or punishment simultaneously on prisoners who disobeyed Transport Board or depot instructions. An example where three such simultaneous sanctions were at least threatened was provided in a letter from Edinburgh to the Transport Board in May 1811 from one of its own members, Commissioner James Bowen, who was reporting on a visit he had made the previous day to Valleyfield depot, where the prisoners had refused to bring out their hammocks to air.[76]

A heavier sanction or punishment than any of the three threatened by Commissioner Bowen, and one which was normally automatic in the case of recaptured escapers, was confinement, which might be solitary, in the depot's cachot or black hole. The confinement might be for several days or (as for many or most recaptured escapers) a couple of weeks. A few prisoners, however, were kept in the cachot for several weeks or even months. That was why the Transport Board more than once expressed its concern about the state of health of prisoners subjected to lengthy terms in such confinement.[77] The cachot was also the usual punishment for prisoners who assaulted depot turnkeys or other staff, or indeed other prisoners.

Though records must have been kept by the depot agents of their sentences to confinement in the cachot, none is known to survive for any

Scots depot. Descriptions do survive, however, of several of the cachots or black holes in the Scots depots. At Valleyfield, according to Charles Cowan, son and nephew of the millowners, it was 'a strong building of hewn ashlar work'.[78] A prisoner sentenced along with a companion to eight days in the cachot there after their failed attempt at escape was Lieutenant Marote-Carrier. 'The Black Hole,' he recalled, 'was a cellar or vault underneath the guardhouse and divided into several dungeons. We were both put into the same dungeon but we were separated from one another by a partition made of planks not quite the height of a man, so that without being able to get together we could at least communicate. Although the punishment of the Black Hole included being chained we were left unshackled. We had straw for our bed.'[79] At Greenlaw, according to Captain Kaald, the cachot or black hole seems to have been in (perhaps underneath) the guardroom.[80] One of its earliest known inmates, the nature of whose offence is not known, was the subject of an order from the Transport Board to the agent in July 1808, 'to put the prisoner Antoine Delabroux into the Cachot and to keep him there until further orders.'[81] At Perth the cachot appears to have consisted of 'some strong dark cells' in the 'high embattled tower for observation', with its flagstaff, in the centre of the depot market-place. There must have been quite a few of those strong dark cells there, or, if there were not, serious overcrowding in them, when in mid-September 1813 the Perth cachot held no fewer than 35 inmates.[82] It was at Perth, too, that for one unnamed prisoner confinement in the cachot imposed as late as two months after the war had ended was further compounded: '... approve,' the Transport Board told the agent on 17 June 1814, 'of your having put the prisoner who threw the stone at Mr Johnston [the depot chief clerk] into the cachot and of your keeping him on short allowance, and not discharging him [i.e., repatriating him to France] until the last of the prisoners.'[83]

It was, however, at Edinburgh Castle that the cachot or black hole seems to have been, in the probably well justified view of the Transport Board and the depot authorities, the most oppressive and punitive of those in Scotland. For it was often to the cachot at the Castle that prisoners at most other Scots depots who were guilty of some of the more serious breaches of rules and regulations were sent, at least from early in 1811. Indeed, when on 4 March that year the Castle for the first time in the Napoleonic Wars resumed the role it had played in earlier wars as a depot for prisoners of war, its and its cachot's first seven inmates were recaptured escapers from Esk Mills. Four other *mauvais sujets* from Esk Mills joined them in the cachot later that same week. It was then, too, that the Transport Board instructed its agent at Esk Mills to send no fewer than 48 prisoners 'of bad character' from there to the Castle, 'to be confined in the cells there'. That instruction appears, however to have been superseded ten days later, on 14 March, by another that 30 prisoners 'concerned in outrageous proceedings at Esk Mills Prison' were to be sent to the Castle and kept there 'in solitary cells, on short allowance of provisions,' as were four French officers already sent who had been ring-leaders in those proceedings.[84] Five months later, in August, the Board told its agent at Edinburgh Castle 'to send the four prisoners stated by you to have been long in close confinement for bad conduct, to Greenlaw.' It is not certain that these four, whoever they were, were among the originals from Esk Mills who had been suffering the rigours of solitary confinement in the Castle cachot. But seven at least of the original eleven *mauvais sujets* in the cachot may have remained in it for five months. If they did, then to survive incarceration so long in those depressing conditions they must indeed have been exceptionally hardy and determined warriors.[85]

What seems to have been an unusual case of transfer from the frying pan into the fire occurred later that year when the Transport Board ordered the agent at Greenlaw 'to send the whole of the Prisoners in the Black Hole to Edinburgh Castle, unless there should be one or two of them whom you may think sufficiently punished.'[86] From Greenlaw, too, a month later several other prisoners who had been caught 'excavating, with a View to their Escape', were sent 'for better security to Edinburgh Castle, to be confined in the Cachot there', on short allowance of course, to pay for the structural damage they had caused at Greenlaw.[87]

From Valleyfield likewise there were prisoners whose offences were considered serious enough to justify their being sent to the cachot at the Castle. Among them in the spring of 1811 were Jean Joseph Watigny, Jean Baptiste Leboube, François Louis Furson (or Purson), and two named Savignon (or Savrignon) and Penne (or Pene). The two latter were evidently 'perpetrators of the inhuman act' of marking the face of Jacques Perrot, a fellow prisoner at Valleyfield. Though details are lacking it is likely that Perrot was an informer or perhaps a thief. At any rate in April 1811, after all the prisoners at Valley-field had been put on short allowance of rations until Perrot's attackers were given up, Savignon and Penne consequently found themselves in the cachot at the Castle. Their 'principal part' in marking Perrot's face (presumably with the word 'informer' or 'thief', or whatever had seemed to them apt) was the subject of 'a declaration by a prisoner named Mansard at Valleyfield.' Mansard's declaration appears to have been that it was he, perhaps under duress by Savignon and Penne, who had actually marked or tattooed Perrot's face. At any rate his declaration apparently brought him punishment rather than reward: 'Mansard and the two Prisoners in Edinburgh Castle are to be kept in the cachot on short allowance until further orders. If the Prisoner Perrot chooses, you will cause Mansard to obliterate the marks made by him on the Face of the Former, if possible.' For reasons unexplained, but perhaps because he had acted under duress, Mansard was put in the cachot not at the Castle but at Valleyfield, where the agent was told three months later by the Transport Board: 'The prisoner Mansard is to be discharged from the Black Hole and you are upon his discharge to admonish him as to his future conduct, apprising him that if he should again offend, the Term of his late Confinement will be doubled.'[88] Another case (or what appears to be a case other than Perrot's) of a prisoner at Valleyfield being tattooed was recounted 25 years after the war by Andrew Johnston, who had been chief clerk there: 'A Prisoner, a Seaman, was here tatooed [sic] by a fine young solder Victor Cretien, who was compelled to do it. He was marked round the upper lip and chin with the words in French "I sold (or informed upon) my brethren aboard the Ponton [hulk] *Le Vigilant*" [at Portsmouth], with the date. He was also kicked about and trampled upon, when to save his life he was taken into the Hospital as a nurse. Even here he was ill-used, so strong is their malice against informers ... The soldier [Cretien] was ordered by the [Transport] Board to be put in irons in the Cachot, to be kept on 2/3 [rations], and to be the last to be sent home. I soon relieved him of his irons, but when I left Valleyfield for Perth [in Jul. 1812] he was reduced to a skeleton and I believe afterwards died there in the Cachot.'[89]

Savignon (after his recapture) and Penne seem still to have been in the cachot at the Castle the following month when François Louis Furson (or Purson) was sent there from Valleyfield. Furson, aged 28, born at Fontainebleau, and a soldier in the 63rd infantry regiment who had been captured off Brest in November 1807, arrived at the Castle on 10 May: 'Notorious rascal. Struck a turnkey. Abused and attempted to strike the agent.'[90] Another prisoner at Valleyfield, who was 'Discharged 7 April 1811 [to] Edinburgh Castle for Striking the Turnkey', was Jean Baptiste Leboube, a soldier of the 14th line regiment, who had been captured on St Domingo in 1806 and who in March 1811 was among the 2,400 or so prisoners sent to Valleyfield from Esk Mills.[91] The band of prisoners sent in those spring weeks to the cachot at the Castle from Valleyfield was further enlarged by the arrival on 23 April of Jean Joseph Watigny. Watigny, aged 24 and born in Gaudeloupe (or, according to another source, Martinique) was a seaman who had already suffered six years of captivity since his capture with other survivors from the privateer *Général Ernouf* in 1805. He was sent to the Castle 'for insolent behaviour'.[92]

There appear, on the other hand, to have been no prisoners sent from Perth to the cachot at Edinburgh Castle. If that was so, the reasons were probably twofold. First, by the time Perth depot opened in August 1812, the Castle had ceased to be used for prisoners of war to anything like the extent it had been the previous year. Second, Perth was thirty miles from Edinburgh as the crow flies, not a mere ten as were the depots at Penicuik, and the difficulties and costs of marching one or two *mauvais sujets* at a time that distance and (unless their march was via Stirling) of arranging a boat for them to cross the Firth of Forth made such removals impracticable.

For some more serious offences against good order and discipline at the depots, especially where criminal law became involved, prisoners were transferred into the hands of the Civil Power, i.e., the sheriff. That meant they found themselves, as has already been observed in the case of those suspected or accused of forging banknotes, for a time in the Edinburgh city gaol or Tolbooth.[93] A prisoner using a degree of violence amounting to serious assault or even attempted murder in, for example, attempting escape from a depot could also find himself in the Tolbooth. Such a prisoner was Jean Baptiste Destrais, alias Pierre Calmain. Destrais was variously said to be a soldier captured at the capitulation of the Saintes in 1808 but also a seaman who had been captured on the frigate *L'Amphitrite* at Martinique in 1809. Born at Joigny and aged 22, he had arrived at Valleyfield in September 1811 from Plymouth, on board the frigate HMS *Latona*. He was said to be 5 feet 7 inches tall, of thin build, with an oval face, pale complexion, dark hair, hazel eyes, and no marks or wounds. On 22 July 1813 he was sent from Valleyfield to the Edinburgh Tolbooth 'for Stabbing a Soldier'. The stabbing, reported in the *Caledonian Mercury* that day, had occurred a week earlier during 'a daring attempt ... by some French prisoners to escape from the depot at Penny-cuick [i.e., Valleyfield]. They had by some means or other, contrived to get a false bottom affixed to one of the carts which carries away the filth from the prison. In this the three secreted themselves and got without the walls for some way, when the driver being accidentally stopped by an acquaintance, they came from their lurking hole and were proceeding to a wood, which they had nearly reached when they were met by a soldier who immediately seized one, who drew a dagger which he had concealed about him and wounded the soldier in the neck, and afterwards stabbed him in the left side. The soldier, having been allowed to go to work in the neighbourhood when off duty, was unfortunately unarmed at the time. Fainting through loss of blood he was obliged to let the prisoner go. But the whole three were afterwards apprehended owing to the alarm raised by the scuffle. The soldier ... lies dangerously ill, if not already dead.' A letter of 24 August from the procurator fiscal at Edinburgh to the crown agent said that the soldier's life had indeed been 'put in the utmost danger' but the victim had by then recovered. The fiscal, after reporting that Destrais had been brought to Edinburgh, examined, and committed to the Tolbooth, and that declarations had been taken from several witnesses, added: 'I shall hope to hear from you soon whether the King's Counsel mean to proceed against Destrais—for if it is not meant to do so he will fall to be disposed of in another way and removed to some other place.' No other information about legal proceedings has been found. Destrais, like his fellow prisoners of war suspected or accused of forging

banknotes and who had also been detained in the Tolbooth, was never indicted or brought to trial for stabbing the soldier.

In Destrais' case, however, and one or two others where more serious offences had been committed by prisoners, especially towards what proved to be
the end of the war in the spring of 1814, another sanction or punishment was
applied by the Transport Board and the depot authorities. Destrais remained
in the Tolbooth for almost a year until 14 June 1814, when he was returned
to Valleyfield as prisoner No. 7,650, the last to be entered in its General
Entry Books. As part of the general release of prisoners he was repatriated to
France the next day—a day after the last of all the others, except for a score
of Poles, had departed. So Destrais on account of his offence was kept back,
like the unnamed prisoner in the Perth cachot, until, and in his case even a
day beyond, the end of the general release.[94]

The punishment for capital offences by prisoners of war found guilty in
civil courts was normally, of course, execution. In England several prisoners of
war were executed during the Napoleonic Wars for murder or stabbing (mainly
during escapes) or, as has already been observed, for forging banknotes.[95] But
none were for any offence committed in Scotland. Of course, those prisoners in Scotland who did commit such capital offences could hardly be sure
when they did so that, even if or when convicted, they would not suffer the
full penalty of criminal law.

Prisoners in Scotland who committed serious offences against either the
criminal law or the Transport Board regulations to which they were subject
could and sometimes did, however, find themselves transferred to the hulks
at Chatham, Portsmouth or Plymouth. The hulks, like the cachot at Edinburgh Castle, were clearly considered by the Board to be among the heavier
sanctions that could be employed against *mauvais sujets* at the depots. Many
of the prisoners in the Scots depots had already spent part of their captivity in the hulks and probably few of them wanted ever to return there. An
exception, at least for a time when things were going particularly badly for
him at Valleyfield, appeared to be Marote-Carrier. He had passed the first
couple of months of his captivity on the hulk *Glory* at Chatham. 'Without a
doubt,' Marote-Carrier later recalled, 'that was a horrible form of captivity,
those floating prisons where men were so tightly crammed together, where
they breathed so foul an air, where they only had to sustain their miserable
existence such disgusting and skimpy food. But still there was there some
hope of liberty. Men could at night throw themselves through the portholes
into the sea, and escape pursuit under cover of darkness ... But in [Valleyfield
depot] in Scotland, bent under the yoke of the closest captivity, no means of
escape was left to us.'[96] Marote-Carrier's near nostalgia for the prospect of
escape from the hulks and his pessimism about the lack of such a prospect
at Valleyfield were both exaggerated: his recollection of the miseries of life

on the hulks was almost certainly far more widely shared among those of his fellow prisoners in Scotland who had experienced them, than was his pessimism, temporary as it proved, about escape from an inland depot.

It was far from the case that every prisoner transferrred from depots in Scotland to the hulks had been guilty of some breach of the civil or criminal law or Transport Board rules and regulations. From Greenlaw, for instance, in the years between 1807 and 1811 at least 300 Danish and French prisoners were sent to the hulks: 282 'Danes' (who included many Norwegians) were said in the two depot General Entry Books devoted to them to have been sent to Chatham, and one of the other Entry Books indicates that at least 27 Frenchmen were sent there, too. That indefatigable note-taker Sergeant Major Beaudoin noted the departure between 30 March and 25 July 1809 of 171 prisoners from Greenlaw to Chatham, and although the implication is that they were French they may in fact have been a mixture of French and Danes.[97] Transfers such as these were not the result of any offence committed by the prisoners but simply of Transport Board policy, which at that period vacillated over making Greenlaw a depot solely for Danes or for French.[98]

Sergeant Major Beaudoin himself, after the transfer of 100 men on 25 July 1809 from Greenlaw to Chatham, wrote: 'I am distressed by this evacuation, following a letter that one of our companions in misfortune has just received from Chatham. He says they are worse off than at Greenlaw. First, the food is worse, except that the bread is a little better; besides, there is no work to do and all the people of the town come to see them on board the hulks. I am afraid to go there.' But to go there Beaudoin himself was duly obliged by order of the Transport Board. 'Only 40 of us French remained at Greenlaw,' he noted in his diary ... 'On 31 October 1809 (the eve of all Saints' Day) the rest of us left for Chatham.' Arrived by sea at Sheerness on 18 November, 'We were put at once on the *Magnanimous*, the flag ship. This vessel is specifically for receiving prisoners from here and there. The crew consists of disabled men. The English service is very hard on sea and land; at the least fault they are given two dozen lashes on the back with a rope.' After a few days on the *Magnanimous*, during which he worked away making his rings from hair, '... several of them for the pretty young ladies there were on board', Beaudoin and some other prisoners were put on board the hulk *Bristol*. He noted nine hulks containing prisoners, one of them the *Sampson*, 'where the *mauvais sujets* are put', and another the *Bahama*, 'which is full of Danes'. Beaudoin, one of the hundreds of prisoners sent from Scotland to the hulks without having committed any offence against either civil or criminal law or depot rules and regulations, then declared: 'The difference between the land prisons and the hulks is very great: there is no space for a walk; we are packed in one on top of the other. No one comes to see us, we are like marooned men. No work to do except menial tasks. We have to hoist up water for our needs ... besides we have to scrape in winter and wash in summer the places where we lie down. In a word, it was enough merely to see them [the hulks]. They represented a place of horror.'[99] It was that horror which, the Transport Board hoped, would act as a deterrent to any prisoner who contemplated making any serious breach of depot regulations or civil or criminal law. If nonetheless that deterrent failed, then their transfer to the hulks of at least some of those who committed such breaches would be an appropriate punishment.

From among those prisoners who were sent as a punishment from Scots depots to the hulks, there survives what seems to be a unique letter, written to a friend and fellow prisoner still then at Perth depot and conveying an impression of at least some aspects of the transfer or descent from depot to hulk. The writer was Michel Chanteleuse; the surname or first name of his friend at Perth, who has not been further identified, was Pascal: it is possible he was Barthelemy Pascal, recipient, as has been observed, of £60 in March 1813 in the Perth Payments Ledger. A second lieutenant of the 4th Legion (or, according to one source, 4th light infantry regiment), captured at Vigo in March 1809, Chanteleuse was born at Lyons and was aged 26. His was an eventful captivity. In Scotland it began at Cupar, Fife, where in March 1811 he arrived as a parole prisoner. Transferred in December that year to Dumfries he and two fellow prisoners who had also been at Cupar with him, Lieutenants Louis Diruit of the 15th light infantry and J. J. Vidal of the 122nd line regiment, broke their parole in May 1812 and escaped, apparently on horseback. Recaptured the same day 21 miles away at Moffat, Chanteleuse and his two companions were put first into Dumfries gaol then sent into close confinement at Valleyfield. Transferred in September that year to Perth, Chanteleuse, with Diruit and Vidal, was sent in November 1813 to Edinburgh Castle and from there at the end of that month he and Diruit (Vidal having escaped two days earlier from the Castle) were embarked with two dozen other prisoners on HMS *Alexandre* and sent to the hulks at Chatham. Chanteleuse wrote from the hulk *Canada* at Chatham to 'my dear Pascal' at Perth depot that he had arrived there eleven days earlier after a 'pleasant' voyage from Leith. 'The next day the group of us were distributed among several of the hulks. Those who remain on board the *Canada* are the two brothers Dague [or Dagues], the two Mussards, Messers Marty, Blatter, Shurman [Scheurman or Scheurmann], Petry, Diruit and I. I have postponed writing you until now because the first few days we were here none of us knew where to lay our heads. We have been obliged to pay very dear for very bad places to do so. A piece of luck has fallen only to Diruit and me, who enjoy the incomparable advantage of a gunport, in return for five shillings. We are surrounded by privateer officers who are excellent neighbours, etc., with whom we shall consequently live in perfect understanding. The others have paid 18 shillings for places in the middle of the hulk and near the latrines. You who have lived in a real place can judge as well as me how disagreeably placed they are! Captain Marty, Blatter, Diruit and I take our meals together for the time being. Our food is limited to tea or coffee, unless we can procure for ourselves other food on board: the cost of everything is exorbitant. I have not yet received news from home—probably I shall be a long time in receiving any because of the detour our letters will have to make to reach the hulk here, and my parents will know only in a couple of months' time that I am here.'[100]

How commonly applied in the Scots depots was the sanction or punishment of handcuffing prisoners is not clear. The infrequent references in the official records to handcuffs perhaps suggest their use was not common. Abell, without giving his source, asserts that 'A prisoner who wounded a turnkey was to be kept handcuffed, with his hands behind him, for not less than twelve hours, and for not more than twenty-four.'[101] Marote-Carrier, as has been observed,[102] said when he was put into the black hole at Valleyfield that it was normal also to be placed in chains there. So far as the limited evidence at the Scots depots goes it indicates that unruly or violent prisoners, and in some cases recaptured escapers while being marched back whence they had come, might find themselves handcuffed. Thus at Perth in April 1813, a few days after a violent attack on an informer among the prisoners by some whose attempt at escape they were convinced the informer had been guilty of frustrating, the agent was told by the Transport Board: 'We approve of your procuring one dozen pairs of hand cuffs.'[103] When at Valleyfield in the early winter of 1812-13 the agent complained of certain prisoners whom he asked to be removed to another depot, the Transport Board told him: 'We cannot give orders for the removal of the Prisoners of bad character mentioned by you to another Depot on any account whatever, but you must punish them by confinement and hand cuffing if necessary in the usual manner.'[104] It was at Valleyfield, too, that prisoners said to have been put to work on an adjacent farm at Cornbank were reported to have worked in manacles.[105] At Greenlaw, the only reference found to handcuffs also contained one to leg-irons and was in a letter from the Transport Board to the agent in January 1812: '… approve of your having put the 8 prisoners thereinmentioned on short Allowance. If they should again burke their Hand Cuffs you are to get stronger Irons for their Hands and also for their Legs.'[106] Finally, when that remarkable escaper François Petit had been recaptured in November 1811 at Stirling and was being marched back through Falkirk to Valleyfield under an escort of militiamen 'he was handcuffed from one place to the other.'[107]

If the cancellation of depot markets, sales of their goods at which they depended on for some income, was, as has already been seen, another sanction that the prisoners might find themselves subjected to, so also in some cases were their transfers from one depot to another within Scotland. Transfers between depots there, as has been repeatedly observed, were very common from early in 1811, when Greenlaw ceased to be the only depot north of the Border, until the end of the war in 1814. The reasons for such transfers were not usually stated in the Entry Books or even in surviving official correspondence, nor are they always obvious. Some were no doubt intended to relieve overcrowding at one depot and fill available space at another. It is likely that some transfers were intended to prevent any over-familiarity or fraternisation between prisoners and their guards. Some other transfers, even if not to the cachot of another depot such as Edinburgh Castle, appear to have been intended to dissolve what the depot authorities and the Transport Board considered troublesome, or potentially troublesome, associations between certain individual prisoners or among groups of prisoners. Although the Transport Board refused in December 1812, for example, to grant the request by the agent at Valleyfield to transfer from there to some other depot some 'Prisoners of bad character', the Board's veto appears not to have been applied consistently in all such cases. When, for instance, at the beginning of September 1812, less than a month after its opening, Perth depot received an intake of 107 prisoners from Greenlaw and Valleyfield (40 from the former, 67 from the latter) two thirds of them were privateeersmen, mainly officers or petty officers. The other third consisted of a dozen navymen (about half of them officers), half a dozen others who were either merchant navymen, clerks, or passengers, and about a dozen army officers. Many, perhaps most, of the 107 were *mauvais sujets*, including parole breakers and escapers. One of those *mauvais sujets* from Greenlaw, for example, was David Fourneau, privateer lieutenant. Described as a 'ringleader' in the troubles at Esk Mills, Fourneau, as has been seen, had escaped from that depot in February 1811 but on his recapture had been sent a few days later to the cachot at Edinburgh Castle, the first prisoner in its Entry Book. From the Castle he had been transferred in August that year to Greenlaw. After 19 months at Perth depot Fourneau was discharged at the end of April 1814 to Leith for reasons that will be discussed in a later chapter.[108] Another from Greenlaw was Valerian Feraud (or Ferand), a naval ensign captured in 1809 in the West Indies. Feraud was successively an inmate of every depot in Scotland except Valleyfield. Arrived at Edinburgh Castle from Esk Mills in March 1811 he had been in the mass escape a month later from the Castle, but after his recapture had been sent to Greenlaw. Feraud was transferred along with a dozen other *mauvais sujets* on 3 November 1813 from Perth to Edinburgh Castle, evidently en route to the hulks in the south of England, but three weeks later he escaped for the second time from the Castle and seems not again to have been seen or heard of.[109] The 67 transferred in September 1812 to Perth from Valleyfield included Marote-Carrier. Before his transfer to Perth Marote-Carrier had, of course, already spent some time in the cachot at Valleyfield following his attempted escape.[110] Among others transferred then with him to Perth who also no doubt were regarded as *mauvais sujets* or troublemakers at Valleyfield were Lazar Cairel, captain of the privateer *Marie Louise*, and Captain Joseph Grimaldi, said in different official sources to be in the Artillery or the 2nd Legion of Reserve. Cairel was a curious character whose three different names or aliases reflected, as already observed, his evidently three separate careers in Napoleon's armed forces. Captain Grimaldi, a Corsican, had been captured in August 1808 while serving with General Dupont's army in Andalucia (although another official source says he was captured then at Madrid). He began his captivity in Scotland in May 1812 as a parole prisoner at Greenlaw in Berwickshire. But three months later he was transferred to Valleyfield for breaking his parole by going beyond the mile perimeter. Grimaldi, who was aged 44 and described under the heading 'Marks and wounds' as having 'bald head', appears to have impressed the depot authorities and the Transport Board by his good behaviour at Perth, however, and was restored to parole in February 1813, although not at Greenlaw, Berwickshire, but at Sanquhar, Dumfriesshire.[111]

Postponement of a prisoner's prospect of exchange or release for his breach of certain Transport Board or depot rules and regulations was another sanction that lay within the armoury of the authorities. As the wars dragged on, however, and recurrent negotiations in 1803-05, 1806, 1808, and 1809-10 between the British and French governments in search of an agreement on a general exchange or release of prisoners broke down, that was a sanction whose use or threatened use had a diminishing effect on the prisoners, particularly after 1810, which of course was precisely the period during which the number of prisoners in Scotland increased from a few hundreds to many thousands. An example of the sanction, however, was provided in a Transport Board circular to depot agents in September 1809: if prisoners undermined or otherwise damaged depot buildings during attempts to escape then not only would all the prisoners in the building concerned be put on short rations until the culprits were found, but also the culprits as well as enduring a period of confinement in the cachot would be 'put upon a list to denote that they shall not be exchanged till the end of the war.'[112] Prisoners who exchanged their names and identities on the eve of their transfer from one depot to another, or between hulks and depots, were, according to a similar circular issued in March 1811, 'to be placed at the bottom of the list for exchange.'[113] Even at the end of the war, when arrangements were being made for the general release and repatriation of all the prisoners, the Board approved of measures taken by the agent at Valleyfield 'to prevent the Prisoners from disposing of their Bedding and Clothing and to keep such as may have disposed of these articles until the last.' So also, the same agent was told, were to be 'any Prisoners detected in changing their Names and Turn of Release...'[114]

A more insidious and demoralising means used by the depot authorities to maintain control over the prisoners was the employment or encouragement among them of informers. Half way, as it proved, through the war the Transport Board in 1809 circularised depot agents on the matter thus: 'In order to prevent the inconveniences which have sometimes arisen ... both to those who have the care and charge of them, and to the prisoners themselves, the Agents are hereby directed to give out in Public Notice, That such prisoners as shall discover to the agent of the depot any attempt to introduce or manufacture offensive weapons calculated for murder or insurrection, or any plot for undermining or breaking down the boundaries of the prison for the purpose of escape or mischief, shall, upon satisfactory proof or evidence of the same, be entitled to his [sic] liberty and also conveyance to the Continent by the first favorable opportunity, and in the mean time his information and name shall be carefully concealed by the agent, to whom alone such information or discovery should be made ...'[115]

For informers, as one prisoner already mentioned at Valleyfield was and another, Jacques Perrot, may have been,[116] the consequences of being found out by fellow prisoners were of course likely to prove serious. 'There being at the Depots several French Prisoners,' the Transport Board informed the Admiralty in June 1812, 'who have given Information of their Fellow Prisoners concerned in Forgery, or in committing Depredations at the Prisons and on board the Prison ships; and as the Lives of these Prisoners would be endangered if they were not kept separate from the others, or even if they were sent to France, to which they strongly object; we submit ... whether it may not be adviseable to allow these Informers to be released to serve on board Merchant Vessels, not more than one of them being sent to any one vessel.' When in response to that letter the Admiralty asked the Board to say how many prisoners were 'in danger of ill treatment, in consquence of having given information of their fellow prisoners', the numbers reported from each depot by the agents were not stated in the surviving copy of the Board's reply.[117]

Informers among the prisoners existed not only in the depots in Scotland but sometimes even on the ships which transferred the prisoners there. 'Anthony Suett and Francis Goddard, French prisoners, came aft and gave information of a plot rase amongst them to brake out the Prison and take charge of the Ship,' as the entry said in the log of HMS *Gorgon* for 25 February 1811, as it brought some 300 prisoners from Portsmouth to Leith.[118]

At Greenlaw, after Laurent Barbe or Barbet had informed on an attempt to escape by several fellow prisoners in September 1811 they were put in the cachot on two-thirds allowance of rations while he was sent for safety to Edinburgh Castle, where he promptly applied to join the Royal Navy.[119] In another case, however, the following month which, although no details are known, apparently involved an informer or informers at Greenlaw the Board was prompted to tell the agent: 'We think it necessary to caution you against giving too much credit to the plausible statements of French prisoners informing against their fellow prisoners.'[120]

At Esk Mills in March 1811 an unnamed prisoner who had informed the agent of intended escapes was evidently released and repatriated to the continent.[121]

At Valleyfield informing appears to have been a minor industry. 'The spies insinuated themselves among us,' Marote-Carrier, confined there in 1811-12, long afterward recalled, 'took part in our conversations, all the time looking out for the most innocent in order unjustly to accuse us.'[122] Four months after the case of Jacques Perrot and two months before that of the Dutch boy who informed on a prisoner who had allegedly forged banknotes,[123] the agent was told by the Board in August 1811: 'You will apply to the Admiral respecting John Clom, the Prisoner mentioned to have given you correct Intelligence and to be desirous of serving in the Navy.'[124] A year later, in a reference apparently to certain prisoners, the Board assured the agent that 'if any of them will give useful information their Cases will be favourably considered.'[125] At the beginning of that same year, following the escape of Guillaume Mariote, a soldier in the 66th regiment of the Line, it seems informers had again been busy at Valleyfield. Written on the official return concerning Mariote's escape were these comments: 'Supposed to have Escaped by the Gate in workman's dress. This man arrived in Scotland under the denomination of a soldier, but from the information of his Comrades he is a Lieutenant in the French Navy, and is one of those who attempted to seize the *Brune* on the passage—came from the *Generaux* [i.e., *Généreux*] prison ship at Plymouth.'[126]

If informers were thus encouraged by the Transport Board and the depot authorities the hatred they aroused among their fellow prisoners was particularly violently demonstrated in April 1813 at Perth. Some prisoners there were discovered attempting to escape by digging a tunnel. 'A prisoner who was in the [depot] hospital being suspected of having given information was ... immediately after his dismission from the sick list assailed by his comrades and very severely handled. They seem to have had an intention of cutting off his ears but from his resistance they had succeeded only in almost severing one of them from his head. He also received a number of cuts on the body with a knife. A rope was afterwards put about his neck, by which he was dragged through the water in the canal [surrounding the depot], and while in this situation some of his companions leapt with all their force upon his body. Their proceedings were at last observed and a party of the Durham militia marched into the prison yard and relieved the sufferer from his tormentors. The man who was thus obnoxious is not only a Frenchman but a Parisian. He has been taken all possible care of in hospital and is likely to recover.' In October that year a prisoner named L. Lemoine was released from captivity at Perth into the Royal Navy, 'he being in danger of his life among the Prisoners from information that he has given [the depot agent].' At Valleyfield, too, although evidently not actually assaulted, 'Savary Gautche, a native of Malta', was reported by the agent to the Transport Board in December 1811 'to be in danger of his life in consequence of information given by him', and the Board approved a proposal by the agent to release Gautche (said in another source to be a native of Genoa) into the Royal Navy.[127]

In addition to the authorities' use of informers and such a wide range of sanctions in maintaining control over the prisoners as the sending of trouble-some prisoners to the cachot within their own depot, or to Edinburgh Castle, the hulks in the south of England, or in a few cases to the sheriff or 'Civil Power', as well as reductions of rations, the use of handcuffs or leg irons, cancellation of depot markets, and postponement of their prospective turn of exchange or release, there were also the daily roll-calls of the prisoners.

The second article of the code of rules laid down by the Transport Board for all prisoners of war to observe declared that 'All the prisoners are to an-swer to their names when mustered, and to point out to the agent any error they may discover in the lists with which he may be furnished, in order to prevent the confusion which might result from erroneous names; and such prisoners as shall refuse to comply with this regulation shall be put on half allowance.'[128]

A description of the daily musters or roll-calls of prisoners at Greenlaw was provided by the Norwegian diarist Captain Paul Andreas Kaald. 'At 11.30 a.m.,' Kaald wrote, 'the guard comes marching outside, to relieve the other guard. Every watch consists of 40-50 men. Therefore, there are a lot of soldiers just outside the prison to be at hand in an emergency. When the changing of the guard has taken place we are taken through a little door one by one, between the 2nd officer and 5-6 soldiers with swords, and if the count isn't correct they chase us in and out 2 or 3 times until it is correct. Then everybody collects his food for dinner. At 3 p.m. we are turned out and called in again.'[129] When in June 1810 one man was missing during the roll-call, 'We had to be turned in and out so many times,' wrote Kaald. 'Finally the clerk came and called out our names. One after the other we had to walk in between a whole row of soldiers and into the prison. But one man (an old woodcutter) by the name of Hendrick Petersen from the crew of the privateer *Dorothea Catharinas* from East Risoer was missing. None of the staff, the officers or jailers are able to find out how he got out of the prison, which pleased us assembled prisoners very much.'[130] Kaald added that Petersen 'had disappeared yesterday evening by creeping under a toilet tub, when we were all chased from the courtyard without being counted. He lay under there until about 11 p.m.' His successful escape then over the palisade without being seen by the guards made Petersen 'the first to gain freedom from this damn prison in this way.' Nine months earlier, in September 1809, there were frantic roll-calls, and considerable amusement among the prisoners, following another escape, this time by a fellow privateer captain and friend of Kaald named Richelieu, who had in fact been carried out from the depot concealed in a box. 'The count was taken here at lunchtime and in the afternoon, but both times the count was correct. We had of course summoned a boy earlier to be available for the first count and then to creep out of the window in the corridor. He was counted in the same way twice and all was well.' It was only the next day, two days after Richelieu's escape, when the count was again taken, that the guards found there was one prisoner short. 'We were turned out and counted three times, but there was still one missing. ... Then the clerk came and we fell into line in between a row of soldiers when our names were called out. He continued calling out the names until he came to Captain Richelieu's name. But no one came. The prisoners began to laugh and shout with all their might on Captain Richelieu. But no one came.'[131]

It was, as Charles Cowan, son and nephew of the Cowan brothers, former owners of the papermills at Valleyfield, long afterwards wrote about these roll-calls, 'an important matter for the authorities to ascertain the number of the poor wretches accurately in passing to or from the prisons'. The agent at Valleyfield may therefore have believed he had found a solution to that problem by the appointment there as a turnkey in June 1811 of Henry Miles. Miles, as Cowan recalled, 'had been previously much among sheep, and especially in taking account of the number in the flocks.'[132] Alas, Miles as turnkey and specialist in counting sheep lasted only fifteen months at the depot: '... direct you,' the Transport Board told the agent there in September 1812, 'to dismiss Henry Miles from his Employment immediately.'[133] At Perth, too, the prisoners were subjected to similar daily roll-calls, as Marote-Carrier, an inmate successively at both depots, later recalled. 'The daily routine began again much as it had been at Valleyfield. We were roused at dawn, and counted man by man as we went into the yard.'[134]

An ultimate sanction in the armoury of the Transport Board and the depot authorities for maintaining their control over the prisoners was of course the presence and deployment of the military guards, about which more will be said in the next chapter. At Greenlaw, the first depot (excluding the Edinburgh bridewell in 1803-4) established in Scotland, the particular controversy will be recalled concerning two fatal shootings by guards. The deaths of Charles Cottier in January 1807 and of Simon Simonsen in July 1810 resulted in the trials at the High Court of Justiciary in Edinburgh of respectively Ensign Maxwell of the Lanarkshire Militia and Private James Inglis of the Edinburgh Militia, both young men in their early twenties, their conviction for culpable homicide, and the sentencing of Maxwell to nine months' imprisonment but of Inglis to 14 years' transportation to the penal settlements in Australia.[135] The comments about trigger-happy guards by those two diarists among the prisoners at Greenlaw, Sergeant Major Beaudoin and Captain Kaald, who were there at the time of one or other of those shootings, have already been quoted.[136] The example of these cases (which were distinct from those in which prisoners actually engaged in escaping were liable legitimately to be fired on if seen by the depot guards) and the consequent clarifications or tightenings up of the orders for the conduct of the guards on duty at the depot no doubt contributed to the absence (so far as is known) of any similar cases of shootings of prisoners at any of the other and later depots in Scotland. The concern expressed by the army commander in Scotland, Lieutenant General Lord Cathcart, at the time of those shootings at Greenlaw, arose not least from the danger that the French government might retaliate on British prisoners of war in its hands.[137]

French and British prisoners of war held by the two opposing states were in effect hostages for the acceptable behaviour of each of those states toward its prisoners of that nationality. The punishments inflicted on prisoners in the depots in Scotland (and in those, and on the hulks, in England) therefore could not be, or at least could not reasonably be considered to be, so drastic as to provoke retaliation by the French authorities. The only overt and official retaliation that did occur in Britain took place in November 1811 and it affected Valleyfield as well as four depots in England. 'The Lords Commissioner of the Admiralty,' a Transport Board circular of the 5th of that month declared to the agents at Valleyfield and those other depots, 'having ordered all the French prisoners of war of the same description as midshipmen in the British navy to be sent into close confinement as a measure of retaliation on account of the French Government having deprived the latter of their paroles and confined them in unwholesome prisons in France; we acquaint you that the numbers of prisoners of that description stated on the other side hereof will be sent in to your custody from the places expressed against them.' Thus Valleyfield was ordered to open its gates to receive from the three Scots parole towns listed 13 French midshipmen or *aspirants* marched under guard from Peebles, eight from Kelso, and three from Jedburgh.[138] These prisoners did not, however, languish long at Valleyfield. 'Having received a communication from the French Government,' the depot agent was told by the Transport Board three weeks later,'stating that the British midshipmen prisoners of war in France had been restored again to their parole of honour in consequence of the remonstrance of this Department, we direct you to restore to their parole immediately all the French aspirants who were sent into your custody as a measure of reprisal, informing them of the cause of their being so restored to their parole. You will send them off to London [sic] in 2 or 3 divisions, allowing a space of three days between the marching of each division …'[139]

Not all discipline emanated from the Transport Board and depot authorities: from time to time the prisoners exercised some of their own. Informers, as has been observed, could suffer severely if found out by their fellow prisoners. So also could thieves. Hence the case of the prisoner among the first intake at Perth in August 1812 who was court-martialled by his fellow prisoners and sentenced to a flogging of two dozen lashes with the end of a hard rope for stealing mortcloths from Inchture Church en route to the depot.[140] At Perth, too, according to Marote-Carrier, a prisoner and former shipmate of his who had established himself as a money-changer having welched on his fellow prisoners they tried and condemned him, as already observed, to a punishment of 200 lashes.[141] An even more savage flogging in that it proved fatal was meted out by his fellow prisoners to Jean Joseph Niquet at Valleyfield. Niquet, a trooper in the 3rd Dragoons, born at Avignon and aged 31, had been captured at Coimbra in Portugal in October 1810 and arrived eleven months later at Valleyfield. In a bundle of official proforma slips reporting deaths at the depot occurs this one dated 29 November 1812 for Niquet: 'Died in consequence of being severely flogged by his fellow Prisoners, he having been detected by them stealing. They also cut off one of his ears. Reported to Vice Admiral Otway.'[142]

Thieves among the prisoners at Greenlaw were likewise flogged by their fellow prisoners but fortunately never, unlike the flogging of trooper Niquet at Valleyfield, with fatal results. Captain Kaald, that source of so much information about events at Greenlaw, recorded several cases there of theft and its punishment. 'Today,' he wrote on 28 November 1808, 'one of Captain Knudtzon's crew was punished with 27 lashes for stealing.' One apparently persistent thief suffered no fewer than 117 lashes for two successive offences in July and August 1809. He was Hans Dahl, a seaman from Kaald's own former privateer ship *Den Kjaekke*. Dahl was given 36 lashes on 6 July. Then seven weeks later, on 22 August, 'Hans Dahl was tied to the post and given three times 27 or 81 lashes for stealing.' On the latter day also, Kaald wrote, a boy, no doubt a ship's boy, was given six lashes 'for some trifling theft.'[143]

Fortunately, flogging was not among punishments to which the prisoners were subjected by the Transport Board or the depot authorities. Nonetheless, with so many other sanctions and punishments which, as has been seen, could be imposed on them, the prisoners in the depots in Scotland may not have had much sympathy to spare for those of their guards who fell foul of British military law and were sentenced to savage floggings. One such militia soldier, for example, who almost certainly was a guard at Greenlaw, for striking his officer was sentenced by a court martial at Musselburgh in April 1807 to 800 lashes.[144]

As their guards—militiamen for the most part—along with the turnkeys, clerks, interpreters, nurses, lamplighters, labourers, and others of the agent's staff were for the prisoners an aspect of daily life in the depot, some discussion of them is now timely.

18

Guards; Uprisings; General Simon; Depot Staffs

The prisoners in the Scots depots were occasionally guarded or escorted in the earlier years of the Napoleonic Wars by soldiers from regiments of the regular army. In October 1805, for example, 'a party of the 71st Regiment brought eleven prisoners-of-war from Glasgow and lodged them at Greenlaw.' To Greenlaw also, when survivors from the Dutch frigate *Utrecht*, shipwrecked early in 1807 on Sanday in Orkney, were landed as prisoners of war at Leith, the captain and eight of his officers were taken by coach, escorted by 'a party of the Scots Greys'.[1] As late as May 1809 Captain Paul Andreas Kaald noted in his diary at Greenlaw that 'Today the Militia Guard was replaced and the 75th Highland Regiment are here again for some days.'[2] Amid all the intensive preparations in the winter of 1810-11 to house far more prisoners in depots and parole towns in Scotland, hundreds were escorted from Leith to Penicuik by militiamen but also by 'a party of dragoons'.[3] The increasingly heavy demands on the regular army from 1808, however, to provide troops for the Peninsular War then beginning, and for other campaigns such as that in 1809 on Walcheren, confirmed the employment normally of militiamen as guards at, and escorts to and from, the depots. It was thus with militiamen and their officers, far more often than with regular troops, that prisoners in the Scots depots had more or less daily contact or at least sight of.

Contemporary accounts, particularly local newspaper reports, indicate that between 1803 and 1814 soldiers from almost 30 different regiments of militia were involved at one time or another in guarding or escorting the prisoners of war at the Scots depots. The guards and escorts provided by the 15 Scottish regiments of militia, which included Aberdeenshire, Argyll and Bute, Ayrshire, Edinburgh, Fife, Forfarshire (Angus), Kirkcudbrightshire and Wigtownshire, Lanarkshire, Perthshire, Renfrewshire, and Stirlingshire, were supplemented or replaced from time to time by those provided by such English, Welsh or Irish regiments of militia as the Cambridgeshire, Durham, East Yorkshire, Norfolk, Northampton, Westminster, Wiltshire, Caernarvonshire, and Antrim. An official list of militia regiments in 1811 showed the total number of men then enrolled in the 15 Scots regiments was 11,127.[4] Guarding and escorting the prisoners of war north of the Border were thus duties which at any given time occupied considerable numbers of militia. At Perth alone there were normally three or four regiments of militia providing guards and escorts for the prisoners there, with 300 soldiers on guard duty every day.[5] Even at Greenlaw, a very much smaller depot than Perth or Valleyfield, Captain Kaald observed that 'Every watch consists of 40 to 50 men. Therefore, there are a lot of soldiers just outside the prison to be at hand in an emergency.'[6]

There were also some artillerymen among the depot guards, at least at Perth and Penicuik. At the former, according to Marote-Carrier, 'a garrison of artillerymen' had ten 18lb guns always loaded and aimed at the depot gates, and 'an artilleryman on guard stood watching there with match ready lit.'[7] At Penicuik there appears to have been a battery of artillery stationed at the tented camp 'in a large field on the high ground to the west of the village of Kirkhill, ... held ready in case of a general rising of the prisoners.'[8]

The barracks occupied by the militia responsible for guard and depot duties at the Scots depots were, in Edinburgh, those at the Castle and sometimes Queensberry House, Canongate; for Penicuik, those at Dalkeith and Musselburgh, apparently some quarters at Roslin, the cavalry barracks in Penicuik itself and the tented camp at the adjoining village of Kirkhill, as well as, after its evacuation as a depot in March 1811, Esk Mills; in Perth, the former cavalry barracks, where 'the stables are now converted into soldiers' rooms, and several officers' rooms have been fitted up in the higher storey. The whole will accommodate 1,000 men, which is nearly the amount of the troops at present there.'[9] The marching back and forth from those barracks or camps by companies of militiamen going on or returning from guard or escort duties was a familiar sight in Edinburgh, Perth, and in Midlothian at or around Penicuik.

As in all wars, relations between the prisoners and their guards varied from place to place and from time to time, and between individuals or groups. Examples at one extreme were the shooting at Greenlaw of the prisoners Cottier in 1807 and Simonsen in 1810 by panicky or trigger-happy guards, and the apparently brutal behaviour of some guards escorting prisoners in November 1812 from their landing place in Fife overland to Perth depot.[10] On the other hand, when at Valleyfield Marote-Carrier and a fellow prisoner were serving a sentence in the cachot or black hole, sympathetic treatment and and friendly advice were given them by the sergeant of the guard.[11]

In the early days of the war the Transport Board had laid down rules governing contacts between the prisoners and their guards. In a letter to Colonel Clinton, military secretary to the commander-in-chief, the Duke of York, the Board said it had 'given strict orders to our agents at all the depots ... not to allow any person whatever to enter into the prisons or to have any communication with the prisoners, excepting the officers of the Guard and such persons as may be employed in the service of the prisons, and to take care that neither the guards nor any of the persons employed about the prisons have any other intercourse with the prisoners than what the service may absolutely require.'[12] These orders appeared during the war to be ideals; the daily realities at the depots were often somewhat different.

Toward what proved to be the end of the war, a routine meeting in early October 1813 of Perthshire landowners, presided over by the Duke of Atholl, expressed concern, as has been seen, about some recent events at Perth depot—including what one speaker described as 'too easy intercourse between the prisoners and the public, such as throwing forged bank notes into circulation, providing themselves with arms, and getting possession of the silver coin of the district.'[13] Soon after the landowners' meeting the Duke of Atholl, as lord lieutenant of Perthshire, wrote about these complaints to the home secretary, who asked the Transport Board for their comments. The Board in its slightly tart reply explained that 'the care and custody of prisoners of war under the direction of the Lords Commissioner of the Admiralty is vested in this Board by patent under the Great Seal, and the regulations which are now objected to by the Duke of Athol [sic] and which are in force at every depot in the kingdom, have been formed after long experience and are established by His Majesty's Order in Council, nor does it appear to us that what His Grace proposes would be any improvement whatever. With respect to the proposed increased intercourse between the prisoners and the sentinels we have had too many instances of irregularities, even under the present restricted intercourse, to recommend that the sentinels should be the only medium of communication with the prisoners.'[14] No doubt the kinds of irregularities the Transport Board had in mind included not only the recently reported further case of banknote forgery, this time involving Private Thomas Gray, a militia guard at Valleyfield, but also numerous cases of complicity by guards in smuggling in or out of the depots straw and straw plait, and (more so in England) the taking of bribes from prisoners intent on escaping.[15]

How many guards at the Scots depots were offered bribes, and how many accepted them, to enable prisoners to escape it is impossible to say. At Valleyfield Marote-Carrier one day about December 1811 entered into conversation with a sentry who, expressing sympathy for his plight, added: 'If you had some money I would try to let you escape.' The outcome was that Marote-Carrier paid in advance the sum the sentry asked for and careful preparations were made for him and six other prisoners, including Lieutenant Jacques Adam, to escape. The sentry, however, had been deliberately leading them on. He reported their plans to his superior officers, and as Marote-Carrier and his companions prepared to depart via a hole in the wall bayonets were thrust through at them from the other side. Five of the would-be escapers succeeded in running back into their beds before the guards rushed into their room but Marote-Carrier and one of his companions were caught red-handed, if not barefooted, and marched off to the cachot.[16] Nor was that the only projected escape where guards acted as agents provocateurs. There was a similar deception practised on prisoners at Perth in April 1813, for example, by a guard in the Durham Militia who in return for a promised bribe connived at six of them getting over the depot wall by a rope ladder. There they were promptly pounced on by 'a strong party of soldiers' and carried off to the cachot. 'In this affair it seems to have been diamond cut diamond, for the prisoners had intended to cheat the soldier of his reward. What they gave him for doubloons as they passed his [sentry] station, were only three-shilling pieces, and the bank notes only waste paper.'[17] On the other hand, again at Perth, two soldiers in the Renfrewshire Militia were arrested along with a woman in February 1813 and detained in prison by the sheriff, all three suspected of having aided in the successful escape from the depot of three prisoners who had made their way to Broughty Ferry and sailed off in the smack *Nancy*.[18] Several months later, in June 1813, when Joachim Souaris, a Portuguese, escaped with two other prisoners from Perth he was soon recaptured. In return for a promise by the depot agent that he would be released and allowed to join His Britannic Majesty's forces, Souaris 'confessed that three sentries had been bribed to favour their Escape, which three with the whole of the [guard] Reliefs of the Night at those Posts have been in confinement ever since.'[19] From Edinburgh Castle a Danish prisoner claimed to have escaped with seven others in 1812 by bribing the sentries.[20]

The corruptibility, actual or potential, of some guards was obviously a subject of concern for the depot authorities and the Transport Board.[21] That concern no doubt helps explain the fairly frequent changing of the militia regiments mounting guard at the depots.[22]

Concern indeed was constant on the part of the army authorities, who (not the Admiralty or the Transport Board) were primarily responsible for guarding the prisoners in order to prevent their escape, especially any mass break-out. That concern was heightened by the arrival in Scotland in 1811-12 of greatly increased numbers of prisoners, the opening then as depots successively of Esk Mills, Edinburgh Castle, Valleyfield, and Perth, and the increase during 1810-12 in the number of parole towns from one (Peebles) to thirteen.[23] The obvious danger confronting the authorities was that any mass break-out by the prisoners, accompanied by their seizure of weapons, might immediately create tumultuous conditions favourable to a possible invasion of Britain by Napoleon. If hundreds, not to say thousands, of such veteran rank and file fighting men could break out from the depots, and if simultaneously from nearby parole towns hundreds or even scores of Napoleon's veteran army or naval officers simply marched off and placed themselves at the head of those rank and file prisoners, then the nightmare of a co-ordinated uprising and invasion might indeed become a reality. If the prisoners of war were hostages for the reasonable treatment of British prisoners in France, they were thus also potentially a Trojan horse for Napoleon to employ in an invasion of Britain. It was, after all, that nightmare of co-ordinated uprising by prisoners in the south of England and simultaneous invasion by Napoleon, as reported by the black prisoner Garçon Baptiste at Portchester Castle depot in September 1810, which had prompted the hurried and extensive removal shortly afterward of thousands of prisoners to Scotland.[24] These anxieties are also plainly audible in a letter from the Transport Board in August 1812 to Mr R.H. Crewe, secretary of the Board of Ordnance, concerning 'a powder magazine near Perth depot, in which is deposited a very considerable quantity of gunpowder belonging to the merchants of Perth and to several Local Militia corps, to which access is allowed in a very negligent and dangerous manner', and asking if the Board of Ordnance 'consider that the public should be at the expense of removing this magazine, or what other mode should be adopted to prevent the danger so much to be dreaded under the present circumstances.'[25]

It was that same concern which in the autumn of 1811 made the army commander in Scotland, Lieutenant General Lord Cathcart, 'apprehensive that the Depot for parole prisoners at Peebles is too near that for the prisoners confined at Valleyfield, and that the parole town of Cupar [Fife] is too near the sea coast and the new depot at Perth.' All the parole prisoners, including of course many veteran army and naval officers, were consequently removed in November that year from Peebles to Dumfries (and a score of them soon afterwards from Dumfries to Sanquhar), and from Cupar to Lanark.[26]

Another eminent, although civilian, person in Scotland who expressed concern about the potential dangers posed by the prisoners of war was the Wizard of the North himself, Sir Walter Scott. In May 1812 Scott, who was sheriff-depute of Selkirkshire, was 'very apprehensive' that militia weapons stored in an unguarded warehouse at Kelso might be seized by parole prisoners there, acting with others from Jedburgh and Selkirk. At the same time Scott, strongly Tory, was alarmed by what he saw as subversive activities among handloom weavers at Galashiels. He had found, he told Robert Southey, the poet, in June 1812, that the Gala weavers were in touch with a weavers' committee at Manchester which 'corresponds with every manufacturing town in the South and West of Scotland, and levies a subsidy of 2s.6d. per man—(an immense sum)—for the ostensible purpose of petitioning Parliament for redress of their grievances, but doubtless to sustain them in their revolutionary movements.' Southey, Scott considered, was 'quite right in apprehending a *Jacquerie*; the country is mined below our feet.'[27]

Scott might have been even more alarmed had he known of certain reports reaching the Home Office and the Transport Board during that troubled summer of 1812, when at least some of the authorities and members of the upper classes were fearful of a revolutionary outbreak.[28] The Luddite movement in England was at its height and there were more British troops deployed against it than had been sent under Wellington in 1808 to Portugal at the beginning of the Peninsular War.[29] The price of wheat and hence of bread reached its highest level in the whole of the 19th century, and there were food riots—for example, in Edinburgh in August.[30] The prime minister, Spencer Perceval, had been assassinated in May at the House of Commons. The power and prestige of Napoleon, whose Grande Armée invaded Russia in June, appeared still at an apogee.

One of those reports to the Home Office—apparently reliable since it came from Lieutenant General the Hon. Thomas Maitland, in command of the troops in the north of England—was that evidence had been found of a connection between Luddites and French prisoners of war on parole. Sergeant James Lawson, a deserter from the Surrey Militia who proved to be a distinctly dubious character, informed (and convinced) the authorities that he had made his way into the central councils of the Luddite movement, and that a joint uprising of Luddites and Irish republicans was being organised in which French prisoners of war were also involved. Lawson also gave the Home Office in August reports of a similar kind, including information that the Luddites were planning a rising in December with the object of liberating the prisoners of war, and that his colleague Matheson had gone to Scotland to identify places where arms from France could be landed. Lawson was the subject of a considerable three-way correspondence that autumn between the home secretary, General Wynyard, army commander in Scotland, and the Lord Advocate. Described in the correspondence as 'a suspicious character', Lawson (whose allegations had meantime led to a score of arrests) came eventually to be regarded by the Home Office as a far from reliable source of information; and with the decline of Luddite disturbances the authorities' fear of a possible uprising by the prisoners of war diminished.[31]

Apart from the reference to Matheson, another intriguing one concerning Scotland was contained in a letter in April 1813 from John Beckett, under-secretary at the Home Office, to Francis Freeling, secretary to the General Post Office. The letter referred to 'cancelling warrants for detaining letters mentioned in the lists below'—and one of those mentioned on 'A list of intercepted letters' was 'Morrison, Private of the Aberdeenshire Militia, Dalkeith. No letter.' The cancellation appears to have been dated 28 December 1812.[32]

The authorities' fear of an uprising was not entirely allayed after 1812. Nor can it have been diminished by a mutiny in February 1813 by some militiamen in several of the regiments stationed at Perth. There is no evidence, nor was there likelihood, of contact, still less of collusion, between the mutineers and the prisoners of war in the depot. Nonetheless that some among the guards themselves were in a state of mutiny cannot have been other than a source of fear for the authorities that the contagion might spread to the prisoners. The prisoners themselves appear likely to have learned of the mutiny more or less as soon as it took place (not least since it included a fracas just outside the walls of the depot), although no reference has been found to their doing so or to their reactions to it.[33]

'It had been confidently anticipated,' declared a local newspaper a week after the militiamen's mutiny broke out at Perth on 19 February, 'from the clear, decided and anxious opinion pronounced by the great law officers of the Crown on the claims of the militia substitutes, that the country should hear no more of the subject. It was therefore with surprise and pain that the inhabitants of the city witnessed on Friday last a sudden burst of mutiny among the Renfrewshire Militia, a regiment which had hitherto united utmost propriety of conduct with a degree of discipline excelled by few regiments of the line.'[34] The main events of the mutiny and its outcome were reported in the press. Within a few hours of its outbreak a troop of the 6th Dragoon Guards was sent from Piershill barracks in Edinburgh to Perth. 'We have also heard,' the *Caledonian Mercury* reported, 'that correspondence has been detected, carried on between some of the regiments, relative to the late application to Government on the subject of the limitation under which some of the militiamen enrolled themselves.' The *Perth Courier* carried particularly full accounts. 'We had drawn up and sent to the press,' it informed its readers on 25 February, 'a minute account of the military disturbance which took place in this city on Friday last [19 February], but have been induced to suppress it for the present, in consequence of having received the following statement from authority. We were sorry to observe a very disgraceful occurrence that took place in the streets of this town, on Friday, the 19th instant. Many men from the Renfrew, and some from the Fife, regiments of Militia, after being dismissed from the Garrison parade that morning, about 11 o'clock proceeded in the most riotous and disorderly manner to the prison, with the determination of liberating a private of the Perth Militia, who was really not in prison but only ordered to appear before the Sheriff for examination and was actually on the street at the time. The Officers did everything in their power to check the men, and with the assistance of the Durham [Militia] Regiment succeeded in getting the men to the Barracks ... The ringleaders who had been secured were instantly sent off in post chaises, under a proper escort, to Edinburgh; and to prevent the immediate recurrence of the outrage, two of the regiments were marched off the same evening, one of them to Dundee, and the other to Crieff and

Dunkeld. It was truly gratifying to witness the good order and regularity in which they left the town, after the moment of delusion was past and their minds were actuated by more soldierly dispositions. It is but justice to mention that during the whole of the riot the Durham Regiment of militia, to a man, behaved with the greatest coolness and steadiness and seemed resolved to suffer everything rather than disgrace their military character. The whole of the officers of the different regiments behaved with the greatest intrepidity and in many cases incurred considerable personal risk in securing the offenders and restoring subordination. The Fifeshire regiment was recalled [to Perth] on Saturday; the Renfrewshire is still quartered in Dundee.' The further march of events was reported in the *Dundee Advertiser* on 26 February: 'The regiment of Renfrewshire Militia, which arrived here [in Dundee] at a late hour on Friday [19 February] last, was yesterday ordered to return [to Perth]. It marched accordingly about midday, and after proceeding a few miles from the town the regiment was drawn up ... in the position [which was] everywhere commanded by detachments of the 6th Dragoon Guards, artillery, and Durham and Fife Militia, which had been marched from Perth at an early hour in the morning. Here the Renfrewshire were commanded to pile their arms and to deliver up seven of their number, whose names were specified. The arms were instantly piled, and the seven soldiers at once surrendered themselves. They were handcuffed, and carried forward under an escort for Edinburgh. But the [Renfrewshire] regiment received its arms again and was ordered back to Dundee. In the meantime, a strong detachment from the 70th Regiment, from Montrose and neighbourhood, had entered the town on the east and taken possession of the barracks before the return of their morning tenants. These manoeuvres have all been executed adroitly and without any accident.' The Renfrewshire Militia were marched away from Dundee three weeks later and posted to Pembrokeshire in south Wales, and the Fife Militia were sent at the same time from Perth to Berwick.

Almost effusive thanks offered to those militiamen and regiments which had not taken part in the mutiny or had helped in its repression were reported during the weeks following it. The Durham Militia, for instance, 'received the thanks of the General for the alacrity and steadiness they displayed in represssing the late disturbance at Perth, and the Magistrates of that town have presented to the men of the regiment a handsome gratuity in testimony of their service ...' Not everyone in Perth shared those views, for as the *Perth Courier* reported on 11 March: 'On Saturday se'ennight [i.e., 27 February] a soldier in the Durham Militia was shot at, and on examining his knapsack found it pierced by a bullet. The magistrates ... have issued hand bills and taken other measures for discovering the intended assassin.' In an advertisement in the same and succeeding issues of the *Courier* the Perth magistrates and the Durham Militia each offered a reward of 25 guineas to anyone giving information that would lead to the arrest and conviction of the offender. Whether the repression of the mutiny generated ill feeling which persisted for several months between some Perth citizens and the Durham Militia is not certain, but that may be the explanation for what, as late as 16 September that year, the *Perth Courier* reported were recent 'childish and indecent riots' in which 'several were knocked down' in the streets during 'tumults … from some quarrel between the town's people and the English militia.' 'Parties of the English militia,' the *Dundee Advertiser* reported of these tumults, had been 'parading the streets, and knocking down with bludgeons all who had the misfortune to fall in their way. Nay, respectable and unoffending citizens were assaulted even in their own shop-doors.' The Kirkcudbrightshire Militia, it was reported concerning the meeting in February, 'were not connected with some of the late proceedings in the militia corps and … have declared their abhorrence of such conduct.' The Ayrshire Militia likewise received the thanks of the Earl of Eglinton and the county of Ayr 'for their loyal, and soldierlike conduct in abstaining from, and expressing abhorrence of, the mutinous spirit manifested by many of the Scots Militia regiments.' The colonel of the regiment was invited by the commander-in-chief to choose 'whatever place he is pleased to select in Scotland as the headquarters of his regiment' in gratitude for its 'good conduct' during the mutiny. The Prince Regent himself approved the regiment in future being titled H.R.H. the Prince Regent's Royal Regiment of Ayrshire Militia. The Edinburgh and the Dumfriesshire Militia regiments were also said to have 'behaved in the most exemplary manner when called upon by other regiments to unite in obtaining redress for past grievances as militiamen. The men of the Dumfriesshire regiment, on receiving letters [from aggrieved fellow militiamen] on the subject, immediately delivered them up to the commanding officer, declaring that they would have nothing to do with the business.'

That the mutinous and riotous militiamen did not, however, lack sympathy and support from some citizens of Perth, as appears to have been further exemplified a week later by the firing of the shot at a Durham militiaman, was clearly demonstrated on the day of the mutiny itself. 'When the chaise in which Hally, a mutineer, was conveyed to Edinburgh was leaving Perth,' the *Caledonian Mercury* reported on 6 March, 'some of the inhabitants were imprudent enough to interest themselves in his favour by throwing stones at the carriage; and the lamps and glasses being broken, and the populace seeming determined to persist in their opposition, the chaise was forced to return for a stronger guard. A man named John Stewart who was conspicuous in the riot was apprehended and held to bail to take his trial for the offence.' No other mention of a mutineer named Hally has been found, but John Stewart, a weaver at Earl's Dykes, Perth, was tried at the High Court in Edinburgh on 15 March for mobbing by throwing stones at soldiers escorting Hally in a chaise from Perth. The *Perth Courier* reported witnesses at the trial describing how a crowd consisting 'chiefly of young men, boys and girls' had thrown stones at the chaise between Perth and the prisoner of war depot a few hundred yards away on the South Inch and forcing it to return for a guard. One soldier witness said he had 'kepped [caught] nearly 100 stones with his hand, held up his hand and caught them like cricket balls'; and an officer in the Durham Militia testified that he had ordered the 40 men under his command 'to load with ball in order to intimidate the mob.' Several witnesses gave Stewart 'an excellent character, both as to moral and religious practices', but the jury unanimously found him guilty, although with a strong recommendation to mercy, and he was sentenced to four months in Perth gaol and to find 600 merks security for his behaviour for three years. Stewart's trial coincidentally delayed until that same day at the High Court the sentencing in the historic conviction of the Scottish Handloom Weavers' Association leaders, William M'Kimmie, president, James Johnstone, treasurer, and almost a dozen others, including Alexander Richmond (although several of the weavers were not sentenced until a day or two later), for illegal combination or conspiracy in seeking an increase in weavers' wages. Coincidentally also, the mutiny by militiamen at Perth took place one month after a decision by the Perth magistrates not to grant a petition by the city's own handloom weavers to fix a rate of wages for them of about 12 shillings per week, although Francis Jeffrey, counsel for the weavers, had pointed out to the magistrates that weavers' wages had recently 'suffered a depression altogether unprecedented and that the depression has been greater in this district than in others', leaving wages at 7s. or 8s. a week for a working day of 14 or 15 hours [i.e., 84 to 90 hours per week], and that 'since 1792 [when a general rate of wages had been adopted] provisions have risen nearly two-thirds and wages instead of rising have sunk in the same proportion.' In giving their decision the magistrates' chairman told the weavers that 'The cause of your distress is the conduct of Bonaparte, and his enmity to commerce.' A week after the magistrates' decision at Perth, 14 convicted Luddites were hanged at York.

A general court martial, presided over by the Earl of Home, colonel of the Berwickshire Militia, and whose other members were 13 officers from the Ayrshire, Perthshire, Fife, East Yorkshire, Cambridge and Lancashire Militia, with Gilbert Hutcheson, Judge Advocate, as prosecutor, assembled at Edinburgh Castle on 3 March to try the militiamen charged with mutiny and riot. The proceedings lasted a month. Ten private soldiers from three militia regiments were found guilty—eight for being concerned in the riot and disturbance at Perth on 19 February, the other two for taking an active part in 'proceedings and meetings of a mutinous and seditious nature, and for endeavouring to excite and cause a mutiny and sedition by writing and sending two mutinous, seditious and inflammatory letters.' The eight were

James Fairlie, Fife Militia, Robert Watson, Peter Macartney, William Miller, David Stewart, John Boyle, Andrew Morris, and Robert Alexander, all of the Renfrewshire Militia; and the other two were Privates James Gillanders and David Taylor, both of the Perthshire Militia. Fairlie, Watson, Gillanders and Taylor were sentenced to 1,000 lashes each on their bare backs with a cat o' nine tails. The other six were sentenced to six months' solitary confinement. Subsequently, a petition by Fairlie, Watson and Gillanders for permission to serve abroad for life rather than suffer 1,000 lashes each was granted. Taylor, however, 'was marched from the Castle on Monday [26 April] to his regiment, there to receive his punishment.' It is not known whether he survived such a savage flogging.[35]

Two other examples of the continuing nervousness of the authorities about a possible mass break-out and uprising by the prisoners were provided at Perth in autumn 1813. First, on the night of 11-12 September, in an occurrence significant enough to attract a report in *The Times*, a tunnel 'was discovered in the floor of the officers' prison (or No. 6) at the depot. The iron hoops had been cut, and an excavation of sufficient diameter to admit a man had been carried 19 feet perpendicularly downwards and 30 feet horizontally outwards. A detachment of the guard having marched into the prison after this discovery, the men were stoned by the prisoners, among whom the sentries fired three muskets but without doing any injury.' The next night at 11 p.m. the guard, alarmed by the sight of 40 prisoners 'strolling about in the airing ground of No.3 [prison],' and 'apprehending a general attempt at escape, rushed towards the place where the prisoners were assembled, and having seized 24 drove the rest back into the prison. Three of the prisoners were wounded in the tumult, and immediately conveyed to the hospital. The 24 who had been seized were lodged in the *cachot*, where they at present remain, together with eleven retaken fugitives.' Next morning at roll call 28 of the prisoners were missing—having departed via a tunnel 'which communicated with the great sewer of the depot.'[36] The *Courier* blamed 'the great commotion' (as the *Dundee Advertiser* of 17 September described it) on 'The 800 prisoners who were lately transferred from Pennicuick [and who] are, it is said, of a much more turbulent and ungovernable character than the rest.' The *Dundee Advertiser* for its part provided a few more details about the major escape on the Sunday night: 'By means of keys which they had made for themselves, one of the prison doors was opened from the inside. A great number of prisoners rushed forward in a body, apparently with the intention of effecting their escape by force; and before they could be reduced to obedience some of them, we believe, were wounded.'

Second, the decision by Major-General Graham, army commander at Perth, to march some 1,500 troops into the depot there on 11 October 1813 in order to conduct a thorough search for arms among the prisoners was no doubt a result partly of the continuing nervousness among the authorities about a possible armed uprising; partly a reaction to the criticism by the *Perth Courier* (reproduced in *The Times*) of the 'very lenient' punishments inflicted on the prisoners and the need for 'a general increase of vigilance and severity in the management of the Depot'; and partly an outcome of the specific anxieties expressed a few days earlier at the meeting in the city of Perthshire landowners, presided over by the Duke of Atholl. 'Having made a large detachment suddenly enter the airing ground of each prison,' the local newspaper reported, 'the prisoners were turned out and the prisons strictly searched. The persons of the prisoners were also searched when they were turned in. We understand that no offensive weapons or anything of much consequence was discovered. General Graham ... intimated to the prisoners that so long as they gave no trouble they should be mildly treated, but that if they continued their restless projects of escape to the disquiet of the country, they might expect the severest measures to be adopted.'[37]

When, two and a half years earlier, some 23 prisoners at Esk Mills had undertaken what appeared to be a particularly 'restless project of escape', followed a few days later by an apparent attempt at mass escape by flattening the surrounding palisade by the sheer weight of their numbers rushing against it, not only were of course the depot guards turned out but also 'large detachments' of troops were summoned by bugle from Roslin and field artillery guns were galloped down to deal with it. According to Andrew Johnston, depot clerk, a mass escape was prevented 'by the military surrounding the entire stockade with fixed bayonets pointed through the openings of the Palisade ... and two field pieces loaded with grape were placed on the heights above the prison so as to command the whole yard.'[38] Whatever the individual or personal contacts between the prisoners in the Scots depots and their guards, the ultimate defining function of the latter was illustrated by that overwhelming firepower.[39]

Apart from during those 'commotions' at Esk Mills and Perth there were no other major interventions by troops at the depots in Scotland. But the threat of bringing in the guards to deal with disobedience or turbulence among the prisoners was from time to time voiced: '... if the prisoners should be refractory we direct you to call in the aid of the military,' Lieutenant Priest, agent at Greenlaw, was told, for example, in August 1811 by the Transport Board. A similar order was given Captain Brown, agent at Valleyfield, by the Board in March 1813: '... you will on no account suffer yourself to be deterred by the threats or riotous conduct of the prisoners but not lose a moment in calling in the aid of the Military if necessary.'[40]

Intervention by armed guards raised, of course, as in the shooting at Greenlaw of Cottier in 1807 and of Simonsen in 1810, the issue of the circumstances in which they could open fire on the prisoners. According to evidence given at the trial at the High Court of the militiaman found guilty of the culpable homicide of Simonsen, orders for the guard made it clear that sentries were not to fire except when prisoners were escaping or attempting to escape. But what were the rules concerning troops firing on prisoners engaged in 'riotous or tumultuous proceedings'? [41] When in April 1813, arising from difficulties with prisoners at Valleyfield, the agent there sought guidance from the Transport Board about relevant orders given the troops at the depot, the Board corresponded on the question with Colonel Henry Torrens, military secretary of the commander-in-chief of the army, the Duke of York. The Board sent Torrens a copy of a letter from the Deputy Adjutant General at Edinburgh to Major General Sir John Dalrymple, 'by which it appears that in case of any riotous or tumultuous proceedings on the part of the prisoners, it is expected that the extreme measure of firing upon the prisoners shall only be resorted to at the requisition of the agent of this Board at the said depot.' The Board asked if the commander-in-chief could consider 'how far it may be proper thus to leave to the determination of the agent … when it may be proper to fire upon the prisoners … [as] the Board from experience are of opinion that when the agent may have occasion to call in the aid of the military in any case of emergency, the officer commanding the guard is the most proper person to determine in what manner that aid is to be given, and particularly when it may become necessary to fire upon the prisoners.'[42] No reply to the Board's letter or any further correspondence by it on the issue has been found.

If the fears of the authorities and of Sir Walter Scott and other members of the upper classes had in fact proved well founded and a rising of prisoners in Scotland ever had taken place in, say, 1812-13, whether or not in some supposed association with Luddites in England or with handloom weavers north of the Border who were then agitating over wages and prices, a leader might have been available from March 1812 onwards for such a rising, could he have been somehow prised out of his enforced residence in Dumbarton Castle. He was General Edouard-François Simon, baron of the French Empire and, with Adjutant General Charles Prévost De Boissi, the most senior army officer in captivity in Scotland during the Napoleonic Wars.

Born in 1769 at Troyes, Simon had risen from the rank of second lieutenant in the 1st regiment of the Line at the outbreak of the French Revolutionary Wars in 1792 to brigadier-general at the time of his capture at the battle of Busaco in Portugal in September 1810. By the time he found himself confined in Dumbarton Castle Simon thus had not only two decades' experience of warfare but also had twice been made a prisoner of war. The first occasion had been in October 1798 when, as chief of staff to its commander General Hardy,

Simon, and others in the French expeditionary force to Ireland, had been captured on board the invasion fleet after a battle off the coast of Donegal with the Royal Navy. Simon had, however, soon afterwards been exchanged and he continued on active service in the French army until the end (as it then seemed) of the wars in 1802. In June that year his career was suddenly brought to a halt when, as chief of staff to General Bernadotte, he became involved in a conspiracy by the latter and General Moreau against Napoleon as First Consul. Fearing discovery, however, Simon had panicked and divulged the plot to the Consulate authorities. Sentenced to confinement for several years on the island of Oléron in the Bay of Biscay near La Rochelle, Simon appealed to Napoleon for a pardon and was restored to his rank in the army, although it was not until after the outbreak of the Peninsular War in 1808 that he was able to re-establish his career.[43]

As senior brigadier-general in General Loison's division at the battle of Busaco on 27 September 1810, Simon was advancing at the head of his troops against the British lines when, according to Lieutenant Doisy de Villargennes, himself later a parole prisoner at Selkirk, who was a subaltern in one of the infantry regiments under Simon's command, Simon 'was knocked off his horse, with a ball in his neck, and left on the field for dead.'[44] In fact, Simon's wounds, though bad enough, were not mortal as Doisy had believed. None other than Wellington himself observed the wounded Frenchman on the battlefield, a victim of the recently introduced Shrapnel shell. Wellington consequently wrote to Lord Liverpool: 'My opinion in favor of these shells has been much shaken lately. First, I have reason to believe that their effect is confined to wounds of a very trifling description; and they kill nobody. I saw General Simon, who was wounded by the balls from Shrapnel's shells, of which he had several in his face and head; but they were picked out of his face as duckshot would be out of a face of a person who had been hit by accident while out shooting ...'[45] When despite repeated attempts his valet had failed to reach Simon to tend him, the young and pretty *vivandière* (a woman authorised to sell the troops food, drink, clay pipes, toiletries, etc.) of Doisy de Villargennes' regiment mounted her donkey, got through the fighting unharmed, and looked after Simon for several days until his valet was able to rejoin him.[46]

Although the Transport Board told their agent at Edinburgh a month after Simon's capture in Portugal that he and other officers were being sent to Leith and from there were to be sent on to one of the proposed new parole towns 'such as Roxburgh, Selkirk and Melrose', Simon in fact was sent on parole to Odiham, midway between Aldershot and Basingstoke in Hampshire.[47]

Simon was experienced not only as a general but also as a plotter, as his confinement by Napoleon on the island of Oléron indicated. He had not been long at Odiham when the authorities discovered he had been in secret correspondence with the French government. A fellow prisoner at Odiham named Dutache, unable to find enough money to join several other prisoners there who were able to escape back to France with the help of an organised group of English escape agents based at Folkestone, had subsequently informed the authorities of their arrangements. As a reward Dutache was granted his release from captivity and was repatriated to France. Simon, however, in secret correspondence with the French authorities, reported Dutache's activity, and on his arrival at the port of Morlaix in Brittany Dutache was executed.[48] Shortly afterwards, in November 1811, Simon in his captivity was created a baron of the French Empire.[49] The Transport Board, however, intercepted letters to Simon and then in early January 1812 seized his papers, which showed he had violated his parole by 'carrying on a correspondence with France through the mediation of several Frenchmen resident in London some of whom we have already apprehended.' The Admiralty sanctioned the Board's proposal that Simon should be 'immediately sent into close Confinement for such a gross Breach of his Parole Honour.' But before the Board could take that action Simon, realising his secret correspondence had been uncovered, escaped from Odiham.[50]

Simon's correspondence, part of which with a certain Monsieur Tannier, an alien living in London, was said by the Transport Board to be 'of a dangerous Tendency', appeared to contain evidence of various conspiracies. Other letters found in his papers led to their writers, all eight of them officers on parole at Odiham and Alresford in Hampshire or Thame in Oxfordshire, being sent into confinement at Portchester Castle.[51] J. B. Sugden, translator at the Transport Office of Simon's correspondence, declared in his report of 28 January to the Transport Board concerning the conspiracies in which it appeared Simon was engaged: 'To leave this unpunished would be subversive of all Order amongst Prisoners of War.'[52] It was Sugden who was apparently the 'Gentleman belonging to the Transport Office' and who, according to *The Times*, 'discovered the traitorous correspondence of General Simon and Surgeon Boiron with the French Government respecting the landing of a considerable number of troops on the coast of Cornwall. General Simon, it is said, undertook to arrange with the prisoners here to join them.'[53] What seemed to confirm and compound Simon's guilt was that, as Sir Rupert George, chairman of the Transport Board, wrote to Lord Melville, First Lord of the Admiralty, 'There are not any papers in this Office of General Simon but what are in Masonic characters, and a few statements of the number of Troops in Spain, and Prisoners in England and his Correspondence which is partly Masonic and partly of such a nature as to induce the Board to reserve them for the present ... The General when on parole was elected Grand Master of Masons at Portchester Castle, for purposes, no doubt, hostile to this country.'[54] All this convinced the authorities that, although an officer, and a senior one at that, General Simon was no gentleman—or, as the historian Abell long afterwards put it, he was 'thoroughly bad'.[55] J. B. Sugden's report on Simon said: 'It is evident that General Simon, on the seizure of his Papers, wrote to his numerous Correspondents in London, and various Parole Towns, advising them to destroy their Papers.' Consequently, only one of Simon's letters was among his papers seized. 'This,' wrote Sugden, 'is much to be regretted, as, from the general Tenor of the Correspondence, there is no Doubt that information of much more Importance would have been obtained from his Letters to his Agents than from their Letters to him ... The whole of the Evidence, therefore, which is in the Possession of this Board, against General Simon, and those who have been concerned with him, has been procured from his Papers alone.' Sugden referred to Simon's having corresponded via Sweden, and to more than 1,000 letters being brought from France to Simon on one occasion by a man named L'Ami Gilles, whose actual name was William Gilles. It was Gilles, said Sugden, who had taken to the French minister of police the general's letter denouncing M. Dutache. An escaped French parole prisoner from Wantage in Berkshire named Boutony or Boutmy had also been 'concerned in forwarding the General's correspondence.' Simon had also, said Sugden, 'connived at the Escape of Prisoners of War'.[56]

For such a prominent captive to abscond and to do so in breach of his parole inevitably aroused keen public interest, and the search for Simon and Philip Boiron, the surgeon and fellow prisoner who had escaped with him, was widely reported in the press, not least in *The Times*. The Transport Board offered a reward of £100 for the recapture of Simon and ten guineas for that of Boiron. In the Board's description of him in its advertisement in *The Times*, Simon was said to be 'called a Baron and Chevalier of the French Empire', was 40 years of age, 5 feet 10 inches tall, with 'black hair, hazle [sic] eyes, oval visage, swarthy complexion, and has a scar on the left cheek.'[57]

Simon remained at large only a couple of days. 'By the exertions of Vickery and Lavender, the Bow Street Officers,' *The Times* reported on 18 January, 'the French General Simon, who is charged with the breach of his parole from Odiham, and with being guilty of traitorous correspondence, was traced on Thursday evening [16 January] to a house in Pratt Street, Camden Town, where they apprehended him. They also took into custody in the same house M. Boiron, a surgeon in the French army, who is charged with being concerned with the general. They were taken ... to Tothill-fields Bridewell, and safely lodged.' A French woman at the house in Pratt Street was also arrested and taken to Bow Street, where she was questioned about concealing the two escapers. Referring to the execution at Morlaix by the French authorities of the repatriated prisoner Dutache, *The Times* added that 'His sole offence ... was that he expressed himself ashamed of the manner in which many French officers had violated their parole of honour. These expressions were conveyed to Buonaparte, who ordered him to be shot instantly.'

A further report of the affair which appeared two days later in *The Times* added that as a result of the activity of the Bow Street runners 'a number of Frenchmen who corresponded with General Simon have been lodged in Tothill-fields Bridewell and were on Saturday [18 January] removed thence to a prison-ship at Chatham.'[58]

The same day as that report in *The Times* the Home Secretary, Richard Ryder, wrote to the army commander in Scotland, Lieutenant General Lord Cathcart, that Simon was 'to be kept in close military custody ... [in] one of the forts in Scotland.' Fort George, near Inverness, was, Ryder believed, 'in a state perfectly fit for the reception of General Simon'. Cathcart's view, which was invited, was, however, that there were 'strong objections' to Fort George. So it was decided that Simon be confined in Dumbarton Castle.[59]

Dumbarton Castle, built on a volcanic rock rising almost 250 feet above the river Clyde, had been for six centuries during the early middle ages the centre of the kingdom of Strathclyde. From the 11th century onward the castle was an important stronghold of the kingdom of Scotland, but at the time of General Simon's arrival there most of the castle buldings dated only from the 18th century. Apart from half a dozen veteran gunners headed by a recently appointed master gunner who rejoiced in the name of Romeo Drysdale (and who retained that appointment at the Castle until his death in 1849 at the age of 84), there was in garrison at the barracks at the Castle a company of militia, all of them under the command of the lieutenant-governor, Colonel (later Major-General) Ilay Ferrier.[60]

The Transport Board, duly instructed by the Home Secretary about Simon's destination, had 'directed two Rooms to be prepared' for his confinement in the Castle. By 20 February the rooms were ready for him. Next day the Admiralty approved Simon's immediate departure there, and instructed the Board to ascertain from the Home Secretary whether 'the place is quite secure and a proper guard prepared ... and also into whose charge the general and his servant are to be delivered in Dumbarton Castle.' A few days later the Board was able to inform Vice Admiral Otway at Leith and Lieutenant General Lord Cathcart that Simon 'is about to be sent, with his servant Pierre La Doure, into confinement at Dumbarton Castle, where they will be delivered into the Charge of the Governor or Commanding Officer, by Messrs Vicking [i.e., Vickery] and Lavender, Police officers, who will attend them thither in the Glasgow Mail Coach of Friday next [6 March].[61] A further letter to General Lord Cathcart followed, expressing the Transport Board's view of the conditions to which Simon should be subject at the Castle: '... we leave it entirely to your Lordship to give such orders as you may think proper for the security of the General and his servant; but we think it highly necessary and advisable that General Simon should be confined to his apartment excepting when permitted to walk in a limited space attended by an escort, as General Rochambeau and other French Generals have been before equally strictly confined; and we see no necessity whatever for employing any person in a civil capacity to attend the General, it being intended that he should remain entirely in military custody. If, however, your Lordship will appoint a person belonging to the garrison to pay him the subsistence money which is to be allowed to him (being 2s.9d. per diem for himself and his servant), we will make a reasonable allowance to the person who may be so appointed for his trouble. We think it proper to add that it appears advisable that no persons whatever excepting those in whose immediate custody he may be should be allowed to have any communication with the General, and that all letters addressed to him and written by him should pass through this office.'[62]

'This morning,' reported the *Glasgow Courier* on 10 March, 'arrived at the Star Inn [Glasgow] the French General Simon, under charge of Messrs Vickery and Lavender, two Bow Street officers, on his way to Dumbarton Castle ... He is attended by one servant.' That same day Simon 'was conducted from Glasgow to Dumbarton Castle. He appears to be in bad health. When he stepped out of the carriage he was seized with a fit of violent bleeding at the nose.'[63]

A few other miscellaneous scraps of information survive about Simon's confinement at the Castle until the end of the war. The week after his arrival there the Transport Board relieved the anxieties of the Barrack Board on the subject by informing it that 'no allowance of coals or candles is to be made to General Simon at the expense of Government but that any additional expenses incurred for lamps and lanterns ... will be defrayed by this Department.' In August that year, when the barrack master at the Castle found himself 'at a loss how to account for the bedding now in the use of the servant of the French General Simon and the Provost Serjeant', the Transport Board asked the Barrack Board 'to furnish such articles of bedding as may be necessary for the accommodation of these persons.'[64] That same summer Simon appears to have addressed to the recently appointed First Lord of the Admiralty, Lord Melville, son of Henry Dundas, some complaints about aspects of his treatment in confinement. Melville took up with Sir Rupert George, chairman of the Transport Board, points evidently made by Simon about his personal papers, as well as his receiving in error papers belonging to another prisoner, and about a poignard or dagger. 'The Poignard,' Sir Rupert replied, 'was ordered to be sent to the Governor of Dumbarton Castle but the General was in such a hurry to receive it that he wished to have it hastened to him, which the Board ordered; and by a misconstruction of their letter it was delivered to the General, of which he has no great cause to complain.'[65]

According to a local historian (who, however, does not give his sources) who was almost contemporary with the general's captivity there, Simon was confined in a two-storey building next to the barracks in 'a suite of rooms with iron-stanchioned windows,' and was 'vigilantly guarded by two soldiers with loaded arms and fixed bayonets.' He was allowed exercise twice a day, from 10 am to 12 noon and from 4 to 6 pm, by walking to the top of the eastern peak of the Castle rock and back again. 'The regular undeviating track of the General's ... walks, being at first covered with soft and verdant grass, became at length a beaten pathway, a yard beyond which he dared not venture, by reason of the strict military orders given his accompanying guards.'[66]

When in the winter of 1813-14 Simon's wife complained in France to Monsieur Rivière, head of the 5th Division of the French Ministry of Marine, the principal official concerned with French prisoners in Britain, about the 'severity of the confinement' experienced by her husband at Dumbarton Castle, Rivière sought from the Transport Board the readmission of Simon to parole. The Board obtained a report (no copy of which appears to have survived) from General Wynyard, who had by then succeeded General Lord Cathcart as army commander in Scotland, on the conditions in which Simon was confined at the Castle. But in sending a copy of Wynyard's report to the Admiralty the Board added: '... from the use which General Simon made of the liberty he at first had in this country we cannot recommend any additional liberty to be given to him at present.' The Board's view must have been strengthened if, as seems certain, it knew of Simon's activities in Scotland as recounted a century later by Abell (though without giving his sources): 'From Dumbarton he appears to have carried on a regular business as an agent for the escape of paroled prisoners, for, at his request, the Transport Office had given permission for two of his subalterns, also prisoners on parole, Raymond and Boutony by name, to take positions in London banks as French correspondents, and it was discovered that these men were actually acting as Simon's London agents for the escape of prisoners on parole. It was no doubt in consequence of this discovery that in 1813 orders were sent to Dumbarton that not only was Simon to be deprived of newspapers, but that he was not to be allowed pens and ink, "as he made such a scandalous and unbecoming use of them."' General Simon remained in captivity at Dumbarton Castle until several weeks after the end of the war.[67]

Prisoners in the Scots depots generally came more into contact day by day with at least some members, such as turnkeys, of the depot staffs who worked under the control of the agent, than they did with the militia guards. The agents themselves, who, with the exception of Malcolm Wright at Greenlaw and Edinburgh Castle, were naval officers, no doubt appeared to most of the prisoners as rather remote and even (as Marote-Carrier found in his interviews with Captain Moriarty, agent successively at Valleyfield and Perth) haughty figures. Because of the paucity of surviving letters from the agents to the Transport Board, it is possible to glean only an impression, which may well not be all that accurate, of their characters, their efficiency, and their attitudes to the prisoners in their charge. The characters and attitudes of Malcolm Wright and of Captain Moriarty have already been suggested above.[68] Those of two other agents, Captains Pellowe and Heddington, are additionally difficult to determine because of the short periods of their service in Scotland; nor is it possible to offer more than a very tentative indication of those of the two remaining agents, Captain Andrew Brown at Valleyfield in 1812-14, and Lieutenant Joseph Priest at Greenlaw in 1811-14. Priest was the only lieutenant who served as a depot agent in Scotland (though other naval lieutenants were among the parole town agents), and an impression left by the Transport Board's correspondence with him is that the Board treated him with rather less respect than it did his fellow agents north of the Border who were captains. Priest appears, however, as an agent who was on the whole not unsympathetic in his treatment of the prisoners, although the crumbling and sometimes distinctly cramped accommodation at Greenlaw presented at times particular difficulties there for him. Captain Brown at Valleyfield, especially in what appears to have been his consistent concern for the clothing of the miserables among the prisoners, leaves an impression of being a humane man.

The agents, as employees of the Transport Board, were all expected to apply systematically and consistently the rules and regulations governing the custody of the prisoners of war in their charge. Despite the obvious problems of communication at such a distance between Scotland and the Transport Board in London, the Board moreover tried, especially once the number of prisoners increased so greatly from early in 1811, to keep a close eye and grip upon the agents' management of their respective depots. Nonetheless the agents were at least sometimes in a position to make rather more or rather less trying the conditions the prisoners had to endure. Malcolm Wright, for example, in his idiosyncratic way, did apparently seek to make life at Greenlaw a little easier, at least for some of the officers in captivity there, as the diary of Captain Kaald testifies.[69]

At the outbreak of the war in May 1803 the Transport Board's concern that its depot agents 'be fit persons and attend to their duty', had led it then to propose to the Admiralty that 'the agents at all the principal depots should be commissioned officers in the Royal Navy.' It was, however, as late, as has been seen, as the end of 1811, with the final pushing overboard then of Malcolm Wright, that that proposal, which the Admiralty had appeared to accept eight years earlier, actually became fully implemented at the depots in Scotland.[70] The Board had maintained its view in the intervening years. 'We take this opportunity of submitting to their Lordships,' its members wrote to the Admiralty in November 1810, when the transfer of thousands of prisoners from England to new depots and parole towns in Scotland was about to begin, 'that, upon the fitting of Mr White's Building [i.e., Esk Mills], or any other place in Scotland, as a principal depot for the confinement of prisoners of war, it would be advantageous to the Service to appoint a Captain of His Majesty's Navy to be Agent there, and to appoint lieutenants as Agents to the inferior depots; all of which officers we beg to suggest on account of the many and various duties to be committed to them should be men of approved activity and possessing a competent knowledge of business.'[71] Indeed, the Admiralty then and afterward appointed as agents for close or confined (though not parole) depots in Scotland, apart from their existing agent Malcolm Wright (who had served as their agent, too, in the French Revolutionary Wars and who clearly must have had an influential patron) and Lieutenant Priest at Greenlaw, only naval captains. The Transport Board, on the suggestion of James Bowen, one of its members, sought for its part to enhance the authority of its agents appointed from the navy by sending all of them this circular in the summer of 1811: 'It being considered advisable, in order to insure a due degree of respect to the officers of His Majesty's navy employed under this Department as agents for prisoners of war that they should constantly wear their naval uniforms ... you are hereby required and directed to conform to this regulation accordingly immediately upon the receipt of this Order.'[72] Whether the wearing by the agents of their naval uniforms had any discernible effect on the prisoners in their charge is another of the many aspects of life in the Scots depots about which no evidence survives.

Of the depots in Scotland Perth, the largest, had unsurprisingly the largest staff to administer the aggregate of 7,700 prisoners confined there between its opening in August 1812 and the end of the war in 1814. Yet that staff, commanded by the agent, Captain Edmund J. Moriarty, RN, appears not to have numbered at any time more than about 30.[73] Next in seniority on the staff to the agent was the surgeon, James Gillies. Gillies had originally been the surgeon at Valleyfield when it opened as a depot in March 1811 but had become assistant there for a time to John Macansh when the latter was transferred from Esk Mills the month following its closure.[74] An assistant surgeon or hospital mate, John Beatty, was also appointed, evidently at the request of the agent, in November 1812.[75]

The chief or first clerk at Perth was Andrew Johnston.[76] Four other clerks, increased from January 1813 to five, were also employed at the depot—three of them described as extra (the work of one of whom was to supervise the sale of small beer in the canteen), and two others as hospital clerks or assistant dispensers. One of the latter, John Lewis, was also depot interpreter.[77] The dispenser appointed at the opening of the depot was Thomas Tripe, who had previously occupied that position first at Esk Mills and then after the latter's closure at Valleyfield.[78]

The most numerous section of Perth depot staff, hardly surprisingly, were the turnkeys or jailers, in whose numbers there appears to have been a gradual increase by the end of the war to ten.[79] A few weeks before the depot opened its agent was asked by the Transport Board to report whether three turnkeys who had lost their jobs at Esk Mills on its closure the previous year 'be now willing to go to Perth and are fit for the Service.' Those three apart, two turnkeys had by then already been appointed to Perth.[80] Before the depot opened early in August two more turnkeys had been appointed, and another two were added toward the end of that month.[81] By November that year the number of turnkeys appeared to have increased by two more to eight, and with the appointment of a ninth successfully proposed by the agent.[82] The first dismissal and replacement took place in January 1813, a second in April that year.[83] What appears to have been an additional appointment was made in May, making the total ten.[84] Another replacement occurred near the end of the war, in February 1814.[85]

The other members of the depot staff at Perth were labourers, lamplighters, a messenger, a hospital steward, a matron and a sempstress. The jobs of matron and sempstress were, the Transport Board told the agent, 'entirely intended for the widows of surgeons and other officers who have died in the service.'[86] There appears to have been one hospital steward;[87] other references to stewards seem to have been to prison stewards or chief turnkeys.[88] Likewise there appears to have been one messenger employed at the depot.[89] Thomas Miller had been appointed as labourer even before the opening of the depot, evidently to sail with the first intake of prisoners arriving on the transport vessel *Mathilda* and 'take charge of the stores on the passage' from Plymouth to Dundee.[90] The agent was authorised in December 1812 by the Transport Board to appoint two additional labourers.[91] Two lamplighters were employed at the depot at its opening, and two additional men were authorised by the Board in October that year.[92]

The staff establishment, including the agent, at Perth depot at any given time between its opening in 1812 and the end of the war in 1814 therefore appears to have between a couple of dozen and 31 or 32 at the maximum.[93]

At Greenlaw, Esk Mills, Edinburgh Castle and Valleyfield the categories of staff employed were similar, though not identical, to those at Perth for, except at Valleyfield, the numbers of their staffs were correspondingly smaller or much smaller.

Valleyfield, though with fewer prisoners than Perth at any given time during 1813-14, had almost as many staff. Between April and August 1811 it had both a surgeon and an assistant surgeon, and although the evidence is incomplete and contradictory it had, or may have had, two surgeons again from the end of 1811 until the end of the war, plus in 1813-14 a French assistant surgeon. It appears that the original intention to appoint a hospital mate or mates was not carried out, but a French surgeon (whose name has not been found) from among the prisoners was appointed to assist the surgeon from December 1812.[94]

As for clerks, the evidence is sometimes tenuous but Valleyfield appears to have had either four, five or even six at certain periods between 1811 and 1814. Alexander Munro, a hospital clerk at Norman Cross depot in England since 1803, was appointed chief or first clerk at Valleyfield in December 1810 and remained at the depot (apart from a period in 1811 when he was employed at Edinburgh Castle) until after the end of the war. From August 1812 Munro was also the official interpreter there.[95] The number of clerks over whom Munro (or, in 1811-12, Andrew Johnston) presided appears to have varied between three and five.[96]

How many turnkeys were employed at Valleyfield at any given period is likewise difficult to specify. The undated (but post-1811) Abstract, already referred to, of the staff establishment at the depot says Valleyfield had eleven turnkeys, including those transferred c. December 1811 from Edinburgh Castle, plus a carpenter-cum-turnkey. When in March and April that year the staff of Esk Mills on its closure had been transferred to Valleyfield those transferred appear to have included six turnkeys. There are, however, other references to three, and possibly more, turnkeys who had been at Esk Mills losing their jobs later.[97] A preliminary estimate may therefore suggest that there were at Valleyfield in its first three or four months from March to June 1811 between four and (including the maximum of six transferred from Esk Mills) twelve turnkeys; and that (assuming three or four of the Esk Mills transferees lost their employment in or about the summer of 1811) the number remained somewhere between four and eight or nine until the end of the war. If in fact Valleyfield had as many as twelve turnkeys at any time between 1811 and 1814 then it had two more than the considerably larger depot at Perth. A more tenable estimate, given the watchfulness of the Transport Board, may therefore be that Valleyfield had a maximum of eight to ten turnkeys at any given time, except perhaps that there may have been briefly a couple more after the closure of Esk Mills in the spring of 1811 and after the running down of the staff at Edinburgh Castle at the end of that year.

Other members of the Valleyfield staff consisted of lamplighters, labourers, a messenger, a dispenser, a hospital steward or stewards, a sempstress, and a matron.[98] The evidence is inconclusive about the employment at Valleyfield of a hospital steward or stewards, but at least one appears to have been transferred there on the closure of Esk Mills, although how long he remained at Valleyfield is a matter of surmise; and a cryptic reference in May 1813 may indicate that two prisoners were employed around that period at the hospital as stewards.[99] The dispenser at the depot hospital from March or April 1811 was Thomas Tripe, formerly dispenser at Esk Mills, and who had as his assistant at both depots successively John Lewis. Tripe, on his appointment to Perth in summer 1812 (when John Lewis was also transferred there), was succeeded by James Lauder.[100] A messenger appears to have been employed at the depot from at least the beginning of 1812.[101] The first reference to labourers at the depot was in March 1811, when two described as 'labourers, gravediggers', arrived among staff transferred from Esk Mills. Whether those two remained at Valleyfield until the end of the war is uncertain, but the meagre evidence suggests there was probably always more than one labourer employed at the depot.[102] A lamplighter was apparently transferred to Valleyfield on the closure of Esk Mills in March 1811, but he was almost at once replaced. An additional lamplighter was employed from September 1811.[103]

The staff establishment, including the agent, employed at Valleyfield between 1811 and 1814 therefore appears to have varied between a minimum of about 20 and a maximum of about 29.

At Esk Mills, on whose closure early in March 1811 the staff appear wholly or mainly to have been transferred to Valleyfield, the Transport Board had decided to appoint under the agent a surgeon, a dispenser and an unspecified number of hospital mates, a matron, a sempstress, and a hospital steward, a chief clerk and two ordinary clerks, a prison steward and six turnkeys, a messenger, two labourers and a lamplighter. But during its short existence the depot also employed several others on its staff.[104] Thus the staff establishment at Esk Mills appears in fact to have been, or during its short existence became, about twenty. If that were so, the number seems disproportionately high in comparison with those employed at Valleyfield and Perth, which had respectively from twice to almost three times as many prisoners as Esk Mills ever held.

At Edinburgh Castle any account of the staff establishment has to follow a particularly tortuous path. Under Malcolm Wright as Transport Board agent, the Castle, earlier an overnight staging post for some prisoners on their way to or from Greenlaw, began to function as a depot in March 1811, simultaneously with Valleyfield. For some refractory prisoners, including its first few arrivals then from Esk Mills, the Castle was also, as has been seen, a place of punishment. Housing at the most between 500 and 1,000 prisoners in its first five or six months as a depot, the Castle appears to have had a smaller staff even than Greenlaw and a much smaller one than Esk Mills, Valleyfield or Perth. On its opening a naval surgeon on half pay was appointed surgeon at the Castle depot. He also acted as dispenser. As early as August that year, when the number of prisoners confined in the Castle had been greatly reduced, the surgeon was discharged, although the Transport Board undertook to 'enter his name on the list for immediate employment.'[105] In the summer of 1813 the Castle again held more prisoners of war, and Vice Admiral Otway at Leith, exercising his general supervision over the Scots depots, appointed a surgeon there temporarily—which proved to be until mid-January 1814.[106]

The much smaller scale of the depot at the Castle was further illustrated by the Transport Board's order to the agent some weeks before its opening, 'to nominate a fit person to be clerk at Edinburgh Castle and two persons to be turnkeys.'[107] The Board undertook a week before the opening of the depot 'to appoint an additional turnkey in a few days who is also able to act as interpreter.'[108] It appears, however, that these two appointments were in fact kept separate.[109] By autumn 1811 the number of prisoners in the Castle had again fallen, and in September the surgeon and also the interpreter, Alexander Drummond, were discharged, leaving only one clerk and one turnkey. That the two latter, along with the agent, constituted the authorised revised staff establishment was confirmed the following month by the Board, though it told the agent that if he 'find occasion the person appointed as turnkey is to be employed as a messenger.' In November the Transport Board re-emphasised to the agent that 'no more than one turnkey can be allowed for the establishment', and the following month rejected an apparent suggestion by him for an increase in staff: '... we see no reason whatever for altering the establishment at Edinburgh Castle.' By January 1814 the Transport Board appears to have decided to transfer all staff remaining at Edinburgh Castle to Valleyfield.[110] No reference has been found to the presence among the Castle depot staff at any stage in 1811-14 of any matron, sempstress, labourer, hospital steward, or lamplighter. The staff, therefore, appears to have been at a maximum of about half a dozen during those spring and summer months in 1811 when it held its largest number of prisoners, but afterward to have declined even from that small number. In the last few months of the war there may only have been one or two staff, or even none at all, remaining in that ancient and dominating fortress which, towering high above Edinburgh, to many of the prisoners of war who trudged into it must have appeared a particularly disagreeable and sinister depot.[111]

Greenlaw, which served three times longer than any other in Scotland during the war as a depot for prisoners, had, as has been seen, two successive agents: Malcolm Wright, from its opening on 31 March 1804 until his appointment at the end of December 1810 as agent at Edinburgh Castle, and Lieutenant Joseph Priest, RN, who arrived at Greenlaw in January 1811 and remained agent until the end of the war. In the same decade the depot had three, possibly four, successive surgeons.[112]

There appear to have been two (or perhaps more accurately one and a half) clerks at Greenlaw until the end of 1809, but only one thereafter, except for six months in 1811-12 when there were again two. The small number reflected the fact that of the five depots in Scotland Greenlaw had (with the intermittent exception of Edinburgh Castle) the smallest number of prisoners.[113] Of turnkeys at Greenlaw there appear to have been either two or three at any given time.[114] A lamplighter and a messenger appear to be the only other categories of staff employed at Greenlaw, the work of storekeeper and interpreter being taken on first by the agent (reluctantly) and later, in the case of interpreter, by the clerk. As at Edinburgh Castle, there appear never to have been employed at Greenlaw either a matron or a sempstress.[115] The staff establishment at Greenlaw therefore appears to have numbered between a minimum of about six, including the agent, in the years from 1804 to 1811, and a maximum of about ten on occasions during the last three or four years of the war. In the last year of the war, when accommodation at Greenlaw was undergoing a massive extension, many prisoners were transferred to Valleyfield and Perth and, although the evidence is sketchy and contradictory, it appears that several of its staff were also then temporarily transferred to Valleyfield.[116]

Three aspects of the staffing of the depots in Scotland which in conclusion may therefore deserve some emphasis are the smallness of numbers employed relative to the number of prisoners, the frequency of dismissals or threats of dismissals, and the payment and in some cases accommodation provided.

For the agents and surgeons, and in most cases also the clerks and turnkeys, accommodation was provided within or near the depot, or lodging allowance was given. In the case of the agents successively in charge at Edinburgh Castle evidence is lacking about any accommodation provided for them within the Castle. It seems more likely that, except in the case of Malcolm Wright, himself a local merchant and once a city magistrate, who appears to have lived at home, they (i.e., Captain Heddington and Lieutenant Priest) lived in civilian rented accommodation near the Castle. At Greenlaw Malcolm Wright, as agent between 1804 and early 1811, evidently never was resident and it is doubtful if he ever did reside nearby at Roslin either, where accommodation appears originally to have been arranged for him.[117] His successor Lieutenant Priest was told on his appointment early in 1811 by the Transport Board that 'it is indispensably necessary that he should reside constantly as near to Greenlaw as possible.'[118] As the weeks passed the Board tightened the screw on Priest and also on the depot surgeon by asking (and threatening) 'whether a Lodging for Lieutenant Priest be not procurable in Pennycuick or any neighbouring Village, as unless this can be done so that the Agent and Surgeon at Greenlaw may be constantly on the Spot, we shall abolish that establishment entirely.'[119] A week later the screw was exchanged for a carrot dangled in front of Priest: '… if you can procure lodgings near the prison at Greenlaw the Board will allow you half a guinea per week'; and soon afterward it approved of his lodging at a place (unnamed in the surviving correspondence) he had mentioned to it. Nonetheless difficulties continued during March, when Priest was again told, 'it is indispensably necessary that you should provide yourself with a lodging close to the Prison, and that you cannot be allowed more than 10s.6d. a week for lodging money', and even well into April: '... the Board ... cannot recommend your taking your Family to Greenlaw at present.'[120] Amid the great extension of Greenlaw depot being built in 1813-14, Priest was told by the Board that although it was hastening on 'the finishing of the new house building for your residence at Greenlaw, ... we are not able to give you any assurance of your continuing at Greenlaw.'[121] The Board did, however, at the end of January 1814 approve of Priest 'having ordered coals to be furnished for the purpose of airing the house recently erected for the agent's residence at Greenlaw', and (apart from whatever intervening weeks he appears to have spent at Edinburgh Castle while the extension of Greenlaw was nearing completion) he was no doubt able to occupy the house until he ceased to be agent at Greenlaw about five months later, after the end of the war.[122]

At Esk Mills, six weeks before the opening of the depot in February 1811, the agent was told by the Transport Board that 'We consider it proper that the House at Esk Mills should be divided from the foundation upwards between you and the surgeon, leaving sufficient apartments for the dispenser and the first clerk.' The arrangement, however, did not suit the agent: '... we cannot remove you to Valleyfield,' he was told by the Board, 'but if you be not satisfied with the apartment allotted to you ... we have no objection to your providing yourself with lodgings as the Agents at Portchester Castle, Plymouth and Chatham do, but no allowance can be made to you on this account.' Whether the agent did move into lodgings is not known, and the question was overtaken by the closure of Esk Mills as a depot a few weeks later.[123]

At Valleyfield an estimate was approved by the Transport Board in June 1811 for building houses for the agent and the surgeon.[124] It appears that at first the two men were accommodated in the two houses formerly occupied by the two Cowan brothers as millowners, but later those two houses were gutted and converted into a depot hospital.[125] At the opening of the depot the agent was told by the Transport Board that 'part of the dwelling house at Valleyfield should be appropriated to the accommodation of the First [or chief] Clerk.'[126] A lodging allowance of 12s.6d. weekly was paid to the depot dispenser, but the clerks were refused any such allowance by the Transport Board on the grounds that no depot clerks anywhere in Britain were eligible for it. Five months later, in October 1811, the agent was told by the Board that 'although the clerks and stewards have been allowed apartments at the depot whenever there have been any that could be appropriated for them, yet it has never been usual to allow them lodging money when they have not had apartments in the prison'—so their request for an allowance was again refused.[127] Even the agent, Captain Pellowe, was at first refused lodging allowance while his house at the depot was being made ready but eventually in July 1811 he was granted a guinea a week backdated to the closure of Esk Mills, and his successor Captain Moriarty was granted the same amount two months later.[128] When in the winter of 1812-13 the agent asked for an allowance for coal, the Board replied: 'No allowance for coals can be made to you, as you have the same allowance as any other Agent, and indeed some of the Agents have not even Houses allowed to them.'[129]

At Perth, 'there was a square immediately within the outer entrance gate, where were the Agent's house on the right, and the surgeon's on the left, each of two storeys .... Further inwards, but without the inner gate, were four buildings, of one storey high, for officers of the establishment.'[130] No clear evidence has been found that the chief clerk, Andrew Johnston, was resident at the depot but it seems very likely he was, as may have been at least some of the rank and file clerks, as well as the dispenser, matron, sempstress, and hospital steward.

The salaries or wages of depot staff ranged, with certain variations for time, place, or rank, from the 30 shillings (£1.50) per day paid to agents, along with the provision of their accommodation and an allowance of £10.10.0 (£10.50) a year for stationery, down to 12s. (60 pence) a week paid to a labourer and a lamplighter.[131]

About members of the depot staffs other than the agents little is known beyond (in most cases) their names, the appointments they held and for how long (or how briefly). A list, undated but almost certainly compiled in 1813, of eleven clerks employed at Perth, Valleyfield and Greenlaw shows that two (John Lewis at Perth and Alexander Manson at Valleyfield) were perhaps surprisingly elderly, being aged respectively 67 and 68, while two others (Francis Wharton at Greenlaw and James White at Valleyfield) were perhaps surprisingly young, being respectively 22 and 19. The other seven were aged between 26 and 54. Several members of the staffs were related: for example, James and Frances Rushmore, who were successively at Esk Mills and Valleyfield, the two John Thorntons, father and son, at Greenlaw and Perth, and John Macansh, surgeon, and his brother Alexander, clerk, at Valleyfield. William Hill, surgeon at Greenlaw in 1811-13, had himself been a prisoner of war of the French from April 1804 to November 1809 at Verdun. James Strachan, hospital clerk at Perth from January 1813, was a former quartermaster sergeant in the 90th regiment of infantry, and it was not unlikely that some other members of the depot staffs, particularly perhaps turnkeys, messengers, labourers, and lamplighters, were former soldiers or navymen.[132]

That some members of staff did indeed hold their appointments briefly was due to their falling short of the depot rules and regulations or otherwise of the discipline that the agents and, from its base in London, the Transport Board sought to exert. Casualties were notably numerous among the turnkeys. At Greenlaw, for example, at least three turnkeys (Cameron, Rose and Ormeston) were dismissed within a period of less than two years in 1809-11; at Valleyfield between June 1811 and September 1812 two (James Wilson, for unspecified 'Mal Practices', and Henry Miles, whose skill in counting acquired from having previously been 'much among sheep' did not save him) were dismissed and three others (William Geddes, Lounie or Lowrie, and Younger) threatened with dismissal; at Perth, two (John Duncan, for 'repeated drunkenness', and Donald Campbell) were dismissed in the four months January-April 1813, and a third (Robert Robertson) may have been so in February 1814.[133] But it was not only the turnkeys who suffered from such occupational hazards. Even one agent (Malcolm Wright), after several years of skating on thin ice first at Greenlaw then at Edinburgh Castle, at the end of 1811 finally fell through it; a second (Lieutenant Priest at Greenlaw) was threatened with dismissal by the Board at least twice, and a third (Captain Heddington at Valleyfield) may have regarded himself as a victim of constructive dismissal. The Greenlaw surgeon William Hill was dismissed in June 1813 for negligence. Clerks, too, suffered dismissal: at Valleyfield, two (John Lauder for 'neglect of Duty', in November 1811, and 15 months later John Macfarlane 'for his very gross and repeated misconduct'); at Perth, two (John Ramsay, in December 1812, for reasons unstated; Patrick Miller, in June 1813, 'for attempting to introduce a profligate woman into one of the prisons') were dismissed and a third threatened with being dropped overboard (the 67-year-old John Lewis, hospital clerk and interpeter, who in December 1813 was told: '... the [Transport] Board cannot do more for you than has already been done and therefore unless you be satisfied you may resign.'); and at Greenlaw, one (Alexander Fraser, in December 1809) forced to resign, and another (Francis Wharton, in January 1811) evidently dismissed but reinstated. Among the labourers, lamplighters and messengers employed at the Scots depots at least two—both lamplighters at Valleyfield (James Blackwood in March 1811, and one named Cranstoun in October that year)—were dismissed.

Being a member of staff in one or other of the Scots depots may therefore, at least at times, have seemed to some incumbents a rather insecure occupation. If a sense of insecurity did exist among staff it may well have become enlarged if also they were aware that applications for appointments were not infrequently received by the agents or the Transport Board from outside the gates of the depots: 'There is a long list of candidates,' the Board told the father of one young man hopeful of being appointed a steward at Greenlaw in February 1814, '... therefore the Board cannot make any Promise to you.' Such applications appear sometimes, however, to have been rejected with brutal rudeness. 'The services of your wife as a sempstress at the Depot,' the Board replied to an enquiry or application from David Murray of Perth in November 1812, 'are not wanted.'[134]

Whether the turnover of, and any sense of insecurity among, some members of staffs in the depots in Scotland affected in any discernible ways the thousands of prisoners they were employed to administer there, is a question which, in the absence of any specific evidence, is easier to ask than to answer. Such meagre evidence as there is might be interpreted to suggest that occasionally in one depot or another a turnkey, a clerk or a lamplighter, from whatever resentment or financial or other motive he harboured, succumbed to temptation to be more than sympathetic toward prisoners—as, for example, was perhaps the clerk Patrick Miller in 'attempting to introduce a profligate woman into one of the prisons' at Perth. But there is no evidence of any such sympathy or helpfulness by staff (as distinct from that by some militia guards) extending to helping prisoners forge or utter bank notes or counterfeit coins, still less to escape. There was perhaps a whiff of implied corruption among some clerks or stewards to be sniffed in the circular from the Transport Board in June 1811 concerning provision and sales of small beer to prisoners. There was an unmistakable odour of corruption and breach of depot rules arising from the smuggling into 'Valleyfield, Pennycuick, Greenlaw and Perth' of spirituous liquors which prompted the Board to urge in September 1812 that excise officers should occasionally search 'the turnkeys and their lodges'.[135]

What is striking about the staffs at the Scots depots are their apparently small numbers. The number of prisoners was so greatly increased with the opening successively as depots of Esk Mills, Edinburgh Castle, and Valleyfield in 1811 and of Perth in 1812, that, in contrast with the few hundreds at most who had been confined at Greenlaw at any time between 1804 and 1810, there were (not including those in the parole towns) in Scotland in the last two years of the war some 12,000 or 13,000 prisoners. Yet, excluding the very few prisoners employed on assorted and often very occasional or temporary tasks, the aggregate establishment of staffs at the Scots depots—agents, surgeons, dispensers, matrons, sempstresses, clerks, turnkeys, stewards, interpreters, messengers, labourers, and lamplighters—varied in those years 1811-14 between a minimum of some 71 and a maximum of about 96. At the lowest ratio there appears therefore to have been approximately one member of staff employed during those three years for every 183 prisoners and, at the highest, one for every 125. Neither ratio suggests that the prisoners were swamped by a mass of administrators.

19

Quarrels Among the Prisoners; Health and Sickness; Deaths and Burials

As among prisoners in other wars, there were sporadic tensions, quarrels and conflicts among some of those confined during the Napoleonic Wars in the depots in Scotland. With hundreds of prisoners, as at Edinburgh Castle or Greenlaw, and thousands, as at Esk Mills, Valleyfield and Perth, crowded together in bleak, cold, or stuffy conditions, inadequately fed, many or most with little or nothing to do, locked in their rooms or wards (as Captain Kaald found at Greenlaw) for up to 17 hours a day with fellow captives, some of whom 'have had little upbringing, others again are some extreme ... pigs',[1] with in many cases little or no contact with their families at home, and above all not knowing when the protracted war might end and their liberty be restored, it was inevitable that the nerves of some became frayed and that from time to time quarrels erupted.

Many or most such quarrels were no doubt personal—two or more prisoners falling out over one or other from among a myriad of disagreements concerning attitudes or behaviour, such as cadging, cheating, bullying, stealing, personal habits or idiosyncracies. Outbreaks of such disagreements took one or more of many forms, ranging from angry words to exchanges of blows, occasionally even duelling.

Sergeant Major Beaudoin, confined at Greenlaw from 1804 to 1809, noted among his fellow prisoners there several quarrels, some personal, others with a nationalist or chauvinist tinge, a few taking a particularly violent turn. 'There are also among our prisoners Spaniards to the number of forty,' he wrote, ostensibly before the outbreak of the Peninsular War in 1808 but perhaps with some later revision to take account of the breakdown in that year of the alliance between France and Spain. 'It's lucky for us that we [the French prisoners] are the strongest [group]; they threaten us daily with their knives. They fight very often with knives among themselves, and more often treacherously than bravely. One day, in the evening, we were being counted. A Spaniard placed himself beside the door with his knife hidden under his greatcoat. The man he was waiting for arrived at the door to make his way in like the others, unaware of anything. The other man brought out his knife from under his greatcoat and as he was passing stabbed him in the face. The guard at once arrested him and put him in the black hole but it had no effect on him. The Spaniards themselves said it was well done; moreover, it's their way of fighting. Another day an Italian and a Spaniard fought each other. The Italian, with a blow of his knife, cut the arm of the Spaniard, and the prison surgeon was obliged to cut the arm again higher up. On another day again a Spaniard was to pour the soup ... another came behind him and stabbed him on the arm ... They fought in public in the yard; the guard did not stop them from doing so. The man who had dealt the treacherous blow received one himself on the arm, and that was the end of the affair.'[2]

At Greenlaw, too, though fortunately it seems without any of the violence noted by Beaudoin on the part of some of the Spanish prisoners there, 'a great noise', according to Captain Paul Andreas Kaald, arose in December 1808 between the French and Danish prisoners when the former, believing they were about to be transferred elsewhere and having sold off cheaply to the latter their tools and spare clothes, learned their transfer had been cancelled and then sought to recover the items they had parted with.[3]

Formal duels between a pair of quarrelling prisoners were rare in the Scots depots. The earliest surviving evidence for what may have been a duel (if it was not merely a friendly exercise in fencing) concerns the encounter at Edinburgh Castle in the summer of 1811 in which Lieutenant Auguste Belisaire Bourignons of the 65th regiment of the Line, aged 20, lost his life. After breaking his parole at Thame in Oxfordshire Bourignons had been sent to Esk Mills, and from there he was transferred in March 1811 along with some 450 other prisoners to Edinburgh Castle, where he soon applied to be readmitted to parole, on the plea that his breach of it had been due to ill treatment at Thame. Before a decision on his application was reached by the Transport Board, however, Bourignons was dead 'from a wound suffered in fencing with another prisoner.'[4] Bourignons's death, and that of another prisoner at a depot in England, prompted the issue of the circular a few days later by the Transport Board to agents at all depots in Britain: 'In consequence of our having this day received reports of two French prisoners having been killed at different Depots by foils which they have been in the habit of using, we direct you in future strictly to prohibit the use of all metal foils by the prisoners in your custody, taking care also to destroy all those now in possession of the prisoners.' The instruction appears not, however, to have been carried out to the letter, at least at Perth depot.[5]

For if there is uncertainty whether it was a duel or a fencing accident which had caused Bourignons' death at the Castle, there is none about an encounter that took place two years later between two unnamed French officers at Perth. 'On Tuesday,' the *Perth Courier* reported two days later on 20 May 1813, 'a dispute having arisen between two of the French officers confined in the Depot, a challenge was the consequence and they fought with sharpened foils. The contest was carried on in the most fair and gentlemanly manner, till one of them being wounded in the body the other immediately came up and shook him by the hand, expressing his sorrow for what had happened. The wounded combatant was conveyed to the hospital, where the greatest attention was paid to him and we understand that he is likely to recover.'

A more curious case of duelling between two prisoners occurred at Valleyfield in the last days of the war, in March 1814. The depot General Entry Book says that Etien Giro was 'Killed in a Duel' and died there on 21 March. A soldier in the 32nd regiment of the Line, Giro, born at Clermont and aged 26, had been captured in Portugal in March 1809. He had arrived two years later at Valleyfield from Esk Mills. Giro (or Giero, Giraud or Girard—his surname, like his prename Etien or Etienne, is varyingly spelled in different sources) was said to have 'Died in consequence of a wound in the breast which penetrated through both sides of the aorta. It appears he was wounded in a duel with a comrade. They fought with the blades of a pair of scissors fixed on the ends of two sticks.' The duel appears to have been due to the belligerence of Giro. But that he, rather than his opponent, Louis Albertini, a soldier in the 2nd Italian regiment, should have been killed in it is surprising, since Giro was said to be by profession a fencing master. The note written on 29 March by the Crown Agent Hugh Warrender on the back of a letter sent him by the procurator fiscal along with witnesses' declarations commented: 'Probably some previous Quarrel had been between the parties not here Explained. As the evidence however stands Mr Defunct seems to have been the aggressor without provocation and Albertini in a manner therefore acting only in self-preservation, and on the whole rather not seeming a matter for further investigation and affording to the prisoners a lesson not to be quarrelling.' The initialled comment by the Advocate Depute, H. Home Drummond, on the Crown Agent's remarks was: 'I am quite of the same opinion.'[6] In his precognition or declaration, signed with his mark as he was illiterate, Albertini said that on 18 March Giro had met him in the middle of the yard or airing ground and pushed him. When Albertini turned to ask him why he had done so, Giro had struck him in the eye and declared: 'You must fight with me.' Giro had then gone and got two pieces of scissors, fixed them to two sticks, and said one or other man must be killed. Albertini refused to fight, but Giro 'said if he did not take the weapon and stand on his guard he would run him through.' Albertini continued to refuse to fight, 'saying he did not understand fighting', and it was only after Giro stabbed him in the shoulder that 'he was under the necessity of standing on his defence. He had no malice towards Giro and did not even know him, he belonged to another Regiment. The second or third lunge he wounded Giro in the right breast ... [and he] was then taken to the hospital.' Of two prisoners at the depot who were witnesses one, Joseph Cheland or Chaillante, a pilot from the cutter *Pirate*, who was Giro's second in the duel, said Giro had 'ill used Albertini but not content with that he struck him in the eye.' Albertini had run away but Giro got the sticks with scissors fixed to them and insisted on fighting, which Albertini refused to do 'as Giro was a fencing master and he [Albertini] did not so well understand it ... Giro was a very quarrelsome man and sought every day to pick quarrels with other prisoners.' Albertini's second in the duel, François Godebert, a seaman from the French man-of-war *Swiftsure*, said that 'Girard [sic] is a very bad character.' John Macansh, Royal Navy, depot surgeon, said Girard was brought into the hospital on 18 March and while there had said 'he was sorry he was wounded by such a Bungler and vowed Revenge whenever he got again into the prison', but had died on Sunday morning two days later.[7]

Two other sources of quarrels and even fracas among the prisoners in the Scots depots were each more significant, however, than the kind of personal belligerence shown by Giro the fencing master. One source was the vicissitudes of the war, especially in 1813-14, when Napoleon's empire was crumbling and some continental states found themselves in changing circumstances, amid shifts, even reversals, of alliances. When even earlier Spain, erstwhile ally of France, had found itself in 1808 invaded and occupied by Napoleon's forces, most Spanish prisoners of war then confined in depots in Scotland or England were soon freed and repatriated to join the forces of the Junta opposed to the French.[8] It is likely that it was then or later that the strictures by Sergeant Major Beaudoin on Spanish prisoners at Greenlaw were consequently intensified. 'The Spanish,' he wrote, 'possess all the good qualities. First, they are excessively lazy, dirty, treacherous, gamblers and thieves like magpies. Those then are the best qualities with which they are invested. The French wanted to get stuck into them but the agent forbade us to do so, recommending us to keep calm every time they fought among themselves. "... if they attack you," he told us, "I allow you to punish them yourselves."'[9] In what proved to be the last year of the war the recruitment of many German, Italian and Dutch prisoners in the Scots and other depots into the forces of their native rulers on the continent who were opposed to Napoleon hardly contributed to endearing them to their French fellow prisoners.

A second main source of conflict among the prisoners in the depots in Scotland, as in England, was the willingness shown throughout the war by numbers of them to be recruited into His Britannic Majesty's forces, even though these volunteers' native states remained in some cases allied with Napoleon. Such volunteers were inevitably seen as traitors by the mass of loyal Bonapartists among the prisoners. This was why the Transport Board consistently did its best to ensure that such volunteers were physically and otherwise fit to serve, as it explained as early as 3 December 1806 in its letter to Lieutenant Colonel Willoughby Gordon, military secretary to the commander-in-chief, the Duke of York: 'Very serious inconveniences having been found to arise from persons confined among the prisoners of war in this country being returned again into custody after having been enlisted for His Majesty's army, we request you will move His Royal Highness the Commander-in-Chief to give the necessary orders to the officers employed in the recruiting service at the depots for prisoners of war not to receive any prisoner as a volunteer who may not be previously found fit in every respect for service, as well as to prevent the inconveniences above referred to, as the danger attending the lives of men so returned from the resentment of their infuriated countrymen or fellow prisoners.'[10]

What was described as an 'Insurrection' by French prisoners at Greenlaw early in January 1811 to prevent Danish and Swedish fellow prisoners leaving to enter the British navy as volunteers, resulted in a series of orders from the Transport Board to the agent, Malcolm Wright. 'Rear Admiral Otway [at Leith] having represented to us that the Danes and Swedes at Greenlaw who had volunteered for His Majesty's Navy had been prevented leaving Greenlaw Prison by an Insurrection of the French Prisoners, we direct you to report fully on this Circumstance, and to make arrangements for removing all the refractory French prisoners under a strong Guard as soon as possible.' Three days later, the Board ordered Wright 'to separate the Danes who volunteered for His Majesty's Service but afterwards refused to leave the Prison, from the French Prisoners as soon as possible.' The following day the Board told Wright that 'It is desirable that all French prisoners should be immediately removed to Edinburgh Castle.' Three days afterward the Board altered their destination to Esk Mills, later adding that Greenlaw was 'intended in future for Danish prisoners only.' Finally the Board reaffirmed the following week to Wright that, 'All the French prisoners at Greenlaw are to be immediately removed to Esk Mills. The Danes and Swedes mentioned by you may be released for His Majesty's Navy, if Admiral Otway will receive them.' Thus the first 192 inmates of Esk Mills, who arrived there from Greenlaw on 4 February 1811, included an unstated but perhaps considerable number of French prisoners who had so recently been in 'insurrection' against fellow prisoners—a further factor that perhaps helps explain the brief but troubled history of Esk Mills as a depot. Moreover, the quarrels at Greenlaw among prisoners over the issue of volunteering into His Britannic Majesty's forces had become so serious as to prompt the Transport Board to resolve (though the resolution appears never to have been fully carried out) that in future that depot should contain prisoners of only one nationality. An outcome, however, of those quarrels among the prisoners was a number of press reports a few weeks later that '300 Danish prisoners were marched into Leith yesterday from Penicuik under an escort, to be embarked on board the *Romulus* frigate for

Portsmouth. We hear that the constant quarrels betwixt the French prisoners and these men is the reason for sending them thither.'[11]

Thus were the miseries of captivity in the depots in Scotland compounded by sporadic changes in alliances among states, by the despair (or conversely the hope of an eventual chance of escape and return home) that drove some prisoners to volunteer themselves into the armed forces of Britain or its allies, by certain chauvinist attitudes that sparked conflict among some of the prisoners, and by some personal animosities.

Prisoners in the Scots depots who needed medical treatment for bruises, cuts, broken bones or other wounds suffered in quarrels, fracas, assaults, or duels with fellow prisoners were, however, a minuscule proportion of those who found themselves on the sick lists there. The vast majority of the sick in the depots were suffering from ill health contracted either in those areas of Europe, the Americas, Asia, or Africa, or on the seas around those continents, where they had been captured (and in not a few cases wounded), or since their confinement in the depots, overcrowded, stuffy or cold as these so often were, and where the diet, especially for those subjected to it over a long period, was hardly conducive to robust health.

At least two among the thousands of prisoners sent to depots in Scotland died on the voyage there. The names of the two are unrecorded. One was a seaman, aged 25, captured between Fraserburgh and Peterhead in May 1808 with the rest of the crew on board the Norwegian privateer *Wovchalfen*. Badly wounded, he died from his wounds en route to Leith and confinement at Greenlaw, and 'was decently interred in North Leith Churchyard.'[12] The other was a prisoner among the first 400 bound in August 1812 for the new depot at Perth. He died on board the transport ship *Mathilda* bringing them from Plymouth, and when the ship berthed at Dundee his body was brought ashore for burial.[13] Whether the privateer pilot Arendt, the very fat prisoner whom Marote-Carrier said appeared to be suffocating during the rough passage from Chatham in January-February 1811 of HMS *Vanguard* with prisoners for Esk Mills, survived the voyage is unknown.[14] No other reference to prisoners dying en route has been found, but it may be that several others did not survive similar voyages to the landing places at Leith, Kirkcaldy, Burntisland, or Greenock.[15]

On at least three occasions several prisoners landed at Burntisland or Leith were sent not to the depots but, because of their wounds or medical condition, straight to Edinburgh Royal Infirmary. Thus two members of the crew of 53 from the captured Norwegian privateer *Wovchalfen*, landed with their colleagues at Leith on 27 May 1808, were so badly wounded that they had to be 'carried on men's shoulders to the Royal Infirmary ...' Twice in autumn 1812 there were similar admissions to the Infirmary. First, 'six or seven of the sick' among 850 prisoners for Perth landed at Burntisland on 12 October from four transports and their escort the small frigate *Rosamond*, 'were brought over to Leith to be put into sick quarters.' Second, after the transport vessel *Latona* had landed 223 prisoners for Perth at Burntisland on 11 November, it had to sail across the Firth of Forth to Leith in order to land there no fewer than 25 prisoners who 'appeared to be in a very languid and debilitated state' and who were then 'conveyed in carts to the Royal Infirmary.' How many of these three dozen prisoners survived and were eventually discharged from the Infirmary to the depots is not known; the archives of the Infirmary appear to contain no reference to them.[16]

What is known is that some prisoners, their health already undermined, died within a few days or weeks after their arrival at the depots. That was the case, for example, at Perth in the last few weeks of 1812. The damning criticisms voiced by Vice Admiral Otway and Major General Ferguson concerning the brutal treatment of sick and dying prisoners landed from the transport vessel *Latona* at Burntisland on 11 November that year and marched to Perth (criticisms apparently confirmed by local press reports and by the contemporary Perth historian George Penny, who may himself have seen the contingents of prisoners concerned), appear further borne out by the two relevant General Entry Books which recorded the arrival at the depot between 15 October and 3 December of some 2,786 prisoners. Of those 2,786, 31 (1.1 per cent) had died by the end of December. Some 1,812 prisoners of the 2,786, arrived at the depot between 15 November and 3 December, and of those 16 (0.8 per cent) had died by end of December. But of the 223 landed from the *Latona* on 11 November, 13 (5.8 per cent) died within five weeks of their arrival at the depot—a significantly higher percentage.[17] At Valleyfield, too, where some 2,486 prisoners arrived on 11 March 1811 or shortly afterward from Esk Mills as a result of its closure, 13 (0.52 per cent) died between 20 March and 30 April inclusive. At Esk Mills itself, excluding one shot while attempting to escape and two others trampled to death in the panic of 11 March, six prisoners died during the five weeks the depot existed.[18]

A glance at Appendix 8 below shows that even in the brief random selection presented there of wounds and physical marks from among the thousands of relevant entries in the General Entry Books of the Scots depots, there were some prisoners who had arrived there with physical or health problems which were more than trifling, such as 'Hump Back', 'Ruptured', 'Only one Eye', 'Blindness left Eye', 'Lost use of left Arm', 'Maimed right Hand', 'broken Hip', 'right Arm broken', 'left Arm broke', 'Wounds in head', 'right Leg amputated', 'left Shoulder broken', 'Wants left Hand', 'wounded in right Eye', 'lost right Hand', 'left Knee broke',

'Very Deaf', 'Blind left Eye and different Wounds on Body', 'Short right thigh', 'Blind right Eye, Ruptured', 'Lame of right Leg', 'Lame of left Foot', 'Broken Thigh', 'Lost his right Eye', 'Scrofula'. As about 17 per cent of all the depot prisoners in Scotland appear to have had smallpox scars of one extent or another, subjection to that disease could have left numbers of them susceptible to other maladies.[19]

Rather than enemy bullets, cannon balls and shells, bayonets, swords or lances, it was disease—a hydra-headed monster that flourished amid neglect, dirt, defective and inadequate medical knowledge or care—that was the greatest single cause of death among combatants in the Napoleonic Wars. It has been calculated, for example, that of the 240,000 French troops who died in Spain during the Peninsular War, 1808-13, the deaths of 45,000 were due to 'direct battle action', 76,650 to guerrillas, and the other 119,000 or so to 'disease and accidental causes'.[20] Nor, of course, did disease attack only land forces: 'Disease ... killed off more naval men than any other cause ...'[21] Many prisoners of war, too, were victims of disease which, ticking away within them like a time bomb, might take months or years before claiming their lives.

Concern about the number of sick prisoners of war being sent to Britain was expressed more than once by the Transport Board. Writing to the Admiralty in December 1810, for instance, about a proposal by Admiral Berkeley, British naval commander at Lisbon, to send several shiploads of prisoners from there, the Board declared: '... we beg to state to their Lordships that the number of sick prisoners already brought to this country from Portugal has not only completely filled our hospitals but also spread contagion to a very considerable degree among the prisoners who were before in health; and as any further increase of prisoners of this description must be attended with very great inconvenience and expence, we submit to their Lordships whether it be not adviseable to give directions for the prisoners of war in Portugal to be kept there for the present, rather than to be sent to this country.'[22] As late as October 1813, even after the war in the Peninsula had ended, the Transport Board again expressed to the Admiralty its concern about the 'great number of sick and wounded prisoners lately received from Spain.'[23]

The Transport Board sought to limit the number of sick prisoners sent to Scotland. 'We direct you,' it instructed its agent at Portsmouth in mid-August 1812, 'upon the arrival of Transports with French prisoners from Spain and Portugal to apply to the Admiral of the Port for convoy for them either to the Tay, if the wind and weather should permit, or to Kirkcaldy in the Firth of Forth, first landing or trans-shipping such of them as from ill health or wounds are unfit to proceed.' Three months later the Board sent the agent a similar instruction: '... the *Freya* has arrived at Spithead, having under convoy three Transports from Lisbon with French prisoners on board, and ... these [two other] ships are to proceed immediately [to the Firth of Forth], after the sick prisoners shall have been taken out and their complement filled up with healthy prisoners from the prison ships.' The Board at the same time, as has already been seen, assured Vice Admiral Otway at Leith, in response to his criticism about the brutal treatment of sick and dying prisoners landed at Burntisland from the *Latona*, that it had given 'the most strict orders for removing all the sick' from among such prisoners embarked at Lisbon 'in the most wretched and exhausted condition, and the greater part in a state of absolute nakedness', replacing them by healthy prisoners and completely reclothing all of them before they were sent on to depots in Scotland.[24] Nonetheless, despite such instructions from the Transport Board, numbers of sick and at least semi-disabled prisoners, as well as some who were dying, did arrive at the Scots depots.

The provision for treating sick prisoners at the depots consisted of three main elements: the surgeons and their staffs, the hospitals, and the medicines and other medical or surgical supplies either sent as a result of applications to the Transport Office or bought locally.

The number and identity of the surgeons and their staffs, their payments and accommodation, have already been indicated.[25] The appreciation expressed by Lieutenant Marote-Carrier successively at Esk Mills and Valleyfield for the sympathetic and skilled treatment he received there from John Macansh as surgeon contrasts with the comments on the Greenlaw incumbent Robert Renton made by Captain Paul Andreas Kaald when he fell ill there in December 1808. 'I feel sickly,' Kaald noted in his diary on the 14th of that month, and then next day: 'Today I have a headache and sickness in my whole body and am afraid I must lie in bed. God take care of the sick in this unhealthy prison.' After things became no better the following day, Kaald wrote: 'Today I have taken to my bed and am terribly sick in all of my body. I can't enjoy any kind of food. The Doctor came to me and gave me a large emetic which completely took my strength away and left me feeling my head was crushed … The sickness continued, got worse and not better. There is a strong pain in my stomach on top of all else previously. The Doctor absolutely wants to bleed me, but I won't allow it in any way whatsoever, since I have never been bled. I received no other help.' On Sunday, 18 December Kaald observed: 'A very unpleasant Sunday, when I find myself dreadfully sick and the Doctor wants to send me to hospital. I managed to put this off also, otherwise I got no help.' 'My sickness is the same, not better,' he noted the following day. 'It is using up my energy. Patience is the best thing just now for me.' Next day something of a crisis occurred: 'I am very sick as before and now pray to God that He will with his good means help me, as I strongly fear for my life since it is deteriorating so quickly.' The crisis passed and next day Kaald wrote: 'Today, thank God, I am a little better. Got a laxative powder from the Doctor—a whole basin full of some kind of stuff, God knows how old it was. Everybody has to admit that this man is a good Doctor—for the well and healthy, but God must help the sick. This laxative powder hasn't worked in the least ... It is lying in my stomach now and simmering.' Finally, on 22 Dcember, Kaald noted: 'Today, thank God, I am much better and have started to eat a little, which pleases me immensely.'[26]

The surviving correspondence between the Transport Board and the depot agents in Scotland (or at least, given the loss or destruction of the agents' letters to the Board, the letters which survive only for 1808 to 1814 from the Board to the agents), contains many references to the monthly applications from the latter or their surgeons for medical supplies. The agent at Valleyfield, for example, in April 1811, was told by the Board to provide the hospital at Greenlaw with '5 bottles port wine, 5 lbs soft sugar, 1 bottle sweet oil, 2 lbs soap, 2 bottles vinegar.'[27] The medicinal value of port wine appeared to be appreciated by the Board when, a few months later, it instructed its agent at Greenlaw to 'Procure three gallons of port wine from Leith for the use of the [depot] hospital.' On the other hand, he was told that 'No trusses are to be supplied for the use of prisoners afflicted with hernia.'[28] The agent was authorised by the Board in April 1813 to procure for the depot hospital four dozen quart bottles (empty, it appears), four dozen quart corks, ten yards each of linen and cotton cloth and of flannel.[29]

References to procurement of medical supplies at Valleyfield ranged across a much wider spectrum of items, including 'Edinburgh Porter, in small casks', 'a quarter cask of port wine from Leith,' '100 lbs surgeon's tow, 50 lbs sacking ditto, 4 gross quart bottle corks, 1 ream Bolus paper, 1 ditto common tea brown paper', 'A Small Thermometer, 2 Gross ½ pint bottles, 2 cases of common Bougies [candles]', '8 Gallons Olive Oil, 50 lbs Moist Sugar, 2 Gross Gallipots, 12 Skins of Leather', lint, '9 gallons vinegar, 1 bolus knife, 2 ditto twine small', calico, a hogshead of red wine, '50 lbs raw Sugar, 10 gallons Vinegar, 20 lbs Hoggs lard', '3 lbs honey, 2lbs cammomile flavours, 20 leather skins.' More parsimonious tendencies were no doubt reflected when in March 1812 condemned bunting for use as bandages in the depot hospital was requested by the Board from the naval yard at Leith. Lemon juice at Valleyfield appeared to be even more in demand than port wine at Greenlaw: two cases of the juice were ordered from the naval stores at Deptford in June 1812, 18 gallons in August, a further 18 gallons in November, and still another 18 gallons and a case in September and October 1813.[30]

There were similar requests for and provisions of medical and surgical supplies at Perth depot, including oatmeal for poultices, old bunting for bandages, and feather pillows. At the opening of the depot in August 1812, the agent was told that 'if there are two sets of surgeon's instruments at Valleyfield one of them must be sent to Perth.'[31] At Edinburgh Castle medicines were sent on at least one occasion from 'Apothecarys Hall'; in the later stages of the war, the Board's instruction was that supplies were to be sought from Valleyfield.[32]

The impression left by the surviving correspondence of the Transport Board is that, despite the parsimonious use of condemned bunting for bandages, the provision of medical supplies for the depot hospitals in Scotland appears to have become both more wide ranging and more generous in the later years of the war.

Wide ranging also were the medical or surgical problems presented at the Scots depots by the prisoners. Many of those problems proved curable (as were those, for instance, of Lieutenant Marote-Carrier for which in February 1811 he was treated in Esk Mills hospital), or at least did not result in the prisoner dying in the depot; but some others among the problems did not. Some indication of the range of the more serious, indeed mortal, problems is contained in the proforma returns that survive from among those submitted weekly to the Transport Office concerning deaths of prisoners in the depots. Certain of these stated or ostensible causes of death were particularly common.[33]

At Greenlaw, as at other Scots depots, not all the prisoners who died had the ostensible causes of their deaths recorded. Of the information available on the subject for Greenlaw, some is contained in a register purporting to be of Danish prisoners who died at the depot, 'commencing January 1811'. In fact, of the 30 prisoners the register lists, 15 died at the depot between April 1805 and March 1809; one died from phthisis not at Greenlaw but at Edinburgh Castle; and far from all 30 prisoners being Danish or even Scandinavian, only two appear to have been so. Of the 15 who died in 1805-9, all but two were said to have died of consumption (pulmonary tuberculosis). Of those two, one (Charles Cottier, in January 1807) was shot by a sentry; the other died from causes 'uncertain'. Of the fourteen who died in 1811-13, six died from consumption, five from fever, one from dysentery, one from gangrene, and one from apoplexy. Of a further 14 prisoners who died at Greenlaw between 1804 and February 1811 and whose deaths are recorded in surviving weekly proforma, but not in the 'Danish' register mentioned above, five died of consumption, three of typhus, two from 'uncertain' causes, one of apoplexy, one of 'Hymaptysis and of spitting of blood', one (Jan de Rymer, a seaman, in May 1809) was shot while attempting to escape, and the cause of death of one other was not stated.[34] There were two further deaths of prisoners at Greenlaw not recorded in those sources: Simon Simonsen, shot on 27 July 1810, and François Couvertier, a seaman, who died on 20 May 1806 from cause unstated.[35] The range of causes given for these 45 deaths at Greenlaw was therefore:

Consumption:	20
Pulmonary Consumption:	1
Phthisis:	1
Consumption or 'Uncertain':	2
Fever:	5
Typhus:	3
'Uncertain':	3
Shot:	3
'Hymaptysis [i.e., haemoptysis] and of spitting of blood':	1
Gangrene (or fever):	1
Dysentery:	1
Apoplexy:	2
Not stated:	2
Total:	45

Of nine prisoners who died at Esk Mills during its brief existence in February-March 1811, the cause of death was given as: 'Deseased liver' 1, 'Phthsis Pulmonatio' [pulmonary tuberculois] 1, dysentery 1, fever 1, dysentery and fever 1, trampled to death [in the panic of 11 March] 2, shot while attempting to escape 1, 'Died suddenly in prison' 1.[36]

The four prisoners who died at Edinburgh Castle had the ostensible cause of their death recorded. One died from a wound suffered in fencing, perhaps in a duel, another from a fractured spine as a result of falling 150 feet down the Castle rock while attempting to escape, the third from 'Abscess in the Lungs', and the fourth from phthsis (tuberculosis).[37]

At Valleyfield and Perth, the two largest depots by far in Scotland, the range of stated causes of prisoners' deaths was consequently wider than at the other three. For Valleyfield, as at most of the other Scots depots, the sources differ concerning the total number of those who died. But there it appears to have been at the most 300. Of the 300 the deaths of six are the subject of contradiction in some sources, which say four of them were repatriated to France at the end of the war, one was repatriated in 1812, and one was transferred to Perth two years after his 'death' at Valleyfield. The six were the one who was said to have hanged himself, one said to have died from cold after repeatedly selling his clothes and hammock, two said to have died from pneumonia, and another two said to have died from fever. But the causes of death of these six have been included in the table below. On the other hand the causes of death of 10 among the maximum of 300 were not recorded in any of the surviving sources. For the 290 prisoners the stated causes of whose deaths were recorded on the weekly proforma returns submitted from Valleyfield to the Transport Office between the depot's opening in March 1811 and the end of July 1814, the range appears to have been this:[38]

Phthsis:	103
Phthsis Pulmonales:	2
Consumption:	31
Fever:	50
Fever and Infirmity:	1
Fever and Debility:	1
Pneumonia:	43
Debility from the Effect of selling [his] Provisions and Clothes:	7
Debility:	5
Debility from selling his Rations:	2
General Debility:	1
General Debility, Phthisis:	1
From the Effect of Want of due Substance, having gambled away his Rations in 14 Days:	1
From the Effect of Cold, having repeatedly sold their Clothes and Hammocks:	4
From the Effect of Cold:	2
Dysentery:	7
Chronic Dysentery:	2
Hipatitis [sic]:	2
Typhus:	1
Enteritis:	1
Erisipilas [sic]:	4
Lumber Abcess [sic]:	3
Abcess [sic]:	1
Dropsy:	2
Apoplexy:	2
Mortification [Gangrene]:	1
Mortification of the Thigh:	1
Ulcer:	1
Deseased [sic] Liver:	1
Cutans: [Some unstated disease affecting the skin, possibly, e.g., Erysipelas]	1
Died suddenly in the Prison:	1
Suddenly in Convalescent Ward:	1
Died in consequence of a Wound in the Breast [i.e., in a duel]:	1
Died in consequence of being severely flogged by his Fellow Prisoners, he having been detected by them stealing:	1
Shot in attempting to escape:	1
Hanged himself in a fit of Derangement:	1
Total:	290

Tuberculosis and fever, in their various forms, and pneumonia thus appear to have accounted for about 71 per cent of all the stated or ostensible causes of deaths of prisoners at Valleyfield.

At Perth, there are more numerous contradictions in the surviving sources than at Valleyfield concerning the number of prisoners who died. As Appendix

11 indicates, the maximum number of deaths at Perth appears to have been 215. But as that Appendix also indicates, conflicting evidence raises doubts concerning no fewer than 30 of those 215 deaths. Of the 215, weekly proforma death certificates survive for 206 prisoners who died between 27 October 1812 and 10 June 1814 inclusive, and these certificates give the causes of those 206 deaths thus:

Consumption:	66
Phthisis Pulmonalis:	3
Fever:	53
Inflammatory Fever:	30
Atrophia:	4
Tabes Mesinturica [i.e. Mesenturica]: In a Compleat State of Atrophy:	1
Atrophia & Nostalgia:	3
Suddenly:	1
Suddenly in Prison No.2:	2
Suddenly in Prison No.3:	2
Suddenly in Prison No.4:	3
Suddenly in Prison No.5:	1
Suddenly in removing to the Hospital:	1
Suddenly in Convalescent Ward:	2
Extreme Debility:	3
Scurvy & Extreme Debility:	2
Scurvy and the …. [indecipherable] State of Debility:	2
Fever and great Debility:	1
Suddenly from Inanition and extreme Debility:	1
Sudden Death from Inanition:	2
Died suddenly of Starvation & consequent Debility:	2
Gangrene of the lower Extremities and General Debility:	1
Mortification:	1
Lumbar Abscess:	3
Abscess:	1
Abscess Thigh & consequent Hectic Fever:	1
Violent Contusion and Abscess on the Head, extending to the Neck and Shoulder:	1
Dropsy:	2
Found Dead in his Bed of Apoplexy:	2
Inanition in consequence of Mental Derangement:	1
Scalded to Death by falling into the Boiler:	1
Peripneumonia:	1
Scirrhous Pyloras [Hard cancer of the lower exit of the stomach]:	1
Haematemisis [i.e., Haematemesis (vomiting of blood)]:	1
Tabes Dorsalis [Literally, wasting of the back]:	2
Iliac Passion [Intestinal obstruction caused by one or other of several diseases]:	1
Anasarca [A form of dropsy]:	1
Total:	206

On the basis of those 206 death certificiates, fever therefore appears to have been the largest single cause of death at Perth, followed closely by tuberculosis (consumption and phthisis), and the two together accounted for three-quarters of the deaths among the prisoners at the depot.[39]

Although it may be argued that some at least of the miserables or *rafalés* who died in captivity in the Scots depots in effect committed suicide by selling their rations or their clothing and losing their will to continue living, only one prisoner was officially stated to have committed suicide. He was Julian Manecan (or Manceau or Manecau), born at Vitré and aged 22, a drummer in the 15th (or 16th) Line regiment, who had been captured in Spain in July 1810, had arrived at Valleyfield from Plymouth at the beginning of October 1811, and who at the depot on 20 November 'hanged himself in a fit of derangement.'[40]

If between 535 and 573 prisoners died in the Scots depots it appears safe to assume, despite the survival of only limited evidence, that the overwhelming majority of them died in the depot hospitals. A key question is what was the rate of cure for those who were admitted to those hospitals. The surviving evidence concerns the hospitals at Esk Mills and Greenlaw. It is contained in a General Entry Book titled 'Edinburgh, 1813, Various', which was used for recording information about prisoners admitted to and returned from Esk Mills and Greenlaw hospitals, as well as about prisoners employed there and at Edinburgh Castle, at varying periods between February 1811 and December 1813.[41] For Valleyfield, Perth and Edinburgh Castle depot hospitals no such registers are known to survive, though for Perth hospital there are some press reports, details of the numbers of patients in which indicate they were written from information issued by the depot authorities.

The first half dozen pages of the Entry Book list 142 'Sick French Prisoners of War sent to and returned from the Hospital' at Esk Mills between 4 February and 18 April 1811. The Book shows admissions to the hospital were thus:

4 Feb.:	8
5 Feb.:	6
6 Feb.:	1
7 Feb.:	23
8 Feb.:	5
9 Feb.:	5
10 Feb.:	5
11 Feb.:	5
12 Feb.:	5
13 Feb.:	1
14 Feb.:	2
17 Feb.:	6
18 Feb.:	13

19 Feb.:	1
21 Feb.:	9
22 Feb.:	4
23 Feb.:	3
26 Feb.:	2
27 Feb.:	4
28 Feb.:	4
1 Mar.:	1
2 Mar.:	1
3 Mar.:	2
4 Mar.:	1
5 Mar.:	4
6 Mar.:	2
7 Mar.:	4
8 Mar.:	2
9 Mar.:	4
10 Mar.:	1
11 Mar.:	8
Total:	142

Of the 142 admitted to the depot hospital five (3.5 per cent) died there.[42] All the other 137 patients are said to have been 'Returned to the Prison' seriatim between 8 February and 18 April, by which latter date of course Esk Mills itself had been closed as a depot for more than five weeks, 2,486 or so of its inmates having been transferred to Valleyfield and the other 460 or so to Edinburgh Castle. Given the seriousness of some of the maladies from which prisoners were said to be suffering when admitted, and the state of medicine and surgery in the era, that appears to have been a commendable rate of recovery. On the other hand, the first three Valleyfield General Entry Books, in which were listed the 2,486 or so prisoners who came there in March (or April, in the case of some who had remained on as patients in the hospital) 1811 from Esk Mills, indicate, as already observed, that 13 died at Valleyfield between 20 March and 30 April. Although five of the 13 were said to have come to Valleyfield from Esk Mills hospital only one of these five (Isidore Boucherie—see No. 13 in the Valleyfield list in Appendix 11) appears in the lists of patients at the hospital. Marius Ponchina or Pinchina, aged 13, captured on the naval sloop *Jean Honorè* in 1808, who is said to have died from an abscess in his lungs on 18 April 1811 at Edinburgh Castle, to which he had been transferred five weeks earlier on 11 March from Esk Mills, seems never to have been a patient in the hospital at the latter.[43]

Three other sections in the 'Edinburgh, 1813, Various' Entry Book deal with the admission of sick prisoners to Greenlaw depot hospital. The first of these sections, filling nine pages, lists 186 patients admitted in the year between 14 August 1811 and 28 August 1812 inclusive. Unlike Esk Mills hospital, where there were often several admissions on any one day (on one occasion 13, and on another as many as 23), these admissions at Greenlaw were almost always of either one or two patients only on each of three or four days of most weeks during the year they cover. The only exceptions were on 9, 10 and 20 December 1811 and 4 January 1812, on each of which days three were admitted, and on 23 March, when admissions were four. Of the 186 prisoners admitted, six (3.2 per cent) were recorded as having died, 19 (10.2 per cent) 'Sent as Incurable to France', and seven (3.7 per cent) 'Sent to Valleyfield Hospital'. The remaining 154 (82.7 per cent) were said to have been 'Returned to the Prison' or 'Discharged', presumably cured of their ailments.

The second section in the Entry Book fills less than half a page and lists six American prisoners, all merchant seamen, admitted to the depot hospital between 7 November and 2 December 1812 inclusive—one on 7, two on 26 and two on 27 November, and one on 2 December. The first is said to have been 'Returned to the Prison' on 14 November, seven days after his admission; the other five were all 'Discharged to Leith' on 3 December, along with all the other 32 American merchant seamen sent off that day from Greenlaw en route to a hulk or depot in the south of England.[44]

Finally, the third section in the Entry Book fills ten pages and lists 202 'French' prisoners admitted to Greenlaw hospital between 13 November 1812 and 6 July 1813. Of the 202, eight (3.9 per cent) died, four (1.9 per cent) were 'Sent as Incurable to France', 26 (12.8 per cent) 'Sent to Valleyfield Hospital', four others (1.9 per cent) 'Sent to Valleyfield Depot', a further 24 (11.8 per cent) 'Sent to Valleyfield', three (1.4 per cent) are described as 'Entered as a Patient', one (0.49 per cent) has only incomprehensible initials against his name in the relevant column. The remaining 132 (65.1 per cent) were 'Returned to Prison' or 'Discharged', presumably cured. Whether the 28 sent to 'Valleyfield' or 'Valleyfield Depot' were sent in fact to the hospital there is uncertain; if they were, then those transferred from the one hospital to the other totalled 54 (26.7 per cent). Of those specifically said to have been sent to the hospital at Valleyfield 18 were sent on 29 November 1812, the other eight on 5 July 1813. The four 'Sent to Valleyfield Depot' were all sent on 28 November 1812, the 24 'Sent to Valleyfield' on 12 January 1813. As no register of admissions to Valleyfield hospital has survived no further analysis of the cure rate at Greenlaw hospital is possible beyond the relevant evidence of deaths recorded in the Valleyfield Entry Books, which indicates that two of the prisoners transferred on 28 November 1812 from Greenlaw to Valleyfield hospital died at the latter soon afterward.[45] Their deaths increase to ten, therefore, the total number of Greenlaw prisoners in the third section of the Entry Book who appear to have died in hospital.

For Valleyfield, although no similar register of prisoners in hospital has survived, an extant note made by Andrew Johnston, the chief clerk, appears to offer a rather opaque snapshot of at least the number of patients in the depot hospital on a given day, when it may have been between about 40 and 116.[46]

For Perth depot hospital it is possible to conclude from successive reports in the local newspaper concerning the number of patients that, despite the deaths of at the most 215 prisoners during 1812-14 (an average of two per week), the rate of cure of sick prisoners, as well perhaps as the success of preventative health measures, was nonetheless impressive. If the hospital could indeed accommodate 150 sick prisoners,[47] then it does seem remarkable that on a day in July 1813, within a year of its opening, 'the whole number of sick, including the convalescents, … amounted to 24, only four of whom were so much indisposed as to be confined to bed.' Six weeks later there were reported to be 'only 16 in the hospital', the number during the two previous months having apparently varied between 14 and a maximum of 30. By early September the number was reported to have fallen to 11, by the end of October to 10, and even in the depth of winter in February 1814 it varied between 10 and a maximum of 20; and on a day that month when the *Perth Courier* reporter had called at the depot, 'though it was among the coldest days we have had, there was not a single individual among the 7,000 [prisoners] confined to bed.' When the great repatriation began in June 1814 after the ending of the war, there were only two prisoners in the hospital 'and for the present incapable of being sent to France.'[48] It may be that as the only purpose built depot in Scotland Perth had a distinct advantage over the other four north of the Border which helps explain its apparently having so relatively few of its inmates in hospital.

Whatever the variations between them in the numbers of sick and hospitalised prisoners, and the number or ratios of deaths, fortunately none of the Scots depots suffered the terrible epidemics that raged in at least two depots in England. In six months during 1809-10 one such epidemic of measles cost the lives of 500 prisoners out of 5,000 at Dartmoor, and in five months during the winter of 1800-1, toward the end of the French Revolutionary Wars, an epidemic of typhoid or enteric fever at Norman Cross in Huntingdonshire had cost the lives of about 1,000 prisoners.[49]

Certain relevant regulations of the Transport Board, and certain measures the Board took from time to time (even if only after representations by other authorities such as Admiral Otway at Leith or suggestions by its own agents at the depots), may have contributed to some extent to making the lives of the prisoners less miserable and less unhealthy than otherwise they would have been, given overcrowding and inadequate diet.

The importance, for instance, of prisoners crowded together in their particularly claustrophic quarters at Edinburgh Castle being obliged to get into the fresh air by day was emphasised by the Board when in February 1811 the Castle again became a depot. 'Mr Reid [crown architect in Scotland] having informed us that he has recommended to you,' the Board told Malcolm Wright, its agent at the Castle, 'that the prisoners ... should be as much as possible excluded from their sleeping rooms in the day time, we desire your attention to this suggestion.'[50]

The airing grounds or exercise yards at all the Scots depots were intended to make an important contribution toward maintaining, or at least diminishing any decline or further decline in, the health of the prisoners. The bigger the airing ground the more scope there was for exercise by the prisoners. At Greenlaw, however, a proposal by the agent toward the end of 1808 apparently to extend the airing ground was turned down by the Transport Board without reason given: 'We do not think it proper to change the airing ground at Greenlaw at present.'[51] Ten months later the subject arose again at the depot, when that informative inmate Captain Paul Andreas Kaald noted in his diary: 'Today Mr Wright [the agent] and Mr Fraser [depot chief clerk] were up here to decide how far the palisade will be moved out around the prison. This has been talked about for four or five years I hear, and is to be discussed for another two or three years yet.'[52] Kaald describes the daily routine for providing the prisoners with some fresh air and opportunity for exercise: 'At 10 o'clock [in the morning] all the prisoners are turned out or chased out of the prison, out into the prisoners' courtyard, which is a place of about some twenty fathoms square.' At noon the guard counted the prisoners one by one as they filed back into the depot building and, Kaald says, if the numbers did not tally the prisoners might be chased out again two or three times into the airing ground until the tally was met. Another dose of fresh air was administered to them by their being sent out on to the airing ground at 3 p.m., after which they were called back in again for counting before being all locked up in their rooms from about 4 p.m. until the following morning at 10.[53] Three months before his release and repatriation in August 1810 from Greenlaw Kaald was, however, able to record that '... we finally now have our beloved courtyard extended. That is now very good. They are working here daily to repair the palisade as well as the courtyard itself, with gutters and paving ...'[54] At Esk Mills, where Lieutenant Marote-Carrier was confined in February-March 1811, there was a similar routine each morning of counting of the prisoners by a gaoler as they passed out into the airing ground or courtyard 'where, despite the cold, we had to pass a good part of the morning [though] We were allowed to remain in the building in the evening because of the snow which fell in big flakes.' Transferred successively from Esk Mills to Valleyfield, then in September 1812 to Perth, Marote-Carrier found at the latter a similar daily routine: 'We were roused at dawn and counted man by man as we went into the yard. We stayed in the rooms at meal times or when bad weather did not allow us to remain outside.' At Valleyfield, he recalled 'three courtyards to which all our promenades were restricted.'[55]

The airing ground at Esk Mills appears to have been particularly inadequate for the 2,817 or so prisoners confined at that depot. '... if the airing ground be considered too small,' the Transport Board told its agent there, 'you are to enlarge it by taking in the Garden ...'[56]

Whether, and if so how, personal cleanliness was achieved or maintained by the prisoners themselves or ensured by the depot authorities is not clear, given the absence of references to washing or bathing. '... I was crawling with vermin,' Sergeant Major Beaudoin noted in his *cahier* or notebook when in June 1804 he arrived at Greenlaw. His was hardly a unique experience among the prisoners in the Scots depots. It seems to have been as late as 1812, eight years after the depot opened, before even the hospital at Greenlaw acquired a tub for bathing: 'I ... shall procure a Bathing Tub for the use of the Hospital, agreeably to your directions,' wrote the agent to the Board on 14 March that year.[57]

So far as his clothes were concerned, however, Beaudoin, no doubt like most other prisoners, was able to wash them thoroughly—in his case once a kindly fellow prisoner had loaned him some other garments to change into.[58] There were in addition the washermen among the prisoners who, in return for payment of the appropriate fee in their tariff of charges, provided a laundry service of sorts for their fellow inmates.[59] There were also barbers among the prisoners who, similarly for a small payment, shaved and trimmed the hair of their fellow captives.[60] At Edinburgh Castle, for example, that curious General Entry Book titled 'Edinburgh, 1813, Various' indicates that there were either two barbers or one and no fewer than six washermen employed in the depot in the early summer of 1813, and evidently three washermen and one barber in the depot hospital. At Esk Mills hospital, in March-April 1811, one barber and two washermen were employed; in Greenlaw hospital from November 1812, a barber and two washermen; and likewise at Perth (and no doubt also at Valleyfield), washermen (and almost certainly also barbers) were employed.[61]

At Valleyfield, the report of the prisoners' defiance of Commissioner Bowen of the Transport Board when he ordered them in May 1811 to bring out their hammocks to air, illustrated another of what Bowen described as the Board's 'orders and regulations that were adopted for the benefit of their health and comforts'.[62]

A clean and adequate supply of water was obviously an important factor in the health of the prisoners, but this is another aspect about which relatively little significant information is available. At Greenlaw, for instance, where the prisoners were said in the depot's earlier years to 'fetch their water' from a pond, the agent was instructed by the Transport Board in February 1812 to 'report what has been done respecting the procuring of Water within the Prison Palisade; and also what would be the Cost of a sufficient Number of Barrels to be carried on Poles by Five Prisoners, and sufficiently large to contain at least 30 Gallons each.' A week later the Board told the agent that it had asked for a report from Robert Reid, architect, about 'procuring of a supply of water for Greenlaw Prison, by sinking a Well in the Prison Yard as proposed by you', and also that 'We consider that 6 Barrels would be very sufficient for the purpose of conveying water; and we direct you to procure that number accordingly.'[63] The decision in the latter stages of the war greatly to enlarge the depot resulted in Commissioner Douglas writing from Edinburgh to his colleagues on the Transport Board: 'This morning I went to Greenlaw to ascertain from whence a supply of water for a large Depot could be obtained, the spring at Greenlaw not affording a sufficient quantity for a large body of men. About a mile from the prison, on the upper road to Valleyfield, there is a very strong spring of good water that is not applied to any use whatever. The ground on which it rises is the property of Sir George Clerk, and I have desired Mr Reid [architect] to inquire through whose grounds the drain must be carried to convey water to the Depot … I have also desired a clause may be inserted in the deeds giving the Board possession of the Greenlaw estate, that will entitle them to carry a drain for water for the use of the Depot through Mrs Trotter's land.'[64] If not in August 1812, Douglas's letter may have been written in 1811, during the spring of which the Board were negotiating unsuccessfully with the landowner, Mrs Trotter, to buy the Greenlaw estate. After abandoning their attempt then to do so the Board succeeded in buying the whole estate for £10,000 in November 1812, and prepared then greatly to extend the depot so that it would hold, not as previously a mere 500 or 600 prisoners, but several thousands. The exact number of prisoners the extended Greenlaw depot was intended to hold is uncertain. The Transport Board's plan submitted for approval to the Admiralty in February 1813 referred to 5,000 prisoners, with the cost of the extended buildings, made of wood but with stone foundations, totalling £72,990. Macbeth Forbes quoted John Cowan of Beeslack as stating £113,000 had been spent on extending Greenlaw to hold 7,000 prisoners. An unidentified press cutting dated 16 September 1899 concerning Glencorse Barracks declared that the Greenlaw extensions in 1813 cost £100,000 and were intended to accommodate 6,000 prisoners. A Penicuik local historian more recently claimed the number of prisoners was to become 8,000.[65] As early as May 1810 Captain Kaald had, however, noted cryptically in his diary what may have been an improvement in the depot's amenities: '… built on the south-west corner of the courtyard is a very brilliant waterhouse, made of stone and with two doors, both on the front corner, and eight stone steps with a grille round about it.'[66] Problems concerning water supply at Greenlaw appear to have continued until virtually the end of the war.[67]

For Valleyfield there are fewer references than for Greenlaw to water supply—perhaps an indication that at the former there was no notable difficulty.[68]

Some questions also arose about water supply at Perth depot. Within two or three weeks of the opening of the depot in August 1812, the Board wrote to Commissioner Douglas, one of its members who was then in Scotland, about damages 'said to be awarded to the farmers through whose grounds the water pipes for the depot ... are conveyed, which damages and attendant expenses are stated to amount to £216.3.2., and we request that you will make particular enquiry and report your opinion on this subject ... we are surprised at so large a demand being made, it being clearly understood that the farmers would be benefited rather than detrimented by the water being conveyed in pipes sunk under their grounds, instead as formerly of passing in open drains or sewers. We also request your opinion on the subject of a supply of water from the depot at Perth, Captain Moriarty [the depot agent] having in his letter to us of the 24th inst. expressed his strong fears that there will be much want of water for the use of the prisoners in the dry season, a communication which appears to us to be very extraordinary.'[69] Whatever the basis for Moriarty's fears, they appear not to have been allayed by whatever report Commissioner Douglas submitted. For in April 1813 Moriarty again raised 'the probable scarcity of water' at the depot with the Board, which agreed to consult Robert Reid on the issue. Reid's comments have evidently not been preserved, but when Moriarty returned to the subject in two successive letters to the Board in June and July it told him: 'While the prisoners are so well supplied with water as you state them to be there there does not appear to us to be any reason for an alarm lest there should be a deficiency of that article.'[70]

Sanitation was another important issue in maintaining, or at least avoiding deterioration or further deterioration in, the health of the prisoners, given the confinement of so many hundreds at Greenlaw and Edinburgh Castle and of thousands at Esk Mills, Valleyfield and Perth. Privies or latrines, supplemented by night or jack tubs for use in the rooms into which, as Captain Kaald found at Greenlaw, the prisoners were locked for up to 17 hours overnight, were the usual offices provided.[71] Privies and privacy were hardly synonymous, but at least at Valleyfield the privies were enhanced within a few weeks of the opening of the depot: 'We ... direct you,' the Transport Board wrote the agent, 'to cause Doors to be immediately placed, agreeably to your Suggestion, on the outside of the Privies.'[72] More generally, what was usually referred to euphemistically as 'the Prison Soil', of which a great deal was daily produced by the prisoners, was for local landowners and farmers a desirable commodity for spreading as manure on their fields and might at the same time become an agreeable if marginal source of revenue for the

Transport Board. 'We direct you,' the Board told its agent at Greenlaw, for instance, 'not to allow Mrs Trotter's Servant to take away any more of the Prison Soil, but to see on what Terms the occupiers of the Grass Land belonging to Government will take it away.' The occupiers, however, appeared unable or unwilling to pay for the privilege of acquiring the prison soil, and the Board told the agent they could take it away free so long as they spread it on the adjoining farmland leased by the government.[73] The occupiers proved unwilling to do so, because they claimed the 'carts will considerably injure the pasture wherever they are drawn over,' and also that 'the Dung … could be of no service to them as they cannot till the ground or even cut the grass.' The agent was then instructed by the Board to 'hire or engage a Man and Horse to come every day to the Prison and carry out the carts with the Soil', for spreading on the government's fields. The agent reported that after asking several farmers around the depot, 'I only found One willing to undertake it, and who at present demands 2 shillings per day.'[74] The following year, however, by which time the government had bought the Greenlaw estate from Mrs Trotter, the agent was told by the Board to allow her to take away the manure.[75] At Perth, the local historian Sievewright indicated that that task was one of the functions of the ten feet wide moat or canal built around the depot partly as a deterrent to potential escapers. At Valleyfield, the canny Cowan brothers, former owners of the paper mill, used the prison soil as manure on their adjoining fields but complained in October 1811 about their 'great difficulty in removing the dung from the new North Prison at Valleyfield as it is in so fluid a state that the carts cannot retain it altogether … [because] the prisoners are throwing down great quantities of water to remove dung from the boards [in the privies], which have been placed too flat.'[76] An incidental attraction for the prisoners of the use of carts to remove a depot's night soil was the possibility they might offer of escape.[77]

One other health measure evidently taken, however tardily, by the authorities at least at one Scots depot is referred to once by Captain Kaald at Greenlaw. When in September 1809 some 50 new prisoners entered the depot they were, says Kaald, 'put into quarantine, after having spent the night with the rest of us.' They remained in quarantine for 16 days.[78]

Whatever the prisoners themselves might do, and the depot authorities, especially the hospital staffs, and the Transport Board by their regulations and medical and other provision might contribute, to maintain their health by taking as much fresh air and exercise and eating as well as the circumstances of their captivity allowed, nonetheless between 535 and 573 prisoners (between 4.1 and 4.4 per cent) out of an estimated net total of about 13,000 confined at one time or another between 1803 and 1814 in the depots in Scotland died there. It is difficult, because of contradictions and some gaps in some of the relevant sources, to establish precisely the number of deaths at each of the five depots. But, as has been seen above, the respective totals appear at the most to have been: Greenlaw 45, Esk Mills nine, Edinburgh Castle four, Valleyfield 300, Perth 215. The names and other details of those who died are entered, depot by depot, in chronological order of death in Appendix 11 below. Additionally, an unknown number among the hundreds of prisoners repatriated from the Scots depots during the war because their wounds or illnesses were considered too serious for them ever again to fight in Napoleon's forces, no doubt died even before the end of the war in 1814.

'So very many prisoners had not been able to survive this long series of persecutions and miseries,' wrote Lieutenant Marote-Carrier of one of the most depressing stages of his captivity at Valleyfield. 'We had been decimated by the maladies and sufferings of captivity. It was first those with feeble and sickly constitutions that succumbed; then the robust and strong were slowly undermined ... Each day one saw a victim fall, and there formed around us a vast enclosure of death that was known locally as the cemetery of the French.'[79]

Seven years earlier even than at Valleyfield, those prisoners confined at Greenlaw had begun to bury their dead in ground near the depot that would remain forever France—or Norway, Denmark, Netherlands, Germany, Italy, Spain, or whichever was the homeland of the deceased. The first prisoner to die at Greenlaw, and indeed the first to die at any Scots depot, appears to have been Alexander Linde, a Danish seaman aged 18 captured on the Dutch 16-gun brig *L'Union* off the coast of Norway in May 1804 by the frigate HMS *Ethalion*. Of the crew of *L'Union* landed at Leith, 77, including Linde, were marched out to Greenlaw. He died there five weeks later on 18 June, 'of consumption, occasioned by a fall from the main mast of *L'Union*.' Where exactly he was buried is not known but it was perhaps in ground at the back of the depot, on the banks of the river North Esk, near where long afterward Auchendinny railway station was built. It was there that almost all the prisoners who died at Greenlaw after Linde appear to have been buried.[80] Macbeth Forbes says that when the railway was being built there years later the skeletons of between 60 and 70 prisoners were found and reburied near their original graves. Their discovery inspired a Penicuik poet, Walter Howden, to write these lines:[81]

> O, ye shades of bygone Frenchmen,
> Why will they not let you lie?
> Was it not enough that exiles,
> Far from home and friends, should die?

At least two prisoners who died at Greenlaw were not, however, buried there but in the churchyard of old Glencorse Church. One of them was

Charles Cottier or Cotier, victim of the shooting at the depot in January 1807 for which in the High Court Ensign Maxwell of the Lanarkshire Militia was convicted of culpable homicide and sentenced to nine months' imprisonment.[82] The other was a prisoner mentioned in his diary by Captain Paul Andreas Kaald. 'Today,' Kaald wrote on 10 March 1809, 'a Danish captain, Nils Wilkensen from Arendal, was buried. He died yesterday. The burial was fairly quiet. The mourners consisted of Captain Greff, Captain Sande, Captain Knudtzen, Captain Haaverson, Captain Paal, his mate, and six mates carried the coffin. The oldest of the mourners sprinkled earth on it, and three sang one and a half verses of a psalm over the grave. It is 1½ English miles to the graveyard.'[83]

Conversely, it may be that some prisoners who had died at Valleyfield were buried at Greenlaw in the depot cemetery on the banks of the North Esk river. When in the autumn and winter of 1812 'the very small Spot at Present used as a Burying Ground' at Valleyfield became full, the Transport Board instructed Captain Brown, its agent there, to negotiate with the Cowan brothers about their letting or selling a piece of adjoining ground for use as a depot cemetery. The Board said it was willing to pay a rent of £5 a year for the ground, but if the Cowans declined then 'we will cause the Prisoners to be buried at Greenlaw.' Ten days later, on 21 December, Brown was instructed 'to consult with Mr Reid [architect] on the subject of a spot of ground for burying prisoners of war at Greenlaw, each corpse to be conveyed by 8 prisoners on a bier which you will provide for that purpose. The messmates of the deceased are to be thus employed under an escort.' Whether burials of Valleyfield prisoners did thereafter take place at Greenlaw is not certain. But the discrepancy of some two dozen between the known deaths at Greenlaw and the number of skeletons in that depot's burial ground uncovered by the later railway builders at Auchendinny station, may indicate that that number of Valleyfield dead were indeed buried there.[84]

At Valleyfield the burying ground appears to have been a source of concern to the authorities from the outset. The day after the depot opened, its agent was instructed by the Transport Board 'To report if there be not sufficient Ground for a Burial Place for the Prisoners at Valleyfield, beyond the Stockade.' A week later, after receiving the agent's reply, the Board wrote to him again: '… we intended that deceased prisoners should be buried in the purchased ground outside of the Stockade and not in Mr Cowan's Ground. It is our Intention that the Piece of Ground under the Hill on the Right of the New Road leading from Esk Mills to Pennycuick, shall be allotted as a burial place.'[85] The question seems not to have become active again until May 1812, when the Valleyfield agent reported the burying ground 'to be nearly full', and in September Commissioner Douglas of the Transport Board, along with Admiral Otway, visited both Greenlaw and Valleyfield. At Valleyfield, as

Douglas wrote to the secretary of the Board, 'There is a want of burial ground ... a part is so low [that] water rises when dug to a foot from the surface, and the higher part is nearly filled with coffins. I strongly recommend a fence being made round the burial ground. Mr Reid [architect] informs me a small piece of ground adjoining the present burial ground might be easily obtained, and I have desired him to enquire at what price.' It appears to have been Douglas's report which led the Board a few days later to write as it did to its agent at Valleyfield about the burial ground.[86]

At Esk Mills also there were problems about the amount of ground available for a cemetery: '... appropriate such part of the Garden,' the agent was told by the Transport Board within two days of the depot opening, 'as you may think to a Burying ground if there be not sufficient room between the Wall and the River.' Three weeks later, when, as has been seen, the airing ground, too, was proving inadequate for the number of prisoners packed into it, the Garden had to be incorporated into it rather than into the cemetery, and the Board instructed the agent to '... report on what terms a piece of ground can be procured for burying the prisoners who may die.' Whatever further problems might have arisen concerning ground for burials were overtaken, however, early the following month by the closure of the depot.[87]

Where at Edinburgh Castle prisoners of war who died were buried is not stated in surviving sources concerning them. At least one, however, was buried not at the Castle but half a mile away in Greyfriars churchyard. He was Joseph Mulart, aged 25, born in Quernifery (?), a soldier of the 26th regiment of the Line, captured in Martinique, who arrived at the Castle on 21 December 1813 from Perth depot as an invalid being repatriated to France. He never reached home: he died from phthisis at the Castle a week later.[88]

At Perth, the 'place of interment was beyond the boundaries of the prison grounds proper, between the north boundary wall and the Cow Inch, ... quite near to where the water engine stood. There were a certain number of layers in whch bodies were laid in consecutive order ...'[89]

Apart from Kaald's description of the funeral of Captain Wilkensen, little is said in any of the sources about rites and ceremonies observed when prisoners were buried at the Scots depots. 'Eleven shillings and three pence each is the greatest price ever paid for coffins at any of the depots in England and no more can be allowed for coffins at Esk Mills,' the Transport Board told the agent there, and it added: 'No charge is made at those depots for digging the graves, this being done by the prisoners. Cannot Robert Aitken, turnkey, who is a carpenter be employed to make the coffins, he being furnished by you with the materials?' The only other reference found concerned arrangements two years later at Valleyfield: 'Approve of your procuring,' the Board told its agent there in May 1813, 'a piece of common black cloth to be used at the burial of prisoners.'[90]

429

20

They Have Their Exits: Transfers, Invalids and Aged, Boys, Allies, Neutrals, Exchanges and Other Releases, Parole, Volunteers

Death was, fortunately, by no means the only way, short of the war at last ending, by which prisoners might make their exit from the depots in Scotland. If the Grim Reaper beckoned between 535 and 573, many hundreds of other prisoners before the end of the war passed outward through the gates of their depots in response to the beckoning fingers of other forces, mainly those of the Transport Office and the Admiralty, certifying surgeons, and the recruiting sergeant. There were also considerable numbers of prisoners who stood not upon the order of their going but, responding to the clarion call of freedom, passed from their depot not usually through its gates but over, under, or through its palisades or walls. Thus the populations of the depots were far from static, although many prisoners did remain at one or other of the two largest depots, Valleyfield and Perth, throughout their captivity in Scotland.

One of the most common of those exits was simply by unsolicited transfer from one depot to another within Scotland—from the frying pan into the fire. Sometimes the transfer was, even less agreeably, as Sergeant Major Beaudoin found after his five years at Greenlaw, from a depot in Scotland to the hulks at Chatham, Plymouth or Portsmouth. Transfers must often have been felt by those prisoners involved in them as an uprooting away from comrades and friends, familiar faces and routines, into a bleak unknown. Depression, misery and despair were hardly strangers in any of the depots; but the physical conditions of captivity at Edinburgh Castle and Esk Mills appear to have been even worse than at Greenlaw, Valleyfield or Perth. An especially daunting experience therefore for those who had to endure it, was to be transferred, for breaches of discipline, from Esk Mills, Greenlaw, Valleyfield or Perth to the cachot at Edinburgh Castle. On the other hand, as Lieutenant Marote-Carrier, for example, found on his transfer from Valleyfield to Perth in September 1812, not only might some comrades and friends be transferred in the same contingent but also acquaintance might be renewed with other old comrades and friends already confined at the depot of destination. Other compensations, too, might offer themselves: the food, for instance, as Marote-Carrier found also at Perth, might be not as bad as at the previous depot.[1]

Occasionally transfers were en masse. Five or six such took place during the war from depots in Scotland. First, there were those hundreds of 'Danish' and French prisoners, such as Beaudoin, transferred in 1808-11 from Greenlaw to the hulks. Second, there were the 2,800 or so prisoners marched away on its closure on 11 March 1811 from Esk Mills, the great majority to Valleyfield, the remainder to Edinburgh Castle. Third, after the mass escape of 12 April 1811 from the Castle and the series of further escapes or attempted escapes in the following weeks, there was the removal from there in August that year of almost all its 365 prisoners to Greenlaw. Fourth, when work on building a huge extension to Greenlaw depot began in 1812, more than 550 of its inmates were transferred on 1 September that year to Valleyfield. Finally, in a six week period between June and August 1813, some 866 prisoners were transferred from Valleyfield to Perth, and a more or less identical number from Perth to Valleyfield.[2]

But also, as has been seen, there were numerous other smaller transfers between the Scots depots involving either individual prisoners or groups varying in number from two or three to a couple of hundred. Marote-Carrier, for example, was one of almost 70 prisoners transferred on 2 September 1812 from Valleyfield to Perth, where 43 other prisoners arrived simultaneously from Greenlaw. Conversely, 177 prisoners were transferred between 29 July and 4 August 1813 from Perth to Valleyfield. The first inmates of Esk Mills depot were the 192 prisoners transferred there on 4 February 1811 from Greenlaw.[3] And the first inmates of Greenlaw itself in the spring of 1804 were the 70 or so prisoners confined until then in the Edinburgh bridewell. Some prisoners were transferred from time to time from Greenlaw or Edinburgh Castle to Valleyfield for hospital treatment.

Thus several thousands among the prisoners in the Scots depots were moved around from one depot to at least one other during their captivity north of the Border. Marote-Carrier, as has been seen, passed his three years in Scotland successively at Esk Mills, Valleyfield and Perth. His fellow privateersman Lieutenant David Fourneau, recaptured after escaping from Esk Mills in February 1811, was then sent to the cachot at Edinburgh Castle, from there in August that year transferred to Greenlaw, and from there in September 1812 to Perth. Jacques Adam, a naval lieutenant, was one of a select band who were prisoners successively in each of the Scots depots, the last of them in his case from September 1812 being Perth where he remained until the end of the war.[4] On the other hand, among that mass of prisoners at Valleyfield who spent their captivity in Scotland in only that depot an example was Jean Genest, alias Yves Leguoine, a soldier in the 82nd infantry regiment. Captured on Martinique in 1809, he was among the first intake of prisoners to enter Valleyfield after the arrival of the original 2,400 or so transferred in March 1811 from Esk Mills. Arriving from Plymouth in

September that year, Genest remained at Valleyfield until June 1814, a couple of months after the end of the war. At Perth, the first prisoner registered in the General Entry Book when the depot opened in August 1812 was Jean Chaseau, a soldier in the 64th infantry regiment, captured the previous year in the Peninsular War. Chaseau was among the thousands for whom Perth was their only experience of a Scots depot before their repatriation to France after the end of the war.[5]

The motives of the authorities in moving prisoners from one depot to another were various, even if by no means always recorded or obvious. As at Greenlaw, with the movement in and out of French and 'Danish' prisoners in 1808-11, the purpose might occasionally be to concentrate a particular nationality in one depot. Sometimes it might be to lessen the risk of prisoners becoming over familiar or friendly with their militia guards. On other occasions, as appears, for instance, to have been the case with the transfer of Marote-Carrier, David Fourneau, Jacques Adam and other officers from Valleyfield and Greenlaw to Perth in September 1812, the purpose was to separate actual or potential leaders from rank and file prisoners where it was considered they had been together too long.[6] In other cases again, no doubt transfers were ordered simply to fill vacant places as previous inmates were moved elsewhere. In the case of Esk Mills and Edinburgh Castle mass transfers of prisoners became unavoidable when each of these depots showed how insecure and vulnerable it was.

Although almost all transfers between depots were unsolicited by the prisoners concerned and were on the orders of the Transport Office or Admiralty, evidence does survive of at least three applications for transfer to other depots made by rank and file prisoners in Scotland themselves. Prisoners were permitted to submit applications on a wide range of matters to the agent of their depot. At Perth, for example, Marote-Carrier found that 'There was a box at the barrier in which the prisoners deposited their letters, which were picked up by a gaoler. I put my petition [i.e., his application for an interview with the agent] there ...'[7] Whenever the subject was one (as was usually the case) which the agent himself had not the authority to decide he sent on the application for decision by the Transport Office in London. The registers of these applications maintained by the Transport Office, and now preserved in The National Archives, indicate that most submitted by prisoners in Scotland came from officers who were either living in the parole towns, such as Peebles, Kelso, Jedburgh, Lanark, etc., or were confined in the depots at Valleyfield, Perth, Edinburgh Castle, Esk Mills or Greenlaw because they had not previously been granted parole and were applying for it, or because they had breached their parole and were anxious to regain it. A few applications survive from rank and file prisoners, however, in the confined depots, and two of these are applications for transfer to another place of confinement. In addition a third request survives which is not preserved in the register but reference to which occurs in a letter of 8 June 1812 from the Transport Board to its agent at Greenlaw: '… the Two Prisoners Joseph Neil and François Guinet dit [i.e., alias] Neil may be removed to Valleyfield agreeable to their request.'[8]

The two applications preserved in the register were both made by prisoners at Valleyfield. The first, dated 6 November 1812, gives no names but is said to be from 'Prisoners at Valleyfield' who request 'To be sent to some other depot.' The prisoners, whoever they were, had evidently by then been languishing in captivity for many years, 'Having been taken at the commencement of the war.' Their plea was that, confined as they were in Scotland, far from the traditional places of captivity centred in previous wars in the south of England at or around Plymouth, Portsmouth and Chatham, they were 'excluded from all partial exchanges [of prisoners of war] on account of their distance from [those] Ports.' Whether their application for transfer to depots or hulks in the south of England was successful is unknown but it seems unlikely.[9]

The second application from Valleyfield was dated 2 April 1813 and was made jointly by Joseph Busse or Bussy, a soldier in the 119th line regiment, and his cousin L. Cormorant, a seaman, captured on *L'Intrépide*, probably but not certainly the man-of-war destroyed as a result of the battle of Trafalgar in 1805. Their application was, the depot agent told the Transport Office, 'To be allowed to join the father of Busse, who is also uncle of Cormorant, now at Portsmouth.' The cousins' application was in order 'to render his captivity easier, he being an aged and infirm man.' Under the heading 'Remarks', a Transport Office official wrote on the application: 'Agent certifies them to be well behaved, quiet men.' If 'Portsmouth' meant a hulk, rather than the neighbouring land prisons of Portchester Castle or Forton, the familial concern of Busse and Cormorant was the more commendable since they were applying to be transferred from Valleyfield to the almost certainly even more dismal conditions of captivity on a hulk.[10]

Aged and infirm prisoners, such as the father of Busse and uncle of Cormorant, were themselves often justified in hoping for a speedier exit not merely from their depot but from their captivity. So, too, were prisoners not necessarily aged (which officially meant over the age of 50) but who had wounds, illnesses or disabilities that might be certified by the depot medical authorities as being sufficiently serious and chronic as to preclude them from being able in future to take up arms against His Britannic Majesty. The government's motives for repatriating invalid prisoners were not purely humanitarian: a letter in 1807 from the Transport Board to the Admiralty supported their repatriation as a means of avoiding the 'very great expence attending their maintenance in Hospital.'[11] Throughout the war there were in Scotland, as in England, many successive selections for the repatriation of such aged, infirm or invalid prisoners.[12] In the opening weeks of the war the Admiralty had in fact instructed the Transport Board to direct the depot agents to 'send lists of … infirm seamen who may be of no use to the enemy.'[13] Captured infirm seamen were soon joined, of course, in the depots and on the hulks by infirm captured soldiers. For several months in 1808, 1809, and 1811-12, when negotiations between the British and French governments concerning general exchanges of prisoners broke down, and there was also a failure or refusal by the French government to repatriate invalid British prisoners, the repatriation of invalids from Britain was stopped—at least of those who were French: repatriation of invalid prisoners who were Dutch or 'Danish', for example, appears to have continued. Those months apart, repatriations of invalids, as well as of the aged and infirm, took place on a fairly frequent if not regular basis throughout the war, and certainly did so from each of the Scots depots.[14]

As early as April 1804, toward the end of the first year of the war, four prisoners at Greenlaw who were described as being 'totally unfit for further service civil or military by land or sea', were the subject of a letter from the Transport Board to the Admiralty, as a result of which the latter directed the Board to 'take all opportunities that may present themselves for sending the persons in this list to any of the ports of Holland.' Three of the prisoners had been captured on the merchant vessel *La Flore* in the North Sea on 5 August 1803. One, Julian Rapideau, aged 23, was suffering from consumption; another, as already observed, Pierre Rideau, aged 70, from 'imbecility and rheumatism' and 'has been suffering from this for some years'; the third, Quentin Boileau, aged 65, had also succumbed to 'age and imbecility'. The fourth invalid, who had a diseased liver, was Arnold Nolmers (or Volner), a Dutchman, aged 37, captured on the merchant ship *Neptune* in the North Sea on 18 July 1803. Nolmers was repatriated from Greenlaw on 12 July 1804.[15] When in February 1807 the Dutch frigate *Utrecht* was shipwrecked on Orkney and the survivors arrived the following month at Greenlaw, 24 among them were reported by Malcolm Wright, the depot agent, to be suffering so badly from frostbite as to be 'in a state totally unfit for any further service.' Had not all the survivors (apart from those who volunteered into the British armed forces) been repatriated shortly afterwards to Holland as an act of humanity by the Transport Board and the Admiralty, it seems very probable that at least the 24 invalids would have been so.[16] While reliable statistics for this aspect at the depot are, as for so many other aspects there, difficult to establish, it appears from the evidence of the Entry Books that between 147 and 200 aged and infirm and younger invalid prisoners, plus the 24 frostbitten Dutchmen from the *Utrecht*, were repatriated during the war from Greenlaw.[17]

The Esk Mills Entry Book, incomplete as it is, provides no evidence of any aged and infirm or younger prisoners being invalided home, and the very brief existence of the depot makes it most unlikely that any were. But numbers of former Esk Mills prisoners were repatriated as invalids in the course of the three years following their transfer in March-April 1811 to Valleyfield. Repatriations of invalids during the war from Edinburgh Castle are even more difficult to establish, given the problems, already described, presented by its Entry Books. Despite, however, the lack of positive evidence, and the relatively short time the Castle functioned as a conventional if small depot, it seems likely that at least a handful of its inmates were sent home before the end of the war as aged or invalids. In addition there were those, such as Joseph Mulart, who died at the Castle on 28 December 1813 after arriving a week earlier with other invalids from Perth on their way to France, who were sent to the Castle for overnight or other brief staging from other depots in Scotland before being carried as aged or invalids on to a homeward bound vessel from Leith.[18]

Their General Entry Books indicate that from Valleyfield no fewer than 456 prisoners were invalided home between 1811 and the end of the war in 1814, and from Perth in 1812-14 at least 18 but perhaps as many as 50. Among one group of nine invalids repatriated from Perth on 26 August 1813, for instance, was Pierre Caly, aged 22, born in Antwerp, who had been a drummer or tambour player in the 88th regiment of the line when captured at Badajoz in April 1812, and who is described in the Entry Book as 'blind'. Sergeant Theo Thuillin, 4th line regiment, aged 31, born in Paris, captured at Coimbra in October 1810, was among another group of invalids being repatriated from Perth who were lodged for a few days at Edinburgh Castle on their way home in December 1813. He had had his right leg amputated.[19]

Only two formal applications for repatriation from invalid prisoners confined in one or other of the five depots in Scotland have been found. Whether this is because very few, perhaps even only these two, such applications were made by prisoners, or, perhaps more likely, because those that were made failed to escape the loss or destruction that befell some other sources such as almost all the letters and reports written by the depot agents to the Transport Office, is not known. Both the surviving applications were made in 1812 by prisoners at Valleyfield. One, in February that year, was by a prisoner named Gouillard, a surgeon, about whom otherwise nothing is known, except that at the time of his application he was either employed at the depot hospital or was a patient there. His application was simply 'to be discharged as an invalid', his plea 'That he grows worse.' The Transport Board's decision was equally terse: 'He cannot be released at present.' The other application, in October, from N.G. Le Montagnes, described as Agent Comptable or accountant, captured on the brig *Sylphe*, no date or place given, made the same request, and pleaded '... his weak state of health, having been taken as a non-combatant, also [he had been] on the Tiverton list of invalids.' The last phrase indicated Le Montagnes had been on parole at Tiverton in Devon before his arrival at Valleyfield. The Board's decision on Le Montagnes's application is unknown.[20]

Whether an instruction given by the Transport Board in September 1811 to Lieutenant Priest, agent at Greenlaw, was standard practice in selecting invalids for repatriation is not clear but the instruction seemed logical and was perhaps not unreasonable. On the other hand, there must have been prisoners in all the Scots depots who were, or considered themselves to be, sufficiently and chronically infirm, ill or disabled to merit repatriation but who were excluded from consideration by the instruction. 'The selection of invalids,' Priest was told, 'is to be made from the prisoners confined in the hospital only.'[21]

Even once it was granted to the aged and infirm and to younger invalids repatriation did not always proceed smoothly. After medical examination and certification by their depot surgeon and agent invalids were usually subject to further examination by Transport Office medical authorities at Portsmouth or the nearby depot of Forton before the last stage of their voyage home. This additional hoop through which invalids had to pass showed the concern of the Transport Board to prevent repatriation of prisoners who might be merely swinging the lead or who, even if obviously ailing or disabled, might nonetheless recover sufficiently to become employed again by Napoleon against Britain's armed forces. The agent at Valleyfield, for example, was sent by the Transport Board in October 1812 an extract of a letter from Captain Woodriff, RN, agent at Portsmouth and Forton, 'respecting the Prisoners lately sent from Scotland as invalids, and to desire that more care may be used in making similar selections in future.'[22] A sharper difference of view on the issue arose in mid-summer 1813, when the Transport Board actually sent back to the agents at Valleyfield and Perth their lists of invalid or 'unserviceable' prisoners recommended for repatriation. The agents were told by the Board to make 'another selection ... in lieu thereof, according to the terms of our letter dated 24th April last, in which you were directed not to select any who may possibly become capable of serving again in any capacity, civil or military. It is evident that there are many on the list sent by you who may be able to serve again, and it is therefore absolutely necessary that a more strict survey should be made, agreeable to the above direction, and a certificate be signed by you and the surgeon at the foot of the list in the annexed form. In making the selection care must be taken that cases of rupture, lameness of the left hand, and afflictions of the chest (too hastily denominated consumptions) should not be considered as invalids, unless in the latter disease it be most completely established and ascertained by expectoration of purulent matter and a corresponding loss of health. All other diseases must be of such a character and in such stages as to be deemed incurable. We have further to observe that the great trouble and expense attending the removal of invalids from Scotland renders it absolutely necessary that none should be sent from thence who are likely to be detained at Portsmouth as not being fit objects [for repatriation].'[23] While the Valleyfield agent apparently bowed to the Board's strictures, Captain Moriarty, agent at Perth, proved more reluctant and his reply to the Board appeared to be somewhat disrespectful. '… your Report on the cases of the persons selected as invalids,' the Board told Moriarty on 7 July, 'is by no means satisfactory … With respect to your remark of no prisoner being fit to be considered as an invalid who has not lost his arms and legs we have only to remark that there is a very great difference between such persons and some of those selected by you and Mr Gillies [Perth depot surgeon] who are young men and have only lost a finger or two of the left hand.' The Board's dissatisfaction with the list of Perth invalids led it to request Vice-Admiral Otway at Leith to '… be so obliging as to ask a surgeon to resurvey those prisoners …'[24]

The prospect of being repatriated as an invalid proved, as no doubt in all wars where such repatriation was accepted practice, an irresistible temptation to some quite healthy prisoners to feign or even deliberately develop some qualifying malady. Marote-Carrier, for example, while at Valleyfield in 1811-12, was among those who tried to pass himself off as an invalid. 'Each year,' he afterwards recalled, 'were sent to France and their respective countries those termed the Incurables. They were prisoners whom age or infirmity had rendered unfit for military service and from whom England no longer had anything to fear. Towards the end of the year everyone had to take part in a sort of visit before the doctors of the prison, and those who were declared incurable were liberated. Each convoy was escorted as far as Leith, where they were embarked.' If only money sent him by his wife in France had reached him in time, Marote-Carrier believed he would thus have had a chance to shake the dust of Valleyfield, and indeed of captivity, from his feet—though he may have overlooked the need to pass through the final medical hoop at Portsmouth. 'One of the incurables who was due to leave that year had agreed to give me his name and his place. We had agreed on thirty louis that I was to pay him on the day of departure, and I had given him two francs a week a month in advance … The day for the departure of the incurables arrived …' But not the money Marote-Carrier awaited from France. So '… in despair I saw the man set off whom I had intended to take the place of and who had sold me his chance of liberty.'[25]

Sergeant Major Beaudoin, a prisoner at Greenlaw in 1804-9, successfully feigned illness and was repatriated—although not from Greenlaw but from the hulk at Chatham to which he had been transferred in October 1809 and where he languished afterward for almost three years. It is difficult to believe that no prisoners at Greenlaw itself ever attempted there what Beaudoin did at Chatham. On the hulk Beaudoin made up his mind to risk his life rather endure captivity any longer: 'You had to love liberty to take such a big risk.' When an inspection of invalids for repatriation became imminent on the hulk he decided 'to cut down on my food, reducing my sustenance a little each day. I began to eat only three quarters of my ration for six days. Then I put myself on half-rations, and put the idea in the heads of my comrades that I was ill, saying the illness entirely took away my appetite. I often lay all day in my hammock, to strengthen that belief on the part of my comrades.' He complained daily of a sore stomach. As the day for inspection of invalids approached, Beaudoin cut down further on his intake of food and became so weak he could hardly stand up. He pretended to faint, the hulk surgeon was called and he ordered Beaudoin's removal to hospital. By then he was so weak he was scarcely able to eat anything at all. Nonetheless it remained uncertain that he would be selected as sufficiently disabled to merit repatriation. Beaudoin became desperate. 'I took some tobacco to chew in my mouth. I swallowed all the juice it produced. It was such a nasty liquid that it made me vomit twice immediately. I was so crushed I could do no more.' When the visiting inspector came on board the hulk to make the selection of invalids he found the list, to which Beaudoin had still not succeeded in having himself added, contained only privateersmen, and these he refused to accept. Beaudoin seized his chance and impressed on the inspector that he was not a privateersman but a soldier captured at Saint Domingo eight years earlier. 'You have had a lot of misfortune in this country,' said the inspector, and 'Without further questions he had me listed to go to France.' It was a close run thing. Beaudoin had so undermined his health that he felt himself 'in the last extremity. To make matters worse, fever gripped me. Then I lost hope. Death would be the compensation for my sufferings. Nothing would stay in my body, my stomach was quite overwhelmed.' Fortunately, a friendly fellow prisoner who was a surgeon nursed him back to better health. The fever lasted eight days. After that Beaudoin began to be able to eat some bread, soup and eggs that he bought with money he had saved. On 2 June 1812, after eight years of captivity, Beaudoin was repatriated to France as an invalid.[26]

Unlike Marote-Carrier, a Valleyfield prisoner who did apparently feign invalidity successfully at least once was Jacques Lavil, alias Guillaume Mailine. Lavil was the subject of an enquiry in November 1811 from the Transport Board to Captain Moriarty, the depot agent. Lavil, the agent at Portsmouth had complained, had been 'among the old and infirm and unserviceable Prisoners' sent there from Valleyfield but, making a remarkable and speedy recovery, had 'run off with the Buoy Boat from Portsmouth and was afterwards captured in Command of the French privateer *Point du Jour.*' Sent again to Valleyfield, Lavil had now been returned once more to Portsmouth, this time under his alias Mailine—though whether again he had been designated 'unserviceable' is not clear. Moriarty's response to the Board's enquiry has not survived.[27]

Marote-Carrier testifies that at Perth, where he was confined in 1812-14, 'Several prisoners feigned certain ailments in order to receive permission to leave with the incurables.' He cites the example of 'a French officer whom we saw was always morose and taciturn. One day when we were all gathered in the room he took a sort of outburst of furious madness, and he began to chase us as if he had a weapon in his hand and threatened us with being mercilessly sliced in two. Then he seized a cane, rushed into the yard and ran straight to the stalls at the gate and stopped suddenly in front of one of them, with a wild look about him, his eyes in a fixed stare. He seized one of those bladders filled with peas that children are given to play with, attached the end of it to his cane, and began to run round the yard waving it about and uttering inarticulate cries punctuated with bursts of laughter. Then he dressed himself up in a bizarre costume in which he continued to caper about. Commandant Moriarty [the depot agent] was alerted about this incident, came to see him and, considering the officer to be mad, ordered that he should be taken to the hospital. He let himself be led away without a struggle, all the time laughing uncontrollably. But when he reached the gate of the yard leading to the hospital he stopped suddenly. Marching straight up to the Commandant and looking at all of us with an air of bewilderment, he brandished his cane and, addressing Moriarty, cried out in French: "What are you going to do here, wretch? Do you want to confront my army? Do you not see my cannons pointed at you? Do you not know that an order from me is enough to blow you to bits?" He continued to speak in this way, and when the Commandant saw how angry he was and feared he might become violent toward him, he was about to order him to be pinioned when the officer suddenly burst out laughing and began to sing at the top of his voice a drinking song. He then let himself be led quietly away to the hospital. Although all this madness was feigned, he had played his role so admirably that the English, wary and distrustful as they were, were taken in. He was treated as a madman. He had the courage to carry on in this role as a madman for six months. At last the doctors, seeing that they were making no progress and that his illness resisted all their remedies, declared him incurable and sent him off with a convoy to Brest. We watched him set off clothed in soiled garments, his beard long and unkempt, his face so changed and wild that we ourselves came to believe that under the pressure of acting as a madman his brain had indeed become deranged.'[28]

Invalid prisoners repatriated appear usually to have been accompanied on their voyage homeward by a surgeon or surgeons from among their fellow prisoners, whether from the depots or parole towns. A surgeon named Carpentier, on parole at Jedburgh, was, for example, to be 'embarked on the transport [ship] conveying the worst cases' from among a group of prisoners invalided home from Valleyfield in December 1812, and he was to be given 'a small supply of medicines in order that he may afford them medical assistance on the passage.' Four months earlier when another group of invalids from Valleyfield was being repatriated the depot surgeon recommended they be accompanied by two nurses (evidently fellow prisoners) from the depot hospital. But the Transport Board's decision was that 'no Prisoners who are in Health can be allowed to go.'[29]

The Board asked for a report from its agents at Valleyfield and Perth, as well as from its transport agent at Leith, when in May 1813 it received from the French government a complaint from 'French prisoners last sent from Scotland as invalids that many of them were removed in a dying state in carts to which they were bound and that some of them died on the journey.' The reports received from the agents evidently denied there was any foundation for the complaint, and the Board's response to the French authorities consequently assured them that 'the greatest possible Care [of the invalids] was taken to provide for their safety and comfort during their Removal.' There is indeed no surviving evidence that appears to justify the complaint about the treatment of repatriated invalids en route from Scotland. The French authorities may have confused those allegations with the earlier attested maltreatment of some prisoners who were marched in the winter of 1812-13 to Perth after being landed in Fife, and which has already been discussed above.[30] Trenchant criticism of the treatment of repatriated invalids was expressed, however, by the French historian Jean Morvan. The British government, Morvan wrote, disembarked them like ghosts on the coasts of France, where often they received a poor reception. On one occasion 57 such invalids, French or French allied, were disembarked in the Low Countries and would have died of hunger, as the French Ministry of War refused them bread, had it not been for the help given them by civilians. No one in authority would take responsibility for them, and they were locked up in such a state of nakedness in the jail at Maastricht that they could not be allowed out like other prisoners of both sexes for daily exercise and fresh air. Whether any invalids repatriated from Scots depots were among those who suffered such treatment is not known. Peter Bussell, a British prisoner of war then in captivity at Besançon in the east of France, recorded of French invalids arriving there in the winter of 1811-12 after repatriation from Britain: '... as bad as they are with respect to wounds, many of them who were soldiers were forced to join the Army again.'[31]

Sometimes quite sizeable contingents of invalids were embarked at Leith for the first stage of their journey homewards, and the local press often carried reports of their going. The Transport Board commissioner J. Douglas reported to his Board from Edinburgh on 29 August 1812, for instance, that '205 invalids are to embark on Monday at Leith for Portsmouth'—166 of them from Valleyfield and the other 39 from Greenlaw. Among 120 prisoners embarked on the frigate *Regulus* at Leith for Portsmouth on 22 October 1811 were many 'sickly, old and infirm' from the depots at Penicuik; a further 150 made the same voyage from Leith in early January 1813. Repatriation of a much smaller contingent was reported in the *Perth Courier* on 26 August in the latter year: 'This morning nine invalids who are pronounced incapable of military service were sent off from the [Perth] depot, to be conveyed to France.'[32]

At the other end of the range of ages from those prisoners aged over 50 who were or might be considered for repatriation were boys aged under 12. Captain Paul Andreas Kaald has already been observed writing in his diary at Greenlaw one day in September 1809: 'Mr Fraser [the depot clerk] was up here and wrote down all the boys' ages—those under 12 years of age and all the old over 50.' In April the following year Kaald wrote: 'Today names of all the boys that are only 12 years old were written down. They through time, when answer or order comes from the Transport Board, will be sent home.'[33] Some boys, although the precise number is elusive, as with so many other statistics concerning that depot, were indeed sent home from Greenlaw as under age. Of the 920 prisoners listed in the first of the depot's two 'Danish' Entry Books for the years from 1807 to 1811, 24 were repatriated as boys under 12 years of age. In October 1809, for instance, the agent was directed by the Transport Board to release not only 28 Danish prisoners aged over 50 but also eight boys aged under 12.[34] The other six Entry Books listing ostensibly French, 'Danish', Dutch, Spanish and some American prisoners at Greenlaw (although some other nationalities such as Swedes and Prussians were also among them), indicate a score described as 'Boy', but none of them appears to have been under 12 years old, although at least one, Michel or Martial Champagne or Champaigne, was actually aged 12. Michel had been captured on a privateer in 1809 when he was 9 or 10 years old. For young boys like Michel there was always a danger, given the lapse of time before the authorities actually reached a decision, that the age barrier of 12 would descend and disqualify them. That appears to have been the misfortune also, as already noticed, of Jean Perrine at Valleyfield.[35]

At Valleyfield, Esk Mills, Edinburgh Castle and Perth there were certainly some boys aged under 12 but by no means all of them were repatriated before the war ended. At Esk Mills the Entry Book gives the ages of only 25 out of the 2,817 prisoners there—and the youngest of the 25 listed was aged 17. Once all the Esk Mill prisoners were transferred, however, in March-April 1811 to Edinburgh Castle and Valleyfield their ages were inserted in the Entry Books of those two depots.

At the Castle there were five boys under 12 who had come from Esk Mills, but the Castle Entry Book does not say that any of them were repatriated from the Castle as under age. Two of them, Brutus Camus, aged 10, and Jean Baptiste Gubert, aged 11, both of whom had been captured at sea (Brutus on a privateer in 1808, when he was presumably 7 years old, Jean Baptiste on a cutter in 1807, also presumably aged 7), were transferred a fortnight after their arrival at the Castle to Valleyfield. Where the other three boys were sent from the Castle is not stated in its Entry Book but one of them was Michel or Martial Champagne or Champaigne, whom a Greenlaw Entry Book shows came there from the Castle on 11 August 1811. Of the two other boys, Jean Marie Harve and Vincent Failés, both aged 10, the latter appears to have been transferred to Valleyfield, from which he was sent back to the Castle in autumn 1813.[36] Jean Marie Harve has not been further traced. In addition to those five there were five others who arrived at the Castle after, or in the case of four of them long after, the intake from Esk Mills. The first of these was Sven Larsen, said to be 'not quite 12', who arrived at the Castle on 10 July 1811, having been captured four days earlier in the North Sea on the privateer *Le Figaro*. The Castle Entry Book is blank concerning Sven's subsequent movement. But in a Greenlaw Entry Book he, like Michel Champagne, is shown to have arrived at that depot from the Castle in August 1811. Sven ended his captivity the following month by joining the British navy. The other four boys, C.I. Romont and Antoine Ghemar, both aged 11, Joseph Olivier, aged 10, and René (or Pierre) Vasseur (or Vapeur), aged 9, were all captured on the privateer *Ravisseur* off the coast of Norway on 18 February 1813, arrived at the Castle on 8 March, and were eventually transferred on 5 July to Valleyfield.[37]

Valleyfield was where no fewer than 24 boys under the age of 12 were gathered at one time or another between 1811 and 1814 and it was there they learned how His Britannic Majesty, or at any rate His Admiralty and Transport Board, had decided to deal with them. According to the sometimes incomplete information about them provided in the depot Entry Books, 13 of the 24 were repatriated to France in 1812 or 1813, and a further two, (described simply as 'Discharged'), probably were during one or other of those two years. Two others joined the British navy, two the British 60th regiment, and one was transferred from Valleyfield to Perth. Four remained in captivity at Valleyfield until the end of the war in 1814.[38]

It can only be surmised that the four boys aged, or ostensibly aged, 11 who remained in captivity at Valleyfield until the end of the war had already reached the age of 12 before their repatriation was or might have been considered. As the Transport Board told Captain Brown, agent at Valleyfield in September 1812: '… no Boys can be released whose Age exceeds 12 years on any Account whatever.'[39]

In the case of Nicolas Le Roy, aged 10, who was transferred to Perth in September 1812, the explanation presumably for his non-repatriation before the end of the war was that he shared his captivity at both depots with his father.[40]

At Perth there were only two prisoners, other than Le Roy junior, who were aged under 12. One was Melon Pain, aged 11, born in Paris, a ship's boy captured on the privateer *Le Pilotin* at the Aland Islands in the Baltic in October 1812, and who arrived at Perth the following month. The other was Gabriel Legrand, also aged 11, evidently a soldier in the 11th Battalion of miners, who had been captured at Madrid in August 1812 and had arrived in December that year at Perth. Like Le Roy junior, though not for the same reason, neither of these boys was repatriated before the end of the war. It may be that they were already aged 12 by the time their cases could be considered; whatever the reason, they both remained in captivity at Perth until July 1814.[41] If their reaching the age of 12 was indeed the reason, then Melon Pain and Gabriel Legrand were not alone in their misfortune. Among other youthful prisoners who remained in captivity at Perth until after the war ended was one already encountered above—Jean Vigneron, alias Durand, a musician in the 1st regiment of the Garde de Paris, captured at Baylen in Spain in July 1808. Aged 15 when he arrived at Perth in January 1813, he had presumably been only 10 or 11 years old at the time of his capture. But like so many other young boys he had no doubt passed the age of 12 before any case for his repatriation was or might have been considered.[42]

Altogether therefore there were repatriated from the Scots depots before the end of the war between 37 and 42 boy prisoners under 12 years of age.

Another small and distinctive group of prisoners, which the surviving sketchy evidence makes it difficult to be precise about but of which at least some members might have expected their captivity to be curtailed by repatriation, were fishermen. Their position as prisoners and the repatriation or temporary release of several of them from Greenlaw and Valleyfield have already been outlined above.[43] Although there were press reports of the capture of Dutch, Danish and German fishermen in the North Sea and of their implied confinement at Greenlaw and Valleyfield, they appear somehow to have escaped being recorded as such in depot Entry Books. Perhaps this was because they were regarded by the authorities as not really prisoners but merely odd fish caught up in the nets of war and soon to be released homewards. Thus the *Caledonian Mercury* reported on 8 May 1806 the capture and sending into Leith of the Emden fishing vessel *Good Intent*. Four Dutch fishing vessels, one with a crew of 14, were taken in the North Sea in May 1809, and at least three of the vessels were sent into Leith. Along with the five or six captured Dutch or German Papenburg doggers, two-masted fishing vessels, sent in July 1810 into Leith as prizes, was a Greenland ship 'with eight fish'—presumably a whaler. Nineteen Dutch and Danish fishermen captured on two vessels off the Dogger Bank, were sent in July 1813 from Aberdeen to Leith. But only half a dozen prisoners at Greenlaw, Esk Mills and Valleyfield have been found who were described in the Entry Books as fishermen. Two fishermen, André Dematte and Jean Lascalles, captured in the West Indies were landed at Greenock on 26 July 1805 and 'discharged same day to Caledonia'—presumably a ship; but no further trace of these men has been found.[44]

An altogether larger group than the captured fishermen who might have looked with some hope to the changing fortunes of war to bring about their repatriation from the depots in Scotland before the conflict ended were those prisoners whose states or homelands were either neutral, or had been allies of Napoleon but were no longer so, or had become members of one or other of the successive coalitions against him, or were conquered by Britain or its allies. Thus those prisoners who were Swedes, Finns, Prussians, Austrians, Russians, Portuguese, or (after the events in Spain in the summer of 1808) Spanish, as well as, before the War of 1812-14, any citizens of the United States of America not captured on board French or other enemy privateers, or subjects of much smaller neutral states such as the duchy of Oldenburg near Bremen on the North Sea coast of Germany, formed the great majority of those who might not unreasonably have entertained such hopes. Some examples of such repatriations that actually occurred have already been observed in Chapter 11.[45]

Thus a sudden change in the political or military situation during the war might result in prompt repatriation for certain prisoners. 'We direct you to send *immediately* all the Spanish prisoners in your custody (being actually natives of Spain) to Gravesend ... to present themselves to Lieutenant Arnold, the Agent for Transport at that place, who will have orders for sending them on to Spain,' Malcolm Wright, agent at Greenlaw, was told, for example, on 1 July 1808 by the Transport Board, on the heels of the Spanish national uprising against the French occupation of their country. Some 30 of the Spanish prisoners at Greenlaw thus ended their captivity.[46] Some prisoners from among other nationalities so affected, such as 'Antonio and 8 other Portuguese seamen' and 'Alexey and others, Russian seamen', did not sit dumbly waiting at Greenlaw or Valleyfield or their other depot in Scotland but firmly applied through its agent and the Transport Board for their repatriation.[47] In terms of numbers, excluding altogether the repatriations of masses of Dutch, Germans, and Italians and of smaller numbers of certain other nationalities in the last few months of the conflict when Napoleon's empire was rapidly crumbling, the largest such repatriation from any of the Scots depots during the war was that from Greenlaw in mid-February 1807 of 'Prussian' seamen, of whom 160 had been confined there in June the previous year, when Britain had declared on that kingdom what proved to be a very brief war.[48] But there were other smaller repatriations, sometimes even of individual prisoners, from the Scots depots during the war as a result of some switch in alliances or conquest or reconquest of territory. Home to Mauritius in June 1813 from Perth depot was sent, for example, Leopold Dauphin, aged 20, a soldier in the 66th line regiment who had been captured at Oporto in 1809, Mauritius (or Ile de France) having meantime been captured by British forces from the French in 1810.[49] A more persistent applicant for repatriation, Deronty Deroland, aged 26 and described as an inhabitant of Ile de Bourbon (Réunion), was, however, unsuccessful. As a civilian passenger on the man-of-war *Marengo*, Deroland had been captured along with Alexis Pissaro. First visible as a prisoner in Scotland in April 1811 at Edinburgh Castle, Deroland applied unsuccessfully from there that month for 'His Liberty. Is a civilian, etc.' Transferred from the Castle in August 1811 to Greenlaw, he was sent a year later to Perth, from which in the winter of 1812-13 he again applied for his release on the grounds that he was a native of the Ile de Bourbon, which had been captured from the French by British forces in 1809. His application was referred back to the depot agent 'for report.' The outcome, though not stated at the time, was shown when, still at Perth, in September 1813 he applied a third time for his repatriation. On this occasion his application appears to have become bureaucratically muddled with that of some other applicant as it described Deroland as a native of Guadeloupe and the decision that month by the Transport Board upon it was: 'Application must be made to the Secretary of State for the Colonies by the Governor of Guadeloupe, as the Transport Board has no authority to allow any person to proceed to a British colony.' Deroland remained a prisoner at Perth until April 1814.[50]

Among those taken prisoner who belonged to countries that were neutral in the great struggle between Napoleonic and British imperialism were some subjects of, for example, the north German duchy of Oldenburg. '… it is not known at this office that any Oldenburghers are detained as prisoners in this country, any natives of that country having been released from time to time as application has been made for them,' the Transport Office told an enquirer in February 1807, 'but … if any such persons were known to be confined they would of course be released …'[51] The Transport Board shortly afterwards, however, informed the Admiralty that the consul for Oldenburg had earlier applied for the release from captivity in Britain of fifteen of its subjects, of whom three confined at Greenlaw, Karl Dohnan, G. Bargending and H. Meyer, had consequently been released the previous December.[52] In 1810-11 Greenlaw held at least a further three Oldenburgers. Two of them, Carsten Wickman (or Curstin Wrickman) and Namen Broren (or N. Braun), both seamen captured on merchant vessels in the North Sea in April and May 1809 respectively, were the subject of a report early in December 1810 requested by the Admiralty from the Transport Board, and both men were then promptly repatriated on the 10th of that month.[53] From Greenlaw, too, on an unspecified day in 1811 was repatriated another Oldenburg seaman named Asmus Pederson, who had been captured in October 1810 in the North Sea on the Danish privateer *Norske-Tas*.[54] At Valleyfield there were several Oldenburgers among the prisoners. Their experiences of captivity were more mixed than those of their fellow countrymen at Greenlaw. Frederick Sprenger, for instance, may have been repatriated as invalid as much as Oldenburger. A privateer seaman, Sprenger, as already observed, had suffered the loss of his right hand, and was repatriated from Valleyfield in October 1811. The previous month his fellow countryman Jan Van Den Hewal, aged 24, who had been captured in November 1810 in the English Channel on the privateer *Barbier de Seville*, and had, like Sprenger, arrived at Valleyfield in March 1811 from Esk Mills, had apparently repatriated himself to Oldenburg by escaping 'by North Necessary.' The experience of Jan Witte Koomen, aged 33, an Oldenburg merchant seaman who had been captured on his ship by the French privateer *La Jeune Louise*, date and place unstated, was different again. Finding himself a prisoner in Scotland first at Esk Mills and then from March 1811 at Valleyfield, Jan Koomen, perhaps frustrated and depressed by the absence of any sign of the restoration of his liberty, volunteered himself in May 1812 into the British navy. Another Oldenburg seaman, J.H. Lettosen, captured on the privateer *Le Figaro* in the North Sea in July 1811, and who arrived in September 1812 from Greenlaw at Valleyfield, was repatriated in December 1813. Finally, Johann Vandenberg, aged 25, a privateer seaman, never saw Oldenburg again: he died on 22 April 1812 at Valleyfield from 'Debility from the Effect of selling [his] Provisions and Clothes.'[55]

The prospect of being repatriated as a neutral was, of course, a magnetic attraction to certain prisoners whose mendacity could match their audacity. Two such at Perth depot were the privateersmen Frederik Haultz, aged 32, a lieutenant on *Le Vengeur*, and who had arrived at Perth in September 1812 from Greenlaw; and that familiar figure from Esk Mills and Valleyfield who had entered Perth the same day as Haultz: Jean Baptiste Carrier, alias Henri-Ferdinand Marote, 1st lieutenant of *L'Aventurier*.[56]

Marote-Carrier, although born in 1784 in Ostend and therefore a Belgian (or, to avoid anachronism, originally a subject of the Austrian Netherlands but which territory had for almost twenty years past been annexed to France), had claimed from the outset of his captivity in 1810 that he was a native of Oldenburg. After languishing for a year or so at Perth Marote-Carrier therefore decided boldly to apply for his repatriation as an Oldenburger. He was sure Captain Moriarty, the depot agent, did not even suspect that his claim was false. It was only after his third written application for an interview, however, that Moriarty agreed to see him. When a gaoler ushered him into the agent's office Marote-Carrier was wearing 'a large frock-coat, clogs, and my prisoner's woollen bonnet. The gravity of the complaint I was about to make, my fear that the Commandant [i.e., agent] might see through my hoax, and also his characteristic severity of manner did not fail somewhat to intimidate me. He received me with the cold indifference which was habitual to him. … Moriarty … had had an arm fractured in a naval combat and it had been impossible for him to resume his naval career. … Although at the time of which I speak he was aged about seventy he was well preserved and was a handsome, robust old man.[57] He asked me what was the reason that was so important as to make me solicit an interview in such a pressing manner. I submitted to him my complaint concerning repatriation. He appeared to suspect nothing of my ruse, and had the register of information on the prisoners brought to him, where he saw that I was indeed set down as an Oldenburger. He spread out a map on the table, produced a fat volume that appeared to be an encyclopedia and began to turn its pages. "Your complaint is correct," he said to me, "and seems justifiable. It will be set right. It can only be by an oversight that you have not already been liberated. … But as many prisoners have deceived me on that subject, I make a practice of questioning them all before giving them their travel papers."'

The last remark made Marote-Carrier feel momentarily nervous. But 'although I had never been to Oldenburg I felt I could rely on my memory. My father in telling me stories of his experiences had imparted knowledge of the place to me, and also I had made the acquaintance in the depot of several Oldenburg seamen whom I had carefully questioned.' Moriarty began, however, by asking him how it was that money sent him by his wife was sent from France. Marote-Carrier explained that his wife was herself French and in his absence as a prisoner of war she had gone to France to rejoin her own family there. Moriarty appeared to accept his explanation and then began to interrogate him in detail about Oldenburg—its boundaries, adjoining territories and towns, local rivers, the size of its population, its principal trades, whether the town of Oldenburg was fortified, the depth of water and the tides in the harbour, how many seamen there were, whether Marote-Carrier knew the Duke of Oldenburg, what the principal religion of the inhabitants was. At each of Marote-Carrier's answers Moriarty consulted his map or the encyclopedia. When Moriarty asked, 'Is there some remarkable building there?' Marote-Carrier's detailed answer clearly impressed him: 'There is quite a high tower but which cannot be seen far out to sea because of the distance and the mountainous nature of the country.' 'On what building is the tower?' 'On the Protestant chapel.' Observing Moriarty's astonishment at his detailed knowledge, Marote-Carrier took further heart and declared: 'I ought to tell you that that chapel is the former Catholic cathedral, whose tower no one wanted to destroy as it was its most beautiful feature. As for the present Catholic church, it is a big building in very bad taste, supported by pillars and very much resembling a storehouse.' Marote-Carrier felt sure that his grasp of the general information given him by Oldenburg fellow prisoners had been sound and that his own plausibility had carried him successfully through the more detailed points. Moriarty, apparently not noticing any slips in his performance, 'appeared well satisfied with my replies and said to me: "I can no longer doubt the genuineness of your application. I give you my word as a gentleman that within the next fifteen days you will be out of here." I left his office transported with joy after thanking the Commandant a thousand times.' Frederik Haultz was inspired by Marote-Carrier's success to submit a similar application to Moriarty and he, too, although subjected to even closer interrogation than Marote-Carrier had been, succeeded in persuading the agent that he really was an Oldenburger.

On 17 February 1814, nine days after their interrogation, Marote-Carrier and Haultz, accompanied as far as the gate by Andrew Johnston, the depot chief clerk, and two guards, were sent on their way to walk, via Falkland and Kirkcaldy, to the ship at Leith that was to carry them back to the continent. Johnston warned the two repatriates that 'our descriptions had been sent to Edinburgh, and that we should present ourselves as soon as possible at the office of the agent for prisoners of war in that town.' Johnston, 'who was after all an excellent man', had just stepped outside the gate to see them off when 'suddenly we heard cries behind us and stones came rolling at our feet. Some prisoners, envious of the success of our ruse, were trying to denounce us and ensure its failure. Loudly they cried in French: "They're French! They're not from Oldenburg!" There were a thousand similar shouts and yells accompanied by the throwing of stones. I had a terrible fear that Johnston would realise what was going on.' However, Marote-Carrier's and Haultz's luck was in: Johnston appeared to accept their explanation that the outcry from their fellow prisoners arose from bitter envy, 'and he left us after wishing us bon voyage.' After prolonged delays en route Marote-Carrier at last disembarked in his home town of Ostend on 21 June, 'where I had the good fortune to find again my entire family.' Although no other inmate is known to have left any similar account it seems unlikely that Marote-Carrier and Haultz, among all the thousands of prisoners in the depots in Scotland desperate to recover their liberty, were unique in succeeding in such an elementary ruse.[58]

In all the Scots depots there were some prisoners who felt aggrieved at not being repatriated despite the terms under which their surrender had been agreed. How many of them succeeded in securing their repatriation before the end of the war is far from clear but the scanty evidence suggests very few did. There were in particular four notable surrenders or capitulations whose terms provided for prisoners being repatriated or exchanged:

on St Domingo in the West Indies in 1803, at Baylen in Spain in 1808, the Convention of Cintra resulting from the battle of Vimeiro in Portugal in 1808, and on Guadeloupe and Martinique in 1809-10. The terms of surrender at St Domingo, at Baylen, and on Martinique have already been outlined above.[59] The main provision of the Convention of Cintra, made after the victory by British forces over General Junot's French army at Vimeiro, was for the repatriation of his 25,000 troops to France. But several hundred French soldiers were either ill in hospital or kept prisoner by the Portuguese or British when Junot's army was taken back to France in British ships.[60] Some of those French soldiers left behind in Portugal later found themselves prisoners in depots in Scotland. At least two among them who applied for repatriation were at Valleyfield. Jacques Bellarde and Alexandre Calligny (or Coligny or De Colloigny), soldiers in the 15th light infantry regiment, applied in October 1812 for their release from captivity '… under the capitulation of General Junot. Plea: They state that they fell sick at Lisbon and were left behind, that they were taken up by the [vessel] *Amazon* to be brought to England and sent home when recovered, but touching in at Vigo and taking up other prisoners there they had by mistake been noted as taken at Vigo.'[61] Bellarde and Calligny may have been among prisoners referred to a year earlier in a reply from the Transport Board to Vice Admiral Otway at Leith, who had sent its members a letter 'from some Prisoners at Valleyfield captured in the Battle of Vimeiro in August 1808, claiming the Benefit of the Capitulation made subsequently to that Affair; and in return acquaint you that the said Prisoners are not intitled to their Release under that Convention, and that we caused the same to be signified to them.' But Calligny at least appears to have secured his release late in 1813 as the result of an exchange.[62]

Four other prisoners at Valleyfield, Jean B. Rousan or Bauzan, André Oudry (or Audry or André), Louis Patatrand, all described as under-officers, and Pierre Chercau or Chevau, a sergeant in the 7th line infantry regiment, all of whom had apparently been captured at St Domingo, where the French commander in chief had been General Rochambeau, applied in August 1811 for 'their liberty as per Rochambeau's capitulation.' The outcome of their application appears to have been unsuccessful; but, as will be shown below, these four men later secured their release by exchange. A letter in February 1812 from the Transport Board to the agent at Valleyfield refers to three applications received from prisoners there 'claiming their release under the Capitulation of General Rochambeau, and we desire you will report their Cases and those of any other Prisoners in your Custody who may have similar Claims. You will observe that no Prisoner is intitled to his Release on this Ground who was not actually at Cape François [on St Domingo] on the 30th of November 1803 and Capitulated with General Rochambeau at that Place.' Nothing more about these applications has been found. Only two prisoners are specifically shown in depot records to have succeeded in securing their repatriation 'under General Rochambeau's Capitulation' or 'the Capitulation of Cap François'. One was Louis Boulogne, aged 25 (or 29), born at Brest, an infantryman, regiment unstated, captured on St Domingo on 2 September 1803, and who, after eight and a half years of captivity, was sent on 22 February 1812 from Greenlaw to Valleyfield and from there reached France on 6 April that year. The other was François Berwinkels, a soldier, aged 30 and born at Troyes, regiment unstated, captured at St Domingo in August 1803, and who had arrived from the south of England at Valleyfield in October 1811. Berwinkels was released home to France on New Year's Day 1812.[63]

The terms of another though smaller capitulation, concerning the captured garrison of the castle on the island of Ischia near Naples, were quoted as justification for his repatriation, in an application from Perth depot in March 1813 by Sergeant Major Ignacia de Simone. 'Plea: By virtue of a capitulation entered into between General Stuart and Prince Stigliano that all Neapolitans should be exchanged and sent home. Remarks: States he is the only one remaining in this country.' The result of the sergeant major's application is also not known.[64]

The reasons for repatriation of a few other prisoners are not given in the Entry Books, seem not to fall into any of the categories discussed above, and usually can only be guessed. One, however, who was a beneficiary of an ad hoc arrangement for the release or exchange of prisoners was Louis Montreuil, a seaman, aged 34, born at Rochefort, who had been captured on the frigate *Caroline* in September 1809 at Ile de Bourbon (Réunion) in the Indian Ocean. Montreuil was transferred from Valleyfield to Edinburgh Castle on 25 June 1811 and three days later was discharged from the Castle to 'Bishop's Waltham [Hampshire], to go to Continent.' The explanation for his liberation can be found in a letter sent three months earlier from the Transport Board to Malcolm Wright, agent at Edinburgh Castle: Montreuil had been sent to Scotland from Portsmouth before an order for his release under a cartel or agreement made in the East Indies had reached Portsmouth.[65] Whether, in return for making wooden desks for Andrew Johnston, when he was clerk at Valleyfield in 1811-12 or chief clerk in 1812-14 at Perth, Sergeant Lelade's appeal that he and nine of his regimental comrades be placed in the first batch for repatriation was one intended to be carried out either before or when the war ended, is not clear. But Lelade seems to have been still at Perth on 17 May 1814, when he appears to have been one of some 40 signatories among the prisoners to a pro-Bourbon petition.[66]

Informing on fellow prisoners, particularly about their attempted escape, might hold out the prospect of a passport to freedom, or at least an exit from the depot, for those prepared to stoop to such action. Several cases, as has already been observed, occurred at Greenlaw, Esk Mills, Valleyfield and

Perth.[67] How many of these informers received repatriation as their reward is uncertain—but in their case a return home might obviously prove fatal if the reason for it became known. From Greenlaw, Laurent Barbe or Barbet was not repatriated, although he did succeed in ending his captivity in September 1811 by informing on an attempted escape by fellow prisoners: 'We approve the prisoner Barbet being permitted to enter His [Britannic] Majesty's Navy,' the Transport Board told its agent at Edinburgh Castle, where Barbet had been sent for his own safety from Greenlaw.[68] At Esk Mills, the unnamed prisoner who informed in March 1811 on intended escapes there by fellow prisoners did secure a return to the continent (although perhaps not to his home) as the reward for his action. 'We have … directed Captain Pellowe [agent at Esk Mills] to release the prisoner … who has given him information relative to the escape of prisoners,' the Transport Board informed Malcolm Wright in mid-March 1811, 'and we desire that you will endeavour to procure a conveyance for him to the continent, communicating with Captain Pellowe on the subject.'[69] At Valleyfield, informers may have been the subject of a cryptic sentence in another letter in May 1811 from the Board to Pellowe, by then agent at that depot: 'Direct you to remove the two Frenchmen now in the Guard-House to Greenlaw, reporting the information given by them and whether it be correct.'[70] If the two were informers their later movements are, however, unknown. At Valleyfield later that year the prisoner John Clom, like his fellow informer Laurent Barbet at Greenlaw, was not repatriated as a reward for his services to the authorities but he was allowed to join the Royal Navy.[71] How many prisoners who, it was hoped a year later at Valleyfield, might give 'useful information' to the authorities actually did so is as unknown as whether any reward given them extended to repatriation.[72] Whether, following the escape at New Year 1812 from Valleyfield of Guillaume Mariote, apparently naval lieutenant but also soldier in the 66th Basque line regiment, the information provided by 'his Comrades' about his double identity and his part in an attempt by prisoners to seize control of the ship *Brune* bringing them from Plymouth to Scotland, resulted in any informers securing their own release and repatriation is likewise unknown.[73] Finally, the severe maltreatment meted out at Valleyfield by fellow prisoners in the spring of 1811 to Jacques Perrot has already been noticed. But whether Perrot was an informer or perhaps a thief is as uncertain as whether his subsequent discharge to Leith signalled his repatriation.[74] At Perth, too, in the one surviving documented case of an informer, in which he was lucky to survive with his life after being severely mauled in April 1813 by enraged fellow prisoners, it is also not known whether after his recovery he was rewarded with repatriation.[75]

A unique case of repatriation from any depot in Scotland (though several prisoners in the Scots parole towns were released for similar reasons) appears to have been that of a French soldier at Perth in October 1812. 'On Tuesday,' the *Caledonian Mercury* reported, '... a brave and humane soldier ... obtained not only liberty but the goodwill and respect of every Briton who knows his story. The gallant [British] General Walker, while storming Badajoz at the head of his brigade, was found by this young Frenchman lying wounded and bleeding in the breach. He took our wounded General in his arms and carried him to a French hospital where he was taken care of by the medical department. The General gave [him] his address, with a promise to serve his deliverer if ever in his power. The Frenchman, at last a captive, applied to General Walker, who lost no time in procuring for him the precious reward of liberty.' The repatriated hero, described in the depot Entry Book as simply 'Discharged 13 October 1812 to Leith', was Constant Derilevaux, aged 32, born at 'Ex La Chapel' (Aix La Chapelle or Aachen), of the 9th light infantry regiment, captured at Badajoz on 7 April 1812, and who had arrived at Perth on 29 August.[76] Two other claims, apparently of a similar, if less dramatic or heroic, nature, were made by prisoners at Esk Mill and Valleyfield but neither claim produced the same result as for Derilevaux at Perth. At Esk Mill the repatriation of a prisoner named J.T.C Dunez was petitioned for by a British friend or sympathiser named Mr Edward Gilchrist. 'You will be pleased to inform their Lordships,' the Transport Board replied on 1 May 1811 to J.W.Croker, secretary of the Admiralty, who six days earlier had sent a letter and a petition from Mr Gilchrist, 'that we do not consider the proper Conduct of Monsieur Dunez to his Prisoners as represented by Mr Gilchrist by any means a sufficient Reason for releasing this Prisoner without Exchange [with a British prisoner in France].'[77] The Valleyfield application was made in December 1812 by an unnamed Dutch prisoner 'who alledges that he has been instrumental in saving the lives of some British subjects.' When the depot agent, Captain Brown, subsequently reported on the case to the Transport Board its decision was that 'The Dutch prisoner ... cannot be released on account of the circumstances stated by him.' The agent was rebuked for sending the Board the Dutchman's application without enclosing any proof of his claim 'together with your own opinion on the subject and the grounds upon which such opinion is founded.'[78]

Among the score and more of non-French, mainly 'Danish' or Dutch prisoners, who were fortunate enough to be given employment away from the depots—or, at least, away from Greenlaw and Valleyfield depots—it is virtually certain that several were in effect taking their first step toward repatriation. When, for instance, in August 1809 the Transport Board ordered the agent at Greenlaw to release three Danish prisoners 'for the purpose of instructing certain Highlanders in the manufacture of Tar,' Mr John Scott, their employer, who was evidently based in London, undertook responsibility for the prisoners' good conduct while travelling to, living in, and also, significantly, returning from the Highlands. But it is not at all clear that these three prisoners ever did return to Greenlaw or indeed to captivity in any other depot, or on the other hand that they were soon afterward repatriated. Hyndhert Davus, the Dutch prisoner released from Valleyfield in December 1813 to assist the fisheries at Greenock, was clearly not expected to set foot again inside that or any other depot. Nor presumably were the 22 Danish and Icelandic seamen released from Greenlaw in 1810-11 to help sail various merchant vessels.[79]

Among repatriations which appeared to involve neither any balancing exchange of British prisoners of war in Danish hands nor any of the other factors already observed, was that from Greenlaw in August 1810 after two years of captivity of the diarist Captain Paul Andreas Kaald. Kaald's repatriation, when many of his crew captured with him in 1808 on the privateer *Den Flinke* remained prisoners of war for several more years, appears to have been due largely to wire-pulling by his shipowner, Johan Christian Vogelsang of Trondheim, and a local politician there named Jorgen Knudtzen. Which wires they pulled are not revealed but they seem at any rate to have opened the gates of Greenlaw to Kaald—and not to Kaald alone, for several other Norwegian or Danish privateersmen confined there were evidently repatriated on other occasions by the same group of influential friends at home.[80] Nor did his two years' experience of captivity deter Kaald from resuming privateering after his repatriation: after several voyages in 1810-13 as captain of merchant vessels, he became prizemaster in autumn 1813 on the *Anna Bruun*, one of the largest Norwegian privateers, commanded by his old shipmate and fellow prisoner Captain Sigismund Richelieu, who had escaped from Greenlaw in September 1809 in a chest.[81] Wires even more glittering were pulled to open the gates of Valleyfield in April 1812 for Dominique Saulnier, aged 21, born at St Requet, a sergeant in the 3rd Artillery regiment, captured on Martinique in 1809, who had arrived at the depot in October 1811. Saulnier's release, bearing, it seemed, some resemblance to a fairy tale, was first signalled in a letter of 8 April 1812 from the Transport Board to Admiral Otway at Leith, requesting him to order 'a Passage on board any of His Majesty's Ships or Vessells proceeding to the River [Thames] for Dominique Saulnier, a French Prisoner of War, whom we have directed Captain Moriarty [agent at Valleyfield] to send to London.' On 27 April the Board wrote again to Moriarty: 'As Dominique Saulnier ... does not appear to have been discharged from Valleyfield, ... you will state the cause of the Delay, and if there should be no Opportunity of his proceeding as above mentioned you will allow him to take his Passage on board one of the Leith passage Vessels, instructing him to present himself at this Office on his Arrival in London. Inclosed is a Letter for him inclosing the Sum of £6 to defray his expenses.' Whatever the reasons for the delay, Saulnier at last passed outward through the gates of Valleyfield on 1 May. The register of prisoners released or exchanged shows that he was 'Released in consequence of an Application on his behalf by the Duke del Infantado to Sir Rupert George [chairman of the Transport Board], and by Order of Lord Melville [First Lord of the Admiralty], 7th April 1812.' Who or what was Saulnier that he attracted such patrician support for his release and presumably his repatriation? That is yet another addition to the myriad of unanswered questions concerning prisoners in the depots in Scotland.[82]

'The Report alluded to by you,' the agent at Valleyfield was told by the Transport Board in December 1812, 'of an Exchange of Prisoners captured prior to October 1805 having taken place at Portsmouth is totally void of Foundation and we direct you to inform the Prisoners in your Custody accordingly.'[83] If, as Thomas Carlyle remarked, history is a distillation of rumour, much history ought to have been distilled among the prisoners in the Scots depots. There rumours of exchanges, such as that denied in 1812 by the Transport Board, circulated frequently. The prospect of being exchanged for British prisoners in French hands was one that until the last year or two of the war many prisoners clung to. 'It is ... said here today,' Captain Paul Andreas Kaald, for instance, noted in his diary on Hogmanay 1808 at Greenlaw, 'that the French prisoners will be exchanged between England and France. This pleases us a lot since there has to be a solution soon for us Danes and Norwegians.' Three months later, Kaald wrote: 'There is great chat in the prison about the papers reporting recently that an English commissioner has gone to France in order to receive the English prisoners of war, and to make a general exchange between France and England ... God grant that this must be true, then we too could expect some solution. But here nothing can be believed.' In August 1810, only a fortnight before he received the news of his own release—though his was not as the result of any exchange—Kaald wrote: 'One now hears a nice tale about the exchanging of prisoners between Denmark and England. The same was made public in the papers two days ago. ... One can't believe this.'[84]

The system of exchanging prisoners, which had developed in the 18th century, especially between Britain and France, largely broke down in the Napoleonic Wars.[85] Virtually every year between 1803 and 1810 there were proposals by, even negotiations as in 1810 between, the two governments about a general exchange of prisoners. As late as 1811-13 one or other was still voicing suggestions or proposals on the subject. But no general exchange resulted. The reason for the breakdown was fundamentally the mutual mistrust between Napoleon and the British government. Neither side was convinced the other would fully carry out whatever agreement might be reached. But also any prospects of a general exchange being agreed were further dimmed by several other clouds. One, for instance, was the problem presented by the imbalance in the respective numbers of prisoners held: an aggregate of

16,000 British in France, compared with 122,000 French or French allied in Britain. Two among many other clouds included the British government's duplicity as early as 1804 in implementing the terms of surrender of French forces at St Domingo,[86] and Napoleon's attempt to equate for purposes of exchange British prisoners held in France with Hanoverian troops captured by his forces at the outset of the war, on the grounds that the Hanoverians were subjects of the elector of Hanover—who happened also to be the king of Britain. '…the troops belonging to the Electorate of Hanover cannot be comprehended in a cartel for the exchange of prisoners belonging respectively to His Majesty's United Kingdom and the French Republic,' Lord Hobart, secretary at war, told the Admiralty as early in the war as December 1803, 'but His Majesty is willing to establish a general cartel, to be regulated upon the basis of that which was in force between the two countries during the late [French Revolutionary] war.'[87] That attempt in 1803 to establish a general exchange of prisoners between Britain and France, and its breakdown, were repeated several times in the course of the war, and no such general exchange took place before 1814.[88] Those repeated failures to reach agreement helped explain the rumours on the subject that arose in the depots in Scotland and the alternating optimism and depression among the prisoners which was illustrated, for instance, in the diary Captain Kaald kept at Greenlaw. Moreover, absence of agreement upon a general exchange contributed to numbers of the escapes or attempted escapes by depot and parole prisoners in Scotland, as south of the Border, and also to some of the volunteering by depot prisoners into the British armed forces. On the other hand, exchanges of prisoners, somewhat unbalanced in terms of numbers though they generally proved, between Britain on the one side and Holland and the kingdom of Denmark on the other, did take place throughout the war.

This general picture concerning exchanges may at least be illustrated from the experiences of French, Danish, Dutch, and some other nationalities among the prisoners in the Scots depots. Of these latter exchanges, as in so many other aspects, it is difficult if not impossible to draw a comprehensive and wholly accurate picture. The relevant column in the depot General Entry Books headed Exchanged, Discharged, Died, or Escaped, sometimes fails to differentiate between prisoners discharged—transferred to another depot or hulk or released altogether as, e.g., invalids—and those who were specifically exchanged for a British prisoner or prisoners in French or French allied hands.

Thus at Greenlaw in the years between 1804, when the depot opened, and the summer of 1812 only two French prisoners appear to have been released through an exchange. They were Louis Boulogne, who, as has been seen above, was captured on St Domingo in 1803 and who was exchanged in April 1812 for a British passenger named Jason; and Louis Thiebaud (or Thibault), a seaman, aged 26, born at Nantes, captured on the privateer *Le Camy*, in the English Channel in 1810, and who was exchanged in June 1812 for a British seaman named Michael Murphy.[89] There was an application for release by exchange in summer 1812 by a third prisoner at Greenlaw, Lieutenant Antoine Lepelletier, captured in October 1806 in the English Channel on the privateer *Clarisse*. Lepelletier, who was born at St Malo and was aged 27, claimed release on the ground that his exchange had been arranged at sea by the captain of the French privateer *Milan* in return for the release from captivity in France of a Mr Hippesley, said to be a lieutenant in the British army. Lepelletier had earlier applied for his release on these same grounds while he was confined at Edinburgh Castle in April 1811. His application from Greenlaw was forwarded to the Transport Board by Vice Admiral Otway at Leith. In its reply of 4 September, two days after Lepelletier had been transferred from Greenlaw to Perth, the Board informed the admiral that '... the original Treaty of Exchange has been received at this Office, but that as the rank of M. Lepelletier (being taken as Lieutenant of a French Privateer) was not equivalent to that of Mr Hippesley, who held no rank whatever in the British Army at the time of his capture, the Exchange could not consistently with the established Regulations be effected, a French Passenger was therefore released and permitted to return to France in exchange for Mr Hippesley. In consideration, however, of the circumstances of M. Lepelletier we have given directions for his being included in the first Exchange.' When Lepelletier tried again in December 1812 to seek his exchange, his depot agent was instructed by the Transport Board to tell him that '... the Lords Commissioner of the Admiralty have determined not to ratify any agreement for the exchange of prisoners of war entered into at sea by individual subjects of Great Britain and France.' Lepelletier applied yet again in the spring of 1813 for his release by exchange. He was unsuccessful, and remained a prisoner at Perth until his release on 2 June 1814.[90]

At Valleyfield in late autumn 1812 there was a release, uniquely large in Scotland, of prisoners through exchange. 'Monday,' the *Caledonian Mercury* reported five days later on 21 November, '24 prisoners of war belonging to the *Piedmontaise* French frigate were released from Greenlaw [in fact, it was Valleyfield] ... in exchange for 24 seamen belonging to His Majesty's schooner *Laura*, given up at sea by the *Diligent*, French privateer.[91] Whether the *Piedmontaise* men exchanged actually numbered 24 or 26 is hardly important; what was striking was that so many as two dozen achieved their release simultaneously by exchange during a war where exchanges of French and British prisoners were relatively rare and, when they did occur, were usually of only one or two individuals at a time.

The other handful of exchanges, or ostensible exchanges, as distinct from releases on other grounds, of French prisoners at Valleyfield took place also in

1812-13. Some ambiguities and uncertainties concerning them arise from a reference in correspondence in February 1812 between the depot agent and the Transport Board to six of these (unnamed) prisoners being released by exchange under the terms of the capitulation of 1804 at Cape François on St Domingo.[92] The following month the Board asked Admiral Otway at Leith to arrange as soon as possible for seven French prisoners at Valleyfield 'who have been exchanged' to be conveyed by sea to Portsmouth where they would be embarked for France. No names are given in that letter either: were the six of February the same six plus one by March? [93] Nor is any light thrown in the Valleyfield Entry Books by references to exchanges. These uncertainties and ambiguities appear to be resolved, however, by two other sources, a register titled 'Partial Exchanges: French', and another titled 'Released, 1812-13', both preserved in The National Archives. These two registers provide names and other details which cast light on what otherwise would remain dark corners. Four entries in the first register refer to the release through exchange in or soon after February 1812 of five seamen and an army sergeant at Valleyfield. The first entry concerns L. Patatrand, A. Oudry (or Audry or André) and Joseph (or Th.) Olivier, who had been captured on the French frigate *La Vertu* off Cape François, and who were exchanged for James Winsborrow, master of the vessel *Commerce of Dartmouth*. The second entry concerns the exchange of J.B. Rousan or Bauzan, steersman of *La Vertu*, for a British seaman from the *Commerce of Dartmouth*; the third, that of Sergeant J. Chercau or Chevau at Valleyfield for James Bowman, master of the British vessel *Noah*; and the fourth, the exchange of P. Vermersck, clerk on the privateer *Braconnier*, for a British seaman.[94] If these six were the prisoners referred to in the Transport Board's letter to Captain Moriarty, then the seventh, referred to in the Board's letter to Admiral Otway, appears to have been Antoine Castinelle, a seaman at Valleyfield who had been captured on the French gun-brig *Surveillante* at St Domingo in November 1803, and who in or soon after February 1812 was exchanged for a British seaman.[95]

A further two exchanges took place at Valleyfield, according to the same two registers, between June and November 1812, and one more as late as November 1813. These were, first, of Fortune Noréal (or Moréal), maréchal des logis (cavalry quartermaster sergeant or corporal) in a regiment unstated, who was exchanged in June for two British seamen; second, of Cyprien Guerin, aged 26, master's mate captured on the man-of-war *Duquesne* off St Domingo in July 1803, who was exchanged in September for a British seaman; and third, Alexandre Calligny (or Coligny or De Colloigny), aged 19, fourier (quartermaster-sergeant or corporal), regiment unstated (but apparently 15th Light), said to have been captured at Vigo (and whose application for release under the Convention of Cintra has already been observed above), who was exchanged in November 1813 for J. Kinlay, a Briton captured while a passenger at sea.[96] Several of these exchanges seem to contradict the statement on policy concerning exchanges which was reiterated in June 1813 by the Transport Board to the agent at Valleyfield: 'We direct you to acquaint Sir James Hall that it is the determination of His Majesty's Government not to ratify or recognise any agreements for the exchange of prisoners made at sea by individuals.'[97]

At Perth, only one prisoner appears to have been exchanged: Cyprien Guerin, consideration of whose case, as has been seen, had begun at Valleyfield before his transfer on 2 September 1812 from there to Perth. Guerin left Perth for home on 13 October, along with the liberated soldier Constant Derilevaux, saviour at the siege of Badajoz of the wounded General Walker.[98]

Among prisoners at Edinburgh Castle, apart from the initial application, already noticed, by Lepelletier in April 1811 for his exchange to be carried out, only two other similar applications have been found. They, too, were made in April 1811. One was by Lieutenant Pierre Passicousset, aged 35, born at Bayonne, who had been captured on the privateer *Invincible Napoléon* the preceding February. Passicousset applied for parole until he was exchanged: 'He has been exchanged at sea by himself and expects to be soon released.' Passicousset was not, however, released, or even granted parole. Instead he found himself transferred with several hundred other prisoners in August 1811 from the Castle to Greenlaw. From Greenlaw on 16 October he escaped. There is no account of his motives in doing so. But is it mere speculation to conclude that Passicousset was one of many prisoners in the Scots depots during the following two and a half years who became convinced that the prospect of exchange was illusory and who therefore decided to try to repatriate themselves? The other application ('His liberty or his parole. Was exchanged by General Decaen, etc.') came from Jean Canet, aged 33, born at Marseilles, a naval lieutenant on *Les Deux Frères Unis* who had been captured in 1810 at the surrender by the French General Decaen on the Ile de France (Mauritius). Canet was sent home to France from the Castle on 24 June 1811.[99]

The total number of specifically French (not Danish, Dutch, or other) prisoners released from the Scots depots through exchange with British prisoners in France appears therefore to have been only 36 or 38.

As for Danish and Dutch prisoners, far more of them than French benefited from exchanges. So far as exchanges of Dutch prisoners were concerned, as early in the war as November 1804 the Transport Board sent the Admiralty 'an extract of a letter which we have this day received from the Council of the Batavian [Dutch] Navy at the Hague, dated the 25th of last month, proposing to enter into a general cartel for the exchange of prisoners of war, on the same footing in all respects as that which was in force between this country and France during the late [French Revolutionary] war; and ... it is our intention, with their Lordships' [of the Admiralty] approbation, to conclude such a cartel with as little delay as possible, and also to send immediately to Holland Dutch prisoners in exchange for the British prisoners in that country, in the manner proposed by the Batavian government.'[100] That exchanges of Dutch and British prisoners were not frustrated during the war as were those of French and British was illustrated by a comment almost four years later in a letter from the Board to the Admiralty that the '… Dutch government … have always shewn a disposition to promote the exchange of prisoners of war as far as lay in their power.'[101]

At Greenlaw, among the first entries in Sergeant Major Beaudoin's diary after his arrival there in June 1804 was: 'Exchange of Dutch prisoners on 26 December 1804, among them a Frenchman who slipped in among them and succeeded in getting out of the prison.'[102] The relevant Greenlaw Entry Book bears out in more detail Beaudoin's terse note, and shows that from the depot were then discharged via Leith on 'The *Mary* tender for the Texel' in north west Holland no less than 46 Dutch seamen and marines. Most of the 46 had been captured on the Dutch frigate *L'Union* in the North Sea the previous May. They included the frigate's captain Simon Theunesse, the 1st and 2nd lieutenants, two surgeons, secretary, a midshipman, and a lieutenant of marines, as well as the bosun, bosun's mate, purser, blacksmith, a steward, eleven seamen, and 13 marines, including two sergeants, two corporals and a tambour or drummer. But also among the 46 were several merchant seamen, including Sjourd Petmans, captain of the *Norstan*, captured in Aberlady Bay a year earlier, and Hendrik Smit, a seaman captured in July 1803 in the North Sea on the *Neptunis*.[103] If press reports, however, are to be believed there were no fewer than 155 Dutch prisoners being exchanged at that time via Leith. Both the *Caledonian Mercury* and the *Edinburgh Evening Courant* reported on 10 January 1805 that, in addition to what they said were 75 Dutch prisoners on the *Mary* cartel ship, a further 80 on a brig also named *Mary*, 'employed in the service of the [Royal Navy] impress at Leith', were sailing to Holland to be exchanged 'for part of the crew of the *Romney*.' Where the 29 additional prisoners on the first vessel, and the 80 on the second, had come from is not clear but at least by implication they had all come from captivity somewhere in Scotland—possibly the 80 from the admiral's flagship at Leith. The *Caledonian Mercury* further reported a week later that on 11 January 'a cartel from the Texel, with about 112 English prisoners, who had been confined in different prisons in Holland, had landed at Scarborough. We believe this to be the first exchange since the commencement of hostilities.'[104]

The 'Dutch' Entry Book at Greenlaw covers only the first two years of the war in 1803-4. But there were certainly numbers of other Dutch prisoners at Greenlaw after 1804, as there were in the other Scots depots from 1811 onwards. Between 1804 and 1811, the repatriation of the survivors of the crew of the Dutch frigate *Utrecht*, shipwrecked in Orkney in February 1807, was not, however, part of an exchange but was due to the humanity of the Transport Board and the Admiralty.[105] More or less simultaneously with their repatriation in spring 1807 the Admiralty had approved a proposal by the Transport Board 'that we should send immediately the whole of the Dutch prisoners in this country to Holland.' At that stage there cannot have been many Dutch left in captivity either at Greenlaw or in England as the cartel ship that was to repatriate them was '... the *Fancy* cutter, a small vessel which ... is now ready at Chatham to receive them.'[106] Indeed, the following month, after the repatriation of *Utrecht*'s crew, the Board informed the Admiralty that they had been 'the only Dutch prisoners ... in this country.' Moreover, the Board said it had 'no knowledge of any British prisoners being in Holland.' So the Dutch-British exchanges of prisoners were, or appear to have been, by then complete. One result, however, was that, more Dutch having been taken prisoner in 1803-07 by the British than British by the Dutch, Britain was considerably in credit: there was a balance due Britain of 780 prisoners who might in future be taken.[107] Even in 1808, when Franco-British exchanges broke down completely after the British cartel vessel attempting to enter the harbour at Morlaix in April with repatriated invalid prisoners and thousands of letters home from French prisoners in Britain was fired on by the French garrison and had to return to Plymouth with the invalids and the letters, exchanges of Dutch prisoners appear to have continued.[108] Eighteen months after the firing at Morlaix, Lord Castlereagh, secretary for war and colonies, informed the Admiralty in October 1809 that the king had approved a private suggestion from the Dutch admiral Winter for an exchange of all Dutch prisoners in Britain for all British in Holland, both Dutch and British to be placed 'on board fishing boats so that they should not be objects of public notice.' Castlereagh added that he had learned from the Transport Office that since the beginning of the war 2,700 Dutch prisoners had been repatriated from captivity in Britain, but only 821 British from Holland. There were then in autumn 1809 313 Dutch prisoners 'in England' [presumably he meant Britain] and an estimated 700 British in Holland. Castlereagh stated that King George III 'will, as long as Holland shall pursue a fair system of cartel, be willing to act to that country in the most liberal manner.'[109] The abdication in 1810 of Louis Bonaparte as king of Holland and that country's annexation then by France no doubt ended the exchanges of Dutch and British prisoners. But so far as Dutch prisoners at Greenlaw or, from 1811, at the other Scots depots are concerned no evidence of exchanges has been found after that in 1807 of the crew of the *Utrecht*.

Spain, which as an ally of France was at war with Britain from 1805 to 1808, was another country hundreds of whose seamen or soldiers found themselves during those years in captivity in Britain. Like the Dutch and the Danish, the Spanish government was willing as in earlier wars to exchange prisoners with Britain. By March 1806, however, the imbalance in the number of Spanish prisoners released from depots in Britain compared with that of British from captivity in Spain led the Admiralty to instruct the Transport Board to release no more of the former for the time being.[110] Greenlaw depot had, as has been seen, an Entry Book specifically for Spanish prisoners, of whom 48 were shown there to have arrived at the depot between July 1805 and March 1806. No fewer than 35 of them were sent in January 1806 to Portsmouth, but whether this was the first stage of their release through exchange or perhaps merely their transfer to captivity on a hulk, is not stated. About the disposal of all but four of the other dozen the Entry Book is silent; the four joined His Britannic Majesty's armed forces.[111] With that list of 48 Spanish prisoners there is clearly duplication in a longer list of 68 who arrived at Greenlaw between July 1805 and October 1808 and which is to be found in the hybrid Entry Book ADM 103/115 preserved at The National Archives. The repatriation from Britain of many, though not all, Spanish prisoners in the summer of 1808, when Napoleon's occupation of Spain converted its government from hostility to alliance with Britain, was not an exchange but, as the Greenlaw Entry Book put it, 'the discharge of Allies.'[112] The Spanish prisoners who remained in Britain after the summer of 1808 were, or were regarded as, *Afrancesados* ('Frenchifiers') or *juramentados*—supporters or collaborators of the French and King Joseph Bonaparte. Perhaps inevitably for them there was no exchange.[113]

Much more numerous than any releases by exchange of Spanish prisoners from the Scots depots must have been those of 'Danes' (who included Norwegians) from Greenlaw. The difficulty in establishing how many 'Danes' were in fact exchanged from there, as distinct from being repatriated for other reasons, is one already familiar in considering so many other aspects of Greenlaw. The depot's two 'Danish' Entry Books, which cover four and a half years from 1807, when the kingdom of Denmark entered the war against Britain, to 1811, list almost exactly 1,000 prisoners.[114] As might be expected, however, given the idiosyncratic administration of the then agent Malcolm Wright, the word Exchanged is never once written against the name of any prisoner in the column headed 'Exchanged, Discharged, Died, or Escaped', but only one or other of the other three words, or occasionally also 'Released'. If all those listed as escaped, died, sent on parole, volunteered into the British armed forces, boys under the age of 12, repatriated as aged, invalids, or neutrals, sent to Chatham or the Nore, as well as various others who may be assumed not at any rate to have been exchanged, are deducted from the 1,000, some 480 are left. Where some 200 of these went is not clear. Of the remaining 276, the Entry Books declare 42 were 'To go Home', 53 are described simply as 'Discharged', and a further 181 were discharged to such destinations as Denmark, Bergen, Stavanger, and Trondheim. If the assumption were made that these last 276, or most of them, were actually exchanged that might provide a minimum figure for 'Danes' repatriated from Greenlaw for that reason. At the other extreme, it could be that some, many, or even all 200 sent to Chatham or the Nore were exchanged from those places—which would bring the total number of exchanges from or at least originating at Greenlaw to 476—virtually half of the total of 1,000 'Danish' prisoners listed in the two Entry Books. Perhaps the most conservative guesstimate, based on the numbers 'To go Home' plus discharged to specified destinations in Scandinavia, may be closest to the actual number of exchanges: about 220, or more than a fifth of the total number of 'Danish' prisoners at Greenlaw.

That considerable numbers of 'Danes', unlike French, were exchanged is testified by official statistics. A statement, for example, sent by the Transport Board to the Admiralty early in 1812 showed that since the outbreak of war between the two states in 1807, 3,490 more Danes had been repatriated by exchange than had British prisoners in Danish hands.[115] Some of those repatriations through exchange of 'Danes' were certainly from Greenlaw, whatever the difficulties in determining precise numbers. Glimpses of such repatriations, even if the numbers or proportion among them of exchanges as distinct from releases on other grounds are unknown, were reported occasionally in the press. 'Sailed from Leith Roads,' the *Caledonian Mercury* reported, for instance, on 8 September 1808, 'the *Laura* tender with Danish prisoners for Stromness'—no doubt on the first stage of their voyage to Stavanger, Bergen, Trondheim, or elsewhere in Norway or Denmark. Three years later another report in the *Mercury*, was that 'The *Pitfour* cartel sailed on Wednesday [from Leith] for Norway with 30 Danish prisoners.'[116]

From the Scots depots, but above all from Greenlaw, there were therefore it appears several hundred prisoners altogether, mainly 'Danes' and Dutch, who in the course of the war were released from captivity by being exchanged.

There were also considerable numbers who, even if not repatriated before the war ended, at least were able to shake the dust of Esk Mills, Edinburgh Castle, Greenlaw, Valleyfield, or Perth depot from their feet by being granted or re-granted parole. Parole still meant captivity, but passed as it was in civilian lodgings in parole towns such as Peebles, Selkirk, Kelso, Dumfries, Lanark, Biggar, and Cupar Fife, although subject to curfew and town limits, it was a much less disagreeable form of captivity than confinement in the depots. Those eligible for parole were commissioned officers of the army and navy, chief surgeons and naval chaplains, pursers and midshipmen, the captains and second captains of merchant vessels, and in the case of privateer ships the captain, second captain and surgeon, plus one lieutenant for every hundred men in the crew, provided that at the time of capture the ship had had more than 14 cannons of a minimum four pound calibre. Naval officers taken prisoner in merchant or privateer vessels were not, however, considered commissioned officers. Civilians, at least those from the middle and upper classes, made captive usually while passengers aboard ships were normally also eligible for parole if the ships were not privateers. In all the Scots depots there were some prisoners who had not hitherto had parole but considered they were, or hoped they might be, entitled to it; and some others who through some breach of it had lost their parole but sought to regain it. A few prisoners in the depots, although eligble for parole, may have chosen not to take it since a condition of parole was an undertaking not to attempt escape.[117]

'Today,' Captain Paul Andreas Kaald noted in his diary at Greenlaw on Sunday, 19 February 1809, '14 Danes left here on parole'; and four months later Kaald noted that 'Captain Wraamand, his mate and six other skippers were sent to Peebles on parole' from Greenlaw.[118] One even more fortunate Dane there was the unnamed gunner of a vessel who had been sent away from Greenlaw on parole by the depot agent, Malcolm Wright. The Transport Board told Wright that in doing so he had exceeded his instructions but that it would not insist on the gunner being returned to confinement at Greenlaw.[119] Less fortunate were two other Greenlaw prisoners, Captains M. Berg and Jacob Burman, on whose behalf Messrs Soltan & Co., presumably merchants or a shipping company, had written to the Admiralty asking they be sent to Peebles on parole. The view of the Transport Board, when sought by the Admiralty, was that neither Berg nor Burman was entitled to parole.[120]

Although Esk Mills functioned as a depot for only a few weeks in February-March 1811, several prisoners there nonetheless applied for the grant or regrant of parole. Joseph Roustan and A.V. Barbe (or Barbel), for example, respectively second captain and first lieutenant of the privateer *Duguay Trouin* applied for parole as soon as they arrived at Esk Mills. Their plea, supported by Rev. Palmer, chaplain of HMS *Ajax*, was that 'They were promised their parole as soon as any ship sailed with Prisoners for Scotland', and Captain Pellowe, agent at Esk Mills, had advised them to inform the Transport Board of this promise. The Board, however, decided that if their vessel was the one of that name captured in January 1810, 'neither of their names are on the Role d'Equipage [crew list] … Decision: Not entitled [to parole].'[121] Four other prisoners, including one of the two most senior officers in captivity in Scotland, were, however, more successful at Esk Mills and all four were sent on parole from there to Kelso. Jean C. Brimont or Bremont was one of them. Clerk on the privateer *Somnambule*, captured in October 1810 off Tréport, Brimont was among the first prisoners to enter Esk Mills on 5 February 1811. He at once applied for parole, which was granted him, and on 16 March he stepped out through Esk Mill's gates en route to Kelso. There, too, ten days later from Esk Mills proceeded that notable applicant, this time not for the grant but for the restoration of parole: Charles Prévost De Boissi, Adjutant General in the French army.[122]

At Edinburgh Castle more than a score of prisoners applied for parole or its restoration to them. The outcome of many of their applications is unstated. One such was L. Panot, described simply as 'Inhabitant, Walcheren.'[123] One among a number of unsuccessful applicants, as has already been seen, was François Le Prince, who in March 1811 had arrived from Esk Mills at the Castle. Another of the select band who were successively held in each of the five Scots depots, Le Prince was sent on 8 November 1813 by order of Vice Admiral Otway to the hulks at Portsmouth 'for breach of parole.' As Le Prince had not enjoyed parole since he had been deprived of it in Malta at least three years earlier, his case illustrated how slowly at times ground the mills of the Transport Board, the Admiralty, and their agents.[124] An applicant who was either too impatient to await at the Castle a decision on his application for the restoration of his parole or had had it rejected was Pierre Woemeseuil or Wormeseul, a midshipman, captured in 1808. In his application, incautiously worded, in March 1811, which apparently was made on behalf of other prisoners, too, Woemeseuil said that 'the agent at Wantage [a parole town in Berkshire] so ill-used them that he forced them to desert. He says they would never have broken their parole if the Government had protected them from the Agent.' As already observed, Woemeseuil died at the Castle on 14 April having, it appears, fallen down the rock while taking part two days earlier in the mass escape along with 48 or 49 other prisoners.[125] Among those whose applications at the Castle for parole were granted, however, in April 1811 were no fewer than 'Ten surgeons, etc., of the Army of Portugal,' who '... inclose a list of the value of their rank in the military service by which they appear to prove they are entitled.' There is again a discrepancy in numbers since only nine, not ten, can be found in the Entry Book to have been discharged on parole to Kelso on 15 April and who appear to have been the successful applicants concerned. On the other hand three other applicants, all lieutenants—one army and two sea-going—were also sent from the Castle on parole that same day to Kelso.[126]

For Valleyfield fewer applications survive than for Edinburgh Castle by prisoners who applied for parole or its restoration. Of six applications extant, three (including the fresh ones from the two former Esk Mills applicants, Joseph Roustan and A. V. Barbe (or Barbel), were rejected, the outcome of another by two privateersmen captured on *L'Intrépide*, Barthelémy Messière, first lieutenant, and Jean Glise or Glisse, surgeon, and who, like Roustan and Barbe, had also applied at Esk Mills, is not known. The application, however, by Simon Timon, second captain or first mate on the merchant vessel *Ange Raphael*, succeeded and he was sent in August 1811 on parole to Selkirk.[127] A survey of the Valleyfield Entry Books indicates that only seven other prisoners were sent from that depot on parole (excluding about 70 who were at the depot only very briefly either because they were midshipmen sent there in October 1811 in retaliation for the treatment of British prisoners in France, or because in that same month they were there overnight on their way from landing at Leith to parole at Selkirk, or because they had come from Scots parole towns to Valleyfield hospital for medical treatment before returning whence they had come or to other parole towns).[128]

The number of surviving applications for parole by prisoners at Perth is similar to that for Valleyfield but, as there, is exceeded by the number to whom parole was actually granted or restored. Among those who were granted parole was Hubert Gronnier or Grouinier, aged 20, born at Laffain, described in the Entry Book as a sergeant major in the 113th line regiment, who had been captured in January 1812 at Ciudad Rodrigo. Grouiner's plea was that '… it is by mistake he is called Sergeant Major, that his rank is Adjutant', and he submitted a certificate from officers in his regiment that he really was an adjutant. Gronnier stepped out through the gates of Perth on 15 November 1812, having been sent on parole to Biggar.[129] Marie Stanislaus Sabatier, aged 21, born in Paris, purser on a naval gun brig when captured in September or November 1811 in the English Channel, was one who regained his parole while at Perth. Sent first in December 1811 on parole to Lauder, Sabatier had broken his parole there in June 1812 by escaping. Recaptured at Dalkeith, 'He was deranged in Mind and sent to Valleyfield Hospital', until transferred in September that year to Perth. There Sabatier at once applied '… to be sent back to Lauder, his parole place. Plea: He was sent to Valleyfield for medical treatment, being deranged, is now recovered. The agent at Lauder has a gold watch and other effects belonging to him.' Sabatier's application was accepted and he was discharged from Perth on 29 November to Leith—but to which parole town, if it were in Scotland, he went from Leith no indication has been found. The Lauder Entry Book certainly does not record his return there.[130]

Subject to the familiar difficulties of establishing complete accuracy, it appears therefore that the number of prisoners in the five Scots depots who were granted parole, or had it restored to them, was approximately: at Greenlaw 149, Esk Mills 4, Edinburgh Castle 14, Valleyfield 8, Perth 12. Thus while the war dragged on, these 187 or so prisoners were able to leave their respective depots and enjoy a less restrictive and depressing existence, even though it was still captivity, in one or other of the parole towns.

Among others who did so were a fortunate handful of Other Ranks prisoners who, although *ipso facto* not themselves entitled to parole, were sent from the depots as servants to some higher ranking officers in the parole towns. An official return in June 1812 showed that there were then in Britain 149 servants to officer prisoners of war on parole. The number in Scotland was only a fraction of that total.[131] Among that fraction was, as observed in the discussion of employment for prisoners in Chapter 16 above, Charles Chalet at Valleyfield, described as secretary, 1st Regiment Horse, and who had been captured in Spain in 1808. 'You will send Charles Chalet on parole to Northampton as servant to Captain Berar,' the Transport Board told the Valleyfield agent in May 1811, 'and we enclose the necessary papers to enable you to do so, his Master having engaged to defray the expenses of the journey.'[132] At Valleyfield, too, a boy captive who was eventually equally as fortunate as Chalet was another already encountered: Michel or Martial Champagne or Champaigne. 'We direct you,' the Transport Board told the agent in September 1812, by which time the boy was aged 12, 'to allow Martial Champagne, a sailor taken in the Privateer *Countess Laura*, to proceed to Kelso to reside on Parole as the Servant to General De Boissi.'[133] From Perth, there was at least one prisoner whose good fortune it was to be sent away, even if late in the war, to the parole town of Oswestry in Shropshire. 'Send M. Steiner to Oswestry to act as servant to General Nielund,' the depot agent was instructed by the Transport Board at the end of November 1813. 'M. Steiner', according to the spelling in the depot Entry Book, was in fact Christophe Estingre, a soldier described as a 'domestique', no regiment given, who had been captured in April 1812 at Badajoz and had arrived five months later at Perth. Aged 40, born at Troifontain (sic), Estingre or Steiner duly set out from the depot on 6 December 1813 to begin what for him was no doubt a distinctly more agreeable period as a prisoner at Oswestry.[134]

More numerous than the 187 or so prisoners granted or regranted parole from the Scots depots were those others who in the course of the war were enabled to march out through the gates by volunteering themselves into the ranks of His Britannic Majesty's armed forces or into the crews of British merchant vessels. Some, probably many, of these volunteers were no doubt motivated by hope of a speedier arrival home thereby, as volunteering might sooner or later offer some prospect of escape, rather than further languishing in the depots until the war ended. Others no doubt volunteered without reflecting too deeply on possible consequences of their action but in the belief they would at least be restored meantime to paid activity or employment.

Encouraging and facilitating such volunteering by prisoners in the depots was a policy followed throughout the war by the British authorities.[135] With cynical hypocrisy the British government, while thus actively encouraging the recruitment of prisoners of war to its own or, particularly in the last months of the war, its allies' forces, threatened with execution as traitors members of its own forces taken prisoner who subsequently volunteered to join the enemy's forces. As early as October 1807 a royal proclamation had declared that all British seamen voluntarily serving on board enemy ships of war were guilty of high treason and would be subjected to 'the utmost Severity of the Law.' Among several consequent executions were those of seven British seamen found guilty in February 1812 by a special Commission of Oyer and Terminer in Surrey of having, while prisoners of war in Ile de France (Mauritius), joined the French army. The seven were sentenced to be hanged, drawn and quartered.[136] Donations widely contributed by church congregations and other groups and individuals throughout Britain and sent to France for the benefit of British prisoners of war there amounted to considerable sums. One of the hopes embodied in these donations was to save those prisoners from an 'unnatural alternative'. Thus '£13,000, collected from different quarters of the United Kingdom,' as the *Edinburgh Evening Courant* reported in July 1809, 'were last year sent over to the prisoners of rank and by them distributed among their more indigent brethren, when 6,000 received occasional relief. Of these, several were snatched from the jaws of the grave, and others were saved from the unnatural alternative of engaging in the service of the enemy.'[137]

Within a few weeks of the renewal of the war in 1803, Lord Hobart, secretary of war, informed the Admiralty of '… His Majesty's pleasure that you should give orders to the Commissioners for the Charge of Prisoners of War for permitting Colonel Diecken, who has received His Majesty's permission to raise a foreign corps and to enlist for that purpose all foreigners, excepting French, Italians and Spaniards, to recruit from among the Prisoners of War detained in this country.'[138] Those stated exceptions, intended primarily to preclude likely attempts at escape or desertion, were clearly substantial. But even as early as that in the war potential recruits from nationalities other than those three were also to be found among the prisoners, as a letter in January 1804 to the Admiralty from the Earl of Camden, Lord Hobart's successor in office, illustrated: 'The Master General of the Ordnance having requested that permission might be given to Major Macquart, who commands a corps attached to His Majesty's Royal Regiment of Artillery, to recruit from amongst the Dutch, German and Polish Prisoners of War such men as may be disposed to enlist with him, I am to signify to your Lordships the King's pleasure that your Lordships should give the necessary orders for enabling Major Macquart or any officer having authority from him to recruit from the prisoners in the several depots, it being understood that no Frenchman, Spaniard or Italian is to be engaged.'[139] Although the general prohibition on French prisoners being accepted as volunteers into the British armed forces was maintained during the war, there were numerous exceptions made to it by the authorities, as the evidence of the depot Entry Books and other documents indicates.[140] Inevitably, the recruitment of prisoners other than

the principal proscribed nationalities of French, Italians and Spanish, encountered difficulties as some prisoners of the latter nationalities, intent
on attempting to quit their depots by one means or another, claimed to
be other than they were. For that reason the Transport Board continued to
have distinct reservations about General Merck's recruiting activities at the
depots. In autumn 1806 the Board had instructed its depot agents to allow
the General 'to recruit for the army, from amongst the Germans, Swiss and
Poles in their custody', but 'We also, in consequence of the very incautious
manner in which the General appeared to have admitted recruits, many being
undoubtedly Frenchmen, found it necessary subsequently to give directions
to the agents not to permit any natives of the countries which were allowed
by the last Treaty of Peace [i.e., Treaty of Amiens, 1802] to form a part of the
French dominions to enlist.' Merck, however, continued 'to consider himself
entitled to recruit from among persons natives of Flanders and of the country
formerly called the Austrian Netherlands [i.e., Belgium]...'[141] The problem
of ensuring volunteers from among the prisoners were not French or of other
excluded nationalities continued throughout the war. In November 1811,
for example, when the Deputy Adjutant General asked the Transport Board
to compile for the commander-in-chief a list of such 'Germans, Austrians,
Prussians, Dutch, Flemish, Poles and Swiss as are confined at the several
depots and may be found on inspection fit for service', the Board replied:
'This Department has not the means of making the selection required with
any degree of accuracy, having only the prisoners' own assertions, which for
the most part are found to be false.'[142] And in a letter to the Admiralty the
previous month, the Board reported that '... very great Confusion and Disorder has taken Place in the late selection of Italians ordered by His Majesty's
Secretary of State, by Prisoners changing their Names and Characters, and
that much Deception must always be expected on such Occasions.'[143]

Inducements were offered prisoners to enlist. The honeyed words spoken
by Lieutenant John Flinn, RN, Transport Board agent, to potential recruits
among the prisoners at Fort George in the autumn of 1803 were no doubt
much the same as those voiced at Scots and English depots in many later
attempts by other recruiters.[144] The bounties offered recruits varied between
one corps or regiment and another of those few into which most volunteers
among the prisoners appear to have been enlisted. In 1805, for instance,
when the Royal Marines' bounty to foreigners enlisting was the large sum
of 14 guineas, the 60th infantry regiment was 'only permitted to give three
guineas.' Generally, '... the bounty given by the Army to Prisoners of War
never exceeds 3 guineas, which is mainly to enable them with necessaries, as it is considered sufficient indulgence to a Prisoner to be allowed his
freedom.'[145] Bounties appear to have been payable also to prisoners of war
volunteering themselves into the Royal Navy.[146] As for the merchant navy,

volunteers from among Danish (or Norwegian) prisoners, and perhaps those of other permitted nationalities as well, were subject to quotas. 'Should any natives of Denmark in your custody be desirous of serving on board British merchant vessels,' the Transport Board informed its depot agents in April 1808, 'we direct you to allow them to do so, as opportunities shall offer, but you will observe that not more than 10 can be allowed to an East India ship, more than one to a ship of under 300 tons, and 2 to any other above that tonnage.'[147]

If the War Office, the Admiralty, and the Transport Board looked upon sections of the prisoners of war as potential recruits for the army, the navy, and for merchant vessels, those authorities were also well aware of the risks of escape or desertion by such volunteers. Some prisoners, for example, recruited in 1808 by General Merck who had declared themselves to be Swiss or Piedmontese had done so not in order to fight King George's enemies but 'evidently to facilitate their return to France or Italy.'[148]

So far as prisoners in the Scots depots then are concerned there is abundant evidence of their volunteering and recruitment into the British armed forces or merchant navy from the opening stages of the war in 1803 until its end in 1814. The earliest example, already noted, appears to have been that undertaken at Fort George by Lieutenant Flinn, RN, in early autumn 1803. But more or less simultaneously the five seamen who escaped on 25 October that year from the Edinburgh bridewell were reported to have 'lately expressed a strong desire to be permitted to enter into our navy.'[149] From the bridewell in January 1804 Jan Rutvelt, a Dutch seaman captured six months earlier in the North Sea on the merchant vessel *Neptunis*, volunteered himself into the Royal Navy.[150] Eight other members of the crew of the *Neptunis*, all of them with Dutch or German names, preferred to serve in the army and volunteered at the bridewell to enlist into Major Halkett's corps.[151] But what is interesting and significant about volunteers from the bridewell is that a further 14 seamen there, all apparently French, were accepted as recruits into the Royal Navy despite their ostensible official ineligibility.[152]

At Greenlaw, the only depot in Scotland from April 1804 until the opening of Esk Mills in February 1811, the number of volunteers was unsurprisingly much larger than at the Edinburgh bridewell. Of the 97 prisoners in the 'Dutch' Entry Book for Greenlaw, 39 joined the British navy and two others the militia.[153] In addition to those volunteers, from the 132 survivors of the crew of the Dutch frigate *Utrecht* shipwrecked the previous month in Orkney and who arrived at Greenlaw in March 1807 no fewer than 21 enlisted within a few days into His Britannic Majesty's Land Service and a further six into the Royal Navy.[154]

The two 'Danish' Entry Books for Greenlaw, covering the years between November 1807 and July 1811, show that as many as 60 prisoners volunteered:

41 into the Royal Navy, six into the Royal Marines, two into His Majesty's Land Forces, two more into, less specifically, 'HM's Service', six to serve on a merchant vessel, and three 'to assist in navigating a lobster vessel'.[155] One of these volunteers incurred the displeasure of a fellow prisoner and fellow Norwegian at Greenlaw, Captain Paul Andreas Kaald. 'Johan F. Trudevind,' Kaald wrote in his diary on 12 November 1808, 'had come to Leith as an able seaman [captured] on a small Kristiansand privateer *Haevneren* ... But [he] had as an excuse that he was scared of the way of life in the prison and could now live better by ending up as an able seaman on board the [British] frigate. In my opinion a poor show by a Norwegian.' Almost exactly a year later Kaald noted that 'There were a number of Marine sergeants here today, offering the service to anyone who wanted to join (except the Danes). They took six men back with them ... under drum and pipe [fife?] music. Among these was Ivar Ronning, who had sailed on the privateer *Den Kjaekke*.' Encouraged, the Marines' recruiters returned to the depot a fortnight later, but with less success: 'Some Marines were up here today in order to recruit for the English Service,' noted Kaald. 'They recruited just two people, because not many have the desire to wear that red coat.' In May 1810, for example, volunteers among the prisoners at the depot were sought to help man merchant ships: 'Today,' wrote Kaald on the 13th of that month, 'a list was made of all the able-bodied and experienced seamen, as well as the boys and ships' mates, who wanted to enter the English merchant service and go to the East and West Indies.'[156]

In the 'Spanish' Entry Book at Greenlaw, two prisoners are shown to have volunteered themselves into the Royal Navy, and two others 'to serve in the Band of the 27th Regiment.'[157]

Of particular significance are the Greenlaw 'French' Entry Books, since French prisoners were officially considered to be ineligible for volunteering into HM's forces. Of the three 'French' Books, which taken together cover the years 1804-12, one listing 214 prisoners (three-quarters of whom were officers) who arrived at the depot in the month of November 1810 shows none at all volunteering into the British armed forces or merchant navy.[158] The two other 'French' Entry Books, one covering the years 1804-9 and the other 1811-12, list (although a marginal allowance has to be made for duplication of entries for recaptured escapers, etc.) an aggregate of 1,356 prisoners. The earlier of these two Books shows that 40 prisoners joined the Royal Navy, 15 others the army or militia. The first three prisoners to exchange captivity at Greenlaw for service in the navy left the depot as early as 10 July 1804. One of the three was Pierre Digurt, a civilian, or at any rate a steerage passenger when captured on the merchant vessel *La Flore* in the North Sea in August 1803 and who had spent the following six months in the Edinburgh bridewell. Of the 15 who volunteered into the army or militia (or in one less specific case into His Majesty's Land Service), nine enlisted in the 27th regiment. Toussaint Giraud, a seaman captured at Cuba in December 1804 on the privateer *Regulus*, arrived at Greenlaw in September the following year but emerged from captivity there three months later, having been discharged 'To the Midlothian Militia, order of Earl Moira.' A more curious case was that of four other seamen, including two named Miviel who were probably brothers or father and son, from three privateer ships captured in the West Indies between July and December 1804, who arrived at Greenlaw on 24 September 1805 and who by 12 October had presumably been able so impressively to demonstrate their musical talents that they were then discharged 'To the band of the Aberdeenshire Militia.'[159]

In the remaining Greenlaw 'French' Entry Book 39 prisoners are shown to have volunteered in 1811 into the Royal Navy: five on 21 August, 17 on 16 September, and the remaining 17 on 26 November. But as a salutary reminder of the difficulties of classifying the volunteers by nationalities, three of the latter 17 were in fact Dutch seamen who had been captured at North Queensferry on the retaken vessel *Fame*. The case of one of the others in this latter group of 17 illustrates the fact that even if a volunteer were French and moreover a proven troublemaker or *mauvais sujet* during his captivity he was not necessarily debarred from enlistment into the British armed forces. The prisoner concerned was one already encountered—Jean Joseph Watigny, a privateer seaman, who was among the mass of prisoners transferred in March 1811 from Esk Mills to Valleyfield. From there the following month he was transferred to Edinburgh Castle 'for insolent behaviour': 'assaulted a Centinel [sic], and one of the Turnkeys.' From the Castle he was sent in August that year to Greenlaw, from which he briefly escaped in October. With the approval of the Transport Board and of Vice Admiral Otway at Leith, Watigny passed out through the gates of Greenlaw on 26 November to join the Royal Navy.[160]

If (although it seems unlikely given the brief existence of the depot in February-March 1811) there were any volunteers into the British armed forces from among the 2,800 prisoners at Esk Mills, their going was not recorded in the distinctly incomplete Entry Book. At Edinburgh Castle, given particularly the incompleteness of its main Entry Book concerning discharges, the number of volunteers among the prisoners is likewise difficult to establish, but 28 have been found. One of these was Laurent Barbe or Barbet, whose enlistment into the Royal Navy from the Castle in September 1811 was really an outcome of his activities as an informer on fellow prisoners at Greenlaw.[161] Two other recruits from the Castle to the navy a month earlier than Barbet were prisoners named Talise and Gesima, respectively a Swede and a Dutchman. No fewer than 14 emerged from the

Castle to join the navy on 6 April 1813. All fourteen were members of the crew of the privateer *Ravisseur*, captured off the coast of Norway seven weeks earlier. One of them was a Dutch seaman, Daniel Hoft. Hoft had escaped from the Castle on 2 April but was recaptured next day at Penicuik (not perhaps an ideal place for an escaper to try to pass through). His view, like that of several other recaptured escapers, might have been: if you can't beat 'em, join 'em. At any rate he enlisted, along with 13 of his shipmates, in the Royal Navy within three days of his recapture. A further eleven volunteers from the Castle enlisted in the 60th regiment of the British army between 30 September and 20 October that year.[162]

At Valleyfield the Entry Books for 1811-13, supported by some relevant references in the official correspondence, provide generally clear guides to the number, as well as the range and variety, of volunteers among the prisoners. These sources, like those for Perth depot, also show the later mass enlistments of prisoners in autumn and winter 1813-14 into the armed forces of Britain's continental allies as Napoleon's empire contracted and crumbled. Excluding altogether, however, these later enlistments, some 157 prisoners volunteered from Valleyfield between March 1811 and summer 1813 into the British armed forces. No fewer than 149 of the 157 enlisted in the Royal Navy, four in the King's German Legion, and the remaining four in 'Army'. There were particularly large enlistments in the navy by prisoners in April and August 1811 and in May 1812—perhaps as a result of energetic recruiting at the depot by naval representatives at those periods.[163] The variety and range of prisoners among the 157 volunteers was exemplified by one already observed, Gilles or Gilus Gronwoud. Born at Amsterdam, described as a seaman, and 4 feet 10½ inches tall, Gilles was only 11 years old when he had arrived at Valleyfield from Esk Mills on 11 March 1811. Only six weeks later, however, on 25 April, he was 'Discharged to Royal Navy, per Order of Rear Admiral Otway.'[164] Pierre Lerouge, who volunteered into the navy in May 1812, appears to have been a French Canadian, having been born at Quebec. A seaman aged 35, he had been captured in 1809 and had arrived from Esk Mill at Valleyfield. Isac (sic) Richard, a seaman aged 22, born in Providence [? Rhode Island or Kentucky?] was one of several Americans among the volunteers at Valleyfield. Described, in the customary language of the period, under 'Marks and Wounds' in the Entry Book as 'Negro', he had been captured on the privateer *Roi de Naples* in 1810, and had passed from Esk Mill to Valleyfield where he enlisted in the Royal Navy in August 1811. Danzig, Memel (Klaipeda), Corfu, Warsaw, St Domingo, and Cadiz were among the birthplaces of some other volunteers from Valleyfield into the navy. Montevideo in Uruguay was the home of two of the four volunteers into 'Army': Joseph Garel and André Mondin, both soldiers captured in 1809 and who left Valleyfield together in September 1811 to exchange their prisoners' clothing for the scarlet tunic. 'Approve of your discharging the Prisoners thereinmentioned for His Majesty's Service,' the Transport Board told the agent at Valleyfield in April 1812 in reply to one of his letters, 'but you are to take very particular care that no Frenchman be thus released.' Yet Frenchmen were certainly also among the volunteers from the depot: Alexis Benoit, alias Pierre La Place, for instance, a soldier in the 82nd regiment when captured at Martinique in 1809, was accepted as a volunteer into the Royal Navy in May 1812 although he was a Frenchman born at Chartres. Another Frenchman, though he claimed on occasion to be French Canadian, and whose exploits will be more fully discussed in a chapter below, also volunteered into the navy: François Petit, privateersman, was discharged from Valleyfield on 1 April 1813 to Vice Admiral Otway at Leith. Nor were Italians absent from the volunteers, despite their official exclusion, too, by previous Transport Board instructions: Savary Gautche, for example, a soldier captured while serving in the Légion Irlandaise at Flushing in 1809 and who volunteered into the Royal Navy in December 1811, was said to be a native of Genoa (though, in another source, of Malta). As early as July 1811, indeed, within four months of the opening of Valleyfield, 20 Piedmontese prisoners at Valleyfield had written to the Transport Board 'requesting to be allowed to enter His Majesty's Service.' An army officer was consequently sent to the depot to enlist Piedmontese there, but no more information about his visit or its success has been found.[165]

At Perth depot, excluding the extensive recruitment of prisoners there in the late summer and autumn of 1813 and during the following winter into the armies of Britain's continental allies such as the Prince of Orange and the king of Sardinia as Napoleon's empire entered its final phase, there appears to have been markedly little volunteering into the British army or navy. Much of the explanation for that difference from the larger numbers of volunteers at Valleyfield or Greenlaw may have been that the depot at Perth did not open until as late in the war as August 1812. Whatever the reasons, only a handful of volunteers appear to have stepped forward there within the depot's first year. Yet official exhortations to volunteer were made to at least some prisoners there during those twelve months. 'Such Germans as chuse to enter into the British Service,' Captain Moriarty, agent at Perth, announced to the inmates on 5 March 1813, 'are desired to send in their names, with their number on their Tickets, and the Number of their Prison. The British Government are inclined to offer Service to them, but they must embrace this offer in the course of three days or they will not be received afterwards.'[166] The outcome was apparently what was reported in the *Perth Courier* a fortnight later: 'An officer from the General Staff of Scotland has enlisted from amongst prisoners confined in the Depot a considerable number of Germans in the King's German Legion.'[167] Unfortunately, however, there is no confirmation in the depot Entry Books of any prisoners being discharged specifically into the King's German Legion. That is not to say none were: it may be their departures from the depot were described instead as 'Discharged to Valleyfield', where some 865 prisoners certainly were sent from Perth between 29 July and 4 August 1813. But such an explanation seems improbable: would prisoners apparently volunteering and recruited in March have been kept waiting four months at Perth before being sent off to their chosen branch of the British armed forces? At any rate a mere handful of prisoners at Perth are clearly shown in the Entry Books to have volunteered between the opening of the depot in August 1812 and early summer 1813. The earliest to do so appears to have been one named Roustasin, whom the Transport Board six weeks after the opening of the depot 'permitted to serve on board a merchant vessel.'[168] Eugène Guchant, 'Being a native of Switzerland', who had been captured on the naval corvette *Hebe* in January 1809, was, however, unsuccessful in his application, made at Perth toward the end of 1812, to 'enter into His [Britannic] Majesty's Service', and remained a prisoner there until his release in February 1814.[169] But for Theodore Desmoulins, aged 15, who had been in the first batch of prisoners to enter Perth in August 1812, the trumpet did indeed sound in June 1813, and although the walls of the depot did not fall down its gates at any rate opened then for him to leave and resume his military musicianship, this time in the British army. Theodore, born at Tell, a lad of slight build and only 5 feet 1 inch tall, had been a trumpeter in the French 47th line regiment when captured in March 1811 at Sabougal in Portugal. He was 'the prisoner applied for by Colonel Tilly ... to serve in the band of the [British] 16th Regiment of Foot under the usual conditions.'[170] The only other volunteer at Perth shown in the Entry Books was a seaman or carpenter said to have been sent off to Leith on 5 July 1813 to serve in the Royal Navy.[171] Thus from Perth, excluding the hundreds of prisoners who were enlisted in the armies of Britain's continental allies in the last six or so months of the war, it appears that only four volunteers were found for Britain's own armed forces—and of those four one was not actually enlisted and another one may not have been.

Two other minor sources of volunteers into the Britsh armed forces from among the prisoners of war in Scotland were not actually depots but landing places or staging posts for prisoners in transit. One was Greenock, the other the admiral's flagship at Leith. The only surviving Entry Book for prisoners arriving at Greenock (all of them captured in the West Indies, and all but five of them sent on to Greenlaw depot) covers the years 1804-05. Of the 86 prisoners listed not one is shown to have volunteered from there into the British armed forces or merchant navy. But in letters to its agent, Mr J. Colquhoun, at Greenock, in September 1808 the Transport Board approved his having allowed three unnamed men, one Spanish and two Portuguese, all three of whom were presumably prisoners of war or, in the case of the Spanish man, had been so until the uprising that summer against the French occupation of Spain, 'to enter His [Britannic] Majesty's Service.' Another letter to Colquhoun from the Board almost two years later illustrates prevailing attitudes to race which deprived at least some black prisoners of the right to volunteer and subjected them to compulsion: '… there is no objection to the [unnamed] prisoner … being impressed for His Majesty's Service, as according to the General Rule, any Black Man or Man of Colour … among the prisoners of war may be allowed to serve.'[172]

21

Escapes

'Darkness prevented us from taking clear note of the places that day,' Lieutenant Marote-Carrier long afterward recalled of the day of his arrival in February 1811 at Esk Mills depot, 'but the next day we had nothing more urgent to do than to go round everything and see if we could find some way out; unfortunately nothing could favour an attempt at flight.' Similar preliminary surveys of prospects and means of escape were no doubt made by many other prisoners newly arrived at the depots in Scotland. At Greenlaw House one of the first notes about the depot Sergeant Major Beaudoin had made in his diary on his arrival there in June 1804 was that 'This house is surrounded by two rows of palisades, with sentries all around; at the side is a little wood that sometimes benefits escapers.'[1]

At least Marote-Carrier and his fellow prisoners on the hulks at Chatham at that time had been given the choice of remaining in captivity there or of being transferred to a depot in Scotland. 'Many among us, even most of us,' he recalled, 'were afraid of finding in Scotland a still more miserable existence and of falling from Charybdis to Scylla. It was also further from France, and in case of escape the chances of arriving there were very much less.'[2] Escape nevertheless was, or at least could appear to be, the most obvious means by which inmates of the Scots depots between 1803 and 1814 might soonest regain their freedom and their homes.

Apart from those prisoners involved in large-scale attempted escapes on the vessels, such as HMS *Gorgon* early in 1811, transporting them from the south of England to Scotland, at least two or three individuals sought to escape en route on their own initiative even before they arrived at their depots north of the Border. Thus among the first batch of 399 prisoners for the new depot at Perth sent on board the *Mathilda* from Plymouth for disembarkation at Dundee on 5 August 1812, two 'whose names are not known at this office,' the Transport Office told the depot agent two days earlier, 'having seized a boat and escaped from that ship were afterwards retaken and the reward of one guinea each has been paid for their recapture. Upon the arrival of this ship [at Dundee] you will enquire the names of the two prisoners in question and put them on short allowance to make good the reward.'[3]

Unlike that attempt, a successful and apparently unique escape by another prisoner en route like himself from Leith to Esk Mills depot in February 1811 was recalled by Marote-Carrier. 'Among us,' he said, describing his landing at Leith early that month along with other prisoners from the hulks at Chatham, 'there was a seaman from Amsterdam named Hummel. He was one of the most miserable among us. Clothed in a long frock coat down to his feet, shabby and threadbare, wearing big torn shoes, a hat enveloped in a coarse and dirty cover, he had the most pitiable appearance. One might have said he was half frozen, so much did he shiver and so much did he try to wrap himself up better. From time to time he uttered groans which the expression of suffering on his face indicated were genuine. In passing [with the other captives] through Leith and Edinburgh Hummel appeared to march only with laboured and pained efforts. As I knew him slightly, and captivity had thrown us closer together, I had watched him with a great deal of interest and had shared in his sufferings, which had suddenly become acute. I say "suddenly", because during our voyage from Chatham he had not appeared to show them so openly. Far from that indeed, he was one of those who had borne their troubles most bravely; rarely had he uttered a complaint or even a murmur. I had been very surprised to see him suddenly change character and lose the resignation he had shown until then. So I had done my best to cheer him up and had supported him so he could march along with less difficulty.'

Arrived at Parliament Square beside St Giles' Cathedral and the Old Tolbooth in the High Street of Edinburgh, the column of prisoners, surrounded by their guards and by a large crowd of curious onlookers, halted for a brief rest before resuming their march to Esk Mills. 'After the guards' weapons had been loaded,' Marote-Carrier recalled, '... we remained, without shelter from the cold, exposed like a spectacle to public curiosity, for the crowd did not cease to form a circle round us despite the shoving and use of their rifle butts by the soldiers, who roughly pushed back those who came too close to us. Hummel, during this time, continued to complain bitterly. I spoke to him sympathetically and did all I could to give him courage. Suddenly he grasped my arm and whispered, "Do you want to save me? " "What?!" I said, utterly surprised. "Come! " he replied.

'The square formed by the guards left free a big enough space between them and us who were enfolded like sheep within this impassable barrier. Hummel and I were in the front rank of the prisoners and until then we had been fully in view of the guards and the crowd. But after his question to me Hummel pulled me into the middle of the prisoners and we were swallowed up so well among our 600 companions that we could not be seen from outside. The Dutchman stopped, and without a word cast off his old frock coat and appeared clothed in a costume so fine that he looked as if he'd stepped straight out of a tailor's shop. He shook off his big shoes and showed he was wearing brilliantly polished boots. He grasped his hat, pulled off its soiled cover, and appeared quite transformed. His transformation was so complete and so fresh and fine was his appearance that it seemed like a miracle. I leave you to imagine the general astonishment this sudden metamorphosis, of which the English had failed to catch sight, caused among us. But that astonishment grew still more when Hummel, plunging his hand into his pocket, withdrew from it a handful of coins which he began to hand out generously left and right to the prisoners. 'Here you are, take it, my poor people,' he said, speaking in faultless English and moving as he did so toward our guards. Arriving among the prisoners on the fringes, he moved out of the circle, raising his voice and continuing to cast alms into everyone's hands. The soldiers at once saw this man who was clearly by his appearance a real gentleman, so generous with his money and speaking in such cultured tones. They immediately approached him: "What the devil are you doing there? Who allowed you to go in there? What are you doing among the prisoners? Get along with you! Quick! Out of there!" And they pushed him along in front of them with redoubled oaths and blows from their rifle butts. Our man was not difficult to persuade. He put up no resistance and let himself be thrust out of the square, fearful only that the English might see through his ruse and change their attitude. I have never seen a man's face more expressive than was Hummel's at that moment. We saw him glancing slyly at us, smiling at each blow that fell on his shoulders. Fear and hope, joy and anxiety chased each other across his face. Thanks to the zeal the soldiers showed in separating us prisoners from every outsider, Hummel was soon pushed outside our ranks. Hardly was he driven out than he lost himself in the crowd of spectators, walking away with lengthened strides, elbowing people out of his way, in a great hurry to distance himself from us as soon as he could. I stood amazed by Hummel's audacity. But I was delighted to see him succeed so completely.

'Everything turned out well for Hummel. Three months later I received [at Valleyfield] the following letter from him which I still have today [in 1840]. "Amsterdam, 11 April 1811. It is indeed from Amsterdam that I write to you, my dear friend. Thanks to heaven I arrived here safe and sound, and nothing diminished the good fortune that favoured me from the time of my escape in Parliament Square. ... my precautions were well enough taken to allay every suspicion during the brief stay I was forced to make in Scotland."' Hummel had strode rapidly away from the crowd of spectators and from the prisoners in the Square. '"Who could have confused me with those prisoners, wretched as they were, so deprived of everything, whereas I was as elegant as most of those dandies who walk up and down in front of Parliament House?"' Hummel had booked himself into an hotel in Edinburgh, eaten a good dinner, and slept soundly all night before going down next day to Leith where he boarded a Dutch ship, whose captain he knew and which was bound for Amsterdam. The ship's lieutenant had died on the voyage to Leith and Hummel was taken on in his place. During the two days he remained on board the vessel at Leith until it sailed he was thus able to avoid the hue and cry arising from his escape, the more easily because the authorities apparently possessed no adequate description of him: "'All that was known about me was that I had worn a long and threadbare frock coat and a hat with a cover. As soon as I was taken on by the [Dutch] captain I had donned the uniform of the deceased ship's lieutenant ... and during the visit made to us by the Scots police my rank went unquestioned.'[4]

Only two recorded escapes by prisoners being transferred between depots within Scotland have been found. One was that by Philip Lefebvre, a seaman, aged 20 and born at Calais, who had been captured on the merchant vessel *Providence* in 1807. Lefebvre got away from his escort on the way from Valleyfield to Perth in July 1813, but he was recaptured a few days later at Dalkeith and had to resume his trudge to Perth, where he remained until the end of the war. The other escaper was Felix Delille, aged 24, captured in 1808 as a midshipman on the man-of-war *Le Héros*, and who had been sent in November 1810 from Greenlaw on parole to Peebles. When midshipmen on parole were sent a year later into confined depots as a measure of retaliation against the treatment of captured British midshipmen in France, Delille escaped from his escort en route from Peebles to Valleyfield. But he soon gave himself up and was duly sent into Valleyfield. Like all the other midshipmen so dealt with, he was restored to parole in December 1811—though not at Peebles but at Lauder.[5]

Hummel's escape on the way to Esk Mills, one of only three recorded examples as it was of an escape by a prisoner en route for the first time to a depot in Scotland, and unique as some of its other aspects appear to have been, nonetheless illustrated several, although by no means all, of the obvious problems confronting any escaper or intending escaper from the Scots depots. The most obvious problem of all was, of course, one that had not confronted Hummel, Lefebvre, or the two unnamed prisoners who had made off en voyage from the *Mathilda*: how to get out of the depot itself. Even once that problem had been resolved there remained innumerable others confronting escapers. They included the need to have at least some money, some iron rations of food, and suitable clothing. Then there was the desirability of being able to understand and speak at least some English. Possession of a relevant map or at least sketch of the chosen route was also clearly desirable, as was a watch and more so a compass, although many or most seamen escapers might doubtless be able to find their directions, at any rate on clear nights, by the stars. Names and addresses of any civilians, whether sympathetic or merely mercenary but at least trustworthy, whether native Scots, English or aliens, able and willing to provide overnight lodging, concealment or guidance en route, or other practical help, were no doubt also invaluable to any escaper. Not least, too, among the problems were the hazards arising from the distances to be covered in Scotland or England before the intended coast or harbour of embarkation could be reached. Above all there was the problem of finding eventually on whatever coast in Britain or Ireland to which escape was directed a boat or ship which would carry the escaper safely at last to the continent. Yet another issue to be considered was whether it was best to escape and travel alone or with a companion or companions and, if the latter, how many. All escapes had obviously to be undertaken in the knowledge that they involved hazards to life and limb, including the possibility of being fired on by the depot sentries, that descriptions of the escapers would be circulated or advertised by the depot authorities within hours or days, rewards would be offered for recapture, and in the event of recapture punishment would have to be endured—normally by confinement for a period in the cachot and by reduced rations of food, but in some cases by confinement in the particularly unpleasant cachot at Edinburgh Castle or even transfer to the hulks in the south of England. Clearly then, escape was more likely to be successful if the escaper was audacious but also cautious, determined and resourceful, well equipped for his journey, well informed about his route, able to speak English well, with sufficient money and with some sympathetic civilian contacts to call upon en route. Getting out of the depot was difficult enough. The realistic escaper, however, had to expect to encounter thereafter many other difficulties, some of them unforeseen or even unforeseeable, before he could hope to set foot again on the continent of Europe. Perhaps, above all, the escaper had to have as his companion sheer luck.

Two of the many categories into which escapes might be separated were the planned and the unplanned—either the culmination of days, weeks or even months of preparation and sometimes hard physical toil, or the apparently spontaneous seizure of some unforeseen opportunity.

It was almost axiomatic that mass, or attempted mass, escapes by a score or more of prisoners from the Scots depots were the outcome of at least some degree of planning and preparation. Several such escapes, from Esk Mills in February and March 1811 and from Edinburgh Castle in April and July that year, have already been discussed in some detail.[6] It was possible, however, that one aspect of the crisis of 9-11 March at Esk Mills was in fact an unplanned attempt at mass escape arising from the panic caused by the apparent collapse of the depot buildings, when, according to the clerk Andrew Johnston, 'several attempts were made to level the Stockade by the Prisoners rushing in large bodies against it.' At any rate, the limited evidence clearly indicates that the mass escape in 1811 from the Castle on 11-12 April and from Esk Mills on 19 February were both preceded by planning and preparation, even if four of the 23 escapers from Esk Mills had arrived at the depot only on the day before the escape. The escape from the Castle by the 49 prisoners had been planned, according to press reports of statements made by some of the recaptured escapers, for a month beforehand. It is also clear that at Perth an attempted mass escape by tunnel-digging in mid-September 1813, in which Lieutenant Marote-Carrier himself took part and which will be more fully discussed below, was planned and toiled for during a period of about two months.[7]

Little evidence, however, survives concerning planning and preparation of other mass, or attempted mass, escapes at the two other depots, Greenlaw and Valleyfield. Nor is it even certain that any mass escape actually took place at Greenlaw. There, according to Andrew Johnston, depot clerk successively at Esk Mills, Valleyfield and Perth, 'Early in a morning of June 1810 about 30 prisoners got out by a mine. The Pennycuick Volunteers were beat to arms to assist the military. They were all retaken in the course of the day. Three were severely wounded, one a Russian by a bayonet in the breast, and two shot by an Aberdeen soldier while secreting themselves ... under a tree. The ball went through the thigh of one and lodged in the hip of the other. They all recovered from their wounds.'[8] Although Johnston provides these circumstantial details there is unfortunately no confirmation in any other source of any such mass escape from Greenlaw. Captain Paul Andreas Kaald, a prisoner at Greenlaw at that time, makes no mention of it in his diary, and it is difficult to believe he would have failed to do so had there been such an escape from his depot. Nor is there any relevant reference in the surviving official archives or in the contemporary press. So did Johnston err in stating that it was from Greenlaw in June 1810 that the mass escape took place? Johnston himself was not appointed as a depot clerk until early in 1811—and his appointment was to Esk Mills, not Greenlaw. It may be Johnston misstated either the place or the date, or both, of the escape he mentions. If such a mass escape indeed took place at Penicuik (other than those at Esk Mills in February-March 1811—and Johnston is clearly not referring to those escapes or attempted escapes) then it must have been from Valleyfield—but Valleyfield of course did not become a depot until March 1811.

What did occur at Greenlaw, not in June 1810 but on 30 April that year, according to the reliable testimony of the diarist Kaald, was the discovery in the cachot or black hole by the depot authorities of 'a hole which lay right under the ceiling' and also of 'a mountain of topsoil'. Kaald recorded that three days earlier 'some of the prisoners here started to dig a hole through which they could come out and attain their freedom. After having dug 7 feet down they started to dig outwards, and had already come about 2 fathoms outside of the palisade. So with 2 days' more work they were already far

481

enough outside it to be able to escape on the first dark and rainy night. The workers hadn't been able to store the topsoil anywhere else, otherwise they would have been found out.' Ten prisoners who were caught working in the tunnel 'were seized and transferred to the guardhouse, but since there wasn't room for them all there, 5 were brought back here [into the prison rooms] in the evening.' If as many as ten prisoners were together at work in the tunnel were there also some others not working there at the time of its discovery who were involved in the project? [9]

At least three mass or attempted mass escapes did indeed take place at Valleyfield, although in the case of the first of these little evidence about it has been found beyond a brief press report, still less about whatever planning or preparation preceded the escape. It appears to have occurred on the night of 12 February 1812 and was reported in the *Caledonian Mercury* three days later thus: '... between ten and 11 o'clock, during a violent storm of rain, about 30 of the French prisoners ... made their escape, all of whom, however, were after a short time recovered and brought back to their former place of confinement.'[10]

Evidence for a second attempted mass escape later that same year at Valleyfield appears to survive only in a letter which the banker-historian Macbeth Forbes, without providing any details of its provenance, says was written to a friend by the agent at Valleyfield, Captain Andrew Brown, on 17 October 1812. The letter, which Macbeth Forbes appears to reproduce in his notes, says: 'Sir George Clerk [the leading landowner at Penicuik] also called and pressed us very much to dine with him on the Wednesday and lucky it was I did not go, as an attempt at a general escape was made the same night. Indeed, I had been looking for it and it was truly the cause of my refusing Sir George's invitation. They had very nearly effected their purpose when fortunately observed by one of the sentries, when the guard was turned out and they (eight in number) were secured. These eight, had they succeeded in cutting through the stockade, were to have made way for the general sally which [sic], had it succeeded, I have no doubt many lives would have been lost. The eight were all armed with short dirks, which some miscreants had carried into the prison to them, and next day I ordered a search for weapons and found a good many of the same kind. It was, however, happily prevented and everything is now quiet and orderly. Weather has been dreadfully bad indeed.'[11]

The third mass escape from Valleyfield took place on 19 November 1813, when no fewer than 30 prisoners made off from the depot. How they did so is not stated in any of the official sources or in press reports. It seems almost certain, however, that, despite the absence of dates and of any specific mention of Valleyfield and certain other apparently differing features in his account, this was the escape recollected from his boyhood in Peebles by William

Chambers, the later publisher and lord provost of Edinburgh. According to Chambers, 23 recaptured escapers from Penicuik, whom he vividly recalled being marched back there from Peebles, had broken out from their depot by means of a tunnel they had dug—clearly an escape into which had gone both planning and much strenuous labour.

Chambers's account, which appears to be based on information about the escape which he must have acquired at that time or in later years, touches on many of the salient aspects of escapes from the Scots, or any other, depots during the Napoleonic Wars or indeed during other wars before or since. He recalled that it was 'One afternoon, on coming out of school, and emerging on the main street [in Peebles], my companions and I were startled with the spectacle of a party of French prisoners of war under a military escort. Even to boys, who are not very sensitive, it was an appalling scene; something at least which I can never forget. The poor wretches in their miserable attire, mostly without shoes, and faint from hunger, walked slowly and painfully within the circle of soldiers towards the county jail, the only place of security in the town. There they were immured for the night, and succoured with some provisions, which they thankfully received. Soon it became known that they had escaped from Penicuik, and in a way interesting to record. From one of the barrack-like buildings in which they were confined at night, they contrived to excavate a tunnel beneath the courtyard, the palisades, and the outer promenade for sentries, as far as the woody bank beyond. There were some serious difficulties in the undertaking. The excavators had to work with imperfect tools, such as bits of the iron hoop of a barrel. A greater difficulty consisted in getting rid of the excavated earth without exciting suspicion. This caused a great deal of trouble, but somehow the pocketsful of loose stuff that were brought to the surface were happily got rid of. There was another very serious difficulty. Digging the tunnel in the required direction, and just as wide as would allow a man to creep through, it was almost impossible to determine on the point where the exit could be safely effected. By burrowing too far, they would get under the steep bank, and be unable to emerge to the surface. If they emerged too soon, even by a few feet, they would be exposed to the fire of the sentry. The whole enterprise was critical. It was a matter of death or life, and only certain daring spirits, ardently sighing for liberty, would engage in the terrible risk. One may imagine the months of agonising labour, digging night after night in that hideous tunnel, the dimensions of a common drain—the constant apprehensions of discovery—the trouble in carrying away and concealing the excavated material—the fears, the hopes attending the final issue. So skilfully were matters managed, that none of the guards or prison officials was aware of the bold attempt at escape that was to be made. The tunnel was completed; everything was ready for bursting forth. So far there had been an extraordinary success: the worst was to come. All things considered, the idea of getting clear off was little better than madness. The party were 23 in number. All were dressed in the yellow prison garb, which would everywhere reveal their character. They were unacquainted with the country. No more than two or three of them could speak English. The project was absurd, pitiable. ... the party selected a moonlight night for the enterprise. With the prime engineer and leader in advance, the party, in single file, crouching down, and following close at one another's heels, stealthily crept through the tunnel to its extreme end, where it was thought to be safe to burst into the open air. The calculation as to the proper spot for issuing just within the loose scattered wood on the bank had been pretty correct. The leader, having cautiously loosened the earth until he saw the glimmer of the moonlight, pushed the incumbent mass upwards with his back, and in an instant was on his feet on the open ground, and hastening away among the trees up the acclivity. The others, one by one, followed, but not with equal success. The nearest sentry, seeing the torrent of fugitives, levelled his musket and fired, killing one dead on the spot. The alarm being thus given, other sentries fired. Following in pursuit, five were captured and taken back to prison. The fugitives were now reduced to seventeen. ... It appears that one of the party, named Deschamps, had at times, under escort of a soldier, been permitted to visit shops in the village on errands connected with the prison, and had thus, by looking about him, and talking to the natives, learned the nature of the country around. His knowledge so acquired was now brought into use. After pausing for a few minutes to gain breath in the woods to the west of the village, he represented the propriety of pushing on in a southerly direction, across a wide moory plain, full of peat-mosses, where some refuge could be obtained; and thereafter by crossing a hill get into a valley, in which was a small river tributary to the Tweed. His guidance was implicitly followed. Before dawn the party had ensconced themselves in the deep cuttings of the moss, where, in momentary apprehension, and peering across the heather, they were on the watch for pursuers. The only food they had was a little bread, which they carried in their pockets, supplemented by morsels of a raw turnip, which one of them had picked from a field in the course of his flight. So passed over the first day, without any cause for alarm.'[12] The 'wide moory plain, full of peat-mosses' was presumably Auchencorth Moss, three miles south-west of Penicuik; and the small tributary to the Tweed, the Cairn Burn or perhaps Lyne Water, into which the Burn flows. Several points in Chambers's account of the escape differ from or are contradicted by those in the Valleyfield Entry Books and in Transport Board correspondence, as well as in the very succinct press reports. The Entry Books and the press reports agreed that 30, not 23 prisoners as Chambers says, escaped; and the clothing worn by most of the escapers, who were mainly seamen, was described in the press as 'seamen's clothes', not the yellow prison garments mentioned by Chambers.[13] No prisoner named Deschamps is listed in the Entry Books as among the escapers, but one of them was a privateer seaman named Dujardin. Is it conceivable that Chambers confused the two names, roughly translateable as Fields and Garden? Or is it possible the name Deschamps was an alias not recorded in the Entry Books, or conversely that it was the actual name of one of the escapers who, however, was listed in the Valleyfield Entry Books under an alias? Despite such discrepancies and contradictions Chambers's recollection was almost certainly of the escape from Valleyfield by 30 prisoners on 19 November 1813. The Entry Books and the press reports agree that five of the escapers were recaptured on the day of their escape and a further three the following morning, thus reducing the total then still at large to 22—which was practically identical with the number recalled by Chambers.

At Perth depot there were or appear to have been as many as nine mass or attempted mass escapes during its two years' existence from 1812 to 1814. It is probable, however, that two or three of the nine were really extensions or continuations, either genuine or bogus and intended to mislead the depot authorities, of the same attempt rather than entirely separate and independent attempts. Whatever the correct number, it appears at least certain that all of them necessarily involved planning and most of them laborious tunnelling as well.

The earliest mass escape appears to have been attempted only two months after the opening of the depot. 'On Tuesday,' the *Perth Courier* reported two days later on 8 October 1812, 'an attempt by the prisoners in the Depot to effect their escape was discovered and prevented. A mine on which they had been employed for three days was excavated from within a privy of the prison allotted to the petty officers and had been pushed as far as the outer wall, on the inside of which the earth gave way and occasioned a detection of the stratagem. The digging had been carried on through the day, and at night when the prisons are inspected, the stones which had been removed were so neatly and regularly replaced as to prevent suspicion. The petty officers are confined in the upper story of their prison, through the floor of which they had cut a hole by which they might pass to the lower. They had afterwards cut out the lock of the door which opens to the yard, and consquently to the entrance to their mine.'

A second attempt at a probable mass escape was discovered on Christmas Day 1812. According to press reports, some of the prisoners had 'begun an excavation from one of the necessaries [latrines], and after piercing a thick wall had carried their mine laterally about five yards. Five of them were found at work and were put in close confinement.' Nothing more, however, about either the planning or preparation for this attempted escape has been found.[14]

Within eight months of its opening, attempts at escape from Perth depot by tunnelling had already become so frequent that the local correspondent of the *Dundee Advertiser* told its readers in April 1813 that 'he would stop reporting escape attempts unless they had some extraordinary feature.' As another local newspaper commented later that year: 'The depot [at Perth] is certainly a splendid building and was erected at great expence; but it should seem that either the foundations are insufficient or the ground very favourable for mining.' It was not only the nature of the ground, however, but almost certainly the presence among the prisoners there of almost 100 miners, sappers and engineers (compared with 27 at Valleyfield, the next highest number at any other Scots depot) which helped explain Perth escapers' partiality for tunnelling.[15]

The next attempt at mass escape from Perth took place in the spring of 1813 and it may either have been a particularly ambitious and co-ordinated undertaking which sought to use two tunnels, or perhaps more probably it was two independent although more or less simultaneous attempts made from separate blocks at the depot. 'On Friday morning,' the *Perth Courier* reported six days later on 1 April, 'the prisoners were detected in an attempt to prepare for their escape from the Depot by means of an excavation. A mine of 3 feet square had been carried from the necessary of the Prison No. 3 to such a distance under the walls (its length being 42 feet) that the work of an hour or two would have been sufficient for its completion. It was intended to have opened close to the base of the outer wall, bounding the military way, and along which the fugitives might have skulked off unobserved by the sentinels.' Nothing more has been found about this attempt or the number of prisoners engaged in it. Nine days later, on Sunday, 4 April, '... the prisoners in the Depot were detected in another attempt to escape. They had dug a pit to the depth of 20 feet from the floor of the prison No. 2, at some distance from the bottom of which they had just begun a lateral cut. The space below was intended to receive the water, and the mine was to have been directed obliquely upwards, that the water might run off into this receptacle.' Again nothing more has been found about the numbers or plans of those engaged in digging this second tunnel—except that its discovery by the depot authorities convinced the prisoners that an informer among them had betrayed their attempt, with the results already described in an earlier chapter above.[16]

More information is, however, available about the actual mass escape of 23 prisoners from Perth in August 1813 and their ostensible lack of planning for their course of action once their break-out had taken place. 'On Tuesday morning,' the *Perth Courier* reported two days later on 26 August, 'a number of prisoners escaped from the Depot through a mine which they had dug from the necessary of No. 2 to the bottom of the outer wall where it faces the

South Inch. It is supposed that they had begun to issue from the aperture of its passage about two in the morning but as they preserved a profound silence, and the night was very dark, they were not observed by the sentinel till one of them, in attempting to leap the stream which skirts the north side of the Depot, fell into the water with considerable noise. The nearest sentry then fired towards the point from which the sound proceeded, and the adjoining sentries, having discharged their muskets in the same direction, an alarm was given and parties of the guard went in pursuit of the fugitives. Ten of them were soon apprehended and we understand that thirteen are still amissing. They seem to have had no plan for proceeding after finding themselves at liberty. Several of them were taken near the river [Tay], which we suppose the previous rise of the tide had prevented them from crossing. Two endeavoured to conceal themselves in a vessel at the shore but quitted it on being called to by the master from below. One of them afterwards climbed a tree, where he was discovered by the soldiers. Another fugitive plunged into the water and swam until his strength began to fail, when he called for help, when he was taken up by a sloop's boat. Those who were taken were immediately committed to the cachot.'[17]

Whether that escape, however unsuccessful as it seems eventually to have proved for virtually all those who took part in it, inspired other prisoners at Perth to begin digging tunnels, or whether preparations for these other attempts were already under way in August 1813, is uncertain. But the following month there were, or there appear to have been, a spate of attempts at mass escape from the depot. Again, as in March-April that year, it is not clear whether those attempts were independent of each other, or whether at least a couple of them may have been allied or co-ordinated, two sides of one coin. A detailed account of the attempts on the two successive nights of 11-12 and 12-13 September has already been given above.[18] Of the 28 prisoners who escaped on the night of 12-13 September, two were recaptured within 24 hours at Bridge of Earn, and a further three a couple of days later.[19]

It had indeed been an eventful week at the depot, for as the *Courier* pointed out in its same issue in an addition to its report about the tunnelling from Nos 6 and 3 prison blocks: '... yesterday [Wednesday, 15 September] the weight of the water in the canal [surrounding the depot] being increased by the rain, a part of the bottom fell into an excavation which had been directed beneath it, and which was traced to the necessary of No.1.' The *Courier*, so informed no doubt by the depot authorities, suggested that an explanation for these mass escapes and attempted mass escapes was that 'The 800 prisoners who were lately transferred from Pennicuick are, it is said, of a much more turbulent and ungovernable character than the rest ...'

Among 'turbulent' prisoners transferred from Penicuik to Perth—although not in the preceding weeks but a year earlier—was Lieutenant Marote-

Carrier. It appears to have been in mid-September 1813, however, that he and a sizeable group of fourteen of his associates took part in an attempt at escape from Perth, which, all going well, would have been a mass escape since other prisoners, although not directly involved in the planning or preparation, were expected to follow them out beyond the walls. It may well have been the tunnelling by Marote-Carrier's group that explained the fall of part of the bottom of the surrounding canal or ditch.

Along with such 'ungovernable' captives as the naval or merchant vessel lieutenant Jacques Adam, the hussar lieutenant Auguste Petry, as well as the privateer surgeon De Kuyper of Ghent (who had sought to play an active part in the projected rising by prisoners on the ship bringing Marote-Carrier and others from the hulks at Chatham to Esk Mills early in 1811), Marote-Carrier had, according to his own account, been placed in prison No.1 at Perth on his arrival there from Valleyfield in September 1812. Marote-Carrier later recalled that, 'Despite all the obstacles to overcome and all the surveillance to thwart', the idea of escaping was taken up by him and his associates at Perth not long after their arrival there. His uniquely detailed account of how their escape was planned and prepared suggests how some of the other mass escapes about which little or no detailed information has survived may also have been carried out. 'It was,' he said, 'Monsieur Adam who discovered the possibility of doing so. Behind the building we inhabited there was a vast latrine built directly against the palisades which lined the surrounding ditch. We decided to dig the ground and make a hole deep enough to give us passage and lead us beyond the wall. We had so often failed at the very moment of success that we took all necessary precautions so that no one might even suspect our project and that the carrying out of it might be as speedy as possible. We reached an agreement with some [French army] miners from the company recently come from Spain. We gave each of them six sous a day and a ration of bread. In order easily to cover the cost of the enterprise without exhausting our resources, fifteen of us clubbed together.

'The first difficulty was to procure the means of digging. Some Scots workmen were still working on completing some inside masonry and joinery works. We stole some of their tools without their noticing, and we hid them so well that no one could discover them, however painstaking the daily visits of the turnkeys. The excavation work began and continued without interruption for fifteen days, despite the proximity of the sentries, who heard nothing of the sounds being made underground. We had lifted two paving stones in the latrine. Each time work was suspended they were carefully replaced so that suspicion was never aroused on the part of anyone not in the secret.

'To begin with, digging went on only in the morning and evening, and there was only one miner at a time. But the earth was crumbly. Soon the hole was deep enough and wide enough for two men to go down and work in it at their ease. Then work went on throughout the day. So that the absence of the miners might not be noticed we forbade them to work too long at a time. Each of those involved took a turn of keeping watch. Only one worked at a time. One of us accompanied him to the latrine, the workman went down into the hole, then the paving stone was replaced over him. An hour later he was fetched out and another man replaced him. In the evening the earth was thrown down in the latrine.

'But soon the ground became more difficult to dig, the tools struck enormous stones that it was necessary to take out first but which afterward we did not know how to transport and dispose of. The inventive mind of Monsieur Adam came to our help. Among the thousand forms of trade the prisoners carried on there was one that served us marvellously. Several of them ran about the rooms and the yards carrying and selling cooked potatoes enclosed in a sort of tin boiler that was quite sizeable and had a lid. We bought a certain number of these boilers that we carried empty from the room to the place of excavation without rousing suspicion. There we filled them with stones. The big ones were broken up by the workmen so that they could easily be put into them.

'We had more trouble finding a suitable place to dispose of the excavated material. After a lot of looking around we thought about the ceiling of our prison. It was recalled that our building was exceptional in not having an upper storey, and for all its height was only a single room. The ceiling was made of beams spaced about two feet apart and so placed that there were a big space between the roof and the planks that covered them. This place, which was inaccessible by ordinary means, served no purpose, so there was no fear of it being visited [by the depot authorities]. One of our group got up to the ceiling by a rope ladder and there made a hole in the board from where the planks could be easily lifted and replaced. He reported there was enough space up above there to hold an immense quantity of stones. From that point onward we were saved.

'We went to fill our tubs, and from the ceiling he dropped down a rope wth a hook. We hung them on it one after the other, he pulled them up to him, emptied their contents and sent them back to us. So that the English would not take us by surprise while we were carrying out this dangerous operation, we had taken care to barricade the door with the bulk of our hammocks, placed one on top of another. If someone arrived unexpectedly the hammocks were lifted aside but not too swiftly, so that whoever was up high had time to pull up the rope and replace the board. As for the windows, they were much too high up for anyone to reach them from outside; moreover, they were fitted with bars and a metal trellis so finely meshed that it prevented sentries on guard on the wall from making out what was going on inside.

'When the tubs were all empty, the board was put back, the door opened and the man charged with pulling them up remained on the floor while we went off again to fill them, but one by one and without fuss. Then the operation began all over again.

'This routine succeeded so well that in one evening the hole was completely cleared. It had a depth of about fourteen feet, but did not yet go down below the bed of the ditch which had to be crossed by a sort of tunnel before we could arrive beyond the surrounding wall. A further four feet were dug but the air became so thin and so foul that it was possible to breathe only with difficulty. To overcome this new obstacle we made out of the uppers of boots and bits of old leather kinds of pipes or nozzles—tubes long enough to help the breathing of whoever was at the bottom of the hole. This expedient proved successful and the works continued without mishap. We went down into the diggings by a sort of ladder cut into the earth and stones.

'About the middle of August, when the waters were running very low, we began to dig horizontally underneath the ditch, which was about ten feet wide. In eight days the gallery was driven through. The water foamed about three or four feet above the passage, which was not high or wide but through which anyone crouching could easily pass. The stones served here as pillars to support the roof, for fear that the weight of water above might break it down.

'It was from the other side of the ditch that we met the most serious obstacle that we had yet come up against. This was the foundations of the enormous surrounding wall that was eight feet thick and was sunk to a great depth below the bed of the ditch. It was necessary to make a new ladderway in order to get below this foundation, then a new gallery, and finally a stairway to get up again on the other side.

'The enterprise was happily terminated in the first days of September, after more than six weeks of hard work and extraordinary fatigues. The miners, taking the utmost precautions not to arouse the attention of the sentries, pierced upwards through the surface a little opening that came out in a field of oats about five or six feet beyond the wall.

'It may seem astonishing that we had thus reached the end of the work without being betrayed by any of the prisoners in our room whom we had necessarily all let into the secret by the carrying of the excavated materials up into the ceiling. But every one of them, above all the poorest among them, were more or less directly interested in its success, for they hoped that once we had escaped they would follow the same route as us, and they were delighted that it was we who had borne all the essential expense.

'… we decided that if we delayed carrying out our project an unforeseen accident could cause it to fail. We decided to make a run for it that very evening. There were fifteen of us, and we proposed to form three groups of five men each who would set off at half-hourly intervals. We drew lots for the order of our going. I was third and thus became a member of the first group

Two pages from the uniquely surviving Perth depot ledger of payments of monies received for prisoners of war there in 1812–14 from their families, friends or bankers. The first prisoner shown on the first page is Lieutenant Auguste Petry. Amounts each prisoner received are shown in the second column from the left and, in the fourth column, the weekly instalments paid to them. © Reproduced by permission of Perth Museum & Art Gallery, Perth & Kinross Council.

The gravestone in Glencorse parish churchyard of Charles Cottier, a young French prisoner, shot in 1807 by a sentry at Greenlaw depot. Courtesy of Mr Hugh McCaig, Glencorse House.

François-Frédéric Billon, a French officer on parole as a prisoner of war at Jedburgh and Selkirk, and one of only two or three in Scotland to leave an account of their voyage to captivity there.

Dumbarton Castle, in which General Edouard-François Simon was held captive from 1812 to 1814. Courtesy of West Dunbartonshire Libraries.

Falkland Palace, Fife, in whose cellars many prisoners were lodged for a night en route to Perth depot. © RCAHMS

On guard: an infantry grenadier of Napoleon's Imperial Guard. Courtesy of Réunion des Musées Nationaux (Musée de L'Armée de la Terre), Paris, Ref. 06-518108.

Two French infantry grenadiers of the Line. Courtesy of Réunion des Musées Nationaux (Musée de L'Armée de la Terre), Paris, Ref. 06-526465.

Two drummers of the French light infantry. Courtesy of Réunion des Musées Nationaux (Musée de L'Armée de la Terre), Paris, Ref. 06-524279.

A trooper of the French 1st Regiment of Dragoons. Courtesy of Réunion des Musées Nationaux (Musée de L'Armée de la Terre), Paris, Ref. 06-526396.

A French naval lieutenant. Courtesy of the Musée de la Marine, Paris, Ref. PH 2792.

A sergeant of a French battalion of seamen. Courtesy of the Musée de la Marine, Paris, Ref. PH 2829

Three French naval warrant officers: from left, a master, a quartermaster carpenter, and a quartermaster sailmaker. Courtesy of the Musée de la Marine, Paris, Ref. PH 14862. BN Estampes.

A Commercial Bank of Scotland one-pound banknote forged by prisoners of war at Greenlaw depot, dated 12 November 1810

Banknote forgers' equipment made from bones from their rations by prisoners of war at Penicuik. Courtesy of the Governor and Company of the Bank of Scotland.

A work box made from straw by prisoners of war at Perth depot in
1812–14. The illustration on the underside of the lid is of depot buildings.
© Reproduced by permission of Perth Museum & Art Gallery, Perth &
Kinross Council.

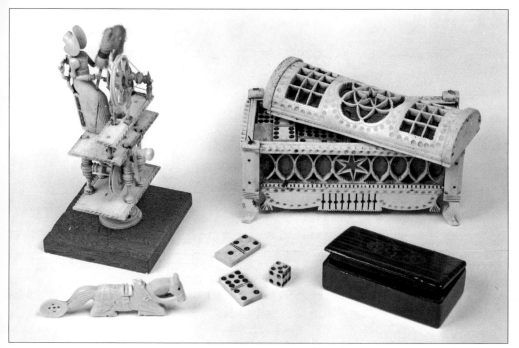

The highly skilled work by some of the prisoners of war in the Scots depots is illustrated by these items they made at Perth from bone or wood: the model of a woman seated at a spinning wheel, the box with dominoes, the snuff ladle (bottom left), and the wooden snuff box (bottom right). © Reproduced by permission of Perth Museum & Art Gallery, Perth & Kinross Council.

An oblong wooden box made by prisoners of war at Edinburgh Castle. Courtesy of National Museums of Scotland, Ref. Acc. No. H.UD.63.

A tobacco or snuff box made from bones by prisoners at Greenlaw depot. Courtesy of National Museums of Scotland, Ref. Acc. No. H.NQ.268.

Model of a barque, made from bones, with a straw-work base, by a prisoner of war at Greenlaw depot. Courtesy of National Museums of Scotland, Ref. Acc. T.1925.25.

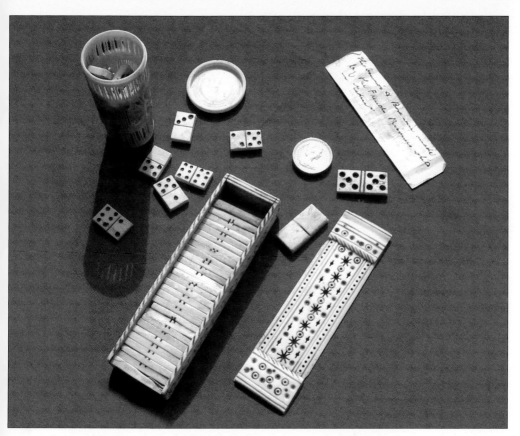

A box and a small tub, both containing dominoes and all made from bones, with a handwritten note in ink that they were the work of prisoners of war at Edinburgh. The present-day one-pound coin indicates the size of the items. Courtesy of private owner.

A comb, and a model of Napoleon, believed to have been made from bone by French prisoners of war. Courtesy of private owner.

A petite boite d'amitié or vanity case, made by prisoners of war at one of the Penicuik depots. Courtesy of National Museums of Scotland, Ref. Acc. No. M.1993.583.

The earliest known sketch of Penicuik, drawn in 1810 by Captain Paul Andreas Kaald, Norwegian prisoner at Greenlaw. At the centre rear of the sketch is St Mungo's parish church from the edge of whose churchyard about 1811–12 the boy William Chambers looked down on the prisoners at Valleyfield in the natural bowl behind the buildings to the right. Courtesy of Trondelag Folkemuseum, Trondheim, Norway.

Spain and Portugal during the Peninsular War, 1808–13.

The monument to the 300 or so prisoners of war who died at Valleyfield depot in 1811–14, and the slope behind it from the top of which the boy William Chambers watched the prisoners one Sunday. Houses were built in the 1990s on the site of the depot and paper mills.

of five. Monsieur Adam, as the instigator of the project and its architect, had acquired the right to go first. Our departure was due to begin at midnight, after the changing of the guard.

'When we were all back in the prison block and the doors were shut for the night, we lifted a stone and removed two bars to give us passage into the yard. During the day it had been excessively warm, but the sky had remained clear and it was only towards evening that some dark clouds appeared on the horizon.

'We got ourselves ready to set off. Each of us was well clothed and had pulled over his boots black stockings in order to make the least possible noise when walking. As for all those of my belongings that I could not take with me, I confided them to a man from Provence, a former quartermaster, who had been taken prisoner at Trafalgar. I begged him, in the event of the project proving abortive and our being recaptured, to send me them in the prison to which I would be taken. I added that if I succeeded in arriving in France and at the end of three months he received no news from me, then everything would belong to him.

'We had posted at the windows and beneath the roof look-outs who were to tell us the state of the weather and the precise timing of the changing of the guard. We emptied several bottles of rum in bidding our friends goodbye. I had met with all the men who came from Ostend and I had taken their messages and their letters and I promised to speak to their families about them.

'Once outside the prison we counted on finding ourselves in the first village on the route from Perth to Falkland. There we would procure coaches at whatever the price and leave for Montrose, where we would arrive the following evening. We planned to embark from that town if we found a vessel due to sail either that night or the day following. If that did not prove possible we proposed to seize a small vessel which had only a handful of crew, cut its cables under cover of darkness, overpower the sailors on board, and once we were out on the open sea and as there were fifteen of us get them to help us reach France or Holland.

'Those who had to leave in the first group with me were Messieurs Adam, the Chasseur lieutenant Petry, Leroi, a scholarly mathematician who had more than sixty pupils in the depot and had sacrificed everything for liberty, and finally his son aged 14, who had been a prisoner the same length of time as his father.

'We were not the only ones counting on benefiting from the tunnel. A large number of other prisoners donned their clothes and prepared to follow us. We had agreed to allow them to do so, on condition that they took the utmost care and only began to set off half an hour after our own last group had left.

'So that the English might not suspect our departure, we brought together all the musicians in our room. They began to play their instruments, and we to sing and dance, in order to create a great uproar. The sentry outside wasted no time in ordering the lights to be put out. We carried on for some time nonetheless, but as he then threatened to resort to force and we were afraid he might come into the room, we fell silent, speaking only quite softly so that we could not be heard outside, while impatiently awaiting the moment when the guard would be relieved.

'Meanwhile the clouds which had appeared on the horizon in the evening grew blacker and blacker and threatened a storm. A storm might have favoured our flight. The noise of the thunder might have prevented the sentinels hearing us. Heavy rain might have driven them back into their sentry boxes, and their look-out might not have been as sharp or easy as on a calm night. On the other hand, should we not fear the wind, the mud and the slushy holes in the road might slow our progress? Might not a flash of lightning, suddenly lighting up the area around the depot, reveal one of us in full daylight and give away the escape of all the others? Finally, would not our footprints be easy to follow, imprinted as they would be in the wet soft earth? All these thoughts made us even more fearful of the storm.

'But to us the sky paid no attention. About ten o'clock (we were due to leave at midnight), thunder was heard, muffled at first then loud, and the rain fell with extraordinary violence. The wind rose and it blew in such terrible gusts that the whole prison shook. This dreadful weather caused us some frustration but it did not cause us to abandon our project: after all it could have its advantages, too.

'We heard at intervals through the noise of the storm the cries of the sentries as they called to each other, "All's well!", and they moved further and further away.

'An hour and a half passed. The moment for our flight neared. We were all prepared! Then suddenly the alarm burst forth. The general summons to arms was beaten. The whole depot came to life. Several musket shots were heard. Instinctively, we realised that all was lost. Automatically we took our clothes off and climbed into our hammocks.

'For ten minutes we waited, our hearts wrung with anguish and terrible uncertainty. Alas! We were not mistaken! All really was lost! The work into which had been put the most courageous and unwearying patience, the work to which we had devoted all our resources, was blown to the sky. An inexplicable fate had laid everything bare. All our hopes had vanished at one blow. The turnkeys, accompanied by soldiers, burst into our barracks. They pulled off the covers from all the hammocks, but they didn't find a single prisoner with his clothes on. They did discover the two broken bars and the stones raised from the wall. But each prisoner expressed his astonishment at these, and accused all his fellow prisoners while protesting his own innocence. So, despite all the enquiries the English made, they never learned who were the authors of the attempted escape.

'Here is how all our precautions had been rendered vain by a wretched chance. At all hours of the night a picket of 25 soldiers made the rounds of the outside of the depot walls in order to see if all the sentries were at their posts and that there was no cause for concern. That procedure we knew about, so we had taken care to make the opening of the exit from the tunnel very small and to plan everything so that the hole was concealed by the oats in the field at the point where it was made. It really was impossible to spot it. But the storm had made the ground waterlogged, so much so that when the patrol had arrived opposite our prison block the soil had suddenly caved in, and the sergeant who was in charge of the patrol just as suddenly disappeared underground along with the lantern he was carrying. Great was the fright suffered by the patrol, who did not at first grasp what had befallen its leader. But the alarm was immediately given by the sentry. The sergeant, who had fallen to the bottom of the underground passageway, uttered loud wails and begged for help. None of the patrol, however, was brave enough to venture down there beside him, fearful of finding a sizeable number of prisoners who might do a rescuer injury. However, when they saw no one emerging from the hole and that the unfortunate sergeant's continual bellowing proved he was still alive, the English assumed the escape had already taken place. Some then began to help their sergeant while others hastily beat up the surrounding area and fired at random into the fields of oats that surrounded the depot. Of course, they found no one. They soon stopped their searches outside and went instead inside the depot to look for those who were the guilty ones. But there they had no greater luck and were unable to find any. The sentry reported how we had sung and made music for part of the evening and that there had been no sign of a general plot to escape.

'The deputy commandant [i.e., chief clerk] Johnston, who had immediately got out of bed, had us all driven out into the yard, although the rain fell still in torrents. We were counted one by one to make sure none of us had escaped. Then we were sent back into the prison. Johnston told us coldly that we would pay dearly for our attempt.

'The next day the bell rang and we were told that the damage having been estimated at £96, the ration [of food] would not be distributed to the prisoners until that deficit was made good. But our gaolers mellowed and reduced the penalty to a half ration. This measure having been applied not to us [in our block] particularly but to everyone … shut up at Perth, there were recriminations and a general uprising of all those poor devils who saw themselves forced to go without food [because of those of us who had tried to escape]. To calm down this anger we chose four ambassadors whom we made responsible for pleading our cause in all the prison rooms or blocks. These ambassadors asked the other prisoners if they had been in our place would they not have attempted what we had. They argued that the punishment would not be inflicted on everyone for long, whereas we, their brothers, would suffer ten times longer if we had to bear the punishment alone. At length the ambassadors did so well that in the twenty rooms the number of those who approved our action and out of a sense of goodwill toward us agreed to being deprived of half their ration, was very much larger than those who blamed us and refused to help us. The half ration lasted for two days, then our life resumed its normal course.

'The failure of our plan for escape that had been so long in preparation, so carefully arranged, left us in a state of despair. My own resources were almost entirely exhausted. I fell into a dismal state of apathy and made up my mind to put up with captivity as long as it pleased God to make it last, for He seemed to have decided that the day of liberty would never dawn for me.'[20]

If Marote-Carrier and his associates felt, at least for the time being, so despondent their despondency was not shared by other prisoners at Perth. 'On Friday evening,' the *Perth Courier* informed its readers on 30 September, a fortnight or so after the attempt described by Marote-Carrier, 'a mine was discoverd at the Depot. It was begun, as usual, from the necessary, but in a corner most remote from the sewer, which it was carried in a circuitous direction to meet. The aperture had been carefully covered up at every interval of working. While some of the prisoners were thus employed others kept crowding, on pretence of amusing themselves, round the place so as to interrupt the view of it from the sentries. A person, however, unknown to the prisoners had been appointed to watch in a turret with a loop-hole, and he observed a number of them successively bringing buckets of earth to the well, where they pumped water upon their contents till the earth and water flowed away together by the sewer. Intimation of this circumstance being given, a search was made and the excavation discovered.' Neither the number of prisoners involved nor any other aspect of it has been found about this attempted escape.

The last recorded attempt at what appears to have been a mass escape from Perth depot was reported in the *Perth Courier* on 7 October 1813, two days after its discovery. 'On Tuesday, one of the sentries at the depot, having observed the prisoners carrying buckets of earth from No. 6 [block], made an immediate intimation to the captain of the guard, who on searching the prison found about 30 cart loads of earth heaped up in the two ends of the cock-loft immediately under the roof. This had no doubt been collected from the excavations made by the prisoners, and must have been deposited there since the time when these were detected. Considering the constant vigilance which the impatient activity of the prisoners has rendered necessary, we are surprised that the discovery should not have been made at an earlier period, and that it should have been occasioned at last by the fears of the prisoners themselves lest the earth, when swelled with the damp admitted through the ventilators, might burst the roof of the apartment and endanger their lives.' There are ambiguities in the *Courier*'s report, but again no further clarification of this attempted escape has been found in any other source.

If these actual or attempted mass escapes from the Scots depots involved almost always some or much planning and preparatory work, on the other hand some other escapes by individual or small groups of prisoners were, or (given the general lack of surviving detailed evidence) at least appear to have been, spontaneous seizures of some unforeseen opportunity. Even apparent spontaneity in these cases, however, was no doubt founded on a fundamental and possibly long-harboured determination to escape as soon as some such unforeseen opportunity might present itself. Did one present itself, for example, to Joseph Gascourin, a seaman who had been captured in August 1803 on the merchant ship *La Flore* in the North Sea? One among the earliest escapers from any Scots depot, Gascourin departed from the Edinburgh bridewell on the afternoon of 4 March 1804 'by leaping the wall'.[21] Whether a similar leap by an unnamed prisoner at Perth in November 1812 was the result of a sudden decision in favour of freedom is not certain either. 'Yesterday,' the *Perth Courier* reported on 5 November, 'one of the prisoners made his escape from the Depot by leaping over the wall of his own gaol into the area of the one adjacent, which is yet unoccupied. He marched past the sentinels unsuspected, but the alarm being immediately given he had not gone far beyond the outer gate when he was seized and brought back to his old quarters.' Was likewise the escape in December 1810 of Joseph Gascourin's shipmate Felix Guigougeux, a prisoner at Greenlaw, simply opportunistic? Guigougeux, a merchant seaman captured also on *La Flore* in August 1803, was one of those prisoners permitted under the idosyncratic administration of Malcolm Wright as agent at Greenlaw to make visits outside the depot to local families. On Good Friday, 20 April 1810, when Captain Paul Andreas Kaald, a similarly privileged prisoner at Greenlaw, was about to dine at the home nearby of the then owner of Esk Mills, Mr John White, and his wife, son and daughters, 'Mr Guigougeux, a French prisoner, came in giving the girls information in French.' Evidently even by then a familiar visitor to the Whites, Guigougeux clearly must have continued to be welcome there, for on Christmas Eve that year, accompanied by Francis Wharton, depot clerk at Greenlaw, he went 'to drink tea at the White's'. Whether the Whites' tea proved decisively stimulating can only be speculated upon, but the outcome of his visit was that Guigougeux took himself off from the Whites' house and was never again seen at Greenlaw.[22]

What may also have been a spontaneous and sudden decision to seize an unforeseen opportunity of escape was that taken at Greenlaw in 1809 by Captain Paul Andreas Kaald's privateer shipmate and friend Captain Sigismund Richelieu. On Saturday 9 September that year, as Kaald noted in his diary, 'About 4 o'clock in the afternoon a wagon came to the prison loaded with pit coal. My friend Richelieu was sitting in our room speaking to me when he went down and came back 5 minutes later in a great hurry, saying 'Here is the opportunity. I must leave.' Kaald and his colleague Captain Locke at once cleared out a heavy chest in their room and put Richelieu in it along with some of his clothes. Kaald then dragged the chest from their room out into the corridor, where two men carried it down to the wagon, whose load of coal had meantime been unloaded, and placed the chest aboard it. Ross, one of the depot turnkeys, appeared and enquired about the chest and its destination but showed no suspicion of what was afoot. The wagon then drove off with the chest, the lid of which was fixed in such a way as to appear from the outside to be locked but it could be opened whenever necessary by Richelieu from inside. Kaald and Locke celebrated Richelieu's undiscovered departure with '2 bottles of warm beer with sugar and butter added'. The expected hazard at the counting of the prisoners that evening did not arise as the count was for some reason cancelled. Even when it was taken the following day at midday and again in the afternoon the total appeared to be correct: Richelieu's absence was concealed on both occasions by a boy prisoner who agreed to creep unnoticed in and out of a window in order to be counted twice over. It was only two days later, on 11 September, that the guard, after three recounts, found that one prisoner was definitely missing. 'The officers and the turnkeys went crazy,' Kaald noted in his diary, 'and threatened to put the missing prisoner in the black hole for a whole month—if they found him.' The depot clerk came and took a roll-call count and it was only then that Richelieu's absence was discovered. For several days afterward there were rumours and counter-rumours of Richelieu's escape from Leith or of his recapture. On 19 and 21 October, however, Kaald received letters from Captain Richelieu from Gothenburg, where he had arrived safely less than a fortnight after his departure in the chest from Greenlaw.[23]

There were several other escapes from the Scots depots where the degree of spontaneity or opportunism may have exceeded that of any longer term planning or preparation. That may have been so, for instance, at Greenlaw in June 1811 when two unnamed prisoners in what was an ostensibly unique case escaped from the depot hospital. If the two escapers were already in the hospital as genuine patients, and were neither prisoners working as nurses there nor escapers from the main prison block who had merely crept or run through the hospital and out to freedom, then their case was indeed unique in depots north of the Border. Yet again, however, no further information about this escape, which took place before a palisade or stockade had been built around the hospital, has been found.[24] Was it their prompt recognition of an opportunity rather than any considered planning which enabled three prisoners—Louis Petitchamp (an alias—his real name was Adrien Victor Tavernier), aged 29, born at St Omer, an ensign captured with Lieutenant Marote-Carrier on the privateer *L'Aventurier* in the English Channel in December 1810, Ferdinand Lambert, a merchant seaman, aged 24, born at St Valery, captured on the *Beaupère* as early in the war as June 1803, and François Petit, privateersman (about whom more will be said in the next chapter)—all to escape on 3 January 1812 from Valleyfield 'through the Gate while the Turnkeys were inside counting'? [25]

Through, over, under: these three prepositions describe how prisoners might hope to escape from the Scots, or indeed other, depots. Through the gate, as at Valleyfield Louis Petitchamp, Ferdinand Lambert, François Petit and Guillaume Mariote somehow succeeded in passing, or through it and the wall, as a few other escapers equipped with some kind of cutting tool undertook to pass; over the wall, as at the Edinburgh bridewell Joseph Gascourin in 1804 had leapt, and others might pass by means of ropes or ladders or simply scaling; under the wall, as so many of the mass escapers or attempted mass escapers tunnelled. Those classic means of exit from captivity are not comprehensively itemised for the Scots depots in any surviving official record. One that involved the use of a ladder, the provenance of which is unexplained, was recorded, however, as having taken place at Perth in 1813 'On the night betwixt Wednesday and Thursday [2-3 June, when] three French prisoners made their escape from the depot ... by breaking the iron bars from the window of their prison and afterwards making their way over the wall by means of a scaling ladder. One of the runaways was known by the name of Captain Massy. He is a genteel looking man and speaks very good English.'[26]

The Valleyfield Entry Books in particular provide examples of prisoners' departures through, over and under. Two privateer seamen and a soldier, for instance—Pierre François Laurent, aged 21 and born at Rouen, who had been captured on *L'Heureuse Etoile* in the English Channel in 1809, Louis Moreau, aged 18, from Besancourt, captured in 1810 in the Channel on *Le Vengeur*, and Louis François Bouillard, a soldier (or a seaman), aged 27, born at Rouen, and captured in 1811 off the coast of France—all escaped from that depot on 8 September 1812 'by water run East Yard'. Louis Casteur, a seaman, aged 20 from Dunkirk, captured in 1807 on the privateer *Le Décidé* in the North Sea, on 12 September 1811 did so 'by stockade'. Matu Bronzan, alias Baptiste Hidgy, seaman, on 12 February 1812 got away, as already observed, 'over stockade'. No fewer than six prisoners—Yves Joseph Robin, seaman, aged 33, born at Cherbourg, captured on the privateer *Vengeur* in 1810 in

497

the English Channel, Louis Macqueron, seaman, aged 23 and also born at Cherbourg, captured in the Channel in February 1810 on the privateer *La Modeste*, Antonio Moreno, aged 32, born at New Orleans, captured, date and place unstated, on the naval vessel *Golette*, a soldier, Louis Ameline, aged 37, born in New Orleans also, who had been captured in 1810 on the troopship *L'Aimable Nelly*, Jacques Le Prieur, a seaman, aged 30, captured also on *Vengeur*, and Joseph Ernel, surgeon, aged 27, born at Pasque, captured also on *La Modeste*—all on 24 August 1811 got out 'by contractor's store room'. Jan Van Den Hewal, a privateer seaman from Oldenburg, on 19 September 1811, as already observed, took himself off 'by North Necessary', and Pierre Duran, a merchant seaman aged 35, from Granville, captured in 1809 on the *Lunon*, on 17 October 1811 'by the necessary'. Constant Yvert, a passenger captured within a few days of the beginning of the war in 1803 on a merchant vessel, nine years later on 10 July 1812 found his way out by 'Market Gate'.[27]

If cutting through palisades, gates or doors is not mentioned specifically in reports of escapes from Valleyfield (except in the case of the second attempted mass escape there in September 1812, and except also for the possibly relevant comment by Andrew Johnston, clerk there, that in the early weeks of the depot 'Dayly complaints were made by the workpeople of their tools being stolen'), Esk Mills or Perth, it is mentioned in the case of a couple from Greenlaw and Edinburgh Castle. From Greenlaw on the night of 4 November 1811, two seamen, Joseph Rafey, aged 37 and born at St Andero, captured in 1809 on the privateer *Jesus Maria*, and Henry Carrier, aged 24 and born at Nantes, captured on the frigate *Minerve* off Rochefort in 1806, escaped 'by cutting one of the palisades.' Four months earlier, on 15 July, Jean Raymot, purser's clerk, aged 21, who like Henry Carrier at Greenlaw had been captured on the *Minerve*, escaped from the Castle having 'Cut through the prison door.'[28]

That Constant Yvert, one of the very few civilians to escape from any Scots depot, did so from Valleyfield by 'Market Gate' is a reminder, if any is needed, that some prisoners regarded the depot markets themselves as occasions on which might be gathered scraps of information, as well as money from their goods sold, that could prove useful to them in possible escapes. The market days themselves might even present opportunities for escape. At Valleyfield, according to Abell, apparently quoting from notes made by Macbeth Forbes, who, however, does not give his sources, 'It was at the daily market when the country people were brought into acquaintance with the prisoners, that many attempts to escape were made, despite the doubling of the guards.'[29]

But the role of markets in escapes or attempted escapes is much more evident at Perth. 'When the noise of the market was most likely to prevent their being heard,' five prisoners 'were caught at work, with pretty good mason tools, about 11 o'clock forenoon,' digging a tunnel on Christmas Day, 1812.[30] Four months later the depot market was the occasion for an attempted escape, which was also one of several in which clothing was employed as a disguise: 'Yesterday,' the *Perth Courier* reported on 29 April 1813, 'three of the prisoners at the Depot found their way by means of false keys to an empty cellar under the tower. They had with them suits of black with crapes [sic] for their hats, in which they intended to have dressed themselves, over their prison jackets, and to have walked out with the crowd at the hour of market. They were discovered, however, by a person who had gone into their place of concealment to examine the water pipes. Had they escaped discovery two more were to have joined them.' A similar attempt was made just over a month later when 'Three more very well dressed fellows attempted to escape on Thursday morning [3 June] by passing through the gate in the throng of the market, but the turnkey observed and stopped them. One of them wore a pair of neat false whiskers, in imitation no doubt of certain leaders of the English *haut ton*.'[31] It seems hardly surprising after these successive attempts by escapers to use the market as a screen for their departures that 'On Tuesday [6 July] the usual traffic at the Depot was prohibited and no admittance allowed to the public. This, we understand, was owing to an apprehension of a design on the part of some of the prisoners to effect their escape by mixing with the multitude of people who were expected for the mid-summer market.'[32] After the mass and attempted mass escapes from Perth in mid-September 1813 there were demands in the press for an example 'of intimidatng harshness—a stop to all communication between the prisoners and the public', and it was complained that the prisoners had been too leniently treated in having had the market closed in July for only one day.[33]

Not every escape through the gates was made on foot. Captain Sigismund Richelieu's departure on wheels from Greenlaw in September 1809 hidden inside a heavy chest which was trundled out through the gates on the back of a coal cart had a few later parallels or attempted parallels, even if most of these appear to have been distinctly malodorous. 'A remarkable thing happened today,' Captain Paul Andreas Kaald noted on 10 July 1810 in his diary at Greenlaw. 'A farmer who drives topsoil and dirt out of the prison came to load his cart today. But one of the prisoners by the name of Johannes Lauser took the farmer with him into the prison and showed him around all the rooms. Meanwhile a prisoner named John Muth crept into the cart and two or three prisoners filled it full of topsoil and dirt. When the farmer came out he was extremely pleased at the prisoners' helpfulness and thanked them a lot. He then drove out of the prison without noticing that there was something brewing. To our great surprise the cart was stopped outside the gate, however. What had happened was that when a soldier on guard came near the cart he saw the topsoil move. As there was a spade and a fork lying on top of the load, the guard and the farmer took these tools and dug into the soil, whereupon the body buried under it immediately popped his head up in the air. The guard and the farmer got a great shock, took a step back and cried out: "Oh, Lord! What is this?" Muth and the farmer were both placed in the black hole over in the guard house.'[34] The nature of the 'dirt' Kaald mentioned, as distinct from the topsoil, is not specified, but in what at least appears to have been an attempted escape by similar means from Esk Mills noted by Andrew Johnston, depot clerk there, its nature was clear enough: '4 March [1811, was] sent to the cachot for 10 days on two-thirds allowance [of food] a prisoner [unnamed] for concealing himself behind the necessary cart at lock-up time.'[35] Whether a bare reference to a reward being paid at Valleyfield in May 1811 'to the driver of the soil cart for the recapture of the [unnamed] prisoners' betokened a similar attempted escape there that month is not certain.[36] But an attempt two years later in July 1813 by three prisoners to escape from Valleyfield by cart makes clear that the cart on this occasion was indeed the one which removed from the depot latrines what was euphemistically described as 'the soil' or 'night soil' which was then spread on the fields as manure.

Yet another escape by cart at Penicuik—though whether Valleyfield or Greenlaw is unstated—was described by Macbeth Forbes, but without providing either his sources or much detail: 'One countryman who did business with [the prisoners] hid a Frenchman in his cart among the straw and got him safely to Leith from whence he escaped to France.'[37] The Penicuik local historian J.L. Black, however, asserted, although without providing any date, that it was from Valleyfield that an attempted escape by cart ended in death: '… the prisoner had made arrangements with the carter who came every morning to remove the rubbish. He was to get into the cart, be covered up with the refuse, and lie still till they got to the field up the Bog Road. He was then to get up and run for the brushwood at "Lowrie's Den". All went well and they got out the gate in safety, up Bridge Street … and half-way along West Street. But here they met another cart driven by a friend who hailed his neighbour with a loud "Hullo! Whaur are ye gaun?" The prisoner, taking this for the signal, jumped out. The sentry-box was right opposite, and in the excitement the sentry fired and shot the prisoner dead. This caused a great sensation, the people blaming the military for not trying to secure the man without bloodshed.' It is possible, even probable, although evidence is absent from the depot Entry Book about the precise place and other details of his death, that this shooting was of the Valleyfield prisoner Pierre Chuchere, alias Jean David Dominique Jance, a seaman, aged 21, born at St Ouve, who under his first name had been captured both in October 1810 on the privateer *Somnambule* in the English Channel, and also, no place and no date given, under his alias on the privateer *Grand Napoléon*. On 24 May 1813 Chuchere was 'Shott [sic] Attempting to Escape'.[38]

A vehicle much less mundane than a cart, and in the mind of whose designer there was also perhaps some notion of its further development for use in an escape, appeared from among the prisoners at Perth on the occasion in August 1813 of their celebration of the birthday of Napoleon. It was a balloon. There is no certainty, of course, that thought of escape had entered the head of the prisoner who had designed and constructed the balloon. But he happened to be that 'meritorious young gentleman of Ghent' (as the *Perth Courier* described him in its reports of the celebration), Monsieur De Cuyper or De Kuyper. He has already been encountered as a leading figure in the projected shipboard rising on the vessel bringing Marote-Carrier and other prisoners to Esk Mills in February 1811. It is pure conjecture that this birthday balloon devised by De Cuyper might have been intended at least as a *ballon d'essai*, which, all going well and perhaps granted also a very large if unlikely measure of naivety on the part of the depot authorities, might have become the prototype for a later attempt at escape from Perth depot by air. The balloon's first public appearance did not, however, prove a stunning success; nor of course was there any opportunity to correct its faults and perfect its ascent before Napoleon's next birthday, by which time the Emperor had become an exile on Elba and all the prisoners at Perth, as at other depots, had been repatriated. But as the *Perth Courier* reported on 19 August 1813, 'About three in the afternoon a numerous crowd of people assembled in the South Inch to see the balloon ascend but were disappointed by an unlucky accident. The balloon, which was large and elegant ... after its inflation by air, which had been rarified by straw burnt underneath it, Monsieur De Cuyper having stepped aside to prepare the car, flags and other ornaments, its ascending force became so powerful from a hasty increase of the fire with a view to preserve its upright position against the force of the wind, that it burst the strings which fastened it to the hoop, and rising without ballast for giving it steadiness, or the necessary apparatus for continuing the rarification of the air, it soon descended and was torn against a tree. We regretted this accident,' the *Courier* continued, 'both on our own account, as we saw that the ascent of the balloon would have otherwise been extremely splendid, and on account of its ingenious artist, whose acquaintance we have the pleasure to boast, as without any error of his own he was disappointed in the result of his labour, after repeated and uniform success in similar experiments.'

If there had indeed been any successful attempt to develop the balloon as a vehicle of escape it would no doubt have inflated the anger of critics concerned by the apparent frequency of escapes from the depot. No escape by balloon ever did take place from Perth, but even as so many eyes were raised skyward to watch the ascent of De Cuyper's balloon on Napoleon's birthday, other prisoners, almost under the feet of the balloon watchers, were hard at work digging the tunnel from which issued forth 23 escapers ten days later.[39]

If balloons then bore no captives aloft to freedom, but exits, or attempted exits, on several occasions were undertaken by concealment in a cart the latter was nonetheless probably less frequent a means than exit greased by bribery, or attempted bribery, of the guards or sentries. Cases of bribery or alleged bribery at Edinburgh Castle, Valleyfield and Perth of which reports or recollections survive have already been discussed in an earlier chapter above.[40] In the nature of such transactions it is likely that more were broached or completed at the Scots depots between escapers and sentries than were ever recorded or reported.

Although there were a few thefts of boats from harbours or shores and no doubt more than a few thefts of turnips or other vegetables growing in fields en route, cases of violence or other offences committed by escapers either in the course of actually departing from the Scots depots or after they had set foot on the road to freedom beyond the walls or gates, appear to have been very rare. The earliest occasion found on which at least a show of violence was offered was in March 1804 when two escapers from the Edinburgh bridewell were recognised and stopped near Glasgow by a soldier in the Argyll militia, who had served as a guard at the bridewell. The two made 'a shew of resistance with their sticks', but when the militiaman drew his bayonet they gave themselves up to him without further ado.[41] The second attempted mass escape from Valleyfield, which appears to have taken place on or about 19 or 20 September 1812, seems to have been marked, as has been observed above, by the possession of 'short dirks' by all eight of those prisoners acting as leaders, and that fact persuaded the depot agent that if the attempt had succeeded 'many lives would have been lost.'[42]

It was, as already observed, at Valleyfield, too, in July 1813 that the case occurred, uniquely serious at any Scots depot, of the use of violence by a prisoner while attempting to escape. It was six days after the attempted escape on 16 July that the *Caledonian Mercury* and the *Edinburgh Evening Courant* both reported it; and that even *The Times* also did so, although not until a fortnight after the event, illustrated the significance of the violence used. The stabbing of a soldier by one of the three escapers, Jean Baptiste Destrais, alias Pierre Calmain, might well have resulted, if the stabbing had proved fatal, in Destrais becoming the only prisoner of war in Scotland during the Napoleonic Wars to be convicted of murder, and hanged.[43] Destrais and his two fellow attempted escapers were not entered as such in the depot Entry Book, and the identities of the other two have not been established.[44]

After the strong expressions of concern by the Perthshire landowners at the beginning of October 1813 about escapes from Perth depot, the sending a few days later by Major-General Graham of 1,500 troops of the garrison into the depot and their searching of all the prisoners and all the prison blocks for offensive weapons nonetheless resulted in the discovery of 'no offensive weapons or anything of much consequence.'[45]

Apart from Destrais' stabbing of the soldier at Valleyfield, only two other reported cases of violence, threatened but not actually perpetrated, by escapers have been found. One took place near Arbroath on 4 September 1813, and was reported in the *Dundee Advertiser* six days later, thus: 'Four of the French prisoners who lately escaped from the Perth depot were discovered on Saturday last within a mile of Arbroath by a seaman belonging to the custom house yacht stationed there. He, with the aid of some labourers who were at a little distance, attempted to apprehend them; upon which they drew their knives and threatened to stab anyone who should lay hold of them. But on the arrival of a recruiting party and other assistance, the Frenchmen submitted.' The second case occurred at Peterhead on 1 October that same year, when three prisoners who had escaped the previous month from Perth were discovered by Aberdeen militiamen 'in a petty public house near the north end of the town, and at first they endeavoured to resist ...'[46]

Allegations or suppositions, however, were made that the perpetrators of the robberies in 1813 of two civilians, one near Perth, the other in Lanarkshire, were escaped French prisoners of war. According to the *Edinburgh Evening Courant* of 28 January that year, 'John Taylor, a mason at the Depot at Perth, on his way from Newburgh to Perth, was stopt [sic] by three men about 9 o'clock on Monday night [25 January] at the Cots of Fenzies [near Rhynd, four miles south-east of Perth] and robbed of £1.18.6d., being all the money he had upon him. One of the men wore a corduroy jacket, the other two dark coloured coats, and had the appearance of farm servants.' Abell, however, concluded that 'it seems quite likely' the three robbers were in fact escapers that day from the depot. The second robbery, an armed one marked by violence upon the victim, took place in December and was reported almost a fortnight after the event by the *Glasgow Courier*. 'On Monday 6th instant, about 8 o'clock at night, as Mr Buchanan, horse dealer, Douglas, was returning from Kirk o' Shotts market he was attacked on the road near to Mr Meek's of Fortesset by two tall men dressed in blue great coats and armed with pistols. He instantly laid hold of the one nearest to him and threw him on the ground, when he called on his companion to fire at Buchanan, which he did not do, but struck him several blows on the head with the butt end of the pistol, which for a short time rendered Buchanan insensible. During this period they dragged him to some distance from the road and robbed him of two one-pound notes and eight shillings in silver. As it was clear moonlight at the time he had a distinct view of their persons, from which and their manner of speaking he supposed them to be two of the French prisoners who lately escaped from Edinburgh Castle.'[47] The three actual escapers from

Perth appear to have been successful in reaching the continent. If the two armed robbers in Lanarkshire were indeed also escapers, and if they were recaptured, their identities have not been established nor was any prosecution for robbery, armed or otherwise, brought against any recaptured escapers from Edinburgh Castle.

If the use or even threat of violence by escapers from the Scots depots appears to have been so rare, on the other hand escapers themselves might obviously become victims of its use against them by sentries, pursuers, local inhabitants, or others. Every escaper ran a risk of being shot or bayoneted by sentries as he passed, or attempted to pass, through, over or under the gates, palisades or walls. There was an equally obvious risk from pursuers even after exit had been achieved from the depot itself. There was likewise risk of injury or death from the collapse of a tunnel, a fall from the walls (or down the Castle rock at Edinburgh), or perhaps from drowning (as in the case of the escaper rescued by a sloop's boat from the Tay at Perth after the mass escape on 24 August 1813).[48] Even after all the hazards to life and limb that might present themselves during both the first phase—escape from the depot itself, and the second phase—the journey to whichever coast or harbour, near or far, where embarkation on some boat or ship might be achieved, there remained those of the third phase—crossing the sea or Channel before at last landing safely on the continent itself.

At Greenlaw, as the *Edinburgh Evening Courant* reported three days later on 18 May 1809, '… a Dane attempting to make his escape … was shot by the centinel [sic] on duty.' Captain Paul Andreas Kaald, who as a Norwegian himself presumably knew best, noted in his diary that day that the escaper had in fact been a Prussian. Kaald's account of this escape has already been noted.[49] It was probably the escape of which the local Penicuik historian J.L. Black said he had been told by an eye-witness whose '… father was ploughing in the field below Maybank Farm in full view of [Greenlaw House], and the boy was sent out with his father's breakfast. As the farmer sat on the stults of the plough supping his porridge, with the boy standing by his side, they saw a big stir going on … soldiers running and spreading themselves out and carrying their rifles. They then caught sight of a man running down the dykeside and crouching as he ran. His aim appeared to be to cross the Esk and get into shelter amongst the bushes, but before he got over he was seen and a volley was fired, and they saw him fall as he touched the other side.' In his manuscript notes on the shooting Black wrote that 'The poor fellow had hidden in some bushes but had incautiously got up to see if the coast was clear. Finding the soldiers close at hand he took to his heels, and was shot down.' Black also mentioned another escape, although without giving it a date, which ended in death at Greenlaw: 'For many years a tree near Pathhead House was known as "the prisoner's tree" from the circumstance that a prisoner, in attempting to escape, had taken shelter in the branches ... and was shot there.'[50] As already noticed, Andrew Johnston, depot clerk successively at Esk Mills, Valleyfield and Perth, claimed in his recollections that in a mass escape by 30 prisoners from Greenlaw in June 1810 three were severely wounded, one by a bayonet, the other two shot respectively in the thigh and hip; but happily all three recovered.[51]

At Esk Mills, Edinburgh Castle and Valleyfield there were also, as has already been seen, fatalities among escapers. At Esk Mills the privateer Lieutenant Nicolas (or Henri) Boulet (or Boulais), who was Marote-Carrier's 'tea captain', was shot dead by a sentry on 19 February 1811 during the mass escape. At the Castle the midshipman Pierre Woemeseuil or Wormeseul died on 14 April 1811 from a fractured spine suffered in a fall down the Castle rock while escaping in the mass break-out of prisoners two days earlier.[52] At Valleyfield Pierre Chuchere was shot on 24 May 1813 during his attempted escape. Perth and, during its use for a few months in 1803-4, the Edinburgh bridewell appear to have been the only Scots depots where no prisoners at all were killed during escapes.

As for non-fatal wounds or injuries suffered by escapers, the few references to these which have been found would no doubt have to be multiplied several times to create a more accurate tally of the number of broken bones, torn ligaments, twisted ankles, badly cut feet or legs, gunshot or bayonet wounds, etc., suffered in clambering over depot walls, creeping through tunnels, descending the towering rock at Edinburgh Castle, or fleeing from sentries, not to speak of other mishaps that befell escapers en route between depot and coast or harbour. One of the few reports found of injuries or wounds thus suffered appeared in the *Montrose Review* following the recapture on 22 April 1811 in the wood of Charleton near Montrose of five of the escapers in the mass break-out from Edinburgh Castle ten days earlier. One of the five, the paper reported, '... has suffered much from the bruises he sustained in dropping from Edinburgh Castle, having been the next in succession on the rope to the unfortunate man [Pierre Woemeseuil] who was killed in the attempt to escape.'[53] It will be recalled that at Perth, in the melee arising on 12 September 1813 when the guard, fearful that a mass escape was about to take place, rushed into the airing ground at No. 3 prison, seized 24 prisoners and drove the others back indoors, three prisoners wounded in the tumult had to be 'immediately conveyed to the hospital'.[54] Deschamps [or Dujardin?] leader of or scout for the 30 escapers who broke out from Valleyfield on 19 November 1813, had (according to William Chambers's recollection of what appears to have been that event), south of Penicuik, somewhere between Auchencorth Moss and Eddleston Water, '...slipped down a rocky bank, and lacerated one of his legs so badly that he was scarcely able to walk.'[55]

If escapers' difficulties in getting out of the depots were even in the early years of the war numerous, substantial and dangerous enough, they were compounded as the war continued by the addition of such other preventative measures as the placing of lamps on the walls or at the gates, collective punishment of all prisoners in some cases of escape or attempted escape, daily inspections of the prison blocks in search of any signs of tunnelling, and an increase in the number or strength of bars across doors and windows. In August-September 1809, for instance, after an attempted escape at Greenlaw, the Transport Board approved 'some additional lamps to be placed' at the depot, as well as approving the agent's having put '367 of the Prisoners in your Custody on Short Allowance for five days, to make good the expence attending the damage done ...' There, too, in May 1810, according to the diarist Captain Paul Andreas Kaald, after the discovery of a tunnel being dug by prisoners, 'Mr Wharton [depot clerk] ordered that all pit coal, water barrels and stones that were in the rooms should be carried out into the courtyard ... [and he] searched all the rooms very thoroughly.' Similarly at Perth in October 1813 the Transport Board ordered the agent to report 'how the prisons are inspected daily to discover any attempt at mining, etc.' On at least two occasions within the year 1811-12 iron bars were placed on doors and windows further to deter escapes from Greenlaw. As late as September 1813 the agent at Perth was instructed by the Transport Board that 'It having been recommended by Lieutenant General Wynyard and Major General Graham that Government should purchase a certain space of ground round the depot ... in order to guard against the future attempts of prisoners to escape, we direct you to enquire and report how much ground would be required for this purpose and at what price it can be procured.' The agent duly reported it would be both undesirable and 'impossible' to carry out the generals' recommendation, and suggested instead the building of an additional guardhouse—but his suggestion seems not to have been acted upon. The agent, who had also suggested within a month of the opening of the depot in August 1812 that its deterrents against possible escapes should include chevaux de frise, was asked by the Transport Board in February 1813 to provide an estimate of the cost of constructing wooden ones, but no other information on this aspect has been found.[56]

The hazards that could confront escapers from the Scots depots during what might be termed the middle passage—from the depot to the coast or harbour of proposed embarkation—were hardly less numerous or formidable. Maps, for example, were obviously very desirable for escapers to possess, especially if their middle passage to the coast or harbour where they might find a boat was intended to be less familiar or more lengthy than, say, from any of the Penicuik depots to Leith, or from Perth to Dundee, Kirkcaldy or Burntisland. Very few references indeed have been found, however, to escapers' possession of maps. If, as its historian reported, prisoners at Norman Cross depot at Huntingdonshire were said to make 'Maps of England showing the best lines of escape ... [which] sold at twenty francs each', no sign of any such impressive provision has been found for escapers from any depot in Scotland.[57] Indeed the only reference found to any escapers from the latter having maps was contained in a press report concerning one group of ten or so from among the 49 who escaped in the mass break-out on 12 April 1811 from Edinburgh Castle: 'They had procured information of the nearest place of embarkation, and being furnished with maps and that part of the almanack containing the principal roads through the country, they bent their way to Grangemouth, where they were to have gone on board some foreign vessels lying there.'[58] It may be that, as the absence of any other evidence to the contrary may suggest, most escapers had to make do (as William Chambers said Deschamps [or Dujardin?], a leader of what appears to have been the mass break-out from Valleyfield on 19 November 1813, had done) by gleaning information about roads and surrounding countryside from local inhabitants or others they might be able to overhear or discreetly question. No doubt depot markets could present some such opportunities to intending escapers. But where escapers had been able to obtain little or no information about roads or directions before setting out on the middle passage, their prospects of success were likely to be diminished. Moreover, as no reference to possession of compasses by escapers from any Scots depot has been found, it must be presumed that, either without any or with only inadequate maps or sketches of their route, their dependence on the sun and the stars for direction and progress must have been more frequent than not. Marote-Carrier and his fourteen intending fellow escapers by tunnel from Perth in mid-September 1813 appear to have been unique in resolving, once they reached Falkland in Fife, 'to procure coaches at whatever price, and to leave for Montrose' in search of a boat that would carry them to the continent.[59] At least for escapers from Greenlaw depot, drove roads played an important part in their flight—according to an article in a local newspaper a century later, which, however, provided no evidence for the assertion. On this aspect, as on several others concerning escapes from the Scots depots, there is a distinct lack of evidence.[60]

About the clothing worn by escapers some limited evidence has, however, survived. The 'two shirts of coarse linen waste, a pair of trousers, a shortened jacket, and a waistcoat, all coloured yellow so that the thing might be more extraordinary and that it might be easier to spot us in case of escape' with which Lieutenant Marote-Carrier and other prisoners at Perth, as at the other Scots depots, were issued were indeed hardly likely, if worn by escapers, to facilitate their successful getaway, even less so since these colourful garments bore, as Marote-Carrier put it, 'imprinted in oil [i.e., ink?], the two ritual letters TO [Transport Office].'[61] What the limited evidence indicates is that while some prisoners absconded still clothed in those conspicuously distinctive garments, others had apparently been able to obtain or retain some ordinary civilian clothing. Seamen particularly, so many of whom as merchantmen or privateersmen did not wear formal uniforms as soldiers did, were perhaps more likely to retain at least some of their own clothing and hence be less conspicuous en route to the coast or harbour in search of a boat. The first prisoner to escape from Perth depot, for example, little more than a month after its opening was Dominique Dewatre, a privateer lieutenant. According to the depot Entry Book Dewatre 'escaped over the wall'. The *Perth Courier*, on the other hand, reported on 10 September 1812, the day of his escape, that he had 'slipped past the turnkey in opening the door of the iron railing … The alarm was immediately given,' the *Courier* continued, 'but he had gained considerably on his pursuers and had reached the Friarton Toll. But finding himself closely pursued he turned into a field of wheat and, attempting to conceal himself, was soon discovered and reconducted to his former habitation. He was genteelly dressed in black and might have got forward had he not been constantly in view.' How exactly Dewatre, who despite a second attempt to escape in March 1813 remained in his 'habitation' at Perth until after the end of the war, had equipped himself with 'genteel' black clothing for his first attempt is, however, nowhere explained. Nor was the possession of 'suits of black with crapes [sic] for their hats, in which they intended to have dressed themselves over their prison jackets', by the three other prisoners who during the depot market on 28 April 1813 attempted to escape from Perth.[62] The similar unsuccessful attempt during the depot market five weeks later at Perth by three more prisoners described in press reports as 'very well dressed fellows' ended without any elaboration upon what they were actually wearing or how they had come by their clothes.[63]

A handful of the surviving proforma reports of escapes sent by the agents at the Scots depots to the Transport Office in London do include brief references to clothing worn by escapers. When, for example, Louis Petitchamp, an ensign captured on the privateer *L'Aventurier*, and Ferdinand Lambert, a merchant seaman captured on the *Beaupère*, escaped from Valleyfield on 3 January 1812 the proforma completed by the depot agent recorded 'One dressed in a Blue the other in a Green Coat.' A month later another seaman who escaped from Valleyfield, Matu Bronzan, alias Baptiste Hidgy, was said to be 'Dressed in blue jacket and trousers with red worsted comforter round his neck.' Constant Ivert, as a civilian passenger captured on a merchant vessel, was presumably able to retain some of his own clothes, for when he escaped from Valleyfield on 11 July 1812 he was 'Supposed to be dressed in a blue coat, light vest, breeches and leather leggins.' Louis F. Bouillard and Louis Moreau, captured respectively on the privateers *L'Ambuscade* and

Le Vengeur, who escaped together from Valleyfield on 8 September that year were 'Dressed in Patched Jacket and Trowsers' in Bouillard's case, and in Moreau's, 'Blue Jacket and Trowsers'. Less a description of their clothing perhaps than a lament for careless treatment of Transport Office property was the additional comment passed on them by the depot agent: 'Lost both their Hats.' When on Boxing Day 1812 Pierre F. Giscard, a soldier of the Imperial Guard, absconded from Valleyfield he was dressed not in the standard yellow prisoner of war garb with its large initials TO stamped on it but 'in Grey Jacket and Trowsers.' Two escapes from Greenlaw provided some terse information about clothing the absconders wore. First, two privateersmen, Captain Johan Jonsen of the *Popham* [sic] and Wilhelm Watry, a seaman, of the *Norske Tas*, both of whom had been captured in autumn 1810, escaped on 2 or 3 March 1811 from the depot and were 'supposed to have proceeded for Leith or Grangemouth ... dressed in blue jackets and trowsers.' Second, the description of Adolphe Douzon, a midshipman captured in 1809 on the packet vessel *La Mouche*, when he escaped on 5 March 1812 from Greenlaw was more question begging: '...[he] has the appearance of a Travelling Jew.'[64]

In most other cases, newspaper press reports provide at least some descriptions of escapers' clothing. Of the 49 prisoners who escaped, for example, in the mass break-out from Edinburgh Castle on 12 April 1811, five recaptured ten days later in the wood of Charleton at Montrose were reported in the local newspaper to be 'in great want of many necessary articles of dress.' When, early on Sunday morning, 19 July 1812, seven French prisoners of war confined in the Edinburgh Tolbooth on suspicion of forging banknotes escaped, the description of one of them—Carlos Gonsalvez, a seaman captured in 1806—which was advertised a few days later in the press, said he had been 'seen dressed in black clothes after his escape.'[65]

A few escapers, apart from Hummel in his fine clothes at Parliament Square in Edinburgh while on his way to Esk Mills and the attempted absconder from Perth on 3 June 1813 who sported '... a pair of neat false whiskers', may well have been disguised as workmen or other civilians or perhaps even as depot staff or British soldiers, but again there is very little confirmatory evidence of any such cases. One that was mentioned, however, by the depot clerk Andrew Johnston concerned a prisoner at Esk Mills named Louis François Beheut (or Behut), a privateersman captured on *Le Barbier de Seville* (or *Brocanteur*), who was sent to the cachot on 7 March 1811 'for attempting to escape by the gate as a carpenter. Workmen were still employed in the depot and Beheut came out with an Apron, a wright's plane in his hand, and chips and shavings in his apron.'[66] Among many escapers, however, who did not succeed in acquiring, or may not even have tried to acquire, civilian clothes were, according to William Chambers, the 23 whom he saw as a schoolboy at Peebles after their recapture following their break-out from Valleyfield, 'dressed in the yellow prison garb' and 'mostly without shoes...'—although press reports of what appears to have been this same escape on 19 Novembr 1813 refer to 'seamen's clothes' being worn by most of the escapers.[67]

If suitable clothing was important for escapers no less so was food, especially for those whose trek to coast or harbour was much longer than the mere ten miles between the Penicuik depots and Leith or than the long stone's throw between Edinburgh Castle and the latter. Saving scraps of food which would remain edible for a few days from the meagre depot rations could hardly have been easy for escapers. The paucity or absence of any such scraps that could have helped stave off the pangs of hunger once the depot was left behind increased the hazards that could arise from attempting en route either to buy or to steal food. The few references found to this aspect of escapes from the Scots depots mainly concern the dependence of escapers on turnips they found in the fields as they passed along. From among the 49 prisoners, for example, who escaped from Edinburgh Castle on 12 April 1811 the recapture of one group of ten became virtually inevitable when they stopped at night at Linlithgow 'to get some refreshment [and] they were challenged as prisoners who had made their escape, when they took to their heels and were found next morning, after a diligent search by the local militia, in the plantations near Polmont [in Stirlingshire], quite exhausted with hunger.' Another group of five from the 49, recaptured on 22 April in the wood of Charleton near Montrose, were 'in a most deplorable condition, without food or clothes, and emaciated and spent with fatigue.' Six of a later group of nine escapers from the Castle in December 1811 were recaptured also near Linlithgow, 'skulking among Lord Hopetoun's plantations.....
They had subsisted for three days on raw turnips.' During an escape which proved more successful by three prisoners from Perth on 20 January 1813 they entered a house in Broughty Ferry 'in quest of provisions. The leader of the party bought up all the bread that the house afforded and presented a leathern bottle to be filled with spirits. His accent was remarked to be foreign; but those who remarked it seem to have had no suspicions.' Almost two months later two other escapers from Perth on 27 March were recaptured four days afterward on a barge in Dundee harbour 'and confessed ... that they had skulked about the fields, subsisting solely on turnips for three days past.' Four of the escapers from Perth in the mass break-out on 12 September that year were recaptured almost three weeks later at Peterhead, where, as has been observed above, 'Three of them were got in a penny public house near the north end of the town ...' As for the escapers whom William Chambers recalled seeing as a boy recaptured at Peebles after the mass break-out from Valleyfield on 19 November 1813 they had had, he wrote, 'nothing to eat but turnips'. Their hunger had driven them in desperation to enter a barn at the farm-steading of Winkston whose farmer, when asked to sell them some

bread and milk, responded by locking them in and sending for the troops at Penicuik to seize them.[68]

Money was hardly less desirable for escapers to have than suitable clothing and a supply of food. When he and his half-dozen associates, including Lieutenant Jacques Adam and Meynder Dow, sought to escape from Valleyfield after, as they believed, finding a bribable sentry, Marote-Carrier had the considerable sum of 27 louis which he had taken the precaution of sewing as if they were buttons to his coat and trousers, and Meynder Dow did likewise with the coins he carried.[69] A year or so later, in mid-September 1813, Marote-Carrier and his fourteen intending fellow escapers from Perth must have possessed among them considerable sums of money since, as has been observed, they had resolved once they reached Falkland in Fife 'to procure coaches at whatever price' to take them on to Montrose, where they hoped to find a boat. In press reports only one reference has been found to the possession of money by escapers from the Scots depots. When a sentry at Perth in February 1813 pretended to be amenable to bribery by seven prisoners who believed they had persuaded him to turn a blind eye while they scaled the wall with ladders, the body search of the seven on their consequent arrest complete with ladders revealed 'an excellent gold watch, 29 pieces of foreign gold coin and a considerable sum of bank notes'.[70] The ledger of payments to prisoners of war at Perth, the only source of its kind that survives for any Scots depot, provides, however, several examples of the sums of money that some escapers from that depot carried upon them. Dominique Dewatre (or Delvatre), whose two unsuccessful escapes in September 1812 and March 1813 have already been mentioned, was found on his first recapture to be carrying £4.9.6. As observed in Chapter 17 above, a group of four prisoners who attempted to escape on 22 February 1813 had an impressive array of coins upon them, even if most of these were perhaps unlikely to be readily presentable to local inhabitants or traders encountered en route to the coast. When he attempted unsuccessfully to 'Escape by the Gate, 27 March 1813' Jean Baptiste Lobe had £7.2.0. in paper money and 13 shillings in silver taken from him. Finally, an unnamed prisoner (whose signature for the later phased return to him of his money appears, however, to be L. Ingerlec) had '3 Double Louis Taken from him in an attempt to Escape, 1 May 1813.'[71] But how many of the escapers from the Scots depots carried money which could help smooth their passage en route is a question to which, like so many other questions concerning the prisoners at Perth, Valleyfield, Edinburgh Castle, Esk Mills and Greenlaw, any answer would be merely a guess.

It is equally difficult to offer other than impressionistic answers to the questions of how many escapers from the Scots depots were able understand and speak English, to what extent that ability contributed to or ensured successful escapes, and how far, if at all, lack of English deterred prisoners who might otherwise have attempted escape. It might appear likely to prove an advantage for any escaper to possess such an ability, above all if he could speak fluently and without a noticeable foreign accent. That advantage of course might not prove crucial in avoiding recapture, given all the other hazards that might be encountered en route to coast or harbour. Too little information was recorded, or has survived, about the precise circumstances of most recaptures en route to enable firm conclusions to be drawn about how many were due to escapers' difficulties in speaking or understanding English.

Very few other escapers, no doubt, possessed the advantage enjoyed, as already observed, by two apparently successful absconders from Esk Mills on 7 March 1811, each of whom according to the solemn entry in the depot register 'Speaks English fluently'. Their command of the language was hardly surprising: both were Americans—Matthew Reilly, 'a native of Baltimore', and Elisha Adams, 'a native of Sprentfield'.[72] On the other hand, there were certainly examples of successful escapes by prisoners who had little or no English at all. That he only 'Speaks a little English' did not deter Matu Bronzan, alias Baptiste Hidgy, from escaping successfully on 12 February 1812 from Valleyfield.[73] Still less that he 'Does not speak a word of English' was Pierre François Giscard, captured in 1808 as a soldier in Napoleon's Imperial Guard, deterred from escaping from Valleyfield four years later on Boxing Day 1812 nor, after his recapture a week afterward and his transfer in July 1813 to Perth, from escaping from there, too, early the following year.[74] From Greenlaw, too, Frank Brown, lieutenant on the privateer *Le Petit Edouard*, escaped successfully on 28 January 1812 although he 'Speaks bad English' (no doubt because, despite his name, he was evidently a Belgian, born in Brussels). Brown's senior shipmate on *Le Petit Edouard*, Captain Pierre Jean Landau, departed with him from Greenlaw that same day, at the age of 52 one of the older escapers from a Scots depot, and he like Brown was never seen there again although he, too, 'Speaks bad English.'[75] Brown and Landau were followed over, under or through the walls or gates of Greenlaw a few weeks later also successfully by Adolphe Douzon, a midshipman captured on a small vessel *La Mouche* in 1809. A previous escape by Douzon from Edinburgh Castle, part of the mass break-out there on 12 April 1811, had, however, ended in his recapture although he 'Speaks English tolerably well.'[76] Likewise, that he 'Speaks English very well' did not ensure success for Jean Raymot, purser's clerk, when he escaped from the Castle on 15 July 1811: he was recaptured at Queensferry and returned to the Castle four days later.[77]

Nor is a great deal of information available about attempts by escapers from the Scots depots, once they reached a coast or harbour, to find boats which would carry them safely back to the continent. Most of the evidence that survives on this aspect concerns prisoners from Perth depot. Of those who escaped successfully from Edinburgh Castle, or from any of the three Penicuik depots, particularly Greenlaw or Valleyfield, an unknown though probably small number no doubt succeeded, like Kaald's former shipmate and friend Captain Sigismund Richelieu at Greenlaw in September 1809 and Marote-Carrier's companion Hummel en route to Esk Mills in February 1811, in finding at Leith or some lesser harbour on the southern shores of the Forth a vessel which carried them safely home to the continent. From among the 49 prisoners who escaped in the mass break-out on 12 April 1811 from Edinburgh Castle, 'Four ... two of whom were officers ... were apprehended at Banff, which place they had reached after a painful journey across the hills. On the evening on which they were to cut a vessel out of the harbour in order to effect their escape, their intention was frustrated by the smoke of a fire they had kindled in the wood of Mountcoffer, which excited alarm and led to [the discovery of] their place of concealment.'[78] An unnamed prisoner who had 'lately escaped from the Castle', but the date of whose escape was not otherwise specified in a press report at the end of June 1811, had 'reached Liverpool, stole a fishing boat and put to sea. After being five days and nights on the water, he was driven into Aberystwyth in Wales, where he was secured and sent to the house of correction.'[79] Their acquisition of a boat was one of the most striking aspects of what apparently proved to be a very successful escape made by three prisoners from Perth depot on 20 January 1813 'during the extremely thick fog' [that night]. The three, who were the same well organised three already observed whose leader bought up bread and presented a leathern bottle to be filled with spirits there, 'got undetected to Broughty Ferry, from whence they stole a small sloop belonging to Mr Grubb; and as nothing further has been heard of them it is supposed they have got clear off. We understand that the prisoners [first] went to Dundee and took some refreshment without seeming to dread any disturbance. They afterwards proceeded directly to the sloop, which is about 13 tons burthen, and was provisioned for ten days.' At nine o'clock in the evening the sloop, the *Nancy*, was seen by some inhabitants at Broughty Ferry to be under weigh, 'but as she was known to be prepared for next morning's excursion of fishing or of pleasure, even this passed unheeded by.'[80] The seizure of the *Nancy* by the escapers raised an issue which was considered successively by H.M. Treasury and the Transport Board. When James Grubb, manager of the Tay Shipping Company, owners of the *Nancy*, sought compensation from the government for the loss of the ship the Treasury passed his appeal to the Board. A dusty answer was passed back to Mr Grubb: '... many cases of a similar nature have occurred,' the Board wrote, 'but ... no compensation whatever has been made by Government for the loss sustained by the owners of Boats taken away by prisoners of war, and we consider that it would be highly improper to make any such compensation, it being the duty of the owners of vessels to take care of them, and public notice has been given by this Department, cautioning the owners of boats to be upon their guard against the seizure of their boats by prisoners of war.' Three years earlier the Admiralty had also warned owners of boats on beaches not to leave masts, oars and tackle in them.[81] The master of an empty barge used to transport stones from Mylnfield quarry, and which was riding at anchor in Dundee harbour at the end of March 1813, was surprised to find 'on removing a sail from what seemed to be a mass of inert matter [that] two lively French instantly jumped up on deck.' They were the escapers Faillant and Dewatre from Perth depot, already noticed, who had 'skulked about the fields, subsisting solely on turnips for three days past.'[82] Four other escapers from Perth in August 1813 were distinctly less successful in their efforts to secure a boat. They were the four, already observed above, who were recaptured near Arbroath on 4 September. 'They stated that on Thursday night [2 September] they were on board a vessel at Dundee but which they were unable to carry off, as the neap tide prevented her floating.'[83] A fortnight or so later three other escapers from Perth depot, pressing on still further up the east coast, 'came to the village of Findon, Kincardineshire, and seized one of the fishing boats there, into which they put some provisions, etc., they had collected and several water casks from the boats lying in the harbour. They made off in the middle of the night and have not since been heard of.'[84] Even further up the north-east coast, four other Perth escapers, three of whom have already been encountered above 'in a petty public house' and all four of whom were part of a group of eleven who had been seen near the fishing village of Boddam two miles south of Peterhead, were recaptured on 1 October by local militiamen. '... it appears that if they had not been apprehended they intended to have taken a small vessel from the north harbour and proceeded to sea during the night.'[85]

The 'middle passage' for escapers, from the walls or gates of the Scots depots to coast or harbour in their search for a boat, could vary in distance from two or three miles, or less, to several hundred. If that is yet another aspect not brightly illuminated by surviving sources, nonetheless rather more evidence survives about it than about some other aspects of the escapes. Examples of distinctly short distances achieved in the pursuit of freedom were provided at all the Scots depots. Of the 49 escapers, for instance, who slid down the precipitous rock from Edinburgh Castle by means of a rope on the night of 12 April 1811, five were promptly recaptured. Their exact place of recapture is nowhere mentioned, but if it was not within the shadow of the Castle itself it could not have been much beyond it. When Wilhelm Watry, a privateer seaman, escaped on 2 March the following year from Greenlaw he was recaptured three days later only two miles away at Loanhead. Nor was the simultaneous flight from that depot by the privateer Captain Johan

Jonsen longer than the two miles to Roslin, where next day he was retaken and marched back under escort to his former quarters. Even less distance than that was achieved by the privateer Lieutenant Dominique Dewatre who on 16 September 1812, in the first of his two escapes from Perth depot, was 'retaken in the adjoining field'; and it appears that Pierre Chuchere, a privateer seaman at Valleyfield, was shot on 24 May 1813 during an attempt to escape concealed in a cart in a street in Penicuik only a few hundred yards from the depot.[86]

Most escapers, however, covered more or much more than such short distances in their flight from their depot. Among the earliest escapers from captivity in Scotland were the eleven prisoners who between October 1803 and March 1804 broke out from the Edinburgh bridewell. Five or six of the eleven appear likely, from lack of evidence to the contrary, to have succeeded in reaching the continent. Of the others, one in a stolen boat had reached St Abbs Head in Berwickshire when he was recaptured, and two more were retaken a few miles east of Glasgow—all three of them about 40 miles from the Edinburgh bridewell.[87] Of the 49 escapers from Edinburgh Castle on 12 April 1811, some 14 were retaken at Linlithgow, 10 near St Andrews, four at Dundee, a further four at Glasgow and Greenock, and half a dozen at Montrose. The four who reached Dundee succeeded in escaping from there, too, and trudged as far north as Banff on the Moray Firth before they were again recaptured. Even as the crow flies (and the rutted, muddy, or otherwise difficult state of many contemporary roads or tracks the fleeing prisoners followed might have made some of them wish they had themselves been crows) those were distances from Edinburgh Castle of respectively 15, 30, 35, 40, 60, 55, and at least 120 miles.[88] Of the 50 or so prisoners who escaped from Perth depot in the two mass break-outs of 24 August and 12 September 1813, three succeeded in covering more than 30 miles northward before they were recaptured 'in the Highlands above Blair [Atholl]', three others the 30 miles east-south-east to St Andrews, four about 35 miles north-eastwards to Arbroath, and three more, who, unlike those others, were not recaptured, the 65 or so miles north-east to the fishing village of Findon on the coast of Kincardineshire.[89] From among the score of prisoners who escaped in the mass break-out on 19 February 1811 from Esk Mills two, Pierre François Le Couche (alias Barbouche) and Jean Baptiste Cabouche, both privateer seamen and shipmates captured in the English Channel on *Le Vengeur* the previous autumn, reached four days later Maxwellheugh at Kelso, some 40 miles away, before they were retaken and sent back to Esk Mills and from there to Edinburgh Castle.[90] Even from these few examples it is obvious that escapers fled from the Scots depots in almost all directions. More than one from Perth depot, for instance, reached Edinburgh, while one or two who absconded from Penicuik depots were retaken at Perth.[91] A few other escapers from Edinburgh Castle and Valleyfield headed south-west. Thus, for example, as already observed, a Danish prisoner of war named Peter Scieves was arrested about 80 miles away in August 1812 by some Kirkcudbrightshire militiamen at Gatehouse of Fleet about two months after he and seven other prisoners had escaped by bribing sentries at Edinburgh Castle. Four days after the mass break-out of 19 November 1813 from Valleyfield, '... two men of the Dumfriesshire militia were returning to Dumfries from furlough [when] they came up with four men at Tweedsmuir [25 miles from Valleyfield] who, on observing the red jackets, took to their heels. This circumstance exciting suspicion, the militiamen followed and, obtaining the assistance of some shepherds, after a long pursuit they overtook and secured them, when they proved to be French prisoners of war who had escaped from the depot at Pennycuick. They were ... lodged in Dumfries jail.'[92]

A few prisoners are recorded as having put even greater distances than those already observed between themselves and their depot in Scotland once they had passed over, under or through its walls or gates. It seems probable, despite the absence of precise information about the ports or beaches of embarkation of most of those who it may be presumed did succeed in crossing the seas surrounding Britain and regaining the continent, that some others, in unrecorded cases, also covered similarly long distances. Four of the escapers, for instance, in the mass break-out from Edinburgh Castle on 12 April 1811 reached Tynemouth in Northumberland, almost 150 miles away, where they were recaptured six weeks later 'endeavouring to get on board an American ship.'[93] Even further down into England in the early winter of 1810 pressed an escaper from Greenlaw named Louis Pineau, described in some sources as an ensign but (assuming it was the same prisoner) in the depot Entry Book as a seaman captured on the merchant ship *La Flore* in August 1803. According to T. J. Walker, the historian of Norman Cross depot in Huntingdonshire, Pineau 'made his way south until he was retaken and lodged in Northampton Gaol, whence he was sent to Norman Cross.' With characteristic negligence Malcolm Wright, depot agent at Greenlaw, had failed to report to the Transport Office the escape of Pineau and another prisoner, and was duly rebuked by the Board after Pineau's recapture.[94] Several other escapers from Scots depots made their ways even further south than Pineau. Two who reached London after escaping on 18 December 1812 from Edinburgh Castle were both privateer seamen: Etienne (or Emanuel) Bouvaist (or Bouvaint), born in Abbeville and aged 25, from *Le Rodeur*, and Baptiste Moussu, born at St Malo and aged 21, from the *Marsouin*. But in London both were recaptured on 12 January and sent to the hulks at Chatham.[95] Further yet than London was the achievement of two escapers on 6 April 1811 from Valleyfield. Both were privateersmen: Philippe Mulard, aged 34, who had been captured a year earlier as 2nd captain of the *Capricieux*, and Jacques Coterix, a gunner or master gunner on *L'Aigle*, captured in 1808. Theirs was yet another case of so near yet so far: both were sent to the hulks at Chatham after being recaptured at Dover.[96] No less remarkable were the distances covered by two other escapers. One was the unnamed prisoner, already observed, who escaped from Edinburgh Castle in the summer of 1811, reached Liverpool, stole and put to sea in a fishing boat, but who after five days and nights on the Irish Sea was driven into Aberystwth in mid-Wales, arrested, and sent to the house of correction. The other escaper was L'Imbert (or Louis or Jacques) Altier, an army lieutenant sent from Valleyfield on 1 April 1812 to the Edinburgh Tolbooth or gaol, as one of seven French prisoners suspected of forging banknotes. The escape on 19 July that year of Altier and the other six suspects from the Tolbooth was marked by his arrest about a fortnight later in Dublin. He was held there in Kilmainham Jail for a couple of weeks and then shipped off to Plymouth, no doubt to the hulks there.[97]

Although the surviving evidence concerning this aspect of escapes from the Scots depots is again very limited, yet there is enough to indicate that a few prisoners did not in fact attempt, or did not persevere in attempting, to make their way to harbour or coast determined to find a boat that would take them to the continent. Instead they appear to have gone to earth, at least for some time, in this country. The *Kelso Mail* of 4 March 1811, for instance, reported such a case in England that was probably typical of a few also in Scotland: the arrest just over the Border at Berwick-on-Tweed a few days earlier of 'a person of rather suspicious appearance ... who upon examination said that he was a French lieutenant of marines, and had made his escape from Colchester where he was a prisoner four years ago. Since that period he had skulked about the country and had never found an opportunity of returning to France.' The case of another prisoner who escaped successively from Esk Mills and Valleyfield and 'skulked' or, as one depot agent put it, was 'rambling through the country' in Scotland for some months, will be discussed in the next chapter.

But also there was the case of Lieutenant Auguste F. L. Beaurepas of the 26th Dragoons. Beaurepas, aged 25 and born at Alençon, had been captured in October 1810 at Coimbra in Portugal, and appears to have arrived in the summer of 1812 on parole at Kelso. For 'an Attempt to Violate his Parole of Honour', however, he was sent on 9 July 1813 to Valleyfield and from there a couple of days later to Perth. Early in November that year he was one of a group of officers in breach of their parole who were transferred from Perth to Edinburgh Castle en route to the hulks in the south of England. But on 25 November Beaurepas escaped from the Castle. Ten weeks later, on 2 February 1814, he surrendered himself at Valleyfield. How and where precisely throughout those ten weeks, during which he had written several letters to, and apparently received several from, the authorities, had he been able to remain in hiding in Edinburgh? Were there citizens there who, knowingly or unknowingly, gave him shelter as an escaped prisoner?

Beaurepas evidently considered himself unfairly deprived of his parole at Kelso and then unfairly consigned to the hulks in England. On the day of his escape from Edinburgh Castle he had written to the Transport Board and a few days later, it seemed, from wherever he was in hiding, to Rear Admiral Hope, naval commander based at Leith, and also to Mr J. Smith, parole agent at Kelso, asking that his parole be restored. The Transport Board on 30 November instructed Lieutenant Priest, its agent for Edinburgh Castle, to undertake a search for Beaurepas. In its reply to a letter about him from Admiral Hope, the Board declared on 18 December that Beaurepas 'has been informed that if he will deliver himself up at the depot at Valleyfield his case will be taken into consideration.' Smith at Kelso was also asked by the Board to 'communicate this to the prisoner for his guidance.' Beaurepas appears to have written again, indeed more than once, to the Board by the beginning of the New Year, for on 5 January 1814 the Board instructed Lieutenant Priest that '… it appearing by letters which have been received at this office from M. Beaurepas that he is still at Edinburgh … you will cause him to be advertised in the Edinburgh newspapers, describing his person and offering a reward of 20 guineas for his apprehension.' Rather less than a month later Beaurepas gave himself up at Valleyfield. He was then sent, via Admiral Hope's flagship at Leith, to England—but it is not known whether on his arrival there he resumed his former status as a parole prisoner or instead became an inmate of one of the hulks.[98]

To what extent inhabitants of Scotland knowingly helped prisoners of war escape from their depot, or once they had escaped assisted them en route toward embarkation at port or coast, or alternatively helped them go to earth, and in any such cases what their motives were, are likewise questions easier to ask than to answer. In England there were certainly numbers of such individuals as well as of organised groups, mainly professional smugglers or other inhabitants similarly chiefly intent on making money from the considerable numbers there of escaping prisoners of war and their need to complete without being recaptured both the 'middle passage' and the voyage to the continent. Such activity in aiding escapes south of the Border had become so notorious by 1812 that the government felt it necessary to introduce and pass that year an Act of Parliament 'for the more effectual punishment of persons aiding prisoners of war to escape from His Majesty's dominions.'[99] In Scotland there was only one prosecution under this Act—that of a Selkirk brother and sister convicted in 1813 of assisting in the escape of three parole prisoners from Lanark.[100]

One case of aiding prisoners in Scotland to escape, although it was dealt with not under the Act of 1812 but by other means, involved a notorious

English professional escape organiser named Thomas Feast Moore whose activity had consequences for several parole prisoners at Kelso, one of whom was the said Lieutenant Auguste Beaurepas. The affair was indeed the origin of the subsequent successive transfers of Beaurepas from Kelso to Valleyfield, from Valleyfield to Perth and from there to Edinburgh Castle en route for the hulks, and then of his escape. But since that particular Thomas Feast Moore case was essentially one involving parole, not depot, prisoners, a more detailed account of it will be given in a projected separate volume dealing with the parole prisoners of war in Scotland. It can be noted here, however, that the precognitions taken in that case show first, if his statements were true, that Moore lodged in Edinburgh for a couple of days in June 1813, and second that Beaurepas may well have been wrongly suspected or accused, because of some circumstantial evidence about clothing marked with his initials, of breaching his parole by becoming involved in the projected escape of parole prisoners that month from Kelso in which Moore certainly was involved.[101] It is also certain, however, that if any civilians were involved either in Beaurepas's escape from Edinburgh Castle in November that year or in his subsequent going to earth in Edinburgh for ten weeks Moore could not have been one of them.

Edinburgh, and Leith, are at the centre of a tantalising reference, although not to native inhabitants but to two apparently French residents, in Transport Board corrrespondence in April 1812, when the Board sent Lieutenant Glinn, RN, its transport agent at the port, 'the annexed Names and Addresses of certain Foreigners in Edinburgh whom there is Reason to believe from Papers found on a French prisoner are in the habit of harbouring escaped Prisoners of War.' The Board instructed Glinn 'that you will look after these Persons in Case of any Escape of Prisoners in Future: Margerie d'Olivier, going up the Street which leads to the Castle, in a House painted sky Blue in the first Floor on the right Hand ... [and] ... Jean Bratiche, Commissionaire de Police, at St Andrews Street, Leith.'[102]

There survives a similarly cryptic and tantalising reference ten months earlier in a letter from the Transport Board to Rear Admiral Otway at Leith concerning 'Papers found on Hypolite de Cruise, one of which contains Names and Addresses of Persons who appear to assist Prisoners of War in their Escape'. De Cruise or Decreuse was the prisoner apparently prominently involved in the attempted shipboard rising by prisoners being brought to Leith on HMS *Gorgon* early in March 1811, and who after his escape on 12 April that year from Edinburgh Castle and subsequent recapture was sent to the hulks at Chatham. What is not clear is whether the names and addresses found on Decreuse were of people in Edinburgh, Leith or elsewhere in Scotland, or instead perhaps in England.[103]

From most if not all of the Scots depots there were escapes which at least appear to have been helped by civilians. The circumstances, for instance, in which three escapers from Perth depot got clean away from Broughty Ferry in January 1813 in the sloop *Nancy* created, according to the *Perth Courier*, 'strong ground for suspecting that they had been assisted in their escape by persons who had given them information of the means which they adopted.' Consequently, as the *Courier* reported, 'A woman, and two soldiers of the Renfrewshire miltia, have been apprehended on suspicion that they aided the three prisoners who escaped from the depot in effecting their object. They have been repeatedly examined, and though we do not know the result of their examinations it has been such as as to induce the Sheriff to detain them in prison.' A later issue of the *Courier* carried an advertisement offering a reward for the recapture of three civil prisoners and a deserter from the Black Watch, who had escaped in early February from Perth gaol after wounding and overpowering the gaoler and taking the prison keys from him. But the paper appeared to reduce the two suspected Renfrewshire militiamen to one by adding in an accompanying report that: 'The soldier of the Renfrew militia, who was imprisoned under suspicion of aiding the escape of the prisoners of war from the [Perth] depot, might have accompanied the rest in their flight, but says he declined doing so from a consciousness of innocence.' Nothing more has been found about this case.[104]

The group of escapers from Valleyfield who after their recapture were seen at Peebles by the boy William Chambers and his schoolmates had sought as they had made their way southward from the depot over very rough ground, '... if possible to reach a humble cottage, known as the Clay House, at Acrefield, in the immediate neighbourhood of ... [Peebles], and where by some private understanding prisoners of war were received and aided in escaping from the country.' Chambers added that the Clay House was 'obscurely situated away from the main thoroughfare', but he says nothing about who the occupants or owners of the Clay House were or what were or might have been their motives in helping prisoners of war to escape.[105]

Oral tradition has preserved an account of help given by a local family to another escaper from a Penicuik depot—though from which of the three depots there is not known, nor is the date of his escape. The tradition concerns a Dutch prisoner, said to have been a surgeon, named Van Beck (though he may have used an alias while a captive), who after escaping from the depot was harboured by a Penicuik family, whose daughter he later married. He and his wife are said to have settled after the Napoleonic Wars first at Dalkeith then at Musselburgh.[106] In one or two other cases prisoners at Penicuik appear to have escaped with the help of local inhabitants such as Macbeth Forbes's 'countryman who did business' with the prisoners and who was said to have helped the escape of one by hiding him in his cart.[107]

The motives of local inhabitants and others in apparently aiding escapes by prisoners from the Scots depots no doubt varied. The Penicuik family said to have helped the Dutch prisoner Van Beck escape may have acted simply out of sympathy for him. If the three who escaped from Perth and sailed off from Broughty Ferry in the *Nancy* were indeed helped by a local woman and one or two militiamen the latter's motives were perhaps more likely to be financial, given that some escapers carried with them appreciable sums of money. Although no evidence has been found of any political motive arising from any lingering support among some more radical Scots for the earlier universal ideals of the French Revolution, it may nonetheless be worth bearing in mind that in the cities of Edinburgh, Perth, Dundee, and Glasgow, but also at Penicuik and at nearby Dalkeith, Lasswade and Loanhead, as well as in more than a score of other towns and villages in Lowland Scotland there had existed in the early 1790s the reforming Societies of the Friends of the People, members of which were influenced to one extent or another by the ideals of the French Revolution. Leaders of the Friends of the People—Thomas Muir, the Rev. Thomas Fyshe Palmer, and William Skirving—as well as Maurice Margarot and Joseph Gerrald as delegates to the Scots reformers from the London Corresponding Society, had been sentenced to transportation to the penal settlements in Australia a decade before the Napoleonic Wars began in 1803. The Societies of the Friends of the People had melted away by the middle 1790s, the more radical United Scotsmen by about 1802. Is it conceivable, however, that here and there in the towns and villages of Scotland, especially in those near the depots for prisoners of war in 1803-14, there remained some old members, or sympathisers with the ideals of the Friends of the People or the United Scotsmen who may have been willing to help French and other prisoners of war escape from their captivity at Penicuik, Edinburgh or Perth?

Although stopping short no doubt of any action or even inclination to help prisoners escape, there certainly were demonstrated among some Scots feelings of sympathy for the plight of the prisoners. Several examples have already been observed above, including the handing out of clothing by bystanders to prisoners landed at Kirkcaldy and Leith, and the throwing of coins to those who included Marote-Carrier and the Dutch escaper Hummel as they trudged under escort from Leith en route to Esk Mills.[108] But two examples of strong feelings of sympathy aroused among some local inhabitants for escaped, though recaptured, prisoners specifically were provided by William Chambers in his recollection of the recapture of the 23 or so whom as a boy he saw at Peebles on their way back to their depot at Penicuik. After spending a night in Peebles town gaol the recaptured prisoners were brought out from it in the morning about nine o'clock and, Chambers recalled, '... by the military officer in command were ordered to march back to Penicuick. From the crowd of boys and townsfolk who were spectators of the scene there arose something like a cry of horror. The unfortunate wretches could not march; they could barely stand, and piteously implored compassion. Deschamps [Dujardin?], who had figured as a leader, presented a sight which is fresh in my remembrance after an interval of more than sixty-four years. Drawing up the leg of his ragged trousers, he, with dramatic gesture, called the officer's attention to the state of his limb. It was a universal ulceration. Though speaking in French, he required no interpreter. The words were the voice of nature, which all could understand. The officer felt the force of the appeal. He ordered carts to be procured. There was accordingly a lull in the proceedings until the carts and horses made their appearance.' Chambers described the scene: 'In the centre, in front of the jail, stood or sat on the street the woe-begone prisoners. Hanging about on their skirts, but ready for action, were the soldiers, the officer with sword drawn pacing backwards and forwards. Outside, at a respectable distance, were the miscellaneous onlookers. Among these was May Ingram, a tall woman of masculine character, who, though married, was known only by her maiden name. In the "dear years" she had headed a meal-mob. Yet May, with all her exterior roughness of character, had in her the milk of human kindness. On this memorable morning she put to shame persons of higher pretensions. Perceiving that Deschamps was helpless, and suffering from a frightful sore, May rushed away to her poor home in quest of rags and emollient salve; and returning in time, bound up the wound, and aided in imparting a degree of comfort to the unfortunate Frenchman. The carts arrive. The cavalcade moves off, and we see it disappear round the corner at the east end of the town, on its way to Penicuick. In the throng who linger behind, May Ingram pathetically expatiates on the nature of her surgical operation and the sufferings of the poor creatures generally. French as they were, she observed, "They were aye somebody's body!" Looking back on this occurrence in my boyish days, the painfulness of the recollection is assuaged by a remembrance of this poor woman's truly Christian act of charity to a totally friendless being.'[109]

Another totally friendless being, however, consequently became the farmer who had refused the escapers' appeal to sell them some bread and milk and instead had locked them in his barn at Winkston the previous day and summoned from Penicuik an escort of militiamen to take them back to their depot there. William Chambers recalled 'How this hard-hearted man—whose name I suppress—was for years afterward execrated throughout the neighbourhood! Conscious, perhaps, of the disrepute into which he had fallen, on account of his cruelty to the poor Frenchmen, he shrunk into a gloomy recklessness of character. The simple people about said he was "under a feydom"—a familiar Scottish phrase only to be translated by saying that he was "under the domination of fees or fairies", something supernatural. At all events, this unhappy person had a dismal ending. One night, he madly attempted to cross the Tweed on horseback at a particularly dangerous ford, when the river was roaring "from bank to brae" in full flood, and was swept away and drowned.'[110]

If the prisoners in the Scots depots observed open and closed seasons for escapes it is not entirely obvious which those seasons were. It may be that in some of the more carefully planned escapes, particularly perhaps those involving the toil of tunnelling, among the factors determining the time of a break-out were the dark nights of autumn, winter and early spring. Seasonal weather may also have been taken into account. Heavy rain or snow, for example, although likely to increase the physical discomforts of escape, might on the other hand make pursuit more difficult. The 'extremely thick fog', for instance, which gratuitously shrouded the depot when three prisoners absconded from Perth in mid-January 1813 must have helped them in what appears to have been otherwise a carefully planned escape involving their acquisition at Broughty Ferry of the sloop *Nancy*, on which they were last seen setting out for home on the continent. A survey of the timing of escapes indicates, however, that on the whole these began soon or very soon after each depot was opened, whatever the season, and, at those still in use, continued almost irrespective of the seasons or of dark or light nights until virtually the end of the war in 1814. At Greenlaw, the depot longest in use, April and May appear to have been the only months in any year between 1804 and 1814 when no escapers passed over, under or through the gates or the walls. Was the absence of those two months from the calendar of escapes due to careful avoidance of lighter nights or merely to chance? The latter seems the more likely, for there were certainly escapers from Greenlaw in the long light months of June, July, August and September. At Perth, although there appear to have been no successful escapers in any February, May, July or December, there were certainly at least some prisoners who attempted escapes in one or other of those months, such as that in February 1813 when seven sought unsuccessfully to bribe a sentry. At Valleyfield, on the other hand, no month in one year or another failed to be chosen by escapers during the depot's existence from March 1811 until the summer of 1814, although some 40 per cent of all its escapers absconded in November. At Esk Mills all 27 escapers chose to depart in February or March 1811—but inevitably so, as those were the only two months the depot was in use. Similar was the timing of escapes from the Edinburgh bridewell, which was in use for prisoners of war from only September 1803 until March 1804. At Edinburgh Castle, with its fitful and often very limited use as a depot between early 1811 and the end of the war, of the grand total of some 90 escapers, no fewer than 60 took to their heels from it in the month of April 1811—some 49 of them on the night of the 11th/12th. The mass descent by rope down the Castle rock that night by 49 escapers seems less likely to have been determined by light or dark nights or any other considerations than by their conviction that even the few weeks of captivity they had endured there since its opening as a depot were sufficient to justify speedy departure from its particularly claustrophobic, dismal and depressing accommodation.

The number of identified escapers from the Scots depots is inevitably somewhat smaller than the total, or probable total, number of escapers. The discrepancy is a result of the familiar gaps, contradictions and other shortcomings in the General Entry Books and other surviving official sources, as well as the general absence of prisoners' names in press reports of escapes. Of the 49 escapers, for example, from Edinburgh Castle on 11/12 April 1811, four were unidentified in any surviving official record, as were about 30 in two later escapes there. For some unexplained reason the Perth General Entry Books failed to record about 30 of those who, according to press reports, escaped from that depot, nor do the standard proforma returns made by other depot agents to the Transport Office concerning escapes appear to have survived in more than three or four cases for Perth. But excluding such exceptions, which in the case of the other depots and of the Edinburgh bridewell all the available evidence suggests were either very few or non-existent, and excluding also the seven suspected of forging banknotes who escaped on 19 July 1812 from the Edinburgh Tolbooth, the number of identified escapers (as distinct from escapes) appears to have been:

Edinburgh bridewell:	11
Greenlaw:	39
Esk Mills:	27
Edinburgh Castle:	62
Valleyfield:	64
Perth:	32
Total:	**235**

An analysis of these identified escapers indicates that the number in the three categories sea-going, army, or civilian was:

	Sea-going	Army	Civilian	Uncertain
Edinburgh bridewell:	11	Nil	Nil	
Greenlaw:	37	2	Nil	
Esk Mills:	25	1	1	
Edinburgh Castle:	53	9	Nil	
Valleyfield:	45	18	1	
Perth:[111]	25	10		
Totals:	**196**	**40**	**2**	**Nil**

Of the two civilians who escaped, the one at Esk Mills was J. Pierre Chauvin, aged 36, captured as a passenger on the vessel *La Santa Maria Nova*, date unstated, and who on 7 March 1811 'Absconded betwixt night and morning. Course of his route has not been discovered.' The other, at Valleyfield on 10 July 1812, was Constant Yvert.[112]

Even if there are added to the total number of escapers from the Scots depots the approximately 30 from Edinburgh Castle and the 30 from Perth whose
names and other details have not been found, and a further nominal aggregate
of 10 for the other depots and the Edinburgh bridewell who may have gone
officially unrecorded and also unreported in the press, it is clear that a huge
majority of escapers in Scotland were sea-going and that army escapers were in a
distinct minority. There were approximately five times more sea-going prisoners
who escaped than those who were army men. Even if all 60 or so unidentified
escapers from Perth and Edinburgh Castle and the possible further 10 or so at
the other depots were army and not sea-going, the latter would remain far more
numerous among the total number of escapers. Excluding those 70, no fewer
than 196 identified escapers were sea-going, and a maximum of 40 were army.
At the Edinburgh bridewell all the identified escapers were merchant seamen.
At Greenlaw out of a total of 39 escapers all but two army men were sea-going;
and at Esk Mills all but one soldier and one civilian were sea-going out of the
total of 27 escapers. At Valleyfield out of a total of 64 escapers 45 were sea-going, one civilian, and 18 army. At Edinburgh Castle there was an even heavier
predominance of sea-going prisoners among the escapers—85.4 per cent of the
total of 62, of whom only nine were army men. Even at Perth, where there was a
huge majority of army prisoners compared with sea-going, out of the 32 identified
escapers approximately two-thirds were sea-going and only one-third army. In
the very unlikely event that all 30 or so unidentified escapers from Perth proved
to be army, the resultant proportions would still not have reflected closely those
of the army and sea-going prisoners confined at the depot.

That sea-going captives in all the Scots depots heavily predominated
among identified escapers appears likely to have been due largely to their
greater confidence that they would be able to secure by one means or another
the essential sea passage home to the continent (or, in the case of two or
three of the escapers, to the United States of America). Among the sea-going
escapers themselves there was in turn a heavy majority of privateersmen, as
the following table shows:

Identified sea-going escapers					
	Total sea-going	Naval	Privateer	Merchant	Category uncertain
Edinburgh bridewell:	11	Nil	Nil	11	Nil
Greenlaw:	37	3	20	6	8
Esk Mills:	25	1	24	Nil	Nil
Edinburgh Castle:	53	17	33	1	2
Valleyfield:	45	5	34	6	Nil
Perth:[111]	22	2	19	Nil	1
Totals:	**193**	**28**	**130**	**24**	**11**[113]

What, apart from presumed confidence in securing a vessel for their passage home to the continent, explained the heavy preponderance of privateersmen among identified escapers from the Scots depots? Was part of the explanation their relative freedom from inhibition about respect for naval or military discipline, a residual tendency to obey which (even when the discipline was imposed by an enemy state) may have deterred many naval or army prisoners from becoming escapers? Was there among army or naval prisoners of war some sense of security in captivity—that so many of them who had experienced and survived the horrors of war on land and at sea had no wish to escape in order to return home where they would be obliged to resume fighting? Was it that privateersmen, if they could repatriate themselves by escaping, were more likely to make money from the resumption of their form of war service than were army or navy men? Whatever the explanation, the disproportionate number of privateersmen who escaped from the Scots depots is striking.

An analysis of the ranks of the identified escapers based on the depot Entry Books and escape proformas and other surviving official sources provides this table:

Ranks of identified escapers[114]					
	Total	Sea-going	Army	Civilians	Category uncertain
Edinburgh bridewell:	11	mv officer: 1 mv seamen: 9 mv other: 1	Nil	Nil	Nil
Greenlaw:	39	mv seamen: 6 priv.officers: 11 priv.seamen: 6 priv.others: 3 nav.officer: 1 nav.seamen: 2 seamen of unstated category: 8	sergeant: 1 soldier: 1	Nil	Nil
Esk Mills:	27	priv.officers: 12 priv.others: 3 priv.seamen: 9 naval. r.u.: 1	soldier: 1	1 (a passenger)	Nil

Edinburgh Castle:	62	mv officer: 1
		 priv.officers: 12
		 priv.others: 5
		 priv.seamen: 16
		 nav. officers: 9
		 nav. seamen: 6
		 nav.others: 2
		 sea-goers of category unstated:
		     officer: 1
		     seamen: 1
			officers: 5
			 sergeants: 2
			 soldiers: 2
				Nil	Nil

Valleyfield:	64	mv seamen: 6 priv.officers: 4 priv.others: 2 priv.seamen: 28 nav.seamen: 5	sergeant: 1 corporal 1 soldiers: 16	1 (a passenger)	Nil
Perth:[111]	32	priv.officers: 6 priv.others: 1 priv. seamen: 12 nav. seamen: 2 seaman of category unstated: 1	sgt-major: 1 sergeant: 2 soldiers: 7	Nil	Nil

Thus of the 235 identified escapers from the depots in Scotland around 170 were Other Ranks—the rank and file and the middle-ranking petty, non-commissioned and warrant officers. Excluding the two civilians, the remaining 63 or 64 other identified escapers (almost 27 per cent of the total) were officers: 5 army, 2 merchant vessel, 10 naval, 45 privateer (or 46, if P. F. Drieu, an escaper from Perth, was indeed not really a soldier but a privateer officer), and one (Lieutenant Jacques Adam) who was probably a naval, but may have been a merchant, officer. Because they were officers confined in the depots, having lost, declined, or never been granted the greater freedom accorded fellow officers who passed their captivity in the parole towns in Scotland, England or Wales, those 63 or 64 no doubt felt little or no compunction about escaping from their depots at Greenlaw, Esk Mills, Edinburgh Castle, Valleyfield, Perth or in one case, in the opening year of the war, from the Edinburgh bridewell.

It was no doubt unlikely that more than a handful of the 63 or so officers and even fewer among the 170 or so rank and file identified escapers from the Scots depots had ever heard of Robert the Bruce, king of Scotland, and still fewer of John Barbour, Scots medieval poet, scholar, 'father' of Scottish history and author of the national epic *The Brus*. All these 235 escapers, however, whatever their rank, as they passed over, under or through the walls or gates of their depots might well have echoed Barbour's much quoted declaration that 'Freedom is a noble thing!'

22

If at First You Don't Succeed …

Freedom, however, for many escapers from the Scots depots proved short lived. It is difficult, for all the familiar reasons, to present an accurate number or proportion of even identified escapers who were recaptured. It does appear, however, that almost two thirds of the latter were soon escorted back to their depots again. The following table of recaptures almost certainly underestimates the number of identified escapers who did not succeed in passing safely through their 'middle passage' between depot and coast or their final passage across the sea to the continent. There may also have been two or three escapers who eluded recapture but who for one reason or another did not return to the continent (or wherever else their homes were) and until the end of the war went to ground in Scotland or south of the Border.

Identified escapers recaptured		
	Total identified escapers	Recaptured
Edinburgh bridewell:	11	5
Greenlaw:	39	7
Esk Mills:	27	13
Edinburgh Castle:	62	60
Valleyfield:	64	47
Perth:	32	19
Total:	**235**	**151**

Thus out of 235 identified escapers 84 were not, or appear not to have been, recaptured. The table excludes certain recaptured escapers already mentioned: the four unidentified escapers who were recaptured within an hour or two of the mass break-out from Edinburgh Castle on the night of 11/12 April 1811, the five identified recaptured from among the seven prisoners of war suspected of forging banknotes who escaped in July 1812 from the Edinburgh Tolbooth, the 30 or so who appear from press accounts to have escaped from Perth but who were not identified in that depot's Entry

Books or in surviving escape proformas submitted to the Transport Office. Excluding all those, and a further guesstimate of perhaps 40 unrecorded or unidentified escapers from other Scots depots, the table shows that even at a conservative calculation almost two thirds, or some 64 per cent, of the identified escapers it lists were recaptured. Identified escapers from Greenlaw evidently had the best prospect of not being recaptured, those from Edinburgh Castle and Valleyfield the least, those from the Edinburgh bridewell and Esk Mills enjoyed at best a fifty-fifty chance of succeeding in reaching home, and those from Perth appreciably less than a fifty-fifty chance of doing so. It was the series of hurdles—including, as already observed, distances, language, clothing, supplies of food and drink, money, and securing passage by boat—over which escapers had to leap which defeated so many en route to coast or continent.

Although metaphorically Barbour's stirring cry so swiftly died away in the ears of so many escapers, at least 14 out of the identified 151 who were recaptured were far from discouraged. They attempted again to escape, some of them successfully. Of these 14 several thus escaped more than once from a particular depot, some from more than one depot.

In the first category was, for example, Lieutenant Dominique Dewatre, whose escape 'over the wall' from Perth on 10 September 1812 and recapture, 'genteelly dressed in black', in a field adjoining the depot have already been observed.[1] Dewatre, as has also been seen, escaped again from Perth on 27 March 1813 and was recaptured on a barge at Dundee.[2] He remained a prisoner at Perth until in April 1814, at the end of the war, he was 'sent to Leith.' Likewise at Valleyfield there was Louis François Bouillard, a soldier (or a seaman) captured on the privateer *L'Ambuscade* in 1811, in the month of October of which year he arrived at Valleyfield. On 8 September 1812 Bouillard escaped from the depot but he was recaptured at Musselburgh and sent back to Valleyfield. Within a month he escaped again, this time 'by Stockade back of Hospital'. But Bouillard's luck was out and he was again recaptured, place this time unstated. He remained a prisoner at Valleyfield until the general release at the end of the war, in June 1814.[3]

If both Bouillard at Valleyfield and Dewatre at Perth were among those prisoners who twice responded to the call of freedom Bernard Gassione at Valleyfield did so thrice. Gassione, a soldier in the 82nd regiment when captured on Martinique in February 1809, was aged 28 and born at Lyons. He had arrived at Valleyfield in September 1811 from Plymouth. His first escape from Valleyfield was on 3 December 1812. He was recaptured at a place unstated in the records and taken back to Valleyfield six days later. He escaped again on 24 May 1813. He was recaptured almost three weeks later at Dunbar. His third escape from Valleyfield, along with a score of other prisoners, was on 19 November 1813. This time he was at large for a month until he was recaptured at Eyemouth. He entered Valleyfield on 22 December for the fourth time. Gassione remained there until he was repatriated in the general release on 6 June 1814.[4]

Among those fourteen or so escapers who escaped more than once, the second category—those who escaped from more than one depot in Scotland— included, for example, François Armand, who escaped twice from both Valleyfield and Perth. A seaman aged 22, born at Gravelines, and captured on the privateer *Grand Rodeur* in the Mediterranean in 1808, Armand was among the prisoners transferred in March 1811 from Esk Mills to Valleyfield. He escaped from the guardhouse at Valleyfield on 1 June 1812. But he was recaptured two days later five miles away at Dalhousie Mains farm and marched back under escort to Valleyfield. From there Armand was transferred in July 1813 to Perth. He was there less than a month when on 24 August he escaped. He was recaptured three days later 30 miles to the north at Blair Atholl. He was scarcely back in Perth depot when on 13 September he escaped again. This time he headed not north but south-westward to Glasgow, where a couple of weeks later he was recaptured and put into the city gaol. From Glasgow gaol Armand was sent back not to Perth but to Valleyfield, where he arrived on 9 October. He was in Valleyfield barely six weeks when on 19 November 1813, along with a score of other prisoners, he escaped again. But within ten days or so he was 'Retaken near Lanark' and again sent back to Valleyfield. There Armand remained until in the general repatriation after the end of the war he was at last restored to freedom on 7 June 1814.[5]

Of two members of Napoleon's Imperial Guard who escaped from Scots depots one, as has been seen, was J. P. (or Pierre François) Giscard, who had arrived from Portsmouth at Valleyfield in October 1811. On Boxing Day 1812 Giscard escaped from Valleyfield 'over the Stockade.' But he was recaptured within a few days. Transferred in July 1813 from Valleyfield to Perth, Giscard was issued on 25 January 1814 at Perth with a pair of shoes and, although no date is given in the Entry Book, at some time thereafter he escaped. He appears this time to have got away successfully, his path eased perhaps by his new shoes.[6]

As an escaper successively from Edinburgh Castle and Valleyfield, Roland Demazelly or Demazilly, described in the Entry Books as a seaman, born in Paris, and captured on the privateer *Point du Jour* in the English Channel in November 1808, appeared remarkable, not least on account of his apparent youthfulness. He was said in the Castle Entry Book to be 13 years old, although in some other sources he was said to be 20. At 4 feet 11 inches tall, of stout build, with a round face, fresh complexion, sandy hair and blue eyes, and with some smallpox scars, Roland may have been the youngest escaper from any of the Scots depots. Arrived at Edinburgh Castle on 20 November 1811 from Greenlaw, he was one of a group of eight escapers from the Castle a month later on 18 December. But he and several of the others were recaptured four days later and sent on 3 January 1812 to Valleyfield. Six weeks later, on 12 February, he escaped from Valleyfield 'over the Stockade.' But within four days, recaptured it seems at Leith, he was back in Valleyfield. Persistence paid: on 26 April 1813 Roland escaped once more from Valleyfield—this time, it appears, successfully.[7]

The most remarkable escaper from the Scots depots was undoubtedly, however, François Petit. Petit first appeared as a prisoner of war in Scotland at Greenlaw. On 17 November 1810 he arrived there along with other prisoners brought by the frigate HMS *Venus* from the hulks at Portsmouth. Petit and his companions had been landed at Leith and, as the *Caledonian Mercury* reported, marched under escort through Edinburgh on their way to the depot. In the Greenlaw Entry Book Petit was said to be a seaman, captured on the privateer *Le Vengeur* in the English Channel a month earlier on 17 October. His description gave his age as 25, his height 5 feet 2¾ inches, and he was said to have black hair, black eyes, long visage, a good complexion, stout build, and with no marks or wounds. No place of birth was given. Two and a half months later, on 4 February 1811, Petit was transferred along with 191 other prisoners to Esk Mills, the first inmates of that new depot.[8]

At Esk Mills Petit was listed in the Entry Book as prisoner No. 35 and his physical description was entered in exactly the same terms as it had been at Greenlaw. He did not, however, remain long at Esk Mills. On 7 March, a month after he had arrived in the depot, Petit disappeared from it, 'Supposed to have escaped in the evening with the workmen coming out of the prison.' The escape proforma submitted by Captain Richard Pellowe, depot agent, to the Transport Office reporting Petit's disappearance referred to him as Pierre Petit, with François Petit said to be his surprisingly unimaginative alias.[9]

Nothing more was heard of Petit for eight months after his escape from Esk Mills. Where was he during all those months? If he had been attempting to make his way back to France he certainly did not succeed.

The next mention of Petit came in a letter on 6 November 1811 sent by the Transport Office to Captain Moriarty, agent at Valleyfield depot. By this time Esk Mills depot had long been closed—indeed its closure had taken place less than a week after Petit's escape from it. 'A foreigner named F. Petit,' the Transport Office told Moriarty, 'apprehended under suspicious Circumstances having been for some time detained in the County Gaol at Stirling, we acquaint you that we have applied to the Commander of the Forces in North Britain to order an Escort to conduct him to Valleyfield Prison.'[10]

Petit's adventures can then be followed in surviving papers of the Lord Advocate. A petition dated 3 December 1811 by Robert Sconce, writer or lawyer in Stirling, to the procurator fiscal explained that 'F. Petit, a French prisoner for some time in Stirling jail, was sent from Stirling on the 12th of

November … under an escort of a party of the Kirkcudbrightshire Militia, on a route to Edinburgh Castle; that the party with their prisoner halted at Falkirk' that same night, … 'when Sergeant Duncan MacIntosh and Private George Baird, two of the escort, were violently assaulted and knocked down, and obstructed in their duty, by which means the French prisoner effected his escape.' Sconce's petition asked the procurator fiscal to grant a warrant to search for and arrest Andrew Turner, a labourer in Falkirk, whom Sconce declared he had 'good reason to suspect, and to charge Turner, one of the persons guilty of the said assault, obstruction and rescue … at least as being art and part.' A warrant had already been issued on 22 November against Andrew Hutton, a flesher or butcher in Falkirk, who was likewise accused of assaulting and obstructing the Kirkcudbrightshire militiamen escorting Petit from Stirling to Edinburgh Castle, and of aiding and abetting Petit in making his escape.[11]

In his precognition taken on 6 December, Andrew Hutton declared he was entirely innocent of the crime laid to his charge. He said that two or three weeks earlier he had 'happened to be in the house of John Brown, a messenger and changekeeper [inn or alehouse keeper] in Falkirk, between 11 and 12 o'clock at night, in company with Andrew Turner … when some soldiers came in in uniform. He did not observe the soldiers had any arms … there was a man in plainclothes along with them who appeared to be a Frenchman. He had no conversation either with the soldiers or the Frenchman, nor did he drink with any of them. He would not have known they were in Brown's house if one of the soldiers, or two of them, had not looked into the room where he [Hutton] was sitting.' About half an hour after the soldiers and the Frenchman had left Brown's house, Hutton said he and Andrew Turner also left it to go home to their beds in the Kirkwynd. In the Kirkwynd, however '… the Frenchman came up to them and asked the road to Stirling and offered Hutton and Turner half a mutchkin [rather less than a half pint] if they would accompany him out of the town and put him on the road to Stirling. They agreed and accordingly went in with the Frenchman to the house of Charles Grindlay, changekeeper in Falkirk, where the Frenchman treated them with some rum for which he paid eighteen pence or two shillings. After leaving Grindlay's the Frenchman proposed to them that if they would accompany him a mile or two on the road he would give them another half mutchkin. So they accompanied him to Camelon on the road towards Stirling, where the Frenchman treated them with spirits in the house of Robert Paterson, cooper in Camelon, for which the Frenchman paid eighteen pence or two shillings.' Hutton denied that he ever said to Grindlay or to Paterson that he and Turner had assisted the Frenchman to make his escape, or that he had shown either of them how he and Turner had tripped up the heels of the sergeant or the soldiers in order to rescue the Frenchman.

The latter, Hutton said, had left Hutton at Paterson's house and had gone on the Stirling road 'saying he was going to see his wife at Stirling.' How did a French prisoner who had escaped from Penicuik come eight months or less later to have a wife at Stirling? [12]

In his precognition Andrew Turner, the accused labourer, gave much the same account as Hutton. When a man had come up to him and Hutton in Kirkwynd he, Turner, had observed that he 'had a broken language and he has since heard that he was a Frenchman.' There was, however, one additional piece of information Turner provided. When he had left him and Hutton at Camelon the stranger had gone 'forward on the Stirling road saying he was going to see his wife at Stirling whose name was Turnbull.'[13]

A somewhat different account was given in his precognition by Robert Paterson, the cooper in Camelon, who recalled that about two o'clock on the morning of 4 December he had been 'wakened while in bed by a loud knocking at his door and his dog barking, which lies in the house.' When Paterson had opened the door Andrew Hutton instantly came into the house followed by two other persons who were unknown to Paterson. Hutton had immediately said, 'Here is a French Prisoner', and had called for some whisky to drink. After about an hour, during which Hutton and Turner drank two gills of whisky, Turner fell asleep on his chair but Hutton and the French prisoner went out, Hutton remarking 'that he would just convey the prisoner a short way on the road to Stirling and return for his companion.' Paterson declared that '… the person called the French Prisoner, who indeed acknowledged himself to have been such, was seemingly quite sober, and drank none of the whisky. Hutton was a little the worse of liquor, but the other person [Turner] was very drunk. Hutton … bragged of his cleverness in rescuing the prisoner from the soldiers, saying to the prisoner, "Did I not act manfully in retrieving you?" At the same time Hutton showed Paterson the way in which he tripped with his foot and knocked over one of the soldiers. Hutton also told Paterson that the other person … seized the other soldier and his bayonet, whereby the prisoner's escape was effected … Hutton returned to Paterson's house after he had been away about fifteen minutes and took away his companion [Turner]. On Hutton's return he had shown Paterson a written paper he said he had got from the Frenchman, being the address of the prisoner's wife in Stirling, on whom if he Hutton called he would be kindly entertained for the service he had done to the prisoner.'[14]

Other witnesses in their precognitions added some further pieces to the colourful mosaic of Petit's escape from his escort at Falkirk. Agnes Galbraith, for example, wife of James Galbraith, yet another changekeeper or alehouse owner in Falkirk, declared that the four soldiers who arrived from Stirling with a French prisoner came with the prisoner into her husband's alehouse and drank spirits. Jean Galbraith, daughter of James and Agnes, testified similarly but added that when the soldiers came into her father's alehouse they 'appeared to be drunk and particularly the sergeant.' The Frenchman had paid her sixpence or a shilling for the reckoning. 'When the prisoner came in he had no shackles on his hands nor while he was in the house nor when he went out of it.' The changekeeper John Brown also testified that the prisoner had had no shackles on his hands when he and the corporal of the escort had entered his alehouse and drank some beer until the sergeant of the escort had taken the prisoner away. John Carmichael, waiter to Mr Carmichael, vintner in Falkirk, said four soldiers had entered his master's house with a French prisoner and had called for half a mutchkin of whisky. After it was drunk they all left and went into the alehouse of Andrew Young which was opposite. They remained there upwards of an hour. Carmichael observed that the sergeant of the escort was becoming drunk and he went and told him 'that if he did not behave himself the populace would perhaps liberate the prisoner.' The sergeant had told Carmichael that the prisoner had about £50 upon him. It was the prisoner who had paid the reckoning to Carmichael, who affirmed also that the prisoner had had no shackles on. Carmichael added that whilst they were in the inn the prisoner and the soldiers had enquired of him 'where they could get a wench or whore.' While they were in Andrew Young's alehouse Carmichael had seen the sergeant with a French watch in his hands and when it was opened Carmichael had observed the word 'Paris' on it. He had also seen the prisoner make one of the soldiers a present of a penknife. Christine Douglas or Hutton, in whose house in Falkirk the sergeant and a private soldier of the escort were to be billeted overnight, declared that they took the shackles off the prisoner in the afternoon and gave them to her to keep. They had all returned that evening about eight o'clock to her house along with another private soldier. The soldiers and the sergeant were very drunk, 'behaving very improperly, called the prisoner a French Buggar, and asking spirits from him. The shackles and the soldiers' arms lay in her house two days after.' She saw the sergeant had a gold watch which she understood belonged to the prisoner. Although she had given the party victuals upon her own account when they first came into her house, 'when she had gone out of the room the soldiers took away a greater part of a Gloucester cheese and … behaved very rude and impertinent to her.'[15]

As for Sergeant MacIntosh of the Kirkcudbrightshire militia, he explained in his precognition that he had been ordered on 11 November to escort Petit next day from Stirling to Edinburgh. He and the three private soldiers of the escort had duly arrived in mid-afternoon with Petit at Falkirk, where they were under instructions to remain that night. When he found there was no jail or guardhouse at Falkirk, MacIntosh had applied to the billet master to provide him with billets in one house, but that had not proved possible and two of the soldiers had had to be lodged in a different quarter of the town. MacIntosh's testimony about seeking refreshment in a public house when they could obtain none in their own lodgings was much as other witnesses had indicated. About 10 pm, when Petit had asked to be allowed to go to the door of Galbraith's alehouse, MacIntosh went with him, 'holding the prisoner by the breast', while the soldier of the escort with him had his drawn bayonet in his hand. Just as they reached the door they were surrounded 'by a number of people who placed themselves between MacIntosh and the door and immediately laid hold of [the soldier's] bayonet and endeavoured to rescue the prisoner.' MacIntosh and the soldier were knocked down and Petit was rescued and immediately ran off. The half dozen rescuers also ran off. MacIntosh and the three soldiers had searched the public houses and elsewhere in Falkirk and the adjoining woods but failed to find Petit. MacIntosh later learned that Petit had been seen next day about eight miles west of Falkirk.[16]

If the testimonies of several of those witnesses were reliable, the behaviour, and particularly the salutations to Bacchus, at Falkirk of the escorting militiamen were hardly conducive to good order and military discipline. As John Carmichael said he had warned, these activities contributed to the escape of Petit at Falkirk. No doubt that was what Petit, who seems to have paid the reckonings, had hoped; and it was noticeable that, apart from some beer which the alehouse keeper John Brown recalled him drinking, Petit himself apparently did not share in any of the libations consumed by the members of his escort. Moreover, the motives of the rescuers—said to number half a dozen—raise perhaps interesting, if unanswerable, questions. Were they moved merely by expectation of personal gain in drink, money, or goods from Petit? Or were any of them moved by political, or anti-authority, anti-war or anti-army views or feelings? The judge at the subsequent trial of Hutton and Turner seems to have found none of these latter motives present.

In what was a rare surviving precognition by a prisoner of war in any Scots depot, Petit gave his own account of his escape at Falkirk, but also of some aspects of his life. His account, which was recorded on 12 March 1812, four months after his escape from Falkirk, suggests Petit was not without certain resemblances to Walter Mitty. First, Petit appears to have given Brest as his place of birth. Brest, however, was later crossed out by whoever took his precognition and in its place was written Havre de Grace [Le Havre]. As will be seen shortly, it is possible that Brest had indeed been the scene of some notable events in Petit's life—but not, it seemed, of his birth. Second, he claimed that at the time of his capture a year earlier he had been second captain of *Le Vengeur*, when all the evidence is that his rank on that ship was seaman.[17]

Some highly significant information, however, about himself which Petit did give in his precognition and whose accuracy there is no reason to doubt, was that 'He was bred a gun and locksmith.' What more useful skill for any prisoner to possess than that of locksmith?

His account of the circumstances of his escape at Falkirk confirmed that he had reached there with his escort after being recaptured at Stirling following his escape in March 1811 from Esk Mills. He had been handcuffed from Stirling to Falkirk but the handcuffs had been removed at the latter by Sergeant MacIntosh on arrival at the house of John Hutton, a barber, where they were to lodge for the night. Hutton's house was next door to the premises of Mr and Mrs James Galbraith. With some differences, the main one of which was that he himself had taken part with Sergeant MacIntosh and the other members of his escort in drinking in various ale houses, Petit's version of events was similar to those of the other witnesses already mentioned. His version reads, however, in places almost like an extract from scenes in a popular comedy or farce. In the course of the evening's drinking, Petit recalled, he and Sergeant MacIntosh found themselves drinking with two men, one of them a butcher, whom MacIntosh informed that Petit was a French prisoner. At a house near Hutton the barber's, the sergeant, one of his soldiers and Petit were still drinking at midnight, this time in the company of 'three bad women.' When about one o'clock in the morning they all left this house, Petit said, 'they were attacked in the street by some men, one of whom was the butcher and his companion.' Petit saw the butcher knock the sergeant down. Petit declared that 'nothing passed between him and the butcher and his companion when they met first in the public house about rescuing Petit from the sergeant and his party. But when the butcher and his companion and others attacked the sergeant and his comrade on the street ... the butcher knew perfectly well that Petit was in custody of the sergeant and his party and endeavoured to pull Petit out of the sergeant's hands. In so doing he tore Petit's jacket, and not having succeeded in his pulling, the butcher knocked down the sergeant and desired Petit to run off. The butcher's companion laid hold of the other soldier and gave Petit a kick in the breech and desired him to run away. Petit then got away. But soon afterward the butcher came up to Petit, who agreed to give him whisky in a public house. There they met up with the butcher's companion again. The butcher, said Petit, advised him to go to Glasgow but Petit wished rather to return to Stirling. The butcher accompanied Petit westward along the road for some distance but before leaving Petit he took from him 'his watch and a bundle containing a pair of grey stockings and a handkerchief and he at the same time took two dollars (of four shillings and six pence each) out of Petit's breeches pocket.' Petit proceeded towards Stirling, where 'he remained about two days ... concealed.' Unfortunately, his precognition did not divulge his place of concealment.[18]

The next part of Petit's precognition illustrates his remarkable audacity. He said that 'he sent a woman with a note to the provost of Stirling describing the watch and other articles which had been stolen but he, Petit, never recovered them.' How many escaped prisoners of war on the run would have thus ventured to complain to a civic head?

After two days, Petit left Stirling and went to Perth, 'where he was apprehended and sent back to the depot. And all this Petit declares to be the truth.' If it was indeed the truth then he seems likely to have been the only escaping prisoner of war in Scotland who had been helped on his way by a kick in the breech from an unexpectedly altruistic inhabitant.

Petit's escape at Falkirk concluded with two trials. One was the court-martial at Edinburgh Castle early in December 1811 of Sergeant Duncan MacIntosh. He was charged with allowing the escape of Petit and also for being drunk while carrying out his escort duty. MacIntosh was acquitted of being drunk or of any connivance in the escape, but he was sentenced to be reduced to the rank and pay of private. The second trial, held in April 1812 at Stirling, was of Andrew Hutton and Andrew Turner. They were unanimously convicted by a jury of unlawfully aiding and assisting Petit in making his escape at Falkirk. But the judge, 'being satisfied from the evidence that the offence proceeded chiefly from ignorance and thoughtlessness, and want of sober habits and not from any previously concerted scheme or malicious design, and considering that the prisoners had already been some time in confinement, sentenced them to the mitigated punishment of two months' imprisonment in the jail of Stirling.'[19]

Captain Moriarty, the agent at Valleyfield, in writing to the Crown Agent two days before the trial of Hutton and Turner to confirm that Petit would be sent to attend it as a witness, added in a postcript: 'He is a very Slippery fellow and a Dangerous Cunning Character and requires to be well watched.'[20]

That that very slippery fellow had himself indeed been apprehended at Perth early in December 1811 was confirmed not only in surviving official sources but also in the *Perth Courier*. 'On Thursday evening,' the *Courier* reported one week later on 12 December, 'while the Constables were in search of some suspected persons, they met with a foreigner who confessed himself to be a prisoner of war that had escaped from Penicuik. He was immediately secured in this jail.' Some checking of the identity of this foreigner, as well as some correspondence concerning it, appears to have followed. Two days after Christmas, Captain Moriarty at Valleyfield (the depot to which, had he not escaped from Esk Mills on 7 March, Petit would have been transferred along with 2,400 or so other prisoners on 11 March, unless he had then been sent to Edinburgh Castle), wrote to the Transport Board about Petit's arrest at Perth. 'François Petit,' the Board replied on 31 December, 'is to be kept in custody as a prisoner of war.' That instruction proved almost immediately to be an expression of groundless optimism.[21]

For Petit, having arrived at Valleyfield on Boxing Day, escaped from it eight days later on 3 January 1812, 'through the gate while the Turnkeys were Inside counting.'

Though he had not lingered long at Valleyfield Petit was there long enough at least to have his physical description inscribed in the depot's Entry Book. In this description there were changes, at least one of them significant, compared with that inscribed at Greenlaw and at Esk Mills. First, he was now said to have been born not at Le Havre but at Quebec. Was Petit claiming to be French Canadian? Second, he was said to be 22, not 25. Third, he was still described as of stout build but his height was now 5 feet 4 inches, not 5 feet 2¾ inches, his hair and his eyes were no longer black but respectively brown and hazel, his face, formerly long, was now oval, his 'good' complexion was now ruddy. Perhaps some of these changes in his physical appearance were the result of Petit's enjoyment of eight months of fresh air and sunshine after his escape from Esk Mills. On the other hand, whereas formerly no marks or wounds on him had been recorded, he was now said to be 'Strongly marked on side of nose with Small Pox' and, more significantly, with 'A variety of marks, with Ink on Breast and Arms, particularly the left Arm under which is the word "Mariette".' Finally, due to his having perhaps 'gone native' for seven or eight months in or about Stirling, it was recorded that Petit 'Speaks English.'

Why had the smallpox scars and the 'variety of marks' and 'Mariette' gone unnoticed in the two previous formal descriptions of Petit in the Greenlaw and Esk Mills Entry Books? Was it due to haste or carelessness on the part of the clerks there? Or was it that Petit had suffered smallpox and had also had the 'variety of marks' and Mariette's name tattooed on himself during his lengthy sojourn in or about Stirling and thus after his description had been inscribed at Greenlaw and Esk Mills? In that case was Mariette the woman at Stirling who had been referred to as 'his wife'? Was her full name Mariette Turnbull? Or had Mariette, a French rather than a Scots name, been a lady of Petit's acquaintance before his capture on *Le Vengeur* in October 1810? As with so many other aspects of the life of this remarkable escaper, such questions are easier to ask than to find reliable answers to.[22]

There was some additional interesting information about Petit provided by Captain Moriarty at Valleyfield when he submitted to the Transport Office a proforma report on Petit's escape from the depot on 3 January 1812. 'Dressed in sailor's blue jacket and trousers,' Moriarty wrote, 'with boots under a good hat [sic], check shirt and handkerchief. Carries an oval tin snuff box about him with the word Petit on the cover. Passes for a watchmaker and a native of Quebec and has been rambling through the country at Glasgow, Stirling and Perth.' In addition to his training and skill as gunmaker and locksmith Petit had apparently claimed also those of watchmaker. The Entry Book, in recording his recapture at Perth and arrival at Valleyfield in December 1811, had indeed mentioned cryptically that he had arrived there not from Perth but from Glasgow. It seems unlikely that he would have been escorted from Perth to Valleyfield via Glasgow. So had he perhaps, in an otherwise unrecorded further escape, absconded from custody at Perth or while on his way from there directly to Valleyfield and had reached Glasgow only to be recaptured there after a few days and then taken to Valleyfield? Or did Captain Moriarty's reference to Glasgow simply mean that while Petit had been at large for seven or eight months after escaping from Esk Mills in March 1811 he had passed some time not only at Stirling but also at Glasgow? These are further unanswerable questions.[23]

Having journeyed for sure to or through Stirling, Falkirk and Perth, and also apparently Glasgow, during his first and second escapes respectively from Esk Mills and Falkirk, Petit after his escape from Valleyfield in January 1812 had made his way to Aberdeen. It was there that he was recaptured about two months later. What had he been doing during those two months? Had he spent all or most of that time in Aberdeen itself? Wherever he had spent it was there someone who had helped conceal him? Why if he still had a wife at Stirling had he apparently not gone there? Or had his wife there joined him at Aberdeen? No answers can be offered to such questions either since there is no surviving evidence about how, where and perhaps with whom Petit spent his time during this third escape. The available scraps of information show only that after his recapture Petit was confined in Aberdeen gaol, that for Petit's subsistence there the agent at Valleyfield had to pay £1.0.3., that the cost of Petit's removal from Aberdeen to Valleyfield was £3.7.0., and that once back at the depot Petit was kept as a matter of course on short allowance or rations of food until he had made good the reward for his recapture. It was exactly on the anniversary of his first escape from Esk Mills that he was brought back from Aberdeen and marched into Valleyfield again on 7 March 1812.[24]

There he remained longer than on his first entry to the depot two months earlier—but not much longer. For on 1 June he escaped a second time from Valleyfield—this time, it appears, from the guardhouse.[25]

On this second escape from Valleyfield Petit again disappeared from sight or sound until a month later the *Montrose Review* informed its readers that 'On Saturday [27 June] a French prisoner of war of the name of François Petite [sic] was apprehended in the vicinity of this town by a party of the local militia ... and is now in gaol. He gives various accounts of himself and says he escaped from Pennycuick.'[26] He would hardly have been Petit if he had not given 'various accounts of himself'. Having previously gone westward to Stirling (and apparently to Glasgow) and north to Aberdeen, Petit must have decided again to try his luck northwards. Had he gone back again as far north as Aberdeen before turning back southward to Montrose? Or had he been at Montrose during that month, perhaps seeking a boat that would take him to the continent? Again all is speculation concerning his movements or his intentions.

The next instalment of the story appeared in the following issue of the *Montrose Review*. 'Monsieur Petite, the French prisoner of war who was apprehended and lodged in gaol here last week, escaped from thence on Saturday morning, having unscrewed the locks from three doors that confined him. He was furnished with the necessary implements by an old woman, an inhabitant of this town.' How and why the old woman had passed the necessary implements to Petit was not explained.[27]

Petit then appears to have headed south-westward from Montrose, through either Brechin or Forfar and Kirriemuir. A fortnight or more after his escape from Montrose gaol he had reached the boundary between Angus and Perthshire at Ruthven. There at the printfield 'after a hard run over hedge and ditch he was caught … by some gentlemen who were viewing the field. He was brought in safely and lodged in his old quarters in Perth gaol (he was there about a year ago). The little gentleman having been ordered over to the depot at Pennycuick, a Serjeant and seven or eight men were sent to escort him. On their arrival at Kirkcaldy, where they were to halt for the day, he was deposited for the time in the prison there. But Monsieur Petite did not like the house, and left it quietly during the night. He has not since been heard of.'[28]

This report, even if (like the previous one in the *Montrose Review*) it misspelled Petit's name, illustrated at least three points. First, it indicated that the authorities were so concerned by Petit's repeated escapes that they sent not merely a sergeant and three soldiers, as on the occasion of his recapture the previous year at Stirling, but a sergeant and seven or eight soldiers to fetch him back from Perth to Valleyfield. Second, it again demonstrated the apparent ability of Petit to escape from custody virtually at will. Third, the newspaper report itself appeared to show a degree of amused indulgence toward the escape of an enemy prisoner which perhaps reflected the not unsympathetic attitude of some, perhaps many, people in Scotland to the prisoners of war and even to escapers among them, an attitude which has already more than once been observed in earlier chapters. Petit's escapades in the summer of 1812 coincided with a strong tide of escapes by French prisoners of war, particularly of officers, several of them generals, from parole towns in England. Since January that year, when General Simon had broken his parole and absconded from Odiham, General Lefebvre-Desnoettes had escaped in May from Cheltenham, and General Phillippon at the beginning of July from Oswestry. It was therefore the more remarkable that the mighty Thunderer itself, *The Times*, which had reported these and other escapes, and in mid-July had denounced 'the scandalous breaches of parole among the French prisoners', and had also reported on 24 July the second reading of the government's Bill for 'better preventing the escape of prisoners of war', should have published word for word the report about Petit's escapes at Montrose and Kirkcaldy quoted above from the *Montrose Review* and the *Caledonian Mercury*. François Petit thus became the only prisoner of war in any Scots closed depot to be mentioned by name in a news report in *The Times*. His fame, or his notoriety, was spreading.[29]

After his departure from the gaol at Kirkcaldy, Petit headed south. At the beginning of August he was recaptured in the Borders, as the crow flies about 45 miles south-east of Valleyfield, at Jedburgh. He was marched back to Valleyfield again on 6 August. Similar questions to those before arise about Petit's activities during these two months following his second escape from Valleyfield as in the two months of his previous escape from that depot. Once more there is no surviving evidence on which to base possible answers.[30]

After his second escape from Valleyfield and his successive recaptures even the apparently indefatigable Petit appears to have begun to tire of his repeated failure to achieve lasting freedom from captivity. Immediately after his recapture at Jedburgh and on the day of his return then to Valleyfield Petit must have informed Captain Andrew Brown, who had succeeded Captain Moriarty the previous month as agent at the depot, of his willingness to volunteer into His Britannic Majesty's navy or army. For it was on that same day, 6 August, that Brown wrote to the Transport Board on the matter. 'We cannot,' the Board replied four days later, 'allow François Petit to enter His Majesty's Service nor can he be received into His Majesty's Navy.' Whether this decision disappointed Petit is not certain. But certainly Captain Brown appears to have been dismayed by the prospect of having to continue to deal with this particularly troublesome prisoner. For on 18 August Brown wrote again to the Transport Board, this time recommending that Petit be transferred from Valleyfield to a prison hulk in the south of England, 'it being impossible for him to keep [Petit] secure.' Brown's dismay was no doubt deepened when several days later the Board's reply reached him: 'François Petit cannot be removed from Valleyfield but you will take such Measures for the better Security of this Prisoner as you may think necessary.'[31]

Baulked of the prospect of being permitted to enlist in the British armed services, and recovering his determination to regain his freedom, Petit escaped for the third time from Valleyfield on 11 October 1812. On this occasion he departed 'by the stockade at back of Hospital.' This proved, however, a relatively brief escape: Petit was recaptured nine days later, at place unstated, and escorted back yet again to the depot.[32]

There was an unusual silence in the official records and in the press about François Petit thereafter until March 1813, when a cryptic reference was made in correspondence between the Valleyfield agent and the Transport Board about the re-capture of an escaped prisoner named Petit, but neither his first name nor any other circumstantial detail about the escaper was given. If this escaper were indeed François Petit then it was his last escape.[33] Then Captain Brown, the depot agent, who had written the Transport Board a few days earlier on the subject, received from the Board a reply dated (perhaps aptly) 1 April, which declared that 'the prisoner François Petit may be allowed to volunteer into the Navy.' The decision might seem a curiously inconsistent one, given the policy of the Board that no French prisoners of war (as distinct from those of most other nationalities) could be allowed to join His Britannic Majesty's forces. Was the Transport Board, like Captain Brown himself, glad to seize the chance to be rid at last of this 'Slippery Dangerous Cunning' prisoner? Petit for his part had evidently abandoned his earlier determination to keep on trying to escape and had instead concluded that, in the popular phrase of a later century, if you can't beat 'em, join 'em.[34]

Whatever the explanations, Petit duly stepped out from Valleyfield depot at last on 7 April 1813 on his way to Leith, by order of Vice Admiral Otway there, apparently to join the crew of HMS *Adamant*. The muster list of that vessel indeed shows Petit duly came aboard that day and became No. 374 of the crew. He appears, however, to have been discharged from the *Adamant* next day, presumably to some other vessel—but if so it was not identified. Thereafter no sign of Petit has been found in any official record or newspaper report. It may not be improbable that from that time or soon afterward he achieved anonymity by assuming an alias more effectual than his previous one of Pierre.[35]

Petit was thus the most frequent escaper from any Scots depot. In the two years between March 1811 and March 1813 he had escaped seven, and possibly even eight, times. In March 1811 he had escaped from Esk Mills, in November that year at Falkirk, in January 1812 from Valleyfield, in June again from Valleyfield, in July first at Montrose then at Kirkcaldy, in October once more from Valleyfield, and possibly, though not certainly, for a fourth time from that depot in March 1813. Captain Moriarty's reference as early as January 1812 to Petit's 'rambling through the country' appeared even more justified as time passed, since Petit not only escaped from such a variety of places but was recaptured at Stirling, Perth, Aberdeen, Montrose, Ruthven, Jedburgh, and two other places unstated.

Was there, however, in captivity at Valleyfield another escaper like Petit? The question arises from the recollections of that familiar inmate successively in 1811-14 at Esk Mills, Valleyfield and Perth—Lieutenant Marote-Carrier. In Marote-Carrier's recollections an entire chapter is devoted to a mysterious character known simply to his fellow prisoners at Valleyfield as The Galérien. A galérien was a convicted criminal sentenced to forced labour. In earlier centuries galériens had been literally galley slaves, chained with other convicts to the benches athwart galleys and forced to row those vessels. The Galérien, whoever or whatever he really was or had been besides being a captive at Valleyfield, had made a strong impression on Marote-Carrier. The latter's recollection of The Galérien's skill, for instance, in entertaining his fellow prisoners in the depot by story-telling has already been observed above.[36]

The Galérien's ability to catch and hold the attention of his audiences, who, according to Marote-Carrier, occasionally included even depot sentries, was not, it seems, due to his having 'something pleasing in his outward appearance or prepossessing in his face. Far from it. Short and thick-set, he crouched awkwardly on the ground. His fiery red hair, tousled, dishevelled, stood all bristly upon his head or hung over his forehead, the narrowness of which appeared still more striking. Whenever the devilish smile habitual to him did not wrinkle his face it presented an expression of the most indescribable ingratitude.'

No one, Marote-Carrier said, knew The Galérien under any other name. 'His name was a mystery as much for the prisoners as for the English. He himself confided it to no one; and although he was incomparably cynical in confessing to having committed a thousand infamies, where he came from or who he was no one ever knew. … he passed whole days recounting his adventures to those who gathered round him and he was never at a loss for words.'[37]

What his fellow prisoners, or at least those of them who were absorbed in listening to his stories, learned about him from these, Marote-Carrier said, was that The Galérien had been condemned to forced labour in perpetuity at the age of 22. 'He had been sent to serve his sentence at the convict prison at Brest. He remained there ten years, while making a thousand attempts to escape and seeing them miscarry.

'He was a locksmith by trade … One night he did so well, thanks to the help of his companion in chains, that he managed to open a concealed door and the two men quietly escaped together… The darkness was profound. The other condemned man belonged to Brest. He guided The Galérien by a thousand little alleys that were little used, passing along with measured tread, slowed by the ball and chain attached to the right leg of each man, taking care to avoid making the slightest noise, and also avoiding places that were watched by sentries.'[38]

The two escaped convicts thus arrived at the house in Brest of The Galérien's companion, who also was a locksmith. His son had taken over his work, but he still knew perfectly the lay-out of his workshop, which was next door to his house. The man from Brest helped himself to a file, and he and The Galérien then walked away from the town. Once they were at a safe distance from it they filed away at the chain that linked them together and at the rivets on the two balls. Once they had filed their way through their shackles they separated and each went his own way. The Galérien found refuge for some time in the countryside, amid the woods, rocks and moors, stealing food and money by night from peasants' houses. After a time, when it seemed at last safe to do so he went to St Malo and got new clothing, cut his moustache and let his hair grow. Assured that his whole appearance was changed, The Galérien went into a cafe to see if by overhearing the conversations of other customers he could find a vessel for which crew were being sought. While thus engaged he noticed a newspaper with a report of his escape and that of his companion from Brest, whose name was published in the paper, and whose recapture was also reported. The Galérien then found that his own description and a reward for his recapture were the subject of a poster pinned up everywhere in St Malo. 'It was remarked,' Marote-Carrier recalled, 'that each time he told this story he did not mention his own name, nor spoke of the crime for which he had been condemned. Sometimes when he was asked about his silence on these points he seemed not to hear the question and went on with his story.'[39]

The Galérien, emphasising his skill as a locksmith, and his robust appearance convincing its captain that he would make a good fighting man, was able to join the crew of a privateer ship at St Malo. Marote-Carrier recalled that the name of this privateer ship was *L'Indomptable*. But *L'Indomptable* was soon captured by the same British frigate, *Royalist*, which had captured Marote-Carrier's own privateer ship *L'Aventurier*, and The Galérien became a captive on the hulks at Chatham. 'As he was not, however,' said Marote-Carrier, 'on the same hulk as us there, I did not see him and knew him only at Valleyfield where each day that passed put me in involuntary contact with him.'[40]

Story-telling was not the only activity in which The Galérien passed his days at Valleyfield. 'Far from it. Very often he was seen alone, walking, silent and preoccupied, dragging his right foot—an incriminating reminder of the ball which had once been riveted there. ... he seemed to be keeping away from the society of the other prisoners; a careworn wrinkle puckered his brows. At other times he went rummaging in all the corners, picking up scrap iron and anything metallic that he found. Then, whenever bad weather prevented us going out the prison block, The Galérien established himself near the fire, heating and fashioning his bits of iron, to which he gave strange forms without explaining to us the use which he wished to make of them. He stubbornly refused to reveal his purpose and did not answer questions put to him on that subject.

'Nimble and dexterous without equal in all bodily exercises, The Galérien had the secret of overcoming obstacles that appeared insuperable. I will cite only one example. One day that we had formed a project for escaping the question arose of prising up an iron bar in one of the windows of our room. It had to be done without a sound, for fear of alerting the guards, and also without making a visible breach so that the damage would not be discovered on the rounds made each day before nightfall by the guards. So we had recourse to The Galérien. Nothing was easier, he told us, and he agreed to do the work on condition that we did not try to discover the method by which he managed it. … He took a rope of average thickness and passed it round the bar in question, then he asked five or six of our group to heave with all our might on the rope when he gave the signal. Above it he stretched a cover in front of the window so that we could see nothing of his work. These preparations duly made, he silently began the work, and at the end of a few seconds he said "Pull!". The six men all heaved together and the bar yielded at the first pull, broken clean off, and so neatly that it seemed as if cut by a razor. That done, The Galérien took the bar and put it back in its place so well that the most practised eye could not spot the break. We never did learn how he had done it.'[41]

Marote-Carrier recalled several escapes made by The Galérien. One was by his hiding in the cart that every evening at dusk took away the night soil from the depot necessaries or latrines. Of The Galérien thereafter nothing was seen or heard for about three months until one day a troop of soldiers appeared escorting him back to Valleyfield. The other prisoners learned then that The Galérien, dressed thanks to his plentiful resources as 'a real gentleman', during those months had 'wandered about Scotland and England. Then one fine day when his purse was empty, he had presented himself at a master locksmith's in London. There he had worked for several months, distinguishing himself by the well finished character of his work and demonstrating quite extraordinary skill.' The Galérien 'had assumed a false name … But his face was unfortunately too distinctive—the colour of his hair, which was a particular shade of red, and the sparkle in his greenish eyes, that gleamed like those of a cat.' One day a policeman, struck by The Galérien's distinctive features, remembered a description on a wanted poster he had seen and on checking it found that the details were identical. The policeman went back unnoticed to The Galerién's place of work at the locksmith's to check on a reference in the poster to his dragging of his right leg as a result of his years as a convict, and confirmed that that feature, too, was identical. The Galérien's recapture then and his return to Valleyfield made him determined to regain 'his liberty whenever the opportunity presented itself.'[42]

The Galérien's next escape from Valleyfield, Marote-Carrier recalled, arose out of the trade in straw goods made by many of the prisoners but to which there was strong objection by some British manufacturers and consequently a prohibition by the Transport Board and the destruction of some of the straw goods by the depot authorities.[43] It was one evening when a pyre of some of these straw goods was therefore blazing in the exercise yard at Valleyfield that '… a very fashionably dressed gentleman presented himself successively at the three gates in the wall surrounding the prison and opened them with a key that he carried, without the sentries, who took him for one of the visiting strangers from Edinburgh [connected with the straw trade], challenging him. It was only next morning the English to their great chagrin found that The Galérien had again escaped.' Marote-Carrier says The Galérien walked all night. Then, believing he had outpaced any immediate pursuit, he 'decided to resume his old status as locksmith, as he had done on his first escape. But made more careful by the troublesome consequences of his sojourn in London, he took the decision to withdraw into a little town where the police would not be so active … as in the capital. He went to … [blank], a township in Scotland, far from all the big towns, and engaged himself as a worker with the master locksmith of the place, saying he came from London, where he had done his apprenticeship, and that he was Scots. The ease with which he spoke the mountain patois led his future employer to believe that he was from the Highlands. The skill with which he carried out some tasks given him as a trial provided the most impressive notion of his cleverness, and the locksmith admitted him into his little forge, proud to have so good a worker. For a month The Galérien lived happily and without anxiety. He believed he was shielded from enquiries. But he had counted without his host. His master had a young and pretty daughter, a girl of unique qualities, and The Galérien, finding her to his taste, began assiduously, with the permission of her father, to pay court to her. The father, far from finding that unacceptable, gave him every encouragement, and announced that he would grant him as son-in-law a dowry for his daughter—his workshop, whose prosperity the talent of this worker would ensure. As for the girl, although young and charming, by one of those inexplicable caprices of the human heart, she fell in love with The Galérien and responded to his advances, so much so that marriage was soon considered as all settled. Love is indiscreet and blind. While keeping quiet about his previous experiences in France, The Galérien confided to his mistress the story of his escape from Valleyfield and urged her to keep it an absolute secret. The girl promised to do so and for a month afterward the fugitive had no cause to regret his confidence.

'Unfortunately, the ease with which he had made himself loved by the locksmith's daughter speedily turned The Galérien's head. He told himself that before his marriage he could enjoy a final fling. He was flighty and unfaithful. He neglected his fiancée for a Hebe in a tavern. The matter remained a secret for some time, but his future wife was not slow to notice it, and in a moment of exasperation and vengeance, she went and denounced the escaped prisoner to the police of the place. … Once the alarm was raised, the policemen began to search for The Galérien, and his marriage was abruptly broken off by his arrest, following which he was carried off to Edinburgh, where his identity was established and from which he was sent a second time to rejoin his former companions in captivity.'[44]

His recapture did not, however, discourage The Galérien from again attempting his escape from Valleyfield. Unobserved by the sentries, he sawed a hole in the palisades one evening and, in the gathering darkness and during a downpour of rain which drove the sentries into their boxes for shelter, he ran off. But he was recaptured at daybreak and again escorted back into Valleyfield.[45]

The Galérien's next escape was, in Marote-Carrier's view, 'the most brilliant of all.' On an evening of heavy snow, when the sentries had made their regular rounds in the exercise yard and elsewhere to check that no prisoners had concealed themselves, and those members of the guard not on sentry duty were sheltering in the guardhouse, the food contractor of the depot arrived on horseback at his usual time. The turnkey opened the three doors of the stockade for the contractor, and gave the keys back to the sentry, asking him to keep them until the return of the contractor. The latter dismounted from his horse and passed the horse over to the care of the sentry, who because of the severity of the cold began to walk the animal in the yard. Not far from the depot gate there was a kind of little shed that was never visited. The Galérien, however, had noticed it and had slipped into it that afternoon. A quarter of an hour after the contractor had entered the kitchens, The Galérien crept stealthily out of hiding, unseen in the darkness. He was, as usual on the days of his escapes, very well dressed. Walking boldly up to the sentry he called to him to open the gate. The sentry, seeing this well turned out man and hearing his order delivered in such an authoritative voice to make way for him, understandably assumed he was the contractor, attached the horse to a post, went to open the gate, then helped The Galérien to mount the horse and opened the three gates for him. In good English, The Galérien thanked the sentry, slipped a shilling into his hand, and galloped off, while the sentry covered him with thanks, closed the gates behind him and returned to his post.

Without looking back the Galérien fled on horseback until the following afternoon. By then he had arrived in a small town on the road to London. At a small inn in the town he ate a hearty meal, then saw in the distance a troop of soldiers in pursuit of him. Abandoning his horse, which had not yet recovered from the lengthy ride of the previous hours, The Galérien abruptly left the inn, plunged into a narrow muddy alley, and disappeared. 'We never saw him again at Valleyfield,' said Marote-Carrier.[46]

Marote-Carrier did himself, however, come across The Galérien once more. In February 1814 Marote-Carrier, having been transferred seventeen months earlier to Perth depot, had eventually convinced both Captain Moriarty, agent at Perth, and the Transport Board that he ought to be released as a subject of Oldenburg. From Perth on his way home therefore he duly arrived at Leith, where he had to report to a British frigate moored in the harbour. 'What was my astonishment,' Marote-Carrier long afterwards recalled, 'when, among the first persons I met on board, I recognised The Galérien from Valleyfield. He was cook for the [frigate's] officers.' After escaping on the contractor's horse and eluding his pursuers, The Galérien had eventually been recaptured and thrown into prison. 'The commandant then told him that the English government was tired of his escapades, and that he had to choose either to pass the rest of his days in the cachot or to take service on board a British warship. The Galérien had [therefore] broken with his true homeland and adopted England instead as his homeland. He had become cook on the frigate where he was still and was, he said, very happy with his position. For although he could not go ashore he lacked for nothing on board and he had as wife the most lively and pretty Scotswoman imaginable. They understood each other so well, although she was only seventeen and he was over forty.'[47]

The obvious question that arises from these recollections by Marote-Carrier is: was The Galérien in fact François Petit? On the one hand, there are some striking differences in the physical descriptions of the two men, as well as in some other aspects. Petit according to official sources was 22, or at least apparently in his early or mid-twenties. The Galérien, Marote-Carrier says, was condemned to the galleys at the age of 22, had spent ten years as a convict, and that in 1814 he was over forty years old. Petit's hair was black or dark brown, The Galerien's fiery red. Petit's eyes were black or (in a later official description) hazel, The Galérien's greenish. Marote-Carrier referred more than once to the dragging movement of The Galérien's right leg, to which in his convict days had been attached a ball and chain. No description of Petit refers to any such gait. Petit was captured as a seaman on board the privateer *Le Vengeur* and had spent some time on a hulk at Portsmouth before arriving successively at Greenlaw, Esk Mills and Valleyfield. Marote-Carrier says The Galérien had been captured on board the privateer *L'Indomptable* and, like himself, had passed some time on the hulks at Chatham before he came across him at Valleyfield.

On the other hand there appear to be some striking similarities between Petit and The Galérien. They apparently shared a gift for story-telling or, in Petit's case, for imaginative reconstruction of facts. Both men were locksmiths. One apparently had, and the other at first claimed to have, a connection with Brest: Petit, initially, that he had been born there; The Galérien that he had spent ten years there as a convict. Both escaped several times from Valleyfield, and Petit from several other ostensibly lockfast places as well. Both spent some months working as locksmiths during periods of escape—Petit once, it would appear, at Stirling; The Galérien, once in London and once in an unnamed town in Scotland 'far from all the big towns'. Both took up with the young daughter of their employer. Both ended the war in the British navy.

Do the apparently obvious differences between Petit and The Galérien make the conclusion inescapable that they really were two different men? Was it that they just happened both to be locksmiths, just happened both to be at Valleyfield at around the same period, just happened both to escape so often, just happened both to take up with the daughter of a master locksmith in Scotland who gave them employment during escapes, and just happened both eventually and roughly at the same period to join the British navy at Leith?

Or should these apparent coincidences point rather to the opposite conclusion, that Petit and The Galérien were in fact one and the same man? Was it conceivable that Marote-Carrier was deliberately attempting, even so long after the Napoleonic wars, to conceal the real identity of Petit by disguising him as The Galérien? If in the 1840s, when those recollections of Marote-Carrier were recorded, Petit (who certainly never tried to conceal his own surname) was, for all Marote-Carrier knew, still alive and perhaps again living in France, then the revelation by a former fellow prisoner of war of Petit's having 'broken with his true homeland' while the war was still being waged and joined the British navy might possibly have had some embarrassing or even more serious consequences for Petit. Is it indeed possible that Marote-Carrier did know at the time of recording his recollections that Petit was still alive, and therefore sought to disguise him sufficiently to shield him from awkward consequences though without making Petit unrecognisable to those who had shared his captivity at Valleyfield or earlier at Esk Mills, Greenlaw and on the hulks at Portsmouth? At the end of the day these are, like so many others concerning either François Petit or The Galérien, unanswerable questions.

23

The Ending of the War and the Great Repatriation

'Public news,' Sir Walter Scott wrote from Abbotsford to his brother-in-law Charles Carpenter on 3 September 1813, 'continue favorable; the great victories of Lord Wellington in Spain & the determined powers of resistance exhibited by the Continental powers seem to augur a favorable termination of the war. Yet I think while Bonaparte lives & reigns peace is hardly to be hoped for. Sebastian one of his favourite Generals who knew his character well told a friend of mine that if Europe Asia & Africa were at Bonapartes feet he would be miserable until he had conquered America, and I do not think his spirit is of that kind which learns moderation from adversity otherwise his disasters in Spain & Russia must have taught it.'[1]

Although the causes, spread and prolongation of the Napoleonic Wars were surely due to more than the megalomania of Napoleon, there was no doubt much perspicacity in Scott's comments. By the time Scott wrote that letter, and mainly for the reasons he mentioned in it, Napoleon's power was clearly in decline and the prospect was beginning to emerge of an end at last to the war. During the following seven months to the spring of 1814 the challenges confronting Napoleon indeed multiplied and deepened until he was obliged to abdicate and accept exile to Elba. If those challenges began with the destruction of his Grande Armée in the catastrophic Russian campaign of 1812 (although by mid-1813 he was able to assemble in Germany an army of some 450,000 but less experienced troops), they were compounded by a mushrooming of other challenges which included the alliance against him from February 1813 by Russia and Prussia which extended the one already formed by Britain, Russia, Spain and Portugal, and developed into the Sixth Coalition against France. That alliance was joined six months later by Austria and embraced also Sweden, (where Napoleon's former marshal Bernadotte had been elected heir apparent to the king). The success of the British army, in alliance with Spanish and Portuguese forces, in the Peninsular War, culminating in June 1813 in the decisive defeat of the French army at Vitoria, was followed in early October by Wellington's invasion of France itself. That invasion in turn was followed within a few days by the decisive defeat of Napoleon at Leipzig by the allied armies of Russia, Prussia, Austria, and

Sweden, (and by his old German allies or client states Saxony, Bavaria and Wurtemberg abandoning him and changing sides), and the consequent collapse of his power in Germany. The battle of Leipzig and its consequences sparked off a revolt in November by the Dutch and their restoration to power of the House of Orange. In December 1813 Switzerland also broke away from Napoleon's control, and further blows the following month were the withdrawal from the war of his hitherto faithful ally Denmark, and the allying of his marshal and brother-in-law Murat, king of Naples, with Austria, an alliance which speeded the ending of the French empire in Italy, where throughout the war the islands of Sardinia and Sicily had been the respective bases, protected by British forces, of the two old regime kings Victor Emmanuel of Piedmont-Sardinia and Ferdinand of Naples. Early in March 1814 the four major allied powers bound themselves by the Treaty of Chaumont to remain allied for twenty years and presently to offer Napoleon peace terms but if he rejected them (as he did), to fight the war to the end.

Despite his brilliant campaign in France in the opening months of 1814 to hold the invading allies at bay, Napoleon's power was broken by events in the first week of April. First, the French legislature decided then to depose him and, a few days later, to call to the throne Louis XVIII, brother of the guillotined Louis XVI. Second, Napoleon's marshals, gathered with him at Fontainebleau, refused any longer to follow him and urged him to abdicate in favour of his three-year-old son. That advice was immediately followed by the desertion to the allies of Marmont, one of the marshals, who took his troops with him, leaving Fontainebleau and Napoleon himself undefended. Tsar Alexander I of Russia then delivered the coup de grâce by demanding the unconditional abdication of Napoleon, which took place on 6 April.[2]

On the heels of some of those events between the summer of 1813 and spring 1814 followed the transfer of certain prisoners between the depots in Scotland, as well as from there to depots, hulks or in some cases to ports of embarkation in England. There also followed the release during those months of some of the non-French nationalities among the prisoners, although in many, if not most, cases their release was from confinement in the Scots depots straight into the ranks of the armed forces either of Britain or of their rulers at home who were allied with Britain against Napoleon.[3]

Even as early as March 1813 a confidential circular had been sent to all depots by the Transport Board, instructing the agents to 'report with the least possible delay for the information of the Lords Commissioner of the Admiralty the number of Germans and Italians respectively among the prisoners of war in your custody.' A reminder was sent a fortnight later to the agent at Greenlaw, who had evidently failed to respond to the Board's request.[4] During the three following months there was some conflict of view between the Secretary at War, Lord Bathurst, and the Admiralty about the transfer and concentration in one depot of the German and Italian prisoners and their separation from French prisoners. The Admiralty, which had received from the Transport Board 'a report ... upon the proposed separation of German and Italian prisoners of war from those who are natives of France,' agreed with the Board's view 'that collecting the German and Italian prisoners together in one depot would be attended with much inconvenience and great expence ...' Lord Bathurst, however, concerned with facilitating the enlistment of German and Italian prisoners into the British or allied armed forces of the prisoners' own rulers, pressed both for their being gathered together in one depot in England, to which those in the Scots depots should be gradually transferred, and also for their enjoying better conditions than French prisoners.

The outcome of these differences of view is not entirely clear but, so far as at least the prisoners in the Scots depots were concerned, it appears to have been a compromise. For in July the Admiralty instructed the Transport Board that 852 German and Italian prisoners reported held at Perth should be sent to Valleyfield, and at the latter the agent was instructed by the Transport Board to transfer to Perth the same number of French prisoners. An instruction two days earlier by the Board to its agent at Perth that from there some at least of the German and Italian prisoners be sent to Admiral Otway at Leith where he would send them on to Portsmouth, appears to have been overtaken a week later, however, by a message from the Transport Board to Otway that the Admiralty had decided 'that the German and Italian prisoners in Scotland are to remain where they are for the present.'[5]

The Perth Entry Book confirms that in three successive contingents on 31 July, 4 and 6 August some 858 prisoners arrived there from Valleyfield; and the Valleyfield Entry Book likewise confirms that on those same three days in successive contingents (the first of which included 204 men from the Hesse-Darmstadt regiment, all of whom had been captured at Badajoz in April 1812) 854 German and Italian prisoners arrived at that depot from Perth.[6]

Between the Entry Books and Transport Board correspondence there are some differences in the respective numbers of German and Italian prisoners composing the 854 transferred then from Perth to Valleyfield. But it seems there were between 460 and about 510 Italians and between 350 and 390 Germans. There are, however, indications that, if the criterion of nationality used were simply place of birth, some of those 'Germans' were actually Dutch, and a few among the 'Italians' were in fact French. As observed earlier, there were also reported, before those transfers from Perth, already in captivity in mid-July 1813 at Valleyfield 181 Italians and 238 Germans. So those transferred from Perth appeared to make the total assembled at Valleyfield by early August at least 641 Italians and 588 Germans.

Of the 350 to 390 Germans transferred from Perth to Valleyfield, the latter's Entry Books show that between 20 September 1813 and 15 February 1814, 111 enlisted: 88 in the British 60th regiment, a further four (of whom two appear to have been born in France) in the King's German Legion, and 19 in the 1st Dutch regiment. Of the Italians from Perth, the Valleyfield relevant Entry Book indicates that as many as 506 were released from the latter depot in successive contingents on 14, 15, 16, 18, 25 and 28 March 1814. Although the surviving evidence may leave some room for doubt, their release was almost certainly not to their homes and families but into the armed forces of the king of Sardinia.[7]

Of the remainder of the 237 or so at Valleyfield from the 854 Germans and Italians transferred from Perth, three Italians were released (probably as invalids) to France between August and December 1813, one Italian (François Le Prince, aide major, born at Turin and captured at Baylen in 1808) was sent in November to Edinburgh Castle en route to the hulks at Portsmouth for an earlier breach of his parole, one other Italian was sent in August to Edinburgh Castle for reasons unstated, and four Germans and two Italians died and were buried at Valleyfield between October 1813 and March 1814. The other 226 of the 854 Germans and Italians from Perth, so far as can be seen, remained at Valleyfield until they were released in the general repatriation of prisoners in June 1814.[8]

The difficulties in offering reliable totals for Italian and German prisoners assembled at Valleyfield by early August 1813 are further compounded by a report on 23 August from the Transport Board to the War Office that the German prisoners then totalled 627. An assessment of the number of Italians at Valleyfield, based on the relevant Entry Book and on press reports in March 1814 of their release then from the depot, suggest the number was not between merely 641 and about 690, but between 900 and 1,000.[9] A survey of the depot's other Entry Books indicates that in those successive contingents on 14, 15, 16, 18, 25 and 28 March 1814 some 450 Italians were released from Valleyfield—in addition to the 506 or so also released then who had been transferred there in July-August 1813 from Perth. All these releases of Italians appear again not to have been to their homes and families but into the armed forces of the king of Sardinia as an ally of Britain.[10]

On 2 March, having been directed two days earlier by the Duke of York, commander-in-chief of the British army, to release from the Scots depots prisoners from Sardinia, Piedmont and Genoa, the Transport Board confirmed that these prisoners would be sent to Leith and embarked for Harwich; and on 18 March the Board sought the Admiralty's instructions on a suggestion forwarded by the War Office that 'as the number of Piedmontese and Genoese prisoners of war in this country are now sufficient to complete the Legion about to be formed that the natives of the north of Italy ... may be allowed to enter into His Sardinian Majesty's service.'[11] Four Piedmontese officers indeed had arrived in Scotland early in March to recruit at the Scots depots prisoners belonging to Sardinia, Piedmont and Genoa. The four officers almost at once complained that many of the prisoners were being 'deterred from enlisting by the fear of being ill-treated by the other prisoners'; and the Transport Board consequently circularised its agents at the depots instructing them to give 'every facility' to these recruiting officers 'and that the natives of those countries may be separated from the French prisoners as much as possible, particularly after their enlistment.'[12] Nor did the release of almost 1,000 Italian prisoners from Valleyfield on those successive days during March 1814 shortly before the abdication of Napoleon, go unreported in the local press. 'Three hundred of the Italian prisoners ... liberated ... by an order of the Government,' the *Edinburgh Evening Courant* informed its readers on 24 March, 'embarked at Leith on Tuesday [22 March], 500 yesterday, and the remainder today.'

From Perth, too, a further 51 Italian prisoners, presumably overlooked in the count made the previous year by the depot authorities, were released on 30 March, 'discharged to the Service of the King of Sardinia.'[13]

Toward the end of November 1813, four months after the transfer of the 854 Germans and Italians from Perth to Valleyfield, one month after the decisive defeat of Napoleon at Leipzig, and five days after the Dutch uprising against him and their recall of the Prince of Orange, a much more peremptory order had been received from the Transport Board by depot agents: '... transmit to this Office *immediately* a return of the number of all the Germans in your custody, whether belonging to the left or right Bank of the Rhine, together with a *separate* statement of the number of "Flimingers" [sic]. P.S. We also direct you to send a statement of the number of subjects of all other states excepting Frenchmen and Italians.'[14]

Concerning any consequent further releases of Germans from Valleyfield or Perth before the end of the war and the general repatriation in early summer 1814, the evidence is limited. But one group of German prisoners about whose suggested release the Transport Board that same month of November 1813 sought instructions from the Admiralty were those who were natives of Hesse-Darmstadt, several hundreds of whom had been serving in that regiment when captured at Badajoz in 1812 and, as has already been observed, had subsequently found themselves confined first at Perth and then transferred in July-August 1813 to Valleyfield.[15] There appears to have been a distinct reluctance, however, on the part of at least some of those prisoners to gain their release at the expense of finding themselves obliged again to fight—this time against their erstwhile comrades in arms, the French. 'There being several prisoners in confinement at Valleyfield belonging to the Hesse Darmstadt Regiment, who have declined coming forward as volunteers from their not being particularly informed by their own officers of the actual state of their country,' the Transport Board wrote to its parole agent at Jedburgh in February 1814, 'we direct you to inform the officers under your care who belong to that Regiment of this circumstance, suggesting to them the propriety of their writing to the prisoners at Valleyfield, apprizing them of the actual situation of their country.'[16] The reluctance among some at least of those Hesse Darmstadt men at Valleyfield must have been prolonged, for as late as 28 April the Board ordered its agent at Valleyfield 'to send to Leith such subjects of Hesse Darmstadt as remain in his custody,' for onward transfer to The Hague.[17]

Another group of German prisoners in the Scots depots who appear not to have been released until the summer of 1814 were 183 men from Anhalt Dessau, of whom 133 were still held at Perth and 50 at Valleyfield as late as June that year. Indeed of the 50 at Valleyfield, as the agent there reported to the Transport Board, '8 only are willing to return home'; and the Board felt obliged to ask the Admiralty whether 'persons declining to return home should be compelled to go thither.'[18]

There appear to have been fewer difficulties in the release early in 1814 of those German prisoners who were Prussians—though in their case questions arose about some who were really Poles belonging to those areas acquired by Prussia during the successive partitions of Poland in the late 18th century. The Transport Board had sought from the depots, including Valleyfield and Perth, as early as September 1813 the number of prisoners who were Prussian. Although no return on this occasion has been found for Perth, Valleyfield reported then having 24 soldiers and 10 seamen who were Prussians. By January 1814, perhaps by the extraction of those considered to be Poles, the number of Prussians in the Scots depots had greatly declined: Valleyfield had 14, Perth only one. The Board suggested to the Admiralty that the cost of keeping Prussian prisoners could be ended either by allowing them to enter the service of His Britannic Majesty, or their helping to crew British merchant ships, or by handing them over to the official representatives of Prussia in Britain. This last proposal was supported by Earl Bathurst, Secretary at War, early in January 1814. The outcome was that a month later the Admiralty ordered the release of the 15 Prussians held at Valleyfield and Perth, and they were duly embarked at Leith for Helvoetsluys in Holland en route for home.[19]

The Dutch revolt against Napoleon in November 1813 and their recall to power of the Prince of Orange resulted within three months in further releases from the Scots depots. The numbers of Dutch involved in these releases were, however, much smaller than those of Italian or German prisoners. The revolt of the Dutch resulted, moreover, in public manifestations of support in Scotland, a few at least of which were reported in the press, and parts of some of which may have been audible, though probably not visible, to prisoners who happened to be held in Edinburgh Castle at the time. On the morning of 25 November, for example, the guns of Edinburgh Castle, as the *Caledonian Mercury* reported, were fired 'to celebrate the liberation of Holland from the French.' The *Perth Courier*, apparently lifting a report from some other unacknowledged Edinburgh journal, offered its readers a more detailed account than did the *Caledonian Mercury* of the celebrations that day. 'When the glorious news of the emancipation of Holland reached Leith on Thursday morning last [25 November], the Prince of Orange's Flag, with the words *Oranje Booven!* Orange for Ever!, was displayed from the counting-house of Messrs Denouan, the Dutch agents. The crews of the Dutch vessels, under charge of these gentlemen, old and young, immediately collected and saluted their favourite standard with loud huzzas! They were then called up to the counting-house and had their hats dressed with orange ribbons, bearing the words *Oranje Booven*, and having been furnished with two of the Prince's flags, proceeded to Edinburgh, and after giving three cheers at the Royal Exchange, returned to Leith, amid the acclamations of a vast crowd of spectators. They were regaled at the expense of the above gentlemen and spent the evening with the utmost conviviality and satisfaction.'[20]

Was it coincidence, or did the Transport Board know of the imminence of the Dutch revolt when, a fortnight before it took place, the Board sent out a circular marked 'Private' to all depots asking their agents to report '... what is the probable number of Dutchmen among the prisoners of war in your custody', and adding: 'It is desirable that this enquiry should be made by you as privately as possible.'?[21] By the end of November there was an unusually rapid exchange of letters between the Board and the Admiralty about the release of Dutch prisoners. As early as 26 November the Transport Board informed Admiral Hope at Leith that the Admiralty had 'directed that all such Dutchmen ... at Perth and Valleyfield as are willing to enter into the service of His Serene Highness the Prince of Orange are to be released and sent to the Nore', and the same day the Board instructed its agents accordingly at Valleyfield and Perth. On the 29th the Board sent the Admiralty, though without naming the depots concerned, 'three petitions which have been addressed to us by Dutch prisoners in this country, requesting to be liberated for the purpose of serving under ... the Prince of Orange.' That same day the Admiralty instructed the Board that Dutch volunteers were to be assembled not at the Nore but at Yarmouth.[22] A further circular by the Board on 24 December ordered its depot agents to report the numbers of prisoners they held who were natives of a dozen specified districts in the Netherlands and certain adjoining areas, 'who are willing to swear allegiance to the Sovereign Prince of the United Netherlands.'[23]

From the beginning of December Dutch prisoners thus began to be released homeward from Perth and Valleyfield to join the forces of the Prince of Orange.

On the 1st of that month 20 were marched away from Perth on the first stage of their journey to Yarmouth 'to join the large brigade of their countrymen at present forming' there. As the *Dundee Advertiser* reported, their release aroused great emotion among many of their non-Dutch fellow captives at the depot. 'On this occasion a vast number of prisoners came forward, anxious to be marched off with their companions, and calling out that they too were Dutchmen. Poor fellows! This ruse was unsuccessful; yet we trust the time is not far distant when the prison doors shall be opened and all the unfortunate captives of war restored to the domestic bliss from which the cruelty of ambition [Napoleon's was the ambition the *Advertiser* meant] has taken them.' Other problems arose when two days later from Valleyfield 'a considerable number' of released Dutch prisoners were marched to Leith 'to embark for the continent.' According to a letter from the Transport Board to its agent at Valleyfield, these Dutch volunteers were 'in a most miserable state in regard to clothing, and in particular are deficient in shoes and stockings.' The agent was asked to explain why he had sent them forth in that condition; his reply has not survived.[24]

In mid-January 1814, in what appears to have been another, if ambiguously phrased, order from the Transport Board to depot agents they were told 'to permit Colonel Sanbury to recruit from among the prisoners of war in your custody natives of the Low Countries whose language is entirely German.' Was the gallant colonel the Dutch officer who was reported by the press to have arrived a month later at Perth 'under the authority of Government to recruit such of the prisoners of the Depot as were natives of Holland, Germany or Flanders.'? Whoever that officer was, his efforts provided the citizens of Perth with 'the pleasure of seeing about 130 Netherlanders marched off from the depot [on 18 February] … to join their brethren already in arms to resist the domination of Bonaparte. They all seemed very pleased to go—as much for the cause of their liberation as for the blessing of liberty itself.'[25] From Valleyfield a week later 'nearly 200 natives of Holland, the Netherlands, and various parts of Germany, who have long been prisoners at Pennycuick marched from Edinburgh Castle to Leith where they embarked to join the armies of the allies on the continent.'[26]

Even if their figures and dates are not exactly the same as those given in press accounts, the Perth and Valleyfield Entry Books confirm that considerable numbers of prisoners were released on 14, 15 or 19 February 1814 as recruits to the 1st Dutch regiment. From Valleyfield the Books show 74 to have been thus discharged on 14 and 15 February, and from Perth 122 on 19 February. Differences from the dates occurring in press reports may be explained by sojourns at Edinburgh Castle for a day or two before embarkation at Leith en route for the continent.[27]

There were also released before the general repatriation in the summer of 1814 the much smaller numbers of several other nationalities among the prisoners in the Scots depots. The withdrawal of Switzerland from the war in December 1813, for instance, was soon followed by a decision by Earl Bathurst, Secretary at War, that all Swiss prisoners be released. The decision, relayed to the Admiralty on 20 January 1814, was presented by it in turn that same day as an order to the Transport Board, which next day directed its agents at Valleyfield and Perth to send their Swiss prisoners to Harwich for embarkation for the continent.[28] The number of Swiss held in the two Scots depots and released from Perth on 1 February and from Valleyfield the following day, was in fact very small: only five at Perth and six at Valleyfield.[29]

When in January 1814 Napoleon's loyal ally Denmark also withdrew from the war, the Admiralty on the 27th of that month directed the Transport Board to arrange the release of Danish prisoners of war. Earlier in the war many hundreds of these, as has been seen, had languished in captivity in Scotland, above all at Greenlaw. They had, however, long since been sent to depots or hulks in England, or had joined the British navy, or (as in the case, for example, of Captain Paul Andreas Kaald) had been repatriated. Two questions which soon arose in early 1814 were successively submitted by the Board to the Admiralty for decision. First, were Danes 'taken under the French flag' to be released? Second, were 'Danish prisoners to be released indiscriminately, or only such as are actually natives of Denmark'? [30] Whatever the replies of the Admiralty may have been, they have not been found. Uncertainty continued, however, about the release of 'Danes'. They had hitherto included Norwegians, as Norway was part of the kingdom of Denmark until given up by its king to Sweden by the Treaty of Kiel in January 1814, a transfer confirmed 17 months later by the peace Treaty of Vienna. On 3 March the Transport Board asked the Admiralty for instructions on even 'whether ... we should discontinue to release such Danes as may volunteer to serve in the usual proportions on board of East India [merchant] Ships', since the Board had just been told not to release any Danish prisoners 'until we shall have received a communication to that effect from [the]... Secretary of State for War and Colonies.'[31]

As for the Scots depots, although it is difficult to believe there were no Danish or Norwegian prisoners held there by early 1814, almost no firm evidence has been found of the presence of any at Valleyfield, Perth or Edinburgh Castle after November 1813. In that month there was a bare reference in a letter from the Transport Board to its agent at the Castle about keeping separate accounts for 'the Danish prisoners'. Since the transfer in or by 1811 of those from Greenlaw, most 'Danish' prisoners had been held at Chatham, Portsmouth and Plymouth. These are the only three places mentioned from 1813 in the accounts of a support fund for them.[32] A survey of releases and of places of birth in the Entry Books for all three Scots depots has found only one Dane apparently released as a result of the Admiralty's directive on the subject to the Transport Board on 27 January. He was one already encountered as a recaptured escaper in December 1811 from Edinburgh Castle and who had been sent the following month to Valleyfield: Brutus du Crot, a seaman, captured on the privateer *Figaro* off Norway in July 1811. Aged 20 and described as 'born Denmark', du Crot was released from Valleyfield to Leith on 25 February 1814. Even then he was said in the Entry Book to have been discharged not to Denmark but to France.[33] The last Transport Office return found listing the number of Danish prisoners in depots in Scotland and England was dated 26 June 1812, and it showed there were then 1,832 (excluding a further 36 on parole). It may be that many or most of those had been released on one ground or another by the time Denmark withdrew from the war early in 1814. On the other hand, so far as those who were actually Norwegian were concerned, the fact that their country was in the process of being transferred in 1814-15 from the kingdom of Denmark to that of Sweden appears to have delayed their release from captivity not merely, like that of the mass of French prisoners, until the summer of 1814, but even into autumn of that year. As late as September, five months after the end of the war and almost eight months after the decision to release the 'Danish' prisoners, there were still 603 Norwegian prisoners of war in captivity in Britain. But none of the 603 was held in any Scots depots, all of which had by then been closed.[34]

Norwegians were not the only non-French group of prisoners delays in whose release from captivity occurred in 1813-14. Some Portuguese, Spanish and Polish prisoners were also affected by political or diplomatic factors before gaining their release. The case of certain Poles in Scotland will be discussed below. So far as Portuguese and Spanish prisoners were concerned, most if not all of those held in Scots depots, especially at Greenlaw, before the French invasion and occupation of Portugal and Spain in 1807-8 had been released in the latter year or, through exchanges, even earlier.[35] But some of either nationality captured since 1807-8 while fighting as part of Napoleon's forces (in the case of the Spanish, as Afrancesados or Juramentados) were still in captivity as the war, first in the Peninsula and then elsewhere in Europe, drew toward its close.

In May 1812, a month after the fall to Wellington's forces of the vital fortress of Badajoz on the Portuguese-Spanish frontier, the Transport Board had instructed its agents at Valleyfield, Greenlaw, and in England 'to transmit to us without delay, for the information of the Lords Commissioner of the Admiralty, a List of all the Portuguese now in your Custody.' The depots' returns showed that out of a total of 91 in depots or hulks in Britain there were then 13 Portuguese at Valleyfield, but none at Greenlaw. The 13 at Valleyfield were released on the orders of the Admiralty at the beginning of July.[36] A further enquiry, this time addressed to its agents at Perth and Valleyfield, was made in September that year by the Transport Board about Portuguese prisoners. No return appears to have been made from Perth, but seven Portuguese soldiers were reported then to be held at Valleyfield. The following month the Board suggested to the Admiralty that it might be 'advisable to relieve the public of the burthen of maintaining these persons' [as well as some other prisoners belonging to three other nationalities] by either handing them over to their government's representatives in Britain, or allowing them to enter the British armed forces or merchant navy. In December that year the Portuguese consul applied for the release of seven Portuguese prisoners held at Perth, a report on one of whom, Manuel Antonio Correa, had been sought by the Board from the agent there the previous month.[37]

Spanish prisoners, no more numerous than Portuguese in the Scots depots in the last months of the war, appear to have had not dissimilar experiences to theirs in those months, although even less information has been found about their repatriation. When in September 1813 the agents at Valleyfield and Perth were instructed by the Transport Board to report on the number of Spanish captives they held, they were asked to distinguish 'such as are Juramentados.'[38] Again no return was submitted from Perth, but Valleyfield was reported to have, out of a grand total of 257 held in various depots in Britain, four Spanish seamen and two soldiers. How many, if any, of these six were Juramentados was not stated, but the Board suggested to the Admiralty the burden on British taxpayers of maintaining such Spanish prisoners might be removed in the same way as suggested for the Portuguese prisoners. What befell those six, and when, is unknown. Only two other references to Spanish prisoners at the end of the war have been found and neither concerns any Scots depot: one, in a letter of 7 June 1814 from the Transport Board, reminded the Admiralty that the Board awaited a reply to its earlier enquiry of 27 May about what to do with 'upwards of one hundred Spaniards taken in the service of Joseph Bonaparte ... [who] still remain a Burthen to the Public on board His Majesty's Prison Ship *Assistance*' [at Portsmouth]; the other reference was in a letter of 9 July from the Board to the Admiralty, explaining that Forton depot, near Portsmouth, still held prisoners 'mainly on Account of the Spaniards taken in the Service of Joseph Buonaparte, amounting in Number to 135.' Were six among those 135 the Spanish captives from Valleyfield, or had the six by then been repatriated? If they did return home to Spain their return appears unlikely to have been a joyful one, given the thoroughly reactionary and vindictive character of the restored Spanish monarchy under king Ferdinand VII.[39]

Non-French nationalities among all the many thousands of prisoners still languishing in 1813-14 in the depots in Scotland and England (as well as on the hulks in the latter) were, however, heavily outnumbered by those who were French. It was the repatriation of the latter rather than of the much smaller groups such as Germans, Italians, Dutch, Swiss, Danes and Norwegians, Spanish and Portuguese, which particularly occupied the Transport Board as the war ended and the settlement of post-Napoleonic Europe proceeded.

French prisoners in the Scots depots (as in those, and on the hulks, south of the Border) during those months had obvious difficulties, including no doubt the unreliability of much of whatever news was passed to them by word of mouth by their militia guards, in learning and keeping abreast of, as well as coming to terms with, the successive deadly blows dealt to Napoleon's empire. Although it was at that period the least populated Scots depot (apart from Greenlaw, which had been emptied of its inmates in summer 1813 as reconstruction and extension works there were pushed ahead to convert it into a much larger depot),[40] at least Edinburgh Castle provided in 1813-14 successive and official, not to say deafening, announcements of allied victories. By these announcements, the deterioration in Napoleon's power must have impressed (and for those loyal to Napoleon, depressed) prisoners at the Castle.

Those announcements took the form of celebratory cannonades from the Castle's battery of guns, as well as by the hoisting of flags. 'The Castle guns were fired at eight o'clock on Tuesday morning,' for example, the *Edinburgh Evening Courant* informed its readers two days later on 8 July 1813, 'and the flag displayed, in honour of the victory obtained by Lord Wellington [at Vitoria, on 21 June]. The flag was also displayed on Nelson's Monument [on Calton Hill], and all the mail coaches were dispatched with colours flying.' That particular cannonade was also heard by some 300 prisoners who, the *Courant* reported, had arrived at the Castle the previous day from Penicuik en route to Perth. But, unless the prevailing south-west wind veered round completely, it was unlikely that any cannonades at the Castle were heard ten miles away by the prisoners at Penicuik itself.

Five weeks later there was another salvo from the guns at the Castle. 'This morning at 8 o'clock,' the *Caledonian Mercury* reported on 19 August, 'the flag was hoisted on the Castle and a round of the great guns were fired, in honour of the victories made [over Marshal Soult in Spain] by the Marquis of Wellington. The music bells were set a-ringing at the same time.'

The salvoes recurred at the Castle at frequent intervals during that autumn and winter and into the spring and early summer of 1814. In September they resounded for Wellington's capture of San Sebastian and for allied victories in eastern and central Europe, in October for the British crossing of the Pyrenean river Bidassoa and hence the invasion of France itself, in early November (when also 'the bells were set a-ringing') to salute the allied victory at the 'Battle of the Nations' at Leipzig, a salute followed two days later 'by a very general and brilliant illumination' of Edinburgh, when 'the bands of the 1st regiment of the Royal Edinburgh Volunteers and of the Antrim, Northampton and Norfolk militia paraded the streets, playing national and favourite airs', and a few days later by another thunderous cannonade to mark the surrender by the French of the major fortress of Pamplona, Napoleon's last toehold in Spain.[41] Toward the end of November the Castle guns boomed twice more. The first booming was 'to announce the joyful tidings from Holland' where, Charles Lebrun, Napoleon's administrator of that country, having evacuated Amsterdam in the wake of the French defeat the previous month at Leipzig, the Dutch revolted on 17 November against the long established French hegemony over their country, and immediately recalled to power the Prince of Orange. The second booming, two days later, was to celebrate the restoration of Hanover.[42] Between New Year's Day and 11 April 1814, the guns of the Castle were fired on seven more occasions, to celebrate successively Wellington's victories in southern France over Marshal Soult, peace with Denmark, a Prussian victory over the French at Laon and another by Wellington at Orthez, the surrender of Bordeaux and then of Paris, and finally the abdication of Napoleon, which was marked also by the ringing of the bells throughout the city of Edinburgh.

Those thunderous discharges and clangorous peals were not the only forms that rejoicings in the city took upon the ending of the war and the return of peace. On 12 April 'a large bonfire was kindled on the top of Arthur's Seat, and a variety of fine fireworks displayed, to celebrate the fall of Bonaparte, and the restoration of the legitimate Sovereign of France'. Three evenings later there was a general illumination of Edinburgh, as urged by the lord provost and magistrates, when, as the *Evening Courant* put it next day, 'The pleasure which the prospect of returning peace has so universally diffused, was most conspicuously manifested in the rejoicings of last night. The streets were crowded to excess by people of all ages and all ranks, every one eager to contribute to the general happiness. Bands of music paraded the street, and one was stationed in a balcony erected at the Tron Church, playing national and patriotic airs. Everyone wore the white cockade [of the Bourbons], the ladies on their breasts, the gentlemen on their hats. A royal salute from the Castle at eight o'clock was the signal for the illumination, which was brilliant beyond any former example ... After the salute, the soldiers in the garrison fired a *feu de joye* [sic] from the ramparts.' To the top of Arthur's Seat, over 800 feet high, were conveyed 'with much labour, [a] great quantity of coals and some tar barrels ... and [they] blazed during the whole evening with sublime effect.'[43]

At Perth celebrations of these events appear to have been much fewer than at Edinburgh Castle. Press reports have been found for only two celebrations. The first of these, arising from 'a very popular order of the Magistrates', were the 'public rejoicings' on 8 November 1813 (an illumination as part of which was said to be the first such at Perth since the celebration eight years earlier of Nelson's victory at Trafalgar), upon 'the glorious success of the Allies near Leipsic [sic]. At one the bells began to ring, which was repeated after every hour during the day. In the evening all the houses in the town and its vicinity were splendidly illuminated ... Though a heavy rain fell during the whole time of the illumination, the streets were crowded with spectators who, being obliged by the weather to exhibit themselves in a variety of grotesque costumes, enhanced the brilliancy of the scene with a sort of carnival or street masquerade.' The second occasion was on the abdication of Napoleon in April 1814, when the *Perth Courier* reporter found it '... impossible to describe the sensation and expressions of pleasure which have been excited by the late intelligence from France. On Monday [11 April] we had the gratification of travelling in the coach which brought the account of Bonaparte's dethronement, and of witnessing the sudden burst of loyalty and delight which was propagated through the country as it advanced. It was decorated with flags, and the intelligence written in large characters on both panels. At Kinross [12 miles south of Perth] it was instantly surrounded by almost the whole population, who drew it from one end of the town to the other. At Perth it was conducted through the streets with similar exaltation. The bells were set a-ringing, and an illumination was expected, but none was ordered. Next day, when assurance of the intelligence [of Napoleon's abdication] had been made doubly sure, a similar expectation was expressed, but Perth, the ancient metropolis of Scotland, remained as dull and dark, with the exception of two houses in Rose Terrace, as if it had been a moment of the deepest mourning ... An illumination has been ordered for the present evening [14 April] ... The bells have been ringing since midday and flags flying in various quarters.' In fact, according to the *Dundee Advertiser* a week later, Perth on the evening of 14 April 'was one continued blaze of splendour and the display of fireworks and transparencies was rich beyond example ... every face shone with joy.'[44]

There were some prisoners' faces, however, which did not shine with joy—or, if they did, it was joy at the prospect of repatriation alternating with dismay at the ending of Napoleon's power. Evidence of the reaction of the prisoners in the Scots depots to these events is limited. Those invaluable sources of information from among the prisoners, Sergeant Major Beaudoin and Captain Paul Andreas Kaald, had long since gone from Greenlaw, and Lieutenant Marote-Carrier, as a self-styled Oldenburger, had been released from Perth in February 1814. Nonetheless at Perth, Edinburgh Castle and Valleyfield there were among the prisoners, as the war at last ended, some discernibly mixed feelings. If on the one hand it may be safe to assume there were few if any prisoners there who did not rejoice at the ending of the war and their imminent release home, on the other hand the abdication of Napoleon, the end of his empire and the restoration of a Bourbon monarchy in France were for some, perhaps even many if not most, of the prisoners a source of distinct chagrin.

While the prisoners down in the natural bowl at Valleyfield were no doubt out of sight and sound of the rejoicings described at Edinburgh, let alone Perth, it is difficult to believe that those immured either in Edinburgh Castle, at least until shortly before the end of the war, or in far larger numbers and throughout those months at Perth, could fail themselves to hear or see at least some of those celebrations. At Perth indeed, the news of the ending of the war was, according to the *Perth Courier*, 'immediately communicated to the prisoners, by whom it was received with acclamations of joy. They soon after sent a respectful message to Captain Moriarty [the depot agent], requesting permission to illuminate the prisons, in token of their delight at the prospect of peace and liberation. This was granted, but as they had too little time for preparation, only the northernmost prison was completely lighted up. The Tower was illuminated by order of the Governor [Moriarty].'[45]

For Edinburgh Castle no reports of such rejoicings by prisoners at the end of the war have been found. The surviving evidence suggests that by the time the news of Napoleon's abdication five days earlier was received in Edinburgh on 11 April there were no prisoners actually in the Castle. Although its Entry Books throw no light on their removal, those relatively few who had been there appear all to have been transferred to Perth or Valleyfield before the middle of March.[46] If the celebratory cannonades of the six or so preceding months had filled the ears of the prisoners then held in the Castle, there were apparently no prisoners still there in early April to hear, see, or themselves to take part in, the celebrations that marked the arrival of peace. Two instructions on 4 April from the Transport Board, one to Lieutenant Glinn, their transport agent at Leith, the other to Lieutenant Priest, agent at Greenlaw, appear to confirm that the Castle by then contained no prisoners of war. Glinn was instructed to 'cause the apartments in Edinburgh Castle lately occupied by Prisoners of War to be immediately cleansed and fumigated.' The instruction to Priest, who had until then been based at the Castle during the reconstruction work at Greenlaw, declared that 'A representation having been made to the Board that the Casemates in Edinburgh Castle lately occupied by Prisoners of War were left in so filthy and dirty a Condition as to produce unwholesome Effects among the Inhabitants of the [sic] Edinburgh Castle, I am directed to desire you to report the Cause of the Casemates having been left in the above State.'[47]

At Valleyfield, too, where their keeping up with the news of events in the last months of the war is perhaps likely to have been more difficult than at

Edinburgh Castle or Perth, no evidence has been found of any celebrations by the prisoners upon its ending. That does not necessarily mean none took place. But there certainly is evidence, to be presented presently, that even almost a fortnight after Napoleon's abdication many, perhaps most, of the Valleyfield prisoners had still not been able to come to terms with the course of events in France.

It may be the feelings of some of the prisoners in the Scots depots in the spring of 1814 were not dissimilar to those expressed by that Edinburgh soldier, Captain John Kincaid of the Rifle Brigade. Learning, as he and his battalion reached Toulouse, that the war had ended, Kincaid declared: 'The news of the peace, at this period, certainly sounded ... strangely in our ears ... for it was a change that we never had contemplated. We had been born in war, reared in war, and war was our trade; and what soldiers had to do in peace, was a problem yet to be solved among us.'[48]

The momentous changes by April 1814, including the end at last of the more or less continuous warfare in which France had been engaged since 1792, were understandably difficult for many prisoners at Perth and Valleyfield to come to terms with. For younger prisoners—those aged, say, 25 or less—the only regime they had really been conscious of was that of Napoleon. Nor perhaps for the middle-aged and older prisoners, who had lived through the last years of the old regime of the Bourbon monarchy, the Revolution of 1789, and the flow of momentous events since then, were adjustments any easier to make. For those prisoners who, despite their ordeals in battle and in captivity, remained loyal still to Napoleon, acceptance of the greatly altered situation in the spring of 1814 was especially difficult. That loyalty and that difficulty were certainly exemplified among some of the prisoners at both Perth and Valleyfield.[49]

Preparations by the Transport Board for the general repatriation of French prisoners once the war ended may have been begun as early as November 1812. It was then that the Board instructed all its depot agents to 'cause an alphabetical list of all the French prisoners in your custody to be prepared up to the end of the present year upon the forms which will be forwarded to you by coach this day. You are to employ on this service an intelligent prisoner who writes a clear legible hand [and] to whom an allowance will be made at the rate of 6d for every hundred names, if they be correctly written.' The agents were told that the lists were to be compiled and returned 'without fail' to the Transport Office by 20 January 1813.[50]

If preparations for the general repatriation really were proceeding from 1812-13 at the Transport Office only one overt sign of them before the end of the war has been found. That sign was political. A year after its demand in November 1812 for alphabetical lists of French prisoners, the Transport Board sent another circular, this time to its agents at Valleyfield and Perth as well as at six depots in England. The circular informed them that 'By the coach of this day will be forwarded to you copies of a publication in the French language called '*L'Ambigu*', in order that the contents of the same may be judiciously made known to all the French prisoners in your custody through the medium of the most intelligent prisoners who may chuse to read them, by their being lent to them by you, but they are not to be lent to any one who is likely to destroy them.' The number of copies of the pamphlet sent to each depot appears very small indeed: only 11 to Valleyfield and 15 to Perth. A month later another circular, made necessary apparently by the lack of response to the earlier one, was sent by Alexander McLeay, secretary of the Board, asking the depot agent concerned to report 'what effect he considers to have been produced among the prisoners by the circulation of the pamphlet *L'Ambigu*.' If either circular produced replies from the agents in Scotland concerned, those replies appear not to have survived. But the subject with which the pamphlet evidently dealt was the restoration of a Bourbon monarchy in France.[51]

The next relevant, if negative, reference appears to have been an announcement in the press on 24 March 1814 that 'Government has given orders to liberate all the prisoners of war at the different depots, with the exception of those who are natives of France.'[52] The basis of the announcement is not clear: no evidence for it has been found in any of the archives of the Transport Board.

As the British government had long been inclined to favour the restoration of the Bourbons in France once Napoleon was defeated, the surrender without a fight of Bordeaux in mid-March to Wellington's forces by royalist supporters of that restoration transformed the government's inclination into a policy decision, which from the end of that month was supported by the other major allied governments. It was therefore with the deposition of Napoleon by the French legislature on 2-3 April, followed by his abdication on 6 April and the recall of the Bourbon monarchy in the person of Louis XVIII, that more, and more traceable, steps began to be taken by the Transport Board to prepare for the repatriation of the thousands of French prisoners. The day after Napoleon's abdication, the Board ordered its agents at Valleyfield and Perth, as well as those at six depots in England, to 'report by return of post whether the late change of affairs in France appears to have had any and what effect on the French prisoners in your custody and whether any and what number of them have declared in favour of the Bourbons, or are likely so to declare themselves if separated from the other prisoners.'[53] The repatriation from Britain to France of tens of thousands of prisoners of war many or most of whom either were or might prove to be strong supporters of Napoleon could present obvious dangers to the stability of the restored Bourbon regime.

From Valleyfield the reply on 14 April from Captain Brown, the agent, appears remarkably optimistic, not to say naive, concerning its inmates' support for the Bourbons. Brown 'Stated that there were about 2,000 of the Prisoners in his custody ready to come foward and faithfully serve the Bourbons, but that it would be necessary to allow them to volunteer with the rank they held at present.' As there were then at Valleyfield about 4,000 prisoners, the agent's estimate was almost certainly a sizeable exaggeration—a figure he had perhaps plucked out of the air, or had had provided to him by pro-Bourbons among the prisoners. As communications between the Board and the Scots depots normally took about three or four days to arrive, Brown must have penned his reply on the day, or the day after, the Board's enquiry reached him—hardly time for him to have made any serious investigation of loyalties or inclinations and numbers.[54]

Brown's estimate, moreover, seems at odds with his observations in a letter he sent a few days later to the Transport Board and which it received on 20 April, a fortnight after Napoleon's abdication. His letter, summarised in the Board's minutes, reported that 'the Prisoners at this Depot could not be convinced of the present State of Affairs [in France], and that they had been parading about the Prison with the Imperial Flag. [Brown] Requested that some official Document might be sent, as they [the prisoners] considered everything in the Newspapers as a mere Fabrication.' The Board ordered that same day that Brown be informed '… that if they will not believe the Statements in the Newspapers the Board do not consider that any Document would convince them, and that they may remain in Confinement until they be altered in their Opinion.'[55]

Whatever the numbers or proportions of pro-Bourbons and pro-Bonapartists among the prisoners at Valleyfield, feelings among them during those weeks in April were running high, according to a press report that seems unlikely to have been 'a mere Fabrication'. As the *Caledonian Mercury* reported on 23 April, '… differences of opinion on the late political events in France have been exhibited at the Pennycuick depot [i.e., Valleyfield] and on some occasions the parties have with difficulty been prevented from proceeding to violence.'

At Perth some more specific, even if far from comprehensive, information has survived about prisoners' reactions to the changed state of affairs in France in April 1814 and also about consequent steps taken by the depot authorities and the Transport Board. The earliest reported indication of prisoners' reactions at Perth was on 21 April, a fortnight after Napoleon's abdication. 'This morning,' reported the *Perth Courier* that day, 'six prisoners in the south prison of the Depot hoisted a white [Bourbon] flag, when almost the whole of their fellow captives clambered over the walls from the other prisons and threatened them with the most violent treatment. By the interference of the guard, they were saved from actual injury, and for their greater security were removed to the hospital.'[56]

That same day Captain Moriarty, agent at Perth, reported to the Transport Board 'the names of 12 French prisoners who had hoisted the White Flag, and recommended them to the notice of the Board, by being first discharged.' Moriarty enclosed with his letter a 'copy of a Notice which he had ordered to be stuck up in the Prison.' Moriarty's notice has not survived. But it seems likely that it warned all prisoners at the depot that riotous behaviour of the kind which had taken place on 21 April against the pro-Bourbon demonstration would result in delaying the repatriation of those involved. Whatever the content of his notice, when Moriarty's letter reached the Board on 25 April it immediately ordered 'that he be directed to release these Twelve Prisoners and send them immediately to Lieutenant Glinn at Leith, who is to send them to Gravesend.' Thus the dozen pro-Bourbonists at Perth appear to have become the first French prisoners to be released from any Scots depots after the end of the war.[57]

Apart from there apparently being, according to the agent's account, not six but a dozen pro-Bourbon prisoners involved in the demonstration on 21 April, there is no reason to doubt the general accuracy of the press report about it. What the report suggests is that the active or committed pro-Bourbons among the prisoners at Perth were in a small, even tiny, minority. It does not necessarily indicate that the overwhelming majority of the prisoners were committed Bonapartists. Numbers of prisoners may have been anti-Bourbon but not supporters of Napoleon. On the other hand, no surviving source mentions specifically prisoners having republican or liberal sympathies—other possible political views upon which some might perhaps have acted that day. Whatever the political views of the mass of the prisoners—and given their celebration at the depot the previous August of Napoleon's birthday, there were clearly a sizeable number who were willing to demonstrate their loyalty to him then—the passions aroused on 21 April by the pro-Bourbon demonstration appear to have abated within a few days. 'We understand the prisoners at the Depot who had engaged in the tumult which we mentioned last week,' the *Perth Courier* reported on 28 April, 'have written a penitential letter expressing regret for their conduct on that occasion.' The penitential letter seems likely to have been a result of the pinning up on 21 April of Captain's Moriarty's warning notice.

One pro-Bourbon prisoner who wrote to Captain Moriarty on 28 April explained his own position, which, although his letter contains some ambiguities, may mean that, unlike the dozen demonstrators on 21 April, he was not put into the depot hospital for his own safety. The writer was a shipmate of Lieutenant Marote-Carrier (who, however, nowhere mentions him in his recollections). He was Louis Petitchamp, ensign, captured on the privateer *L'Aventurier* in 1810 in the English Channel. Petitchamp had arrived at Perth in September 1812 from Valleyfield, from which he had escaped on 3 January that year 'through the gate while the Turnkeys were inside counting', but had been recaptured at Saltoun in East Lothian. Petitchamp's letter throws a little additional light on the position at Perth in the weeks following Napoleon's abdication. 'After the good news you were so good as to inform us of on the 12th of this month,' he told Captain Moriarty, 'I was filled with joy. But it was even greater when I learned that our dynasty had changed and that our ill-fated family the Bourbons reigned. I was totally filled with joy. And wanting my comrades to see the happiness we were going to enjoy, I was the first to shout in elation Long Live Peace, Long Live Louis XVIII. And this for the justified reason that several of my relatives belong to the old nobility, which I can prove to you. But the joy and satisfaction was dearly paid for by the abuse and rudeness of several prisoners, for I believe you [know? (a word or words illegible)] ... what happened. I thought I was going to suffer the fate of my fellow countrymen but it appears that when they were at the hospital they forgot me. I place myself in your hands and dare to beg you to allow me to change the name by which I am known at the Depot, which is Louis Petitchamp, which is an assumed name. My own name is Adrien Victor Tavernier, aged 26, a native of Paris.'[58]

It was on 30 April, two days after Tavernier-Petitchamp wrote his letter to Captain Moriarty that the twelve pro-Bourbon prisoners were 'marched from the depot ... ornamented with white cockades and other Bourbon insignia', on their way to Leith, there to embark for Gravesend and from there home to France.[59] Whether Tavernier-Petitchamp himself was one of the twelve is, however, for two reasons uncertain. First, of the twelve named prisoners three have not been found in the Perth Entry Books. It is possible that one of these, named Paranti, had his name so misspelled in the Board's letter of 25 April to its agents at Perth and Leith that it was really intended to be Tavernier (or Petitchamp). Second, in the Entry Book the date and reason for release of Tavernier are not given at all. If Paranti was not Tavernier, then the latter was not among the twelve Bourbonists who shook the dust of Perth from their feet on 30 April. Indeed, Tavernier may have been among the approximately 40 prisoners at Perth depot who signed a loyal address to the restored Bourbons on 17 May.

Of the twelve named in the Board's letter those nine found in the depot Entry Books included several familiar but perhaps surprising individuals. One of these was Bernard Charlot, aged 25, captured in 1810 as prizemaster on board the privateer *Phoenix*. Transferred in March 1811 from Esk Mills to Edinburgh Castle, Charlot had been one of the 49 escapers from the Castle on the night of 12 April 1811 but had been recaptured and sent to Greenlaw, from which he was transferred in September 1812 to Perth. Was there any significance in Charlot's place of birth being Bordeaux, which city royalists had handed over in March 1814 to Wellington without a fight? Two others were those companions in escape, both born at Calais and both aged 22, Lieutenant Dominique Dewatre (or Duvatre) and 2nd Captain P. Faillant, both captured on the privateer *Le Figaro* in 1811. Both men had escaped from Perth on 27 March 1813 but both had been recaptured. Dewatre had also escaped earlier from the depot—the first prisoner to do so—in September 1812, when he had been recaptured, 'genteelly dressed in black', in an adjoining field. But perhaps most surprising of all to find among the Perth Bourbonists was Lieutenant David Fourneau, like Dewatre and Faillant aged 22 and born at Calais, captured in 1810 on the privateer *Le Barbier de Seville*, and when transferred as a 'ringleader' in the troubles at Esk Mills, from which he had escaped on 19 February 1811, the first prisoner to be enrolled in the Entry Book at Edinburgh Castle. Later sent from the Castle to Greenlaw, Fourneau had been transferred from there in September 1812 to Perth. Apart from the three otherwise unidentified men out of the twelve released, all except three of the nine were privateersmen. Jacques Dubois, alias Billon, was a soldier, aged 30, born at Pigoly, who had been captured at Badajoz in April 1812 while serving in the 88th line regiment; Jacques Baland was also a soldier, in the 27th Chasseurs cavalry, born, like Bernard Charlot, at Bordeaux, and captured in July 1812 at Tardesilias [Tordesillas?] and had arrived at Perth two months later; and D. Deroland, who has previously been encountered, was aged 26 and born on the island of Bourbon (Réunion), had been captured in 1806 as a passenger on board the man-of-war *Marengo*, and had arrived from Greenlaw in September 1812 at Perth.[60]

Prisoners such as Fourneau, Dewatre, Faillant and Charlot could hardly be regarded by the depot authorities or the Transport Board as model captives who had earned early release through consistently exemplary behaviour. On the contrary, with their records of escape they were from the official point of view classic cases of *mauvais sujets*. In the spring of 1814 the importance of their professed political views, however, superseded their earlier records at the Scots depots and brought them and their eight companions their early release home from Perth on 30 April.

From these dozen early releases from Perth at least five questions arise, but unfortunately none of the five can be answered for lack of evidence. First, did their fellow captives know these dozen men even from their earlier years in captivity to be pro-Bourbon? Second, if so, did their pro-Bourbon views lead even before the end of the war to quarrels with, and perhaps even ostracism by, their fellow prisoners? Third, did those views arouse such animosity among their fellow prisoners that that animosity became a factor in, even perhaps the main reason for, the attempts at escape by Fourneau, Dewatre, Faillant and Charlot? Fourth, if that were so in the case of any of those four prisoners, were there other escapers or attempted escapers (such as Petitchamp-Tavernier) from the Scots depots who were similarly motivated? Fifth, and on the other hand, were all twelve men genuine adherents of the Restoration in France, or were some at least among them opportunists who had no qualms about genuflecting toward Louis XVIII if to do so would restore more speedily their liberty and their repatriation?

There were two other small groups of French prisoners who gained, or at least were recommended for, early release home. One was those belonging to Dunkirk, the other those from Romorantin, a small town 40 miles south of Orleans. As early as 9 April the Transport Board had ordered all its depot and parole agents 'to transmit immediately to this Office a list of all the natives of Dunkirk under your care, in order that measures may be taken for their being sent home.' No reason was given for the order, and no lists of those Dunkirk men in the Scots depots appear to have survived. But the explanation for the order appears in a letter written to Alexander McLeay, secretary of the Board, a month later by four Dunkirk prisoners at Perth. 'The Town of Dunkirk,' wrote the four, after denouncing Napoleon's despotism in forcing so many to serve in his unjust cause, 'has been one of the first in France to show its complete devotion [to the restored Bourbon monarchy.] Our fellow citizens have displayed the White [Bourbon] flag and given the signal for peace ...' The four, whose names appear to have been Simcas (?), Widons, Requetz, and Lacueil, then appealed to McLeay to use his good offices to grant them promptly their liberty.[61] Not every prisoner belonging to Dunkirk, however, appears to have enjoyed earlier release than the mass of French prisoners. Jean Pierre Le Maire, alias Pierre Tarvelet, for example, a seaman captured in 1806 on the privateer *La Prospère*, and who arrived from Esk Mills in March 1811 at Valleyfield, was not released from there until the general release on 6 June 1814; and Jean Baptiste Josin, alias N.B. Jansens, seaman, captured in 1805 on the privateer *La Lionesse*, was not released from Valleyfield until 15 June that year; while at Perth, Joseph Françoise, for instance, a seaman captured in 1808 and who had arrived in the first intake at the depot in August 1812, was repatriated only amid the general release on 3 June 1814. Early release for Dunkirk men may well have depended on whether their political loyalties were Bourbon.[62]

Ten days after its circular to its agents about Dunkirk prisoners, the Transport Board wrote to the Admiralty strongly recommending a request it had received from Major-General Lord Blayney. Blayney had been taken prisoner at Malaga near Gibraltar in 1810 and had proceeded at a very leisurely pace lasting nine months through Spain and France to captivity at Verdun. Among the places en route where he had sojourned may have been

Romorantin, south of the Loire. At any rate, the war over, his lordship wrote to the Transport Board 'reporting the humane conduct of the inhabitants of Romorantin towards British Prisoners of War and requesting in consequence thereof that certain natives of that place now detained as Prisoners in this country may be released.' The Board consequently recommended to the Admiralty the immediate release of such prisoners. If, as seems very probable, the Admiralty agreed, how many prisoners in the Scots depots who were natives of Romorantin promptly benefited from Lord Blayney's request before the repatriation of the mass of French prisoners, is unknown.[63]

There were a handful of other early releases the grounds for which are not stated in the official records and can only be surmised. One such from Valleyfield was that of Benjamin Delarue, 'a French prisoner', whom the agent was told on 21 May to release and to give him a 'Passeport to enable him to proceed to France by the way of Brighton.'[64] Another, from Perth, was Louis Brunet, described as a servant in the army, who had been captured on St Domingo as early in the war as November 1803, and had arrived at Perth in August 1812. Brunet, aged 26, born at Leimonge [? Limoges], 'Speaks good English and a marked character' (as the Entry Book put it somewhat ambiguously), was the subject of an instruction on 27 May 1814 from the Transport Board to the Perth agent, to release him 'and allow him to come to London, delivering him a Passport for his Protection and instructing him to present himself at this Office immediately upon his Arrival.' The next day, however, the Board amended its instruction: Brunet was to proceed not to London but to Edinburgh, 'presenting himself on his arrival to John Murray, Esq., 122 George Street.'[65] John Murray was in fact Sir John Archibald Murray, Lord Murray (1779-1859), joint editor of the *Edinburgh Review*, a distinguished Whig advocate, later active in the Great Reform Bill agitation in 1830-2, elected unopposed as MP for Leith in 1832, and Lord Advocate, 1835 and 1837, until appointed in 1839 a judge in the Court of Session. Why Brunet should have been instructed to present himself to Murray is another question concerning the prisoners in Scotland to which no answer has yet been found.[66]

Another French prisoner of much more exalted rank than Louis Brunet and who proceeded to Edinburgh shortly before him en route to France was General Simon, one of the two most senior French officers in captivity in Scotland during the Napoleonic Wars. As the *Glasgow Courier* reported on 19 May of his release from confinement, 'The French General Simeon [sic], who has been long a prisoner in Dumbarton Castle, passed through this town [Glasgow] yesterday on his way to France.' Further details were added four days later in the *Edinburgh Evening Courant*: Simon, 'who has been confined about two years in Dumbarton Castle, for breaking his parole, arrived in town [Edinburgh] on Thursday [19 May], accompanied by Major Bell, of the East

York Militia, on his way to France. We understand that the general, before his departure, gave a ball to the inhabitants of Dumbarton.'[67]

These and the other early releases of French prisoners already noticed involved, however, very small numbers compared with the thousands of those at Valleyfield and Perth who continued to wait through the months of April and May 1814 for news of their repatriation. During those two months discussions were taking place at government level, the Admiralty and the Transport Board were reaching certain policy or practical decisions concerning the mass repatriation, including the provision of transport vessels; and among the prisoners themselves there were continuing signs of feeling for and against, as well as incredulity concerning, the new state of affairs in France, where also the Peace Treaty of Paris between the allied powers and the new Bourbon French government was signed on 30 May. Among the prisoners, too, practical preparations for release were being undertaken, such as the saving of money sent them by their families at home: at Perth, for example, as has been seen in an earlier chapter, some 919 payments of such monies were recorded in the special depot ledger for that purpose during the three months ending 26 May.[68]

Orders having been given by the French government in mid-April for the release of all British prisoners of war in France, a request made on 19 April by Monsieur Rivière, the French government official dealing with the matter, for the 'immediate liberation' of a list of named French prisoners was received a week later by the Transport Board. The Board sought the Admiralty's instructions on the request, and there appears then to have been discussion between the Admiralty and the War Office. On 29 April Lord Bathurst, Secretary at War, asked the Admiralty 'to instruct the Commissioners of Transports to signify to the proper authorities in Paris that as the Count de la Chatre [ie., Count de Chartres] is now residing in London as the accredited Minister of His Majesty Louis XVIII no selection of individual prisoners could with propriety be made unless the application came through His Excellency.' The names of the prisoners listed by M. Rivière appear not to have survived in the archives. It seems most unlikely they included those of any rank and file prisoners confined in the depots, but rather they were of senior officers confined in the parole towns and perhaps also General Simon. Two French government commissioners, Vice Admiral de Sercey and Monsieur de la Boulaye arrived in London the first week in May to arrange the release of all French prisoners of war in Britain. But about the arrival of the commissioners there is ambiguity in the relevant Transport Board circulars, which were addressed to its parole but not to its depot agents. If the mechanics of the arrangements proposed by the two French commissioners are not documented the general direction of policy concerning the mass repatriation appears nonetheless clear enough from the announcements of the Admiralty and the Transport Board in the weeks before June and July when at last it actually took place.[69]

Even before the arrival of the two French government commissioners, the Board on 22 April had assured Rear Admiral Hope, successor to Admiral Otway as naval commander based at Leith, that 'a general Arrangement for the Release of Prisoners of War is in Progress.' By then, too, the Board had told its agent at Perth that 'as the prisoners may be expected to be shortly released we do not consider it necessary to order the articles demanded by you at present.'[70] A little more than a month later, the *Perth Courier* reported it understood 'intimation has been received at the [Perth] Depot from Commissioners nominated by the French Government, that the prisoners of war will begin to be removed in June, and the whole conveyed to France before the end of July. Those who have been longest in captivity will be liberated first.' The first part of the *Courier*'s understanding proved correct, the second also appears generally to have proved so, although in the final part there were at both Perth and Valleyfield a number of unexplained exceptions.[71]

Among the practical preparations, several even of the most apparently mundane of which also had political connotations, made or approved by the Transport Board before the great repatriation of French prisoners from the Scots depots began in June, was one concerning the prisoners' footwear. Clearly, it would hardly help the peaceable re-establishment of the Bourbons in France if thousands of prisoners of war arrived home either barefoot or wearing merely list or selvage shoes made of cloth. As early as 14 April the agent at Valleyfield reported to the Board 'that he had only 512 pairs of leather shoes in store and requested further supply in the event of the release of the prisoners.' The Board replied that a supply of leather shoes would be sent to Valleyfield, 'but if orders should arrive in the meantime for the Discharge of the Prisoners they may be supplied with List Shoes.' Upon this the agent commented 'that he did not think that it would be possible for the Prisoners to march in List Clogs.' So the Board then assured the agent on 25 April that 'a supply of 3,000 Pairs Leather Shoes has been ordered to be sent to him.'[72] In mid-May two further circulars with practical instructions, however, from the Board to the agents at Valleyfield and Perth, as well as at depots in England, had no bearing upon the restoration of the Bourbons. 'You will immediately stop all works that are going on [at your depot],' the first circular, dated 12 May, declared, 'reporting what remains to be done of any works now in hand.' Simultaneously, the second circular instructed the agents 'to allow the contractors to issue the salt beef and biscuit in store in the usual manner to the prisoners so as to prevent any large quantity of provisions being left on hand when the prisoners are sent away.'[73]

Another question raised with the Admiralty by the Transport Board itself on 25 April was that concerning the acquisition by French prisoners of 'guineas and other gold coin of the realm to a very considerable amount', as a result of their sales of paper, bone, wood, straw, hair, and other items of handicraft they had made during their captivity. 'As it is probable … the prisoners in question may be speedily released,' the Board wrote, 'we beg to be informed whether it be their Lordships' pleasure that we should take measures for preventing such coin from being carried out of the country by giving the prisoners foreign coin in lieu thereof, or otherwise.' The Admiralty's reply to this enquiry has not been found, nor has any other evidence that the prisoners were obliged to exchange their British gold coins for other money.[74]

At the very end of the period of preparations before the mass repatriation began at the beginning of June, the Transport Board granted a concession that seems likely to have become among the prisoners a source of wry amusement if not derision. 'Any Prisoners in your Custody,' the Board instructed the agents at Valleyfield and Perth on 31 May, 'who may be willing and able to return to France at their own expense may be allowed to do so.'[75]

Two other aspects of the repatriation dealt with more or less simultaneously by the Board had obvious political, as well as some humanitarian and practical, implications. On 30 May the Board had received a letter from the French government, anxious to ward off political criticism and hence threats to its own stability, asking that 'no prisoners shall be sent to France who are not real subjects of that country, but be delivered over to their respective Consuls or sent directly from England to the countries where they belong.' The Board consequently sent a circular on 6 June to its agents at Valleyfield and Perth, as well as at depots in England, ordering that 'you will not discharge any prisoners to be embarked for France excepting such as are subjects of that country.' That was why many non-French prisoners released were disembarked at, for example, Helvoetsluys in Holland.[76] So far as sick prisoners were concerned, the Board first instructed its agent at Valleyfield on 24 May that once the transports assembling at Leith were ready to begin the great repatriation, sick prisoners, accompanied by 'Medical Officers and a supply of medicines, etc.' should also be put on board them. But a week later when the agent had apparently enquired about the release of the more seriously ill prisoners, the Board told him that 'only such of the sick Prisoners as are not likely to die on the Passage are to be sent to France.'[77]

Among the more overtly political aspects of the preparations for the great repatriation from Valleyfield and Perth in June and July was a visit made early in May by Admiral Hope at Leith to Valleyfield where, as he reported, no doubt rather optimistically, to the Transport Board, he had found the prisoners 'perfectly satisfied with the present alteration of affairs in France, and transmitted Five Letters from them to be laid before the Count de Chartres', the French ambassador in London.[78] The admiral's visit coincided more or less with the arrival of a Transport Board circular at Valleyfield, as well as at Perth and depots in England, directing the agents 'to release from the cachot all the prisoners now confined therein who can in your opinion be allowed to mix again with the prisoners in general without endangering the security or quiet of the Depot. We also direct you to remit [i.e., to waive payment of] all such sums of money as may remain to be made good by any of the prisoners whether on account of breach of parole or otherwise, causing the parties to whom these indulgencies are granted to understand that it is in consequence of the happy restoration of the Bourbon family to the throne of France.'[79]

The circular about releases from the cachots was followed a few days later by a letter from the Transport Board to its agents at both Valleyfield and Perth, instructing them to 'deliver the enclosed address to some of the most respectable of the Prisoners under your Care in order that it may be communicated to the rest of the Prisoners, and you will report to the Board how it may be received.' Neither the address itself nor the agents' reports appear to have survived. But presumably the address was another attempt to persuade the prisoners to reconcile themselves to the restored Bourbon regime in France.[80] It seems likely, too, that that was the purpose of a circular on 24 May from the Transport Board to twelve of its parole agents in Scotland, including those at Kelso, Lanark, Selkirk, Hawick and Dumfries, asking them 'to select from among the French prisoners under your care intelligent officers of good character and instruct them to proceed to Perth or Leith as you may be required by Captain Moriarty [agent at Perth] or Lieutenant Glinn [the Board's transport agent at Leith], in order that they may proceed to France with the prisoners about to embark from those places.'[81]

A source of comfort to the Transport Board in its efforts to influence the political views of the prisoners and minimise any dangers for the Bourbon restoration in France from the mass repatriation was no doubt the address or petition signed on 17 May by some 40 prisoners at Perth, evidently including some officers of the navy or of merchant vessels as well as some soldiers, including at least one sergeant and two fouriers or corporals, expressing their loyalty to the Bourbons. It is curious that no reference to this petition appears to exist in the Admiralty or Transport Board archives, and no report of it has been found in the press. Yet it is difficult to believe the depot agent at Perth and the Transport Board were not informed of it. Addressed to the two French commissioners, Vice Admiral de Sercey and Monsieur de la Boulaye, sent to Britain to arrange the exchange of prisoners, the petitioners declared: 'By a happy event, we learn that our beloved country has just regained the state of peace which it should never have lost. We undertake the task of testifying to you gentlemen, as representatives of our country, our joy at that news. We do not know how to express to you our gratitude to the kindly hand which has achieved such a great task in so short a time. As simple subjects of the kingdom we can only make it known by our feelings of loyalty and devotion that we are eager to swear to the august sovereign who will rule us …' The signatures are not all legible, nor did the signatories give their Entry Book numbers as prisoners; consequently it is not possible to identify them with any certainty. At least two signatures may have been those of prisoners already encountered: Adrien Victor Tavernier (alias Louis Petitchamp), ensign captured on Marote-Carrier's privateer *L'Aventurier*, and Sergeant Lelade, maker of desks for Andrew Johnston, chief clerk at Perth. A third signature may have been that of Joseph Feraud, aged 28, a seaman captured on the *Berwick* at the battle of Trafalgar, who had come to Perth from Valleyfield in July 1813, and who was repatriated on 2 June 1814.[82]

As well as arranging the early release, already described, of pro-Bourbon prisoners, the Transport Board took steps in the opposite direction by delaying the repatriation of certain other prisoners. A secret and confidential circular sent on 17 May by the Board to its agents at Valleyfield and Perth, as well as those at depots in England, referred to 'the orders which you have received for the discharge of prisoners', and declared that 'any whom you may know to be persons of dangerous character should be detained in order that they may hereafter be sent home separately from the body of the prisoners, and you will report to the Board the names of prisoners who may be so detained by you.'[83] No lists of whichever names were submitted from Valleyfield and Perth appear to have survived. It may well be surmised that in the Board's view 'dangerous' meant, or at least included, politically dangerous. On the other hand, there were at least two prisoners at Perth who appear to have had their release delayed until the last batch left the depot on 13 July but who, so far as the very limited evidence indicates, had not held or expressed subversive political views. One was the last prisoner listed in the depot Entry Books: No. 7760 (a clerical error for No.7761) Nicolas Etienne Jennat, a soldier, aged 28, captured in March 1808 on the privateer *Renois*, and who had arrived at Perth in August 1812. Jennat, who had a lame leg, had escaped from the depot on 4 June 1814 but was apparently recaptured the same day. A letter dated 21 June that year survives which was written by Jennat evidently from the cachot, appealing to the agent to restore him his liberty. But it was not restored to him until he was released with the last batch of prisoners from the depot on 13 July. The unanswerable question is: what had driven Jennat, after more than six years in captivity, to try to escape on the eve of his repatriation? [84] The second prisoner at Perth whose repatriation was delayed, like Jennat's, until the last contingent on 13 July was unnamed. 'Approve,' the Transport Board told the agent on 17 June, in reply to his letter of the 13th, 'of your having put the prisoner who threw the stone at Mr Johnston [depot chief clerk] into the cachot and of your keeping him on short allowance, and not discharging him until the last of the prisoners.' Was this prisoner as a thrower of stones at persons in authority regarded by Board and agent as a real or potential danger to the stability of the restored Bourbon monarchy in France? Or, perhaps more likely, was he thus punished for breaching the depot's own good order and discipline? [85] There was no implication that at Valleyfield, from which the last contingent of French prisoners left on 14 June 1814, Jean Baptiste Destrais, alias Pierre Calmain, had his release delayed until the following day because he held politically dangerous views. Destrais-Calmain was the prisoner who, during an attempted escape from the depot in July 1813, had stabbed a soldier who as a result had come near to death. Narrowly avoiding becoming the first prisoner in any Scots depot to be charged with murder, Destrais-Calmain had spent the intervening year in gaol in the Edinburgh Tolbooth before being returned to Valleyfield and repatriated next day.[86] Another prisoner released from Valleyfield even later than Destrais-Calmain was Pierre Mousse, aged 45, born at Brescia, a sergeant in the 2nd Italian regiment, captured off Corfu, date unstated, and who had arrived from Esk Mills at Valleyfield in March 1811. Mousse was not released until 5 July 1814. Although the reason for the delay was unstated it seems more likely to have been because until then he was recovering from illness in the depot hospital than that he constituted any kind of political danger to the post-war restoration either in France or in Italy.[87]

Other prisoners threatened with delayed repatriation, but who could hardly be considered politically dangerous, were some of the so-called 'Miserables'. The Transport Board approved action taken by the agent at Valleyfield when he found, perhaps unsurprisingly, the 'Miserables' there had 'begun to make away with and convert their Clothing and Blankets to other purposes.' He had warned them 'that they would not be released until they had produced their Complement of Bedding.' The Board instructed him 'to keep such as may have disposed of these Articles until the last.'[88] Other prisoners at Valleyfield likewise not politically dangerous but who were 'detected in changing their Names and Time [? Turn] of Release are to be kept back till the last,' the Board instructed the agent as late as 6 June.[89]

While many of these decisions were being taken the Transport Board was also organising the ships needed to convey to the continent the mass of French prisoners from Valleyfield and Perth once they were released. The Board ordered its transport agent at Leith, Lieutenant Glinn, on 29 April to enquire 'on what Terms the Leith Smacks will engage to carry Prisoners of War to the nearest Port in France, and to victual them on the Passage, agreeable to the Ration stated', which latter was 1½ lbs of bread, ¾ lb of beef, and two quarts of beer. But when Glinn duly reported the terms offered, the Board told him they were 'inadmissable' and that 'Transports will be sent for this service.'[90]

As the month of May progressed a greater sense of urgency began to permeate the Board's correspondence with its depot and transport agents in Scotland. It was becoming clear that contracted transport vessels alone would be unable to cope with the mass repatriation and that some Royal Navy ships would also be needed. On the 20th the Board told its agent at Valleyfield that as the Admiralty had directed port admirals 'to furnish all the assistance in their power from the vessels under their orders for the conveyance of French Prisoners to France', he should ask Admiral Hope at Leith 'if he has any Vessels under his Command that can be appropriated to that Service, and in that case ... you will lose no Time in embarking such prisoners as can be received on board without waiting for further instructions. Transports are in preparation to be employed as Cartels [i.e., unarmed vessels officially recognised by both the British and French governments] and will be sent round to Leith with as little Delay as possible.'[91]

Further orders were sent to its agent at Valleyfield four days later, after the Board had received from him a letter which has not survived. '...release and send away, as usual,' the agent was told, 'the Prisoners ... referred to [in his letter], as soon as Lieutenant Glinn shall inform you that he is prepared to embark them on board transports which are under orders to convey French prisoners to France, putting on board with the Sick Medical Officers and a supply of medicines, etc. The whole of the Prisoners in your Custody are to be released and sent away from time to time in like Manner, or as Rear Admiral Hope may have opportunities of His Majesty's ships, and you will communicate with the Rear Admiral and Lieutenant Glinn on the subject. It is desirable that five officers should go to every 100 men; but the Service is not to be delayed on this Account.' The officers concerned were the 'intelligent' ones who were the subject of the Board's circular that same day to parole agents in Scotland.[92]

Simultaneously the Board instructed Lieutenant Glinn that 'Having ordered the transports ... *Ann* (120 tons), *Agnes* (135 tons), *Marytam* (278), *Royal Briton* (237), *Union* (260), *Malvina* (266), *Ruby* (226), *Harliston* (314), *Flora* (244), *Emperor Alexander* (196), *Milbank* (193) ... to be appropriated for the Conveyance of Prisoners of War from Leith to France, we direct you to make Arrangements for embarking the Prisoners from Valleyfield immediately on their Arrival. You are to inform Captain Brown when and in what Number Prisoners may be sent for Embarkation, Captain Brown having been directed to send them off as you may require. Five officers are to go with every 100 Men and if possible a Surgeon in each ship but the Vessels are not to be detained on this Account if the Officers should not have arrived in Time. The Agents for Parole Prisoners have been directed to send officers in such Numbers as you may require. ... the Masters of the Transports ... are to be ordered to return immediately to Leith and on their return you will again put Prisoners on Board without waiting for further Orders. You will observe that invalid prisoners are to be embarked at the rate of one man per ton and Prisoners in Health at the rate of three men to two tons.'[93]

The royal naval frigate HMS *Solebay* and the sloop HMS *Porpoise* were ordered by the Admiralty to join the small fleet of transports at Leith and to take prisoners from there to Dunkirk, and the Transport Board ordered its agent at Valleyfield on 27 May to embark prisoners on the two naval ships 'without loss of time'.[94]

From Valleyfield the great repatriation of French prisoners began on 1 June. Those like the prisoner Marcher, who thirty years later as a veteran inmate of the Invalides in Paris told John Cowan of Beeslack that Valleyfield had been a 'terribly cold' depot, perhaps felt it wryly appropriate their departure took place when, as the *Caledonian Mercury* reported next day, 'The weather has been exceedingly cold here for some time past. Yesterday morning there was ice of considerable thickness on the pools in the neighbourhood.' The *Mercury* went on to report that 'Yesterday a considerable number of French prisoners passed through here [Edinburgh] from Pennycuick, to embark at Leith for their native country. Many who were not able to walk were conveyed in artillery waggons and other carriages fitted up for the purpose.'

The Penicuik local historian J.L. Black, writing long afterward about the repatriation, was able to quote from aged inhabitants who had witnessed it. 'That was a great day in Penicuik when the men imprisoned in Valleyfield Mills were to march into Leith to be shipped to France. The scene has been described to me by men and women who were spectators, and some of them old enough to take notes and form their own opinions. The streets were densely lined, and all the way into Edinburgh the people were gathered to watch their departure. Most of the prisoners had parcels; as much as they could carry—and rare parcels some of them were. One man had a large cage with two tame rats he had trained to play tricks. At Thorburn Terrace—then a row of one-storey houses—a large crowd had collected, chiefly women, who gave expression to their feelings in a way far from complimentary. This was answered back by one of the Frenchmen who had picked up some Scotch, and who kept bawling, "Bawbee Penicuik! Cauld kail and soor dook!" This enraged the women and there threatened to be a riot, but the military silenced the offender.'[95]

An Edinburgh witness who long afterward recalled the passage of the released prisoners through the city streets to Leith was the distinguished Scots engineer James Nasmyth (1808-1890). In his autobiography, published in 1883 and edited by Samuel Smiles, Nasmyth recalled that 'At the peace of Amiens [sic], which was proclaimed in 1814 ... the liberation [of the French prisoners] confined in Edinburgh Castle was accompanied by an extraordinary scene. The French prisoners marched down to the transport ships at Leith by torchlight. All the town was out to see them. They passed in military procession through the principal streets, singing as they marched along their revolutionary airs *Ça Ira* and *The Marseillaise*. The wild enthusiasm of these haggard-looking men, lit up by torchlight and accompanied by the cheers of the dense crowd, which lined the streets and filled the windows, made an impression on my mind that I can never forget.' [96]

After the first contingent on 1 June there was a delay of five days before further columns of prisoners, amounting to well over a thousand, released from Valleyfield marched on 6, 7 and 8 June to Leith to embark for France. The Transport Board was concerned at the delay. It instructed the depot agent 'to employ additional assistance to make out the Embarkation Lists.' Two further contingents, amounting to more than 800, were marched under escort from Valleyfield to Leith on 10 and 11 June. They were followed on the 13th, 14th and 15th by another 1,500 or so. 'We believe,' commented the *Caledonian Mercury*, 'that nearly the whole that were at this depot are now sent away.' The *Mercury*'s belief was well founded. Valleyfield by then was almost emptied of its inmates. [97]

If the release from the depot between 1 and 15 June of the successive contingents, totalling around 4,000, and their embarkation at Leith appear reasonably speedy they did not appear to the Transport Board to be nearly speedy enough. On 15 June, by which date all the prisoners from Valleyfield, except for a score or so of Poles and a number of Germans and Italians, had been marched down to Leith and embarked for France, the Board wrote to Lieutenant Glinn, its agent at Leith, to express 'our surprise at the very great Delay which has taken place in the Service of Embarkation, more especially as you reported in your Letter of the 1st Inst. that Tonnage had then arrived in Leith Roads capable of receiving nearly the whole of the French at Valleyfield, the Embarkation of whom we are of opinion might have been affected [sic] in two or three Days at furthest. We desire you to report to us on the Subject, and hasten the Embarkation as much as possible.' The Valleyfield agent was written to in similar terms next day and also asked to report to the Board on the question. [98]

The two agents' reports have not survived, but whatever the reasons for the delays the Board had complained of it accepted the explanations the agents offered. It also expressed its gratitude to a Mr Kelly and two unnamed men for their 'Exertions in embarking the Prisoners', and it instructed Lieutenant Glinn to pay Mr Kelly a guinea and the other two a half guinea each. The Board thanked Rear Admiral Hope at Leith 'for the obliging Manner in which you have directed the Service of embarking the French prisoners from Valleyfield, as also our Satisfaction that the Conduct of the Officers [Glinn and Brown] under this department has been such as to merit the high appreciation to have been bestowed upon them.' [99]

So far as the release of the prisoners from Valleyfield was concerned, the final instructions by the Transport Board were issued in the last days of June to Captain Brown and Lieutenant Glinn. 'You will report by the Return of Post,' the Board ordered Brown on 24 June, 'the present State of the Sick French prisoners remaining in your custody and when it is probable they will be sufficiently recovered to be sent away. A Transport appointed to convey Germans from the Tay to Helvoetsluys has been ordered to call at Leith and on her arrival the Germans in your Custody are to be immediately put on board her. The Piedmontese remaining in your Custody are to be sent to France by the way of Gravesend in the usual manner.' The next day Lieutenant Glinn was instructed to send 'some Piedmontese now at Valleyfield to Gravesend in Smacks in the usual Manner unless any of them should choose to leave the Country for France or Holland by any other route at their own expense.' Finally, Captain Brown was instructed on 27 June that 'the Italians and Genoese in your Custody are to accompany the Piedmontese. You will hear from us in a Day or two, relative to the Disposal of the Poles.'[100]

There was a similar flurry of orders issued by the Board in the month between 25 May and 24 June to its agent at Perth. The names of several of the transport vessels contracted to embark them there may have brought a wry grimace to the faces of the released prisoners. 'Having ordered the Transports *Willing Minds* (118 tons), *Harmony* (127 tons), *British Volunteer* (144 tons), *Trial* (187 tons), *Moscow* (176 tons), *Economy* (137 tons), to proceed to the Tay for the purpose of conveying the prisoners of war at your depot to France,' the Board instructed the agent on 25 May, 'we direct you to make arrangements for embarking the prisoners in your custody immediately on the arrival of these vessels …' As with those released from Valleyfield, medical officers and medicines were to be put on board with those who were sick, and five officers were to accompany every 100 men, and if possible a surgeon was to be on each ship, but embarkation was not to be delayed if officers released from the Scots parole towns did not arrive in time. If any Royal Navy vessels became available to take prisoners from the Tay then they should be sent on board them, and the agent should communicate with Admiral Hope and Lieutenant Glinn at Leith on this subject. The masters of the transports were to return immediately to the Tay after landing the prisoners in France, and the agent was to put other contingents of prisoners on board them without awaiting further orders. By the last day of May, however, unspecified difficulties had arisen. On that date the agent, Captain Moriarty, wrote the Board about these, and in its reply to him on 4 June the Board expressed surprise 'that there should have been any difficulty in embarking the prisoners as you might have employed a clerk and one of the turnkeys to accompany the prisoners with the Guard. The masters of the Transports also will follow such instructions, and give such assistance as you may desire. Lieutenant

Priest [until then agent at Greenlaw and also based previously for a time at Edinburgh Castle] has been ordered on this service but if he should not have arrived, or be in bad health, the above plan is to be adopted.'[101]

As at Valleyfield, the first contingent of released prisoners passed out through the gates of Perth depot on 1 June. 'Yesterday,' the *Perth Courier* reported next day, 'upwards of 120 were carried down the river [and Firth, to Newburgh, on the southern or Fife shore] in boats. A great number of spectators attended their embarkation and greeted them with repeated cheers on their departure. They were also cordially cheered from the walls of the Depot, which were crowded by their fellow captives. This day, though the number in the Depot still exceeds 6,000, only two are in the hospital and for the present incapable of being sent to France.' If a report in the *Dundee Advertiser* was accurate, the efforts of the Transport Board and the depot authorities to smooth the path of the restored Bourbon monarchy in France had not been successful among those first 120 repatriates. 'The news of the defeat and dethronement of Bonaparte,' the *Advertiser* reported, 'had been pronounced by them, up to the very last day of their confinement, to be entirely false, and a fabrication of the English Government.'[102]

The 6,000 or so were further reduced the following day, 2 June, when 'about 400 prisoners ... were marched from the Depot on their way to France. They were to embark at Newburgh, about 10 miles down the river, on board six transports which arrived there on Tuesday [31 May]. They are to be landed at Dunkirk, Calais or Boulogne, as may be found most convenient at the moment.'[103]

Another contingent of 700 or so prisoners were marched the next day, 3 June, to Newburgh 'where they joined their companions who had been removed on the two preceding days. The transports, including in all above 1,200 (including 30 who had arrived from Leith), dropt down the river to Dundee on Sunday morning [5 June] and sailed on Tuesday. At Newburgh the prisoners were allowed to go at large, and we are glad to find that the people of that place speak highly of their behaviour. As soon as they arrived they exhibited their articles for sale on the quay and much traffic went on between them and the inhabitants of the vicinity. All, however, was conducted honourably, and the additional graces of French *politesse* seem to have made a deep impression on the natives of Fife, both male and female.'[104] Among commercial activities which prisoners were reported to have undertaken on their way to their embarkation was the sale of 'a considerable number' of Testaments in French, which had been sent some weeks earlier 'from Edinburgh to a gentleman in this city [Perth], with special instructions to distribute them among the French prisoners of war on their leaving the Depot for their native country. The instructions were attempted to be complied with but they (the prisoners) with a few exceptions sold the Testaments for a trifling consideration ... The distribution was immediately stopped and the remaining copies were sent direct to France on board the transports, and given to the prisoners on their landing, which fulfilled the design of the benevolent donors, viz., their circulation in France.'[105]

At Dundee, too, many of the prisoners were allowed ashore from some of the transports. 'Our streets on Sunday and Monday [5 and 6 June],' the *Dundee Advertiser* reported, 'presented the novel scene of numerous parties of Frenchmen walking about at large, purchasing provisions, and followed by crowds of townspeople, attracted by curiosity to view them. Six transports from Newburgh, with upwards of a thousand prisoners of war lately confined in the depot at Perth but now liberated and sent home, were detained in the Roads by contrary winds, and it was from some of those ships that the strangers were landed. Making allowance for their long confinement and for certain peculiarities of visage to which we are little accustomed here—such as the huge mustachoes on the upper lip—the appearance of the Frenchmen was healthy, interesting and agreeable. Some of them were men of education and refinement. One *pauvre diable*, in purchasing necessaries, having paid a pound note which turned out to be a forged one and being unable to make restitution, he was on the point of being seized when Mr Daraux [a French civilian, probably a refugee, resident in Dundee], with a feeling of generosity and kindness to his countryman of which we have formerly seen instances, paid the money and tore the fraudulent note. Strong symptoms of discontent, which might have ended in open mutiny, were manifested in the transports on Sunday, in consequence of spirits being prohibited. The Provost of Dundee was sent for and went on board, accompanied by Mr Daraux as interpreter; and it took all the patience of the latter gentleman, all the authority [?] of weight among themselves, to persuade the prisoners that wine and spirits were withheld by an order from the Transport Board. The incredulity of these [prisoners] to the late events in France is remarkable. Some of them were convinced for the first time on the testimony of their excellent countryman Daraux. To "Louis XVIII règne maintenant?", Daraux assured them there was no doubt of it. If the fidelity to their new master shall bear any proportion to their attachment to Bonaparte, no Prince in Christendom has such devoted subjects as Louis XVIII.'[106]

An interval of six days appears to have passed before the next contingent of some 300 to leave the depot marched out to Newburgh on 9 June, following the arrival there the previous evening of two transport vessels. The 300 appear promptly to have been joined by a further 400, and all 700 to have sailed away on 14 June on four vessels. The number of prisoners left in the depot was said then to be 'little more than 4,000.'[107]

While the number of prisoners at the depot was thus diminishing, Captain Moriarty, the agent, was bombarded almost daily with instructions and comments by the Transport Board. On 7 June it signalled its approval of his having sent the first batch of 120 released prisoners by boats down the river Tay to Newburgh for the reasons he had written to explain upon their departure. Two further letters sent Moriarty by the Board on 10 and 13 June about other aspects of the releases were followed by one on the 14th that 'the Board are satisfied with the exertions of Lieutenant Priest, but it has not been found expedient or necessary to employ a naval officer in the removal of the prisoners from the depot at Norman Cross although those prisoners had had to undergo two embarkations after the performance of a march.'[108]

A further 650 or so prisoners marched to Newburgh in two contingents on 21 and 22 June and sailed off early on 23 June on three transports. A fourth transport, a brig named *Venus*, whose master was said to have refused the services of a pilot, was lost temporarily to the work of repatriation when it ran aground on the river bank near Flisk, six miles north-east of Newburgh.

Over 1,000 more prisoners marched from the depot for Newburgh on 30 June, 1 and 4 July and embarked on several transports which had arrived there. By 7 July the number of prisoners left in the depot was said to be 'about 2,000.'[109] Next day some 400 marched from Perth to Dundee, where they were embarked on the frigate HMS *Solebay*, which sailed the following day. More or less simultaneously, no fewer than eight transport vessels arrived at Newburgh and to there on 10, 11, 12, and 13 July, in four successive daily contingents of about 400 or 500 each, all the remaining prisoners were marched from Perth. The depot was at last empty.[110]

Thus the French government commissioners' statement, reported on 26 May in the *Perth Courier*, that the repatriation of the French prisoners would begin in June and be completed by the end of July, had proven correct both at Perth and even more so at Valleyfield, the last of whose French inmates had departed as early as 15 June. But was the commissioners' further reported statement that 'Those who have been longest in captivity will be liberated first', borne out also at the two depots? A document among papers of the Perth depot chief clerk Andrew Johnston which are preserved in the National Library of Scotland, appears to suggest that the principle of 'first in, first out' was followed at that depot. The document, dated 14 June 1814, signed by Johnston, and said to be issued by order of the agent, Captain Moriarty, declared: 'No. 5 prison is to be evacuated and the men put as follows—The remainder of 1810 and as many of 1811 to No.1 [prison] as makes 1035. The rest of 1811 and first part of 1812 to No.2 [prison], another 1035. Next to go off of 1812—to No. 3 [prison], another 1035. The last of 1812—to No. 4 [prison], another 1035. [Total]: 4140.' The total corresponds with that reported in the *Perth Courier* to be still at the depot on 14 June.[111]

Given the close control the Transport Board sought to maintain at the depots concerning the arrangements for the repatriation, it seems unlikely that such a scheme at Perth was not also applied at Valleyfield, for which, however, no similar document is known to survive. Both at Valleyfield, where the releases were completed between 1 and 15 June, and even at Perth, where they extended from 1 June to 13 July, there was little scope within such short periods for any distinctively early release for those who had been longest in captivity. Perhaps it did not matter much anyway to those who by the summer of 1814 had been prisoners for eleven, or ten, nine, eight, seven, or half a dozen years that they were released only two or three weeks earlier than those fellow inmates who had been prisoners for fewer years than theirs. At Perth, from the aggregate of some 7,700 prisoners of all nationalities held during 1812-14, of whom around 5,300 (68.8 per cent) had been captured as late in the war as 1811 or 1812, there were only about 487 (6.3 per cent) who had been captured during the years 1803-08. At Valleyfield, on the other hand, from the aggregate of some 7,600 held in 1811-14 the numbers (1,637, or 21.4 per cent) who had been captured in 1811 and 1812 were almost exactly equal to those (1,641, also 21.4 per cent) captured during the years 1803-08.[112] A glance through the Perth Entry Books suggests that while there appears generally to have been some correlation between capture before 1810 and release in the earlier days of June 1814, and also between capture from 1810 and release in the month or so to mid-July 1814, there were some unexplained exceptions, and that the principle of 'first in, first out' was not strictly, certainly not rigidly, observed. For example, why was Jean Raffat or Raphard, aged 39, born at St Maxonnery, a soldier from an unnamed regiment who had been captured on a warship off Rochefort as relatively late in the war as November 1811 released on 1 June 1814? Was he perhaps a professed Bourbon loyalist? On the other hand, why did Nicolas Le Roy, aged only ten, have to wait with his father, also a prisoner at Perth, until 10 June for their release when they had been captured in September 1810? Was it because Le Roy senior was captain of a privateer, the *Hirondelle*, when he and his son were captured? Why was another prisoner of tender years, Melon Pain, aged 11, captured on the privateer *Le Pilotin* in October 1812, not released until as late as 13 July 1814? [113] At Valleyfield, a similar glance through the Entry Books suggests that there, too, although there appears generally to have been a correlation between year of capture and date of release, some unexplained exceptions occur. Why, for example, was Pierre Mari [sic] Sevenot, a seaman who had been captured at St Domingo on the man-of-war *Créole* as early in the war as 29 June 1803 not released until 7 June 1814, which was half-way through the fortnight of French repatriations from the depot? By contrast, two soldiers, André Duvoine and Germain Doucin, both of the 2nd line regiment and both of whom had been captured on the man-of-war *Le Berwicke* at the battle of Trafalgar on 21 October 1805, almost two and a half years after Sevenot's capture, were released four days before him on 3 June 1814. Why also did François Roger, described as a seaman although aged only 11, who had been captured in October 1808, have to wait for his release until 14 June 1814, second last day of the general repatriation of French prisoners from the depot? As has already been observed above, Jean Baptiste Josin, alias N.B. Jansens, a seaman aged 28 and born at Dunkirk, who had been captured as early as February 1805, did not enjoy the concession of early release evidently granted some other prisoners belonging to that town, and had to wait for his until the last day, 15 June 1814.[114]

A few non-French prisoners at Valleyfield had to wait even longer for their repatriation. Some German prisoners still at Perth, and some Germans and Italians still at Valleyfield, appear to have been repatriated in the last days of June, but there remained even then some Poles at Valleyfield.[115] On 8 June a Transport Board circular to depot agents had instructed them to send as soon as possible 'a list of all the Poles in your custody.' What the response was from Valleyfield and Perth is unknown as no such list from either depot seems to have survived. The next day Lieutenant Glinn, the Board's transport agent at Leith, was instructed to detain until further orders 'Any natives of Poland who may arrive' there, and to send a list of 'such Persons' to the Transport Office without delay. The Board, as has been seen, instructed its agent at Valleyfield on 27 June, by which time all the French prisoners had been gone from the depot for almost a fortnight, that 'You will hear from us in a Day or two, relative to the Disposal of the Poles.' On 6 July the Board instructed its agent at Gravesend in Kent that 'two natives of Poland have been embarked at Leith on board the *Fife* smack for Gravesend ... and on their arrival ... you will send them back to Leith by the first opportunity, in order that they may be sent to their own country.' The next surviving reference to the continuing presence of Poles at Valleyfield occurred in a letter of 8 September from the Board to the Admiralty. Referring to an order from the Admiralty on 20 July, the Board informed their Lordships 'that in consequence thereof the Poles therein mentioned [at Valleyfield] have been kept at the disposal of Count de Kruckowucki at that depot and repeated applications have been made to the Count for their removal. But having no prospect of his taking them away we directed our agent at Leith on 22nd August and again on 3rd inst. to engage a conveyance for these Poles by a Baltic trader without delay, and immediately upon their removal the establishment [at Valleyfield] will be abolished.'[116] So at last Valleyfield was emptied of all its inmates when on 16 September 1814 'A few Poles, the last of the prisoners of war, were ... marched to Leith, to embark for their own country. They were mostly stout well looking men.'[117]

The 12,000 or so prisoners of war, most of them French, released in 1814 from the Scots depots constituted about one sixth of all those released then from depots and hulks in Britain as a whole. If that total of 72,000 or so released from Britain included approximately 60,000 who were French, then those 60,000 were hardly one third of all the released French prisoners of war who poured back into France in 1814 from other countries where they had been held captive, including Spain, Italy and Germany. Those 200,000 or so were, as the French historian Georges Blond put it, a real Grande Armée. The misery of their captivity was scarcely expunged by the absence of welcome or provision made for them by the new government authorities in France: '"Here's your leave, all you have to do is go home." Along the roads they formed long processions of down and outs in rags and tatters. As they passed, the villagers shut their doors and windows.'[118] As the *Caledonian Mercury* commented on 28 May on the eve of the great repatriation from the Scots depots: 'It is not a favourable omen for the future tranquillity of France that a great proportion of prisoners now returning into her bosom still remain with perverse blindness attached to the interest of Bonaparte.'

24

All Men Are Brethren

The attachment 'with perverse blindness' to the interest of Napoleon of which the *Caledonian Mercury* had warned was not confined in 1814-15 to many of the released French prisoners of war only. That attachment, however, was by no means the sole factor in the return of Napoleon from Elba to France on 1 March 1815. The following Hundred Days, when he gathered an army of some 126,000 and attempted to defeat one at a time the two separate allied armies stationed in Belgium and led respectively by Wellington and the Prussian Marshal Blücher, culminated in Napoleon's decisive defeat on 18 June at Waterloo. About 7,500 of his troops were taken prisoner there. It seems certain that some at least of those who had been prisoners in the Scots depots until 1814 joined Napoleon's army in the Hundred Days and fought at Waterloo. But the only one who has been positively identified was Marcher, who had been a prisoner at Valleyfield, where he complained of the cold and praised the large cabbages, and whom Mr John Cowan of Beeslack met at the Invalides in Paris in 1845. Marcher had lost an arm at Waterloo.[1]

In June 1814, when from Valleyfield depot the French prisoners had been released and had moved in long columns along the road to Edinburgh and their embarkation at Leith, they had passed close to the newly reconstructed and extended depot at Greenlaw on whose completion building tradesmen were still at work. To them the passing prisoners had shouted in derision, 'No more prisoners come!'[2] And none did. Nonetheless some might have come after Waterloo to Greenlaw, Valleyfield, and Perth if certain preliminary recommendations made then to the Admiralty by the Transport Board had actually been carried out.

Only four days after the battle of Waterloo the Transport Board wrote to the Admiralty about the reception 'of French Prisoners of War which are likely to be immediately brought from Flanders to this Country.' The Board suggested that six prison hulks be used—two each at Chatham, Portsmouth and Plymouth—until the prisoners could be sent to land depots. '... as it is proper that no time should be lost in preparing some of the depots for the reception of prisoners and in making contracts for victualling them,' the Board's letter continued, 'we ... recommend that the Depots at Valleyfield,

Greenlaw and Perth in Scotland, together with Norman Cross, may be forthwith prepared and that their Lordships may be pleased to appoint officers
to take charge of them under this department, and surgeons to superintend
them.'[3] Their lordships of the Admiralty replied next day, expressing the
hope that at least for the present there would be no need to house prisoners
in the hulks at Chatham, Portsmouth or Plymouth. The arrangements the
Admiralty proposed, which it considered 'will be most advantageous both in
point of convenience and economy', were to send 5,000 of the prisoners to
Dartmoor, 2,000 to Mill prison at Plymouth, and 2,000 or 3,000 to Stapleton. The Admiralty said it believed Greenlaw and Valleyfield could 'contain
10,000 men—Greenlaw only wants to be cleared of Stores & Valleyfield is
stated to be quite ready. My Lords will therefore direct to this latter depot
the first prisoners that it may be expedient to send to the Northward. Perth,
estimated to [be able to] receive 7,000 Men, will be also ready when cleared
of Stores, which is to be forthwith done; but it seems inexpedient to have
recourse to it until both Valleyfield and Greenlaw are full. It is therefore their
Lordships' direction that you immediately proceed to carry into effect the
foregoing arrangements, and not to lose a moment in preparing for the reception of about 7,000 Men, who will be distributed to Dartmoor, Stapleton and
probably Valleyfield.'[4] A week later the Board informed the Admiralty that
Robert Reid, crown architect in Scotland, had on the Board's instructions
inspected Greenlaw and Valleyfield depots, and that the Board supported
Reid's recommendation that 'Greenlaw may be firstly occupied, and that
Captain [Andrew] Brown may be directed to take charge of it.'[5] Contracts for
victualling prisoners of war at Greenlaw, Valleyfield and Perth, as well as at
Plymouth and Stapleton, near Bristol, were to be advertised in the press.

In the event, however, no prisoners at all were sent after Waterloo to any
depot in Scotland.[6]

Napoleon himself, according to one Scots local historian, following his
surrender after Waterloo might have become a prisoner of war in Scotland.
Andrew Mair, in his history of Dumbarton Castle, asserted, although without
identifying the source of his claim, that 'the British Government had under
consideration, among other places, Dumbarton Castle as a suitable prison
for the fallen Emperor. Napoleon himself was in hopes that he would be
allowed to settle down as a country gentleman, or at the worst be interned
in the old fortress.'[7] The *Edinburgh Evening Courant* in its leading article on
27 July 1815 presciently informed its readers that: 'Conjecture has been
extremely busy in fixing Bonaparte's future residence. Fort George, Edinburgh Castle, and Dumbarton Castle in Scotland—the Tower of London,
and Sheerness, have all been mentioned; but the most general credit seems
to be attached to the statement that the British Government intend to
send him to St Helena.'

As after every war, there were enquiries after the fall of Napoleon about prisoners whose fate remained unknown to their families. At The National Archives in London is preserved a box of papers, dated mainly between 1827 and 1830, and consisting chiefly of such enquiries by the British and French authorities. Nothing in the box concerns any missing prisoners in any Scots depot between 1803 and 1814. In the Macbeth Forbes collection in the National Archives of Scotland, however, there is a letter from the Transport Office and three from the Victualling Office replying to enquiries made as late as 1825-7 about four prisoners—three at Perth and one at Greenlaw. Three of the four letters were addressed to Monsieur Halgan, evidently a French government official. The first letter, from the Transport Office and dated 10 August 1825, concerned Henry Joseph Narote, taken prisoner in 1809 and said to have been discharged from Perth depot in 1813. The Transport Office said no prisoner of that name had been found on any lists for Perth, though there had been at the depot one named Jean Louis Narotte, captured in 1810 and repatriated to France on 13 June 1814. The second letter, dated 4 November 1825 and, like the remaining two, from the Victualling Office, concerned a prisoner named Jacques Roger, described as a Neapolitan gendarme. The Office suggested that the prisoner in question was Jacques Rogier or Roche or Rocher, described variously as a soldier and as a gendarme, who had been captured in Calabria in July 1806, taken to Malta in September that year, then two years later to Portsmouth, and sent from there in August 1812 to Perth, from which he had been released to France on 3 June 1814. The third letter, dated 12 April 1827, concerned 'the fate of' François Julien Nasbreek, soldier, 1st Colonial Battalion, confined at Perth in December 1813 and who 'appears to have been released from Perth to return to France on the 9th June 1814.' The fourth letter, dated 29 November 1830, was in reply to a request from Baron de Mackan, French minister of Marine and Colonies, for a death certificate for Jean Ayrand (or Airo, or Aycand), captured on the man-of-war *Jupiter* in 1806 and who had died two years later as a prisoner at Greenlaw. It appears likely that at least a few more captives confined in Scots depots were not heard of again by their families after the war. Was that the case perhaps with René Jezequel, for example, who may have been confined at Esk Mill? It appears certainly to have been so with M. J. Silas Priere, who died at Valleyfield in May 1814.[8]

A letter from 1812 which is preserved in the National Library of Scotland may serve as an illustration, if any is needed, of the anxiety and grief which so many tens of thousands of families suffered during and after the war about sons, husbands, fathers, or other loved ones who had been taken prisoner or had gone missing, or at least of or from whom nothing had been heard. The letter, signed 'Widow Raphael' and dated from Morlais [Morlaix, in Brittany], 12 June 1812, was addressed to 'Monsieur Damson [Johnston], Second Commissaire [chief clerk] of Valleyfield Depot, near Penicuic [sic], in England, in

Scotland.' Widow Raphael wrote: 'Sir, I take the liberty of writing these lines in order to implore your kindness toward my son Alexis Pierre Marie Raphael. Your goodness of which the prisoners who came from his depot have told me dares me to beg you if always it is possible to have consideration for my poor child and [a word illegible] his fate, I would have for you, Monsieur, all the recognition of a true mother for her child. I beg you to excuse me, Monsieur. I close, Monsieur, with respect, your very humble servant, Widow Raphael.' It appears that Madame Raphael's appeal to Andrew Johnston was success-ful. At any rate her son survived the war, and on 3 June 1814, at the time of his release and repatriation from Perth, Alexis Raphael wrote to Johnston inviting him to visit him at his mother's house in Morlaix.[9]

Only two or three prisoners from the depots are known, or said, to have remained in Scotland after the war, though of course it is possible some others also did so. One, already noticed in an earlier chapter above, was the Dutch-man Van Beck, who was said to have escaped at Penicuik with the aid of a local family a member of which he later married. Another, whose name, however, has not been found, who apparently had also been a prisoner at Penicuik, was said after the war to have become a shepherd and settled on a farm in Midlothian near the Moorfoot hills.[10] About a third prisoner who stayed on in Scotland a note written as late as 25 August 1848 by Mr (later Sir) John Cowan of Beeslack at Penicuik, which he penned on the back of the list compiled in 1821 of prisoners who had died at Valleyfield, says: 'Champvray called. Was here from 1809 to 1814. Has supported himself since by travelling thro' the Lowlands sharpening knives. A brother of his died here but having been in the army he very probably gave a false designation. The knife sharpener seems a decent man and has been here [to Beeslack House] before.'[11]

The end (as it appeared then to be) of the war in 1814 was followed not only by the repatriation of all the prisoners in the Scots depots, as in those and on the hulks in England, but also by the closure of the depots themselves and the end of the employment of their staffs. The establishment at Perth depot, from which as has been seen the last of the prisoners had been released on 13 July, was reported in the press to have 'broken up, partly on the 16th and partly on 31st July.' That almost all the staff ceased to be employed there on or by either of those two days appears confirmed by references in the official archives and other sources. On the other hand, Andrew Johnston, as first or chief clerk appears to have remained at the depot until 13 August; and one of his clerks, John Mathew, evidently found new employment there until 31 December that year.[12]

Captain Moriarty, the depot agent, and James Gillies, the depot surgeon, were both honoured by the conferment on them by the provost and magis-trates of Perth of the freedom of the city. Moriarty lived on, in retirement so far as is known, until 1833.[13]

Other members of Perth depot staff appear not to have been so well treated. Of six, including Andrew Johnston, the chief clerk, who applied for pensions or gratuities, four were wholly or partially unsuccessful and the incompleteness of surviving documentation leaves it impossible to know if the remaining two had any greater success.

Johnston's application for a pension was strongly supported by Captain Moriarty in a letter of 17 July 1814 to the Transport Board. 'It is with the greatest delicacy,' wrote Moriarty, 'that I beg leave most anxiously to call your attention to my first Clerk, whose indefatigable exertions in seconding me in the arduous and anxious charge of 7,000 Prisoners, in which situation he has acted for four years, and the time under me I must acknowledge. He often endured the greatest dangers and hardships—night after night [having to rise] from his Bed, often knocked down by the Prisoners, and lately nearly killed—but his zeal and perseverance has carried him through with the highest credit and Honor to Himself and the Service, as well as to my admiration and satisfaction. Permit me to add he had eight children, and without your Humanity in taking His case into consideration, will retire a poorer man than when he first entered. I must entreat your excuse [sic], I shall be truly grateful for anything you can do for him, and I well know I cannot do better than place him on your Humanity.' Moriarty's advocacy failed, however, to win approval of Johnston's application. 'With respect to your recommendation of Mr Johnston,' replied J. Dixon on behalf of the secretary of the Transport Board on 21 July, 'I am directed to inform you that many persons of great merit and long service are of necessity now discharged from the employ of this Department but that the Board have not the power of making any pecuniary recompense to them.'[14] Seven years after the closure of the depot Johnston applied for a gratuity, but the outcome of his application is uncertain as the surviving documentation is incomplete. In a comment by an unidentified official on the memorial submitted by Johnston on 25 August 1821, there is a reference to Johnston's employment as a clerk or first clerk successively at Esk Mills, Valleyfield and Perth from 1 March 1811 to 13 August 1814, throughout which time his conduct had been 'highly satisfactory'. The comment continued: 'It has not been usual to allow gratuities for so short a service, but in consideration of the injuries sustained by him in the execution of his duty it is probable that the Lords Commissioner of HM Treasury might be disposed to consider his case favourably. Whether the Board shall judge it expedient to recommend him to their Lordships, or merely in the first instance to refer him to that department and reserve their report on his cause until it may be called for by their Lordships, is submitted …'[15] Andrew Johnston died in 1844 at the age of 73. His son William, founder in 1825 with his brother Alexander of the publishing firm W. & A. K. Johnston, was elected lord provost of Edinburgh in 1848 and was knighted in 1851.[16]

Of the three other members of the depot staff who also failed (in their case, to win a gratuity for their services), Mrs Dovey, who had been matron at the hospital from January 1813 to July 1814, and whose 'conduct appears to have been satisfactory', was unsuccessful when she applied in 1819 because 'the shortness of the period [of her service] must prevent her from being considered entitled to any gratuity.' The same shortness of service of Jasper Armstrong, a turnkey at Perth for two years till July 1814, likewise defeated his application in November 1821.[17] The application in January 1819 by John Duncan, who had been a turnkey successively at Norman Cross, Dartmoor and Perth, was given short shrift when the correspondence files revealed he had been dismissed at Perth on 17 January 1813 for repeated drunkenness.[18]

The outcome is unknown, because of incomplete documentation, of the application in early 1819 for a gratuity by John Lewis, who had been assistant dispenser and interpreter at Perth for two years until July 1814, before which he had been similarly employed at Valleyfield and before that as assistant dispenser, but not also interpreter, at Esk Mills from December 1810. His conduct in those employments had been 'highly satisfactory' and he had moreover sustained 'considerable loss by being shipwrecked on his return' [presumably from Perth southward].[19]

For the same reason the outcome is unknown of an application for a pension made toward the end of 1818 by John Mathew. Mathew was said to have been employed as a clerk at Perth depot from July 1813 to 31 December 1814, and later, from December 1815 to the end of January 1818, as keeper of the depot premises at Greenlaw, throughout which years 'his conduct appears to have been satisfactory.'[20]

That John Mathew's employment at Perth depot continued for five months even after the prisoners had been released in the summer of 1814 was due to the use to which the buildings were then put by the authorities. Although in early May that year reports had appeared in the press that the government intended 'to convert the depot at Perth into artillery barracks' after the prisoners had gone, it was decided before the end of June that the depot would in fact be given up to the Storekeeper General of the Ordnance Department, for use as a store for military clothing and other stocks. The depot appears accordingly to have been handed over soon after 30 August. The Perth historian George Penny later wrote that consequently 'The whole prison was filled with clothing and various articles for the army. A great number of women and boys were employed in brushing and cleaning them. To such an extent were they employed, that the value of the articles would soon have been paid for by their keeping. The scheme was therefore given up, and the stores sent back to London.' Abell, though without giving his source, said the depot remained a military clothing store until 1833. The latter date appears to fit in with Penny's statement, in his history of Perth published in 1836, that 'The Prison has since been either empty or let for granaries, for which it is admirably adapted.' Penny added that in or by 1836 only two persons were employed at the former depot—'the governor and one man.' Penny urged, presciently as it proved, that the buildings 'might be far better occupied as a national bridewell—where convicted felons, instead of being sent out of the country [i.e., transported to Australia] at so great an expense, could be employed in labour to maintain themselves.' After undergoing some reconstruction, the depot did become in 1840-1 the General Prison for Scotland, and it has remained a prison since then. Writing about the former depot in 1849, David Peacock, another historian of Perth, declared: 'This establishment ... has within these ten years been converted into a General Prison or Penitentiary for Scotland. Formerly it was a neat and rather ornamental adjunct to the town; it is now a huge unseemly excrescence; and its object, as a means of moral reformation chiefly, is admitted to have been comparatively a failure.'[21]

Edinburgh Castle, as has been seen, apart from being a place of confinement during 1811-14 for some of the more troublesome French and other prisoners and an occasional staging post for prisoners in transit, had been used only during most of 1811 as a general, if relatively small, depot. It had ceased altogether to be a depot, for punishment or otherwise, for prisoners of war shortly before the end of the war in April 1814. Although there appears to have been a proposal during the Second World War that prisoners of war might be confined in the Castle, it was in fact never again used for that purpose after the Napoleonic Wars. It remained an army barracks and also the headquarters of Scottish Command until 1955, when the latter moved to Craigiehall on the outskirts of Edinburgh.[22]

Esk Mills, which during the Napoleonic Wars had had an even shorter existence as a prisoner of war depot than Edinburgh Castle, after the war resumed its earlier function as a place of manufacture. But whereas its original function from the later 18th century had been cotton spinning and then additionally, before its conversion in 1810-11 into a depot for prisoners of war, paper making, Esk Mills was bought after the war by Messrs Haig of Lochrin and associates 'and fitted up with paper-making machinery.' But their business soon failed, and the mills were bought in 1821 by one of the creditors, James Brown, and were then converted into a larger paper-making mill, which under successive owners and managers, continued to produce paper as James Brown & Co. until its closure in 1968. All the mill buildings have since then been demolished.[23]

At Greenlaw, earliest (apart from the temporary use in 1803-4 of the Edinburgh bridewell) of the Scots depots in the Napoleonic Wars, the agent, Lieutenant Priest, had been ordered on 5 May 1814 to deliver all the depot stores to his senior colleague Captain Brown, at Valleyfield and to submit to the Transport Board his final accounts 'with as little delay as possible.' A week later, however, the Board instructed Captain Brown that Priest was 'to remain until the whole Business at Greenlaw is finally arranged.' When exactly Priest departed as agent from the depot is not certain but it appears to have been during June when, as has been seen, he was ordered by the Transport Board to help with the repatriation of the prisoners from Perth. There is no evidence that his departure from Greenlaw was accompanied by any expression of thanks to him by the Board.[24]

In early July the *Edinburgh Evening Courant* reported it was 'the intention of Government to convert the buildings lately completed at Greenlaw into barracks.' But it was only in March 1816 that the Admiralty formally ordered the transfer of the depot buildings to the Barrack Department and it was three months after that that the transfer actually took place. For two years from December 1815 John Mathew, formerly a clerk at Perth depot, was in charge of the premises at Greenlaw. But the premises remained otherwise untenanted and apparently unused until 1846, when Greenlaw, with the addition of some wooden buildings, became the military prison for Scotland and remained so until 1888. A decade or so before the latter date Greenlaw also became what it is has since remained, an army depot and barracks. At the end of the 19th century most of the buldings which had housed or, following the substantial extensions built in 1813-14, had been intended to house prisoners of war were demolished, as were the wooden extensions of 1846. The only parts of the older buildings surviving in the early 21st century are the octagonal stone guard house and some of the boundary wall. To avoid confusion with Greenlaw in Berwickshire, the name of the barracks was changed toward the end of the 19th century to Glencorse.[25]

At Valleyfield Alexander Munro, who had been first clerk there from December 1810, as well as from August 1812 interpreter, until September 1814, remained after the war as keeper of the premises until their sale by the government in 1820. From 1803 until December 1810 Munro had been employed as a clerk or hospital steward at Norman Cross depot in England. His long service appears to have won for him better post-war provision than that enjoyed by any other member of any Scots depot staff. In November 1815 he was granted a gratuity equal to one year's pay, and it appears he was also granted a pension from the end of 1818.[26]

Valleyfield, the largest depot in Scotland from 1811 until the opening a year later of Perth, was put up for sale after the end of the war in 1814. But it consistently failed to attract any offers except successively lower ones made by the two canny brothers Duncan and Alexander Cowan, owners of the paper mill there until they had sold it in 1810-11 to the government for use as a depot. As Robert Reid, crown architect in Scotland, explained in a letter in July 1817 to the Commissioners of the Royal Navy Victualling Board, there was a clause in the sale agreement with the Cowans that the latter were 'bound to repurchase them at £6,000 if called upon to do so within ten years. But it was likewise stipulated that in the event of the premises being redelivered to Messrs Cowan for £6,000 the same were previously to be re-stored to their original state by the Commissioners of the Transport Board.' That clause, wrote Reid, was 'the great obstacle,' to the sale of Valleyfield after the end of the war, because the alterations and additions to the origi-nal buildings undertaken by the Transport Board in 1811-14 to enlarge the depot 'rendered it, in great measure, impracticable to comply literally with this clause.' Moreover, the Cowans had not at the time of the sale in 1810-11 given up their ownership of the water supply to the mill, and without that no other post-war bidder would have been able to run the mill. As Charles Cowan, son of one of the brothers and nephew of the other, recalled years later in his autobiography, 'The prisons continued unoccupied until 1820, when they were repurchased by my father and uncle for, I think, £2,200, after they had been exposed repeatedly for sale by tender or auction. My father offered always a few hundred pounds less than he had done on each preced-ing occasion, as, owing to exposure to the weather, non-occupancy, and want of protection, the buildings greatly deteriorated in value. My impression is, that if my father's offer in 1815 or 1816 had been accepted, the Government would have obtained about double the price realised in 1820.' Valleyfield thus resumed from 1820 the production of paper which had been carried on at the mill from 1709 until the Napoleonic Wars. Valleyfield mill remained in the ownership of the Cowans until some years before production ceased in 1975, after which the mill was completely demolished. During the 1990s houses were built on the site of the mill and prisoner of war depot.[27]

Upon Scotland and its people the presence of the thousands of French and other prisoners of war immured at one period or another during 1803-1814 in the depots at the Edinburgh bridewell, Greenlaw, Esk Mills, Edinburgh Castle, Valleyfield or Perth, left only limited and largely ephemeral traces. The goods the prisoners made in straw, paper, wood, hair or bone for sale to frequenters of the depot markets remain in some cases still in possession of descendants of their then or later purchasers, as well as in the store rooms or exhibition cabinets of some Scots national or local museums or other institu-tions.[28] Any other legacies they left, even in or around Edinburgh, Penicuik or Perth where they were confined, are more or less indiscernible. Only two or three cases of marriage with Scotswomen (as apparently in the case, for instance, of the Dutch escaper Van Beck, as well as, briefly, of Marote-Car-rier's soi-disant fellow subject of Oldenburg who was his companion on his departure early in 1814 from Perth, and, as Marote-Carrier also testified when he found him happily established as cook on a naval vessel at Leith, of that prince of escapers the Galérien—perhaps alias François Petit) or of any permanent post-war settlement in Scotland (again as in the case of Van Beck, as well as of that of Champvray the knife-sharpener and of the unnamed prisoner said to have become a shepherd in the Moorfoots) hardly constituted a significant gain to Scotland of French or other European peoples or of their traditions and culture.[29]

Since only a very small handful were sent out from the Scots depots to work—as were, for example, the three Danes from Greenlaw in August 1809 'for the purpose of instructing certain Highlanders in the manufacture of tar', and the Dutch seaman from Valleyfield in December 1813 'to assist Mr Dugald Fergusson of the Cod and Herring Fishery at Greenock'—the prisoners left no discernible legacies, still less monuments, in manufacturing, civil engineering or building.[30] If prisoners of war were driven in ancient times as slaves to build pyramids in Egypt, and in the Second World War British and other prisoners were forced by the Japanese to build the Burma-Siam railway, there was no such brutal exploitation, nor even unexceptionable employment, of the prisoners in the depots in Scotland (or England) during the Napoleonic Wars. Persisting local traditions that French prisoners then had built the walls round the Duke of Buccleuch's estate at Dalkeith Palace or those round the Duke of Roxburghe's estate at Floors Castle, are mere legends.

Rarely indeed were the French or other Napoleonic War prisoners in Scotland the subject of, or even referred to in, literary works. The chief exceptions to this dearth have been Robert Louis Stevenson's eponymous adventure story *St Ives*, whose hero, a French prisoner in Edinburgh Castle, escapes by rope down the rock as some fifty prisoners had actually done on the night of 11-12 April 1811; a chapter in *The Life of Mansie Wauch, Tailor in Dalkeith*, where also an escaped prisoner of war in that town near Penicuik figures; and the passage in Scott's *Waverley* quoted in an earlier chapter.[31]

The presence of the prisoners at Penicuik, Perth and Edinburgh in 1803-1814 did, on the other hand, have some impact on contemporary local employment, farmland values and obviously on the profits of contractors and others concerned in supplying the depots. Building workers and labourers, many or most of them local men, were employed at one time or another between 1803 and 1812 in the fitting up as depots successively of Greenlaw, Esk Mills, and Valleyfield, and above all in the construction of Perth, as well as in the big extensions to Greenlaw in 1813-14. Although little or nothing is known of their backgrounds or previous experience, at least a few of the lower ranks of the depot staffs (such as perhaps Henry Miles, a turnkey at Valleyfield for fifteen months until his dismissal in September 1812, who was apparently taken on there for his ability to count heads at roll-calls of the prisoners, as he 'had been previously much among sheep') appear likely to have been employed from among local people.[32] There appears to be more visible evidence of a contemporary rise in the value of farming land near the depots, and in the prices of farm products such as vegetables and grain, especially at Penicuik and Perth. The 'very high price' paid for turnips, for instance, by the rations contractor for Perth depot in January 1813 was merely one illustration of how the presence of several thousand prisoners of war and of the hundreds of militiamen guarding them provided incentives to local farmers in producing crops that figured in the Transport Board's lists of daily or weekly rations. That same example was also indicative of the profits that could be made by the depot contractors themselves. The depots with their thousands of mouths to be fed pushed upward the value of local farmland. When, for instance, the letting of Mains of Glencorse farm was advertised toward the end of 1813 in the *Edinburgh Evening Courant*, the advertisement contained not only a glowing description of the farm's attractions, including impressive fences, ditches, and good shelter for enclosures provided by thriving plantations of trees, but also emphasised that 'as the lands are only a quarter of a mile distant from the large depot just now building at Greenlaw, which is to contain 8,000 prisoners, they will, of course, command a ready market in the immediate vicinity for both farm produce and cattle.'[33] Depot staffs and guards also spent money, mainly no doubt on food and drink, in hostelries and for other services elsewhere in the immediate vicinity of their depots; and some at least of the prisoners fortunate enough to possess some money were no doubt able to buy some extra food from local sources, probably fetched into the depot for them by members of the depot staff or militia guards who were either sympathetic and/or were paid for their trouble by the prisoners.[34] The Rev. Scott Moncrieff, parish minister of Penicuik, in writing his contribution in the 1830s to the *New Statistical Account*, admitted that at Penicuik the depots had given 'unusual life and activity to the place, and had enriched some of its inhabitants.'[35]

The presence of the depots appears likely to have had some other effects, too, on surrounding communities, although those effects appear to be documented only for Penicuik. Those effects arose, however, not so much from the presence of the prisoners, strictly confined as they were within the walls or palisades, as from that of the depot staffs and militia guards and their activities off-duty. As James Anton, the militiaman on guard at Greenlaw in its earlier years as a depot, recollected in his memoirs published almost thirty years after the war: 'The inhabitants of Pennycuik and its neighbourhood, previous to the establishment of this depot of prisoners, were as comfortable and contented a class of people as in any district in Britain. The steep woody banks of the Esk were lined with prospering manufactories; neat houses and cleanly cottages rose on each side of the road leading to the village and overlooking the windings of the river. All these were tenanted by an industrious thriving community, principally paper-makers. At these manufactories the young as well as the old obtained employment according to their abilities, and liberal wages were given. Their hours of labour were generally from three or four in the morning until the same in the afternoon. This rendered it unnecessary to light candles during any part of the evening, either in summer or winter; and the leaving off work so early in the afternoon, afforded sufficient time for domestic labour or rural sports. The cleanliness required in some of the departments of these manufactories, particularly that assigned to the women, was attended with the best effects, and displayed itself in the superior neatness and comfort of their dwellings; and no place could boast of women so decently, so genteely, yet so unostentatiously dressed, as those on the lovely banks of the Esk. At that time there were only one or two public-houses in Pennycuik, and none in Kirkhill, which contained nearly as many inhabitants; in short they were a thrifty, thriving, sober, well-disposed, kindly-hearted people. When the soldiers (militiamen) were first quartered here, they met with a welcome reception and were hospitably entertained; this was too frequently but poorly requited; and in the course of a few years, those kindly people began to consider the quartering of soldiers upon them more oppressive than they at first anticipated. Trade declined as prisoners increased; and instead of tradesmen's shops starting up into notice, public-houses were springing up, displaying the ill-drawn outlines of frothing jugs to the passengers and thirsty soldiers; while the latter, getting their provisions at a reasonable rate from the inhabitants, expended their pay in these houses, and too often led astray the younger branches of the families on whom they were billeted; and a laxity in the moral feelings and orderly habits of the rising generation visibly crept in. One of the principal factories (Valleyfield) was afterwards converted into another depot for prisoners, and Esk-mills into a barrack for the military; this gave a decisive blow to trade, and several of the most active industrious young men emigrated to America, while others left their native home to carry the knowledge of their craft to other parts of the kingdom.' Anton underestimated, however, the effects of the war itself on the paper-making industry at Penicuik.[36] Similar criticism of some of the social effects of the presence of the depots at Penicuik was expressed long after the war by the parish minister, the Rev. Scott Moncrieff. 'This occurrence,' he wrote of the depots, 'could not fail to produce results very unfavourable to the social and religious well-being of the parishioners. The peaceful artisan gave way to the soldier, and the din of a camp, with its attendant irregularities, prevailed where formerly nothing had interrupted the orderly occupations and Sabbath solemnities of a Scottish village.' Not even as late as the 1830s, when he was writing these criticisms, the Rev. Scott Moncrieff believed, 'have the unfavourable effects then produced ... quite disappeared.'[37]

While Edinburgh Castle, Esk Mills and Valleyfield Mill reverted to their pre-war functions, the two other depots, as has also been seen, were respectively transformed in the decades after the Napoleonic Wars into an army barracks and depot which have remained so to the present day, in the case of Greenlaw or Glencorse, and in that at Perth into a civil prison for Scotland which has likewise remained so for the past century and a half. These two sets of buildings, although both have been greatly altered and reconstructed since they were depots for prisoners in the Napoleonic Wars, are (excluding Edinburgh Castle) the largest remaining visible legacies of the presence in Scotland between 1803 and 1814 of those thousands of captives from France but also from so many other countries in Europe and even, in a few cases, from other continents.

Between 535 and 573 of the prisoners died in the Scots depots in 1804-14 and were buried there. At Greenlaw and at Esk Mills those who died lie in unmarked graves whose precise locations even appear to have been lost in the passage of time. At Perth, those who died in captivity were officially commemorated by a plaque unveiled on a wall of the civil prison more than a century later in September 1930 by the then secretary of state for Scotland, William Adamson. The plaque said: 'Near this spot was interred a number of French prisoners of war who died in military captivity at Perth about the year 1812.'[38]

At Valleyfield there survives not a mere plaque but a substantial monument, unique in Scotland, to those prisoners of war who died and were buried there in 1811-14. The monument was built in 1830 and paid for (apart from a nominal contribution of five shillings from a local watchmaker, arranged so that its inscription could truthfully say the monument had been 'erected by certain inhabitants of the parish' and would not appear to be due only to one person) by the Valleyfield millowner Alexander Cowan. The monument bears an inscription in English and in French and also a line in Latin, suggested by Sir Walter Scott, by the Roman poet Sannazarius: 'Pleasing it is to lie at rest in one's own country, but all the world is a tomb.' The inscription in English and in French reads: 'The mortal remains of 309 prisoners of war, who died in this neighbourhood between 21st March 1811 and 26th July 1814, are interred near this spot.'[39]

To the inscription these lines were contributed by the French poet Alphonse de Lamartine:

> 'Born to bless the marriage vows of mothers growing old.
> Called away by fate,
> To become lovers, loved, spouses, and fathers,
> They died in exile.

The inscription on the monument declares that the reason for its erection was the desire to 'remember that all Men are Brethren'.

Appendix 1

THE 23 ESCAPERS FROM ESK MILLS DEPOT, 19 FEBRUARY 1811

The relevant sources, contradictory and incomplete as they often are, concerning these 23 escapers are the Esk Mills General Entry Book TNA ADM 103/124, the main Entry Books for French prisoners at Edinburgh Castle (TNA ADM 103/110-114), a 'Register of descriptions of ... French Prisoners at Edinburgh' (TNA ADM 103/116), a ledger listing escapers in alphabetical order (TNA ADM 103/491), miscellaneous lists of prisoners, including those who died in captivity, in TNA ADM 103/648, and the Valleyfield Entry Books TNA ADM 103/432 and /433, plus the Valleyfied prisoners in TNA ADM 103/113, Nos 6445-7479 inclusive. Each prisoner's number below is that given in the Esk Mills Entry Book, and where any other number is given him in other relevant sources it also is shown below. For abbreviations and contractions, see above, p.ix.

1. No. 458 Nicolas (or Henri) Boulais (or Boulet), 1st lieut., aged 35, b. St Valery en Caux, capd 16 Nov. 1810 on *Le Barbier de Seville* priv. off Norway (or n.d. on *Le Vengeur* priv. off Hastings), arr. EM from Chatham 7 Feb. 1811, 'died 19 February 1811 at 2 o'clock in the Morning, Shot by a Centinel on duty in the act of Escaping with others.' TNA ADM 103/124; ADM 103/648, No 1007.

2. No. 573 Marc Butel (or Buttel or Butelle), bosun (or seaman), 35, b. Graveline, capd 4 Dec. (or 11 Oct.) 1810 on a prize to *La Josephine* priv. in the English Channel; arr. EM from Chatham 7 Feb. 1811; h. 5ft 6ins, stout build, oval face, fresh complexion, dark brown hair, hazel eyes, no marks or wounds. 'Escaped by the Stockade ... retaken 5 March and put in the cachot on two-thirds allowance [of food] until he made good One Guinea for his recapture.' Sent 11 Mar. 1811 to V, Butel escaped from there 19 Nov. 1813 but was recapd near Selkirk within a couple of days, along with nine other escapers. He was rel. and repatriated 10 Jun. 1814. TNA ADM 103/124; ADM 103/432, No. 784; ADM 103/113, No.7426.

3. No. 42 Jean Baptiste Cabouche (or Caboche), seaman, 34, b. Dunkirk, capd 17 Nov. 1810 on *Le Vengeur* priv. off Cherbourg; arr. EM from G 4 Feb. 1811; h. 5ft 7½ins, slender (or stout) build, long (or oval) visage, good complexion, brown (or dark red) hair, hazel (or black) eyes, no marks or wounds. Recapd at Kelso on 24 Feb., Cabouche was sent 5 Mar. to EC and from there 14 Aug. 1811 to G, from G 21 Dec. 1812 to V, where he was rel. and repatriated 14 Jun. 1814. TNA ADM 103/124; ADM 103/491, unnumbered; ADM 103/112, No.6; ADM 103/157, No.6; ADM 103/114, No.901; ADM 103/435, Nos 5615 and 6252.

4. No. 246 Etienne Duplessy (or Duplessay), capd 8 Oct. 1808 on *Janet* (or *Jenet*) corvette 'in Bengal', arr. EM from Chatham, 5 Feb. 1811. Duplessy appears to have succeeded in his escape. TNA ADM 103/124; ADM 103/491, unnumbered.

5. No. 20 Jerome (Geriani) Favali, 28, ensign, capd n.d. n.p. on *Le Vengeur* priv.; arr. EM from G 4 Feb. 1811; h. 5ft 5½ins, long visage, good complexion, black hair, black eyes; recapd and sent to V 30 Mar. 1811. TNA ADM 103/124; ADM 103/491, unnumbered.

6. No. 459 David Fourneau, 2nd lieut., 22, b. Calais, capd 15 Nov. 1810 on *Le Barbier de Seville* priv. off Norway; arr. EM from Chatham 7 Feb. 1811; h. 5ft 6ins, stout build, round face, good complexion, brown hair, gray [sic] eyes, wound on right wrist.

Recapd 22 Feb., Fourneau was sent 4 Mar. to EC, from there on 14 Aug. 1811 to G, and from there 2 Sep. 1812 to P, from which he was dischgd to Leith on 30 Apr. 1814 and repatriated. TNA ADM 103/124; ADM 103/491, no No.; ADM 103/112, No.1; ADM 103/157, No.1; TNA ADM 103/263, No. 1094.

7. No. 594 Joachim (Jean) Halnes, prize master, capd 17 Dec. 1810 on *L'Aventurier* priv. off St Valery; arr. EM from Chatham 7 Feb. 1811. Halnes appears to have succeeded in his escape. TNA ADM 103/124; ADM 103/491, unnumbered.

8. No. 108 Gabriel Iusset (or Iasset), pilot, capd 12 Sep. 1810 on *Le Phoenix* priv. n.p.; arr. EM from G 4 Feb. 1811; h. 5ft 6¼ins, stout build, long visage, dark complexion, black hair, brown eyes, no marks or wounds. Iusset appears to have succeeded in his escape. TNA ADM 103/124; ADM 103/491, unnumbered.

9. No. 40 Pierre François Le Couche (alias Barbouche or Bourbouche), seaman, 31, b. Caen, capd 17 Oct. 1810 on *Le Vengeur* priv. off Cherbourg; arr. EM from G 4 Feb. 1811; h. 5ft 3¾ins, stout build, oval face, dark hair, black eyes, no marks or wounds. Recapd at Kelso 24 Feb. 1811, Le Couche was sent 5 Mar. to EC (where the Entry Book describes him as 5ft 3ins, slender build, sharp face, black hair, and hazel eyes). Transferred to G, he arr. from there 21 Dec. 1812 at V (in which month he seems also to have been briefly at EC), and from V he was sent 29 Jul. 1813 to P. TNA ADM 103/124; ADM 103/491, unnumbered; ADM 103/112, No. 7; ADM 103/114, No. 902; ADM 103/435, Nos 5616 and 6253.

10. No. 37 Louis J. Lepine (or Lepin), seaman, 32, b. Cherbourg, capd 17 Oct. 1810 on *Le Vengeur* priv. off Cherbourg; arr. EM from G 4 Feb. 1811; h. 6ft 1in., stout build, long face, good complexion, dark brown hair, blue eyes, maimed right hand. Recapd 22 Feb. 1811, sent 4 Mar. to EC (where the Entry Book says he had an oval face, brown hair, grey eyes, and no marks or wounds). Later he was sent to G and from there 21 Dec. 1812 to V, from which he was rel. and repatriated 14 Jun. 1814. TNA ADM 103/124; ADM 103/491, unnumbered; ADM 103/112, No.3; ADM 103/435, Nos 5613 and 6250.

11. No. 641 Pierre Malfoy (or Malsay), capt., capd 18 Dec. 1810 on *L'Héro du Nord* priv. at Texel. Arr. EM from Chatham 7 Feb. 1811. Malfoy appears to have succeeded in his escape. TNA ADM 103/124; ADM 103/491, unnumbered.

12. No. 428 Charles Marechal, soldier, capd 11 Oct. 1810 on *Somnambule* priv. off Tréport; arr. EM from Chatham 5 Feb. 1811. Marechal appears to have succeeded in his escape. TNA ADM 103/124; ADM 103/491, unnumbered.

13. No. 442 Antoine Morel (or Moret or Morete), lieut., 29, b. Cherbourgh [sic], capd 14 (or 8) Oct. 1810 on *Sans Souci* priv. at Dogger Bank, arr. EM from Chatham 5 Feb. 1811; h. 5ft 4½ ins, stout build, round face, good complexion, brown hair, grey eyes, no marks or wounds. Recapd 22 Feb. 1811, Morel was sent 4 Mar. to EC, transferred 14 Aug. to G and from there 1 Sep. 1812 to P. TNA ADM 103/124; ADM 103/491, unnumbered; ADM 103/112, No. 2; ADM 103/157, No.2.

14. No. 1488 Geo. Muller (or Miller), 2nd lieut., capd 20 Nov. 1810 on *Le Général Toussaint* priv. at Beachy Head; arr. EM via HMS *Ruby* 18 Feb. 1811. Muller appears to have succeeded in his escape. TNA ADM 103/124; ADM 103/491, unnumbered.

15. No. 1442 Pierre Jean Noets, 2nd capt., capd 25 Oct. 1810 on *La Comtesse de Hambourg* priv. at Dogger Bank, arr. EM via HMS *Ruby* 18 Feb. 1811. Noets appears to have succeeded in his escape. TNA ADM 103/124; ADM 103/491, unnumbered.

16. No. 9 P. J. Pierre Nosten, 2nd capt., 31, b. Dunkirk, capd n.d. n.p. on *Adolphe* priv.; arr. EM from G 4 Feb. 1811; h. 6ft, stout build, round face, fresh complexion, brown

hair, brown eyes, smallpox a little. Nosten appears to have succeeded in his escape. TNA ADM 103/124; ADM 103/491, unnumbered.

17. No. 119 A. Pagliano (or Pagliam), capt., capd 14 May 1810 on *La Beille* priv. n.p.; arr. EM from G 4 Feb. 1811; h. 5ft 5ins, stout build, oval face, good complexion, black hair and eyes, no marks or wounds. Pagliano appears to have succeeded in his escape. TNA ADM 103/124; ADM 103/491, unnumbered.

18. No. 391 Pierre Rabeau, lieut., capd 2 Oct. 1808 on *Le Dorade* priv. off Nantes; arr. EM from Chatham 5 Feb. 1811. Rabeau appears to have succeeded in his escape. TNA ADM 103/124; ADM 103/491, unnumbered.

19. No. 19 Frederik Reimer (or Rumer), ensign, 28, capd n.d. n.p. on *Le Vengeur* priv.; arr. EM from G 4 Feb. 1811; h. 5ft 6½ins, stout build, oval face, good complexion, brown hair, brown eyes, no marks or wounds. Recapd, Reimer was sent 30 Mar. 1811 to V. TNA ADM 103/124; ADM 103/491, unnumbered.

20. No. 566 Jean François Ruy, seaman, 31, b. Christiansand (or Narbonne), capd 10 Dec. 1810 on *Mameluke* priv. off Dover; arr. EM from Chatham 7 Feb. 1811; h. 5ft 9ins, stout build, oval face, good complexion, brown hair, grey eyes, 'wants part of both forefingers'. Recapd 22 Feb. 1811, Ruy was sent 4 Mar. to EC. Later he was transferred to G and from there 21 Dec. 1812 to V, from which he was rel. and repatriated 14 Jun. 1814. TNA ADM 103/124; ADM 103/491, unnumbered; ADM 103/112, No. 5; ADM 103/435, Nos 5614 and 6251.

21. No. 545 Jean Talise Simonsen, bosun, 23, b. Christiansand, capd 10 Dec. 1810 on *Mameluke* priv. off Dover; arr. EM from Chatham 7 Feb. 1811; h. 5ft 7ins, stout build, oval face, good complexion, fair hair, grey eyes, no marks or wounds. Recapd 22 Feb. 1811, Simonsen was sent 4 Mar. to EC, then 14 Aug. to G, where 21 Aug. 1811 he was rel. into the RN. TNA ADM 103/124; ADM 103/491, unnumbered; ADM 103/112, No.4; ADM 103/110, No. 4; ADM 103/157, No. 4.

22. No. 1201 Henri Vanvelier (or Vanvelior or Vanveilen), 1st lieut., capd 1 May 1808 on *Le Passepartout* priv. in the North Sea; arr. EM via HMS *Ruby* 18 Feb. 1811. Vanvelier appears to have succeeded in his escape. TNA ADM 103/124; ADM 103/491, unnumbered.

23. No. 1499 Arent Vanveen, prizemaster, capd 25 Oct. 1810 off the Texel on a prize to *Etoile* or *Eliza* priv.; arr. EM via HMS *Ruby* 18 Feb. 1811. Vanveen appears to have succeeded in his escape. TNA ADM 103/124; ADM 103/491, unnumbered.

Appendix 2

THE 44 ESCAPERS FROM EDINBURGH CASTLE DEPOT, 11-12 APRIL 1811

The advertisement placed by Malcolm Wright, agent, in the *Edinburgh Evening Courant* on Monday, 15 April 1811, is reproduced below. Physical descriptions it gave of the escapers varied in some cases from those given in the Edinburgh Castle Entry Book. Additional information gathered from other sources concerning those prisoners is given below in italics. All those escapers were, or appear to have been, recaptured within six weeks; five others not included in the advertisement were recaptured within a few hours; and one escaper (who may or may not have been one of those five but was almost certainly Pierre Woemeseuil or Wormeseul) died on 14 April from his injuries in falling down the Castle rock.

ESCAPE OF PRISONERS OF WAR
Office of the Agent, Prisoners of War,
Edinburgh Castle, April 13, 1811.

Whereas the several FRENCH PRISONERS here under named and described, having effected their escape from this place, in the course of last night, notice thereof is hereby given, and that the usual Reward, together with all necessary expenses, will be paid for retaking all or either of the said Prisoners, on application to Mr Wright, Agent for Prisoners of War, at this Office.

No.1. Ls Debausset, 27 years of age, 5 feet 8 inches high, slender made, sharp visage, good complexion, black hair, and hazel eyes. *Louis Debausset (or Debasset), b. Nantes, lieut., 5th Light infantry (or 2nd Artillery), capd 26 Feb. 1809 on Martinique, arr. EM from Portsmouth 27 Feb. 1811. One of the four mauvais sujets sent from EM to EC 9 Mar. 1811, after his recapture Debausset, by order of Admiral Otway, was sent on board HMS Aquilon at Leith on 30 Apr. for Sheerness, evidently to be confined on the hulks at Chatham. TNA ADM 103/112, No.8; ADM 103/124, No. 2,061; CM, 2 May 1811.*

2. H. Decroze, 23 years of age, 5 feet 10 inches high, slender made, sharp visage, good complexion, fair hair, and grey eyes. *For Hipolyte Decreuse (or Decroze or Decruise), who after his recapture was sent to the hulks at Chatham, see above, pp.94, 95, and below, 703.*

3. H. Foucault, 23 years of age, 5 feet 8 inches high, stout made, sharp visage, good complexion, black hair, hazel eyes, and has a cut on his upper lip. *For Honoré Foucault, see also above, pp.94, 95.*

4. J. Befey, 37 years of age, 5 feet 4½ inches high, stout made, round visage, sallow complexion, black hair, and hazel eyes. *Joseph Befey, b. St Andero, seaman, capd 20 Sep. 1809 on Jesus Maria priv. 'at sea', arr. EC from EM 11 Mar. 1811. EC Entry Book says he had 'cut on the upper lip'. TNA ADM 103/112, No. 16.*

5. F. Melee, 28 years of age, 5 feet 4 inches high, well made, round visage, fair complexion, black hair, and black eyes. *François Melee (or Melle), b. St Malo, seaman, capd n.d. n.p. on Le Brilliant m.o.w., arr. EC from EM 11 Mar. 1811. TNA ADM 103/112, No.17.*

6. J. Silvestre, 23 years of age, 5 feet 5¼ inches high, stout made, oval visage, dark complexion, black hair, and dark brown eyes. *Jacques (or Jacob) Sylvestre, b. Bordeaux, seaman, capd 3 Sep. 1803 on La Félicité priv. 'at sea', arr. EC from EM 11 Mar. 1811, and was described in EC Entry Book as aged 28, of slender build and with smallpox scars; after his recapture Sylvestre was sent 21 Aug. 1811 to G, but from G on 20 Nov. 1811 back to EC, from which he again escaped on 18 Dec. but was recapd 22 Dec. and sent 3 Jan. 1812 to V. TNA ADM 103/110, No. 322; ADM 103/112, Nos 128 and 538.*

7. Pre. Desbois, 24 years of age, 5 feet 3 inches high, slender made, long visage, pale complexion, black hair, and dark eyes. *Pierre Desbois, b. Nantes, lieut., capd 15 Oct. 1808 on Friedland priv., arr. EC from EM 11 Mar. 1811. Recapd, probably at Montrose, Desbois arrived back at EC 21 May. TNA ADM 103/112, Nos 48 and 469.*

8. J. Briant, 23 years of age, 5 feet 7½ inches high, stout made, oval visage, sallow complexion, brown hair, and blue eyes. *Joseph Briant, b. Dieppe, seaman, capd 25 Jan. 1808 on Général Canclaux priv. off Portsmouth, arr. EC from EM 11 Mar. 1811. TNA ADM 103/112, No.49. See also below, Appendix 11, V, No.216.*

9. Jn Savrignon [or Savignon], 28 years of age, 5 feet 6 inches high, slender made, oval visage, brown complexion, black hair, and hazel eyes. *Jean Savignon [or Savrignon],*

b. Bordeaux, seaman, capd 3 Oct. 1803 on L'Aventure frig. 'at sea', arr. EC from EM 11 Mar. 1811. Details of his recapture are lacking, but he was back in EC by 1 May, when he was issued with a blanket, and he was still there on 7 Aug. 1811, when he received shoes. TNA ADM 103/112, No.53.

10. Brd Charlot, 25 years of age, 5 feet 2¼ inches high, stout made, oval visage, fresh complexion, brown hair, and blue eyes. *Bernard Charlot, b. Bordeaux, prize master, capd 12 Sep. 1810 on Phoenix priv. 'at sea', arr. EC from EM 11 Mar. 1811, EC Entry Book says he was 5ft 7ins with black hair and a scar on his right cheek. Recapd (probably at Montrose), Charlot arr. back at EC 21 May and was later sent to G, from which in Sep. 1812 he was sent to P, where he was rel. and repatriated on 30 Apr. 1814. TNA ADM 103/112, Nos 89 and 470; ADM 103/263, No. 1122.*

11. Bt Foucard, 24 years of age, 5 feet 8 inches high, stout made, oval visage, dark complexion, black hair, and blue eyes. *Baptiste (or Bernard) Foucard, b. Rouen, lieut., capd 6 Nov. 1810 on Le Surcouf priv. in the English Channel, arr. EC from EM 11 Mar. 1811; EC Entry Book says he was aged 34, with a fresh complexion, dark brown hair, and grey eyes. Recapd (probably at Banff or Montrose), he arr. back at EC 25 May. TNA ADM 103/112, Nos 90 and 471.*

12. Thomas Jque Samson, 36 years of age, 5 feet 4¼ inches high, stout made, round visage, fresh complexion, dark brown hair, and grey eyes. *Thomas Jacques Samson, b. Malta, clerk, Le Surcouf priv., capd 6 Nov. 1810 in the English Channel; arr. EC from EM 11 Mar. 1811. Recapd (probably at Banff or Montrose), he arr. back at EC 25 May. TNA ADM 103/112, Nos 99 and 472.*

13. G. [sic] Emens, 29 years of age, 5 feet 2½ inches high, well made, oval visage, fresh complexion, brown hair, and hazel eyes. *Stanislaus Emens, b. Le Havre, lieut., capd 27 Dec. 1807 on L'Aigle priv. in the English Channel, arr. EC from EM 11 Mar. 1811; EC Entry Book says he had smallpox scars. Recapd (probably at Banff or Montrose), he arr. back at EC on 25 May. TNA ADM 103/112, Nos 103 and 473.*

14. Ns Kambrun, 23 years of age, 5 feet 8 inches high, stout make [sic], round visage, fair complexion, light brown hair, and grey eyes. *Nicholas Kambrun, b. Treguier, lieut., capd 29 Oct. 1807 on Requin priv., arr. EC from EM 11 Mar. 1811. TNA ADM 103/112, No. 104.*

15. F. Ricard, 24 years of age, 5 feet 7 inches high, stout made, oval visage, fresh complexion, brown hair, and hazel eyes. *J. François Ricard, b. St Valery, bosun, capd n.d. n.p. on Iris m.o.w., arr. EC from EM 11 Mar. 1811; EC Entry Book says he had a dark complexion, with black hair, blue eyes, and smallpox scars. TNA ADM 103/112, No. 397.*

16. Pre Heuze, 28 years of age, 5 feet 7 inches high, stout made, round visage, fresh complexion, brown hair, and blue eyes. *Pierre Heuze, b. Honfleur, lieut., capd 27 Oct. 1807 on Requin priv. in the English Channel, arr. EC from EM 11 Mar. 1811. TNA ADM 103/112, No. 111.*

17. C. Pour, 32 years of age, 5 feet 5 inches high, stout made, oval visage, fresh complexion, brown hair, and hazel eyes. *Charles Pour, b. Boulogne, lieut., capd 4 Apr. 1808 on Active priv. 'at sea', arr. EC from EM 11 Mar. 1811. TNA ADM 103/112, No. 161.*

18. J. Clemence, 31 years of age, 5 feet 8 inches high, slender made, oval visage, swarthy complexion, brown hair, and grey eyes. *Jacques Clemence, b. Dieppe, captain, capd 4 Apr. 1808 on Active priv. 'at sea', arr. EC from EM 11 Mar. 1811. TNA ADM 103/112, No. 163.*

19. Trousset Drouaux, 32 years of age, 5 feet 8½ inches high, stout made, round visage, fair complexion, light brown hair, and grey eyes. *Captain, b. Dieppe, capd 25*

Apr. 1808 on Général Canclaux priv. 'at sea', Drouaux arr. EC from EM 11 Mar. 1811. TNA ADM 103/112, No.164.

20.   Xr Malavois, 19 years of age 5 feet 8½ inches high, slender made, oval visage, sallow complexion, brown hair, and hazel eyes. *Xavier H. Malavois (or Malavais), b. Isles (sic) of France (Mauritius), midshipman (or passenger), capd 3 Sep. 1810 on Confiance m.v. at or off Nantes, arr. EC from EM 11 Mar. 1811, but has not been found in EC Entry Book. Recapd, he was sent 14 Aug. 1811 from EC to G, where the Entry Book says he was 26, with long visage, swarthy complexion, dark brown hair, dark eyes, and a small scar under his left eye. In a TO list, 31 Dec.1812, Malavois is said to have been recapd after breaking his parole and absconding—but presumably in England, before he came to EM from Portsmouth 5 Mar. 1811. From G, Malavois was dischgd to Portsmouth 31 Aug. 1812 as an invalid, and was presumably repatriated from Portsmouth to France soon afterward. TNA ADM 103/124, No. 2178; ADM 103/157, No. 114; ADM 105/61, TO list, 31 Dec. 1812.*

21.   Bote Lartigue, 46 years of age, 5 feet 5½ inches high, stout made, round visage, fresh complexion, black hair, and grey eyes. *Benedict Lartigue, b. Villeneuve, seaman, capd 6 Feb. 1806 on Brave m.o.w., arr. EC from EM 11 Mar. 1811. The EC Entry Book adds that he had smallpox scars. TNA ADM 103/112, No.170.*

22.   J. Bote Labe [or Lobe], 34 years of age, 5 feet 7¼ inches high, stout made, round visage, dark complexion, black hair, and hazel eyes. *Jean Baptiste Lobe (or Lobé), b. Boulogne, lieut., capd 5 Nov. 1809 on L'Etoile naval sloop, n.p., arr. EC from EM 11 Mar. 1811. The EC Entry Book said he was 'pockmarked'. Transferred from EC to G, then in Sep. 1812 to P, Lobe escaped from P in Mar. and Sep. 1813 but was recapd each time. TNA ADM 103/112, No.204; ADM 103/263, No.1103.*

23.   J. Declire [or Declite], 28 years of age, 5 feet 5¼ inches high, stout made, round visage, fresh complexion, brown hair, and hazel eyes. *François Declire (or Declare), b. Dunkirk, lieut., capd 27 Dec. 1807 on Réciprocité naval sloop 'at sea', arr. EC from EM 11 Mar. 1811. TNA ADM 103/112, No. 205.*

24.   Mathieux Jean, 21 years of age, 5 feet 6 inches high, well made, oval visage, swarthy complexion, brown hair, and hazel eyes. *Joseph Mathieux, b. Corse (Corsica), prize master, capd 20 Aug. 1805 on Régulateur naval sloop 'at sea', arr. EC from EM 11 Mar. 1811. TNA ADM 103/112, No. 206.*

25.   J. B. Callop, 27 years of age, 5 feet 9 inches high, stout made, round visage, fair complexion, brown hair, and hazel eyes. *Jean Baptiste Callop, b. Granville, prize master, capd 4 Oct.1810 on Speculateur priv. in the English Channel, arr. EC from EM 11 Mar. 1811. After his recapture, Callop was sent to G, and from G on 2 Sep. 1812 to P, from which he was repatriated to France 1 Jun. 1814. TNA ADM 103/112, No. 210; ADM 103/263, No. 1106.*

26.   Jn Mil. Lescallier, 30 years of age, 5 feet 7 inches high, stout made, oval visage, fair complexion, black hair, and grey eyes. *Jean Marie Lescallier, b. Cherbourg, capt., capd 22 Mar. 1808 on Renais priv. in English Channel (or 26 Sep. 1807 on Espérance priv. 'at sea'), arr. EC from EM 11 Mar. 1811. TNA ADM 103/112, No. 211.*

27.   Manl Bouvet, 25 years of age, 5 feet 10 inches high, stout made, oval visage, fresh complexion, brown hair, and blue eyes. *Manuel Bouvet, b. Abbeville, seaman, capd 1 Nov. 1808 on Rodeur priv. 'at sea', arr. EC from EM 11 Mar. 1811. TNA ADM 103/112, No. 236. See also Appendix 3, No. 3.*

28.   Ml Hamblin, 37 years of age, 5 feet 7½ inches high, well made, round visage, fair complexion, dark grey hair, and hazel eyes. *Michel Amelin (or Hamblin), b. Honfleur, seaman, capd 8 Feb. 1808 on Furet priv. 'at sea', arr. EC from EM 11 Mar. 1811. The EC*

Entry Book said he had an oval face, fresh complexion, and 'scar left eye'. TNA ADM 103/112, No. 237.

29. St. Georges, 20 years of age, 5 feet 4½ inches high, well made, round visage, fair complexion, brown hair, and blue eyes. *St. Georges, b. Calais, seaman, capd 21 Nov. 1808 on an unnamed retaken prize vessel 'at sea', arr. EC from EM 11 Mar. 1811. The EC Entry Book says he was aged 25. TNA ADM 103/112, No. 239.*

30. Jn Smith, 22 years of age, 5 feet 11 inches high, stout made, oval visage, fresh complexion, sandy hair, and blue eyes. *Jean Smith, b. Calais, seaman, capd 24 Oct. 1808 on Eliza retaken prize 'at sea', arr. EC from EM 11 Mar. 1811. TNA ADM 103/112, No. 246.*

31. J. Bt Broton, 25 years of age, 5 feet 10 inches high, stout made, round visage, fresh complexion, light brown hair, and blue eyes. *Jean Baptiste Le Broton, b. Bordeaux, seaman, capd 6 Feb. 1806 on Alexandre m.o.w. 'at sea', arr. EC from EM 11 Mar. 1811. TNA ADM 103/112, No.251.*

32. Ml Tullier, 32 years of age, 5 feet 8 inches high, stout made, oval visage, sallow complexion, black hair, and hazel eyes. *Michel Tullier, b. Bordeaux, seaman, capd 10 Jan. 1806 on Atalante frig. 'at sea', arr. EC from EM 11 Mar. 1811. TNA ADM 103/112, No. 259.*

33. Jn Pre Fortier, 18 years of age, 5 feet 9 inches high, slender made, oval visage, fair complexion, black hair, and dark eyes. *Jean Pierre Fortier, b. Honfleur, soldier, capd 3 Mar. 1808 on Virginie storeship in the English Channel, arr. EC from EM 11 Mar. 1811. TNA ADM 103/112, No.261.*

34. Pre L. Raquet, 34 years of age, 5 feet 6¼ inches high, stout made, long visage, sallow complexion, light brown hair, and grey eyes. *Pierre Louis Raquet, b. St Valery, capd 12 Jan. 1806 on L'Espérance priv. off Cherbourg, arr. EC from EM 11 Mar. 1811. Later Raquet was sent to P, from which he escaped but recapd at Burntisland and sent 7 Oct. 1813 to EC, from which he was sent back to Perth on 19 Oct. TNA ADM 103/112, No. 271; ADM 103/114, No. 1323.*

35. John Colas, 28 years of age, 5 feet 5½ inches high, well made, oval visage, sallow complexion, dark hair, and hazel eyes. *Jean Colas, b. Granville, seaman, capd 12 Feb. 1809 on Joseph priv. in the English Channel, arr. EC from EM 11 Mar. 1811. TNA ADM 103/112, No. 287.*

36. Ant. Goudicheau [or Goudieheau], 46 years of age, 5 feet 2½ inches high, stout made, oval visage, dark complexion, grey hair, and blue eyes. *Antoine Goudicheau, b. Bordeaux, capt., capd 10 Jan. 1809 on Général Mathieu priv. 'at sea', arr. EC from EM 11 Mar. 1811. After recapture, Goudicheau was sent to G, then 22 Oct. 1811 dischgd to Portsmouth as an invalid and presumably repatriated soon afterward to France. TNA ADM 103/112, No. 288; ADM 103/110, No. 206.*

37. Jn Noel, 35 years of age, 5 feet 6¾ inches high, stout made, oval visage, ruddy complexion, brown hair, and hazel eyes. *Jean Noel, b. Lupcourt, sergeant, 65th Line regt, capd 15 Aug. 1809 at Flushing, arr. EC from EM 11 Mar. 1811. Recapd at Banff, Noel arr. back 25 May at EC. TNA ADM 103/112, No. 290.*

38. Jacques Adam, 40 years of age, 5 feet 4 inches high, well made, long visage, fair complexion, dark hair, and blue eyes. *Adam, b. Granville, naval lieut. but capd 10 Feb. 1810 as a passenger on Duc de Wagram m.v. at Guadeloupe, arr. EM from Portsmouth on HMS Gorgon 5 Mar. 1811, and arr. EC from EM 11 Mar. After recapture, Adam was sent to G but was transferred again on 17 Dec. 1811 to EC, from which he escaped again next day. In a similar newspaper advertisement after this second escape from EC his age was given*

as 45, and he was said to be of slender build, thin visage, dark complexion, brown hair, and 'pitted with the small pox.' Recapd four days after his second escape from EC, Adam was sent 3 Jan. 1812 to V. Marote-Carrier, also a prisoner at V, recalls 'Monsieur Adam of St Malo' as one of his friends there and that he had been taken prisoner at the battle of Trafalgar: if that were so, then Adam must presumably have already escaped from captivity before being taken prisoner at Guadeloupe in 1810. Perhaps that earlier escape explains his inclusion in a TO list dated 31 Dec. 1812 of French officers who had broken their parole and escaped. Adam and Marote-Carrier were associates in abortive attempts at escape not only from V but also later from P to which they were both transferred 1 Sep. 1812. TNA ADM 103/124, No.2306; ADM 103/110, No. 211; ADM 103/112, Nos. 296 and 540; ADM 103/435, No. 5311; ADM 103/263, No. 1171; ADM 105/61 (TO list, 31 Dec. 1812); CM, 21 Dec. 1811.

39. A. Dowzon, 21 years of age, 5 feet 7½ inches high, stoutish made, oval visage, sallow complexion, dark brown hair, and grey eyes. *Adolphe Douzon (as his surname is spelled in all other references to him), b. Ponticherry (presumably Pondicherry, near Madras, India) midshipman, capd 8 Mar. 1809 on schooner or packet La Mouche No.13 'at sea', arr. EC from EM 11 Mar. 1811, described in EC Entry Book as having light brown hair. Recapd, Douzon was sent back from Banff to EC 25 May, then transferred 14 Aug. 1811 from EC to G, from which he escaped, evidently successfully, on 5 Mar. 1812. TNA ADM 103/110, No. 275; ADM 103/112, Nos 304 and 476; ADM 103/157, No 275; ADM 105/45, unnumbered; ADM 103/489, unnumbered.*

40. Augt Garzin, 27 years of age, 5 feet 6 inches high, stout made, sallow complexion, dark hair, and hazel eyes. *Auguste Garsin (or Garcin or Garzin), b. St Malo, aged 20, prize master, capd 18 Sep. 1811 (sic) on Le Bon Interet, a retaken vessel, off St Malo, arr. EC from EM 11 Mar. 1811. Recapd, Garsin was sent 14 Aug. from EC to G, from which he escaped 3 Oct. 1811. TNA ADM 103/110, No.237; 103/112, No.369; ADM 103/157, No.237; ADM 103/491, unnumbered.*

41. Pre Dechevery, 24 years of age, 5 feet 6 inches high, slender made, oval visage, dark complexion, and black hair. *Pierre Decheverry (or Dechevry), b. Isle de France (Mauritius), ensign, capd n.d. n.p. on La Mouche naval sloop, arr. EC from EM 11 Mar. 1811, is said in EC Entry Book to be of stout build, with a ruddy complexion, brown hair, blue eyes and smallpox scars. Recapd, Decheverry appears later to have been sent to G. In a TO list dated 31 Dec. 1812 he is said to have broken his parole and absconded, and the date 3 Dec. 1809 is given—but whether that was when he was originally capd or broke his parole or first arr. at Greenlaw is not clear. TNA ADM 103/112, No. 371; ADM 105/61 (TO list, 31 Dec. 1812).*

42. Pre Trochery, 30 years of age, 5 feet 5 inches high, round visage, fair complexion, fair hair, and grey eyes. *Pierre Trochery (or Trocherie), b. Granville, sergeant, Imperial Guard, capd 19 Jul. 1808 at Baylen, Spain (or 'Cadiz'), arr. EC from EM 11 Mar. 1811; said in EC Entry Book to be 5ft 7ins, stout build, and with blue eyes. Recapd, Trochery was sent 14 Aug. 1811 to G (where the Entry Book said he had 'Lost front teeth'), from there 1 Sep. 1812 to V, from which he was sent back 14 Nov. 1812 to G. He seems to have remained in captivity until the end of the war. TNA ADM 103/112, No. 381; ADM 103/157, Nos 247 and 801; ADM 103/435, No. 5764.*

43. Et. Tiebaud, 31 years of age, 5 feet 7 inches high, stout made, oval visage, fresh complexion, dark hair, and dark eyes. *Etienne Tiebaud, b. Boulogne, capt., capd Mar. 1810 on Général Furinet m.v. in the English Channel, arr. EC from EM 11 Mar. 1811; the EC Entry Book said he was aged 26, 5ft 3½ins tall, thin build, sandy hair and grey eyes. Recapd, Tiebaud was sent back to EC 25 May 1811 from Banff. TNA ADM 103/112, Nos 390 and 474.*

44.   V. Ferand, 30 years of age, 5 feet 7 inches high, well made, long visage, fresh complexion, brown hair, hazel eyes, and marked with the small pox. *Valerian Feraud (or Ferand), b. Marseilles, naval ensign, capd 18 Feb. 1809 on recapd prize vessel in the Antilles, arr. EC from EM 11 Mar. 1811; the EC Entry Book described him as aged 27, 5ft 11ins and with smallpox scars. Recapd, Feraud was sent to G and from there 2 Sep. 1812 to P. Transferred 3 Nov. 1813 from P to EC, Feraud escaped again 25 Nov. from EC. TNA ADM 103/112, No. 84; ADM 103/263, No. 1099.*

Appendix 3

THE 14 ESCAPERS FROM EDINBURGH CASTLE DEPOT, 18-19 DECEMBER 1811

A similar advertisement to that in Appendix 2 was placed by Malcolm Wright, agent at the Castle, in the *Caledonian Mercury* of 21 December 1811 concerning the escapers of 18-19 December and is reproduced below exactly as it was printed in the *Mercury*. Some further information, gathered from other sources, about the nine advertised but also about five others who escaped that night but who for some unexplained reason were not included in the advertisement, is added in italics.

NAMES AND DESCRIPTIONS

P.M. BELANGER, seaman of the *Napoleon* privateer, aged 26, five feet seven inches high, slender made, oval visage, fresh complexion, brown hair, hazle eyes, pitted with the small pox. *Pierre Marie Belanger (or Bellanger), b. St Vallery (sic), capd 19 Sep. 1807 (or 21 Oct. 1808) in the English Channel, arr. G from EC 14 Aug. 1811, sent to EC from G 20 Nov. 1811. Recapd 22 Dec. 1811, Belanger was sent 3 Jan. 1812 to V, and from V 20 Feb. 1812 by order of Admiral Otway to HMS Adamant at Leith. In the EC Entry Book Belanger's age was said to be 19, in the V Entry Book his birthplace was given as Calais, his age 23. TNA ADM 103/112, No. 531; ADM 103/435, No. 5305; ADM 103/110, No. 161.*

Rd. DEMAZELLY, seaman of the *Petit du Jour* privateer, aged 17, four feet eleven inches high, stout made, round visage, fresh complexion, sandy hair, blue eyes, pitted with the small pox. *Roland Demazelly (or Demazilly), b. Paris, capd 16 Nov. 1808 in the English Channel, arr. G from EC 14 Aug 1811, sent to EC from G 20 Nov. 1811. Recapd 22 Dec. 1811, Demazelly was sent 3 Jan. 1812 to V, from which he escaped 12 Feb. 'over the Stockade'. But recapd at Leith, he was sent back to V 16 Feb. He escaped again from V 26 Apr. 1813, this time evidently successfully. In the EC Entry Book Demazelly was said to be aged 13, in the V Entry Book 20. TNA ADM 103/112, No. 532; ADM 103/435, Nos 5306 and 5359; ADM 103/491, unnumbered; ADM 103/110, No. 160.*

El. BOUVAINT, seaman of *Le Roduir* privateer, aged 28, five feet ten inches high, slender made, oval visage, fresh complexion, brown hair, blue eyes, cut on the chin. *Emanuel (or Etienne) Bouvais, b. Abbeville, capd 1 Nov. 1808 on Le Rodeur 'at sea', arr. G from EC 14 Aug.1811, sent to EC from G 20 Nov. 1811. Recapd 12 Jan. 1812 in London, Bouvais was 'Sent to Chatham' (i.e. to the hulks). See also Appendix 2, No. 27. TNA ADM 103/112, No.533; ADM 103/491, unnumbered; ADM 103/110, No. 165.*

Jn Bte ZOUTIN, seaman of the *General Canclaux* privateer, aged 24, five feet seven inches high, stout made, red visage, fair complexion, brown hair, blue eyes. *Jean Baptiste Zoutin (or Soutin), b. Oldenburg, capd 25 Jan. 1808 in the English Channel, arr. G from EC 14 Aug. 1811, sent to EC from G 20 Nov. 1811. In the EC Entry Book Zoutin's visage was described as round, not red, his age 21. TNA ADM 103/112, No. 534; ADM 103/110, No. 171.*

P. Me. CAMUS, seaman of the *Le Esperance* privateer, aged 22, five feet four inches high, stout made, long visage, dark complexion, light brown hair, blue eyes. *Pierre Camus, b. Cherbourg, capd 20 Dec. 1807 in the English Channel, arr. G from EC 14 Aug. 1811, sent to EC from G 20 Nov. 1811. Recapd 22 Dec. 1811, Camus was sent 3 Jan. 1812 to V, and from V sent 20 Feb. 1812 by order of Admiral Otway to HMS Adamant at Leith. The EC Entry Books said Camus was aged 17 and 5 ft tall; the V Book that he was 21, 5 ft 7 ins, and had grey eyes. TNA ADM 104/110, No. 190; ADM 103/112, No. 535; ADM 103/435, No. 5307.*

Bte MOUSSU, seaman of the *Marsouin* privateer, aged 21, five feet five inches high, stout made, red visage, fresh complexion, brown hair, grey eyes. *Baptiste Moussu, b. St Malo, capd 25 Dec. 1807 off Ushant, arr. G from EC 14 Aug. 1811, sent to EC from G 20 Nov. 1811. Recapd 12 Jan. 1812 in London, Moussu was 'Sent to Chatham' (i.e., to the hulks). TNA ADM 103/112, No. 536; ADM 103/110, No. 193; ADM 103/491, unnumbered*

Louis CLAIRET, seaman of *Le Figaro* privateer, aged 45, five feet four inches high, slender made, oval visage, dark complexion, black hair, black eyes. *Clairet (or Cloiret), b. Lorraine, capd 6 Jul. 1811 'at sea', arr. G from EC 14 Aug. 1811, sent to EC from G 18 Nov. 1811. Recapd 22 Dec. 1811, Clairet was sent 3 Jan. 1812 to V. TNA ADM 103/112, No.537; ADM 103/110, No. 313.*

Jacques SYLVESTER, seaman of *La Felicite* privateer, aged 30, five feet one fourth inches high, slender made, oval visage, dark complexion, black hair, dark brown eyes, pitted with the small pox. *For Sylvester, see Appendix 2, No.6.*

Jacques ADAM, Lieutenant of the *Duc de Wagram* merchant vessel, aged 45, five four four inches high, slender made, thin visage, dark complexion, brown hair, blue eyes, pitted with the small pox. *For Adam, see Appendix 2, No. 38.*

The other five escapers from the Castle on the night of 18-19 December 1811, according to the EC Entry Book, were:

Louis (or Jacques) Imbert Altier, b. Mulere (or Mutere or Montero), aged 28, lieutenant, French army (no regt stated), capd 18 Jun. 1808 in Portugal (Oporto), arr. EM Mar. 1811 and sent a few days later to EC, from which 14 Aug. he was sent to G, and from there 17 Dec. 1811 back to EC. H. 5ft 10ins, stout build, long visage, sallow complexion, black hair, hazle eyes, no marks or wounds. Recapd 22 Dec. 1811 and sent 3 Jan. 1812 to V, sent from V to sheriff, Edinburgh, 1 Apr. 1812, escaped from Edinburgh Tolbooth, 19 Jul. 1812, recapd at Dublin and sent Aug. 1812 to Plymouth (presumably to hulks). TNA ADM 103/112, No. 539; ADM 103/435, No. 5310; ADM 103/110, No. 197; EEC, 25 Jul. 1812; National Archives of Ireland, Kilmainham Jail Register, 1812, No. 80.

J. Nicolas Mordet, lieutenant (or seaman), capd 28 Jul. 1808. on Requin naval sloop 'at sea', arr. G from EC 14 Aug. 1811, sent to EC from G 17 Dec. 1811. Recapd 22 Dec. 1811, Mordet was sent to V 3 Jan. 1812. TNA ADM 103/110, No.241; ADM 103/112, No. 541.

François Noel, variously described as lieut. or 2nd capt., or as a soldier, capd 22 Mar.1808 on Renais priv. at St Domingo (or 'at sea') (or 'by Lord Nelson's Fleet, on 20 Sep. 1809 at Trafalgar'); b. Alsace, aged 20, 5ft 4ins, stout build, oval face, fresh complexion, black hair, blue eyes, mark on back of right hand. Noel arr. at V from EM 11 Mar. 1811, was sent from V to EC 7 Apr. 1811 for attacking a turnkey, arr. G from EC 14 Aug. 1811, sent from G to EC 17 Dec. 1811. Recapd 22 Dec. 1811, Noel was sent to V 3 Jan. 1812. TNA ADM 103/110, No. 263; ADM 103/112, Nos 462 and 542; ADM 103/432, No. 143.

Joseph Boutefeu, seaman, capd 24 Dec. 1805 on La Libre frig. off Rochefort, arr. G from EC 14 Aug. 1811, escaped from G 2 Nov. 1811, recapd and sent back to G 3 Dec., arr. EC from G 17 Dec. 1811. Recapd 22 Dec. 1811, Boutefeu was sent to V 3 Jan. 1812, then 20 Feb to HMS Adamant at Leith. TNA ADM 103/112, No. 543; ADM 103/110, Nos 207 and 697; ADM 103/435, No. 5314.

Brutus du Crot, seaman, capd 6 Jul. 1811 on Le Figaro priv. in North Sea, arr. G from EC 14 Aug. 1811, dischgd 16 Sep. 1811 to RN; arr. EC from HMS Sarpedon 30 (sic—13 ?) Dec. 1811. Recapd 22 Dec. 1811, du Crot was sent 3 Jan. 1812 to V. Evidently a Dane, du Crot was rel. from V to France in Feb. 1814 after Denmark had withdrawn from the war. TNA ADM 103/112, No. 544; ADM 103/110, No. 296; ADM 103/435, No.5,315.

Appendix 4

REGIMENTS OR CORPS OF SOLDIERS AMONG THE PRISONERS IN THE SCOTS DEPOTS

The table below indicates the regiments, corps, or other units to which belonged those among the prisoners in the depots in Scotland who were soldiers. The number of such prisoners shown at each depot is the aggregate there from that regiment or corps (at Greenlaw in 1803-14, Edinburgh Castle in 1811 only, Esk Mills in Feb.-Mar. 1811, Valleyfield in 1811-14, and Perth in 1812-14). The sources for these listings are the depot Entry Books. These Books cannot, however, be regarded as entirely reliable in identifying each prisoner's regiment, their accuracy being sometimes doubtful in distinguishing, for example, between line and light infantry regiments. The abbreviations used below are: G—Greenlaw; EC—Edinburgh Castle; EM—Esk Mills; P—Perth; V—Valleyfield:

	G	EC	EM	P	V
A. Imperial Guard:	2	1	1	1	35
B. 'King Joseph's Guard' ('Garde Roi', 'Garde de Corps'):				1	2
C. French infantry regiments:					
Line (Ligne):					
1st:		1	2	31	48
2nd:	4	1	22	33	16
3rd:			2	5	12
4th:	11	1	8	32	44
5th:			1	20	84
6th:	10	3	14	81	70
7th:	3		8	3	4
8th:				72	7
9th:	2		1	35	5
10th:				5	1
12th:	1		2	13	
13th:	2	1	2	13	12
14th:	1	1		46	23

	G	EC	EM	P	V
15th:	24		12	109	47
16th:				6	5
17th:			1	36	11
18th:				7	
19th:				13	2
20th:				4	1
21st:				7	7
22nd:	5		14	119	54
23rd:				1	
24th:				19	
25th:				31	8
26th:	2	3	47	205	331
27th:	3		1	54	15
28th:	6		1	61	12
29th:				4	
30th:					1
31st:	6		16	24	38
32nd:	9		17	6	25
34th:	1			203	43
36th:	2			42	16
37th:				1	
38th:				1	
39th:	5		1	60	16
40th:				99	26
42nd:				2	
43rd:				3	
44th:				5	2
45th:	3	4	9	63	21
46th:				10	2
47th:			5	40	32

	G	EC	EM	P	V
48th:	1	2	26	43	35
50th:	7			171	28
51st:	3			13	6
52nd:				1	
53rd:				1	1
54th:			6	44	8
55th:	1			13	4
56th:				2	1
58th:	5	12	13	152	99
59th:	6			133	31
60th:				1	2
61st:				1	
62nd:	3			45	6
63rd:	3	1		3	3
64th:				84	10
65th:	7	11	77	168	125
66th:	4			195	74
67th:				3	12
69th:	2			75	20
70th:	2			116	54
72nd:	1	1	6	35	31
75th:	3			25	7
76th:	2		1	58	18
79th:					1
82nd:	10	5	153	289	
84th:				3	
85th:					1
86th:	2	12	12	64	22
88th:				197	60
92nd:					3

	G	EC	EM	P	V
94th:				3	
95th:				6	
96th:				16	3
100th:				28	3
101st:	3			67	6
103rd:	2			147	30
105th:	1			1	
108th:					2
113th:				114	87
116th:				3	
118th:				4	
119th:	67			42	268
120th:					12
122nd:				15	19
126th:					1
148th (sic):			1		
French infantry regiments (contd):					
Light (Léger or *Chasseur):*					
1st:	1			22	4
2nd:	4		4	66	26
3rd:					1
4th:	4		4	74	33
5th:		1		1	5
6th:				223	26
7th:				1	
8th:				4	4
9th:	23			247	62
12th:	2	1	1	11	8
13th:	2	1		6	13
14th:			8	2	7

	G	EC	EM	P	V
15th:	2			120	25
16th:				13	7
17th:	1			88	30
18th:					4
19th:				19	2
20th:	2				
21st:				12	2
22nd:			3	66	2
23rd:				2	2
24th:				3	1
25th:	1			35	4
26th:				17	3
27th:	2			32	5
28th:	3			244	49
29th:				3	
31st:	2			18	31
32nd:				1	3
34th:				139	6
36th:				61	1
39th:				16	
Chasseurs (but unstated whether infantry or cavalry):					
1st:					1
4th:				4	
13th:				2	3
14th:				1	1
21st:				2	
24th:				1	
25th:				3	
26th:				2	
27th:				1	

	G	EC	EM	P	V
'French':					4
'Carabiniers' (no regt given):			5		
'Carabiniers, Russian':			2		
Other French infantry:					
Chasseurs Rentrés:				6	32
'Chasseurs of Mountain', 3rd Bn:				5	
Garde de Paris:	6			9	1
Légions:					
– 1st:	23			5	2
– 2nd:				1	1
– 3rd:	16			3	2
– 4th:	17			5	2
– 5th:				3	
– 46th (sic):				1	
– Unspecified:				1	
Provisional Regts					
(Provisoire):					
1st:				1	1
8th:	2				
Other French infantry regts:					
Basque Regt: [NB This *seems* to be in fact the 66th Line Regt]				1	
Colonial Regt:			5		
– 1st Bn:			28	16	32
– 4th Bn:				1	
– Unspecified Bn:					9
Navarre Regt [Otherwise unidentified]:			11		
D. French cavalry regiments:					
'Cavalry' (Category unstated):					
1st Regt:			2		4
2nd Regt:					7

	G	EC	EM	P	V
3rd Regt:				1	
4th Regt:			25		
6th Regt:				8	
11th Regt:			1		1
12th Regt:					1
13th Regt:				1	
14th Regt:					1
15th Regt:			1	3	11
16th Regt:				1	1
17th Regt:				1	
18th Regt:					3
20th Regt:				1	
21st Regt:				5	
22nd Regt:				1	5
Chasseurs à Cheval:					
1st Regt:				1	2
2nd Regt:				1	3
4th Regt:				3	5
5th Regt:				1	
10th Regt:				2	
11th Regt:				1	
12th Regt:				1	4
13th Regt:				8	
14th Regt:				3	
15th Regt:				3	
20th Regt:				2	
21st Regt:				3	
22nd Regt:				6	
24th Regt:				1	2
27th Regt:				8	1

	G	EC	EM	P	V
29th Regt:					1
Regt unspecified:				1	9
Cuirassiers:					
2nd Regt:	1				
10th Regt:				1	
Dragoons:					
1st Regt:			23	2	
2nd Regt:				4	1
3rd Regt:				3	4
4th Regt:				6	12
5th Regt:				4	
6th Regt:	1			26	3
7th Regt:				1	
8th Regt:			26	5	21
9th Regt:				1	1
10th Regt:				5	11
11th Regt:				13	5
12th Regt:				1	1
13th Regt:	1			5	1
14th Regt:	1			2	5
15th Regt:			30	20	8
16th Regt:			1		
17th Regt:				27	1
18th Regt:				10	3
19th Regt:	1			1	
20th Regt:				20	5
21st Regt:				2	2
22nd Regt:					1
25th Regt:				14	4
26th Regt:				21	1

	G	EC	EM	P	V
27th Regt:				40	1
Unspecified Regt:					10
'Horse': (Category unstated)					
1st Regt:					8
8th Regt:					3
Hussars:					
1st Regt:				4	1
2nd Regt:				7	1
3rd Regt:	3			9	2
5th Regt:				7	2
10th Regt:				21	2
Lancers:					
1st Regt:				1	
E. French artillery regiments, etc.					
1st:	2		2	122	35
2nd:	3	1		6	1
3rd:	1	1	1	29	20
4th:	2		21	70	31
5th:				60	7
6th:			1	55	2
9th:				3	
10th:				2	
12th:				3	1
13th:				2	
Regt not stated:			4	3	3
2nd Company:				3	
79th Company:				1	1
à Cheval (Horse):					
– 2nd:				3	1
– 5th:					1

	G	EC	EM	P	V
– 22nd Flying (sic):					1
'1st Regt Inf.':				1	
Train:	3			14	2
– 2nd Bn:				1	
– 5th Bn:				2	
– 6th Bn:					2
– 11th Bn:				6	
– '2 Waggon':				2	
– '5 Waggon':				16	
Armourier, 2nd Coy:				5	
Ouvriers (Artificers, Journeymen, et al.):					
– Artificers					2
– Artificers, 3rd Coy					1
– Journeymen, 2nd Bn: 1				1	
– Labourer: 1				1	
– Military Workmen:				2	5
– Ouvriers, 1st Coy:				8	
– Ouvriers, 16th Coy:				6	1
Pontonniers, 1st Bn:				6	
F. French Engineers, Miners and Sapeurs:					
Engineers:					
– 2nd Regt:				1	
– 4th Regt:				1	
– 5th Regt:				1	
Mineurs:					
– 2nd Bn:				26	3
– 6th Bn:					3
– Unspecified Bn:				17	
Sapeurs:					
– 1st Bn:	1			2	

	G	EC	EM	P	V
– 2nd Bn:	3			32	18
– 3rd Bn:					1
– 4th Bn:				12	
– Unspecified Bn:				5	2
G. French transport and supply units:					
Trains des Equipages Militaires ('Baggage Waggoners'), 1st Bn:				5	1
Unspecified Bns				12	7
H. French Medical Services:					
'Hospital Dept': (? Depot)	1			1	1
'Hospital Staff':				1	
'Hospital at Fort Desaix, Martinique':				1	
Ambulance:				5	6
I. Gendarmes:					
3rd Bn:				3	
6th Bn:				6	
17th Bn:				3	
Unspecified Bn:	2			4	
J. Administration:					
Militaire:	1				
des Postes:	1				
Unspecified:				1	
K. Pionniers:					
– 2nd Regt (or Bn):				72	
– 3rd Regt:		1			
– 4th Bn:				14	
'Pioneers Infantry, 2nd':				1	
'Pioneers Infantry, 4th':				1	
L. Veterans:					
6th Regt:				1	
Unspecified regt:				2	

	G	EC	EM	P	V
M. Naval troops:					
'Marines' (i.e., seamen)					
– 4th Bn:			1		1
– 43rd Bn:				2	
– 44th Bn:				7	22
– Unstated Bn:			1	1	
– Artillery,					
1st Regt:				1	
2nd Regt:					1
N. Miscellaneous:					
'Bourgeois':				1	
Courier:					1
'Followers of the Army':				4	
Servants/Domestics:				5	
O. Colonial Regts:					
Island of Bourbon (i.e., Réunion) Regt:				7	5
Isle of France (i.e., Mauritius) Regt:				1	1
1st West Indian Regt:					2
P. Foreign Regts:					
Dutch, 1st:			1		1
Dutch, 3rd:				2	6
Dutch, 5th:			11	2	16
Dutch Artillery, 1st:					4
Dutch Artillery, 5th:					2
Dutch Cavalry:					1
Dutch Marines:	12				
Dutch Mineurs:				1	
Zealand Regt:			3		
Etrangers Regts:					
– 1st:				3	12

	G	EC	EM	P	V
– 4th:				1	
Unstated Regt:				10	
German Regts:					
'German Battn, 4th':				3	1
Hanoverian Legion:			2	11	15
Hanoverian Legion, 1st:	1				
Hanoverian Legion, 2nd:	1				
Hesse-Darmstadt Regt:				203	209
Jager, 1st:			1		
Nassau Regt:					1
Prussian Regt:				5	11
– 1st:	1		3	4	6
– 4th:				1	
– 12th:	1				
– 14th:	2				
'12th Regt of the Rhine':				1	
Grec/Grecian Regt, 2nd:					13
Irlandais (Irish) Légion/Regt/Bn:			2		16
Italian Legion/Regts:					
– Italian Horse:				1	2
– Italian Legion, 2nd:			22	4	
– Italian Legion, 3rd:			6		
– Italian Regt, 2nd:			6		86
– Italian Regt, 3rd:			1		2
– Italian Regt, 4th:				3	6
– Italian Regt, 5th:					5
– Italian Regt (sic):					3
– Légion Piémontaise: (or du Midi)	1			7	6
– Napoleon's Dragoons:				3	
– Neapolitan Dragoons:					1

	G	EC	EM	P	V
– Neapolitan Infantry, 1st:					1
– Neapolitan (Regt):				1	
– Neapolitan Regt, 12th:					1
Royal Corsican Regt:					4
Polish Regts:					
– Polish Infantry, 2nd:	7				
– Polish Lancers, 1st:	2				1
– Polish Regt, 1st:				22	30
– Polish Regt (unspecified):				1	
Portuguese Regts:					
– Porto (sic) Regt:					1
Swiss Regts:					
– 1st Regt:				1	1
– 2nd Regt:	1			1	2
– 3rd Regt:	11			1	1
– 4th Regt:	9			4	2
– Regt (unspecified):				2	
O. Undifferentiated or unidentified:					
Flushing Army:				45	168
5 Corps:				1	
'8 Comn Dambatn':				1	
Others:	370	23	224	172	573

Appendix 5

THE RANKS OF THE PRISONERS IN THE SCOTS DEPOTS

Ranks are given as in the column in the General Entry Books headed 'Quality'. Abbreviations used below are: N—naval, P—privateer, M—merchant vessel, T—transport vessel, U—uncertain. The numbers for Edinburgh Castle are, as in several other aspects, less comprehensive and reliable than those for the other depots.

(a) SEA-GOING PRISONERS
Greenlaw: 'Danes': [Source: TNA ADM 103/152, /153]

Captain: 29 (16 P, 12 M, 1 T)
2nd Captain: 18 (15 P, 1 M, 2 T)
Master: 45 (2 P, 41 M, 1 T, 1 U)
2nd Master: 2 (P)
3rd Master: 3 (P)
1st Lieutenant: 2 (P)
2nd Lieutenant: 1 (N)
Lieutenant: 1 (P)
Lieutenant and Comm. (sic): 1 (N)
Mate: 68 (2 N, 3 P, 62 M, 1 T)
2nd Mate: 3 (1 P, 2 M)
Prize Captain: 1 (P)
Prize Master: 9 (P)
Surgeon: 4 (1 N, 3 P)
Master of the Crew: 1 (P)
Boatswain: 2 (1 N, 1 P)
Purser: 1 (N)
Gunner: 8 (1 N, 7 P)
Carpenter: 14 (1 N, 4 P, 9 M)
Cooper: 1 (P)
Cook: 4 (3 P, 1 M)
Steward: 1 (P)
Clerk: 2 (P)
Scryver: 2 (P)
Boy: 38 (23 P, 15 M)
Seaman: 701 (51 N, 358 P, 241 M, 41 T, 10 U)

Greenlaw: 'Dutch': [Source: TNA ADM 103/154]

Captain: 2 (1 N, 1 M)
1st Lieutenant: 1 (N)
2nd Lieutenant: 3 (1 N, 1 P, 1 U)
Surgeon: 1 (N)
2nd Surgeon: 1 (N)
Midshipman: 1 (N)
Master: 1 (N)
Pilot: 1 (N)
Boatswain: 1 (N)
Boatswain's Mate: 1 (N)
Purser: 1 (N)
Secretary: 1 (N)
Carpenter: 2 (N)
Smith: 1 (N)
Sailmaker: 1 (N)
Cook: 2 (N)
Steward: 1 (N)
Seamen: 63 (46 N, 13 M, 4 U)
Marines:
    Lieutenant: 1
    Sergeant: 2

Corporal: 2
Tambour: 1
Soldier: 6

Greenlaw: 'Prussian': [Source: TNA ADM 103/115]

Captain: 25 (M)
Mate: 19 (M)
Boy: 9 (M)
Seamen: 78 (M)

Greenlaw: 'French': [Source: TNA ADM 103/155. In this Entry Book it has not proved possible to analyse the numbers who were either naval or merchant or privateer officers and crew—apart from the first 130, of whom none was N, 74 were M, 1 P, none T, and 55 U.]

Captain: 7
2nd Captain: 8
1st Lieutenant: 3
2nd Lieutenant: 2
3rd Lieutenant: 1
5th Lieutenant: 1
Mate: 1
Surgeon: 4
Prize Captain: 1
Conductor of Prizes: 1
Midshipman: 1
Cap. d'Armes: 1
Maître d'Equipage: 2
2nd Maître d'Equipage: 2
Sail Master: 1
Maître Voilier: 2
Contre Maître: 1
Quartermaster: 3
Dispenser de Vivres: 1
Armourier: 1
Gunner: 6
Salter: 2
Carpenter: 3
Cooper: 2
Cook: 1
Clerk: 1
Ecrivain: 1
Volunteer: 3
Novice: 2
Boy above Age: 4
Boy: 17
Sailor: 16
Seaman: 311

Greenlaw: 'French' [Source: TNA ADM 103/157]

Captain: 5 (3 P, 2 M)

2nd Captain: 2 (P)
Lieutenant or 1st Lieutenant: 27 (2 N, 24 P, 1 T)
2nd Lieutenant: 1 (P)
3rd Lieutenant: 1 (P)
Surgeon: 5 (1 N, 4 P)
Prizemaster: 5 (P)
Ensign: 8 (4 N, 4 P)
Midshipman: 9 (N)
Master-at-Arms: 3 (P)
Boatswain: 1 (N)
Gunner: 1 (P)
Carpenter: 2 (1 N, 1 P)
Cooper: 1 (P)
Cook: 2 (P)
Steward: 2 (P)
Interpreter: 1 (P)
Clerk: 4 (1 N, 3 P)
Volunteer: 1 (P)
Boy: 4 (P)
Seaman: 233 (86 N, 138 P, 4 M, 5 U)

Greenlaw: American: [Source: TNA ADM 103/157]

Master: 4 (M)
1st Mate: 6 (M)
2nd Mate: 3 (M)
Seaman: 35 (M)

Greenlaw: 'Spanish' [Source: TNA ADM 103/115 and ADM 103/158]

2nd Mate 1 (N)
Gunner 2 (N)
Seamen: 111 (1 N, 51 P, 22 M, 37 U)
Boy 2 (P)

Esk Mills: [Source: TNA ADM 103/124]

Commissaire of Marine: 1 (N)
Captain: 21 (2 N, 15 P, 4 M)
2nd Captain: 13 (1 N, 11 P, 1 M)
1st Lieutenant: 53 (4 N, 47 P, 2 M)
2nd Lieutenant: 13 (1 N, 12 P)
3rd Lieutenant: 6 (P)
4th Lieutenant: 2 (P)
Surgeon: 12 (P)
Ensign: 22 (5 N, 16 P, 1 M)
Midshipman: 11 (10 N, 1 M)
Prizemaster: 29 (1 N, 28 P)
Mate: 7 (2 N, 3 P, 2 M)
3rd Mate: 1 (M)
Master's Mate: 2 (1 N, 1 P)
Quartermaster: 38 (14 N, 24 P)
Master-at-Arms: 10 (2 N, 7 P, 1 M)

Captain of Arms: 5 (P)
Pilot: 16 (6 N, 9 P, 1 M)
Boatswain: 24 (2 N, 22 P)
Maître d'Equipage: 1 (M)
Boatnmate (sic) (Bosun's Mate): 6 (3 N, 3 P)
Boat's Mate: 2 (1 P, 1 M)
Purser: 1 (P)
Gunner: 45 (29 N, 16 P)
Armourier: 2 (N)
Carpenter: 13 (4 N, 7 P, 2 M)
Carpenter's Mate: 4 (1 N, 3 P)
Sailmaker: 11 (5 N, 5 P, 1 M)
Cooper: 3 (N)
Caulker: 1 (M)
Maître d'Hotel: 1 (M)
Interpreter: 2 (P)
Clerk: 11 (1 N, 10 P)
Purser's Clerk: 1 (N)
Cook: 9 (3 N, 6 P)
Steward: 12 (2 N, 9 P, 1 M)
Servant: 2 (N)
Volunteer: 33 (P)
Novice: 1 (M)
Boy: 61 (20 N, 34 P, 6 M, 1 U)
Seaman: 1,219 (528 N, 621 P, 65 M, 4 T, 1 U)

Valleyfield: [Sources: TNA ADM 103/432, /433, /434, /435, and ADM 103/113, Nos 6445-7479 inclusive]

Commissaire de Marine: 1 (N)
Captain: 14 (1 N, 10 P, 3 M)
2nd Captain: 22 (4 N, 15 P, 2 M, 1 U)
Lieutenant/1st Lieutenant: 38 (2 N, 33 P, 2 M, 1 T)
2nd Lieutenant: 2 (P)
3rd Lieutenant: 1 (P)
Sous Lieutenant: 1 (U)
Sub Lieutenant: 1 (N)
'Officer', 1 (M)
Ensign: 7 (3 N, 4 P)
Enseigne/Enseigne de Vaisseau: 2 (N)
Midshipman: 30 (N)
Pilot: 5 (1 N, 3 P, 1 M)
Surgeon: 25 (5 N, 19 P, 1 U)
3rd Surgeon: 1 (N)
Mate: 3 (2 P, 1 U)
Master's Mate: 1 (N)
Prizemaster: 15 (P)
Master-at-Arms: 6 (1 N, 5 P)
Quartermaster: 4 (2 N, 2 P)
Purser: 6 (4 N, 2 P)

Boatswain: 5 (1 N, 4 P)
Bosun's Mate: 2 (P)
Owner of Vessel: 1 (P)
Master Cannonier: 1 (N)
Gunner: 10 (6 N, 3 P, 1 M)
Gunner's Mate: 2 (N)
Cannonier: 1 (P)
Armourier: 1 (N)
Maître Cordnr: 1 (N)
Carpenter: 6 (2 N, 4 P)
Sailmaker: 1 (P)
Cooper: 1 (N)
Cook: 1 (P)
Steward: 5 (1 N, 4 P)
Servant: 2 (1 P, 1 M)
Interpreter: 2 (P)
Clerk: 15 (P)
Apprentice: 8 (3 N, 4 P, 1 M)
Novice: 1 (U)
Boy: 24 (4 N, 17 P, 1 M, 2 U)
Volunteer: 14 (P)
Tambour: 1 (N)
Seaman: 1,655 (659 N, 910 P, 66 M, 20 U)

Edinburgh Castle: [Sources: TNA ADM 103/110, /112]

Captain: 12 (8P, 4M)
2nd Captain: 2 (P)
Lieutenant/1st Lieutenant: 70 (7N, 63P)
2nd Lieutenant: 1 (P)
3rd Lieutenant: 1 (P)
Ensign: 11 (7N, 4P)
Midshipman: 18 (14N, 3P, 1M)
2nd Pilot: 1(N)
Surgeon: 5 (P)
Master: 2 (N)
Mate: 1 (N)
Prizemaster: 9 (P)
Master at Arms: 5 (P)
Bosun: 2 (N)
Gunner: 2 (P)
Carpenter: 4 (1N, 3P)
2nd Cooper: 2 (P)
Cook: 4 (P)
Steward: 4 (P)
Interpreter: 2 (P)
Clerk: 8 (2N, 6P)
Purser's Clerk: 2 (N)
Boy: 19 (1N, 18P)
Volunteer: 2 (P)

Seaman: 447 (159N, 269P, 7M, 3T, 9U)

Perth: [Sources: TNA ADM 103/263, /264, /265, /266]

Captain: 8 (P)
2nd Captain: 6 (P)
Lieutenant/1st Lieutenant: 35 (2 N, 30 P, 3 U)
2nd Lieutenant: 2 (P)
3rd Lieutenant: 1 (P)
'Officer': 1 (P)
Enseigne de Vaisseau: 4 (N)
Ensign: 5 (1 N, 4 P)
Midshipman: 8 (N)
Aspirant: 1 (N)
Surgeon: 8 (P)
Assistant Surgeon: 1 (N)
'Py Mr' (? Prizemaster): 4 (P)
Quartermaster: 1 (U)
Purser: 5 (1 N, 4 P)
'2nd M.Arms': 1 (P)
'Master Mate': 1 (N)
Armourier: 1 (N)
Carpenter: 1 (P)
Cooper: 1 (N)
Interpreter: 1 (N)
Clerk: 6 (1 N, 5 P)
Servant: 1 (M)
Boy: 1 (P)
'Marin': 1 (U)
Seaman: 165 (54 N, 102 P, 7 M, 2 U)

(b) PRISONERS FROM ARMIES
Greenlaw: [Sources: TNA ADM 103/155, /156, and /157]

Captain: 24
Lieutenant: 63
2nd Lieutenant: 51
Ensign: 2
Surgeon: 20
Adjutant-Major: 2
Sergeant Major: 9
Sergeant: 31
Corporal: 25
Fourrier: 2
'Garde Magne' (Magazine Guard): 1
Cannonier: 1
Boulanger: 1
Drummer: 2
Boy: 1
Soldier: 568

Esk Mills: [Source: TNA ADM 103/124]

Adjutant General: 1
Captain: 16
Chief Apothecary ('rank of Captain'): 2
Storekeeper ('rank of Captain'): 4
Lieutenant: 7
Civil Officer ('rank of Lieutenant'): 2
2nd Lieutenant: 3
Adjutant: 1
Sergeant Major: 4
Sergeant: 31
Corporal: 47
Fourrier: 1
Trumpeter: 1
Drummer: 14
Gunner/Cannonier: 2
Bowyiou (?) (or Bourjoin ?): 1
Servant: 2
Boys (Artillery Journeymen): 17
Soldier: 903

Valleyfield: [TNA ADM 103/432, /433, /434, /435 and ADM 103/113, Nos. 6445-7479 inclusive]

Captain: 12
Lieutenant/2nd Lieutenant: 24
'Officer': 1
Inspecteur des Services: 1
Director of Hospitals: 2
Surgeon: 6
Ensign: 5
Sub-Lieutenant: 1
Sous-Lieutenant: 1
Adjutant: 4
Sergeant Major: 44
Quartermaster: 7
Maître de Logis: 3
Sergeant: 214
Aide-Major: 1
Corporal: 241
Fourrier: 4
Brigadier: 2
Gunner: 10
Cannonier: 2
Armourier: 4
Artificer: 5
Master Shoemaker: 1
Shoemaker: 1
Tailor: 1
Baker: 8

Cook: 1
Storekeeper: 1
Nurse: 1
Secretary: 2
Trumpeter: 2
Drummer: 57
Musician: 3
Courier: 1
Workman: 3
Labourer: 1
Waggoner: 4
Servant: 31
Boy: 1
'Launcier'/Lancer: 2
Chasseur (Light inf.): 1
No rank given: 4
Soldier: 3,367

Edinburgh Castle: [Sources: TNA ADM 103/110 and ADM 103/112]

Captain: 1
Chief Apothecary: 3
Lieutenant: 16
Adjutant Major: 1
Adjutant: 1
Sergeant: 8
Garde Magazin: 2
Storekeeper: 4
Soldier: 172

Perth: [Sources: TNA ADM 103/263, /264, /265, and /266]

Captain: 5
Lieutenant: 11
Surgeon: 2
Adjutant Major: 1
'2nd Master' (Infantry): 2
Quartermaster: 2
Maître de Logis: 3
Sergeant Major: 50
Maréchal de Logis: 3
Sergeant: 308
Brigadier: 16
Corporal: 403
Fourrier: 27
Cavalier [17th Light Regt]: 1
Carabinier: 85
Chasseur: 244
Chasseur à Cheval: 1
Lancier: 1
Dragoon: 17
Hussar: 9

Cuirassier: 1
Train (i.e., Artilleryman): 2
Cannonier: 52
Gunner: 10
Sappeur (sic): 20
Fusilier: 166
Voltigeur: 107
Grenadier: 86
Artificer: 4
Baker: 3
Boulanger: 2
Pioneer: 2
Multier (sic): 1
Waggoner: 4
Storekeeper: 1
Musician: 2
Musicman: 1
Bugle Man: 2
Trumpeter: 6
Drummer: 31
Tambour: 21
Nurse: 6
Servant: 12
Habinger (sic): 1
Inhabn (sic): 1
D.N. (? D.M.) (sic): 1
Inpervner (? Infervner) (sic) [Infirmière ? = nurse ?]: 1
Rank not given: 5
Soldier: 5,718

(c) CIVILIANS (Mainly passengers captured on ships)
Greenlaw: 'Danes': 32 [Sources: TNA ADM 103/152 and /153]
   'French': 18 [Sources: TNA ADM 103/155 and /157]

Esk Mills: 12 [Source: TNA ADM 103/124]

Valleyfield: 21 [Sources: TNA ADM 103/432, /433, /434, /435, /436, and ADM 103/113, Nos. 6445-7479 inclusive]

Edinburgh Castle: 5 [Sources: TNA ADM 110 and ADM 103/112]

Perth: 19 [Sources: TNA ADM 103/263, /264, /265, and /266]

Appendix 6

'PLACES OF NATIVITY'

The following are random selections from the depot General Entry Books of some of the better known places of birth of prisoners confined in the Scots depots, with place names spelled as in the Entry Books:

(a) **Greenlaw:** 'Danes' [Source: TNA ADM 103/153]

Bergen, Copenhagen, Stavanger, Arendal, Trondheim, Flensburg, Hamburg, Rostock, Friedrichstadt, Christiana, Bornholm Island, Bremen, Helsingfors, Faroes, Lerwick, Wisby, Gothenburg, Aarhus, Tonsberg, Sonderburg, Holstein, Jutland, Oldenburg, Memel, Finland, Emden, Lubeck

Greenlaw: Americans [Source: TNA ADM 103/157]

New Bedford, Long Island, Dartmouth, Middleburgh, Beverley, Manchester, Boston, Nobleport, Eastport, Newburgh, Marblehead, Ipswich, Pennsylvania, Plainfield, Salem, Norfolk, Dover, Barnstable, Philadelphia, New York, Rhode Island, Nantucket, Christiansand [Norway], Middlesex, New London.

Greenlaw: 'French' [Source: TNA ADM 103/157]

Calais, Cherbourg, Christiansand, Narbonne, Dunkirk, Caen, Paris, Marseilles, Bordeaux, St Malo, Liège, Sette, Toulon, Abbeville, Le Havre, Hamburg, Dieppe, Limoges, Sedan, Naples, Tuscany, Fécamp, Angres, Rochefort, Switzerland, Isle of Elba, Sardinia, Nantz, Angoulême, Rouen, Dinan, Falaise, Barcelona, Bourbon, Morlaix, Trieste, Venice, Ponticherry [presumably Pondicherry, India], Piedmont, Flanders, Isle de France [Mauritius], Boulogne, Lorient, Granville, St Valery, Brest, Corsica, Turin, Montevideo, Painboeuf, Konigsberg, Oldenburg, Besançon, Brienne, Honfleur, Léon, Malage [presumably Malaga, Spain], Florida, Valenciennes, Alençon, Germany, Grenoble, Bayonne, Blaye, Alsace, Fontainebleau, Lubeck, Pernamburg [Pernambuco, Brazil], Ferrol, Emden, Lisbon, Norway, Carthagena [not clear whether Spain or Colombia], Copenhagen, Manilla, Neort, Martinique, Burgundy, Normandy, Languedoc, Picardy, Memel, Gothenburg, Amsterdam, Hague, Milan, Chartres, Coutances, Arras, Nancy, Metz, Strasbourg, Bar le Duc, Douai, Evreux, Troyes.

(b) **Esk Mills** (See below, Edinburgh Castle (i) and Valleyfield (i).

(c) **Edinburgh Castle:** [FOOTNOTE: Source: TNA ADM 103/112]

(i) Prisoners who came in March 1811 from Esk Mills: Orleans, Bayonne, Quimper, France, Istria, Perigord, Hougue, Pontichery [presumably Pondicherry, India], Metz, Painboeuf, Valenciennes, Montero, Florida, St Valery en Somme, Cognac, Ancona, Oldenburg, Konisberg [Konigsberg], Oléron, Isle de Bas, Fécamp, St Germain, Grenoble, Strasbourg, Franconia [central Germany], Bezière, Reims, Montpellier, Brest, Constant, Granville, Condé, St Servan, Villeneuve, Isle of France [Mauritius], Boulogne, Maine, Flanders.

(ii) Other than from Esk Mills: Alsace, Bordeaux, Martinique, Fontainebleau, Nantes, Rouen, Malta, Boulogne, Rochefort, Christiansand, Lupcourt, Pontichery, Oldenburg, Havre de Grace, Lubeck, Rio de Janeiro, Caligari, Penambuco [Pernambuco, Brazil], Ferrol, Emden, 'Santa Caterina, South America' [Santa Catharina, Brazil], Gravelines, Lushaven [Norway], Pappenberg [Papenburg, north Germany], Cronen [Holland], St Omer, Carthagena [not clear whether Spain or Colombia], Copenhagen, Havana, Lorain [Lorraine], Cherbourg, Condé, Isle de Bas, St Trope [? St Tropez], Blaye, Granville, Sardinia, St Maloe, Aix, Isle of Rhé, Marseilles, Honfleur, Paris, Dieppe, Santes, Calais, St Vallery, Abbeville.

(d) **Valleyfield:** [FOOTNOTE: Sources: TNA ADM 103/432, /433, /434, /435, /436, and ADM 103/113, Nos. 6445-7479]

(i) Prisoners who came in March/April 1811 from Esk Mills: Arras, Dieppe, Marseilles, Compiègne, Picardy, Toulouse, Dunkirk, Caen, Ostend, Nantes, Brussels, Neufchateau, Morlaix, Lyons, Brittany, Paris, Colmar, Lorient, Nancy, St Malo, Guadeloupe, Auge, Vannes, Angoulême, Castillon, Chalons, Angers, Contamines, Rouen, Drome, Somme, Sweden, St Valery, Philadelphia, Virginia, Portugal, Namur, Granvilliers, Calvados, St Brieux, Evreux, Blangy, Lunéville, Toulon, Gravelines, Orleans, Oldenburg, Abbeville, Venice, Genoa, Savoie, Charlesville, Oporto, Bayeux, Puillac, Bordeaux, New York, Amsterdam, Luxembourg, Calais, Villeneuf, St Domingo, Granville, Boulogne, Konigsberg, Honfleur, Montevideo, Avranches, Copenhagen, Bruges, Hague, Hamburg, Lorraine, Strasbourg, Rochefort, Cherbourg, Lisle Adam, Leghorn, Sardinia, Messina, Milan, Majorca, Mayence, Liège, Quebec, Bray, Orbec, Soissons, Versailles, Dijon, Alsace, Garonne, Finisterre, Rotterdam, Prussia, Norway, Brazil, Auvergnac, Jura [Département de], Agene [? Agen], Azores, Lisieux, Modena, Ancona, Pavia, Levant, Corsica, Turin, Dordogne [Département of], Bayonne, Perigord, Languedoc, Istria, Corfu, Fiume, Sicily, Painboeuf, Amiens, Poitou, Bergerac, Figueras, Asturias, Castille, Villefranche, Rome, Berlin, Dauphiné, Perignac, Loire [Département of], Maine, Flanders, Charente, Montpellier, Fruges, Pontoise, Martinique, Minorca, Montreal, Clermont, Gothenburg, Trieste, Cette, Cologne, Naples, Stockholm, Spain, Holland, Artois, Grenoble, Verdun, Rochelle, Melun, Danzig, Bremen, Memel, Malta, Providence, New Orleans, Friesland, Utrecht, Blankenbergh [probably Blankenberge, near Bruges, rather than Blankenburg near the Harz mountains in Germany], Emden, Portsmouth ['North America'], Norfolk [probably Virginia], Varsovie [Warsaw], Stavanger, Morea [Greece], Ceuta [Spanish Morocco], Alexandria, Blois, Bergamo, Stettin, Asti, Lausanne, Masteric [? Maastricht], Lisle de Res [Ile de Rhé], Bizanson [Besançon], Brescia, Neufchatel, Barcelona, Dreux, Dauphiné, Lisbon, St Nazaire, Deuville [? Deauville], Brabant, Tarbe [Tarbes], Normandy, Ollarone [Ile d'Oléron], Avignon, Cadiz.

(ii) Prisoners other than from Esk Mills: Harlingen, Midelburg, Hamburg, Guadeloupe, Breda, Paris, Rouen, St Malo, St Roper, Piedmont, Milan, Bayonne, Chartres, Amiens, Joigny, Harnhem [? Arnhem], Orange, Poland, Morlaix, Prussia, Westphalia, Italy, Bologna, France, Troyes, Granville, Lemberg [Lvov or L'viv], Angres, Portoferio, La Rochelle, Orleans, Varseau [Warsaw], Angers, Genoa, Flanders, Brabant, Nancy, Marseilles, Montebello, St Omer, Dijon, Nantes, Austerlitz, Caen, La Flèche, Liège, Autun, Toulon, Verdun, Angoulême, Versailles, St Morice, Beauvais, Tréport, Toulouse, Metz, Elbeuf, Boulogne, Picardy, Luxembourg, Turcoing, Vannes, Compiègne, Condé, Grenoble, Utrecht, Friesland, Montdidier, Vienna, St Domingo, Martinique, Havre de Grace, Moulins, Palma, Switzerland, Dunkirk, Verona, Amsterdam, Montreux, Ghent, Dieppe, Loraine, Berlin, Strasbourg, Brest, Bessières, Ostend, Briançon, Libourne, Bordeaux, Gascony, Morlaix, Turin, Blois, Montereau, Dompierre, Tarascon, Montauban, Dole, Bourgoine, Spa, Luxeil, Avignon, Leyden, Zutphen, Flessingen [Vlissingen—Flushing], Champagne, Lyons, Corsica, Vitrie [? Vitry], Poitiers, Arras, Rhennes [? Rennes], La Chapel, Agens [Agen], St Denis, Sallin [Departément de ? Ivret], St Dize [? St Dizier], Courtray, Péronne, New Orleans, Germany, Le Mans, Dinan, Antwerp, Norway, Blaye, Mastrick [Masstricht], Hanover, Denmark, Rotterdam, Barcelona, St Pol de Léon, Sette, Alsace, Tours, Sedan, Besançon, Berne, Blankenberg, Auxonne, Artois, Charleville, Osnaburg, St Lo, Pontarlier, Amboise, Fougère,

Pavia, Narbonne, Vire, Onzin, Sicily, Provence, Canne, Marengo, Namur, Lunéville, Auxerre, Cazale, Isle of France (Mauritius), Saarlouis, Rochefort, Lucerne, Geneva, Vesoul, Worms, Cleves, Hungary, Pressburg, Munster, Cologne, Fuldau, Aix la Chapelle, Rostock, Coblentz, Speier, Ansbach, Baden, Brandenburg, Saxony, 'Alexandria in Italy', Pisa, Florence, Parma, Liverno, Sienna, Piacenza, Valence, Modena, Chambéry, Leghorn, Alba, Romagna, Tuscany, Castiliglione, Asti, Fiorli, Nice, Rome, Como, Padua, Venezia, Argentan, Bretagne, Chaumont, Ardennes, Auvergne, Limoges.

(e) **Perth** : [FOOTNOTE: Sources: TNA ADM 103/263, /264, /265, /266]

Bourges, Piedmont, Nice, Valence, Vierzon, Dijon, Parma, Toulouse, Rouen, Mastrick [Maastricht], Lyon, Grenoble, Berne, Tours, Paris, Fontainebleau, St Valery, 'Turneau, 6 leagues from Paris', Poland, Ostend, Arras, 'Lanuville devant Bayonne', Astie, Briard, Brussels, Villefranche, St Denis, Anvers, Colmar, Provins, St Sulpice, Choisy, Loup, Pisa, St Omer, Coulomier, Ligourno, Schelling, Donato, Grasse, Boulogne, Nemour, Dunkirk, Villeneuve, Anger, Fulda, Neuchateau, Rotterdam, Montigny, Boneval, Maçon, Marseilles, Fontevraux, Liège, Cologne, Tachebry [? Tinchebrai], Amiens, Crevecoeur, Frévent, Bayeux, Lemoge [? Limoges], Dax, Meuse, Joinville, Geneva, Turin, Genoa, Florence, Verdun, Metz, Blois, Luxemburgh, St Julien, Sienna, Strasbourg, Versailles, Havre de Grace, Besançon, Meaux, Morlaix, Fécamp, Anzin, Bordeaux, Amsterdam, Chateauroux, Meung, Melun, Vienna, Sicily, Caen, Toulon, Altona, La Rochelle, Nantes, Corsica, Rome, Montpellier, Grandville, Dieppe, Oldenbourg, Cherbourg, Brest, Naples, Calais, Norway, St Malo, Isle of Bourbon [Réunion], Trieste, Hamburg, Chartres, Rennes, Tuscany, Laon, Orleans, Honflur, Cahors, Marie Galante, Dinant, Dampierre, Vannes, Ex la Chapel [Aix-la-Chapelle], Chateau Renau [Chateau-Renault], Hungary, Dordogne, Burgos, Aix, Poitiers, Warsaw, Lille, Guise, Louvain, Arles, Montfaulcon, Namur, Berry, Auvergne, Bapaume, Cambrai, Nancy, Mons, Vervin, Dauphiné, Montargis, Chinon, Clermont, Modena, Vicenza, Brabant, Tarascon, Pavia, Flandre, Milan, Lorraine, Mitau, Calvados, Champagne, Perigord, Berlin, St Symphorien, Bruges, Stenay, Malines, Alba, Barbary, Chaumont, Coblenz, Lichtenburg, Leghorn, Alsace, Chambéry, Rhé, Lubignan, Florence, Felino [Appenines], Ponte Mole [Appenines], Marengo, Courtray, 'Bazle in Switzerland', Vallensien [Valenciennes], Brie, Pont Leveque, Auxerre, Beauvais, Speier, Avignon, Epinal, Falaise, Lisieux, Vire, Bar, Commercy, Alexandria [Italy], Vendée, Charleroi, Carcassonne, Treves, Troyes, Beaume, 'Oldenham near Antwerp', Philippeville, Agen, Nimes, Tournai, Montreuil, Hague, Castel Franca, Mezières, Dusseldorf, St Etienne, Orbec, Como, Gropo Genoa, Nivelle, Verona, Padua, Brion [? Brionne], Perigueux, Mobeuge [Maubeuge], Abbeville, Jamaica, Bocage, Grenade, Nogent, Lens, Damstadt, Chalons, Hessel, Rheims, St Quentin, Jemappes, Laigle [L'Aigle], Montebello, Saumur, Poitou, Vienne, Blainville, Soissons, Gand [Ghent], Vichy, 'Isles in Flanders', Vouvray, Hesse, Betune [Bethune], Perpignan, Vitry, Napoleonville, Hasbach, Sarbrock [Saarbrucken], Quimper, Germany, France, Friesland, Baden, Britany, Kaiserslautern, Indre et Loire [Département of], Depte de Lot, Dpt du Nord, Ile de Rhé, Nice, Senlis, Laneuville le Roi, Prundnitz, Pistoya, Lachapelle Villefort, Thionville, Département of Haut Rhin, Switzerland, Martinique, Péronne, Fougère, Artois, Provence, 'Palme—positively asserts St Vallery', Albi [Languedoc], Allier, St Brienne, Menin, Picardy, Po [near Bayonne], Bergerac, Sluy, Barcelonete [Département des Bas Alpes], Anjou, St Brieuc, Guadeloupe, Mayenne, Chatillon, Département de Vosges, Marocque, Fribourg, Isle de Bas, Flushing, Chateauneuf, St Servan, Choire [Swizerland], Le Mans, Condé.

Appendix 7

SOME SWEDISH PRISONERS

(Abbreviations and contractions used below: arr.—arrived; capd—captured; dischgd—discharged; G—Greenlaw; n.d.—no date; rel.—released)

(a) **At Fort George, in late summer 1803:** [Source: TNA ADM 1/3743, correspondence between Transport Board and Admiralty, 30 Aug.-14 Sep. 1803. See also above, p.5.

One unnamed seaman or passenger 'From the King of Sweden's dominions', among 86 other prisoners taken by the British privateer *St Joseph*, all of whom were landed at Ullapool then marched overland to captivity in Fort George.

(b) **At Greenlaw:** [Sources: TNA ADM 103/152, ADM 103 /153, ADM 103/115, and ADM 103/155]

The following were said to have been released 'as Swedish subject':
Johan Moller, 3rd Master, capd off Norway, 30 Mar. 1808, on privateer *Gordenskiold*, arr. G 6 Apr. 1808, dischgd home 21 Jun.1808.
Sven Sodergreen, seaman—as for Johan Moller.
Charel Gramand, seaman—as for Johan Moller.
Jonas Bruyne, seaman—as for Johan Moller.
Peder Dalmann, seaman—as for Johan Moller.
Hans Lund, seaman—as for Johan Moller.
Jacob Berngstrem, seaman, capd off Scotland, 25 May 1808, on privateer *Weghals*, arr. G 27 May 1808, dischgd home 21 Jun. 1808
Johanes Ustreberg, seaman, capd off Jutland, 11 Sep. 1809, on merchant vessel *Neptunes*, arr. G 10 Oct. 1809, dischgd to Wisby, Sweden, on (?) 31 Jul. 1810.

The following, listed in the 'French' Entry Book ADM 103/155, were released, 'Being Swede', as subjects of a state allied with Britain, on 21 Jun. 1808:

No. 367 Johan Engstroom, seaman, captured off Norway, 2 May 1808, on privateer *Passepartout*, arr. G 17 May 1808.
No. 374 Hans Koelberg—as for Johan Engstroom.
No. 379 A. Ketler—as for Johan Engstroom.
No. 381 P. Eriksen—as for Johan Engstroom.
No. 386 A.Ryberg—as for Johan Engstroom.
No. 390 J. Laarsen—as for Johan Engstroom.
No. 396 A. Norborn—as for Johan Engstroom.

The following among the 130 'Prussian' seamen sent to Greenlaw between Apr. and Jun. 1806 were released as 'Swedish Subject': [Source: TNA ADM 103/115, Nos 30, 31, 90-93, 114-116]:

Johan Kroon, seaman, merchant vessel *Romulus*, capd in the North Sea, 21 Apr. 1806, arr. at G 7 Jun.1806, rel. 10 Nov. 1806.
John Schersing, seaman—as for Johan Kroon.
Michel Wolfcam, seaman—as for Johan Kroon, except he arr. at G 9 Jun. 1806.
Fredrick Jenberg, seaman—as for Michel Wolfcam.
J.H. Shellink, seaman—as for Michel Wolfcam.

Jan Hernis, seaman, merchant vessel *Vrow Wilske*, capd in the North Sea, 26 Apr. 1806, arr. G 9 Jun. 1806, rel. 14 Feb. 1807.

Anderis Scoburg, seaman, merchant vessel *Diana*, capd Aberdeen, 17 Apr. 1806, arr. G 22 Jun. 1806, rel. 10 Nov. 1806.

Daniel Westenberg, seaman—as for Anderis Scoburg.

Hendrik Bronkhorst, seaman—as for Anderis Scoburg, except he was rel. 14 Feb. 1807.

The following appear to have been Finns (Finland was part of the kingdom of Sweden until the Swedish-Russian war of 1809, when it passed to Russia), who, according to entries in TNA ADM 103/152, were discharged to Helsingfors (Helsinki) either on (?) 22 May 1810 or (in Rasmus Andersen's case) no date given, but who, according to entries in ADM 103/153, were on the contrary sent on 5 Apr. 1811 to Chatham, presumably to the hulks there:

Rasmus Andersen, seaman, capd off Jutland, 9 Aug. 1808, on man-of-war *Fama*, arr. G 19 Sep. 1808, dischgd n.d. to Helsingfors.

Abram Sarlin, seaman, capd off Scotland, 19 Oct. 1808, on privateer *Fremkomsten*, arr. G 8 Nov. 1808, dischgd to Helsingfors on (?) 22 May 1810.

Christian Andersen, seaman—as for Abram Sarlin.

Berent Andersen, seaman—as for Abram Sarlin.

The following appear to have been Finns who were sent to Chatham on 20 Jul. 1811 (and therefore probably *not* then released):

Jan Grinder, seaman, capd off Norway, 9 May 1811, on privateer *Klempa*, arr. G 17 May 1811.

G. Nettiness, seaman—as for Jan Grinder.

(c) **At Edinburgh Castle:** [Source: TNA ADM, 98/277, letter, 13 Aug. 1811, from TB to Capt. Heddington, its agent at the Castle.]

Although it seems very probable there was more than one Swede in captivity at the Castle during 1811, one specifically mentioned was Jean Talise, a 'native of Sweden', who was released in Aug. that year, having volunteered to join His Britannic Majesty's navy and serve on HMS *Nightingale* based at Leith.

(d) **At Valleyfield:** [Sources: TNA ADM 103/432, Nos 525-36; ADM 103/433, Nos 1104, 1105]

Fourteen Swedish seamen from privateers were all, except one, dischgd to Leith, on 5 Oct. 1811. The exception was No. 526 Matthew (or Mathias) Castelin (or Castellin), aged 41, capd on the privateer *Mameluke* off Dover, 28 Dec. 1810, who was said to have been 'Delivered to Swedish Consul, 28 Jul. 1812' and dischgd 28 Jul. 1813 [sic]. The other thirteen were:

No.525 Joseph Salin, seaman, aged 26—ship and details of capture as for Castelin.

No.527 Peter Askland, seaman, aged 20—ship and details of capture as for Castelin.

No.528 Keneth Berstrom, seaman, aged 28—ship and details of capture as for Castelin.

No.529 Jan Lindgwis, seaman, aged 56—ship and details of capture as for Castelin.

No.530 Jan Halstrom, seaman, aged 35, capd in North Sea, 17 Oct. 1810, on privateer *Héro du Nord.*

No.531 Joseph Hrmnitz, seaman, aged 23—ship and details of capture as for Halstrom.

No.532 William Nillson, seaman, aged 19, capd in North Sea, 17 Oct. 1810, on privateer *Roy de Naples.*

No.533 L. Peter Sodeystrom, seaman, aged 19—ship and details of capture as for Nillson.

No.534 William Dodricksen, seaman, aged 36, capd in the English Channel, 7 Dec. 1810, on a prize to the privateer *Le Petit Rodeur.*

No.535 Torras Sickstrom, seaman, aged 32, capd, n.p., .n.d., on a prize to the privateer *Josephine.*

No.536 Mathew Borgeson, seaman, aged 18, capd in the English Channel, 17 Oct. 1810, on the privateer *Aventurier.*

No. 1104 François Hendriks, aged 28—ship and details of capture as for Borgeson.

No. 1105 Hans Anderson, aged 26—ship and details of capture as for Castelin.

A letter of 12 Sep. 1812 (in TNA ADM 98/279) from the Transport Board to Capt. A. Brown, agent, Valleyfield, asking him to report on the case of Matthew Castelin, referred also to Eric Murberg and Carl Sandill, two other Swedish subjects said to be at Valleyfield; but no more information about these two men has been found.

(e) and (f): **At Esk Mills and at Perth:**

The 14 Swedish prisoners listed above at Valleyfield had all come there on 11 March 1811 from Esk Mills, and from the latter there may have been some other Swedes marched also that day to Edinburgh Castle. No evidence has been found of the presence of Swedes among the prisoners at Perth, but that does not necessarily mean none were there. As Swedish prisoners identified at the other Scots depots were virtually all seamen, the relatively small number of seamen, compared with soldiers, at Perth depot suggests that if any Swedes were indeed there it is unlikely they numbered more than one or two.

As late as Oct. 1813 a letter (in TNA ADM 1/3765, FOL. 480-4, 18 Oct. 1813) from the Transport Board to the Admiralty reported there were in the depots in Britain 157 prisoners who were Swedes—but none of them appeared to be then in Scots depots.

Appendix 8

MARKS OR WOUNDS

The following is a random selection from the actual descriptions recorded in the Entry Books of the depots in Scotland concerning prisoners' marks and wounds. (Sources: TNA ADM 103/153, Nos. 1-45, 352-431; ADM 103/157 passim; ADM 103/124, Nos. 1-192 passim; ADM 103/112 passim; ADM 103/114 passim; ADM 103/432, /433, /434, /435 passim; ADM 103/113, Nos. 6445-7479 passim; ADM 103/263, /264, /265, /266 passim).

Scar under Chin; Smallpox; Scar under Left Eye; Hump Back; Smallpox, little; Scar Forehead; Hare Lip; Small Pox much; Wants Parts of both Fore Fingers; lisps; squints

Left Eye; wrinkled; Moles on right Cheek; Mole on right Cheek and lost 1st Joint from Finger right Hand; large Cut left Side of Mouth; freckles; lost front Teeth; Mark left Eye; Smallpox and Mole right Side of Chin; Mark over right Side Eye; Mark left Side of Nose; Mark on both Eyes; 2 Moles on right Cheek; Cut first Finger right Hand; roundshouldered; sore Eyes; Pimples Right side Nose; Ruptured; Only one Eye, Scar left Cheek; Red Whiskers; flat Nose; Lost front Teeth upper Jaw; long Nose; Bridge of Nose broken; Blindness left Eye; Bald; Lame right Arm; Wound left Leg; Squints right Eye; Scar Throat; Lame 3rd Finger left Hand; Squints and smallpox a little; Blind left Eye and Smallpox; wounded Wrist; lost Joint of middle Finger, left Hand; Smallpox a little and a Large Nose; Smallpox and Bald; Wants 2 Fingers Left Eye; Dimples Cheek; Lost Use of left Arm; Hair very thin; Very hoarse in Speech; Lost left Thumb; Smallpox; Blind left Eye; Wounded right Arm; Maimed right Hand; Wounded right Arm; Wound in Breast; broken Hip; Wound in right Knee; right Arm broken; lame in left Foot; Wounded in left Arm; left Arm broke; Wound near left Ear; Wounds in Head; Lump on left Eye; wants left Thumb; scar over the left Eyebrow; ruptured (also smallpox); Great Hoarscress; Scar on Forehead; right Leg amputated; Mole upper Lip; Scar right Side of Mouth; Scar left Side Nose; Right Hand and Left Knee; Wound left Leg; Speckle, Corner of left Eye; crooked Nose; Cut Nose; blind left eye, diff. Wos Body [different wounds on body]; wound right Thigh; bald Spot back Head; Wound left Side; Scar Neck; Contusion Nose and Freckles; Moles and Freckles; fractured Nose; scar Face, Head partly bald; Scar right Temple; Wound Shoulder; Wound left Leg; Wound Head; Wound right Hand; Wound left Hand; Wound left Arm; wounded Hands; Wound left Leg and Freckles; Scar under right Ear; Moles under Lip; Mole Forehead; Wound right Knee; lost front Tooth; Wounds Head and Back; Wound Thighs; Wound right left; Wound Neck, cut Ear; Cut on Head and left Hand; Wound left Foot; Wound right Breast; left Shoulder broken; Cut on Chin; Wounded slightly right Shoulder; Wound Side Shoulder and Head; lost Finger right Hand; Cuts left Hand and Mouth; Wounded right Hand and left Thigh; large Nose; Wound Ankle; Wants two of his Teeth in front above; Mark back of right Hand; Wound left Elbow; Wants left Hand; greyish Eyes with black Spots on the Eyeballs; wounded in right Eye; Blind left Eye and Cut under right Eye; wants fore Teeth; red Mark on Nose; wants little Toe left Foot; lost right Hand; wound Nose; Gunpowder Marks in Face; first Joint of Fore Finger [sic]; Marked Face; left Knee broke; Wound on the Belly; little Finger on left Hand crooked; Very Deaf; wounded Finger on left Hand; Wound right Foot; Wound right Hip; Lost the Top of Fore Finger right Hand; Musquet Ball through Calf of right Leg; Ball through left Thigh; Wart on right Cheek; Mark on the right and left Cheek; Marked on right Thumb; Red Mark right Hand; Scar right and left Legs; Wounds Neck Face and Back; Smallpox, cut left Eye, squints; Cut upper Lip and left Wrist; Cut left Fore Finger; Several Moles on Face; Summer Freckled; Lost second Finger left Hand; Wart Corner left Eye; Blind left Eye and different Wounds on Body; Pockmarked and Moles; Wants 1st Joint 3rd Finger left Hand; Short right Thigh; Lost Points of Toes left Foot; Wants half right Ear and Wound right Hand; Lost part of both Forefingers; Wants 2nd Finger left Hand; Hernia; Wound both legs; Bald Forehead; Variety of Marks on Breast and Arms particularly the left on which is the word Mariette, strongly marked on Nose with Smallpox; Anchor on right Hand; Long Nose; Little Finger contracted; Hair very thin; The Top of the Thumb of his left Hand cut off; Excrescence right Side of Nose; Wounded left Leg, wounded Head; Blind right Eye, Ruptured; Wounded Body and left Foot; Wounded both Legs; Wounded right Ankle; Wounded right Leg and Thigh and different Parts of Body; Scar on Finger; Wounded Breast; Wounded left Hand severely; Mole on Hip; Wounded in

Head and Body; Wounded in the Face; Wounded Ears; Lame of right Leg; Pimples on the Chin; Lame of left Foot; Broken Thigh; Roman Nose; Broad Nose; Cast Eye; Lost his right Eye; Large Lump in the Chin; Brown Speck in each Eye; Two Scars on Breast; Ball under Chin, speaks Thick; Crooked Nose; Scrofula.

Appendix 9

THE HEIGHTS OF 7,322 PRISONERS AT VALLEYFIELD, AS SHOWN IN THE DEPOT'S ENTRY BOOKS:

[Sources: TNA ADM 103/432, /433, /434, /435, /113 (Nos 6445-7479), and /436].

Height	No. of prisoners	Height	No. of prisoners	Height	No. of prisoners
6 ft 4 ins:	1	5 ft 7½ ins:	258	5 ft 1½ ins:	60
6 ft 3 ins:	2	5 ft 7¼ ins:	42	5 ft 1¼ ins:	4
6 ft 2 ins:	4	5 ft 7 ins:	615	5 ft 1 in:	102
6 ft 1½ ins:	2	5 ft 6¾ ins:	51	5 ft 0¾ ins:	7
6 ft 1 in:	6	5 ft 6½ ins:	347	5 ft 0½ in:	26
6 ft 0½ in:	5	5 ft 6¼ ins:	46	5 ft 0¼ in:	2
6 ft 0¼ in:	1	5 ft 6 ins:	806	5 ft:	83
6 ft:	22	5 ft 5¾ ins:	59	4 ft 11¾ ins:	1
5 ft 11½ ins:	8	5 ft 5½ ins:	371	4 ft 11½ ins:	4
5 ft 11¼ ins:	4	5 ft 5¼ ins:	59	4 ft 11 ins:	24
5 ft 11 ins:	49	5 ft 5 ins:	751	4 ft 10½ ins:	2
5 ft 10¾ ins:	4	5 ft 4¾ ins:	60	4 ft 10 ins:	10
5 ft 10½ ins:	47	5 ft 4½ ins:	357	4 ft 9 ins:	6
5 ft 10¼ ins:	8	5 ft 4¼ ins:	45	4 ft 8 ins:	5
5 ft 10 ins:	115	5 ft 4 ins:	677	4 ft 7 ins:	3
5 ft 9¾ ins:	5	5 ft 3¾ ins:	42	4 ft 6½ ins:	1
5 ft 9½ ins:	77	5 ft 3½ ins:	238	4 ft 6 ins:	2
5 ft 9¼ ins:	18	5 ft 3¼ ins:	29	4 ft 5½ ins:	2
5 ft 9 ins:	264	5 ft 3 ins:	391	4 ft 4 ins:	1
5 ft 8¾ ins:	20	5 ft 2¾ ins:	22	4 ft 3½ ins:	1
5 ft 8½ ins:	158	5 ft 2½ ins:	127		
5 ft 8¼ ins:	23	5 ft 2¼ ins:	22		
5 ft 8ins:	425	5 ft 2 ins:	246		
5 ft 7¾ ins:	38	5 ft 1¾ ins:	9	*Total:*	**7,322**

Appendix 10

THE PRISONERS' RATIONS AND DIET

(1) **Comments on the prisoners' rations in the Scots depots, by Michael Clapham, Lecturer Nutrition, Queen Margaret University College, Edinburgh:**

5 days

Bread (wholemeal) 1½ lb (675g)	3,375g
Fresh beef ½ lb (225g)	1,125g
Barley 1 oz (28g)	140g
Onion ¼ oz (7g)	35g
Cabbage 8 oz (225g) x 3	675g
or	
Turnip 8 oz (225g) x 2	450g
Salt 1/3 oz (9g)	45g

2 days

Bread (wholemeal) 1½ lb (675g.)	1,350g
Potatoes 1 lb (450g)	900g
Herring 1 lb (450g) x 1	450g
Cod fish 1 lb (450g) x 1	450g

I have taken 1 oz to be equal to 28 grammes.

I have calculated the nutritional composition of the above rations or diet of the prisoners by calculating 7 days' intake and then dividing by 7 to give an average daily intake. This is assuming the prisoners received all their rations.

Overall, the diet of the prisoners is low in energy, riboflavin, and very low in Vitamin A, these having respectively only 45 per cent and 5.5 per cent of each prisoner's nutrient intake. The energy content of these rations would provide only 80 per cent of the daily requirement of 2,550 Kcals of energy per day for a sedentary, non-active male. Each man's energy requirement varies according to his level of activity and his basal metabolic rate. Due to the assumed very low levels of activity of the prisoners, however, it is difficult to say just how much of their individual body weight the men on these rations would lose. We can safely say that the vast majority of the men in the prison depots would be extremely thin.

Riboflavin deficiency would be relatively common amongst the prisoners. The symptoms that would be seen would include angular stomatitis (cracks and redness at the corners of the mouth). The deficiency could also lead to anaemia due to riboflavin's interaction with other vitamins. This would not be fatal but would grind the men down into a low level of health status and leave them feeling very lethargic.

With an estimated intake of 38 μg of vitamin A (reference nutrient intake being 700 μg), a deficiency in that vitamin would be common amongst the prisoners. The main symptoms of vitamin A deficiency are night blindness, changes in skin, and reduced resistance to infection. In the early times of nutritional science vitamin A was termed the 'anti-infective' vitamin, based on the increased number of infections noted in vitamin A deficient animals and humans. Vitamin A is required to maintain healthy epithelial cells (which line many of our tissues), that help fight infection by preventing the invasion of bacteria and viruses. Vitamin A also plays a direct role in the immune system itself. In the lungs, for example, the lining cells are unable to remove micro-organisms, cells that fight infection are less able to do so, and therefore the body as a whole is less able to fight infection. What I would expect to see in these prisoners would be an increased rate of infections, particularly chest infections such as tuberculosis, but also diarrhoea.

(2) **The 'Established Diet' for prisoners of war at Norman Cross depot hospital during the Napoleonic Wars**, extracted from T.J. Walker, *The Depot for Prisoners of War at Norman Cross, Huntingdonshire, 1796-1816* (London, 1915), 169-70:

'1st. Full Diet: Tea, or water-gruel with salt, for breakfast, the same for supper. Meat 12 oz., with potatoes or greens, and 1 pint of broth, for dinner. Bread 14 oz., sugar 2oz., beer 2 pints (of beer at 16s. the 38 gallons), and if any other drink is wanted, water, or toast and water.

'2nd. Reduced Diet: Tea, or water-gruel with salt, for breakfast; the same for supper. Meat 6 oz., with potatoes or greens, and 1 pint of broth, for dinner. Sugar 2 oz. The same quantity and quality of bread and beer as on full diet.

'3rd. Low Diet: Water-gruel or tea for breakfast. Water-gruel or barley-water for dinner. The same or rice-water for supper. Bread 7 oz. Patients on low diet are supposed to require no stated meal, drinks only being allowable, or even desirable; a small quantity of beer may be given when anxiously wished for and permitted by their surgeon. The bread is supposed to be chiefly for toast and water, or, should the patient incline, a bit of toasted bread without butter, with a little of his gruel or tea. Sugar 2 oz.

'4th. Milk Diet: Milk, 1 pint, for breakfast. Rice-milk, 1 pint-and-a-half (sweetened with sugar when desired), for dinner. Milk, 1 pint, for supper. Bread 14 oz. Drink—water, barley-water or rice-water. Sugar 2 oz.

'5th. Mixed Diet: Milk, 1 pint, for breakfast. Meat, 4 oz., with potatoes or greens, and 1 pint of broth, for dinner. Milk, 1 pint, for supper. Bread 14 oz. Drinks as on milk diet. Sugar 2 oz. Beer 1 pint.

'Notes: The meat mentioned in the different diets to be beef and mutton alternately. Should any patient particularly require a mutton-chop or beefsteak, instead of either the beef or mutton boiled and made into broth, the surgeon may direct it accordingly. The Matron is allowed to purchase ripe fruit, or any other article not comprehended in the several diets, by permission and direction of the surgeon. Sago, when particularly ordered by the surgeon, will be furnished in the quantity equal to the value of one day's ordinary diet, but then for that day the matron is to supply nothing else, save toast and water, water-gruel or barley-water, and any bread which may be ordered by the surgeon. No beer is to be issued to any patient in the hospital until after dinner, unless particularly ordered by his surgeon, and no patient is allowed to give his allowance of beer to another, for when he does not choose the whole, or any part of it, it is to remain with the matron.'

Appendix 11

PRISONERS WHO DIED IN CAPTIVITY IN THE SCOTS DEPOTS

Details, contradictory and varying in fullness between sources as they sometimes are, of those prisoners of war who died are presented here in chronological order of their deaths, depot by depot. The details are drawn from the General Entry Books of the depots and from surviving proforma returns of deaths sent weekly or at other intervals from the depots to the Transport Office in London. The surviving returns are in TNA ADM 103/624 and ADM 103/648; and where these give a serial or entry number for a prisoner it is, unless otherwise stated below, the same as his number in the Entry Book. The special list concerning Valleyfield compiled in March 1821 by the Victualling Department of the Admiralty, and which is now preserved in the National Archives of Scotland (NAS), provides several names additional to those in the Entry Books. Although that 1821 list purports to contain 309 names, the compiler omitted listing any between Nos. 181 and 189 inclusive; hence its actual total is 300, not 309. The spelling, generally preserved as it appears in the sources, of some names and places of birth is not infrequently phonetic. For abbreviations and contractions used, see above, p.ix.

GREENLAW

1. Alexander Linde, seaman, 18, b. Denmark, capd 10 May 1804 on *L'Union* Dutch brig of war, North Sea, arr. G 16 May 1804, d. 18 Jun. 1804: 'consumption, occasioned by a fall from the main mast of *L'Union*.' TNA ADM 103/154, No. 53; ADM 103/648.

2. Cornelius Loorsen, seaman, 36, p.o.b. u., capd n.d. on *Contents Increase*, a prize to *Contre Amiral Majon* priv., 'off Foleybridge', arr. G 17 Nov. 1804 from Greenock, d. 15 Apr. 1805: consumption. TNA ADM 103/155, No. 155; ADM 103/624.

3. Alexandre Sec, seaman, 44, b. Cassel, capd n.d. on *Vigilant* m.o.w. in the West Indies, arr. G 16 Mar. 1805 from Greenock, d. 16 Sep. 1805: consumption. TNA ADM 103/155, No.171; ADM 103/624.

4. Jean Flouret, seaman, b. Barcelona, capd Mar. 1804 on *Félicité* priv. in the West Indies (Cuba?), arr. G 24 Sep. 1805 from Greenock, d. 18 Oct. 1805: consumption. TNA ADM 103/155, No.215; ADM 103/624.

5. François Couvertier, seaman, priv. *Gascoungade*, arr. G 3 Mar. 1806, d. 20 May 1806, cause of death unstated. TNA ADM 103/115, No. 40.

6. Jean Laxal (or Lascal), seaman, 30, capd Jul. 1803 on a fishing boat at St Pierre, Newfoundland (or n.d. on an u. ship in the West Indies), arr. G 2 Aug. 1805, d. 13 Jul. 1806: consumption. TNA ADM 103/155, No. 199; ADM 103/624.

7. Charles Cottier (or Cotier), seaman, 19, b. Dunkirk, capd 11 Jul. 1803 on *Elizabeth* m.v. in the North Sea, arr. G 31 Mar. 1804 from Edinburgh bridewell, d. 8 Jan. 1807 '... in consequence of a shot fired in the prison.' TNA ADM 103/155, No. 7; ADM 103/624.

8. Pierre Gachigarre, seaman, 35, b. Saintes, capd 30 Nov. 1803 on *Clorinde* frig. in the West Indies, arr. G 22 Jul. 1804, d. 12 Apr. 1807: consumption. TNA ADM 103/155, No. 105; ADM 103/624.

9. F.F. Xavier Frederic, 2nd lieut., 51, b. Dunkirk, capd 26 Jan. 1807 on *Adolphe* priv. in the North Sea, arr. G 4 Feb. 1807, d. 25 Sep. 1807: consumption. TNA ADM 103/155, No. 287; ADM 103/624.

10.   Ollivier Offier (or Offret), seaman, 37, b. Lorient, capd 25 Jul. 1803 on *Duquesne* m.o.w. off St Domingo, arr. G 19 Aug. 1804, d. 29 Jan. 1808: consumption. TNA ADM 103/155, No.119; ADM 103/624; ADM 103/648.

11.   Jean Genaudeau (or Genodeau), seaman, 36, b. Department of Nantes, capd n.d. on *Cerf* m.o.w. in the West Indies, arr. G 22 Jul. 1804, d. 14 Mar. 1808: consumption. TNA ADM 103/155, No.104; ADM 103/624; ADM 103/648.

12.   Jorgen Blank, Boy, 20, p.o.b. u., capd 30 Mar. 1808 on *Gordenskiold* priv. off Norway, arr. G 6 Apr. 1808, d. 27 Apr. 1808: 'Consumption of the lungs.' TNA ADM 103/152, No. 160; ADM 103/648.

13.   Jean Ayrand (or Airo, or Aycand), seaman, 39, b. Bordeaux, capd 6 Feb. 1806 on *Jupiter* m.o.w. off St Domingo, arr. G 30 Aug. 1806 from Greenock, d. 20 May 1808: consumption. TNA ADM 103/155, No. 243; ADM 103/624; ADM 103/648 (which says he died on 20 Aug. 1808).

14.   Pierre Jacques Senne, seaman, 35, p.o.b. u., capd Jul. 1804 on *La Liberté* priv. off Jamaica, arr. G 24 Sep.1805 from Greenock, d. 10 Jul. 1808: consumption. TNA ADM 103/155, No.206; ADM 103/624; ADM 103/648 (where cause of death is given as 'uncertain').

15.   Etienne Girot, seaman, 22, b.Toulon, capd 25 Jul. 1803 on *Duquesne* m.o.w. off St Domingo, arr. G 19 Aug. 1804, d. 6 Aug. 1808: 'cause uncertain'. TNA ADM 103/155, No. 129 (which says he had 'been brought from the Prison Ship at Jamaica to the Clyde'); ADM 103/624; ADM 103/648 (Both latter sources say Girot was capd in the *East* Indies, which is incorrect if he was on the *Duquesne*).

16.   Lars Arneson, Boy, 18, b. Norway, capd 27 Jul. 1808 on *Christiania* priv. in the North Sea, arr. G 6 (or 10) Aug. 1808, d. 9 Sep. 1808: 'cause of death uncertain'. TNA ADM 103/152, No.332; ADM 103/648.

17.   Berent Jacobsen, seaman (or quartermaster), 35, b. Copenhagen, capd 26 Jan. 1807 on *Adolphe* priv. in the North Sea, arr. G 4 Feb. 1807, d. 15 Sep. 1808: consumption. TNA ADM 103/155, No. 296; ADM 103/624; ADM 103/648 (which says cause of death 'uncertain').

18.   Jean Verron (or Verren), seaman, 26, p.o.b. u., capd 6 Feb. 1806 on *Brave* m.o.w. off St Domingo, arr. G 7 Oct. 1806, d. 30 Nov. 1808: consumption. TNA ADM 103/155, No. 259; ADM 103/624; ADM 103/648.

19.   Surns Sandersen, seaman, 25, p.o.b. u., capd 19 Oct. 1808 on *Fremskomisten* priv. off Scotland, arr. G 8 Nov. 1808, d. 1 (or 2) Feb. 1809: consumption. TNA ADM 103/152, No. 408; ADM 103/648.

20.   Niels Wilkensen, 30, b. Norway, master m.v. *Vron Christina*, capd 1 Aug. 1808 off Jutland, arr. G 19 Sep. 1808, d. 9 Mar. 1809: 'cause uncertain'. TNA ADM 103/152, No. 350; ADM 103/648.

21.   Jean Loiserel [or Loizeret or Loireret], soldier, 33, p.o.b. u., capd n.d. on *Mary Ann* trans. in the West Indies, arr. G 31 Mar. (or 18 June) 1804, d. 16 Mar. 1809: consumption. TNA ADM 103/155, No. 102; ADM 103/624; ADM 103/648.

22.   Jan de Rymer, seaman, 23, p.o.b. u., capd 18 Apr. 1809 off Jutland on a ship capd by *Prosper* priv., arr. G 9 Mar. 1809, d. 15 May 1809, '…in consequence of a shot fired, attempting to make his escape.' TNA ADM 103/152, No. 514; ADM 103/648.

23.   Andreas Embroug, seaman, 23, p.o.b. u., capd 22 Jul. 1809 on *Maria Catherina* m.v. off Norway, arr. G 14 Aug. 1809, d. 18 Nov. 1809: 'Hymaptisis and of spitting of blood.' TNA ADM 103/152, No. 603; ADM 103/648.

24. Rasmus Hemmingsen, seaman, 21, b. Copenhagen, capd 5 Sep. 1807 on *Fryhling* m.v. off Norway, arr. G 12 Nov. 1807, d. 21 Dec.1809: consumption. TNA ADM 103/152, No. 47; ADM 103/648.

25. Simon Simonsen, seaman, age and p.o.b. n.k., capd 30 Mar. 1808 on *Gordenskiold* priv. off Norway, arr. G 6 Apr. 1808, d. 30 Jul. 1810, shot in the head by a sentry. TNA ADM 103/152, No. 137.

26. Volkert Ares, seaman, 54, b. Amsterdam, capd 26 Oct. 1810 on 'ship uncertain' in the North Sea, arr. G 17 Nov. 1810, d. 17 Dec. 1810: consumption. TNA ADM 103/152, No. 859; ADM 103/648.

27. Jean Lambert, volunteer, 19, b. Dieppe, capd 17 Oct. 1810 on *Vengeur* priv. in the English Channel, arr. G date n.k., d. 11 Jan. 1811: typhus fever. TNA ADM 103/648, No.522. (Lambert has not been found in the Greenlaw Entry Books TNA ADM 103/155 or ADM 103/157).

28. A.M. Lagarde, soldier, 15th line regt, 22, b. Rouen, capd 13 Apr. 1810 (Marshal) 'Massena's army' (n.p., but Portugal or Spain), arr. G date n.k., d. 12 Jan. 1811: typhus fever. TNA ADM 103/648, unnumbered. (Lagarde has not been found in the Greenlaw Entry Books TNA ADM 103/155 or ADM 103/157).

29. Louis Picard, volunteer, 26, b. Picardy, capd 17 Oct. 1810 on *Vengeur* priv. in the English Channel, arr. G date n.k., d. 19 Jan. 1811: typhus fever. TNA ADM 103/648, No. 553. (Picard has not been found in the Greenlaw Entry Books TNA ADM 103/155 or ADM 103/157).

30. Peder Skophamer, seaman, 27, b. Bergen, capd 30 Mar. 1808 on *Gordenskiold* priv. off Norway, arr. G 6 Apr. 1808, d. 19 Feb. 1811: cause of death unstated. TNA ADM 103/152, No. 123; ADM 103/648.

31. Bore Sunderberg, 42, b. Copenhagen, 2nd capt. of *Drestyhaden* priv., capd 6 Oct. 1810 off Norway, arr. G 17 Nov. 1810, d. 21 Feb. 1811: apoplexy. TNA ADM 103/152, No. 824; ADM 103/648.

32. Jean Druet, seaman, 43 (or 46), b. Nantes, capd 6 Feb. 1806 on *Brave* m.o.w. off St Domingo, arr. G 14 Aug. 1811 from EC, d. 11 Oct. 1811: consumption. TNA ADM 103/157, No. 93; ADM 103/117, No. 92 (sic); ADM 103/624; ADM 103/648.

33. Jean Papau, soldier, 37, b. St Jean de Marienne, capd 4 Nov. 1805 on *Mont Blanc* m.o.w. off Cape Ortegal, arr. G 17 Nov. 1811 from V hospital, d. 20 Nov. 1811: phthisis. TNA ADM 103/157, Nos 371, 665 and 688; ADM 103/117, No. 688; ADM 103/648.

34. Nicolas Devilliers, soldier, 27, b. Besançon, capd 4 Mar. 1806 on *Volontaire* frig. at Cape of Good Hope, arr. G 30 Sep. 1811 from V hospital, d. 14 Mar.1812: consumption. TNA ADM 103/157, No. 668; ADM 103/117, No. 668; ADM 103/624; ADM 103/648.

35. Philippe [? Pierre] Savasse [or Lavasse], soldier, 'French army depot', 35, b. Piedmont, capd 21 Oct. 1805 at Trafalgar (or 4 Nov. 1805 at Cape Ortegal), arr. G 27 Feb. 1812 from V hospital, d. 26 May 1812: pulmonary consumption. TNA ADM 103/157, No. 700; ADM 103/117, No. 700; ADM 103/624; ADM 103/648.

36. Jean Baptiste Depotte [or Dechotte, Dechatte, or Dehotte], soldier, 'French army', 50, b. Constance (or Coutance), capd 4 Nov. 1805 on *Formidable* m.o.w. off Cape Ortegal, arr. G 26 Sep. 1811, d. 23 Jul. 1812: consumption. TNA ADM 103/157, No. 382; ADM 103/117, No. 382; ADM 103/624; ADM 103/648.

37. Pierre Antoine Bor, soldier, 'French army', 31, b. Falaise, capd 9 Oct. 1810 in Portugal, arr. G 26 Sep. 1811, d. 13 Aug. 1812: consumption. TNA ADM 103/157, No. 636; ADM 103/117, No. 636; ADM 103/624; ADM 103/648.

38. Jean Jacquet, soldier, 101st (or 22nd) line regt, 29, b. Piedmont, capd 7 Apr. 1812 at Badajoz (or 18 Jul. 1812 at Salamanca), arr. G 13 Nov. 1812, d. next day: fever. TNA ADM 103/110 (unnumbered); ADM 103/157, No. 789; ADM 103/117, No. 789; ADM 103/624.

39. Jacques Jerlan, cannonier, 'French army', 48, b. Paris, capd 18 Jul. 1812 at Salamanca, arr. G 13 Nov. 1812, d. 19 Nov. 1812: fever. TNA ADM 103/110 (unnumbered); ADM 103/157, No. 791; ADM 103/117, No. 791; ADM 103/624; ADM 103/648.

40. Antoine Leolle, soldier, 9th light infantry, 23, b. Piedmont, capd 7 Apr. 1812 at Badajoz, arr. G 30 Nov. 1812, d. 2 Dec. 1812: fever. TNA ADM 103/157, No. 839; ADM 103/117, No. 839; ADM 103/624.

41. Louis Lombrun, soldier, 105th line regt, 32, b. Piedmont (or Metz), capd 18 Jul. 1812 at Salamanca, arr. G 1 Dec. 1812, d. 5 Dec. 1812: dysentery. TNA ADM 103/110 (unnumbered); ADM 103/157, No. 869; ADM 103/117, No. 879; ADM 103/624; ADM 103/648.

42. Jean Baptiste Fenard (or Fenaro or Penarel), soldier, 76th line regt, 26, b. Metz, capd 18 Jul. 1812 at Salamanca, arr. G 30 Nov. 1812, d. 5 Dec. 1812: fever. TNA ADM 103/110 (unnumbered); ADM 103/117, No. 864; ADM 103/157, No. 864; ADM 103/624; ADM 103/648.

43. Louis Huguet (or Houguet), soldier, 28th light infantry, 28, b. Metz, capd 7 Apr. 1812 at Badajoz, arr. G 30 Nov. 1812, d. 6 Dec. 1812: fever. TNA ADM 103/157, No. 856; ADM 103/117, No. 856; ADM 103/624; ADM 103/648.

44. Pierre Colichet (or Collichet or Callichet), sergeant, 22nd line regt, 46, b. Bretagne, capd 18 Jul. 1812 at Salamanca, arr. G 1 Dec. 1812, d. 8 Dec. 1812: gangrene (or fever). TNA ADM 103/157, No. 884; ADM 103/117, No. 884; ADM 103/624; ADM 103/648.

45. Nicolas Devallé (or Devalle), maitre d'équipage (bosun), 46, b. Granville, capd 18 Feb. 1813 on *Le Ravisseur* priv. off Norway, arr. EC 8 Mar. 1813, sent 8 Jun. 1813 to Greenlaw hospital and d. there that same day: apoplexy. TNA ADM 103/114, No. 1259; ADM 103/117, No. 1259; TNA ADM 103/624; ADM 103/648.

ESK MILLS

1. Jean Moulin (or Meullin), soldier, 26, b. St Valery, capd 11 Oct. 1810 on *Somnambule* priv. off Le Tréport, arr. EM from Chatham 5 Feb. 1811, d. 10 Feb. 1811: dysentery. TNA ADM 103/124, No. 421; ADM 103/648.

2. Nicolas Boulet, 1st Lieut., 35, b. St Valery en Caux, capd n.d. on *Vengeur* priv. off Hastings, arr. EM from Chatham 7 Feb. 1811, d. 19 Feb. 1811 'at 2 o'clock in the Morning, Shot by a Centinel (sic) on duty in the act of Escaping with others.' TNA ADM 103/648, No. 1007; ADM 103/124, No. 458 (which gives: Henri Boulais, 1st lieut., *Le Barbier de Seville* priv., capd 16 Nov. 1810 off Norway).

3. Jean Ledieu, boats (bosun's?) mate, 52, b. Brest, capd 6 Feb. 1806 on *Jupiter* m.o.w. off St Domingo, arr. EM from Chatham 5 Feb. 1811, d. 20 Feb. 1811 'Suddenly in prison.' TNA ADM 103/124, No. 218; ADM 103/648.

4. Antoine Baillie, volunteer, 41, b. Dieppe, capd 17 Oct. 1810 on *Vengeur* priv. in the English Channel, arr. EM from G 4 Feb. 1811, d. 2 Mar. 1811: fever. TNA ADM 103/124, No. 67; ADM 103/117, No. 67; ADM 103/648.

5. Charles de Charles, seaman, priv. *Grand Napoléon*, (no other details given), d. 11 Mar. 1811: 'Trampled to Death this morning by the Prisoners in rushing to the doors on an alarm that the Prison was falling.' TNA ADM 103/648, unnumbered.

6. Eloy, soldier, 4th Regt of Marins (seamen). No other details given. Died 11 Mar. 1811: 'Trampled to Death this morning by the Prisoners in rushing to the doors on an alarm that the Prison was falling.' TNA ADM 103/648, unnumbered.

7. César Geneaux (or Genau or Genot), 2nd lieut. (or soldier), age and p.o.b. u., capd 2 Oct. 1808 on *Somnambule* priv. off Neivers, arr. EM from Chatham 5 Feb. 1811, d. 15 Mar. 1811: dysentery and fever. TNA ADM 103/124, No. 397; ADM 103/117, No. 397; ADM 103/648.

8. Jean Baptiste Pinson (or Puison), seaman, 21, b. Dieppe, capd 3 Jan. (or 3 Feb.) 1809 on *L'Iris* corvette in the North Sea, arr. EM 18 Feb. 1811, d. 23 Mar. 1811: 'Phthisis Pulmonatio.' TNA ADM 103/124, No. 1191; ADM 103/117, No.1191; ADM 103/648.

9. Christophe Andrée (or Charles Arnott or C. Arnol), seaman, 28, p.o.b. n.k., capd n.d. (or 19 Oct. 1808) on *Pylade* corvette at Cayen (Cayenne, French Guiana), arr. EM 18 Feb. 1811, d. 7 Apr. 1811: 'Deseased liver.' TNA ADM 103/124, No. 1255; ADM 103/117, No. 1255; ADM 103/648.

EDINBURGH CASTLE

1. Pierre Woemeseuil (or Wormeseul), midshipman, 20, b. Bordeaux, capd 28 Jul. 1808 on *Requin* brig-corvette off Corsica, arr. EC from EM 11 Mar. 1811, d. 14 Apr. 1811: 'Fractured Spine.' TNA ADM 103/112, No. 379; ADM 103/648.

2. Marius Ponchina (or Pinchina), Boy, 14, b. Marseilles, capd 2 May 1808 on *Jean Honore* naval sloop off Sicily, arr. EC from EM 11 Mar. 1811, d. 18 Apr. 1811: 'Abscess in the Lungs.' TNA ADM 103/112, No. 14; ADM 103/648.

3. Auguste Belisaire Bourignons, lieut., 65th line regt, 20, b. Saintes (or Santes), capd 15 Aug. 1809 at Flushing Fort, arr. EC from EM 11 Mar. 1811, d. 25 July 1811: ' betwixt the hours of 6 & 7 in the Morning By a wound from a fencing foil…' TNA ADM 103/112, No. 167; ADM 103/648.

4. Joseph Mulart, soldier, 26th line regt, 25, b. Quisnefage [? Quernifery], capd n.d. at Martinique, arr. EC from P 21 Dec. 1813, d. 28 Dec. 1813: phthisis. Buried at Greyfriars. TNA ADM 103/114, No. 1365; ADM 103/648.

   (See also above, No. 45, Nicolas Devalle, on the list of those who died at Greenlaw. Some evidence appears to suggest that Benois (or Benoit) Jordan (or Jourdant) died on 5 Jan. 1814 at Edinburgh Castle; but the weight of evidence indicates he died on that date at Valleyfield—see No. 256 on the Valleyfield entries below).

VALLEYFIELD

1. Sebastien Surina, seaman, 48 (or 56), b. Minorca, capd 21 Oct. 1810 on *Somnambule* priv. off Dieppe, arr. V from EM 11 Mar. 1811, d. 20 (or 21) Mar. 1811: 'Fever & Infirmity'. NAS Adm. list, 1821, No. 285; TNA ADM 103/432, No. 221, and ADM 103/648, No. 13.

2. Remi Barré (or Barri), seaman, 33 (or 28), b. Martinique (or 'St Jean de Lon near Dijon'), capd 1810 on *La Caroline* priv. off Jamaica (or Cuba), arr. V from EM 11 Mar. 1811, d. 26 Mar. 1811: pneumonia. NAS Adm. list, 1821, No.13; TNA ADM 103/432, No. 222, and ADM 103/648, No.16.

3.   Pierre Morin (or Morill), seaman, 35, b. Caen, capd 1810 on *La Caroline* priv. off Jamaica (or Cuba), arr. V from EM 11 Mar. 1811, d. 31 Mar. 1811: fever. NAS Adm. list, 1821, No.227; TNA ADM 103/432, No.223, and ADM 103/648, No.28.

4.   Nicolas Bruno, soldier, 82nd line regt, 26 (or 36), b. 'supposed near Fécamp', capd 24 Feb. 1809 at Martinique, arr. V from EM 11 Mar. 1811, d. 1 Apr. 1811: fever. NAS Adm. list, 1821, No.51; TNA ADM 103/432, No.224, and ADM 103/648, No.48.

5.   Clement Huteau, seaman, 18, b. Bordeaux, capd n.d. on *Le Décidé* priv. in the North Sea, arr. V from EM hospital 31 Mar.1811, d. 5 (or 9) Apr. 1811: pneumonia. NAS Adm. list, 1821, No. 153; TNA ADM 103/434, No. 2453 and ADM 103/648, No. 49.

6.   Mathias Guilers, seaman, 38, b. Livourne (or Livonia), capd n.d. on *La Stella* priv. in the Mediterranean, arr. V from EM hospital 31 Mar. 1811, d. 9 Apr. 1811: pneumonia. NAS Adm. list 1821, No.142; TNA ADM 103/434, No. 2454, and ADM 103/648, No. 55.

7.   Jean Jacques Gué (or Guet), soldier, 82nd line regt, 23, b. Salon, capd 24 Feb. 1809 at Martinique, arr. V from EM on 11 Mar. 1811, d. 10 Apr. 1811: pneumonia. NAS Adm. list, 1829, No. 139; TNA ADM 103/433, No.2050, and ADM 103/648, No. 70.

8.   William Sigala, seaman, 58, b. Amsterdam, capd n.d. on *Sans Souci* priv. in the English Channel, arr. V from EM hospital 31 Mar.1811, d. 13 Apr. 1811: fever. NAS Adm. list, 1829, No. 279; TNA ADM 103/434, No. 2455, and ADM 103/648, No. 83.

9.   Hubert Castillon (or Castellenau or Castellnan), lieut., aged 39, b. Calais (or St Pierre et Miquelon), capd 10 Oct. 1810 on *Téméraire* priv. in the English Channel, arr. V from EM 11 Mar.1811, d. 14 April 1811: fever. NAS Adm. list, 1821, No. 60, TNA ADM 103/432, No.166, and ADM 103/648, No.79.

10.   Pierre Alexis, soldier, 1st Colonial Bn, 28, p.o.b. n.k., captd 16 Aug. 1809 at Flushing, arr. V from EM 11 Mar. 1811, d. 19 Apr. 1811: fever. NAS Adm. list, 1821, No.2; TNA ADM 103/434, No. 2314, and ADM 103/648, No.72.

11.   Guillaume Terret, soldier, 82nd line regt, 24, b. Normandy, capd 24 Feb. 1809 at Martinique, arr. V from EM hospital 31 Mar. 1811, d. 23 Apr. 1811: fever. NAS Adm. list, 1821, No. 287; TNA ADM 103/434, No. 2456, and ADM 103/648, No.78.

12.   Henri (or Charles) Lantern (or Lendin, Lentin, or Lantein), seaman, 39, b. Dunkirk, capd 17 Oct. 1810 on *Le Vengeur* priv. in the English Channel, arr. V from EM 11 Mar. 1811, d. 25 Apr. 1811: 'suddenly in the Prison.' NAS Adm. list, 1821, No. 170; TNA ADM 103/434, No.2149, and ADM 103/648, No.1505.

13.   Isidore Boucherie (or Boussière), seaman, 30, b. Briançon, capd 21 Oct. 1805 on *Swiftsure* m.o.w. at Trafalgar, arr. V from EM hospital 31 Mar. 1811, d. 30 Apr. 1811: fever. NAS Adm. list, 1821, No. 40; TNA ADM 103/434, No. 2450, and ADM 103/648, No. 106.

14.   Jean Baptiste Teleque (or Telyca), prizemaster (or seaman), 54, b. Ghent, capd 14 Nov. 1807 on *Friedland* priv. in the North Sea, arr. V from EM 11 Mar. 1811, d. 1 (or 2) May 1811: fever. NAS Adm. list, 1821, No. 288; TNA ADM 103/434, No.2250, and ADM 103/648, No.80.

15.   Léonard Riviere, seaman, 45, b. Libourne, capd n.d. on *Le Huron* priv. at St Domingo, arr. V from EM hospital 31 Mar. 1811, d. 7 May 1811: fever. NAS Adm. list, 1821, No. 262; TNA ADM 103/434, No. 2457, and ADM 103/648, No.21.

16.   Jean Cabon, seaman, 25, b. Gascony, capd n.d. on *Friedland* m.o.w. in the North Sea, arr. V from EM hospital 31 Mar. 1811, d. 7 May 1811: fever. NAS Adm. list, 1821, No. 52; TNA ADM 103/434, No.2458, and ADM 103/648, No.110

17.   Jean Corderon, soldier, 32nd line regt, 24, p.o.b. n.k., capd n.d. in Portugal, arr. V from EM hospital 31 Mar. 1811, d. 8 May 1811: fever. NAS Adm. list, 1821, No. 76; TNA ADM 103/434, No.2459, and ADM 103/648, No.54.

18.   Charles Chastel, seaman, 60, b. Morlaix, capd 10 Oct. 1810 on *Le Téméraire* priv. off Brest (or in the English Channel), arr. V from EM hospital 31 Mar. 1811, d. 18 May 1811: 'General Debility, Phthisis.' NAS Adm. list, 1821, No. 65; TNA ADM 103/434, No. 2460, and ADM 103/648, No.105.

19.   Jean Brasset (or Brosset), soldier, 6th line regt, 23, b. Perigord (or Deuville—Deauville?), capd 5 Nov. 1807 on *La Providence* m.v. off Corfu, arr. V from EM 11 Mar. 1811, d. 22 May 1811: 'hipatitis.' NAS Adm. list, 1821, No.44; TNA ADM 103/433, No.1805, and ADM 103/648, No.176.

20.   Gilles Pierre Cadet, seaman, 34, b. La Rochelle, capd 6 Feb. 1806 on *La Vertu* frig. off St Domingo, arr. V from EM 11 Mar. 1811, d. 31 May 1811: phthisis. NAS Adm. list, 1821, No.55; TNA ADM 103/434, No.2448, and ADM 103/648.

21.   Yves Pierre, seaman, 36, b. Brittany, capd 10 Jul. 1806 on *La Guerrière* frig. off Faroe, arr. V from EM 11 Mar. 1811, d. 31 May 1811: cutans. NAS Adm. list, 1821, No.245; TNA ADM 103/433, No.2136, and ADM 103/648.

22.   Jean Vandercourt (or Fandercort), soldier, 5th Dutch regt (or Dutch Cavalry), 39, b. Amsterdam, capd 2 Aug. 1809 at Flushing, arr. V from EM 11 Mar. 1811, d. 2 Jun. 1811: apoplexy. NAS Adm. list, 1821, No. 297; TNA ADM 103/434, No.2215, and ADM 103/648.

23.   Guillaume Croisat, seaman, 31, b. Bessières, capd 21 Oct. 1805 on *Berwicke* m.o.w. at Trafalgar, arr. V from EM 11 Mar. 1811, d. 4 Jun. 1811: phthisis. NAS Adm. list, 1821, No.81; TNA ADM 103/434, No. 2447, and ADM 103/648.

24.   Jean Menesse (or Menese or Menesel), soldier, 27th Chasseurs, 21, b. Morlaix, capd 15 Aug. 1809 at Flushing, arr. V from EM 11 Mar. 1811, d. 12 Jul. 1811: phthisis pulmonales. NAS Adm. list, 1821, No. 213; TNA ADM 103/432, No.1036, and ADM 103/648.

25.   Jean Charles Duquesne, seaman, 26, b. St Valery, capd 29 Oct. 1807 on *Le Requin* priv. in the English Channel, arr. V from EM 11 Mar. 1811, d. 18 Jul. 1811: hepatitis. NAS Adm. list, 1821, No. 104; TNA ADM 103/432, No.363, and ADM 103/648.

26.   Dominique Caujeon (or Conjon), soldier, 3rd Italian (or light infantry) regt, 24, b. Terasso, capd 26 Aug. 1809 at Fort Cortillas, arr. V from EM 11 Mar. 1811, d. 3 Aug. 1811: dysentery. NAS Adm. list, 1829, No.61; TNA ADM 103/434, No.2483, and ADM 103/648.

27.   Jean Joseph Canivet, seaman, 45, b. Brest, capd 25 Apr. 1806 on *Finisterre* priv. off Finisterre, arr. V from EM on 11 Mar. 1811, d. 10 Aug. 1811: fever and debility. NAS Adm. list, 1821, No. 56; TNA ADM 103/434, No. 2428, and ADM 103/648.

28.   Bernard Henault (or Heneau), 34, b. Alavet, master at arms (or soldier, 1st Artillery), capd 26 Mar. 1805 on *Le Voltigeur* priv., n.p., arr. V from EM 11 Mar. 1811, d. 23 Aug. 1811: fever. NAS Adm. list, 1821, No. 146; TNA ADM 103/433, No. 2029, and ADM 103/648.

29.   George Audinot (or Aubino), soldier, 12th cavalry regt, 24, b. Montreux (or Montreaux), capd 27 Dec. 1807 (sic—1809?) in Spain, arr. V from EM 11 Mar. 1811, d.

26 Aug. 1811: debility. NAS Adm. list, 1821, No. 9; TNA ADM 103/434, No.2232, and ADM 103/648.

30. Giovanni Boldrini, soldier, 3rd Italian regt, 20, b.Verona, capd 27 Aug. 1809 in the Gulf of Venice, arr. V from EM 11 Mar. 1811, d. 6 Sep.1811: pneumonia. NAS Adm. list, 1821, No.34; TNA ADM 103/434, No.2173, and ADM 103/648, No.2149.

31. François Favet, seaman, 22, b. St Malo, capd 19 Jul. 1808 on *Le Serpent* m.o.w. in the North Sea, arr. V from EM 11 Mar. 1811, d. 23 Sep. 1811: phthisis. NAS Adm. list, 1821, No.107; TNA ADM 103/433, No. 1517, and ADM 103/648.

32. François Forteau, seaman, 28, b.Toulon, capd 21 Oct. 1805 on *L'Intrépide* m.o.w. at Trafalgar, arr. V from EM hospital 31 Mar. 1811, d. 28 Sep. 1811: phthisis. NAS Adm. list, 1821, No. 115; TNA ADM 103/434, No.2484, and ADM 103/648.

33. Nicolas Bertaux, seaman, 20, b. Grand Caen (or Grandeau), capd 24 Feb. 1809 on *L'Amphitrite* frig. at Martinique, arr. V from EM 11 Mar. 1811, d. 2 Oct. 1811: phthisis. NAS Adm. list, 1821, No. 26; TNA ADM 103/433, No. 1425, and ADM 103/648.

34. Pierre François Stevano, soldier, 82nd line regt, 30, b. Dole, capd 24 Feb. 1809 on Martinique, arr. V from Plymouth 2 Sep. 1811, d. 19 Nov. 1811: 'suddenly in convalescent ward'. NAS Adm. list, 1821, No. 283; TNA ADM 103/434, No. 2851, and ADM 103/648.

35. Julien Manecan (or Manceau or Mancau), drummer, 15th (or 16th) line regt, 20, b. Vitré, capd 7 Jul. 1810 in Spain, arr. V from Plymouth c. 7 Oct. 1811, d. 20 Nov. 1811: 'hanged himself in a Fit of Derangement'. NAS Adm. list, 1821, No. 205; TNA ADM 103/435, No. 4331, and ADM 103/648, No. 4331. [NB: The death certificate gives that as the cause of death, while the Valleyfield Entry Book does not record Manecan's death at all but says he was released from there on 14 Jun. 1814.]

36. Henri Sertier, soldier, 26th line regt, 34, b. Isle of Bourbon (Réunion), capd 24 Feb. 1809 on Martinique, arr. V from Plymouth c. 7 Oct. 1811, d. 22 Nov. 1811: phthisis. NAS Adm. list, 1821, No.278; TNA ADM 103/648, No. 4379.

37. Etienne (or Pierre) Masurier, soldier, 2nd line (or light infantry) regt, 25, b. St Disant Conac, capd 7 Oct. 1808 in Portugal, arr. V from EM 11 Mar. 1811, d. 4 Dec. 1811: dysentery. NAS Adm. list, 1821, No. 210; TNA ADM 103/433, No. 1694, and ADM 103/648.

38. George Leonard (or Leonard Iet), soldier, 82nd line regt, 33, b. Moyran, capd 24 Feb. 1809 on Martinique, arr. V from Plymouth 2 Sep. 1811, d. 4 Dec. 1811: pneumonia. NAS Adm. list, 1821, No. 194; TNA ADM 103/434, No.2693; ADM 103/648. [NB: The death certificate gives the cause of death, while the Valleyfield Entry Book does not record Leonard's/Iet's death at all but says he was released from captivity on 8 Jun. 1814].

39. Jean Sausse, seaman, 34, b. Dunkirk, capd on *Le Mameluke* priv. off Dover, 10 Dec. 1810, arr. V from EM 11 Mar. 1811, d. 8 Dec. 1811: enteritis. NAS Adm. list, 1821, No. 276; TNA ADM 103/433, No. 1730, and ADM 103/648.

40. Jean Charpentier, seaman, 50, b. Nantes, capd n.d. on *La Caroline* priv. off St Domingo, arr. V date n.k., d. 11 Dec. 1811: pneumonia. NAS Adm. list, 1821, No. 64; TNA ADM 103/648, No.2287.

41. Pierre Monard, soldier, 22nd line regt, 21, b. St Denis, capd 28 Mar. 1809 at Vigo, arr. V from Portsmouth 1 Oct. 1811, d. 19 Dec. 1811: pneumonia. NAS Adm. list, 1821, No. 223; TNA ADM 103/434, No. 3971, and ADM 103/648.

42. Louis Chaillot (or Challon), soldier, 1st Legion, 20 (or 39), b. Posin (or Vitry), capd at Flushing (or at the capitulation of the Saintes), 1809, arr. V from Plymouth 30 Sep. 1811, d. 19 Dec. 1811: pneumonia. NAS Adm. list, 1821, No. 62; TNA ADM 103/434, No. 3529, and ADM 103/648, No. 4812.

43. François Gabereaux, alias Martineau, soldier, 82nd line regt, 24, b. Montauban, capd 24 Feb. 1809 on Martinique, arr. V from Plymouth 2 Sep.1811, d. 21 Dec. 1811: fever. NAS Adm. list, 1821, No. 121; TNA ADM 103/648, No.2668. [NB: The Valleyfield Entry Book ADM 103/434, No.2668, says Gabereaux was dischgd to Perth on 4 Aug. 1813.]

44. Augustin Lamarre, soldier, 20th line regt, 22, b. Dijon, capd 20 Mar. 1809 at Reggio, Calabria, arr. V from Portsmouth 1 Oct. 1811, d. 26 Dec. 1811: pneumonia. NAS Adm. list, 1821, No. 167; TNA ADM 103/434, No. 3835, and ADM 103/648.

45. Louis Maha (or Maho), soldier, 82nd line regt, 38, b. Vergon, capd 24 Feb. 1809 on Martinique, arr. V from Plymouth c. 7 Oct. 1811, d. 26 Dec. 1811: fever. NAS Adm. list, 1821, No. 202; TNA ADM 103/648, No.4613. [NB: The Valleyfield Entry Book ADM 103/435, No. 4613, says Maha was released from there on 13 Jun. 1814.]

46. Gabriel Abel (or Ribel), Isle de France (Mauritius) regt, 45, b. Auria, capd 8 Jul. 1810 on the Isle of Bourbon (Réunion), arr. V from Portsmouth 1 Oct. 1811, d. 30 Dec. 1811: pneumonia. NAS Adm. list, 1821, No.1; TNA ADM 103/434, No.4265, and ADM 103/648.

47. Jean Baptiste Fievé, soldier, 1st line regt (or 1st Colonial Bn), 24, b. Etru, capd 15 Aug. 1809 at Flushing, arr. V from Portsmouth 1 Oct. 1811, d. 2 Jan. 1812: pneumonia. NAS Adm. list, 1821, No. 111; TNA ADM 103/648, No.3985. [NB: The Valleyfield Entry Book ADM 103/434, No. 3985, says Fievé was released from the depot and repatriated on 11 Jun. 1814.]

48. Jean Trouvé, seaman (or 'soldier, no regiment'), 25, b. Rennes, capd 22 or 23 Jan. 1809 on *Topaze* frig. off Guadeloupe, arr. V from Plymouth 30 Sep. 1811, d. 2 Jan. 1812, cause of death unstated. NAS Adm. list, 1821, No.294; TNA ADM 103/434, No. 3662. [NB: No death certificate for Trouvé seems to have survived.]

49. Charles Baudouin, soldier, Basque 66th regt, 21, b. Bouasse, capd 13 Nov. 1809 on a m.o.w. off Ireland, arr. V from Plymouth 19 Sep. 1811, d. 8 Jan. 1812: phthisis. NAS Adm. list, 1821, No. 14; TNA ADM 103/434, No.3272, and ADM 103/648.

50. Jean Baptiste Casimer, sergeant, 76th (or 70th) line regt, 22, b. Soissant [Soissons?], capd 15 Sep. 1809 at Bailem, arr. V from EM 11 Mar. 1811, d. 9 Jan. 1812: phthisis. NAS Adm. list, 1821, No. 59; TNA ADM 103/432, No.162, and ADM 103/648.

51. Jan (Jean) Peterskough, seaman, 22, b. Amsterdam, capd 2 Dec. 1810 on *Le Renard* priv. in the North Sea, arr. V from EM 11 Mar. 1811, d. 13 Jan. 1812 'From the effect of want of due sustenance, having gambled away his rations in 14 days.' NAS Adm. list, 1821, No. 243; TNA ADM 103/432, No.342, and ADM 103/648.

52. Louis Marvin (or Maurin), soldier, 82nd line regt, 24, b. Brozal, capd 28 Feb. 1809 on Martinique, arr. V from Plymouth c. 3 Oct. 1811, d. 13 Jan. 1812: phthisis. NAS Adm. list, 1821, No.209; TNA ADM 103/435, No. 4637, and ADM 103/648.

53. René Dumont, soldier, 1st Colonial Bn, 24, b. Aumé (or Reimé), capd 15 Aug. 1809 at Flushing, arr. V from EM 11 Mar. 1811, d. 20 Jan. 1812: dropsy. NAS Adm. list, 1821, No. 102; TNA ADM 103/433, No.2042, and ADM 103/648.

54. Joseph Vilard (alias Jean Velien), soldier, 21st line (or light) regt, 22, b. Lanonabull (or Lanerbule), capd 1808 at the capitulation at Baylen, arr. V from Plymouth 19 Sep. 1811, d. 24 Jan. 1812: apoplexy. NAS Adm. list, 1821, No. 303; TNA ADM 103/434, No. 3290, and ADM 103/648.

55. François Moneron, soldier, 26th line regt, 32, b. Longuiere, capd 24 Feb. 1809 on Martinique, arr. V from Plymouth c. 1 Oct. 1811, d. 25 Jan. 1812: dysentery. NAS Adm. list, 1821, No. 224; TNA ADM 103/435, No. 4381, and ADM 103/648.

56. Louis Jean Rossay (alias Jarosé), soldier, 15th light infantry (or 15th cavalry), 25, b. Chaux, capd 21 Dec. 1808 in Spain, arr. V from EM 11 Mar. 1811, d. 29 Jan. 1812: phthisis. NAS Adm. list, 1821, No. 155; TNA ADM 103/432, No. 754, and ADM 103/648.

57. François Bousquet (or Bosquet), soldier, 26th line regt, 28, b. Agens, capd 24 Feb. 1809 on Martinique, arr. V from Plymouth c. 1 Oct. 1811, d. 29 Jan. 1812: 'Deseased Liver.' NAS Adm. list, 1821, No. 39; TNA ADM 103/435, No. 4421, and ADM 103/648.

58. Jean Baptiste La Fleur (alias Lefevre), corporal, 82nd line regt, 25, b. Montauban, capd 24 Feb. 1809 on Martinique, arr. V from Plymouth 2 Sep. 1811, d. 30 Jan. 1812: phthisis. NAS Adm. list, 1821, No. 176; TNA ADM 103/434, No.2848, and ADM 103/648.

59. Pierre Romain, soldier, 30th line regt, 22, b. Bourgoine (Burgundy), capd 31 Jan. 1809 in Spain, arr. V from Plymouth 2 Sep. 1811, d. 2 Feb. 1812: phthisis. NAS Adm. list, 1821, No. 268; TNA ADM 103/434, No. 2882, and ADM 103/648.

60. Antoine Delaborde (or Delabarde or Delabare or Delbare), corporal, 5th Dutch regt, 41, b. Leyden, capd 31 Jul. 1809 at Campvere, arr. V from Plymouth 19 Sep. 1811, d. 5 Feb. 1812: fever. NAS Adm. list, 1821, No. 94; TNA ADM 103/434, No.3090, and ADM 103/648.

61. Jean Mercier (or Merceuil), seaman, 22, b. Portesse, capd 1809 on *Le Décidé* priv. in the English Channel, arr. V from EM 11 Mar.1811, d. 12 Feb. 1812: phthisis pulmonales. NAS Adm. list, 1821, No. 214; TNA ADM 103/433, No. 1577, and ADM 103/648.

62. Nicolas Belval, aged 31, b. Falaise, soldier, regt n.k., capd 28 Mar. 1809 at French army depot, Vigo, arr. from G in V Hospital on 8 and again on 24 Oct. 1811, d. 17 Feb. 1812: phthisis. NAS Adm. list, 1821, No. 20; TNA ADM 103/157, No.646, ADM 103/435, No. 5241, and ADM 103/648, No. 5241.

63. Louis François Roquelore (or Roclore), seaman, 33, b. Marseilles, capd 19 Oct. 1810 on *La Caroline* priv. in the West Indies, arr. V from EM 11 Mar. 1811, d. 19 Feb. 1812: phthisis. NAS Adm. list, 1821, No.269; TNA ADM 103/432, No. 1015, and ADM 103/648.

64. Michel Leroi (or Le Roy), soldier, 82nd line regt, 26, b. Montier, capd 21 Aug. 1808 in Portugal, arr. V from EM 11 Mar. 1811, d. 23 Feb. 1812: phthisis. NAS Adm. list, 1821, No. 195; TNA ADM 103/434, No. 2349, and ADM 103/648.

65. Pierre Minel, soldier, 82nd line regt, 46, b. Piedmont, capd 24 Feb. 1809 on Martinique, arr. V from Plymouth 30 Sep. 1811, d. 25 Feb. 1812: erysipelas. NAS Adm. list, 1821, No. 222; TNA ADM 103/434, No. 3453, and ADM 103/648.

66. Amédé Corbeller, seaman, 20, b. St Pierre, capd 27 Dec. 1807 on *La Réciprocité* priv. n.p., arr. V from EM 11 Mar. 1811, d. 26 Feb. 1812: fever. NAS Adm. list, 1821, No. 75; TNA ADM 103/433, No.2018, and ADM 103/648.

67. Hendrick Boolke, seaman, 33, b. Amsterdam, capd 22 Oct. 1811 on *Le Petit Edouard* priv. off Norway, arr. V 30 Oct. 1811, d. 27 Feb. 1812: dysentery. NAS Adm. list, 1821, No. 36; TNA ADM 103/435, No. 5269, and ADM 103/648.

68. Dominique Andry, Director of Hospitals, 24, b. Cailis, capd n.d. in Spain, arr. V from Lanark 26 Dec. 1811, d. 3 Mar. 1812: phthisis. NAS Adm. list, 1821, No. 6; TNA ADM 103/435, No.5363, and ADM 103/648.

69. Pierre Chamblain, soldier, 66th line regt, 42, b. Poitiers, capd 17 Apr. 1809 at the capitulation of the Saintes, arr. V from Plymouth 30 Sep. 1811, d. 4 Mar. 1812: pneumonia. NAS Adm. list, 1821, No. 63; TNA ADM 103/434, No.3578, and ADM 103/648.

70. Dominique Rouffy (or Rousey), soldier, 32nd (or 122nd) line regt, 24, b. Chastene (or Chastave), capd 1809 in Spain, arr. V from Plymouth on 19 Sep. 1811, d. 8 Mar. 1812: pneumonia. NAS Adm. list, 1821, No. 271; TNA ADM 103/434, No. 3060, and ADM 103/648.

71. Yves Bodiot, ensign, 26th line regt, 34, b. Luxeil (or Treillé), capd 24 Feb. 1809 on Martinique, arr. V from Plymouth 2 Sep. 1811, d. 9 Mar. 1812: fever. NAS Adm. list, 1821, No.32; TNA ADM 103/434, No. 2903, and ADM 103/648.

72. Guillaume Thaureux (or Thoreux), seaman, 34, b. Capfickel, capd 8 Mar. 1808 on *Piedmontaise* frig. in the East Indies, arr. V from EM 11 Mar. 1811, d. 11 Mar. 1812: phthisis. NAS Adm. list, 1821, No. 289; TNA ADM 103/432, No. 662, and ADM 103/648.

73. Alexandre (or Alexis Auguste) Hignet, soldier, 4th Chasseurs, 30, b. Caen, capd 10 Jul. 1807 on *Iaseur* at Bombay, arr. V from EM 11 Mar. 1811, d. 14 Mar. 1812: 'Mortification of the Thigh'. NAS Adm. list, 1821, No. 151; TNA ADM 103/432, No. 979, and ADM 103/648.

74. Dominique Culain (or Culine), soldier, 82nd line regt, 24, b. Turin, capd 24 Feb. 1809 on Martinique, arr. V from Plymouth 2 Sep. 1811, d. 16 Mar. 1812: dropsy. NAS Adm. list, 1821, No. 85; TNA ADM 103/434, No.2582, and ADM 103/648.

75. Gaspard Fournier, seaman, 40, b. Dunkirk, capd 22 Oct. 1811 on *Le Petit Edouard* priv. off Norway, arr. V eight days later, d. 19 Mar. 1812: dysentery. NAS Adm. list, 1821, No.117; TNA ADM 103/435, No. 5251, and ADM 103/648.

76. Gerrit Gosling, seaman, 45, b. Rotterdam (or Amsterdam), capd 22 Oct. 1811 on *Le Petit Edouard* priv. off Norway, arr. V eight days later, d. 22 Mar. 1812: 'the effect of cold, having repeatedly sold [his] Clothes & Hammock'. NAS Adm. list, 1821, No. 132; TNA ADM 103/435, No. 5260, and ADM 103/648.

77. Hendrik Meyer, seaman, 26, b. Amsterdam, capd 22 Oct. 1811 on *Le Petit Edouard* priv. off Norway, arr. V eight days later, d. 22 Mar. 1812 'From the effect of Cold, having repeatedly sold [his] Clothes and Hammock.' NAS Adm. list, 1821, No. 216; TNA ADM 103/648, No.5266. [NB: The Valleyfield Entry Book TNA ADM 103/435, No. 5266, says he was 64 and born at Capel. But the reference to his death has been scored through in ink and replaced by: 'Discharged 31 August 1812 France via Portsmouth. Board Order 20 Aug. 1812.']

78. Honoré Rousselet, corporal, 82nd line regt, 50, b. Tolle, capd 24 Feb. 1809 on Martinique, arr. V. from Plymouth c. 1 Oct. 1811, d. 24 Mar. 1812 from 'the Effect of Cold, having repeatedly sold [his] Clothes and Hammock'. NAS Adm. list, 1821, No. 273; TNA ADM 103/435, No. 4547, and ADM 103/648.

79.   Peter Brouwer (or Brower), seaman (or soldier), 20, b. Sneake, capd 8 Nov. 1808
        on *La Jeune Louise* (or *La Belle Louise*, or *Le Brave*) priv. at Doggerbank, arr. V from
        EM 11 Mar. 1811, d. 25 Mar. 1812: '... the Effect of Cold, having repeatedly sold
        [his] Clothes and Hammock.' NAS Adm. list, 1821, No. 50; TNA ADM 103/433,
        No. 1464, and ADM 103/648.

80.   Jean Bavure (or Bauver), sergeant, 82nd line regt, 52, b. Nancy, capd 24 Feb.
        1809 on Martinique, arr. V from Plymouth c. 1 Oct. 1811, d. 25 Mar. 1812: pneu-
        monia. NAS Adm. list, 1821, No. 15; TNA ADM 103/435, No. 4512, and ADM
        103/648.

81.   Barthelemy Fanchon (or Fengeon), soldier, 82nd line regt, 29, b. Campelon, capd
        24 Feb. 1809 on Martinique, arr. V from Plymouth 19 Sep. 1811, d. 27 Mar. 1812
        'from the Effect of Cold.' NAS Adm. list, 1821, No. 106; TNA ADM 103/434,
        No. 3236, and ADM 103/648.

82.   Pierre Augé, soldier, 82nd line regt, 40, b. Dompierre (or Dontpierre), capd 24
        Feb. 1809 on Martinique, arr. V from Plymouth 2 Sep. 1811, d. 28 Mar. 1812:
        dysentery. NAS Adm. list, 1821, No. 10; TNA ADM 103/434, No. 2782, and ADM
        103/648.

83.   Cornelius (or Cornely) de Colony, sergeant (soldier), 5th Dutch regt, 53, b. Breda,
        capd 31 Jul. 1809 at Campvere, arr. V from Plymouth 19 Sep. 1811, d. 28 Mar.
        1812, cause of death unknown. NAS Adm. list, 1821, No. 87; TNA ADM 103/434,
        No. 3135.

84.   Pierre Louis Haynaud, soldier, 26th line regt, 23, b. Biscourt, capd 24 Feb. 1809 on
        Martinique, arr. V from Plymouth c. 1 Oct. 1811, d. 28 Mar. 1812: pneumonia . NAS
        Adm. list, 1821, No.143; TNA ADM 103/435, No. 4457, and ADM 103/648.

85.   Antoine Joly (or Jolly), soldier, 82nd line regt, 26, b. Bus, capd 24 Feb. 1809 on
        Martinique, arr. V from Plymouth c. 1 Oct. 1811, d. 31 Mar. 1813: phthisis. NAS
        Adm. list, 1821, No. 159; TNA ADM 103/435, No. 4757, and ADM 103/648.

86.   Joseph Cusinier, soldier, 82nd line regt, 28, b. Monthereau, capd 24 Feb. 1809
        on Martinique, arr. V from Plymouth 2 Sep. 1811, d. 1 Apr. 1812 'from the Effect
        of Cold.' NAS Adm. list, 1821, No. 84; TNA ADM 103/434, No. 2728, and ADM
        103/648.

87.   Noel Lebon (or Le Bon), soldier, 26th line regt, 30, b. Spa, capd 24 Feb. 1809
        on Martinique, arr. V from Plymouth 2 Sep. 1811, d. 2 Apr. 1812: pneumonia.
        NAS Adm. list, 1821, No. 175; TNA ADM 103/434, No. 2909, and ADM
        103/648.

88.   Jean Martin, soldier, 2nd line regt, 25, b. Persuque, capd n.d. in Spain, arr. V from
        Plymouth 13 or 30 Sep. 1811, d. 5 Apr. 1812: pneumonia. NAS Adm. list, 1821,
        No. 207; TNA ADM 103/434, No. 3677, and ADM 103/648.

89.   Philipe Flint, sergeant, 5th Dutch regt, 42, b. Breda, capd 31 Jul. 1809 at Camp-
        vere, arr. V from Plymouth 19 Sep. 1811, d. 7 Apr. 1812: pneumonia. NAS Adm.
        list, 1821, No. 113; TNA ADM 103/434, No. 3138, and ADM 103/648.

90.   Jean Verdon, soldier, 82nd line regt, 38 (or 28), b. Chesquine, capd 24 Feb. 1809
        on Martinique, arr. V from Plymouth c. 1 Oct. 1811, d. 9 Apr. 1812: dysentery. NAS
        Adm. list, 1821, No. 304; TNA ADM 103/435, No. 4661, and ADM 103/648.

91.   Jacques Bondon, soldier, 26th line regt, 30, b. Filchine, capd 24 Feb. 1809 on
        Martinique, arr. V from Plymouth 19 Sep. 1811, d. 9 (or 11) Apr. 1812: fever. NAS
        Adm. list, 1821, No.35; TNA ADM 103/434, No.3233, and ADM 103/648.

92.	Jean Louis Cabrot, soldier, 1st Prussian regt, 59, b. Utrecht, capd 18 Aug. 1809 at Flushing, arr. V from EM 11 Mar. 1811, d. 10 Apr. 1812: phthisis. NAS Adm. list, 1821, No. 54; TNA ADM 103/432, No. 308, and ADM 103/648.

93.	Alexis Correare (or Courearé), soldier 1st (or 3rd) Artillery, 31, b. Dauphiné, capd 24 Feb. 1809 on Martinique, arr. V from EM 11 Mar. 1811, d. 11 Apr. 1812: debility. NAS Adm. list, 1821, No. 80; TNA ADM 103/433, No. 1385, and ADM 103/648.

94.	Guillaume Herman, soldier, 1st Prussian regt, 32 (or 26), b. Neissau, capd 1 Aug. 1809 at Campvere, arr. V from Plymouth 30 Sep. 1811, d. 11 Apr. 1812: pneumonia. NAS Adm. list, 1821, No. 149; TNA ADM 103/434, No. 3687, and ADM 103/648.

95.	Joseph Maine, seaman, 59, b. Dunkirk, capd 8 Nov. 1808 on *La Comtesse de Hambourg* priv. in the North Sea, arr. V from EM 11 Mar. 1811, d. 12 Apr. 1812: 'Debility from the Effect of selling [his] Provisions and Clothes.' NAS Adm. list, 1821, No. 203; TNA ADM 103/433, No. 1998, and ADM 103/648.

96.	Jean Baptiste Besant (or Bessant or Outand), soldier, 65th line regt, 19, b. Auvergne, capd 15 Aug. 1809 at Flushing, arr. V from the south of England 14 Oct. 1811, d. 16 Apr. 1812: fever. NAS Adm. list, 1821, No. 28; TNA ADM 103/435, No. 4845, and ADM 103/648.

97.	Joseph Gaffé (or Gaffée), soldier, 1st Colonial Bn, 38, b. Arras, capd 17 Apr. 1809 at the capitulation of the Saintes, arr. V from Plymouth 13 or 30 Sep. 1811, d. 17 Apr. 1812: 'Debility from the Effect of selling [his] Provisions and Clothes.' NAS Adm. list, 1821, No. 122; TNA ADM 103/434, No. 3590, and ADM 103/648.

98.	Joseph Le Bie, seaman, 27, b. St Malo, capd 19 Dec. 1807 on *St Joseph* priv. in English Channel, arr. V from EM 11 Mar. 1811, d. 18 Apr. 1812: pneumonia. NAS Adm. list, 1821, No. 174; TNA ADM 103/433, No.1515, and ADM 103/648.

99.	Jérome Grilly (or Grille or Grily), soldier, Chasseurs Rentrés, 46, b. Berlin, capd 16 Aug. 1809 at Flushing, arr. V from EM 11 Mar. 1811, d. 20 Apr. 1812: 'Debility from the Effect of selling [his] Provisions and Clothes.' NAS Adm. list, 1821, No. 136; TNA ADM 103/434, No. 2311, and ADM 103/648.

100.	Antoine Grinder (alias Guindor), soldier, 82nd line regt, 31, b. Blois, capd 24 Feb. 1809 on Martinique, arr. V from Plymouth 2 Sep. 1811, d. 20 Apr. 1812: 'Debility from the Effect of selling [his] Provisions and Clothes.' NAS Adm. list, 1821, No. 137; TNA ADM 103/434, No. 2630, and ADM 103/648.

101.	Jacques Boucau (or Bocquet or Boucal), seaman, 36, b. Havre de Grace, capd 13 Mar. 1806 on *Marengo* m.o.w. in the East Indies (or n.d. *Le Marengo* priv. off Spain), arr. V from EM 11 Mar. 1811, d. 22 Apr. 1812: pneumonia. NAS Adm. list, 1821, No.43; TNA ADM 103/433, No.1473, and ADM 103/648.

102.	Nicolas Lejeune, soldier, 65th line regt, 20, b. Lorraine, capd 15 Aug. 1809 at Flushing, arr. V from EM 11 Mar. 1811, d. 22 Apr. 1812: pneumonia. NAS Adm. list, 1821, No. 180; TNA ADM 103/433, No. 1489, and ADM 103/648.

103.	Johan Vandenberg (or Vanderberghe), seaman, 25, b.Oldenburg, capd 20 Dec. 1810 on *L'Aventurier* priv. in the English Channel, arr. V from EM 11 Mar. 1811, d. 22 Apr. 1812: 'Debility from the Effect of selling [his] Provisions and Clothes.' NAS Adm. list, 1821, No. 298; TNA ADM 103/433, No.1563, and ADM 103/648.

104.	Eugène Vainville (or Vanvulle), soldier, 82nd line regt, 27, b. Hellins, capd 24 Feb. 1809 on Martinique, arr. V from Plymouth 2 Sep. 1811, d. 25 Apr. 1812: 'Debility from the Effect of selling [his] Provisions and Clothes.' NAS Adm. list, 1821, No. 295; TNA ADM 103/434, No. 2577, and ADM 103/648.

105. Frederik De Haas, seaman, 19, b. Emden, capd 25 Oct. 1810 on *La Comtesse de Hambourg* priv. in the North Sea, arr. V from EM 11 Mar. 1811, d. 26 Apr. 1812: 'Debility from the Effect of selling [his] Provisions and Clothes.' NAS Adm. list, 1821, No. 90; TNA ADM 103/432, No. 623, and ADM 103/648.

106. Eugene Jan Soienne, carpenter, 54, b. St Omer, capd 10 Dec. 1810 on *Le Mamelouk* priv. off Dover, arr. V from EM 11 Mar. 1811, d. 26 Apr. 1812: fever. NAS Adm. list, 1821, No. 282; TNA ADM 103/434, No. 2206, and ADM 103/648.

107. Michel Lachet, soldier, 82nd line regt, 26, b. Tarascon, capd 24 Feb. 1809 on Martinique, arr. V from Plymouth 2 Sep. 1811, d. 27 Apr. 1812: consumption. NAS Adm. list, 1821, No. 163; TNA ADM 103/434, No. 2846, and ADM 103/648.

108. Antoine Van Harlem, soldier, 1st (or 5th) Dutch regt, 40, b. Derk, capd 31 Jul. 1809 at Campvere, arr. V from Plymouth 19 Sep. 1811, d. 27 Apr. 1812: pneumonia. NAS Adm. list, 1821, No. 300; TNA ADM 103/434, No. 3113, and ADM 103/648.

109. Antoine Sangreti, seaman, 49, b. Lisbon, capd 1809 on *La Desirée* priv. in the English Channel, arr. V from EM 11 Mar. 1811, d. 30 Apr. 1812: pneumonia. NAS Adm. list, 1821, No. 275; TNA ADM 103/433, No. 1427, and ADM 103/648.

110. C.L.L. Velassier (or Velasière), soldier, 70th line regt, 19, b. Champagne, capd 1809 at Vigo, arr. V from Plymouth 30 Sep. 1811, d. 30 Apr. 1812: 'From Debility from selling his Rations.' NAS Adm. list, 1821, No. 302; TNA ADM 103/434, No. 3371, and ADM 103/648.

111. Marc Joseph Sert, seaman, 20, b. Ostend, capd 19 Oct. 1810 on *L'Héro du Nord* in the North Sea, arr. V from EM hospital 31 Mar. 1811, d. 1 May 1812: 'Debility from selling his Rations.' NAS Adm. list, 1821, No.277; TNA ADM 103/434, No. 2449, and ADM 103/648.

112. François Gentier (or Jeantier), soldier, 82nd line regt, 38, b. Dampiere, capd 24 Feb. 1809 on Martinique, arr.V from Plymouth c. 1 Oct. 1811, d. 1 May 1812: phthisis. NAS Adm. list, 1821, No. 156; TNA ADM 103/435, No. 4493, and ADM 103/648.

113. Maximilien Biernaud (or Biernault), soldier, 4th line regt (or 4th Colonial Bn), 26, b. Brabant, capd 7 Oct. 1810 at Coimbra, arr. V from Portsmouth 14 or 21 Oct. 1811, d. 1 May 1812: phthisis. NAS Adm. list, 1821, No. 30; TNA ADM 103/435, No. 5088, and ADM 103/648.

114. Pierre Galbert, soldier, 82nd line regt, 26, b. St Laurent, capd 24 Feb. 1809 on Martinique, arr. V from Plymouth c. 1 Oct. 1811, d. 3 May 1812: phthisis. NAS Adm. list, 1821, No. 123; TNA ADM 103/435, No. 4751, and ADM 103/648.

115. Jean Guillebeau (or Guilbeau), seaman, 35, b. St Nazaire, capd 13 Mar. 1806 on *Marengo* m.o.w. in the East Indies, arr. V from EM 11 Mar. 1811, d. 4 or 5 May 1812: Mortification (gangrene). NAS Adm. list, 1821, No. 141; TNA ADM 103/433, No. 1666, and ADM 103/648.

116. René Etot (or Hétaud), soldier, 8th line regt, 25, b. Corsica, capd 24 Feb. 1809 on Martinique, arr. V from Plymouth 30 Sep. 1811, d. 4 May 1812: 'Lumber Abcess.' NAS Adm. list, 1821, No. 150; TNA ADM 103/434, No. 3506, and ADM 103/648.

117. Jean Dortence (or Dortense), soldier, 3rd Dragoons, 35, b. Poupel, capd 7 Oct. 1810 at Coimbra, arr.V from Portsmouth 1 Oct. 1811, d. 5 May 1812: fever. NAS Adm. list, 1821, No. 100; TNA ADM 103/434, No. 4215, and ADM 103/648.

118. William De Grasse, soldier, 1st line (or 1st Dutch?) regt, 26, b. Zutphen, capd 31 Jul. 1809 at Campvere, arr. V from Plymouth 19 Sep. 1811, d. 12 May 1812: 'General Debility.' NAS Adm. list, 1821, No. 88; TNA ADM 103/434, No. 3110, and ADM 103/648.

119. Joseph Allione, soldier, 3rd Artillery regt, 50, b. Roman (sic), capd 18 Jun. 1809 on *La Félicité* m.v., n.p., arr. V from Plymouth 19 Sep. 1811, d. 14 May 1812: fever. NAS Adm. list, 1821, No.3; TNA ADM 103/434, No.3032, and ADM 103/648.

120. William Noltzen, sergeant, 5th Dutch Artillery, 40, b. Flushing, capd 31 Jul. 1809 at Campvere, arr. V from Plymouth 19 Sep. 1811, d. 14 May 1812: chronic dysentery. NAS Adm. list, 1821, No. 232; TNA ADM 103/434, No. 3121, and ADM 103/648.

121. Antoine Coujean, seaman, 30, b. St Nion, capd 4 Nov. 1805 on *Scipion* m.o.w. at Cape Ortegal, arr. V from EM 11 Mar. 1811, d. 16 May 1812: phthisis. NAS Adm. list, 1821, No. 77; TNA ADM 103/433, No. 1962, and ADM 103/648.

122. Jean Ringo (or Rigo), seaman, 43, b. Blankenbergh, capd 10 Sep. 1810 on *Mamelouk* priv. off Dover, arr. V from EM 11 Mar. 1811, d. 17 May 1812: fever. NAS Adm. list, 1821, No. 261; TNA ADM 103/432, No. 470, and ADM 103/648.

123. Jean Pierre Jelly (or Jolly), soldier, 82nd line regt, 32, b. Languedoc, capd 24 Feb. 1809 on Martinique, arr. V from EM 11 Mar. 1811, d. 17 May 1812: 'Erisipalas.' NAS Adm. list, 1821, No. 157; TNA ADM 103/433, No. 1420, and ADM 103/648.

124. Guillaume Michelet, seaman, 23, b. Lateste, capd 26 Sep. 1806 on *Le Président* frig. off Brest, arr. V from EM 11 Mar. 1811, d. 18 May 1812: 'Lumber Abcess.' NAS Adm. list, 1821, No. 218; TNA ADM 103/432, No. 852, and ADM 103/648.

125. Julien Prevert, 2nd capt., 44, b. Blankenbergh (or Amsterdam, or Cancal), capd 17 Sep. 1810 on *L'Auguste* priv. in the English Channel, arr. V from Selkirk 1 Feb. 1812, d. 18 May 1812: 'Erisipilas.' NAS Adm. list, 1821, No. 252; TNA ADM 103/435, No. 5355, and ADM 103/648.

126. Jean Pierre Robert, soldier, 47th line regt, 28, b. Avignon, capd 10 May 1809 in Portugal, arr. V from EM 11 Mar. 1811, d. 19 May 1812: phthisis. NAS Adm. list, 1821, No. 264; TNA ADM 103/432, No. 318, and ADM 103/648.

127. Felicien Constantine, soldier, 26th line regt, 36, b. Diome, capd 24 Feb. 1809 on Martinique, arr. V from Plymouth c. 1 Oct. 1811, d. 19 May 1812: phthisis. NAS Adm. list, 1821, No.74; TNA ADM 103/435, No. 4399, and ADM 103/648.

128. Claude Loyez, soldier, 82nd line regt, 42, b. La Ville de Bois, capd 24 Feb. 1809 on Martinique, arr. V from EM 11 Mar. 1811, d. 20 May 1812: pneumonia. NAS Adm. list, 1821, No. 198; TNA ADM 103/433, No. 1250, and ADM 103/648.

129. Charles Langlois (or Langlais), soldier, 4th line (or Artillery) regt, 25, b. Honfleur, capd 24 Feb. 1809 on Martinique, arr. V from EM 11 Mar. 1811, d. 20 May 1812: phthisis. NAS Adm. list, 1821, No. 169; TNA ADM 103/433, No. 1251, and ADM 103/648.

130. Gilbert Signoret, sergeant, 26th line regt, 51, b. Bourbon, capd 23 Feb. 1805 on *La Ville de Milan* frig. in the Atlantic, arr. V from Plymouth 19 Sep. 1811, d. 26 May 1812: phthisis. NAS Adm. list, 1821, No. 281; TNA ADM 103/434, No. 3248, and ADM 103/648.

131. Joseph Leinbourg (or Limbourg), soldier, 82nd line regt, 34 (or 42), b. Gand (Ghent) (or Legemonde), capd 24 Feb. 1809 on Martinique, arr. V from Plymouth 2 Sep. 1811, d. 26 or 27 May 1812: fever. NAS Adm. list, 1821, No. 190; TNA ADM 103/434, No. 2649, and ADM 103/648.

132. François Pénéde, soldier, 82nd line regt, 42, b. Legemonde, capd 24 Feb. 1809 on Martinique, arr. V from Plymouth 2 Sep. 1811, d. 27 May 1812: fever. NAS Adm. list, 1821, No. 240; TNA ADM 103/434, No. 2563, and ADM 103/648.

133. François Lunau, soldier, 65th line regt, 19, b. Tours, capd 15 Aug. 1809 at Flushing, arr. V from the south of England 14 Oct. 1811, d. 28 May 1812: phthisis. NAS Adm. list, 1821, No. 197; TNA ADM 103/435, No. 4862, and ADM 103/648.

134. Nicolas Rose Midoc, soldier, 82nd line regt, 30, b. Reuse, capd 24 Feb. 1809 on Martinique, arr. V from EM 11 Mar. 1811, d. 7 Jun. 1812: phthisis. NAS Adm. list, 1821, No. 219; TNA ADM 103/432, No. 686, and ADM 103/648.

135. Jacques Carron (or Caroux), seaman, 33, b. Painboeuf, capd 28 May 1806 on *Le Diligent* priv. in the English Channel, arr. V from EM 11 Mar. 1811, d. 8 Jun. 1812: phthisis. NAS Adm. list, 1821, No. 57; TNA ADM 103/432, No. 492, and ADM 103/648.

136. Jean Louis Caron (or Carron), soldier, 75th line regt, 21, b. Berne, capd 4 Jun. 1810 in Spain (St Herme or St Florence), arr. V from Portsmouth 14 or 21 Oct. 1811, d. 8 Jun. 1812: chronic dysentery. NAS Adm. list, 1821, No. 58; TNA ADM 103/435, No. 5112, and ADM 103/648.

137. Jacques Bouchange (or Bosange), soldier, Island (i.e., Bourbon [Réunion]) regt, 45, b. Behen (or Beheu), capd 8 Jul. 1810 on Bourbon, arr. V from Portsmouth 1 Oct. 1811, d. 11 Jun. 1812: phthisis. NAS Adm. list, 1821, No. 37; TNA ADM 103/434, No. 4261, and ADM 103/648.

138. Louis François Boisseau (or Boiseau), drummer, 82nd line regt, aged 27 (or 37), b. Joeant (or Nojiant) [Nogent?], capd 24 Feb. 1809 on Martinique, arr. V from Plymouth c. 1 Oct. 1811, d. 15 Jun. 1812: fever. NAS Adm. list, 1821, No. 33; TNA ADM 103/435, No. 4707, and ADM 103/648.

139. Thomas Roblot, seaman, 32, b. Nantes, capd 27 Nov. 1808 on a vessel prize to *Iena* m.o.w. in the English Channel, arr. V from EM 11 Mar. 1811, d. 18 Jun. 1812: consumption. NAS Adm. list, 1821, No. 265; TNA ADM 103/432, No. 1007, and ADM 103/648.

140. Claude Ravie, gunner, 50, b. Martues, capd 17 Apr. 1809 on *D'Hautpoul* m.o.w. off the Saintes, arr. V from EM 11 Mar. 1811, d. 18 Jun. 1812: pneumonia. NAS Adm. list, 1821, No. 256; TNA ADM 103/433, No. 1387, and ADM 103/648.

141. Pierre Chevalier, seaman (or gunner), 59, b. Libourne, capd 21 Oct. 1805 on *Swiftsure* m.o.w. at Trafalgar, arr. V from EM 11 Mar. 1811, d. 21 Jun. 1812: 'Ulcer.' NAS Adm. list, 1821, No. 68; TNA ADM 103/434, No. 2241, and ADM 103/648.

142. François Houllier (or Houlier), soldier, 1st Regt on Shore (sic) (or 13th line regt), 19, b. Bressier (or Beiziers), capd 16 Aug. 1809 at Flushing, arr. V from the south of England 14 Oct. 1811, d. 21 Jun. 1812: pneumonia. NAS Adm. list, 1821, No. 152; TNA ADM 103/435, No. 4817, and ADM 103/648.

143. Dominique Paion, soldier, 1st Artillery, 25, b. Venice, capd n.d. on Corfu, arr. V from EM 11 Mar. 1811, d. 22 Jun. 1812: pneumonia. NAS Adm. list, 1821, No. 233; TNA ADM 103/432, No. 881, and ADM 103/648.

144. François Gavelle (or Garelle), soldier, 31st line regt, 27, b. Ansis, capd 28 Mar. 1809 at Vigo, arr. V from Plymouth 19 Sep. 1811, d. 24 Jun. 1812: consumption. NAS Adm. list, 1821, No. 126; TNA ADM 103/434, No. 3132, and ADM 103/648.

145. Barthelemy Artifoni, corporal (or soldier), 2nd Italian regt, 30, b. Viliman, capd 3 Oct. 1809 on Zante, arr. V from EM 11 Mar. 1811, d. 26 Jun. 1812: consumption. NAS Adm. list, 1821, No. 8; TNA ADM 103/433, No. 1593, and ADM 103/648.

146. Auguste Delavalle (or Delaval), soldier, 26th line regt, 26, b. Pocapaille, capd 24 Feb. 1809 on Martinique, arr. V from Plymouth c. 1 Oct. 1811, d. 30 Jun. 1812: pneumonia. NAS Adm. list, 1821, No. 92; TNA ADM 103/435, No. 4371, and ADM 103/648, No. 4361 (sic).

147. Pierre Valette, soldier, 82nd line regt, 35, b. Domart, capd 24 Feb. 1809 on Martinique, arr. V from Plymouth 2 Sep. 1811, d. 12 Jul. 1812: consumption. NAS Adm. list, 1821, No. 296; TNA ADM 103/434, No. 2583, and ADM 103/648.

148. Antoine Signé, soldier, 82nd line regt, 25, b. Argenta, capd 24 Feb. 1809 on Martinique, arr. V from EM 11 Mar. 1811, d. 19 Jul. 1812: pneumonia. NAS Adm. list, 1821, No. 280; TNA ADM 103/432, No. 576, and ADM 103/648.

149. Jean Marie Gourvenec (or Gouvernec), seaman, 20, b. La Nelis, capd 18 Jun. 1809 on *La Félicité* armed supply ship in the Mediterranean, arr. V from EM 11 Mar. 1811, d. 21 Jul. 1812: pneumonia. NAS Adm. list, 1821, No. 135; TNA ADM 103/433, No. 1634, and ADM 103/648.

150. Pierre Torchet, soldier, 82nd line regt, 22, b. Bouves, capd 24 Feb. 1809 on Martinique, arr. V from Plymouth 30 Sep. 1811, d. 23 Jul. 1812: pneumonia. NAS Adm. list, 1821, No. 291; TNA ADM 103/434, No. 3702, and ADM 103/648.

151. Sebastien Blee, soldier, 65th line regt, 19, b. Grampont (or Gran Pont (sic)), capd 15 Aug. 1809 at Flushing, arr. V from south of England 14 Oct. 1811, d. 24 Jul. 1812: pneumonia. NAS Adm. list, 1821, No. 31; TNA ADM 103/435, No. 4838, and ADM 103/648.

152. Jean Baptiste Guange, sergeant (or soldier), 1st line regt, 22, b. Grangulies, capd 15 Aug. 1809 at Flushing, arr. V from Portsmouth 1 Oct. 1811, d. 6 Aug. 1812: consumption. NAS Adm. list, 1821, No. 138; TNA ADM 103/434, No. 3989, and ADM 103/648.

153. Jacques Auguste Belle, seaman, 15, b. Calais, capd 12 Nov. 1810 on *General Dorsin* priv. in the North Sea, arr. V from EM 11 Mar. 1811, d. 7 Aug. 1812: fever. NAS Adm. list, 1821, No.18; TNA ADM 103/433, No. 1794, and ADM 103/648.

154. Jacques Fontaine, soldier, 26th line regt, 34, b. Audincourt, capd 24 Feb. 1809 on Martinique, arr. V from Plymouth c. 1 Oct. 1811, d. 8 Aug. 1812: consumption. NAS Adm. list, 1821, No. 114; TNA ADM 103/435, No. 4395, and ADM 103/648.

155. Antoine Fortier (or Fortière), drummer, 82nd line regt, 33, b. Rouen, capd 24 Feb. 1809 on Martinique, arr. V from Plymouth 2 Sep. 1811, d. 12 Aug. 1812: consumption. NAS Adm. list, 1821, No. 116; TNA ADM 103/434, No. 2647, and ADM 103/648.

156. Jean Baptiste Pierre Parmentier, soldier, 70th line regt, 24, b. Lesquelles, capd 30 Jul. 1810 at Cazales, arr. V from Portsmouth 21 Oct. 1811, d. 19 Aug. 1812: pneumonia. NAS Adm. list, 1821, No. 234; TNA ADM 103/435, No. 5208, and ADM 103/648.

157. Etienne Rossigni, seaman, 16, b. Dieppe, capd on *La Modeste* priv. in the English Channel, arr. V from EM 11 Mar. 1811, d. 24 Aug. 1812: consumption. NAS Adm. list, 1821, No. 270; TNA ADM 103/432, No. 869, and ADM 103/648.

158. François Paul, soldier, 26th line regt, 31, b.Vannes, capd 24 Feb. 1809 on Martinique, arr. V from Plymouth c. 1 Oct. 1811, d. 1 Sep. 1812: consumption. NAS Adm. list, 1821, No. 237; TNA ADM 103/435, No. 4367, and ADM 103/648.

159. Toussaint Mahé, soldier, 4th Chasseurs (or 4th line regt), 34, b. Villeneuf, capd 24 Feb. 1809 on Martinique, arr. V from EM 11 Mar. 1811, d. 9 Sep. 1812: consumption. NAS Adm. list, 1821, No. 201; TNA ADM 103/432, No. 843, and ADM 103/648.

160. Pierre François Cockan, soldier, regt u. (probably 82nd line), 20, b. Arras (or Aron), capd 24 Feb. 1809 on Martinique, arr. V from Plymouth 30 Sep. 1811, d. 21 Sep. 1812: consumption. NAS Adm. list, 1821, No. 71; TNA ADM 103/434, No. 3458, and ADM 103/648.

161. Pierre Yonies, soldier, regt u., 26, b. Ronci, capd 28 Mar. 1809 at Vigo (or 7 Apr. 1809 at the Saintes), arr. V from Plymouth 30 Sep. 1811, d. 27 Sep. 1812: phthisis. NAS Adm. list, 1821, No. 308; TNA ADM 103/434, No. 3392, and ADM 103/648.

162. Solomon Sybrand, soldier, 5th Dutch regt, 26, b. Amsterdam, capd 31 Jul. 1809 at Campvere, arr. V from Plymouth 19 Sep. 1811, d. 27 or 28 Sep. 1812: phthisis. NAS Adm. list, 1821, No. 286; TNA ADM 103/434, No. 3128, and ADM 103/648.

163. Jean Depla, soldier, 5th Dutch regt, 42, b. Flushing, capd 31 Jul. 1809 at Campvere, arr. V from Plymouth 19 Sep. 1811, d. 1 Oct. 1812: consumption. NAS Adm. list, 1821, No. 97; TNA ADM 103/434, No. 3151, and ADM 103/648.

164. Jean L. Belecque, seaman, 23, b. Breton (sic), capd 29 Jan. 1807 on *Le Grand Napoléon* priv. (or on a prize to it) off Dungeness, arr. V from EM 11 Mar. 1811, d. 14 or 19 Oct. 1812: cause of death not stated. NAS Adm. list, 1821, No. 16; TNA ADM 103/432, No. 174.

165. Joseph Julien, seaman, 23, b. Marseilles, capd 30 Oct. 1809 on *Le Président* priv. in the English Channel, arr. V from EM 11 Mar. 1811, d. 24 Oct. 1812: cause of death unstated. NAS Adm. list, 1821, No. 161; TNA ADM 103/432, No. 1027.

166. Jean Payon, quartermaster (or 2nd master), 29, b. La Hougue, capd 10 Feb. 1809 on *Junon* frig. in the East Indies, arr. V from EM 11 Mar. 1811, d. 14 Nov. 1812: pneumonia. NAS Adm. list, 1821, No. 238; TNA ADM 103/432, No. 10, and ADM 103/648.

167. Frederik (or Joseph) Prunet (or Prunel), solder, 58th line regt, 20, b. Melin, capd 21 Aug. 1808 in Portugal, arr. V from Portsmouth 1 Oct. 1811, d. 14 Nov. 1812: phthisis. NAS Adm. list, 1821, No. 254; TNA ADM 103/434, No. 4254, and ADM 103/648.

168. Jacques Gourins, soldier, 50th line regt, 20, p.o.b. n.k., capd 14 Aug. 1812 at Madrid, arr. V 'from Leith for medical assistance' 13 Nov. 1812, d. 15 Nov. 1812: typhus. NAS Adm. list, 1821, No. 134; TNA ADM 103/435, No. 6197, and ADM 103/648.

169. Antoine Lemoine, soldier, regt u., 33, b. Amby, capd 4 Nov. 1805 on *Formidable* (or *Mont Blanc*) m.o.w. off Rochefort, arr. V from G 1 Sep. 1812, d. 20 or 22 Nov. 1812: cause of death unstated. NAS Adm. list, 1821, No. 192; TNA ADM 103/435, No. 5858.

170. Claude Dugueuse (or De or Du Goussel), soldier, 50th regt, 22, b. St Omer, capd 15 Aug. 1812 at Madrid, arr. V 'from Leith for medical assistance' 13 Nov. 1812, d. 20 Nov. 1812: fever. NAS Adm. list, 1821, No. 89; TNA ADM 103/435, No. 6198, and ADM 103/648.

171. Auguste Crumet, gunner, 37, b. Dieppe, capd 17 Oct. 1810 on *Le Vengeur* priv. in the English Channel, arr. V from EM 11 Mar. 1811, d. 22 Nov. 1812: fever. NAS Adm. list, 1821, No. 83; TNA ADM 103/434, No. 2244, and ADM 103/648.

172.   Jean Joseph Niquet, soldier, 3rd Dragoons, 31, b. Avignon, capd 5 Oct. 1810 at Coimbra, arr. V from Plymouth 19 Sep. 1811, d. 29 Nov. 1812 'in consequence of being severely flogged by his fellow Prisoners, he having been detected by them stealing, they also cut off one of his ears. Reported to Vice Admiral Otway.' NAS Adm. list, 1821, No. 231; TNA ADM 103/434, No. 3072, and ADM 103/648.

173.   François Lagneau, seaman, 35, b. Oléron, capd 25 Sep. 1806 on *L'Armide* frig. off Brest, arr. V from EM 11 Mar. 1811, d. 30 Nov. 1812: pneumonia. NAS Adm. list, 1821, No. 165; TNA ADM 103/433, No. 2077, and ADM 103/648.

174.   Pierre Jean Devaux (or Devaud), soldier, 39th line regt, 26, b. Nantes (or La Lampatrie), capd 14 Aug. 1812 at Madrid, arr. V from G 29 Nov. 1812, d. 1 Dec. 1812: fever. NAS Adm. list, 1821, No. 99; TNA ADM 103/435, No. 6211, and ADM 103/648.

175.   Urvain Robert, soldier, 65th line regt, 19, b. St Jean Delamotte, capd 15 Aug. 1809 at Flushing, arr. V from the south of England 14 Oct. 1811, d. 9 Dec. 1812: fever. NAS Adm. list, 1821, No. 263; TNA ADM 103/435, No. 4854, and ADM 103/648.

176.   Antoine Dupont, soldier, 101st line regt, 31, b. Neville, capd 27 Jun. 1812 at Salamanca, arr. V from G 29 Nov. 1812, d. 17 Dec. 1812: pneumonia. NAS Adm. list, 1821, No. 103; TNA ADM 103/435, No. 6224, and ADM 103/648.

177.   Jacques Le Sit (or Le Set or Le Fie), soldier, 48th line regt, 26, b. Cherbourg, capd 15 Aug. 1809 at Flushing, arr.V from EM 11 Mar. 1811, d. 18 Dec. 1812: consumption. NAS Adm. list, 1821, No. 177; TNA ADM 103/432, No. 675, and ADM 103/648.

178.   Chaidon Brezwrilz (or Brezivritz), seaman (or soldier, no regt stated), 23, b. La Chappel (sic), capd 10 Jun. 1809 on *La Regouine* trans. off Portugal, arr. V from Plymouth 13 or 30 Sep.1811, d. 18 Dec. 1812: fever. NAS Adm. list, 1821, No. 45; TNA ADM 103/434, No. 3722, and ADM 103/648.

179.   Jean Baptiste Poyard, soldier, 6th light infantry regt, 31, b. Layon (or Lajon), capd 25 Mar. 1809 in Portugal, arr. V from EM 11 Mar. 1811, d. 19 Dec. 1812: pneumonia. NAS Adm. list, 1821, No. 251; TNA ADM 103/433, No. 1524, and ADM 103/648.

180.   Marcel Chevalier, soldier, 82nd line regt, 23, b. Normandy, capd 21 Aug. 1808 in Portugal, arr. V from EM 11 Mar. 1811, d. 22 Dec. 1812: pneumonia. NAS Adm. list, 1821, No. 67; TNA ADM 103/433, No. 1940, and ADM 103/648.

181.   Jean Lailleau (alias Ratail), seaman, 38, b. Libourne, capd 17 Apr. 1809 on *D'Hautpoul* m.o.w. off the Saintes, arr. V from EM 11 Mar. 1811, d. 29 Dec. 1812: fever. NAS Adm. list, 1821, No. 166; TNA ADM 103/433, No. 1486, and ADM 103/648.

182.   Ernout Vergnot (or Vergnout), soldier, 82nd line regt, 32, b. Perigord, capd 24 Feb. 1809 on Martinique, arr. V from EM 11 Mar. 1811, d. 30 Dec. 1812: fever. NAS Adm. list, 1821, No. 305; TNA ADM 103/433, No. 1809, and ADM 103/648.

183.   Charles Richard (or Richarde), seaman, 18, b. Gravelines, capd 6 Jul. 1811 on *Le Figaro* priv. in the North Sea, arr. V from G 21 Dec. 1812, d. 3 Jan. 1813: cause of death unstated. NAS Adm. list, 1821, No. 260; TNA ADM 103/435, No. 6249.

184.   Jean Baptiste Bernardin, soldier, 15th line regt, 43, b. Dreux, capd 12 May 1809 in Portugal, arr. V from EM 11 Mar. 1811, d. 4 Jan. 1813: cause of death unstated. NAS Adm. list, 1821, No. 24; TNA ADM 103/433, No. 1295.

185. Jean Michel, soldier, Chasseurs Rentrés, 29, b. Lamberg, capd n.d. (1809?) at Flushing, arr. V from Plymouth 19 Sep. 1811, d. 10 Jan. 1813: fever. NAS Adm. list, 1821, No. 217; TNA ADM 103/434, No. 3157, and ADM 103/648.

186. Jean Vincent, soldier, 26th line regt, 23, b. Bourgogne, capd 24 Feb. 1809 on Martinique, arr.V from Plymouth c. 1 Oct. 1811, d. 17 Jan. 1813: phthisis. NAS Adm. list, 1821, No. 307; TNA ADM 103/435, No. 4464, and ADM 103/648.

187. Pierre Amble (or Amblé), soldier, 82nd line regt, 25, b. Nantes, capd 24 Feb. 1809 on Martinique, arr. V from Plymouth 2 Sep. 1811, d. 23 Jan. 1813: fever. NAS Adm. list, 1821, No. 4; TNA ADM 103/434, No. 2580, and ADM 103/648.

188. Vincent Mutin, 'Baker to the Army', 36, b. Tousi, capd 22 Jul. 1809 on a trans. near Ancona, arr. V from Portsmouth 1 Oct. 1811, d. 27 Jan. 1813: debility. NAS Adm. list, 1821, No. 228; TNA ADM 103/434, No. 4190, and ADM 103/648.

189. Antoine Beroire, soldier, 2nd line regt, 28, b. Meng, capd 4 Nov. 1805 on *Formidable* m.o.w. off Rochefort, arr. V from G 1 Sep. 1812, d. 31 Jan. 1813: phthisis. NAS Adm. list, 1821, No. 25; TNA ADM 103/435, No. 5881, and ADM 103/648.

190. René Bourier (or Bourrier), soldier, 119th line regt, 21, b. Tellier, capd 21 Jun. 1812 at Le Quito, arr. V from Portsmouth 21 Jul. 1812, d. 11 Feb. 1813: phthisis. NAS Adm. list, 1821, No. 42; TNA ADM 103/435, No. 5506, and ADM 103/648.

191. Alexandre (or Alexis) Damon (or Danion), soldier, Imperial Guard, 32, b. Orleans, capd 6 Jul. 1810 at St Antonio, Spain, arr. V from Plymouth 19 Sep.1811, d. 12 Feb. 1813: phthisis. NAS Adm. list, 1821, No. 86; TNA ADM 103/434, No. 3310, and ADM 103/648.

192. Etienne Benoit (or Benoist), soldier, Bourbon Island regt (or Colonial Bn), 33, b. St Dize, capd 8 Jul. 1810 on Bourbon (Réunion), arr. V from Portsmouth 1 Oct. 1811, d. 20 Feb. 1813: debility. NAS Adm. list, 1821, No. 21; TNA ADM 103/434, No. 4268, and ADM 103/648.

193. Jean Heilbory (or Hielbouri), seaman, 26, b. Painboeuf, capd 25 Jul. 1805 on *Prosperité* priv. in the English Channel, arr. V from EM 11 Mar. 1811, d. 10 Mar. 1813: fever. NAS Adm. list, 1821, No. 144; TNA ADM 103/433, No. 1113, and ADM 103/648.

194. Martin Pastello (or Patelo), soldier, 66th line regt, 32, b. La Brie, capd 17 Apr. 1809 at the capitulation at the Saintes, arr. V from Plymouth 30 Sep. 1811, d. 13 Mar. 1813: fever. NAS Adm. list, 1821, No. 236; TNA ADM 103/434, No. 3594, and ADM 1093/648.

195. Julien Rohot, soldier, 26th line regt, 37, b. Roumiers, capd 24 Feb. 1809 on Martinique, arr. V from Plymouth c. 1 Oct. 1811, d. 15 Mar. 1813: pneumonia. NAS Adm. list, 1821, No. 267; TNA ADM 103/435, No. 4407, and ADM 103/648.

196. Claude Hulier (or L'Hullier), soldier, 8th Dragoons, 27, b. Renaville (or Gienaville), capd n.d. in Portugal, arr. V from EM 11 Mar. 1811, d. 16 Mar. 1813: fever. NAS Adm. list, 1821, No. 196; TNA ADM 103/433, No. 1182, and ADM 103/648.

197. Prosper Verdier (or Vidier), soldier, 4th Artillery, 20, b. Vitrie, capd 27 Jun. 1812 at Salamanca, arr. V from G 12 Jan. 1813, d. 19 Mar. 1813: fever. NAS Adm. list, 1821, No. 306; TNA ADM 103/435, No. 6309, and ADM 103/648.

198. Jean M. Perotté (or Pirotte or Perot), soldier (or sergeant), 47th (or 45th) line regt, 28, b. Liège, capd 15 Aug. 1809 at Flushing, arr.V from Portsmouth 1 Oct. 1811, d. 24 Mar. 1813: pneumonia. NAS Adm. list, 1821, No. 242; TNA ADM 103/434, No. 3994, and ADM 103/648.

199. Pierre Millebois, soldier, 82nd line regt, 21, b. Machy, capd 24 Feb. 1809 on Martinique, arr. V from Plymouth 2 Sep. 1811, d. 25 Mar. 1813: fever. NAS Adm. list, 1821, No. 220; TNA ADM 103/434, No. 2611, and ADM 103/648.

200. Etienne Henocque (or Henacque), soldier, 26th line regt, 23, b. Biscourt, capd n.d. on Martinique, arr. V date n.k., d. 25 Mar. 1813: cause of death unstated. NAS Adm. list, 1821, No. 147. [Henocque has not been found in the Valleyfield Entry Books nor any record of his death among the certificates in TNA ADM 103/648].

201. Lorenzo (or Laurent) Garbelli, soldier, 5th Italian (or 5th line) regt, 27, b. Lonti, capd 24 Aug. 1807 at Corfu, arr. V from EM 11 Mar. 1811, d. 4 Apr. 1813: phthisis. NAS Adm. list, 1821, No. 125; TNA ADM 103/433, No. 1388, and ADM 103/648.

202. Louis Replot, soldier, 34th line regt (or 6th Legion), 23, b. Sedan, capd 9 Oct. 1810 at St Herme (or St Herene), arr. V from Portsmouth 21 Oct. 1811, d. 4 Apr. 1813: phthisis. NAS Adm. list, 1821, No. 257; TNA ADM 103/435, No. 5026, and ADM 103/648.

203. Jean Coumont (or Commone), soldier, 82nd line regt, 29, b. Metz, capd 24 Feb. 1809 on Martinique, arr. V from Plymouth 19 Sep. 1811, d. 5 Apr. 1813: phthisis. NAS Adm. list, 1821, No. 79; TNA ADM 103/434, No. 3199, and ADM 103/648.

204. Orne De Vaux (alias Arné Devaus Yvon), soldier, 48th line regt, 23, b. Cretoul, capd 21 Aug. 1809 at Flushing, arr. V from EM 11 Mar. 1811, d. 6 Apr. 1813: phthisis. NAS Adm. list, 1821, No. 309; TNA ADM 103/432, No. 964, and ADM 103/648.

205. Jean Lequelles (or Sickerts), soldier 1st line (or 1st Prussian) regt, 32, b. Kamitz, capd 31 Jul. 1809 at Campveere, arr. V from Plymouth 19 Sep. 1811, d. 20 Apr. 1813: fever. NAS Adm. list, 1821, No. 191; TNA ADM 103/434, No. 3159, and ADM 103/648.

206. Alexis Barbet, soldier, 82nd (or 12th) line regt, 38, b. Amiens, capd 24 Feb. 1809 on Martinique, arr. V from Plymouth c. 1 Oct. 1811, d. 21 Apr. 1813: phthisis. NAS Adm. list, 1821, No. 12; TNA ADM 103/435, No. 4710, and ADM 103/648.

207. Alexandre (or Alexis) Meugnier (or Meunier), soldier, 119th line regt, 21, b. Terreau (or Terraw), capd 21 Jun. 1812 at Fort Le Quito, arr. V from Portsmouth 21 Jul. 1812, d. 21 Apr. 1813: 'Lumber Abcess.' NAS Adm. list, 1821, No. 215; TNA ADM 103/435, No. 5491, and ADM 103/648.

208. Sulpice Soriman (or Surimant), soldier, 27th light infantry, 20, b. Polignan, capd 15 Aug. 1809 at Flushing (or Gulf of Venice, n.d.), arr. V from Portsmouth 21 Oct. 1811, d. 2 May 1813: fever. NAS Adm. list, 1821, No. 284; TNA ADM 103/435, No. 5189, and ADM 103/648.

209. Gilles François Nicolas, seaman, 32, b. St Malo, capd 27 Nov. 1808 on *Swallow*, a prize to *Iena* m.o.w., in the English Channel, arr. V from EM 11 Mar. 1811, d. 3 May 1813: phthisis. NAS Adm. list, 1821, No. 230; TNA ADM 103/432, No. 1008, and ADM 103/648.

210. Jean Malerati (or Malgrati), soldier, 82nd line regt, 24, b. Auvignac, capd 24 Feb. 1809 on Martinique, arr. V from EM 11 Mar. 1811, d. 5 May 1813: phthisis. NAS Adm. list, 1821, No. 204; TNA ADM 103/432, No. 593, and ADM 103/648.

211.   Jean François Tonellier (or Tondelier), sergeant (or soldier), 3rd Artillery, 21, b. Doucoeur, capd 8 Mar. 1809 on Martinique, arr. V from Portsmouth 1 Oct. 1811, d. 15 May 1813: fever. NAS Adm. list, 1821, No. 290; TNA ADM 103/434, No. 4004, and ADM 103/648.

212.   Pierre Madie, soldier, 82nd line regt, 21, b. La Rochelle, capd Oct. 1810 at Coimbra, arr. V from Plymouth 19 Sep. 1811, d. 17 May 1813: phthisis. NAS Adm. list, 1821, No. 200; TNA ADM 103/434, No. 3327, and ADM 103/648.

213.   Jean Pierre Giraudon, soldier, 82nd line regt, 28, b. Domais, capd 24 Feb. 1809 on Martinique, arr. V from Plymouth 19 Sep. 1811, d. 17 May 1813: phthisis. NAS Adm. list, 1821, No. 131; TNA ADM 103/434, No. 3235, and ADM 103/648.

214.   Albert Anton (or Antone), soldier, 1st Colonial Bn, 25, b. Giebets (or Giebetz), capd 15 Aug. 1809 at Flushing, arr. V from EM 11 Mar. 1811, d. 21 May 1813: phthisis. NAS Adm. list, 1821, No. 7; TNA ADM 103/433, No. 2039, and ADM 103/648.

215.   Pierre Chuchère (alias Jean David Dominique Jance or Janie), seaman, 21, b. St Ouve (or St Auve), capd 19 Oct. 1810 on *Somnambule* (or n.d. on *Le Grand Napoléon*) priv. in the English Channel, arr. V from EM 11 Mar. 1811, d. 24 May 1813: 'Shott Attempting to Escape.' NAS Adm. list, 1821, No. 69; TNA ADM 103/433, No. 1708, and ADM 103/648.

216.   Joseph Briant, seaman, 31, b. Dieppe, capd n.d. on *Général Canclaux* priv. in the English Channel, arr. V from G 1 Sep. 1812, d. 24 May 1813: phthisis. NAS Adm. list, 1821, No. 48; TNA ADM 103/435, No. 5638, and ADM 103/648.

217.   Dominique De Regel (or De Kegel), soldier, 82nd line regt, 28, b. Flanders, capd 24 Feb. 1809 on Martinque, arr. V from Plymouth c. 1 Oct. 1811, d. 6 Jun. 1813: phthisis. NAS Adm. list, 1821, No. 91; TNA ADM 103/435, No. 4693, and ADM 103/648.

218.   Giuseppe Ferrari, soldier, 2nd Italian regt, 28, b. Caravaggia, capd 29 Sep. 1809 in the Gulf of Otranto, arr. V from EM 11 Mar. 1811, d. 8 Jun. 1813: phthisis. NAS Adm. list, 1821, No. 108; TNA ADM 103/434, No. 2165, and ADM 103/648.

219.   Jean Pelias, soldier, 26th line regt, 31, b. Rouen, capd 6 Feb. 1809 on Martinique, arr. V from EM 11 Mar. 1811, d. 9 Jun. 1813: phthisis. NAS Adm. list, 1821, No. 239; TNA ADM 103/432, No. 547, and ADM 103/648.

220.   Michel Cabon, seaman, 25, b.Croise, capd 17 Apr. 1809 on *D'Hautpoul* m.o.w. off the Saintes, arr. V from EM 11 Mar. 1811, d. 10 Jun. 1813: consumption. NAS Adm. list, 1821, No. 53; TNA ADM 103/432, No. 1018, and ADM 103/648.

221.   Jean Pierre Chassier, soldier, 82nd line regt, 33, b. Montoul, capd 24 Feb. 1809 on Martinique, arr. V from EM 11 Mar. 1811, d. 13 Jun. 1813: consumption. NAS Adm. list, 1821, No. 70; TNA ADM 103/433, No. 2118, and ADM 103/648.

222.   Arnold Hellewarst (or Helluvardt), sergeant major, 1st line (or 1st Dutch?) regt, 39, b. Arnheim, capd 31 Jul. 1809 at Campveere, arr. V from Plymouth 19 Sep. 1811, d. 18 Jun. 1813: consumption. NAS Adm. list, 1821, No. 145; TNA ADM 103/434, No. 3104, and ADM 103/648.

223.   Valentin Friquet, soldier, Basque 66th regt, 20, b. Lantage, capd 13 Nov. 1809 on a naval vessel off Ireland, arr. V from Plymouth 19 Sep. 1811, d. 18 Jun. 1813: consumption. NAS Adm. list, 1821, No. 120; TNA ADM 103/434, No. 3279, and ADM 103/648.

224. Joseph Jolli, drummer, 48th line regt, 27, b. Angoulême, capd 15 Aug. 1809 at Flushing, arr. V from Portsmouth 1 Oct. 1811, d. 19 Jun. 1813: fever. NAS Adm. list, 1821, No. 158; TNA ADM 103/434, No. 3924, and ADM 103/648.

225. Jean Etienne, soldier, 65th line regt, 19, b. Lacoux, capd 15 Aug. 1809 at Flushing, arr. V from the south of England 14 Oct. 1811, d. 21 Jun. 1813: consumption. NAS Adm. list, 1821, No. 105; TNA ADM 103/435, No. 4865, and ADM 103/648.

226. Simon Brento, soldier, 1st Legion, 21, b. Charenton, capd 17 Apr. 1809 at the capitulation of the Saintes, arr. V from Plymouth 30 Sep. 1811, d. 22 Jun. 1813: consumption. NAS Adm. list, 1821, No. 46; TNA ADM 103/434, No. 3651, and ADM 103/648.

227. Laurent Gautier, soldier, 119th line regt, 25, b. St André, capd n.d. at Le Quito, arr. V from G 1 Sep. 1812, d. 26 Jun. 1813: consumption. NAS Adm. list, 1821, No. 127; TNA ADM 103/435, No. 6137, and ADM 103/648.

228. Toussaint Pinker, soldier, 72nd line regt, 20, b. Plekat, capd 15 Aug. 1809 at Flushing, arr. V from Portsmouth 21 Oct. 1811, d. 28 Jun. 1813: consumption. NAS Adm. list, 1821, No. 247; TNA ADM 103/435, No. 5188, and ADM 103/648.

229. Jean M. Plodome, soldier, 82nd line regt, 31, b. Ilveyade, capd 24 Feb. 1809 on Martinique, arr. V from Plymouth 2 Sep. 1811, d. 11 Jul. 1813: fever. NAS Adm. list, 1821, No. 249; TNA ADM 103/434, No. 2507, and ADM 103/648.

230. Jean Cougner, soldier, 82nd line regt, 38, b. Arleray, capd 24 Feb. 1809 on Martinique, arr. V from the south of England 14 Oct. 1811, d. 13 Jul. 1813: consumption. NAS Adm. list, 1821, No. 78; TNA ADM 103/435, No. 4733, and ADM 103/648.

231. Pierre Pion, soldier, 82nd line regt, 28, b. Cheppo, capd 24 Feb. 1809 on Martinique, arr. V from Plymouth c. 1 Oct. 1811, d. 16 Jul. 1813: fever. NAS Adm. list, 1821, No. 248; TNA ADM 103/435, No. 4708, and ADM 103/648.

232. Jean Baptiste Revoir, soldier, 34th line regt, 26, b. Artois, capd 27 Nov. 1811 at San Martin, Spain, arr. V from G 5 Jul. 1813, d. 17 Jul. 1813: consumption. NAS Adm. list, 1821, No. 258; TNA ADM 103/435, No. 6432, and ADM 103/648.

233. François Legère (or Leger), soldier, 82nd line regt, 34, b. Dijon, capd 24 Feb. 1809 on Martinique, arr. V from Plymouth 2 Sep. 1811, d. 27 Jul. 1813: consumption. NAS Adm. list, 1821, No. 178; TNA ADM 103/434, No. 2554, and ADM 103/648.

234. Benoit Landesse (or Landes), corporal (or soldier), 26th line regt, 31, b. Alasse, capd 24 Feb. 1809 on Martinique, arr. V from Plymouth c. 1 Oct. 1811, d. 27 Jul. 1813: consumption. NAS Adm. list, 1821, No. 168; TNA ADM 103/435, No. 4390, and ADM 103/648.

235. Pierre Moral (or Morell), soldier, Prussian regt (or Chasseurs Rentrés), 25, b. Besançon, capd 16 Aug. 1809 at Flushing, arr. V from Portsmouth 21 Oct. 1811, d. 30 Jul. 1813: consumption. NAS Adm. list, 1821, No. 226; TNA ADM 103/435, No. 5066, and ADM 103/648.

236. Claude Chavant, sous-lieutenant (or lieut.), 12th Dragoons, 28, b. Auxonne, capd 23 Jul. 1808 at Baylen, arr. V on 6 Jan. 1813 from Lanark 'for medical Assistance', d. 8 Aug. 1813: consumption. NAS Adm. list, 1821, No. 66; TNA ADM 103/435, No. 6256, and ADM 103/648.

237. Louis M. Bellec, soldier, 13th Legion, 23, b. Rhennes, capd 15 Aug. 1809 on Walcheren, arr. V from Portsmouth 1 Oct. 1811, d. 9 Aug. 1813: consumption. NAS Adm. list, 1821, No. 17; TNA ADM 103/434, No. 4179, and ADM 103/648.

238. François Lemonier, soldier, 66th line regt, 30, b. Auvre, capd 3 Apr. 1811 at Ciudad Rodrigo, arr. V from G 5 Jul. 1813, d. 10 Aug. 1813: consumption. NAS Adm. list, 1821, No. 193; TNA ADM 103/435, No. 6431, and ADM 103/648.

239. Hyacinth Croisé, seaman, 17, b. La Hougue, capd 17 Oct. 1810 on *Le Vengeur* priv. in the English Channel, arr. V from EM 11 Mar. 1811, d. 11 Aug. 1813: consumption. NAS Adm. list, 1821, No. 82; TNA ADM 103/432, No. 9, and ADM 103/648.

240. Louis Tortai, soldier, 22nd line regt, 19, b. Tourigny, capd 15 Aug. 1809 at Flushing, arr.V from Portsmouth 21 Oct. 1811, d. 31 Aug. 1813 from 'Abcess.' NAS Adm. list, 1821, No. 292; TNA ADM 103/435, No. 4981, and ADM 103/648.

241. Victor Hermann (alias Honoré Verstorf), soldier, 15th line regt, 26, b. Cologne (or 'Boulogne'), capd 7 Apr. 1812 at Badajoz, arr. V from P 31 Jul. 1813, d. 4 Oct. 1813: phthisis. NAS Adm. list, 1821, No. 148; TNA ADM 103/113, No. 6676, and ADM 103/648.

242. Jean Tinette (or Trenette), seaman, 37, b. Bordeaux, capd 4 Feb. 1809 on *L'Amphitrite* frig. at Martinique, arr. V from EM 11 Mar. 1811, d. 5 Oct. 1813: 'Erisipilas.' NAS Adm. list, 1821, No. 293; TNA ADM 103/434, No. 2145, and ADM 103/648.

243. Basile Balli, soldier, 34th line regt, 21, b. Herard, capd 7 Sep.1810 at St Herme, Spain, arr. V from Portsmouth 21 Oct. 1811, d. 15 Oct. 1813: phthisis. NAS Adm. list, 1821, No. 11; TNA ADM 103/435, No. 5027, and ADM 103/648.

244. Louis Marie Gouastoué, seaman, 36, b. St Malo, capd 6 Feb. 1806 on *Jupiter* m.o.w. off St Domingo, arr. V from EM 11 Mar. 1811, d. 15 Nov. 1813: fever. NAS Adm. list, 1821, No. 133; TNA ADM 103/433, No. 1958, and ADM 103/648.

245. François Lardin, soldier, Basque 66th regt, 20, b. Pomsaux (or Panissan), capd 13 Nov. 1809 on a naval vessel off Ireland, arr. V from Plymouth 19 Sep.1811, d. 19 Nov. 1813: phthisis. NAS Adm. list, 1821, No. 173; TNA ADM 103/434, No. 3277, and ADM 103/648.

246. Jean Rodost, soldier, 6th line regt, 35, b. Dukensi, capd 24 Aug. 1807 on *Notre Dame de Grace* trans. in the Mediterranean, arr. V from Portsmouth 1 Oct. 1811, d. 21 Nov. 1813: phthisis. NAS Adm. list, 1821, No. 266; TNA ADM 103/434, No. 4016, and ADM 103/648.

247. Isidore Colombo (or Colombi), soldier, 16th line regt, 25, b. 'Save in Piedmont', capd 7 Apr. 1812 at Badajoz, arr. V from P 31 Jul. 1813, d. 22 Nov. 1813: phthisis. NAS Adm. list, 1821, No. 73; TNA ADM 103/113, No. 6863, and ADM 103/648.

248. Johannes Barto (or Berthaud), soldier, 1st Artillery, 40, b. Palma (or Amsterdam or Utrecht), capd Jul. 1809 at Campvere, arr. V from Plymouth 19 Sep. 1811, d. 12 Dec. 1813: phthisis. NAS Adm. list, 1821, No. 27; TNA ADM 103/434, No. 3118, and unnumbered death certificate in ADM 103/648.

249. Victor Bouvrais (or Bouré), soldier, 66th line regt, 20, b. Portmoc (or Portmec), capd n.d. at Coimbra, arr. V from Portsmouth 21 Oct. 1811, d. 16 Dec. 1813: phthisis. NAS Adm. list, 1821, No. 41; TNA ADM 103/435, No. 5040, and ADM 103/648.

250. Antoine Monier, seaman, 31, b. Marseilles, capd 4 Nov. 1805 on *Duguay Trouin* m.o.w. off Cape Ortegal, arr. V from EM 11 Mar. 1811, d. 17 Dec. 1813: phthisis. NAS Adm. list, 1821, No. 225; TNA ADM 103/432, No. 1037, and ADM 103/648.

251. Pierre Quel, soldier, 82nd line regt, 34, b. Honceau (or Honcault), capd 24 Feb. 1809 on Martinique, arr. V from Plymouth c. 1 Oct. 1811, d. 20 Dec. 1813: phthisis. NAS Adm. list, 1821, No. 255; TNA ADM 103/435, No. 4658, and ADM 103/648.

252. Pierre Feret (or Ferete), soldier, 19th Dragoons, 27, b. Angers, capd 1809 at Vigo, arr. V from G 1 Sep. 1812, d. 22 Dec. 1813: phthisis. NAS Adm. list, 1821, No. 109; TNA ADM 103/435, No. 6020, and ADM 103/648.

253. Guillaume Poulmard, seaman, 34, b. Brest, capd 6 Feb. 1806 on *La Bellone* priv. in the West Indies, arr. V from EM 11 Mar. 1811, d. 23 Dec. 1813: phthisis. NAS Adm. list, 1821, No. 250; TNA ADM 103/434, No. 2431, and ADM 103/648.

254. Herman Bugel (or Beugles), sergeant, Hanoverian Legion, 40, b. Munster, capd 7 Apr. 1812 at Badajoz, arr. V from P 31 Jul. 1813, d. 28 Dec. 1813: phthisis. NAS Adm. list, 1821, No. 29; TNA ADM 103/113, No. 6674, and ADM 103/648.

255. Jean Millet, seaman, capd on *Le Figaro* priv., no other details given, d. 1 Jan. 1814: cause of death unstated. NAS Adm. list, 1821, No. 221. (Millet has not been found in the Valleyfield Entry Books or among the death certificates in TNA ADM 103/648).

256. Benois (or Benoit) Jordan (or Jourdant), soldier, 31st light infantry (or line regt), 25, b. Wolgram, capd 7 Oct. 1810 at Coimbra, arr. V from EC on date u. (c. Dec. 1813?), d. 5 Jan. 1814: phthisis. NAS Adm. list, 1821, No. 160; TNA ADM 103/436, No. 7610, ADM 103/648, No. 7610, and ADM 103/114, No. 1081.

257. Jean Baptiste Dubois, seaman, 32, b. Bordeaux, capd 1804 after the shipwreck of *L'Atalante* frig. at the Cape of Good Hope, arr. V from G 1 Sep. 1812, d. 16 Jan. 1814: fever. NAS Adm. list, 1821, No. 101; TNA ADM 103/435, No. 5747, and ADM 103/648.

258. Jean Pierre Legossi (or Legosse or Legofe), seaman, aged 16 (or 19), b. Brittany (or Broons), capd Oct. 1810 on *La Caroline* priv. in the English Channel, arr. V from EM 11 Mar. 1811, d. 22 Jan. 1814: debility. NAS Adm. list, 1821, No. 179; TNA ADM 103/432, No. 954, and ADM 103/648.

259. Pierre Lapousse, soldier, 3rd line regt, 32, b. Sardatz, capd 19 Nov. 1810 in Portugal, arr. V from Plymouth 19 Sep. 1811, d. 28 Jan. 1814: pneumonia. NAS Adm. list, 1821, No. 172; TNA ADM 103/434, No. 3323, and ADM 103/648.

260. Jean Pierre Martin, soldier, 6th line regt, 33, b. Lompon, capd 24 Aug. 1807 on a trans. off Corfu, arr. V from Portsmouth 21 Oct. 1811, d. 2 Feb. 1814: phthisis. NAS Adm. list, 1821, No. 208; TNA ADM 103/435, No. 5196, and ADM 103/648.

261. Joseph Vandresteraelen (or Vanderstralen), soldier, 82nd line regt, 22, b. Huysee, capd 24 Feb. 1809 on Martinique, arr. V from EM 11 Mar. 1811, d. 10 Feb. 1814: phthisis. NAS Adm. list, 1821, No. 299; TNA ADM 103/433, No. 1327, and ADM 103/648.

262. Dominique Gerrullot (or Guerrillot), soldier, 15th line regt, 22, b. Dotusinère (or Dotasiner), capd 13 Apr. 1810 in Spain, arr. V from EM 11 Mar. 1811, d. 13 Feb. 1814: phthisis. NAS Adm. list, 1821, No. 140; TNA ADM 103/433, No. 1189, and ADM 103/648.

263. Etienne Gautier (or Gautière), soldier, 6th line regt, 27, b. Maresplay (or Mane-splay), capd 27 Aug. 1807 on *Notre Dame de Grace* trans. in the Mediterranean, arr. V from Portsmouth 1 Oct. 1811, d. 20 Feb. 1814: phthisis. NAS Adm. list, 1821, No. 128; TNA ADM 103/434, No. 4030, and ADM 103/648.

264.   Pierre Sylvestre Lanfranc, seaman, 27, b. Marseilles, capd 14 Mar. 1806 on *Marengo* m.o.w. in the East Indies, arr. V from G 5 Jul. 1813, d. 1 Mar. 1814: phthisis. NAS Adm. list, 1821, No. 164; TNA ADM 103/435, No. 6390, and ADM 103/648.

265.   Paul Gantini (or Gantilli), soldier, 9th light infantry, 24, b. Volpiano, capd 3 May 1811 at Almeida, arr. V from P 31 Jul. 1813, d. 2 Mar. 1814: phthisis. NAS Adm. list, 1821, No. 124; TNA ADM 103/113, No. 6994, and ADM 103/648.

266.   Claude (or Louis) Marchand, soldier, 82nd line regt, 30, b. Lyons, capd 24 Feb. 1809 on Martinique, arr. V from Plymouth 30 Sep. 1811, d. 4 Mar. 1814: phthisis. NAS Adm. list, 1821, No. 206; TNA ADM 103/434, No. 3451, and ADM 103/648.

267.   Pierre Noel Saillot, seaman, 20, b. Dieppe, capd 28 Oct. 1807 on *Le Requin* priv. in the English Channel, arr. V from EM 11 Mar. 1811, d. 6 Mar. 1814: phthisis. NAS Adm. list, 1821, No. 274; TNA ADM 103/432, No. 868, and ADM 103/648.

268.   Jacob Krensember (or Kremsember), soldier, 48th line (or Porto (sic)) regt, 30, b. Mons, capd 7 Apr. 1812 at Badajoz, arr. V from P 31 Jul. 1813, d. 11 Mar. 1814: cause of death unstated. NAS Adm. list, 1821, No. 162; TNA ADM 103/113, No. 6715, and ADM 103/648, No. 1715.

269.   Etienne Giro (or Giero or Giraud), soldier, 32nd line regt, 26, b. Clermont, capd 10 Mar. 1809 in Portugal, arr. V from EM 11 Mar. 1811, d. 21 Mar. 1814: 'in consquence of a wound in the breast which penetrated through both sides of the aorta. It appears he was wounded in a duel with a comrade. They fought with the blades of a pair of scissors fixed on the ends of two sticks.' NAS Adm. list, 1821, No. 129; TNA ADM 103/432, No. 879, and ADM 103/648.

270.   Charles Fremon, seaman, 50, b. Granville, capd 15 Dec. 1808 on *Iena* m.o.w. in the East Indies, arr. V from EM 11 Mar. 1811, d. 29 Mar. 1814: phthisis. NAS Adm. list, 1821, No. 118; TNA ADM 103/432, No. 368, and ADM 103/648.

271.   Pierre Paquet (or Pasquet or Pacquet), soldier, regt u., 24, b. Genongal, capd 4 Nov. 1805 on *Formidable* m.o.w. off Cape Ortegal, arr. V from G 1 Sep. 1812, d. 2 Apr. 1814: fever. NAS Adm. list, 1821, No. 235; TNA ADM 103/435, No. 5861, and ADM 103/648.

272.   Louis Vasseur, seaman, 21, b. Spikar, capd 4 Dec. 1810 on *Le Roi de Naples* priv. in the English Channel, arr. V from EM 11 Mar. 1811, d. 3 Apr. 1814: phthisis. NAS Adm. list, 1821, No. 301; TNA ADM 103/433, No. 1492, and ADM 103/648.

273.   Bertrand Roulet (or Bernard Roulette), soldier, 12th light infantry, 24, b. Tarbe, capd 21 Aug. 1808 in Portugal, arr. V from EM 11 Mar. 1811, d. 3 Apr. 1814: phthisis. NAS Adm. list, 1821, No. 272; TNA ADM 103/433, No. 1942, and ADM 103/648.

274.   Jacques Amoureux, soldier, 44th Marin Bn, 21, b. St Herse, capd 7 Oct. 1810 at Coimbra, arr. V from P 31 Jul. 1813, d. 3 Apr. 1814: phthisis. NAS Adm. list, 1821, No. 5; TNA ADM 103/113, No. 7457, and ADM 103/648.

275.   Louis Brochard, soldier, 1st Colonial Bn, 35, b. Strasbourg, capd 16 Aug. 1809 at Flushing, arr. V from EM 11 Mar. 1811, d. 10 Apr. 1814: phthisis. NAS Adm. list, 1821, No. 49; TNA ADM 103/434, No. 2310, and ADM 103/648.

276.   Jacques Desfarges, soldier, 86th line regt, 19, b.Villebanois, capd 21 Mar. 1810 on *La Necessité* frig. or sloop 'at sea', arr. V from Portsmouth 21 Oct. 1811, d. 10 Apr. 1814: phthisis. NAS Adm. list, 1821, No. 98; TNA ADM 103/435, No. 5173, and ADM 103/648.

277. Joseph Muzard, seaman, 21, b. Pontoise, capd 19 Oct. 1810 on *Somnambule* priv. in the English Channel, arr. V from EM 11 Mar. 1811, d. 16 Apr. 1814: phthisis. NAS Adm. list, 1821, No. 229; TNA ADM 103/432, No. 233, and ADM 103/648.

278. Jacques Mayer, soldier, 2nd line regt, 32, b. Angers, capd 4 Nov. 1805 on *Formidable* (or *Mont Blanc*) m.o.w. off Cape Ortegal, arr. V from G 1 Sep. 1812, d. 21 Apr. 1814: phthisis. NAS Adm. list, 1821, No. 212; TNA ADM 103/435, No. 5872, and ADM 103/648.

279. Nicolas Gilot (or Gilau), soldier, 48th line regt, 21, b. Lorraine, capd 15 Aug. 1809 at Flushing, arr. V from EM 11 Mar. 1811, d. 22 Apr. 1814: phthisis. NAS Adm. list, 1821, No. 130; TNA ADM 103/434, No. 2298, and ADM 103/648.

280. Theodore Fouqueur (or Fouqueux) (alias Pierre Laporte), prizemaster, 23, b. Dieppe, capd 1 May 1809 on *La Princesse de Boulogne* priv. in the English Channel, (or aged 32, b. Tréport, soldier, 3rd Artillery, capd n.d. on Martinique), arr. V from EM 11 Mar. 1811, d. 25 Apr. 1814: phthisis. NAS Adm. list, 1821, No. 171; TNA ADM 103/432, No. 5, and ADM 103/648.

281. Jean Pierre Gaillet (or Jaillier), soldier, 1st Artillery, 23, b. Sallin, département of Jura, capd 10 Feb. 1809 on *Junon* frig. off the Saintes, arr. V from Portsmouth 1 Oct. 1811, d. 26 Apr. 1814: phthisis. NAS Adm. list, 1821, No. 154; TNA ADM 103/434, No. 4152, and ADM 103/648.

282. Jean Baptiste Demasure (or De Mausure), soldier, 2nd light infantry, 23, b. Brabant, capd 21 Aug 1808 in Portugal, arr. V from EM 11 Mar. 1811, d. 28 Apr. 1814: phthisis. NAS Adm. list, 1821, No. 96; TNA ADM 103/433, No. 1948, and ADM 103/648.

283. Bernard Perin (or Perrin), sergeant (or soldier), 26th line regt, 39 (or 44), b. Rissaucourt (or Resancourt), capd 24 Feb. 1809 on Martinique, arr. V from Portsmouth 1 Oct. 1811, d. 1 May 1814: phthisis. NAS Adm. list, 1821, No. 241; TNA ADM 103/434, No. 4077, and ADM 103/648.

284. Jacques Bretin, soldier, 82nd line regt, 35, b. Artilly (or Artilie), capd 24 Feb. 1809 on Martinique, arr. V from the south of England 1 Oct. 1811, d. 1 May 1814: phthisis. NAS ADM list, 1821, No. 47; TNA ADM 103/435, No. 4619, and ADM 103/648.

285. Jean De La Touche, soldier, 82nd line regt, 30, b. Muel, capd 24 Feb. 1809 on Martinique, arr. V from Plymouth 2 Sep. 1811, d. 3 May 1814: phthisis. NAS Adm. list, 1821, No. 93; TNA ADM 103/434, No. 2836, and ADM 103/648.

286. Jean Nicolas Fervagné, soldier, 26th line regt, 26 (or 30), b. Amiens (or Ameyn), capd 24 Feb. 1809 on Martinique, arr. V from Plymouth 1 Oct. 1811, d. 10 May 1814: phthisis. NAS Adm. list, 1821, No. 110; TNA ADM 103/435, No. 4372, and ADM 103/648.

287. Jacob Fischback, soldier, Hesse-Darmstadt regt, 30, b. Ambidoeuf, capd 7 Apr. 1812 at Badajoz, arr. V from P 31 Jul. 1813, d. 10 May 1814: phthisis. NAS ADM list, 1821, No. 112; TNA ADM 103/113, No. 6645, and ADM 103/648.

288. François Morillon (or Maurillon), sergeant, 50th line regt, aged 40, b. Tours, capd 12 Mar. 1811 at Pombal, arr. V from G 5 Jul. 1813, d. 12 May 1814: phthisis. NAS Adm. list, 1821, No. 211; TNA ADM 103/435, No. 6371, and ADM 103/648.

289. Nicolas Pierre, lieut., 26th line regt, 40, b. Couranvoie, capd 24 Feb. 1809 on Martinique, arr. V from Hawick 24 Apr. 1814 'for medical Assistance', d. 14 May 1814: phthisis. NAS Adm. list, 1821, No. 246; TNA ADM 103/436, No. 7648, and ADM 103/648.

290. Louis Emanuel (or Emile) Bernard, seaman, 16 (or 22), b. Havre, capd 8 Feb. 1808 on *Le Furet* priv. 'at Sea', arr. V from EM 11 Mar. 1811, d. 16 May 1814: phthisis. NAS Adm. list, 1821, No. 23; TNA ADM 103/433, No. 1479, and ADM 103/648.

291. Jean Baptiste Billoc (or Belloc), soldier, 122nd line regt, 20 (or 24), b. Auxonne (Auson), capd Mar. 1809 at Vigo, arr. V from Plymouth 19 Sep. 1811, d. 16 May 1814: phthisis. NAS Adm. list, 1821, No. 19; TNA ADM 103/434, No. 3337, and ADM 103/648.

292. Pierre Coline (or Colin), soldier, 65th line regt, 19 (or 25), b. Brier (or Brière), capd 15 Aug. 1809 at Flushing, arr. V from the south of England 14 Oct. 1811, d. 17 May 1814: phthisis. NAS Adm. list, 1821, No. 72; TNA ADM 103/435, No. 4851, and ADM 103/648.

293. Leonard Fraideau, soldier, 6th line regt, 21 (or 28), b. Agens (or Gentz), capd 11 Jan. 1808 on *St Nicolas* trans. 'at Sea', arr. V from Portsmouth 1 Oct. 1811, d. 19 May 1814: phthisis. NAS Adm. list, 1821, No. 119; TNA ADM 103/434, No. 3810, and ADM 103/648.

294. Albain Lugue, seaman, 23 (or 29), b. Lorient, capd 30 Jan. 1809 on *Charlemagne* m.o.w. 'at Sea', arr. V from EM 11 Mar. 1811, d. 20 May 1814: phthisis. NAS Adm. list, 1821, No. 199; TNA ADM 103/433, No. 2051, and ADM 103/648.

295.   Joseph Dalmat (or Antoine Delmas), soldier, 31st line regt, 20 (or 23), b. Montdoive (or Montdoui, or Mondovi), capd n.d. in Portugal, arr. V from Plymouth 30 Sep. 1811, d. 25 May 1814: phthisis. NAS Adm. list, 1821, No. 95; TNA ADM 103/434, No. 3666, and ADM 103/648.

296. Louis Bossy (also known as Bossie, Canope, Borgnes, and Jean Berquet), seaman, 20, b. Painboeuf, capd 18 Feb. 1808 on *Malvina* priv. off the Azores, (and/or soldier, 82nd line regt, 36, b. Bessières, capd n.d. on Martinique), arr. V from EM 11 Mar. 1811, d. 27 May 1814: phthisis. NAS Adm. list, 1821, No. 22; TNA ADM 103/432, No. 138, and ADM 103/648.

297. M. Joseph Silas Priere, seaman, 26 (or 31), b. Havre, capd 24 Feb. 1809 on *L'Amphitrite* frig. off Martinique, arr. V from EM 11 Mar. 1811, d. 27 May 1814: phthisis. NAS Adm. list, 1821, No. 253; TNA ADM 103/434, No. 2197, and ADM 103/648.

298. Gervais Richard, soldier, 47th regt, 24 (or 26), b. Compiègne, capd n.d. (1809?) at Vigo, arr. V from G on (probably) 1 Sep. 1812, d. 27 Jun. 1814: phthisis. NAS Adm. list, 1821, No. 259; TNA ADM 103/435, No. 6088, and ADM 103/648.

299. Pierre Peuchrot (or Pucherot), soldier, 59th line regt, 23, b. Marcourt, capd 7 Jul. 1810 at St Antonio, Spain, arr. V from Plymouth 19 Sep. 1811, d. 24 Jul. 1814: phthisis. NAS Adm. list, 1821, No. 244; TNA ADM 103/434, No. 3315, and ADM 103/648.

300. Antonio Bosco (or Bosca), soldier, 82nd line regt, 28, b. St George, capd 24 Feb. 1809 on Martinique, arr. V from Plymouth c. 1 Oct. 1811, d. 31 Jul. 1814: phthisis. NAS Adm. list, 1821, No. 38; TNA ADM 103/435, No. 4568, and ADM 103/648.

PERTH

NB: Those marked (+) have had the entry in the Entry Book recording their death scored through lightly in pencil or ink: the deletion may have been intended simply to signify their reduction from the total number of prisoners or, perhaps less likely, that they had not in fact died in captivity at Perth. For those marked (*) no death certificate survives in TNA ADM 103/648.

1. Toussaint Basin (or Bazin), soldier, 88th line regt, 23, b. 'Turneau 6 Leagues from Paris', capd 7 Apr. 1812 at Badajoz, arr. P from Portsmouth 14 Oct. 1812, d. 27 Oct. 1812: 'Scurvy and ... state of debility.' TNA ADM 103/263, No. 2085; ADM 103/648.

2. Gaspard Potpaune (or Potpaume), soldier, Hesse-Darmstadt regt, 23, b. Ampt Asfeld, capd 7 Apr. 1812 at Badajoz, arr. P from Portsmouth 14 Oct. 1812, d. 28 Oct. 1812: 'Scurvy and the ... state of debility.' TNA ADM 103/263, No. 2077; ADM 103/648.

3. André Lambert, fusilier, 1st line (or light infantry) regt, 28, b. Grace, capd 22 Jul. 1812 at Salamanca, arr. P from Portsmouth 15 Oct. 1812, d. 4 Nov. 1812: 'Scurvy & Extreme Debility.' TNA ADM 103/264, No. 2284; ADM 103/648.

4. (+)(*) Augustin Constant, brigadier, 21st Chasseurs, 36, b. Florence, capd 7 Apr. 1812 at Badajoz, arr. P from Portsmouth 13 Oct. 1812, d. 6 Nov. 1812: cause of death unstated. TNA ADM 103/263, No. 1613.

5. (*) Pierre Michel, cannonier, 1st Artillery, 24, b. Paris, capd 19 Jan. 1812 at Ciudad Rodrigo, arr. P from Portsmouth 14 Oct. 1812, d. 7 Nov. 1812: cause of death unstated. TNA ADM 103/263, No. 2041.

6. (*) M. Plansaier, corporal, 103rd line regt, 26, b. Skeda, capd 7 Apr. 1812 at Badajoz, arr. P from Portsmouth 14 Oct. 1812, d. 9 Nov. 1812: cause of death unstated. TNA ADM 103/263, No. 1953.

7. (*) Jean Lebrave, soldier, 17th cavalry regt, aged 37, b. St Germain, capd 17 May 1809 at Oporto, arr. P from Portsmouth 20 or 21 Aug. 1812, d. 11 Nov. 1812: cause of death unstated. TNA ADM 103/263, No. 488.

8. Ludwig (or Ludovic) Histchin (or Hestien or Hestetrien), soldier, 5th Artillery Bn, 30 (or 22) b. Arras (or Bouffia), capd 7 Apr. 1812 at Badajoz, arr. P from Plymouth 25 or 26 Sep. 1812, d. 13 Nov. 1812: 'Extreme Debility.' TNA ADM 103/263, No. 1379; ADM 103/648.

9. Jean Michels (or Alitchell), soldier, Hesse-Darmstadt regt, 24, b. Arras (or Herheigen), capd 22 Jul.1812 at Salamanca, arr. P from Portsmouth 12 Nov. 1812, d. 13 Nov. 1812: 'Extreme Debility.' TNA ADM 103/264, No. 3063; ADM 103/648.

10. Jean Spetherin (or Spetheron), soldier, 17th line (or light) regt, 31, b. Alignon Nante (or Rogue), capd 22 Jul. 1812 at Salamanca, arr. P from Portsmouth 12 Nov. 1812, d. 15 (or 17) Nov. 1812: 'Extreme Debility.' TNA ADM 103/264, No. 3036; ADM 103/648.

11. Jean François Vilbert, sergeant, 103rd line regt, 25 (or 42), b. Ostend (or 'Damientz, Saone'), capd 7 Apr. 1812 at Badajoz, arr. P from Portsmouth 14 Oct. 1812, d. 18 Nov. 1812: 'Scurvy & Extreme Debility.' TNA ADM 103/263, No. 2070; ADM 103/648.

12. Joseph Chambon, chasseur, 9th light regt, 22, b. Toulon, capd 7 Apr. 1812 at Badajoz, arr. P from Portsmouth 15 Oct. 1812, d. 21 Nov. 1812: fever. TNA ADM 103/264, No. 2177; ADM 103/648.

13. Nicolas Joseph Darigneux (or Jean Baptiste Derimaux), soldier, 50th line regt, 34, b. Toulouse, capd 14 Aug. 1812 at Madrid, arr. P from Portsmouth 12 Nov. 1812, d. 21 Nov. 1812: 'Inflamatory Fever.' TNA ADM 103/264, No. 2995; ADM 103/648.

14. Pierre Villier, soldier, 36th line regt, 40, b. Picardy, capd 14 Aug. 1812 at Madrid, arr. P from Portsmouth 15 Nov. 1812, d. 21 Nov. 1812: 'Suddenly in Convalescent Ward.' TNA ADM 103/264, No. 3250; ADM 103/648.

15. Joseph Peiglasses, chasseur, 13th Chasseurs, 31, b. Paris, capd 21 Apr. 1812 at Castelblanco, arr. P from Portsmouth 13 Oct. 1812, d. 23 Nov. 1812: fever. TNA ADM 103/263, No. 1612; ADM 103/648.

16. Joseph Dujy, soldier, 22nd light (or line) regt, 26, b. Lorient, capd 22 Jul. 1812 at Salamanca, arr. P from Portsmouth 12 Nov. 1812, d. 23 Nov. 1812: 'Suddenly in Prison No. 5.' TNA ADM 103/264, No. 2882; ADM 103/648.

17. Jean Baptiste Castelle (or Castello), soldier, 101st line regt, 21, b. Piedmont, capd 22 Jul. 1812 at Salamanca, arr. P from Portsmouth 15 Nov. 1812, d. 23 Nov. 1812: 'Inflamatory Fever.' TNA ADM 103/264, No. 3339; ADM 103/648.

18. Jean Baptiste Simon, dragoon, 17th Dragoons, 24, b. Lorient, capd 11 Apr. 1812 at Lerena, arr. P from Portsmouth 13 Oct. 1812, d. 24 Nov. 1812: fever. TNA ADM 103/263, No. 1616; ADM 103/648.

19. Henning (or Henry) Thaufré, soldier, Hesse-Darmstadt regt, 24, b. Strasbourg, capd 7 Apr. 1812 at Badajoz, arr. P from Portsmouth 12 Nov. 1812, d. 24 Nov. 1812: 'Inflamatory Fever.' TNA ADM 103/264, No. 2908; ADM 103/648.

20. Ambrose Ambrosio, soldier, 2nd light (or line) regt, 26, b. Marengo, capd 14 Aug. 1812 at Madrid, arr. P from Portsmouth 12 Nov. 1812, d. 24 Nov. 1812: 'Inflamatory Fever.' TNA ADM 103/264, No. 2910; ADM 103/648.

21. Pierre Paulcel (or Bomsill), soldier, 1st light (or line) regt, 27, b. Turin, capd 14 Aug. 1812 at Madrid, arr. P from Portsmouth 15 Nov. 1812, d. 24 Nov. 1812: 'Inflamatory Fever.' TNA ADM 103/264, No. 3164; ADM 103/648.

22. Mathieu Boudeloche (or Martin Bodelong), soldier, 51st line regt, 34, b. Leous (Laon?) (or Liens—Lyons?), capd 14 Aug. 1812 at Madrid, arr. P from Portsmouth 12 Nov. 1812, d. 25 Nov. 1812: 'Fever & great Debility.' TNA ADM 103/264, No. 2979; ADM 103/648.

23. F. Jeveneux (or Feveneux), soldier, 101st line regt, 23 (or 40), b. Arras (or Verdun), capd 22 Jul. 1812 at Salamanca, arr. P from Portsmouth 12 Nov. 1812, d. 25 Nov. 1812: 'Suddenly in Convalescent Ward.' (or 'Suddenly in Convulsion'). TNA ADM 103/264, No. 3052; ADM 103/648.

24. Philippe Aine (or Ainé), soldier, 15th Dragoons, 30, b. Arras, capd 22 Jul. 1812 at Salamanca, arr. P from Portsmouth 12 Nov. 1812, d. 26 Nov. 1812: 'Inflamatory Fever.' TNA ADM 103/264, No. 3062; ADM 103/648.

25. Jean Baptiste Actioie (or Actiau), corporal, 88th line regt, 29, b. Piedmont, capd 7 Apr. 1812 at Badajoz, arr. P from Portsmouth 14 Oct. 1812, d. 27 Nov. 1812: 'Inflamatory Fever.' TNA ADM 103/263, No. 2081; ADM 103/648.

26. Jean Monmezar (or Dominique Aubrio), soldier, 36th (or 101st) line regt, 22, b. Normandy, capd 14 Aug. 1812 at Madrid (or n.d. at Badajoz.), arr. P from Portsmouth 15 Nov. 1812, d. 27 Nov. 1812: 'Inflamatory Fever.' TNA ADM 103/264, No. 3251; ADM 103/648.

27. Charles Romanie, soldier, 118th line regt, 26, b. Leon (Laon?), capd n.d. at Salamanca; d. 27 Nov. 1812: 'Inflamatory Fever.' TNA ADM 103/648, No. 3694. (No date for Romanie's arrival at Perth is given on the death certificate. Romanie has not been found in the Perth Entry Book, where in TNA ADM 103/264, No. 3694 is A. Cochard, a soldier, 1st Artillery, 23, b. Maux, captd 7 Apr. 1812 at

Badajoz, arr. P. from Portsmouth 29 or 30 Nov. 1812, and dischgd to France Jul. 1814.)

28.   Jean Labrot, soldier, 62nd line regt, 27, b. 'Toulouse in Gascony', capd 22 Jul. 1812 at Salamanca, arr. P from Portsmouth 12 Nov. 1812, d. 28 Nov. 1812: 'Inflamatory Fever.' TNA ADM 103/264, No. 2934; ADM 103/648.

29.   Louis Girard (or Gerard), soldier, 66th line regt, 24, p.o.b. n.k., capd 22 Jul. 1812 at Salamanca, arr. P from Portsmouth 15 Nov. 1812, d. 30 Nov. 1812: 'Suddenly in Prison.' TNA ADM 103/264, No. 3217; ADM 103/648.

30.   François Bastien, soldier 2nd light (or 36th line) regt, 26, p.o.b. n.k., capd 14 Aug. 1812 at Madrid, arr. P from Portsmouth 15 Nov. 1812, d. 1 Dec. 1812: 'Suddenly in Prison No.4.' TNA ADM 103/264, No. 3348; ADM 103/648.

31.   Jean Antoine Christol (or Crissiole), grenadier, 62nd line regt, 26, b. Anvers (Antwerp), capd 22 Jul. 1812 at Salamanca, arr. P from Portsmouth 16 Nov. 1812, d. 2 Dec. 1812: 'Inflamatory Fever.' TNA ADM 103/264, No. 3457, and ADM 103/648, No. 3414.

32.   Pierre Rosier, soldier, 59th (or 101st) line regt, 24, b. Bomme, capd 14 Aug. 1812 at Madrid, arr. P from Portsmouth 15 Nov. 1812, d. 3 Dec. 1812: 'Inflamatory Fever.' TNA ADM 103/264, No. 3353; ADM 103/648.

33.   Jean Gradel (or Gradet), corporal (or soldier), 50th line regt, 26, b. Metz ('German' is written in pencil on the Entry Book), capd 14 Aug. 1812 at Madrid (or n.d. at Salamanca), arr. P from Portsmouth 12 Nov. 1812, d. 4 Dec. 1812: 'Inflamatory Fever.' TNA ADM 103/264, No. 2897; ADM 103/648.

34.   Antoine Bourguignon, soldier, 59th line (or Chasseurs) regt, 38 (or 22), b. Chateau (or Roctoi—Rocroi?), capd 6 Jul. 1812 (sic) at Madrid, arr. P from Portsmouth 3 Dec. 1812, d. 4 Dec. 1812: 'Inflamatory Fever.' TNA ADM 103/265, No. 4712; ADM 103/648.

35.   François Guisen (or Gisen), soldier, 39th (or 30th) line regt, 32 (or 22), b. Nantes (or Mecklenburg), capd 14 Aug. 1812 at Madrid, arr. P from Portsmouth 12 Nov. 1812, d. 5 Dec. 1812: 'Inflamatory Fever.' TNA ADM 103/264, No. 2900; ADM 103/648.

36.   Antoine Sasinius, soldier 62nd line regt, 32, b. Caleason (or Galeason), capd n.d. at Madrid, arr. P date n.k., d. 5 Dec. 1812: 'Inflamatory Fever.' TNA ADM 103/648, unnumbered.

37.   Isaac Favekers (or Vauveckers), 113th (or 103rd) line regt, 28 (or 21), b. Aras (sic) (or 'Boornic in Flanders'), capd 7 Apr. 1812 at Badajoz (or n.d. at Madrid), arr. P from Plymouth 25 or 26 Sep. 1812, d. 6 Dec. 1812: 'Inflamatory Fever.' TNA ADM 103/263, No. 1574; ADM 103/648.

38.   Jean Baptiste Mayeurs (or Mayeur), fusilier, 34th line regt, 22, b. Arras, capd 28 Oct. 1811 at Rio Molino (or n.d. at Salamanca), arr. P from Portsmouth 13 Oct. 1812, d. 7 Dec. 1812: 'Inflamatory Fever.' TNA ADM 103/263, No. 1831; ADM 103/648.

39.   Choumack Matis (or M. Shoemaker), soldier, 4th light (or 27th line) regt, 26, b. Florence, capd 14 Aug. 1812 n.p. (probably Madrid) (or n.d. at Salamanca), arr. P from Portsmouth 2 Dec. 1812, d. 8 Dec. 1812: 'Inflamatory Fever.' TNA ADM 103/265, No. 4559; ADM 103/648.

40.   Armand Varraguier (or Varotin), soldier, 59th line regt, 35 (or 30), b. Anvers (or Picardy), capd 22 Jul. 1812 at Salamanca, arr. P from Portsmouth 3 Dec. 1812, d. 8 Dec. 1812: 'Sudenly'. TNA ADM 103/265, No. 4755; ADM 103/648.

41.   François Vilingua, soldier, 101st line regt, 25, b. Alexandri (sic), capd n.d. at Madrid, arr. P, date and from place unstated, d. 10 Dec. 1812: 'Suddenly in Prison No. 2.' TNA ADM 103/648, No. 3395. (Vilingua has not been found in the Perth Entry Books: No. 3395 in the Entry Book TNA ADM 103/264 is not Vilingua but Louis Gavand, grenadier, 59th line regt, who returned to France in Jul. 1814).

42.   Pavola Lunati, soldier, Dragons Napoléone, 28, b. Milan, capd n.d. at Badajoz, arr. P, date and from place unstated, d. 11 Dec. 1812: fever. TNA ADM 103/648, No. 4212. (Lunati has not been found in the Perth Entry Books: No. 4212 in TNA ADM 103/264 is not Lunati but François Huteaux, soldier, 59th line regt, who returned to France in Jul. 1814).

43.   Theodore Vaissier, soldier, 66th line regt, 31, b. Dol, capd n.d. at Madrid, arr. P, date and from place unstated, d. 12 Dec. 1812: fever. TNA ADM 103/648, No. 3698. (Vaissier has not been found in the Perth Entry Books: No. 3698 in TNA ADM 103/264 is not Vaissier but Pierre Norge, soldier, 6th Artillery, who returned to France 6 Jul. 1814).

44.   Jean Bien, soldier, 50th line regt, 22, b. Dinar (sic), capd n.d. at Madrid, arr. P from Portsmouth 3 Dec. 1812, d. 12 Dec. 1812: 'Suddenly in Prison No.3.' TNA ADM 103/648, No. 4762. (Perth Entry Book TNA ADM 103/265, No. 4762, says Bien was aged 44, b. Fontenay, and was released to France Jul. 1814).

45.   Jean Baptiste Boucon, soldier, 2nd light (or line) regt, 29, b. St Brieux, capd 14 Aug. 1812 at Madrid, arr. P from Portsmouth 15 Nov. 1812, d. 13 Dec. 1812: fever. TNA ADM 103/648, No. 3202. (Perth Entry Book TNA ADM 103/264, No. 3202, says Boucon was aged 44, b. Marsilly, and was released to France Jul. 1814).

46.   Guillaume Quintelle (or Kentel or Rentel), soldier, 62nd line regt (or 27th Dragoons), 21 (or 30), b. Piedmont (or Colmar), capd 22 Jul. 1812 at Salamanca, arr. P from Portsmouth 15 Nov.1812, d. 13 (or 30) Dec. 1812: 'Mortification' (gangrene). TNA ADM 103/264, No. 3342; ADM 103/648.

47.   Pierre Ornet (or Cornct), soldier, 27th light (or line) regt, 26 (or 35), b. Arras (or Bayens), capd 14 Aug. 1812 at Madrid, arr. P from Portsmouth 15 Nov. 1812, d. 15 Dec. 1812: fever. TNA ADM 103/264, No. 3326; ADM 103/648.

48.   André Garré, soldier, 15th line regt, 32, b. Lianoir, capd n.d. at Madrid, arr. Perth date and from place unstated, d. 15 Dec. 1812: fever. TNA ADM 103/648, No. 4314. (Garré has not been found in the Perth Entry Books: No. 4314 in TNA ADM 103/264 is not Garré but Jacques Besserant, soldier, 82nd line regt, dischgd to France Jul. 1814).

49.   Louis Nicolas Gilles, soldier, 88th line regt, 21, b. St Omer, capd n.d. at Madrid, arr. P date and from place unstated, d. 15 Dec. 1812: fever. TNA ADM 103/648, No. 4684. (Gilles has not been found in the Perth Entry Books: No. 4684 in TNA ADM 103/265 is not Gilles but Jean François Decot, soldier, 2nd Company Armourers, rel. to France Jul. 1814).

50.   Pierre Schmidt, soldier, 15th line regt, 30, b. Strasburgh (sic), capd n.d. at Salamanca, arr. P date and from place unstated, d. 16 Dec.1812: fever. TNA ADM 103/648, No. 4631. (Schmidt has not been found in the Perth Entry Books: No. 4631 in TNA ADM 103/265 is not Schmidt but Antoine Proes (or Pronesse), soldier, 28th light infantry, rel. to France 14 Jul.1814).

51.   François Peyre (or Perrer), soldier, 101st line regt, 29, b. Arras, capd 22 Jul. 1812 at Salamanca, arr. P from Portsmouth 3 Dec. 1812, d. 17 Dec. 1812: 'Inflamatory Fever.' TNA ADM 103/648, No. 4738. (Perth Entry Book TNA ADM 103/265, No. 4738, says Peyre or Perrer was rel. to France Jul. 1814).

52. Jean Baptiste Cabourdin, soldier, 76th (or 59th) line regt, 31, b. Granger, capd 14 Aug. 1812 at Madrid, arr. P from Portsmouth 3 Dec. 1812, d. 17 Dec. 1812: 'Inflamatory Fever.' TNA ADM 103/648, No. 4798. (Perth Entry Book TNA ADM 103/265, No. 4798, says Cabourdin was dischgd to V 29 Jul. 1813).

53. Louis Allar (or Allier or Hallard), soldier, 22nd line (or light) regt, 22, b. Bayone (sic), capd 22 Jul. 1812 at Salamanca, arr. P from Portsmouth 3 Dec. 1812, d. 17 Dec. 1812: 'Inflamatory Fever.' TNA ADM 103/648, No. 4843. (Perth Entry Book TNA ADM 103/265, No. 4843, says he was rel. to France Jul. 1814).

54. (*) Jean Baptiste Lainhard, soldier, 50th line regt, 26, b. Inck, capd 14 Aug. 1812 at Madrid, arr. P from Portsmouth 12 Nov. 1812, d. 18 Dec. 1812: cause of death unstated. TNA ADM 103/264, No. 2970.

55. Nicolas Servière, sapper, 2nd Infantry Pioneers, 32, b. Amiens (or Paris), capd 7 Apr. 1812 at Badajoz, arr. P from Portsmouth 29 or 30 Nov. 1812, d. 18 Dec. 1812: 'Inflamatory Fever.' TNA ADM 103/648, No. 3954. (Perth Entry Book TNA ADM 103/264, No. 3954, says Servière was rel. to France Jul. 1814).

56. Charles Dupère (or Dupeyre or Duperoz), sergeant, 28th light infantry, (or soldier, 48th line regt), 24 (or 30), b. Coutance (or Modano), capd n.d. at Madrid, arr. P from Portsmouth 2 Dec. 1812, d. 19 Dec. 1812: 'Inflamatory Fever.' TNA ADM 103/648, No. 4608. (Perth Entry Book TNA ADM 103/265, No. 4608, says he was rel. to France Jul. 1814).

57. Pierre Vaisse (or Fesso), soldier, 9th light (or line) regt, 30 (or 24), b. Genev (sic) (or Blaye), capd 7 Apr. 1812 at Badajoz, arr. P from Portsmouth 13 Oct. 1812, d. 20 Dec. 1812: 'Inflamatory Fever.' TNA ADM 103/263, No. 1682; ADM 103/648.

58. Jean Laurand, soldier, 86th line regt, 30, b. Pontarson, capd n.d. at Badajoz, arr. P date and from place unstated, d. 20 Dec. 1812: 'Inflamatory Fever.' TNA ADM 103/648, No. 4662. (Laurand has not been found in the Perth Entry Books: TNA ADM 103/265, No. 4662, is not Laurand but Jean Choisy Dupin, sergeant major, 58th line regt, who was released to France Jun. 1814).

59. Charles Maigre (or Negro), soldier, 9th line (or light) regt, 28 (or 23), b. Dinan (or Piedmont), capd 7 Apr. 1812 at Badajoz, arr. P from Portsmouth 15 Oct. 1812, d. 22 Dec. 1812: 'Inflamatory Fever.' TNA ADM 103/648, No. 2180. (Perth Entry Book TNA ADM 103/264, No. 2180, says he was dischgd 2 Aug. 1813 to V).

60. Joseph Coilit (or Coury), alias Koehly, 33, b. Dol, soldier, Gendarmes, capd 14 Aug. 1812 at Madrid, arr. P from Portsmouth 2 Dec. 1812, d. 22 Dec. 1812: 'Suddenly in Prison No.2.' TNA ADM 103/265, No. 4490; ADM 103/648.

61. Mukjor (or Theodore) Winterosi (or Winteroh, Winteroft, or Wilthof), soldier, Hesse-Darmstadt regt, 29, b. Erlinghausen, capd 7 Apr. 1812 at Badajoz, arr. P from Plymouth 6 Aug. 1812, d. 23 Dec. 1812: 'Inflamatory Fever.' TNA ADM 103/648, No. 253. (Perth Entry Book TNA ADM 103/263, No. 253, says he was dischgd 29 Jul. 1813 to V).

62. Jean Corsière (or Le Kosker), alias Yves Cuillier or Culier, soldier, 50th line regt, 24 (or 31), b. Korbeke (or Dunkirk), capd 14 Aug. 1812 at Madrid, arr. P from Portsmouth 12 Nov. 1812, d. 24 Dec. 1812: fever. TNA ADM 103/648, No. 3002. (Perth Entry Book TNA ADM 103/264, No. 3002, says he was rel. to France 1 Jun. 1814).

63. Marien Boile (or Boille), soldier, 2nd Bn Miners, 26 (or 29), b. Aras (sic) (or Clermont), capd 7 Apr. 1812 at Badajoz, arr. P from Portsmouth 29 or 30 Nov. 1812, d. 24 Dec. 1812: fever. TNA ADM 103/648, No. 3754. (Perth Entry Book TNA ADM 103/264, No. 3754, says he was dischgd 4 Aug. 1813 to V).

64. Johan Behm (or Joseph Behmer), soldier, 17th line (or Hesse-Darmstadt) regt, aged 31 (or 24), b. Hanover (or Horbeke), capd 7 Apr. 1812 at Badajoz, arr. P from Plymouth 6 Aug. 1812, d. 27 Dec. 1812: fever. TNA ADM 103/648, No. 158. (Perth Entry Book TNA ADM 103/263, No.158, says he was dischgd 29 Jul. 1813 to V).

65. Jean Baptiste Ribeau (or Ribot), soldier, 101st line (or 1st Artillery) regt, 28, p.o.b. unstated, capd n.d. at Badajoz (or 19 Jan. 1812 at Ciudad Rodrigo), arr. P from Portsmouth 3 Dec. 1812, d. 27 Dec. 1812: fever. TNA ADM 103/648, No. 4734. (Perth Entry Book TNA ADM 103/265, No. 4734, says he was dischgd 4 Aug. 1813 to V).

66. Antoine Ferrand (or Ferand), soldier 62nd (or 50th) line regt, 46 (or 29), b. Mouchantile (or Caen), capd 22 Jul. 1812 at Salamanca, arr. P from Portsmouth 3 Dec. 1812, d. 27 Dec. 1812: 'Inflamatory Fever.' TNA ADM 103/265, No. 4788; ADM 103/648.

67. Walter Bergens, soldier, 13th Dragoons, 22, b. Dol, capd n.d. at Almeida, arr. P on date and from place unstated, d. 29 Dec. 1812: 'Inflamatory Fever.' TNA ADM 103/648, No. 2740. (Bergens has not been found in the Perth Entry Books: No. 2740 in TNA ADM 103/264 is Gruelle Brutus, trumpeter, 13th line regt, dischgd to France Jul. 1814).

68. Paul Parquer (or Partier), soldier, 88th line regt, 22, b. Saine Sur Marme (sic) (or Lannion), capd 7 Apr. 1812 at Badajoz, arr. P from Portsmouth 29 or 30 Nov. 1812, d. 31 Dec. 1812: fever. TNA ADM 103/264, No. 4017; ADM 103/648.

69. Joseph Drolands (or Drolance), soldier, 76th line regt, 27, b. Liège (or La Rochelle), capd 27 Jun. 1812 at Salamanca, arr. P from Plymouth 30 Nov. or 1 Dec. 1812, d. 31 (or 17) Dec. 1812: fever. TNA ADM 103/264, No. 4169 (which says he died on 17 Dec. 1813); ADM 103/648.

70. Antonio Matteat (or Antoine Macet), chasseur, 9th light regt, 28 (or 35), b. Arras (or Paris), capd 7 Apr. 1812 at Badajoz, arr. P from Portsmouth 13 Oct. 1812, d. 1 Jan. 1813: fever. TNA ADM 103/263, No. 1685; ADM 103/648.

71. Pierre Levegue (or Levecque), soldier, 45th line regt, 19 (or 21), b. Ange (or Auray), capd 15 Aug. 1809 at Flushing, arr. P from Portsmouth 21 or 22 Oct. 1812, d. 1 Jan. 1813: fever. TNA ADM 103/264, No. 2767; ADM 103/648.

72. Firmin Bonnefoi, soldier, 101st line regt, 27, b. Vire (or Crenel Lain), capd n.d. at Salamanca, arr. P from Portsmouth 15 Nov. 1812, d. 1 Jan. 1813: fever. TNA ADM 103/648, No. 3133. (Perth Entry Book TNA ADM 103/264, No. 3133, says Bonnefoi was rel. to France Jul. 1814).

73. (*) Jacques Pierre, soldier, 5th Artillery, 23, p.o.b. unstated, capd 7 Apr. 1812 at Badajoz, arr. P from Portsmouth 29 or 30 Nov. 1812, d. 2 Jan. 1813: cause of death unstated. TNA ADM 103/264, No. 3641.

74. Clement Bigourd, sergeant (or soldier), 2nd Bn Sappers, 32, b. Calais (or Arras), capd 6 Apr. 1812 at Badajoz, arr. P from Portsmouth 3 Dec. 1812, d. 2 Jan. 1813: fever. TNA ADM 103/265, No. 4665; ADM 103/648.

75. Pierre Le Grand, soldier, 5th Artillery, 36, b. Messe, capd n.d. at Badajoz, arr. P date and from place unstated, d. 2 Jan. 1813: fever. TNA ADM 103/648, No. 4719. (Le Grand has not been found in the Perth Entry Books).

76. Liev. (or Livain) Vanderdone, soldier, 27th Dragoons, 29 (or 32), b. Anvers (or Tournai), capd 11 Apr. 1812 at Irena, arr. P from Portsmouth 29 or 30 Nov. 1812, d. 9 Jan. 1813: fever. TNA ADM 103/264, No. 3820; ADM 103/648.

77. Pierre Delaunay, soldier, 86th line regt, 30, b. Fidlers (or Fidlor), capd 14 Aug. 1810 at Cazalet, arr. P from Portsmouth between 8 and 11 Jan. 1813, d. 11 Jan. 1813: 'Suddenly in Prison No.3.' TNA ADM 103/265, No. 4970; ADM 103/648.

78. Antoine (or Alex.) Legrand (or Le Grand), soldier, 62nd (or 55th) line regt, 26 (or 29), b. Salvacourt (or Orliac), capd 22 Jul. 1812 at Salamanca, arr. P from Portsmouth 3 Dec. 1812, d. 13 Jan. 1813: fever. TNA ADM 103/265, No. 4790; ADM 103/648.

79. François Victor Boitel (or Beautel), soldier, 50th line regt, 31, b. Hensar, capd 14 Aug. 1812 at Madrid (or Qualpino), arr. P from Portsmouth 12 Nov. 1812, d. 15 Jan. 1813: fever. TNA ADM 103/264, No. 2993; ADM 103/648.

80. Jean Louis Pontonnier, soldier, 15th light (or line) regt, 26, b. Carron, capd 22 Jul. 1812 at Salamanca, arr. P from Portsmouth 15 Nov. 1812, d. 16 Jan. 1813: fever. TNA ADM 103/264, No. 3345; ADM 103/648.

81. Louis Palaron (or Paul Desanos, according to his death certificate), soldier, Royal Etrangers (or 9th line regt), 32, b. Chantigny, capd 16 Aug. 1812 at Goulacara (or Salamanca), arr. P from Portsmouth 3 Dec. 1812, d. 16 Jan. 1813: fever. TNA ADM 103/265, No. 4754; ADM 103/648.

82. Christophe Gros, nurse (or soldier), 'Follower of the Army', 50, b. Loraine (sic), capd 19 Jan. 1811 at Ciudad Rodrigo, arr. P from Plymouth 6 Aug. 1812, d. 18 Jan. 1813: fever. TNA ADM 103/263, No. 74; ADM 103/648.

83. André Lenoir, soldier, 88th line regiment, aged 24/29 (sic), b. St Valery Rosier, capd 7 Apr. 1812 at Badajoz, arr. P from Portsmouth 14 Oct. 1812, d. 18 Jan. 1813: fever. TNA ADM 103/263, No. 2090; ADM 103/648.

84. Pierre N. Bouan, soldier, 6th line regt, 26, b. Trieste, capd n.d. at Badajoz, arr. Perth, date and from place u., d. 18 Jan. 1813: fever. TNA ADM 103/648, No. 4652. (Bouan has not been found in the Perth Entry Books, where TNA ADM 103/265, No. 4652 is Julien Gouillon, soldier, 4th Artillery, rel. to France Jul. 1814. It seems unlikely two prisoners named Bouan should die the same day: it is possible, but by no means certain, that Bouan was in fact the same man as No. 85, Michel Bouan).

85. (*) Michel Bouan, carabinier, 6th light infantry, 26, b. Lyons, capd 23 Jul. 1812 at Salamanca, arr. P from Lisbon 9 Jan. 1813, d. 18 Jan. 1813: cause of death not stated. TNA ADM 103/265, No. 5760.

86. Albert Bigourd, sergeant major, 2nd Bn Sappers, 31 (or 36), b. Calais (or Arre), capd 6 Apr. 1812 at Badajoz, arr. P from Portsmouth 3 Dec. 1812, d. 20 Jan. 1813: fever. TNA ADM 103/265, No. 4664; ADM 103/648.

87. Blaise Herel, soldier, 50th line regt, aged 35, b. Fontainebleau, capd n.d. at Badajoz, arr. P, date and from place u., d. 24 Jan. 1813: Anasarca (dropsy). TNA ADM 103/648, No. 3638. (Herel has not been found in the Perth Entry Books; but No. 3638 in TNA ADM 103/264 is Blaise Haye, sergeant, 5th Artillery, 33, b. Fontainebleau and capd 7 Apr. 1812 at Badajoz, arr. P. from Portsmouth 29 or 30 Nov. 1812, rel. to France Jul. 1814. The two names are not unalike: this may be another case of identity or other documentation confused by the depot clerks).

88. François Guilleux (or Guieux), soldier, 22nd light infantry, 22 (or 25), b. Versailles (or Perigord), capd 22 Jul. 1812 at Salamanca, (or n.d. at Badajoz), arr. P from Portsmouth 3 Dec. 1812, d. 30 Jan. 1813: fever. TNA ADM 103/265, No. 4749; ADM 103/648, No. 4708 (sic).

89. Jacques Charles Monamir (or Bonami), soldier, 8th line regt, aged 21, b. Haut Rhin, capd 18 Mar. 1811 in Portugal, arr. P from Portsmouth 12 Jan. 1813, d. 30 Jan. 1813: fever. TNA ADM 103/265, No. 6239; ADM 103/648, No. 6060.

90. Bernard Chazer (or Hazer), soldier, 17th light (or line) regt, 21 (or 28), b. Arras (or Vilerre), capd 22 Jul. 1812 at Salamanca, arr. P from Portsmouth 15 Oct. 1812, d. 6 Feb. 1813: 'Suddenly in removing to the Hospital.' TNA ADM 103/264, No. 2192; ADM 103/648.

91. Aimard Harault (or Hemar Arault), soldier, 9th light (or line) regt, 25, b. Valence, capd 7 Apr. 1812 at Badajoz, arr. P from Portsmouth 29 or 30 Nov. 1812, d. 9 Feb. 1813: fever. TNA ADM 103/264, No. 3786; ADM 103/648.

92. Julien Jefroy (or Geffroi), soldier, 26th Dragoons, 27, p.o.b. n.k., capd 4 Jan. 1812 at Fontalmestre, arr. P from Plymouth 6 Aug. 1812, d. 11 Feb. 1813: fever. TNA ADM 103/263, No. 27; ADM 103/648.

93. Baptiste Monier (or Monnier), soldier, 116th (or 11th) line regt, 25, b. Carcassonne, capd 8 May 1810 at Valla...n (sic) (or Valanciennes (sic)—Valencia?), arr. P from Portsmouth 11 or 12 Jan. 1813, ('Raffalée' is pencilled in on Entry Book), d. 12 Feb. 1813: fever. TNA ADM 103/265, No. 5821; ADM 103/648.

94. Pierre Sentoyen (or Saintouin), soldier 101st line regt, 25, b. Valence, capd 22 Jul. 1812 at Salamanca (or n.d. at Badajoz), arr. P from Portsmouth 3 Dec. 1812, d. 15 Feb. 1813: fever. TNA ADM 103/265, No. 4785; ADM 103/648.

95. Jean Norega (or Noriga), soldier, 86th line regt, 22, b. St Leon, capd 21 Feb. 1810 on the sloop *La Nécessité* 'at sea', arr. P from Portsmouth 8, 9 or 11 Jan. 1813, d. 18 Feb. 1813: fever. TNA ADM 103/265, No. 4916; ADM 103/648.

96. Pierre (or Jean) Sarrazin, soldier, 54th line regt, 29, b. Lusignan, capd 5 Mar. 1811 at Cadiz, arr. P from Portsmouth 20 or 21 Aug. 1812, d. 27 Feb. 1813: fever. TNA ADM 103/263, No. 723; ADM 103/648.

97. Jean Baptiste Dupair, soldier, 22nd light (or line) regt, 27, b. Vilame, capd 22 Jul. 1812 at Salamanca, arr. P from Portsmouth on 3 Dec. 1812, d. 28 Feb. 1813: fever. TNA ADM 103/648, No. 4815. (Perth Entry Book TNA ADM 103/265, No. 4815, says Dupair was rel. to France Jul. 1814).

98. Silvestre Pioie (or Pivie), soldier, 6th Artillery, 28, b. Bordeaux, capd 19 Jan. 1812 at Ciudad Rodrigo, arr. P from Plymouth 25 or 26 Sep. 1812, d. 5 Mar. 1813: fever. TNA ADM 103/263, No. 1504 ADM 103/648.

99. Edmé Hisson (or Konsin), soldier, 4th Artillery (or 4th Dragoons), 31, b. Paris, capd 28 Jun. 1812 at Salamanca, arr. P from Portsmouth 29 or 30 Nov., d. 12 Mar. 1813: fever. TNA ADM 103/264, No. 4008; ADM 103/648.

100. Severin Midy (or Midi), corporal, 88th line regt, 22, b. Saine la Marine (sic), capd 7 Apr. 1812 at Badajoz, arr. P from Portsmouth 29 or 30 Nov. 1812, d. 12 Mar. 1813: fever. TNA ADM 103/264, No. 4014; ADM 103/648.

101. Jean Baptiste Marchand, soldier, 88th line regt, 23, b. Chartres, capd 7 Apr. 1812 at Badajoz, arr. P from Portsmouth 13 Jan. 1813, d. 15 Mar. 1813: fever. TNA ADM 103/266, No. 6563; ADM 103/648.

102. Mathieu (or Jean) Fabre, soldier, 6th light (or line) regt, 22, b. Authen, Département de Digne, capd 19 May 1812 at Pont Almaras (or n.d. at Badajoz), arr. P from Portsmouth 16 Nov. 1812, d. 16 Mar. 1813: fever. TNA ADM 103/264, No. 3436; ADM 103/648.

103. Remé Gutin, fusilier and cannonier auxiliaire, 75th line regt, 28, b. Pontarme, capd 14 Aug. 1812 at Madrid, arr. P from Lisbon 9 Jan. 1813, d. 17 Mar. 1813: fever. TNA ADM 103/265, No. 5662; ADM 103/648.

104. Claude Birotte (or Birau), soldier, 16th light (or line) regt, 26, b. Manarn (or Mancoin), capd 16 May 1811 at La Guarda, arr. P from Portsmouth 20 or 21 Aug. 1812, d. 20 Mar. 1813: fever. TNA ADM 103/263, No. 645; ADM 103/648.

105. Joseph Leroy, fusilier, 36th (or 59th) line regt, 24, b. Inbercour Dinan (sic) (or Inberiour), capd 19 Mar. 1811 at Coimbra, (or n.d. at Badajoz), arr. P from Portsmouth 13 Oct. 1812, d. 20 Mar. 1813: fever. TNA ADM 103/263, No. 1836; ADM 103/648.

106. Auguste Faran (or Augstin Favrier), soldier, 21st light (or 4th line) regt, 22, b. Evresy, capd 15 Apr. 1811 at Olivencia, arr. P from Portsmouth 8, 9 or 11 January 1813, d. 21 Mar. 1813: fever. TNA ADM 103/265, No. 5173; ADM 103/648.

107. Jacques Jacob (or Jacquau), soldier, 88th line regt, 25, b. Hte Saone, capd Apr. 1811 in Spain (or n.d. in Portugal), arr. P from Portsmouth 13 Jan. 1813, d. 22 Mar. 1813: fever. TNA ADM 103/265, No. 6276; ADM 103/648.

108. Antoine Simon, soldier, Artificers (or 4th Artillery), 26, b. Brase, capd 7 Apr. 1812 at Badajoz, arr. P from Portsmouth 29 or 30 Nov. 1812, d. 23 Mar. 1813: fever. TNA ADM 103/264, No. 3731; ADM 103/648.

109. Barthelemy Sord, chasseur, 31st light infantry, 33, b. Bueneta, capd 22 Jul. 1812 at Salamanca, arr. P from Portsmouth 15 Oct. 1812, d. 30 Mar. 1813: fever. TNA ADM 103/264, No. 2276; ADM 103/648.

110. Pierre Brisson (or Brison), soldier, 103rd (or 28th) line regt, 28, b. Tisau (or Pisau), capd 7 Apr. 1812 at Badajoz, arr. P from Portsmouth 29 Aug. 1812, d. 31 Mar. 1813: fever. TNA ADM 103/263, No. 904; ADM 103/648.

111. Dominique Choquet, soldier, 82nd line regt, 22, b. Soissons, capd 7 Jun. 1812 at Salamanca, arr. P from Portsmouth 29 or 30 Nov. 1812, d. 4 Apr. 1813: 'Suddenly in Prison No.4.' TNA ADM 103/264, No. 3524; ADM 103/648.

112. Nicolas Joseph Jance (or Iance), soldier, 22nd light infantry (or ouvrier militaire), 29, b. Bresolle, capd 15 Aug 1809 at Flushing, arr. P from Portsmouth 8, 9 or 11 Jan. 1813, d. 11 Apr. 1813: dropsy. TNA ADM 103/265, No. 4927; ADM 103/648.

113. Jean A. Reversham (or Reverchon), soldier, 25th line regt, 23, b. Boisdomont, capd 11 May 1811 at Almeida, arr. P from Portsmouth 11 or 12 Jan. 1813, d. 12 Apr. 1813: consumption. TNA ADM 103/265, No. 5902; ADM 103/648.

114. Jean François Barroire, soldier, 55th line regt, 28 (or 24), b. 'in Florence' (or Buraix), capd 16 Mar. (May?) 1811 at Albuera, arr. P from Portsmouth 12 Nov. 1812, d. 15 Apr. 1813: consumption. TNA ADM 103/264, No. 2886; ADM 103/648.

115. Charles Gazen (or Gasen), soldier, 11th Dragoons, 27 (or 23), b. Paris (or Sternay), capd 23 Jul. 1812 at Salamanca, arr. P from Portsmouth 16 Nov. 1812, d. 15 Apr. 1813: consumption. TNA ADM 103/264, No. 3483; ADM 103/648.

116. Nicolas Mautelers, ('German'), soldier, 10th Dragoons, 23 (or 26), b. Svistring (or Lrestring), capd 28 Oct. 1811 at Rio Molino, arr. P from Portsmouth 21 or 22 Oct. 1812, d. 24 (or 25) Apr. 1813: consumption. TNA ADM 103/264, No. 2561; ADM 103/648.

117. Antoine François Perrine, soldier, 15th line regt, 26, b. St Lambert, Calvados, capd 12 May 1811 at Almeida, arr. P from Portsmouth 21 or 22 Oct. 1812, d. 24 Apr. 1813: consumption. TNA ADM 103/264, No. 2845; ADM 103/648.

118. Prosper Marielle Martello, soldier, 70th line regt, 28, b. Antwerp (or Piedmont), capd 22 Jul. 1812 at Salamanca (or n.d. at Madrid), arr. P from Portsmouth 2 Dec. 1812, d. 28 Apr. 1813: consumption. TNA ADM ADM 103/265, No. 4369; ADM 103/648.

119. Etienne Ponand, soldier, 5th Dragoons, 21, b. Haut Rhin, capd 5 May 1811 at Almeida, arr. P from Portsmouth 13 Jan. 1813, d. 4 May 1813: consumption. TNA ADM 103/265, No. 6449; ADM 103/648.

120. Edmé Goure, soldier, 17th light (or line) regt, 33, b. Montigny, capd 27 Jun. 1812 at Salamanca, arr. P from Portsmouth 11 or 12 Jan. 1813, d. 6 May 1813: 'Suddenly of Starvation & consequent Debility.' TNA ADM 103/265, No. 5991; ADM 103/648.

121. Pierre Alexandre, soldier, 72nd line regt, 20, b. Nancy, capd 15 Aug 1809 at Flushing, arr. P from Portsmouth 8, 9 or 11 January 1813, d. 7 May 1813: consumption. TNA ADM 103/265, No. 4919; ADM 103/648.

122. Louis Nicolas Charpentier, soldier, 50th line regt, 24, b. Arras (or Moulin), capd 14 Aug. 1812 at Madrid, arr. P from Portsmouth 2 Dec.1812, d. 8 May 1813: consumption. TNA ADM 103/265, No. 4486; ADM 103/648.

123. Charles Romier (or Remier), soldier, 64th line regt, 28, b. Orleans, capd 16 May 1811 at Albuera, arr. P from Chatham 13 Jan. 1813, d. 8 May 1813: peripneumonia. TNA ADM 103/266, No. 6584; ADM 103/648.

124. Jean Baptiste Thomas, soldier, 21st line regt, 24, b. Paris, capd 19 Jul. 1808 at Baylen, arr. P from Portsmouth 11 or 12 Jan. 1813, d. 10 May 1813: 'Suddenly of Starvation and consequent Debility.' TNA ADM 103/265, No. 5931; TNA ADM 103/648.

125. (+) Jean Lacome (or Lacombe), soldier, 70th line regt, 28, b. Florence (or Rennes), capd 7 Oct. 1810 at Coimbra, arr. P from Portsmouth 14 Oct. 1812, d. 13 May 1813: consumption. TNA ADM 103/263, No. 2093; ADM 103/648.

126. Constantin (or Constant) Dumarque, soldier 86th (or 36th) line regt, 25, b. Detain, capd 28 Mar. 1809 at Vigo, arr. P from Portsmouth 14 Jan. 1813, d. 17 May 1813: consumption. TNA ADM 103/266, No. 6863; ADM 103/648.

127. Joseph Durant, soldier, 34th line regt, 30, b. 'Arras Morvin' (or Bery), capd 19 Jan. 1812 at Ciudad Rodrigo, arr. P from Portsmouth 14 Oct. 1812, d. 21 May 1813: 'Suddenly in consequence of Inanition.' TNA ADM 103/263, No. 2068; ADM 103/648.

128. Jean Baptiste Martin, carabinier, 6th light infantry, 27 (or 33), b. Paris (or Chevecy), capd 23 Jul. 1812 at Salamanca, arr. P from Lisbon 9 Jan. 1813, d. 21 May 1813: consumption. TNA ADM 103/265, No. 5769; ADM 103/648.

129. Jean Baptiste Charles, carabinier, 6th light infantry, 26 (or 33), b. Anvers (or Maubeuasse), capd 23 Jul. 1812 at Salamanca, arr. P from Lisbon 9 Jan. 1813, d. 31 May 1813: 'Iliac Passion.' TNA ADM 103/265, No. 5782; ADM 103/648.

130. Nicolas Lemreux, soldier, 86th line regt, 20, b. Breteville, capd 21 Feb. 1810 on the sloop *La Nécessité* 'at sea', arr. P from Portsmouth 8, 9 or 11 Jan. 1813, d. 4 Jun. 1813: consumption. TNA ADM 103/265, No. 4914; ADM 103/648.

131. Louis Ribaut, soldier, 34th line regt, 26, b. Chautrecourt, capd 19 Jan. 1812 at Ciudad Rodrigo, arr. P from Portsmouth 9 Jan. 1813, d. 4 Jun. 1813: consumption. TNA ADM 103/265, No. 5552; ADM 103/648.

132. Julien Foret (or Foiret), soldier, 88th line regt, 26, b. Ferici (or Fevici), capd 7 Apr. 1812 at Badajoz, arr. P from Portsmouth 29 Aug. 1812, d. 11 Jun. 1813: 'Scalded to Death by falling into the Boiler.' TNA ADM 103/263, No. 885; ADM 103/648.

133. Pierre Mahaut, soldier, 70th line regt, 21, b. Chaumont, capd 30 Jul. 1810 off Cazalet, arr. P from Portsmouth 8, 9 or 11 Jan. 1813, d. 21 Jun. 1813: consumption. TNA ADM 103/265, No. 4944; ADM 103/648.

134. Alexandre Piedleux (or Predeleu), soldier 4th light (or line) regt, 25, b. Ennery, capd 14 Aug. 1812 at Madrid, arr. P from Portsmouth 15 Nov. 1812, d. 27 Jun. 1813: consumption. TNA ADM 103/264, No. 3199; ADM 103/648.

135. Jacques Roudine, soldier, 82nd line regt, 28, b. Carrio, capd 14 Aug. 1812 at Madrid, arr. P from Portsmouth 15 Nov. 1812, d. 29 Jun. 1813: consumption. TNA ADM 103/264, No. 3139; ADM 103/648.

136. Pierre Berte, soldier, 26th line regt, 21, b. Rouen, capd 7 Oct. 1810 at Coimbra, arr. P from Portsmouth 12 Jan. 1813, d. 29 Jun. 1813: consumption. TNA ADM 103/265, No. 6188; ADM 103/648.

137. Jean Mesonier, soldier, 66th line regt, 21, b. St Messan (or St Meissan), capd 7 Oct. 1810 at Coimbra, arr. P from Portsmouth 20 or 21 Aug. 1812, d. 2 Jul. 1813: consumption. TNA ADM 103/263, No. 657; ADM 103/648.

138. Cazimir Leblanc, soldier, 9th light infantry, 25, b. Mezieres, capd 7 Apr. 1812 at Badajoz, arr. P from Portsmouth 29 or 30 Nov. 1812, d. 3 Jul. 1813: Tabes Dorsalis (literally, wasting away of the back). TNA ADM 103/264, No. 3848; ADM 103/648.

139. Samuel Cornu, soldier, Royal Etrangers, 27 (or 61), b. Anvers (or 'Aujle (or Ausle) en Suisse'), capd 16 Aug. 1812 at Goudalazama (or Goudalazara), arr. P from Portsmouth 3 Dec. 1812, d. 3 Jul. 1813: 'Sudden Death from Inanition.' TNA ADM 103/265, No. 4718; ADM 103/648.

140. Louis Prevost, drummer, 15th line regt, 24, b. Lisieux, capd 27 Jun. 1812 at Salamanca, arr. P from Portsmouth 11 or 12 Jan. 1813, d. 4 Jul. 1813: 'Abscess Thigh & consequent Hectic Fever.' TNA ADM 103/265, No. 5995; ADM 103/648.

141. Jean Nauden (or Naudin), soldier, 66th line regt (or 1st Legion), 24, b. Bourges, capd 8 Feb. 1810 at Guadeloupe, arr. P from Portsmouth 21 or 22 Oct. 1812, described in the Entry Book as a 'Raffalé', d. 7 Jul. 1813: Tabes Dorsalis (literally, wasting away of the back). TNA ADM 103/264, No. 2724; ADM 103/648.

142. Antoine André, soldier, 65th line regt, 28, b. Anvers (or Hazel, Département de Lot), capd 18 Jun. 1812 at Salamanca, arr. P from Portsmouth 16 Nov. 1812, d. 10 Jul. 1813: 'Violent Contusion and Abscess on the Head, extending to the Neck and Shoulder.' TNA ADM 103/264, No. 3508; ADM 103/648.

143. Dominique Petrain (alias Petragne), soldier, 3rd Artillery, 29, b. Bugnie, capd 8 Mar. 1809 at Vigo (or n.d. Martinique), arr. P from Portsmouth 14 Jan. 1813, ('Madman' is written in pencil in the Entry Book), d. 23 Jul. 1813: consumption. TNA ADM 103/266, No. 6880; ADM 103/648.

144. Michel Moulin (or Pierre Meulin), soldier, 50th line regt, 30, b. Layas (or Vassieu), capd 22 Jul. 1812 at Salamanca, arr. P from Portsmouth 16 Nov. 1812, d. 24 Jul. 1813: atrophia. TNA ADM 103/264, No. 3427; ADM 103/648.

145. Jacques (or Jean François) Lecoure (or Lacour), soldier, 88th (or 28th) line regt, 24, b. Marseilles, capd 7 Apr. 1812 at Badajoz, arr. P from Portsmouth 21 or 22 Oct. 1812, d. 3 Aug. 1813: atrophia. TNA ADM 103/648, No. 2665. (Perth Entry Book TNA ADM 103/264, No.2665, says Lacour was rel. to France Jul. 1814).

146. Jean Somelet, soldier, 25th light regt, 28 (or 24), b. Dunkirk (or Tournon), capd 14 Aug. 1812 at Madrd, arr. P from Portsmouth 15 Nov. 1812, d. 17 Aug. 1813: haematemesis (vomiting of blood from the stomach). TNA 103/264, No. 3349; ADM 103/648.

147. Jean Leonard, soldier, 82nd line regt, 32, b. Paris, capd n.d., 'Sent in by H.M. Ship *Pompée*,' arr. P from Plymouth 6 Aug. 1812, d. 20 Aug. 1813: atrophia. TNA ADM 103/263, No. 391, and ADM 103/648.

148. François Hondin, soldier, 64th line regt, 25, b. Meurchy, capd 16 May 1811 at Albuera, arr. P from Portsmouth 13 Jan. 1813, d. 20 Aug. 1813: phthisis pulmonalis. TNA ADM 103/265, No. 6407; ADM 103/648.

149. Pierre Charman, soldier, 4th light (or line) regt, 25, b. Anvers (or Vereresne), capd 22 Jul. 1812 at Salamanca, arr. P from Portsmouth 15 Nov. 1812, d. 27 Aug. 1813: 'Atrophia & Nostalgia.' TNA ADM 103/264, No. 3167; ADM 103/648.

150. Jean Pradet, soldier, 31st light (or line) regt, 21, b. Clermont, capd 17 Mar. 1811 at Almeida, arr. P from Portsmouth 20 or 21 Aug. 1812, d. 30 Aug. 1813: 'Atrophia & Nostalgia.' TNA ADM 103/263, No. 601; ADM 103/648.

151. Pierre Merique, soldier, 70th line regt, 24, b. Moulins, capd 7 Oct. 1810 at Coimbra, arr. P from Portsmouth 8, 9 or 11 Jan. 1813, d. 30 Aug. 1813: 'Atrophia & Nostalgia.' TNA ADM 103/648, No. 5202. (Perth Entry Book TNA ADM 103/265, No. 5202, says Merique was rel. to France 13 Jun. 1814. A note, signed by Thomas Gillies, Surgeon, and preserved in the weekly returns, commenting on Merique's and the two preceding deaths above, states: 'The cases which have terminated in Death lately are confined to the Italian and Piedmontese Prisoners, partaking of that characteristic among the Swiss Nation, Maladie du pays.').

152. François Pissano (or Pichoneau), soldier, 22nd (or 25th) line regt, 19, b. Beaufort, capd 15 Aug. 1809 on Zealand, arr. P from Portsmouth 12 Jan. 1813, d. 6 Sep. 1813: consumption. TNA ADM 103/648, No. 6141. (But the Perth Entry Book TNA ADM 103/265, No. 6141, says he was rel. to France 3 Jun. 1814).

153. Alexandre Fauveau, fusilier, 15th light (or line) regt, 28, b. Naujean (Nogent?), capd 22 Jul. 1812 at Salamanca, arr. P from Portsmouth 15 Oct. 1812, d. 7 Sep. 1813: consumption. TNA ADM 103/264, No. 2214; ADM 103/648.

154. Jacques Gille, soldier, 20th Dragoons, 30, b. Guiche, capd 28 Jun. 1812 at Pampeluna, arr. P from Plymouth 25 or 26 Sep. 1812, d. 18 Sep. 1813: consumption. TNA ADM 103/263, No. 1217; ADM 103/648.

155. Jean Anclaine, soldier, 18th light infantry (or 18th Dragoons), 30, b. Pouso, capd 23 Jul. 1811 at Talavera, arr. P from Portsmouth 21 or 22 Oct. 1812, d. 19 Sep. 1813: consumption. TNA ADM 103/264, No. 2355; ADM 103/648.

156. Alexandre Romtin (or Rometin), alias Romutin, soldier, 88th line regt, 27, b. Dunkirk, capd 7 Apr. 1812 at Badajoz, arr. P from Portsmouth 14 Oct. 1812, d. 22 Sep. 1813: 'Tabes Mesinturica. In a Compleat State of Atrophy.' TNA ADM 103/263, No. 1918; ADM 103/648.

157. Jean Desbot (or Desbote), soldier, 82nd line regt, 27, b. Castillneu (or Castleneuve), capd 2 Mar. 1809 at Martinique, arr. P from Portsmouth 21 or 22 Oct. 1812, d. 25 Sep. 1813: 'Phthisis Pulmonalis.' TNA ADM 103/264, No. 2453; ADM 103/648.

158. Jean Baptiste Autrot, soldier, 19th light infantry (or 19th Dragoons), 26, b. Anvers (or Signy), capd 22 Jul. 1812 at Salamanca, arr. P from Portsmouth 15 Nov. 1812, d. 25 Sep. 1813: dropsy. TNA ADM 103/264, No. 3334; ADM 103/648.

159. Jean Jacques Pondand (or Pendant), soldier, 6th Dragoons, 30, b. Chevron (or Cherron), capd 9 Mar. 1811 at Aleria, arr. P from Portsmouth 21 or 22 Oct. 1812, d. 26 Sep. 1813: 'Phthisis Pulmonalis.' TNA ADM 103/264, No. 2827; ADM 103/648.

160. Jacques Portier, soldier, 39th (or 34th) line regt, 26, b. Département Pre Soucie, capd 19 Jan. 1812 at Ciudad Rodrigo, arr. P from Portsmouth 29 Aug. 1812, d. 8 Oct. 1813: consumption. TNA ADM 103/263, No. 869; ADM 103/648.

161. Benoit Pairin (or Perine), soldier (or seaman), 36, b. Ville Fera, capd 12 Apr. 1809 on *Varsovie* m.o.w. at Rochefort, arr. P from Portsmouth 14 Jan. 1813, d. 12 Oct. 1813: consumption. TNA ADM 103/266, No. 6839; ADM 103/648.

162. Joachim Rell, soldier, 113th line regt, 24, b. Pistoya, capd 19 Jan. 1812 at Ciudad Rodrigo, arr. P from Portsmouth 13 Jan. 1813, d. 17 Oct. 1813: consumption. TNA ADM 103/265, No. 6454; ADM 103/648.

163. Jean Baptiste Ridon (or Redon), cannonier, 1st Artillery, 31, b. Berne, capd 7 Apr. 1812 at Badajoz, arr. P from Portsmouth 15 Oct. 1812, d. 23 Oct. 1813: consumption. TNA ADM 103/263, No. 2108; ADM 103/648.

164. Thomas Rodelais, soldier, 45th line regt, 27, b. Rouselar (Roulers), capd 6 Mar. 1811 near Cadiz, arr. P from Portsmouth 8 Jan. 1813, d. 27 Oct. 1813: consumption. TNA ADM 103/265, No. 5396; ADM 103/648.

165. François Le Couste (or Le Coustie), soldier, 34th line regt, 24 (or 34), b. Calais, capd 28 Oct. 1811 at Rio Molino, arr. P from Portsmouth 29 or 30 Nov. 1812, d. 30 Oct. 1813: consumption. TNA ADM 103/264, No. 3617; ADM 103/648.

166. François Guidou (or Gidoux), soldier, 45th line regt, 25, b. Angers, capd 23 Apr. 1811 at Salamanca, arr. P from V 6 Aug. 1813, d. 30 Oct. 1813: consumption. TNA ADM 103/266, No. 7531; ADM 103/648.

167. Louis Le Cointre (or Lequiete), soldier, 66th line regt, 21, b. Baumont Larouce, capd 11 May 1811 at Almeida, arr. P from Portsmouth 29 Aug. 1812, d. 2 Nov. 1813: 'Lumbar Abscess.' TNA ADM 103/263, No. 966; ADM 103/648.

168. Isabelle Massique, chasseur, 9th light regt, 35, b. Valence, capd 7 Apr. 1812 at Badajoz, arr. P from Portsmouth 13 Oct. 1812, d. 3 Nov. 1813: 'Suddenly, from Inanition and extreme Debility.' TNA ADM 103/263, No. 1657; ADM 103/648.

169. Jean George Hussard, soldier, 9th line regt, 24, b. Lorraine, capd 7 Apr. 1812 at Badajoz, arr. P from Plymouth 25 or 26 Sep. 1812, d. 10 Nov. 1813: consumption. TNA ADM 103/263, No. 1446; ADM 103/648.

170. François Royall (or Reyall), surgeon (or soldier), 69th line regt, 42, b. Sariou, capd 7 Oct. 1810 at Coimbra, arr. P from Portsmouth 21 or 22 Oct. 1812, d. 20 Nov. 1813: 'Was in Apparent Good health in the Prison over night and was found dead in his Hammock of Apoplexy in the morning.' TNA ADM 103/264, No. 2404; ADM 103/648.

171. Nicolas Brasseur, sergeant, 5th Artillery, 32, b. Luxembourg, capd 7 Apr. 1812 at Badajoz, arr. P from Portsmouth 29 or 30 Nov. 1812, d. 27 Nov. 1813: consumption. TNA ADM 103/264, No. 3636; ADM 103/648.

172. Joseph (or Jacques) Dessaux, soldier, 28th light (or line) regt, 22, b. Rouen, capd 7 Apr. 1812 at Badajoz, arr. P from Portsmouth 29 or 30 Nov. 1812, d. 30 Nov. 1813: consumption. TNA ADM 103/264, No. 3918; ADM 103/648.

173. Louis Autin, soldier, 28th light (or line) regt, 28, b. Pays de Calais, capd 7 Apr. 1812 at Badajoz, arr. P from Portsmouth 2 Dec. 1812, d. 30 Nov. 1813: consumption. TNA ADM 103/265, No. 4625; ADM 103/648.

174. Mathias (or Mathieu) Cornelis, soldier, 26th line regt, 28, b. Liège, capd 24 Feb. 1809 on Martinique (or n.d. at Salamanca), arr. P from V 6 Aug. 1813, d. 30 Nov. (or 13 Dec.) 1813: consumption. TNA ADM 103/266, No. 7648; ADM 103/648.

175. (*) P. Soucasse, soldier, 62nd line regt, 27, b. Lacourt, capd 22 Jul. 1812 at Salamanca, arr. P from Portsmouth 12 Nov. 1812, d. 5 Dec. 1813: cause of death unstated. TNA ADM 103/264, No. 3043.

176. (*) Charles Rozanier, chasseur, 17th light regt, 26, b. Genoa, capd 7 Apr. 1812 at Joncia, arr. P from Portsmouth 13 Oct. 1812, d. 7 Dec. 1813: cause of death unstated. TNA ADM 103/263, No. 1692.

177. Claude François Bordé, soldier, 58th line regt, 23, b. Chateau Chinon, capd 7 Apr. 1812 at Badajoz, arr. P from Plymouth 30 Nov. or 1 Dec. 1812, d. 13 Dec. 1813: consumption. TNA ADM 103/264, No. 4192; ADM 103/648.

178. Jean François Potel, soldier, 66th line regt, 24, b. Paris, capd 17 Apr. 1809 at the capitulation of the Saintes, arr. P from Plymouth 6 Aug. 1812, d. 16 Dec. 1813: consumption. TNA ADM 103/263, No. 346; ADM 103/648.

179. Jean Colas, soldier, 58th line regt, 23, b. Nevers, capd 7 Apr. 1812 at Badajoz, arr. P from Portsmouth 29 or 30 Nov. 1812, d. 18 Dec. 1813: 'Scirrhous Pyloras' (stomach tumour). TNA ADM 103/264, No. 3555; ADM 103/648.

180. Mathieu Classet (or Clausset), soldier, 26th line regt, 25, b. Tupie, capd 24 Feb. 1809 on Martinique (or n.d. at Flushing), arr. P from V 6 Aug. 1813, d. 18 Dec. 1813: consumption. TNA ADM 103/266, No. 7505; ADM 103/648.

181. Pierre Fenand, soldier, 27th Chasseurs, 22, b. Fesher Band, capd 18 Mar. 1810 in Spain, arr. P from Portsmouth 21 or 22 Oct. 1812, d. 20 Dec. 1813: consumption. TNA ADM 103/264, No. 2457; ADM 103/648.

182. Pierre Metivier, carabinier, 9th light infantry, 38, b. Courbray (or Courtray), capd 7 Apr. 1812 at Badajoz, arr. P from Portsmouth 13 Oct. 1812, d. 5 Jan. 1814: consumption. TNA ADM 103/263, No. 1647; ADM 103/648.

183. Jean Jacques Debaste, soldier, 34th line regt, 28, b. St Omer, capd 28 Oct. 1811 at Rio del Molino, arr. P from Plymouth 6 Aug. 1812, d. 7 Jan. 1814: 'Lumbar Abscess.' TNA ADM 103/263, No. 6; ADM 103/648.

184. Michel Couliaux, soldier, 45th line regt, 28, b. Neuville, capd 6 Mar. 1811 at Cadiz (or St Maria), arr. P from Portsmouth 20 or 21 Aug. 1812, d. 29 Jan. 1814: consumption. TNA ADM 103/263, No. 725; ADM 103/648.

185. François Favreux (or Faviers), chasseur, 17th light (or line) regt, 24, b. Lanior, capd 27 Jun. 1812 at Salamanca, arr. P from Portsmouth 13 Oct. 1812, d. 4 Feb. 1814: 'Inanition in consequence of Mental Derangement.' TNA ADM 103/263, No. 1693; ADM 103/648.

186. François Lambre (or Lambré), soldier, 25th Dragoons, 26, b. Arras (or Vitry), capd 22 Jul. 1812 at Salamanca, arr. P from Portsmouth 3 Dec. 1812, d. 12 Feb. 1814: 'Gangrene of the lower Extremities, and general Debility.' TNA ADM 103/265, No. 4705; ADM 103/648.

187. Jacob Fouate, soldier, 3rd (Italian?) regt, 22, b. Mentcher, capd 13 Mar. 1811 at Bellone, arr. P from Portsmouth 11 or 12 Jan. 1813, d. 12 Feb. 1814: consumption. TNA ADM 103/265, No. 5939; ADM 103/648.

188. Pierre Noblet, soldier, 2nd Infantry Pioneers (or Sappers), 29, b. Saintes, capd 7 Apr. 1812 at Badajoz, arr. P from Portsmouth 29 or 30 Nov. 1812, d. 20 Feb. 1814: consumption. TNA ADM 103/264, No. 3952; ADM 103/648.

189. René Lacosta (or Lacourte), soldier, 2nd line regt, 33, b. St Goutabout, capd 24 Feb. 1809 on the trans. *Revanche* at Martinique, arr. P from V 6 Aug. 1813, d. 3 Mar. 1814: consumption. TNA ADM 103/266, No. 7733; ADM 103/648.

190. Claude Grenot (or Grenet), soldier, 59th line regt, 30, b. Pontaye sur Soane (sic), capd 14 Aug. 1812 at Madrid, arr. P from Portsmouth 12 Nov. 1812, d. 5 Mar. 1814: consumption. TNA ADM 103/264, No. 2983; ADM 103/648.

191. Auguste (or Augustin) Merlette, sergeant major, 2nd Bn Sapeurs (or Mineurs), 42, b. La Neuville le Roi, capd 7 Apr. 1812 at Badajoz, arr. P from Portsmouth 2 Dec. 1812, d. 8 Mar. 1814: 'Found dead in his Bed of Apoplexy.' TNA ADM 103/265, No. 4554; ADM 103/648.

192. Jean Monnery, soldier, 50th line regt, 25, b. Toumalin, capd 12 Mar. 1811 at Pombal, arr. P from Plymouth 6 Aug. 1812, d. 10 Mar. 1814: 'Psoas Abscess.' TNA ADM 103/263, No. 95, and ADM 103/648.

193. Pierre Delanau, soldier, 3rd Artillery, 29, b. Tours, capd 8 Mar. 1809 at Martinique, arr. P from Portsmouth 14 Jan. 1813, d. 15 Mar. 1814: consumption. TNA ADM 103/266, No. 6888; ADM 103/648.

194. Philippe Lefrance, soldier, 70th line regt, 25, b. Anvers, capd 7 Oct. 1810 at Coimbra, arr. P from Portsmouth 8, 9 or 11 Jan. 1813, d. 16 Mar. 1814: consumption. TNA ADM 103/265, No. 5200; ADM 103/648.

195. Ambrose Millerot, soldier, 10th Hussars, 41, b. Lachapelle Villeforet, capd 16 Apr. 1811 at Los Santos, arr. P from Portsmouth 8, 9 or 11 Jan. 1813, d. 22 Mar. 1814: consumption. TNA ADM 103/265, No. 5089; ADM 103/648.

196. Rouss (or Roux) Mayelle, soldier, 70th line regt, 22, b. Valensoles, capd 30 Jul. 1810 off Cazalet, arr. P from Portsmouth 8, 9 or 11 Jan. 1813, d. 25 Mar. 1814: consumption. TNA ADM 103/265, No. 4942; ADM 103/648.

197. Pierre Delanger, alias Pierre Beauchel, soldier, 86th line regt, 29, b. Thionville, capd 17 May 1809 at Oporto, arr. P from Portsmouth 11 or 12 Jan. 1813, d. 25 Mar. 1814: consumption. TNA ADM 103/265, No. 5940; ADM 103/648.

198. Pierre Bert, soldier, 2nd Infantry Pioneers (or Sappers), 35, b. Virieux, capd 7 Apr. 1812 at Badajoz, arr. P from Portsmouth 29 or 30 Nov. 1812, d. 27 Mar. 1814: consumption. TNA ADM 103/264, No. 3978; ADM 103/648.

199. René Pepat (or Pierre Pipat), soldier, 86th line regt, 24, b. Rocford (sic), capd 21 Feb. 1810 on the sloop *La Nécessité* 'at sea', arr. P from Portsmouth 8, 9 or 11 Jan. 1813, d. 1 Apr. 1814: consumption. TNA ADM 103/265, No. 4909; ADM 103/648.

200. Jean Cousin, soldier, 1st line regt, 27, b. Condé, capd 12 Apr. 1809 on *Varsovie* m.o.w. at Rochefort, arr. P from Portsmouth 14 Jan. 1813, d. 2 Apr. 1814: consumption. TNA ADM 103/266, No. 6835; ADM 103/648.

201. Joseph Grosse (or Groche), soldier, 2nd Bn Train, 26, b. Lyons, capd 23 Jul. 1812 at Salamanca, arr. P from Portsmouth 15 Oct. 1812, d. 19 Apr. 1814: consumption. TNA ADM 103/263, No. 2129; ADM 103/648.

202. Joseph Montobio, soldier, 64th line regt, 22, b. Marengo, capd 21 May 1811 at Badajoz, arr. P from Portsmouth 20 or 21 Aug. 1812, d. 1 May 1814: consumption. TNA ADM 103/263, No. 612; ADM 103/648.

203. Bernard Lajons (or Lajoue), soldier, 40th line regt, 26, b. Salens (or Salins), capd 16 May 1811 at Ebora, arr. P from Portsmouth 20 or 21 Aug. 1812, d. 2 May 1814: consumption. TNA ADM 103/263, No. 608; ADM 103/648.

204. Benoit France, soldier, 4th light (or line) regt, 21, b. Chaget, capd 21 Aug. 1808 in Portugal, arr. P from Portsmouth 20 or 21 Aug. 1812, d. 3 May 1814: fever. TNA ADM 103/263, No. 469; ADM 103/648.

205. Jean Paul Dupont, soldier, 82nd line regt, 27, b. Toulouse, capd 27 Jun. 1812 at Salamanca, arr. P from Portsmouth 29 or 30 Nov. 1812, d. 17 May 1814: 'Atrophia.' TNA ADM 103/264, No. 3518; ADM 103/648.

206. Jean Baptiste Mathieu (or Mothiu), soldier, 39th line regt, 28, b. Amiens, capd 29 May 1812 at Almeria, arr. P from Portsmouth 29 or 30 Nov. 1812, d. 20 May 1814: consumption. TNA ADM 103/264, No. 3585; ADM 103/648.

207. Nicolas Costard (or Castard), soldier, 70th line regt, 24, b. Coutances, capd 7 Oct. 1810 at Coimbra, arr. P from Plymouth 30 Nov. or 1 Dec. 1812, d. 20 May 1814: consumption. TNA ADM 103/264, No. 4303; ADM 103/648.

208. François Felix, soldier, 34th line regt, 26, b. St Moris (or St Noris), capd 19 Jan. 1812 at Ciudad Rodrigo, arr. P from Portsmouth 29 Aug. 1812, d. 21 May 1814: 'Lumbar Abscess.' TNA ADM 103/263, No. 899; ADM 103/648.

209. Joseph Rouvsère (or Rouvière), soldier, 1st (line? Italian?) regt, 27, b. Naples, capd 3 Jan. 1807 on the naval sloop *Le Creole* at Dominica (or n.d. in Calabria), arr. P from Portsmouth 20 or 21 Aug. 1812, d. 25 May 1814: consumption. TNA ADM 103/263, No. 404; ADM 103/648.

210. Nicolas Chameau, soldier, 3rd line regt, 34, b. Main, capd 7 Oct. 1810 at Coimbra, arr. P from Portsmouth 21 or 22 Oct. 1812, described in Entry Book as 'Raffalé, d. 25 May 1814: consumption. TNA ADM 103/264, No. 2705; ADM 103/648.

211. Paul Antoine Baulany, soldier, 17th light infantry, 26, b. Serjant, capd 27 Sep. 1810 at Coimbra, arr. P from Portsmouth 11 or 12 Jan. 1813, d. 27 May 1814: consumption. TNA ADM 103/265, No. 5977; ADM 103/648.

212. Jean Pierre Talouard (or Talicr), soldier, 54th line regt, 20, b. Cornesson, capd 15 Aug. 1809 at Flushing, arr. P from Portsmouth 12 Jan. 1813, d. 27 May 1814: consumption. TNA ADM 103/265, No. 6148; ADM 103/648.

213. Jean Grangeau (or Granjean), soldier, 70th line regt, 22, b. Bordeaux, capd 7 Oct. 1810 at Coimbra, arr. P from Portsmouth 21 or 22 Oct. 1812, described in Entry Book as 'Raffalé', d. 28 May 1814: consumption. TNA ADM 103/264, No. 2733; ADM 103/648.

214. Antoine Buisson, chasseur, 6th light infantry, 28, b. Gregni, capd 23 Jul. 1812 at Salamanca, arr. P from Lisbon 9 Jan. 1813, d. 1 Jun. 1814: consumption. TNA ADM 103/265, No. 5800; ADM 103/648.

215. Eugène Hanotan, soldier, 6th light infantry, 20, b. Messières, capd 24 Feb. 1809 at Martinique, arr. P from V 4 Aug. 1813, d. 10 Jun. 1814: consumption. TNA ADM 103/266, No. 7357, and ADM 103/648.

Notes

For abbreviations and contractions used, see above, p.ix.

INTRODUCTION

1. See, e.g., Geoffrey Best, *War and Society in Revolutionary Europe 1770-1870* (Stroud, 1998), 114; Eric Hobsbawm, *The Age of Revolution. Europe 1789-1848* (London, 1962), 92-4.

2. Francis Abell, *Prisoners of War in Britain, 1756-1815* (Oxford, 1914), 43; Thomas J. Walker, *The Depot for Prisoners-of-War at Norman Cross, Huntingdonshire, 1796-1816* (London, 1915), 248; Michael Lewis, *Napoleon and his British captives* (London, 1962), 53.

3. Georges Lefebvre, *Napoleon* (London, 1969), Vol.1, 179. See also, e.g., Geoffrey Bruun, *Europe and the French Imperium 1799-1814* (New York, 1963), 36-62 passim; George Rudé, *Revolutionary Europe 1783-1815* (London, 1964), 201-4, 228, 242-3; Franklin L. Ford, *Europe 1780-1830* (London, 1971), 189-203 passim; J. Steven Watson, *The Reign of George III 1760-1815* (Oxford, 1960), 406-14 passim; Felix Markham, *Napoleon* (London, 1963), 103-8 passim.

CHAPTER 1: THE FIRST YEAR OF THE WAR, 1803-1804

1. William James, *The Naval History of Great Britain* (London, 1859), Vol. III, 169; *Caledonian Mercury* (henceforth *CM*), 23 May 1803; *Edinburgh Evening Courant* (henceforth *EEC*), 26 May 1803.

2. The Board's staff at 31 Jan. 1807 included its secretary (annual salary £1,000), several sectional chief clerks and their assistants, and two accountants and their assistants—a total of 49, which by 3 Feb. 1813 had grown to 87. The National Archives (henceforth TNA), ADM 1/3750, fol. 440; ADM 1/3764, fols 78-85.

3. Abell, *Prisoners of War in Britain*, op. cit., 3, 4; J. Macbeth Forbes, 'The French Prisoners-of-War in the Border Towns, 1803-1814', in *Transactions of Hawick Archaeological Society, 1912*, 17; J. N. Tonnessen (ed.), *Pa Kapertokt og i Prisonen 1808-1810. Av. Kaptein Paul Andreas Kaalds, Etterlatte Papirer* (*Privateer Cruising and in Prison 1808-1810. From Captain Paul Andreas Kaald's Posthumous Papers*) (Trondheim, 1950), 98 (henceforth Kaald).

4. *EEC*, 8 Sep. 1803. Barbed wire, invented in the United States about 1867, began to be widely used only from about 1874. *Encyclopedia Britannica*, 15th ed., Vol. I (Chicago, 1990), 887.

5. W. Branch-Johnson, *The English Prison Hulks* (London, 1957), 45, 46; Patrick Crowhurst, *The French War on Trade: Privateering 1793-1815* (London, 1989), 177-80, 211. Branch-Johnson, op. cit., 45, and Lewis, *Napoleon and his British captives*, op. cit., 59, say the Admiralty (henceforth Adm.) provided a total of more than 60 hulks for the purpose during the French Revolutionary and Napoleonic Wars. But that total presumably included hulks used in the West Indies and elsewhere.

6. See, e.g., TNA ADM 105/59 for 35 Dutch prisoners at Edinburgh Castle, 1796-9, and ADM 103/585 for 65 parole prisoners at Peebles, 1798-9.

7. Walker, *The Depot at Norman Cross*, op. cit., 247. Portchester Castle, used as a depot for prisoners of war since the War of Austrian Succession in the mid-18th century,

appears not have been used as such in the Napoleonic Wars until 1810, a letter dated 21 May 1803 from the Duke of York, Commander-in-Chief, to Lord Hobart, Secretary-at-War, having warned against massing prisoners so close to the naval arsenal at Portsmouth. TNA WO 1/625, fol. 217; Abell, *Prisoners of War in Britain*, op. cit., 166, 167.

8. TNA ADM 99/149, 9 and 20 Jun. 1803; N.G. Allen, 'The French Prisons in Edinburgh Castle', in *Book of the Old Edinburgh Club* (Edinburgh, 1985), Vol. XXXV, Part II, 164; TNA ADM 99/150, ltr, 1 Sep. 1803, TB to Wright; *CM*, 8 Sep. 1803; TNA ADM 98/191, ltr, 23 Aug. 1803, TB to Kerr; Sheila Scott, *Peebles during the Napoleonic Wars* (n.p. (Peebles), 1980), 6; J.W. Buchan (ed.), *A History of Peeblesshire* (Glasgow, 1925), 92, 106, 351-2, 554.

9. TNA ADM 99/149, ltrs, 6, 26 and 28 Jul. 1803; ADM 99/150, ltrs, 19 Aug. and 5 Sep. 1803; ADM 99/151, ltrs, 15 Oct. and n.d. (c. 22 Oct.) 1803. As Colquhoun told the Board that 'there was no place at Greenock proper for the confinement of prisoners of war', they were kept there on the guard ship HMS *Tourterelle* until they could be escorted to Edinburgh. (TNA ADM 99/152, ltr, 7 Nov. 1803). Colquhoun resigned in Jan. 1807 and was succeeded by his son John as the Board's agent at Greenock. (TNA ADM 99/175, fol. 35). A surviving register, or General Entry Book, of prisoners at Greenock lists 86 during 1805. They appear all to have been captured in the West Indies or on ships in the Atlantic. Except for a dozen soldiers or marines, five passengers, and two fishermen, all were seamen. All these prisoners, excepting half a dozen whose disposal is not clear, were sent on to Malcolm Wright, agent at Edinburgh. TNA ADM 103/159 passim.

10. TNA ADM 99/149, ltrs, 22 Jun., 28 Jul. and 4 Aug. 1803.

11. TNA ADM 99/150. A ltr in ADM 98/129, 23 Jan. 1807, TB to Lieut. Col. Gordon, War Office (henceforth WO), says the Board's request at the beginning of the war had been refused.

12. TNA ADM 99/150, ltr received 25 Aug. 1803 by TB from Wright.

13. Ibid., ltrs, 4, 13 and 25 Aug. 1803.

14. Fort George, intended as a military bulwark against any further Jacobite risings, had been designed and built between 1747 and 1770 by the distinguished architects William and John Adam. It had held some state prisoners after the Irish rebellion of 1798.

15. TNA ADM 1/3743, fol. 317-19, 379-82; ADM 1/3744, ltrs, 3 and 6 Oct., 15 and 28 Nov. 1803; ADM 99/150, ltrs, 26, 27, 29, 30 Aug., 2, 5, 10, 11 Sep. 1803; ADM 99/151, ltrs, 14, 17, n.d. (17 or 18), 18, n.d. (c. 20) Sep. and 3 Oct. 1803.

16. TNA ADM 99/151, ltr, 25 Sep. 1803, from Adm. enclosing copies of ltrs from Generals Brownrigg and Vyse; ADM 1/3743, ltr, 1 Oct. 1803; ADM 99/152, fol. 165, ltr, 21 Dec. 1803, M. Wright to TB.

17. J. Macbeth Forbes, 'French Prisoners of War in Scotland, and Bank Note Forging', in *Bankers' Magazine*, Mar. 1897, 396-8; Allen, op. cit., 161-3.

18. TNA ADM 105/44, report by Serle, 10 Jul. 1799.

19. TNA ADM 99/150, ltr, n.d., c. 7 or 8 Sep. 1803; *CM*, *Glasgow Courier* and *EEC*, 22 Sep. 1803.

20. TNA ADM 99/153, fol. 38.

21. John Howard (1726-1790), English prison reformer, himself a prisoner of war in France during the Seven Years' War, 1756-63, had visited Edinburgh Castle on his

tour of prisons in Britain in 1779 during the American War of Independence, and had persuaded the lord provost of the city to hold a competition for plans for building a prison. The competition was won by the distinguished architect Robert Adam (1728-1792), who had studied the 'panopticon' or prison designed by the utilitarian and reformer Jeremy Bentham (1748-1832). The Edinburgh bridewell, consequently built in 1791-5 on Calton Hill, was said at that time to have approximately 150 cells. Serle's reference to the possibility of 2,000 prisoners of war being confined in it therefore appears distinctly optimistic, unless either presumably serious overcrowding was envisaged (which hardly squares with his denunciation of conditions at the Castle), or the cells were unusually commodious, or (more likely) an error was made by a clerk in the Transport Office (henceforth TO) in copying that figure in his report. *Edinburgh Magazine*, Dec. 1797; *EEC*, 10 and 28 Sep. 1795; Abell, *Prisoners of War in Britain*, op. cit., 271-2; TNA ADM 105/44, report by Serle, 10 Jul. 1799; see also Joy Cameron, *Prisons & Punishment in Scotland* (Edinburgh, 1983), 101 (quoting *Reports of the Burgh Commissioners, Local Report, Part I*, 306, where the bridewell was said to have '52 working cells and 129 sleeping cells.').

22. TNA ADM 99/151, ltrs, 17 and 18 Sep. 1803, from Wright, and n.d. (probably c. 20 Sep.), TB to Wright; ADM 105/44, report, 10 Jul. 1799, from Serle to TB. One of the criticisms Serle had made of Wright in this report in 1799 was that he had delegated to Alexander Fraser as his clerk too much of his own responsibility.

23. TNA ADM 99/151, ltr, 26 Sep. 1803, Wright to TB.

24. Ibid., 21 Sep. 1803.

25. Ibid., ltr, n.d. (but probably c. 30 Sep. 1803), TB to Wright; ibid., ltrs, 28 Sep. and 7 Oct. 1803, Wright to TB.

26. Louis Simond, *Journal of a tour and residence in Great Britain during the years 1810 and 1811* (Edinburgh, 1817), 2 vols, Vol. 1, 358-9.

27. That is the net total after deducting five re-entries in the registers for recaptured escapers who were given new numbers.

28. TNA ADM 103/154 and ADM 103/155. The first of these two General Entry Books indicates that 13 prisoners described as Dutch, all seamen capd in the North Sea on 18 Jul. on the m.v. *Neptunis*, arr. in the bridewell on 29 Sep. 1803, and one, a Dutch officer (evidently not granted parole), from an unspecified priv. capd in the North sea, arr. in Feb. 1804. The second Entry Book, said to be of French prisoners, lists 96 men held captive in the bridewell at one time or another between 19 Sep. and the end of Mar. 1804. Entry Books that Malcolm Wright as agent was responsible for keeping are less clear and comprehensible than those of later TB agents in Scotland.

29. TNA ADM 103/115, No.1.

30. *EEC*, 28 Nov. and 3 Dec. 1803, reported, however, that on 17 Nov. a boat with only one man in it had tried to evade a revenue service vessel off St Abbs Head, north of Berwick-on-Tweed. Taken into Berwick the man (unnamed in the *Courant*) claimed at first to be a (neutral) Danish seaman. 'But he was proved not to speak Danish but to speak Dutch fluently.' The man later admitted he was an escaped prisoner of war from the Edinburgh bridewell. 'It appears that after breaking from prison he had entered as a sailor on one of the vessels at Leith, and had made his escape after stealing a boat, a watch and some money from the ship ... and was creeping along the shore [at St Abbs Head] in hopes of meeting some neutral vessel. He was brought to Edinburgh on Tuesday [22 Nov.].' If he was not one of the five Belgians

he must have been another prisoner whose escape went unrecorded in Malcolm Wright's register.

31. TNA ADM 103/155, No. 70.

32. Ibid., No 7 is Cottier.

33. *EEC*, 8 Mar. 1804. Nor did the two escapers of 24 Feb., François Rokes and Jean Perneil, both seamen, long enjoy their freedom. They were recognised a few miles east of Glasgow on 5 Mar. by a soldier of the Argyll militia who had been one of their guards at the bridewell. 'Though alone, he instantly challenged them, upon their making a shew of resistance with their sticks, he threw away his bundle and drew his bayonet, when they submitted, and were conducted to Glasgow jail. When ... the Argyll man was asked if he was not afraid to attack two such men, one of them a Russian by birth, being remarkably stout, he answered, 'Hoot, damn—after I had stickit the one I could surely have secured the other.' *Glasgow Courier*, 10 Mar. 1804. How the two escapers had coped during the ten days they were at large was not reported.

34. TNA ADM 99/151, ltrs, 9 and n.d. (12?) Oct. 1803; ADM 99/152, ltr, 1 Nov. 1803, from Wright.

35. TNA ADM 99/152, fol. 114; ADM 99/153, fol. 38.

36. In fact, the cost of immediately preparing Greenlaw as a depot proved to be 'upwards of £2,000'. TNA ADM 98/129, ltr, 23 Jan. 1807, TB to Lieut. Col. Gordon, WO.

37. TNA ADM 99/153, fols 100, 151, 154, 173; ADM 99/154, fols 47 and 81; ADM 99/155, fol. 9; NAS E886/79, Tack, 10 and 17 Feb. 1804, betwixt HM Commissioners of Transport and Robert Trotter, Esq.; *EEC*, 2 Apr. 1804.

CHAPTER 2: GREENLAW

1. TNA ADM 105/44, report by Serle, 10 Jul. 1799. Andrew Johnston, clerk or chief clerk successively at Esk Mills, Valleyfield and Perth depots during the Napoleonic Wars, stated in his unpublished recollections that there were French prisoners in Greenlaw mansion house in 1796. No evidence has been found, however, to support his statement. See 'Recollections of the Depots for French Prisoners in Scotland, written by Andrew Johnston in 1839', in National Library of Scotland (henceforth NLS), MS Acc. 5811/1/63, p.1.

2. A writer in the *Peeblesshire Advertiser*, 15 Apr. 1905, recalled a conversation he had had many years earlier with 'someone who as a child remembered looking through the palisade at the prisoners.' An illustration in Major R.C. Dudgeon, *History of the Edinburgh or Queen's Regiment Light Infantry Militia, (now) Third Battalion, the Royal Scots* (Edinburgh, 1882), is a copy of the original drawing of Greenlaw Mansion in 1803 which was in the possession of Col. Trotter of The Bush, Midlothian.

3. The two sketches by Kaald are included in his diary, preserved in Trondheim museum and edited by J. N. Tønnessen, op. cit., 94, 97. Copies of the other two sketches are in National Archives of Scotland (henceforth NAS), GD1/405/4 (Macbeth Forbes Coll.).

4. Midlothian Local Studies Library, Loanhead (henceforth ML), Black Collection, vol. 2(c), pp. 3, 4.

5. TNA ADM 103/635 Part I, ltr, 18 Jul. 1812, A. Greig, Edinburgh, to TB.

6. Another clause in the tack provided that: '... whatever Dung is made on the premises

either by horses, cows or other Bestial, the Prisoners or other Persons belonging to the Depot, or in any other manner during the foresaid lease, the same shall be laid on the grounds hereby let.'

7. NAS E886/79.

8. TNA ADM 103/635 Part I, ltr, 14 Mar. 1812, Lieut. Joseph Priest, agent, Greenlaw, to TB.

9. ML, Black Coll., vol.2(c), p.2; TNA ADM 103/155, No. 97.

10. *Carnet d'Etapes et Souvenirs de Guerre et de Captivité du sergent-major Philippe Beaudoin de la 31e demi-brigade de ligne*, in *Carnet de la Sabretache* (Paris, 1909), Second series, no.201, Sep. 1909, 632-4 (henceforth Beaudoin); TNA ADM 103/155.

11. The Danish registers are TNA ADM 103/152 and ADM 103/153; the Dutch registers ADM 103/110 (the first 38 pages) and ADM 103/154; the French registers ADM 103/155, /156 and /157; and the Spanish ADM 103/158.

12. TNA ADM 103/155, Nos 140 (Corbeau), 158 (Gerrin), and 260-9.

13. TNA ADM 103/154, Nos 16-92; *EEC*, 17 May 1804. Whether some or all of the 13 detained were suspected of being British seamen serving with the Dutch navy, is not clear.

14. TNA ADM 103/155, Nos 282-320.

15. *CM*, 26 Feb. 1807, reported the firing two days earlier of 'the great guns' from Edinburgh Castle and from ships at Leith in celebration of the news, newly received, that Curaçoa had been capd by a British naval squadron on 1 Jan. James, op. cit., Vol. IV, 275-8.

16. Orkney Archives, D1/48; *CM*, 15, 19 and 30 Mar., and 2 and 9 Apr. 1807.

17. *EEC*, 30 Mar. 1807.

18. TNA ADM 99/176, fols 91, 111, 113, 118, 121, 122 and 124; ADM 99/177, fols 129, 131, 132, 149, 152 and 156; ADM 103/110; *EEC*, 21 and 30 Mar., 6 and 23 Apr. 1807. Bernard Humbert, one of the *Utrecht* prisoners who volunteered himself into the British army, was soon discovered to be in fact Clement Guillon, 'a French prisoner and a native of France', and was sent back to Greenlaw. One who enlisted in the Royal Navy (henceforth RN) was named Daniel Robertson, but no question appears to have arisen about his *bona fides*.

19. TNA ADM 103/158, Nos 1-7.

20. TNA ADM 103/115, another ambiguous General Entry Book that purports to be of French prisoners at Edinburgh between 1803 and 1812, but seems in fact to be of men at Greenlaw. After an initial group of 620, there are 30 blank pages followed by a list of 68 prisoners, many of whom are clearly Spanish seamen, received into custody at the depot between 21 Jul. 1805 and 28 Oct. 1808. Against some of the entries occurs the phrase 'To go home' from Jul. 1808—the month in which Spain ceased to be Napoleon's ally and became Britain's.

21. H.W. Koch, *A History of Prussia* (London, 1978), 155-60; J.A.R. Marriott and C.G. Robertson, *The Evolution of Prussia* (Oxford, rev. ed. 1946), 207-11; Georges Lefebvre, *Napoleon*. Vol. II: *From Tilsit to Waterloo, 1807-1815* (London, 1969), 251-5.

22. *Glasgow Courier*, 26 Jun. 1806. An advertisement in *EEC* on 23 Oct. announced the sale at Leith of 17 impounded Prussian m.vs or fishing smacks. The names of 131 prisoners in a separate section of the ambiguous General Entry Book TNA ADM 103/115 that purports to be of French prisoners at Edinburgh in 1803-12 indicate that they, or most of them, were in fact the Prussian seamen who were confined in

Greenlaw. All 131 arrived between 7 Jun. and 14 Nov. 1806, and their names all appear to be German, Dutch or Scandinavian—crews of Prussian ships were no doubt as cosmopolitan as those of merchant ships of many other countries.

23. *CM*, 16 Feb. 1807; *EEC*, 19 Feb. 1807; TNA ADM 99/175, fol. 65, ltr, 17 Feb. 1807, M. Wright, Greenlaw, to TB, enclosing a list of 42 Prussian prisoners discharged. Thirteen, or 10 per cent, of the original 131 'Prussians' had volunteered into His Britannic Majesty's navy. TNA ADM 103/115.

24. T. K. Derry, *A History of Scandinavia* (London, 1979), 202-3.

25. One of the passengers, Anders Iversensand, capd off Norway on the m.v. *Else Kierstine* on 7 Oct. 1807, is described as 'passenger and owner'. TNA ADM 103/152, No. 79.

26. Kaald, op. cit., 11-17, 82, 83.

27. TNA ADM 103/156; ADM 103/596.

28. TNA HO 28/38, fol. 97, ltr, 18 Oct. 1810, J. Barrow, Adm., to J. Beckett, Home Office (henceforth HO), enclosing copy of a ltr, 24 Sep. 1810, about Greenlaw from Adm. to TB.

29. TNA ADM 103/596. The Peebles Entry Book lists some 190 prisoners received from Greenlaw on parole between Aug. 1805 and Dec. 1810. ADM 98/114, ltr, 19 Nov. 1808, to Hon. W.W. Pole, Adm.; ADM 98/115, ltr, 20 Oct. 1809, to J. W. Croker, Adm.; ADM 103/152 passim and ADM 103/153 passim; Beaudoin, op. cit., 636, 639.

30. For escapes and deaths in that period, see TNA ADM 103/115, and ADM 103/152-/156 passim; and particularly above, Chapter 21 and Appendix 11.

CHAPTER 3: SHOOTINGS AND 'SERIOUS ABUSES' AT GREENLAW

1. TNA HO 28/34/149. Sir William Cathcart (1755-1843), an advocate from 1776, joined the army in 1777, served in the American War of Independence and became acting Quarter Master General in America; a strong Tory, he was elected a representative peer for Scotland, 1788; he fought in the Netherlands and Germany, 1794-5, lieut. general from 1801, army commander in Ireland, 1803-5, commanded a British army at Bremen, 1805-6, army commander in Scotland from 1806; commanded, 1807, the British expeditionary army to Copenhagen; created Viscount Cathcart, 1807; in 1812 promoted general and appointed British military commissioner with the army of the Tsar and also, until 1820, ambassador to Russia; created Earl Cathcart, 1814.

2. *The Times*, 23 Jun. 1807.

3. Adam Gillies (1760-1842), an advocate from 1787, a judge as Lord Gillies from 1811. Francis Jeffrey (1773-1850), an advocate from 1794, a founder, 1802, and editor until 1829, of the *Edinburgh Review*, a Whig MP, 1830-4, Lord Advocate, 1830-4, a judge as Lord Jeffrey, 1834-50. The Lord Advocate was Archibald Campbell-Colquhoun (died 1820), advocate from 1768, Lord Advocate from Mar. 1807, Tory MP, 1807-20, Lord Clerk Register from 1816. David Boyle (1772-1853), an advocate from 1793, Solicitor-General from May 1807, Tory MP, 1807-11, a judge as Lord Boyle from 1811, Lord President of the Court of Session, 1841-52. William Erskine (1769-1822), an advocate from 1790, an advocate-depute from Mar. 1807, a close friend of Sir Walter Scott, and appointed a judge as Lord Kinneder in 1822 shortly before his death.

4. *EEC*, 18 Jun. 1807.

5. Ibid., 15 and 18 Jun. 1807; *CM*, 18 Jun. 1807.

6. NAS, Justiciary Court JC 26/334.

7. Ibid.; Kaald, op. cit., 88.

8. *The Manual of Military Law* (War Office, London, 1887), Chap. VIII, 208.

9. TNA ADM 103/155, No. 7 (Cottier).

10. *CM*, 16 and 19 Feb. 1807; *EEC*, 19 Feb. 1807; Henry Cockburn (1779-1854), an advocate from 1800, Advocate-Depute, 1807-10, Solicitor-General, 1830-4, a Whig who played a leading role in drafting the Scottish Reform Bill; from 1834 a judge as Lord Cockburn; author of *Memorials of his Time* and other works.

11. *EEC*, 28 Aug. 1810.

12. TNA ADM 98/116.

13. *Ance a Bailie Aye a Bailie. An Account of the 800 year long history of the Edinburgh Bailies* (Edinburgh City Museums, 1974), ii, 2, 23.

14. *Williamson's Edinburgh Directory 1790-2* (Edinburgh, 1792), 104; Ibid., *1794-6* (Edinburgh, 1796), 157; *Aitchison's Edinburgh Directory* (Edinburgh, 1793-4), 129; Ibid. (1794-5), 190; Ibid. (1795-6), 181; Ibid. (1796-7), 141; Ibid. (1797-8), 198; Ibid. (1799-1800), 258.

15. James Anton, *Retrospect of a military life* (Edinburgh, 1841), 29-31, 39. After two tours of duty guarding the prisoners at Penicuik, Anton enlisted in the 42nd infantry regt (the Black Watch), in which he later became quartermaster.

16. Beaudoin, op. cit., 638-9. The prisoners' letter to the authorities appears not to survive. The black hole was the cachot or close confinement cells into which were put prisoners who breached depot regulations.

17. Kaald, op. cit., 182-4.

18. A TB ltr to the Adm. as early as 1 Oct. 1803 had declared that 'the most strict orders are given to all our Agents not to allow any person whatever, except the officer of the guard, to have any communication with the prisoners in their custody.' TNA ADM 1/3744.

19. Kaald, op. cit., 130.

20. Ibid., 147.

21. Ibid., 152. Kaald was unlikely to have been aware that Sir George Clerk's great uncle John Clerk of Eldin had published an article in 1782 on naval tactics. These tactics, which he had worked out on the pond at Penicuik House, where Kaald skated a generation later, included a plan for breaking the long single line astern formation adopted in battle by contemporary warships—a plan that Nelson carried out at Trafalgar. John J. Wilson, *The Annals of Penicuik* (Stevenage, new ed. 1985), 157.

22. Kaald, op. cit., 160-2. Mrs Annadell or Annandale was almost certainly the same woman who in Apr. 1812 was employed as an assistant sempstress at Valleyfield depot. TNA ADM 98/278, ltrs, 21 and 29 Apr. 1812, TB to Capt. Moriarty, RN.

23. Johnston, 'Recollections', op. cit., p.1.

24. TNA ADM 98/276, ltr, 7 Sep. 1809, to Wright.

25. Ibid., ltr, 6 Oct. 1809, to Wright, and ADM 99/199, ltrs, 19, 22 and 29 Sep. and 3 Oct. 1809.

26. TNA ADM 99/199 and ADM 99/200 passim; ADM 98/276, ltrs, 6 Oct. and 29 Nov. 1809, TB to Wright.

27. Kaald, op. cit., 141.

28. TNA ADM 99/205, ltr, 29 Oct. 1810, Adm. to TB.

CHAPTER 4: THE 'NEW ARRANGEMENTS'

1. The list is in NAS, Melville Castle Muniments, GD 51/2/783.

2. TNA HO 28/40, ltr, 26 Aug. 1811, TB to J. Beckett, HO.

3. The totals for the years to 1810 are based on the lists in the General Entry Books for the Edinburgh bridewell, Greenlaw and Peebles; those from 1811 on the two latter and on the Entry Books for the new depots and parole towns. For the estimates for Mar. 1810 and May 1814, see Guillaume Lévêque, *Les Prisonniers de Guerre Français en Grande Bretagne, 1803-1814*, (2 vols), University of Paris unpublished Mémoire de Maitrise, 1988, Annexe 13. A TO list dated 4 Aug. 1812, in TNA HO 42/126, fol. 164B, gives as at 30 Jul. that year a grand total of 49,629 prisoners in depots and hulks in Britain, of whom 5,620 (11.1 per cent) were in confined depots in Scotland (640 at Greenlaw and 4,980 at Valleyfield). In addition the list shows there were then in Britain 3,356 parole prisoners, of whom 1,305 (38.9 per cent) were in 12 parole towns in Scotland. Abell, op. cit., 118, estimated that in 1814 there was a total of 72,000 prisoners of war in Britain, with spare capacity for holding almost 10,000 more—i.e., up to 45,000 in land depots, 35,000 on the hulks, and 2,000 on parole.

4. Sir Charles Oman, *A History of the Peninsular War, 1807-1814* (Oxford, 1902-1930), Vol. III, Sep. 1809—Dec. 1810, 385, 411-12, 461.

5. *The Despatches of Field Marshal The Duke of Wellington* comp. by Lieut. Col. Gurwood (London, 1835), contain many references to Wellington's concern about the safety of French prisoners in Spain and Portugal. 'It would be advisable,' Wellington wrote on 29 Apr. 1810, for example, to his younger brother Henry Wellesley, then secretary to the British embassy in Spain and from 1811 ambassador to the junta or regency at Cadiz, 'for the Regency to offer a reward for every Frenchman, or soldier in the French service, brought in alive to any post occupied by any of the allied troops. This measure was adopted with some success by [the Spanish] General Cuesta. The peasants refrained from the murder of the French soldiers, and many consequently deserted.' *Despatches of The Duke of Wellington*, Vol. VI, 62.

6. Ibid., Vol.VII, 200. George Berkeley (1753-1818), British naval commander on the coast of Portugal and in the Tagus, Dec. 1808-May 1812; promoted admiral in Jul. 1810 and became Lord High Admiral of Portugal.

7. Walker, *The Depot at Norman Cross*, op. cit., 250.

8. J. Fortescue, *A History of the British Army* (London, 1912), Vol. VII, 1809-1810, 16, 19-24, 80.

9. *The Times*, 13 Oct. 1809.

10. Basil Thomson, *The Story of Dartmoor Prison* (London, 1907), 9-10.

11. Roy Bennett, French Prisoners of War on Parole in Britain (1803-1814). Unpublished Ph.D. thesis, University of London, 1964, p. 212.

12. For these attempts, see Bennett, op. cit., pp. 15-36 and 148-58.

13. Escapes or attempted escapes by officers on parole increased from 55 in 1808 to 126 in 1809 and to 209 in 1810. Thus the total, which in the years 1803-07 had been 117, was 390 in 1808-10. Bennett, op. cit., pp.196-7.

14. For example, General Osten escaped from Lichfield in Feb. 1810. In the same year, another general, eight colonels or lieutenant colonels, and seven naval captains, also escaped. Bennett, op. cit., pp. 197 and 205.

15. TNA HO 28/38, ltr, 5 Sep. 1810, to TB from Capt. C.M. Paterson, agent, Portchester Castle.

16. Ibid., ltr, 7 Sep. 1810, to TB from Capt. Paterson.

17. Ibid. The Portchester Castle depot General Entry Book, TNA ADM 103/333, gives as No. 1,624 Henry Catalin, alias Catala, surgeon, capd 'at sea' in Nov. 1806 on the priv. *Décidé*. Catalin or Catala had arr. at Portchester Castle on 10 Jun. 1810 from Odiham, where he had been on parole. The only other information about him in the Portchester Castle Entry Book is that he was dischgd on 11 Sep. 1810 back to Odiham. The Odiham General Entry Book, TNA ADM 103/563, No. 244, says Henry Catalac (sic), capd on the *Décidé* (but in Nov. 1807, not 1806), had arr. there on 2 Dec. 1807 from Chatham and was sent to Portchester Castle. It also confirms that Henry Catalo (sic) arr. back on parole at Odiham on 12 Sep. 1810 from Portchester Castle, and adds that he was re-entered as No. 363 and then he was sent on 11 Aug. 1811 via Forton depot on parole to Selkirk. A TB alphabetical list of parole prisoners (TNA ADM 103/611) confirms that Catala was No. 142 at Selkirk (where the General Entry Book for parole prisoners was one of several of those for Scots parole towns that appear not to survive). There Catala's involvement in Freemasonry continued, as he was recorded as being either a member of or at least a visitor to the Scotch Lodge at Selkirk on 9 Mar. 1812. John T. Thorp, *French Prisoners' Lodges. A brief account of fifty lodges and chapters of Freemasons, established and conducted by French prisoners-of-war in England and elsewhere, between 1756 and 1814* (Leicester, 1935, 2nd. ed.), 266. Catala was also one of the parole prisoners in the town who borrowed books 'as freely and as often as they chose' from the Selkirk Subscription Library which had been founded in 1772. *Southern Reporter*, 23 May 1901, which lists the names of 89 borrowers of the books among the prisoners.

18. TNA HO 28/38/97.

19. TNA HO 28/38/95-6.

20. TNA ADM 98/131, ltr, 10 Oct. 1810, TB to Bowen.

21. TNA HO 28/38/99-102.

22. TNA ADM 99/205. Sir John Sinclair (1754-1835), b. at Thurso; MP, 1780-1811, president, Board of Agriculture, 1793-8 and 1806-13.

23. Bowen had been commended by Lord Castlereagh, Secretary of State for War, for his 'judgement, activity and perseverance … upon this arduous occasion' as commissioner sent to Spain to organise the re-embarkation at Corunna of the British army led by General Sir John Moore after its retreat to that port in Jan. 1809. TNA WO 6/156, ltr, 4 Feb. 1809, Lord Castlereagh to TB.

24. TNA ADM 98/131.

25. TNA ADM 98/132, ltrs, 13 and 16 Jul. 1811, TB to Mr Yorke, Adm., and to Bowen.

26. TNA ADM 99/205, ltr, 24 Oct. 1810, Adm. to TB, and ADM 98/131, ltr, 25 Oct. 1810, to Bowen. As already noted, 25 per cent of all parole prisoners *were* in Scotland by 1814, though not all other prisoners taken from 1811 onwards were in fact sent there.

27. TNA ADM 98/119, ltr, 15 Jul. 1812, TB to Adm.; Melville Castle Muniments, in NAS GD 51/756/1-2, memorandum, 13 Mar. 1811, by David Steuart, Edinburgh; TNA ADM 98/132, ltr, 14 May 1811, TB to Bowen; ADM 98/131, ltrs, 10 Oct. and 5 Nov. 1810, TB to Bowen; ADM 98/133, ltr, 5 Mar. 1812, TB to Mr J. Merry; ADM

99/206, ltr, 3 Nov. 1810, Adm. to TB; NLS, Melville papers, MS Acc. 1075/222-6, ltr, 24 Dec. 1810, Lord Melville (Henry Dundas) to the brother of Sir Rupert George, chairman, TB.

28. The source of Napier's comments, quoted by J. Macbeth Forbes in his 'French Prisoners of War in Scotland and Bank Note Forging', op.cit., 394, was not given, but they appear not to have been made in Napier's *History of the War in the Peninsula and the South of France 1807-1814* (London, 1834-40 (and later editions)), 6 vols.

29. TNA ADM 98/132.

30. TNA ADM 98/131, ltr, 5 Nov. 1810, TB to Bowen.

31. Serle's report of 10 Jul. 1799 is in TNA ADM 105/44.

32. NAS, Melville Castle Muniments, GD 51/756/1-2.

33. TNA ADM 98/119, ltr, 15 Jul. 1812, TB to Adm.

34. TNA ADM 98/133, ltr, 5 Mar. 1812, TB to Mr J. Merry.

35. TNA ADM 98/132, ltrs, 14 May, 4 and 24 Jun. 1811, TB to Bowen. In the last of these letters there is also a reference to land offered at Penicuik by Messrs Haig and Philp, who by this time appear to have succeeded Messrs White as owners of Esk Mills; and Messrs Stark, Craig & Co., merchants, Elbe Street, Leith, offered the TB their premises at Kirkhill, adjoining Penicuik, for £10,000. But both offers were declined as 'not now wanted'. TNA ADM 99/207, ltrs to TB, 17 May 1811, from Mr Wardlaw, Edinburgh, and 26 May 1811, from Capt. Pellowe, Valleyfield; ADM 99/206, ltr, 11 Dec. 1810, from Stark, Craig & Co.; *The Post Office Annual Directory* (Edinburgh, 1811), 321.

36. NLS, Melville Papers, MS Acc. 1075, fols 222-6. Henry Dundas (1742-1811), 1st Viscount Melville, Scots advocate and politician, MP, 1774-90, for Midlothian, and 1790-1802, for Edinburgh; Solicitor-General, 1773-5, Lord Advocate, 1775-83, a leading lieutenant and friend of the Younger Pitt as prime minister from 1783-1801 and 1804-06, Home Secretary, 1791-4, Secretary at War, 1794-1801, Treasurer of the Navy, 1782, 1783-1800, First Lord of the Admiralty, 1804-6, and political manager of Scotland for thirty years from 1775. He died on 28 May 1811.

37. TNA ADM 105/44, report, 10 Jul. 1799, to TB by Serle; *EEC*, 8 Sep. 1803; *CM*, 5 Sep. 1803.

38. TNA HO 28/38/99-102.

39. TNA HO 28/38/124, fols 126-7. Robert Reid, principal government architect in Scotland, was titled from 1808 King's Architect and Surveyor in Scotland.

40. TNA HO 28/38/122-7, ltr, 3 Nov. 1810, J. Barrow, Adm., to J. Beckett, HO; ADM 98/131, ltrs, 14, 22, 23 and 29 Nov. and 6 Dec. 1810, to Bowen from TB; ADM 105/44, ltr, 3 Dec. 1810, Bowen to TB; ADM 103/635 (Part II), ltr, Sir T. Livingstone to Bowen; HO 28/39/34, ltr, Greig to TB.

41. TNA HO 28/39. George Hamilton-Gordon (1784-1860), 4th Earl of Aberdeen, whose guardians Henry Dundas and William Pitt had become on the death of his father in 1791; a Tory Scots representative peer, 1806-13; among British signatories of the Treaty of Paris, May 1814; Foreign Secretary, 1828-30 and 1841-6, Secretary of War, 1834-5, Prime Minister, 1852-5.

42. NLS MS Acc. 353 fols 98-103, ltr, 18 Mar. 1811. Robert Dundas (1771-1851), 2nd Viscount Melville and, 1812-30, First Lord of the Admiralty.

43. The Lord President, 1808-11, was Robert Blair (1764-1811) of Avontown, near Linlithgow.

44. NLS MS Acc. 353 fols 98-103, ltr, 18 Mar. 1811.

45. *The Letters of Sir Walter Scott, 1811-1814*, ed. by H.J.C. Grierson (London, 1932); *Waverley* (Everyman, London, 1906 ed.), 293.

46. TNA ADM 98/117, ltr, 18 Apr. 1811, TB to Adm.; HO 28/39/146, ltr, 1 May 1811, Charles Yorke, First Lord of the Admiralty, to Richard Ryder, Home Secretary, enclosing the Earl of Aberdeen's ltr of 31 Mar., and informing Ryder 'that the plan for forming a depot there ['at Linlithgow Castle'] has been given up.'

47. In another letter he wrote dated 3 Oct. without the year but almost certainly written that same day and dealing with accommodation in Scotland for prisoners of war, Lord Cathcart admitted to Lieut. General Robert Brownrigg, the Quarter Master General, that '... great doubts exist in my mind of the expediency of applying any of the Castles, forts or barracks to the purpose in question.' NLS MS 9819 fols 43-4. In a letter in NAS GD 1/405/2-3 to J. Macbeth Forbes, C.M. Fraser, writing from India on 20 Sep. 1893, says '... an old lady can recollect as a girl being taken out to see French prisoners at Fort George as curiosities, and purchasing basket-work from them, which they executed very tastefully.' The old lady's recollection was presumably of the prisoners of war held at Fort George for some months from Aug. 1803.

48. TNA HO 28/38/126-7.

49. TNA ADM 98/131, ltr, 22 Nov. 1810, TB to Bowen; ADM 98/117, ltr, 30 Nov. 1810, TB to Adm.: 'It being understood that the ... Lords ... of the Admiralty have relinquished the idea of occupying Stirling Castle as a depot for prisoners of war ...'

50. See, e.g., TNA ADM 98/129, ltr, 23 Jan. 1807, TB to Lieut. Col. Gordon.

51. Ltr of that date from Lord Cathcart to TB, in TNA HO 28/38/99-102.

52. TNA ADM 98/131, ltr, 10 Oct. 1810.

53. TNA HO 28/38/126.

54. TNA ADM 105/44.

55. TNA ADM 98/131.

56. Ibid.

57. TNA ADM 98/117.

58. TNA ADM 98/131, ltr, 3 Dec. 1810, TB to Bowen; ADM 99/206, ltr, 14 Dec. 1810, George Harrison, HM Treasury, to Adm.; ADM 98/117, ltr, 21 Dec. 1810, TB to Adm.

59. TNA ADM 99/206, ltrs: 17 Dec. 1810, Robert Reid to TB, and 28 Dec. 1810, Adm. to TB; ADM 98/117, ltrs, 21 and 28 Dec. 1810, TB to Adm.; ADM 98/276, ltr, 4 Jan. 1811, TB to Wright.

60. *EEC*, 31 Dec. 1810.

61. TNA ADM 98/131, ltrs, 28 Dec. 1810, TB to G. Harrison, HM Treasury, and to Lieut. Col. Torrens, Office of the Commander-in-Chief; ADM 99/206, ltrs, 25 Dec. 1810, Reid to TB, and 29 Dec. 1810, General Hope to TB; ADM 98/117, ltr, 31 Dec. 1810, TB to Adm..

62. TNA ADM 98/117, a draft ltr dated 21 Jan. 1811, preserved loose in the bound pages of the letterbook.

63. TNA ADM 99/205, ltr, 3 Oct. 1810, to TB.

64. TNA ADM 98/116, ltrs, 21 Sep. and 21, 26 and 29 Oct. 1810, TB to Adm.; ADM 99/206, ltrs, 28 and 29 Dec. 1810, Adm. to TB; ADM 103/156, General Entry Book,

French prisoners, Greenlaw, Nos 1-214; ADM 103/110, note at p. 40; *CM*, 10, 12, 17 and 19 Nov. 1810.

65. TNA ADM 98/276, ltrs, 3, 4 and 31 Jan. 1811, TB to Priest, Capt. R. Pellowe and M. Wright. Priest, a lieut. since 1793, was serving on the *Salvador de Mundo* flag ship at Plymouth when appointed agent at Greenlaw. D. Syrett and R.L. DiNardo, *The Commissioned Sea Officers of the Royal Navy, 1660-1815* (Navy Records Society, 1994), 367; TNA ADM 98/278, ltr, 22 Feb. 1812, TB to Priest.

66. TNA ADM 98/131.

67. TNA ADM 99/207, ltr, 17 May 1811, Bowen to TB; ADM 98/132, ltrs, 25 Apr. and 14 May 1811, TB to Bowen.

68. TNA ADM 99/207, ltrs, 31 May, 4, 12 and 21 Jun., between Bowen and TB.

69. Charles Cowan, *The Reminiscences of Charles Cowan* (Edinburgh, 1878), 11. Cowan (1801-1889), son of Alexander and nephew of Duncan Cowan, the two brothers who owned and lived at the nearby Valleyfield Mills, and who was Liberal MP for Edinburgh, 1847-59, recalls that 'In my boyish days Messrs White [then owners of Esk Mills] carried on cotton-spinning and paper-making.'; the Rev. Thomas M'Courty, parish minister of Penicuik, wrote in the *Old Statistical Account*, 1794, Vol. X, 422, that the Mill 'at present employs about 500 hands, though sometimes more.'; Wilson, *Annals of Penicuik*, op. cit., 119.

70. Wilson, *Annals of Penicuik*, ibid.

71. *EEC*, 7 and 21 Apr. 1804, and 8 Apr. 1805.

72. TNA HO 28/38/99-102; ADM 98/131, ltr, 10 Oct. 1810, TB to Bowen.

73. TNA ADM 98/116, ltr, 23 Oct. 1810, TB to Adm.; ADM 99/206, ltr, 12 Nov. 1810, Adm. to TB.

74. TNA ADM 98/133, ltr, 25 May 1812, TB to Commissioners for Barracks; ADM 98/277, ltr, 25 May 1811, TB to Capt. Pellowe; Johnston, 'Recollections', op. cit., pp. 3-4, where Johnston says the annual rent for Esk Mills paid by the government was £2,500. Johnston himself was appointed a clerk at Esk Mills depot on 1 Mar. 1811. TNA ADM 98/276, ltr, 1 Mar. 1811, TB to Capt. Pellowe; ADM 98/131, ltr, 30 Oct. 1810, TB to Bowen.

75. TNA ADM 98/131, ltr, 16 Nov. 1810, TB to Bowen; ADM 1/3761, ltr, 27 Dec. 1810, TB to Adm.; *EEC*, 10 Dec. 1810.

76. Cowan, *Reminiscences*, op. cit., 10; TNA ADM 99/206, ltrs, 3 and 7 Dec. 1810, Bowen to TB; ADM 103/635 Part I, ltr, 31 Jul. 1817, Robert Reid to Commissioners for Victualling HM's Navy. There was a clause in the agreement for sale of the mills that 'Messrs Cowans [were] bound to repurchase them at £6,000 if called upon to do so within ten years. But it was likewise stipulated that in the event of the premises being redelivered to Messrs Cowan for £6,000 the same were previously to be restored to their original state by the Commissioners of the Transport Board.' The two canny Cowan brothers in their agreement with the Board also 'reserved to ourselves the waterfall, so that if contrary to expectation Government should retain the place after peace, we would be enabled, by altering the situation of the waterfall (that is, carrying it a little further up) to erect our works again to the same extent … our object is only to have a certainty of being able to re-erect our works, when times more favourable to papermaking return.' Ltr, 19 Dec. 1810, the Cowans to Sir George Clerk of Penicuik, in NAS, Cowan of Valleyfield Papers, GD 311/2/36.

77. TNA ADM 99/206, ltr, 17 Dec. 1810, Robert Reid to TB, and 18 Dec. 1810, Adm.

to TB; ADM 98/276, ltr, 2 Jan. 1811, TB to Capt. Pellowe; *EEC*, 29 Dec. 1810.

78. TNA HO 28/38/99-102 and 126-7.

79. TNA ADM 98/132, ltrs, 6, 14 and 30 May, 1, 15, 21 and 24 Jun., and 16 Jul. 1811, TB to Bowen; ADM 98/118, ltrs, 16 and 30 May, and 27 Jul. 1811, TB to Adm. The lowest estimate tendered was £96,012.13.0; *EEC* and *CM*, 29 Jun. 1811; *Glasgow Courier*, 2 Jul. 1811; *Perth Courier*, 4 and 11 Jul. and 5 Sep. 1811.

CHAPTER 5: ESK MILLS, AND THE VOYAGE FROM ENGLAND TO SCOTLAND

1. TNA ADM 1/3761.

2. TNA ADM 99/206, ltr, 29 Nov. 1810, and ADM 1/3761, ltr, 20 Dec. 1810, Pellowe to TB.

3. TNA ADM 1/3761; ADM 99/206, 26 Dec. 1810.

4. TNA ADM 98/131, ltr, 27 Dec. 1810, TB to G. Harrison, HM Treasury, and 28 Dec. 1810, TB to Lieut. Col. Torrens, WO; ADM 98/117, ltr, 2 Jan. 1811, TB to Adm.; ADM 99/206, ltr, 29 Dec. 1810, Adm. to TB; ADM 98/276, ltrs, 28 Dec. 1810, 19 and 23 Jan. and 5 Feb. 1811, TB to Wright and Lieut. Priest.

5. TNA ADM 99/206, ltr from Pellowe and Board's undated reply to it.

6. TNA ADM 98/276.

7. Ibid., 12 Jan. 1811, TB to M. Wright.

8. TNA ADM 103/124, No. 1.

9. Cowan, *Reminiscences*, op. cit., 16. Cowan indicates Aucum's 'parole' was at Valleyfield depot but this appears to be a confusion with Greenlaw.

10. Warships were classified or rated according to the number of guns (cannons) they had. Thus ships of the line were 1st rate if they had 100 or more guns, 2nd rate with between 90 and 98 guns (both 1st and 2nd rates had three decks), and 3rd rate with between 64 and 80. The 4th rate was an intermediate class with between 50 and 60 guns (both 3rd and 4th rates had two decks). Then came frigates rated 5th and 6th class, with respectively between 32 and 40, and 20 and 28 guns. Of smaller naval vessels sloops had 16 or 18, and gun-brigs, cutters and others between 6 and 14 guns. See Piers Mackesy, *The War in the Mediterranean, 1803-1810* (London, 1957), xiii.

11. TNA ADM 103/124; Greenlaw General Entry Books ADM 103/152, /154, /155, /156, and /158, and ADM 103/115; *CM*, 4, 7, 9, 11, 14 and 18 Feb. 1811.

12. TNA ADM 103/124, Nos 1,590, 1,591. There is some ambiguity about Lambare: written in ink against his name in the Greenlaw Entry Book, TNA ADM 103/156, No. 171, is that he was transferred that day to Esk Mills but, written in pencil, 'Remains at Greenlaw'.

13. TNA ADM 103/124; *CM*, 21, 23 and 28 Feb. and 2 and 7 Mar. 1811; *EEC*, 2 Mar. 1811.

14. The blasphemous might have added that even Christ was among the prisoners at Esk Mills: No. 2,075, George Christ, soldier, regt unstated, who arr. via HMS *Gorgon* from Portsmouth on 5 Mar. The Customs House officer was No. 1,477, R. Colignon, 'captured on shore at Waren by English boats on 2 August 1810', and who arr. at Esk Mills on 18 Feb. via HMS *Ruby* and Edinburgh Castle. TNA ADM 103/124 passim.

15. TNA ADM 98/276, ltrs, 24 and 27 Dec. 1810, 12 and 22 Feb. and 1 Mar. 1811, TB

to Pellowe. Johnston says in his 'Recollections', op. cit., p.4, John White resigned on 13 Feb. and he himself was appointed in White's place on 14 or 16 Feb. After the dramatic events at the depot in Feb. and early Mar., the TB agreed to the appointment of two extra clerks named Turner and Macfarlane. TNA ADM 98/277, ltr, 18 Mar. 1811, TB to Pellowe.

16. TNA ADM 103/491, a TB ledger that lists escapers alphabetically from 1811 onwards; Lothian Muniments, in NAS GD 40/9/239/8.

17. *EEC*, 25 Feb. 1811; *CM* and *Kelso Mail*, 28 Feb. 1811.

18. Johnston, 'Recollections', op. cit., pp. 9-10.

19. TNA ADM 103/124, No. 577; *Souvenirs d'un Corsaire 1811-1814. Souvenirs de H.F. Marote, Lieutenant du Corsaire L'Aventurier* (Comp. and ed. by Léon Wocquier (Liège, 1845) (henceforth Marote-Carrier), vii-viii.

20. The Berlin Decree declared the British Isles to be in a state of blockade, that therefore no vessel whose voyage originated in Britain or its colonies would be admitted into the ports of the French Empire, and that all British goods found in territories occupied by France or its allies would be confiscated. The decrees of Fontainebleau and Milan declared that colonial goods were to be considered British unless there could be provided for them a certificate of origin, that any ships that touched in at Britain would be confiscated with their cargoes, and that any neutral vessel complying with the British Orders-in-Council would itself be considered British and thus liable to seizure. The series of British Orders-in-Council in Nov. and Dec. 1807 obliged any neutral vessel sailing to or from an enemy port to unload its cargo in one of a number of named British ports and to be subject to customs duties and also to be obliged to take out a special licence if it proposed to trade with the enemy. Neutral vessels were also forbidden to import certain goods, such as cotton and quinine, into France. Lefebvre, *Napoleon* Vol. I, op. cit., 261, and Vol. II, op. cit., 6, 11.

21. Marote-Carrier, op. cit., x-xi.

22. Ibid., 85-8.

23. This is an example of Marote-Carrier being mistaken about a date, unsurprisingly after the passage of so many years since the events he is recalling; but also there appear to be contradictions in dates concerning him in an official record. The mass escape he proceeds to relate took place on 19 Feb. The Esk Mills Entry Book of Sick Prisoners of War (TNA ADM 103/117, Nos 13 and 126), however, says (a) he was sent to the depot hospital on 5 Feb. (presumably an error for 7, 8 or 9 Feb., since he did not arrive at Esk Mills till 7 Feb.) and he remained in the hospital until he was returned to the prison on 10 Feb.; and (b) he was again a patient in the hospital from 7 to 25 Mar. inclusive.

24. While a prisoner on the hulk *Glory* at Chatham Marote-Carrier had established a daily study class in navigation which a dozen fellow prisoners attended and for which they paid him a small fee. Marote-Carrier, op. cit., 56-7. No prisoner named De Backen has been found in the Esk Mills General Entry Book—but perhaps he was entered there, like Marote-Carrier himself, under an alias or *nom de guerre*.

25. Marote-Carrier, op. cit., 88-90.

26. Ibid., 91.

27. Ibid., 91-2.

28. Ibid., 93-4. Since the priv. lieut. Nicolas (or Henri) Boulet (or Boulais) was the only escaper shot, he must have been Marote-Carrier's 'tea captain'.

29. It seems to have been the sight of the Pentland Hills to the west and north as he had trudged out with other prisoners from Edinburgh to Esk Mills depot that had convinced Marote-Carrier he was in the highlands of Scotland, and that the inhabitants of Midlothian were highlanders. Ibid., 84-5.

30. The good peasants may rather have been only too well aware their clients were escaped prisoners but to have been intent on making hay from them while the sun shone.

31. Ibid., 94.

32. His lordship's letter was dated 20 Feb.—so the five may have been recaptured then rather than on 22 Feb.

33. See above, Appendix 1, for some further details of the 23 escapers.

34. TNA ADM 103/124.

35. TNA ADM 98/277, ltrs, 4 Mar. 1811, TB to Wright and Pellowe.

36. TNA ADM 98/276, ltr, 23 Feb.1811, TB to Pellowe.

37. TNA ADM 98/277. By the time it journeyed from Esk Mills to the Board's offices in London the sample seems likely to have become more brick than loaf.

38. TNA ADM 103/124; *CM*, 9 Mar. 1811. *EEC*, 7 Mar., had two slight variants in its report, which said the plot had been discovered only half an hour before it was due to be carried out, and that 'Two of the ringleaders, one of them an officer, were strongly guarded on their way to Greenlaw [i.e., to Esk Mills].' The identity of the two ringleaders is not known but the officer may have been Hipolyte Decreuse (or Decroze or Decruise), a lieut. on the French naval sloop *Friedland*, capd in Mar. 1808. Decreuse, No. 2,315 in the Entry Book, arr. at Esk Mills from HMS *Gorgon* on 5 Mar. and was transferred four days later to Edinburgh Castle. He escaped from the Castle on 12 Apr. but was recapd. Born at Aix, and aged 23, Decreuse, after his recapture, was the subject of a letter on 7 Jun. 1811 from the TB to Rear Admiral Otway at Leith, in which there is this reference to the attempted shipboard rising: 'In addition to the bad conduct of M. de Cruise on board the *Gorgon*, for which he is to be sent to Chatham by direction of the Lords Commissioner of the Admiralty, this prisoner was previously to his being sent to Scotland concerned as a ringleader in a riot at Thame where he was on parole, for which offence he was sent into confinement at Portsmouth.' *EEC*, 7 Mar. 1811; TNA ADM 53/574, Log of HMS *Gorgon*, 13 Sep. 1808-29 Feb. 1812; TNA ADM 98/277, ltr, 7 Jun. 1811, TB to Admiral Otway; ADM 103/112, No. 10, and ADM 103/124, No.2,315.

39. *CM*, 4 Feb. 1811. Actually, Marote-Carrier, op. cit., 61, says it was 29 Jan. 1812, but he is a year in advance in all the dates he gives at that period.

40. TNA ADM 103/124, No. 557. These points illustrate the difficulties in achieving complete accuracy that are presented by these and some other sources concerning the prisoners.

41. TNA ADM 103/648, escape report on Mariote; ADM 103/434, No. 3,275 (Mariote); *EEC*, 5, 6 and 21 Sep. 1811; *CM*, 5 and 19 Sep. 1811; TNA WO 1/645, ltr, 29 Sep. 1810, Capt. Sotheby to J.W. Croker, Adm. A search for relevant information in logs of HMS *Brune* and *Vanguard* proved unsuccessful.

42. In the General Entry Book for HMS *Glory* Marote-Carrier is listed as No. 12,074, Jean Carries (sic), capd off St Valery, 17 Dec. 1810, and arr. on the prison hulk twelve days later. He is said to have been b. at Oldenburg, was aged 32, 5ft 6ins tall, well made, with an oval face, fair complexion, brown hair, blue eyes, and with no marks or wounds, and was dischgd to Leith on 22 (sic) Jan. 1811.

43. Marote-Carrier, op. cit., 59-66. De Kuyper, De Cuiper or De Cuyper appears to have been L. J. or L. I. De Cuyper, lieut., capd on the *Friedland* priv. in the North Sea, Dec. 1807, b. in Ghent, aged 28, 5ft 6ins tall, of stout build, with an oval face, fresh complexion, black hair, hazel eyes, and with no marks or wounds. In the Esk Mills Entry Book, he was described as Henry De Cuiper, seaman, *Friedland*, who had arr. at that depot on 7 Feb. 1811 from Chatham via HMS *Vanguard*. Transferred 11 Mar. 1811 to Valleyfield, he was transferred again on 1 Sep. 1812 to Perth, where he was said to have been surgeon on the *Friedland*. He was dischgd from Perth, 19 Feb. 1814, into the 1st Dutch Regt. TNA ADM 103/124, No. 685; ADM 103/434, No. 2,477; ADM 103/263, No. 1,191.

44. Marote-Carrier, op. cit., 66-7.

45. Ibid., 69-70.

46. Ibid., 70-2.

47. Johnston, 'Recollections', op. cit., p.6; TNA ADM 103/648.

48. There were several De Cuypers among the prisoners at Perth, but the one referred to here by Johnston appears to have been the one described in Note 43 above.

49. Johnston, 'Recollections', op. cit., pp. 6-7. Rushing en masse against a depot wooden fence or wall in a concerted effort to escape had been attempted in Sep. 1807 by a phalanx of 500 prisoners of war at Norman Cross depot in Huntingdonshire, a depot largely built of wood. They had succeeded in thus flattening one section of the enclosure and were beginning on the next when they were charged by the depot guards, and more than 40 of the prisoners were severely wounded. None escaped. A 14 feet high brick wall was afterwards built to replace the wooden one. It would be interesting to know if any prisoners at Esk Mills in Mar. 1811 had been active in those events at Norman Cross in 1807. *EEC*, 1 Oct. 1807. Grape or grapeshot was ammunition for artillery and consisted of a canvas tube holding clusters of small iron balls that scattered after being fired—usually at men en masse.

50. Cowan, *Reminiscences*, op. cit., 17-18.

51. Marote-Carrier, op. cit., 97-100. Marote-Carrier appears mistaken in recalling four dead bodies: all the other evidence is of two prisoners trampled to death. Perhaps the other two he recalled seeing on stretchers were injured men who survived.

52. Johnston, 'Recollections', op. cit., p.6.

53. Ibid., p.7.

54. TNA ADM 103/434. Once more there are contradictions and, apparently, some inaccuracy in Marote-Carrier's recollection of dates. The second Valleyfield Entry Book, TNA ADM 103/433, shows Marote-Carrier as No. 1,973. No date is given in this Entry Book for the arrival of any prisoner at the depot except for the first, No. 1,072, who arr. on 11 Mar. from Esk Mills, and two on the last page, Nos 2,137 and 2,142, who arrived from Esk Mills hospital on 11 and 18 Apr. respectively. But according to an entry in the Esk Mills hospital register (TNA ADM 103/117, No. 126), Marote-Carrier (although described as 'seaman', not lieut., and his number in the General Entry Book given as 1,081, not, as previously, 577) was in the hospital from 7 to 25 Mar. inclusive, and so it appears to have been 25 Mar. 1811 when he arr. at Valleyfield. As so often, Marote-Carrier got the date wrong: he believed he had entered Valleyfield on 10 Mar. 1812. Marote-Carrier, op. cit., 100-1.

55. TNA ADM 98/277. The name of the informer is not in fact given in the margin of the surviving letterbook copy.

56. TNA ADM 98/277; Johnston, 'Recollections', op. cit., pp. 6-8.

CHAPTER 6: VALLEYFIELD AND EDINBURGH CASTLE

1. TNA ADM 103/432, No. 1.
2. TNA ADM 98/131, ltr, 27 Dec. 1810, TB to G. Harrison, HM Treasury.
3. *EEC*, 29 Dec. 1810.
4. TNA ADM 98/276, ltrs, 22 and 27 Feb. 1811, TB to Heddington.
5. TNA ADM 98/117, ltr, 4 Mar. 1811, TB to Adm.; ADM 103/434.
6. TNA ADM 98/117, ltr, 27 Mar. 1811, TB to Adm.; ADM 98/118, ltr, 12 Aug. 1811, TB to Adm.; ADM 103/635 Part I, ltr, 31 Jul. 1817, Robert Reid to Commissioners for Victualling HM's Navy; *EEC*, 25 Nov. 1811.
7. TNA ADM 98/118, ltr, 12 Aug. 1811, TB to Adm.; ADM 98/277, ltr, 12 Aug. 1811, TB to Pellowe; ADM 103/432, ADM 103/434 and ADM 103/435.
8. Cowan, *Reminiscences*, op. cit., 11, 12. Parts at least of the Valleyfield mill buildings were probably relatively new at the time of their sale to the government in Dec. 1810, as a fire in May 1802 had destroyed 'the vatt-house [sic], finishing house, counting house, and drying lofts' and the whole of the 'ingeniously constructed' mills would then have been destroyed but for a fortuitous change in the direction of the wind from east to west. *EEC*, 22 May 1802. At the time of their sale the mills employed 98 workers: 26 ragwomen, 28 women pickers, and 44 men, including a foreman, vatmen, porters, layers, dryworkers, couchers, sizers, pressers, a fireman, a feltcaster, two engineers and three millwrights. NAS Cowan Papers, GD 311/4/2 (wages book). Until its demolition in 1897 one of the original casernes or blocks for prisoners was used as a rag store by the restored paper mill. Abell, op. cit., 197. Joy Deacon, a Penicuik local historian, found signs of the presence of the prisoners which had remained until the demolition of Valleyfield mills in the mid-1970s. She considered that the old mill stamping house, with walls three feet thick, small windows high up on the walls fitted with vertical and horizontal bars and with wooden shutters outside, 'was probably used for cells.' Joy Deacon, ed., 'History of Penicuik', (Penicuik Historical Society, n.d. (c.1985)), Vol. 5, p. 11.
9. Marote-Carrier, op. cit., 103-4.
10. The prisoner, named Marcher, then resident in the Invalides in Paris, and who had lost an arm at Waterloo, recalled his experiences for Mr John Cowan of Beeslack, Penicuik, when he visited the Invalides in 1845. Abell, op. cit., 199-200.
11. Marote-Carrier, op. cit., 75-7, 81.
12. See Appendix 1, No. 6.
13. For a description of Decreuse see above, Appendix 2, No. 2.
14. Ibid., No. 3.
15. TNA ADM 103/124, No. 2,061 (De Beausset), No. 2,313 (Duhenot-Grandjean); ADM 103/110, No. 8 (Duhenot), 103/112, No. 9 (Duhenot), and ADM 103/157, No. 8 (Duhenot); ADM 99/210, ltr, 19 Sep. 1811, Lieut. Priest to TB.
16. TNA ADM 98/277, ltr, 14 Mar. 1811, TB to M. Wright, agent, Edinburgh Castle. A ltr, ibid., of 4 Mar. 1811 from TB to Wright had informed him that Capt. Pellowe at Esk Mills had been told to send 48 prisoners 'of bad character' from there to the Castle, 'to be confined in the cells there'—but in the margin of the copybook where this letter is entered is written 'Cancelled'.

17. Allen, 'The French Prisons in Edinburgh Castle', op. cit., 160, a study to which everyone interested in the subject will remain indebted.

18. 'By 1811, the eastern vaults held stores rather than captives. The western sub-vaults, unlike their counterparts to the east, do appear to have been in constant use.' Ibid., 163-4. Allen appears, however, to be mistaken in believing that 'The vaults were to be used as prisons throughout the wars of the Napoleonic era, holding particularly large numbers of prisoners until 1811.' They did hold considerable numbers of prisoners in 1811 but few if any between 1803 and then, and (apart from overnight or brief staging for prisoners in transit between, for example, Valleyfield and Perth or the converse) not many either from 1812 until the end of the war in 1814. A paper in TNA ADM 103/635 Part II titled 'Descriptive Inventory of the fixtures and other matters in and Connected with the Apartments in Edinburgh Castle lately occupied by Prisoners of War', and headed in red ink: 'Received in Mr Reid's [the architect's] letter, 9 Dec. 1815', appears to refer to the sub-vaults when it states that: 'These Apartments consist of Three Rooms above, and Four places below, together with a Cooking House entering from the Yard and an Airing Ground. They are situated under the Barrack Building forming the west side of the Square ...'

19. TNA ADM 98/129, ltr, 23 Jan. 1807, TB to Lieut. Col. Gordon.

20. TNA ADM 105/44, report, 10 Jul. 1799.

21. That was approximately the number of prisoners of war then held in Britain. See, e.g., TNA ADM 98/118, ltr, 16 Dec. 1811, TB to J.W. Croker, Adm.

22. Simond, *Journal*, op. cit.,Vol. II, 52-6; *CM*, 18 Feb. 1811; TNA ADM 103/124.

23. *EEC*, 15 Apr. 1811. The advertisement, with some additonal information in italics, is reproduced at Appendix 2 above.

24. The Entry Book records the deaths of only three prisoners but not the causes of their deaths, which are, however, given elsewhere in the TB archives: TNA ADM 103/648, proforma returns recording deaths of prisoners. All three of these prisoners had come from Esk Mills on 11 Mar. One was an army lieut., Auguste B. Bourignons, whose death on 25 Jul. was 'in consequence of a wound received in fencing with another prisoner.' (TNA ADM 98/208, ltr, 25 Jul. 1811, Heddington to TB; and ADM 103/648, return for week ending 25 Jul. 1811). Another was Marius Pinchina or Ponchina, a boy aged only 13, capd on the naval sloop *Jean Honore* in Jul. 1808, and who died on 18 Apr. from 'Abscess in the Lungs'. (TNA ADM 103/648, returns for week ending 18 Apr. 1811). The cause of his death appears most unlikely to have arisen from a fall down the Castle Rock. Woemeseuil, Wormeseul or Wormselle, whose death was due to 'Fractured Spine', must surely therefore have been the victim of the fall of some 150 feet down the rock. TNA ADM 103/648, returns for week ending 18 Apr. 1811; and ADM 103/112, Nos 14, 167 and 379; James Grant, *Old and New Edinburgh* (London, n.d.), Vol. I, 71.

25. *CM*, 20 Apr. 1811. *EEC*, 15 Apr. 1811, said 10 of the escapers were recapd at Linlithgow.

26. *CM*, 22, 27 and 29 Apr. 1811; *EEC*, 15, 20, 25 and 27 Apr. and 2, 11 and 23 May 1811. The *Perth Courier* reported on 25 Apr. that the four prisoners recapd at Dundee on 18 or 20 Apr. and put into Perth gaol had escaped from there next day. 'By cutting some planks out of the partititon of their apartment, they made their way to the court room, from the window of which they descended to the street. On their table was found a letter, expressing their gratitude to the magistrates and inhabitants of Perth for the civilities they had received, and promising a return of kindness

to any Scotchmen whom they might find among the British prisoners in France.' A letter of 24 May in TNA ADM 98/277 from the TB to M. Wright, agent at the Castle, makes it clear that those were the four later recapd at Banff. The *Montrose Review* reported on 26 Apr. the recapture four days earlier in the wood of Charleton there of five of the escapers, one of whom 'has suffered much from the bruises he sustained in dropping from Edinburgh Castle, having been the next in succession on the rope to the unfortunate man who was killed in the attempt to escape.' TNA ADM 103/112 says that Pierre Desbois and Bernard Charlot (Nos 469 and 470) arr. back at the Castle on 21 May from Montrose, and Etienne Tiebaud, Jean Noel and Adolphe Douzon (Nos 474, 475 and 476) on 25 May from Banff.

27. And, if the *Mercury's* report was accurate, by the same route and means. There is no indication either in the General Entry Books or escapes proforma for the Castle of the names of the dozen prisoners who escaped, however briefly, on 26-27 Apr.

28. *Glasgow Herald*, 20 Apr. 1811.

29. TNA ADM 98/277, ltr, TB to Wright. Wright's reply, if he had time to send one, has not been preserved.

30. TNA ADM 98/277, ltrs, 29 Apr. and 9 May 1811, TB to Wright.

31. TNA ADM 105/44.

32. TNA ADM 98/277. It may be that a patron, if not the patron, of Wright was Sir Patrick Murray, Bart, who sent to the Adm. early in 1812 a memorial from Wright 'praying under the circumstances stated that he may be granted some relief.' TNA ADM 98/119, ltr, 1 Feb 1812, TB to Adm.

33. The Castle Entry Books and other official sources do not identify the escapers or provide information about their recapture, with one exception. The one not so promptly recapd was Jean Raymot, purser's clerk, aged 21, b. at Niort, capd originally on the frig. *Minerve*, Sep. 1806, off Rochefort. But even Raymot was recapd a couple of days later at Queensferry, and was transferred on 14 Aug. from the Castle to Greenlaw, from which on 10 Feb. 1812, he was 'Delivered over to the Civil Power', presumably accused or suspected of forging banknotes. TNA ADM 103/110, No. 318 (Raymot), and ADM 103/157, No. 318 (Raymot); ADM 99/208, ltr, 15 Jul. 1811, Heddington to TB.

34. TNA ADM 98/277, ltrs, 7 and 9 Aug. 1811, TB to Heddington; ADM 103/157, Nos 1-365. The Greenlaw Entry Book shows the report in *EEC* on 17 Aug. that 'all the French prisoners of war in the Castle' had been marched to Greenlaw earlier that week was an anticipation of the fact, as a further 39 followed the same road on 26 Aug. and five more on 7 Sep. The first prisoner listed in that Greenlaw Entry Book was David Fourneau, lieut., priv., *Le Barbier de Seville*, one of the escapers from Esk Mills on 19 Feb., who following his recapture had been confined in the Castle since 4 Mar. (See above, Appendix 1, No. 6). Others included No. 114 Xavier Malavois or Malavais and No. 275 Adolphe Douzon, both among the recapd escapers of the mass outbreak from the Castle on 12 Apr. (See above, Appendix 2, Nos 20 and 39).

35. Walker, *The Depot at Norman Cross*, op. cit., 326, Appendix E; TNA HO 28/40, fol. 120, ltr, 26 Aug. 1811, TB to J. Beckett, HO; ADM 98/119, ltr, 1 Feb. 1812.

36. TNA ADM 98/277, ltrs, 9 and 22 Aug. 1811, TB to Pellowe. Heddington appears to have been disgruntled for a long time with his appointments in Scotland and by what he considered his unsympathetic treatment by the TB, and as late as Aug. he had still not carried out his legal obligation to give the Board securities for the performance of his duties as an agent, though the Board had asked him to do so in

Jan. 1811. (See TNA ADM 98/118, ltr, 19 Aug. 1811, TB to Adm.). Commissioner Bowen was critical of Heddington, who had not enhanced his reputation at the TB by his lengthy (almost three months') leave of absence in England at this period: 'I hope their Lordships [of the Adm.] will not transfer Heddington to the Castle,' Bowen had written on 24 May. 'Wright is a much better man.' If that opinion was sound what more telling criticism could there be of Heddington? (See TNA ADM 105/44, ltr, 24 May 1811, Bowen to A. McLeay, secretary, TB). The TB ensured Pellowe accepted the appointment at Plymouth: it told him that if he did not accept it, Heddington would be given the job. ADM 98/277, ltrs from TB: 9 Aug. 1811, to Pellowe, and 22 Aug. 1811, to Heddington; ADM 98/118, ltrs, 2 and 19 Aug. 1811, TB to J.W. Croker, Adm.

37. TNA ADM 98/277, ltrs, 13 and 19 Sep. 1811, TB to M. Wright, and 7 Oct. 1811, TB to Vice Admiral Otway; ADM 98/278, ltrs, 16 Nov. and 12 Dec. 1811, TB to Lieut. Priest; ADM 103/112, Nos 531-543; for Jacques Adam, see above, Appendix 2, No. 38. For an example of a parole prisoner sent to the Castle in that period, see ADM 98/204, ltr, 7 Nov. 1811, TB to John Smith, parole agent, Kelso, instructing him to send 'the prisoner Galabert in proper custody to Edinburgh Castle, where he must remain until he gives security for the maintenance of his [illegitimate?] child.'

38. *CM*, 19 Dec. 1811. The prisoners who escaped are listed in Appendix 3 above.

39. TNA ADM 98/278. The Valleyfield Entry Book, ADM 103/435, Nos 5,305-5,315, shows that two lieuts and nine seamen arrived there on 3 Jan. 1812: they were 11 of the recapd escapers from the Castle on 18-19 Dec.

40. TNA ADM 98/278, ltr, 28 Dec. 1811.

CHAPTER 7: PERTH DEPOT

1. A TB return dated 19 Mar. 1810 gives the total number of French prisoners of war then in Britain as 43,683, of whom 2,572 were on parole. Another Board return, dated 26 Jun. 1812, shows there were then 54,517 French and Dutch prisoners, of whom 3,267 were on parole. TNA ADM 1/3760, fol. 161; *Parliamentary Papers*, Vol. IX, 1812, 301.

2. *The Post Office Annual Directory 1811-1812* (Edinburgh, 1811), 252, 322, gives John Thin, builder, 1 Howe Street, Edinburgh, but also James Thin, builder, Bonnington, Leith.

3. TNA ADM 98/135, ltr, 25 Aug. 1814, TB to G. Harrison, HM Treasury.

4. George Penny, *Traditions of Perth* (Perth, 1836), 91.

5. *Perth Courier*, 5 Sep. 1811.

6. An advertisement in the *Perth Courier* that same day, 12 Dec., was less lyrical: 'MASONS WANTED. At the Depot, Perth. Good encouragement will be given to masons of every description, by applying to the Contractor or Foreman at the works.' The difference in the texts of the Perth and Edinburgh advertisements (the latter of which were carried also in the *Caledonian Mercury*) was no doubt because there was a much larger pool of stonemasons in the capital city to appeal to. On the other hand, it appeared for a time after New Year 1812 as if the services of a few of the masons might be lost to the depot. 'During the last month,' the *Perth Courier* reported on 6 Feb., 'several masons at the depot were examined on suspicion of having been connected in the outrages in Edinburgh. We do not hear, however, that any important discovery has been made.' The 'outrages' were the assaults and robberies around the

Tron on Hogmanay by an organised gang of young men, including some apprentices, upon some two dozen 'gentlemen' among the crowds celebrating New Year, during which the gang had murdered a police watchman. Three of the gang found guilty at the High Court of murder and robbery were hanged and two others transported for life. See K. J. Logue, *Popular Disturbances in Scotland 1780-1815* (Edinburgh, 1979), 187-90.

7.   *Perth Courier*, 5 Mar. 1812.

8.   *New Statistical Account*, Vol. X, *Perth* (Edinburgh, 1845), 85.

9.   Penny, *Traditions of Perth*, op. cit., 91.

10. The 'ingenious and unusual' mode of ventilation was not explained, but as Robert Reid had also been responsible for preparing Valleyfield as a depot it appears that a system of ventilation there, as described by the Penicuik local historian Joy Deacon, op. cit., p. 12, although without naming her sources, resembled the one at Perth: 'The roof had a series of hollow beams which opened to the outside and had holes below. There were a series of hollow pillars in the walls, studded with holes, which connected with the hollow pillars in the roof. The ventilation system presumably removed the need for the large windows which were kept shuttered. A series of such beams supported the roof of the second machine house until 1926.' J.L. Black, an earlier Penicuik local historian, commenting in 1928 on a report in *EEC*, 11 Jul., 1812, which had been taken from that quoted in the *Perth Courier* above, declared: 'This system is still to be seen at Valleyfield, 1928.' ML, Black Coll., vol. 2(d), p.30.

11. *Perth Courier*, 9 Jul. 1812.

12. TNA ADM 98/120, ltr, 24 Sep. 1812.

13. Abell, op. cit., 166, 167, 168, 208, 212; Thomson, *Dartmoor*, op. cit., 7, 9-10, 111; *The Times*, 5 Nov. 1810, which reported that Portchester Castle was 'completely filled', with 'upwards of 6,000' prisoners; Walker, *The Depot at Norman Cross*, op. cit., 13, 14, 21, 48, 67; Willliam Sievewright, *Historical Sketch of the Old Depot or Prison for French prisoners-of-war at Perth* (Perth, 1894), 2.

14. David Peacock, *Perth: its annals and its archives* (Perth, 1849), 496-7.

15. Sievewright, *Depot at Perth*, op. cit., 3-6.

16. Marote-Carrier was No. 1,166 in the depot's first General Entry Book, TNA ADM 103/263.

17. Marote-Carrier, op. cit., 153-4.

18. TNA ADM 98/119, ltr, 4 Jun. 1812, TB to Adm.

19. TNA ADM 98/278, ltrs, 8 Jun. 1812, TB to Moriarty and Gillies.

20. Ibid., ltrs, 20 Jun. and 10 Jul. 1812, TB to Moriarty. A request by Capt. Andrew Brown, RN, who had been appointed Moriarty's successor as agent at Valleyfield, that he should be made agent at Perth and Moriarty remain at Valleyfield, was rejected by the TB: '... we see no reason whatever for proposing this change to the Lords Commissioner of the Admiralty.' Ibid., ltr, 9 Jul. 1812, TB to Brown.

21. NAS GD 157/2004, Scott of Harden Muniments, containing a copy of *The Star* newspaper, 16 May 1812. See also the advertisement in *EEC*, 11 May 1812, and *Perth Courier*, 14 and 21 May 1812.

22. TNA ADM 98/278, ltrs, 10 and 13 Jul. 1812, TB to Moriarty.

23. TNA ADM 98/278.

24. Ibid.

25. TNA ADM 98/119, ltrs, 13 and 28 Jul. 1812, TB to Adm. Benjamin Waterhouse,

a young American surgeon capd at sea the following year during the war between Britain and the United States of America, and sent with other captives on board the *Regulus* to the hulks at Chatham, later wrote bitterly of their treatment on board her: '... the filth, the semi-starvation, the vermin, the sleeping on the stone ballast, the lack of air owing to the only opening to the lower deck being a hatchway two feet square, the brutal rule of allowing only two prisoners to go on deck at a time, and the presence in their midst of the only latrine. The captain, a Scotsman, would only yield to constant petitions and remonstrances so far as to sanction the substitution of iron bars for the hatchway.' Quoted by Abell, op. cit., 82, from *The Journal of a Young Man of Massachussetts* (1816), by Waterhouse. Lieut. François-Frédéric Billon, 14th regt of the line, and previously a private in the Imperial Guard, who had been present at Napoleon's coronation as emperor in 1804 and had fought in the battles of Austerlitz, Iena, Eylau and Friedland before being capd in Spain, was transferred with other parole prisoners from England in 1811 to Scotland, for parole at Jedburgh, on the frigate HMS *Romulus*, commanded by Captain Lord Balgonie (later Earl of Leven and Melville), whom Billon declared the prisoners would long remember, for Balgonie was 'a Scotsman worthy of being a Spaniard: England could well entrust him with escorting its criminals to Botany Bay. This young lord, lacking any nobility of character, treated us pitilessly ... When we disembarked from the *Romulus* we resembled people who had escaped from hell.' F.F. Billon, *Souvenirs d'un Vélite de la Garde sous Napoléon Ier* (Paris, 1905), 254; TNA ADM 103/611, No. 105 (Billon). Balgonie (1785-1860) was a vice admiral by the time of his death. No more evidence seems to survive about how shipboard conditions experienced by the thousands of other prisoners brought on the *Regulus* and other ships to depots in Scotland compared with those described here, and earlier (on HMS *Vanguard* between Chatham and Leith in 1811) by Marote-Carrier.

26. TNA ADM 98/278, ltr, 27 Jul. 1812, TB to Moriarty.

27. Ibid., ltrs, 1 and 12 Aug. 1812, TB to Moriarty; *Perth Courier* and *CM*, 20 Aug. 1812.

28. *Dundee Advertiser*, 7 Aug. 1812.

29. Ibid.; *Perth Courier*, 6 Aug. 1812; Penny, *Traditions of Perth*, op. cit., 92; *The Times*, 15 Aug. 1812.

30. Among innumerable examples of the looting so common in the Peninsular War was one recalled by Rifleman Harris on the battlefield of Vimeiro in Portugal in 1808, when he found a dying French soldier with 'a bundle containing a quantity of gold and silver crosses, which I concluded he had plundered from some convent or church. He looked the picture of a sacrilegious thief, dying hopelessly, and overtaken by Divine wrath. I kicked over his cap, which was also full of plunder ...' Christopher Hibbert, ed., *The Recollections of Rifleman Harris* (London, 1970), 37. Looting was hardly a monopoly of the French and French allied or satellite forces in the Peninsula: there are also many recorded examples of its practice by British troops there.

31. *Perth Courier*, 13 Aug. 1812; TNA ADM 98/278.

32. TNA ADM 103/263, No.1.

33. NAS GD 1/405/2, ltr, 16 Feb. 1893, to Macbeth Forbes from Charles Holland (?), Falkland; TNA ADM 103/263, Nos 400-1,093; *CM*, 20 and 27 Aug. 1812; TNA ADM 98/278, ltrs from TB: 4 and 5 Aug. 1812, to Admiral Otway, and 5 Aug. 1812, to Lieut. Glinn, RN, at Leith.

34. TNA ADM 98/278, ltr, 18 Aug. 1812, TB to Moriarty; ADM 103/263, Nos 1,094

(Fourneau), 1,099 (Feraud), 1,106 (Callop), 1,166 (Marote-Carrier), 1,168 (Charles de Kuyper), 1,191 (L.I. De Kuyper), and 1,171 (Adam); Watson, *Reign of George III*, op. cit., 552.

35. TNA ADM 103/263-6 (Perth General Entry Books) passim.
36. TNA 98/120, ltr, 11 Jan. 1813; *CM*, 14 Jan. 1813.
37. TNA ADM 103/266, Nos 6,892-7,761; Lewis, *Napoleon and his British captives*, op. cit., 58.
38. TNA ADM 103/263-6 passim.

CHAPTER 8: PLACES, DATES, AND CIRCUMSTANCES OF CAPTURE, RECAPTURES, AND LENGTH OF CAPTIVITY

1. 'Some Early Recollections', in *Chambers's Journal*, No. 600, 26 Jun. 1875 (Edinburgh, 1875), 402.
2. TNA ADM 103/152 and ADM 103/153 passim. For the two pressed men see ADM 103/152, Nos 98 and 99.
3. TNA ADM 103/154, No. 15.
4. TNA ADM 103/110, Nos 98-214.
5. TNA ADM 103/158.
6. TNA ADM 103/155. The Entry Book actually runs from No. 1 to No. 452, but eight 'entries' are blank. Nos 1-96 were in aggregate those who had been held prisoner before Apr. 1804 in the Edinburgh bridewell.
7. The name of the boy has not been found, nor the nature of any reward given him by the authorities. Of the six privateersmen made prisoners of war, Jan Peters, prizemaster, was dischgd from Greenlaw depot to Portsmouth in Feb. 1812 as an invalid—presumably for repatriation to France or Hamburg. At least three of the five Dutch seamen within a month of their capture volunteered to serve in the British navy. *CM*, 2 and 7 Nov. 1811; TNA ADM 103/157, General Entry Book, Greenlaw, Nos 682-7.
8. Moreover, there appears to be a difference of some 144 between the net total (after deducting 25 escapers, deaths, and transfers on parole or to Edinburgh Castle as punishment) of the apparently 2,792 prisoners at Esk Mills at its closure and the 2,486 transferred then or soon afterward from there to Valleyfield, plus the 450 sent to Edinburgh Castle, according to the Entry Books of the two latter depots.
9. TNA ADM 103/124 passim, and ADM 103/432-4 passim.
10. Four French warships, *Formidable*, *Mont Blanc*, *Scipion* and *Duguay-Trouin*, commanded by Rear Admiral Dumanoir le Pelley in the vanguard of the Franco-Spanish fleet at Trafalgar had succeeded toward the end of the battle in making their way westward in the Atlantic. On their voyage back to France on 4 Nov. they were intercepted off Cape Ortegal, north-west Spain, by a British squadron commanded by Sir Richard Strachan and, after losing 750 men killed and wounded in that encounter, forced to surrender. The 124 prisoners at Esk Mills sent to Valleyfield who had been capd at Trafalgar or off Cape Ortegal came from the following warships: *Achille* (six), *L'Aigle* (16), *L'Argonaute* (one), *Berwicke* (17), *Duguay-Trouin* (two), *Formidable* (two), *Fougeux* (11), *L'Intrépide* (14), *Le Pluton* (one), *Redoutable* (three), *Scipion* (30), *Swiftsure* (21). The musket shot which mortally wounded Nelson was fired from *Redoutable*. Ibid.; James, *Naval History*, op. cit., Vol. III, 433-7, 444-5, and Vol. IV, 1-11.

11. TNA ADM 103/433, No. 2,069. Muchet, b. in Brussels and aged 43, remained in captivity at Valleyfield until the general release of prisoners in Jun. 1814. ADM 103/432, No. 781. Lewis, b. at Konigsberg (presumably in East Prussia—now Kaliningrad), was aged 40 and he, too, remained in captivity at Valleyfield until 1814, when in Feb. that year he was released and 'sent to Leith'. The Esk Mills Entry Book ADM 103/124, No. 1589, says Lewis was bosun on the m.v. *L'Aurore* when capd, n.p., 8 Feb. 1808.

12. TNA ADM 103/112 passim.

13. Of these 169 prisoners, 146 (all but two of them soldiers) had been taken on the warship *Formidable*. The others came from the *Achille* (three, of whom one was a soldier), *Argonaute* (one), *Berwicke* (one), *Duguay-Trouin* (one), *L'Intrépide* (three), *Mont Blanc* (nine, of whom six were soldiers), *Pluton* (one), *Scipion* (one), and *Swiftsure* (three, of whom one was a soldier). TNA ADM 103/434-6 passim. Thus at Valleyfield, including the 124 who had arrived in Mar.-Apr. 1811 from Esk Mills, there were altogether 293 prisoners who had been capd at Trafalgar or the subsequent naval encounter off Cape Ortegal. That fact may help explain some of the mischievous enjoyment young boys from Penicuik are said to have taken in shouting derisively down to the prisoners from the high banks above the depot: 'The French fleet is a' sunk! Ten thoosand mair prisoners are ta'en!' J. L. Black, *Penicuik and Neighbourhood* (Edinburgh, n.d., 2nd ed.), 22.

14. Another, described simply as 'Impressed' (presumably another catch found in the nets of the RN press gang), whose place of capture is not given, was Jean Simon, a seaman, b. in Paris, aged 32, who remained in captivity at the depot until the general release of prisoners in Jun. 1814. TNA ADM 103/435, No. 5,734.

15. The prisoner taken off Guadeloupe was No. 5,311 in the fourth Valleyfield Entry Book, Lieut. Jacques Adam—see above, Appendix 2, No. 38.

16. TNA ADM 103/434-6 passim, and ADM 103/113, No. 7,119.

17. TNA ADM 103/112 passim. One additional prisoner, Louis Carron, a seaman capd, n.d., on a priv. in the West Indies, was entered, but without a number, between Nos 243 and 244, and was said to have been 'Left at Esk Mills'.

18. TNA ADM 103/263, No. 396.

19. James, *Naval History*, op. cit., Vol. III, 399-401, 426, 441-2.

20. Beaudoin, op. cit., 627-32.

21. Marote-Carrier, op. cit., 15-16.

22. Ibid., 16-26.

23. Ibid., 26. If nine of *L'Aventurier's* 20 cannons had indeed been thrown overboard as Marote-Carrier says, there seems to be one too many in the total reported by the *Royalist* midshipman. Under the rules and conventions governing the taking of prisoners, the captain, second captain, and surgeon of a privateer ship were granted parole, and so was one lieutenant for every hundred men in its crew—all provided the ship had more than 14 four-pounder cannons. These senior officers remained parole prisoners (subject to their obeying the rules governing parole) until their exchange with similar prisoners taken by their own state could be arranged, or until certain factors, such as chronic illness or old age, might bring their release from captivity. The throwing overboard of eight or nine of *L'Aventurier's* 20 cannons thus precluded the grant of parole status. '... no parole has for many years been granted to officers of privateers having less than 14 guns actually mounted at the time of capture and that no guns less than 4 pounders are admitted, nor any guns allowed

that are found in the hold, or thrown overboard in chace [sic]; but as it is possible that notwithstanding our endeavours to procure correct information on this subject from the ports into which privateers are carried, some mistake may occur owing to the captors misrepresenting the strength of the privateers in the *Gazette*, to which we have recourse when other information is wanting, we submit whether some orders on this subject should not be given by their Lordships, and whether captors might not be directed to give information to this Board of the number and calibres of guns, actually mounted at time of capture, and the number of men found on board.' TNA ADM 98/117, ltr, 19 Nov. 1810, TB to Adm. Marote-Carrier himself says that it was the first and second captains, the lieutenant, and the two prizemasters of privateer ships who were entitled to parole, provided the ship carried at least 18 cannons. Marote-Carrier, op. cit., 27. See also Bennett, op. cit., p.10.

24. Marote-Carrier, op. cit., 29, 30.

25. TNA ADM 103/156 and ADM 103/157 passim. The defeat and surrender in Jul. 1808 of General Dupont's army at Baylen in Andalusia to Spanish forces appeared to have great military and political significance. It seemed to prove Napoleon's armies were after all not invincible. It encouraged the resistance of the mass of the Spanish people to the French conquest and occupation of their country. Spanish resistance contributed also, as the war continued, to the resistance of other peoples, including those of Germany and Russia. The atrocious treatment meted out to many of the 17,500 or so French and allied troops (including Swiss, Poles and Italians), most of whom were not 'the invincible troops of Austerlitz and Friedland', as Spanish patriots boasted, but were in fact raw young conscripts, taken prisoner by the Spanish forces at Baylen, seems certain to have been suffered by some at least of those who eventually found themselves in captivity at Greenlaw and other depots in Scotland. After the Spanish government or Junta refused to carry out the terms of surrender agreed between the two armies at Baylen (which had provided for the repatriation of Dupont's army by sea to France) the prisoners, subjected en route to brutal treatment, including murderous attacks on them by local inhabitants outraged by looting and other breakdowns in discipline that had marked the French invasion of Andalusia, were sent to languish in terrible conditions first on hulks in the bay of Cadiz then, in 1809, without shelter, almost without water, and without adequate and regular provision of food, on the small uninhabited Mediterranean island of Cabrera, ten miles south of Majorca. Cannibalism among the prisoners was one of many consequent horrors that took place on Cabrera. A small minority, mainly officers and non-commissioned officers, of the prisoners were fortunate to be transferred in 1810 to captivity in Britain: a TO ltr of 16 Aug. 1811 to the Adm. reported that there were then in captivity in Britain, 223 officers and 1,674 other ranks who had been capd at Baylen. But, although Napoleon considered on at least three occasions between 1810 and 1813 their rescue from Cabrera by his forces, the other thousands of prisoners remained a dwindling band there until the end of the war, when only two or three thousand broken men survived to be repatriated to France. See, e.g., Oman, *Peninsular War*, op. cit., Vol. I, 107, 126-205 passim; Reprinted and paraphrased with the permission of The Free Press, a Division of Simon & Schuster Adult Publishing Group, from SWORDS AROUND A THRONE: Napoleon's Grande Armée by John R. Elting. Copyright © 1988 by John R. Elting. All rights reserved. (London, 1989), 618-19; *Correspondance de Napoléon Ier* (Paris, 1858-70), Vol. XX, 462-3, Vol. XXIII, 35, and Vol. XXV, 118; TNA ADM 98/118, ltr, 16 Aug.1811.

26. TNA ADM 103/432-4 passim. At the capitulation of the French colony of Martinique to British forces in Feb. 1809, 155 officers and over 2,000 other ranks, plus a further 500 in hospital with wounds or fever, became prisoners of war and, under the terms of surrender, were to have been sent back to France and exchanged with British prisoners of war there. But Napoleon refused to release any of his British captives and the French prisoners were sent instead into captivity in Britain. Fortescue, *British Army*, op. cit., Vol. VII, 16.

27. TNA ADM 103/112 passim.

28. Ibid. In an obvious clerical error, one soldier was said to have been captured in Apr. 1806 on a sloop at Verdun.

29. TNA ADM 103/434-6 passim; ADM 103/113, Nos 6,445-7,479 passim.

30. In his account of the battle of Salamanca on 22 Jul. 1812, Sir Charles Oman, op. cit., Vol. V, 445-53 and 475-81, describes how the French General Thomières having been killed in the fighting, 'his divisional battery [of artillery] was captured whole; of his two leading regiments the 101st Line lost 1,031 men out of 1,449 present; its colonel and eagle were both taken with many hundred unwounded prisoners; the 62nd Line lost 868 men out of 1,123.' As a result of a charge by British cavalry on two battalions of the French 66th infantry regiment, '... some hundreds cast down their muskets, raised their hands, and asked quarter. The rear ranks scattered and fled southward across the plateau.' And another British cavalry charge '... made a complete wreck of the left wing of the French army. The remnants of the eight battalions ... broken fled eastward in a confused mass, towards the edge of the woods, becoming blended with the separate stream of fugitives from Thomière's division. The [British] 5th Division swept in some 1,500 prisoners from them, as also the eagle of the 22nd Line.' British eye-witness accounts of the battle quoted by Oman say that '... a mass of their routed infantry ... in the wildness of their panic and confusion, and throwing away their arms, actually ran against our horses, where many of them fell down exhausted, and incapable of further movement', and '... hundreds of men frightfully disfigured, black with dust, worn out with fatigue, and covered with sabre-cuts and blood, threw themselves among us for safety.' The next day, in a unique action, heavy dragoons of the [British] King's German Legion pursuing French forces after Salamanca broke into a defensive square formed at Garcia Hernandez by two French infantry regts and destroyed or captured a whole battalion of one of them, the 76th regt, and the other, the 6th Light regt, suffered losses almost as heavy. There were prisoners from these regts at Perth who had been made captive at Salamanca. One was Jean Labrot, soldier, 62nd regt, who arr. at Perth on 12 Nov. 1812. A native of Toulouse, Labrot was aged 27. He died and was buried at the depot a fortnight later. TNA ADM 103/264, No. 2,934. There were 21 other men from Labrot's regt held captive at Perth, 170 from the 66th regt, 36 from the 76th, and 37 from the 101st. From the 6th Light regt there were some 223 prisoners at Perth and of these at least 140 appear to have been capd at Garcia Hernandez. TNA ADM 103/263-266 passim.

31. For repatriation during the war on grounds of age, wounds, illness, and these other reasons, see particularly Chapters 20-22 above.

32. How long all these 1,000 'Danes' (many of whom were Norwegians), whose kingdom was at war with Britain from 1807 until 1814, remained in captivity it is not possible to say without a great deal more detailed research. The two Greenlaw Entry Books TNA ADM 103/152 and ADM 103/153 indicate that before the end of 1811 about

107 of them were sent from there on parole to Peebles, about 576 to the hulks at Chatham, and well over 100 were, for a variety of reasons, repatriated.

33. TNA ADM 103/154.

34. TNA ADM 103/158.

35. TNA ADM 103/155, /156 and /157. ADM 103/157, although a 'French' General Entry Book, also lists separately 48 American seamen taken prisoner betwen Aug. and Nov. 1812, following the declaration of war earlier that summer by the United States on Britain. These 48 Americans are not included in this table.

36. TNA ADM 103/432-4.

37. TNA ADM 103/112, Nos 1-461.

38. TNA ADM 103/434-6; ADM 103/113, Nos 6,445-7,479.

39. TNA ADM 103/263-6. The total number of prisoners listed in the four Perth General Entry Books is actually 7,761. That eight are missing from the table constructed here illustrates the difficulty of arriving at an entirely accurate figure. Moreover, in most General Entry Books the difficulty in attempting to construct wholly accurate tables is compounded by the re-entry under a different serial number of a few former inmates, including some recapd escapers.

40. *Supplementary Despatches, Correspondence, and Memoranda of Field Marshal Arthur, Duke of Wellington, K.G.* Ed. by his son, the Duke of Wellington (London, 1861), Vol. VIII, 515.

41. Simond, *Journal*, op. cit., Vol. II, 55.

42. The decision of the Board on Paulon's application was: 'Cannot be allowed, he being taken in a privateer.' But soon afterward the Board relented: 'Paulon ... to be allowed to go to Odiham [a parole town in Hampshire] on his parole.' TNA ADM 105/53/147 and 198 (Registers of Prisoners' Applications, 1810-11), and ADM 105/44/33.

43. TNA ADM 103/434. The contradictions are not diminished by the apparent death of Hermann at Valleyfield on 11 Apr. 1812 (see above, Appendix 11, Valleyfield, No. 94). Was there simply a confusion between two Guillaume Hermanns at the depot, one of whom was alias J.B.C. Traut?

44. TNA ADM 103/263, No. 947; C. Northcote Parkinson, *War in the Eastern Seas 1793-1815* (London, 1954), 274.

45. TNA ADM 103/264, No. 4,106.

46. TNA ADM 103/265, No. 5,190.

47. TNA ADM 103/265, No. 5,155.

48. Marote-Carrier, op. cit., 184-5.

49. TNA ADM 103/263, No. 1,133.

50. *Glasgow Courier*, 28 Nov. 1811.

51. Members of the crew of the *Ravisseur* priv. (including Louis Lamargant, its owner, and a surgeon, a lieut., a prizemaster, a bosun, 24 seamen, a clerk, a steward, and four ship's boys two of whom were aged 11, one 10, and one, René or Pierre Vasseur, 9) capd off Norway on 18 Feb. that year, they entered Valleyfield in Jul. The owner and the surgeon were soon sent on parole respectively to Biggar and Lanark, and the four boys, all natives of Dunkirk, were sent home to France in Aug. TNA ADM 103/435, Nos 6,394-6,438 passim.

52. Marote-Carrier, op. cit., 158-9.

53. Ibid., 146-7. Breskens, on the southern shore of the Scheldt estuary, is three and

a half miles south of Walcheren; Cassant, or Cassandria, lies to the south-west of Walcheren, on the western tip of the mainland province of Cadsand, south across the Scheldt from Flushing; L'Ecluse, now known as Sluis, a town in Zeeland province in the south-west of the Netherlands, about 13 miles south-west of Flushing. Was the poor Fleming Joseph De Vau (or De Vaus or De Vaux), capd at Flushing on 18 Aug. 1809, described as 'Labourer', b. 'Fleming' and aged 43, who arr. at Valleyfield from Esk Mills in Mar. 1811, and who volunteered and was dischgd on 14 Feb. 1814 into the 1st Dutch Regt? TNA ADM 103/433, No. 1,106 (De Vaus).

CHAPTER 9: SEAMEN, SOLDIERS, CIVILIANS, SHIPS, REGIMENTS, CORPS, AND RANKS

1. Merchant seamen were civilians, too; privateersmen might be described as civilian combatants. 'Seamen' had two meanings: sea-going, as distinct from military or army; but also a specific rank, distinct from, e.g., bosuns, pursers, et al.
2. TNA ADM 103/152 and ADM 103/153.
3. TNA ADM 103/154. The 159 officers and crew of the shipwrecked Dutch navy frig. *Utrecht*, briefly held captive at Greenlaw in Mar.-Apr. 1807, are not included in these figures. Most of the men from the *Utrecht* are listed in TNA ADM 103/110, Nos 98-214.
4. TNA ADM 103/115 and ADM 103/158.
5. TNA ADM 103/115.
6. TNA ADM 103/155.
7. TNA ADM 103/157.
8. Ibid.
9. TNA ADM 103/124.
10. TNA ADM 103/112. Of the naval prisoners 145, of priv. 171, of m.v. six, and all 24 'uncertain' came in Mar. 1811 to the Castle from Esk Mills. The remainder came to the Castle from elsewhere between Apr. and Dec. 1811, when it ceased to be a depot except for prisoners in transit or for *mauvais sujets* sent as a punishment.
11. TNA ADM 103/432-6 passim, and ADM 103/113, Nos 6,445-7,479. These are the aggregate totals of seamen at Valleyfield and include those seamen among the 2,486 prisoners who came there in Mar.-Apr. 1811 from Esk Mills.
12. TNA ADM 103/263-6 passim.
13. With all the usual reservations arising from misspellings in the depot General Entry Books of ships' names, and contradictory information there about the categories of vessels and their places and dates of capture, there appears to have been a net total of some 232 captured or destroyed naval vessels from which prisoners came to Scotland.
14. TNA ADM 103/434, Nos 2,231 (David) and 2,293 (Gauvin). David, a seaman, b. at St Valery and aged 30, arr. from Esk Mills at Valleyfield on 11 Mar. 1811 and remained there until his release in Jun. 1814. Where Gauvin, purser on the *Impérial*, had been before he entered Valleyfield is not stated, nor when he arr. there, but his number in the Entry Book indicates he must have come from Esk Mills, almost certainly in Mar. 1811. Born in Cherbourg and aged 34, he was transferred to Perth in Sep. 1812. The other four French line-of-battle ships destroyed or captured with *Impérial* in that naval action in 1806 were *Alexandre, Brave, Diomède* and *Jupiter*, from all of

which also there were prisoners in the depots in Scotland. James, *Naval History*, op. cit., Vol. IV, 88-103 passim.

15. For Douzon, see also above, Appendix 2, No. 39. For Molinière and Soberg see TNA ADM 103/157, Nos 204 and 365 respectively, and for Soberg (or Soeberg) see also TNA ADM 103/110, No. 365.

16. Abell, op. cit., 54-5.

17. '... the indulgence of parole ... [does] ... not extend to any officers of a merchant vessel beyond the captain and second captain ...' TNA ADM 98/111, ltr, 20 Oct. 1803, TB to W. Marsden, secretary, Adm.

18. What may have been the smallest priv. vessel of the Napoleonic Wars certainly failed to meet these criteria on its capture in summer 1809: 'Wednesday arrived [at Leith] a small row-boat privateer of two guns ... captured by the *Childers* sloop near the ... coast of Norway.' *Glasgow Courier*, 12 Aug. 1809.

19. TNA ADM 1/3764, Admiralty Secretary's Department, in-letters from TB.

20. TNA ADM 103/432 and ADM 103/433; Marote-Carrier, op. cit., 16.

21. For *Héro du Nord* crew men, see TNA ADM 103/432-4. Three other capd priv. ships were named *Le Vengeur*, 19 of the members of whose crews were then also confined at Esk Mills. TNA ADM 103/124 passim.

22. TNA ADM 103/155, Nos 357-400; ADM 103/157.

23. There were very much larger numbers of soldiers from the same regts also in captivity together in depots such as Perth and Valleyfield; yet these soldiers do not seem to have been impelled by the same determination to escape as were many privateersmen. As already observed, Marote-Carrier, op. cit., 16, recalled, however, 'a sizeable number' of the crew of his own privateer *L'Aventurier* were old soldiers of the French Wars since 1792 who, after their discharge from the army, had out of boredom signed on *L'Aventurier* as volunteers. How many other privateer crews may have been similarly composed is a matter of conjecture.

24. See Appendices 1 and 2 above. A major factor in the decision by the authorities in autumn 1810 to send far more prisoners of war to Scotland was the report then by the informant Garçon Baptiste at Portchester Castle of a projected mass uprising by prisoners there and on the hulks at Portsmouth. The leader of the projected mass uprising was said to have been a privateer captain.

25. TNA ADM 98/280. Lieut. Gen. Wynyard was Commander of the Forces in North Britain.

26. TNA ADM 105/53, Register of Prisoners' Applications, Nos 371-81, 27 Oct. 1811; ADM 98/277, ltrs, 17 Oct. 1811, TB to M. Wright and Capt. Moriarty.

27. TNA ADM 103/434, Nos 2,960-4.

28. '... no Prisoner taken in a Privateer can be recognised as a non-combatant.' TNA ADM 98/279, ltr, 30 Mar. 1813, TB to Lieut. Priest, agent, Greenlaw.

29. TNA ADM 103/152 and ADM 103/153 passim. Priv. ships after capture were often sold off to civilian bidders at public auctions. The Danish 64-ton priv. *Alvor*, for instance, brought into Leith by HM sloop *Egeria*, was among five capd Danish vessels advertised in Apr. 1812 for sale there. Some of its armaments, including '14 guns, 26 muskets, and 20 cutlasses', were also put up to auction. *CM*, 16 Apr. 1812. Although almost all enemy priv. ships brought as prizes into ports in Scotland had been capd by ships of the Royal Navy (a few others by British privateers) there was an unusual case in 1811 of one capd by fishermen. 'On ... 4 October, three fishing

smacks off Peterhead, sailing north for the fishing grounds off the coast of Orkney, saw a privateer sloop about three miles away, chased it for three hours, during which it threw overboard three guns, forced the privateer to strike her colours but could not board her because of stormy weather. ... the privateer made many attempts to escape, but the smacks kept her surrounded and boarded her next day. The privateer ... was ... [the] *Tack For Sidst*, of Bergen, Captain Andreas Orn, sixteen men, three guns, and a number of small arms. The crew was taken off and the smacks brought her into Stromness harbour the next day.' *Glasgow Courier*, 24 Oct. 1811.

30. Two of these American privateering seamen were Matthew Reilly and Elisha Adams, both capd aboard the French priv. *Phoenix* in the English Channel in Sep. 1810. Reilly was aged 33, Adams 22. TNA ADM 103/487.

31. TNA ADM 103/154, Nos 1-13, (Volner was No. 12, Smit No.7). Some other merchant seamen of various nationalities had of course found themselves prisoners for a time in late summer and early autumn 1803 at Fort George.

32. Derry, *Scandinavia*, op.cit., 204. Derry points out that Danish farmers, however, greatly profited from high wartime corn prices, and Danish traders from 'highly profitable undercover contacts ... maintained with the British, who had seized Heligoland in 1807 for commercial access to the mainland [of Europe] and two years later safeguarded their shipping routes by occupying the little island of Anholt in the middle of the Kattegat.' Norwegians, then subjects of the kings of Denmark, were worse, or even worse, affected by the war, which also cut off their previously predominant overseas trade with British markets and drastically curtailed their essential corn imports from Jutland as a result of blockade by the British navy, although king Frederick VI for some years did modify his obligations under Napoleon's Continental System by issuing licences to his Norwegian subjects to export timber to Britain in return for British manufactures and an easing of the blockade on Danish corn ships. Some of these developments are reflected in the diary that the Norwegian privateer captain Paul Andreas Kaald kept at Greenlaw during his captivity there in 1808-10.

33. Among numerous examples at Leith were 17 Prussian prize m.vs and fishing smacks put up for sale in Oct. 1806, and 13 Danish vessels of between 14 and 81 tons, and the cargoes of ten of them, including 'rye, barley, malt, butter, beef, deals, rock moss, herrings, stock fish, soap, Norwegian timber, etc.' advertised for sale in May 1812. *EEC*, 23 Oct. 1806; *CM*, 14 May 1812.

34. The distribution of naval prize money was amended by the government in 1808. The total amount of prize money remained divisible as before into eight parts, but the captain's share (though still subject to part of his share being passed on to his admiral) then declined from 3/8ths to 2/8ths; two groups of ship's officers and principal warrant officers or equivalent ranks had equal shares in a further 2/8ths as previously, and a third and very much larger group (midshipmen, lesser warrant officers and marine sergeants, who had previously had equal shares in 1/8th, but which group from 1808 also embraced all the lower or rank and file members of the ship's crew, who had previously had equal shares in 2/8ths) had equal shares in the remaining 4/8ths. Michael Lewis, *A Social History of the Navy, 1793-1815* (London, 1960), 318.

35. The aggregate total of civilian prisoners (excluding merchant seamen) in the Scots depots appears to have been about 100, but after adjustments for transfers between depots and other factors the net total was about 60.

36. TNA ADM 98/279, ltr, 10 Sep. 1812, TB to Capt. Andrew Brown; ADM 103/152, Nos 79, 102, 462 and 463.
37. TNA ADM 103/124, No. 4, and ADM 103/581, No. 133.
38. TNA ADM 103/155, Nos 114 (Baille snr) and 115 (Baille jnr); ADM 103/115, Nos 114 (Baille snr) and 115 (Baille jnr).
39. TNA ADM 103/155, No. 37.
40. TNA ADM 103/432, No. 827. Another passenger who had done so from Esk Mills in Mar. the previous year was J. Pierre Chauvin, aged 36, who had been capd aboard the vessel *La Santa Maria Nova*. TNA ADM 103/487.
41. TNA ADM 103/124, No. 1,477.
42. TNA ADM 103/263, Nos 1,187 (La Coste) and 1,188 (La Borde); ADM 103/124, No. 2,721 (La Coste, said there to have been capd on a m.v.); ADM 103/432, Nos 134 (La Coste) and 159 (La Borde).
43. TNA ADM 98/111, ltr, 26 Jun. 1804, TB to Adm. The Dutch agent, Mr Apostool, had written the Adm. from his office in the Strand on the issue on 14 Sep. 1803. TNA ADM 1/3743/383.
44. TNA ADM 98/116, ltr, 13 Mar. 1810, TB to Adm.
45. *Glasgow Courier*, 16 May 1809; *CM*, 21 Jul. 1810.
46. TNA ADM 98/121, ltr, 15 Sep. 1813, TB to Adm.; ADM 1/3765, fols 60 and 65; ADM 98/121, ltr, 29 Jul. 1813, TB to Adm.; *Montrose Review*, 23 Jul. 1813; *Glasgow Courier*, 27 and 29 Jul. 1813.
47. Edinburgh City Archives, Register of Aliens, ltr, 14 Jan. 1813, from Mr Denovan, Police Office, Leith.
48. TNA ADM 103/124, No. 1,182 (Bernard); ADM 103/434, No. 2,473 (Walinck); ADM 103/432, No. 572 (Briant); ADM 105/53, No. 238 (Briant).
49. TNA ADM 98/122, ltr, 29 Nov. 1813, and ADM 103/496; ADM 98/134, ltr, 8 Nov. 1813, TB to James Buller.
50. The degree of error in these and other statistics presented in this study, based as they are on the information, sometimes contradictory, occasionally demonstrably incorrect, in the General Entry Books, is at most perhaps five per cent. Between attempts to compile such statistics about the prisoners in the Scots depots in 1803-14 and the counting of votes in parliamentary or local elections there may appear to be some similarity: each recount tends to result in a somewhat different total.
51. TNA ADM 103/152 and ADM 103/153.
52. TNA ADM 103/154.
53. TNA ADM 103/115.
54. TNA ADM 103/158 and ADM 103/115.
55. TNA ADM 103/157.
56. TNA ADM 103/155, ADM 103/156, and ADM 103/157.
57. TNA ADM 103/124.
58. TNA ADM 103/112. Of these, 116 arrived at the Castle from Esk Mills in early Mar. 1811, the other nine from elsewhere between Mar. and Dec. 1811, when the Castle ceased to be an ordinary depot.
59. TNA ADM 103/432-6 and ADM 103/113, Nos 6,445-7,479. Of that aggregate number about 935 came to Valleyfield in Mar.-Apr. 1811 from Esk Mills on its closure.
60. TNA ADM 103/263-6.

61. David Chandler, *Dictionary of the Napoleonic Wars* (Ware, 1999), 208. Oman, *Peninsular War*, op. cit., Vol. I, 111, says that in 1813 the French army had 156 Line and 36 Light infantry regts.

62. Oman, ibid., 111-12, says in that year the French army had altogether 12 regts of cuirassiers (heavy cavalry, mounted on big horses, and whose soldiers wore metal breastplates and backplates, carried a long straight sword, pistols, and later in the war a carbine), two of carabiniers (similar to cuirassiers), 30 of dragoons (originally mounted infantrymen, armed with a sword, pistols, a musket and bayonet, the dragoons had by this period evolved into medium or light cavalrymen), 10 of hussars and 26 of *chasseurs à cheval*, both latter groups light horsemen whose main weapons were the sabre and the pistol but many of whom were also armed with carbines. See also Chandler, *Dictionary*, op. cit., 85.

63. For a table, presented with the usual reservations, of the regts and corps from which the soldiers among the prisoners came to the depots in Scotland, see above, Appendix 4.

64. The Valleyfield Entry Book TNA ADM 103/434, Nos 4,112-4,134, gives 21 Dec. 1808 as their date of capture; but Oman, *Peninsular War*, op. cit., Vol. I, 549-50, describes the British cavalry action led by Lord Paget that resulted in the capture of these 23 men (along with 59 others) and their General Lefebvre-Desnouëttes, as taking place on 29 Dec. Chandler, *Dictionary*, op. cit., 49, says 100 French prisoners were taken in the action that day and their capture 'took place under the eyes of Napoleon himself, who watched from an eminence on the southern bank of the river.'

65. The Perth Entry Book states he had been capd on 20 Aug. 1808. TNA ADM 103/435, Nos 5,000 and 6,279, and ADM 103/266, No. 7,119.

66. TNA ADM 103/265, No. 4,564 (Bellus); ADM 103/113, No. 7,162 (Bellus); ADM 103/436, No. 7,606 (Denis). The Valleyfield General Entry Book does not give dates of arrivals there for prisoners Nos 7,480-7,632.

67. TNA ADM 103/124, Nos 1,334 and 1,335. Perhaps the regt was not one of infantry but of cavalry; even so, it remains so far unidentified.

68. Alan Forrest, *Conscripts and Deserters: The Army and French Society during the Revolution and Empire* (New York, 1989), 70.

69. Elting, *Swords Around a Throne*, op. cit., 435.

70. The carabiniers listed in Appendix 4 above as prisoners at Esk Mills appear to have been not cavalrymen but five infantrymen whose rank that was but whose regt is not given, and the two 'Russian Carabiniers' already mentioned but not otherwise identified.

71. TNA ADM 103/156, No. 141 (Navetier); and ADM 103/263, No. 399 (Meunier).

72. TNA ADM 103/263, No. 119. His name and place of birth suggest he was more likely to have been in the 1st Regt of Polish Lancers than in any French regt of lancers.

73. TNA ADM 103/265, Nos 5,612-6 and 5,618.

74. TNA ADM 103/266, No. 6,539.

75. TNA ADM 103/435, No. 5,363; ADM 103/600, No. 111; see also above, Appendix 11, Valleyfield, No. 68.

76. TNA ADM 103/265, No. 4,490.

77. TNA ADM 103/263, Nos 73-6.

78. TNA ADM 103/435, Nos 5,648 and 5,651; E.H. Jenkins, *A History of the French Navy*

(London, 1973), 270; Elting, *Swords Around a Throne*, op. cit., 308-9; Oman, *Peninsular War*, op. cit., Vol. III, 410-12.

79. Elting, *Swords Around a Throne*, op. cit., 709.

80. TNA ADM 98/278, ltr, 4 Mar. 1812, TB to Vice Admiral Otway.

81. Lucien Bonaparte (1775-1840), a younger brother of Napoleon, had played a leading role in the coup d'état of 18th Brumaire 1799 and afterwards became Minister of the Interior, but later fell out with Napoleon. In 1810 while on his way to America he was capd by a British warship and spent the remainder of the war as a parole prisoner at Ludlow and Worcester. Abell, op. cit., 448; Markham, *Napoleon*, op. cit., 72-7; TNA ADM 103/124, No. 2,816; ADM 105/54, Register of Prisoners' Applications, No. 180, 6 Mar. 1811; ADM 98/277, ltr, 23 Mar. 1811, TB to Capt. Pellowe; ADM 103/581, No. 132.

82. Marote-Carrier, op. cit., 104.

83. Peacock, *Perth: its annals and its archives*, op. cit., 496-7.

84. *Perth Courier*, 13 Aug. 1812.

85. Lewis, *Napoleon and his British captives*, op. cit., 141.

CHAPTER 10: WOMEN AND CHILDREN; AGES

1. Marote-Carrier, op. cit., 159. Lévêque, op. cit., p. 57, gives examples of women who shared their menfolk's imprisonment in depots or on the hulks in England. Quoting French government sources, he shows that in Jun. 1812 there were 37 women and children accompanying the 49,418 prisoners then in the closed depots in Britain. 'There being in custody … at Forton [a depot near Portsmouth] a Spanish and a Portuguese Woman,' the TB wrote to its agent at Portsmouth in Oct. 1812, 'who having been brought to this Country by French Prisoners of War have been since abandoned by them, we direct you to send them by the first Opportunity to Corunna and Lisbon respectively, causing them to be victualled on the Passage. The Spanish Woman has an infant with her.' TNA ADM 98/187, 24 Oct. 1812.

2. TNA ADM 98/191.

3. On the eve of his defeat of the Prussian army in Oct. 1806 at Iena and Auerstadt, Napoleon, 'desiring that the evils of war be diminished as much as possible', declared that all women and children, surgeons, and administrators made captive would be released, 'not being considered as prisoners of war.' *Correspondance de Napoléon Ier*, op. cit., Vol. I, 341. Numbers of their wives or partners who accompanied the French troops in their invasion of Spain in 1808 became captives there with their menfolk; and of those women four or five, according to François-Frédéric Billon, himself a prisoner on that island for a time before becoming a parole prisoner in Scotland, were among the French captives sent by the Spanish government that year to the uninhabited island of Cabrera in the Balearic Islands. Billon, *Souvenirs*, op. cit., 231. Some wives also accompanied their husbands in the Grande Armèe during Napoleon's invasion of Russia in 1812-13. Sergeant Bourgogne of the Imperial Guard describes how Madame Dubois, his regimental *cantinière*, was feeding her baby during the Grande Armée's disastrous retreat from Moscow that winter when 'suddenly we heard a cry of anguish. The infant was dead, and as stiff as a piece of wood.' The child's father and a sapper dug a grave for the baby in the snow: 'he kissed the baby, and placed it in its tomb. It was covered with snow, and all was at an end.' *Memoirs of Sergeant Bourgogne*, ed. P. Cottin and M. Hénault (London,

1899), 72. When thousands of Spanish prisoners of war were marched to captivity in France after the outbreak of the Peninsular War in 1808 they were accompanied by multitudes of their womenfolk. But Napoleon 'knew them [the women] by reputation and ordered "that none of them be allowed to enter [France]."' J. Lucas-Dubreton, *Napoléon devant L'Espagne* (Paris, 1946), 488. In the British army 'only six wives were allowed to travel on service with each company. The women drew lots as to which should go, and this casting of lots was usually left until the last evening before a regiment embarked for the war. Tickets inscribed "To go" and "Not to go" were put in a hat, and when the moment of suspense and destiny arrived, most affecting, pathetic scenes occurred, because wives left behind often faced starvation or charity, though individual regiments did give allowances to carry the women and children home.' Antony Brett-James, *Life in Wellington's Army* (London, 1972), 271. The anonymous Edinburgh *A Soldier of the 71st*, ed. Christopher Hibbert (London, 1975), 31, described how, during the terrible retreat by Sir John Moore's army to Corunna in the bitterly cold winter of 1808-9, 'From the few remaining wagons we had been able to bring with us, women and children, who had hitherto sustained, without perishing, all our aggravated sufferings, were, every now and then, laid out upon the snow, frozen to death. An old tattered blanket, or some other piece of garment, was all the burial that was given them.' Although to do so was breaching regulations, some women accompanied their menfolk to sea aboard warships, and a woman named Jane Townshend was on board HMS *Defiance* at the battle of Trafalgar. Lewis, *Social History of the Navy*, op. cit., 282-3.

4. TNA ADM 98/277.

5. TNA ADM 98/278. Louis Diédont, capd on 13 Apr. 1811 in Spain as a servant in the 67th Line regt, had arr. at Valleyfield on 10 Jan. 1812 from the *Zealous*. In pencil after his name in the Entry Book is written: 'avec Cathareine Diedont sa femme'. Born at Mayenne and aged 37, Diédont remained in captivity at Valleyfield until his release on 14 Jun. 1814. TNA ADM 103/435, No. 5,326.

6. NAS Macbeth Forbes coll., GD 1/405/2. Macbeth Forbes gives no source for this information.

7. Marote-Carrier, op. cit., 159-61. The unnamed Spanish woman hussar (it seems odd that if she was a hussar she had fought beside her husband in the artillery) was not the only female who fought in the Napoleonic Wars. According to the *EEC*, 30 Nov. 1812, a young woman named Virginie, from 'a respectable family' near Lille, with the eventual consent of her parents, took the place of her sickly brother when he received his notice of conscription to Napoleon's army. Dressed in her brother's clothes she hoodwinked the recruiting officer and was sent to serve with a French regiment in Portugal, where she was soon promoted to sergeant. Twice she saved the life of her captain although wounded herself. A later wound from a bayonet 'led to the discovery that she was a woman. She was conveyed to Burgos, and having again recovered, the officer whose life she had twice preserved, feeling the full force of love and gratitude, married her. They both returned to France and enjoyed, in the bosom of her family, the happiness due to love and intrepidity.' Elting, *Swords Around a Throne*, op. cit., 611, quotes the case of another Frenchwoman who at age 14 joined the French army as a drummer and, unlike Virginie of Lille, did not try to conceal that she was female—a fact which in due time led her to take defensive action against the advances of male comrades in her regiment, culminating in her challenging them to a duel. Napoleon placed her under his personal protection. She

continued to serve in the army until badly wounded at Waterloo. Nor were women combatants confined to one nation only: *The Times*, 22 Aug. 1808, reported that 'A young lady of quality in Russia, having been pressed by her family to enter into a matrimonial engagement contrary to her inclinations, abandoned her home and, disguised in male attire, entered a Polish regiment, in which she served at the battle of Austerlitz. She likewise served in the late campaign, was promoted to the rank of corporal, and received the little cross of the Order of St George for some act of heroism. She was at length discovered by her family, and was ordered to Petersburg by the Emperor [the Tsar], who made her considerable presents.'

8. Penny, *Traditions of Perth*, op. cit., 92.

9. These printed proformas are preserved in TNA ADM 103/267, titled 'Perth 1812-14 Various'.

10. *EEC*, 6 Dec. 1813; TNA ADM 103/263, Nos 931 and 813.

11. The Perth Entry Book TNA ADM 103/263, No. 879, gives Joseph Elène (sic) as soldier, 82nd Line regt, capd 27 Jan. 1812 at Salamanca, and arr. at Perth on 29 Aug. that year via HMS *Freya*. Born in Piedmont, he was aged 27. On his arrival at the depot he was provided with a hammock, bed and blanket; a month later with a hat, jacket, waistcoat, trousers, shirt, and shoes; on 10 Jan. 1813 with shoes and stockings; and on 23 Jun. that year with a shirt. On 2 Aug. 1813 he was transferred to Valleyfield. ADM 103/263, No. 832, lists Pierre Etienne Lebrun as a soldier in the 6th Artillery, capd 27 Jun. 1812 at Salamanca, and who arr. at Perth on 29 Aug. 1812 via HMS *Freya*. Aged 31, he was born at Cueire. On his arrival at the depot Lebrun was provided with a hammock, bed and blanket, but interestingly he was given another hammock three weeks later, as well as a hat, jacket, waistcoat, trousers, shirt, and shoes; on 7 Apr. 1813 he received stockings, on 29 Jul. that year another shirt, and on 11 Feb. 1814 another blanket. He was rel. on 1 Jun. 1814 after the end of the war.

12. TNA ADM 103/263, No. 1,906, gives André Millet as a sergeant in the 28th Line regt, capd 7 Apr. 1812 at Badajoz, and who arr. at Perth on 14 Oct. 1812 via the *Golden Fleece* trans. from Portsmouth. Born at Valence, Millet was aged 31. Against his name is written in pencil: 'In the Hospital'. He was provided a few days after his arrival at the depot with a hammock, and on 31 Jan. 1814 with a hat, jacket, waistcoat, trousers and a shirt. He was rel. on 4 Jun. 1814.

13. TNA ADM 103/265, No. 4,518, gives Pierre Dévery (sic), soldier, 50th Line regt, capd at Madrid 14 Aug. 1812, and said to have arr. at Perth 2 Dec. 1812 via '*Jane & Ariel* Transports'. Born at Lavre [? Le Havre], Dévery or Dervi was aged 23. He was issued at the depot two days after his arrival with a hammock; on 17 Nov. 1813 with shoes; and on 21 Jan. 1814 with a blanket, hat, jacket, waistcoat, trousers, shirt, and another pair of shoes. He was dischgd from the depot into the 1st Dutch regt 19 Feb. 1814.

14. Peuxe is listed in TNA ADM 103/265, No. 5,668, as b. at Meulon and aged 30.

15. TNA ADM 103/263, Nos 931-6, and ADM 103/265, Nos 4,520 (Catherine Latyce) and 5,611 (Marie Manuel); *EEC*, 31 Aug. 1812; *Perth Courier*, 15 Oct. 1812; *Glasgow Courier*, 1 Dec. 1812. The Entry Book says HMS *Freya* had come from Lisbon; the *Glasgow Courier*, 9 Jan. 1813, that the *Freya* had arr. from Portsmouth. The two statements are not necessarily incompatible. But whether Marie Manuel and her husband had spent some time in captivity at Portsmouth on their way to Perth, or had not even been disembarked during a brief halt at Portsmouth on the voyage from Lisbon, is not clear.

16. TNA ADM 98/279.

17. TNA ADM 103/263, No. 813 (Vanherff).

18. About Maria Martin's date of leaving Perth, however, there is ambiguity. The Entry Book says she was dischgd to France 1 Jun. 1814, but the proformas in TNA ADM 103/267 say she was dischgd with all the other five women (excluding Marie Manuel) and the two Lantigny infants to Leith for Portsmouth and then to France, on 8 Jan. 1813. The later date for her repatriation would appear to enhance the significance of the issue of bedding, clothing and footwear uniquely to Marie Manuel, who alone among these seven women may have been considered by the depot authorities and TB to be actually a prisoner of war. It is also possible that as he was recalling these events some thirty years afterward, Marote-Carrier was mistaken in believing his 'Andalusian' was a hussar when in fact she was in or had been associated with the artillery; and that he was also mistaken in recalling the fainting fits as those of the 'Andalusian' when in fact they were suffered by Catherine Latyce or Leliot.

19. Examples abound: Admiral William Albany Otway (1756-1815), naval commander, based at Leith, of the east coast of Scotland from Aug. 1810 to Nov. 1813, had joined the navy in 1765 at the age of nine. *The Naval Chronicle* (London, 1814), Vol. XXXI, 442. Nelson himself had joined the navy in 1771 at the age of 12. General Karl von Clausewitz (1780-1831), military historian and theorist, posthumous author of the classic study *On War*, joined the Prussian army at the age of 12 and as an ensign fought against the French the following year. He, too, for a time after the battle of Auerstadt in 1806 was a prisoner of war. James J. Sheehan, *German History 1770-1866* (Oxford, 1989), 230-1; Chandler, *Dictionary*, op. cit., 95. Among Napoleon's marshals, Berthier and Sérurier were in the army at the age of 12, Grouchy at 13, Davout, Jourdan, Poniatowski, Marmont, and Moncey at 15, Soult, Victor, and Pérignon at 16. David Chandler, *The Campaigns of Napoleon* (London, 1966), 1,122-5. Lieut. General Sir John Moore, son of a Glasgow doctor, was a commissioned officer in the army at the age of 15. Marote-Carrier, prisoner at, and source of information about, successively Esk Mills, Valleyfield and Perth, had begun his career as a merchant seaman at the age of nine; Paul Andreas Kaald, the diarist, a prisoner at Greenlaw in 1808-10, had first gone to sea at the age of 14. Similarly youthful British captives could be found in France during the Napoleonic Wars. Alexander Stewart (1790-1874) of Kirkcaldy, who ran away to sea as a boy, was a prisoner of war in France from the age of 14 for almost a decade until the end of the wars. *The Life of Alexander Stewart. Prisoner of Napoleon and Preacher of the Gospel. Written by himself to 1815, abridged by Dr Albert Peel to 1874* (London, 1948), passim. An English boy aged five, against wartime regulations taken to sea by, and captured in Jul. 1803 with, his father, a Royal Navy carpenter on HMS *Minerve*, spent his captivity in three successive French prison depots in the second of which his father was brutally killed while attempting to escape. In an earlier unsuccessful attempt the father had tried to swim across the Rhine with the boy on his back. Lewis, *Napoleon and his British captives*, op.cit., 147, 254.

20. Beaudoin, op. cit. 706, 708.

21. Apart from the failure or inability of depot clerks to enter some ages in the Entry Books, a few prisoners themselves appear to have been unsure of their age. One of several such at Perth, for example, was Pierre Godron, voltigeur (light infantryman), 22nd Light regt, capd by Wellington's army at Alligosse in Jun. 1812, and who arr. at the depot in Oct. that year. Godron said he was either 29 or 39. TNA ADM 103/263, No. 1,801.

22. TNA ADM 103/153.
23. TNA ADM 103/153, Nos 400 (Stevensen) and 410 (Stolls).
24. TNA ADM 103/157.
25. Ibid., Nos 6 (Cook), 25 (Smith) and 43 (Clark).
26. TNA ADM 103/157.
27. Ibid., No. 694. There was at Greenlaw in its early months as a depot in 1804 a prisoner even older than Armand Kreyer. A letter of 13 Apr. that year from the TB to the Adm. enclosed a list of prisoners 'totally unfit for further service civil or military by land or sea', one of whom at 'Edinburgh' (i.e., Greenlaw) was Pierre Rideau, a seaman capd on the m.v. *La Flore* the previous Aug. Rideau, said to have been suffering for some years from 'imbecility and rheumatism', was rel. from the depot on 12 Jul. 1804, 'Being unfit for Service.' He was then aged 70. TNA ADM 1/3745.
28. TNA ADM 103/112, No. 516.
29. TNA ADM 103/157, Nos 314 (Larsen) and 259 (Champagne); ADM 103/112, No. 394 (Champagne); ADM 103/435, No. 5,771 (Champagne); ADM 98/279, ltr, 18 Sep. 1812, TB to Capt. Brown.
30. This table further illustrates some of the difficulties in presenting entirely accurate statistics about the prisoners. The Esk Mills General Entry Book lists an aggregate of 2,817 prisoners of whom, as already seen, by the time of the depot's closure on 11 Mar. 1811 some 25 had either escaped, died, been sent away on parole, or (in the case of 11) removed as a punishment to Edinburgh Castle. So there remained a net total of some 2,792. Of these 450 were then sent to Edinburgh Castle, making the total there who had come from Esk Mills 461. According to its first three General Entry Books Valleyfield took in (or appears to have taken in) from Esk Mills in Mar.-Apr. 1811 2,486 prisoners, not 2,494 as the table shows. The surplus of eight is an error (of 0.32 per cent) for which pardon can perhaps be sought by again drawing exculpatory analogies with recounts in parliamentary or local elections. Wherever that surplus of eight sprang from it was not from among the youngest or oldest age groups shown. The very large influx of prisoners into Valleyfield in its opening weeks as a depot appears to have overwhelmed the clerks compiling the Entry Books, since between prisoners Nos 206 and 1,071 inclusive no entry was made of either the date on which or place from which they had come, although the implication is certainly that all of those prisoners, as apparently was the case with Nos 1-205 and 1,072-2,486, came from Esk Mills. But also if it sent 2,486 prisoners to Valleyfield and 461 to Edinburgh Castle, Esk Mills must have held not 2,817 but 2,947 prisoners. TNA ADM 103/112, Nos 1-461; ADM 103/432-4, Nos 1-2,486.
31. TNA ADM 103/432, No. 750 (Brasse); and ADM 103/434, No. 2,293 (Baladier).
32. TNA ADM 103/434, No. 2,243.
33. TNA ADM 103/432, No. 213 (Floriot), ADM 103/433, No. 1,554 (Decrock), and ADM 103/434, No. 2,235 (Fleurette).
34. Vincent Failés's case illustrates the difficulties in tracing some of the prisoners or even of being sure of their identities. In Sep. 1813 the TB instructed its agent at Valleyfield to send Vincent Fitte or Fitti [sic] to Edinburgh Castle, 'in order that he may join his father, who is confined at that place.' The Valleyfield Entry Book duly records the transfer of Vincent Fairy [sic] to the Castle, but describes him as a seaman capd on the *Hebe* m.o.w. in 1809 off Bordeaux, of which city he was a native, that his age was 19, his height 5ft 4½ins, and his physical description more or less

the same as that of the 10-year-old Vincent Failés, except for having blue eyes. The Edinburgh Castle Entry Book describing him in Sep. 1813, says Vincent Fetti, aged 21 and 5ft 6 ins, was capd on *Hebe* in Feb. 1809 in the West Indies. So were the two one and the same person but made to appear not so through clerical errors in the Entry Books? TNA ADM 103/112, No. 282; ADM 98/280, ltr, 17 Sep. 1813, TB to Capt Brown; ADM 103/435, No. 5,740 (Faity); ADM 103/114, No. 1,318 (Fetti).

35. TNA ADM 103/112.

36. Ibid., No. 208.

37. TNA ADM 103/112, No. 508.

38. TNA ADM 103/432-5, and ADM 103/113, Nos 6,445-7,479. No ages for the 171 prisoners entered in it are given in the remaining Valleyfield General Entry Book, ADM 103/436, nor are they given for the first 31 of the 1,035 listed in ADM 103/113, Nos 6,445-7,479; and in the four other Entry Books (ADM 103/432-5) ages are not entered for a further 114 prisoners. On the other hand, there are approximately 29 double entries—for recapd escapers et al. The table is therefore 99 per cent accurate, on the basis of the information given in the Entry Books.

39. TNA ADM 103/432, No. 213; ADM 103/433, No. 1,554; ADM 103/434, Nos 2,235 and 3,101.

40. TNA ADM 103/432-5 passim.

41. TNA ADM 103/435, No. 4,761.

42. TNA ADM 103/434, No. 2,243.

43. TNA ADM 103/432, Nos 44, 673, 750, 950; ADM 103/434, Nos 2,203 and 2,425; ADM 103/435, Nos 5,254, 5,267, 5,258 and 5,252.

44. TNA ADM 103/435, Nos 5,243-73 and 6,394-6,419, 6,423, 6,427-30, 6,435-8. According to the *Demographic Year Book 2000* (United Nations, New York, 2002), 136-40, the expectation of life at birth of males in 2000 in virtually all the states of western and northern Europe was between 73 and 77 years (an exception was Portugal: 71.98 years). In eastern Europe, it was 68.83 years in Poland and 59.93 in the Russian Federation.

45. TNA ADM 103/263-5. The total number of prisoners listed in the Perth Entry Books, after subtracting the seven women and two little girls Lantigny, was 7,752. The total number of prisoners listed in this table is 7,739, so on the basis of the information given in the Entry Books it falls short by 13. The two totals of 7,752 and 7,739 are aggregates, which both include a very small number of duplicated entries for recapd escapers. The ages of six of the seven women listed in the Entry Books were given but have not been included in the table as the women (or at least six of the seven) were not prisoners of war.

46. TNA ADM 103/263, No. 1,161 (Nicolas Le Roy) and No. 1,160 (Antoine Le Roy).

47. TNA ADM 103/264, No. 3,072.

48. TNA ADM 103/263, Nos 427-45, 447 and 451. At Valleyfield there was a similar group of older men from the 1st Polish regt, capd also in Calabria in 1806. On the other hand, at Valleyfield also there was a group of 67 prisoners, all aged 19 (and therefore almost certainly all conscripts), who had been capd more or less on the same day at Flushing in Aug. 1809. TNA ADM 103/434, Nos 4,220-48, and ADM 103/435.

49. TNA ADM 98/128.

50. Walker, *The Depot at Norman Cross*, op. cit., 35, quoting *Notes and Queries*, 8th series, Vol. x, 197.

51. *The Life of Alexander Stewart*, op. cit., 24-5.

52. Kaald, op. cit., 120, 134, 168.

53. TNA ADM 98/170 and 98/276. The Entry Book ADM 103/152 for 'Danes' at Greenlaw gives a total of 24 boys 'Discharged as a boy under age', and two prisoners discharged as 'Old man'. Commissioner J. Douglas, TB, writing from Edinburgh to the Board's secretary, Alexander McLeay, on 4 Sep. 1812, says: 'In my letter of the 2nd I omitted to mention to the Board there are a few boys in the Prison at Valleyfield. I have desired Captain Brown [the agent there] to send a return of them, their ages, etc., as Admiral Otway [at Leith] is desirous that they may be permitted to return to France, and I suppose the Board will not object.' The Board informed the Admiral on 10 Sep. that it had directed that 'such of these Boys as are not more than 12 years of Age [are] to be put on board the *Matilda* ... in order that they may be sent to France from Plymouth.' TNA ADM 105/44 and ADM 98/279.

CHAPTER 11: RACE AND NATIONALITY

1. The other six were: John Allen, from the *Dido*, detained in Aug at the Faroe Islands, aged 25, b. in Boston, 5ft 7½ins tall; Lymus W. Little, from the *Cygnet*, capd in Aug. at the Little Belt in the Baltic, aged 32, b. at Plainfield (New Jersey, rather than Wisconsin?), 5ft 1¾ins; Nicolas Vensen and Benjamin Johnston, both from the *Cuba*, likewise capd in Aug. at the Little Belt, were aged respectively 32 and 22. Vensen, b. in New York, and Johnston, b. in Rhode Island, were both 5ft 4ins. The remaining two were James Derry and Jacob Robinson from the *Joseph Ricketson*, detained in Aug. at the Faroes, and aged respectively 28 and 21. The former was b. at Menland (?), the latter at New London (whether Connecticut or Ohio is unstated). James Derry was 5ft 7ins and had 'Left Nostril Split'; Jacob Robinson was 5ft 8ins. TNA ADM 103/157, list of American prisoners, Nos 6, 17, 31, 38, 39, 46 and 47.

2. TNA ADM 103/116, No. 642 (Smatt). Jacob Smatt appears in this Entry Book among 'Danish' prisoners and is described as aged 23, 5ft 8½ins tall; Ferdinand Antonia was 5ft 4ins, Charles Gittet 5ft 9ins. ADM 103/124, Nos 57 (Antonia) and 115 (Gittet).

3. TNA ADM 103/114, No. 1,277. Abraham Levie was aged 20, b. in Demerara, 5ft 6ins tall, and 'Scar left side of mouth'.

4. Isac Richard, aged 22, b. in Providence (whether Rhode Island or Kentucky is unstated), was 5ft 7ins. Charles Fille, b. in Philadelphia, was aged 31, and 5ft 6½ins. He was rel. in Oct. 1811 from Valleyfield and sent to France, presumably either as an invalid or an American citizen and thus of what was still then a neutral state. Jean Baptiste Moreau was aged 19, and 5ft 4ins. Moreau had been b. in New Orleans, part of the vast French colony of Louisiana until the end of the Seven Years' War in 1763 when it became a Spanish possession. Reacquired from Spain in 1800 in a secret treaty made by Napoleon as part of his plan to create a new French colonial empire in America, Louisiana was, however, sold off in Apr. 1803 by Napoleon to the United States for 12 million dollars (or 55 million francs), his attempt to reconquer St Domingo (Haiti) as an essential first step in his American expansionist policy having meantime been defeated by the resistance of the former black slaves on the island, led by Toussaint L'Ouverture and his successors. Other factors in Napoleon's

decision to sell Louisiana were the imminent prospect of renewed war with Britain, the likelihood that British naval superiority would result in the loss by France of New Orleans and indeed Louisiana, the attraction of receiving so much cash for the sale at such a time, and the possibility that without the sale the United States might draw closer to Britain. Whether these historic events meant that Jean Baptiste Moreau at Valleyfield was a French, Spanish, or American subject or citizen is not clear but perhaps it became so by the time he departed from the depot in the general release of prisoners in Jun. 1814. ADM 103/432, Nos 942 (Richard), 949 (Fille), and 1,039 (Moreau); S. E. Morison and H. S. Commager, *The Growth of the American Republic* Vol. I: 1000-1865 (New York, 1962), 379-81; Bernard DeVoto (ed.), *The Journals of Lewis and Clark* (Boston, 1997), xxviii-xxxii. Dominique Chartran was himself b. in Martinique. He was aged 22, at 6ft unusually tall among the prisoners. His description as 'Mulatto' occurs in the Entry Book under the heading not of Marks and Wounds but Visage and Complexion. He remained at Valleyfield until the general release in Jun. 1814. Charles Soil, aged 28, was another American, b. in Philadelphia, and 5ft 7ins. François Julien, b. in St Domingo (Haiti) was aged 27, and 5ft 4ins. Both Charles Soil and François Julien left Valleyfield in order to enter the RN, Soil in Aug. 1811, Julien in May 1812. TNA ADM 103/433, Nos 1,463 (Chartran) and 1,111 (Soil); ADM 103/434, No. 2,419 (Julien).

5.   Abell, op. cit., 352; TNA ADM 98/203, ADM 98/279, and ADM 103/435, No. 6,324; Macbeth Forbes, 'The French Prisoners-of-War in the Border Towns', op. cit., 18. A list compiled by Macbeth Forbes a century ago apparently from an Entry Book for parole prisoners at Hawick in the TB archives in the TNA (which Book, however, if it did survive then, along with those for several other parole towns in Scotland, appears no longer to be available) gives Ile de France (Mauritius) as Antoine Figaro's birthplace and 16 as his age in 1812. Macbeth Forbes's list is in NAS GD1/405/1.

6.   TNA ADM 103/265, No. 4,722.

7.   TNA ADM 103/112, No. 486, and ADM 103/157, No. 294.

8.   TNA ADM 1/3744. Colonel Lebertre, a French parole prisoner who escaped in 1811 from Alresford but was recapd and sent as a punishment to the *Canada* hulk at Chatham, complained that 'officers in the hulks were placed on a level with common prisoners, and even with negroes'. His complaint was taken up personally by Napoleon, who in 1802 had reintroduced slavery in the French colonies after its abolition (only sporadically implemented, however) eight years earlier by the French Revolutionary Convention. At Dartmoor, white American prisoners successfully petitioned early in 1814 that 'the blacks should be confined by themselves as they were dirty by habit and thieves by nature'. There, too, a black general was confined, having been refused parole because of the colour of his skin. At Portchester Castle the black prisoner Garçon Baptiste gave as his reason for informing the authorities about a projected mass rising of the prisoners that the French among them were 'very hostile to the Blacks and Americans, and that in the event of a general rising he has but very little doubt but they would put them all to death.' Abell, op. cit., 75, 251; Macbeth Forbes, 'French Prisoners of War in Scotland, and Bank Note Forging', op. cit., 395; Thomson, *Dartmoor*, op. cit., 17, 114; Georges Lefebvre, *The French Revolution from 1793 to 1799* (London, 1964), 130; Lefebvre, *Napoleon* Vol. I, op. cit., 171.

9.   Prisoners taken at the capitulation harboured a well justified grievance which was expressed in their petitions to the TB for years afterward. The terms of the capitulation

had provided for the shipment of the surrendered troops to Europe. The prisoners believed this meant they were being transported home to France—but Europe included Britain, and it was into captivity in Britain they discovered en voyage that they were being sent. Of the eleven transport ships on which the prisoners sailed from Jamaica, 'ostensibly for Morlaix' in France, as the TB later explained to the Adm., seven arrived in Britain. Two of the eleven were wrecked on the coast of America (where the prisoners on one of them were said to have 'dispersed'). On another of the vessels the prisoners seized control when they learned how they had been deceived 'and [it] was carried into France by the prisoners there detained'. When the remaining vessel was wrecked at Havana in Cuba the prisoners on it were transferred to another ship 'but this vessel proving leaky on her passage to Europe, all the prisoners and crew were taken out of her by a French cruiser which fell in with her, and the crew are still detained as prisoners of war.' TNA ADM 98/112, ltr, 3 Mar. 1806, TB to William Marsden, secretary, Adm.

10. Beaudoin, op. cit., 221-4, 273-5.

11. Paul Andreas Kaald, the Norwegian priv. captain at Greenlaw, confided to his diary on 11 Jul. 1809, for example: '31 French prisoners left here for Sheerness—only 21 [of them] are now left.' Kaald, op. cit., 118.

12. TNA ADM 103/263, No. 1,256.

13. The seven Greenlaw Entry Books, although each contains ostensibly one nationality, illustrate this point.

14. One historian of the subject says more of these prisoners in Britain as a whole were Norwegians than Danes. Carl Roos, *Prisonen Danske og Norske krigsfanger i England 1807-1814* (Copenhagen, 1953), 20.

15. A TB letter of 7 Jul. 1810 to the Adm. said there were then 2,104 Danish prisoners in Britain; and a TO return in Jun. 1812 shows a total of 1,832. TNA ADM 98/116; Walker, *The Depot at Norman Cross*, op. cit., 202.

16. TNA ADM 103/152 and 103/153.

17. *EEC*, 6 Apr. 1807; *CM*, 9 Apr. 1807. Even earlier, there were also 32 prisoners who proved to be 'From the King of Denmark's dominions', then a neutral state, among the 87 taken in Aug. 1803 on board what were described as three Dutch Greenland ships and who were sent then into confinement at Fort George.

18. TNA ADM 103/112, No. 4; ADM 103/435, No. 5,254.

19. TNA ADM 103/263, No. 1,134; ADM 103/432, No. 19.

20. Derry, *Scandinavia*, op. cit., 205-6.

21. TNA ADM 1/3760, ltr, 10 Apr. 1810, TB to J.W. Croker, secretary, Adm.; ADM 103/152, Nos 43 (Christian), 54 (Gero), 548 (Johanesen).

22. TNA ADM 98/277, ltr, 14 Mar. 1811, TB to Lieut. Priest.

23. Kaald, op. cit., 142-3. The Greenlaw Entry Book for 'Danes', TNA ADM 103/152, Nos 748-59, lists 12 prisoners who arrived that day, capd by *Fancy* on the m.v. *Diana*. The 12 were a second mate, a carpenter, four seamen-passengers, and six seamen. One seaman, Johannes Nickesen, was released from Greenlaw almost a year later, on 31 Oct. 1811, 'as a boy under age'. The other 11 were dischgd on 19 Sep. 1811—but to where is not stated in the Entry Book.

24. TNA HO 28/40, ltr, 3 Oct. 1811, Adm. to J. Beckett, HO.

25. TNA ADM 103/153, Nos 78, 114-20, 358-60, 373-4, 379-80. The absence of places of birth for many of the other 'Danes' in that Entry Book, and of all such information

in the smaller format Entry Book ADM 103/152 for 'Danes', makes it likely that the actual number born in Shetland was considerably more than 15.

26. TNA ADM 1/3743, fols 317-19 and 379-82, correspondence, 25-30 Aug and 7 and 14 Sep. 1803, between TB, Adm., and WO. See also Appendix 7 above.

27. TNA ADM 103/152, Nos 110, 115, 124, 133, 140, 196 and 696; ADM 103/115, Nos 30-1, 90-3, and 114-16; ADM 103/155, Nos 367, 374, 379, 381, 386, 390, 396; ADM 98/117, ltr, 30 Mar. 1811, TB to Adm., concerning four Swedes at Valleyfield: P.J. Eikman, Joseph Salin, Mathias Castelin and Peter Askelund (or Askland); ADM 98/279, ltr, 12 Sep. 1812, TB to Capt. Brown, agent, Valleyfield, concerning Mathias Castelin and two other Swedes there, Eric Murberg and Carl Sandill; ADM 103/432, Nos 526 M. Castelin (who was 'Delivered over to Swedish Consul', 28 Jul. 1813) and 952 Jan Alstas, dischgd to Leith in Oct. 1811, presumably for release home; ADM 103/433, No. 1,685, Charles Sandel (Carl Sandill?), a seaman who, though his place of birth was said to be Strasbourg, was also 'Delivered over to Swedish Consul' on 28 Jul. 1813. For further details of these Swedish prisoners see Appendix 7.

28. The release of the four Swedish prisoners at Valleyfield (P.J. Eikman, Joseph Salin, M. Castelin, and Peter Askelund), for instance, was sought by Mr Grill. In Sep. 1812 the Board, in a circular to all its depot agents, directed them 'to permit M. Claes Grill … together with a Swedish clergyman, to visit the prisoners in your custody in order to ascertain whether any Swedish subjects are confined whom it may be proper to restore to their country, taking care that they be as is usual in similar cases accompanied by an officer of this Department.' TNA ADM 98/170, 5 Sep. 1812. An Edinburgh merchant named Robert Wight had been appointed Swedish vice-consul at Leith and for other ports on the Firth of Forth early in 1805. Although no other mention of him by name has been found (except that on 31 Oct. 1807 the *Caledonian Mercury* reported Wight had been instructed by the Swedish government 'to supply with necessaries of every kind the Swedish frigate which conveys His Majesty Louis XVIII [of France] to this country'), it may be it was Wight at Leith rather than Grill in London to whom released Swedes were 'delivered over' from the depots in Scotland. *Glasgow Courier*, 21 Feb. 1805. *CM*, 24 Mar. 1808, reported that 'the Swedish Consul is collecting all the straggling Swedish seamen he can find in order to send them home to man the fleets of their magnanimous Sovereign'; and the same paper three months later on 23 Jun. reported that 'Thirteen Swedes, who were lately taken on board of a privateer, have been liberated from the depot at Greenlaw and are to go immediately to Gottenburgh.' There are also references in TB correspondence in Jan. 1811 with Malcolm Wright, its agent at Edinburgh, to Swedes at Greenlaw who had volunteered to serve in His Britannic Majesty's navy, but their names and number were unstated. TNA ADM 98/276, 12 and 28 Jan. 1811.

29. For details of these Finns see Appendix 7.

30. A request to the Adm. by the Prussian consul for the release of the Prussian subjects at Fort George was the subject of a note dated 18 Nov. 1803 from Sir Evan Nepean, secretary, Adm., to the TB concerning those of the 87 prisoners still held at the Fort: '… discharge such of the prisoners as appear to be subjects of neutral states and were not taken in arms.' TNA ADM 1/3744.

31. *EEC*, 12 Jul. 1804.

32. A letter of 11 Jun. 1806 from TB to Adm., acknowledging the latter's instructions that 'the crews of all the Prussian ships detained in the ports of Scotland be re-

moved to ... Greenlaw', added: '... it appears that the said crews are a mixture of the different northern Continental states'. The three Oldenburgers (Karl Dohnan, G. Bargending, and H. Meyer) among the 'Prussians' were released from Greenlaw on 7 Dec. 1806. TNA ADM 1/3749, fol. 61; ADM 1/3751, fol. 105.

33.   Kaald, op. cit., 113. The Prussian (No. 514 in ADM 103/152, an Entry Book of 'Danes') was Jan de Rymer, seaman, aged 23, capd off Jutland, Apr. 1809. De Rymer was one of the Germans whose arrival at Greenlaw six days earlier was noted by Kaald. See also the official proforma, signed by M. Wright, agent, Greenlaw, of de Rymer's death, in TNA ADM 103/648.

34.   TNA ADM 103/153, No. 413

35.   TNA ADM 103/112, No. 534.

36.   TNA ADM 103/433, Nos 1,563 (Vandenberg) and 1,574 (Sprenger).

37.   TNA ADM 103/113, Nos 6,445-6,648.

38.   TNA ADM 103/435, No. 5,380; Edmund Burke, *Reflections on the French Revolution* (London, 1905 ed.), 71.

39.   TNA ADM 98/170, circular, 12 Mar. 1813; ADM 98/121, ltr, 10 Jul. 1813, TB to Adm.; ADM 98/134, ltr, 23 Aug. 1813, TB to Maj. Gen. Darling, Horse Guards.

40.   TNA ADM 103/263, Nos 121-299.

41.   Ibid., No. 2,100

42.   Ibid., No. 2,077.

43.   Ibid., No. 1,193.

44.   Owen Connelly, *Napoleon's Satellite Kingdoms* (New York, 1969), 50-2. Connelly points out that no fewer than 30,000 Italian troops fought in the Peninsular War in Spain and Portugal, of whom only 9,000 survived. Oman, *Peninsular War*, Vol. I, op. cit., 105-6, mentions that, for instance, between Oct. 1807 and May 1808 four bns of Italians and two of Neapolitans (i.e., from the kingdom of Naples) formed part of the French forces in Spain and Portugal, and these six bns formed a complete division in the army of Catalonia. Some of the cavalry regts were then also composed of Italians and Neapolitans.

45.   TNA ADM 103/157, Nos 700, 659, 305, and passim; ADM 103/110, No. 575 (Savasse—whose first name is given there as Philippe, not Pierre, and who is said to have been capd at Vigo in Mar. 1809); ADM 103/112, No. 508 (Castel). A report in *CM* on 17 Mar. 1814, however, appears to refer to Valleyfield at 'Pennycuick', rather than to Greenlaw: '... about 700 prisoners arrived [at Leith on the three preceding days] from the depots at Pennycuick and Perth. They consist of Savoyards, Piedmontese, Sardinians, Genoese, Neapolitans, etc. They are to be sent to their own countries to join their countrymen in arms against the French.'

46.   TNA ADM 103/113, No. 7,272; ADM 103/114, No. 1,315; ADM 103/436, No. 7,631.

47.   TNA ADM 103/114, No. 1,355. The Perth Entry Book ADM 103/263, No. 1,129, gives Le Prince's rank as adjutant major, shows he had come in Sep. 1812 to Perth from Greenlaw and was dischgd in Aug. 1813 to Valleyfield. The Valleyfield Entry Book ADM 103/113, No. 7,273, says Le Prince was an Aide Major and became a prisoner at the capitulation of General Dupont's army at Baylen, Jul. 1808. ADM 105/53, Register of Prisoners' Applications, includes one dated Edinburgh 19 Apr. 1811 from Le Prince, described as an adjutant major in the Calabrian Guards, asking for parole: 'He enjoyed his parole at Malta but was deprived of it for sleeping out of

his room one night.' Le Prince was confined successively in every depot in Scotland between Mar. 1811, when he had originally arr. at Esk Mills from Portsmouth on HMS *Gorgon*, and Nov. 1813, when he was returned whence he had come. ADM 103/124, No. 2,222; ADM 103/110, No. 141.

48. TNA ADM 98/170, 12 Mar. 1813; ADM 98/121, 10 Jul. 1813.

49. TNA ADM 103/432-5 passim. There was some doubt expressed in the Valleyfield Entry Book ADM 103/435 about one prisoner ostensibly born in Sicily—No. 6,205 Jean Claude Morin, aged 22, soldier, 66th Regt, capd near Talavera, Jun. 1812, and who had arr. at Valleyfield in Nov. that year from Greenlaw: 'Place of Nativity Sicilly—Doubtful. Calls himself a frenchman.' Whatever his place of birth, Morin continued his peregrinations with his transfer in Aug. 1813 from Valleyfield to Perth.

50. TNA ADM 103/432, No. 121.

51. TNA ADM 103/434, No. 2,871 (Tépateau); ADM 103/433, Nos 1,888 (Guariano), 2,065 (Signori) and 2,103 (Robiche).

52. TNA ADM 103/434, No. 2,172.

53. TNA ADM 103/263-6 passim.

54. TNA ADM 103/263, No. 1,179; ADM 103/435, No. 5,383; ADM 103/114, No. 1,343.

55. TNA ADM 103/263, No. 577.

56. Ibid., No. 404.

57. TNA ADM 103/265, No. 4,564.

58. TNA ADM 105/54, Register of Prisoners' Applications.

59. TNA ADM 103/263, No. 932.

60. TNA ADM 103/154.

61. For example, in the 'Danes' Entry Book TNA ADM 103/152, three prisoners were repatriated from Greenlaw to Rotterdam; and in the 'French' Entry Book ADM 103/157 were entered the five Dutch seamen capd on the retaken prize vessel *Fame* at North Queensferry in Oct. 1811. Moreover, at Greenlaw were briefly confined until their repatriation (apart from those who volunteered to join His Britannic Majesty's forces) 159 or so officers and crew of the Dutch frig. *Utrecht*, shipwrecked in Feb. 1807 on Sanday in Orkney.

62. TNA ADM 103/157, No. 359 (Bernick).

63. TNA ADM 103/648, No. 859.

64. TNA ADM 98/277, ltrs, 13 Aug. 1811, TB to Admiral Otway, Capt. Heddington and Lieut. Priest.

65. TNA ADM 103/114, Nos 1,258 (Bontaus), 1,260 (Latx), 1,262, 1,265, 1,267, 1,269, 1,270, 1,273, 1,275-7 (1,276: Hoft), 1,279, 1,286, 1,309.

66. TNA ADM 103/432-4, Valleyfield Entry Books, Nos 1-2,486 passim.

67. TNA ADM 103/432, No. 271 (Gronewoud); ADM 103/433, Nos 1,355 (Van Weltingen), 1,358 (Vilser/Fisher), and 1,983 (Happers).

68. TNA ADM 103/434, No. 310.

69. Ibid., Nos 3,086 (Press), 3,146 (B. Schmidt) and 3,142 (J. Schmidt).

70. TNA ADM 103/435, Nos 4,830 (Jansens), 6,423 (Vanderham) and 5,260 (Gosling).

71. TNA ADM 103/267, bundles 37, 41 and 42 passim. It appears certain, however, that

a number of those 149 'Dutch' prisoners, as well as some others likewise released from other Scots depots for that purpose in those months, were in fact Belgians or Flemings.

72. TNA ADM 103/263, Nos 813 (Vanherff) and 931 (Kaiserlich).

73. Another was Pierre Digurt, capd in Aug. 1803 on m.v. *La Flore*, who volunteered into the RN in Jul. 1804 from Greenlaw. TNA ADM 103/155, No. 37.

74. TNA ADM 103/263, Nos 1,158 (Prucenar), 1,163 (Volbracht), 1,198 (Amand/Hams), 6,999 (Jansens).

75. *EEC*, 25 Oct. 1803.

76. TNA ADM 105/45, Nos 693 (Colas) and 695 (Brown).

77. TNA ADM 103/114, No. 1,317; ADM 103/266, No. 7,541. In the Perth Entry Book Colas was said to have been capd on the m.o.w. *Manilla* at Rochefort, 1809, his p.o.b. Senny.

78. TNA ADM 103/433, No. 1,948.

79. TNA ADM 103/435, Nos 4,829 (Destroop) and 4,831 (Rottiers).

80. TNA ADM 103/264, No. 3,072.

81. TNA ADM 103/265, No. 4,755.

82. TNA ADM 103/158, Nos 1 (Gomes), 22 (Crevis), 38 (Costes) and 44 (Detarre).

83. TNA ADM 103/624, No. 215.

84. TNA 103/155, Nos 163 (Bages), 167 (Rodriguez), 170 (Issou), 223 (Delavrou).

85. TNA ADM 103/157. The prisoner b. in Cartagena was No. 310 Joseph Pero, seaman, aged 37, capd on *Le Figaro* priv. in the North Sea, Jul. 1811. Arr. at Greenlaw from Edinburgh Castle in Aug. 1811 Pero was rel. three months later as a volunteer into the British navy.

86. TNA ADM 103/115. The 68 are entered in this curious Entry Book between the first group of 620 evidently French prisoners and the following group of 132 'Prussians'.

87. TNA ADM 103/112 passim.

88. TNA ADM 103/432-5 and ADM 103/113 passim.

89. TNA ADM 103/434, No. 2,472.

90. TNA ADM 103/433, No. 1,801 (Fourcholle); ADM 103/435, No. 5,662 (Columba). Although Spain was from summer 1808 an ally of Britain, Spanish prisoners could be found in the depots until the end of the war. Some were *Juramentados*—Spanish sympathisers with or supporters of the French and recruited to King Joseph Bonaparte's regts but who had been capd by British or allied troops. In Oct. 1813, at the end of the Peninsular War, a survey by the TB showed there were then 257 Spanish soldiers and sailors in the depots, of whom 176 were *Juramentados*. There were then at Valleyfield two soldiers and four sailors, but whether any of those six were *Juramentados* is not clear. TNA ADM 98/122, ltr, 18 Oct. 1813, TB to Adm.

91. TNA ADM 103/432, No. 221.

92. TNA ADM 103/263, No. 773.

93. Ibid., No. 934 (Maria Martin); ADM 103/265, No. 5,611 (Marie Manuel).

94. TNA ADM 103/156, Nos 117-23, 127-8.

95. TNA ADM 103/433, Nos 1,493 (Libare), 1,107 (Showwisky), and 1,636 (Pooloski).

96. TNA ADM 103/434, No. 3,158.

97. TNA ADM 103/435, No. 6,323.
98. TNA ADM 103/434, Nos 3,801 and 4,220-48. Foutz appears to exemplify two characteristics of many Polish soldier prisoners in Scots depots: their greater than average age and height. The ages of 30 Polish prisoners from the 1st Regt at Valleyfield were: 25 (1), 29 (3), 30 (1), 34 (1), 35 (2), 36 (1), 38 (3), 40 (5), 43 (1), 45 (1), 46 (2), 48 (1), 49 (1), 50 (4), 51 (1), 55 (1), 56 (1).
99. TNA ADM 103/263, Nos 427-45, 447 and 451.
100. TNA ADM 103/263, Nos 481 (Cowalsky) and 614 (Patersky).
101. Traditionally a provider of mercenary troops to foreign states, Switzerland, by a convention made with Napoleon in 1803, had agreed to provide France with four infantry regts, each of 4,000 men, and not to provide troops to any other state. Between Oct. 1807 and May 1808 Napoleon sent no fewer than seven bns of Swiss troops into Spain, where eventually some of them fought against Wellington's army. Some 7,000 Swiss troops took part in the Grande Armée's invasion of Russia in 1812-13. Numbers of other Swiss served from 1810 in the French 11th Light Infantry regt. Swiss troops who had been serving in the Spanish army until 1808 were transferred by the end of that year into the French regt Royal Etranger which was serving in Spain. Wellington, writing to Admiral Berkeley at Lisbon on 19 Aug. 1810, pointed out 'the surrender by capitulation of a Swiss battalion at La Puebla de Sanabria. This battalion, consisting of about 450 men, including officers, has been marched to Corunna, from whence it is desirable that they should be removed to England at an early period.' Elting, *Swords Around a Throne*, op. cit., 375-8; Oman, *Peninsular War*, op. cit., Vol. I, 105, and Vol. II, 2; *Wellington's Despatches*, ed. Gurwood, op. cit., Vol. VI, 343.
102. Another possible indication was, of course, the membership of some prisoners of specifically Swiss regts—although not every man who served in a Swiss regt was necessarily Swiss (any more than, as has been seen above, every soldier in the Irish Bn or Legion of the French army was Irish).
103. TNA ADM 103/433, No. 1,120.
104. TNA ADM 103/156, Nos 89-107. Blatter was No. 93, Scheurmann No. 104.
105. TNA ADM 103/124, No. 2,084; ADM 103/157, No. 52; ADM 103/435, No. 5,651; ADM 103/266, No. 7,092.
106. TNA ADM 103/113, No. 1,312; ADM 103/266, No. 6,896; ADM 103/600, No. 96.
107. TNA ADM 103/432, No. 346 (L'Amy); ADM 103/433, Nos 1,699 and 6,325 (Choulie), Nos 1,741 and 7,408 (Elie).
108. TNA ADM 103/435, No. 5,112.
109. TNA ADM 103/263, No. 944. Though he addressed his letter from 'Edinburgh Prison' and gave his prison number as 1,667, it appears to have been Guchant who wrote in English ('... as I can speak, write and read the English tongue well enough') on the day of his arrival at Perth to the agent there, seeking employment as a hospital nurse or storekeeper at the depot, or as a servant to the agent himself, and adding in a postscript: 'Native from Basle in Switzerland and written down as a Frenchman by mistake of the French Clarks when I entered in prison.' NLS MS Acc. 5811/1/17. Guchant may well not have been the only Swiss prisoner in a Scots depot whose nationality was incorrectly set down in the Entry Books as French.
110. TNA ADM 103/263, Nos 999 (Mudri) and 2,108 (Ridon); ADM 103/648, No. 2,108.

111. TNA ADM 103/263, No. 750, shows one to have been W. Kanigh, soldier, 4th German Bn, capd on 29 May 1812 at Almera Bridge, who was aged 30 and arr. via HMS *Regulus* from Portsmouth on 20 or 21 Aug. 1812 at Perth and remained there until transferred on 29 Jul. 1813 to Valleyfield. TNA ADM 103/434, No. 3,832, Juste Artrue, soldier, 'French Army', was another possible Austrian, born like Kanigh at Vienna. Capd 13 Aug. 1809 at Flushing, he was aged 34, arr. via HMS *Diadem* at Valleyfield on 1 Oct. 1811 and was repatriated the following Aug. to France.

112. TNA ADM 103/434, No. 4,167.

113. TNA ADM 103/432, No. 494 (Bronzan); ADM 103/433, No. 1,107 (Vocowihi).

114. TNA ADM 105/53.

115. TNA ADM 103/432, Nos 549-59. The other ten also all had Italian rather than Greek names, and all of them had been born in such unGreek places as Turin, Ancona, Pavia and Modena.

116. TNA ADM 103/114, No. 1,018.

117. TNA ADM 103/432, No. 499 (Pereri); ADM 103/433, Nos 1,827 (Espira Selencia), 1,828 (Andria Bastianela), and 1,830 (Gregorio Antonio).

118. TNA ADM 103/263, No. 783; ADM 103/113, No. 6,664.

119. TNA ADM 103/265, No. 6,498 (Filiare); ADM 103/264, No. 3,636 (Brasseur); ADM 103/648, No. 3,636.

120. See above, Appendix 2, No.12.

121. TNA ADM 103/432, No. 914.

122. TNA ADM 103/433, No. 1,421.

123. TNA ADM 105/53, Nos 311 and 341.

124. TNA ADM 1/3763, fols 279-81; ADM 103/157.

125. TNA ADM 1/3765, fols 480 and 484.

126. TNA ADM 103/433, No. 1,427.

127. TNA ADM 98/280.

128. TNA ADM 98/276.

129. Johnston, 'Recollections', op. cit., p.2.

130. TNA ADM 105/54, No. 208.

131. See above, e.g., pp.121, 178.

132. TNA ADM 103/433, Nos 1,371 (Nicolson) and 1,374 (Bays).

133. TNA ADM 103/157, No. 196.

134. TNA ADM 103/432, Nos 713 (Lerouge) and 220 (Jongh).

135. TNA ADM 103/112, No. 492 (Jozé); ADM 103/114, No. 1,277 (Levie).

136. TNA ADM 103/110, Nos 152 and 681.

137. TNA ADM 103/112, No. 483.

138. TNA ADM 103/263, No. 948.

139. TNA ADM 105/54, No. 290.

140. TNA ADM 103/434, No. 2,395.

141. TNA ADM 103/112, No. 517.

142. TNA ADM 103/265, No. 4,722.

143. TNA ADM 105/54, No. 310.

144. TNA ADM 103/157, No. 315.

145. TNA ADM 103/433, No. 1,777.
146. TNA ADM 103/432, No. 551.
147. TNA ADM 103/433, No. 1,836.
148. TNA ADM 103/263; ADM 103/266.
149. TNA ADM 103/157, No. 695 (Brown); ADM 103/124, No. 1,589 (Lewis), and ADM 103/432, No. 781 (Lewis); ADM 103/124, No. 1,158 (Simon); ADM 103/433, No. 1,371 (Nicolson); ADM 1/3745, ltr, 5 Jun. 1804, TB to W. Marsden, Adm. One with a distinctively Irish name has been found among the prisoners in Scotland—he was, however, not in a closed depot but on parole: H. Fitzgerald, a surgeon, capd in 1809 on the naval vessel *L'Aquillon* and who was among the first prisoners to arrive at Kelso in Nov. 1810, but about whom nothing more is known. There is some contradiction in the surviving sources concerning another parole prisoner in Scotland with a possibly Irish surname: François Conor, midshipman, capd in 1808 on *Neptune* m.o.w., spent a year at Peebles, was then transferred in Nov. 1811 to Dumfries, and from there four months later to Sanquhar. But in a letter of 30 Mar. 1812 to James (father of William) Chambers at Peebles, a French parole prisoner at Dumfries named L. Motin referred to the recent transfer to Sanquhar of 'our friends Walther and O'Conor [sic]'. It may appear likely Motin would know the spelling of the latter's name better than the parole agents at those towns. TNA ADM 103/581, No. 63 (Fitzgerald); ADM 103/596, No. 29 (Conor), ADM 103/599, No. 63 (Conor), NLS MS Dep. 341/29 (O'Conor). At Valleyfield, among the dozen captives from the Irish Bn were: Carlo Widekind, Larenth Klasovsky, and Mathew Kitzlerost—men perhaps likely to have been more familiar with Lublin than Dublin. See ADM 103/434, Nos. 2,890-2,900, and No. 3,758 (Kitzlerost). In a paper preserved in TNA ADM 105/61 and headed 'The cases of seven Irishmen and three Englishmen taken as French prisoners at the surrender of Flushing [in 1809] and now confined on board the *Sampson* prison ship at Chatham', one of the seven Irishmen, Robert McCagae, gives an account of his experiences that were no doubt similar to those of many other Irish rebels exiled following the failure of the 1798 rebellion: 'I was banished from Ireland the 1st May 1798, was sent to the King of Prussia, remained there six years; was taken by the French; ran from them [perhaps at or following the battles of Iena and Auerstadt against the Prussians in Oct. 1806] and went to the Austrians, where I remained two years and a half; the 23 April last [1809, following the re-entry that month of Austria into war against France] was taken by the French and sent forcibly to Flushing, was eleven days there before the English landed. Had no arms or cloaths at that time. When the town surrendered was marched out with the rest of the [French] troops.' A note at the bottom of McCagae's statement says he 'has a wife with him, a native of Prussia.' One of the three Englishmen captured at Flushing, William Salter, states: 'I belonged to the [British] 23rd Regiment of Foot; was taken [prisoner] at Corunna the 15 January 1809, marched into France, from then to Flushing the 27 of July 1809. They wished to make me join a [French] Regiment. I refused and they put me in prison. Remained there till the 16 of August when the English took possession. Was marched out as a prisoner of war. [I] Had no arms.'

CHAPTER 12: MARKS OR WOUNDS; HEIGHTS, AND ALIASES

1. See, e.g., Forrest, *Conscripts and Deserters*, op. cit., 136-7.
2. TNA ADM 103/266, No. 6,631.

3. TNA ADM 103/434, No. 2,818, and ADM 103/266, No. 7,695.

4. TNA ADM 103/434, No. 3,141.

5. TNA ADM 103/157, No. 60.

6. TNA ADM 103/435, No. 5,304.

7. *Glasgow Courier*, 3 Nov. 1804.

8. Louis Bergeron, *France under Napoleon* (Princeton, 1981), 112.

9. Elting, *Swords Around a Throne*, op. cit., 292, 293.

10. Abell, op. cit., 86, 254; Thomson, *Dartmoor*, op. cit., 133; Crowhurst, *French War on Trade*, op. cit., 190.

11. TNA ADM 103/157 passim, and ADM 103/153 passim.

12. TNA ADM 103/124, Nos 1-192.

13. TNA ADM 103/112 passim.

14. TNA ADM 103/114 passim.

15. TNA ADM 103/432-5 passim; ADM 103/113, Nos 6,445-7,479 passim; ADM 103/263-6 passim.

16. Elting, *Swords Around a Throne*, op. cit., 323, 210, 186, 209.

17. TNA ADM 103/157, Nos 1-359, 361-761.

18. TNA ADM 103/116.

19. Ibid., Nos 464 (Larsen), 887 (Olsen).

20. TNA ADM 103/435, No. 4,836.

21. See above, pp.170, 172, 173.

22. TNA ADM 103/434, Nos 3,280 (Giraux) and 3,597 (Landria).

23. For the heights of prisoners at Perth see the depot's four Entry Books TNA ADM 103/263-6 passim.

24. TNA ADM 103/264, No. 2,411.

25. TNA ADM 103/263, No. 1,161 (Nicholas Le Roy); ADM 103/265, No. 4,834 (Gabriel Legrand); ADM 103/264, No. 3,248 (August Devot); ADM 103/266, No. 6,539 (Nicolas Dausseur). Nicolas Dausseur may not have been the shortest prisoner at Perth. Pierre Peraulaun, soldier, 40th infantry regt, capd at Rio de Molino on 28 Oct. 1811, and who arr. at Perth on 9 Jan. 1813 on HMS *Freya* from the prison hulk *Veteran* at Portsmouth, is clearly described in the Entry Book as being 2ft 8½ins in height. Was this a clerical error and Peraulaun's height should perhaps have read 5ft, 4ft, or even 3ft 8½ins? Aged 26, b. at Caramant, and described as well made, with a round face, sallow complexion, brown hair, hazel eyes, and with 'Wounded Calf Right Leg', Peraulaun remained in captivity at Perth until rel. in Jun. 1814 after the end of the war. TNA ADM 103/265, No. 5,567; Crowhurst, *French War on Trade*, op. cit., 180.

26. TNA ADM 103/155, Nos 157 (Gillevere) and 158 (Gerrin).

27. TNA ADM 103/124, Nos 35 (Petit), 757 (Mascara), 1,631 (Lecheneau), 1,651 (Sepinetly), 1,804 (Scagliano), 2,198 (Billiard), and 2,427 (Barbel); ADM 103/487 (Petit).

28. TNA ADM 103/114, No. 1,145; ADM 103/113, No. 7,396.

29. TNA ADM 103/432, No. 494.

30. TNA ADM 103/433, Nos 1,708 (Chuchère), 1,358 (Vilser); ADM 103/434, No. 3,527, and ADM 103/436, No. 7,650 (Destrais).

31. TNA ADM 103/434, Nos 2,211 (Mathieu) and 2,395 (Jofroi).

32. TNA ADM 103/264, No. 2,723 (Lavy), ADM 103/266, No. 7,206 (Mouszin), and No. 6,805 (Vigneron).

33. TNA ADM 103/266, No. 7,240.

CHAPTER 13: BEDS AND BEDDING, AND CLOTHING

1. Lewis, *Social History of the Navy*, op. cit., 271.

2. NAS GD1/405/2.

3. Kaald, op. cit., 86, 88, 90.

4. *Kelso Mail*, 14 Mar. 1811.

5. Sievewright, *Depot at Perth*, op. cit., 4, 6. Overcrowding was not unique to depots in Scotland. On at least the *Bahama* hulk at Chatham, and at Dartmoor and Millbay depots, the most demoralised among the prisoners, many with little or no clothing or bedding, huddled closely together on the deck or floor in the 'spoon fashion' mentioned by Sievewright. At midnight every night an officer on duty shouted out the order, 'Turn to your right side.' Then at 3 a.m. he shouted, 'Turn to your left side.' Abell, op. cit., 59, 60, 229, 245. Louis Garneray, a French seaman capd in 1806 who developed his talents as a painter during his eight years of captivity and became a professional artist after the war, was imprisoned at Portsmouth successively on the hulks *Prothée*, *Crown* and *Vengeance*. In his memoirs Garneray described sleeping conditions on the *Prothée* thus: 'As we were nearly four hundred on each deck and as each deck was only 130 feet long by 40 feet wide and 6 feet high at the most, hammocks could not be slung in a single row; so half of them had to be slung above the others. The richer prisoners had a kind of swinging cradle made for them on which they could place a mattress, and so they made sure of a certain amount of comfort, but they still had to put up with the stench and with the vermin ... At six in the morning in summer and eight in winter the warders opened the scuttles and portholes, but the air by this time had become so foul from the great number of prisoners breathing it that as soon as their round was done they retreated hastily to avoid the pestilential stench. In summer they sometimes left them open, to save us from utter suffocation.' Louis Garneray, *The French prisoner.* Trans. by Lawrence Wood (London, 1957), 7, 8. 'If we were to look inside,' wrote an historian of Dartmoor depot, 'we should find on every floor five hundred men packed into the space now [i.e., a century later, in 1907, in the civil prison there] allotted to forty. Two alleyways run from end to end, and on either side of them the hammocks are stretched taut from hooks let into a stout timber framing—three tiers, closely packed together.' Thomson, *Dartmoor*, op. cit., 63. When there were as many as 6,000 prisoners or more in Norman Cross, the prison buildings, each block of which was 100 feet long by 22 feet wide, 'were absolutely packed, 300 in the lower chambers, which were 12 feet high, and 200 in the upper chambers, the height of which was 8 feet 6 inches.' The prisoners there slept in hammocks arranged in three tiers in the lower and more lofty of the rooms, one above the other, and suspended between posts 8 feet apart; and in two tiers in the upper room, where the roof was below the regulation height for three tiers. Two feet in width appears to have been allowed for each hammock. Walker, *The Depot at Norman Cross*, op. cit., 90, 91. When at Portchester Castle depot the number of prisoners increased the shortage of sleeping space obliged some to lie nightly not in hammocks but on straw on the floor. *Hampshire Notes and Queries* (Winchester, 1900), Vol. X, 74. For many, even most, of the prisoners of war in the depots in Scotland

and England overcrowded sleeping conditions were no doubt not a new experience, although not such a prolonged one as in the depots. In Napoleon's armies regulations prescribed a maximum of two soldiers per bed. Elting, *Swords Around a Throne*, op. cit., 587. That 'Soldier of the Empire', Captain Jean-Roch Coignet of the Imperial Guard, when in 1803 first admitted as a new rank and file grenadier to that corps, although he was marginally under the regulation height, shared a bed with a regimental comrade who was six feet four inches tall. *The Note-Books of Captain Coignet, Soldier of the Empire* Ed. by Sir John Fortescue (London, 1929), 96.

6. Cowan, *Reminiscences*, op cit., 11, 12.

7. No comparable statistic for temperatures within the prisoners' accommodation in any Scots depot is known to exist, but a medical inspection of Dartmoor depot in Feb. 1815 found 'the temperature inside the buildings to be 25 degrees warmer than it was outside, which was due partly to the cooking stoves, but mainly to the animal heat of 1,200 human bodies, for there was no heating apparatus.' Thomson, *Dartmoor*, op. cit., 87.

8. TNA ADM 98/117, ltr, 10 Dec. 1810.

9. See Kaald, op. cit., 97.

10. TNA ADM 98/276.

11. Ibid.

12. TNA ADM 98/170.

13. Ibid.

14. TNA ADM 98/187.

15. TNA ADM 98/278.

16. Ibid.

17. TNA ADM 98/279; and ibid., ltr, 21 Nov. 1812, TB to Glinn.

18. TNA ADM 98/276, ltr, 11 Feb. 1811, TB to M. Wright, Edinburgh, concerning a complaint received by the Board that day from Capt. Pellowe, agent, Esk Mills. The TB's responsibilities also included monitoring conditions for British prisoners of war in enemy hands, and among many letters exchanged on that subject between the Board and Monsieur Rivière, French government agent for prisoners of war, were the two following, which indicate not only the normal provision to prisoners of war in Britain but also that, at least at times, conditions appear to have been even more spartan for British prisoners in French hands. First, in May 1804 the Board wrote to M. Rivière that 'It has been represented to us that the British Prisoners of War confined in France are not provided with any Bedding by the French Government, whereas in this Country, every Prisoner is furnished with a Hammock and a good Blanket.' Second, on 7 Jan. 1809, the Board wrote to M. Rivière that, 'Having received Information that in consequence of an order from the French Government the sheets allowed as part of the Bedding of British Prisoners in France have been for some time past withheld from them by which the hardship of their situation has been much increased; we think it proper to refer you to our letter dated 27 August 1804 in which we stated the Allowances of Bedding made to French Prisoners of War confined in this country to be as mentioned on the other side hereof [i..e., 1 Hammock, 1 Paillasse, 1 Blanket] and to your letter in reply dated 28th Brumaire An 12 [18 Nov. 1804] informing us that one Paillasse, one Pair of Sheets and one Blanket (or 'Couverture') would in future be supplied to each British Prisoner similarly situated. As no Alteration whatever has been made in the Supply of Bedding stated

in our said Letter, and the Order given by the French Government for withholding the Sheets was stated to be a Measure of Reciprocity, we trust that if this Order should be persisted in, the French Government will see the Justice and Necessity of causing either Hammocks or Bedsteads to be furnished as an Equivalent free of Expense to the Prisoners, it being understood that they are now obliged to pay a certain Sum for the Hire of the latter Article.' TNA ADM 98/300, fols 63-5, ltrs, TB to M. Rivière, 10 May and 27 Aug. 1804 and 7 Jan. 1809. Alexander Stewart, the Kirkcaldy boy who remained a prisoner of war for ten years until 1814, indicates that at Sarrelibre, where he and other prisoners were held in French army barracks, each bedstead, with a straw mattress and one blanket, was shared by two prisoners. Previously, Stewart had been confined with other prisoners at Sarrelibre in a former hospital, where most had bedsteads with straw mattresses and one blanket but others, because of the lack of bedsteads, slept on the floor on their mattress with their blanket. *The Life of Alexander Stewart*, op. cit., v, 26, 31, 32.

19. TNA ADM 103/157.
20. TNA ADM 103/124 passim.
21. TNA ADM 103/112 passim.
22. TNA ADM 103/435, No. 5,304; ADM 103/113, Nos 7,304 and 7,431.
23. TNA ADM 103/263-6 passim; for Walle, TNA ADM 103/263, No. 511. Only a handful of prisoners listed in that first Entry Book at Perth appear to have received the same amount of bedding as Walle did. See also, e.g., Nos 329-32, 334 and 1,168.
24. TNA ADM 103/263, No. 1,161.
25. TNA ADM 103/263, No. 1,187.
26. TNA ADM 103/266, No. 6,839.
27. TNA ADM 103/266, No. 7,760.
28. TNA ADM 103/265, No. 5,611.
29. This seems to have been the kind of bed Louis Garneray described the richer prisoners on the hulk *Prothée* at Portsmouth providing themselves with.
30. TNA ADM 105/44.
31. Kaald, op. cit., 98; TNA ADM 98/277, ltr, 6 Aug. 1811, TB to Priest.
32. Kaald, op. cit., 99.
33. TNA ADM 98/132, ltr, 19 Oct. 1811, TB to John Trotter, Esq.
34. TNA ADM 98/276, ltr, 26 Apr. 1809, TB to M.Wright.
35. Beaudoin, op. cit., 638.
36. Simond, *Journal*, op. cit., Vol. II, 53. Though Simond describes Col. Maghee as 'commanding at the fort', or Castle, he has not been identified in other sources consulted.
37. Chambers, 'Some Early Recollections', *Chambers's Journal*, No. 600, op.cit., 402.
38. Ibid., 403.
39. Cowan, *Reminiscences*, op. cit., 17.
40. R. L. Stevenson, *Vailima letters to Sidney Colvin, November 1890—October 1894* (London, 1895), 324-5.
41. Marote-Carrier, op. cit., 95.
42. NAS AD/14/12/63, precognitions by Christian Hutton and Agnes Galbraith.
43. Marote-Carrier, op. cit., 163, 164.
44. TNA ADM 98/117, ltr, 10 Dec. 1810.

45. Beaudoin, op. cit., 636, 638.

46. *Perth Courier*, 3 Dec. 1812.

47. The archives of the Royal Infirmary appear to contain no reference to these 25 prisoners.

48. By François-Frédéric Billon, for example, who says the prisoners were stripped of all their clothing except trousers and shirt. Billon, *Souvenirs*, op. cit., 173. Wounded at Salamanca in Jul. 1812 by a Scots sergeant, Lieut. Alphonse D'Hautpoul, another veteran of Eylau and Friedland, lay all night without help on the battlefield after two squadrons of cavalry had passed over him but without their horses touching him. 'Next day,' D'Hautpoul recalled, 'some Spanish guerrillas who had not appeared during the action threw themselves on us like vultures on their prey. I was made as naked as a worm. One of these vultures, in order to take my boots, put a foot on my stomach and pulled them off me.' Found by British troops on the battlefield, D'Hautpoul's life was saved by a British surgeon and afterwards he was sent to Lisbon in a cart with other prisoners too weak to walk. En route there 'the Portuguese, remembering what they had suffered [from the invading French army], threw themselves on the carts which were transporting us and massacred several of my companions in misfortune. I would probably have had the same fate if I had not known my prayers. Three or four peasants came up to me with an unequivocally hostile attitude. They asked me if I was a Christian and I replied I was. They asked me to make the sign of the Cross and recite the *Credo*, which I did. They took pity on me and told me they could see I was one of those unfortunates whom the great robber (as they called Napoleon) had taken by force. The English soldiers who ought to have escorted us had abandoned us to the care of the cart drivers. This act of cold barbarity was aimed at getting rid of us, because they knew well that the vengeance of the Portuguese would put an end to our troubles.' *Mémoires du Général Marquis Alphonse D'Hautpoul, Pair de France, 1789-1865* (Paris, 1906), 14, 21-4, 69, 70-4, 80. The experiences of D'Hautpoul, who later became a parole prisoner at Bridgnorth in Wales, and of Billon were no doubt similar to those of many rank and file prisoners in the depots in Scotland who had been capd in the Peninsular War. See also Oman, *Peninsular War*, op. cit., Vol. I, 280-3, and Vol. IV, 175, for discussion of why some French prisoners arrived in Britain almost naked: '... the [French] Army of Portugal [in Mar. 1811] was also in desperate straits for boots and clothing. In many regiments a third or a quarter of the men had no footgear but "rivlins" or mocassins made every few days from the hides of cattle. The uniforms were in rags; many soldiers had nothing that recalled the regulation attire but the *capote* [overcoat] that covered everything.'

49. Beaudoin, op. cit., 636.

50. TNA ADM 98/279. General Sir Ronald Ferguson of Raith (1773-1841), a distinguished and highly experienced soldier, who fought in the French Revolutionary and Napoleonic Wars, Whig MP for Kirkcaldy Burghs, 1806-30, and Nottingham, 1830-41.

51. Ibid.

52. Penny, op. cit., 92.

53. TNA ADM 98/280.

54. Marote-Carrier, op. cit., 26.

55. Chambers, 'Some Early Recollections', *Chambers's Journal*, No. 600, op. cit., 402.

56. TNA ADM 98/276, ltr, 18 Feb. 1811, TB to Capt. Pellowe, agent. What description of headgear these caps were remains an unanswered question.

57. Kaald, op. cit., 103.

58. TNA ADM 98/276.

59. TNA ADM 98/280.

60. A complaint about prisoners being dischgd from a depot in Scotland without shoes and stockings was the subject of a letter by the TB in early Dec. 1813 to Capt. Brown, agent, Valleyfield: '… a representation having been made to us that the Dutch volunteers [to fight for the restoration of the Prince of Orange in the Netherlands as Napoleon's empire there crumbled and fell] discharged from your depot are in a most miserable state in regard to clothing, and in particular are deficient in shoes and stockings, we direct you to explain the cause of your having discharged these men without shoes or stockings.' Whatever Brown's explanation, the Board told him a week later they were perfectly satisfied with it. TNA ADM 98/280, ltrs, 4 and 11 Dec. 1813, TB to Brown.

61. TNA ADM 98/279, ltr, 16 Nov. 1812, TB to Brown, and 28 Apr. 1813 to Moriarty.

62. TNA ADM 98/279.

63. TNA ADM 98/276. Wright's reply has not survived.

64. TNA ADM 98/276, ltrs, 27 Feb. 1811, TB to Capt. Pellowe at Esk Mills and Capt. Heddington at Valleyfield.

65. NLS MS Acc. 5811/1/7, Andrew Johnston Coll. These notes are: Statement of the Expense of Materials and Labour for making Clog Shoes for the Use of the Prisoners.

List Slippers:

List 560 lbs at 11½d. per lb	£26.16. 8
Carriage of the above from London	£2.16.19
Making the Slippers by the Prisoners, 1,000 Pairs at 1½d. each	£6. 5. 0
	£35.18. 5

Wooden Clogs:

Blocks for making the Clogs, 1,000 Pairs at 4d. per Pair	£16.13. 4
Making the Clogs by the Prisoners, 1,000 Pairs at 1d. per Pair	£4. 3. 4
	£20.16. 8
Leather straps 1,000 sets at 6½d. per set	£27. 1. 8
Hemp for sewing the Straps to the Slippers	£1. 6.10
Wax and Thread	3.10
Nails for nailing the Slippers to Clogs	£5. 4. 0
Labour to complete the Shoe by nailing the Slippers to the Clogs, done by the Prisoners at 8/- per Hundred Pairs	£4. 0. 0
	£94.11.5
Deduct 81 lbs List remaining	£3.17.7
Cost of 1,000 Pairs complete being 21¾ 24/1000 per pair.	*£90.13.10*

Among stores held at Valleyfield at the end of the war but then transferred for storage to Greenlaw were 1,326 'Pairs of Wood for Clog Soles'. TNA ADM 103/635 Part I, 'Inventory of Stores and Articles Lately belonging to the Depot at Greenlaw, now deposited in the Offices of Path Head House, the Agent's Residence ... July 10th 1816.'

66. TNA ADM 98/279, ltrs, 21 Oct. and 14 Dec. 1812, TB to Capt. Moriarty.

67. TNA ADM 98/278, ltr, 2 Jan. 1812, TB to Capt. Moriarty.

68. Kaald, op. cit., 87.

69. TNA ADM 98/277, ltrs from TB: 21 Mar. 1811 to M. Wright and Admiral Otway, and 25 Mar. 1811 to Otway.

70. Kaald, op. cit., 151, 152.

71. TNA ADM 98/280, ltr, 11 Dec. 1813.

72. TNA ADM 98/279, ltrs, 25 Aug. and 25 Sep. 1812, TB to Capt. Moriarty.

73. Kaald, op. cit., 87. There are also references at Edinburgh Castle and Esk Mills, as well as at Greenlaw some others than Kaald's, to washermen; but at the Castle six washermen mentioned were evidently employed specifically in the depot hospital, as were the two mentioned at Greenlaw. At Esk Mills two prisoners (Jean Tant, seaman, capd on the *Mameluke* priv., and Louis Patatrand, gunner, capd on *La Vertu*) appear to have been washermen, not patients, in the hospital. TNA ADM 103/117, Nos 555 (Tant) and 1,062 (Patatrand), and pp. 13 and 16.

74. Abell, op. cit., 49, 50.

CHAPTER 14: FOOD AND DRINK

1. The tender, in the form only of photostated typescript whose provenance is uncertain but which seems to have been copied from Miller's archive, is in the National War Museum of Scotland (henceforth NWMS) at Edinburgh Castle, ref. French Forces 808.1

2. *EEC*, 5 Nov. 1808.

3. TNA ADM 1/3743, ltr, 23 May 1803, TB to Adm. Nothing further about the Board's recommendation has been found.

4. B.R. Mitchell and P. Deane, *Abstract of British Historical Statistics* (Cambridge University Press, 1962), 488; G.D.H. Cole, *A Short History of the British Working-Class Movement 1789-1947* (London, new ed. 1947), 135; G.D.H. Cole and R. Postgate, *The Common People 1746-1946* (London, 4th ed., 1949), 119; Asa Briggs, *The Age of Improvement* (London, 1959), 164-5.

5. TNA ADM 98/117, ltr, 10 Dec. 1810. Sergeant Major Beaudoin, a prisoner at Greenlaw from 1804 to 1809, complained that 1 lb (or 16 oz.) was 'the equivalent of only fourteen French ounces.' Beaudoin, op. cit., 637.

6. Simond, *Journal*, Vol. II, op. cit., 53.

7. TNA ADM 98/132, ltr, 21 Oct. 1811, TB to G. Harrison, HM Treasury.

8. Crowhurst, *French War on Trade*, op. cit., 187. For his professional comments by Michael Clapham, Lecturer Nutrition, Queen Margaret University College, Edinburgh, on the prisoners' rations, see above, Appendix 10.

9. Two mentions of butter at Greenlaw are made by Kaald, op. cit., 88, 163.

10. John Burnett, *Plenty and Want. A Social History of Diet in England from 1815 to the Present Day* (Harmondsworth, 1968), 25, 26.

11. TNA ADM 98/132, ltr, 21 Oct. 1811, TB to G. Harrison, HM Treasury.

12. Burnett, op. cit., 25, 26; Denys Forrest, *Tea for the British. The Social and Economic History of a Famous Trade* (London, 1973), 82, 134.

13. Marote-Carrier, op. cit., 89, 91.

14. TNA ADM 103/635, Part I, 'Inventory of Stores ... Lately belonging to the Depot at Greenlaw ... July 10th 1816'.

15. TNA ADM 98/170, 2 Jul. 1808.

16. Ibid., 11 Mar. 1809.

17. Ibid., 2 Nov. 1810.

18. Ibid., 5 Jun. 1811.

19. Ibid., 21 Dec. 1811 and 3 Jun. 1812.

20. Ibid., 9 Sep. 1813.

21. See, e.g., TNA ADM 98/276, ltr, 21 Dec. 1809, TB to M. Wright, Greenlaw: '... [Board] approve of the money tendered to the two soldiers for the purchase of spirits for the prisoners, but which they detained and delivered up to the officer of the guard, being given to the sentries who acted in so proper a manner.'; ADM 98/277, ltr, 6 Apr. 1811, TB to Capt. Pellowe, Valleyfield; ADM 98/133, ltr, 4 Sep. 1812, TB to Adam Pearson, secretary, Excise Office, Edinburgh: '... there is reason to believe that much smuggling of spirituous liquors takes place at the several depots for prisoners of war at Valleyfield, Pennycuick, Greenlaw and Perth, and ... request that some Excise officers may be directed to search occasionally all persons attending at the markets of the prisons and also the turnkeys and their lodges.'

22. Kaald, op. cit., 117, 155, 165.

23. TNA ADM 98/279, ltrs, 9 Sep. and 11 Nov. 1812; ADM 98/280, ltrs, 27 Oct. 1813, TB to Capt. Brown, Valleyfield, and 2 Nov. 1813, TB to Capt. Moriarty, Perth.

24. TNA ADM 98/278, ltr, 10 Jun. 1812, TB to Capt. Moriarty.

25. NLS MS Acc. 5811/1/3.

26. TNA ADM 98/117, ltr, 10 Dec. 1810, TB to Adm. Alexander Stewart, the young Kirkcaldy seaman who was a prisoner of war at Sarrelibre, later recalled how: 'Here we had 1 lb of brown bread per day, a little meat, nominally half a pound, but really not half that weight, for all the heads, legs, livers and other offal were counted in the weight. Though the liver and lights were often putrid and full of little bladders, yet so great was our hunger that we could eat almost anything. We were allowed also a few French beans per week, with five farthings [i.e., 1¼d.] in money, but a great part of this was deducted, under pretence of paying for damages done, as well as to buy brooms to sweep the place, tubs for washing and—coffins for those that died, for French feeling contained no such sympathy for the English dead, as would meet such a case. With our pence, most of us purchased potatoes, onions, turnips, milk and cheese. Some of these we had with our meat, others with our French beans, to give them at least some taste.' *Life of Alexander Stewart*, op. cit., 26, 27.

27. Of men in the Royal Navy, Lewis, *Social History of the Navy*, op. cit., 402, says, 'Their diet was bad, their food and drink usually vile—sometimes unnecessarily but generally unavoidably, since the preservation of food and water was an almost unknown art.'

28. Ibid., 404.

29. Christopher Lloyd, *The British Seaman 1200-1860* (London, 1968), 254. Lloyd's account of naval daily rations appears to differ somewhat in certain items from the official

scale of 1808, in that he says each man was provided with 1 lb of salt pork or 2 lb of beef on alternate days, and weekly with three pints of oatmeal, 8 oz. of butter and 1 lb of cheese.

30. Abell, op. cit., 77, 78.
31. Beaudoin, op. cit., 658.
32. Marote-Carrier, op. cit., 57, 58, 59.
33. TNA ADM 98/113, ltr, 2 Sep. 1807, TB to W.W. Pole, secretary, Adm.
34. *Correspondance de Napoléon Ier*, op. cit., Vol. XIX (1866), 3, 4, Item 15207; Elting, *Swords Around a Throne*, op. cit., 576, 577. Another list presented by Elting indicates that daily rations of soldiers in Napoleon's army were 24 oz. of bread, 8 oz. of meat, either 1 oz. of rice or 2 oz. of dried beans, peas or lentils, a quart of wine, about an eighth of a pint of brandy, and about a tenth of a pint of vinegar. 'The average French soldier had grown up accustomed to simple living: *Soupe* and bread with a little wine and brandy kept him happy, so long as there was enough of them ... Besides his bread ration the soldier, while in camp or barracks, usually had two meals a day: Around noontime, *soupe*, a bit of boiled beef or mutton, and vegetables; in the evening, potatoes or some other vegetable, with or without trimmings.' Elting, *Swords Around a Throne*, op. cit., 575.
35. Jean Morvan, *Le Soldat Impérial* (Paris, 1904), Vol. I, 428, says Napoleon increased the soldier's bread ration from 1 Aug. 1810 so that, at least on paper, it became 750 grammes of bread or 550 of biscuit, 200 grammes of salt beef, 30 of rice or 60 of dried vegetables, 16 of salt, a quarter litre of wine, and a sixteenth of a litre of brandy or one twentieth of a litre of vinegar.
36. Abell, op. cit., 47; TNA ADM 98/170, TB circulars to depots, 9 and 16 Jul. 1808.
37. E.g., the naval sloop *Alert* sailed from the Downs, on the Sussex coast of the English Channel, to Leith in Apr. 1814 in 44 hours—'the shortest [i.e., speediest] passage ever known.' Even a coach service between Edinburgh and Lanark (a distance of 30 miles) instituted in summer 1813 took six hours in each direction. *CM*, 23 Apr. 1814 and 5 Aug. 1813.
38. TNA ADM 98/170, from TB to depots, 16 Aug. 1810, 11 Jan. and 17 Dec. 1811. The circular of 11 Jan. 1811 enclosed standing orders and regulations, partly set out above, that were supplementary to the printed instructions for every depot agent.
39. Ibid., 28 Sep. 1813.
40. Ibid., 11 Jan. 1811.
41. Ibid., 18 Sep. 1812.
42. Ibid., 28 Jul. 1813.
43. TNA ADM 98/277, ltr, 21 Mar. 1811, TB to M. Wright.
44. Kaald, op. cit., 86.
45. Ibid., 117.
46. TNA ADM 98/276, ltr, 10 Jul. 1810, TB to M. Wright.
47. TNA ADM 98/279, ltr, 12 Feb. 1813, TB to Lieuts Priest and Glinn.
48. Ibid., ltrs, 26 Apr. 1813, TB to Lieut. Priest and Capt. Brown.
49. TNA ADM 98/277, ltr, 4 Mar. 1811, TB to Capt. Pellowe.
50. Ibid., ltr, 26 Mar. 1811, TB to Pellowe.
51. Ibid., ltr, 29 Apr. 1811, TB to Pellowe.
52. Ibid., ltr, 12 Aug. 1811, TB to Pellowe.

53. TNA ADM 98/278, ltr, 14 Apr. 1812, TB to Capt. Moriarty.
54. TNA ADM 98/279, ltr, 25 Aug. 1812.
55. Ibid., ltrs, 16 and 21 Jan. 1813, TB to Capt. Brown.
56. Ibid., ltr, 22 Jan. 1813, TB to Otway.
57. Ibid., ltr, 13 Feb. 1813, TB to Capt. Brown.
58. Ibid., ltrs, 15, 25 and 29 Mar., 2, 19, and 22 Apr. 1813.
59. Marote-Carrier, op. cit., 106, 117.
60. *Dundee Advertiser*, 26 Mar. 1813. If the quality and quantity had been as 'sufficient', even 'excellent', as the depot authorities and/or the contractors claimed, it is not obvious why the prisoners should have become 'disorderly' and even 'in a state of mutiny'.
61. TNA ADM 98/279.
62. TNA ADM 98/170, 18 Nov. 1809.
63. Ibid., 5 and 15 Sep. 1810.
64. Ibid., 7 May 1811.
65. Ibid.
66. TNA ADM 1/3751, 19 May 1807. Two tables of rations, said to be for French and Spanish prisoners respectively, formed an appendix to the Board's letter. The rations, consisting of ½ lb of bread, ½ lb of pilchards or 1 lb of herrings, or alternatively 1 lb of potatoes, were the same for both nationalities, except that Spanish prisoners were allotted a quart of beer, the French none.
67. Kaald, op. cit., 86.
68. Ibid., 117.
69. Ibid., 174, 175.
70. TNA ADM 98/277, ltr, 26 Aug. 1811.
71. See above, pp.63, 64, 82-6.
72. TNA ADM 98/277.
73. Simond, *Journal*, Vol. II, op. cit., 53; TNA ADM 98/277, ltrs, 21 Mar. 1811, TB to Otway and M. Wright.
74. TNA ADM 98/277, ltr, 26 Mar. 1811, TB to Capt. Pellowe.
75. TNA ADM 98/276.
76. TNA ADM 98/277, ltr, 15 Jul. 1811, TB to Capt. Pellowe.
77. TNA ADM 98/278, ltr, 2 Nov. 1811, TB to Capt. Moriarty.
78. TNA ADM 98/279, ltrs, 2 Feb. and 11 Sep. 1813, TB to Capt. Brown.
79. Kaald, op. cit., 86, 98.
80. TNA ADM 98/128, ltr, 2 Aug. 1804, TB to Commissioners for Sick and Wounded Seamen.
81. Deacon, 'History of Penicuik', op. cit., p.13, says there was 'a plot close to James the Less Church [on the other side from the depot of the main Penicuik-Peebles road], known as "Cabbage Hall", and there are mentions of other plots. One is described as "the park behind the Manse", possibly meaning a plot close to the South Kirk Hall—a French army button was found in the garden of the South Kirk Hall.'
82. Black, *Penicuik and Neighbourhood*, op. cit., 328; NAS GD 1/405/2, p.4; Deacon, op. cit., p.13.
83. NAS, Cowan Papers, GD 311/2/36, ltrs, 29 Dec. 1810, to Somerville Lyall & Co.,

Wine Merchants, Edinburgh—'Offered to them turnips, delivered at Eskmills Depot, 50 and [?] 100 tons or whatever we have to spare at 1/9d. per cwt, without shaws or tails'; 22 Jul. 1811, to George Stone, Haughhead—'We are willing to give you all our Cabbages plus overheads at 6/8d. per hundred, containing 120, to be counted now, and to be delivered at the Depot, as you may require them. If this does not suit you we must give them to you by weight, but they will not likely attain size for that purpose before September. I am sorry that we cannot engage to supply you with cabbage and turnips overhead, having nothing at present to begin with. We may probably be able to do it after September is over.'; 10 Aug. 1812, to Lyall & Stone: 'We ... propose to you that in future while we supply you with cabbages, that everything of them shall be weighed and that we shall make you an allowance of, say, ten plants for waste from the gross weight'; 11 Aug. 1812, to Lyall & Stone: '... you will recollect yourself as to the conversation which passed between us yesterday forenoon. When an allowance of ten per cent was talked of we were not speaking of a second deduction but we had calculated that we had suffered a loss of 300 cwt of vegetables @ 4/6d. per cwt or £120 or £130. This is the loss at the first weighing. The loss at the second weighing may have been 3 cwts not exceeding 5 cwts @ 4/6d. is 22/6d. How is it possible that you can think us liable to any deduction after the first? Certainly not for when they are once out of our hands we are unquestionably not bound to make up any loss that may arise in again weighing them out to the prisoners. This you have yourself repeatedly acknowledged and you have added that we are only bound to see them weighed over to you, and not to satisfy the prisoners either at first or afterwards. How then could you propose that we should be liable to a second deduction of 10 per cent, or how could it be supposed that I would agree to any such thing is what I cannot conceive, and what I must leave you to reconcile, for although we are liable to the second deduction, still 10 per cent could more than ten times pay it judging from what it has hitherto been ... I think I must have convinced you that you were in a mistake when you supposed that the ten per cent could apply to anything else than to the state in which the cabbages commonly arrive, but I have no wish to take any advantage of an offer so hastily made and perhaps without sufficient reflection upon the circumstances. If therefore you wish it we shall give up the idea of the 10 per cent and try to make some other arrangement. Perhaps the shortest way now would be for us to be responsible for satisfying the prisoners, and this we will do if you will agree to make the price 5/- in place of 4/6d. per cwt for the whole period. If this does not suit you, we must next propose to weigh them over to you and that you shall object to nothing by [? but] the decayed leaves.'; 13 Sep. 1813, to Somerville Lyall & Co., Edinburgh—'In reply to yours of yesterday we offer to supply you with Potatoes for Valleyfield Depot to 1st June next at 3/3d. per cwt or for four months longer, say to 1st October following at 3/9d. per cwt for the whole period.'

84. Sievewright, *Depot at Perth*, op. cit., 7.
85. *Perth Courier*, 21 Jan. 1813.
86. TNA ADM 98/277, ltr, 20 May 1811, TB to Capt. Pellowe; ADM 98/280, ltr, 31 Jan. 1814, TB to Capt. Brown.
87. TNA ADM 98/277, ltr, 17 Jul. 1811, TB to Capt. Pellowe.
88. Nor was it only unscrupulous professional contractors who profited out of the misery of the prisoners. Abell, op. cit., 201, 202, writing at the beginning of the 20th century, recounts how an elderly woman at Lasswade, five miles from Penicuik,

recalled from her childhood an old farmer who was said to have 'made his fortune by providing oatmeal to the prisoners at Valleyfield of an inferior quality to that for which he had contracted.'

89. TNA ADM 1/3743, ltr, 27 May 1803, TB to Adm.

90. TNA ADM 98/170, circulars, 2 Dec. 1813 and 7 Nov. 1811, TB to contractors.

91. Difficulties that Lyall & Stone, for example, had in 'conveying the Provisions for the Prisoners to the Depots in North Britain' were the subject of two letters in late summer 1812 by that company to the TB, but the nature of the difficulties is unstated in the surviving correspondence. See TNA ADM 98/279, ltr, 1 Sep. 1812, TB to Capt. Brown, agent, Valleyfield.

92. See, e.g., TNA ADM 98/277, ltr, 22 Oct. 1811, TB to Lieut. Priest, Greenlaw: '... approve of your having purchased two wheelbarrows for the service mentioned by you.' ADM 98/279, ltr, 29 Apr. 1813, TB to Capt. Brown, agent: 'You will report how the old brooms at the Depot at Valleyfield are disposed of.' Ibid., ltr, 22 Apr. 1813, TB to Capt. Moriarty, agent: 'The consumption of birch brooms at [Perth] appearing by your accounts to be very great, we desire you to let us know what measures of precaution are used to prevent them being consumed as fuel or otherwise destroyed instead of being fairly worn out. ... if the stumps of the worn out brooms were received before new brooms were issued, a very considerable reduction would be made in the expenditure of them. We also desire to know in whose charge the brooms are kept and in what number and under what Regulation they are now issued.' Once Moriarty had reported, the Board wrote him again a week later: '... state how the hicks and humps of the old brooms are disposed of. Report if brooms cannot be procured at a cheaper rate than the contract price.' Ibid., 30 Apr. 1813.

93. TNA ADM 98/277, ltr, 21 Mar. 1811, TB to Otway.

94. TNA ADM 98/170, 7 Nov. 1811.

95. See, e.g., a reply on 29 Oct. 1811 (in TNA ADM 98/277) from the Board to Malcolm Wright, then its agent at Edinburgh Castle: 'If the contractor refuses to victual the prisoners ... we will prosecute him for the penalty of his bond and in that case you are to apply to the contractor for victualling the prisoners at Greenlaw.'

96. TNA ADM 98/280, ltr, 28 Jul. 1813, TB to Capt. Brown. Abell, op. cit., 49-50, in excoriating the corruption in which contractors were deeply immersed, declares: '... we know that the war-prison contract business was a festering mass of jobbery and corruption, that large fortunes were made by contractors, that a whole army of small officials and not a few big ones throve on the "pickings" to be had. Occasionally, a fraudulent contractor was brought up, heavily fined and imprisoned; but such cases are so rare that it is hard to avoid the suspicion that their prominence was a matter of expediency and policy, and that many a rascal who should have been hanged for robbing defenceless foreigners of the commonest rights of man had means with which to defeat justice and to persist unchecked in his unholy calling.'

97. Kaald, op. cit., 92; and Carl Roos, *Prisonen*, op. cit., 180.

98. Beaudoin, op. cit., 637.

99. Johnston, 'Recollections', op. cit., p.10.

100. Marote-Carrier, op. cit., 163, 164.

101. TNA ADM 98/199, ltr, 7 Apr. 1809, TB to James Cairns, Peebles. If some prisoners sold their rations other prisoners bought them. Marote-Carrier, op. cit., 146, recalled how at Valleyfield in 1811-12 some prisoners sold their daily rations of food for money

they spent on playing billiards. Much more seriously, Abell, op. cit., 143, quotes a report from the agent at Norman Cross depot, Huntingdonshire, in 1801, toward the end of the previous war, which describes a practice whose complete absence from depots in Scotland during the Napoleonic Wars would be surprising: 'There are in these prisons ... some men—if they deserve that name—who possess money with which they purchase of some unfortunate and unthinking fellow-prisoner his ration of bread for several days together, and frequently *both bread and beef for a month*, which he, the merchant, seizes upon daily and sells it out again to some unfortunate being on the same usurious terms, allowing the former *one-half penny worth of potatoes daily* to keep him alive.'

102. Marote-Carrier, op. cit., 157, 158.
103. Ibid., 168.
104. Kaald, op. cit., 87, 88.
105. Anton, *Retrospect of a military life*, op. cit., 31.
106. Kaald, op. cit., 88.
107. Ibid., 98, 163.
108. Ibid., 147-63 passim.
109. TNA ADM 98/131, ltr, 29 Nov. 1810.
110. Kaald, op. cit., 86.
111. TNA ADM 98/278, ltr, 20 Feb. 1812, TB to Capt. Moriarty.
112. Chambers, 'Some Early Recollections', *Chambers's Journal*, No. 600, op. cit., 402.
113. Marote-Carrier, op. cit., 156, 157.
114. TNA ADM 98/276, ltr, 16 Feb. 1811. It is significant that in his detailed list of the 'entire Establishment' of staff at Esk Mills, Andrew Johnston, depot clerk, included turnkeys, a steward, labourers-gravediggers, and a lamplighter—but no cooks: surely indicative that the latter were prisoners. Johnston, 'Recollections', op. cit., p.8.
115. *CM*, 19 Jun. 1813; TNA ADM 103/263, No. 885; ADM 103/648, lists of deaths, Perth, week ending 17 Jun. 1813, No. 885. On his death bed Foret 'made over to F. Corvesin', a fellow prisoner, the considerable sum of £9.10.0., which was paid in instalments to Corvesin by the depot authorities between 19 and 30 Jun. Foret's bequest may suggest that non-hospital cooks at the depots were also paid. Perth Museum & Art Gallery, Perth Depot Payments Ledger, Item 89/22/G1935, No. 885.
116. TNA ADM 103/117, Nos 50 (Fauché), 799 (Dastillon) and 894 (Boisdefray).
117. Kaald, op. cit., 149.
118. Quoted in Walker, *The Depot at Norman Cross*, op. cit., 63. Kaald also noted in his diary on 10 May 1810 that he was in the Greenlaw cookhouse that day as a supervisor.
119. Both lists are in TNA ADM 103/117, Nos 1,179 (François Joseph Mallet), 1,190 (J.A. Marriet), 908 (François Picard), 907 (Jacques Vié), 800 (M. Tullier), and 798 (A. Ranfart). Mallet, Picard, Tullier and Ranfart appear in both lists.
120. TNA ADM 98/279, ltr, 22 Jan. 1813, TB to Vice Admiral Otway.
121. TNA ADM 98/279.
122. Ibid.
123. Kaald, op. cit., 91, 92, 94, 95, 96.
124. Ibid., 167, 170.
125. TNA ADM 98/276, ltrs, 28 Jan. and 21 Aug. 1809, and 4 May 1810, TB to M. Wright;

ADM 98/277, ltr, 7 Mar. 1811, TB to Lieut. Priest; ADM 98/278, ltr, 11 Feb. 1812, TB to Lieut. Priest.

126. TNA ADM 98/277, ltr, 14 Mar. 1811, TB to M. Wright.

127. Ibid., ltr, 24 Oct. 1811, TB to M. Wright.

128. TNA ADM 98/276, ltr, 23 Feb. 1811, TB to Capt. Pellowe.

129. Ibid., ltr, 26 Feb. 1811.

130. TNA ADM 98/277, ltr, 4 Mar. 1811, TB to Capt. Pellowe.

131. Ibid., ltr, 8 Apr. 1811, TB to Capt. Pellowe; ADM 103/432-434.

132. TNA ADM 98/280, ltr, 24 Sep. 1813, TB to Capts Brown and Moriarty.

133. TNA ADM 98/279, ltr, 6 Apr. 1813, TB to Capt. Brown.

134. TNA ADM 98/280, ltr, 11 May 1814, TB to Capt. Moriarty.

135. TNA ADM 98/170, circular, 24 May 1809.

136. Ibid., circular, 29 Mar. 1810.

137. TNA ADM 98/278, ltr, 1 May 1812, TB to Capt. Moriarty. Moriarty's reply has not survived.

138. *CM*, 18 Sep. 1813, reported that at Perth depot that week, when an attempt at mass escape had taken place, at least 35 prisoners were held in the cachot.

139. Marote-Carrier, op. cit., 141-2.

140. Marote-Carrier, op. cit., 95, 101.

141. Marote-Carrier, op. cit., 142-5.

142. Thomson, *Dartmoor*, op. cit., 15-16. Exactly the same hospital diet is given for Norman Cross depot by Walker, *The Depot at Norman Cross*, op. cit., 71. A more detailed breakdown of the varying grades of hospital diet which was also presented by Walker is given above at Appendix 10.

143. NLS MS Acc. 5811/1/2.

144. TNA ADM 98/277, ltr, 2 Mar. 1811, TB to Capt. Pellowe. See also ADM 98/280, ltr, 8 Oct. 1813, TB to Capt. Moriarty, mentioning a quarterly list 'of the French servants victualled in the hospital at Perth'.

145. TNA ADM 98/279, ltr, 2 Jan. 1813, TB to Capt. Brown.

146. TNA ADM 98/277, ltrs, 4 May and 19 Apr. 1811, TB to Capt. Pellowe.

147. TNA ADM 98/279, ltr, 2 Dec. 1813.

148. NLS MS Acc. 5811/1/3.

149. Peacock, *Perth: its annals and its archives*, op. cit., 497.

150. *Perth Courier*, 28 Oct. 1813.

CHAPTER 15: THE SLOW MARCH OF TIME: BOREDOM, ACTIVITY, LETTERS TO AND FROM HOME

1. While Kaald was making such entries in his diary at Greenlaw, the young Fife seaman Alexander Stewart, in captivity more or less simultaneously at Sarrelibre in Lorraine, recalled that among his fellow British prisoners of war there: 'Time hung heavy. We had no employment and but little space and disposition for amusement. Much of our time was spent in bed, and not a little in playing at different games, such as dominoes, drafts [sic], cards, etc., which in many cases led to gambling and that again to fighting. At night we often amused ourselves with tales, anecdotes and

songs racounting [sic] our several histories past and *future*, while a few who had a little genius made ships and other trinkets and sold them. One man got a good few pence from his fellow prisoners for puncturing certain devices on their arms and legs with Indian ink … I do not remember to have seen a book of any kind all the time I was in this place, nor any day in the seven ever having been distinguished by us from the rest; nor ever heard religion, in any sense, so much as once named.' *Life of Alexander Stewart* , op. cit., 28, 29.

2. Chambers, 'Some Early Recollections', *Chambers's Journal*, No. 600, op. cit., 402.

3. Beaudoin, op. cit., 636.

4. Kaald, op. cit., 114, entry for 18 May 1809.

5. *Glasgow Courier*, 12 May 1810. The *Courier* says the prisoners were 'confined at Edinburgh', but Greenlaw, ten miles from the city, was the only depot at that time in Scotland.

6. Anton, *Retrospect of a military life*, op. cit., 31.

7. Simond, *Journal*, Vol. II, op. cit., 53, 54.

8. NAS GD1/405/2-3, postscript to a letter, 2 Jan. 1911, from Francis Abell to Macbeth Forbes: 'A Scots lady not long ago made me a present of a tea caddy made of beautifully patterned and coloured compressed paper, the work of prisoners at Valleyfield.'

9. Black, *Penicuik and Neighbourhood*, op. cit., 19. Black adds that 'quite a number' of such items made by the prisoners at Valleyfield were exhibited by their owners at the International Fisheries Exhibition at Waverley Market, Edinburgh, in 1882.

10. NLS MS Acc. 5811/1/25, ltr, 6 Oct. 1812, Faussié (or Fourtrie) to Johnston; TNA ADM 98/279, ltr, 25 Aug. 1812, TB to Capt. Brown, Valleyfield, instructing him 'to procure a Dozen Rattles for the use of the Turnkeys'; NLS MS Acc. 5811/1/11, ltr, n.d., from Lelade, Prison No. 4, to Johnston. A search of the Entry Books for Valleyfield and Perth has failed to trace Lelade. But a signatory of a loyal address to the Bourbons from Perth depot in May 1814 was a Sergeant Lelade, who may well have been Johnston's maker of desks.

11. TNA ADM 98/279, ltr, 12 Oct. 1812, TB to Capt. Moriarty. These and several other items, including an impressive workbox with a depiction in straw of the buildings of the depot, are preserved in Perth Museum and Art Gallery.

12. Marote-Carrier, op. cit., 156-7.

13. Abell, op. cit., 158, gives no source for this information.

14. Sievewright, *Depot at Perth*, op. cit., 19.

15. *Dundee Advertiser*, 11 Sep. 1812.

16. Beaudoin, op. cit., 637.

17. Kaald, op. cit., 92, 93, 98, entries for 6, 8, 29 and 30 Dec. 1808; Marote-Carrier, op. cit., 126-7, 140, 167.

18. NAS JC 26/334 (papers in the trial of Ensign Maxwell, 1807). The orders were signed by Alexander Mackay, Deputy Adjutant General.

19. Kaald, op. cit., 88; Beaudoin, op. cit., 636.

20. Kaald, op. cit., 141, entry for 11 Nov. 1809.

21. Samuel Smiles (ed.), *James Nasmyth, Engineer. An Autobiography* (London, 1883), 68, 69.

22. NAS GD1/405/2, pencil notes by Macbeth Forbes, p.15; Abell, op. cit., 200; Cowan, *Reminiscences*, op. cit., 12; Black, *Penicuik and Neighbourhood*, op. cit., 18.

23. Black, *Penicuik and Neighbourhood*, op. cit., 19.

24. *Dundee Advertiser*, 11 Sep. 1812; Penny, *Traditions of Perth*, op. cit., 92. According to the *Perth Courier*, 4 Nov. 1813, the market at midday was 'discontinued for the winter' from the beginning of Nov.

25. Marote-Carrier, op. cit., 157, 158.

26. Penny, *Traditions of Perth*, op. cit., 92, 93.

27. Ibid., 93, 94.

28. Rose seems likely to have been William Stewart Rose, Clerk of the Pleas from 1797 to 1837, an officer of the Exchequer. *Officers of the Exchequer*, comp. by J.C. Sainty (London, 1983), 98.

29. TNA ADM 98/113, letter, 2 Sep. 1807. A letter in more or less identical terms had been sent by the Board on 27 Jun. that year to William Huskisson, secretary of the Treasury. TNA ADM 98/129.

30. TNA ADM 98/170, circular, 26 Sep. 1808.

31. Ibid., 11 Jan. 1811. Abell, op. cit., 147-9, says that 'from motives of humanity' prisoners at Norman Cross depot in Huntingdonshire were allowed in 1808 to make baskets, boxes, ornaments, etc., which did not compete with the straw-plaiting work of local poor English labourers, but illicit traffic in straw-plait made by the prisoners continued, despite many courts martial of depot guards involved in it and the trial and conviction in Mar. 1811 of three English civilians, one of whom was sentenced to twelve months' imprisonment, the two others to six months'.

32. NAS GD 51/2/439/8 (Melville Castle Muniments), ltr, 11 Aug. 1812, Lord Melville, First Lord of the Admiralty, to Sir Rupert George, chairman, TB.

33. *EEC*, 15 May 1813.

34. E.g., Beaudoin, op. cit., 636.

35. TNA ADM 98/279, ltr, 21 Sep. 1812, TB to Capt. Brown. Brown had reported to the Board that 'a man residing in Pennycuick is concerned in conveying to the prisoners vast quantities of pipe straw for making straw plait', a large hamper full of which Brown had seized. He had asked the Board if he was authorised to detain the hamper and search the Penicuik man's house for straw. TNA ADM 99/219, ltr from Brown, 16 Sep. 1812.

36. TNA ADM 98/279, ltr, 5 Dec. 1812, TB to Capt. Brown.

37. TNA ADM 98/280, ltr, TB to Capt. Brown.

38. Ibid., ltr, 18 Jun. 1813, TB to Capt. Brown.

39. Ibid., ltr, 21 Jun. 1813, TB to Capt. Brown.

40. Ibid., ltr, 14 Feb. 1814, TB to Capt. Brown.

41. Ibid., ltr, 31 Jan. 1814, TB to Capt. Brown.

42. Abell, op. cit., 149, 203-4. Abell gives no source and does not say if Wingrave was found guilty. No report of Wingrave's trial has been found .

43. *EEC*, 14 Jul. 1814.

44. NLS MS Acc. 5811/1/29 (Andrew Johnston coll.).

45. *Glasgow Courier*, 24 Dec. 1811. Possibly, of course, the toys and work boxes offered for sale by Burton had been made by prisoners on hulks or in depots in England.

46. ML, Black Coll., Vol. 2(c), p.89a. No source is given by Black for this statement.

47. NLS Acc. 5811/1/25, ltr, 6 Oct. 1812, Faussié (or Fourtrie) to Johnston.

48. Anton, *Retrospect of a military life*, op. cit., 32; *Perth Courier*, 9 Sep. 1813.

49. TNA ADM 98/170, 4 Dec. 1810.

50. TNA ADM 98/122, ltr, 25 Apr. 1814.

51. The quotation is from Walker, *The Depot at Norman Cross*, op. cit., 96. Walker adds that the greater part of money made by prisoners of war at that depot from things they made for sale outside the prison 'was either transmitted for safe-keeping to France or Holland, banked with the agent, or hoarded until the hoped-for day of release should come.' Ibid., 126.

52. Chambers, 'Some Early Recollections', *Chambers's Journal*, No. 600, op. cit., 402.

53. Kaald, op. cit., 145.

54. Ibid., 50.

55. TNA ADM 98/277, ltr, 17 Apr. 1811, TB to Wright.

56. TNA ADM 98/170, 29 Jul. 1811.

57. TNA ADM 103/648, proforma reports concerning deaths of prisoners, Edinburgh Castle, week ending 25 Jul. 1811. Among other scraps of information about Bourignons and his death are that he had arr. at Edinburgh Castle on 11 Mar. 1811 from Esk Mills, was b. at Saintes or Santes, was 5ft 4¾ins, had (perhaps significantly) a scar on his left cheek, and that his fatal wound had been suffered in fencing with another (unnamed) prisoner. TNA ADM 103/112, No. 167; ADM 98/208, ltr, 25 Jul. 1811, Capt. Heddington, Edinburgh Castle, to TB.

58. TNA ADM 98/170, circular, 4 Jan. 1814.

59. Walker, *The Depot at Norman Cross*, op. cit., 147. Walker says his father told him that 'in his sixteenth and seventeenth years [he] was living in Perth and was in the habit of going to the prison to take lessons in French and in fencing from one of the officers confined there.'

60. *CM*, 24 May 1813.

61. Kaald, op. cit., 152.

62. NAS GD1/405/2, pencil notes, p.15.

63. Allen, 'French Prisons in Edinburgh Castle', op. cit., 166, quoting C. Mackie, *Historical Description of the Castle of Edinburgh* (Edinburgh, 1832), 36.

64. Marote-Carrier, op. cit., 146. Elting, *Swords Around a Throne*, op. cit., 587, notes that French army barracks usually had 'a billiard parlour and a circulating library'.

65. Kaald, op. cit., 162.

66. Ibid., 145.

67. Marote-Carrier, op. cit., 104.

68. NLS Acc. 3651/68, ltr, 1 Jan. 1814, F. Diotz to Capt. A. Brown.

69. Marote-Carrier, op. cit., 157. Laurencini seems likely to have been Antoine Lorenzini, 24, b. at Trieste, midshipman, naval sloop *Peulié*, capd in the Mediterranean Jun. 1808, who had arr. from Edinburgh Castle in Aug. 1811 at Greenlaw and was transferred from there in Sep. 1812 to Perth. ADM 103/157, No. 236.

70. Marote-Carrier, op. cit., 172.

71. Penny, *Traditions of Perth*, op. cit., 93.

72. TNA ADM 98/170, circular, 8 Oct. 1811.

73. Penny, *Traditions of Perth*, op. cit., 93.

74. Kaald, op. cit., 145, 146.

75. Marote-Carrier, op. cit., 104, 105.

76. Ibid., 121, 122.

77. Kaald, op. cit., 99, 100, entry for 10 Jan. 1809.

78. Ibid., 90, entry for 15 Nov. 1808.

79. Marote-Carrier, op. cit., 106.

80. Kaald, op. cit., 90, 92, entries, 14 and 19 Nov. and 3 Dec. 1808.

81. Ibid., 93, entry, 13 Dec. 1808.

82. Ibid., 99, entry, 8 Jan. 1809, at the time of General Moore's retreat to Corunna.

83. Ibid., 112, 142, 167.

84. NAS, Hannay Coll., GD214/739/1.

85. See TNA ADM 103/156, No. 104 (C. Scheurman); ADM 98/278, ltr, 7 Mar. 1812, TB to Capt. Moriarty; ADM 103/114, No. 1,339; ADM 103/489, Dumfries; ADM 103/491, Scheurman; ADM 103/596, No. 150; Perth Museum & Art Gallery, item 89/22/9 1935, No. 1,173; TNA ADM 103/263, No. 1,173.

86. *Perth Courier*, 5 May 1814.

87. NLS MS 3651 fols 64-5 and 68.

88. Beaudoin, op. cit., 636, 638.

89. Kaald, op. cit., 151, 155, entries for 10 Feb. and 26 Mar. 1810.

90. Ibid., 151.

91. Ibid., 144, 145.

92. Ibid., passim. One of Kaald's correspondents was Capt. Alexander Morison, who had himself apparently been a prisoner of war in Trondheim for almost two years until repatriated in May 1809. Morison wrote to Kaald from Glasgow, Aberdeen, Leith, and Gothenburg. See Kaald, op. cit., 123, entry for 8 Aug. 1809.

93. Ibid., 139.

94. Marote-Carrier, op. cit., 109.

95. NLS MS Acc. 5811/1/31.

96. Marote-Carrier, op. cit., 180.

97. TNA ADM 98/197, circular, 12 Feb. 1808, TB to agents at parole towns.

98. TNA ADM 98/133.

99. Beaudoin, op. cit., 664.

100. Marote-Carrier, op. cit., 109-11, 145.

101. Ibid., 80.

102. Ibid., 92, 171.

103. Ibid., 146, 147.

104. Ibid., 158-9.

105. TNA ADM 98/114, ltr, 22 Feb. 1808, TB to Adm.

106. TNA ADM 98/197, circular, 4 May 1808, TB to all depot and parole agents.

107. TNA ADM 98/116, ltr, 6 Jan. 1810, TB to Adm.

108. TNA ADM 98/280, ltr, 19 Jan. 1814.

109. *Dundee Advertiser*, 6 May 1814.

110. NLS MS Acc. 5811/1/26.

111. TNA ADM 103/434, No. 2,197; NAS GD1/405/2, ltr, from J.C. (John Cowan), said to be in *Scotsman*, May 1881. A search of the *Scotsman* for that month has failed to find the letter; James, *Naval History*, op. cit., Vol. V, 439. Three other letters, two of them in English, from Priere at Valleyfield in 1811-12 survive: the two in English to Andrew

Johnston, depot clerk at Valleyfield, later at Perth, (one of which suggests Priere had, or claimed to have, a usable knowledge of Italian, Spanish and Portuguese), and one in French to a prisoner on the hulk *San Antonio* at Portsmouth. The last of these letters appears not to have been sent and had probably been confiscated by the depot authorities because of such comments in it by Priere as: 'The inhabitants of this country are savages, egoists, of unparalleled dourness', and an implication that the agent had advised the prisoners to 'Buy an halter and hang ourselves.' NLS MS Acc. 5811/1/13, ltr, 26 Jun. 1811, Priere at Valleyfield to Charles Cuisso, 'Assistant Clerk Prisoner of War, His Majesty's Prison Ship *San Antonio*, Portsmouth Harbour, Hants.'

112. Emile Fairon and Henri Heuse, *Lettres de Grognards* (Liège, 1936), xi, 246, 247.

113. Ibid., 260.

114. Ibid., 258.

115. E.H. Kossmann, *The Low Countries* (Oxford, 1978), 65. Kossmann's reference was to the end of the 18th century, but there cannot have been much, if any, improvement in literacy in Belgium before the capture within the following decade of such of its soldiers as Laurent Maquet and Nicolas Terwagne.

116. Elting, *Swords Around a Throne*, op. cit., 392.

117. Jean Morvan, *Le Soldat Impérial*, op. cit., Vol. I, 297. No fewer than 1,322 of those prisoners at Perth depot who received money in 1812-14 from their families or friends at home were illiterate. Of 95 German soldiers of the Hesse-Darmstadt regt confined at the depot who in Oct. 1812 were sent money from home, 38 were illiterate. Payments ledger, Perth depot, in Perth Art Gallery and Museum, item 89/22/G/1935 passim; NLS MS Acc. 5811/1/22-4.

118. Adelbert J. Doisy de Villargennes, *Reminiscences of Army Life under Napoleon Bonaparte* (Cincinnati, 1884), 38-40, 62-4, 74, 75. Georges Blond, *La Grande Armée, 1804-1815* (Paris, 1979), 21, says that most young conscripts recruited in France to the army received no letters from home because their parents were illiterate. Coignet of the Imperial Guard, who eventually became a captain, had first to learn at the age of 33 how to read and write when he was made a corporal, so that he met the basic educational qualifications for that rank. Coignet, *Soldier of the Empire*, op. cit., 158-9.

119. Kaald, op. cit., 138.

120. Beaudoin, op. cit., 708.

121. Marote-Carrier, op. cit., 172. Leroi was almost certainly Antoine Le Roy, 42, b. at Granville, capt. of *Hirondelle* priv. when capd in the English Channel in Sep. 1810, and who, as Marote-Carrier indicates, was father of Nicolas Le Roy, aged 10, taken prisoner also on the *Hirondelle* and who shared his father's captivity successively at Esk Mills, Valleyfield and Perth.

122. Walker, *The Depot at Norman Cross*, op. cit., 147.

123. Such classes were held, for example, at Millbay depot in England. No prisoner north of the Border appears to have emulated Baron Bonnefoux, a former parole prisoner sent as a punishment to the hulk *Bahama* at Chatham, who there published an English grammar book, a copy of which Abell found in the Bibliothèque Nationale in Paris. Abell, op. cit., 229, 60.

124. Kaald, op. cit., 134, entry for 16 Sep. 1809.

125. Ibid., 126, 127, entry for 20 Aug. 1809.

126. Black, *Penicuik and Neighbourhood*, op. cit., 22, 23.

127. NAS GD1/405/2, pencil notes, p. 36. Whether the number of pets kept by prisoners in the Scots depots resembled the huge number of dogs kept by those at Stapleton depot near Bristol, is unknown. As a result of one dog at that depot being thrown into a well, an order was given to destroy no fewer than 710 other dogs there. Abell, op. cit., 213, 214. Abell suspected the dogs were kept not as pets but for eating by the prisoners.

128. *Edward Costello. Adventures of a Soldier. The Peninsular and Waterloo Campagins* (London, 1967), ed. Antony Brett-James, 47, 48.

129. Kaald, op. cit., 87, 96, 163, 181, 182, entries for 13 Nov and 24 Dec. 1808, 21 Apr. and 27 Jul. 1810.

130. Marote-Carrier, op. cit., 158.

131. Ibid., 157.

132. *Perth Courier*, 5, 12 and 19 Aug. 1813. Monsieur de Cuyper or De Kuyper was, or appears to have been, he who had played a part in the projected uprising of prisoners on board the ship bringing Marote-Carrier and other prisoners from Chatham to Leith in Feb. 1811.

133. Ibid., 26 Aug. 1813.

134. *EEC*, 21 Aug. 1813.

135. Kaald, op cit., 150.

136. Marote-Carrier, op. cit., 107-8.

CHAPTER 16: BOREDOM AND ACTIVITY: PHILANDERING, PRAYING, GAMBLING, FORGING, WORKING

1. *Parliamentary Papers*, Vol. IX (London, 1812), 301.

2. See above, pp.159-64.

3. NLS MS Acc. 5811/1/63, p.8; TNA ADM 98/276, ltr, 27 Dec. 1810, TB to Capt. Pellowe; *Morison's Perth and Perthshire Register for 1814 of the Public Offices, Office Bearers, etc., in the City and County* (Perth, 1814), in NLS MS Acc. 5811/1/62, p.63. At Perth, for instance, the matron (aptly named or not) was Mrs Dovey.

4. TNA ADM 98/276, ltr, 22 Jan. 1811, TB to Capt. Pellowe.

5. Macbeth Forbes, op. cit., NAS GD1/405/2, pencil notes, p.19. Macbeth Forbes, writing this a century or so ago, meant by 'Making love through the grille' that prisoners making the acquaintance of women at the markets could only communicate with them by eye, speech, gesture, or possibly handwritten notes, through the small grilles in the wall or fence. It was the scene that the boy William Chambers had described at Valleyfield as '... several prisoners ... stationed at small wickets opening with hinges in the tall palisades, offering for sale articles, such as snuff-boxes of bone...' Chambers, 'Some Early Recollections', *Chambers's Journal*, No. 600, op. cit., 402.

6. TNA ADM 98/280, ltr, 22 Nov. 1813. The agent's letter has not survived and the reason for the woman's exclusion is not stated in the Board's reply.

7. *Perth Courier*, 9 Sep. 1813.

8. Kaald, op. cit., 154, 164, 167.

9. Ibid., 160-2.

10. *Perth Courier*, 28 Jan. 1813; Sievewright, *Depot at Perth*, op. cit., 15.

11. Marote-Carrier, op. cit., 184-5, 188, 189, 190. Marote-Carrier declined, to protect the Dunkirk man's family, to mention his name, but he was Frederik Haultz. They were the only two prisoners dischgd from Perth on 17 Feb. 1814 to Leith. If François Petit was indeed married to a Scotswoman during his somewhat intermittent captivity, then those two bridegrooms had been taken prisoner on the same priv..

12. Hugue's letter in French to Capt. and Mrs Brown, and its accompanying English translation, are in NLS MS 3651 fol.70. The English translation reads thus: 'Captain, Vouchsafe an unfortunate to communicate these words to you. I have the honneur to expose to you that I have sent to Miss your Chamber-maid, my intentions which have always been, Such they are still to put an end to what I have communicated to her, considering the prerogatives your Captainship would honnour me with in the future. Considering the Government business now going on, my little fortune, and not being far advanced in English pronunciation, I therefore dare hope you will not take it as improper that I, by writing, trust you my true intentions, with an inviolable secret. I leave your Captainship to be the judge of the result and success of my dearest wishes. Forgive me, Sir, the boldness I take to trouble you, Praying you to tell her, yourself, that I wish her as good as I can do to what is the dearest object of my wishes, though I had not yet such good luck as to know her name. I have the honour to be with the utmost respect, Captain …'.

13. *Perth Courier*, 8 Jul. 1813. The dismissal of Patrick Miller, store clerk, had been recommended by Capt. Moriarty, depot agent, to the TB on 22 Jun. and approved by the Board four days later. TNA ADM 98/280, and ADM 99/237.

14. Lewis, *Social History of the Navy*, op. cit., 282.

15. It was presumably at least partly to homosexuality that Basil Thomson, an early 20th century historian of the Napoleonic War captives at Dartmoor depot in England, referred when he wrote that among the demoralised prisoners there known as 'the Romans', who had been 'expelled from the society of decent men' among the prisoners, 'the darkest forms of vice were practised … almost openly.' Thomson, *Dartmoor*, op. cit., 45-58. Abell quotes several comments by prisoners confined on the hulks in the south of England which likewise indicate homosexual relations among some of the prisoners who had to endure the terrible conditions on board. Abell, op. cit., 59, 76, 87.

16. TNA ADM 98/127, ltr, 20 Oct. 1803, Sir R. George to John King, Home Office.

17. TNA ADM 98/132, ltr, 19 Oct. 1811, TB to Robert Peel.

18. TNA ADM 1/3763, fol. 331, ltr, 27 Aug. 1812, TB to J.W. Croker, Adm.

19. TNA ADM 98/279, reply, 21 Sep. 1812, from TB to ltr, 15 Sep. 1812, from Capt. Brown.

20. Ibid., ltrs, 27 Jan. 1814, to Capt. Brown and Lieut. Priest. Mr Aikin has not been further identified.

21. NAS GD1/405/2, pencil notes, p.32.

22. *EEC*, 28 Sep. and 21 Oct. 1809, and 13 Jan. 1810. Perhaps one of those Greenlaw prisoners was later the porter whom Charles Cowan met in Paris in 1838 and who had been a prisoner of war at Penicuik (depot unstated). The porter told Cowan that 'while he was at Pennicuick some one, unknown on earth, had presented him with a copy of the Bible, by a persual of which he had become a totally changed and much more happy man.' Cowan, *Reminiscences*, op. cit., 15.

23. Beaudoin, op. cit., 631.

24. Kaald, op. cit., 94, 95, 96, 98, 109, 114, 205.

25. *Perth Courier*, 21 Jul. 1814.

26. Thorp, *French Prisoners' Lodges*, op. cit., preface (unpaginated).

27. Ibid., 277, 279, 280. A photograph of this certificate is in Thorp, op. cit., 278. The certificate measured 14 ins x 12¾ ins, with the figure of Minerva, Roman goddess of wisdom, at the foot. Thorp says it was entirely drawn by hand in ink and sepia and testifies to the skill and patience of the prisoner who drew it.

28. Ibid., 28.

29. Abell, op. cit., 38.

30. Johnston, 'Recollections', op. cit., pp. 9-10.

31. Marote-Carrier, op. cit., 163.

32. Anton, *Retrospect of a military life*, op. cit., 32.

33. Kaald, op. cit., 158.

34. Johnston, 'Recollections', op. cit., p.11.

35. Their forging of banknotes aroused the interest of J. Macbeth Forbes (1846-1913), secretary, Scottish Bankers' Institute, in the history of the prisoners. His article in the *Bankers' Magazine*, Mar. 1897, titled 'French Prisoners of War in Scotland, and Bank Note Forging', leaves everyone interested in these subjects in his debt, as do his articles on 'The French Prisoners-of-War in the Border Towns, 1803-1814' (in *Transactions of the Hawick Archaeological Society, 1912*), and 'French Prisoners on Parole at Dumfries, Sanquhar, Lockerbie, and Lochmaben' (in *Dumfriesshire and Galloway Natural History and Antiquarian Society Transactions*, Third Series, Vol. I, 1913). Francis Abell, a pioneering historian of the French prisoners of war in Britain, acknowledged his debt to Macbeth Forbes, who gave Abell access to his manuscript and typescript notes, compiled between 1890 and his death in 1913, and now preserved in NAS (GD1/405). Macbeth Forbes, born in Perthshire, began work in Perth branch of the Bank of Scotland in 1861, and after working in several county branches, including Aberdeen, was transferred to Edinburgh, where from 1897 until his death he was agent of the Dalry branch. An Edinburgh JP, Macbeth Forbes was also the first treasurer of the Franco-Scottish Society. His obituary is in the *Scotsman*, 16 Jan. 1913.

36. Macbeth Forbes, *Bankers' Magazine*, Mar. 1897, op. cit., 401.

37. Ibid.

38. *CM*, 21 and 28 Sep. 1811; TNA ADM 98/277, ltr, 9 Sep. 1811, TB to M. Wright.

39. TNA ADM 98/277, ltr, 25 Sep. 1811.

40. Ibid., ltr, 27 May 1811, TB to M. Wright, Edinburgh; ADM 103/112, Nos 9 (Duhenot) and 477 (Plantaut), and ADM 103/157, Nos 8 (Duhenot), 68 (Nivelet), 113 (Caron), 152 (Gonsalvez), 276 (Plantaut), and 679-81 (Nivelet, Caron and Gonsalvez); ADM 103/568, Nos 123 (Plantaut) and 124 ((Duhenot); ADM 103/600, Nos 100 (Plantaut) and 101 (Duhenot).

41. TNA ADM 103/157, No. 677.

42. Macbeth Forbes, *Bankers' Magazine*, op. cit., 409.

43. Ibid., 404, 405.

44. Wilson, *Annals of Penicuik*, op. cit., 121; Deacon, op. cit., 14.

45. TNA ADM 98/277.

46. Ibid.; ADM 103/157, No. 677.

47. TNA ADM 98/277, ltrs, 26 Sep. 5 and 12 Oct. 1811, TB to Capt. Moriarty.

48. TNA ADM 98/278.

49. Ibid. The prisoner detected forging banknotes according to the Dutch boy's statement may have been Mathieu Voila, 27, b. at Cosin, soldier, 82nd Line regt, capd on Martinique, 1809, who had arr. at Valleyfield on HMS *Brune* from Plymouth on 19 Sep. 1811. In Dec. that year the Valleyfield agent asked instructions from the TB 'for the disposal of Mathieu Voila, who had been in close confinement since October for forging Bank Notes.' Voila appears consequently to have been rel. from the cachot. He escaped from Valleyfield on 25 Apr. 1813. TNA ADM 99/213, ltr, Capt. Moriarty to TB, received 16 Dec. 1811; ADM 103/434, No. 3,181 (Voila).

50. TNA ADM 98/170.

51. TNA ADM 98/278, ltr, 15 Feb. 1812, TB to Lieut. Priest.

52. TNA ADM 103/157, Nos 113/680 (Caron), 152/681 (Gonsalvez), 77 (Bouyer), 99 (Guillemard), and 318 (Raymot); ADM 105/45; ADM 103/112, No. 520 (Raymot).

53. James Grant, *Old and New Edinburgh* (London, nd. (1882)), Vol. I, 127.

54. *CM* and *EEC*, 13 Feb. 1812; and, e.g., *Dumfries Courier*, 18 Feb. 1812, *Kelso Mail* and *Perth Courier*, 20 Feb. 1812. The advertisement was repeated four or five times during the following five weeks.

55. Allen, 'French Prisons in Edinburgh Castle', op. cit., 167, quoting Bank of Scotland Archives, Directors' Minute Book, 24 Feb. 1812.

56. *Glasgow Courier*, 15 Feb. 1812.

57. Macbeth Forbes, *Bankers' Magazine*, op. cit., 402-4. Macbeth Forbes recorded how one of the banks 'drew up an elaborate report on the whole subject, the pith of which was that all such processes of law should be set agoing at the expense of the procurator fiscal; that banks were public institutions, performing public functions, and as such should be protected by the law; that the felony being a public felony, was committed against the lieges, and that "it originated with the prisoners of war, of whom there is an extraordinary number in this country." In short, this bank, though its notes were forged [in the leading case, tried at the High Court in Sep. 1812, of Private Alexander Thomson, alias John Laurie, of the Aberdeenshire militia, a guard over the prisoners at the Penicuik depots], refused to prosecute. Its action or inaction was tantamount to raising the standard of revolt against what are termed private prosecutions in criminal cases.' Macbeth Forbes does not name the bank concerned but it must have been either the Bank of Scotland or the Commercial Bank, for it was their notes that witnesses at his trial spoke to seeing in the possession of Thomson. See, e.g., *EEC*, 10 Sep. 1812.

58. Macbeth Forbes, *Bankers' Magazine*, op. cit., 403.

59. *EEC*, 25 Jul. 1812, which also reported that day the recapture of the three at Glasgow; Macbeth Forbes, *Bankers' Magazine*, op. cit., 403. For L'Imbert (or Louis or Jacques) Altier see above, Appendix 3, No. 10. On 1 Apr. 1812 Altier, along with Augustin Flour, Pierre Roset or Rosier, and Ferdinand Lefebvre or Lefevre, was dischgd from Valleyfield to the sheriff in Edinburgh. TNA ADM 103/124, No. 2,289; ADM 103/157, No. 197; ADM 103/112, No. 539; ADM 103/435, No. 5,310. Ferdinand Lefebvre or Lefevre, 29, b. at Rouen, drummer, capd on the m.o.w. *Le Brave*, 1806, at St Domingo, had arr. at Valleyfield from Portsmouth on 1 Oct. 1811. Pierre Roset, 26, b. at Rouen, soldier, capd 'at sea' on *Petit Confiance* priv., 1806, had also arr. from Portsmouth at Valleyfield on 1 Oct. 1811. Augustin Flour, 33, b. at Tamboure, seaman, capd on *Le Vengeur* priv., Jan. 1809, had been transferred in Mar. 1811 to Valleyfield

from Esk Mills. TNA ADM 103/434, Nos 4,195 (Lefebvre), 4,165 (Roset) and 2,154 (Flour).

60. *CM*, 6 Aug. 1812; National Archives of Ireland, Kilmainham Jail Register, 1812, No. 80, 'Leuis [sic] Limbert Altier'; Macbeth Forbes, *Bankers' Magazine*, op. cit., 403.

61. NAS GD1/405/2, pencil notes, p.10.

62. TNA ADM 98/279, ltr, 7 Dec. 1812, TB to Capt. Brown.

63. TNA ADM 103/434, Nos 3,046 and 3,840; ADM 103/435, Nos 5,622, 5,627, 5,629, 5,650, 5,711, 5,715, 5,749, 5,870 and 6,097. The 11 prisoners were: on 9 Oct., No. 3,840 Silvetre Marmise or Marmire, 22, b. at Bordeaux, soldier, regt u., capd on the frig. *Minerve*, 1806, off Rochefort, who had arr. at Valleyfield in Oct. 1811 from Portsmouth; No. 5,622 François Soulet, 25, b. at Sette, seaman, capd on the m.o.w. *Mont Blanc*, 1805; on 12 Oct, No. 5,629 Jean Baptiste Pegie, 26, b. at Paris, seaman, capd on the sloop *Tapageuse* in the West Indies, 1805; on 2 Dec., No. 3,046 François Crosmier, 21, b. at Grenneville, soldier, 66th infantry regt, capd at Guadeloupe (n.d., but probably in 1809), who had come to Valleyfield in Sep. 1811 from Plymouth; No. 5,627 Pierre François Labry (or Laby), 34, b. at Paris, seaman, capd on the frig. *L'Armide* off Rochefort, 1806; No. 5,650 Felix Ceas, 21, b. at Marseilles, seaman, capd on the corvette *Bèrgère*, 1806; No. 5,711 Guillaume Merielle, 27, b. at Painboeuf, seaman, capd on the frig. *Belle Poule* at Cape of Good Hope, 1806; No. 5,715 Guillaume Delacroix, 23, b. at Dieppe, seaman, capd on *Point du Jour* priv. in the English Channel, Nov. 1808; No. 5,870 Pierre Destanguer, 22, b. at Mont de Maison, soldier, capd on the m.o.w. *Formidable*, 1805; and No. 6,097, P. Vauchel, 23, b. at Bone, sergeant, 2nd infantry regt, capd in 1811, n.p.; and on 11 Dec., No. 5,749 Pierre Aufavre, 29, b. at Grandville, sergeant, 58th infantry regt, no details of capture. The nine who had all come on 1 Sep. 1811 to Valleyfield from Greenlaw were Soulet, Pegie, Labry, Ceas, Merielle, Delacroix, Destanguer, Vauchel and Aufavre.

64. Macbeth Forbes, *Bankers' Magazine*, op. cit., 404.

65. *CM*, 30 Oct. 1813.

66. *EEC*, 16 Dec. 1813.

67. NAS AD 14/14/56, ltr, G. Dickmans to William Scott.

68. *EEC*, 16 May 1814.

69. *Perth Courier*, Thurs., 26 Aug. 1813.

70. Ibid., 9 Sep. 1813.

71. *EEC*, 9 Oct. 1813; *Edinburgh Almanac for 1813* (Edinburgh, n.d. (1812)), 67.

72. TNA ADM 98/119, ltr, 9 Jun. 1812.

73. TNA ADM 98/170, circular, 11 Jun. 1812.

74. *EEC* and *CM*, 10 Apr. 1813.

75. *EEC*, 10 Sep. 1812.

76. Macbeth Forbes, *Bankers' Magazine*, op. cit., 402.

77. NAS AD 14/12/76.

78. NAS AD 14/14/4. Crombie was indicted to stand trial on 1 Mar. 1813 at the High Court for vending notes, but no report of his trial, which may have been abandoned, has been found.

79. *EEC*, 14 Jul. and 10 Sep. 1814. The forged notes found in Gray's box were said to be two each of the Bank of Scotland and Bank of England for £2, 16 one guinea notes of William Forbes & Co., 10 £1 notes of the Falkirk Bank Co., and five £1 notes of

the Dundee Union Bank, and thus demonstrated an impressive eclecticism on the part of the prisoners who had forged them. In a rare, if not unique, gesture 'The respectable Jury on the trial of Thomas Gray have, with a degree of benevolence and feeling much to be commended, given the seven guineas and a half allowed for their services to his wife.' *EEC*, 16 Jul. 1814.

80. NAS AD 14/13/7. In a letter of 11 Nov. 1813, informing the crown agent in Edinburgh of the arrest and charges against Blair, the procurator fiscal at Inveraray wrote: 'I have notified the apprehension and commitment of the prisoner to these banks [whose notes had been forged] but they appear to decline taking any concern in prosecuting, conceiving this to be the business of His Majesty's Advocate equally as it would be so in any other public crime.' *Scots Magazine*, Feb. 1814, 147-8; *EEC*, 4 Feb. 1814.

81. *EEC*, 17 Mar. 1814. The two men had passed a forged guinea note of the Bank of Scotland in a public house at Stirling Bridge. Beattie said he had been given the note by his employer in Edinburgh. Beattie, arrested after passing another forged note in Glasgow, was found to have a parcel of twenty such notes in his mattress. 'God bless me, what is this?' the searcher had enquired. 'I am afraid,' Beattie had replied, 'this will be a bad job.' Tolmie had apparently declared that when work was scarce Beattie had assured him he could get as many banknotes as he liked for a few pounds.

82. *EEC*, 7 Jul. and 11 Aug. 1814.

83. *EEC*, 16 Jul. 1814; *CM*, 16 Jul. 1814, which says the sentence on Horn was seven years' transportation.

84. *Perth Courier*, 9 Sep. 1813.

85. Ibid. A few days earlier, according to the *Courier*, a man had also been arrested 'for circulating base money at the depot', but nothing more about his case has been found. Ibid., 26 Aug. 1813.

86. *EEC*, 23 Apr. and 5 May 1814; *Scots Magazine*, May 1814, 391-2.

87. William Chambers, in *Chambers's Journal*, No. 607, 14 Aug. 1875, 513-15.

88. Macbeth Forbes, *Bankers' Magazine*, op. cit., 409, where he says that two prisoners were hanged at Winchester on 28 Mar. 1812, three others at Maidstone on 9 Apr. and one at Launceston on 21 Apr. Abell, op. cit., 149, says two at Norman Cross were convicted and sentenced to death but were respited during His Majesty's pleasure, and remained in gaol for nine years until the end of the war in 1814.

89. Macbeth Forbes, *Bankers' Magazine*, op. cit., 409, says: 'The Government was said to intend to shew no lenity to prisoners engaged in forging notes in England ... It would be interesting to know who paid the expense of bringing these poor French prisoners to justice—the Government or the Bank of England. The conjecture may be hazarded that it was the latter, as the public prosecutor was not known then in England. If the former, then it shows that the Bank of England wielded a power which was unknown to the Scottish banks.'

90. TNA ADM 98/120, ltr, 27 Nov. 1812, TB to Adm.; *CM*, 5 Dec. 1812.

91. William Chambers, 'Some Early recollections', in *Chambers's Journal*, No. 607, 14 Aug. 1875, 516.

92. TNA ADM 98/ 276, ltr, 5 Aug. 1809.

93. TNA ADM 103/153, Nos 400 (Stevensen), 410 (Stolls), 413 (Smitt). These three, all capd in May that year, were two elderly men and a boy. Claus Stevensen, 62, a

Norwegian seaman, and Jan Stolls, 14, b. at Memel, have already been mentioned above; the third prisoner was, as also earlier observed, Frederik Smitt, 58, seaman, b. at Konigsberg, East Prussia, and capd on the priv. *Klempa.*

94. TNA ADM 98/134, ltr, 8 Nov. 1813, TB to James Buller. Mr Henderson had given a bond for the security of the Dutchmen.

95. TNA ADM 103/496, 6 Dec. 1813.

96. TNA ADM 103/152, Nos 42, 43, 48, 49, 98 and 99; ADM 103/155, Nos 208 and 329; ADM 98/277, ltr, 14 Mar. 1811, TB to Lieut. Priest.

97. TNA ADM 98/277, ltr, 18 May 1811, TB to Capt. Pellowe; ADM 103/432, No. 586 (Chalet); ADM 103/486; NAS GD1/405/5/1/73; TNA ADM 98/280, ltr, 30 Nov. 1813, TB to Capt. Moriarty.

98. TNA ADM 98/276, ltr, 27 Feb. 1811, TB to Capt. Pellowe.

99. Marote-Carrier, op. cit., 104, 146, 164.

100. Marote-Carrier, op. cit., 158.

101. TNA ADM 98/277, ltrs from TB: 11 Mar. 1811 to Capt. Pellowe, 26 Mar. 1811 to Capt. Heddington.

102. Ibid., ltr, 11 Sep. 1811, TB to Capt Pellowe; ADM 98/280, ltr, 27 May 1813, TB to Capt. Brown.

103. TNA ADM 98/279, ltr, 8 Jan. 1813, TB to Lieut. Priest. It is not clear what tasks captives there were engaged on during the previous month, when the Board told Lieut. Priest: '… the Prisoners employed by you are only to work with Day Light.' Ibid., ltr, 14 Dec. 1812.

104. TNA ADM 98/280, ltrs, 27 May and 5 Jun. 1813.

105. TNA ADM 98/277, ltr, 9 Mar. 1811, TB to Capt. Pellowe. In directing in Dec. 1812 the agent at Valleyfield (where there was difficulty in finding enough ground for burials) to discuss with the crown architect in Scotland the burial of prisoners from that depot a mile away at Greenlaw, the Board declared: '… each corpse to be conveyed by 8 prisoners on a bier which you will provide for that purpose. The messmates of the deceased are to be thus employed under an escort.' But 'employed' in this case presumably did not imply payment. TNA ADM 98/279, ltr, 21 Dec. 1812, TB to Capt. Brown.

106. TNA ADM 103/117, fol. 12; ADM 103/114, No. 1,180.

107. TNA ADM 98/278, ltr, 22 Jul. 1812, TB to Capt. Moriarty.

108. TNA ADM 98/279, ltr, 7 Dec. 1812, TB to Capt. Moriarty.

109. TNA ADM 98/280, ltrs, 22 and 30 Dec. 1813.

110. TNA ADM 98/277 and ADM 98/278, ltrs, 17 Oct., 16 and 25 Nov. 1811, TB to Capt. Moriarty.

111. TNA ADM 98/279, ltrs, 21 Jan. and 25 Mar. 1813, TB to Capt. Brown.

112. TNA ADM 98/280, ltr, 9 Dec. 1813, TB to Capt. Brown.

113. TNA ADM 98/279, ltr, 24 Apr. 1813, TB to Capt. Moriarty.

114. TNA ADM 98/278, ltr, 25 Feb. 1812, TB to Lieut. Priest. The same rate of pay was to be given to 'the men' employed to pick hair. TNA ADM 98/279, ltr, 17 Dec. 1812, TB to Lieut. Priest.

115. TNA ADM 103/117.

116. TB depots regulation No. 8. obliged the appointment of these inspectors.

117. TNA ADM 103/117.

118. TNA ADM 98/277, ltr, 30 Sep. 1811, TB to Capt. Moriarty.

119. TNA ADM 98/279, ltrs, 12 Oct. and 14 Dec. 1812 and 30 Mar. 1813, TB to Capt. Moriarty.

120. Ibid., 24 Nov. 1812.

121. TNA ADM 98/170, 13 May 1811.

122. TNA ADM 98/278, ltr, 13 Jan. 1812.

123. Ibid., ltr, 30 Dec. 1811.

124. TNA ADM 98/280, ltr, 6 Jun. 1814; ADM 98/276, ltr, 27 Dec. 1810, TB to Capt. Pellowe.

125. TNA ADM 98/279, ltr, 24 Nov. 1812, TB to Capt. Moriarty.

126. TNA ADM 98/170, circular from Board, 11 Jan. 1811.

127. Ibid., 22 Jan. 1812.

128. TNA ADM 103/117. The three nurses were Pierre Lebas, seaman, capd on *Le Vengeur* priv., who appears to have worked in the hospital for seven days in Feb. 1811; Barthelemy Pieters and Jean Van Laard, seamen, capd on the priv. *Barbier de Seville*. Pieters worked as a nurse in the hospital for a fortnight in Feb., Van Laard for almost two months to 18 Apr. 1811. The two washermen were seamen, too: Jean Tant, capd on the priv. *Mameluke*, and Louis Patatrand, gunner, *La Vertu*. Tant worked in the hospital for ten days in Feb., Patatrand much longer—from 28 Feb. to 18 Apr. 1811. The cook was Mathias Matiche, soldier, Navarre regt, who worked in the hospital for seven days in Feb.; and the barber Pierre Vaines, seaman, priv. *Barbier de Seville*, who was employed in the hospital from 27 Feb. to 18 Apr. 1811.

129. Ibid.

130. TNA ADM 98/280, ltr, 13 Nov. 1813, TB to Capt. Moriarty.

131. TNA ADM 98/277, ltr, 23 Mar. 1811, TB to M. Wright; ADM 1/3762, fols 406 and 408.

132. TNA ADM 98/276, ltr, 27 Dec. 1810, TB to Capt. Pellowe.

133. Ibid., ltr, 20 Feb. 1811.

134. TNA ADM 98/280, ltr, 31 May 1813, to Capt. Brown.

135. For convalescent prisoners in Valleyfield hospital the TB sanctioned in Jan. 1813 the services of a nurse, a barber and a washerman at wages of 3d. each per day. When Esk Mills opened in Feb. 1811 the agent was told by the Board to pay the nurses and barbers 3d. per day, 'and the cooks, washermen, and other servants necessary for keeping the Hospital clean are to be paid by the contractor 6d. each per diem.' TNA ADM 98/279, ltr, 2 Jan. 1813, TB to Capt. Brown; ADM 98/276, ltr, 16 Feb. 1811, TB to Capt. Pellowe.

136. TNA ADM 98/277, ltr, 2 Mar. 1811, TB to Capt. Pellowe.

137. TNA ADM 98/280, ltr, 8 Oct. 1813, TB to Capt. Moriarty. A note survives in NLS MS Acc. 5811/1/3, the papers of Andrew Johnston, chief clerk at Perth, of the 'Number of Rations for Prisoners in the Hospital, including French Surgeons, Nurses, Washermen, etc.', who were victualled there between 1 Apr. 1813 and 1 Apr. 1814. The list shows that the total numbers of meals fell markedly from 4,760 in Apr. 1813 to 880 in Aug. that year, and to as low as 699 in Jan. 1814, before rising to 877 in Mar. 1814 (the highest number since the preceding Aug.). Unfortunately, the list does not separate the figures for hospital patients and for prisoners employed.

138. NLS MS Acc. 5811/1/17.

139. NLS MS Acc. 5811/1/18.

140. NLS MS Acc. 5811/1/27, ltr, 6 Jan. 1813; TNA ADM 103/263, No. 549.

141. NLS MS Acc. 5811/1/16, ltr, 29 Aug. 1812. That three out of four of the letters quoted here were written from Valleyfield on 29 Aug. 1812, the last of them evidently delivered by Grouet himself, was because the transfer of almost 70 prisoners was then about to take place from that depot to Perth. See TNA ADM 103/263, Perth Entry Book, Nos 1,134-1,200 inclusive.

CHAPTER 17: MONEY; MISERABLES; DISOBEDIENCE AND DISCIPLINE

1. Marote-Carrier, op. cit., 26, 55. A louis, or louis d'or, (which had been replaced by the *napoléon*), was worth about 20 francs.

2. Abell, op. cit., 256, says the US government gave each American prisoner of war at Dartmoor depot an allowance for soap, coffee and tobacco of 2½d. a day. But those at Greenlaw were in the depot only six weeks so it seems unlikely they received any such allowances there.

3. Kaald, op. cit., 98, 99, entries for 27 Dec. 1808 and 6 Jan. 1809.

4. Ibid., 115, entry for 31 May 1809.

5. Ibid., 119, entry for 7 Jul. 1809.

6. Ibid., 136, entry for 30 Sep. 1809.

7. Ibid., 144, entry for 14 Dec. 1809.

8. Ibid., 150, 167, 168, 181, 182, entries for 30 Jan., 19 May and 27 Jul. 1810.

9. Kaald, op. cit., 184, 185.

10. *Glasgow Courier*, 12 May 1810.

11. See, e.g., Robert Garioch, *Two Men and a Blanket. Memoirs of Captivity* (Edinburgh, 1975), 21, 22, 23, 54, 63, 80, 81, 152. The TB instructed Lieut. Flinn, RN, its agent at Leith, in Apr. 1808 to 'transmit to us an account of the payments made by you to the Danes at Leith up to the 31st March last, with an account current.' What payments these were is not clear but they may have been to Danes held captive on the admiral's flagship stationed at Leith. TNA ADM 98/276, ltr, 16 Apr. 1808.

12. Kaald, op. cit., 116.

13. Beaudoin, op. cit., 639. A sol or sou, a twentieth of a livre, was equal to five centimes. During the French Revolution the livre had become the franc; values obviously fluctuated, but 24 livres were worth about £1. Although until the end of the Peninsular War in 1813 occasional sums of money were sent to former regimental comrades in captivity in Britain by the French army in Spain, there is no evidence that any of it was ever sent to French prisoners in depots in Scotland. Bennett, op. cit., 290, gives as an example £106 sent in Feb. 1812 to officers of the 40th infantry regt capd at Arroyo dos Molinos who were on parole at Welshpool, Montgomeryshire. Bennett, op. cit., 286, also points out that from Mar. 1809 Napoleon granted half pay to army officers who were prisoners of war. But this money was not to be paid until the end of the war.

14. Oman, *Peninsular War*, op. cit., Vol. V, 217-64, in his account of the siege and fall of Badajoz to Wellington's troops on 6-7 Apr. 1812, says the garrison, 'all picked men', included two bns of the Hesse-Darmstadt regt amounting to 910 men, which 'had an excellent record'.

15. The list, Rechler's letter and his instructions to the corporal are in NLS MS Acc.

5811/1/22-4. There is uncertainty about the actual number of beneficiaries at Perth of the prince of Hesse-Darmstadt's donation. Even if, as Johnston indicates, there was a further part of the list of the soldiers' names which has not survived, it is not clear what is the basis for his statement that there were about 650 prisoners at Perth from the regt. The depot Entry Books appear to show only 204—and that was almost exactly the number (210) said to be in the regt who were transferred to Valleyfield at the end of Jul. and beginning of Aug. 1813. See TNA ADM 103/263, Nos 121-180 and 186-299, and passim a further score of men said to be 'Duke of Hesse' or 'Hesse Regiment'; ADM 103/264, Nos 2,908, 3,063, 3,507; ADM 103/265, Nos 5,012-14, 5,523-5; and the Valleyfield Entry Books ADM 103/435, Nos 6,440-5, and ADM 103/113, Nos 6,445-6,648.

16. Marote-Carrier, op. cit., 76-7.

17. Ibid.

18. Fairon and Heuse (eds), *Lettres de Grognards*, op. cit., 258.

19. The ledger, preserved in Perth Museum and Art Gallery, item No. 89/22/G.1935, was presented to Perth town council in 1925 by the Rev. John Stirton (1871-1944), a native of Perth, minister of Crathie, chaplain to the king, and author of many historical works.

20. TNA ADM 103/263, No. 1,988. Le Clerc or Leclaire, soldier, 88th line regt, capd at Badajoz, Apr. 1812, was b. at Rouen and was aged 32. He was repatriated on 5 Jul. 1814. Le Soeuf or Soiffe, soldier, 6th line regt, capd at Flushing, Aug. 1809, arr. at Perth from Valleyfield four years later. Aged 22, and b. at St Lot (Saint Lo?), he was rel. to France in Jun. 1814. TNA ADM 103/266, No. 7,694.

21. Aged only 23 at the time of his capture, but partly no doubt because of his affluence and partly also because during the three years he was in Scotland he was confined successively in all the depots except Esk Mills and also for half that period was successively in the two parole towns of Peebles and Dumfries, Petry appears to have become relatively well known among the prisoners in Scotland. He became well known, too, to the authorities as a troublesome prisoner or *mauvais sujet*. In Nov. 1810, a month after his capture, Petry had arrived at Greenlaw with other officers capd in Spain or Portugal but within a few days he had been sent with them on parole to Peebles. From there he was transferred a year later on parole to Dumfries, along with the other prisoners at Peebles, including Charles Hivert, a fellow lieut. in the 3rd Hussars, capd with him in the Peninsula. At Dumfries, Petry, Hivert and two other prisoners, Lieut. Rudolph Blatter, 3rd Swiss regt and Capt. Lashivisky or Laskivisky, 2nd Vistula regt, broke their parole and escaped in Jun. 1812. Petry and his three companions achieved the distinction, rare among prisoners in Scotland, of having their descriptions published in an advertisement by the TO on 6 Jul. on the front page of *The Times*. Petry, b. at Lisle, was 5ft 4½ins, of stout build, round face, fresh complexion, brown hair, hazel eyes, and with a cut on his forehead. Petry, Hivert and Blatter were recapd a fortnight later at Leith and sent to Valleyfield. At Perth Petry was confined in the same block (No. 1) as, and was an associate of, Marote-Carrier, along with whom and a number of other prisoners he became involved in a major attempt at escape by tunnelling. At the beginning of Nov. 1813, Petry, Hivert, Blatter and a score of other parole breakers, were sent from Perth to Edinburgh Castle, and at the end of that month they were embarked on HMS *Alexandria* at Leith, their destination the hulks at Portsmouth. Marote-Carrier, op. cit., 155, 167-75; TNA ADM 103/489 (Escapes—Dumfries, 29 Jun. 1812); ADM

103/435, No. 5,384; ADM 103/596, No. 53; ADM 103/156, No. 144; ADM 103/114, Nos 1,328-52.

22. Petry's payments were £12.8.0 on 23 Sep., £13.11.1 on 22 Oct., £18.3.6 on 25 Nov., £27.1.3 on 17 Mar. 1813, £27.2.9 on 17 Jun., and £36.2.9 on 23 Oct., ten days before he was sent to Edinburgh Castle. Hivert's payments were £53.15.0 on 9 Oct., £27.1.6 on 24 Apr. 1813, and £45.3.7 on 20 Oct. Perth Payments Ledger, op. cit., passim.

23. Ibid., 10 Mar. and 1 Dec. 1813. Pascal has not been found for sure in the Perth Entry Books. Dormier was said in the payments ledger to be No. 4,169—but the Perth Entry Book TNA ADM 103/264 shows No. 4,169 to have been Joseph Drolands (or Drolance), 27, b. at Liège and aged 27, a soldier, 76th line regt, capd Jun. 1812 at Salamanca, who arr. at Perth on 30 Nov. or 1 Dec. 1812 from Plymouth, had a 'Ball in Right Hand', and died at the depot on 17 Dec. 1813. Was Dormier therefore Drolands, with perhaps one of those names an alias, or were these two separate prisoners with whose Entry Book number there was some confusion?

24. W. Hamish Fraser, *Conflict and Class. Scottish Workers 1700-1838* (Edinburgh, 1988), 106, 97, and 91. The wages in the ten trades mentioned were stated in evidence before the Justices of the Peace in Lanarkshire, who had been asked by the handloom weavers to approve a list of prices.

25. Perth Payments Ledger, op. cit., p. 23, No. 1,127; TNA ADM 103/263, No. 1,127.

26. Perth Payments Ledger, op. cit., p. 23.

27. TNA ADM 98/278, ltr, 16 Apr. 1812, TB to Capt. Moriarty.

28. Marote-Carrier, op. cit., 111-14.

29. Ibid., 110-11.

30. NLS MS Acc. 5811/1/34. TNA ADM 103/264, No. 3,835, says Didiot was in the 26th Chasseurs, had been capd, Sep. 1811, near Ciudad Rodrigo and arr. in Nov. 1812 at Perth from Portsmouth. Born at Metz, Didiot was aged 23 and had 'many wounds'. He was rel. to France in Jun. 1814.

31. NLS MS Acc. 5811/1/40. Foux was not in fact No. 4,082 in the Entry Book TNA ADM 103/264 and attempts to trace him have been unsuccessful.

32. Perth Payments Ledger, op. cit., p.23. Michel Dufour, 59, b. at Damien, soldier, 5th Artillery, capd at Valcarnero, Feb. 1812, arr. at Perth in Aug. that year. He was rel. from the depot and captivity in Jul. 1814. TNA ADM 103/263, No. 912.

33. *Lettres de Grognards*, op. cit., 253.

34. The ledger mentions, for example, Sandeman Goodin & Co., London, John Tweedie, an [legal?] agent, Selkirk, John Heath, London, and William Hall & Co, Edinburgh. Marote-Carrier, op. cit., 110, 111, mentions of course John Knighton, English merchant perhaps but embezzler certainly, and also 'an Ostend merchant well known to everyone'.

35. TNA ADM 98/118, ltr, 19 Nov. 1811.

36. TNA ADM 98/170, 14 Dec. 1811.

37. TNA ADM 98/119, ltr, 16 Mar. 1812.

38. TNA ADM 98/170, circular, 28 Mar. 1812.

39. Marote-Carrier, op. cit., 108.

40. TNA ADM 103/263, Nos 1,134-1,200; Marote-Carrier, op. cit., 162.

41. Marote-Carrier, op. cit., 162, 163.

42. *Glasgow Courier*, 27 Jul. 1809. See also Lewis, *Napoleon and his British captives*, op. cit.,

30-1, where he states that the 400 wealthy Britons detained by Napoleon at Verdun during the war, and who transferred some or much of their wealth there from Britain, 'were unconsciously helping the enemy …'

43. Lucas-Dubreton, *Napoléon devant L'Espagne*, op. cit., 385.

44. TNA ADM 98/280, ltr, 13 May 1813, TB to Capt. Brown. Miserables or *rafalés* were certainly also to be found among British prisoners in France during the Napoleonic Wars. Lewis, *Napoleon and his British captives*, op. cit., 140-1, points out that 'The danger to the mass morale of prisoners of war has long since been recognised, and all possible precautions are always taken—now—to prevent any wholesale collapse of it. But—then—such precautions were hardly known.' Lewis considered that the most obvious causes of the collapse of the morale of rank and file prisoners were twofold: their enforced idleness and the separation of officers and men—the men's sudden deprivation of 'their natural leaders', their officers. But since at the Scots depots there were always some officers, whether commissioned in the army or navy or (as, for instance, Capt. Kaald at Greenlaw and Lieut. Marote-Carrier at Esk Mills, Valleyfield and Perth) from priv. or m.vs, confined with the rank and file prisoners, Lewis's second explanation seems to be open to at least some argument.

45. TNA ADM 98/199, ltr, 7 Apr. 1809, TB to James Cairns.

46. Anton, *Retrospect of a military life*, op. cit., 32. Howard was John Howard (1726-1790), prison reformer.

47. TNA ADM 98/280, ltr, 29 May 1813, TB to Capt. Brown.

48. Johnston, 'Recollections', op. cit., p.11.

49. TNA ADM 105/44, ltr, 2 Sep. (no year stated but the context indicates it was 1812), Douglas, at Edinburgh, to TB.

50. TNA ADM 98/278, ltrs, 25 Apr. and 13 May 1812, TB to Moriarty.

51. TNA ADM 98/279, ltr, 9 Sep. 1812, TB to Capt. Brown.

52. TNA ADM 103/648, bundles of lists of deaths at Valleyfield, passim.

53. TNA ADM 98/278, ltr, 13 May 1812, TB to Capt. Moriarty.

54. Ibid., ltr, 20 Jul. 1812, TB to Brown.

55. Ibid., ltrs from TB: 16 Dec. 1811 to Capt. Moriarty, and 11 Aug. 1812 to Capt. Brown.

56. Ibid., ltr, 18 Aug. 1812, TB to Capt. Brown.

57. TNA ADM 98/279, ltr, 16 Oct. 1812, TB to Capt. Brown.

58. Ibid., ltr, 24 Oct. 1812, TB to Capt. Brown.

59. Ibid., ltr, 7 Dec. 1812, TB to Capt. Brown.

60. Ibid., ltrs, 3 and 9 Mar. 1813, TB to Capt. Brown.

61. TNA ADM 98/280, ltr, 11 Sep. 1813, TB to Capt. Brown.

62. Ibid., ltr, 22 Jan. 1814, TB to Capt. Brown.

63. Ibid., ltr, 17 Jan. 1814, TB to Capt. Brown.

64. TNA ADM 98/279, ltr, 24 Oct 1812, TB to Capt. Brown.

65. None of the agents at the Scots depots appears to have followed the example of their colleague at Dartmoor depot where the Romans, as the miserables or *rafalés* there were termed and who numbered at one stage more than 500, were for long a particularly distinctive section among the prisoners. 'From morning till night groups of Romans were to be seen raking the garbage heaps for scraps of offal, potato peelings, rotten turnips, and fish heads, for though they drew the ration of soup at midday,

they were always famishing, partly because the ration itself was insufficient, partly because they exchanged their rations with the infamous provision buyers for tobacco with which they gambled ... Sometimes the continual state of starvation and cold did its work and the poor wretch was carried to the hospital to die, but generally the bodies of the Romans acquired a toughened fibre which seemed immune from epidemic disease.' Eventually, however, 'the scandal of their mode of life was so great' that on 16 Oct. 1813 'the scarecrow battalion of 436 "Romans" was mustered at the gate, decently clothed, and marched under a strong escort to a prison hulk in Plymouth, and kept under strict discipline until the peace.' Thomson, *Dartmoor*, op. cit., 48, 57, 58.

66. TNA ADM 103/263, No. 579 (Levalle); ADM 103/264, No. 3,617 (Le Couste). The other three, all also soldiers, who died are in ADM 103/264, No. 2,214, and ADM 103/265, Nos 5,760 and 5,821.

67. TNA ADM 98/280, ltr, 15 May 1813. Moriarty had informed the Board then that 'the Raffalés now amount to 102.' ADM 99/235, 11 May 1813.

68. Penny, *Traditions of Perth*, op. cit., 93.

69. Marote-Carrier, op. cit., 163-5.

70. TNA ADM 98/280, ltr, 13 May 1813, TB to Capt. Brown; Walker, *The Depot at Norman Cross*, op. cit., 95.

71. See above, Chapter 3 passim.

72. For conscription dodging and desertion from the French army during the Revolution and Empire, see Forrest, *Conscripts and Deserters*, op. cit. For atrocities during the Peninsular War, see, e.g., Oman, *Peninsular War*, op. cit., Vol. I, 68, 130, 131, 315, 530, Vol. II, 8, 12, 20-1, 164-5, 246-8, 260-1, 398, 561, Vol. III, 60, 287-8, 307, 341-2, 396-7; Lucas-Dubreton, *Napoléon devant L'Espagne*, op. cit., 202-5.

73. See above, Chapter 8 passim.

74. See above, pp.264-7.

75. Kaald, op. cit., 91, entry for 28 Nov. 1808.

76. Bowen threatened to stop the prisoners' market and the serving of their soup, as well as removing their hammocks from them. TNA ADM 105/44, ltr, 5 May 1811.

77. See, e.g., TNA ADM 98/170, TB circular, 29 Mar. 1810, to depot agents.

78. Cowan, *Reminiscences*, op. cit., 13.

79. Marote-Carrier, op. cit., 141-2. Marote-Carrier and his companion, as already observed, did not serve their full sentence in the cachot as they were able to feign illness and secure admission to the depot hospital.

80. Kaald, op. cit., 176.

81. TNA ADM 98/276, ltr, 8 Jul. 1808, TB to M. Wright.

82. Sievewright, *Depot at Perth*, op. cit., 4; *CM*, 18 Sep. 1813.

83. TNA ADM 98/280.

84. TNA ADM 98/277, ltrs, 4 and 14 Mar. 1811, TB to M. Wright.

85. Ibid., ltr, 17 Aug. 1811, TB to Capt. Heddington. Of the 11 prisoners, escapers or so called 'ringleaders' from Esk Mills, who between 4 and 9 Mar. 1811 were the first occupants of the cachot at the Castle, seven were transferred on 14 Aug. that year to Greenlaw. They were the priv. lieuts David Fourneau and Antoine Morel, the army lieut. Grandjean Duhenot, alias Benoit P. Grandjean, and the four priv. seamen Louis Jean Lepine or Lepin, Jean François Ruy, Jean Baptiste Cabouche, and Pierre

François Le Couche (alias Barbouche). Of the remaining four, the two naval lieuts Hipolyte Decreuse and Honoré Foucault escaped from the Castle on 12 Apr., the army lieut. Louis De Beausset or Debasset was sent on 30 Apr. to Sheerness, and the priv. seaman Jean Talise Simonsen volunteered on 21 Aug. into the RN. Duhenot, alias Grandjean, was sent a month after his arrival at Greenlaw to Edinburgh gaol or Tolbooth, from which he was rel. on 4 Oct. 1811 and sent, as already observed, on parole to Cupar, Fife. TNA ADM 103/112, Nos 1 to 11 inclusive, and ADM 103/110, Nos 1-8; ADM 103/568, No. 124; see also above, Appendix 1.

86. TNA ADM 98/278, ltr, 16 Nov. 1811, TB to Lieut. Priest.

87. Ibid., ltrs, 12 Dec. 1811, TB to Lieut. Priest and M. Wright.

88. TNA ADM 98/277, ltrs, 8 and 16 Apr. and 12 Jul. 1811, TB to Capt. Pellowe, and 16 Apr. 1811, TB to M. Wright. Perrot (whose first name is given in some sources as Tanques or Tanqui, not Jacques), seaman, 31, b. at Lesmurin (or Lesnevin), had been capd on the frig. *Minerve* off Rochefort, Sep. 1806, and was transferred in Mar. 1811 successively from Esk Mills to Edinburgh Castle then to Valleyfield. He was described as 5ft 3ins, well made, long face, brown complexion, black hair, hazel eyes, and with smallpox marks. He was dischgd to Leith, 4 Aug. 1812, and nothing more about him has been found. Jean Savignon, 28, b. at Bordeaux, and Joseph Penne, 26, b. at Cannes, were, like Perrot, naval seamen, the former capd on the frig. *L'Aventure*, Oct. 1803, Penne on the m.o.w. *Mont Blanc*, Nov. 1805. TNA ADM 103/112, Nos 20 (Penne), 53 (Savignon) and 68 (Perrot). Savignon was among the mass of escapers from Edinburgh Castle on 11-12 Apr. 1811 but, although details are lacking, he appears to have been soon recapd. A search for Mansard in the Valleyfield Entry Books was unsuccessful.

89. Johnston, 'Recollections', op. cit., p.10. There is no reason to doubt Andrew Johnston's recollection, but no prisoner named Cretien has been found among those who died at Valleyfield—perhaps he used an alias. A prisoner of that name is mentioned as a recapd escaper at Perth in Feb. 1813; but if, as Johnston says, Cretien had died at Valleyfield he cannot have been the escaper from Perth. Several other cases on the hulks in the south of England of prisoners being tattooed, as Perrot probably was at Valleyfield, and, in one case, at Millbay depot at Plymouth, being afterward stoned to death, for informing on attempts at escape, are recorded by Garneray, *The French Prisoner*, op. cit., 109, 110, as well as in *Hampshire Notes and Queries*, Vol. X, 1900, 77, and by Abell, op. cit., 231.

90. TNA ADM 103/434, No. 2,373; ADM 103/112, No. 468.

91. TNA ADM 103/434, No. 2,274; ADM 103/112, No. 463. The Castle Entry Book does not say how long Leboube, 20, b. in Alsace, and whose capture is said to have been 'at sea' in Mar. 1807, languished at the Castle but it shows he was still there two months later.

92. TNA ADM 103/432, No. 786; ADM 103/112, No. 466. Watigny, aged only 18 at the time of his capture, must have been among those prisoners in the Scots depots who had had to cope with particularly traumatic experiences. His ship, the *Général Ernouf*, which had formerly been the capd British naval sloop *Lilly*, was in action near Barbados in Mar. 1805 against another British warship, HMS *Renard*, which fired a broadside into her 'with such effect that in 35 minutes the *Général Ernouf* was set on fire, and in 10 minutes more blew up with a tremendous explosion. Every exertion was now made by the British to save the lives of their late enemies ... [and consequently] ... 55 persons [including Watigny] that were floating on the scattered remains of

the wreck, the survivors of a crew of 160, were rescued from a watery grave.' James, *Naval History*, op. cit., Vol. IV, 26, 27. Watigny remained at the Castle until 26 Aug., though whether throughout those four months he remained confined in the cachot is not known. He was then sent along with 47 other prisoners forming the second of three groups totalling 365 who were transferred in Aug.-Sep. from the Castle to Greenlaw. Watigny, whose physical description was then said to include 'sore eyes', escaped from Greenlaw on 16 Oct. but two days later evidently gave himself up, apparently at Edinburgh Castle, on the understanding that 'if Vice Admiral Otway [at Leith] will receive him' he would be 'discharged for His Majesty's Service.' Watigny was duly released from captivity at Greenlaw on 28 Nov. 1811 as a volunteer into the RN, which six years earlier while saving his life had taken him prisoner. TNA ADM 103/157, No. 325 and No. 673; ADM 98/277, ltr, 21 Oct. 1811, TB to Lieut. Priest; ADM 103/110, No. 325; NAS GD1/405/1. At least three other prisoners were sent from Valleyfield to the Castle between 7 Apr. and 25 Jun. 1811: François Noel, variously described as lieut. or 2nd capt., or as a soldier, capd on a priv. in 1808 (or 1809) at St Domingo (or 'at sea'), and who escaped from the Castle on 18 Dec. 1811 but was recapd and sent back to Valleyfield in Jan. 1812; Louis Montreuil, seaman, capd on the m.o.w. *La Caroline*, 1809, off Réunion, and Nicolas Bride, soldier, Chasseurs Rentrées regt, capd at Flushing, Aug. 1809. Noel was sent to the Castle for attacking a turnkey at Valleyfield; but whether the transfers of Montreuil and Bride were also to the cachot at the Castle is unknown. TNA ADM 103/432, Nos 143 (Noel), 350 (Montreuil) and 438 (Bride); ADM 103/112, No. 462.

93. Again, it seems, there were no such removals there from Perth depot: any cases there of forgery were subject to judicial process locally.

94. TNA ADM 103/434, No. 3,527; ADM 103/436, No. 7,650; *CM*, 28 Sep. 1811 and 22 Jul. 1813; NAS AD/14/13/74, ltr, 24 Aug. 1813, William Scot, procurator fiscal, to Hugh Warrender, crown agent.

95. For executions for murder or stabbing, on the hulks or at depots in England such as Forton, Norman Cross, and Portchester Castle, see, e.g., Abell, op. cit., 93, 94, 172, 178, 179, 218, 219.

96. Marote-Carrier, op. cit., 117, 118.

97. TNA ADM 103/152 and ADM 103/153 passim. The 38 American merchant seamen sent from Greenlaw to Leith on 3 Dec. 1812 after their five or so weeks of captivity there were probably en route to the hulks, if not to inland depots, in the south of England. TNA ADM 103/152, /153, /155, and /157 passim; Beaudoin, op. cit., 636.

98. The 'constant quarrels' reported in the press between French and 'Danish' prisoners at Greenlaw seem likely to have been a factor in that policy. *CM*, 6 Apr. 1811.

99. Beaudoin, op. cit., 636, 639, 640.

100. NLS MS Acc. 5811/1/38, ltr, 28 Dec. 1813, from Chanteleuse. All the other prisoners named in the letter were, like Chanteleuse, officers transferred from Scotland after breaching their parole by attempting to escape. Indeed 25 officers in breach of their parole had been sent on 3 Nov. 1813 from Perth to Edinburgh Castle en route to the hulks. Their transfer appears to have originated a month earlier in a letter to the TB from Lieut. General Wynyard, army commander in Scotland, 'representing the inconveniences arising from the confinement at Perth of French prisoners who have broken their parole and prisoners taken in privateers ...' TNA ADM 98/280, ltrs, 5 and 20 Oct. 1813, TB to Vice Admiral Otway. See also ADM 103/267; ADM

103/114, Nos 1,341 (Chanteleuse), 1,342 (Vidal); ADM 103/568, Nos 13 (Diruit), 23 (Chanteleuse), 25 (Vidal); ADM 105/45, Dumfries; *Dumfries Courier*, 26 May and 2 Jun. 1812.

101. Abell, op. cit., 123.

102. Marote-Carrier, op. cit., 141.

103. TNA ADM 98/279, ltr, 13 Apr. 1813, TB to Capt. Moriarty; *Perth Courier*, 8 Apr. 1813. That approval may suggest the depot, which had over 7,000 prisoners, had had till then only a small supply of handcuffs.

104. TNA ADM 98/279, ltr, 3 Dec. 1812, TB to Capt. Brown.

105. NAS GD1/405/2, p.4.

106. TNA ADM 98/278, ltr, 2 Jan. 1812.

107. NAS AD/14/12/63, precognition, 12 Mar. 1812, by François Petit. When Petit's handcuffs were removed at Falkirk by his escort he promptly escaped again.

108. TNA ADM 103/112, No.1; ADM 103/157, No. 1; ADM 103/263, No. 1,094.

109. TNA ADM 103/112, No. 84; ADM 103/263, No. 1,099.

110. Marote-Carrier, op. cit., 141-2.

111. TNA ADM 103/263, Nos 1,149 (Cairel) and 1,183 (Grimaldi); ADM 103/570, No. 52 (Grimaldi); ADM 103/435, No. 5,606 (Grimaldi); ADM 98/279, ltr, 22 Jan. 1813, TB to Capt. Moriarty.

112. TNA ADM 98/170, 20 Sep. 1809.

113. Ibid., 27 Mar. 1811.

114. TNA ADM 98/280, ltrs, 5 May and 6 Jun. 1814, TB to Capt. Brown.

115. TNA ADM 98/170, 20 Sep. 1809.

116. TNA ADM 98/277, ltrs, 8 and 16 Apr. 1811, TB to Capt. Pellowe; Johnston, 'Recollections', op. cit., p.10.

117. TNA ADM 98/119, ltrs, 9 Jun. and 13 Jul. 1812.

118. TNA ADM 53/574. A prisoner recommended by the TB 'for favourable consideration' after he had informed on a similar proposed shipboard rising on the frig. HMS *Success* was Mathew Le Mercier. 'It appears upon enquiry,' the Board, however, told the Adm. in Dec. 1812, 'that the Person who calls himself Le Mercier is Auguste Le Grange, Prize Master of the *Courier* Privateer, who took the name of Le Mercier and embarked in the room of that prisoner for Scotland.' The Board suggested that Le Grange 'be allowed to enter the Navy or merchant navy—if the latter, he should be sent to Chatham from where he can be sent on board an East Indiaman.' Which Scots depot Le Grange arr. at from the *Success* is not stated. TNA ADM 98/120, ltrs, 28 and 30 Dec. 1812, TB to Adm.

119. TNA ADM 98/277, ltrs, 16 and 17 Sep. 1811, TB to Lieut. Priest and M. Wright respectively.

120. Ibid., ltr, 29 Oct. 1811, TB to Lieut. Priest.

121. Ibid., ltr, 14 Mar. 1811, TB to M. Wright.

122. Marote-Carrier, op. cit., 118.

123. See above, pp.316, 358.

124. TNA ADM 98/277, ltr, 8 Aug. 1811, TB to Capt. Pellowe.

125. TNA ADM 98/279, ltr, 27 Aug. 1812, TB to Capt. Brown.

126. TNA ADM 103/648. (The escape return for Mariote was found among reports of the deaths of prisoners).

127. *Perth Courier*, 8 Apr. 1813; TNA ADM 99/244, ltr received 9 Oct. 1813 by TB from Capt. Moriarty; ADM 99/213, ltr, 16 Dec. 1811, Capt. Moriarty to TB.

128. Quoted in Walker, *The Depot at Norman Cross*, op. cit., 62.

129. Kaald, op. cit., 88, entry for 13 Nov. 1808.

130. Ibid., 173-4.

131. Ibid., 130-2, entries for 9, 10 and 11 Sep. 1809.

132. Cowan, *Reminiscences*, op. cit., 13; TNA ADM 98/277, ltr, 26 Jun. 1811, TB to Capt. Pellowe, approving Miles's appointment as a turnkey.

133. TNA ADM 98/279, ltr, 28 Sep. 1812.

134. Marote-Carrier, op. cit., 156.

135. See above, pp.24-9.

136. See above, pp.30-2.

137. TNA HO 28/34/149.

138. TNA ADM 98/170, TB circular, 5 Nov. 1811.

139. TNA ADM 98/278, ltr, 28 Nov. 1811, TB to Capt. Moriarty. The *aspirants* were not, however, to be marched to London, 400 miles from Valleyfield: that was a clerical error for Lauder, a mere 22 miles from the depot as the crow flies. There was also some discrepancy in the numbers of *aspirants* or midshipmen evidently sent to Valleyfield. The depot's Entry Book shows that on 14 or 16 Nov. 11 arr. from Peebles, seven from Kelso, and three from Jedburgh. All of them were sent to Lauder on 9 Dec. These details accord with the entries in the Lauder General Entry Book, which show that 21 midshipmen arrived there from Valleyfield, 11 on 10 Dec. and the other 10 the next day—the first prisoners in fact to arrive on parole at the Berwickshire town. Was the slight discrepancy in the number of parole prisoners who suffered this retaliation explained in the treacly gloss or spin put upon the official statement in the *Edinburgh Evening Courant* that the TB, 'with that humanity and liberality which have always been the characteristic of the British Government,' had ordered 'that if any of the midshipmen should be in such a state of health as to render the journey and confinement prejudicial, they were not to be removed from their place of parole'? TNA ADM 103/435, Nos 5,278-98; ADM 103/580, Nos 1-21; *EEC*, 21 Nov. 1811.

140. *Perth Courier*, 13 Aug. 1812.

141. Marote-Carrier, op. cit., 162-3.

142. TNA ADM 103/648, No. 3,072; ADM 103/434, No. 3,072.

143. Kaald, op. cit., 91, 119, 127, entries for 28 Nov. 1808, 6 Jul. and 22 Aug. 1809.

144. *CM*, 11 Apr. 1807. The punishment was said to have been inflicted on one day: whether the victim survived his punishment was not reported. Nor, of course, were the punishments inflicted on army offenders confined to floggings. In addition to the case of Private James Inglis, sentenced to 14 years' transportation for shooting a prisoner at Greenlaw, Andrew Williamson, a private in the Edinburgh Militia, who also must have spent some of his service on guard at Greenlaw depot, was found guilty in Dec. 1807 by a court martial at Edinburgh Castle 'of desertion on or about 11 November last.' He was sentenced to seven years' transportation to the penal settlements in Australia 'and at the end of that time to be at the disposal of His Majesty for service as a soldier in any of His Majesty's forces at home or abroad, for life or otherwise as His Majesty shall think fit.' *Glasgow Courier*, 16 Jan. 1808.

CHAPTER 18: GUARDS; UPRISINGS; GENERAL SIMON; DEPOT STAFFS

1. *EEC*, 7 Oct. 1805 and 30 Mar. 1807. The Scots Greys' depot, then at Piershill Barracks, Edinburgh, moved in May 1808 to Haddington. *CM*, 26 May 1808.
2. Kaald, op. cit., 113, entry for 8 May 1809.
3. *CM*, 7 and 18 Feb. 1811.
4. TNA WO 1/646, fol. 47.
5. Sievewright, *Depot at Perth*, op. cit., 7.
6. Kaald, op. cit., 88.
7. Marote-Carrier, op.cit., 153.
8. NAS GD1/405/2, Macbeth Forbes's notes, p.4. Macbeth Forbes gives no source for this information.
9. *EEC*, 8 Aug. 1812. The rooms into which the stables at Perth were converted were said to be 'filled with double beds, one above the other, in a very crowded state—which rendered it unhealthy, and filled the place with bugs and fleas to such an extent that they were uninhabitable.' Penny, *Traditions of Perth*, op. cit., 91. Nonetheless the former stables appear to have been where the militiamen remained housed. When Perth opened as a depot in the summer of 1812 there were press reports that 'a considerable number of soldiers are to be encamped in bodies between Inverkeithing and Perth for the more safe and ready conveyance of prisoners of war' to the new depot; but no other reference to any such camp or camps has been found. See e.g., *CM*, 20 Jul. 1812.
10. TNA ADM 98/279, ltr, 20 Nov. 1812, TB to Vice Admiral Otway.
11. Marote-Carrier, op. cit., 141-2.
12. TNA ADM 98/127, ltr, 13 Sep. 1803.
13. *EEC*, 9 Oct. 1813. The speaker was Sir Alexander Muir MacKenzie of Delvin.
14. TNA ADM 98/134, ltr, 17 Nov. 1813, TB to J. Beckett, HO. The Duke's letter, if it survived, has not been found.
15. See, e.g., TNA ADM 98/113, ltr, 2 Sep. 1807, TB to W. W. Pole, secretary, Adm.
16. Marote-Carrier, op. cit., 138-41.
17. *Perth Courier*, 6 May 1813.
18. Ibid., 4 Feb. 1813. Sievewright, *Depot at Perth*, op. cit., 17, indicates that one of the two militiamen arrested escaped from Perth city gaol on 8 Feb. but the other one, 'from a consciousness of innocence', declined to join him in his flight. No more information about this case has been found, although it may be to it Marote-Carrier referred in his recollection of a successful escape by three prisoners from Perth after bribing a guard. Marote-Carrier, op. cit., 175-7.
19. TNA ADM 99/236, ltr, received 10 Jun. 1813 by TB from Capt. Moriarty.
20. ' A few days ago a party of the Kirkcudbright Militia stationed at Gatehouse of Fleet apprehended and brought from thence to Kirkcudbright a person calling himself Peter Scieves, and who, upon examination before the magistrates of the burgh, acknowledged that he was a Danish prisoner of war and that he and seven others, also prisoners of war, had about two months ago, by bribing the sentries, obtained their release from Edinburgh Castle where they were confined. The magistrates committed him to the Tolbooth till otherways [sic] disposed of.' *Dumfries Courier*, 18 Aug. 1812. No further information about Scieves or that escape has been found.
21. Frequent escapes from Norman Cross depot in Huntingdonshire in autumn 1805

were the subject of a letter then from the Board to the military secretary of the Commander-in-Chief, the Duke of York. '... and as,' the letter said, '... there are strong reasons for believing they are aided by some of the soldiers of the regiment now doing duty over the prisoners, many of whom, from speaking the French language and the long time they have been at Norman Cross, have contracted habits of intimacy with the prisoners, we request you will submit to His Royal Highness whether it may not be proper in order at once to check so alarming and increasing an evil to order the guard at present on duty at Norman Cross to be relieved.' TNA ADM 98/128, letter, 28 Oct. 1805. There is evidence of the similar corruptibility of some guards in England on the hulks and at Dartmoor depot. See, e.g., Abell, op. cit., 55, and Thomson, *Dartmoor*, op. cit., 33-4.

22. Deacon, op. cit., 9, without giving her source, says that at Greenlaw the detachment guarding the prisoners was changed 'every month'. Anton, op. cit., the only militiaman known to have left some memoirs of his tour of duty at Greenlaw, does not say for how long his bn provided guards there.

23. There were 15 Scots towns which at one time or another during the war housed parole prisoners, but the maximum number at any one time, reached in 1812-14, was 13, since toward the end of 1811 Peebles had been replaced by Dumfries, and Cupar Fife by Lanark.

24. TNA HO 28/38/95-7.

25. TNA ADM 98/133, ltr, 17 Aug. 1812.

26. TNA HO 28/41, ltr, 2 Nov. 1811, TB to J.W. Croker, Adm.; TNA ADM 103/596 passim; ADM 103/600, Nos 1-113; ADM 103/599, Nos 40-66.

27. *The Letters of Sir Walter Scott* Vol. III: *1811-1814*, ed. H.J.C. Grierson (London, 1932), 111, 125-6. Another factor in the removal of the parole prisoners from Peebles to Dumfries is said to have been 'the terror of a lady of rank in the neighbourhood at so many enemies being near Neidpath Castle, where were deposited the arms of the Peeblesshire Militia.' Abell, op. cit., 333. In the months immediately before Scott's letter to Southey, General Lord Cathcart was asked by the magistrates of Glasgow, the sheriff of Renfrewshire and the lord lieutenant of Ayrshire to send additional troops to those areas to deal with what they considered were threats to public order by large numbers of handloom weavers demanding an increase in wages . A. Aspinall (ed.), *The Early English Trade Unions. Documents from the Home Office papers in the Public Record Office* (London, 1949), 122, 123 (Letter, 4 Jul. 1812, from the Lord Advocate to the Home Secretary).

28. See, e.g., M.I. Thomis, *The Luddites. Machine-breaking in Regency England* (Newton Abbot, 1970), 82-100.

29. Ibid., 144.

30. Cole and Postgate, *The Common People*, op. cit., 119, 120; Fraser, *Conflict and Class*, op. cit., 93.

31. J.L. and Barbara Hammond, *The Skilled Labourer 1760-1832* (London, 1920), 317, 318; Robert Reid, *The Land of Lost Content. The Luddite Revolt, 1812* (London, 1986), 200; TNA HO 79/2 (Home Office private and secret letters), Feb. 1812-Jan. 1817 passim. Writing on 14 Jul. 1812 to J. Beckett, under-secretary, HO, on the subject of those French prisoners of war on parole, General Maitland expressed his view that 'as well from breaking their Paroles in such a shameful manner, as from the general character of their conduct ... the attention of Government ought to be drawn to a more forcible mode of inspecting them and superintending both their

general Conduct and the mode in which they actually maintain their Paroles.' TNA HO 42/125, fols 529-33. An anonymous letter sent that same month to the Home Secretary from 'a well wisher' writing from 'Daypool near Hull', claimed that the writer, who described himself as having been 'too long a dupe to mischiefous men', was a secret Luddite delegate. 'I am sent with others,' he wrote, 'to different parts of the Country, and especially to where French prisoners are, many to some thousands are already sworn in, to rise on a certain day, appointed in all parts of the Kingdom on the 5th day of November next, the Luddites mean to rid themselves of all their Enemys. They reckon on 50,000 French Prisoners, as helpers, as out of all that are sworn, among the French, not one did refuse. … Men are to go to all the places where French Prisoners are, to assasinate the Gards, to get the Prisoners out, to join the Luddites, & then mischief follows. Tho' they are very quiet now … Beware French Prisoners. … I will go so far as to say that the Watch Word on that Day say 5th November next is to be—Liberty and Ludd, for Ever.' TNA HO 42/125, fol. 439. Although a TB circular on 4 Jun. 1812 to parole agents appears to have been confined to those, or some of those, in England, the reference in the text to 'England' may have been intended, as on countless other occasions, to mean Britain. 'It having been represented to His Majesty's Government that French Prisoners of War on Parole in different parts of England act as Agents of the French Government and distribute large Sums of Money among the disaffected persons in this Country, we direct you to make private Enquiry in order to ascertain whether the said representation be correct or not and to report to us the result of your Enquiry.' The results of the enquiries, if duly reported, appear not to have survived. TNA ADM 98/200.

32. TNA HO 79/2, ltr, 1 Apr. 1813.

33. The mutiny appears to have arisen out of the rejection by the War Office, on the advice of the Attorney General and Solicitor General in London, of a petition sent direct to the Prince Regent by some men in the Perthshire Militia. The men, who were serving in the regiment as substitutes, had claimed they were entitled under the Militia Act of 1802 to release from their military service at the end of five or at the most ten years from the date of their enrolment. The law officers concluded the men's claim was 'totally groundless' and that they had misunderstood the distinction made in the Act between those militiamen who were conscripts selected by ballot, and those who as in their own case were substitutes and who served by their own engagement and had received a considerable bounty. Section 35 of the Militia Act fixed the period of service for balloted men at five years. Section 36 fixed it for substitutes, too, at five years—but also prescribed that they would in addition serve as long as the militia remained embodied: and the king had ordered that the militia remain embodied. There had also been similar petitions from substitutes in the Lanarkshire and Berwickshire Militia. TNA WO 1/654, fols 85, 86, 89, 90, 93, 94; *EEC*, 25 Jan. 1813; *CM*, 28 Jan. 1813; *Dundee Advertiser*, 29 Jan. 1813. The deep unpopularity of the Scottish Militia Act, 1797, (37 Geo. III, cap. 103), had resulted during the weeks after its passage in widespread disturbances in Scotland, including a major riot, indeed massacre, at Tranent. There, after the Riot Act had been read, the Cinque Ports and Pembrokeshire cavalry, commanded by Lord Hawkesbury (later, as Earl of Liverpool, British prime minister, 1812-27), appear to have run amok: 12 local people were killed and a further score wounded—a greater loss of life even than in the Peterloo Massacre of 1819. See, e.g., K. J. Logue, *Popular Disturbances in Scotland 1780-1815* (Edinburgh, 1979), 75-115; Sandy Mullay, *Scotland's Forgotten*

Massacre (Edinburgh, 1979); H.W. Meikle, *Scotland and the French Revolution* (Glasgow, 1912), 178-185.

34. *Dundee Advertiser*, 26 Feb. 1813.

35. *CM*, 20 Feb., 6, 15, 18 and 20 Mar., 1 and 12 Apr., and 17 Jun. 1813; *Perth Courier*, 14 and 28 Jan., 25 Feb., 11 and 18 Mar. and 16 Sep. 1813; *Dundee Advertiser*, 26 Feb. and 17 Sep. 1813; *EEC*, 8, 13, 27 and 29 Mar., 5 and 26 Apr. and 1 May 1813; Fraser, *Conflict and Class*, op. cit., 85-96.

36. *The Times*, 25 Sep. 1813. *The Times* had lifted its report, dated 16 Sep. at Perth, from the *Perth Courier* of the latter date.

37. *Perth Courier*, 16 Sep. and 14 Oct. 1813.

38. The *Glasgow Courier*, 12 Mar. 1811, reported that 'An increased supply of ball cartridges has since been delivered to the soldiers ...'

39. Apart from the shooting by guards at Greenlaw of the prisoners Cottier in 1807 and Simonsen in 1810, and of several other individual prisoners at Greenlaw, Esk Mills and Valleyfield during attempts at escape, there were no mass shootings of prisoners at the depots in Scotland such as did occur on a hulk and at Dartmoor depot in England. According to the former Greenlaw prisoner Sergeant Major Beaudoin, during a dispute in May 1811 between the prisoners and the captain of the hulk *Sampson* at Chatham over the quality and quantity of their food the captain ordered the guards to open fire: about 15 prisoners were killed and 20 wounded. Beaudoin, op. cit., 658. Abell, op. cit., 80, 93, says six prisoners were killed then and 'a great many' wounded. At Dartmoor in Jul. 1813 attempts by American prisoners to celebrate Independence Day led to the guard firing on the prisoners and wounding two. Consequent fighting between the American and French prisoners led to the intervention of the guard and to 40 prisoners being badly wounded. Abell, op. cit., 249, 250; Thomson, *Dartmoor*, op. cit., 102. In a further violent incident on 6 Apr. 1815 at Dartmoor the guard fired on and charged with fixed bayonets at American prisoners, killing five and wounding 28. Abell, op. cit., 258-60. Thomson, *Dartmoor*, op. cit., 175-80, says there were 63 casualties: seven killed, two who died later from their wounds, and 54 others wounded.

40. TNA ADM 98/277, ltr, 26 Aug. 1811; ADM 98/279, ltr, 9 Mar. 1813.

41. *EEC*, 28 Aug. 1810.

42. TNA ADM 98/134, ltr, 27 Apr. 1813, TB to Col. Torrens.

43. Georges Six, *Dictionnaire Biographique des Généraux et Amiraux Français de la Révolution et de l'Empire (1792-1814)* (Paris, 1934), Vol. II, 458; Marcellin Marbot, *Mémoires du Général Baron de Marbot* (Paris, 1892), Vol. I, 154-67.

44. Doisy de Villargennes, *Reminiscences*, op. cit., 50-1.

45. Quoted in Julian Rathbone, *Wellington's War* (London, 1984), 191. Marbot, *Mémoires*, op. cit., Vol. I, 167, says that Simon, 'seeking to have his past errors forgotten and make up lost time in his promotion ... was the first to enter the enemy's trenches. But there a shot broke his jaw... He had almost no face left.' Abell, op. cit., 435, quotes George Napier (elder brother of William Napier, historian of the Peninsular War), who fought at Busaco, as saying that: 'We took some prisoners and among them General Simon. He was horribly wounded in the face, his jaw being broken and almost hanging on his chest. Just as myself and another officer came to him a soldier was going to put his bayonet into him, which we prevented, and sent him up as a prisoner to the General.'

46. Marbot, *Mémoires*, op. cit., Vol. II, 395.
47. TNA ADM 98/276, ltr, 24 Oct. 1810, TB to M. Wright.
48. Bennett, 'French Prisoners on Parole in Britain', op. cit., 257-61.
49. *Dictionnaire Biographique des Généraux*, op. cit., 458.
50. TNA ADM 98/119, ltrs, 13 and 16 Jan. 1812, TB to Adm.
51. Ibid., ltrs, 11 Jan. and 31 Mar. 1812, TB to Adm. The eight officers were respectively a colonel, a lieut. colonel, an army capt., a lieut., a surgeon, and three midshipmen. 'The letters of Col. Vaxoncourt were more offensive than those of the other prisoners.' Bennett, 'French Prisoners on Parole', op. cit., 224, says the eight were later sent to the hulks.
52. TNA ADM 1/3763, fols 74-83.
53. *The Times*, 20 Jan. 1812.
54. NAS GD 51/2/439/7 (Melville Castle Muniments), ltr, 14 Jul. 1812. By 'Masonic characters' was meant a masonic practice where letters of the alphabet were substituted for certain words.
55. Abell, op. cit., 435. General Marbot's opinion of Simon was that he was 'a capable man, but irresolute.' Marbot, *Mémoires*, op. cit., Vol. I, 155.
56. TNA ADM 1/3763.
57. *The Times*, 16 and 17 Jan. 1812.
58. Ibid., 20 Jan. 1812. These were no doubt the eight officers on parole at Odiham, Alresford and Thame.
59. TNA HO 79/1, ltrs, 20 and 28 Jan. 1812, Ryder to Cathcart, and 20 Jan. 1812, J. Beckett, HO, to Commissioner J. Bowen, TB.
60. I.M.M. MacPhail, *Dumbarton Castle* (Edinburgh, 1979), 153. The militia company in garrison in 1812 were from the Ayrshire regt, and in 1813 from the East Yorkshire. Dr MacPhail appears mistaken in stating there was also 'a number of French prisoners-of-war' in the Castle. General Simon and his servant were the only ones there.
61. TNA ADM 98/119, ltr, 20 Feb. 1812, TB to Admiralty; ADM 98/133, ltr, 22 Feb. 1812, TB to R.Ryder, Home Secretary; ADM 98/278, ltrs, 4 Mar. 1812, TB to Admiral Otway and General Lord Cathcart.
62. TNA ADM 98/278, ltr, 6 Mar. 1812, TB to General Lord Cathcart. A sadistic mass murderer of black people on St Domingo while he had commanded French forces there, General Donatien Rochambeau, strongly suspected by the TB of attempting while on parole at Ashbourne in Derbyshire to organise risings by prisoners of war in Britain, had consequently been sent in 1804 along with General Boyé, a fellow parole prisoner, into close confinement at Norman Cross depot. Ralph Korngold, *Citizen Toussaint* (Boston, 1944), 326-7; Bennett, 'French Prisoners on Parole', op. cit., 110-21.
63. *CM*, 14 Mar. 1812.
64. TNA ADM 98/133, ltrs, 20 Mar. and 7 Aug. 1812, TB to Barrack Board.
65. NAS GD 51/2/439/7 (Melville Castle Muniments), ltr, 14 Jul. 1812, Sir R. George to Lord Melville.
66. John Glen, *History of the Town and Castle of Dumbarton* (Dumbarton, 1847), 98, 99.
67. TNA ADM 98/280, ltr, 15 Feb. 1814, TB to General Wynyard; ADM 98/122, ltrs, 10 Feb. and 16. Mar. 1814, TB to Adm.; Abell, op. cit., 372. One result of his confinement there in Mar. 1812 was the retaliation promptly inflicted by the French government

on Major General Lord Blayney, a senior British prisoner of war on parole at Verdun. Coincidentally with Simon's arrival at Dumbarton Castle, Blayney was arrested and confined in the citadel at Verdun. Once the TB, however, on the instructions of the Adm., had informed Rivière of the circumstances of Simon's confinement at Dumbarton Castle, had pointed out that Blayney had not been guilty of any similar breach of parole, and had requested Blayney be immediately released from close confinement, the French government promptly complied with the request. TNA ADM 98/119, ltrs, 24 Mar. and 11 May 1812, TB to Adm.; Lewis, *Napoleon and his British captives*, op. cit., 206.

68. For Wright, see particularly above, Chapters 3 and 6; for Moriarty, above, Chapters 7, 17 and 20.

69. Among innumerable examples of the TO's fussy concern with, and tireless supervision of, the minutiae of depot routines and discipline was its order to Capt. Pellowe, agent at Valleyfield, in Aug. 1811: 'You will procure a fresh supply of marking ink', and its approval granted him the following month for '… your having ordered extra candles for the guard on account of the circumstances you have stated.' TNA ADM 98/277, ltrs, 5 Aug. and 6 Sep. 1811.

70. TNA ADM 1/3743, fol. 96, ltr, 27 May 1803, TB to Adm.

71. TNA ADM 1/3761, ltr, 1 Nov. 1810.

72. TNA ADM 98/132, ltr, 22 Jun. 1811, TB to Bowen, and ADM 98/170, circular, 22 Jun. 1811.

73. Biographical information has proved difficult to find about Moriarty and the other agents at the Scots depots. He had become a lieut. in 1776 during the American War of Independence, a commander in 1779, and a capt. in 1809. He died in 1833. Syrett and DiNardo, *Commissioned Sea Officers of the Royal Navy*, op. cit., 320.

74. In Aug. 1811, however, Gillies had been put on half pay by the TB and apparently kicked his heels at home until Perth depot was opened. TNA ADM 98/119, ltr, 4 Jun. 1812, TB to Adm.; ADM 98/278, ltr, 8 Jun. 1812, TB to Gillies; ADM 98/276, ltr, 20 Dec. 1810, TB to Capt. Pellowe; ADM 98/277, ltr, 28 Aug. 1811, TB to Gillies.

75. TNA ADM 98/279, ltrs, 26 Oct. and 20 Nov. 1812, TB to Capt. Moriarty. Beatty was appointed to HMS *Zealous* at the Nore at the end of 1813, and was succeeded at Perth by Duncan McNicoll. TNA ADM 98/280, ltr, 21 Dec. 1813, TB to Capt. Moriarty.

76. Johnston had begun as a clerk at Esk Mills before being promoted to first clerk there a few days before its closure, after which he had become first clerk at Valleyfield. Johnston, 'Recollections', pp. 4, 7; TNA ADM 98/276, ltr, 1 Mar. 1811, TB to Capt. Pellowe; ADM 98/277, ltr, 6 Mar. 1811, TB to Pellowe. It is not clear if Johnston immediately superseded Alexander Munro as first clerk at Valleyfield, or whether the two were jointly first clerks there from Mar. 1811 until Johnston's appointment as first clerk at Perth in summer 1812. In his claim for a pension after the war Munro appears to have claimed he was first clerk at Valleyfield continuously from Dec. 1810 to Sep. 1814, although he was in fact employed at Edinburgh Castle for some time during the second half of 1811. Munro was the TB's original choice as first clerk at Perth but the Board approved an agreement between him and Andrew Johnston that the latter fill that position and Munro be, or continue to be, first clerk at Valleyfield. TNA ADM 105/46; ADM 98/277, ltrs, 24 and 26 Aug. 1811, TB to M. Wright; ADM 98/278, ltr, 13 Jan. 1812, TB to Munro, and 13 and 20 Jun. and 13 Jul. 1812, TB to Capt. Moriarty.

77. Of the three clerks originally appointed in summer 1812 John Ramsay was dismissed as store clerk in Dec. that year for reasons not given. His successor, Mr Mitchell, Cupar, never appeared at the depot to begin work so he was replaced in Feb. 1813 by Patrick Miller. Miller was dismissed in Jun. that year. John Mathew or Matthew replaced Miller. John Thornton, the canteen clerk, previously a clerk at Greenlaw, died in Dec. 1813 and was succeeded as an extra clerk by his son John. John Lewis, one of the hospital clerks or assistant dispensers, had previously been assistant dispenser at Esk Mills and then at Valleyfield, where from Jun. 1811 he had also been depot interpreter until his appointment in Jul. 1812 to carry out both tasks at Perth. TNA ADM 98/278, ltrs, 20 Jun. and 18 Aug. 1812, TB to Capt. Moriarty; ADM 98/279, ltrs, 11 Nov. and 30 Dec. 1812, 6 Jan., 23 Feb., and 26 and 30 Jun. 1813, TB to Moriarty; ADM 98/280, ltr, 6 Dec. 1813, TB to Moriarty; ADM 105/46, ltr, 27 Feb. 1819, from Mr Lushington, HM Treasury, about a gratuity for Lewis.

78. Johnston, 'Recollections', op. cit., p. 8.

79. TNA ADM 98/279, ltr, 11 Nov. 1812, TB to Capt. Moriarty: 'You will let the Board know how you employ the Number of eight turnkeys and how you propose to station an additional one.' Marote-Carrier, op. cit., 154, recalled ten turnkeys 'and each of them had his lodging at one of the ten gates.'

80. The three ex-Esk Mills men were John McDonald, Robert Ritchie and Alexander Lymington, but none of the three appears to have been appointed at Perth. The two already appointed were John Duncan 'from Dartmoor' (who was also described as prison steward, or chief turnkey) and Jasper Armstrong. According to Macbeth Forbes, Duncan had also been a turnkey at Norman Cross depot in Huntingdonshire. TNA ADM 98/278, ltr, 20 Jun. 1812, TB to Capt Moriarty; NAS GD1/405/5/1/150.

81. Donald Campbell and Robert Walker were appointed in Jul., Robert Robertson and David Murray in late Aug. TNA ADM 98/278, ltr, 10 Jul. 1812, and ADM 98/279, ltrs, 25 and 28 Aug. 1812, TB to Capt. Moriarty.

82. TNA ADM 98/279, ltrs, 11, 19 and 27 Nov. 1812, TB to Capt. Moriarty. The names of the seventh and eighth appointed have not been found; the ninth was David Ferguson.

83. John Duncan was sacked in Jan. for 'repeated drunkenness', and James Hewatt 'of Edinburgh' appointed to replace him; Donald Campbell was sacked in Apr. and replaced then by John McEwen. TNA ADM 98/279, ltrs, 13 Jan., 15 and 27 Apr. 1813, TB to Capt. Moriarty; ADM 105/46, comments on ltr, 7 Jan. 1819, from George Harrison, HM Treasury.

84. The new appointee was Francis Dead (Dean? Dear?). TNA ADM 98/280, ltr, 11 May 1813, TB to Capt. Moriarty.

85. Robert Robertson was replaced for reasons unknown by John Sidney. TNA ADM 98/280, ltr, 8 Feb. 1814, TB to Capt. Moriarty.

86. TNA ADM 98/279, ltr, 10 Nov. 1812, TB to Capt. Moriarty. The matron appointed at the opening of the depot was Mrs Priscilla Wakely, widow of a doctor who had been an employee of the TO. She was succeeded in Jan. 1813 by Mrs Elizabeth Dovey, who remained as matron until the end of the war. ADM 98/278, ltrs, 10 and 23 Jul. 1812, TB to Capt. Moriarty; ADM 105/46, ltr, 24 Feb. 1819, Mr Lushington, HM Treasury, to TB about a gratuity for Mrs Dovey. The sempstress was Mrs Annandale, previously employed as such at Valleyfield and evidently the same woman of whom Captain Paul Andreas Kaald had written in his diary at Greenlaw. A proposal by the agent shortly before the depot opened that a second sempstress should also

be employed was vetoed by the TB. TNA ADM 98/278, ltrs, 20 and 29 Jun. 1812, TB to Capt. Moriarty. According, however, to *Morison's Perth and Perthshire Register for 1814* (Perth, 1813), 63, Mrs Doig was sempstress by 1813. May it have been that Mrs Annandale, if indeed a widow, had by then married Mr Doig?

87. TNA ADM 98/278, ltr, 20 Jun. 1812, TB to Capt. Moriarty. He was W. Doig, but no other information about him has been found (unless in fact he became husband to Mrs Annandale).

88. See, e.g., TNA ADM 98/279, ltr, 6 Oct. 1812, TB to Capt. Moriarty.

89. A few days before the opening of the depot the agent was authorised by the TB to engage 'another labourer or messenger'. The messenger engaged was John Stuart or Stewart; when he resigned in Nov. 1812 he was succeeded by Thomas Miller, previously labourer at the depot. TNA ADM 98/278, ltrs, 21 and 30 Jul. 1812, TB to Capt. Moriarty; ADM 98/279, ltr, 9 Nov. 1812, TB to Capt. Moriarty.

90. TNA ADM 98/278, ltr, 21 Jul. 1812, TB to Capt. Moriarty. When Miller became messenger at the depot he was succeeded in Nov. 1812 as labourer by J. McIntyre. TNA ADM 98/279, ltr, 9 Nov. 1812, TB to Capt. Moriarty.

91. TNA ADM 98/279, ltr, 18 Dec. 1812, TB to Capt. Moriarty: 'Walton, the man recommended by Sir T. Graham, is to be employed as one of the above persons if he should be fit for the situation.' Of those two labourers one named James Hutton was replaced in Jan. 1813 by another unnamed. Ibid., ltr, 29 Jan. 1813, TB to Capt. Moriarty. According to *Morison's Perth and Perthshire Register for 1814*, op. cit., 63, there were four labourers in 1813-14 at the depot.

92. TNA ADM 98/278, ltr, 30 Jul. 1812, TB to Capt. Moriarty; ADM 98/279, ltr, 20 Oct. 1812, TB to Capt. Moriarty. When John Morrison resigned in Dec. 1813 as one of the lamplighters he was replaced by David McCask—of the four, the only two whose names are known. TNA ADM 98/280, ltr, 20 Dec. 1813, TB to Capt. Moriarty. *Morison's Perth and Perthshire Register for 1814*, op. cit., 63, also states there were four lamplighters in 1813-14.

93. A few prisoners, as already observed, were also employed, at least from time to time, on a range of tasks by the depot authorities at Perth and the other Scots depots.

94. The agent was told by the TB on 8 Mar. 1811 that there was 'no need to appoint any hospital mate at present'; and when the surgeon proposed in Jun. 1812 the appointment of John Smith, he was told by the Board that 'that Gentleman has not passed the necessary Examination.' A reference by the Board in May 1813 to the French assistant surgeon declared that he 'cannot possibly be allowed to go in and out of the prison.' TNA ADM 98/277, ltr, 8 Mar. 1811, TB to Capt. Pellowe; ADM 98/278, ltr, 10 Jun. 1812, TB to John Macansh; ADM 98/279, ltr, 19 Dec. 1812, TB to Capt. Brown; ADM 98/280, ltr, 31 May 1813, TB to Capt. Brown. That John Macansh, surgeon at Valleyfield from Apr. 1811 after his transfer there from Esk Mills on its closure, was not appointed in the summer of 1812 as surgeon at the new depot of Perth may have been due to a clash of personalities between him and Capt. Moriarty, agent at Valleyfield in 1811-12: Marote-Carrier, op. cit., 142-4. It was not Macansh, although he was the senior of the two, but James Gillies, the original surgeon at Valleyfield appointed in Dec. 1810 but who had become assistant to Macansh at Valleyfield for a few months in 1811, who was appointed surgeon at Perth. According to a reference to staff at Valleyfield in a paper in TNA ADM 103/635, Part II, headed 'Abstract of the Establishment of the several Depots under stated, during the last War', n.d. and unsigned, the depot again had two surgeons as a result of the

transfer to it c. Dec. 1811 of staff who had previously been employed at Edinburgh Castle. On the other hand, as late as 19 Sep. 1811 (TNA ADM 98/277) the TB told Malcolm Wright, then agent at Edinburgh Castle, that the number of prisoners confined there having greatly diminished, '… under the present circumstances it is proper that the present establishment at Edinburgh Castle should be reduced,' and instructed him 'to discharge Mr Stone the surgeon … retaining only your clerk and one turnkey.' The Board added, however, that Stone was to be informed 'that we have entered his name on the list for immediate employment.' Whether Stone, or perhaps some other surgeon, was transferred or appointed soon afterwards to Valleyfield is not certain. If there were another surgeon assisting Macansh at Valleyfield after Gillies's departure in Aug. 1811 his name has not been found.

95.   NAS GD1/405/2, pencil notes, p.38; TNA ADM 98/276, ltr, 28 Dec. 1810, TB to Capt. Heddington. Although the evidence, as for the number of surgeons, is incomplete and contradictory there is a reference in the undated and unsigned 'Abstract of the Establishment [at] … Valleyfield' to there being two first or chief clerks at Valleyfield, including 'the Persons who were employed at Edinburgh Castle and who upon the breaking up of that Establishment, were transferred to Valleyfield'. TNA ADM 103/635, Part II. It seems likely that the other chief clerk, if indeed there were two, was not from Edinburgh Castle but, in 1811-12, Andrew Johnston, who was either co-equal with or, as has been seen, according to some sources had superseded Munro for some 15 months following the closure of Esk Mills and the transfer of its staff to Valleyfield.

96.   In Feb. 1811, a month before Valleyfield opened as a depot, the TB approved the appointment of two clerks (neither of them named but one was John Lauder and the other appears to have been surnamed White), one of whom was also to be interpreter. TNA ADM 98/276, ltr, 2 Feb. 1811, TB to Capt. Heddington. By Apr. 1811 John Lewis had been transferred from Esk Mills on its closure to Valleyfield as hospital clerk and interpreter. Whether White resigned or was dismissed is not clear, but in Jul. 1811 he was succeeded by John Macfarlane. TNA ADM 98/277, ltr, 15 Jul. 1811, TB to Capt. Pellowe. John Lauder was dismissed 'for neglect of Duty' in Nov. 1811 and replaced by James White (who may have been the same White who had been there four months earlier). TNA ADM 98/278, ltr, 15 Nov. 1811, TB to Capt. Moriarty. On the transfer in summer 1812 of John Lewis to Perth as hospital clerk and interpreter, John Macansh, the Valleyfield surgeon, successfully proposed that his own brother Alexander succeed Lewis as hospital clerk. TNA ADM 98/278, ltrs from TB: 13 Jul. 1812 to J. Macansh, 24 Jul. 1812 to Capt. Brown. In Nov. 1812 there occurs a reference to Alexander Manson as canteen clerk or keeper: Manson appears to have been at the depot for at least some months before then. TNA ADM 98/279, ltr, 11 Nov. 1812, TB to Capt. Brown. In Feb. 1813 John Macfarlane was dismissed 'for his very gross and repeated misconduct' (unspecified) and replaced by Cornelius Elliot. TNA ADM 98/279, ltrs, 19 and 22 Feb. 1813, TB to Capt. Brown. James White resigned in May 1814 and was succeeded by James Wilson. TNA ADM 98/280, ltrs, 4 and 13 May 1814, TB to Capt. Brown.

97.   NLS MS Acc. 5811/1/63, p.8; TNA ADM 98/277, ltr, 30 May 1811, TB to Capt. Pellowe; ADM 98/278, ltr, 20 Jun. 1812, TB to Capt. Moriarty. The first turnkey appointed at Valleyfield appears to have been John Laurie in later Dec. 1810, and a second, James Bushmer, was appointed a few days later. TNA ADM 98/276, ltrs from TB: 20 Dec. 1810 to Capt. Pellowe, 29 Dec. 1810 to Capt. Heddington. That same week the TB indicated that there would be six turnkeys on the establishment

at Valleyfield. Ibid., ltr, 27 Dec. 1810, TB to Capt. Pellowe. In Jun. 1811 Robert Aikin or Aitken, who appears to have originally been a turnkey or prison steward at Esk Mills, and whose skill as a carpenter by trade may have been put to use at that depot as a coffin maker, was appointed a steward or turnkey at Valleyfield as replacement for James Wilson, 'discharged for Mal Practices'; and Henry Miles was also appointed a turnkey. TNA ADM 98/277, ltrs, 9 Mar., 22 and 26 Jun. 1811, TB to Capt. Pellowe. In Sep. that year William Geddes became a turnkey at the depot. Ibid., ltr, 25 Sep. 1811, TB to Capt. Moriarty. Two other turnkeys, whose appointment appears to have gone unmentioned in the surviving archives, were the subject of an order sent by the TB to the agent in Dec. that year: '… direct you to reprimand the Turnkeys Lounie [? Lowrie] and Younger, and to apprize them, if they should be again guilty of a similar offence they must be discharged.' TNA ADM 98/278, ltr, 21 Dec. 1811, from TB to Capt. Moriarty. In Jul. 1812 the Board relented on its decision to dismiss William Geddes as a turnkey and instructed the agent 'to continue … Geddes in his Employment but to warn him that if he should give any further Cause of Complaint he will be immediately dismissed.' At the same time the Board approved the employment of 'Hugh Cranstin [? Cranston] as a Turnkey instead of John McDonald, whose appointment is not to take place.' Ibid., ltrs from TB: 15 Jul. 1812 to Capt. Moriarty, 22 Jul. 1812 to Capt. Brown. In Sep. that year the Board ordered the immediate dismissal of Henry Miles as a turnkey at the depot '… for having, without provocation, wounded three of the prisoners with a bayonet.' TNA ADM 99/219, 24 Sep. 1812. Miles appears to have been replaced by John Player, until then a turnkey at Stapleton depot near Bristol. TNA ADM 98/279, ltrs, 28 Sep. and 24 Oct. 1812, TB to Capt. Brown. Finally, in Jul. 1813 Thomas Grindlay was appointed as both turnkey and carpenter at Valleyfield. TNA ADM 98/280, ltr, 26 Jul. 1813, TB to Capt Brown.

98. The matron first appointed appears to have been Elizabeth White (until then a sempstress at Deal hospital in Kent), but if so she appears to have been replaced c. Apr. 1811 by Mrs Mary Ann McMillan, who until then had been matron at Esk Mills. No later reference to Elizabeth White has been found. Mrs McMillan was appointed matron at Perth depot a year before it opened, but after a prolonged leave of absence from Valleyfield in the first half of 1812 she resigned in Jul.—though whether only from her pending employment at Perth or from Valleyfield too is not clear. Only one other reference, in Aug. 1812, to the matron at Valleyfield has been found, but it did not name her. TNA ADM 98/276, ltr, 27 Dec. 1810, TB to Capt. Pellowe; Johnston, 'Recollections', op. cit., p.8; TNA ADM 98/277, ltrs, 15 Apr. and 20 Aug. 1811, TB to Mrs McMillan, and 29 Apr. 1811, TB to Capt. Pellowe; ADM 98/278, ltrs, 14 Feb. and 5 Mar. 1812, TB to Mrs McMillan, and 3 Jun., 10 Jul. and 5 Aug. 1812, TB to Capt. Moriarty. Whether there was a sempstress on the staff at Valleyfield from its opening in Mar. 1811 is not certain, although if there were none in its first few days the depot appears to have acquired one shortly afterward with the transfer of staff from Esk Mills, where Frances Rushmore had been sempstress. Johnston, 'Recollections', op. cit., p.8. It may therefore have been to the suggested appointment of an assistant sempstress that the TB referred in a letter to the depot agent in Oct. 1811, instructing him to inform John Macansh, depot surgeon, '… that if he considers a sempstress to be necessary he must represent the same officially to the Board through you …' TNA ADM 98/277, ltr, 15 Oct. 1811, TB to Capt. Moriarty. The next reference to the subject occurred in a letter from the Board to the agent six months later, which appears to confirm that there was indeed a sempstress at

Valleyfield: '… we direct you to employ Mrs Annandale to assist the sempstress as long as you may find it necessary.' TNA ADM 98/277, ltr, 21 Apr. 1812, TB to Capt. Moriarty. The implication in another Board letter to the agent in Jun. 1812 is that the sempstress then at Valleyfield was Frances Rushmore. 'The Board have no objection to either the Rushmores [James Rushmore, presumably brother, father or son (but not husband) of Frances, was a hospital steward] or Mrs Annandale going to Perth.' It was Mrs Annandale who went to Perth as sempstress, not Frances Rushmore. TNA ADM 98/278, ltr, 29 Jun. 1812, TB to Capt. Moriarty.

99. James Rushmore, formerly hospital steward at Esk Mills, seems to have been employed as such at Valleyfield until at least Nov. 1812 and perhaps until the end of the war. TNA ADM 98/278, ltr, 29 Jun. 1812, TB to Capt. Moriarty; ADM 98/279, ltr, 11 Nov. 1812, TB to Capt. Brown; NLS MS Acc. 5811/1/63, p.8. The two prisoners referred to were named Falise and Savara. TNA ADM 98/280, ltr, 22 May 1813, TB to Capt. Brown.

100. NLS MS Acc. 5811/1/63, p.8; TNA ADM 105/45, ltr, 27 Feb. 1819, Mr Lushington, HM Treasury, to TB; ADM 98/277, ltrs, 18 and 26 Apr. 1811, TB to Capt. Pellowe; ADM 98/278, ltrs, 20 Jun. and 10 Jul. 1812, TB to Capt. Moriarty.

101. The earliest reference found to one, although he is unnamed, is in TNA ADM 98/278, ltr, 17 Jan. 1812, TB to Capt. Moriarty. John Blackie was appointed to the job in Sep. that year; but two months later the messenger was said to be James Muir. ADM 98/279, ltrs, 28 Sep. and 13 Nov. 1812, TB to Capt. Brown.

102. NLS MS Acc. 5811/1/63, p.8. The next reference found to 'a labourer' was in Jan. 1812. TNA ADM 98/278, ltr, 17 Jan. 1812, TB to Capt. Moriarty. In Sep. 1812 James Craig was appointed labourer, but was replaced the following month by James Barrow. ADM 98/279, ltrs, 28 Sep. and 5 Oct. 1812, TB to Capt. Brown. 'Labourers', but unnamed, at Valleyfield were mentioned in a letter from the agent to the TB in Apr. 1813. Ibid., ltr, 13 Apr. 1813, TB to Capt. Brown.

103. James Blackwood, lamplighter, was discharged before the end of Mar. 1811 by the agent at Valleyfield and replaced by George Dickie. William Cranstoun, lamplighter, (presumably the additional lamplighter appointed the previous year) was discharged 'immediately' in Oct. 1812 ('having been detected … conveying spirits to the prisoners in a Bladder'), and replaced the following month by George Dickie, junior, as assistant lamplighter. NLS MS Acc. 5811/1/63, p.8; TNA ADM 98/277, ltr, 26 Mar. 1811, TB to Capt. Heddington, and 6 Sep. 1811 to Capt. Pellowe; ADM 98/279, ltrs, 24 Oct. and 20 Nov. 1812, TB to Capt. Brown.

104. The agent was also told he should appoint 'As many French Assistant Surgeons as may be absolutely necessary', and if necessary a French prisoner, too, as a hospital clerk. A French surgeon was employed as an assistant surgeon or hospital mate three weeks after the depot opened, and so was a prisoner as hospital or surgeon's clerk. For the time being the agent was refused permission by the Board the week after the depot opened to appoint any more clerks, but on 18 Mar., a week after the prisoners had been removed to Valleyfield and Edinburgh Castle but a week or so before the decision to abandon Esk Mills altogether as a depot, two more clerks were appointed. According to a list in the papers of Andrew Johnston, chief clerk at the depot, at the time of its closure and the transfer of its staff to Valleyfield, Esk Mills had in addition to those shown above a supernumerary clerk (Alexander Munro). There is also a reference in mid-Feb. to washer-women keeping the depot hospital clean. Who among all the Esk Mills staff were retained as employees at Valleyfield

is not entirely clear, but the Board on 30 May approved of the agent 'having paid off the remainder of the establishment at Esk Mills agreeably to the directions of Commissioner Bowen.' Those members of the Esk Mills staff in Feb.-Mar. 1811 who are or appear to be identifiable were, besides Capt. Pellowe, the agent: surgeon—John Macansh; chief clerk—John White (succeeded from 6 Mar. by Andrew Johnston); clerks—Mr Leslie, John Lewis, Andrew Johnston (from 1 Mar.), Mr Turner and Mr Macfarlane (both from 18 Mar.); dispenser—Thomas Tripe; hospital steward—James Rushmore; matron—Mrs Mary Ann McMillan; sempstress—Frances Rushmore; turnkeys—Robert Aitken, William Doig, Henry Miles (successor to Doig), John McDonald, Robert Ritchie, and Alexander Lymington; lamplighter—James Blackwood [?]. There was also James Cuthbertson, who was dismissed as a turnkey a fortnight after the depot opened. TNA ADM 98/276, ltrs, 3, 24 and 27 Dec. 1810, 2 Jan., 12, 16, 21 and 23 Feb., and 1 and 6 Mar. 1811, TB to Capt. Pellowe; NLS MS Acc. 5811/1/63, p.8; TNA ADM 98/277, ltrs, 2, 9 and 18 Mar. 1811, TB to Capt. Pellowe, and ltr, 15 Apr. 1811, TB to Mrs McMillan; ADM 98/277, ltr, 20 Jun. 1812, TB to Capt. Moriarty; ADM 98/117, ltr, 21 Nov. 1810, TB to Adm.

105. TNA ADM 98/277, ltr, 19 Sep. 1811, TB to M. Wright. Dr Kellie, a naval surgeon on half pay who tended to sick and wounded seamen at Leith, and who had been surgeon at Greenlaw depot in its earlier years, had been the Board's first nominee in Dec. 1810 for appointment at the Castle but he declined to accept the job. Thomas Stone, another naval surgeon on half pay, was appointed in Feb. 1811, with permission from the Board to employ a paid French prisoner as assistant when necessary. The agent's application to the Board at the end of Mar. 1811 to appoint a servant for the dispensary received a dusty answer: '... we are much surprised ... as there are only sixteen patients in the hospital according to your last weekly return.' TNA ADM 98/117, ltrs, 28 Dec. 1810 and 20 Feb. 1811, TB to Adm.; ADM 98/277, ltrs, 23 Mar., 1 Apr. and 19 Sep. 1811.

106. TNA ADM 98/280, ltr, 9 Jul. 1813, TB to Vice Admiral Otway, and ltr, 31 Jan. 1814, TB to Lieut. Priest. The temporary surgeon was Mr S. Eden.

107. TNA ADM 98/276, ltr, 29 Dec. 1810, TB to M. Wright. Of Wright's two nominations as turnkeys Peter Cameron (who had been dismissed as a turnkey at Greenlaw the previous year) proved unacceptable to the Board: '... after what has passed respecting Peter Cameron's conduct we cannot agree to his reappointment as you propose'; but the other nominee, Alexander McDonnell or Mcdonell, was appointed, along with one surnamed Campbell (presumably Donald or Finlay Campbell). Mr M. Coomb was appointed the agent's clerk. MacDonnell (or Macdonell—the spelling of his name varied at each mention) lasted hardly a month as turnkey and was replaced by Frederick Flower. Coomb (or Combe, as his name was subsequently spelt), too, did not last as clerk more than two or three weeks, and the Board suggested he might be succeeded by Mr Leslie, one of the Esk Mills clerks. It was, however, not Leslie but a Mr Neilson (or Nelson) who then became clerk. Ibid., ltrs, 10 and 18 Jan. and 8 and 15 Feb. 1811, TB to M. Wright; ADM 98/277, ltrs, 4 and 11 Mar. 1811, TB to M. Wright.

108. TNA ADM 98/277, ltr, 4 Mar. 1811, TB to M. Wright.

109. Alexander Drummond was appointed interpreter without anything being said about his acting also as a turnkey; and a week or so later Archibald McDonald was appointed a turnkey. Ibid., ltrs, 11 and 21 Mar. 1811, TB to M. Wright. In Jun. that year James Craigie was appointed a turnkey, but whether as an additional one or, more likely,

as a replacement for McDonald or Flower is not certain. Ibid., ltr, 26 Jun. 1811, TB to Capt. Pellowe. Upon Malcolm Wright's re-appointment in Aug. 1811 as agent at the Castle, given the intended transfer from there of Capt. Heddington back to Valleyfield as agent, John Thornton was to replace Mr Neilson (or Nelson), who 'had neglected his duty', as clerk at the Castle. In fact, however, Thornton was retained at Valleyfield and it was Alexander Munro, intermittent chief clerk at the latter depot, who took over as clerk at the Castle until he could take up his appointment as chief clerk at the new depot then being built at Perth. Ibid., ltrs, 17, 24 and 26 Aug. 1811, TB to M. Wright.

110. Ibid., ltrs, 19 Sep., 15, 19 and 26 Oct. 1811, TB to M. Wright. (By the last date the agent may have been mollified by learning that the Board had 'no objection to your retaining Donald Campbell in the service for the present agreeably to your suggestion': Campbell, of whom this seems to be the first mention since Feb. that year, had presumably by then become the turnkey-messenger); ADM 98/278, ltrs, 26 Nov. and 14 Dec. 1811; ADM 98/280, ltr, 11 Jan. 1814, TB to Capt. Brown.

111. The Castle appears to have finally ceased to hold prisoners of war on or by 18 Mar. 1814. TNA ADM 99/255, ltr, 18 Mar. 1814, Lieut. Priest, RN, to TB.

112. The first, appointed in 1804, was Kellie, the same naval surgeon who, as has been seen, declined at the beginning of 1811 to become surgeon at the depot at Edinburgh Castle. He was succeeded at Greenlaw, date unknown (but certainly by Jan. 1807), by Robert Renton, who in turn was followed in Mar. 1811 by William Hill. Hill was dismissed in Jun. 1813 for negligence. As by then Greenlaw was undergoing a massive extension which might have made it the largest depot in Scotland, the number of its staff and inmates appears to have been reduced while the building work proceeded. It is therefore not certain that Hill had any successor there as surgeon before the end of the war. A French prisoner named Frederick Pevirance (or Peurance) appears to have been employed from Nov. 1811 as assistant surgeon. TNA ADM 98/128, ltr, 2 Aug. 1804, TB to Commissioners for Sick and Wounded Seamen. ADM 98/277, ltrs, 5 Mar. 1811, TB to Lieut Priest, and 29 Mar. 1811, TB to M. Wright; ADM 98/117, ltr, 20 Feb. 1811, TB to Adm.; ADM 98/280, ltr, 23 Jun. 1813, TB to Lieut. Priest; ADM 98/278, ltr, 26 Nov. 1811, TB to Lieut. Priest.

113. Until his resignation in Dec. 1809 under pressure from the TB Alexander Fraser was clerk, with Francis Wharton as his assistant—though when Wharton had been appointed is uncertain: it may have been from the opening of the depot in 1804 but, if so, he must then have been a very young clerk indeed. Fraser was succeeded then by Wharton. Wharton, however, soon appeared as not merely the new occupant of the clerk's chair but also heir to the idiosyncracies which had been practised at Greenlaw by Malcolm Wright as agent and Fraser, and in Jan. 1811 he, too, fell foul of the TB: '… we consider Mr Wharton's conduct as totally unjustifiable in permitting a prisoner to go out of prison or any account or under any pretence whatever without our special order, and … we cannot possibly retain Mr Wharton in the service …' TNA ADM 98/276, ltr, 5 Jan. 1811, TB to M. Wright. But Wharton, as a result it would seem of a plea on his behalf to the Board by the new agent Lieut. Priest, was reprieved from dismissal: 'Board allow you to retain Mr Wharton in his present situation, but he is to be warned of the Consequence of any similar Misconduct in future.' Ibid., ltr, 4 Feb. 1811, TB to Lieut. Priest. At the end of 1811 Wharton fell ill and his work as clerk at Greenlaw was undertaken during his absence by Alexander Munro, seconded from Valleyfield (or Edinburgh Castle); but that period

apart, Wharton appears to have remained clerk at Greenlaw until the end of the war. TNA ADM 98/276, ltrs, 19 Dec. 1811, TB to Lieut. Priest and Capt. Moriarty; ADM 98/278, ltr, 19 Dec. 1811, TB to M. Wright; ADM 98/280, ltr, 13 Jan. 1814, TB to Lieut. Priest. An extra clerk, John Thornton, was appointed at Greenlaw in May 1812 to administer sales of small beer at the depot, but was transferred six months later to do the same work at Perth depot and he does not appear to have had a successor as a clerk at Greenlaw: from then until the end of the war Wharton was sole clerk. TNA ADM 98/278, ltrs, 29 May and 17 Jun. 1812, TB to Lieut. Priest; ADM 98/279, ltr, 11 Nov. 1812, TB to Lieut. Priest.

114. The earliest surviving reference to any of them by name was in Sep. 1809 when the agent was told by the TB to 'immediately discharge the Turnkeys Cameron and Rose ... [and] to propose to us fit Persons to succeed them.' As within a month two named Macdonald and Campbell were appointed they were presumably the replacements. In Jan. 1811 one named Handyside was appointed to succeed Finlay (?Donald) Campbell (presumably the same Campbell who had been appointed in Oct. 1809), who had been transferred to Edinburgh Castle. In Jun. that year Robert Ritchie replaced as a turnkey J. Ormeston, who had been discharged. Whether Ormeston had himself replaced either Macdonald or Handyside, or whether there was always, or at least had been for some time past, an establishment of three turnkeys at Greenlaw is not certain but that the latter was the case is suggested in a letter from the Transport Board to the agent at nearby Valleyfield at the end of the war: 'We ... approve of your discharging the three Turnkeys, Lamplighter and Messenger belonging to the Greenlaw establishment.' TNA ADM 98/276, ltrs, 22 Sep. and 19 Oct. 1809, and 28 Jan. 1811, TB to M. Wright; ADM 98/277, ltr, 25 Jun. 1811, TB to Lieut. Priest; ADM 98/280, ltr, 5 May 1814, TB to Capt. Brown.

115. The lamplighter, whose name is nowhere given, appears to have been employed only from Jun. 1811 but to have continued working at the depot until after the end of the war. The messenger, Andrew Hunter, was employed from Mar. 1811 and was not in fact discharged at the beginning of May 1814 but continued to work at Greenlaw for at least a few weeks longer. TNA ADM 98/277, ltr, 25 Jun. 1811, TB to Lieut. Priest; ADM 98/280, ltrs, 5 and 13 May 1814, TB to Capt. Brown, and 14 May 1814 to Lieut. Priest. When in Aug. and again in Oct. 1811 Lieut. Priest, the agent, sought the permission of the TB to increase the depot staff, first by employing a prison and hospital steward, second an interpreter and storekeeper, the Board's reply to his first request was: 'We do not consider it necessary to appoint a prison and hospital steward, having no such appointment when there were upwards of 600 Prisoners in confinement at Greenlaw'; and to his second: '... as you have already more assistance than Mr Wright [the previous agent] had during the seven years that he had charge of Greenlaw Depot, the Board do not therefore consider it necessary to allow you a storekeeper or interpreter, and you must consequently consider yourself as having charge of the stores.' When Priest again raised the issue of his having to act not only as storekeeper but also as interpreter, he was told by the Board that if he was unable to accept that no more staff would be employed at Greenlaw '... we shall be under the necessity of looking out for an Agent who understands the French language, in order to obviate the inconvenience mentioned by you.' Nor, the following month, did the Board 'consider a Clerk for the Hospital to be necessary', though it granted permission for a French prisoner to be employed as assistant surgeon. It was as late as Dec. 1813 before the Board relented sufficiently on the issue of an interpreter as to authorise the depot clerk, Francis Wharton, to add that task to his work in return

for some extra payment. TNA ADM 98/277, ltrs, 29 Aug., 15 and 30 Oct. 1811, TB to Lieut. Priest; ADM 98/278, ltr, 26 Nov. 1811, TB to Lieut. Priest; ADM 98/280, ltr, 14 Dec. 1813, TB to Lieut. Priest.

116. TNA ADM 98/280, ltrs, 23 Jun. 1813, TB to Capt. Brown and Lieut. Priest. Priest, the agent, was to remain at Greenlaw 'for the purpose of superintending the new works', but under the direction of Capt. Brown, agent at Valleyfield.

117. TNA ADM 99/154, fol. 47.

118. TNA ADM 98/276, ltr, 3 Jan. 1811, TB to Priest.

119. Ibid., ltr, 9 Feb. 1811, TB to Capt. Pellowe.

120. Ibid., ltr, 15 Feb. 1811, TB to Priest; ADM 98/277, ltrs, 2 and 22 Mar. and 19 Apr. 1811, TB to Priest. Priest continued to have difficulties with his housing and domestic arrangements. In Aug. 1811 he was told that '... the Board cannot allow an oven for the use of your house, but you will be allowed two fenders and two setts [sic] of fire irons for your two sitting rooms', and the following month, that 'We cannot authorise any furniture for the private convenience of an agent to be forwarded at the public expence.' TNA ADM 98/277, ltrs, 26 Aug. and 4 Sep. 1811, TB to Priest.

121. TNA ADM 98/280, ltr, 18 Dec. 1813, TB to Priest.

122. Ibid., ltrs, 28 Jan. and 22 Jun. 1814, TB to Priest. In TNA ADM 103/635, Part I, a Home Department paper dated 15 Jul. 1817 refers to the 'Houses formerly occupied by the Agent and Surgeon of the [Greenlaw] Depot.' A letter of 12 Jul. 1817 in the same file but from the Barrack Office to G. Harrison, HM Treasury, indicates that a house named Pathhead House between Auchendinny and Greenlaw had been occupied by the agent and that there was a cottage between the depot and the main road which was to have been let to William Hill, depot surgeon, but in fact was not—presumably because of his dismissal from his appointment in Jun. 1813. Another letter, dated 4 Sep. 1814, from Robert Reid, crown architect in Scotland, to the TB, says, however, that at Greenlaw the 'houses erected for the officers of the Establishment [i.e., presumably the turnkeys and clerks] are without the Great Gateway, and ... that the surgeon's house and the house for the Agent are at some distance from the Depot. The House for the Agent was formerly the Farm house on the grounds.' An unsigned comment in the margin of Reid's letter says: 'All to be given up excepting the late Agent's house and the premises built where the farm house was and which was intended for the residence of the Agent.' A copy of decreet of the division of the valued rent of the lands and estate of Greenlaw, dated 15 Nov. 1813, includes a petition presented by the Trotters of Castlelaw, the earlier owners, and by the TB and Alexander Cowan, paper merchant, which refers to the feu disposition granted in Sep. 1812 by the Trotters to the Board for parts of the estate, one boundary of which was '... the new Turnpike road from Edinburgh to Dumfries by Pennycuick, together also with the house and garden on the east side of the road leading from Auchendinny Bridge to House of Muir presently occupied by the Agent for Prisoners of War.'

123. TNA ADM 98/276, ltrs, 20 Dec. 1810 and 7 Jan. 1811, TB to Capt. Pellowe.

124. TNA ADM 98/132, ltr, 21 Jun. 1811, TB to Commissioner Bowen.

125. TNA ADM 103/635, Part I, ltr, 31 Jul, 1817, Robert Reid, crown architect, to Commissioners for Victualling HM's Navy. Charles Cowan, *Reminiscences*, op. cit., 17, as son and nephew of the two Cowan brothers, confirms that 'The old mansion-house at Valleyfield, the centre part of which was approached by a rather handsome outside staircase of about fifteen steps, with the two wings, was in a great measure rebuilt

and converted into a hospital for the sick and wounded, who had a separate airing-ground to themselves.' An undated, but post-war, paper in TNA ADM 103/635, Part II, shows that the cost of building 'Houses for the Agent, Surgeon, etc.' was part of the whole cost of £48,500 expended on the purchase and fitting up of existing buildings and erection of four new prison buildings at Valleyfield.

126. TNA ADM 98/277, ltr, 8 Mar. 1811, TB to Capt. Heddington.

127. Ibid., ltrs from TB: 18 Apr. 1811 to Capt. Pellowe, 18 May 1811 to Alexander Munro, and 15 Oct. 1811 to Capt. Moriarty.

128. Ibid., ltrs from TB: 26 Jun. and 26 Jul. 1811, to Capt. Pellowe, and 18 Sep. 1811 to Capt. Moriarty.

129. TNA ADM 98/279, ltr, 4 Jan. 1813, TB to Capt. Brown.

130. Peacock, *Perth: its annals and its archives*, op. cit., 497. Marote-Carrier, who arrived with other prisoners transferred from Valleyfield to Perth within a month of the latter's opening, afterwards recalled that 'The commandant's [i.e., agent's] residence was situated to the left of the hospital, not far from the gate giving on to the main road … Ten jailers [turnkeys] were responsible for watching over the entrances and exits, and each of them had his lodging at one of the ten gates.' Marote-Carrier, op. cit., 154.

131. Abell, op. cit., 146; TNA ADM 98/276, ltr, 27 Dec. 1810, TB to Capt. Pellowe. Abell says an agent's salary was the same as that of a junior naval post captain. When Malcolm Wright, a civilian, was appointed agent at Edinburgh Castle depot in Dec. 1810 his salary was set at £200 per year. TNA ADM 98/117, ltr, 27 Dec. 1810, TB to Adm. Other salaries and wages appear to have been: surgeon—£1.1.0. (£1.05 pence) per day, plus £16.16.0. (£16.80) in annual allowances for stationery, coal, candles, etc.; hospital mate (assistant surgeon)—6s.6d. (32½ pence) per day; chief or first clerk—£118 per annum; other clerks—30s.6d. (£1.52½ pence) per week; interpreter—£30 per annum; dispenser—10s. (50 pence) per day; assistant dispenser—30s.6d. (£1.52½ pence) per week; matron—£25 per annum, plus allowances of 1s.3d. (8 pence) per day for provisions and 10s.6d. (52½ pence) a year for stationery; sempstress—4s.6d. (22½ pence) per week, plus allowance of 1s.3d. (8 pence) per day for provisions; turnkey—£50 per year; steward—3s.6d. (17½ pence) per day; messenger 15s. (75 pence) per week. TNA ADM 98/276, ltr, 27 Dec. 1810, TB to Capt. Pellowe; ADM 1/3764, fols 295-8. But also the clerks and stewards received according to their seniority additional payments from the division of profits from the sale of small beer to the prisoners. At Perth, for example, in Nov. 1813 almost £100 was divided according to seniority among the seven clerks and stewards (i.e., hospital stewards and chief turnkeys) in amounts ranging from £7 to almost £18 each; and there were several similar divisions at Valleyfield in 1811-13. TNA ADM 98/280, ltr, 2 Nov. 1813, TB to Capt. Moriarty. The turnkeys and the lamplighters appear to have received rations of food as part of their payment. TNA ADM 98/279, ltr, 13 Nov. 1812, TB to Lieut. Priest.

132. For clerks' ages, see TNA ADM 1/3764, fols 295-8. For Hill, see TNA ADM 1/3762, fol. 408, ltr, 26 Aug. 1811, Hill to TB. For Strachan, see TNA ADM 98/279, ltr, 6 Jan. 1813, TB to Capt. Moriarty, and *Morison's Perth and Perthshire Register for 1814*, op. cit., 63.

133. That the turnkeys' lot was not always a happy one was illustrated in a letter in Sep. 1812 from the Valleyfield agent to the TB, in which he said that a turnkey there while 'examining under the Prisons' had been attacked by prisoners. He had afterward

been given a small dirk to defend himself with, 'but yesterday [the prisoners] took it from him and broke it in pieces.' TNA ADM 99/219, 20 Sep. 1812.

134. TNA ADM 98/280, ltr, 5 Feb. 1814, TB to James Rushman; ADM 98/279, ltr, 24 Nov. 1812, TB to David Murray.

135. TNA ADM 98/133, ltr, 4 Sep. 1812, TB to secretary, Excise Office, Edinburgh.

CHAPTER 19: QUARRELS AMONG THE PRISONERS; HEALTH AND SICKNESS; DEATHS AND BURIALS

1. Kaald, op. cit., 88.

2. Beaudoin, op. cit., 634, 635. French and Spanish prisoners at Edinburgh Castle were said to be 'constantly engaged in feuds.' C. Mackie, *Historical Description of the Castle of Edinburgh* (Edinburgh, 1832), 36. Mackie appears to be discussing the prisoners during the Napoleonic Wars, but that particular reference may rather be to those confined in the Castle in the 1790s during the French Revolutionary Wars.

3. Kaald, op. cit., 92, 98.

4. TNA ADM 105/53, No. 202, application by Bourignons for re-admission to parole.

5. TNA ADM 98/170, circular 29 Jul. 1811.

6. TNA ADM 103/432, No. 879; ADM 103/648 (Deaths at Valleyfield, Mar. 1814); NAS AD 14/14/56.

7. NAS AD 14/14/56.

8. See, e.g., TNA ADM 103/155, Nos 163, 167, 170 and 223, and ADM 103/115 passim.

9. Beaudoin, op. cit., 635. The General Entry Book for Spanish prisoners at Greenlaw shows that of the 48 listed as being there during 1805-6, 35 had been sent to Portsmouth in Jan. 1806, while Spain was still an ally of France. That Beaudoin later revised his notes and inserted some information after or long after the event without ensuring the accuracy of his dating, is suggested by an entry where he states: 'Departure of the Spanish for their country 1st January 1808, having peace with the English'—whereas in fact Spain did not declare war on France and become the ally of Britain until the summer of that year. Ibid.; TNA ADM 103/158.

10. TNA ADM 98/129. The same warning was repeated by the Board on several later occasions—see, e.g., TNA 98/130, ltr, 18 May 1809, TB to Lieut. Col. Gordon; ADM 98/132, ltr, 6 Nov. 1811, TB to Robert Peel; ADM 98/119, ltr, 19 May 1812, TB to Adm.

11. TNA ADM 98/276, ltrs, 12, 15, 16, 19, 23 and 28 Jan. 1811, TB to Wright; *CM*, 6 Apr. 1811. The two depot General Entry Books for 'Danes' show that of the 1,000 or so prisoners listed between Nov. 1807 and Jul. 1811, 251 were sent to Chatham (not Portsmouth), 41 entered the British navy or marines, two the British army, two more an unspecified branch of the British armed forces, 19 were sent to the Nore (which may also have meant to Chatham), and four entered the British merchant navy—a total of 319. TNA ADM 103/152 and ADM 103/153.

12. *EEC*, 28 May 1808. NAS, North Leith Old Parish Register 692 1/7, entry dated 28 May 1808: '... a Dane killed in the Hope Privateer was buried the 27th of May. Killed in battle. Age 25.' Before its capture by the Norwegians the *Wovchalfen* had formerly been the Leith sloop *Hope*, engaged in trading with Shetland.

13. *Dundee Advertiser*, 7 Aug. 1812.

14. Marote-Carrier, op. cit., 67.

15. One who died while voyaging in the opposite direction after being repatriated from Valleyfield as an invalid was Jean Millet, a seaman from *Le Figaro* priv., who died en route to France via Chatham on 1 Jan. 1814. TNA ADM 103/648, Valleyfield proforma returns, No. 5,790.

16. *EEC*, 28 May 1808, and 15 Oct and 14 Nov. 1812; *CM*, 15 Oct., 12 and 14 Nov. 1812. Six prisoners, all soldiers from line regts, who arr. from Leith on 13 Nov. 1812 at Valleyfield 'for Medical Assistance', though whether they were from those landed at Burntisland a month earlier or, more likely, from the *Latona* is unstated, were: J.J. Hurel and P.J. Mercier, both 82nd line, Jacques Gourins and Claude Dugoussel, both 50th, François La Flotte, 51st, and Jacques Guillot, 59th. Hurel was dischgd in Aug. 1813 to France, presumably as an invalid; Mercier was transferred that same month to Perth; Gourins and Dugoussel both died at Valleyfield within a few days of their arrival there; and La Flotte and Guillot remained there until their repatriation as part of the general rel. of prisoners in Jun. 1814. TNA ADM 103/435, Nos 6,195-6,200.

17. *EEC*, 12 Nov. 1812; TNA ADM 103/264, Nos 2,177, 2,284, 2,882, 2,897, 2,900, 2,908, 2,910, 2,934, 2,970, 2,979, 2,995, 3,036, 3,052, 3,062, 3,063, 3,164, 3,217, 3,250, 3,251, 3,326, 3,339, 3,342, 3,348, 3,353, 3,457, 4,017; ADM 103/265, Nos 4,490, 4,559, 4,712, 4,755, 4,788.

18. For Valleyfield, see TNA ADM 103/432, Nos 166, 221-4, ADM 103/433, No. 2,050, and ADM 103/434, Nos 2,149, 2,314, 2,450-1, 2,454-6. For Esk Mills, see ADM 103/124, Nos 67, 218, 397, 421, 1,191 and 1,255.

19. Crowhurst, op. cit., 190.

20. David G. Chandler, *On the Napoleonic Wars. Collected Essays* (London, 1994), 160. See also Hobsbawm, *The Age of Revolution*, op. cit., 92-4.

21. Lewis, *A Social History of the Navy*, op. cit., 402.

22. TNA ADM 98/117, ltr, 6 Dec. 1810.

23. TNA ADM 98/122, ltr, 13 Oct. 1813, TB to Adm.

24. TNA ADM 98/187, ltrs, 15 Aug. and 14 Nov. 1812, TB to Capt C. Patton, RN; ADM 98/279, ltr, 20 Nov. 1812, TB to Admiral Otway.

25. See above, pp.332-3, 394-403.

26. Kaald, op. cit., 94, 95, 96, notes, 14-22 Dec. 1808.

27. TNA ADM 98/277, ltr, 19 Apr. 1811, TB to Capt. Pellowe.

28. Ibid., ltr, 29 Aug. 1811, TB to Lieut. Priest. The popularity certainly, and perhaps even in some cases the efficacy, of port wine as a medical treatment apparently increased as the months passed. By Jan. 1812 the Board approved Lieut. Priest's procurement for use in the depot hospital of six gallons of it, by 7 Dec. 1812 ten gallons, and three days later the Board told Priest it had ordered a further cask of port to be forwarded to him. TNA ADM 98/278, ltr, 15 Jan. 1812, TB to Priest; ADM 98/279, ltrs, 7 and 10 Dec. 1812, TB to Priest.

29. TNA ADM 98/279, ltr, 27 Apr. 1813, TB to Priest.

30. TNA ADM 98/277, ltrs, 4 May and 15 Aug. 1811, TB to Capt. Pellowe; ADM 98/278, ltrs from TB: 15 Apr., 13 May and 16 Jun. 1812, to Capt. Moriarty, and 22 Jul. and 12 Aug. 1812 to Capt. Brown; ADM 98/279, ltr, 5 Oct. 1812, TB to Capt. Brown; ADM 98/280, ltrs, 17 Dec. 1813, 14 Jan. and 8 Feb. 1814, TB to Capt. Brown; ADM 98/133, ltr, 10 Mar. 1812, TB to Commissioners of the Navy; ADM 98/187, ltrs, 16

Jun., 12 Aug., 13 Sep., 9 Oct. and 12 Nov. 1812, and 13 Sep. and 9 Oct. 1813.

31. TNA ADM 98/280, ltr, 13 Apr. 1814, TB to Capt. Moriarty; ADM 98/133, ltr, 17 Aug. 1812, TB to Commissioners of the Navy; ADM 98/278, ltr, 17 Aug. 1812, TB to Capt. Moriarty.

32. TNA ADM 98/277, ltr, 1 May 1811, TB to M. Wright; ADM 98/280, ltrs, 8 and 13 Nov. 1813, TB to Lieut. Priest, and 16 Nov. 1813 to Capt. Brown.

33. Particular thanks are due to Professor I.M.L. Donaldson, FRCP Edin., Honorary Librarian, Royal College of Physicians of Edinburgh, for providing his cautionary comments on this aspect of the history of the prisoners of war at the Scots depots, thus: 'The first very important point to make is that these "causes of death" are not pathological diagnoses and are not causes of death as one understands them from death certificates now. They are presumably records of the most striking, and perhaps the final, signs and symptoms that were observed when the patient was dying. It is not possible to assign a primary disease process to any of them without a great deal more information about the course of the patient's illness—information which is presumably not available.'

34. TNA ADM 103/624 and ADM 103/648.

35. TNA ADM 103/152, No. 137 (Simonsen); ADM 103/115, No. 40 (Couvertier). See also above, Appendix 11, Greenlaw, Nos 5 and 25.

36. TNA ADM 103/648 (proforma for Esk Mills).

37. TNA ADM 103/648, Edinburgh Castle proforma, week ending 25 Jul. 1811, No. 167, A.B Bourignons, and week ending 18 Apr. 1811, No. 379, P. Wormeseul, and No. 14, Marius Ponchina. TNA ADM 103/624, No. 1,365, Joseph Mulart.

38. TNA ADM 103/648. The deaths of 292 Valleyfield prisoners are actually reported in these proforma returns, but in two cases (No. 1,715, Jacob Kremsember, soldier, 48th Line regt, who died 11 Mar. 1814, and No. 5,790 Jean Millet, a priv. seaman, who died 1 Jan. 1814 when he had already left Valleyfield and was en route to Chatham for repatriation as an invalid), the cause of death is not given.

39. TNA ADM 103/648, death certificates for prisoners at Perth; Perth General Entry Books, TNA ADM 103/263-266 passim.

40. TNA ADM 103/648, No. 4,331. That statement on the death certificate appears contradicted by the absence in the depot Entry Book of any reference to Manecan having died, but even more so by the Entry Book recording that amid the general repatriation after the end of the war he was released from Valleyfield on 14 Jun. 1814. TNA ADM 103/435, No. 4,331.

41. TNA ADM 103/117. The Entry Book was evidently taken to Valleyfield from Esk Mills on its closure in Mar. 1811. A note written on a slip of paper pasted on the margin of the tenth page declares: 'The Part here enclosed was in Use at Eskmills. It is requested that this may be preserved for future Inspection. (Signed) Richard Pellowe, Capt, RN, Agent, Valleyfield, 6th July 1811.'

42. That accords with other evidence that of nine prisoners altogether who died at Esk Mills, four died elsewhere in the prison than in the hospital.

43. TNA ADM 103/112, No. 14; ADM 103/432, Nos 166, 221-4; ADM 103/433, No. 2,050; ADM 103/434, Nos 2,149, 2,314, 2,450, 2,453-6.

44. TNA ADM 103/157.

45. The two who died were Pierre Devaud, 23, b. at La Lampatrie, soldier, 39th Line regt, capd Aug. 1812 at Madrid, who died three days after entering Valleyfield hospital,

and Antoine Dupont, 37, b. at Neville, soldier, 101st Line regt, capd in Jun. 1812 at Salamanca, who died on 17 Dec. TNA ADM 103/435, Nos 6,211 and 6,224.

46. Johnston's 'Note of one day's expense and profit on the victualling of the Hospital at Valleyfield, 1810', is misdated, since the depot did not open until Mar. 1811. His table gives:

19 @ 1s.10d.	£1. 15. 7½d.
92 @ 1s.7½d.	£7. 9. 6d.
5 @ 8d.	£0. 3. 4d.
20 @ 1s.10d. (Cooks, Nurses, etc.)	£1. 17. 6d.
	£11. 5. 11½d.

It is not clear how Johnston arrived at some of his prices, but excluding the 20 rations for cooks, nurses, et al., 116 rations apparently remained for patients. Whether that figure ought to be divided by two or even three to allow for that number of meals per day per patient is not clear either. NLS MS Acc. 5811/1 fol. 2. Macbeth Forbes, without giving his source, says that 'Four months after the depot was opened [in Mar. 1811] there were 2,425 prisoners in Valleyfield, of whom 41 were ill.' Whether he means the 41 were in the depot hospital is not certain, though that is implied. If Johnston's 116 rations were divided by three for the number of meals per day they may have represented the result would be close to Macbeth Forbes's 41 sick prisoners. NAS GD 1/405/2, pencil notes, p. 18.

47. Peacock, *Perth: its annals and its archives*, op. cit., 497; Sievewright, *Depot at Perth*, op. cit., 5.

48. *Perth Courier*, 15 Jul., 26 Aug., 2 and 9 Sep. and 28 Oct. 1813, 3 Feb. and 2 Jun. 1814. The *Courier* of 15 Jul. 1813, its ear perhaps caught by the depot authorities, considered that 'So small a proportion of sick among nearly 7,000 close prisoners is a powerful and pleasing evidence of the great care which is bestowed on these unfortunate men, and of the admirable manner in which the medical department of this institution is conducted.' That the number of patients was impressively small appears confirmed, however, by a letter of 13 Nov. 1813 from the TB to the agent, Capt. Moriarty: 'It appearing by your accounts for the last week that although there are only 13 patients in the hospital there are 7 Nurses employed, we direct you to cause the number of Nurses to be immediately reduced ...' TNA ADM 98/280.

49. Abell, op. cit., 44, 241; Walker, *The Depot at Norman Cross*, op. cit., 163.

50. TNA ADM 98/276, ltr, 4 Feb. 1811. Rather greater amounts of fresh air within their quarters than the prisoners probably relished appears to have been the likely result of a decision by the Board concerning Greenlaw when in Nov. 1808 it told its agent there: '... the Windows in the Prison are not to be repaired, unless at the Expense of the Prisoners.' Ibid., ltr, 5 Nov. 1808, TB to M. Wright. At Perth there was an 'ingenious and unusual mode adopted for ventilating and introducing fresh air into the different prison buildings, and other means for ensuring the health and cleanliness of the prisoners.' *Perth Courier*, 9 Jul, 1812. It appears, however, to have been a mode of ventilation already in use at Valleyfield. Deacon, op. cit., 12.

51. TNA ADM 98/276, ltr, 14 Nov. 1808, TB to M. Wright.

52. Kaald, op. cit., 129, entry for 7 Sep. 1809.

53. Kaald, op. cit., 87, 88.

54. Ibid., 170.

55. Marote-Carrier, op. cit., 88, 156, 121.

56. TNA ADM 98/276, ltr, 27 Feb. 1811, TB to Capt. Pellowe. General Lord Cathcart, army commander in Scotland, himself pointed out to the Board that the airing ground was too small; and Andrew Johnston, chief clerk at the depot, considered its inadequacy a factor in making Esk Mills 'a very unfit building for a depot'. ADM 98/277, ltr, 15 Mar. 1811, TB to Capt. Pellowe.

57. Beaudoin, op. cit., 636; TNA ADM 103/635, Part I. This was a relatively rare example of the survival of a letter to the Board from an agent at a Scots depot.

58. Beaudoin, op. cit., 636.

59. Kaald, op. cit., 87.

60. Abell, op. cit., 123, 256, says barbers, like washermen, were paid 3d. per day. Washermen charged ½d. per item, or 1d. if they also provided soap and starch.

61. TNA ADM 103/117, pp. 12-14.

62. TNA ADM 105/44, ltr, 5 May 1811, James Bowen, at Edinburgh, to Alex McLeay, secretary.

63. TNA ADM 98/278, ltrs, 10 and 18 Feb. 1812, TB to Lieut. Priest.

64. TNA ADM 103/635, Part I, ltr, 14 Mar. 1812, Lieut. Priest to TB; ADM 105/44, ltr, 12 Apr. (no year), J. Douglas to TB.

65. TNA ADM 103/635, Part I, ltr, 20 Nov. 1812, A. Greig, Adm. solicitor, Edinburgh, to TB, and 12 Jul. 1817, Barrack Office to G. Harrison, HM Treasury; ADM 98/120, ltrs, 20 Feb. and 5 Mar. 1813, TB to Adm.; NAS GD 1/405/5, pencil notes, p.23; ML, Black Coll., op. cit., item 69, p.3; Deacon, op. cit., p.16.

66. Kaald, op. cit., 170, entry for 29 May 1810.

67. See, for instance, NAS GD 311/2/36, ltrs, 30 Nov. and 21 Dec. 1813, to Robert Reid, architect, from the Cowan brothers, former owners of Valleyfield paper mill, about damage to their adjoining land from pipes being laid by Reid to supply Greenlaw depot with water from Burrowford Burn; and NAS EE 886/81, a lease, dated 3 Nov. 1813, granted by Sir George Clerk of Penicuik to the TB to pipe a water supply from the Law Burn on his estate to Greenlaw.

68. According to Andrew Johnston, chief clerk of the depot, the terms of sale by the Cowans of Valleyfield to the government in Dec. 1810 for £10,000 included 'the reservation of property in the Water, after supplying the Prisons, wet ditch, etc., which after the War, or when the prisons was [sic] evacuated, the right to which returned to the Messrs Cowans.' Johnston, 'Recollections', op. cit., p.4. 'The course of the water run,' Robert Reid, architect, explained after the war, 'formerly used for the [papermaking] machinery, which passed through the centre of the grounds, was changed and continued by a new cut round the whole extent of the premises, serving in some measure as an enclave and boundary to the prison yards.' TNA ADM 103/635, Part I, ltr, 31 Jul. 1817, R. Reid to Commissioners for Victualling HM's Navy. The TB approved of the depot agent in Sep. 1811 'having employed some of the prisoners for cutting the airing ground for a Run of Water.' TNA ADM 98/277, ltr, 11 Sep. 1811, TB to Capt. Pellowe. A cryptic passage in a letter from TB Commissioner J. Douglas to Alex McLeay, secretary, TB, referring to compensation paid to farmers 'for damages occasioned by the water pipes passing through their grounds', appears from the context to refer to the water supply at Valleyfield. TNA ADM 105/44, ltr, 2 Sep. (1812).

69. TNA ADM 98/133, ltr, 28 Aug. 1812.

70. TNA ADM 98/279, ltr, 30 Apr. 1813, TB to Capt. Moriarty; ADM 98/280, ltrs, 26 May and 5 Jul. 1813, TB to Capt. Moriarty. A later letter which does survive from Reid to the Board says that the supply of water for the depot came from the estate of Moncrieffe. TNA ADM 103/635, Part I, 12 Mar. 1815. The contemporary Perth historian George Penny, *Traditions of Perth*, op. cit., 94, appears to justify Moriarty's concern when, noting that 'Great expense had been incurred' in laying on the water supply to the depot, he adds: '… pipes were laid through Magdalene Farm, and the hill above, and the water collected into a reservoir, and thence conducted into a cistern within the buildings; but the supply being found inadequate to the demand, pipes were laid across the Cow Inch to the [river] Tay, and an engine erected on the lade which raised the water into the Depot.'

71. The continuing demand for night tubs appears to have considerably exceeded the original provision. Thus the agent at Greenlaw was authorised by the TB in Dec. 1809 to buy 30 jack tubs, his colleague at Valleyfield in Jun. 1811 the same number of additional tubs, a further 'two large Tubs for Night Tubs' in Nov. 1812 and still more in Sep. 1813, while Capt. Moriarty at Perth was allowed in Dec. 1812 to procure an unspecified number. TNA ADM 98/276, ltr, 10 Dec. 1809, TB to M. Wright; ADM 98/277, ltr, 28 Jun. 1811, TB to Capt. Pellowe; ADM 98/279, ltr, 30 Nov. 1812, TB to Capt. Brown, and 10 Dec. 1812, TB to Capt. Moriarty; ADM 98/280, ltr, 17 Sep. 1813, TB to Capt. Brown.

72. TNA ADM 98/277, ltr, 30 Mar. 1811, TB to Capt. Heddington.

73. TNA ADM 98/278, ltrs, 10 and 24 Mar. 1812.

74. Ibid., ltrs, 10 and 21 Apr. 1812, TB to Lieut. Priest; ADM 103/635, Part I, ltrs, 14 and 28 Mar. and 16 Apr. 1812, Lieut. Priest to TB.

75. TNA ADM 98/279, ltr, 16 Mar. 1813, TB to Lieut. Priest.

76. Sievewright, *Depot at Perth*, op. cit., 8; NAS GD 311/2/36, ltr, 7 Oct. 1811, Cowans to Robert Reid, architect.

77. See examples at Greenlaw and Valleyfield in Chapter 21 above.

78. Kaald, op. cit., entries for 12, 13 and 30 Sep. 1809.

79. Marote-Carrier, op. cit., 117.

80. TNA ADM 103/154, No. 53; ADM 103/648, No. 53; *CM*, 17 May 1804; NAS GD 1/405/2, pencil notes on Greenlaw, p.12.

81. ML, Black Coll., op. cit., vol. 2(c), pp.15-16.

82. *EEC*, 18 Jun. 1807.

83. Kaald, op. cit., 106, 107. For Capt. Wilkensen, see also above, Appendix 10, Greenlaw, No. 20. Although Kaald does not say the burial was in old Glencorse churchyard, which is rather less than the distance he gives from the depot, it seems virtually certain that since that was the parish churchyard that was where it took place. Since Arendal was then, and still is, in Norway Kaald may have meant by 'Danish' that Capt. Wilkensen was, like all other Norwegians at that time, a subject of the king of Denmark.

84. TNA ADM 98/279, ltrs, 29 Sep., 7 and 19 Oct., 11 and 21 Dec. 1812, TB to Capt. Brown.

85. TNA ADM 98/277, ltrs, 12 and 19 Mar. 1811, TB to Capt. Pellowe.

86. TNA ADM 105/44, ltr, 2 Sep. (1812), J. Douglas to A. McLeay, secretary, TB; ADM 99/214, ltr received 25 May 1812 by TB from Capt. Moriarty. The burial ground at

Valleyfield appears therefore to have been at the base of the steep slope at the top of which is St Mungo's church and churchyard, from which the boy William Chambers, future publisher and lord provost of Edinburgh, looked down on the prisoners in the depot airing ground one Sunday, probably around the time those letters about the ground were being written. The monument erected soon after the Napoleonic Wars to those prisoners who died at Valleyfield, stands at the edge of the burying ground.

87. TNA ADM 98/276, ltrs, 6 and 21 Feb. 1811, TB to Capt. Pellowe.

88. TNA ADM 103/114, No. 1,365; ADM 103/624, No. 1,365.

89. Sievewright, *Depot at Perth*, op. cit., 35. According to the *Perthshire Advertiser*, 27 Sep. 1930, reporting the unveiling of a tablet the previous day at Perth Prison by William Adamson, Secretary of State for Scotland, to commemorate the dead prisoners of war, 'the actual position of the French cemetery is where the prison officers' quarters are situated and not where the tablet has been placed.'

90. TNA ADM 98/277, ltr, 9 Mar. 1811, TB to Capt. Pellowe; ADM 98/280, ltr, 22 May 1813, TB to Capt. Brown.

CHAPTER 20: THEY HAVE THEIR EXITS: TRANSFERS, INVALIDS AND AGED, BOYS, ALLIES, NEUTRALS, EXCHANGES AND OTHER RELEASES, PAROLE, VOLUNTEERS

1. Beaudoin, op. cit., 640; Marote-Carrier, op. cit., 155, 156.

2. TNA ADM 103/157, Nos 1-904 passim; ADM 103/266, Nos 6,896-7,761.

3. TNA ADM 103/263, Nos 1,094-1,200; ADM 103/265, Nos 4,335-6,483 passim; ADM 103/124, Nos 1-192.

4. For Adam's movements see above, Appendix 2, No. 38; TNA ADM 103/110, No. 211 (Adam); ADM 103/112, No.1 (Fourneau), No. 540 (Adam); ADM 103/124, No. 2,306 (Adam); ADM 103/157, No. 1 (Fourneau), No. 211 (Adam); ADM 103/263, No. 1,094 (Fourneau), No. 1,171 (Adam); ADM 103/435, No. 5,311 (Adam).

5. TNA ADM 103/434, No. 2,511; ADM 103/263, No.1.

6. The rebuke by the Board to the agent at Valleyfield in Dec. 1812, when he asked for some *mauvais sujets* among the inmates there to be moved to another depot, was hardly consistent with the reasons for certain other transfers between depots within Scotland and from Scotland to the hulks in the south of England that the Board itself sometimes ordered. TNA ADM 98/279, ltr, 3 Dec. 1812, TB to Capt. Brown.

7. Marote-Carrier, op. cit., 180.

8. TNA ADM 98/278. The two men were almost certainly brothers, both born in Granville, although each 'says he is from Condé'. Joseph, 25, was a soldier, regt u., capd Oct. 1804 off Brest on gun boat No. 380; François, 22, a seaman, ship u., capd at Fort Royal, Martinique, Feb. 1809. Both had arr. at Edinburgh Castle in Mar. 1811 from Esk Mills, both came to Greenlaw from the Castle in Aug. that year, and both were duly transferred on 12 Jun. 1812 to Valleyfield. They did not, however, remain together at Valleyfield until quite the end of the war: Joseph volunteered into the 1st Dutch regt and was dischgd to it on 14 Feb. 1814; François remained a prisoner at the depot until his rel. on 6 Jun. 1814. Why the two men wanted to leave Greenlaw for Valleyfield was unstated. ADM 103/110, Nos 123, 124; ADM 103/112, Nos 180, 181; ADM 103/435, Nos 5,377, 5,378.

9. TNA ADM 105/54, Register of Prisoners' Applications, No. 391.

10. Ibid., application No. 461. A search for Busse and Cormorant in the Valleyfield Entry Books was unsuccessful.

11. TNA ADM 98/113, ltr, 9 Apr. 1807.

12. Lewis, *Napoleon and his British captives*, op. cit., 173, found that of all the 17,607 prisoners of war released by the British government during the war more than three-quarters were invalids.

13. TNA ADM 1/3743, fol. 122, ltr, 8 Jun. 1803, Sir Rupert George and Ambrose Serle, TB, to Sir Evan Nepean, secretary, Adm. The quotation is from comments written on the letter by Nepean.

14. A typical circular on the question sent on 18 Nov. 1812 by the TO to agents at nine depots, including Valleyfield and Perth, declared: 'Having received the directions of the Lords Commissioner of the Admiralty to cause a selection to be made of such French invalid prisoners as are unfit for further service, or not likely to become again serviceable, we direct you, in conjunction with the surgeon(s) of the Prison ... to make such selection and taking care that the prisoners be accurately examined so as not to select any who may possibly become capable of serving again in any capacity civil or military; and you will transmit to us a list of such unserviceable prisoners in the inclosed form, signed by yourself and the surgeon(s). The selection is to be made in a manner so careful as to meet the subsequent examination of the Inspectors of Hospitals should the same be judged necessary.' The circular added that 'It is not intended to exclude prisoners taken in privateers from the selection, provided there be nothing particular against their characters, and they be not, in point of ability to serve, in the same state as when captured.' TNA ADM 98/170.

15. TNA ADM 1/3745, ltr, 13 Apr. 1804, TB to Adm.; ADM 103/154, No. 12.

16. TNA ADM 98/113, ltr, 9 Apr. 1807, TB to Adm.

17. TNA ADM 103/152-158 passim. An Adm. order to the TB on 20 Aug. 1812, for example, was that 39 prisoners be released from Greenlaw as they were 'totally unfit for further service.' TNA ADM 99/217.

18. For Mulart, see Appendix 11 above, Edinburgh Castle, No. 4.

19. TNA ADM 103/114, No. 1,366 (Sgt Thuillin); ADM 103/263, No. 2,049 (Caly); ADM 103/432-436 passim for Valleyfield; ADM 103/263-266 passim for Perth. Even for these two latter depots there is a lack of clarity in the Entry Books about how many prisoners dischgd to 'Leith', 'Edinburgh Castle' or 'France' were in fact invalids on the first stage of their way home. One certain major discharge from Valleyfield, however, was an Adm. order to the TB on 20 Aug. 1812 that 166 prisoners at that depot be released as 'totally unfit for further service.' ADM 99/217.

20. TNA ADM 105/53, No. 433; ADM 105/54, No. 363.

21. TNA ADM 98/277, 23 Sep. 1811.

22. TNA ADM 98/279, ltr, 9 Oct. 1812, TB to Capt. Brown.

23. TNA ADM 98/280, ltr, 21 Jun. 1813, TB to Capts Brown and Moriarty.

24. TNA ADM 98/280, ltrs, 7 Jul. 1813, TB to Moriarty and Otway.

25. Marote-Carrier, op. cit., 137-8.

26. Beaudoin, op. cit., 661-6.

27. TNA ADM 98/278, ltr, 26 Nov. 1811.

28. Marote-Carrier, op. cit., 161-2. Another prisoner at Perth, François Quantel, 23, b.

at Allonne, soldier, 80th line regt, capd at Vigo Mar. 1809, has 'madman' pencilled against his name in the depot Entry Book. But he was not repatriated as an invalid and remained at Perth until 1 Jun. 1814. TNA ADM 103/266, No. 6,878.

29. TNA ADM 98/279, ltr, 4 Dec. 1812, TB to Lieut. Glinn, RN, at Leith; ADM 98/278, ltr, 8 Aug. 1812, TB to Capt. Brown.

30. Penny, *Traditions of Perth*, op. cit. 92; TNA ADM 98/280, ltrs, 28 May 1813, TB to Capts Brown and Moriarty, and Lieut. Glinn at Leith; ADM 99/236, ltr, 9 Jun. 1813, TB to M. Rivière, French Ministry of Marine.

31. Jean Morvan, *Le Soldat Impérial*, op. cit., Vol. II, 418; *Diary of Peter Bussell* (London, 1931), 146, quoted in Lewis, *Napoleon and his British captives*, op. cit., 155.

32. TNA ADM 105/44, ltr, 29 Aug. 1812, Douglas to A. McLeay, secretary, TB; ADM 98/119, ltr, 19 Aug. 1812, TB to Adm.; *EEC*, 14 Jan. 1813; *CM*, 24 Oct. 1811.

33. Kaald, op. cit., 136, 159 and 160, entry for 17 Apr. 1810.

34. TNA ADM 103/152, passim; ADM 98/276, ltr, 9 Oct. 1809, TB to M.Wright. In addition to the 24 repatriated in 1807-11, a further three were sent on parole 'To Peebles as being a boy under age.'

35. TNA ADM 103/153-158 passim.

36. TNA ADM 103/435, No. 5,740.

37. TNA ADM 103/112, Nos 208 (Jean Marie Harve), 276 (Brutus Camus), 282 (Vincent Failés), 355 (Jean Baptiste Gubert), 394 (Michel Champagne), 516 (Sven Larsen); ADM 103/157, No. 259 (Michel Champagne), No. 314 (Sven Larsen); ADM 103/114, Nos 1,294 (C.I. Romont), 1,295 (Antoine Ghemar), 1,296 (Joseph Olivier), and 1,297 (Pierre Vapeur).

38. The 13 definitely repatriated from Valleyfield were (a) in Sep. 1812: Pierre Tournelle, aged 11, ship's boy, b. Honfleur, capd on *Voltigeur* priv. Nov. 1809; Michael Floriot, 9, ship's boy, b. Havre, capd on *Sommambule* priv. Oct. 1810; Roelf Van Weltingen, 11, ship's boy, b. Amsterdam, capd on *Sans Souci* priv. Oct. 1810; François Guis, 11, soldier, b. Marseilles, capd on the vessel *L'Ange Raphael* Nov. 1808; Jean C. Keastere, 10, seaman, b. Dunkirk, capd on *Comtesse d'Hambourg* priv. Oct. 1810; Yves Legal, 10, seaman, b. Brest, capd on *Téméraire* priv. Oct. 1810; Pierre Decrock, 9, seaman, b. Dunkirk, capd on *Comtesse d'Hambourg* priv. Oct. 1810; Jean Renault Fleurette, 9, seaman, b. Brest, capd on *Téméraire* priv. Oct. 1810; François Vanderboom, 9, soldier, b. Harlingen, 5th line regt, capd at Campveere Jul. 1809; (b) in Aug. 1813: C. I. Romont, 11, Antoine Ghemar, 11, Joseph Olivier, 10, and René (or Pierre) Vasseur, 9—all four b. Dunkirk, all ship's boy, all capd on *Ravisseur* priv. Feb.1813. The two who were 'Discharged', n.d., probably repatriated, were: Jean Alvaretz, 9½, and Henry Fockeday, 9½, both b. Dunkirk, both ship's boy capd on *Petit Edouard* priv. Oct. 1811. The two who joined the British navy were: Gilus (or Gilles) Gronwoud (or Gronewood), 11, seaman, b. Amsterdam, capd on *Héro du Nord* priv. Oct. 1810, dischgd into RN Apr. 1811; and M. Ramsdoueck (or Ramsdoneck), 11, soldier, 5th line regt, b. Middleburg, capd at Campveere Jul. 1809, dischgd into RN Nov. 1811. The two who enlisted in the 60th regt in Oct. 1813 were: Jean Noré, 11, seaman, b. Dunkirk, capd on *Général Dorsin* priv. Nov. 1810; and Jacob De Klunders, 10, seaman, b. Dunkirk, capd on *Mamelouk* priv. Nov. 1810. The one transferred to Perth in Sep. 1812 was Nicolas Le Roy, 10, b. Granville, passenger on *L'Hirondelle* priv. when captured, Sep. 1810. The four who remained in captivity at Valleyfield until the end of the war were: François Roger, 11, seaman, b. Cherbourg, capd on *Courier de la Mer* priv. Oct. 1808, rel. Jun. 1814; Frederik Boldore, 11, seaman, b. Bordeaux, capd on *La Tonnerre* priv. Oct. 1809, rel. Jun. 1814;

Martin Robiche, 11, ship's boy, b. Venice, cap on m.o.w. *Friedland* Dec. 1807, rel. Mar. 1814; and Pierre Jean Aimé, aged 11, seaman, b. Marseilles, capd on *Le Debordier* priv. Oct. 1810, rel. Mar. 1814. TNA ADM 103/432, Nos 213 (Floriot), 271 (Gronwoud), 820 (Tournelle), 832 (Le Roy); ADM 103/433, Nos 1,355 (Van Weltingen), 1,481 (Roger), 1,546 (Noré), 1,554 (Decrock), 1,574 (Keastere), 1,705 (Boldore), 1,839 (Legal), 1,878 (Guis), 2,087 (De Klunders), 2,103 (Robiche), 2,104 (Aimé); ADM 103/434, Nos 2,235 (Fleurette), 3,101 (Vanderboom), 3,102 (Ramsdoueck); ADM 103/435, Nos 6,435 (Romont), 6,436 (Ghemar), 6,437 (Olivier), 5,270 (Alvaretz), 5,272 (Fockeday), 6,438 (Vasseur).

39. TNA ADM 98/279, ltr, 10 Sep. 1812.
40. Le Roy senior was capt. of the priv. *L'Hirondelle* on which they had both been capd in 1810.
41. TNA ADM 103/264, No. 3,078 (Pain); ADM 103/265, No. 4,834 (Legrand).
42. TNA ADM 103/266, No. 6,805.
43. See above, pp.147, 148-9.
44. *CM*, 20 May 1809 and 21 Jul. 1810; *Glasgow Courier*, 16 May and 21 Jul. 1810; *EEC*, 24 Jul. 1813; TNA ADM 103/159, Greenock Entry Book, 1804-5, Nos 90, 91.
45. See above, especially pp.185-206 passim.
46. TNA ADM 98/276, ltrs from TB: 1 Jul. 1808 to M. Wright, and 5 Jul. and 1 Aug. 1808 to Lieut. Flinn, Leith.
47. TNA ADM 105/53, No. 311, Jul. 1811; ADM 105/54, No. 208, 28 Feb. 1811.
48. *CM*, 9 Jun. 1806 and 16 Feb. 1807.
49. TNA ADM 103/263, No. 492. Less fortunate was Alexis Pissaro, a prisoner at Valleyfield, but of whom no details have been found other than that he had been capd on the m.o.w. *Marengo* in the Atlantic in Mar. 1806. When Pissaro, like Leopold Dauphin, a native of Mauritius, 'Having a wife and family there, being in alliance with this country', applied in Oct. 1812 for repatriation the authorities' decision was: 'Cannot be done.' TNA ADM 105/54, No. 310.
50. TNA ADM 103/157, No. 192; ADM 105/53, Nos 210 and 590; ADM 103/263, No. 1,109.
51. TNA ADM 98/129, ltr, 20 Feb. 1807, TB to General Walpole. As early in the war as Aug. 1803, 13 subjects of Oldenburg had been among the 87 prisoners landed from the British privateer *St Joseph* at Ullapool and marched the 50 miles into confinement at Fort George until rel. three months later.
52. TNA ADM 1/3751, ltr, 11 Mar. 1807, TB to W. Marsden, secretary, Adm.
53. TNA ADM 98/117, ltr, 5 Dec. 1810, TB to Adm.; ADM 103/152, Nos 550 (Broran) and 552 (Wickman).
54. TNA ADM 103/152, No. 856.
55. TNA ADM 103/433, Nos 1,361 (Koomen), 1,563 (Vandenberg), 1,565 (Van Den Hewal), 1,574 (Sprenger); ADM 103/435, No. 5,781 (Lettosen).
56. Haultz is No. 1,133 in Perth Entry Book TNA ADM 103/263.
57. Moriarty's year of birth is not known, but as he died in Sep. 1833 it seems improbable for that and other reasons that at the time of their interview in the winter of 1813-14 he was quite as old as Marote-Carrier, then himself barely 30, says.
58. Marote-Carrier, op. cit., 179-95 passim; TNA ADM 103/263, Nos 1,133 (Haultz) and 1,166 (Marote-Carrier).

59. For St Domingo, for example, see above, pp.728, 729, Note 9.

60. Oman, *Peninsular War*, op. cit., Vol. I, 280-3; Charles Esdaile, *The Peninsular War. A New History* (London, 2002), 101, 102.

61. TNA ADM 105/54, No. 362.

62. TNA ADM 98/278, ltr, 14 Nov. 1811; ADM 103/434, No. 3,364 (Calligny).

63. TNA ADM 105/53, No.339, Aug. 1811; ADM 98/278, ltr, 3 Feb. 1812, TB to Capt. Moriarty; ADM 103/110, No. 214 (Boulogne); ADM 103/435, No. 5,361 (Boulogne); ADM 98/278, ltr, 28 Dec. 1811, TB to Vice Admiral Otway at Leith; ADM 103/434, No. 4,168 (Berwinkels). In Louis Boulogne's case, however, other sources say his release was the result of an exchange for a British seaman: see ADM 103/499, 'Partial Exchanges: French', Apr. 1812.

64. TNA ADM 105/54, No. 458. General Sir John Stuart had landed with a large British force on Ischia on 24 Jun. 1809, and immediately took 180 prisoners while the rest of the enemy forces retreated into the castle, where they were besieged until their surrender a few days later. 'Altogether fifteen hundred prisoners ... were taken.' Fortescue, *British Army*, op. cit., Vol.VII, 293-9.

65. TNA ADM 103/112, No. 478; ADM 98/277, ltr, 27 Mar. 1811, TB to Wright.

66. The petition is in FF2.23B12, Service historique de la marine, Ministry of Defence, Chateau of Vincennes, Paris.

67. See, e.g., Marote-Carrier, op.cit., 118.

68. TNA ADM 98/277, ltrs from TB: 16 Sep. 1811 to Lieut. Priest, and 17 Sep. 1811 to M. Wright; ADM 103/112, No. 221 (Barbet). Barbet, 20, b. at Cherbourg, had been capd, presumably at the age of 12, on *L'Oiseau* priv. Sep. 1803, had been transferred to the Castle from Esk Mills in Mar. 1811, and from the Castle to Greenlaw in Aug., before entering 'His Majesty's Service, 14 Sep. 1811, By Order of Admiral Otway.' Had he informed on his fellow prisoners from desperation at the length of time he himself had spent in captivity?

69. TNA ADM 98/277, ltr, 14 Mar. 1811, TB to M. Wright.

70. Ibid., ltr, 18 May 1811.

71. Ibid., ltr, 8 Aug. 1811, TB to Pellowe.

72. TNA ADM 98/279, ltr, 27 Aug. 1812, TB to Capt. Brown.

73. TNA ADM 103/648, No. 3,275; ADM 103/434, No. 3,275.

74. See above, pp.358, 359.

75. This was the case reported in *Perth Courier* on 8 Apr. that year.

76. *CM*, 17 Oct. 1812; TNA ADM 103/263, No. 908. Such magnanimity was not one-sided: Napoleon himself ordered the freeing of 14 British prisoners of war at Givet who had ensured his safe passage there in Nov. 1811 by volunteering to improvise a chain-ferry that replaced a pontoon bridge swept away in tempestuous flooding by the river Meuse; and at Christmas 1809, when a serious fire at Auxonne was extinguished and inhabitants rescued by British prisoners there, Napoleon had ordered the release and repatriation of 21 of those involved. Lewis, *Napoleon and his British captives*, op. cit., 157, 165-7.

77. TNA ADM 98/118.

78. TNA ADM 98/279, ltrs, 3 and 11 Dec. 1812, TB to Brown.

79. For these releases, see above, p.328.

80. Kaald, op. cit., 13, 18, 19.

81. Ibid., 20, 131-5. One official source indicates that Kaald was repatriated 'on parole', but his discharge in the Greenlaw Entry Book makes no reference to parole. TNA ADM 103/486; ADM 103/152, No. 410.

82. TNA ADM 98/278, ltrs from TB, 8 Apr. 1812 to Admiral Otway, 27 Apr. 1812 to Capt. Moriarty; ADM 103/434, No. 3,999; ADM 103/496. The Duke del Infantado (1773-1841), a Spanish grandee and political leader, close associate of the heir to the throne and later king, Ferdinand VII, was commander of the Spanish army defeated by the French at the battle of Uclés in Jan. 1809.

83. TNA ADM 98/279, ltr, 14 Dec. 1812, TB to Capt. Brown.

84. Kaald, op. cit., 98, 156, 186.

85. Lewis, for example, points out that before the Napoleonic Wars exchange 'covered all prisoners: but in practice the officers benefited from it more than the men; at least, more surely and more quickly. The men almost always had to wait for cartels [i.e., agreements between governments on exchange of prisoners; though cartels also meant the ships used in repatriating exchanged or otherwise released prisoners]; and batches or shiploads, often of many hundreds, had to be assembled and forwarded.' Officers, on the other hand, might expect to be exchanged for an enemy prisoner within days or weeks. Lewis, *Napoleon and his British captives*, op. cit., 39-46.

86. That duplicity remained a festering sore during most of the war.

87. TNA WO 6/149, fol. 201, ltr, 2 Dec. 1803.

88. Of the 16,000 British prisoners in France, Lewis estimated that not more than 40 were exchanged in the course of the war. Lewis, *Napoleon and his British captives*, op. cit., 180.

89. TNA ADM 103/499, 'Partial Exchanges: French'; ADM 103/157, Nos 214 (Boulogne) and 273 (Thiebaud); ADM 103/509, 2 Mar. 1812 (Boulogne). As already seen, there is ambiguity about Boulogne's release, as the Greenlaw Entry Book does not mention exchange but says he was released 'under General Rochambeau's Capitulation.' In the hybrid Entry Book ADM 103/110, for Edinburgh Castle and Greenlaw, Thiebaud, No. 273, is said to be master of *Le Camy*, described as a m.v., not a priv.

90. TNA ADM 98/279, ltrs from TB, 4 Sep 1812 to Admiral Otway, 30 Dec. 1812 to Capt. Brown; ADM 105/53, No. 641; NAS GD1/405/5/1/28; ADM 103/263, No. 1,116.

91. The exchange, with the addition of two men, is testified in the depot Entry Books: TNA ADM 103/432 (where 12 seamen from the *Piedmontaise* are shown to have been exchanged), ADM 103/433, Nos 1,152, 1,158, 1,519, 1,542, 1,742, 1,993-7, 2,130-2, and ADM 103/434, No. 2,469. This last was Yves Nadelicke, 24, seaman, *Piedmontaise*, capd in the East Indies in Mar. 1808, and for whom the exchange may have been doubly fortunate as he appears to have been a native of Morlaix, the cartel port in Brittany where prisoners repatriated to France were landed.

92. TNA ADM 98/278, ltr, 14 Feb. 1812, TB to Capt. Moriarty.

93. Ibid., ltrs, 3 Mar. and 9 Apr. 1812, TB to Admiral Otway.

94. TNA ADM 103/499, 'Partial Exchanges: French'. Applications by Rousan, Oudry, Patatrand and Chercau for release under the terms of Rochambeau's or the St Domingo capitulation, 1803, had been made in Aug. 1811: ADM 105/53, No. 339.

95. Ibid., passim; ADM 103/509, 'Released, 1812-13', passim.

96. TNA ADM 103/434, No. 3,364 (Coligny); ADM 103/499, 12 Jun. 1812 (Noréal), 16 Sep. 1813 (Coligny), Sep. 1812 (Guerin); ADM 103/509, 12 Jun. 1813; NAS

GD1/405/5/1/49. Guerin had been transferred from Valleyfield to Perth on 2 Sep. 1812, while arrangements for his exchange were underway, so it was actually from Perth that his journey home began on 13 Oct. that year. TNA ADM 103/263, No. 1,189 (Guerin).

97. TNA ADM 98/280, ltr, 2 Jun. 1813, TB to Capt. Brown.

98. Press reports (e.g., in *CM*, 17 Oct. 1812) of Guerin's departure from Perth described him as a lieutenant. But the Entry Book TNA ADM 103/263, No. 1,189, says he had been master's mate on the m.o.w. *Duquesne* at the time of his capture.

99. TNA ADM 105/53, Register of Prisoners' Applications, Nos 205 (Passicousset), No. 209 (Canet); ADM 103/110, No. 248; ADM 103/157, No. 248; ADM 103/491 (see Passicousset under Richard, Charles); ADM 103/112, No. 374 (Canet).

100. TNA ADM 98/112, ltr, 8 Nov. 1804, TB to W. Marsden, secretary, Adm.

101. TNA ADM 98/116, ltr, 19 Jul. 1810, TB to J.W. Croker, secretary, Adm.

102. Beaudoin, op. cit., 634.

103. TNA ADM 103/154, Nos 1-97 passim; ADM 103/110, Nos 7-97 passim.

104. *CM*, 17 Jan. 1805.

105. TNA ADM 99/176, fol. 111, ltr, 2 Apr. 1807, TB to M. Wright.

106. TNA ADM 98/113, ltr, 17 Mar. 1807, TB to W. Marsden, secretary, Adm.

107. Ibid., ltr, 9 Apr. 1807.

108. TNA ADM 98/170, circular, 4 May 1808, TB to parole agents.

109. TNA WO 6/150, fol. 259, ltr, 14 Oct. 1809, Castlereagh to Adm.

110. TNA ADM 98/112, ltrs, 24 Apr. 1805, and 3 Mar. and 3 Apr. 1806, TB to W. Marsden, Adm.

111. TNA ADM 103/158, Nos 1-48.

112. According to *The Times*, 7 Jul. 1808, the total number of Spanish prisoners repatriated then from Portsmouth and Plymouth was more than 1,500. From Greenlaw that month 22 Spanish prisoners released were embarked on board trans. vessels at Dunbar and taken to Harwich on the first stage of their journey home. TNA ADM 98/276, ltrs from TB: 1 Jul. 1808 to M. Wright, 5 Jul. 1808 to Lieut. Flinn at Leith, 1 Aug. 1808 to Wright and Flinn. See also ADM 103/115, which confirms that from Greenlaw on 5 Jul. 1808 the almost identical number of 19 prisoners described as 'Spanish Subject' were released 'To go Home'. By mid-Aug. there were only four Spanish prisoners remaining at Greenlaw, whom the Board instructed the agent to transfer 'to the French Account, agreeably to your suggestion.' Ibid., 12 Aug. 1808. These four men, all seamen, have names that certainly suggest they were French, not Spanish. See TNA ADM 103/115, Nos 38 (Jean Delage), 41 (François Bonne), 42 (François Bernier), and 62 (Alexis Durand).

113. According to a letter in TNA ADM 1/3760, fol. 49, dated 30 Mar. 1810, from TB to Adm., there were that month, almost two years after the outbreak of the Peninsular War, 333 Spanish prisoners in Britain. How many, if any, of them were confined at Greenlaw is not stated. In Oct. 1813 a similar letter in ADM 1/3765, fol. 484, shows there were 257 in Britain. Of the latter total four seamen and two soldiers were held at Valleyfield. No figure is given for Perth.

114. TNA ADM 103/152 lists 919 (of whom two are re-entered as recapd escapers) and the second Entry Book, ADM 103/153, lists 431—but 351 of these prisoners are duplicated in the first Book, so the net listing is 80.

115. TNA ADM 98/119, ltr, 12 Mar. 1812, TB to Adm. Abell, op. cit., 34, without specifying his sources, says: 'In the year 1808 the balance due from Denmark to Britain was 3,807. There were 1,796 Danish prisoners in England [whose Border presumably stretched north to include Greenlaw]. Between 1808 and 1813 the balance due us was 2,697.'

116. *CM*, 19 Oct. 1811.

117. TNA ADM 105/61, *Instructions for Agents … respecting the Management of Prisoners of War on Parole* (London, 1809), passim; ADM 98/111, ltr, 20 Oct. 1803, TB to W. Marsden, Adm., and ADM 98/191-196 passim.

118. Kaald, op. cit., 104, 116.

119. TNA ADM 98/276, ltr, 23 Jun. 1809, TB to M. Wright.

120. TNA ADM 98/116, ltr, 1 Aug. 1810, TB to Adm. A privateersman at Greenlaw named James Hardy, capd in Oct. 1810 on *Le Vengeur* and who applied for parole, was equally unsuccessful: the Board told him his vessel had not carried 14 cannons at the time of its capture. NAS GD1/405/1, p.12, 22 Dec. (no year).

121. NAS GD1/405/1, Vol. II, 30, 31, 1 Mar. 1811. Roustan and Barbe, transferred along with most of the other prisoners in Mar. 1811 from Esk Mills to Valleyfield, immediately reapplied for parole from the latter. This time their application was rejected by the Board on the grounds that 'They say she [the *Duguay Trouin*] had 16 guns but the *Gazette* says 5. Not entitled.' TNA ADM 105/53, Register of Prisoners' Applications, No. 227, Apr. 1811.

122. TNA ADM 103/124, No. 429 (Brimont), No. 2,816 (Prévost De Boissi).

123. TNA ADM 105/53, No. 268. Could Panot have been the 'poor Fleming' recalled later at Valleyfield by Marote-Carrier? No prisoner named Panot has been found, however, in the Castle Entry Books and, even allowing for spelling that was often phonetic, it is difficult to believe the applicant could have been another inmate there whose name is given in the Entry Books as Louis Paneau. Though capd on 15 Aug. 1809 at Flushing, Pancau, aged 28, was described as a member of the Bn of Seamen of the French army and his birthplace was said to be Switzerland. TNA ADM 103/110, No. 52, and ADM 103/112, No. 72.

124. TNA ADM 105/53, No. 206, 19 Apr. 1811; ADM 103/124, No. 2,222; ADM 103/114, No. 1,355, where Le Prince is described as a sergeant major capd at Baylen; ADM 103/263, No. 1,129; ADM 103/113, No. 7,273.

125. TNA ADM 105/53, No. 158, 14 Mar. 1811; ADM 103/112, No. 379.

126. The nine, all but one capd at Coimbra in Oct. 1810, were two Civil Officers: Jacques Mabuere and Anastase Chevalier; three Chief Apothecaries: François Graux, Jean Cabanes and Mathieu Dordilly; and four storekeepers: François Parmisson, Jean Baptiste Pouzin, Jean Adolphe Galland, and François Boujon or Bougon. Galland had been capd Jul. 1810 'in Portugal'. The three lieuts were Calixte Real, capd in Portugal Oct. 1810; Louis Planté, capd in the East Indies Apr. 1806 on *Ile de France* priv.; and William Raudestaing, capd 'at sea' Jan. 1811 on the *Dodridge*, a retaken vessel. TNA ADM 105/53, No. 183, 29 Mar. 1811; ADM 103/112, Nos 188-96, 305, 363 and 364.

127. TNA ADM 103/53, Nos 221, 227, 252; NAS GD1/405/1, 10 Aug. 1811 (Timon).

128. TNA ADM 103/432-436 passim, and ADM 103/113 passim.

129. TNA ADM 103/263, No. 1,075 (Gronnier); ADM 105/54, No. 296 (Gronnier); NAS GD1/405/1 (List of prisoners at Biggar).

130. TNA ADM 103/580, No. 23; ADM 103/435, No. 5,381; ADM 98/278, ltr, 19 Jun. 1812, TB to Capt. Moriarty, Valleyfield; ADM 103/491; ADM 103/263, No. 1,177; ADM 105/54, No. 345.

131. *Parliamentary Papers*, Vol. IX, 301, (Return of Prisoners of War at present in the United Kingdom, submitted by the TO to the House of Commons, 26 June 1812).

132. TNA ADM 103/432, No. 586; ADM 98/277, ltr, 18 May 1811, TB to Capt. Pellowe. Capt. Berar was presumably a naval, not an army, captain: officers entitled to servants were normally at least one rank higher than army captains. The Entry Book for Esk Mills, where Chalet had been confined before his transfer in Mar. 1811 to Valleyfield, says he was a servant, 2nd line regt. TNA ADM 103/124, No. 989.

133. TNA ADM 98/279, ltr, 18 Sep. 1812, TB to Capt. Brown. Commissioner Douglas of the TB, who had been visiting parole towns in the Borders the previous month, had informed the secretary of the Board that 'General De Boisy, who is at Kelso, is very anxious to have a French servant. His late servant absconded above a year ago. I wish the Board would grant his request, for from Gout and other infirmities he requires the assistance of a servant, and he says he has written three times to the Board on the subject without obtaining an answer.' TNA ADM 105/44, ltr, 29 Aug. 1812, J. Douglas to A. McLeay, secretary, TB; ADM 103/112, No. 394; ADM 103/435, No. 5,771 (Champagne).

134. TNA ADM 98/280, ltr, 30 Nov. 1813, TB to Capt. Moriarty; ADM 103/263, No. 1,570.

135. The policy, which had been followed in earlier wars, too, was by no means confined to the British authorities but was practised also by other belligerent states. Napoleon, for example, after his decisive defeat of the Prussian army at the battles of Iena and Auerstadt in Oct. 1806, found himself with more than 140,000 prisoners. Some of these were recruited into the French army, others were offered to his client state Holland and his then ally Spain—in the case of the latter, on condition that they were not transported to the Spanish American colonies to labour in the mines. *Correspondance de Napoléon 1er*, op. cit., Vol. XIII, 521-2, ltr, 12 Nov. 1806, to General Dejean.

136. *London Gazette*, No. 16078, 17-20 Oct. 1807, 1,393-4; *EEC*, 22 Oct. 1807; *The Times*, 15 Feb. 1812.

137. *EEC*, 22 Jul. 1809.

138. TNA WO 6/149, fol. 146, ltr, 5 Aug. 1803.

139. Ibid., fol. 335, ltr, 31 Jan. 1804.

140. A broader exception was signalled as early as Nov. 1806, when a letter from the WO to the TB acknowledged the 'apprehension' of the Board's agent for prisoners at Plymouth '… that the French seamen who enlist with General Merck [a leading recruiter] enter only for the purpose of effecting their escape', and requested therefore that General Merck's recruiting should be confined '… to the prisoners of war who have been in the Land Service of France.' TNA WO 6/156, ltr, 7 Nov. 1806, George Shee to TB. An undated paper, written probably in 1811, preserved in the WO archives and headed 'Proposals for Enlisting Recruits from amongst Prisoners of War in England [i.e., Britain] for the King's German Legion', a prestigious corps in the British army formed originally in 1803 from Hanoverians in exile following the French conquest of their homeland, excluded from enlistment prisoners of several nationalities in addition to French, Spanish and Italians. The additional exclusions specified (of Danes, Swedes, Russians, and Portuguese) appear to have been because

recruitment to the Legion was directed toward 'none but such as are natives of Germany, and speak, or at least understand, German'. The paper provided that 'The Transport Office shall prepare a return of the number of Germans, Austrians, Prussians, Dutch, Flemish, Poles and Swiss at the several depots for prisoners of war and the recruits in this case should be approved on the spot ...' Prisoners in the four latter categories were presumably considered more likely to speak or understand German. TNA WO 1/648, fol. 373.

141. TNA ADM 98/113, ltr, 29 Dec. 1806, TB to W. Marsden, secretary, Adm.

142. TNA ADM 98/132, ltr, 2 Nov. 1811, TB to Deputy Adjutant General.

143. TNA ADM 98/118, 18 Oct. 1811.

144. TNA ADM 1/3744, ltr, 3 Oct. 1803, Flinn to TB.

145. TNA WO 1/631, fol. 525, ltr, 27 Dec. 1805, Lieut. Col. Willoughby Gordon, Military Secretary to the Commander-in-Chief, to E. Cooke, enclosing a letter of 26 Dec. 1805 from the Inspector General of the Recruiting Service. Three months later Lieut. Col. Gordon wrote to Sir George Shee concerning the 'near 2,000 Poles among the French prisoners of war' who might be enlisted into the 60th Regt, and confirming the going rate of bounty for each prisoner of war recruited was normally three guineas. TNA WO 1/632, fol. 211, ltr, 18 Mar. 1806. Another letter that same month, however, which indicated the extent of competition for recruits from among the prisoners, was written to Lieut. General Whitelocke by Lieut. Col. D. Rottenburgh at Haslar Barracks, Portsmouth, and mentioned a much higher bounty: 'Sir, The long expected prisoners of war from Plymouth have not as yet arrived, and they will never be brought to Portsmouth as long as there are any Germans remain amongst them to be laid hold of by the Marines. To my knowledge about 2,000 Poles and others not natives of France are at every different prison of the interior, and ... French immigrants are making proposals to Government to form a corps of these men. In my humble opinion it would be safer, cheaper and more advantageous to Government to fill up the 60th Regiment with that description of men, which is not the most desirable and yet better than nothing at all, for since all the recruits enlisted on the Continent are given over to the [King's] German Legion the 60th Regiment cannot expect any recruits from that quarter. If you will be pleased to send me an authority among the French prisoners of war wherever they may be confined ... and with the 8 guineas bounty money allowed to prisoners of war, I shall try what I can do.' Ibid., fol. 219, ltr, 12 Mar. 1806. By Feb. 1807 the bounty paid by the Marines had increased to 16 guineas, which was considered to be 'to the great prejudice of the recruiting for the Army.' TNA WO 1/633, fol. 483, ltr, 6 Feb. 1807, Lieut. Col. Willoughby Gordon to Sir G. Shee. The problem appears to have diminished, however, early in 1810, with a decision by the Adm. that 'the enlisting of prisoners of war for the Royal Marine Service should be discontinued.' TNA ADM 98/170, circular, 2 Mar. 1810, TB to depot agents. By then or soon afterward the bounty given foreign recruits, at least to the King's German Legion, was, according to the undated paper quoted above concerning the Legion, four guineas.

146. Lewis, *A Social History of the Navy*, op. cit., 92, 95.

147. TNA ADM 98/170, circular, 5 Apr. 1808.

148. TNA WO 1/639, fol. 41, ltr, 18 Jul. 1808, Deputy Adjutant General to J. Beckett, HO. Recruits to the German Brunswick Oels Jager regt, composed of German, Polish, Swiss, Danish, Dutch, and Croat volunteers from the prisoner of war depots and hulks in Britain, were among those particularly prone to desert to the French. 'Of

the Brunswick corps,' F.S. Larpent, Judge Advocate General of the British forces in the Peninsular War, wrote in Jul. 1813 in Spain, 'ten went off from picket two nights since to the French, and fourteen from the camp, and others have gone off also, and some have been surprised, so that I believe they are ordered to be sent more to the rear and cannot be trusted; I do not wonder at it, as government have taken men from the French prisons [i.e., depots and hulks in Britain], who were only taken [prisoner] last year, and who, I have no doubt, only enlisted on purpose to desert the first opportunity.' Sir George Larpent, ed., *The Private Journal of F.S. Larpent* (London, 1853), Vol. II, 3, 4; Christopher Hibbert, ed., *A Soldier of the 71st. The Journal of a Soldier of the Highland Light Infantry 1806-1815* (London, 1975), 102. Private Wheeler of the 51st light infantry regt expressed similar views about prisoners enlisted in the Chasseurs Britanniques, a regt formed from volunteers among prisoners of war and deserters from the French forces, including French, Italians, Poles, Swiss and Croats. Writing from Villa Mayor in Spain in Sep. 1811, Wheeler reported that: '... 9 men of the Chasseurs Britannique Regiment were shot for desertion. This Corps was originally formed of French Loyalists [i.e., Royalists, in the 1790s], but the old hands are continually dropping off and they are replaced by volunteers from the French prisons [i.e., depots and hulks in Britain]. A great number of these men enter our service for no other purpose than to go over to their [the French] army as soon as an opportunity occurs (and who can blame them).' B.H. Liddell Hart, ed., *The Letters of Private Wheeler 1809-1828* (London, 1951), 53, 67.

149. *EEC*, 27 Oct. 1803.

150. TNA ADM 103/110, No. 3; ADM 103/154, No. 3.

151. TNA ADM 103/154, Nos 2, 4, 6, 8-11, 13. Seven did so on 6 Oct. 1803, the eighth, Carel Naast, on 3 Nov.

152. TNA ADM 103/155, Nos 6, 46, 47, 51-4, 56, 57, 61, 64, 66, 67, 81. All fourteen were merchant seamen: one from the *Elizabeth*, eight from the *Prudence*, and five from the *Droiture*. Twelve of them left the bridewell for the navy on 27 Jan. 1804, François Tapouren, described as 'Boy above age', on the following day. Jacques Cruys, who must have applied to enlist while he was at the bridewell, had been transferred to Greenlaw on 31 Mar. along with all other prisoners of war until then confined in the bridewell, but he left Greenlaw the next day for the navy. All fourteen are listed in the first 'French' Entry Book for Greenlaw but their dates of discharge from captivity show (with the formal exception of Jacques Cruys) it was from the bridewell, not Greenlaw, they entered the navy.

153. TNA ADM 103/154. Johan Erickson, seaman, capd May 1804 in the North Sea on the Dutch gun brig *Union*, joined the Aberdeenshire militia in Jul. that year; and Jean Martin, a cook, and shipmate of Erickson, the Inverness-shire militia the following month. Ibid., Nos 54, 32.

154. TNA ADM 103/110, Nos 1-132.

155. TNA ADM 103/152 and ADM 103/153 passim.

156. Kaald, op. cit., 87, 141, 142, 167, entries for 12 Nov. 1808, 9 and 23-25 Nov. 1809, and 13 May 1810. TNA ADM 103/152, No. 222, confirms Kaald's note: Ivar Ronning (or Ivert J. Runing) is shown to have been dischgd from Greenlaw on 8 Nov. 1809 into the Royal Marines.

157. TNA ADM 103/158, Nos 1, 22, 38, 44. The two who joined the navy were Pedro Gomes and Jean Crevis, the two the band of the 27th regt Joseph Costes and Joaquin Detarre. All four had arrived at Greenlaw from Greenock, Gomes on 21 Jul. and Crevis on 24

Sep. 1805, Costes and Detarre both on 3 Mar. 1806. Crevis joined the navy only two days after his arrival at Greenlaw, Gomes three months after his. Costes and Detarre both spent only 17 days at the depot before leaving to become army bandsmen.

158. This is the Entry Book TNA ADM 103/156. All these 214 prisoners were transferred from Greenlaw between Nov. 1810 and the beginning of Feb. 1811 either, in the case of the officers, on parole to Peebles or, in the case of the other ranks, to Esk Mills depot.

159. TNA ADM 103/155 passim; Digurt is No. 37, Giraud No. 210, the four other privateersmen are Nos 207-9 and 211. Jannot Miviel (No. 208) and Orphi Miviel (No. 209) had both been capd on the *Chasseur* at Cuba in Aug. 1804.

160. TNA ADM 103/157 passim. For Watigny, see TNA ADM 103/432, No. 786, ADM 98/277, ltrs from TB: 24 Apr. 1811 to Capt. Pellowe, and 21 Oct. 1811 to Lieut. Priest; ADM 103/112, No. 466, and ADM 103/157, Nos 325 and 673.

161. TNA ADM 103/112, No. 221 (Barbet).

162. For Talise and Gesima, see TNA ADM 98/277, ltrs, 13 Aug. 1811, TB to Admiral Otway at Leith and to Capt. Heddington at Edinburgh Castle. For Hoft, see ADM 103/114, Nos 1,309 and 1,276. For the other 13 volunteers into the navy, see ADM 103/114, Nos 1,258-79 passim, 1,286 and 1,309. For the 11 volunteers into the 60th regt, see ADM 103/114, Nos 921, 946, 955, 961, 973, 1,051, 1,121, 1,126, 1,144, 1,175 and 1,176.

163. TNA ADM 103/432-435 passim and ADM 103/113 passim.

164. TNA ADM 103/432, No. 271.

165. Ibid., No. 713 (Lerouge), No. 942 (Richard), No. 806 (Mondin), No. 811 (Garel); ADM 103/432-435 passim; ADM 98/278, ltr, 20 Apr. 1812, TB to Capt. Moriarty; ADM 103/434, Nos 2,518 (Benoit) and 3,948 (Gautche); ADM 103/435, No. 6,194 (Petit); ADM 98/118, ltr, 26 Jul. 1811, TB to J. W. Croker, Adm.; ADM 99/209, ltr 2 Aug. 1811, Adm. to TB; ADM 98/277, ltr, 5 Aug. 1811, TB to Capt. Pellowe. A seaman volunteer into the RN from Valleyfield in Aug. 1811, who was b. in 'Portsmouth, North America' and had been capd, n.d. and n.p., on *Fontaine* m.v., had, as already observed, the distinctly Scots name Neil Nicolson. TNA ADM 103/433, No. 1,371.

166. NLS MS Acc. 5811/1/29.

167. *Perth Courier*, 18 Mar. 1813.

168. TNA ADM 98/279, ltr, 29 Sep. 1812, TB to Capt. Moriarty. No prisoner of that name has been found in the alphabetical index of prisoners at Perth (ADM 103/516), but the Valleyfield Entry Book (ADM 103/432, No. 532) suggests he may have been Pierre Joseph Roustan, 41, b. at Marseilles, 2nd capt. of *Duguay Trouin* priv. when capd May 1810 in the Mediterranean, arr. at Valleyfield from Esk Mills in Mar. 1811, and was transferred to Perth on 1 Sep. 1812.

169. TNA ADM 105/54, Prisoners' Applications, No. 437, 13 Dec. 1812.

170. TNA ADM 98/280, ltr, 27 May 1813, TB to Capt. Moriarty; ADM 103/263, No. 64.

171. TNA ADM 103/267, No. 3,070, and ADM 103/264, No. 3,070. He was Joachim Souaris (or Guillaume Soullard), 29, b. at Caen, capd Oct. 1812 in the Baltic on *Pilotin* priv. But Souaris (or Soullard), according to a comment in red ink in the Entry Book, was 'Found unfit for H.M.'s Service. Ordered to be sent with the Germans and Italians.'

172. TNA ADM 103/159, Greenock Entry Book, passim; ADM 98/276, ltrs, 7 and 20 Sep. 1808, TB to J. Colquhoun; ADM 98/201, ltr, 23 Jul. 1810, TB to Colquhoun; ADM 1/3744, ltr, 16 Nov. 1803, TB to Sir E. Nepean, secretary, Adm.

CHAPTER 21: ESCAPES

1. Marote-Carrier, op. cit., 85; Beaudoin, op. cit., 633.
2. Marote-Carrier, op. cit., 60.
3. TNA ADM 98/278, ltr, 3 Aug. 1812, TB to Capt. Moriarty.
4. Marote-Carrier, op. cit., 77-81.
5. TNA ADM 103/435, No. 6,439 (Lefebvre); ADM 103/266, No. 7,627 (Lefebvre); ADM 99/212, ltr, received 19 Nov. 1811, by TB from M. Wright; ADM 103/596, No. 31 (Delisle); ADM 103/580, No. 21 (Delisle).
6. See above, pp.63-72, 82-6, 98-101.
7. Marote-Carrier, op. cit., 167-75.
8. Johnston, 'Recollections', op. cit., p.2.
9. Kaald, op. cit., 164, 165.
10. The Valleyfield Entry Books show only that two prisoners escaped on 12 Feb. 1812, and the Books' complete absence of reference to any group of 30 escaping may indicate the recapture of the latter was so speedy that it was not considered necessary even to enter them as escapers. The two shown were Roland Demazelly, who was recapd at Leith and returned to Valleyfield on 16 Feb., and Matu Bronzan, alias Baptiste Hidgy, who appears not to have been recapd. Both had escaped 'over the Stockade'. Whether the group of 30 also did so is not known, nor is whether Demazelly and Bronzan were two of the 30 rather than two 'independents' who also chose that day to depart from Valleyfield. TNA ADM 103/432, No. 494 (Bronzan); ADM 103/435, Nos 5,306 and 5,359 (Demazelly).
11. NAS GD1/405/2, pp. 12-13. It may well be to this incident that a letter of 24 Sep. 1812 to Capt. Brown from the TB referred, in which were mentioned prisoners put on short allowance for assaulting turnkeys and the need to call in the guard when making searches or when 'tumult or resistance' by the prisoners was anticipated, as the Board assumed the guard 'will not suffer themselves to be insulted with impunity.' TNA ADM 98/279.
12. W. Chambers, 'Some Early Recollections', *Chambers's Journal*, No. 600, Jun. 26, 1875, op. cit., 403-4.
13. *CM*, 4 Dec. 1813.
14. *Perth Courier*, 31 Dec. 1812.
15. C.M. Kinnear, 'Les Prisonniers de Perth', in *Scots Magazine*, Jun. 1989, 271; *Dundee Advertiser*, 9 Apr. 1813; *Montrose Review*, 3 Sep. 1813.
16. See above, pp.368, 369; *Perth Courier*, 8 Apr. 1813.
17. In the four Perth Entry Books only one prisoner is shown specifically to have escaped on 24 Aug. 1813: Charles Jansens, 20, seaman, b. at Flushing, 'captured on French boats at Flushing' in Aug. 1809, and who had arr. at Perth from Valleyfield a month before his escape. TNA ADM 103/266, No. 6,999. Proforma reports submitted by depot agents to the TB concerning escapes have survived for only five prisoners at Perth: P.F. Drieu, Claude Remis and Jean Baptiste Godfred, all three on 20 Jan. 1813, and D. Dewatre and P. Faillant on respectively 1 and 6 Apr. 1813. See TNA

ADM 103/487, 103/489 and 103/491, and ADM 105/45. But some further information about escapers from the depot, and the recapture of several of them, is provided among the 42 bundles of loose sheets in TNA ADM 103/267, evidently smaller duplicate versions of the four Perth Entry Books. Thus in the 31st bundle, three of those who escaped on 24 Aug. 1813 but were recapd three days later at Blair Atholl are shown to have been: No. 6,975 François Armand, seaman, capd on *Grand Rodeur* priv.; No. 6,976 Jean Baptiste Beaugrand, seaman, capd on *Barbier de Seville* priv.; and No. 7,176 Laurent Negrol, seaman, capd on the m.o.w. *Le Brave*.

18. See above, p.384. The 11 retaken fugitives, lodged in the cachot with the 24 prisoners seized by the guards, appear to have been some of those who had escaped from Perth depot on 24 Aug.

19. *Perth Courier*, 16 Sep. 1813. The 32nd bundle of loose sheets in TNA ADM 103/267 shows that in fact three of the escapers on the night of 12-13 Sep. were recapd on 16 Sep. at the wood of Moormonth, near Bridge of Earn: No. 6,921 François Wimé, seaman, capd on *Revenge* priv.; No. 6,915 Jean M. Delpierre, seaman, capd on *Renard* priv.; and No. 5,585 François Semin, sergeant major, 1st Artillery regt. In addition, in an unnumbered bundle of loose sheets in ADM 103/267 it is said No. 4,106, Pierre Neveaux, alias Firman Lapine, first capd in 1804 as a carpenter on a priv., then at Salamanca in Jul. 1812 as a soldier, having escaped from Perth on 11 Sep. 1813 [? perhaps a misdating for the night of 12-13 Sep.] was recapd n.d. (but evidently several weeks after his escape), at Peterhead and re-entered Perth depot on 28 Oct. 1813. Eight other prisoners who escaped on 13 Sep. were recapd as follows, according to other unnumbered bundles of sheets in TNA ADM 103/267: at Pettycur, Fife, and re-entered Perth depot 21 Sep., No. 6,930, Maurice Houard, seaman, capd on *Roy de Naples* priv.; at St Andrews, Fife, and re-entered Perth 17 Sep., No. 5,386 Manuel Champion, seaman, capd 1809 on *Vengeur* priv. at Flushing, No. 5,817 Etienne Fouche, soldier, capd on the frig. *La Gloire*, No. 6,917 Nicolas Tullet, seaman, capd on a prize to an unnamed priv., and No. 7,000 Jean Baptiste Benard, seaman, capd on *Roy de Naples* priv.; on 16 Oct. at Peterhead, No. 1,103 Jean Baptiste Lobe, lieut., capd on *Etoile* priv., No. 6,920 Louis Codran, seaman, capd on an unnamed prize ship, and No. 7,071 Jean Louis Secullier, seaman, capd on *Ratafia* priv.

20. Marote-Carrier, op. cit., 167-75.

21. Unfortunately for Gascourin his leap to freedom was not long enough: he was recapd and returned to the bridewell two days later. *CM*, 5 Mar. 1804; TNA ADM 103/155, Nos 26 and 94.

22. Wharton was consequently dismissed by the TB but it reinstated him as depot clerk in Feb. 1811. TNA ADM 103/155, No. 30; Kaald, op. cit., 162; TNA ADM 98/276, ltrs from TB: 5 Jan. 1811 to M. Wright, and 4 Feb. 1811 to Lieut. Priest; ADM 103/491 (vide 'G': Guigougeux).

23. Kaald, op. cit., 130-3, 134, 138; TNA ADM 103/152, No. 235.

24. The reference to this escape occurs in a ltr, 14 Mar. 1812, Lieut. Priest, agent, Greenlaw, to TB, in TNA ADM 103/635.

25. TNA ADM 103/432, Nos 124 (Petitchamp) and 920 (Lambert); ADM 103/435, No. 5,304 (Petit). The Entry Book says that the following day, 4 Jan. 1812, Guillaume Mariote, soldier, 66th Basque line regt, escaped from Valleyfield in exactly the same way—it is not improbable that the date given for his escape should read 3 Jan., and that he, Petitchamp, Lambert and Petit all escaped at the same time even if not as a group. TNA ADM 103/434, No. 3,275.

26. *Dundee Advertiser*, 4 Jun. 1813. The *Perth Courier*, 3 Jun. 1813, said the three escapers 'are supposed to have got over the palisade and the walls by a ladder and ropes.' Although the identities of two of these three escapers are not specified in the Perth Entry Books or other sources, 'Captain Massy' was almost certainly First Lieut. Fiacre Masse or Massé, capd in 1812 when 'Driven ashore in a boat from the [priv.] *Incomparable*', who had been in the first intake of prisoners to arrive at Perth two months later, and who is merely said in the Entry Book to have escaped in 'June 1813. Not retaken.' TNA ADM 103/263, No. 396.

27. TNA ADM 103/432, Nos 291 (Laurent), 432 (Casteur), 494 (Bronzan), 667 (Robin), 717 (Moreau), 780 (Duran), and 827 (Yvert); ADM 103/433, Nos 1,227 (Macqueron), 1,373 (Moreno), 1,436 (Ameline), 1,565 (Van Den Hewal); ADM 103/434, Nos 2,463 (Le Prieur), 2,466 (Ernel), 4,164 (Bouillard).

28. NLS MS Acc. 5811/1/63, op.cit., p.12; TNA ADM 103/157, No. 12 (Rafey); ADM 103/487 (Rafey); ADM 105/45 (Rafey, Carrier, Raymot); ADM 103/110, No. 318 (Raymot).

29. Abell, op. cit., 200; NAS GD1/405/2, p15.

30. *Dundee Advertiser*, 1 Jan. 1813; *Perth Courier*, 31 Dec. 1812.

31. *Dundee Advertiser*, 4 Jun. 1813; *EEC*, 7 Jun. 1813; TNA ADM 98/280, ltrs, 7 and 15 Jun. 1813, TB to Capt. Moriarty.

32. *Perth Courier*, 8 Jul. 1813.

33. Ibid., 16 Sep. 1813.

34. Kaald, op. cit., 175, 176. John Muth appears to have been Jan David Mouth, whom the Greenlaw Entry Book shows was successful in a later escape from the depot on 1 Sep. that year. A seaman capd on the Danish priv. *Havneren* off Scotland in Oct. 1808, he had arr. a month later at Greenlaw. Johanes J. Lauser, seaman, had been a shipmate of Kaald himself on the priv. *Den Kjakke*, capd in May 1808 off Trondheim, and had entered Greenlaw a month later. TNA ADM 103/152, No. 377 (Mouth), No. 216 (Lauser).

35. Johnston, 'Recollections', op.cit., p.9.

36. TNA ADM 98/277, ltr, 31 May 1811, TB to Capt. Pellowe.

37. NAS GD1/405/2, p. 35.

38. Black, *Penicuik and Neighbourhood*, op. cit., 19, 20. Black's account, which appears to be based on oral tradition, may be another but more violent version of one or other of the attempted escapes by cart from Valleyfield in May 1811 and Jul. 1813; but it may on the other hand provide circumstantial details missing from the bald statement in the Valleyfield Entry Book about the death of Chuchere. TNA ADM 103/433, No. 1,708 (Chuchere); ADM 103/648, No. 1,708.

39. That such a conjecture about De Cuyper's balloon as a possible vehicle of escape was not beyond the bounds at least of eventual possibility was perhaps strengthened by a similar development a few weeks later among French prisoners on parole at Selkirk. Reporting on 18 Oct. 1813 how the inhabitants there had recently been entertained by the prisoners' performances of concerts, 'setting off balloons, etc.', the *Caledonian Mercury* added: 'A few days ago one of 50 feet dimensions was set off in the presence of a vast concourse of spectators, which ascended in fine style and was to have been accompanied by one of the prisoners, but the agent, thinking the balloon might go to too great a distance, did not think proper to admit him [to it].'

40. See above, pp.376, 377.

41. *CM*, 12 Mar. 1804.

42. NAS GD 1/405/2, p.11, ltr, 17 Oct. 1812, Capt A. Brown, agent, Valleyfield, to a friend.

43. For details of Destrais's case, see above, pp.360, 361.

44. TNA ADM 103/434, No. 3,527, and ADM 103/436, No. 7,650 (where Destrais is said to be a seaman, capd on the frig. *L'Amphitrite* in 1809 at Martinique); NAS AD 14/13/74.

45. *Perth Courier*, 14 Oct. 1813.

46. *Dundee Advertiser*, 8 Oct. 1813.

47. Abell, op. cit., 158; *Glasgow Courier*, 18 Dec. 1813.

48. While, as has been seen, some prisoners in or on their way to the Scots depots might occasionally suffer brutal treatment by escorts or guards, the instruction on 28 Aug. 1813 by the TB to its agent at Perth after the mass escape there four days earlier indicates humane concern: 'Pay the boatman hired by you in order to assist in saving the prisoners therein mentioned from drowning.' TNA ADM 98/280.

49. Kaald, op. cit., 113.

50. Black, *Penicuik and Neighbourhood*, op. cit., 20, 21; ML, Black Coll., op. cit., vol. 2(c), p.72.

51. Johnston, 'Recollections', op. cit., p.2.

52. TNA ADM 103/648, No. 1,007 (Boulet) and No. 379 (Woemeseuil).

53. *Montrose Review*, 26 Apr. 1811.

54. *Perth Courier*, 16 Sep. 1813.

55. Chambers, 'Some Early Recollections', *Chambers's Journal*, No. 600, 26 Jun. 1875, op. cit., 404.

56. TNA ADM 98/276, ltrs, 21 Aug. and 18 Sep. 1809, TB to M. Wright; Kaald, op. cit., 166, 167, entry for 4 May 1810; TNA ADM 98/280, ltr, 16 Oct. 1813, TB to Capt. Moriarty; ADM 98/277, ltr, 7 Mar. 1811, and ADM 98/278, ltr, 10 Mar. 1812, TB to Lieut. Priest; ADM 98/280, ltrs from TB: 3 Sep. 1813 to Capt. Moriarty, 15 Sep. 1813 to Vice Admiral Otway; ADM 98/279, ltrs, 14 Sep. 1812 and 3 Feb. 1813, TB to Capt. Moriarty.

57. Walker, *The Depot at Norman Cross*, op. cit., 157.

58. *CM*, 20 Apr. 1811. A useful guide, had escapers been able only to obtain a copy, might have been, for example, *The Traveller's Guide through Scotland*, published by J. Thomson & Co., Edinburgh, and John Murray, London, which contained a 'travelling map of Scotland [which] contains many new roads … viz. Midlothian, and the road from Edinburgh to Carlisle …', and whose 5th edition was advertised for sale in the press in Sep. 1812. There were also Thomas Brown's *Atlas of Scotland*, containing a general map of Scotland and separate maps of each county, and a *Map of Edinburghshire*, by Mr Knox, Land Surveyor, Edinburgh, publication of both of which was advertised in the press in Feb. 1813. *CM*, 5 Sep. 1812, 1 and 15 Feb. 1813.

59. Marote-Carrier, op. cit., 171.

60. See an anonymous article in *Peeblesshire Advertiser*, 15 Apr. 1905.

61. Marote-Carrier, op. cit., 163, 164.

62. TNA ADM 103/263, No. 1,127; ADM 103/266, No. 6,894; ADM 103/491 (Dewatre); *Perth Courier*, 29 Apr. 1813.

63. See, e.g., *Dundee Advertiser*, 4 Jun. 1813.

64. TNA ADM 105/45; ADM 103/152, No. 817 (Jonsen), No. 854 (Watry); *CM*, 7 Mar. 1811.

65. *Montrose Review,* 26 Apr. 1811; *CM*, 20 Jul. 1812; *EEC*, 25 Jul. 1812; TNA ADM 103/157, Nos. 152 and 681 (Gonsalvez).

66. Johnston, 'Recollections', op. cit., p.9.

67. *CM*, 4 Dec. 1813.

68. Ibid., 20 Apr. 1811; *EEC*, 15 and 20 Apr. and 30 Dec. 1811; *Montrose Review*, 26 Apr. 1811; *Perth Courier*, 4 Feb. and 14 Oct. 1813; *Dundee Advertiser*, 2 Apr. 1813. The two escapers recapd on the barge at Dundee were P. Faillant, 2nd capt., and Lieut. Dominique Dewatre, of *Le Figaro* priv. Dewatre, genteelly dressed in black, had already been an unsuccessful escaper from Perth in Sep. 1812; *Chambers's Journal*, No. 600, 26 Jun. 1875, op. cit., 404.

69. Marote-Carrier, op. cit., 141.

70. *Perth Courier*, 25 Feb. 1813.

71. Perth Payments Ledger, op. cit., passim. Michel Croesec or Croesel, 29, b. at Tanve, was capt. of *Le Pilotin* priv. when capd at the Aland Islands in the Baltic in Oct. 1812. He appears to have succeeded in escaping from Perth on 13 Sep. 1813. TNA ADM 103/264, No. 3,066.

72. TNA ADM 103/487.

73. TNA ADM 103/432, No. 494; ADM 103/489.

74. TNA ADM 103/435, No. 5,000; ADM 103/266, No. 7,119.

75. TNA ADM 103/157, No. 695 (Brown), No. 693 (Landau); ADM 103/489 (Greenlaw entries). The two men had been capd in the North Sea in Oct. 1811.

76. TNA ADM 103/157, No. 275; ADM 103/489 (Greenlaw entries); ADM 103/112, No. 304.

77. TNA ADM 103/112, No. 520; ADM 105/45.

78. *Glasgow Courier*, 13 Jun. 1811.

79. *EEC*, 29 Jun. 1811.

80. *Perth Courier*, 28 Jan. and 4 Feb. 1813.

81. TNA ADM 98/134, ltr, 30 Apr. 1813, TB to G. Harrison, HM Treasury; Abell, op. cit., 383.

82. *Dundee Advertiser*, 2 Apr. 1813.

83. *Dundee Advertiser*, 10 Sep. 1813. The *Advertiser* added: 'Thus three attempts within the space of a few months have been made by these restless neighbours upon our unprotected shipping. The first attempt [i.e., upon the sloop *Nancy* at Broughty Ferry] was successful; the second and third were defeated only by accident.'

84. *Perth Courier*, 23 Sep. 1813.

85. *Dundee Advertiser*, 8 Oct. 1813.

86. *CM*, 13 Apr. 1811; TNA ADM 103/152, No. 854 (Watry), No. 817 (Jonsen); ADM 103/263, No. 1,127 (Dewatre); ADM 103/433, No. 1,708 (Chuchere).

87. *EEC*, 28 Nov. and 3 Dec. 1803; *Glasgow Courier*, 10 Mar. 1804.

88. *CM*, 20, 22, 27 and 29 Apr. 1811; *EEC*, 15, 20, 25, 27 Apr., 2, 11 and 23 May 1811.

89. *Perth Courier*, 2, 16 and 23 Sep. 1813.

90. TNA ADM 103/124, No. 40 (Le Couche), No. 42 (Cabouche); ADM 103/112, No. 6 (Cabouche), No. 7 (Le Couche); *CM*, 2 Mar. 1811.

91. See, e.g., TNA ADM 103/113, No. 1,317, and ADM 103/266, No. 7,541, for Michel Colas, sergeant, capd on a naval or transport vessel in 1809, who had been transferred in Aug. 1813 from Valleyfield to Perth, escaped the following month from the latter, was recapd at Edinburgh, 'lodged' briefly in the Castle, then sent back again to Valleyfield; and *Perth Courier*, 9 Jul. 1812, reporting the recapture at Huntingtower near Perth of an unnamed prisoner from Valleyfield who was then 'lodged' temporarily in Perth gaol.

92. *Dumfries Courier*, 18 Aug. 1812 and 30 Nov. 1813. The four escapers were a soldier, and a privateer and two naval seamen, respectively Pierre Ducrosse, 2nd Swiss regt, Gregoire Godefroy, *L'Aigle* priv., Julian Ganivet, m.o.w. *La Gloire*, and Jean Louis Marocque of the sloop *La Mouche*. All four were sent back to Valleyfield and remained there until the general release of prisoners in Jun. 1814. TNA ADM 103/113, Nos. 7,434-7.

93. *EEC*, 3 Jun. 1811.

94. TNA ADM 103/155, No. 36. Walker, *The Depot at Norman Cross*, op. cit., 195; Charles Cowan, *Reminiscences*, op. cit., 16, 17, says Pineau (whose name he recalls as Pinet or Pinou) '... was very unfortunate. In making his way, a few days after his escape, to London and France by the coach-road, he took refuge from a heavy shower, and was instantly recognised as one of the prisoners of war confined previously at Norman Cross. The poor fellow was doubtless unaware that he was in that neighbourhood.' TNA ADM 98/276, ltr, 18 Dec. 1810, TB to M. Wright.

95. TNA ADM 103/112, No. 533 (Bouvaist), No. 536 (Moussu); ADM 103/491.

96. TNA ADM 103/432, Nos 160 (Mulard) and 161 (Coterix); ADM 103/491.

97. See above, Appendix 3, No. 10, and *CM*, 6 Aug. 1812.

98. TNA ADM 103/611, No. 269; ADM 103/435, No. 6,338; ADM 103/266, No. 6,091; ADM 103/114, No. 1,352; ADM 103/436, No. 7,636; ADM 98/280, ltrs from TB: 30 Nov. 1813 and 5 Jan. 1814 to Lieut. Priest, 18 Dec. 1813 to Admiral Hope, and 7 Feb. 1814 to Capt. Brown; ADM 98/210, ltr, 18 Dec. 1813, TB to J. Smith, Kelso.

99. 52 Geo. III c.156. The penalty for anyone convicted was transportation for seven or fourteen years or for life.

100. Their trial and conviction will be discussed in a future volume, complementary to the present one, which will deal with parole prisoners in Scotland during the Napoleonic Wars.

101. TNA ADM 97/111, letters, papers and precognitions, Jun.-Jul. 1813, concerning Moore and the Kelso parole prisoners.

102. TNA ADM 98/278, ltr, 3 Apr. 1812. About Margerie d'Olivier or Jean Bratiche no more has been found, nor any other references to their alleged aiding of escapers.

103. TNA ADM 98/277, ltr, 7 Jun. 1811.

104. *Perth Courier*, 28 Jan., 4 and 11 Feb. 1813.

105. *Chambers's Journal*, No. 600, 26 Jun. 1875, op. cit., 403.

106. Private information. It seems not improbable that one of their descendants was Charles Vanbeck, who worked as a miner at Prestonlinks colliery, Prestonpans, before the 1914-18 War. NLS MS Acc. 4312, minutes, Mid and East Lothian Miners' Association, 4 Mar. 1911. Several Vanbecks or Van Becks are listed in the current Lothians telephone directory some of whom also may be descendants of the Penicuik prisoner of war.

107. NAS GD 1/405/2, p. 35.

108. *Perth Courier*, 3 Dec. 1812; *CM*, 14 Nov. 1812; Marote-Carrier, op.cit., 76.

109. *Chambers's Journal*, No. 600, Jun. 26 1875, op. cit., 404. Meal-mobs, popular riots and disturbances concerning the supply and price of oatmeal, staple food of the common people in Scotland, were frequent in the 18th and early 19th centuries. See, e.g., Logue, *Popular Disturbances in Scotland*, op. cit., 18-53.

110. *Chambers's Journal*, No. 600, Jun. 26 1875, op. cit., 404. Was an advertisement in the *Caledonian Mercury* on 26 May 1814 too early to be connected with the death of the 'hard-hearted' farmer? It announced the sale of the lands of Winkston, a mile from Peebles, and which lay 'on both sides of the turnpike road to Edinburgh' and included 'a tolerable mansion house'.

111. At Perth, three escapers on 20 Jan. 1813 were said to have come to the depot '… under the Name of Soldiers, but they are Sailors'. All three were said to be privateersmen: Pierre François Drieu, soldier, 88th line regt, but also a priv. officer; Claude Remis, soldier, 16th Artillery regt, but also a priv. seaman; and Jean Baptiste Godfred, soldier, 20th Dragoons, but also a priv. seaman. These three are entered twice in the table as both sea-going and army. TNA ADM 103/489.

112. TNA ADM 103/487 and 103/489; ADM 103/432, No. 827 (Yvert).

113. At Greenlaw, the eight sea-going escapers in the uncertain category were Jacob Miller, who escaped 1 Jun. 1804; Carol Puch, Hendrik Tonks and Ernest Vonck, who all escaped 13 Nov. 1806; Louis G. Pineau, 11 Nov. 1810; Etienne Parfaitinus and Louis Adlophe St Vereau, both of whom escaped 4 Dec. 1810; and Desiré Molinière, 11 Nov. 1811. At Esk Mills, Gabriel Iusset (or Iasset) has been entered as a privateer, although in another official source he was said to have been capd on an 'uncertain vessel'. At Edinburgh Castle, the two whose category is uncertain were: Jacques Adam, who may have been a m.v. officer but was probably a naval officer capd on a m.v.; and Jean Smith, said to be either a naval or a priv. seaman. At Perth, Charles Jansens was the seaman in the uncertain category who escaped on 24 Aug. 1813 from that depot. The three privateersmen mentioned in Note 111 above—an officer (Drieu) and two seamen (Remis and Godfred) have not been included in the Perth figures in this table as they entered that depot as soldiers.

114. Ensigns and midshipmen have been entered in the table as officers. Thus at Edinburgh bridewell Henry Le Hure, who escaped on 16 Mar. 1804, was a m.v. ensign; at Greenlaw, Adolphe Douzon, who escaped on 5 Mar. 1812, was a naval midshipman; at Esk Mills, Jerome (or Geriani) Favali and Frederik Reimer, who both escaped on 19 Feb. 1811, were priv. ensigns; at Edinburgh Castle, four of the nine naval officers were ensigns or midshipmen; at Valleyfield, one of the four priv. officers was an ensign (Louis Petitchamp, alias of A. Tavernier, who escaped on 3 Jan. 1812). 'Other' naval, m.v. or priv. escapers include all those who were not in rank either seamen or officers—carpenters, prizemasters, scryvers, clerks, salters, et al. Thus at Edinburgh bridewell, the m.v. 'other' was Jean de Rycke, salter, who escaped on 25 Oct. 1803. At Greenlaw, the three priv. 'others' were Ludowig Frhen, scryver, who escaped on 2 Sep. 1809, Auguste Garsin (or Garcin or Garzin), prizemaster, who escaped on 3 Oct. 1811, and Hendrick Petersen, carpenter, who escaped on 29 Jun. 1810. At Esk Mills, Jean Halnes and Arent Vanveen, who both escaped on 19 Feb. 1811, were priv. prizemasters, Marc Butel and Jean Simonsen, two other privateersmen who escaped that day, were variously described as seamen but also bosuns—they have both been entered in the table as seamen; and Gabriel Iusset, who likewise escaped on 19 Feb. 1811, and was variously described as a priv. master-at-arms but also as a pilot from

an 'uncertain' vessel, has been entered under 'priv. others'. Etienne Duplessay, who also escaped on 19 Feb. 1811, was described as naval but of rank unstated (r.u.) and is entered thus on the table. At Edinburgh Castle, four of the five privateer 'others' were prizemasters, the other a clerk; and of the two naval 'others' one was a clerk (Jean Raymot, who escaped on 15 Jul. 1811), and the other a bosun (J. François Ricard, who escaped on 12 Apr. 1811). Of the two others who were sea-going but of unstated or uncertain category, one was Lieut. Jacques Adam, probably a naval, but possibly a m.v., officer; and the seaman was Jean Smith, who was likewise either a privateersman or from a m.v. At Valleyfield the two priv. 'others' were a gunner (Jacques Coterix, who escaped on 6 Apr. 1811) and a clerk (J. De La Sauvage, who escaped on 19 Nov. 1813). At Perth the 'other' priv. was a carpenter in rank (Pierre Neveau, alias Firman Lapine, who escaped on 11 Sep. 1813); and the 'other' seaman of unknown service was Charles Jansens, who escaped on 24 Aug. 1813. Three of the 10 soldiers shown in the table were P.F. Drieu, J.B. Godfred, and Claude Remis, who were said in other official sources to be in fact privateersmen—Drieu an officer, and the other two seamen.

CHAPTER 22: IF AT FIRST YOU DON'T SUCCEED …

1. *Perth Courier*, 10 Sep. 1812.
2. *Dundee Advertiser*, 2 Apr. 1813.
3. TNA ADM 103/434, No. 4,164; ADM 103/435, Nos 5,612 and 6,193; ADM 103/489.
4. TNA ADM 103/434, No. 3,206; ADM 103/435, Nos 6,228 and 6,331; ADM 103/113, No. 7,439.
5. TNA ADM 103/432, No. 907; ADM 103/266, No. 6,975; ADM 103/267, No. 6,975; ADM 103/113, Nos 7,304 and 7,431.
6. TNA ADM 103/435, Nos 5,000 and 6,279; ADM 103/266, No.7,119; ADM 103/489. The other Imperial Guardsman who escaped from a Scots depot, though only once, was Sergeant Pierre Trochery—see above, Appendix 2, No. 42. TNA ADM 103/124, No. 2,707; ADM 103/112, No. 381; ADM 103/157, Nos 247 and 801; ADM 103/435, No. 5,764.
7. TNA ADM 103/112, No. 532; ADM 103/435, Nos 5,306 and 5,359. In the Valleyfield Entry Book, Roland Demazelly is said to be aged 20, 5ft 5ins tall, with an oval face, light brown hair and grey eyes.
8. TNA ADM 103/116, No. 507; *CM*, 19 Nov. 1810.
9. TNA ADM 103/124, No. 35; ADM 103/487; ADM 105/45.
10. TNA ADM 98/278. In fact, a letter received by the TO in London on 5 Nov. from Mr Lailjohn (?), a clerk of the peace at Stirling, said Petit had been apprehended 'a month since'. ADM 99/212.
11. NAS Lord Advocate's Papers, AD/14/12/63.
12. Ibid.
13. Ibid.
14. Ibid.
15. Ibid.
16. Ibid.
17. Ibid.
18. Ibid.

19. Ibid., Extract from the proceedings of a General Court Martial held within Edinburgh Castle, 5 Dec. 1811, at the trial of Sergeant Duncan MacIntosh, Kirkcudbrightshire Militia; *EEC*, 19 Dec. 1811 and 18 Apr. 1812.

20. NAS AD 14/12/63, ltr, 16 Apr. 1812, Moriarty to Crown Agent.

21. TNA ADM 98/278.

22. TNA ADM 103/435, No. 5,304; ADM 103/489.

23. TNA ADM 105/45, Valleyfield, 3 Jan. 1812, Petit.

24. TNA ADM 98/278, ltrs, 14 Mar., 11 and 22 May 1812, TB to Capt. Moriarty.

25. TNA ADM 103/435, No. 5,365; ADM 105/45, Valleyfield, 1 Jun. 1812.

26. *Montrose Review*, 3 Jul. 1812.

27. Ibid., 10 Jul. 1812.

28. *CM*, 27 Jul. 1812.

29. See *The Times*, 16 Jan., 7 May, 4, 13, and 24 Jul., and (for Petit) 1 Aug. 1812.

30. TNA ADM 103/435, No. 5,605; ADM 103/491.

31. TNA ADM 98/278, ltr, 10 Aug. 1812, TB to Brown; ADM 99/217, ltr, 18 Aug. 1812, Brown to TB; ADM 98/279, ltr, 22 Aug. 1812, TB to Brown.

32. TNA ADM 103/435, No. 6,194.

33. The Valleyfield Entry Book TNA ADM 103/435, in which he was last entered as No. 6,194, gives no indication, however, that Petit had again escaped in Feb. or Mar. 1813, so there is no clear evidence that he was other than confined in the depot between his recapture in Oct. 1812 and Apr. 1813.

34. The cryptic references are in TNA ADM 99/230, ltrs, 12 Mar. 1813, Capt. Brown to TB, and 15 Mar. 1813, TB to Capt. Brown; see also ADM 98/279, ltrs, 15 Mar. and 1 Apr. 1813, TB to Brown; ADM 103/435, No. 6,194.

35. TNA ADM 37/3502, Muster Lists of HMS *Adamant*, Nov. 1811 to Jun. 1813, Petit, François (no number); ADM 37/3504, Muster Book for HMS *Adamant*, Sep. 1812 to Apr. 1813, No. 374, Petit, François.

36. Marote-Carrier, op. cit., 121, 122.

37. Ibid.

38. Ibid., 122.

39. Ibid., 122-4.

40. Ibid., 125, 126.

41. Ibid., 126, 127.

42. Ibid., 127, 128, 129, 130.

43. See, e.g., TNA ADM 98/170, circular, 11 Jan. 1811, TB to all its agents.

44. Marote-Carrier, op. cit., 130-2.

45. Ibid., 132, 133.

46. Ibid., 134-6.

47. Ibid., 190.

CHAPTER 23: THE ENDING OF THE WAR AND THE GREAT REPATRIATION

1. Grierson (ed.), *Letters of Sir Walter Scott* Vol. III: *1811-1814*, op. cit., 341. Count François H. B. Sebastiani (1772-1851), a fellow Corsican and one of Napoleon's most loyal generals, fought in many of his campaigns, including those in Spain and

Russia and, six weeks after Scott's letter, at the 'Battle of the Nations' at Leipzig, and he joined Napoleon on his return in 1815 from exile in Elba.

2.   This bare summary of some principal explanations for the downfall of Napoleon Bonaparte in 1814 obviously omits others, such as opposition to his Continental System, in France itself widespread war weariness, the unpopularity of the heavy imperial taxation and of the recurring demands in 1813-14 for large numbers of conscripts for the imperial army, and the collaboration with the invading allies by royalists and some other dissidents, collaboration which resulted, for example, in the handing over of the city of Bordeaux to Wellington's forces without a fight. As for Napoleon's marshals, they had become among the wealthiest people in France, richly endowed as they were with land and other grants by the emperor, and ruthless looters as also were several of them, not least during the Peninsular War—as the slogans or graffiti scribbled on the walls of many houses in Spain by rank and file French soldiers fighting there in 1808-13 had proclaimed: 'Spain—death for the soldiers, ruin for the officers, fortunes for the generals.' (See Morvan, *Le Soldat Impérial*, op. cit., Vol. I, 486; and Lucas-Dubreton, *Napoléon devant L'Espagne*, op. cit., 368). By 1813-14 many of his marshals, having fought in so many campaigns during the preceding twenty or so years, wanted peace to enjoy their wealth—hence their advice to Napoleon to abdicate and thus end the war. Bergeron, *France under Napoleon*, op. cit., 122-4.

3.   The deteriorating situation with which he was by then faced, including the loss by defection or by allied conquest of so many parts of his Grand Empire and its client states, led Napoleon in mid-Nov. 1813 to order that except for certain categories including Swiss, Italians, Poles, and some Germans, foreign troops serving with his armies should be disarmed. *Correspondance de Napoléon Ier*, op. cit., Vol. XXVI, 427-8, 15 Nov. 1813. Napoleon's order began: 'We are now at a stage where we cannot rely on any foreigner. That can only be extremely dangerous for us.'

4.   TNA ADM 98/170, 12 Mar. 1813; ADM 98/279, ltr, 29 Mar. 1813, TB to Lieut. Priest.

5.   TNA WO 6/153, ltrs, 16 Apr. and 23 Jun. 1813, H.C. Bunbury, War Dept, respectively to J. Barrow and J.W. Croker, Adm.; ADM 98/280, ltrs from TB: 15 Jul. 1813 to Capt. Moriarty, 17 Jul. 1813 to Capt. Brown, and 23 Jul. 1813 to Admiral Otway.

6.   TNA ADM 103/266, Nos 6,902-7,198, 7,199-7,499, and 7,500-7,760; ADM 103/113, Nos 6,445-7,298.

7.   TNA ADM 103/113, Nos 6,445-7,298 passim.

8.   Ibid.

9.   TNA ADM 98/134, ltr, 23 Aug. 1813, TB to Maj. Gen. Darling, Horse Guards; ADM 103/113, Nos 6,445-7,298 passim.

10.   TNA ADM 103/432-/436 passim.

11.   TNA ADM 98/135, ltr, 2 Mar. 1814, TB to Col. Torrens, Horse Guards; ADM 98/122, ltr, 18 Mar. 1814, TB to Adm.

12.   TNA ADM 1/3766, fol. 310, ltr, 13 Mar. 1814, Lieut. Gen. Wynyard, Edinburgh, to Col. Torrens, Horse Guards; ADM 98/170 circular, 8 Mar. 1814, TB to depot agents.

13.   TNA ADM 103/263—ADM 103/266 passim.

14.   TNA ADM 98/170, circular, 22 Nov. 1813. By 'Flimingers' was apparently meant Flemings or Dutch or both.

15. TNA ADM 98/122, ltr, 26 Nov. 1813, TB to Adm. The Board's letter enclosed one it had received 'from Mr G.L. Engelbach, requesting the release of the natives of Hesse Darmstadt confined among the prisoners of war in this country in order that they may join the forces now raising by the Grand Duke to combat for the good Cause.'

16. TNA ADM 98/210, ltr, 19 Feb. 1814, TB to George Bell, Jedburgh.

17. TNA ADM 98/280, ltr, 28 Apr. 1814, TB to Lieut. Glinn, Leith.

18. TNA ADM 98/123, ltr, 6 Jun. 1814, TB to Adm. See also Board circular to depots, 16 May 1814, in TNA ADM 98/170. The Board reported that at five depots in England there remained in Jun. a further 405 prisoners from Anhalt Dessau.

19. TNA ADM 98/170, circulars, 9 and 11 Sep. 1813; ADM 98/122, ltr, 18 Oct. 1813, TB to Admiralty; WO 6/153, fol. 184, ltr, 3 Jan. 1814, H.C. Bunbury, War Dept, to John Barrow, Adm.; ADM 98/122, ltr, 27 Jan. 1814, TB to Adm.; ADM 98/187, ltr, 3 Feb. 1814, TB to Capt. G. Bowen, RN; ADM 98/280, ltrs, 3 and 11 Feb. 1814, TB to Lieut. Glinn and Capt A. Brown.

20. *CM*, 25 Nov. 1813; *Perth Courier*, 2 Dec. 1813. The *CM* permitted itself on 18 Dec. to print a pun on the subject: 'Bonaparte formerly called the Dutch, as well as ourselves, a nation of shopkeepers. He must at least allow that they know how to manage a *counter*-revolution.' It is unlikely the Leith celebrants would yet have been aware, as *The Times* reported three weeks later on 15 Dec., of 'A patriotic song *Oranje Boven!*, sung at the Grand Dinner in the City of London Tavern yesterday, attended by the Duke of Clarence ... the Prince of Orange, the Dukes of York and Kent and H.M. Ministers and others, Given in Honour of the EMANCIPATION OF HOLLAND, [and] written and composed by John Parry', the first of four verses of which ran:

> "Hark! Hark the voice of Freedom cries,
> Ye brave and gallant Dutchmen rise!
>   Nor longer slaves remain!
> Too long by cruel War distressed
> Too long by hostile France oppressed,
>   Now burst the Gallic chain!
> In lasting bonds of love
> Oh, may your hearts be woven!
> The Tyrant's crest remove,
>   And—ORANGE BOVEN!
> *Chorus*
> Down with the Tyrant—and Oranje Boven!"

There was also in Edinburgh what was advertised in the *Caledonian Mercury* that day as an 'AN ORANJE BOOVEN GREAT BALL' on the evening of 30 Dec. in Corri's Rooms, 'in honour of the EMANCIPATION OF HOLLAND.' To the great ball, arranged 'at the desire of several Ladies and Gentlemen of distinction', there was, needless to say, no evidence of any invitations having been extended to any of the Dutch prisoners of war at Valleyfield or on overnight stays at Edinburgh Castle before their embarkation at Leith.

21. TNA ADM 98/170, 5 Nov. 1813.

22. TNA ADM 98/280, ltrs, 26 Nov. 1813, TB to Admiral Hope, and Capts Brown and Moriarty; ADM 98/122, ltrs, 29 and 30 Nov. 1813, TB to Adm. A copy of the

declaration of loyalty which these Dutch volunteers had to sign is preserved in TNA ADM 103/267, fol. 41. Signed by H. Boclaars, 1st lieut. on *Barbier de Seville* priv., the declaration, counter-signed as personally witnessed by the depot agent Capt. Moriarty, says: 'I, the undersigned, hereby Engage to Serve His Serene Highness the Prince of Orange, Faithfully and Truly and with perfect Allegiance. Perth, 15th December 1813.' The Perth Entry Book TNA ADM 103/263, No. 1,193, gives Boclaars as Frederik Boclard or Boelard, capd in the Channel Nov. 1810, arr. at Perth 2 Sep. 1812 from Valleyfield, aged 29, born 'Rotterdam proper place of Nativity Altona' [sic], discharged to Leith on 15 Dec. 1813.'

23. TNA ADM 98/170. The districts specified were in Dutch Brabant (three), Department of the Two Netherlands (two), Department of the Lower Meuse (three), Department of the Roer (five: Pays de Cleves, de Juliers and de Cologne, and Aix La Chapelle and Guildre Autrichienne).

24. *Dundee Advertiser*, 3 Dec. 1813; *CM*, 4 Dec. 1813; TNA ADM 98/280, ltr, 4 Dec. 1813, TB to Capt. Brown.

25. TNA ADM 98/170, 14 Jan. 1814; *Perth Courier*, 24 Feb. 1814; *Dundee Advertiser*, 25 Feb. 1814.

26. *CM*, 26 Feb. 1814.

27. TNA ADM 103/432-ADM 103/436 passim; ADM 103/113 passim; ADM 103/263-ADM 103/266 passim. Not all those thus released were actually Dutch as some, if their places of birth were the criterion, were German or (as they later became known) Belgian. Those released from Perth, for example, on 19 Feb. included Antoine Franck, soldier, 27th regt of chasseurs, capd at Rio Molino 1811, b. in Liège; Cornelius Diolpho, grenadier, 103rd line regt, capd at Badajoz 1812, b. at Antwerp; and H. Grosse, corporal, 28th light infantry, also capd at Badajoz 1812, and b. at Koblenz. TNA ADM 103/263, Nos 20 (Franck), 182 (Diolpho), and 305 (Grosse).

28. TNA ADM 98/122, ltr, 21 Jan. 1814, TB to Adm.; ADM 98/187, ltr, 21 Jan. 1814, TB to Capt. Bowen, RN, Harwich; ADM 98/280, ltr, 21 Jan. 1814, TB to Lieut. Glinn at Leith. So anxious were the authorities to repatriate all Swiss prisoners promptly that the TB authorised the agent at Valleyfield to waive the normal stoppages due to be paid by two Swiss prisoners there who had been recapd after their recent escape. TNA ADM 98/280, ltr, 7 Feb. 1814, TB to Capt. Brown.

29. TNA ADM 103/263, ADM 103/264, ADM 103/266, ADM 103/433, and ADM 103/434 passim. One of the Swiss released from Valleyfield, for example, was Jean Elie, priv. seaman, b. in Lausanne, capd in 1806, and recapd after his escape from that depot in Nov. 1813; and one released from Perth was Louis Paneau, 29, b. 'Switzerland'. TNA ADM 103/433, Nos. 1,741 and 7,408 (Elie); ADM 103/266, No. 7,092 (Paneau).

30. TNA ADM 98/122, ltrs, 1 and 24 Feb. 1814, TB to Adm. The first question arose from the case of 31 such Danes held not in Scotland but at Portsmouth; the second from a request to the TB from Mr H. F. Horniman, evidently a Danish consul or other official representative, who had asked that Danish prisoners be delivered over to him so they could be sent home.

31. Ibid., 3 Mar. 1814.

32. Roos, *Prisonen Danske og Norske krigsfanger i England 1807-1814*, op. cit., 20.

33. TNA ADM 98/280, ltr, 13 Nov. 1813, TB to Lieut. Priest; ADM 103/435, No. 5,315 (du Crot).

34. For the numbers of 'Danes' in captivity in 1812, see Walker, *The Depot at Norman*

Cross, op. cit., 202. For several months after the Treaty of Kiel in Jan. 1814 the constitutional arrangements for Norway's union with Sweden were a matter of disagreement between the two, during which Norway was invaded by a Swedish army. See, e.g., Derry, *Scandinavia*, op. cit., 212-15; TNA ADM 98/123, ltr, 19 Sep. 1814, TB to Adm. At the end of Jun. the TB, in acknowledging an instruction from the Adm. that Norwegian prisoners at Portsmouth should be transferred to Chatham until they could be released 'in the manner proposed by the Swedish Consul', had suggested it might be 'most advisable to order these persons to be sent in one of His Majesty's ships as we do not consider that it would be safe to send them in Transports, it being well known that many of them have a strong dislike to going to Sweden, of which the Swedish Consul appears to be aware as he did not think it safe to convey them otherwise than in a Ship of War.' Ibid., 30 Jun. 1814.

35. E.g., all Spanish prisoners at Greenlaw were immediately repatriated in Jul. 1808. TNA ADM 98/276, ltr, 1 Jul. 1808, TB to M. Wright.

36. TNA ADM 98/278, ltrs from TB: 12 May 1812 to Capt. Moriarty and Lieut. Priest, and 2 Jul. 1812 to Admiral Otway, Leith; ADM 1/3763, fols 279-81. One of the Portuguese released, for instance, on 8 Jul. from Valleyfield, where he had arr. in Mar. 1811 from Esk Mills, was Jean Baptiste Martinau, seaman, 28, b. at Oporto, and capd at Trafalgar Oct. 1805 on the French m.o.w. *Achille*. ADM 103/433, No. 1,746.

37. TNA ADM 98/170, circulars, 9 and 11 Sep., from TB; ADM 98/122, ltrs, 18 Oct. and 3 Dec. 1813, TB to Adm.; ADM 98/280, ltr, 13 Nov. 1813, TB to Capt. Moriarty.

38. Juramentados were Spanish sympathisers with or supporters of the French.

39. TNA ADM 98/170, circulars, 9 and 11 Sep. 1813, from TB; ADM 98/122, ltr, 18 Oct. 1813, TB to Adm.; ADM 1/3765, fols 480 and 484; ADM 98/123, ltrs, 7 Jun. and 9 Jul. 1814, TB to Adm.

40. TNA ADM 99/237, TB minute, 23 Jun. 1813. A letter of 29 Mar. 1814 from Lieut. Priest, agent, Greenlaw, confirmed that 'there were no prisoners at Greenlaw during the two quarters ending 31st December last.' TNA ADM 99/256.

41. *EEC* and *CM*, 18 and 25 Sep., 21 Oct., 6, 11 and 13 Nov. 1813. According to the *CM* of 11 Nov. 1813, Leith and most of the villages around Edinburgh were also illuminated on 8 Nov., but whether these included Penicuik, where Valleyfield was situated, is not clear.

42. *EEC* and *CM*, 25 and 27 Nov. 1813.

43. *EEC*, 1 Jan., 24 and 26 Mar., and 11, 14 and 16 Apr. 1814; *CM*, 1 and 29 Jan., 21, 24 and 26 Mar., 11, 14 and 16 Apr. 1814.

44. *Perth Courier*, 11 Nov. 1813, 14 Apr. 1814; *Dundee Advertiser*, 22 Apr. 1814.

45. *Perth Courier*, 14 Apr. 1814.

46. On 18 Mar. Lieut. Priest reported from Greenlaw to the TB that in accordance with instructions from Lieut. General Wynyard, commander of the Forces in Scotland, and Capt. Brown, agent at Valleyfield, he had delivered the keys of the depot at Edinburgh Castle to Lieut. Glinn, the Board's transport agent at Leith. TNA ADM 99/255.

47. TNA ADM 98/280. Priest's reply has not survived.

48. J. Kincaid, *Adventures in the Rifle Brigade in the Peninsula, France, and the Netherlands* (London, 1830), 296.

49. Of the devotion and loyalty Napoleon inspired widely among his troops an example

occurred even at the landing at Marseilles in May 1814, a few weeks after the end of the war, of the 3,389 near skeleton survivors of the 16,000 French prisoners, many of them raw young conscripts, taken at the battle of Baylen in 1808 and condemned by the Spanish authorities to an appalling existence on the Mediterranean island of Cabrera. In welcoming back to France these victims of the war, the Royalist general in command at Marseilles attempted to denounce Napoleon as the source of their miseries but they interrupted him with audible murmurs of 'We love him still.' Another example was a recollection years later by a Belgian aristocrat of how, when many of the citizens of Brussels journeyed out the few miles to Waterloo at the end of the battle on 18 Jun. 1815 to help the wounded, they found that 'The fanaticism of that French army for Napoleon was so great that wounded soldiers were seen to throw their amputated arms and legs into the air, crying "Vive L'Empereur!"' Lucas-Dubreton, *Napoléon devant L'Espagne*, op. cit., 484, 485; *Souvenirs du Comte de Merode-Westerloo* (Paris and Brussels, 1845), Vol. I, 352.

50. TNA ADM 98/170, circular, 13 Nov. 1812, TB to all depot agents. The only Scots depot for which any alphabetical list of prisoners survives is Perth (ADM 103/516), although the list appears not to be comprehensive. It may be the origins of that list lie in the circular of Nov. 1812.

51. TNA ADM 98/170, circulars from TB, 25 Nov. and 23 Dec. 1813; G. Lévêque, 'Les Prisonniers de Guerre Français en Grande Bretagne', Vol. I, op. cit., p. 381. Similarly small numbers of copies of *L'Ambigu* were sent to the six depots in England. Attempts to find a copy of *L'Ambigu* in the Bibliothèque Nationale in Paris and in libraries in Britain have proved so far unsuccessful.

52. *EEC*, 24 Mar. 1814. This report, no doubt lifted from the *Courant*, appeared also in the *Glasgow Courier* two days later and in the *Kelso Mail* on 28 Mar.

53. TNA ADM 98/170, 7 Apr. 1814.

54. TNA ADM 99/256.

55. TNA ADM 99/257.

56. There were similar manifestations by prisoners in England who were pro-Napoleon and who came into conflict with those who were pro-Bourbon. As early as 20 Dec. 1813 *The Times* reported that a few days earlier almost 600 men and officers on the prison hulk *Sampson* at Chatham had first quarrelled then come to blows in 'a desperate conflict' over the rival dynasties and had been put in close confinement. A Bourbon government peace commissioner attempting to visit prisoners on a hulk at Portsmouth in Apr. 1814 'had a large basket of filth thrown over him': the punishment imposed on the prisoners on that hulk was that they were the last to be repatriated from England. At Portchester Castle depot the prisoners unanimously refused to hoist the white Bourbon flag, and threw stones at an English officer wearing a white cockade. Abell, op. cit., 182, 183. At Dartmoor in early Apr. many prisoners declared with tears in their eyes they would rather die in prison than serve any master but their emperor, wore tricolour cockades in their hats, and pinned white Bourbon cockades on the dogs that ran about the prison yards. Thomson, *Dartmoor*, op. cit., 117, 118.

57. TNA ADM 99/257, ltr, 21 Apr. 1814, Moriarty to TB; ADM 98/280, ltr, 25 Apr. 1814, TB to Moriarty.

58. NLS MS Acc. 5811/1/46; TNA ADM 103/263, No. 1,172 (which gives Petitchamp's age as 29); ADM 103/432, No. 124 (the Valleyfield Entry Book, which also says he was 29, but b. at St Omer), and ADM 103/435, No. 5,316 (which says Petitchamp

was b. at St Thomas). Like Marote-Carrier, Petitchamp had arr. at Valleyfield from Esk Mills in Mar. 1811.

59. *Dundee Advertiser*, 6 May 1814.

60. TNA ADM 103/263, Nos 1,094 (Fourneau), 1,109 (Deroland), 1,122 (Charlot), 1,126 (Faillant), 1,127 (Dewatre), 1,271 (Baland), and ADM 103/266, No. 6,553 (Dubois-Billon). The others of the 12 released on 30 Apr. 1814 were François Declerc, lieut., priv. *Reciprocité*, capd Sep. 1807, aged 29, b. at Dunkirk, arr. at Perth Sep. 1812 from Greenlaw; Charles Le Maire, seaman, priv. *Le Renard*, capd Sep. 1808, aged 22, b. at Calais, arr. at Perth Jul. 1813 from Valleyfield; and the three not further identified were named Jamar, Paranti, and Victor. ADM 103/263, No. 1,104 (Declerc); ADM 103/266, No. 7,167 (Le Maire).

61. TNA ADM 98/170, 9 Apr. 1814; NLS MS Acc. 5811/1/50. The four writers have not been found in the Perth Entry Books, the alphabetical list for which, as already mentioned, is not comprehensive.

62. TNA ADM 103/433, Nos 1,881 (Le Maire), 1,434 (Josin); ADM 103/263, No. 354 (Françoise).

63. TNA ADM 98/122, ltr, 19 Apr. 1814, TB to Adm.

64. TNA ADM 98/280, ltr, TB to Capt. Brown.

65. TNA ADM 103/263, No. 952; ADM 98/280, ltrs, 27 and 28 May 1814, TB to Capt. Moriarty.

66. *Edinburgh and Leith Post Office Directory 1814* (Edinburgh, 1813-14), 196; *The Faculty of Advocates in Scotland 1532-1943*, ed. by Sir Francis J. Grant (Edinburgh, 1944), 161.

67. It is difficult to imagine anyone less likely than Simon to have given a ball, or indeed anything else, to the inhabitants of Dumbarton. MacPhail, *Dumbarton Castle*, op. cit., 153, in rightly expressing scepticism about another version of largesse allegedly conferred there by Simon, may err merely in underestimating the length of the roots of such legends, given the date of the *Courant*'s report: 'The tradition that on his release he entertained the magistrates and other Dumbarton notables to a banquet in the town's inn is of comparatively late origin and probably derived from the imagination of some soldier guides. The tale of the French General's banquet did not appear in print until the second edition of Donald MacLeod's *Castle and Town of Dumbarton* in 1881.'

68. Perth Payments Ledger, op. cit., pp. 188-230.

69. TNA ADM 98/122, ltr, 26 Apr. 1814, TB to Adm.; TNA WO 6/153, fol. 251, ltr, H.C. Bunbury, War Dept, to J. Barrow, secretary, Adm.; ADM 98/170, circulars, 7 and 11 May 1814, TB to parole agents.

70. TNA ADM 98/280, ltrs, 22 and 18 Apr. 1814, TB to Admiral Hope and Capt. Moriarty respectively.

71. *Perth Courier*, 26 May 1814. The prospect at last of liberty and repatriation inspired the versifying prisoner named Canette at Perth to pen eight verses, translated into English for him by a militia guard and sent to the *Perth Courier* in early May, and which were later reproduced in Sievewright, *Depot at Perth*, op. cit., 43, 45, along with an anonymous and less earnest verse guying Napoleon which was published simultaneously in the paper. The first two and the sixth of Canette's verses ran:

> 'This happy period, long desired,
> Now cheers my breast, and lulls its woes;

A change of fate, with joy I learn,

Will soon my hours of durance close.

Ah, cruel state of bondage here!

One gleam now gilds thy closing days;

I see succeed the horrid storm,

A soothing calm, a cheering ray.

Six years a wretched captive here,

To thee I've kept a faithful heart;

And when I reach thy happy shores,

My sufferings ease—Now I depart!'

The anonymous verse guying Napoleon ran:

'A Monarch there was, and he got a great fall,

Which lost him France, Italy, Holland and all,

Yet now like the cobbler, the same is his doom,

And all that he covets is just *Elba* room.'

72. TNA ADM 99/257, ltrs, 14 and 21 Apr. 1814, Capt. Brown to TB, and 18 and 25 Apr. 1814, TB to Brown.

73. TNA ADM 98/170, circulars, 12 May and n.d. [1814], TB to depot agents: marginal notes in the ledger say both circulars were sent to Valleyfield on 13 May and to Perth on 16 May.

74. TNA ADM 98/122.

75. TNA ADM 98/280, ltrs, 31 May 1814, TB to Capts Brown and Moriarty.

76. TNA ADM 98/123, ltr, 6 Jun. 1814, TB to Adm.; ADM 98/170, circular, 6 Jun. 1814, TB to depot agents.

77. TNA ADM 98/280, ltrs, 24 and 31 May 1814, TB to Capt. Brown. Ten days after the last of the French prisoners at Valleyfield had been released, the Board ordered its agent there to 'report by the Return of Post the present State of the Sick French Prisoners remaining in your custody and when it is probable they will be sufficiently recovered to be sent away.' Ibid., ltr, 24 Jun. 1814.

78. TNA ADM 99/258, ltr, 7 May 1814, Admiral Hope to TB. The Board assured the admiral that the letters, or 'Addresses', as it described them, would be duly forwarded to the ambassador. Ibid., TB to Hope, 10 May 1814. The content of the addresses is not known but presumably they were appeals for speedy release from captivity.

79. TNA ADM 98/170, circular, 3 May 1814.

80. TNA ADM 98/280, ltrs, 14 May 1814, TB to Capts Brown and Moriarty.

81. TNA ADM 98/170.

82. The petition or address is preserved in the Service historique de la marine, Ministry of Defence, Chateau of Vincennes, Paris, in FF2.23B12. For Feraud, see TNA ADM 103/266, No. 6,910.

83. TNA ADM 98/170.

84. TNA ADM 103/266, No. 7,760/7,761; NLS MS Acc. 5811/1/56, letter, 21 Jun. 1814, from Jennat, addressed to 'Mon Commandant'. It seems to be to Jennat to whom a letter of 10 Jun. 1814, from the TB to the agent at Perth refers: 'We approve of

your sending the prisoner whom you report [on 6 Jun.] to have placed in the cachot, among the last prisoners embarked by you.'

85. TNA ADM 98/280.

86. TNA ADM 103/436, No. 7,650.

87. TNA ADM 103/433, No. 1,197.

88. TNA ADM 99/258, ltr, 1 May 1814, Capt. Brown to TB; ADM 98/280, ltr, 5 May 1814, TB to Capt. Brown.

89. TNA ADM 98/280, ltr, 6 Jun. 1814, TB to Capt. Brown.

90. Ibid., ltrs, 29 Apr. and 6 May 1814, TB to Glinn.

91. Ibid., TB to Capt. Brown.

92. Ibid.; ADM 98/170.

93. TNA ADM 98/280, ltr, 24 May 1814, TB to Glinn.

94. Ibid., ltr, 27 May 1814, TB to Admiral Hope.

95. Abell, op. cit., 199-200; *CM*, 2 Jun. 1814; Black, *Penicuik and Neighbourhood*, op. cit., 22, 23. There was, of course, not merely one but a succession of days in Jun. 1814 when contingents of released prisoners were marched from Valleyfield to Leith. Bawbee Penicuik meant ha'penny or tight-fisted Penicuik; and cauld kail and soor dook—cold kail soup and buttermilk or sour milk.

96. *James Nasmyth, Engineer. An Autobiography* Ed. by Samuel Smiles (London, 1883), 69. The accuracy of Nasmyth's recollection, apart from the confusion of the Peace or Treaty of Amiens of 1802 with the Treaty of Paris in 1814, is perhaps open to some doubt. Nasmyth was born in Aug. 1808, so he was not quite six years old when the prisoners were released in 1814. Would a boy of that age have been able to identify whatever songs the prisoners sang—or did an older person tell him either at the time or afterward, or did he find the information years later in some other source? If the prisoners sang (and it is possible, perhaps even likely, they did), there is no other surviving source that says so. Nor is there any reference in any other source to prisoners of war being in Edinburgh Castle in Jun. 1814, though again it is possible some may have been lodged there overnight after marching from Valleyfield. No hours of the day or evening when prisoners marched to Leith to embark are mentioned either in any other source, but given the long light summer evenings it seems perhaps unlikely they would be marching by torchlight in the first half of Jun. 1814.

97. TNA ADM 98/280, ltr, 6 Jun. 1814, TB to Capt. Brown; *CM*, 9, 13 and 16 Jun. 1814.

98. TNA ADM 98/280, ltrs, 15 and 16 Jun. 1814, TB to Lieut. Glinn and Capt. Brown respectively.

99. Ibid., ltrs from TB: 22 Jun. 1814 to Lieut. Glinn, 23 Jun. 1814 to Admiral Hope, and 25 Jun. 1814 to Capt. Brown.

100. TNA ADM 98/280.

101. Ibid., ltrs, 25 May and 4 Jun. 1814, TB to Capt. Moriarty.

102. *Dundee Advertiser*, 3 Jun. 1814.

103. *Perth Courier*, 2 Jun. 1814.

104. Ibid., 9 Jun. 1814.

105. Ibid., 21 Jul. 1814.

106. *Dundee Advertiser*, 10 Jun. 1814.

107. *Perth Courier*, 9 and 16 Jun. 1814.

108. TNA ADM 98/280, see ltrs, 6, 7, 10, 13, 14 (two), 17, 20, 22 and 24 Jun. 1814, TB to Capt. Moriarty.

109. *Perth Courier*, 23 Jun. and 7 Jul. 1814.

110. Ibid., 14 Jul. 1814.

111. NLS MS Acc. 5811/1/4; *Perth Courier*, 16 Jun. 1814.

112. See above, pp.131, 132-3.

113. TNA ADM 103/263, No. 336 (Raffat), No. 1,161 (Le Roy); ADM 103/264, No. 3,078 (Pain).

114. TNA ADM 103/432, No. 453 (Sevenot), Nos 100 and 101 (Duvoine and Doucin); ADM 103/433, Nos 1,434 (Josin) and 1,481 (Roger).

115. The Poles seem to have numbered between 19 and 29.

116. TNA ADM 98/170, circular, 8 Jun. 1814, TB to depot agents; ADM 98/280, ltrs, 9 and 27 Jun. 1814, TB to Lieut. Glinn and Capt. Brown respectively; ADM 98/188, ltr, 6 Jul. 1814, TB to Lieut. Arnold; ADM 98/123, ltr, 8 Sep. 1814, TB to Admiralty. Some information about these Valleyfield Poles was gathered by the banker-historian Macbeth Forbes, but without identifying his sources. He found there were 28 soldiers at the depot belonging to the 1st Polish infantry regt who had been capd in Calabria in Jul. 1806, and there was also an officer's servant at Leith. These 29 Poles, Macbeth Forbes says, 'received two months' pay, the sum of 873 francs 60 c.—equal at the then rate of exchange to £40.9.0.—having been handed over for the purpose to Brigadier General Krakowski [were he and Count de Kruckowucki one and the same?]. The pay certificate was passed at Leith, where the officers were residing, under the signatures of Lieutenants Radwovski, Wyslawski, Slonski and Wiswievski. But General Krakowski, with a paternal regard for the grenadiers and fusiliers of his regiment, as these men were, desired from the French Peace Commissioners on 14 Jul. 1814 the pay of his 29 soldiers since their capture eight years ago. He received in this way 13,805 francs 10c. ... It had been arranged that all the Polish prisoners in Scotland were to assemble at Leith and sail for Dantzig, but the Grand Duke Constantine [brother of Tsar Alexander I, king of Poland under the terms of the peace settlement of 1814-15] said that their accounts would first be settled and paid. At Valleyfield, matters having been put right, the Polish prisoners were free to quit Scotland.' NAS GD1/405/2. There was some disagreement about the precise number of Poles concerned: the *Caledonian Mercury*, 3 Sep. 1814, reported that 'Only 19 Continental [i.e., European, as distinct from American] prisoners of war (who are Poles) now remain in this country.'

117. *EEC*, 17 Sep. 1814.

118. Blond, *La Grande Armée*, op. cit., 485; Abell, op. cit., 118; J. Macbeth Forbes, 'French Prisoners of War in Scotland, and Bank Note Forging', op. cit., pp. 394, 395.

CHAPTER 24: ALL MEN ARE BRETHREN

1. Abell, op. cit., 199-200.

2. ML, Black Coll., vol. 2(c), pp. 82-3.

3. TNA ADM 98/123, ltr, 22 Jun. 1815, TB to Adm.

4. TNA ADM 103/635, Part II, ltr, 23 Jun. 1815, Adm. to TB.

5. TNA ADM 98/123, ltr, 30 Jun. 1815, TB to Adm.

6. NAS GD1/405/2, pp. 23, 38. No advertisement about victualling prisoners has been found in the *Caledonian Mercury*, *Edinburgh Evening Courant* or *Perth Courier*.

7. Andrew Mair, *Dumbarton Castle. Historical and Descriptive Notes* (Dumbarton, 1920), 44.

8. TNA ADM 105/66, box of miscellaneous TO papers; NAS GD1/405/5/1. For Jezequel and Priere, see above, pp.296, 297.

9. TNA ADM 105/66, box of miscellaneous TO papers; NLS MS Acc. 5811/1/15 and 50. Alexis Raphael's was one of the 40 or so signatures on the loyal address on 17 May 1814 to the restored Bourbon dynasty from prisoners at Perth depot.

10. ML, Black Coll., item 69, a cutting dated 13 May 1922.

11. NAS GD1/872.

12. *Perth Courier*, 4 Aug. 1814; NAS GD1/405/5/1, quoting memorial for Johnston, 25 Aug. 1821, and ltr, 27 Nov. 1818, G. Harrison, HM Treasury, to TB.

13. *Perth Courier*, 14 Apr. 1814; Syrett and DiNardo (eds), *Commissioned Sea Officers of the Royal Navy*, op. cit., 320. The freedom of the city was also conferred on Major General Graham (who had ordered the search of the depot in Oct. 1813 for offensive weapons suspected to be in possession of the prisoners), and on two of his captains.

14. NLS MS Acc. 5811/1/5-6.

15. TNA ADM 105/46.

16. NLS MS Acc. 5811/1, note on Johnston.

17. TNA ADM 105/46, ltrs to TB: 24 Feb. 1819, from Mr Lushington, HM Treasury, and 17 Nov. 1821, from G. Harrison, HM Treasury.

18. Ibid., ltrs and reports, 7 Jan. and 20 Feb. 1819, concerning Duncan.

19. Ibid., comments, 6 Mar. 1819, on ltr, 27 Feb. 1819, from Mr Lushington, HM Treasury.

20. Ibid., comments on ltr, 27 Nov. 1818, from G. Harrison, HM Treasury.

21. *EEC*, 7 May 1814; *CM*, 9 May 1814; *Dundee Advertiser*, 3 Jun. 1814; TNA ADM 98/123, ltr, 22 Jun. 1814, TB to Adm. This letter enclosed a copy of one from HM Treasury asking that Perth and two depots in England 'be appropriated temporarily to the Service of the Storekeeper General's Department.' The TB, in seeking the instructions of the Adm. on the matter, enclosed also a copy of a letter of 19 Jun. 1811 from R.H. Crew, secretary, Ordnance Board, 'by which the land on which this depot [Perth] is erected was given up to this Department [i.e., the Transport Office] on the condition that it should revert to the Ordnance Department when no longer required for the object to which it was then intended to be applied.' [i.e., the building of the depot for prisoners of war]. See also ADM 98/132, ltr, 21 Jun. 1811, TB to R.H. Crew; ADM 98/135, ltrs, 14 and 18 Jul. and 30 Aug. 1814, TB to J. Trotter, Ordnance Board; ADM 103/635, Part I, a paper dated 15 Jul. 1817 and titled 'Home Department. A list of Prisons ... or Depots ... lately used for Prisoners of War ... delivered over to other Departments of Government'; Penny, *Traditions of Perth*, op. cit., 94. Presumably John Mathew was employed until Dec. 1814 in administering or supervising the women and boys mentioned; Abell, op. cit., 165. Sievewright, *Depot at Perth*, op. cit., 48, added that 'It is said, whether correctly or not, that a great many arms were also deposited in the Depot, and I have heard it stated as a fact, that when the demand for political justice and rights among the great mass of the people about 1830-31 had become threatening in its aspect, the authorities, alarmed at the prospect of a possible revolution, took means in a stealthy way to have the locks taken from the guns in the Depot and

removed to Sheffield. Of course the passing of the Reform Bill in 1832 put an end to any apprehension of danger.' Penny, *Traditions of Perth*, op. cit., 94; Peacock, *Perth: its annals and its archives*, op. cit., 497.

22. See NAS RHP 35787, 'A scheme to convert Edinburgh Castle to a prisoner of war camp', 1944.

23. Wilson, *Annals of Penicuik*, op. cit., 126; Charles Cowan, *Reminiscences*, op. cit., 11. After its closure as a depot in Mar. 1811 Esk Mills had been used as a barracks for the militia guards at Valleyfield and Greenlaw. An advertisement in *EEC*, 15 Oct. 1814, announced that 'The remaining articles of furniture, fixtures, etc., at the barracks at Eskmills and Valleyfield will be sold at these places on … 7th November.'

24. TNA ADM 98/280, ltrs from TB: 5 May and 22 Jun. 1814 to Lieut. Priest, 13 May 1814 to Brown, and 4 and 14 Jun. 1814 to Moriarty.

25. *EEC*, 11 Jul. 1814; TNA ADM 103/635, Part I, paper dated 15 Jul. 1817 and headed 'Home Department', concerning depots delivered over to other government departments; NAS GD1/405/2, pp. 23-4, where Macbeth Forbes quotes Mr John Cowan, owner of the adjoining estate of Beeslack, on the history of Greenlaw; Abell, op. cit., 197; J.U. Thomson, 'Glencorse', in *Scotland's Magazine*, Dec. 1965, 51.

26. TNA ADM 105/46, ltr, 12 Oct. 1818, to [?] G. Harrison, HM Treasury.

27. The earliest advertisement for the post-war sale of Valleyfield appears to have been that inserted in *EEC*, 26 Nov. 1814. See TNA ADM 103/635, Part I, ltr, 31 Jul. 1817, Robert Reid to Commissioners for Victualling HM's Navy; NAS GD1/405/2, pencil notes, p.38; Charles Cowan, *Reminiscences*, op. cit., 18. Two letterbooks in the Cowan Papers in NAS GD 311/2/36 and 311/2/37 bear out Charles Cowan's recollection. Successive letters from the Cowan brothers to the government authorities concerned with the sale of Valleyfield show that on 9 Dec. 1814 they offered £3,760, on 13 Apr. 1816 £2,800, on 19 Jul. 1816 £2,300, and on 21 Oct. 1817 and again on 26 Jul. 1818, £2,200.

28. Examples include prisoners' banknote forging equipment made from mutton bones which is preserved in the archives of the Bank of Scotland; model ships in the National Museum of Scotland, Chambers Street, Edinburgh; and several items preserved in Perth Museum and Art Gallery, including a box with dominoes, a straw workbox depicting depot buildings,and a model in bone of a woman at a spindle.

29. For Van Beck, see above, pp.520, 521; for Marote-Carrier's companion, Frederik Haultz, who had evidently married a Scotswoman then deserted her, see above, pp.135, 305, 306; for the Galérien as Royal Navy cook, see above, p.548.

30. TNA ADM 98/276, ltr, 5 Aug. 1809, TB to M. Wright; ADM 103/496, Register of Releases, Hyndhert Davus, 6 Dec. 1813.

31. R.L. Stevenson, *St Ives, being the adventures of a French prisoner in England* (London, 1924); D.M. Moir, *The Life of Mansie Wauch, Tailor in Dalkeith, Written By Himself* (Edinburgh, 1913 ed.), Chap. 25, 'Catching a philistine in the coal-hole', 295-313.

32. Charles Cowan, *Reminiscences*, op. cit., 13; TNA ADM 98/277, ltr, 26 Jun. 1811, TB to Capt. Pellowe; ADM 98/279, ltr, 28 Sep. 1812, TB to Capt. Brown.

33. *EEC*, 1 Nov. 1813.

34. For instance, Captain Kaald at Greenlaw used his money to provide himself with 'a good lunch, consisting of a small cup of coffee with egg in it and two boiled eggs with butter and bread.' Kaald, op. cit., 98.

35. *New Statistical Account* (1845), Vol. I, 34.

36. Anton, *Retrospect of a military life*, op. cit., 32-4.

37. *New Statistical Account* (1845), Vol. I, 34, 38. But Rev. Scott Moncrieff's lamentations concerning the wartime fall from grace of Penicuik parishioners should perhaps be seen in the context of comments on the parish made half a century earlier by his predecessor the Rev. Thomas M'Courty, in the *Old Stastistical Account*, Vol. X, 423-4, published in 1794: 'It must be observed that there are too many dram shops, to which the people often resort, and are in danger of destroying themselves by taking too much of that poisonous liquor, cheap whisky, by which both their health and morals are greatly injured, and their families much straitened.'

38. The proposal to erect the plaque at or near the otherwise unmarked burial place in the prison was made in a motion on 7 Jan. 1929 by Bailie Peter Baxter at the meeting of the prison visiting committee. The Bailie, who was also secretary of The Gaelic Society of Perth, had been told of the burials of the prisoners of war by his father, who had been a warder in the civil prison in the 1850s. The Bailie's conclusion after studying the works of the 19th century Perth local historian William Sievewright was that the prisoners' burial place was the Cow Inch or north-east corner of the civil prison, where in 1929-30 the prison laundry was sited. The text of the plaque as erected was suggested, apart from some final minor amendments, by Bailie Baxter. The Prison Commissioners, however, resisted the erection of any plaque, 'as the exact place of burial of these prisoners [of war] is very uncertain, bones having been found in places widely apart …' and also 'particularly as [the plaque] could never be seen by the public, who cannot come inside the Prison Walls.' Another objection put was that the plaque 'might not be beneficial' to the civil prisoners confined at Perth. The prison visiting committee, however, dug in its heels; and G. Anderson, Fife County Council representative on the committee, wrote to William Adamson (himself a former Fife miner and general secretary of the miners' county union there) about his support for the proposal 'as worthy of commendation of the patriotism of the now unknown soldiers'. J. Mackie, governor of Perth prison, also supported the proposal and recommended to Adamson that the plaque be placed 'in the wall at the spot previously agreed on at the back of the Prison Laundry.' According to an undated photograph by the *Perthshire Advertiser* the plaque was actually erected in the wall of 'B' Hall of the civil prison—but that Hall was demolished in Jul. 1948. See file of letters, press cuttings, etc., concerning the plaque in NAS HH 57/203.

39. The precise number of prisoners who died at Valleyfield is, as has been shown in Appendix 11 above, uncertain. The figure 309 came from the list compiled in 1821 from Adm. records; the actual number appears to have been several fewer. Successive generations of the mill-owning Cowans appear to have shown respect for the remains of prisoners who had died in captivity at Valleyfield and were buried there. Abell found that during excavations for a new enamelling house at the mill in 1906 'a dozen coffins were unearthed, all with their heads to the east'; and a Penicuik local historian wrote that in 1923, when several other burials were uncovered, 'Alexander Cowan saw that they were put into coffins and reburied.' Abell, op. cit., 198; Deacon, 'Penicuik—Napoleonic Prisoner of War Camp', op. cit., 19. Veteran Valleyfield papermill workers have told the present writer how, during alterations or extensions to the mill, when skulls or bones of dead prisoners were unintentionally dug up they were on the instructions of the Cowans respectfully reburied. The closure of the mill in 1975 and its subsequent demolition was followed some years later by the

building of houses on the site. Fortunately, the monument survives intact. But the graves of the prisoners of war, which were close to the site of the monument itself, now appear to have been built upon, in so far as they survived the 19th and 20th century extensions to, and later complete demolition of, the mill.

Bibliography

A. MANUSCRIPT SOURCES

1. In The National Archives (TNA) (formerly the Public Record Office (PRO)), Kew, London:

ADM 1/3743-3766: Admiralty Secretary, in-letters from Transport Board

ADM 37/3502: Muster lists, HMS *Adamant*, Nov. 1811-Jun.1813

ADM 37/3504: Muster Book, HMS *Adamant*, Sep. 1812-Apr. 1813

ADM 51/2078: Captain's log, HMS *Adamant*

ADM 53/574: Log of HMS *Gorgon*

ADM 97/111: Transport Board, in-letters from legal officers

ADM 97/126-130: Transport Board, miscellaneous in-letters

ADM 98/111-124: Transport Board, letters to Admiralty

ADM 98/127-135: Transport Board, letters to Public Offices

ADM 98/170: Transport Board, circulars to agents at prison depots and parole towns

ADM 98/186-188: Transport Board, letters to agents at ports

ADM 98/191-211: Transport Board, letters to agents at parole depots

ADM 98/276-280: Transport Board, letters to agents in Scotland

ADM 98/300: Transport Board letters to French agents

ADM 99/149-258: Transport Board, minutes relating to prisoners of war

ADM 100/4: Cash account, 1817-18, of agent at Valleyfield

ADM 103/110: General Entry Book, 'Edinburgh', 1803-1812

ADM 103/112: General Entry Book, 'French' at Edinburgh Castle, 1811

ADM 103/113: General Entry Book, 'French' at 'Edinburgh Castle', 1811

ADM 103/114: General Entry Book, Edinburgh Castle, 1812-13

ADM 103/115: General Entry Book, 'French at Edinburgh, 1803-1812'

ADM 103/116: 'Register of the description of the French prisoners of war at Edinburgh'

ADM 103/117: General Entry Book, 'Edinburgh, 1813, Various'

ADM 103/124: General Entry Book, Esk Mills, 1811

ADM 103/152: General Entry Book, Danish, Greenlaw, 1807-1811

ADM 103/153: General Entry Book, Danish, Greenlaw, 1808-1811

ADM 103/154: General Entry Book, Dutch, Greenlaw [and Edinburgh bridewell], 1803-1804

ADM 103/155: General Entry Book, French, Greenlaw [and Edinburgh bridewell], 1803-1809

ADM 103/156: General Entry Book, French, Greenlaw, 1810

ADM 103/157: General Entry Book, French, Greenlaw, 1811-1812

ADM 103/158: General Entry Book, Spanish, Greenlaw, 1805-1806

ADM 103/159: General Entry Book, Greenock, 1805

ADM 103/263: General Entry Book, Perth, 1812

ADM 103/264: General Entry Book, Perth, 1812

ADM 103/265: General Entry Book, Perth, 1812-1813

ADM 103/266: General Entry Book, Perth, 1813

ADM 103/267: Perth, 1812-1814, 'Various'

ADM 103/333: General Entry Book, Portchester Castle

ADM 103/418: General Entry Book, Stapleton depot

ADM 103/432: General Entry Book, Valleyfield, 1811

ADM 103/433: General Entry Book, Valleyfield, 1811

ADM 103/434: General Entry Book, Valleyfield, 1811

ADM 103/435: General Entry Book, Valleyfield, 1811-1813

ADM 103/436: General Entry Book, Valleyfield, 1813-1814

ADM 103/482: 'Exchanges French & English'

ADM 103/486: 'French in England' [i.e., Britain], 1810-1814

ADM 103/487: 'Descriptions of Prisoners of War [who escaped], 1811-1814'

ADM 103/489: Escapes, 1811-1813

ADM 103/491: Escapes [from 1811 onwards, an alphabetical list]

ADM 103/496: Released/Exchanged, 1811-1814

ADM 103/497: Exchanged, 1810-1811

ADM 103/499: 'Partial Exchanges, French' [1812-1813]

ADM 103/509: Released, 1812-1813

ADM 103/516: Alphabetical list of prisoners at Perth

ADM 103/563: General Entry Book, parole prisoners at Odiham, Hampshire

ADM 103/568: General Entry Book, parole prisoners at Cupar, Fife, 1811-1812

ADM 103/570: General Entry Book, parole prisoners at Greenlaw, Berwickshire, 1812-1814

ADM 103/580: General Entry Book, parole prisoners at Lauder, 1811-1814

ADM 103/581: General Entry Book, parole prisoners at Kelso, 1810-1814

ADM 103/585: General Entry Book, parole prisoners at Peebles, 1798-1799

ADM 103/586: General Entry Book, parole prisoners, 'Edinburgh, etc.,' and Peebles, 1795-1800

ADM 103/596: General Entry Book, parole prisoners at Peebles, 1803-1811

ADM 103/599: General Entry Book, parole prisoners at Sanquhar, 1812-1814

ADM 103/600: General Entry Book, parole prisoners at Lanark, 1811-1814

ADM 103/611: Alphabetical lists (A to K) of parole prisoners

ADM 103/612: Alphabetical list (L to Z) of parole prisoners

ADM 103/613: Alphabetical list (A to K) of parole prisoners

ADM 103/614: Alphabetical list (L to Z) of parole prisoners

ADM 103/624: 'Danish' [mainly French] prisoners who died at Greenlaw, 1805-1813

ADM 103/635, Part I: 'Various Deaths, 1795-1831' [In fact, contains miscellaneous letters, maps, lists, etc., from c.1811 to c.1826]

ADM 103/635, Part II: [A box of miscellaneous letters, papers, lists, etc., from c. 1810 to c. 1816]

ADM 103/648: Death certificates of prisoners [1804-1814]

ADM 105/44: Reports by Transport Board Commissioners, 1799-1812

ADM 105/45: Reports of escapes from depots and parole towns, 1810-1813

ADM 105/46: 'Various reports' to Transport Office, 1810-1821

ADM 105/52: Prisoners' applications, 1810-1813

ADM 105/53: Prisoners' applications, 1810-1813

ADM 105/54: Prisoners' applications, 1810-1813

ADM 105/59: Dutch prisoners at Edinburgh Castle, 1796-1799

ADM 105/60: Miscellaneous Transport Office papers, 1808

ADM 105/61: Miscellaneous Transport Office papers, 1811-1812

ADM 105/66: Miscellaneous Transport Office papers [mainly 1827-1830]

HO 5/35: Home Office Register of applications by Aliens (secret), 1813

HO 28/34-43: Home Office Correspondence: Admiralty, Transport, and Prisoners of War, etc., 1803-1814

HO 79/1: Home Office: private and secret letters, 1806-1812

HO 79/2: Home Office: private and secret letters, 1812-1817
WO 1/625-658: War Office, in-letters, 1802-1814
WO 6/149-153: War Office, out-letters to Admiralty, 1803-1814
WO 6/156-161: War Office, out-letters to Transport Board, 1806-1814

2. In the National Archives of Scotland (NAS):

Justiciary Court/Lord Advocate's Papers:

AD 14/12/63 (Precognitions in the escape at Falkirk in Nov. 1811 by François Petit)

AD 14/12/76 (Papers concerning arrest, 1812, of John Shaw at Edmonstone, Midlothian, with forged banknotes)

AD/14/13/7 (Indictment and other papers, 1813, concerning Nathaniel Blair, alias Sawers, and forged banknotes)

AD 14/13/74 (Letters, etc., Aug. 1813, concerning J.B. Distrait (or Destrais), prisoner of war, in Tolbooth, Edinburgh, for wounding a soldier at Valleyfield)

AD 14/14/4 (Declarations by William Dowie, Aug. 1812, concerning forged banknotes)

AD 14/14/44 (Indictment, precognitions, etc., 1814, concerning James M'Dougal and forged banknotes)

AD 14/14/56 (Precognitions, letters, etc., Mar. 1814, concerning Louis Albertini, who killed a fellow prisoner of war at Valleyfield in a duel)

JC 26/334 (Indictment, list of witnesses, guards' orders, precognition, letters, jury's verdict, etc., in the trial of Ensign Hugh Maxwell for the shooting of a prisoner at Greenlaw, 1807)

JC 26/363 (Indictment, list of witnesses, depositions, jury's verdict, etc., 1813, in the case of Jessie and James Hislop, indicted for helping French prisoners of war escape from Lanark)

GD 1/405 (Macbeth Forbes Collection)

GD 1/872 (List of prisoners who died at Valleyfield, 1811-1814)

GD 40/9/239/8 (Lothian Muniments)

GD 51/2 and GD 51/756 (Melville Castle Muniments)

GD 157/2004 (Scott of Harden Muniments)

GD 174/1534/1 (MacLaine of Lochbuie Collection)

GD 214/739/1 (Hannay Collection)

GD 311 (Cowan of Valleyfield Papers)

E 886/79 (Tack, 1804, concerning Greenlaw, between Transport Board Commissioners and Robert Trotter of Castlelaw)

E 886/80 (Decreet of the division of the valued rent of Greenlaw, Nov. 1813)

E 886/81 (Lease, Nov. 1813, by Sir George Clerk of Penicuik to Transport Board Commissioners concerning water supply for Greenlaw depot)

HH 57/203 (Letters, cuttings, etc., 1929-30, concerning French prisoners of war buried at Perth depot)

North Leith Old Parish Register 692 1/7

RHP 35787 ('A scheme to convert Edinburgh Castle to a prisoner of war camp', 1944)

3. In National Library of Scotland (NLS):

MS 3651, fols 61-79 (Letters, 1812-1814, to and from Capt. Andrew Brown, RN, agent, Valleyfield)

MS Acc. 5811 (Johnston Collection)

MS 9819, fols 43-4 (Letter from Lieut. Gen. Lord Cathcart to Lieut. Gen. Brownrigg, 3 Oct. (no year: 1810))

MS Acc. 353, fols 98-103 (Melville Papers, letter, 18 Mar. 1811, from Lord Melville to Robert Dundas)

MS Acc. 1075, fols 222-6 (Melville Papers, letter, 24 Dec. 1810, from Lord Melville (Henry Dundas) to the brother of Sir Rupert George, chairman, Transport Board)

4. In National War Museum of Scotland:

French Forces 808.1 (Letters and papers, 1808-1813, concerning victualling and rations of prisoners of war at Greenlaw depot)

5. In National Archives of Ireland, Dublin:

Kilmainham Jail register, 1812

6. In Trondelag Folkemuseum, Trondheim, Norway:

The diary of Captain Paul Andreas Kaald

7. In Service Historique de la Marine, Ministère de la Défense, Vincennes, Paris:

FF2.23.B.12 (Loyal address to the restored Bourbons from some 40 prisoners of war at Perth, 17 May 1814)

8. In Edinburgh City Archives:

Register of Aliens, 1808-1814

Applications for passports, 1809-1855 (and associated correspondence)

9. In Midlothian Local Studies Library, Loanhead:

Black Collection (Film 2, item 2 [formerly Vol.2(c)]; film 11, item 9/69)

10. In Orkney Library:

D1/48: (Letter, 14 Apr. 1807, from James Watson, Vice Admiral Depute of Orkney and Shetland, to William Marsden, secretary, Admiralty, concerning the wreck of the Dutch frigate *Utrecht* on the island of Sanday.)

11. In Perth Museum and Art Gallery:

Item 89/22/G/1935 (Ledger of payments to prisoners of war at Perth, 1812-1814)

12. Theses:

Roy Bennett, French Prisoners of War on Parole in Britain (1803-1814). Unpublished Ph.D. thesis, University of London, 1964

Guillaume Lévêque, Les Prisonniers de Guerre Français en Grande Bretagne, 1803-1814 (2 vols). Unpublished Mémoire de Maitrise, University of Paris, 1986-7

B. PUBLISHED CONTEMPORARY SOURCES

1. Official publications, documentary collections, etc.:

Correspondance de Napoléon Ier (Paris, 1858-1870)

Parliamentary Papers, Vol. IX, 1812 [Transport Office return of prisoners of war in the United Kingdom, 26 June 1812]; Vol XIII, 1817 [An account, February 1817, of sums claimed in 1814-15 by the British government from the French government for the maintenance of prisoners of war, and the converse in 1810-1817]

Selection from the private correspondence of the First Duke of Wellington (Roxburgh Club, 1952)

Supplementary Despatches, Correspondence, and Memoranda of Field Marshal Arthur, Duke of Wellington, KG Ed. by his son, the Duke of Wellington (London, 1858-72), Vols VI-IX and XIII

Wellington at War, 1794-1815. A selection of his wartime letters Ed. by Antony Brett-James (London, 1961)

Wellington's Despatches Comp. by Lieutenant Colonel Gurwood (London, 1835), Vols IV-X, 1809-1813

2. Recollections by prisoners of war and by other contemporary soldiers and seamen:

Anon. *A Soldier of the 71st. The Journal of a Soldier of the Highland Light Infantry 1806-1815* Ed. by Christopher Hibbert (London, 1975)

James Anton, *Retrospect of a military life* (Edinburgh, 1841)

Carnet d'Etapes et Souvenirs de Guerre et de Captivité du sergent-major Philippe Beaudoin, de la 31e demi-brigade de ligne in *Carnet de la Sabretache* (Paris, 1909), Nos 193, 195-7, 201-3, Jan.-Nov. 1909

François-Frédéric Billon, *Souvenirs d'un Vélite de la Garde sous Napoléon Ier* (Paris, 1905)

The Note-books of Captain Coignet, Soldier of the Empire Ed. by Sir John Fortescue (London, 1929)

Edward Costello, *Adventures of a Soldier. The Peninsular and Waterloo Campaigns* Ed. by Antony Brett-James (London, 1967)

Adelbert Doisy de Villargennes, *Reminiscences of Army Life under Napoleon Bonaparte* (Cincinnati, 1884)

John J. Vernon, *Reminiscences of a French Prisoner of War at Selkirk, 1811-1814* [Adelbert J. Doisy de Villargennes], in *Transactions of the Hawick Archaeological Society, 1912*

Doisy de Villargennes, Souvenirs Militaires de Ed. by M.G. Bertin (Paris, 1900)

Emile Fairon and Henri Heuse, *Lettres de Grognards* (Liège, 1936)

Louis Garneray, *The French prisoner* Trans. by Lawrence Wood (London, 1957)

G.R. Gleig, *The Subaltern. A chronicle of the Peninsular War* (London, n.d.)

Mémoires du Général Marquis Alphonse D'Hautpoul, Pair de France, 1789-1865 (Paris, 1906)

Michael Glover (ed.), *A Gentleman Volunteer. The Letters of George Hennell from the Peninsular War, 1812-1813* (London, 1979)

Recollections of Rifleman Harris Ed. by Christopher Hibbert (London, 1970)

Pa Kapertokt og i Prisonen 1808-1810. Av. Kaptein Paul Andreas Kaalds Etterlatte Papirer Ed. by Joh. N. Tonnessen (Trondheim Sjofartsmuseum, 1950)

Captain John Kincaid, *Adventures in the Rifle Brigade* (London, 1830)

The Private Journal of F.S. Larpent, Esq., Judge Advocate General of the British Forces in the Pensinular ... from 1812 to its close Ed. by Sir George Larpent, *Bart* (London, 1853), Vols 1 and II

Marcellin Marbot, *Mémoires du Général Baron de Marbot* (Paris, 1892)

Souvenirs d'un Corsaire 1811-1814. Souvenirs de H.F. Marote, Lieutenant du Corsaire L'Aventurier Comp. and ed. by Leon Wocquier (Liège, 1845)

The Autobiography of Sir Harry Smith Ed. by G.C. Moore Smith (London, 1902)

The Life of Alexander Stewart. Prisoner of Napoleon ... Written by himself to 1815, abridged by Dr Albert Peel to 1874 (London, 1948)

The Memoirs of Baron Thiébault Trans. and condensed by A. J. Butler (London, 1896), Vol. II

The Wheatley Diary: Journal and Sketch-book kept during the Peninsular War and the Waterloo Campaign Ed. by Christopher Hibbert (London, 1964)

The Letters of Private Wheeler, 1809-1828 Ed. by Captain B.H. Liddell Hart (London, 1951)

3. Other published contemporary recollections, collections, or primary sources:

William Chambers, *Some Early Recollections* (In *Chambers's Journal*, Fourth Series, No. 597, 5 June 1875; No. 600, 26 June 1875; No. 601, 3 July 1875; No. 607, 14 August 1875)

Charles Cowan, *Reminiscences* (Edinburgh, 1878)

Souvenirs du Comte de Merode-Westerloo (Paris and Brussels, 1845), Vol. I

James Nasmyth, Engineer. An Autobiography Ed. by Samuel Smiles (London, 1883)

New Statistical Account

Old Statistical Account

Louis Simond, *Journal of a tour and residence in Great Britain during the years 1810 and 1811* (Edinburgh,1817) 2 vols

The Letters of Sir Walter Scott. Vol. III: *1811-1814* Ed. by H.J.C. Grierson (London, 1932)

4. Newspapers and periodicals:

Caledonian Mercury
Dumfries Courier
Dundee Advertiser
Edinburgh Advertiser
Edinburgh Evening Courant
Edinburgh Magazine
Edinburgh Star
Glasgow Courier
Greenock Advertiser
Kelso Mail
Montrose Review
Perth Courier
The Naval Chronicle
The Scots Magazine
The Times

C. SECONDARY SOURCES:

1. Histories of prisoners of war and their depots or hulks:

Francis Abell, *Prisoners of War in Britain, 1756-1815* (Oxford, 1914)

N.G. Allen, 'The French Prisons in Edinburgh Castle' (In *Book of the Old Edinburgh Club* (Edinburgh, 1985), Vol. XXXV, Part II.)

Justin Atholl, *The Prison on the Moor. The Story of Dartmoor Prison* (London, 1953)

J.L. Black, *Penicuik and Neighbourhood* (Edinburgh, n.d.)

W. Branch-Johnson, *The English Prison Hulks* (London, 1957)

J.W. Buchan (ed.), *A History of Peeblesshire* (Glasgow, 1925)

Joy Cameron, *Prisons & Punishment in Scotland, from the Middle Ages to the Present* (Edinburgh, 1983)

Joy Deacon, 'Penicuik—Napoleonic Prisoner of War Camp' (In 'History of Penicuik', Vol.5 (Penicuik Historical Society, n.d.(c.1985))

Walter Elliot, *The French in Selkirk 1811-1814* (Selkirk, 1982)

J. Macbeth Forbes, 'French Prisoners of War in Scotland, and Bank Note Forging' (In *Bankers' Magazine*, March 1897)

J. Macbeth Forbes, 'The French Prisoners-of-War in the Border Towns, 1803-1814' (In *Transactions of Hawick Archaeological Society, 1912)*

John Glen, *The History of the Town and Castle of Dumbarton* (Dumbarton, 1847)

Robert Jackson, *The Prisoners of 1914-18* (London, 1989)

C.M. Kinnear, *Les Prisonniers de Perth* (In *Scots Magazine*, June 1989)

Michael Lewis, *Napoleon and his British captives* (London, 1962)

Ian MacDougall, *The Prisoners at Penicuik. French and other prisoners of war, 1803-1814* (Dalkeith, 1989)

I.M.M. MacPhail, *Dumbarton Castle* (Edinburgh, 1979)

Andrew Mair, *Dumbarton Castle. Historical and Descriptive Notes* (Dumbarton, 1920)

Philippe Masson, *Les sépulchres flottants. Prisonniers français en Angleterre sous l'Empire* (Rennes, 1987)

David Peacock, *Perth: its annals and its archives* (Perth, 1849)

George Penny, *Traditions of Perth* (Perth, 1836)

Carl Roos, *Prisonen Danske og Norske krigsfanger i England 1807-1814* (Copenhagen, 1953)

Sheila Scott, *Peebles during the Napoleonic Wars* (Peebles, 1980)

George Sievewright, *Historical Sketch of the Old Depot or Prison for French prisoners-of-war at Perth* (Perth, 1894)

George Sweetman, *The French in Wincanton* (Wincanton, 1897)

Basil Thomson, *The Story of Dartmoor Prison* (London, 1907)

James U. Thomson, 'Glencorse' (In *Scotland's Magazine*, December 1965)

John T. Thorp, *French Prisoners' Lodges* (Leicester, 1935)

Thomas J. Walker, *The Depot for Prisoners-of-War at Norman Cross, Huntingdonshire, 1796-1816* (London, 1915)

John J. Wilson, *The Annals of Penicuik* (Stevenage, rev. ed. 1985)

2. Histories of the Napoleonic Wars and their era:

A. Aspinall (ed.), *The Early English Trade Unions. Documents from the Home Office papers in the Public Record Office* (London, 1949)

Louis Bergeron, *France under Napoleon* (Princeton, 1981)

Geoffrey Best, *War and Society in Revolutionary Europe 1770-1870* (Stroud, 1998)

Georges Blond, *La Grande Armée, 1804-1815* (Paris, 1979)

Antony Brett-James, *Life in Wellington's Army* (London, 1972)

Geoffrey Bruun, *Europe and the French Imperium 1799-1814* (New York, 1963)

Raymond Carr, *Spain 1808-1975* (London, 1982)

David Chandler, *The Campaigns of Napoleon* (London, 1966)

David Chandler, *Dictionary of the Napoleonic Wars* (Ware, 1999)

David Chandler, *On the Napoleonic Wars. Collected Essays* (London, 1994)

Owen Connelly (ed), *Historical Dictionary of Napoleonic France, 1799-1815* (London, 1985)

Owen Connelly, *Napoleon's Satellite Kingdoms* (New York, 1965)

Patrick Crowhurst, *The French War on Trade: Privateering 1793-1815* (London, 1989)

Norman Davies, *God's Playground. A History of Poland* Vol. II (Oxford, 1986)

T.K. Derry, *A History of Scandinavia* (London, 1979)

John R. Elting, *Swords Around a Throne. Napoleon's Grande Armée* (London, 1989)

Charles Esdaile, *The Peninsular War. A New History* (London, 2002)

Franklin L. Ford, *Europe 1780-1830* (London, 1971)

Alan Forrest, *Conscripts and Deserters: The Army and French Society during the Revolution and Empire* (Oxford, 1989)

Alan Forrest, *Napoleon's Men. The Soldiers of the Revolution and Empire* (London, 2002)

J.W. Fortescue, *The County Lieutenancies and the Army, 1803-1814* (London, 1909)

J.W. Fortescue, *A History of the British Army* (London, 1899-1930), Vols VII and XIII

W. Hamish Fraser, *Conflict and Class. Scottish Workers 1700-1838* (Edinburgh, 1988)

David Gates, *The Napoleonic Wars 1803-1815* (London, 2003)

David Gates, *The Spanish Ulcer. A History of the Peninsular War* (London, 1986)

A. Gieysztor et al., *History of Poland* (Warsaw, 1968)

Richard Glover, *Britain at Bay. Defence against Bonaparte, 1803-1814* (London, 1973)

Ian Grimble, *The Sea Wolf. The Life of Admiral Cochrane* (London, 1978)

A. Halecki, *A History of Poland* (London, 1978)

J.L. and Barbara Hammond, *The Skilled Labourer 1760-1832* (London, 1920)

Eric Hobsbawm, *The Age of Revolution. Europe 1789-1848* (London, 1962)

William James, *The Naval History of Great Britain* Vols III-V (1803-1812) (London, 1859)

André Jardin and André-Jean Tudesq, *Restoration and Reaction 1815-1848* (Cambridge, 1988)

E.H. Jenkins, *A History of the French Navy* (London, 1973)

H.W. Koch, *A History of Prussia* (London, 1978)

Ralph Korngold, *Citizen Toussaint* (Boston, 1944)

E.H. Kossmann, *The Low Countries* (Oxford, 1978)

Georges Lefebvre, *Napoleon* Vol. I: *From 18 Brumaire to Tilsit, 1799-1807*; Vol. II: *From Tilsit to Waterloo, 1807-1815* (London, 1969)

Michael Lewis, *A Social History of the Navy, 1793-1815* (London, 1960)

Christopher Lloyd, *The British Seaman 1200-1860* (London, 1968)

Kenneth J. Logue, *Popular Disturbances in Scotland 1780-1815* (Edinburgh, 1979)

J. Lucas-Dubreton, *Napoléon devant L'Espagne* (Paris, 1946)

Piers Mackesy, *The War in the Mediterranean, 1803-1810* (London, 1957)

A.T. Mahan, *The Influence of Sea power upon the French Revolution and Empire, 1793-1812* Vol. II (London, 1892)

Felix Markham, *Napoleon* (London, 1963)

J.A.R. Marriott and C.G. Robertson, *The Evolution of Prussia* (Oxford, 1946)

John Marshall, *Royal Naval Biography* Supplement, Part II (London, 1828)

S.E. Morison and H.S. Commager, *The Growth of the American Republic* Vol. I: *1000-1865* (New York, 1962)

Jean Morvan, *Le Soldat Impérial (1800-1814)* (Paris, 1904), 2 vols

Sir Charles Oman, *A History of the Peninsular War, 1807-1814* (Oxford, 1902-1930), 7 vols

Sir Charles Oman, *Studies in the Napoleonic Wars* (London, 1987)

Brigadier F.C.C. Page, *Following the Drum. Women in Wellington's Wars* (London, 1986)

Julia Page, *Intelligence Officer in the Peninsula. Letters and Diaries of Major the Hon. Edward Charles Cocks, 1786-1812* (Tunbridge Wells, 1986)

C. Northcote Parkinson, *War in the Eastern Seas, 1793-1815* (London, 1954)

Julian Rathbone, *Wellington's War* (London, 1984)

Colonel H.C.B. Rogers, *Napoleon's Army* (Shepperton, 1974)

George Rudé, *Revolutionary Europe 1783-1815* (London, 1964)

Simon Schama, *Patriots and Liberators. Revolution in the Netherlands 1780-1813* (London, 1992)

James J. Sheehan, *German History 1770-1866* (Oxford, 1989)

Georges Six, *Dictionnaire Biographique des Généraux et Amiraux Français de la Révolution et de l'Empire (1792-1814)* (Paris, 1934) 2 vols

David Syrett and R.L. DiNardo, *The Commissioned Sea Officers of the Royal Navy, 1660-1815* (Navy Records Society, 1994)

W.A. Thorburn, *French Army Regiments & Uniforms* (London, 1969)

Jean Tulard, *Napoléon* (Paris, 1987)

J. Steven Watson, *The Reign of George III 1760-1815* (Oxford, 1960)

Isser Woloch, *The French Veteran from the Revolution to the Restoration* (Chapel Hill, 1979)

Index

Virtually all persons shown without designation (except occasionally rank) were POWs. Place names are as given in the principal manuscript sources. Where place names are now changed (e.g., Konigsberg/Kaliningrad), or are different in other languages (e.g., Antwerp/Anvers), the latter form, as well as some suggested possibly correct spellings, is given in brackets, as is a question mark where a place has not, or not yet, been identified.

ABBREVIATIONS USED IN THE INDEX

Adm.	*Admiralty*
Bn	*Battalion*
capd	*captured*
dischgd	*discharged*
Eb	*Edinburgh bridewell*
EC	*Edinburgh Castle*
EM	*Esk Mills*
G	*Greenlaw*
HO	*Home Office*
P	*Perth*
POW(s)	*prisoner(s) of war*
recapd	*recaptured*
regt	*regiment*
TB	*Transport Board*
TO	*Transport Office*
trans.	*transport vessel*
V	*Valleyfield*

Abbotsford, Roxburghshire, 550

Abel (or Ribel), Gabriel, 653

Aberdeen, 20, 145, 203, 293, 444, 539, 542, 754; Banking Co., 318; Bank of Scotland branch in, 758

Aberdeen, Earl of *see* Hamilton-Gordon, George

Aberdeenshire *see* militia

Aberystwyth, 517

Actioie (or Actiau), Jean Baptiste, 674

Adam, John, architect, 690

Adam, Lieut. Jacques, 712; escapes or attempted escapes by, 376, 488, 489, 491, 511, 527, 608, 609, 611, 813, 814; transfers of, 102, 114, 431, 432

Adam, Robert, architect, 691

Adam, William, architect, 690

Adams, Elisha, 512, 718

Adamson, William, Secretary of State for Scotland, 601, 795, 827

Admiralty, 1, 4, 5, 18, 22, 37, 38, 40-58 passim, 102, 103, 180, 184, 185; First Lord of the, *see* Dundas, Henry, 1st Viscount Melville; Dundas, Robert, 2nd Viscount Melville; Yorke, Charles; Secretary of, *see* Croker, J.W; Marsden, W.; Nepean, Sir Evan; Pole, Hon. W.W.; solicitor in Scotland for, *see* Greig, Alexander

Adriatic, 183

Africa, xiii, xv, 550

agents: TB, depot, parole, and transport, 1, 3, 6, 44, 58, 386, 393, 394, 793; characteristics at Scots depots of, 392, 393, 447; Dutch, for POWs in Britain, 147, 719; *see also* individual depots and parole towns

ages, xvii, 11, 22, 60, 97, 121, 164-77, 179, 190, 192, 193, 195, 206, 433, 441, 442, 443, 610, 724-7 passim, 734

Aikin, Rev., Edinburgh, 308, 757

Aimé, Pierre Jean, 798

Aine (or Ainé), Philippe, 674

Airdrie, 16

airing grounds, 422; *see also* individual depots

Aitken, Mr, Canongate tolbooth, 321

Aitken (or Aikin), Robert, turnkey, 245, 429, 782, 784

Aix La Chapelle, 818

Albertini, Louis, 406, 407

Aldershot, Hampshire, 387

Alexander I, Tsar of Russia, 551, 723, 824

Alexander, Robert, militiaman, 384

Bishop's Waltham, Hampshire, 450

black hole *see* cachots

Black, J.L., Penicuik historian, 276, 500, 504, 505, 580

Blackie, John, depot messenger, 783

black POWs, 5, 40, 167, 178, 179, 180, 181, 183, 472, 475, 727, 728

Black Sea, 183

Blackwood, James, depot lamplighter, 402, 783, 784

Blair (alias Sawers), Nathaniel, convict, 325, 761

Blair Atholl, Perthshire, 515, 530, 808

Blair, Robert, Lord President, Court of Session, 50, 698

Blank, Jorgen, 646

Blatter, Lieut. Rudolf, 199, 363, 364, 734, 765

Blayney, Major General Lord, 571, 572, 778

Blee, Sebastien, 661

blindness *see* illness, disease, etc.

Blücher, Marshal Gebhard von, 589

Boddam, Aberdeenshire, 514

Bodiot, Yves, 655

Boelard (or Boclard or Boclaars), Lieut. Frederik, 188, 818

Boile (or Boille), Marien, 677

Boileau, Quentin, 434

Boiron, Philip, parole POW, 388, 389

Boisdefray, Louis, 263, 749

Biggar, Cupar (Fife), Dumfries, Green-
law (Berwickshire), Hawick, Jedburgh,
Kelso, Lanark, Lauder, Melrose, Peebles,
Sanquhar, Selkirk; transfers
Parquer (or Partier), Paul, 678
Parry, John, songwriter, 817
Pascal, Barthelemy, 341, 363 (?), 364 (?),
766
passengers, 20, 22, 119, 120, 122, 126,
134, 144, 146, 194, 570, 690, 694; from
Greenland, released, 184, 185; women
and children as, 157, 175, 226
Passicousset, Lieut. Pierre, 458
Pastello (or Patelo), Martin, 664
Patatrand, Louis, 449, 457, 743, 763
Patersky, Simon, 199, 734
Paterson, Capt. C.M., TB agent, Portches-
ter Castle depot, 40, 41
Paterson Robert, cooper, 532, 533
Pathhead House, by Greenlaw, 504, 787
Patriotic Fund, Lloyd's, 121
Patton, Capt. C., RN, 224
Paul, François, 661
Paulcel (or Bomsill), Pierre, 674
Paulon (or Pauron), J.B., 134, 715
Paumier, Thomas, 89, 230, 235
Pavien (or Pavren or Parren), François, 202
Payon, Jean, 662
Peacock, David, Perth historian, 107, 108,
307, 595
Pearre, Dematre, 201
Pearson, Adam, Excise Office, 744
Pederson, Asmus, 446
Peebles, xviii, 37, 38, 44, 289, 290, 306,
326, 377, 432, 462, 813; all POWs at
transferred to Dumfries, 290, 378, 774;
bonnet laird at, 326, 327; employment
of parole POWs as clerks to TB agent
at, 332; and escapers, 229, 479, 483, 509,
510, 521, 522; in French Revolutionary
Wars, 3, 689; letter to Capt. Kaald from,
293; meal mob at, 522; midshipmen
POWs at sent in retaliation to V, 371, 372,
772; number of parole POWs at, 38, 696,
714, 715; places in or near: Clay House,
Acrefield, 520, Kerfield, 3, gaol, 483, 521,
522, Winkston Farm, 510, 522, 813; POW
at G refused parole at, 260, 350; POWs
sent, 1803-11, on parole to, 4; POW with
Irish name at, 736; TB parole agent at,
3, 332; William Chambers and father at,
116, 482, 736; *see also* parole
Peeblesshire *see* militia

Peel, Robert, Under-Secretary for War and
Colonies, 307
Pegie, Jean Baptiste, 760
Peiglasses, Joseph, 674
Pelias, Jean, 666
Pellowe, Capt.Richard, RN, TB agent for
Scotland, EM and V: accommodation for,
400, 401; character of, 393; experiences
at EM of, 57-63 passim, 70, 72, 87, 88,
224, 235, 251, 255, 451, 463, 531, 739,
791; relations with Capt. Heddington,
RN, 100, 101, 102; at V, 88, 91, 149, 451,
778; and removal of POWs from EM to
EC, 87, 705; transferred as TB agent to
Plymouth, 101, 102, 316, 708
Pembrokeshire, 381
Pénéde, François, 660
Penicuik, 12, 13, 26, 28, 66, 92, 232, 280,
302, 303, 305, 323, 374, 375, 504, 580,
712, 752, 819; and accommodation
for TB agent at G, 399; and banknote
forgeries, 321, 324, 325, 326, 327, 328,
759; 'bawbee', 823; bonnet laird at,
326, 327; children in coal pits at or near,
164; and escapers, 472, 484, 500, 505,
506, 510, 515, 520, 521, 522, 532, 537,
540, 592; Friends of the People at, 521;
guards at, 28, 280, 321, 324, 325, 375,
598, 599, 600, 695, 759, 827; land at
offered for depot, 45, 47, 55, 482, 698;
parish minister of, 599, 600, 700; places
in or near: Auchencorth Moss, 484,
Bank Mill, 315, Beeslack, 222, 580, 589,
592, 705, 826, Bog Road, 500, Bridge
Street, 500, Burrowford Burn, 793,
'Cabbage Hall', 746, cavalry barracks,
375, Cornbank Farm, 257, Glencorse
Barracks, xviii, 424, High Street, 276,
James the Less Church, 746, Kirkhill,
34, 35, 86, 324, 375, 600, 698, Lowrie's
Den, 500, Maybank Farm, 504, Penicuik
House, 34, 283, 695, public park, 257, St
Mungo's Church and churchyard, 116,
117, 795, shops, 116, South Kirk Hall,
746, Thorburn Terrace, 580, Valleyfield
House, 276, West Street, 500; poet
at, 427; POW at undergoes religious
conversion, 757; POWs at G allowed to
visit, 34, 35, 484; POWs at 'more turbulent', 487; POWs staying on post-war
at, 592, 812; William Chambers visits,
116, 117, 208, 326, 327, 328; *see also* Esk
Mills; Greenlaw; Valleyfield

to, 566; Marote-Carrier and, xviii, 118, 127, 141; monument at, 601, 795, 828; number of POWs at, 88-91 passim, 126, 130, 133, 171, 172, 213, 215, 266, 395, 567, 586, 696, 720, 725, 792, seamen, 125, 139, 140, 716, soldiers, 130, 149, 719, *see also* Appendix 4; officer POWs at, 91, 92, 155, 285, 767; palisades at, 91, 116, 117, 271, 303, 428, 482, 483, 497, 529, 530, 531, 541, 547, 610; p.o.b. of POWs at, 182, 636, 637; 'poor Fleming' POW at, 138, 802; post-1814, 589, 590, 591, 596, 597, 705, 709, 826, 827; privies, jack tubs, and 'prison' or 'night' soil at, 425, 426, 500, 545, 794; staff at, 35, 244, 245, 291, 370, 394, 395, 396-7, 401-7 passim, 497, 594, 598, 692, 695, 744, 751, 778-83, 788, accommodation or lodging allowance for, 400, 401, number and categories of, 395, 396-7, 398, 399; transfer of EC staff to, 398; women staff, 304, 695, 779, 780, 782, 783; TB agent at, 89, 91, 290, 291, 292, 306, 343, 344, 365, 385, 392, 393, 402, 482, 531, 537-42 passim, 567, 579, 580, 581, 582, 595, 596, 640, 707, 708, 709, 778, 795, accommodation for, 90, 400, 401, 788, interview with, 343, 344, quarrel with surgeon by, 268, salary of, 58, subordination of, 58, 87, 88, successive appointments as, 58, 91, 100, 101, 102, 708, 709, *see also* Heddington, Capt. T., RN, Moriarty, Capt. E.J., RN, Pellowe, Capt. R., RN; too near Peebles, 378; tricolour flies at, 117; ventilation system at, 709, 792; visited by TB commissioners and admirals, 351, 356, 428, 429, 575; water supply at, 425, 597, 700, 793; William Chambers visits, 116, 117, 138, 139, 208, 229, 234, 262, 271, 272, 282, 284, 305, 326, 327, 756, 795; *see also* Appendices 4, 5, 9; beds and bedding; burials and cemeteries; cachots; capture; contracts and contractors; education, entertainments, etc.; escapes and attempted escapes; exchanges; food and drink; freemasonry; guards; informers; Johnston, Andrew; miserables; nationalities; releases and repatriations; retaliation; shootings; short allowances; transfers; volunteers; women

Valleyfield paper mills, 35, 57, 60, 700, 705; *see also* Cowan, Alexander; Cowan, Charles, MP; Cowan, Duncan; Cowan, John

Vanbeck, Charles, miner, Prestonpans, 812
Van Beck, a Dutch POW at Penicuik, 520, 521, 592, 597, 598
Vandenberg (or Vandenberghe), Johann, 187, 446, 657, 731
van den Berg, Pieter, 148
Van Den Hewal, Jan, 446, 498
Vanderboom, François, 173, 177, 193, 797, 798
Vandercourt (or Fandercort), Jean, 651
Vanderdone, Liev (or Livain), 678
Vanderham, Jan, 193, 732
Vandresteraelen (or Vanderstralen), Joseph, 669
Van Gruthem, a Dutch priv. officer POW, 260, 276, 301
Vanguard, HMS *see* ships
Van Harlem, Antoine, 658
Vanherff, Christian, 161, 164, 194, 724, 733
Van Laard, Jan, 763
Vanveen, Arent, 72, 604, 813
Vanvelier (or Vanvelor or Vanveilen), Lieut. Henri, 72, 604,
Van Weltingen, Roelf, 192, 732, 797, 798
Varraguier (or Varotin), Armand, 195, 675
Varseau (or Varsovie) *see* Warsaw
Vasseur, Louis, 670
Vasseur (or Vapeur), René (or Pierre), 172, 174, 177, 442, 715, 797, 798
Vauchel, P., 760
Vaxencourt, Colonel, parole POW, 777
Veitch, William, outlaw, 326
Velassier (or Velasière), C.L.L., 658
Vensen, Nicolas, 727
Verdier (or Vidier), Prosper, 664
Verdon, Jean, 656
Verdun, 176, 333, 345, 401, 571, 714, 767, 778
Vergnot (or Vergnout), Ernout, 663
Vermersck, P., 457
vermin *see* cleanliness and dirt
Verron (or Verren), Jean, 646
Verté, Julien (alias or nickname Bataille), 218
Vickery, Mr, Bow Street runner, 389, 390, 391
Victor Emmanuel, king of Sardinia, 473, 551, 553, 554
victories, celebrations of, 561-5, 693, 817, 819
Victor, Marshal Claude, 724